Khoi/San Cave Paintings

S0-AZW-562

Footprint

South Africa Handbook

Francisca Kellett & Lizzie Williams

Drifters

"It will never happen again that our country should
seek to dominate another through force of arms,
economic might or subversion. We are determined
to remain true to the vision of a non-racial society,
which asserts the ancient African values of respect
for every person and commitment to human dignity,
regardless of colour or race."

Nelson Mandela, 1994

South Africa Handbook
6th edition
© Footprint Handbooks Ltd
September 2002

Published by Footprint Handbooks
6 Riverside Court
Lower Bristol Road
Bath BA2 3DZ. England
T +44 (0)1225 469141
F +44 (0)1225 469461
Email discover@footprintbooks.com
Web www.footprintbooks.com

ISBN 1 903471 02 8
CIP DATA: A catalogue record for this
book is available from the British Library

Distributed in the USA by
Publishers Group West

Neither the black and white nor
coloured maps are intended to have any
political significance.

Every effort has been made to ensure
that the facts in this Handbook are
accurate. However, travellers should still
obtain advice from consulates, airlines
etc about current travel and visa
requirements before travelling. The
authors and publishers cannot accept
responsibility for any loss, injury or
inconvenience however caused.

Credits

Series editors
Patrick Dawson and Rachel Fielding

Editorial
Editor: Sarah Thorowgood
Maps: Sarah Sorensen

Production
Page layout: Jo Morgan
Maps: Claire Benison, Robert Lunn,
Kevin Feeney
Colour maps: Kevin Feeney
Cover: Camilla Ford
Colour section: Kevin Feeney

Design
Mytton Williams

Photography
Front cover: Impact
Back cover: Impact

Inside colour section:
Alamy: pages 7, 9 (bottom left), 10 (top
left and right), and 15 (top and centre)
Francisca Kellett: pages 4 and 16
gettyone Stone: pages 9 (bottom right),
10 (bottom), and 15 (bottom right)
Robert Harding Picture Library: pages 9
(top and centre), and 10 (centre)
Patrick Syder: page 15 (bottom left)
Lisa Young: pages 12 and 13

Print
Manufactured in Italy by LEGOPRINT

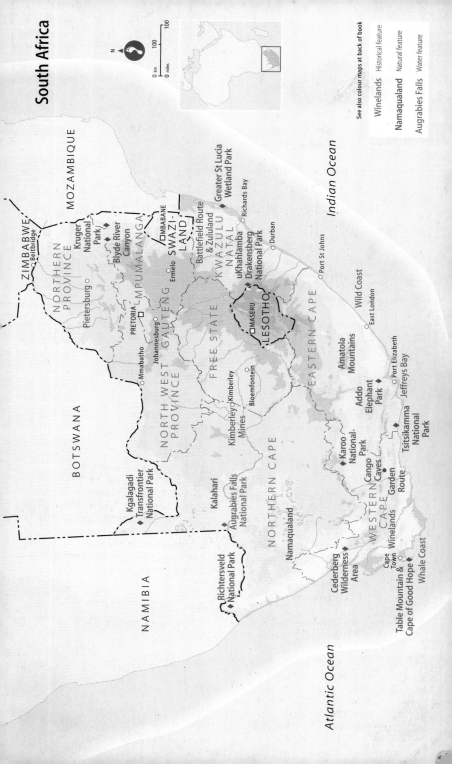

Contents

Left Strolling out in the midday sun on Cape Town's colourful Long Street

Right *Local kids avoid the surf in Jeffreys Bay*

A foot in the door

Highlights

South Africa is celebrated, first and foremost, for its incredible natural beauty. It has some of the most varied and extreme environments in the world, from the tropical coasts of KwaZulu Natal and the sweeping emptiness of the Kalahari Desert, to the snow-capped Drakensberg and the cacti-studded plains of the Karoo. Yet it is its people, a fascinating mix of cultures, religions and ethnicities, that are very pulse of South Africa – and who give meaning to its nickname, 'Rainbow Nation'. Although still struggling to recover from the hangover of apartheid, the country has changed considerably in recent years. Tourism is booming, and ever more visitors are coming to explore South Africa's stunning landscapes, vibrant cities and extraordinary game parks. But its sheer size means that escaping the hoards and discovering sleepy villages, deserted beaches and genuine areas of wilderness is easy.

The famous five One of the main reasons for coming to South Africa is to see the Big Five – the collective term for the big-bucks players of wildlife spotting: elephant, black rhino, Cape buffalo, leopard and lion. South Africa is an excellent place for first-time safaris, with a number of good value game reserves that virtually guarantee you will see all of them. Home to the king of game reserves, Kruger Park, South Africa also offers the opportunity of viewing wildlife in more varied landscapes than any other country in Africa. In the Northern Cape is the spectacular Khalagadi Transfrontier Park, defined by the rolling red sand dunes of the Kalahari; KwaZulu Natal offers contrasting tropical swamps and forests, while Addo Elephant Park stretches through the rolling hills of the Eastern Cape. Similarly, there are almost as many different degrees of comfort, from bumping through the bush in drafty verlander trucks and crashing out in tents, to being driven in private jeeps and sleeping in sumptuous camps.

City life South Africa's lively cities are perhaps even better reasons for visiting, be it for the big-city sophistication of Johannesburg and Pretoria, or the quirky beachside hedonism of Cape Town. The latter is certainly South Africa's most appealing draw, known as the 'Mother City' and one of the most beautiful cities in the world. Its setting, dominated by the soaring presence of Table Mountain and surrounded by the wild Atlantic, is unrivalled. The city itself is an intriguing hotchpotch of grandiose colonial buildings, Victorian suburbs and sprawling townships, with stunning beaches and mountain wilderness on all sides. Johannesburg and Pretoria, despite their bad press, are exciting and intriguing cities with vibrant nightlife and music scenes – not least in the cutting-edge Kwaito clubs. Other coastal urban centres, such as Durban or Port Elizabeth, are major surfing hotspots, while the desert town of Kimberley is the heart of the international diamond industry.

Nice & easy does it Away from the frenetic pace of the cities are vast rural areas with excellent opportunities for exploring sleepy villages, hiking through spectacular mountains or relaxing on wild and deserted beaches. South Africa has an appealingly slow pace of life, so kick back and take a few days to relax into it. In the east lie the magnificent Drakensberg, offering the best hiking in the country, while the Tsitsikamma National Park is a lush forested area fringed by the warm Indian Ocean. The Great Karoo, with its vast stretches of shimmering semi-desert, is perfect for experiencing the slow pace of small-town life, while the traditional Xhosa kraals of the Transkei offer a glimpse of rural Africa. Stunning beaches abound, from the wide, empty stretches of the Wild Coast to the developed seaside resorts of the Garden Route.

Having a vine time South African wines are fast finding their feet in the international market, and the beautiful Winelands in the Western Cape offer the chance of trying some. Within a few hours' drive from Cape Town are over a hundred fine estates, many of which serve up excellent meals in the beautiful surrounds of classic Cape Dutch homes. Around Stellenbosch and Paarl are elegant country hotels, while the Franschhoek Valley has strong French Huguenot traditions. Further from the Cape are a number of lesser-known but often equally good wineries, such as those of the Breede River Valley, set in beautiful countryside and little-visited by tourists.

Left *Few plants can grow to the height of the quiver tree in the arid, unforgiving Richtersveld*
Below *If you climb Lion's Head at sunset you will be rewarded with these views of a glimmering Cape Town*
Bottom right *Protected pachyderms in herds of hundreds at Addo Elephant Park*
Bottom left *The magnificent Winelands shelter countless historic wine estates, like this one at Franschheok*

Right Is today a good day to die? Bungee hell or high at Bloukrans Bridge, the highest jump in the world
Below Riding the 'Cape Doctor' – taking advantage of Cape Town's famous wind at Blouberg Beach

Centre Blyde River Canyon, the third largest in the world, is carved out by the 'river of joy' as it runs off the Drakensberg escarpment to the lowveld
Right Sunset on the sandstone rock formations of Golden Gate National Park, a short sprint from Johannesburg
Next page A lone ostrich surveys the Cape peninsula – 98% of the world's ostriches call the Western Cape home

Geen Heining

Highs and lows

South Africa has in recent years become a major playground for the fast and the furious, offering some of the wildest and best-organized adrenaline sports in the world. It has the varied environments to cater for a wide range of activities, while the outdoors lifestyle of many South Africans has brought about an ever-expanding market for sports fanatics. You can try just about anything here, from the world's highest bungee on the Garden Route and abseiling from the Top of Table Mountain, to white-water rafting in Swaziland or scuba diving a huge range of dive sites.

Things can only get wetter

South Africa is where the Atlantic Ocean meets the Indian Ocean, and its watery attractions are every bit as tempting as those of terra firma. From Sodwana Bay to the Cape are numerous opportunities for scuba diving, with an excellent choice of dives – you can explore wrecks, gently drift over colourful coral reefs or cage dive with great white sharks. The surfing scene is even bigger, focusing on Durban and legendary Jeffreys Bay, or J-Bay, said to have the world's greatest right-hander. Many a traveller has spent months here searching for that elusive, perfect wave, lured not just by the water but by the surprising lack of cliquiness usually found in surfer hangouts. There are also some impressive rapids on South Africa's rivers, with a number of outfits organizing white-water rafting on the Orange and Tugela rivers, where rapids can reach grade 4/5 – not for the fainthearted. Other recent booms include kitesurfing, where you are strapped to a large kite and pulled on a board across the waves at breakneck speed – the southeasterly around Cape Town has made it one of the most popular destinations for this breed of adrenaline fiend. But if you are of a less active persuasion, you can go on boat trips to see seals, sharks and whales, or charter a boat and go deep-sea fishing.

On dry ground

Away from the waters, visitors can try a range of different, but no less exhilarating, activities. One of the most popular developments has been kloofing, also known as canyoning, which involves hiking, boulder-hopping and swimming along mountain rivers. You have to be pretty fit to get the most out of kloofing, and it is very popular along the Garden Route and on and around Table Mountain. Mountain biking is only slowly making an impact – unless you want to go on a leisurely ride around the Winelands – and exciting trails can be limited, although the surrounding countryside and views usually make it worthwhile. Some areas, including smaller game parks and the Cederberg are slowly opening up to mountain bikers, including some good single tracks, but most trails are still rather limited. A more sedate and hugely popular pursuit is hiking, and the industry has boomed in the last 20 years. Just about every part of the country has some sort of hiking trail, including nature reserves, national parks and game reserves. The best area in the country is the Drakensberg, its stark, rugged landscape criss-crossed with hundreds of kilometres of marked trails. Many game parks also offer guided walks with armed guards, an excellent way of seeing the smaller flora and fauna that is usually missed on a game drive – don't expect any run-ins with lions though.

Turn up, drop in and bounce back

The massive backpacker's market in South Africa is bringing about ever bigger, better and wilder adventure sports, and every year a new fad brings in the bucks to operators. Ever popular is bungee jumping, with several jumps dotted around the country, including the world's highest at the Bloukrans Bridge. Newer alternatives include bridge jumping, where you swing rather than bounce from a bridge, while bungee venues become ever more bizarre – the latest offering is a jump from the Table Mountain cable car in Cape Town. More traditional adrenaline sports such as abseiling take on new twists, such as the world's highest commercial abseil, also from Table Mountain. Sandboarding is also getting big press, with trips organized to some impressively large dunes. Aerial pursuits have also remained popular, with a number of skydiving companies offering diverse drop zones – by beaches, over deserts or in the Cederberg. Paragliding is another big hit, with some spots along the Garden Route claiming to have the best thermals in Africa.

Tales of the cities

Though apartheid has been dead for almost a decade, its legacy is often apparent in the country's landscape and the pattern of South African cities and towns. Most cities were – and remain – divided. The Group Areas Act of the 1960s ensured that all prime land was in white hands, while black and coloured communities were, often forcibly, resettled in townships. The vast majority of black and coloured South Africans living in urban areas still live in these townships, which are usually some distance from the city centre. While the colour barriers have long since disappeared, the division between rich and poor remains. Today, this means that visitors often see a very lopsided view of cities. Township tours, however, have become very popular, and provided that they work with the communities they are visiting, can provide a useful insight into what urban South Africa is really all about.

Getting down in Cape Town Cape Town is one of the world's most beautiful cities, with the dramatic backdrop of Table Mountain dominating every view. One of the most spectacular experiences this country has to offer is a chance to witness sunrise from its top, or to watch the blanket of cloud, known as the 'tablecloth', ooze its way over the edge and slowly slide down its sheer walls. The city also has some of the country's most magnificent beaches, as well as a beautiful and vibrant city centre, a lively nightlife and a thriving music scene – not least in the unforgettable Cape Jazz. It is the capital of the South African club scene and has gained the status of being one the great clubbing cities in the world, with a fast-growing reputation for uninhibited hedonism.

Hey, Jo As Cape Town is known for its spectacular backdrop, then it also has to be said that Johannesburg is synonymous with crime and violence. Most people view Jo'burg as an urban nightmare – a crazy mix of Blade Runner and Escape from New York – and a visit here almost carries a government health warning. Much of the hype is just that, however, and those brave, foolish or single-minded souls who spend time in Jo'burg will experience a side of post-apartheid South Africa that is essential to a true appreciation of the country. Jo'burg remains South Africa's financial hub, and is correspondingly hyperactive and full of contradictions. The city centre, once the financial centre, is a now a no-go area with hundreds of hotels and office blocks lying empty or being occupied by squatters. Meanwhile, gentrified suburbs such as Melville are populated by media and arty types who patronize its trendy coffee bars and hip jazz clubs. On the outskirts is the vast residential area of Soweto, which originally stood for South Western Townships, once a hotbed of political struggle and still the best-known of South Africa's segregated areas. Here, kids relate to the newest stars of kwaito, a slow and sexy version of bass-heavy house music.

Every kind of people South Africa is known as the 'Rainbow Nation' and the entire country is a fascinating, and at times bewildering, melting pot of cultures. Every province is unique in terms of language, religion and ethnicity, from the Zulu traditions of KwaZulu Natal, and the Xhosa culture of the Eastern Cape, to the Afrikaaner way of life. This meeting of different cultures is no more apparent than in the cities, which are the most cosmopolitan in all of Africa. The Bo-Kaap district in Cape Town is home to a large Muslim community, its streets lined with spice stalls and the call from mosques filling the air. Durban, the third largest city, is home to the majority of the country's Indian community. At the Victoria Street market, in the colonial heart of Durban, you could be forgiven for thinking you'd taken a wrong turning and ended up in India. Around the mosque are stalls selling spicy curries, exotic spices and colourful silks.

Left *A cool moment in the shade of multi-coloured façades in the Bo-Kaap Malay quarter, Cape Town*
Below *Almost a city – the legendary township of Soweto, breeding ground of political radicalism during apartheid, and now one of South Africa's biggest tourist destinations*
Bottom right *Shiny-new Durban's business district*
Bottom left *Women share a joke at Mbabane market, Swaziland's not-so-seething metropolis*
Next page *Harvesting oranges in Citrusdal, Western Cape*

Essentials

2

18

Essentials

Planning your trip

Where to go

South Africa is arguably one of the most beautiful and varied countries in the world, and as such has more to offer than you could ever see in one trip. The choice of destinations within the country is expanding year by year and it is becoming an increasingly accessible place. South Africa's main attraction is its magnificent natural beauty, represented in a multitude of game reserves and national parks but another major draw is its vibrant cities, resplendent with the cosmopolitan populations you'd expect from the Rainbow Nation. Being outdoors is very much a way of life here, be it hiking and surfing, or trying one of the booming adrenaline sports such as bungee jumping and whitewater rafting. Its history, too, is fascinating and there are numerous historical towns, townships and battle sites worth visiting. In short, the choice of destinations, activities and itineraries is virtually inexhaustible, so careful planning is needed to make best use of your time.

Although South Africa is still a fairly new destination for international travellers, tourism has become a major boom industry in recent years. It is developing fast, and in general you will find the facilities, food and hotels similar to those in Europe or the US. A wide range of travel options is also available. Independent travel is one of the most popular ways of seeing the country and an excellent network of buses, trains and planes. There are also ever-expanding choices of organized tours, taking in the national parks and historical sites, focusing on sports such as scuba diving, or tailored to specific interests such as history or flora and fauna.

South Africa's transport network is one of the best on the continent. Modern highways, efficient trains and internal flights link the main urban centres, while buses connect the larger towns. In more rural areas, however, public transport remains limited to a few buses or trains connecting smaller centres. This is gradually improving, and budget buses such as the *Baz Bus* is opening up some of these areas to travellers. Nevertheless, the best way of getting around is still to hire a car. This gives you a number of freedoms, including exploring more remote areas and having independent access to national parks. Without a vehicle, it is only possible to enjoy safaris and game viewing on an organized tour. Car hire companies have a range of vehicles, from basic hatchbacks and saloon cars, to camper vans and fully equipped four-wheel drives.

Tour ideas
These 5 routes outline some of the most rewarding circuits from South Africa's major cities. All can be completed in 3 weeks or less

Cape Town and the Western Cape The first part of the tour involves a series of day trips from Cape Town, including the drive to the Cape of Good Hope via False Bay. Within **Cape Town** there are numerous historical buildings, beautiful beaches, the botanical gardens of Kirstenbosch, and the famous Constantia wine estate. The best-known wine estates around **Stellenbosch** can be visited on a day trip, although it is worth spending a couple of days here. The second part of the tour involves a drive through contrasting landscapes from the Atlantic to the Indian Ocean. **Langebaan** is by the West Coast National Park, from where the route passes through typical West Coast fishing communities until it reaches **Lambert's Bay**, an important fishing port. The route then turns inland towards the **Olifants River** and follows the valley south to **Clanwilliam** and the rugged **Cederberg mountains** – an excellent hiking region. Continuing south, the road crosses several mountain ranges into the **Tulbagh Valley** and then the **Breede River Valley**, before arriving at the Indian Ocean at **Hermanus**. The coast road back to Cape Town hugs the cliffs and beaches. There is also a worthwhile detour inland to the **Valley of the Huguenots** and Franschhoek, another wine growing region. It is a short drive back into Cape Town from here.

Tour duration: 21 days This route involves a minimal amount of travel with the maximum variety of landscapes

Durban and KwaZulu Natal Starting in **Durban** head north, up the coast road to the upmarket seaside resort of **Umhlanga Rocks**. The route continues along the tropical coast to the **game reserves of Zululand**, and the lakes and beaches at **St Lucia**. Hluhluwe-Umfolozi is home to a large rhino population. Turning inland the route goes via the mountain reserve of **Itala** and on to **Dundee** which is a suitable base for exploring the numerous battlefields and sites relating to the Anglo-Boer War and the Anglo-Zulu War. From **Ladysmith** the route heads

Tour duration: 21 days A circular tour including the principal nature reserves, historical sites and best coastlines in KwaZulu Natal

across the Natal Midlands towards the magnificent mountain chain which forms a natural border with Lesotho – the **Drakensberg**. The Royal Natal Park is the northernmost resort. From here the route follows the foothills southwards, turning into the mountains at Giant's Castle and Underberg. Due to either the lack of roads in the foothills or their poor quality, you often have to return to the main highway between Giant's Castle and Underberg. (At least a day should be spent in **Pietermaritzburg**, a British colonial town.) From Underberg the route leaves the mountains and heads back towards the coast via the small reserve at **Oribi Gorge**. The last segment of the route follows the coast road back to Durban.

Tour duration: 21 days
This tour covers vast distances from one end of South Africa to the other, starting and ending in Pretoria

Wildlife route The nature reserves on this route are regions ranging from typical African lowveld savannah, sub-tropical forests, afro-alpine mountain ranges, to temperate western coastline and the Kalahari desert. The tour starts with **Kruger** where most visitors will spend a couple of days and continues to **Itala**, a mountain reserve with KwaZulu Natal's only herd of tssesebe. **Hluhluwe-Umfolozi** is a world famous reserve for viewing white rhino but it also has large areas of thick riverine forest rich in birdlife. In the **Drakensberg National Park** there is a popular hide at Giant's Castle from where it is possible to view the rare lammergeyer vulture. **Addo** is an excellent park protecting vast herds of Cape elephants. The **Karoo Nature Reserve** is a fascinating area of arid semi-desert inhabited by klipspringers and black eagles, whilst the **Bontebok National Park** has succeeded in bringing this species back from the brink of extinction. The route continues to the **West Coast National Park**, an important bird sanctuary and a base from which to look for whales along this coast. The final stop is at the superb **Kgalagadi Transfrontier Park,** a stunning desert wilderness with a unique ecosystem.

Tour duration: 14 days
This is a shorter tour visiting some of the most popular regions of South Africa

Shorter tour Starting from **Cape Town**, the tour follows the coast along the **Garden Route** stopping off at coastal resorts such as Hermanus, Knysna, George and Tsitsikamma National Park, along the way. Taking an internal flight from Port Elizabeth to **Johannesburg**, the tour then moves into **Mpumalanga. Kruger** is South Africa's premier wildlife destination and it is worth spending a couple of days here. The route then passes through the mountain scenery of the **Eastern Drakensberg** stopping off at **Blyde River Canyon**, one of the deepest canyons in the world. Finally, the tour visits the historic towns of **Pilgrim's Rest** and **Barberton**, two of the most interesting gold rush towns of the region. From here the tour returns to **Johannesburg**.

Tour duration: 2 months
This route is for travellers who want to see more unusual and isolated destinations, as well as the more popular tourist resorts

Grand tour Starting in **Cape Town**, the route heads north up the west coast after visiting the **Winelands**. It then crosses the northern desert region between **Springbok** and **Upington** before heading inland to the historical towns of **Kimberley** and **Bloemfontein**. The route crosses Lesotho from **Maseru** to **Sani Pass**, from where it is possible to visit the **Drakensberg** mountains, though this section is only suitable in a 4 wheel drive vehicle. **Pietermaritzburg** and **Durban** are KwaZulu Natal's main towns. Heading north from Durban the route visits game reserves in **Zululand** and **Maputaland** before crossing **Swaziland**. The gold rush town of **Barberton** is the first stop in Mpumalanga before visiting the mountain resorts at **Graskop** and the **Blyde River Canyon**. Entering the Kruger National Park via the **Phalaborwa Gate** opens up possibilities of seeing less frequently visited areas of the park by heading north to **Punda Maria**. After Kruger the route heads west to **Louis Trichardt** from where it is possible either to travel into Zimbabwe or to continue with the route south through the Limpopo (Northern) Province before exploring a bit of the Northwest: **Sun City** and the **Magaliesberg Mountains**. From **Pretoria** continue south towards the **Eastern Highlands** and **Golden Gate National** Park in Free State. The route circles Lesotho visiting **Rhodes**, one of South Africa's few ski resorts and **Port St Johns**, a relaxed seaside town in the Transkei. The route then follows the N2 down to **Grahamstown** before heading inland to historic **Cradock** and **Graaff-Reinet**. The journey from here to **Knysna** crosses a fabulous semi-desert **Karoo** landscape before ending up at the Garden Route. There are options here of travelling east or west along the Garden Route. The route finishes with visits to **Oudtshoorn**, the Cape Dutch town of **Swellendam** and then follows the coast through **Cape Agulhas** and **Hermanus** back to Cape Town.

When to go

South Africa isn't a destination that has one prime season for visitors. As a country in the southern hemisphere the seasons are in reverse for visitors from Europe and the US, with the coldest weather occurring during the European summer. In spite of this, winter weather from June to September is sunny and warm during the day, though temperatures can drop below freezing at night in the Cape and the Karoo. Snow does fall on the higher mountain peaks. Summer weather, particularly between December and February tends to be hot and humid, this is also when most of the rain falls.

The best times of the year for **game viewing** are during the winter months when vegetation cover is at a minimum and a lack of water forces animals to congregate around rivers and waterholes. Winter is also the best time of year for hiking, avoiding the high temperatures and frequent thunderstorms of the summer months.

The coast around **Cape Town and the Garden Route** is at its best during the spring and summer months. Whales can be spotted between July and November, and although July is the best month for surfing in Jeffreys Bay, further down the coast at Chapman's Bay near Cape Town the waves are good for surfing throughout the summer. One major disadvantage of visiting during the summer is that much of the holiday accommodation is fully booked months in advance for the Christmas holidays, and the coastal towns become horribly overcrowded.

Avoid the popular tourist sites between the middle of December and the middle of January or book accommodation well in advance

If you are travelling from Europe, there are two peak periods: around Christmas, and between July and September. During these periods **air tickets** are more expensive and it is necessary to book your flight at least three months in advance.

It may seem trivial, but the dates of local school holidays can have a significant bearing on your visit. During local holidays the price of accommodation can increase by more than 50%, but of greater concern is the actual availability of rooms. In the most popular destinations, such as Cape Town and the Garden Route, there simply won't be anywhere to stay if you have not made an advance booking. This also applies to national parks accommodation.

*School holidays
The dates below are for the school terms for 2003, not holidays*

Western Cape, Northern Cape, Eastern Cape and KwaZulu Natal 1st term: 22 January-28 March; 2nd term: 8 April-27 June; 3rd term: 21 July-26 September; 4th term: 6 October-5 December.

Gauteng, Free State, Northern Province, Mpumalanga and Northwest Province 1st term: 15 January-22 March; 2nd term: 7 April-20 June; 3rd term: 14 July-19 September; 4th term: 1 October-5 December.

From a weather point of view, the best time to visit rather depends on what conditions you prefer. In the summer, parts of the Northern Cape experience temperatures in the region of 45°C – too hot for most people, and unsafe for hiking. The Western and Eastern Capes rarely get hotter than 30°C, while Gauteng and KwaZulu Natal get very humid. During August and September it can get quite cold in Cape Town at night, with frosts and snowfalls on the higher mountain peaks, while this is the best time to visit the northern desert areas around Upington and the Kalahari. Check the climatic charts within the text for the different rain seasons, but as a general rule it gets progressively drier the further west you travel from the Durban coast. Most of the rain falls in the summer months, although the Cape can remain dry for most of the summer. When it does rain, there are often very heavy storms, wherever you are in the country. If driving in these conditions, you should slow down and pull over if the rain gets too heavy. Also be on the lookout for flash floods, especially if camping. In the interior, the summers are hot and wet; winters are cool with clear sunny days. The best time to visit the game parks, including Kruger, is between May and August. It is not too hot then and because of the dry conditions animals are more easily spotted by the waterholes. During the summer months, October-March, you can expect the average daytime temperature in Kruger National Park to be around the 30°C (86°F) mark. You will only come across truly tropical conditions in the northeast corner of KwaZulu Natal around Kosi Bay and the border with Mozambique.

*Climate
South African Weather Service: T082162
www.weathersa.co.za*

Essentials

Tour operators

In the UK
& Ireland

Abercrombie & Kent, Sloane Square House, Holbein Place, London, SW1W 8NS, T0845-0700610, F0845-0700607, www.abercrombiekent.co.za **Africa Travel Centre**, 21 Leigh St, London, WC1H 9QV, T020-3871211, www.africatravel.co.uk **Cape Tours**, 10 Christian Court, Willen, Milton Keynes, MK15 9HX, T01908-679377, F231362, www.capetours.co.za **Cedarberg Travel**,16A High St, Hampton, Middlesex, TW12 2SJ, T020-8941 1717, F9793893, www.cedarberg-travel.com **Comet Travel**, 21 Newman St, London, W1P 4DD, T020-73234545, F6363907. **Discovery Initiatives**, 51 Castle St, Cirencester, Glos, GL7 1QD, T01285-643333, F01285-885888.

 Executive Travel, Jefferson House, Elington Rd, Donnybrook, Dublin 4, T00-3531-2697488, F2838404. **Gold Medal Travel**, Gold Medal House, Metropolitan Dr, Blackpool, Lancs, FY3 9LT, T01253-792200, F791333, www.goldmedal.co.uk **Jetset Holidays**, Amadeus House, 52 George St, Manchester, M1 4HF, T0161-9530920, F2366693. **Kuoni Travel**, Kuoni House, Dorking, Surrey, RH5 4AZ, T01306-747002, F744683, www.kuoni.co.uk **Okavango Tours & Safaris**, Malborough House, 298 Regents Park Rd, London, N3 2TJ, T020-83433283, F83433287, www.okavango.com

 SAA Holidays, Sandrocks, Rocky Lane, Haywards Heath, West Sussex, RH16 4RH, T0870-4443552, F0870-2400321. **Saga Holidays**, Saga Building, Middleburg Sq, Folkestone, Kent, CT20 1AZ, T01303-711111, F776866, holidays.saga.co.uk **Scotia Air Holidays**, 57 Bothwell St, Glasgow, G2 6RF, T0141-3055050, F3055051, www.scotiatravel.com **South Africa Affair**, George House, 5/7 Humbolt Rd, London, W6 8QH, T020-73815222, F73813919 . **STA Travel**, National call centre, T0870-1600599, www.statravel.co.uk 50 branches in the UK. **Steppes Africa**, 51 Castle St, Cirencester, Glos, GL7 1QD, T01285-650011, www.steppesafrica.co.uk Tailormade tours and safaris. **Sunvil Discovery**, Sunvil House, Upper Square, Old Isleworth, Middlesex, TW7 4BJ, T020-82329777,

F85688330, www.sunvil.co.uk/africa *Superlative Travel*, 43 Woodhurst Rd, London W3 655, T020-74834300, F74833600. *Tana Travel*, 2 Ely St, Stratford-upon-Avon, CV37 6LW, T01789-414200, F414420, www.tana-travel.demon. co.uk *Tim Best Travel*, 68 Old Brompton Rd, London, SW7 3LQ, T020-75910300, F75910301, www.timbesttravel.com *Trailfinders*, 194 Kensington High St, London, W8 7RG, T020-79383939, www.trailfinders. co.uk *Travel Hewetts*, 31 Exchequer St, Dublin 2, Ireland, T0035-31-6770446, F6775168. *Twohigs Travel*, 8 Burgh Quay, Dublin 2, Ireland, T0035-31-6772666, F6772691, info@twohigs.ie

Union Castle *Travel*, 86/87 Campden St, Kensington, London, W8 7EN, T020-72291411, F72291511, info@u-ct.co.uk Specialists in tailor-made luxury tours. *Virgin Holidays*, The Galleria, Station Rd, Crawley, RH10 1WW, T0870-2202788, F536957, www.virginholidays.co.uk *Wild Africa Safaris*, Mauritius House, 1 Portsmouth Rd, Guildford, Surrey, GU2 5BL, www.wildafricasafaris.co.uk *Worldwide Journeys & Expeditions*, 27 Vanston Pl, London SW6 1AZ, T020-73864646, F73810836, www.worldwidejourneys.co.uk

Airtrack Adventures, PO Box 630, Muldersdrift 1747, T011-9572322, F9572465. Hot air balloon *In South Africa* flights over the Kalahari. *Baz Bus Tours*, 8 Rosedene Road, Sea Point, Cape Town, T021-4392323, F4392343, www.bazbus.com The budget bus company recently started organizing good value Cape Peninsula tours from Cape Town. *The Blue Train*, PO Box 2671, Joubert Park, 2044, T012-3348459, F3348464, www.bluetrain.co.za The original luxury train with a reputation for fine food. Now operating on several routes each month. *The Bundu Bus* T011-6750767, www.bundusafaris.co.za Kruger National Park Tours. *Capital Travels* T00268-44143, Swazi Plaza, Mbabane, Swaziland. *Calabash Tours*, 8 Dollery St, Central, T041-5856162, calabash@iafrica.com Tours from Port Elizabeth to Addo Elephant Park and Shamwari Game Reserve. *Day Trippers*, 8 Pineway, Pinelands, Cape Town, T021-5313274, T082-8079522 (mob), www.daytrippers.co.za *Drifters* PO Box 48434, Roosevelt Park 2129, T011-8881160, F8881020. *Durban Africa*, Station Building, 160 Pine St, Durban, T031-3044934, F3043868, www.durbanexperience.co.za, www.bookabedahead.co.za Useful and informative contacts when planning a trip to KwaZulu Natal. *Expeditionary Force*, T012-6672833, historical tours of Johannesburg and Pretoria. *Gold Reef Guides*, T011-4961400, tours of Soweto and Gold Reef City. *Far & Wild Safaris*, 477 Essenwood Rd, Morningside, Durban, T031-2083684, F2074700. Hluhluwe and Umfolozi tours. *Face Afrika Tours*, 104 Burger St, PO Box 245, Louis Trichardt, 0920. T/F015-5162076, facaf@mweb.co.za The best option for anyone keen to explore the Limpopo (Northern) Province. Chris Olivier, who is part of the team, is an expert on tourism throughout the province and a board member of The Limpopo Province Tourism Board. *Greencape Tours*, T/F021-7970166. *Intaba Tours*, T031-866831, F7771405. Day tours around Durban. *Kalahari Adventure Centre*, T054-4510177, www.kalahari.co.za Based close to the Augrabies Falls, offer range of rafting trips and tours to the Khalagadi Transfrontier Park. *Kalahari Junction*, 3 Oranje St, T082-4350007 (mob). Budget tours to the Khalagadi Transfrontier Park, Augrabies Falls and rafting on the Orange River. *Karabo Tours*, T/F011-8805099, karabotours@iafrica.com Affordable in-depth tours around Johannes- burg, Soweto, and Pretoria. Comprehensive website, www.backpackinafrica.com, for all budget travel in Southern Africa right the way up to Nairobi. Any budget traveller is well-advised to check out the website when planning a trip to South Africa. *Legend Tours*, Sea Point, Cape Town, T021-4480625, legend@kingsley.co.za

Pride of Africa, T012-3158258, F3230843, www.rovos.co.za Luxury train between Pretoria and Cape Town (48 hrs) with side excursions in the Karoo, or Pretoria to Durban (55 hrs) stopping for a game drive in Kruger. *Quagga Tours*, 10 Queen Rd, Rondebosch, T/F021-4612231. *Strelitzia Tours* 23 Serpentine Dr, Westville, T031-2669480, 861904, F2669404. Battlefield tours. A comprehensive range of tours in KwaZulu Natal from 1-3 days. *Swazi Trails*, Mantenga Craft Centre, PO Box 2197, Mbabane, Swaziland, T268-4162180, F4161040, tours@swazitrails.co.sz From South Africa phone T011-7041975 for a free international connection. A local tour operator specializing in culture, wildlife and adventure tours throughout Swaziland. All the guides are local Swazis with plenty of knowledge and enthusiasm. *Tekweni Ecotours*, 169 9th Av, Morningside, Durban, T031-3031199, F3094369. Durban's alternative tour operator catering for backpackers. Hluhluwe, Umfolozi and St Lucia game parks, cultural day and overnight trips to Zululand.

Essentials

South African Tourism offices

Head Office *442 Rigel Av South, Erasmusrand 0181, Private Bag X164, Pretoria 0001, T012-3470600, F012-454889.*

Overseas offices

Australia and New Zealand *Level 6, 285 Clarence St, Sydney 2000 NSW, T02-2613424, F2613414.*

Austria *Stefan-Zweig-Platz 11, A-1170, Vienna, T1-47045110, F47045114.*

Benelux Countries *Josef Isrëlskade 48, Postbus 75360, 1070 AJ, Amsterdam, Netherlands, T20-6646201, F6629761.*

Canada *Suite 2, 4117 Lawrence Av East, Scarborough, Ontario, M1E 2S2, T416-2830563, F2835465.*

France *61 rue La Boëtie, 75008 Paris, T01-45610197, F45610196.*

Germany *Alemannia Haus, An der Hauptwache 11, D-60313 Frankfurt/Main 1, Postfach 101940, Frankfurt 60019, T69-9291290, F280950 and Rhein Str 80, 65795 Hattersheim, T06190-71107.*

Israel *14th Flr, Century Towers, 124 Ibn Gvirol St, PO Box 3388, Tel Aviv 61033, T3-5272054, F5271958.*

Italy *Via Durini 24, 20122 Milan, T2-794100, F794601.*

Japan *2nd Flr, Akasaka Lions Building, 1-1-2 Moto Akasaka, Minato-ku, Tokyo 107, T3-3 4787601, F3 4787605.*

Switzerland *Seestrasse 42, CH 8802, Kilchberg, Zurich, T1-7151815, F7151889.*

UK *5-6 Alt Grove, Wimbledon, London, SW19 4DZ, T020-8944 8080, F8944 6705; 24-hour brochure request, T0541-550044.*

USA (Eastern) *500 Fifth Av, 20th Flr, Suite 2040, New York NY 10110, T212-7302929, F7641980.* **(Western)** *Suite 1524, 9841 Airport Blvd, Los Angeles, CA 90045, California, T310-6418444, F6415812.*

Zimbabwe *Offices 9 and 10, Mon Repos Building, Newlands Shopping Centre, Harare, PO Box H9 1000, Highlands, T4-707766, F786489.*

Union Limited Steam Rail Tours, Spoornet Building, 1 Adderley St, T021-4494391, F4494395. Luxury travel on beautifully restored steam trains, most popular route is to Knysna via the Winelands (6 days from US$600 fully inclusive), longer tours are also organized to Pretoria, good standards of service and food, the ultimate treat. *Ventures for Africa*, PO Box 3005, Cresta 2118, T011-4768842, F4761437. Professionally organized hiking tours. *Wilderness Safaris*, PO Box 5219, Rivonia 2128, T011-8071800, F8072110, enquiry@wilderness.co.za An excellent company with some of the best luxury bush camps in South Africa.

Special interest operators
Camping and overlanding *Exodus Expeditions* 9 Weir Rd, London SW12 0LT, T020- 8675 5550, www.exodustravels.co.uk *Guerba Expeditions*, Wessex House, 40 Station Rd, Westbury, Wiltshire BA13 3JN, T01373-826611, F858351, www.guerba.com *Holts Tours*, Golden Key Building, The Plough, High St, Eastry, 15 Market St, Sandwich, Kent CT13 9DA, T01304-612248, F614930. *Sunway Safaris*, T/F8037400. Small group budget overland and camping tours in minibuses, 17 days Johannesburg to Cape Town via Kruger, Swaziland, Drakensberg, Garden Route, from US$995 per person. *Trek International Travel*, 4 Waterperry Court, Middleton Rd, Banbury, Oxon OX16 8QG, T01295-25677, F257399. *Wagon Trails*, T011-9078063, F9070913, wagon.trails@pixie.co.za Some of the best value camping tours to Kruger for anyone who wants an enjoyable as well as informative trip. Further afield adventure tours to Zimbabwe and Mozambique.

Culture *Prospect Tours*, 454-458 Chiswick High Rd, London, W4 5TT, T020-9952151, F87421969.

Disabled *Epic Enabled*, 14 Clovelly Rd, Fish Hoek, Cape Town, T021-7829575, F021-7829576, www.epic-enabled.com The first of its kind in South Africa, fully modified overland trucks for budget travellers, which take 6 wheelchair passengers and 8 non-wheelchair passengers, hydraulic lift, camp assistants and cooks, utilise wheelchair-friendly accommodation. Eight-day Kruger/Mpumalanga camping tours from US$750. Pam and Jeff Taylor run a company called *Disabled Adventure Tours*, T/F021-5574496, T082-4502031 (mob), flamtour@iafrica.com We suggest you contact them for further advice and recommendations.

Useful words and phrases

amabokaboka *a Xhosa/Zulu version of Springbok – the South African rugby team*

bafanabafana *literally 'our boys', refers to the South African football team*

berg *a mountain*

biltong *strips of sun-dried meat, beef but often game*

boer *literally means a farmer, but these days more often used as a disparaging term when referring to Afrikaners*

boerewors *large, well-seasoned beef and pork sausage, frequently cooked over a braai*

boma *a traditional enclosure for cattle, nowadays frequently used at safari lodges to refer to a sheltered area where guests sit outside*

braai *South African equivalent of a barbecue*

bubalarse *a hangover*

burg *a term referring to a borough*

dorp *a small country settlement where a road crosses a dry river bed, or a ford*

dumela *hello/greetings (in SeSotho)*

egoli *refers to the city of Johannesburg, literally 'place of gold' in Zulu*

fynbos *the rich variety of indigenous vegetation growing in the Western Cape where there is winter rainfall*

kunjani *widely used informal greeting meaning 'how is it' in Zulu*

kloof *gorge or a ravine*

koppie *flat-topped hillock, often used to describe outcrops of granite boulders*

laager *literally a defensive position made by drawing wagons into a circle, now often used to describe a defensive state of mind*

rooinek *literally 'redneck', a disparaging term used to describe English-speaking white South Africans*

sawabona *hello/greetings (in Zulu)*

veld *open grasslands*

vlei *shallow lake or swamp*

Essentials

History *Campfire Adventures*, 31 Grosvenor Road, Shaftesbury, SP7 8DP, T01747-855558, www.campfire.co.uk *Midas Battlefield Tours*, PO Box 376, West Byfleet, Surrey KT14 7FB, T01932-349605, F348967, arooney@midas.itsnet.co.uk *Temple World Tours*, 13 The Avenue, Richmond, Surrey TW9 2AL, T020-89404114, F83322456. Archaeology tours.

Sports *Andante Travel*, The Old Telephone Exchange, Winterbourne Dauntsey, Salisbury, Wiltshire, SP4 6EH, T01980-610555, F610002, andante-travels@virgin.net *Sport Abroad*, Deep Dene Lodge, Dorking, Surrey, RH5 4AZ, T01306-744345, F744380. *Teamsports International*, Enterprise Generation Centre, Dane St, Rochdale, Lancashire, OL12 6XB, T01706-715808, F715984.

Wildlife *Discover The World*, 29 Nork Way, Banstead, Surrey, SM7 1PB, T01737-218800, F362341. *Wild Africa Safaris*, Mauritius House, 1 Portsmouth Road, Guildford, Surrey, GU2 5BL, T01483-453731, F532820, was@bctuk.demon.co.uk

Wine tasting and hiking *Wine Trails*, Greenways, Vann Lake, Ockley, Dorking RH5 5NT, T01306-712111, F713504.

Africa Collection, 15 Station Road, Horsham, West Sussex, RH13 5EZ, T01403-256655, F253325, www.africacollection.com. *Africa Exclusive*, 66 Palmerston Rd, Northampton, Northamptonshire NN1 5EX, T01604-628979, F639879, africa@africaexclusive.co.uk *African Ethos*, 15 Station Road, Horsham, West Sussex, RH13 5EZ, T01403-243619, F217558, www.africanethos.com Sabi Sabi Private Game Reserve, Blue Train (South Africa), *Garonga Safari Camp*, *Legacy Hotels and Resorts*, *South African National Parks* and *Tourism KwaZulu Natal*. *KAI (Kartagener Associates)*, 631 Commack Rd, Commack, New York, 11725, United States, T212-4650619, F212-2688299, Kainyc@worldnet.att.net Sabi Sabi Reserve. *South Africa Travel*, 6 Pioneer Business Park, Amy Johnson Way, York, YO30 4TN, T01904-692469, F691340.

International representatives for major South African hotels & game reserves

Finding out more

South African Tourism, has a useful website, www.southafrica.net, with information on special interest travel, maps, latest news, airlines, accommodation, and national parks. Regional tourist boards include: *Gauteng Tourism Authority*, Rosebank Mall, Johannesburg, T011-3272000,

Tourist boards

F3277000, tourism@gauteng.net *Mpumalanga Tourism Authority*, PO Box 679, Nelspruit 1200, T013-7527001, F7595441, www.mpumlanga.com; *Tourism KwaZulu Natal*, PO Box 2516, Durban 4000, T031-3047144, F3056693, www.zulu.org.za; *Western Cape Tourism Board*, PO Box 3878, Tyger Valley 7536, T021-9144613, F9144610, www.wcapetourism.co.za; *Eastern Cape Tourism*, T043-7439511, www.ectourism.co.za; *Northern Cape Tourism Authority*, Private Bag X5017, Kimberley 8300, T053-8322657, www.northerncape.org.za; *North West Parks and Tourism Board*, Military Village, Khupe Complex, Mmabatho, North West Province, T018-3861225-9, F3861158, www. tourismnorthwest.co.za *Northern/Limpopo Province Tourism Board*, PO Box 1309, Pietersburg 0700, T015-2880099, F2880094, www.tourismboard.org.za *Trans Gariep Tourism*, 60 Park Rd, PO Box 639, Bloemfontein, T051-4471362, F4471363, www.fstourism.co.za. This is the regional office for the Free State.

Other useful websites

www.durbanexperience.com This is a useful site for information about Durban and the surrounding region. Hotel and travel details as well as background information.

www.gardenroute.co.za A large site covering one of the most popular tourism regions in South Africa. Unfortunately many of the pages are incomplete. In addition to tourist information you can find out more about the local news plus local business contacts.

www.capeoverberg.co.za The Overberg is a region of the Western Cape. In addition to the usual tourist information you will find details about whale watching and wine regions.

www.putumayo.com Interesting information on South Africa's music scene.

Language

See the guide to slang: www.southafrica.net See also Useful words and phrases box

There are 11 official languages in South Africa: **English, Zulu, Xhosa, Afrikaans, Venda, Swazi, North Sotho, South Sotho, Tswana, Sindebele** and **Shangaan**. English is widely spoken and understood, but it is always a good idea to learn at least a couple of basic phrases in the predominant language of the area that you're travelling in – a simple 'hello' in Xhosa or 'thank you' in Afrikaans can go a long way. There are a few pockets where only Afrikaans is spoken, but people should understand enough English to meet your needs. Having said that, don't be surprised to find white South Africans in the Northern Cape or Northern Province who can barely speak English. Afrikaans is spoken by 60% of the white South Africans, along with the majority of coloured people in the Cape. In addition to this, there are six Asian languages spoken, mostly in KwaZulu Natal. One consequence of having 11 official languages has been a significant reduction in the number of hours of Afrikaans broadcast on television, with a rise in other languages broadcast, particularly Zulu and Xhosa.

Disabled travellers

See also listings under specialist tour operators, page 24

Although the concept of disabled access to museums, hotels and restaurants only recently began to have any significance, things are developing fairly quickly, and a number of guesthouses advertise if their facilities have wheelchair access. Some tourist attractions have been developed for disabled visitors, such as the Braille trail at Kirstenbosch Botanical Gardens, or the easily accessible cable car to the top of Table Mountain. The fact that South Africa is a very car-friendly country should make getting to the major sites no problem and most places have disabled parking right by the entrance. Game parks should also not prove too difficult, although park accommodation and ablution facilities are rarely wheelchair-friendly. Pam and Jeff Taylor run a company called *Disabled Adventure Tours*, T/F021-5574496, T082-4502031 (mob), flamtour@iafrica.com We suggest you contact them for further advice and recommendations.

Gay and lesbian travellers

While homosexuality is not illegal in South Africa, the country lags some way behind Europe in its attitude towards gay and lesbian people. This is a deeply conservative society and overtly affectionate behaviour between gay and lesbian couples may elicit a strong,

South African embassies and consulates

Australia *8 Light House, Sydney 2001, NSW, T02-2338188 and Rhodes Pl, Yarralumla, Canberra ACT 2600, T06-2732424.*

Canada *15 Sussex Dr, Ottawa K1M IM8, T613-7440330 and Suite 2615, 1 Place Ville Marie, Montreal, H3B 4S3, T513-8789217, T8784715.*

Denmark *Gammel Vartov VEJ, No 8, 2900 Hellerup, Copenhagen, T031-180155, F184006.*

Finland *Rahapajankatu 1 A5, 00160, Helsinki, T09-68603100, F68603160.*

France *59 Quai d'Orsay, Paris 75007, T1-53592323.*

Germany *4th Floor, Atrium Building, Friedrichstrasse 60, D-10117 Berlin-Mitte, T30-22073-0, F22073208*

Republic of Ireland *Alexander House, Earlsford Centre, Earlsford Terrace, Dublin 2, T1-6615553, F6615590.*

Israel *Yakhin House, 2 Kaplan St, Tel Aviv 64734, T03-5252566.*

Malawi *Mpico Building, City Centre, Lilongwe 3, T09265-733722.*

Netherlands *36 Wassenaarseweg 2596 CJ, The Hague, T070-3105920.*

Norway *Drammensveren 88c, 0205 Oslo, T022-447910, F443975.*

Spain *Edificio Lista, Calle de Claudio Coello 91, 28006 Madrid, T91-4363780, F5777414.*

Sweden *Linngatan 76, 11523 Stockholm, T08-243950, F6607136.*

Switzerland *Alpenstrasse 29, 3006 Bern, T31-3501313.*

UK *South Africa House, Trafalgar Square, London, WC2N 5DP, T020-70304488, 74517229, F74517284.*

US *3051 Massachusetts Av NW, Washington, DC 20008, T1-202-2324400; there are consulates in Beverley Hills, Chicago and New York.*

Zimbabwe *Temple Bar House, Baker Av, Harare, T04-753150.*

disapproving response, particularly in more remote rural parts. Conversely, there is a flourishing gay scene in Cape Town, where attitudes are more progressive – it is the self-proclaimed 'Gay Capital' of Africa, and an annual Mardi Gras is planned here in the future. A 'Pink Map' of the city is available from the tourist offices.

Student travellers

Anyone in full-time education is entitled to an International Student Identity Card (ISIC). These are issued by student travel offices and travel agencies across the world, and offer special rates on all forms of transport and other concessions and services. The ISIC head office is: ISIC Association, Box 9048, 1000 Copenhagen, Denmark, T45-33939300.

See also page 22, for student tour operators

Women travellers

Aside from unwanted attention from groups of men, South Africa is a relatively safe country for women to travel in. You should not be faced with prejudice when checking into hotels and trying to be served, but it is worth remembering that amongst most communities in South Africa there is a strong macho element. It is often a good idea to cover up in more remote, rural areas – avoiding revealing tops and short skirts should do it.

Before you travel

Getting in

All visitors are issued with a 90-day tourist visa. If you exit to Lesotho or Swaziland you will NOT be issued with a new visa when you re-enter South Africa. **NB** Going to Lesotho or Swaziland and returning to South Africa is not a way to extend your holiday visa. On re entering, South African immigration will scan your original South African entry stamp, on

Visas & immigration

Essentials

which the given date of departure is still valid despite your having left the country for a while. If the date of departure from South Africa has expired whilst you are in Lesotho or Swaziland, South African immigration will extend your visa for between 2-4 weeks, during which time you are expected either to depart or to extend your visa at one of the Home Affairs offices in the major cities. An extension to a holiday visa takes up to 3 weeks and costs (R390). Expect lengthy queues and general disarray at Home Affairs offices and you will need to produce documentation to show when you are leaving the country, such as a flight ticket or tour confirmation voucher, as well as proof of funds. A credit card will usually suffice. *Department of Home Affairs* (visa extensions and information): Cape Town, T021-4624970; Durban, T031-3062740; Johannesburg, T011-8363228; Pretoria, T012-3268081.

Customs & duty free The official customs allowance for visitors over 18 years includes 400 cigarettes, 50 cigars, 250 g of tobacco, two litres of wine, one litre of spirit, 50 ml of perfume and 250 ml of toilet water. Tourists can bring in all personal effects without charge as well as duty-free gifts and souvenirs to the total value of R500. For further information from **Customs and Excise** (Johannesburg International Airport), T011-9759308; Cape Town airport, T021-9340222.

There are extensive duty free shops at Johannesburg, Durban and Cape Town international airports and there are small duty free cabins at most of the major border crossings with Zimbabwe, Mozambique and Botswana, which sell spirits, wines and electrical goods, though the choice is fairly limited and opening times erratic.

Export restrictions CITES The CITES Convention was established to prevent trade in endangered species. Attempts to smuggle controlled products in to countries which are signatories to the convention can result in confiscation, fines and imprisonment. International trade in elephant ivory, sea turtle products and the skins of wild cats such as the leopard is illegal. Restrictions have been imposed on the trade in reptile skins, coral, and certain plants and wild birds. Special import and export permits are available for some products but it is best to check before you buy. The animal products that tourists are most likely to encounter in Southern Africa are ivory, biltong made from antelopes and wallets, shoes, and handbags made from crocodile or snake skins. Many of these products will be freely available for the domestic market; you would not be breaking any laws if you were to buy such an item, but your conscience is your own issue.

Medical preparations
For detailed advice, see page 65; for a basic check list, see page 29

Take out medical insurance including the possibility of medical evacuation by air ambulance to your own country. You should have a dental check-up, obtain a spare glasses prescription and, if you suffer from a longstanding condition such as diabetes, high blood pressure, heart/lung disease or a nervous disorder, arrange for a check-up with your doctor who can at the same time provide you with a letter explaining details of your disability. Check the current practice for malaria prophylaxis (prevention) for the areas you intend to visit.

Vaccinations South Africa requires yellow fever vaccination certificates from travellers who have travelled through the yellow fever zones in Africa or South America. Similarly, even though the unpleasant cholera vaccination is not officially required (nor even recommended by the World Health Organization because its effectiveness is limited) travellers are occasionally asked to produce vaccination certificates if they arrive from cholera endemic areas such as parts of Asia or South America. If you are concerned this may be a problem, but do not want to be given an ineffective vaccine, ask your doctor for a cholera vaccination exemption certificate. The following other vaccinations are recommended: Typhoid (monovalent); Poliomyelitis; Tetanus; Hepatitis A and B. Children should in addition be properly protected against diphtheria, whooping cough, mumps and measles. Teenage girls, if they have not yet had the disease, should be given rubella (german measles) vaccination. Consult your doctor's advice on BCG inoculation against tuberculosis. It is worth remembering that if a vaccination needs renewing during your stay in South Africa, or your travel plans change, there are a number of vaccination clinics in Johannesburg, Cape Town and Durban, where malaria prophlaxis can also be purchased.

What to take

Many visitors are surprised at how cold it can get during the winter months, from May to August. Once the sun goes down you will need a pair of long trousers and a fleece jacket or a thick sweater. Few hotels will have any form of heating, though you can often expect to see log fires in restaurants and lounges. If you are camping during the winter be prepared for frosts; it will freeze most nights in the Karoo and the Drakensberg.

Clothes in general are cheaper in South Africa than in Europe or the US. Locally-made clothes can be real bargains, as can international labels. Remember that during the day, even in winter, the sun will be hot enough to dry any washing within a few hours. For a budget traveller there is no need to pack your rucksack with a different set of clothes for each day.

Sunstroke and sunburn can be a serious problem and a wide-brimmed hat, long sleeved cotton shirt, sunglasses and high-factor sun cream are vital for protection.

Footwear should be as airy as possible for the hot weather; sandals or canvas trainers are ideal. European style leather walking boots can be too heavy for most walks except winter hikes in the Drakensberg. However, if you are planning on hiking for several days a good pair of comfortable boots is essential. Lightweight Goretex boots are so popular that many travellers seem to wear them every day. A good range of South African handmade leather desert boots are sold in sports shops which are great for local conditions, but remember that they will need to be worn in.

Note that not all backpacker hostels include **bedding** and **towels** in the price of a dorm bed, so a towel, cotton sheet and a sleeping bag are recommended for backpackers, though these items can usually be hired for an additional cost. **Mosquito nets** are not generally necessary in towns, but are very useful in wilderness areas, depending on the season, and can be purchased on arrival in South Africa in the many camping shops. Organized safari tours and luxury bush camps usually supply mosquito nets when they are needed.

Air tickets, cash, cheque book, credit cards, passport including visa, passport photographs, photocopies of main documents (keep separate), travellers' cheques, toiletries, comb, concentrated detergent, contact lens solution, deodorant, elastoplast, insect repellent, nailbrush, razor and blades, shampoo, sleeping tablets, soap, sun protection cream, talcum powder, tissues and toilet paper, toothbrush, toothpaste, vaseline/moisturizer.

Other Ear plugs, electric insecticide vapourizer and tablets, electric plug adaptor, folding umbrella, inflatable cushion, multiple outlet adaptor, plastic bags, sewing kit, short-wave radio and batteries, small torch plus batteries, sunglasses, Swiss army knife, traveller's heating jug, water bottle.

Health kit Anti-acid tablets, anti-diarrhoea tablets, anti-malaria tablets, anti-infective ointment, condoms, contraceptives, dusting powder for feet, first aid kit and disposable needles, flea powder, sachets of rehydration salts, tampons, travel sickness pills, water sterilizing tablets.

Clothes
Always take more money and fewer clothes than you think you'll need

All toiletries – medicines, contact lens solution, tampons, condoms, insect repellent and suntan lotion – are widely available from chemists, usually at a fraction of the price you'll pay at home

Checklist

Essentials

Money

The South African currency is the Rand (R) which is divided into 100 cents (c). Notes: R10, R20, R50, R100 and R200. Coins: 1c, 2c, 5c, 10c, 20c, 50c, R1, R2 and R5. **NB** At the time of writing, the South African Mint had announced that they were no longer issuing 1c and 2c coins. You may find that as these coins will be gradually taken out of circulation, and prices will be rounded up to the nearest 5c. The import and export of currency is limited to R1,000 – ensure you keep some receipts for the purpose of reconverting surplus funds at the end of your trip. All currency must be declared on entry.

For long trips it is a good idea to carry your funds in several forms, including travellers' cheques, Rands, credit cards and US dollars or sterling. Don't keep it all in one place! To lessen the harm caused by theft, spread it between your money belt and your luggage.

There is no black market to speak of and visitors are restricted to bringing in R1,000 cash in person. Change any surplus Rand back into your own currency before leaving South

Currency
Moneyline for exchange rates, T0800-111177 See also www.oanda.com US$1 = R10.16 GBP1 = R15.97 Euro 1 - R10.29

Africa. This is a straightforward transaction if completed in the international departure lounge at the airport. There are still some restrictions in place for purchasing foreign exchange, so if you were to try and convert your Rand at a high street bank you would need to produce proof of your initial transaction, and the whole process could take some time. The rates at the airport are very reasonable and it should only take a few minutes to change any unwanted currency.

If you plan on visiting **neighbouring countries**, note that most currencies can only be purchased from within South Africa and not before you leave home. However, Rand can easily be exchanged in these countries on arrival. The Zimbabwe dollar, Malawi kwatcha and Mozambique meticas are not convertible. The Namibian dollar, Lesotho's maloti and Swaziland's lilangeni are all pegged to the South African Rand on a one to one basis. Consequently, Rand is a recognized currency in these countries and can be used equally alongside the local currency. These are, however, not convertible back in South Africa, so ensure you have got rid of the last of the local currency before leaving Swaziland, Lesotho, or Namibia.

ATMs   As long as you have the right type of card and sufficient funds, using an ATM (Automatic Teller Machine) is the most convenient and cheapest way of obtaining funds, assuming your own bank does not charge an excessive fee for foreign ATM transactions.

Nedbank is on the Plus system; *ABSA*, *First National* and *Standard Bank* are on both the Plus and Cirrus systems. ATMs have been installed in most banks, and are available 24 hours a day. You can also use your credit card if you have applied for a PIN. Visa, Mastercard/Eurocard, American Express and Diners' Club are all accepted. The amount you can withdraw varies between systems and cards, but you should be able to take out up to R1,000 on each occasion; full receipts are issued with each withdrawal. **Warning**: theft during or immediately after a withdrawal can be a problem. Never accept a stranger's help with an ATM – nor should you offer help with a transaction if anyone seems to be experiencing problems. Avoid using street side ATMs, rather go into a bank or shopping mall where many banks employ 24-hour guards to watch customers and the machines. Be aware of your surroundings and if you are not comfortable have a friend stand close by or behind you when you make the withdrawal.

Banks &   The following high street banks offer foreign exchange services: *First National*, *Nedbank*,
bureaux de   *Standard*, and *ABSA*. Normal banking hours: Monday-Friday 0900-1530; Saturday 0830/0900
change   to 1030/1100. Some small branches may close for an hour over lunch.

In addition to high street banks, you can change money at branches of *Rennies Travel*, who act as agents for *Thomas Cook*. They have branches in all regional and tourist centres and most shopping malls, and cash Thomas Cook travellers' cheques free of charge.

American Express Foreign Exchange Service have offices in the large cities. They also offer a Poste Restante service to card holders. Johannesburg: Sandton City T011-T8849195; Rosebank T011-8808382; Eastgate T011-6223914; Hyde Park T011-3254424. Pretoria (Brooklyn) T012-3462599. Durban: Pavilion T031-2651455; Musgrave T031-2028733. Port Elizabeth T041-3688000. Cape Town: V&A Waterfront T021-4193917; Thibault Square T021-4089700.

Credit cards   Taking a credit card to South Africa is a sensible option. Not only is it a convenient way to
Always remember   cover major expenses but they offer some of the most competitive exchange rates when
to bring emergency   withdrawing cash from ATMs. They are particularly useful when hiring a car - indeed many
international   companies will only hire a car to foreign visitors if they have a credit card, and if you fill out an
telephone numbers for   open credit slip you will not be faced with the inconvenience of a large cash deposit of
your particular credit   several thousand Rand. Note that credit cards are NOT accepted as payment for petrol, which
card company with   can only be purchased with cash.
you in case of theft

Travellers'   Travellers' cheques can be exchanged at high street banks in most provincial centres. One
cheques   advantage of travellers' cheques is that if they are lost or stolen there is a relatively efficient
system of replacement, which should not cost you anything. Make sure you keep a full record of their numbers and value, and always keep the receipts separate from the cheques. The only drawback with this service is having to collect the replacement cheques, usually only possible in major cities.

Discount flight agents in the UK and Ireland

Council Travel, 28a Poland St, London, W1V 3DB, T020-7437 7767, www.destinations-group.com
The London Flight Centre, 131 Earl's Court Rd, London, SW5 9RH, T020-7244 8000; 47 Notting Hill Gate, London, W11 3JS, T020-7727 4290.
www.topdecktravel.co.uk/flights
STA Travel, central number, T0870-1600599,

www.statravel.co.uk   Have branches in London, as well as in Brighton, Bristol, Cambridge, Leeds, Manchester, Newcastle and Oxford and on many University campuses. Specialists in cheap student/youth flights and tours, and also good for ISIC cards and insurance.
Trailfinders, 194 Kensington High St, London, W8 7RG, T020-7983 3939
www.trailfinders.co.uk

The major disadvantage of travellers' cheques is the time it takes to cash them and the commission charged by the bank. Different branches of the same bank will alter commission rates depending on their distance from major banking centres. Small rural banks that exchange relatively few travellers' cheques will charge a higher commission than busy central banks. Bank charges range between 0.2% and 0.5% commission. The most widely recognized cheques are American Express, Thomas Cook and Visa. US dollars and sterling travellers' cheques can be exchanged at banks throughout the country. Thomas Cook issue South African Rand travellers' cheques. Rand travellers' cheques can be cashed at branches of **Rennies Travel**; no commission is charged. Eurocheques can be cashed at banks.

With the exchange rate as it is, South Africa is excellent value for travellers from Europe or the USA. Even those on a very tight budget will find they can afford to eat out most of the time, while accommodation and transport is generally very reasonable. As a rough guide, backpackers watching their pennies will find they can scrape by on as little as R120 a day. A dorm bed costs from about R70, while a filling meal from a café or fast-food restaurant will set you back about R30. Those with a little more to spend will need between R200-300 per day, including R150-200 for a double room in a guesthouse, and a decent three-course meal with wine rarely costing more than R60. Luxurious boutique hotels or 5-star affairs are markedly more expensive, although by European standards these too are very good value, and even top restaurants in Cape Town or Johannesburg rarely charge more than R150 per person for a three-course meal. The only place that prices can really skyrocket is at private game reserves, where all-inclusive prices per day can be as high as R3,500 per person.

Cost of living

Getting there

Air

There are direct flights to Cape Town and Johannesburg from most European countries, the United States, Australia and neighbouring African states. Until fairly recently most flights arrived in Johannesburg, but these days more carriers fly direct to Cape Town. This is due to the recent rise in Cape Town's popularity, coupled with general security problems in Johannesburg. If you have the choice, it is best to fly into Cape Town and leave via Johannesburg.

South Africa is a very popular destination at the moment, and there is a shortage of flights – during peak periods such as Christmas, flights need to be booked three to four months in advance. Be wary of new airlines – new discount flight companies are repeatedly springing up in the country, only to go bust just months later.

Essentials

 Discount flight agents in North America

Air Brokers International, 323 Geary St, Suite 411, San Francisco, CA94102, T01-800-883 3273, www.airbrokers.com Consolidator and specialist on RTW and Circle Pacific tickets.
Council Travel, 205 E 42nd St, New York, NY 10017, T1-888-COUNCIL, www.counciltravel.com Student/budget agency with branches in many other US cities.
Discount Airfares Worldwide On-Line, www.etn.nl/discount.htm A hub of consolidator and discount agent links.

International Travel Network/Airlines of the Web, www.itn.net/airlines Online air travel information and reservations.
STA Travel, 5900 Wilshire Blvd, Suite 2110, Los Angeles, CA 90036, T1-800-777 0112, www.sta-travel.com Also branches in New York, San Francisco, Boston, Miami, Chicago, Seattle and Washington DC.
Travel CUTS, 187 College St, Toronto, ON, M5T 1P7, T1-800-667 2887, www.travelcuts.com Specialist in student discount fares, Ids and other travel services. Branches in other Canadian cities.

International airports
The three main international airports are at **Cape Town**, **Johannesburg** and **Durban**. An international airport near **Nelspruit** in Mpumalanga is due for completion at the end of 2002, though it is expected to be some time before it features on the international passenger timetable.

From Europe
The cheapest deals are on flights between London and Johannesburg. Although *British Airways* and *South African Airways* are the two main flight operators, competition is increasing and newer operators such as *Virgin* offer some of the cheapest flights to Johannesburg. All of the major European carriers also serve Johannesburg or Cape Town, often at much cheaper prices (although bear in mind that these flights are usually indirect, via another European country).

From North America
South African Airways and *American Airlines* run direct flights from New York to Johannesburg. *South African Airways* also runs directs flight from New York and Atlanta to Cape Town. *Delta Airlines* have a code-sharing agreement with *Air France*. There is a daily non-stop flight between Johannesburg and Paris. This flight connects with Delta's non-stop flights to Atlanta, New York (JFK), Boston, Chicago, LA, San Francisco and Washington.

From Australia & New Zealand
Qantas code shares with *South African Airways*, and between them run flights from Auckland, Melbourne, Perth, and Sydney to Johannesburg. *Malaysia* and *Singapore Airlines* offer the cheapest flights to Johannesburg departing from Melbourne and Sydney, however they do involve a stopover in South East Asia.

From African countries
There are regular flights connecting Harare (Zimbabwe), Lusaka (Zambia), Gabarone (Botswana), Lilongwe (Malawi), Mbabane (Swaziland), Maputo (Mozambique), Maseru (Lesotho) and Windhoek (Namibia) with either Cape Town or Johannesburg.

Road

The Department of Home Affairs in Pretoria can provide up-to-date details of the opening and closing times of border posts, T012-3268081, F3232416

There are good road connections between South Africa and Namibia, Botswana, Mozambique, Lesotho, Swaziland, and Zimbabwe. Long distance bus services, overland trucks and private cars frequently use these routes. If you are crossing in a private car you must be in possession of a registration document, insurance, authority to drive signed by the vehicle's owner, and a driver's licence with a photograph. At quieter border crossings officials can be very inconsistent in their interpretation of the laws.

If driving into Mozambique, make sure there are no defaults on the vehicle and that there are two red warning triangles in the boot. Any minor infringement is likely to result in a high fine. Corruption of the traffic police in Mozambique was notorious but has decreased

Discount flight agents in Australia and New Zealand

Flight Centre, T133133,
www.flightcentre.com.au
Sydney Travel, Reid House Level 8, 75 King
St, Sydney, NSW 2000, T1800 251 911,
www.sydneytravel.com.au
STA Travel, www.statravel.com.au. Australia
head office: 260 Hoddle Street, Abbotsford,

Victoria 3067, T1300-733035. New Zealand
head office: Level 8, 229 Queen St, Auckland,
T0508-782872. Also in major towns and
university campuses.
Travel.com.au, 76 Clarence Street, Sydney
NSW, T02-92495444 (Sydney area), T1300
130 482 (outside Sydney), F02-92623525.

Essentials

dramatically in recent years. However, it does seem to be on the increase in certain parts of South Africa. Particularly in KwaZulu Natal, where police have been known to stop cars with outrageous demands. Road signs have appeared inviting drivers to phone and report incidents of corruption by traffic police. If you do get stopped for a driving offence and asked to pay an on-the-spot fine, insist on getting an official receipt, or even better insist on going to the nearest police station to pay the fine.

The main border crossings between Botswana and South Africa are at: **Pioneer Gate**, open **From Botswana** 0700-2000; **Ramatlabana**, open 0700-2000; and **Tlokweng Gate,** open 0700-2200. The crossing is usually swift and efficient. The R505 from Tlokweng connects with the R27 at Zeerust heading towards Johannesburg. From Ramatlabana there is a road leading to Mafeking which connects with the R52 to Johannesburg.

The main border crossings between Lesotho and South Africa are at **Maseru Bridge**, open 24 **From Lesotho** hours, **Maputsoe Bridge**, open 24 hours, and **Calendonspoort**, open 0600-2200. There are several others such as **Sani Pass** and **Qachas Nek**, that are only open for limited periods and can only be crossed by 4-wheel drive, horse, or on foot.

Trains and buses run from Maputo to Johannesburg via **Komatipoort** and Nelspruit. Trains **From** running between Maputo and Johannesburg transport huge numbers of migrant workers **Mozambique** employed as miners around Gauteng. Luckily the lengthy customs and immigration formalities don't affect most tourists, who are dealt with separately. Visas for Mozambique are now available at the border. *Translux* (see page 42) run a regular coach service between Maputo and Johannesburg via Nelspruit. The journey by road between South Africa and Maputo has recently improved due to the completion of the section of toll road between Nelspruit and Maputo. Travelling time has been reduced dramatically and facilities at the border improved.

The three main frontier posts between Namibia and South Africa are at **Rietfontein**, **From Namibia** **Ariamsvlei**, and **Vioolsdrift**; all are open 24 hours. *Intercape* buses (see page 42) run from Windhoek and Keetmanshoop to Cape Town and Upington.

The main frontier posts between South Africa and Swaziland are at **Ngwenya/Oshoek**, open **From Swaziland** 0700-2200, **Lavumisa**, open 0700-2200, and **Mahamba**, open 0700-2200. The R38 heads from Oshoek to Johannesburg via Carolina and the N4.

The only border crossing between Zimbabwe and South Africa is at **Beitbridge**, open **From** 0530-2230, 24 hours over the Christmas and Easter holiday period. Train and bus services **Zimbabwe** run to Johannesburg from Victoria Falls, Bulawayo and Harare. The border crossing at Beitbridge is notoriously slow during peak periods, long queues and thorough searches by customs take time so expect to spend at least two hours completing border formalities. A customs declaration form will be given to you on which you are required to list all the possessions in your luggage and their estimated value, customs officials concentrate their efforts on local traders smuggling food, clothes and electrical goods from South Africa. As well as your passport, your onward ticket and travellers' cheques may well be inspected. At

Touching down

Business hours Banks: *Monday-Friday 0900-1530, Saturday 0830/0900 to 1030/1100.*
Businesses: *Monday-Friday 0830-1700, Saturday 0830-1400.*
Government offices: *Monday-Friday 0830-1630. Most shut for lunch between 1300-1400.*
Post offices: *weekdays 0830-1600, Saturday 0800-1200. Minor branches have slightly shorter hours.* **International postage**: *postcards to all countries 90c. Stamps can occasionally be bought at CNA stationers, petrol stations and supermarkets, but this has yet to really catch on.*
Shops and supermarkets: *Monday-Friday 0800-1800, Saturday 0800-1300, Sunday 0900-1300. The principal supermarket chains are* **Pick 'n' Pay**, *Monday-Friday 0800-1800, Saturday 0800-1300, the larger branches are open 0900-1300 on Sunday.* **Woolworths**, *Monday-Friday 0900-1700, Saturday 0800-1300, Sunday 0900-1400.* **Shoprite Checkers**, *Monday-Friday*

0900-1800, Saturday 0800-1700, Sunday 0900-1300. **Hyperama**, *Monday-Thursday 0900-1700, Friday 0900-1800, Saturday 0800-1600.* **OK Bazaars**, *Monday-Friday 0830-1700, Saturday 0830-1300, Sunday 0900-1300.*
IDD code *27*
Official time *Despite its size, South Africa only has one time zone: GMT +2 hours, 7 hours ahead of Eastern (USA) Standard Time, 1 hour ahead of Europe; 8 hours behind Australian Eastern Standard Time. There is no daylight saving.*
Useful numbers *International telephone enquiries: T1025; Local telephone enquiries: T1023*
Voltage *220/230 volts AC at 50 Hz, except for Pretoria, where it is 250 volts AC. Most plugs and appliances are 3-point round-pin (one 10 mm and two 8 mm prongs). Hotels usually have two round-pin sockets for razors and hairdryers.*
Weights and measures *The metric system is used.*

present Zimbabwe customs insist upon detaining the long distance bus services for a full baggage check, this affects *Greyhound, Translux* and *Blue Arrow* services. Unfortunately there is usually someone trying to smuggle something and the bus will be further detained while the individual negotiates with customs about how much to pay. Under Zimbabwe's present political climate, do not state your occupation as a journalist or any job involved in the media.

Touching down

Airport information

For tourist information, see page 25 and under each individual town
The three international airports in South Africa are at Cape Town, Johannesburg and Durban. For details on airport facilities, see under those destinations on pages 74, 515 and 386 respecitvely, or visit www.airports.co.za All departure taxes are included in flight tickets.

Local laws and customs

Clothes South African fashions are basically exactly the same as Europe and the US. Day wear tends to be casual and most people on holiday wear shorts, sandals and a T-shirt. If you intend to do any game viewing, clothes in green, muted browns and khaki colours are best. While most restaurants are casual, some have dress codes where sandals, vest and shorts are not appreciated after 1800. In general, bars and restaurants in the major cities are very relaxed, but in more provincial towns it might be a good idea to wear formal clothes. Long trousers, shirts and a good pair of leather shoes will do; only the smartest restaurants will expect jackets. Note that most nightclubs countrywide have dress codes (in particular, no trainers).

How big is your footprint?

The point of a holiday is, of course, to have a good time, but if it's relatively guilt-free as well, that's even better. Perfect eco-tourism would ensure a good living for local inhabitants while not detracting from their traditional lifestyles, encroaching on their customs or spoiling their environment. Perfect ecotourism probably doesn't exist, but everyone can play their part. Here are a few points worth bearing in mind:

■ *Think about where your money goes, and be fair and realistic about how cheaply you travel. Try and put money into local people's hands; drink local beer or fruit juice rather than imported brands and stay in locally owned accommodation wherever possible*

■ *Haggle with humour and not aggressively. Remember that you are likely to be much wealthier than the person you're buying from*

■ *Think about what happens to your rubbish. Take biodegradable products and a water bottle filter. Be sensitive to limited resources like water, fuel and electricity*

■ *Help preserve local wildlife and habitats by respecting rules and regulations, such as sticking to footpaths, not standing on coral and not buying products made from endangered plants or animals*

■ *Don't treat people as part of the landscape, they may not want their picture taken. Ask first and respect their wishes*

■ *Learn the local language and be mindful of local customs and norms. It can enhance your travel experience and you'll earn respect and be more readily welcomed by local people*

■ *And finally, use your guidebook as a starting point, not the only source of information. Talk to local people, then discover your own adventure*

Essentials

Although dressing down is not usually frowned upon, looking scruffy is. A tidy presentation, even if wearing shorts and sandals, is always appreciated. Women may want to cover up in conservative rural areas – avoiding revealing tops or short skirts should do.

Waiters, hotel porters, stewards, chambermaids and tour guides, according to the service, should be tipped 10 to 15%. Away from the big towns and major tourist destinations service can be very poor and at times rude. When leaving tips make sure it goes to the person you intended it to, as there is no guarantee kitty money gets to everyone.   **Tipping**

Responsible tourism

Much has been written about the adverse impacts of tourism on the environment and local communities. It is usually assumed that this only applies to the more excessive end of the travel industry such as the Spanish Costas and Bali. However, it now seems that travellers can have an impact at almost any density and this is especially true in areas 'off the beaten track' where local people may not be used to western conventions and lifestyles, and where natural environments may be very sensitive.

Of course, tourism can have a beneficial impact and this is something to which every traveller can contribute. Many National Parks are part funded by receipts from people who come to see exotic plants and animals. Similarly, travellers can promote protection of valuable archaeological sites and heritages through their interest and entrance fees.

However, where visitor pressure is high and/or poorly regulated, damage can occur. It is also unfortunately true that many of the most popular destinations are in ecologically sensitive areas easily disturbed by extra human pressures. This is particularly significant because the desire to visit sites and communities that are off the beaten track is a driving force for many travellers. Eventually the very features that tourists travel so far to see may become degraded and so we seek out new sites, discarding the old, and leaving someone else to deal with the plight of local communities and the damaged environment.

Fortunately, there are signs of a new awareness of the responsibilities that the travel industry and its clients need to endorse. For example, some tour operators fund local

Essentials

conservation projects and travellers are now more aware of the impact they may have on host cultures and environments. We can all contribute to the success of what is variously described as responsible, green or alternative tourism. All that is required is a little forethought and consideration.

It would be impossible to identify all the possible impacts that might need to be addressed by travellers, but it is worthwhile noting the major areas in which we can all take a more responsible attitude in the countries we visit. These include, changes to natural ecosystems (air, water, land, ecology and wildlife), cultural values (beliefs and behaviour) and the built environment (sites of antiquity and archaeological significance). At an individual level, travellers can reduce their impact if greater consideration is given to their activities. Canoe trips up the headwaters of obscure rivers make for great stories, but how do local communities cope with the sudden invasive interest in their lives? Will the availability of easy tourist money and gauche behaviour affect them for the worse, possibly diluting and trivializing the significance of culture and customs? Similarly, have the environmental implications of increased visitor pressure been considered? Where does the fresh fish that feeds the trip come from? Hand caught by line is fine, but is dynamite fishing really necessary, given the scale of damage and waste that results?

Some of these impacts are caused by factors beyond the direct control of travellers, such as the management and operation of a hotel chain. However, even here it is possible to voice concern about damaging activities and an increasing number of hotels and travel operators are taking 'green concerns' seriously, even if it is only to protect their share of the market.

Environmental legislation Laws are increasingly being enacted to control damage to the environment, and in some cases this can have a bearing on travellers. The establishment of National Parks may involve rules and guidelines for visitors and these should always be followed. In addition there may be local or national laws controlling behaviour and use of natural resources (especially wildlife) that are being increasingly enforced. If in doubt, ask. Finally, international legislation, principally the Convention on International Trade in Endangered Species of Wild Fauna and Flora (CITES), may affect travellers.

CITES aims to control the trade in live specimens of endangered plants and animals and also "recognisable parts or derivatives" of protected species. Sale of black coral, turtle shells, protected orchids and other wildlife is strictly controlled by signatories of the convention. The full list of protected wildlife varies, so if you feel the need to purchase souvenirs and trinkets derived from wildlife, it would be prudent to check whether they are protected. Importation of CITES protected species into these countries can lead to heavy fines, confiscation of goods and even imprisonment. Information on the status of legislation and protective measures can be obtained from *Traffic International*, UK office T01223-277427, F277237, traffic@wcmc.org.uk

Green travel companies & information The increasing awareness of the environmental impact of travel and tourism has led to a range of advice and information services as well as spawning specialist travel companies who claim to provide 'responsible travel' for clients. This is an expanding field and the veracity of claims needs to be substantiated in some cases. The following organizations and publications can provide useful information for those with an interest in pursuing responsible travel opportunities.

Tourism Concern, Stapleton House, 277-281 Holloway Rd, London N7 8HN, UK, T020-77533330, F77533331, www.tourismconcern.org.uk, aims to promote a greater under-standing of the impact of tourism on host communities and environments. *Centre for Responsible Tourism (CRT)*, PO Box 827, San Anselmo, California 94979, USA, co-ordinates a North American network and advises on North American sources of information on responsible tourism. *Centre for the Advancement of Responsive Travel (CART)*, 70 Dry Hill Park Rd, Tunbridge, Kent, TIN 3BX, UK T01732-352757, has a range of publications available as well as information on alternative holiday destinations. *CARE International*, 10-13 Rushworth St, London SE1 0RB, UK, T020-7934 9334, www.careinternational.org.uk Works to impove the economic conditions of people living in developing countries.

Safety

As people come to terms with the new South Africa, there has been a major problem of well-publicised crime, particularly in Johannesburg, frequently dubbed the most dangerous city in the world. Despite the statistics, much of the serious violent crime is gang-based and occurs in areas that tourists are unlikely to visit, such as Cape Town's Cape Flats or the more dubious areas of Soweto. Dangers facing tourists are on the whole limited to traditional mugging or car jacking. Guns are widely available and you should be aware that your assailant may well be armed and any form of resistance could be fatal. The crime rate in many other South African city centres has increased recently and many travellers have reported being mugged in, say, Cape Town after they have survived Johannesburg unscathed. One important reason for this is that they have simply let their guard down.

The average visitor need not worry about their safety outside the inner cities any more than they would in any foreign country. The most simple points to remember are to avoid altogether what are considered to be dangerous areas, not to walk about any urban centres late at night, and make sure you do not drive after dark. If you are going to be travelling alone in a car, it's a good idea to bring (or hire) a mobile phone, helpful in any case if you break down

City centres Horror stories abound amongst travellers passing through Johannesburg. The city centre, Hillbrow, and Yoeville have the worst reputation and the crime rate remains high. There are few facilities or accommodation options in these areas anymore, so it is feasible to avoid them altogether and visit the sights only on an organized tour. Travellers arriving at the **Park City Transit Centre** in Johannesburg should not wander casually into town. Several travellers have lost everything within metres of the terminal. Avoid this fate by taking a taxi directly to your hotel. The crime rate in Johannesburg's suburbs, where most of the hotels, hostels, nightlife, and shops are located, has improved greatly in recent years, due mainly to increased security of property and vehicles, and you should experience few problems in these areas.

Apart from Johannesburg, city centres are generally safe during daylight hours, although listen to advice from locals about which areas to avoid. A number of urban centres (including Cape Town) have recently installed closed-circuit TV cameras and private security guards, making the city centre far safer. After dark, however, the likelihood of being mugged increases sharply. The safest way to travel around cities at night is to take a taxi directly to and from your destination.

Townships It is not safe to visit townships unless you are on a guided tour. Townships are generally located on the outskirts of towns and cities. Few of them are signposted but if you should enter one by mistake leave as quickly as possible.

Problem areas

Transkei There were a number of violent assaults on tourists in the Transkei several years ago, which received international media coverage. These assaults are in reality very rare and the main thing to keep in mind is staying off the roads after dark. Even if you are just passing through Transkei, always plan your journey so that you won't have to travel at night. The roads away from the N2 are rocky and potholed and some can only be negotiated in a four-wheel drive. Umtata can be dangerous at night and many people will eat in their hotels. Hotel owners are aware of the dangers and have been known to give discounts to budget travellers in need of secure accommodation.

Car jacking Car jacking remains a problem in South Africa's cities. The favoured location for this is at red traffic lights on a junction. It is a good idea to travel with the windows closed and the doors locked. When faced with a suspicious situation at a junction, it is general practice to jump the lights and get away as fast as possible. Again, it is important to remember that car jackers are almost always armed and will use their weapons when faced with resistance. The insurance on hired cars in South Africa is correspondingly high.

Drugs

Although smoking marijuana, locally known as *dagga*, is relatively widespread and grown in rural areas such as Transkei and Lesotho, it is illegal, and the same penalties apply as elsewhere. Also note that many young South Africans nowadays are extremely health and image conscious and the dope-smoking hippy image is regarded with disdain in some quarters. (The backpacker circuit and some hostels, however, have the usual drug scene found all over the world.) Since independence there has been an alarming growth in drug-related crime and Cape Town has become a major transit point for drugs en route to Europe and America. Traditionally, poor people have smoked a lethal cocktail of mandrax (buttons) and marijuana (*dagga*), which will almost instantly comatose inexperienced users. Hard drugs such as cocaine and heroin, along with their associated problems, are also now easily available. There is also a thriving rave scene in Cape Town, and clubs are packed with dance fans loved-up on Ecstasy. **NB** Be aware that if you encounter someone who wants to sell you drugs, they will usually be a member of a gang, and under no circumstances should you get embroiled in any dealings with a gang. The process is far more dangerous than you would expect elsewhere and they will often be under police surveillance.

Where to stay

See inside the front cover of the book for our hotel price guide

Popular destinations tend to have a complete range of accommodation to suit all budgets. Many domestic tourists like either to stay in self-catering flats, or camp. At the more expensive end of the market there is a shortage of luxury hotel accommodation away from the major cities, but in its place are some excellent luxury game lodges, with unrivalled degrees of comfort and service in a beautiful rural setting. Larger cities have the ubiquitous large **chain hotels** such as *Holiday Inn* and the national *Protea* chain. A fairly new development is **boutique hotels**; small, exclusive guesthouses with stylish interiors and correspondingly fashionable clientele. There is also a choice of accommodation in the national parks and nature reserves. In the Cape Province and KwaZulu Natal the facilities are always clean and good value, but you will have to be prepared to self-cater in most places. Every town will have at least one hotel of a two- or three-star standard, but where tourists are not expected the service can be poor and dismissive. These hotels tend to be aimed at business travellers and can be set in characterless, modern buildings serving notoriously bland food. There are exceptions, and many small towns have quite delightful historic family-run hotels.

One of the major boom industries in South Africa has been bed and breakfast accommodation, with many private homes opening up a room or two for tourists. These can be extremely good value and allow you to get to know a little more about South African life through your hosts. Local tourist offices usually have a comprehensive list of local B&Bs. The other major growth industry is budget travel, and there is an excellent range of backpacker hostels found around the country.

Backpacker hostels

Apart from camping, backpacker hostels are the cheapest form of accommodation in South Africa. A bed in a dormitory will cost between R50-70 a night, while a double room costs between R120-180. A tent pitched in the garden can cost as little as R30.

Hostels vary widely between run-down houses that look like chaotic student squats, to clean, well-run B&B-type places. Facilities tend to be similar everywhere – you can expect a self-catering kitchen, usually a TV/video room and internet access. Many hostels also have bars and offer meals or nightly braais, plus gardens and plunge pools. Most hostels are a good source of travel information and may act as booking agents for bus companies, budget safari tours and car hire. On the whole, hostels are very safe and security is not a problem. There is sometimes the problem of leaving valuables at reception as they do not always have safes and your property will instead be stored in a locked cupboard. Your fellow traveller remains the greatest threat, especially in dorms in the busy city hostels.

Although hostels are popular with students and younger travellers it is possible to meet all kinds of people travelling through. The *Baz Bus* (see page 42) minibus services caters for backpackers and links most backpacker hostels along the coast between Cape Town and Durban. From Durban there are two alternative routes to Johannesburg and Pretoria via either Swaziland or the Drakensberg. The bus collects and drops off at backpacker hostels so long as you call in advance. At the last count more than 175 hostels were visited along the route.

Bed and breakfast accommodation is a relatively new phenomenon in South Africa where a   **Bed & breakfast**
shortage of hotel rooms has created a demand for pleasant alternative accommodation. Small
towns in South Africa often have only one or two hotels, which in turn cater mainly for business
travellers. Bed and breakfasts start at around R90 per person sharing and can go up to as much
as R300 per person. Assuming you get on with your hosts, they can offer a valuable insight to
local life. In rural areas, farmhouse B&Bs are often in beautiful settings where guests will have
access to a garden and swimming pool as well as to hikes and horse riding. Increasingly, some
establishments are providing TVs, air-conditioning or fans, and have separate entrances for
those who want more privacy away from the owners. The breakfasts are almost always good
and the quantities enough to fill you up for the day. Full English breakfasts are usually served but
it is increasingly common to have a choice of continental breakfast or even traditional South
African – *boerewors*, mince on toast, and mealie porridge.

Prices do vary according to the facilities and a B&B in a Victorian house decorated with
antique furniture will be more expensive than a converted spare bedroom. At the top end of
the market the luxury B&Bs in spectacular locations such as the Winelands outside Cape
Town can charge as much as US$75.

This is the cheapest and most flexible way of seeing South Africa. Every town has a municipal   **Camping &**
campsite, many of which also have simple self-catering chalets. As camping is very popular   **caravan parks**
with South Africans, sites tend to have very good facilities. Many retired South Africans travel
in caravans, so the majority of campsites have power points and a water supply close to
where you might pitch your tent or park the caravan. For most of the year the weather is ideal
for camping, although be prepared for frosts at night in some parts. Note that because
camping is so popular, sites can often be booked months in advance, especially in the most
popular game reserves and national parks during the school holidays (see page 21 for school
term dates). Don't always assume there will be space at a campsite.

The facilities at most sites are excellent. Even the most basic site will have a clean
washblock with hot water, plus electric points and lighting. At the most popular tourist
destinations, campsites are more like holiday resorts with shops, swimming pools and a
restaurant – these can get very busy and are best avoided in peak seasons. Some sites do not
allow tents during busy times, to stop people with caravans from taking up additional space.
If confronted with this problem, point out you are from overseas and don't have a caravan.
Ground sheets are also banned to help protect the grass, but these should not be a problem
for a couple of days. For a small extra fee you can have access to electricity with your site. This
is meant for caravans, but the points are suitable for most electric appliances (you may need
to buy a special adaptor from the camp shop).

Camping equipment is widely available in South Africa and usually at a fraction of the
price found at home. If your time is limited, bring along at least a tent and sleeping bags, but if
you're not on a tight schedule you may want to shop around once you've arrived.
Lightweight tents, sleeping bags, ground mats, gas lights, stoves and cooking equipment can
be bought at excellent prices in all the major cities. The cooking side of camping is generally
the most awkward factor. All sites have braai facilities and charcoal, wood, and fire lighters can
be bought in the camp shop, and some sites have kitchen blocks so your only major concern
is keeping food fresh. We recommend buying a cool box for your trip, and selling it on to a
fellow traveller when you leave.

If you don't want to camp, municipal sites often offer self-catering rooms. These vary in
quality and facilities, from basic rooms with twin beds to chalets with a couple of bedrooms and
fully-equipped kitchens. They can be excellent value, and are often the only budget
accommodation available in a town. Camping fees are divided into per tent/caravan site and
per person, and on average they should be no more than R40 per person and R40 for the tent.

A guesthouse should have no less than four bedrooms and no more than 16. They must not   **Guesthouses**
have a public bar, and they cannot accept permanent residents. The *Guesthouse Association
of South Africa* is a non-profit making association set up by owners to protect their interests.
Guesthouses can vary enormously; much has to do with the character of the owners and the
location of the homes. These days the most luxurious rooms outside the major cities will be

Essentials

found in guesthouses, not hotels. Expect to pay from R120 per person for the simplest of guesthouses, but prices increase steadily along with quality.

Booking by phone in advance guarantees you a room at the end of a day, and at quieter times enables the owners to prepare meals for you if necessary. Note that where an evening meal is served it will be early in the evening, around 1900, and everyone will eat at the same time in a communal environment. It can be a good way to meet South Africans.

Hotels   Cape Town and Johannesburg suffer from a shortage of hotel beds, and you should always book well in advance for these. Once on the road, you're only likely to encounter shortages along the Garden Route during the Christmas holiday period. Generally, hotels booked through agents in Europe will be more expensive than if you contact the hotel direct, due to agent booking fees. It is usually best to contact the hotels directly by email or fax. Many of the more established chain hotels have an online booking service via their websites. Make sure you keep a copy of all correspondence and reconfirm your bookings once you arrive in the country. Be wary if sending advance deposits, or paying in advance by credit card, though sometimes supplying your credit card details is the only way to secure a reservation.

There are many hotel chains operating in South Africa. Details of their head offices and central reservations are listed below. *Satour* graded hotels are given a star rating, but this is usually a reflection of their facilities rather than their character or service. Conference facilities and the number of rooms can result in an extra star rating, while service and food remain very average. Always check your rooms if you are not sure of a place. In general, the *Southern Sun* group manage hotels which are either four or five star. *Protea* have hotels throughout the country, usually close to major tourist attractions, and will be in the two- to five-star range. The *Holiday Inn Crowne Plazas* tend to be four-star, while *Holiday Inn Garden Court* are three-star hotels. The *City Lodge* group represent excellent value, and range from one- to three-star hotels. Reservations for *City Lodge, Town Lodge,* and *Road Lodge* can be made throughout South Africa from any of their hotels. Finally there is the *Formula 1 (Formule 1)* chain from France, a great concept in cheap functional rooms, convenient but characterless and not the sort of place to spend too many nights in a row. The *Protea* group runs a loyalty card which offers discounts and room upgrades after you have stayed a certain number of nights within a 12 month period. If you are a frequent visitor or are spending several months in South Africa it is worth looking into the card terms.

Bed & Breakfast Association, T012-4802001. *City Lodge Hotels Ltd*, Lodgeline, T011-8840660; Head office, T011-8845327, F8833640, www.citylodge.co.za City Lodge, Town Lodge, and Road Lodge are all part of this company. *Classic Retreats*, Po Box 53063, Kenilworth, Cape Town 3120, T021-6712102, F021-6713101, www.classicretreats.co.za *Formula 1*, PO Box 2776, Rivona, Johannesburg 2128, central reservations, T011-8070750, F8073888, www.formule1.co.za (NB There's an 'e' in the web address). *Guest House Association of Southern Africa*, PO Box 18416, Wynberg 7824, T021-7620880, F7973115, www.guesthouseassocation.co.za *Holiday Inns & Southern Sun*, central reservations: toll free, T0800-117711; head office, T011-7800200, F7800262, GMCPSandton@southern.com *The Portfolio Collection*, reservations office: PO Box 132, Newlands, Cape Town 7725, T021-6894020, F6865310, www.portfoliocollection.com *Protea Hotels and Aventura Resorts*, central reservations: T021-4305300, F4305310, www.protea-hotels.co.za *Sun International*, PO Box 784487, Sandton, Johannesburg 2146, central reservations: T011-7807800, www.sun-international.com *Hostelling International South Africa (HISA)*, PO Box 4402, Cape Town 8000, T021-4242511, F4244119. Regional office for the Youth Hostelling Association, representative for over 30 South African backpacker hostels affiliated with YHA.

Luxury Game   The most famous luxury game lodges are on private game farms adjoining Kruger National
Lodges   Park, although there are others around the country. Their attraction is a combination of exclusive game viewing in South Africa's prime wilderness areas, with top-class accommodation, cordon bleu meals, vintage wines and a spectacular natural setting.

The cost of staying in a luxury game lodge varies from US$250 to over US$800 per person each night. This includes all meals, drinks and game viewing trips. In order to get the most from a stay, guests tend to stay for at least two nights. The lodges are often isolated and not easily accessible by road so many reserves have their own airstrips where light aircraft can land. Charter flights save time and avoid long dusty journeys, and can easily be booked through the game lodge or from Johannesburg, Durban or Cape Town.

Before setting off to visit the national parks and game reserves, it is worth contacting the **National parks** central reservations office of the relevant authority; see page 64. All bookings can be made over the telephone, by email or direct through the website. Most international credit cards are accepted (see page 30 for details). If you are staying in a park, the reception will often help make advance bookings for other parks. The central reservations offices are a good source of advice and can help plan your trip in advance. It is quite possible to travel around South Africa and to only ever stay in nature reserves and national parks. While the accommodation may be spartan, it is usually located in a beautiful, natural setting.

South Africans tend to book their accommodation in national parks and nature reserves several months in advance, but outside peak periods you should be able to find rooms in most reserves at short notice, as long as you make the arrangements soon after your arrival in South Africa.

Self-catering flats are particularly popular with South African holidaymakers and there is an **Self-catering** enormous choice, especially along the coast. Prices vary with the seasons: Christmas is the **apartments** most expensive time of year, but off season many resorts are virtually empty and discounts can be negotiated. If you are travelling in a group, a flat could cost as little as R50 a day per person. After several weeks on the road it is often a treat to cook a meal for oneself.

Getting around

Air

There is a far-reaching, safe and efficient domestic service run by *South African Airways (SAA)*. All the major towns can be reached within a couple of hours' flying time from each other. If you make your reservations from overseas, there are some good-value deals available. On popular routes where there is some competition, such as from Durban to Johannesburg, or Johannesburg to Cape Town. The cost of a single ticket is comparable to a luxury bus ticket. When you consider the time saved, taking an internal flight can be a very attractive proposition.

In addition to *SAA*, there are several smaller operators who fly between South Africa's main cities: *SAA*, T011-9781111, in conjunction with *SA Airlink*, T011-9781111 and *SA Express*, T011-9785569, is the largest local carrier and has regular daily flights connecting Johannesburg with other major towns within South Africa. *Comair*, PO Box 7015, Bonaero Park 1622, T011-9210222, F9733913, operate in conjunction with *British Airways*. The cheapest flights between Johannesburg and Durban and Cape Town are with *Kulula.com*, www.kulula.com, South Africa's new no-frills, budget airline.

Rail

All of the major cities are linked by rail, but on some routes there is only one train per week. While this is a very comfortable and relaxing way to travel, it is slow. Refreshments are available on all trains, though most dining cars have been franchised to burger-type chains, so don't expect brilliant food, and on the longer routes it is possible to reserve a sleeping berth.

Since privatization the South African railway network for passengers, *Spoornet*, has slowly been shrinking. The most frequent services are the 'named' trains, which you are most likely to use. These run between the main urban centres, usually on a daily basis. There are also a number of steam trains, organized for enthusiasts and tourists. Finally there are several luxury trains which follow three similar routes: Cape Town to Pretoria; Pretoria to Durban via the Kruger Park region; and from Cape Town through the Winelands to the Garden Route. Occasionally a special train is run through to Victoria Falls in Zimbabwe, Swakopmund in

Namibia, or even Dar es Salaam in Tanzania. All of these trains are like five-star hotels on wheels, and their prices start in the region of US$800 per person.

Luxury trains The *Blue Train*, T012-4494020, www.bluetrain.co.za, and *The Pride of Africa*, (operated by *Rovos Rail*), Pretoria office: T012-3158258, F3230843, www.rovos.co.za These two companies currently run the ultimate in luxury train travel in southern Africa. There is also a slightly less expensive company which is part of the national rail network, *Spoornet*, known as the *Union Limited Steam Rail Tours*, Spoornet Building, 1 Adderley St, T021-4494391, F4494395. *Shongololo Express*, T011-4862824, F4862909, shongo@mweb. co.za, is also a cheaper company equivalent to a three-star hotel rather than top-of-the-range luxury. See also page 546.

Main line 'named' services There are a number of named trains offering services between the major towns such as the Trans Oranje and the Komati. These services stop at stations en route but often arrive at inconvenient times. The long distance services have sleeping compartments, with coupés and compartments in first and second class. Coupés sleep two or three people and have a wash basin, electric point, a fold-away table and bunkbeds; compartments sleep four or six people. Third class sleeping compartments, when available, sleep up to six people, but there is usually only open coach seating. All trains have either a dining car or a trolley selling snacks and refreshments.

Reservations for first and second class travel can be made up to three months in advance. Always book in advance for first and second class compartments, during local holidays (and other times of the year) many trains become fully booked. Reservations are usually not necessary for third class travel. **Reservations**: T011-7732944. Accompanied children under age seven travel free; children between seven and 12 years pay half price.

See also page 61 **Special tourist trains** Excursions on restored vintage steam trains are available on the *Apple Express* in Port Elizabeth; the *Banana Express* from Port Shepstone to Oribi Gorge; the *Outeniqua Choo-Tjoe* between George and Knysna, and the *Umgeni Steam Railway* from Hilton, just outside Pietermaritzburg, to Howick.

Metro Commuter Trains Many of the larger cities such as Pretoria, Johannesburg and Cape Town have a network of Metro Commuter services linking some of the suburbs to the business districts. These are to be avoided at all costs due to regular incidents of robbery and violent assault. In any case, they provide transport between the townships and cities during rush hour and tourists are unlikely to need to use them. The exception is the Metro rail link between Pretoria and Johannesburg, which would seem by all accounts to be the convenient way to travel between the two cities. However, this is *not* the case and taking the bus is a far safer alternative. A high speed direct train link is being planned, connecting Johannesburg International Airport with Pretoria and Johannesburg, but at present this is still at the planning stage and is likely to take several years to complete.

Road

Bus There are three major long distance bus companies which run between towns and popular destinations. There are plenty of buses on each route and seats can be reserved several months in advance. The coaches are air-conditioned and have a toilet; some sell refreshments and show videos. They will stop every four or five hours to change drivers and give the passengers a chance to stretch their legs. For long journeys, the prices are reasonable, but short routes are expensive. These may well come down with more competition. On night routes, bear in mind that you're saving the cost of a hotel room.

See also page 831 for Baz Bus timetables **Budget buses** Several companies offer an alternative bus service specifically designed for the ever-increasing number of backpackers visiting South Africa. The *Baz Bus* is the only company to have continually expanded its services and it remains the most popular and efficient service on the market.

Essentials

The *Baz Bus* service is aimed specifically at backpackers. One of the best aspects of the service is that the bus collects and drops off passengers at their chosen backpacker hostel. There are a few exceptions such as Hermanus, Coffee Bay and Sani Pass, where the bus will drop you off at the closest point on the main road, and the hostels will then meet you for a small extra charge (you must arrange this in advance; the hostels are aware of the timings but you must let them know which day and which direction you are coming from). It is important to remember to call the **Baz Bus** to arrange to be collected; during busy times of the year it is advisable to call as soon as you have decided what your next move will be.

The tickets are priced per segment, for example from Cape Town to Durban. You are allowed to hop off and on the bus as many times as you like along the given segment, but must not backtrack. This is where the great savings are made, since other commercial buses such as **Translux** and **Greyhound** charge high prices for short journeys; while their price for Cape Town to Durban (non-stop) may be similar to that of the *Baz Bus*, you would end up paying four times the price if you were to stop in several towns along the route.

The drivers of each bus are a great source of information, both about the places of interest along the route and what to expect at each hostel. The really bad hostels are swiftly found out, and any new hostels can quickly make a name for themselves once they are on the *Baz Bus* route.

The buses are fairly cramped Mercedes buses, although a trailer at the back has plenty of space for rucksacks, surf boards, etc. If you have access to the internet at home you can find out more about the service and related topics via their web site. *Baz Bus*, 8 Rosedene Rd, Sea Point, Cape Town T021-4392323, info@bazbus.com, www.bazbus.com

Intercity coaches *Greyhound Citiliner*, T011-2498900, www.greyhound.co.za *Intercape*, T021-6544114. *Translux Express*, T012-3154300, www.translux.co.za

These are the three major operators which run luxury buses between most tourist centres and towns in South Africa. For budget travellers, these services are expensive for shorter journeys, but they are an efficient and safe way of travelling. On long journeys the bus will stop at a roadside service station where passengers have the chance to stretch their legs and buy a snack at the fast food outlet or the local shop. Bookings for *Greyhound* and *Translux* can be made directly via their websites, *Intercape* is expected to provide this facility in the future.

Hiring a car for part, or all, of your jouney is undoubtedly the best way to see the country. The roads are generally in good condition, and away from the major urban centres there is little traffic. South Africans are, however, notoriously bad drivers – speeding and drink driving are common. Do not drive at night for safety reasons. The advantage of hiring a car is that you get to explore more isolated areas, as well as seeing the national parks and nature reserves without being tied to a tour. For budget travellers, hiring a car is ideal for carrying camping equipment, and costs come down considerably if you share them between three or four people. Petrol, not a major expense, is available 24 hours a day along the national highways.

Driving is on the left side of the road and speeds range from 60 kmph in built up areas to 120 kmph on the main highways. The police are very strict on drink driving and speed traps with on the spot fines are employed. *Automobile Association*, breakdowns: T0800-010101.

Be wary of out-of-date leaflets in hotel receptions, on hostel notice boards or in local information centres. Car hire is one aspect of your holiday where it is worth making your own enquiries and shopping around after arrival. In general there are two types of deal on offer: a short weekend package including free mileage; or longer-term deals for a week or more. In the first case you can get very good rates for a Group A car, but such a vehicle would not be comfortable for long journeys. Where the company is looking to rent a car out for several weeks their rates for a few days will not be competitive.

If you are planning on having a car for two or three weeks the chances are you will clock up in excess of 3,000 km. Remember that Cape Town to Pretoria is nearly 1,500 km alone. We strongly recommend that you hire at least a Group B car. The extra engine power and space will make for more comfortable and safe driving. Check that the air conditioning unit and cassette deck are working before you sign for a car.

Car hire
National Department of Transport T082-2325600 (mob), provides route planners for all national roads

See also page 37 for security cautions

Many South Africans are careless drivers; they drive fast and dangerously, and blind overtaking is a frequent practice

Essentials

Tourist offices will often only recommend large, international companies such as *Avis* or *Budget*. For a business traveller this may be the most sensible option, but when you are paying for yourself consider one of the many other companies. These tend to have a good fleet of cars and follow-up service. Backpacker hostels are often a good source of information on these and can offer competitive rates. Make sure you have the correct documents from the rental company if you wish to take the car into Namibia, Lesotho or Swaziland. It is not so easy to take a hire car into Mozambique, Botswana or Zimbabwe, see page 32.

If you are intending to visit more remote areas such as Maputaland, the Kalahari and the Richtersveld, consider hiring a four-wheel drive vehicle. There are specialist companies in Cape Town and Johannesburg which hire out fully equipped safari Land Rovers or pickups. Fully equipped camper vans or motor homes represent excellent value for a group or a family as they can save on accommodation. A saloon car can negotiate most roads in South Africa.

Below are the details of the largest rental companies. For a more complete listing check under car hire in our Transport sections for individual towns and popular tourist centres.

Avis Rent A Car, toll-free T0800-021111 for the nearest branch; *Britz Africa*, T011-3961860, camper vans and motorhomes – good all-inclusive deals; *Budget Rent A Car*, central reservations T011-3923929, toll-free T0800-16622; *Europcar*, central reservations T021-4180670, F4398603; *Imperial Car Rental*, central reservations T011-8834352, toll-free 0800-031000; *Tempest*, central reservations T011-3961080, toll-free T0800-031666.

Cycling   Mountain bikes are available for hire at some backpacker hostels, family resorts and the occasional hotel close to a nature reserve. Note, however, that many of the best trails have no nearby facilities for hiring bikes, so enthusiasts should bring their own. When you buy your ticket to fly to South Africa check with the airline what their policy is on transporting bicycles. You will normally be expected to pack the bicycle in a cardboard box (available from cycling shops), take the pedals off and deflate the tyres. The weight will count towards your baggage allowance. One important point to bear in mind is the heat. On long trips it is not advisable to cycle during the hottest part of the day. Beware of dehydration and sunstroke, wear a hat and drink plenty of liquids.

Hitchhiking   Hitchhiking is not uncommon in South Africa, but like many countries it can be unsafe. Women should under no circumstances hitch alone. If you do choose to hitch, always do it in groups of two or more. It is also a good idea to take public transport out of towns and then start hitching once you've passed the townships. Make sure you look as smart as possible – you're more likely to get a lift if you look clean cut. In rural areas you may be expected to pay for a lift if a lorry or a pickup give you a ride.

Taxis   There are few taxi ranks in South African towns and it is not customary to hail a taxi in the street. Instead, taxis must be ordered in advance – make sure you get an advance quote on your proposed journey. Travelling by taxi, especially by night, is one of the safest ways to cross city centres when visiting a restaurant or a nightclub; don't walk just to save a few cents. Remember to check that the meter is working and that the driver sets it to zero.

Minibus taxis The majority of South Africa's population travel by minibus taxis, and in many areas including inner cities, they are the only way of getting around. Unfortunately, the notorious 'Minibus wars' of the late 1990s have put many travellers off using them. The Minibus wars involved rival minibus companies opening fire on each other's buses, on some occasions killing every single passenger on board. This has not happened in quite some time, but many visitors are still frightened of using them.

Minibus taxis remain the cheapest and most extensive form of transport in the country in the country; you could theoretically get just about anywhere by minibus taxi. There are places and routes where there has been little violence, but you should **exercise extreme caution** and always ask people who are in the know before using them. The accident rate is also notoriously high, overcrowded minibuses speed to get to their destination in order to pick up passengers for the return journey before their competitors. Some of the accidents have been horrific and many drivers do not maintain their vehicles sufficiently and so they are often not road worthy. It is probably best if you avoid using minibus taxis other than in areas where you can be sure they are safe. One such place is in central Cape Town where minibus taxis provide an effective (and safe) means of transport into the city centre from places such as Observatory, Rondebosch and Claremont.

An excellent source of maps is ***Stanfords*** at 12-14 Longacre, London WC2E 9LP, **Maps** T0207-8361321. Within South Africa, the ***Shell Road Atlas to Southern Africa***, available at all Shell service stations, is a comprehensive map book that includes maps of major tourist areas marking sights and some accommodation facilities, and detailed city maps.

Keeping in touch

Communications

South Africa is generally well-served by the internet and most companies, hotels, tourist **Internet** offices, guesthouses and individuals have email addresses and websites. There are internet cafés in all major urban centres and many hotels, guesthouses or backpacker hostels offer email access as a service. The notable exception to this is in Johannesburg and the surrounding suburbs, where there does not appear to be a demand for public internet cafés, presumably because most people have home internet connections. Try the backpacker hostels or the occasional Vodacom shop in the shopping malls, which sometimes have a spare computer for the public to log on at. In the more remote regions you are unlikely to see internet cafés unless the town is served by a university or college, and there is a demand for internet access by students.

For a short list of website addresses which have good regional or national information, see page 26. At the start of each chapter the address for the official province website has been listed, some of which are very informative and useful. However, be wary when making use of the practical information, telephone numbers and email addresses are often out of date.

The internal mail service is notoriously slow, but international post is generally reliable if you **Postal services** use Airmail. Surface mail to Europe will take at least six weeks. Letters to Europe and the United States should take no more than a week, although over the busy Christmas season it can take up to a month. There is a 'Speed Service', but this costs significantly more. Parcels have been known to disappear en route, so it's probably best to use registered or insured mail for more valuable items – using a private carrier is the safest bet. Courier services are useful for sending back heavier objects such as wooden sculptures and furniture. *DHL* T0860-345000, toll free for the nearest branch.

Essentials

Telephone services
Country code: 27
When dialling a number in South Africa from abroad drop the first 0 in the area code. All numbers called from within the country must now include the full regional code

The telephone service tends to be very efficient, although numbers seem to change every couple of years. **Note that you now must dial the full regional code for every number, even if you are calling from within that region**. In this book we have not included the code with the number for every listing, but instead have given the code in the margin at the beginning of each town heading, with a note "Always use 3-figure prefix" to remind you that you must always dial the number in full. For example, the code for Cape Town is 021. If you are calling a Cape Town number from within Cape Town, you must still prefix the telephone number with 021.

Card and coin phones are widespread and work well – even in remote national parks there are usually card phones from which one can direct dial to anywhere in the world. Take note that hotels will at least double the usual rates, and even a short international call can become very expensive. There are a number of private companies which offer fax and mail services, but these tend to charge about double the usual rate for calls. Phone boxes found in backpacker hostels, shops and bars are known as 'chatterboxes' and are usually set at a high rate.

Blue call boxes are coin operated telephones, green indicates a card phone – the latter are slowly taking over from coin phones, and are often the only choice in cities. Phone cards are sold for R10, R20, R50 and R100. They are available in larger supermarkets, newsagents, some chemists and Telkom vending machines. A R50 card is sufficient to make an international call to Europe for a few minutes. Cheaper calls, known as 'Callmore Time' are available between 1900 and 0700 on weekdays and from 1900 on Friday until 0700 on Monday. Discounts only apply to national calls. You can usually speak for up to 50% longer for the same charge.

Dialling codes: Johannesburg, (011); Pretoria, (012); Cape Town, (021); Durban, (031); Port Elizabeth, (041); East London, (043); Bloemfontein, (051); Kimberley, (053); Pietersburg/Polokwane, (015); Mafikeng/Mmabatho, (018).
International operator: T0009.
International directory: T0903.
International access code: 09.
Local enquiries: T1023.
Speaking clock: 1026.

Throughout this book, when listing a mobile number, we have added '(mob)' after the number

Mobile phones South Africa uses the GSM system for cellular phones and overseas visitors should be able to use their mobiles here, if arranged with their service provider prior to departure. Mobile numbers consist of 10 digits and start with 082, 083, 084, or 072 depending on the network. Cellular phones and Sim cards are available for hire at each of the three international airports – Cape Town, Durban and Johannesburg. For anyone travelling alone by car, especially women, it is sensible to hire one for emergencies. Along the N4 between Johannesburg/Pretoria and Nelspruit (a popular route for visitors to Kruger National Park) there are few roadside phones.

Media

Newspapers
The **Sunday Times** and **Sunday Independent** are weekly English-language papers with national coverage, although several editions are produced for different areas. The excellent weekly **Mail & Guardian** (with close links to the British Guardian) provides the most objective reporting on South African issues, and has in-depth coverage of international news. Daily English-language newspapers include: **The Star** and **The Citizen** (Johannesburg); **The Daily News** and **The Natal Mercury** (Durban); **The Argus** and **The Cape Times** (Cape Town). **The Sowetan** provides a less white-orientated view of South African news but has the best coverage of international soccer if this is something you are missing from home. There are also a number of papers published in Afrikaans, Zulu and Xhosa.

Magazines
There are a number of publications that travellers will find useful in South Africa. The bi-monthly **Eat Out** lists the best restaurants in the country, though tends to concentrate on the more upmarket eateries. The recently re-launched **SA City Life** issued four times a year, concentrates on listings in Johannesburg, Pretoria, Cape Town and Durban, of anything to movies, theatre, galleries, to street festivals and shopping. The monthly **Getaway** is aimed at

outdoorsy South Africans, usually 4x4 drivers, but has interesting travel ideas and regular reviews of accommodation alternatives and activities throughout Southern Africa.

The following stations are based in Johannesburg, you will not be able to receive them outside of the Gauteng region. (Durban and Cape Town have their own local FM stations.) On the medium wave band you can pick up 1197 kHz throughout the country. In Johannesburg check out 702 Talk Radio. Radio Zulu, 91.5 MHz; Highveld Stereo, 94.7 MHz; Radio 5, 98.0 MHz; Radio 2000, 99.7 MHz.

Local FM Radio

If you are not familiar with short wave radio, read the notes in the manual about reception; a simple attachment can greatly enhance the quality of your signal. Signal strength varies throughout the day, with lower frequencies generally better at night. For programme listings contact BBC, PO Box 76, Bush House, London.

Short wave radio

British Broadcasting Corporation (BBC, London). These bands cover the whole region from Namibia to Mozambique, as well as different times of the day. 90 metre band: 3255 kHz; 49 metre band: 6005 kHz, 6190 kHz; 25 metre band: 11860 kHz, 11940 kHz; 19 metre band: 15400 kHz; 16 metre band: 17885 kHz; 13 metre band: 21470 kHz, 21660 kHz. *Voice of America* (VoA). 25 metre band: 11920 kHz; 22 metre band: 13680 kHz; 19 metre band: 15580 kHz; 16 metre band: 17895 kHz; 13 metre band: 21485 kHz.

The state broadcaster is the **South African Broadcasting Corporation (SABC)**. The service has been significantly restructured to accommodate all 11 official languages. The majority of programmes are in English, followed by Afrikaans, Zulu and Xhosa. There are now four free channels available, known as SABC 1, 2 and 3, and the newer e channel. The latter is the most popular and tends to have better news and entertainment programmes, although SABC 3 has a link with CNN, with live CNN broadcasts on most afternoons. The paying channel, M-Net, is available in most hotels and backpacker hostels, and offers a range of sport, sit-coms and movies. It is available for free from 1700-1900, known as 'open time'. Many hotels also have satellite TV, known as DSTV, with a range of sports, movie and news channels.

Television

Food and drink

The staple diet for most of South Africa's population is a stiff maize porridge known as **pap**, served with a stew. Pap tends to be very bland and unpalatable, although the accompanying stews are often quite tasty. It is not, however, a dish that you are likely to encounter, unless you are invited into an African home.

If you choose to self-cater, it would be very wise to invest in a cool box or bag for fresh produce and ice is widely available. Supermarkets tend to have a similar selection to that found in Europe. Meat is generally significantly cheaper than in Europe, but fruit and vegetables can be relatively expensive. There are a couple of local meat products that non-vegetarians should try: **biltong** and **boerewors**. The former is heavily salted and spiced sun-dried meat, usually made from beef but often made from game such as ostrich, kudu or impala. Boerewors is a highly seasoned sausage that is best eaten after being cooked on a braai out in the bush.

Buying food

South Africa is a great source of fresh fruit. However, much of the top grade fruit is exported to Europe and the United States, while some of the lowest grade of fruit ends up in grocers and supermarkets. Nevertheless, during the summer months you should be able to get a good range of fresh fruit from the better supermarkets (*Woolworth's* is always a good bet), and local produce such as apples in Ceres or pineapples in the Transkei will always be exellent.

Restaurants and cafés vary wildly in quality and service, depending largely on where you are. Small town hotels tend to serve bland meals focusing on standard meat-and-two-veg dishes, while most town restaurants are usually part of a chain such as the *Spur* or *Saddles* steakhouses. The main cities, however, have a good variety of restaurants and South Africa is fast gaining a reputation as a culinary hotspot. Cape Town in particular has experienced a boom in top-class

Eating out

Essentials

restaurants, from traditional Cape Malay cooking to cordon bleu seafood, all at incredibly good prices. Johannesburg and Pretoria also have a wide selection of smart restaurants in the more affluent suburbs. Some of the best restaurants in the country are found in the Winelands around the Western Cape, many of which are part of historical wine estates. Franschoek has a particularly good reputation, with a number of excellent French restaurants, while the Garden Route offers fresh, good value seafood. Because of the Indian influence in KwaZulu Natal, the best curries are found in Durban and the authenticity of the dishes is better than you would expect in Europe. Meat is almost always of a good standard wherever you are, and a number of restaurants offer a variety of game such as springbok, ostrich and kudu.

Vegetarians, however, will find their choice greatly limited. South Africa is a meat-loving country and menus rarely include anything but the most basic dishes for vegetarians. Away from the major cities, you'll have to make do with salads, pasta and chips. Cape Town, Pretoria and Johannesburg have a better range for vegetarians, with some trendy meat-free restaurants appearing on the scene in recent years. Self-catering is often a better option.

With the current exchange rate as it is, eating out is excellent value. Outside the major tourist centres, people eat early and many kitchens will close around 2100, except at the weekend. Private restaurants are often closed on Sunday evenings, when hotel dining rooms or fast food outlets may well be the only choices for eating out.

Braais   One of the first local terms visitors are likely to come across is *braai*, which quite simply means cooking food on a barbecue. Braais are incredibly popular and during summer are a major form of entertainment for South Africans. Every picnic spot, camping site or layby will have at least one permanent grate, and cooking on a braai is seen as something of an art form, particularly for South African men who compliment the great tradition with a few beers.

Drink   South Africa is fast making its mark on the international **wine** market, and produces a wide

Drink-driving is a very   range of excellent wines. The Winelands in the Western Cape produce the best-known labels
serious offence, but   (see the Western Cape chapter for details) but there are a number of other wine routes
remains a problem   dotted around the country. South Africa also produces a range of good **beers**. Major labels
especially in rural areas   include Lion, Black Label, Castle and Windhoek – the last two are probably the most popular at present. Home brewed beer, made from sorghum or maize, is widely drunk by the African population. It has a thick head, is very potent and not very palatable to the uninitiated. Bitter is harder to come by, though brewed at *Mitchell's Brewery* in Knysna and Cape Town, and found at good outlets along the Garden Route.

No liquor may be sold on Sunday except in licensed restaurants with meals. The standard shop selling alcohol is known as a bottle store, usually open Monday-Friday 0800-1800, Saturday 0830-1400 (some may stay open until 1600). Supermarkets do not sell beer or spirits, and stop selling wine at 2000.

Tap water in South African towns is chemically treated and safe to drink. Bottled mineral water is available from most shops. There is also a good range of fruit juices available at most outlets including petrol stations.

There are some excellent **fruit juices** widely available – the *Ceres* brand is the best variety on sale, followed by *Liquifruit*. These fruit juice cartons are ideal for long journeys by train or car, and are also worth taking on shorter hikes.

Another non-alcoholic drink you are likely to see on menus is **Rooibos tea**, literally red bush tea. This is a caffeine-free tea with a smoky flavour, usually served with sugar or honey. The main area producing Rooibos is around Clanwilliam by the Cederberg in the Western Cape.

Shopping

African art and curios are of widely varying quality but can be surprisingly expensive as many are imported from other African countries to the north. It is worth remembering that you will find cheaper curios in the neighbouring countries like Lesotho and Swaziland. Sculptures, baskets, ceramics and other souvenirs start as curios sold at roadside stalls but as the quality and craftsmanship improves these products are reclassified as art, with prices to match. Animal products made from ivory and reptile skins are on sale in some areas but if you take them back home you could well fall foul of CITES regulations (see export restrictions, page 28).

VAT of 14% is levied on most services/goods purchased. All marked prices include VAT. Non-resident visitors on a temporary visit to South Africa qualify for a refund of VAT paid on items purchased in South Africa and taken out of the country on their departure. All items on which a VAT refund is to be claimed must be presented for examination to an official on departure; offices are to be found at Johannesburg, Durban and Cape Town airports, and kiosks at the major border crossings. The minimum value per claim is R250. You should ensure that you obtain a receipt with a VAT number from the retailer or wholesaler. The procedure is simple enough at the airport but allow plenty of time, especially if your flight is at night. At the border crossings such as Beitbridge (Zimbabwe) or Ramotswa (Botswana) the procedure is painstakingly slow, as there are few customs officials to check goods against receipts. Expect lengthy queues.

VAT refund

Essentials

Holidays and festivals

When a public holiday falls on a Sunday, the following Monday becomes a holiday. The majority of businesses will observe the holidays, although some large supermarkets in city centres may remain open.

Public holidays

New Year's Day, 1 January; **Human Rights' Day**, 22 March; **Good Friday**; **Family Day** (Easter Monday); **Freedom Day**, 27 April; **Workers' Day**, 1 May; **Youth Day**, 16 June; **National Women's Day**, 9 August; **Heritage Day**, 24 September; **Day of Reconciliation**, 16 December; **Christmas Day**, 25 December; **Day of Goodwill**, 26 December.

Carnival A New Year's parade staged by the Cape coloured community in the Bo-Kaap district of Cape Town. There is a float procession, minstrel bands and dancers, culminating with a huge competition and carnival held in Seapoint stadium. *Grahamstown Festival* A major cultural event held over two weeks in **July**, including theatre, art, music events, cabaret and comedy. *Splashy Fen* A musical gathering on a farm close to Underberg. This is a mix of popular sounds and jazz bands from all walks of life, more akin to the summer festivals held in Europe with camping and fringe activities. Dates vary between **April** and **May**, check local press for exact dates. *Rustler's Valley* Similar set up to Splashy Fen. Set in the Witteberge Mountains in the Eastern highlands of the Free State. The main music festival is held in **April** or **May**, but a second event is now held at **Christmas**, which is a week-long party to see the New Year in. Contact T/F051-9333939, wemad@rustlers.co.za, for all the details. A hip crowd but fun nevertheless! *Umhlanga Dance* This is held in **August/September**, the annual dance of Swazi maidens before the king. There are a few other Swazi festivals but they are more private and the public are not as welcome. *Oppikoppi* This is a rock festival held between Rustenburg and Thabazimbi (North West Province / Limpopo (Northern) Province border) each year usually in **October** and **Easter**. This is becoming hugely popular with visitors from Gauteng particularly over the long Easter weekend. Check out listings in Johannesburg for what's on, when. *Stellenbosch Wine Festival* Held in **October/ November**, a glorified excuse to drink vast amounts and dress up. Worth visiting to see how South Africans let their hair down.

Festivals

Sport and special interest travel

Archaeology and history

San rock paintings are found throughout South Africa, with a number of copies on display in major museums and art galleries. They are a fascinating introduction to ancient San culture, with the oldest examples having been carbon dated to 27,500 years ago. The most recent

Rock art

paintings show the first white settlers arriving in ox wagons, wearing European dress and hunting with rifles. All paintings are protected under the National Monuments Act of 1969. Some of the best places to see San rock art are in the Drakensberg, the Cederberg Mountains and the eastern Free State.

Museums
Most of the best-known museums in South Africa focus on colonial history, although this is slowly changing, and a couple of more progressive museums have opened in recent years. These include the informative **Nelson Mandela Museum** in Umtata, the disturbing **Holocaust Museum** in Cape Town and the excellent **Apartheid Museum** in Johannesburg. Most provincial museums have collections put together from items left to the town by past residents. These tend to tell similar stories, and once you've visited one it will be difficult to find anything original in other museums. One of the best collections and displays is to be found in Lydenburg in Mpumalanga. The **Kimberley Mine Museum** also has a fine collection. The **Museum of Natal** in Pietermaritzburg is unusual in having an interesting anthropological gallery displaying items from West Africa. However, the best museum in the country relating to African art and culture is to be found in **Tzaneen**, Limpopo (Northern) Province. If you have a serious interest in the history and culture of the region this is a museum well worth a detour.

Birdwatching

With over 700 species of bird recorded in South Africa, birdwatching has become a popular pastime which is easily combined with game viewing. The incredibly diverse ecosystems, ranging from fynbos and semi-desert to rainforest, support a fascinating variety of birds including several rare species that are endemic to South Africa. Highlights include the unusual species such as African penguins by Cape Town and lammergeyers in the Drakensberg.

There is a good selection of books available including *Newman's Birds of Southern Africa* and *Robert's Birds of South Africa*, the two definitive identification guides. Contact: *Southern African Birding*, PO Box 1438, Westville 3630, Durban, T/F031-2665948. Worth contacting for advance expert advice on where to go to see the more elusive species.

Bungee jumping

The most popular location in the region is the old bridge across the Zambezi River at Victoria Falls in Zimbabwe. In recognition of how popular bungee jumping has become several companies now offer jumps in South Africa. The largest operator is *Face Adrenaline*, T021-6977001, www.faceadrenaline.com There are two jumps along the Garden Route. The first at **Gouritz River Bridge** on the Cape Town side of Mossel Bay; the jump is about 60 m. The second is at the **Bloukrans River Bridge** between Plettenberg Bay and Tsitsikamma – this is the highest in the world at approximately 200 m. The first rebound is higher than the full descent at Victoria Falls.

Diving

The convergence of two major oceans' environments provides the South African coastline with a particularly rich and diverse marine flora and fauna. The Agulhas current continually sweeps warm water down from the subtropical Indian Ocean and meets the cold nutrient-rich waters of the Atlantic. This mixing of water temperatures has created a marvellous selection of marine ecosystems, ranging from the tropical coral reefs of KwaZulu Natal through to the temperate kelp forests around Cape Point. The coastline boasts over 10,000 marine species some of which are not found anywhere else in the world.

Diving seasons & conditions
Diving here is regarded by some as challenging due to the launches through heavy surf and erratic weather patterns. The best time of year to dive the east and southern coast is during the South African winter from April to October when the predominant wind comes from the west. Visibility is generally better and the waters calmer. Summertime, October to March, is when you

Tips for responsible diving – adapted from the Marine Conservation Society 'Coral Code'

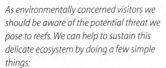

As environmentally concerned visitors we should be aware of the potential threat we pose to reefs. We can help to sustain this delicate ecosystem by doing a few simple things:

Buoyancy Control *Through proper weighting and practice, do not allow yourself or any item of your equipment to touch any living organism.*

Skills Review *If you haven't dived for a while, do a review in the pool or sandy patch before diving around the reef.*

Control your fins *Deep fin kicks around coral can cause damage.*

Avoid kicking up sand *Sand can smother corals and other reef life.*

Never stand on the reef *Corals can be damaged by the slightest touch.*

If you need to hold on to something *Look for a piece of dead coral or rock.*

Know your limits *Don't dive in conditions beyond your skills.*

Avoid temptation *Don't disturb or move things around (eg for photography)*

Do not collect or buy *Shells or any other marine curios (eg dried pufferfish)*

Do not feed fish

Do not ride turtles or hold on to any marine animal *It can easily cause heart attacks or severe shock to the creature.*

Choose your operator wisely *Report irresponsible operators to relevant diving authorities (PADI, NAUI, SSI).*

*See the **Marine Conservation Society** at www.mcsuk.org or contact Communications Officer, T01989-566017, F567815.*

Essentials

can brave the icy waters of the Atlantic for some incredible wreck and kelp dives – visibility often exceeds 20 m. To avoid crowds, avoid South African holidays wherever possible.

Shark attacks According to the International Shark Attack File, in the past 100 years, only 74 fatal attacks on humans have been recorded. None of those were while diving on scuba. Sharks do not mean to eat humans. We are simply not part of their food chain. Most 'attacks' are a case of mistaken identity. It is now on record that sharks are frightened of scuba diver's bubbles. Unless provoked and agitated, a shark will rarely come too close, let alone take a bite.

If you are going to dive in an area where shark encounters are possible, familiarize yourself with shark-diving etiquette – something that should be explained by your local dive-centre or divemaster.

Which wetsuit to wear is explained in the relevant sections. Having your own equipment   **Equipment** considerably reduces costs. **NB** Prior to departure, check your baggage allowance with the airlines and see if you can come to some arrangement for extra weight.

New divers South African waters provide an exciting training ground for first-time divers. PADI, NAUI and CMAS courses available. Five-day entry level courses include theory, pool sessions and four to five ocean training dives. Medical questionnaires must be completed prior to any course and sometimes medical certificates will be required.

Dive facilities The diving community in SA is widespread and the facilities are generally excellent value. The cheapest costs per dive are from R100 without equipment and R150 including equipment. Open Water (beginner) courses, between R1,250 and R2,000 usually include equipment and training manuals. In diving emergencies, recompression chambers are widespread. Dive centres should brief divers on emergency procedures for their areas and carry oxygen and first-aid kits on the boats.

Marine hazards Check with your dive centre for local marine hazards. Here are some common ones, occurring around coral reefs of Northern KwaZulu Natal, and their basic treatments:

Venom of the scorpion fish and stonefish can cause large swelling and intense pain. It is broken down by heat so treat any sting by immersing that part of the body with hot water (50°) for a couple of hours until the pain eases or stops.

Diving jargon used in this section

Visibility *This is how far you can see underwater – measured horizontally.*
Coral Garden *An area of pristine coral with much variety and high concentration.*
Drop Offs *Where a coral reef or shelf drops off into the depths.*
Nitrox *Oxygen Enriched Air – Great value courses available in Cape Town.*
Negative Entries *Entering the water without any air in your buoyancy jacket to enable rapid descent, to avoid strong surface currents and potential shark excitement.*

You can either learn to dive or you can further your diving career with the following organizations: **PADI**, *Professional Association of Dive Instructors;* **NAUI**, *National Association of Underwater Instructors (South African);* **CMAS**, *Confédération Modiale des Activités Subaquatique;* **IANTD**, *International Association for Nitrox and Trimix Divers – specializes in courses for technical diving.*
BSAC, *British Sub Aqua Club*

Fire coral burns must be treated immediately with vinegar or acetic acid (lemons/limes) or large blisters may result.

Jellyfish (blue bottle or sea wasp) stings can also be treated with vinegar, alcohol or urine directly on the sting.

The sting in stingrays' tails can cause severe wounds if trodden on or caught. Clean the wound. Immerse wound in 50° water for two hours, followed by antibiotics and anti-tetanus injection if necessary.

If bitten or stung, immediately notify the medic first-aider on board or at the dive centre. Consult a doctor if pain worsens or treatment is ineffective.

Recommended reading *Two Oceans* – published by David Philip Publishers (Pty) Ltd, available in most bookshops in South Africa. Beautifully presented and very useful identification guides to the marine life of southern Africa.

KwaZulu Natal: **Sodwana Bay** Just south of the Mozambique border, Sodwana Bay is a Mecca for South African divers due to its warmer, clearer waters, wide variety of exciting tropical reefs and rare but magical whalesharks. There are common sightings of turtles, reef sharks, ribbontail and giant stingrays, along with a huge variety of hard and soft corals and colourful reef fish. The two-mile reef is the most visited due to its proximity to shore. Despite the thousands of divers who visit this reef each year, the coral is looking healthy and the fish life overflowing, particularly on *'Antons'* and *'Stringer'* which house resident hanging shoals of humpbacked and many lined snapper, baardmen and bannerfish (coachmen). *Green Tree* at 11 miles is a craggy area riddled with caves and swim throughs. Large bass in the holes and teeming fish life on the top reef. A photographer's dream is *Breaking Waters* (11 miles) – at low tide you can spend an hour at 3 m wide-eyed, just watching and hearing the thunderous waves roll towards and then crash overhead. *Mushroom Rocks* and *Amphitheatre* at 7 miles are popular sites with interesting topography varying in depth to max 25 m. Look closely for little life at 5 miles where the flat reef holds many surprises for the curious. *'Deep Sponge'* off 2 miles is a gently descending seabed from 23 m. Like cactii of the desert, the seafloor is sparsely populated with purples, reds and oranges of small cup and branching sponges. White and black tip reef sharks regularly seen cruising around these flat reefs and during the slow ascent from 30 m, the diver has time to look out for passing eagle rays and shark traffic. Dolphins are regularly spotted on the way back from dive sites and occasionally whalesharks too. If they hang around, most boats will allow you to snorkel with them. Sodwana Bay is well-equipped for divers with a permanent medical station on the beach. Facilities for gear washing available on site and for payment local boys will carry and wash your equipment. Major crime has reduced drastically and is now a problem of the past. Just keep obvious temptation out of reach and don't leave easy pickings lying around.

The Sardine Run

This mass movement of pilchards, anchovy and sardines occurs in June when many of the fish head north from the Western Cape. Following the cold water streams, several shoals congregate about 40 km south of KwaZulu Natal Border. When the water temperature cools, some of these shoals travel north, hugging the Natal coastline so closely that they sometimes beach themselves. The event attracts thousands of people who wait on beaches armed with buckets and nets to scoop up the easy catch. Right on the tails of these shoals are the predators; Humpback Whales, Bottlenose and Common Dolphins, Sharks, Turtles, Game fish, and a host of Marine Birds: White Chinned Petrels, Cape Gannets, Storm Petrels and Albatross to name a few. Boat trips are organised for tourists to view the spectacle.

Essentials

Dive centres *Coral Divers*, T035-5710209, F5710042, www.coraldivers.co.za PADI courses available up to Divemaster level. Costs: five-day dive package included, tented accommodation start from R1250. Basic en suite huts available. Young, sociable atmosphere. Daily KZN Wildlife fees R20 per person. *Sodwana Bay Lodge*, T035-5710095, F5710144, www.sodwanadivelodge. co.za Luxurious accommodation with professionally run PADI dive centre offering a number of all inclusive diving package deals that can be booked in advance from Durban, the courses include transport to and from Durban (toll free T0861-000333).

Water temperature Between 21°C mid-winter and sometimes as high as 30°C mid-summer. You will need 5 mm two-piece wetsuit with hood if you feel the cold. **Seasons** South African winter – April to September. May is the best month for diving. Avoid Easter weekend. **Visibility** Variable. Average 15 m, up to 25 m. **Diving extras** Usually a surcharge of R10-25 is added to cost of dives if visiting further reefs.

Aliwal Shoal lies 5 km offshore, south of Umkomaas. It is roughly 3 km long, has a rich and varied marine life and some interesting dive sites. The annual excitement at Aliwal is during raggie season when a dive between August and November practically guarantees that you will be surrounded by the reputedly docile spotted ragged tooth sharks (also known as grey nurse sharks, or sand tigers). The diving operators below run popular shark courses which include dives with ragged tooth sharks and come highly recommended. *Raggie Cave* lives up to its name during this period with sometimes 20+ sharks around divers. During the summer months, tiger, hammerhead and Zambezi sharks are also seen here along with the odd great white shark (see above for info on diving with sharks). Out of Raggie season but during good diving conditions in May/June, *The Produce* wreck, 176 m long, is a fascinating dive. The Norwegian Bulk carrier sank after hitting Aliwal Shoal. She lies on her starboard side and has gradually formed a reef. She has an entire eco-system living in and around her. Glass fish and lionfish hide in the dark corners along with gigantic brindle bass (Malabar grouper). Humpback whalesong is loud and clear between August and October. 'Sardine Run' trips are organized during the first two weeks of June.

KwaZulu Natal: Aliwal Shoal

Launch site Umkomaas. **Dive centres** There are several: *Andy Cobb Eco Diving*, T031-964239, www.adventurescuba.co.za Runs specialist shark courses and dive tours. *Sea Fever Lodge and Dive Centre*, T039-9731328, F9731285, www.seafever.co.za PADI affiliated. Fully equipped with training pool, three rigid inflatable boats and professional skippers showing an impressive knowledge of the local dive sites and sometimes challenging sea conditions. Costs per dive R130. Nitrox and Trimix Fills. PADI Instructor Development Courses conducted by full time Course Director – Graham Powell. *Aliwal Dive Charters*, T039-9732233, F9732133, www.aliwalshoal.co.za Run PADI, NAUI, CMAS, SSI, BSAC courses to instructor level. A variety of accommodation available. Costs include transfers to beach: Open water course - R1300 Per dive: R120. Dive schools, clubs and tour operators qualify for discount. Contact: Swinny or Sonja. **Water temperature** 19°C (winter) - 24°C. 5 mm

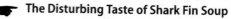

The Disturbing Taste of Shark Fin Soup

Essentials

(The following text, written by Bruce McCoubrey, is based on extracts from a report produced by the Barbara Delano Foundation (US) and Wildlifeline, London. Any queries are to be directed to Bruce McCoubrey at: brucemcc@hotmail.com or T(UK)07940-735644.)

"Fisheries and shark populations in East and Southern Africa are on a long-term collision course. Traditional use of shark meat for protein in developing countries like Tanzania has existed for centuries. However the spiraling trade value of shark fins for export to the Far East has decimated many near shore and reef species, as well as deep-water pelagic sharks.

The highly-prized fins of the Giant guitarfish and sawfish have pushed these species towards local extinction in parts of East Africa. Other reef and coastal species of shark are already overexploited. In Southern Africa, such as Madagascar, Mozambique and South Africa, large-scale industrial tuna fisheries have had untold impacts on pelagic species such as Mako, Blue Shark and Thresher sharks taken as by-catch. The fins are cut off and the shark, often still alive, is discarded at sea.

The large demand for fins reached its peak in the late 80s and early 90s as the Tiger economies of the Far East increased demand for shark fin soup as a status symbol. However, demand from an increasingly prosperous mainland China threatens to make the fin of the shark its very own epitaph."

two-piece wetsuit with hood if you feel the cold. Thermoclines are common. **Depths** Sites vary – for the raggies, 18 m is average. **Visibility** 10–30 m. **Diving seasons** Raggie season - August to November. Best diving conditions - May/June.

KwaZulu Natal:
Protea Banks

Protea Banks lie approximately 8 km offshore from Shelly Beach. Stretching over 10 km, the area for diving is concentrated on the higher pinnacles (Northern and Southern) which cover 3 km. The reef begins at 30 m so experienced divers only. It also helps if you're fit as the currents can be strong at times. A Nitrox (Oxygen Enriched Air) qualification means you'll be able to hang out for longer in places like *Sandshark Gulley* – where 20 or more sharks is usual.

Protea Banks is not yet a protected area or Marine Reserve. The numbers of sharks that visit this area have been tremendous but they're apparently in decline. Likely causes are the foreign long liners who catch them for Shark Fin Soup.

The reef itself is interesting but you'll get a slap from the Divemaster if you start staring at angelfish or nudibranches. Rightly so as you'll have just missed 30 hammerheads cruising above you. Book three or four dives to improve your chances of meeting sharks. Nature is unpredictable and you can't always book the sharks.

Launch site Shelly Beach. **Dive centres** *African Dive Adventures*, T082-4567885 (mob), F039-3171483, www.cybercraft.co.za/dive/ The longest standing dive centre. Professionally run by Roland and Beulagh. Dives led by experienced guides (in English and German). Costs per dive R130-150 including equipment. Highly recommended. **Water temperature** Between 17°C (September) and 24°C (April) with a few icy thermoclines. 5 mm two-piece wetsuit with hood and 7 mm two-piece for mid-winter diving. **Average depth** 40 m but the average depth of the reef is between 29-35m. **Seasons** April/May are the best months for diving Protea Banks but avoid the chaotic Easter weekend. **Marine encounters** Spotted ragged tooth sharks - July to September, Zambezi sharks - October (small) - May (big), schooling scalloped hammerhead sharks, potato bass, gamefish arrive January through to April/May. Large sandsharks and black spotted ribbontail rays are common April/May; eagle rays and manta rays also seen.

Sleeping *Margate Backpackers*, 14 Collis St, Margate, T/F3122176. Dorms, doubles plus camping in the garden, can arrange all diving excursions. For the full list of accommodation see page 410.

Despite low visibility, the sites around PE are magnificent and boast coral colours more vivid than tropical waters. A torch is needed on most day dives. The many gulleys and overhangs make the dives an exciting place for the curious. Outside reefs on the 'Wild Side' - *Thunderbolt, Rie Banks* and *Evans Peak* (near St Croix Island Marine Reserve) are for the more advanced diver due to challenging currents and depth. Pristine reefs with both hard and soft corals and lots of 'little' life, ie colourful nudibranches (pretty sea slugs) and beautiful anemones. *The Haarlem* wreck is littered with leopard and pyjama sharks generally seen lazily flopping over each other in dark crevices. It is not unusual to see huge pods of dolphins, African penguins and southern right whales in the bay.

Launch site Hobie Beach. **Dive centres** *Ocean Divers International*, Boardwalk Centre, T5831790, www.odipe.co.za PADI courses and equipment. *Pro Dive*, Walmer Park, T3687880, T083-6598485 (mob), dive@prodive.co.za 5-star dive centre, courses, charters, equipment hire, one-day 'resort' courses, underwater specialty courses. Costs for a dive, R80-R125 depending on distance from shore. **Water temperature** 16-20° Minimum 5 mm two-piece wetsuit plus hood and gloves. **Seasons** With the Westerlies in winter. Locals dive year round but find September through to mid-November has the most unpredictable weather. **Visibility** Average 5-6 m. Up to 15 m. Rarely 20 m. **Possible marine encounters** Leopard sharks, pyjama sharks (dogfish), red Roman rock cod, colourful nudibranchs, anemones, stingrays, ragged tooth sharks, juvenile hammerhead sharks in December/January, southern right whales in winter, humpback whales all summer. Great white shark is also a possible encounter and not one necessarily to be afraid of.

Sleeping *Lungile Backpackers*, 10 minutes' walk from Hobie Beach. Very cosy home from home. Swimming pool, TV, internet use, washing machine, clean kitchen, bathrooms and friendly staff. Rooms from R50. Camp in the small garden for R20 per person per night. For a full accommodation listing, see page 322.

From the windy city of Port Elizabeth westwards, the Garden Route weather is more than a little changeable. In fact there is a local saying – "What comes after two days of rain? Monday!" If you want four dives a day in 'azure-blue' seas, visit the Maldives instead. You must be game for all conditions, and flexible in your dive planning. If you love exploring the reef for its little life, enjoy wreck diving or just revel in challenging conditions, dive in and you won't regret it.

The Garden Route offers a wide range of dive sites. *The Underwater Trail* at Storms River Mouth camp, Tsitsikamma National Park, is reasonably protected but calmer after a westerly wind. Great for snorkelling. You can dive if you bring own equipment. Spend a good hour pottering amongst the shoals of Steenbras, marvelling at the Gas Flame Nudibranchs (pretty sea slugs), urchins and anemones. Ragged tooth sharks, and the little dogfish (leopard/pyjama sharks) are also seen.

Inside Knysna Lagoon *Tapas Jetty* (shore entry from Thesen's Jetty) invariably a poor-visibility dive, and without much imagination you could miss catching a glimpse of the indigenous Knysna seahorse, amongst other creatures. By searching through the numerous bottles and tyres scattered over the silty bottom, this can be a bizarrely satisfying dive. These have created artificial reefs for the tiny creatures. Look out for blennies' homes in bottlenecks, camouflaged and very shy seahorses, and a variety of nudibranches. Take a local buddy as you won't find seahorses without one. *Paquita* wreck (a shore entry clearly signposted at The Heads) lies broken in the channel just before The Heads. Covered with colourful anemones, soft corals and shoals of white steenbras and strepie. Must dive it half an hour before high tide to avoid strong tidal flow.

Outside the Knysna Heads Superb diving but more dependent on the weather. Main sites; *Bruce Se Bank, Knopie, East Cape*. These are deeper, more challenging dives which can be hectic for novice divers on rougher days. A fairground surge shoots the divers through gulleys and around the rocks and can at times yo-yo divers from 10-20 m in a second or two. Great fun for the experienced but judge your own capabilities.

Gerrickes Point reefs, launching from Sedgefield, are full of gulleys, walls, pinnacles and swim-throughs. Although sometimes rough on top, the surge is gentle enough underneath due to average depth 24-30 m. The life on the reefs is abundant and visibility averages approximately 10 m. Notorious area for great white sharks, the dive-briefings includes rules for reducing the risk of inviting their attention.

Plettenberg Bay is popular with native tourists. It has lots of soft coral reefs. Due to the more sheltered location, these reefs are more frequently accessible than weather-dependent, colourful outer reefs of Knysna and therefore act as a perfect alternative. Home to dolphins and seals, the bay also acts as a nursery to the endangered southern right whales which come to calve in winter and spring (July-December).

Dive centres *Stormsriver Adventures*, T042-2811836, www.stormsriver.com *Pro-Dive* (see above) in Port Elizabeth organizes trips here. Entrance fee R40. **Knysna** *The Heads Adventure Centre*, Bottom Car Park, Knysna Heads, T3840831. PADI courses, equipment rental, daily trips to reefs and to the Paquita wreck in the lagoon. **Plettenburg Bay** *Beyond the Beach*, T5331158, T082-7733344 (mob), runs daily dives and rent equipment; *Diving International*, T5330381, T082-4906226 (mob).

Best time to dive After Westerlies: March-May. Hardy locals will dive year round. **Water temperature** 15° C (brrrrr) up to 23° C in summer. Thick suits needed, preferably 7 mm two-piece wetsuits and hood for winter. **Visibility** Average 5-6 m. Up to 15 m. **Possible marine encounters** As Port Elizabeth, plus endemic Knysna seahorse found inside Knysna Lagoon (see above).

Great white shark cage diving – Dyer Island, off Gansbaai

Dyer Island is located 10 km offshore. Populated by seals, penguins, large gamefish and birds, the area is a natural hunting ground for the most revered of the apex marine predators: *Carcharidon Carcharius*, the great white shark. The great white is a protected species off the shores of Australia, Southern Africa, The Maldives and areas of the US. Shark cage diving raises many questions about teaching sharks to associate humans with food, but for many, cage diving is a chance to witness this magnificent animal in its natural habitat safely.

With the cage diving industry booming in South Africa, there are quite a number of operators all stating 'eco-friendliness'. Just watch out for some who bait the sharks close to swimming beaches, or cleverly pose as a Research Institute attracting high paying volunteers for supposed 'scientific' research.

Recommended operators *White Shark Adventures*, 13 Main Rd, Gansbaai, T028-3841380, T082-8226920 (mob), www.whitesharkdiving.com Member WHISPRA (White Shark Preservation Association). Run by Jackie and Rosemary Smit. Supports marine research at Stellenbosch University. Their boat, *Master of Happiness*, looks small and the cage even smaller, but both are within safety standards and adequate for shark viewing. Salty seadog Jackie is full of entertaining shark tales, has an obvious passion for these creatures and takes great pleasure in educating others. An enlightening and thrilling day out for divers and non-divers.

Baiting sharks Thankfully, *most* operators have nowadays discarded the methods of baiting with boogie boards, and feeding the sharks with meat or seal-meat. The 'chum-mix' generally consists of ground fish and oil. This is continuously piped into the water and scattered by the current to direct the white sharks towards the boat. A strong net bag full of fish then entices the shark closer to the boat so that excited onlookers can snap away to their hearts' content.

Shark viewing and cage diving Shark viewing is a patience game, but with plenty of penguins, seals and flocks of hunting cormorants around Dyer Island, waiting for the sharks is not exactly a boring task. There is roughly a 30% chance of seeing a great white from the cage and 70% from the boat. All diving equipment provided.

Costs High due to expensive tourist boat licenses. One day/night including accomodation/diving R1870; non diving R1410. Check conditions of payment before booking.

Season for great whites Higher chance of viewing from the cage during winter (April to September) when there are more shark sightings and clearer waters.

Cape Town   Many scientists argue about where the Two Oceans actually meet. Logic points to the southernmost tip of Africa at Cape Agulhas but the confusion arises when you see just how different the marine environments are either side of Cape Point. The advantages, from a diving perspective, are obvious; not only can you experience several marine ecosystems, water temperatures and conditions but also if the wind's blowing the wrong way one side, the chances are you can dive on the other.

Launch sites *AO* – Hout Bay; *FB* – Millers Point. **Diving Seasons** *AO* – from October to April with the strong south-easterlies. *FB* – during SA winter May to October. **Water temperature** *FB*: 13-20°C. *AO*: 7-10°C. 7 mm two-piece wetsuits with thick hood and booties is adequate for both sides. Drysuits are even better if you have them. Do not use neoprene drysuits in summer unless you want to lose severe amounts of weight! **Visibility** In season, this can reach 20 m both sides.

'AO' means Atlantic Ocean and 'FB' means False Bay on the Indian Ocean side of Cape Point

There are several types of diving environments and possible marine encounters. **Kelp diving**, in the tall Kelp Forests: the life is prolific and the sighting of playful and inquisitive seals and Shy Sharks (dogfish) common. Also seen are large sluggish cow sharks, cheeky Hottentots and klipfish. **Wreck diving**, The *Smitswinkel Bay* wrecks were scuttled by the Navy in the early seventies. There are two frigates, the *Good Hope* and *Transvaal;* two trawlers *Oratava* and *Princess Elisabeth;* and the diamond dredger the *Rockeater.* All lie at over 30 m, so experienced divers only. Life on the multitude of *shipwrecks* around the Cape vary from the primary colonizers of mussels to colourful soft corals, anemones, sponges, larger fish, crayfish and small sharks (dogfish). A dive on the *Maori* is recommended. This 5,317 tonne British cargo ship ran aground in 1909 carrying explosives, water piping and crockery. She lies between 12-20 m on the Atlantic side, and due to the shelter of the bay, is still fairly intact. **Other marine life**: nudibranches (pretty sea slugs) are abundant on both sides of Cape Point. In one dive you can count at least 25 different species. Great whites have been spotted on occasion. Southern right whales play in False Bay from August to October.

Two Oceans Aquarium If the Cape waters are too cold, you can dive in the predator tank at the aquarium, on the V&A Waterfront. The tank is surprisingly large, with inquisitive ragged tooth sharks, stingrays, turtles and large predator fish. This is an excellent dive and highly recommended as an introduction to shark diving. Other exhibits provide fascinating insights on the biodiversity within the surrounding oceans. Contact Two Oceans on T021-4183823, www.aquarium.co.za for details on tank dives.

Dive centres *Dusky Dive Academy*, T4261622. Beginners' instruction. *Two Ocean Divers International*, 1 Central Parade, Victoria Rd, Camps Bay, T/F7908833, www.two-oceans.co.za Full range of PADI-recognized instruction and equipment hire, as well as organized tours to the best dive sites and great white shark cage dives. *Table Bay Diving*, V&A Waterfront, T4198822, spero@netactive.co.za Organizes night diving, wreck dives and seal dives and sell scuba gear.

Golf

South Africa has always been well-represented in the golf world. First there was Bobby Locke who beat the likes of Hogan and Snead and won the British Open four times. Then there was Gary Player, a name respected throughout the golfing world, a winner of nine majors and seven Australian Opens. Continuing the great tradition is Ernie Els, fast becoming a leading international golfer. This all adds up to some excellent facilities and some stunning courses which help you forget your score. The following are a selection of the country's finest courses: **Milnerton**, Cape Town, championship links course; **Stellenbosch**, enjoy a peaceful round amongst the vineyards in the heart of the Winelands; **Fancourt Country Club**, George, exclusive course designed by Player, ideal for visitors on the Garden Route; **Durban Country Club**, rural course within the city, ideal for anyone on business with little free time; **Houghton**, Johannesburg, venue for SA Open, a real challenge; **Gary Player Country Club**, Sun City, venue for the Million Dollar Classic which has attracted most of the world's top golfers; **Hans Merensky**, Phalaborwa, enjoy a round after game viewing in Kruger; crocodiles and hippos live in the water hazards!

Hiking

See map for location of hiking trails. See under individual hikes for further details

South Africa has an enormous number of well-developed hiking trails, many passing through spectacular areas of natural beauty. These range from pleasant afternoon strolls through nature reserves to challenging hikes in Wilderness Areas. Hiking in South Africa does involve forward planning and permits, but the rewards and the choice of trails are well worth the effort.

The opportunities for hiking begin on the edge of Cape Town on **Table Mountain** with other coastal trails along the Garden Route at **Tsitsikamma**, 65 km, and further along the coast with the **Strandloper Trail**, 93 km. The **Klipspringer Trail**, 40 km, and the **Pofadder Trail**, 72 km, crossing magnificent areas of semi-desert along the Orange River just south of the Kalahari. The **Drakensberg**, bordering Lesotho, is a national park nearly 300 km long where a network of trails (some climbing to over 3,000 m) offer hikers a vast mountain region with undiscovered hiking possibilities comparable to regions of the Himalayas. The **Giant's Cup Hiking Trail**, 60 km, and the hike up to **Mont-aux-Sources**, 20 km, are two of the most popular Drakensberg hiking trails.

Day hikes   Day hikes are very popular, and well-signposted trails can be found in most nature reserves. Such hikes are easy to organize and need little or no special equipment. On the shorter trails you won't even need hiking boots - a pair of trainers will normally be quite adequate.

Hiking trails   These are longer trails, involving at least one night spent in the wild. You should carry backpacks with a sleeping bag, tent, food and other equipment. Depending on the facilities available, nights are either spent in a campsite or an overnight hut. These trails are not guided and hikers will be able to get brochures and maps when they apply for permits.

Wilderness trekking   These are hiking areas where there are no designated footpaths and hikers are free to roam at will. There is usually no specific overnight accommodation – one is left to sleep in rock shelters or to pitch a tent wherever possible. Hikers entering wilderness areas are basically left to their own devices and should have a good knowledge of map reading and have enough experience of hiking to deal with extreme weather conditions if necessary. There are wilderness areas for hikers in the Cederberg and the southern section of the Drakensberg.

Guided wilderness trails   Wilderness areas in the game reserves are designated areas where no human activity takes place except for the hiking trails. The idea behind them is to introduce people to an undisturbed wilderness. The trails concentrate on game viewing walks with a game ranger and are less strenuous than other hiking trails as they cover shorter distances on day walks departing each day from a base camp. These are some of the most expensive trails to go on but all equipment and food is provided. Reservations for places on wilderness trails should be made well in advance as they are extremely popular. That said, it is always worth trying at the last minute as cancellations are common. Wilderness trails are organized in **Kruger**, **Hluhluwe-Umfolozi** and in the **Greater St Lucia Wetland**.

Permits   Permits are necessary on most long-distance trails where hikers will be expected to pay for the use of the trail and the huts en route. There is usually a minimum number of three people who will be allowed on a trail at one time. Please observe the restrictions imposed by permits – they are for your own safety, as well as conservation. In an emergency, search parties will struggle to find you if you have walked elsewhere.

On shorter day trails a permit will simply involve a small fee and signing the hiking register to let the nature reserve staff know how many people are using the trails. This also helps them make sure that everyone has safely returned.

Conditions   It is worth remembering that some of the trails involve conditions which few European hikers will have experienced before – be sure to check on local conditions before setting off. Extremes of weather, from the intense heat of the Karoo to frost and snow in the Drakensberg are not the only factors to take into account. The Wild Coast Hiking Trail will involve crossing shark infested estuaries whilst on the wilderness trails in areas of Kruger and Hluhluwe-

Umfolozi you will be accompanied by an armed guard to protect you from attacks by animals. That said, most problems will be relatively easy to solve with the information and leaflets provided by the trail organizers.

One of the practical problems facing hikers in South Africa is that public transport rarely reaches interesting hiking areas. The alternative is to hire a car to reach the trail head, but this will obviously involve paying for a car for several days while it is not in use. One of the few areas where it is relatively easy to get to the trails is at Underberg and Sani Pass. The Giant's Cup Hiking Trail starts near Sani Pass and ends at Bushman's Nek, it is possible to arrange to be collected at the end of the hike by the owners of hostels or guest houses in the area.

Transport & organization

Hikers new to Southern Africa have the option of joining an organized hike with a specialist tour operator or with a local hiking association. This can help to solve the logistical problems of organizing a hike, and is a good way to meet people and find out about hiking in this region. There is a good range of hiking books available in South Africa with comprehensive maps and detailed information on history and wildlife.

Security is not a major problem for hikers but there are some areas particularly at Mont-aux-Sources and the Wild Coast Hiking Trail where hikers have been mugged. In areas where there is a security problem, hikers should travel in larger groups. Walk with more than just two people whenever possible, and leave valuables in your hotel safe. Most importantly, take heed of local advice, even if it does sound a bit over the top at times. Ironically, the safest trails are probably those in the most remote regions of the Karoo and the Kalahari region where there are virtually no permanent settlements. Elsewhere in the country you may not always be aware of it, but there is usually a collection of homes on a farm nearby.

Security

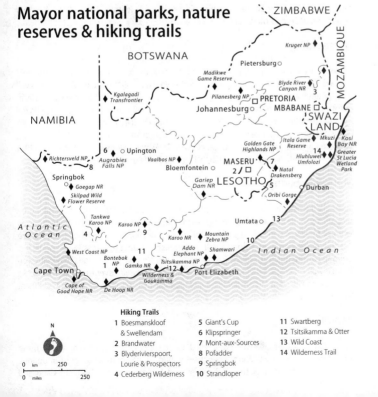

Mayor national parks, nature reserves & hiking trails

Hiking Trails

1 Boesmanskloof & Swellendam	5 Giant's Cup	11 Swartberg
2 Brandwater	6 Klipspringer	12 Tsitsikamma & Otter
3 Blyderivierspoort, Lourie & Prospectors	7 Mont-aux-Sources	13 Wild Coast
4 Cederberg Wilderness	8 Pofadder	14 Wilderness Trail
	9 Springbok	
	10 Strandloper	

0 km 250
0 miles 250

Equipment The equipment required depends greatly on the areas in which you intend to hike. For most day hikes, a pair of lightweight walking boots, shorts, shirt, sunglasses, sun hat and a day pack with food, water and waterproof clothes will be enough. Remember, it is possible to experience a blazing African sun and torrential rain all in one day. For long hikes in the Drakensberg or the Cape in winter the weather conditions will be similar to Europe – take layered clothing with warm fleeces and Goretex outer layers to deal with heavy rains and snow. For longer hikes a lightweight tent and a two or three season sleeping bag will be essential.

A cooking stove and utensils can be useful, as in many wilderness areas hikers are not allowed to make fires. A multi-fuel stove which takes paraffin or petrol is probably the best all-round choice, as Camping Gaz cylinders can be hard to find in rural areas. It is a good idea to buy dried lightweight foods (couscous, pasta, pulses etc) from good supermarkets in the larger cities before you set off on a hike. Rural stores often sell a limited range of tinned foods which are heavy and not always very appetising. Pilchards in tomato sauce on sliced white bread loses its appeal after the first few days.

Survey maps are generally only available in major cities, although designated trails like the Wild Coast Hiking Trail and the Drakensberg Trails have special maps for hikers. Contact hiking organizations to find out about availability – many maps are in the process of being redesigned with new African names for villages and natural features. Most camping equipment can be bought in major cities for a fraction of the price one might pay in Europe. Everyone has their own opinion as to what a backpack should contain, but it pays to at least have the following: map; compass; tent; backpack; sleeping bag, two or three season; sleeping mat; lightweight boots; thick socks, cotton or wool; torch; penknife; cooking stove; cooking utensils; dried foods; sun hat; sunglasses; sunblock; suntan lotion; aftersun lotion; insect repellent; first aid kit; whistle; bathing costume; towel; thermal underwear; fleece jacket; waterproof jacket and trousers; shorts; long sleeved cotton shirt; binoculars.

Useful *National Hiking Way Board*, 643 Leyds St, Muckleneuk, Pretoria, T012-3439770. *Hiking* **addresses** *Federation of South Africa*, T011-8866507.

Horse riding

A popular activity amongst farming communities and in the mountains. On trails lasting more than a day you will be responsible for looking after your horse. In the **Drakensberg** hotels will organize anything from a short morning trot to a six-day mountain safari. This is very popular in **Lesotho** where the pony is the main form of transport in rural areas. Western-style riding in the Maluti Mountains is organized by *Bokpoort Farm* outside Clarens in the Free State. On the **Garden Route** you can ride in the ancient forests close to Knysna, and on the beaches in the **Western Cape**. Contact the *Association of Horse Trails and Safaris of South Africa*, 36 12th Av, Parktown North, Johannesburg 2193, T011-7883923, F8808401.

Mountain biking

Many nature reserves and designated wilderness areas have recently increased their accessibility for mountain bikes. Some excellent routes have been planned out which suit all levels of fitness. The following are some of the best organized regions: **De Hoop Nature Reserve** in the Overberg; **Tulbagh Valley**; **Kamiesberg** close to Garies in Namaqualand; **Goegap Nature Reserve** outside Springbok; and in the mountains around **Citrusdal**. **Cape Town** is well-organized for mountain bikers – contact *Downhill Adventures*, T021-4220388, downhill@mweb.co.za   Rents out bikes and organize tours on Table Mountain, Cape Point Nature Reserve and the Winelands.

Paragliding

South Africa has several world-renowned paragliding locations. Leaping from **Table Mountain** or peacefully wafting above the **Kalahari** are two of the most popular options. Cape Town aside, most of the action is around **Kuruman** in the Northern Cape and

Baberton in Mpumalanga. Climatic conditions in South Africa are ideal - good thermal activity allows one to climb between 6 and 8 m a second and the cloud base is usually at 5,000 m. The best season is between November and February. Distance and height records have recently been set in the country, which has encouraged the growth of the sport.

Courses can now be done in most cities, costing around R1,800, and you need to complete a minimum of 25 flights to get your licence. For a full list of clubs contact the *South African Paragliding and Hang-gliding Association*, PO Box 1993, Halfway House, Centurion 1685 , T/F012-6681219, www.sahpa.co.za.

Steam trains

South Africa's first railways were built in the 1860s in Cape Town and Durban, with Port Elizabeth, East London and Kimberley soon following suit. This had a major effect in opening up the interior of the country, as South Africa's inland mountain barriers and winding rivers had long caused problems for overland transport. Prior to the advent of the train, goods were carried by ox wagons and porters and seldom managed to travel more than 20 km a day – the journey between Cape Town and Kimberley could take over a month.

The concept of developing the railways was promoted by Cecil Rhodes, who dreamed of a railway line stretching all the way from the Cape to Cairo. Their development revolutionized communications in the colonies, which was felt to be essential for effective administration and political control. This was an attitude shared by Paul Kruger who, following the discovery of gold in the Transvaal, attempted to limit British influence by not connecting Pretoria to any of the British controlled ports. Instead, a line crossed the lowveld to Lourenço Marques in Mozambique.

Vintage steam train excursions South Africa attracts many vintage steam train enthusiasts. The best known train tours are the modern diesel electric *Blue Train* and *Rovos Rail*, 'Pride of Africa', which run long distance luxury train safaris. Their rolling stock dates from 1893 to 1970 but the majority of the carriages were built during the 1920s and 1930s (see page 546 for details).

There are several less widely known vintage steam trains which run day excursions through amazing scenery. These locos were built specifically for South Africa and there are some unusual pieces of rolling stock to see including a steam crane, a re-enforced carriage for transporting gold bullion and the original De Beers directors coach built in Chicago.

Tour operators include: the *Apple Express* in Port Elizabeth (not running at time of writing); the *Banana Express* running from Port Shepstone to Oribi Gorge; the *Outeniqua Choo-Tjoe* running between George and Knysna through the wetlands of the Wilderness Nature Reserve; the *Umgeni Steam Railway*, at the Natal Railway Museum in Hilton just outside of Pietermaritzburg; and the old electric tram at Kimberley that runs from outside the city hall to the Kimberley Mine Museum.

Useful numbers *Banana Express*, T039-6824821; *Outeniqua Choo-Tjoe*, T044-8018289 or 044-3821361; *The Blue Train*; T012-3348459; *Rovos Rail Steam Safaris*, T012-3158258; *Umgeni Steam Railway*, T033-3431857; *Union Limited Steam Safari Train*, T021-4494391, F4494395.

Spectator sports

South Africans love watching sport. **Cricket** and **rugby** are largely the preserve of white South Africans, with **soccer** being hugely popular among the black population. Facilities, at least for the former two, are often excellent, with first class stadiums in Bloemfontein (Springbok Park), Johannesburg (Ellis Park), Durban (Kings Park) and Cape Town (Newlands). Soccer is based in Guateng. The national soccer team is known as Bafana Bafana (roughly meaning 'our boys'), and has been gradually metamorphosing into a respectable international side since winning the African Cup of Nations in 1996. The Cricket World Cup is being hosted by South Africa during 2003. South Africa's rugby team, the Springboks, won the Rugby World Cup in 1995 and then-president Nelson Mandela memorably awarded the trophy in a Springbok's jersey – as

Essentials

traditionally white an item of clothing as can be imagined. Since then, however, many South African whites have complained of excessive government intervention in rugby and cricket, with speculation growing that racial quotas will be introduced into the predominantly white national sides. Interestingly, there has less emphasis by the government on introducing racial quotas into the predominantly black soccer teams.

Surfing

South Africa has quickly established itself as a major surfing hotspot, and has some of the best waves in the world. There are, however, two drawbacks to surfing in South Africa. Firstly, the waters are cold, especially around the Cape, and full-length wetsuits are generally essential. Second, there is a small risk of shark attack – but remember that attacks on surfers are very rare, while fatal attacks are almost unheard of. Wherever you surf, be sure to listen to local advice, not just vital for safety, but also for learning about the best local surf spots.

Jeffreys Bay on the south coast of the Eastern Cape is undoubtedly South Africa's surfing Mecca, known for its consistently good surf and host to the annual Billabong surf championships in July. This is also a good place to learn surfing, with a number of courses available and areas of reliable, small breaks which are prefect for learning. The whole southern coast is in fact dotted with good breaks, particularly around **Port Elizabeth** and **East London**. **Cape Town**, too, has an ever-expanding surfing community with some excellent, reliable breaks on the Atlantic and False Bay beaches. Surfing in the Indian Ocean at **Durban** and the **KwaZulu Natal beaches**, is a far warmer experience than the cool oceans of the Cape, though is only permitted at designated areas due to the unpredictable currents. The Golden Mile on Durban's beachfront has good surf, well-protected by lifeguards and the presence of shark nets and is ideal for the beginner. Floodlit night surfing is sometimes arranged in Durban, which is equally entertaining for the spectator.

Safaris

See also wildlife colour section

No visit to South Africa is complete without at least one visit to a major game reserve. The best parks for seeing wild animals are **Kruger**, **Pilanesberg**, **Itala**, **Hluhluwe-Umfolozi** and **Kgalagadi Transfrontier Park**. The game reserves here are not as crowded as the East African game parks and offer visitors the chance of seeing splendid African landscapes and wildlife including the Big Five: elephant, buffalo, rhinoceros, lion and leopard.

South Africa's wildlife parks are well-organized with good facilities for game viewing from well-surfaced roads and hides overlooking waterholes. You have the freedom to explore the game reserves over two or three days either on organized game drives and game walks or with your own transport.

Game viewing

Game viewing in South Africa's game reserves is left to the individual to a much greater extent than in East Africa. Most of the reserves are rarely crowded and you will have the opportunity to drive on an extensive network of surfaced or gravel roads which visit waterholes, hides and the various different ecosystems within the parks. The occasional traffic jam at Kruger is the worst that most visitors experience with overcrowding.

As visitors are largely left to their own devices, it is a good idea to buy one of the wildlife identification books which are available in camp shops. The best times to go viewing game are early in the morning and late in the afternoon. The midday heat is usually too intense for the animals who will rest up in thickets for most of the day. The best season for game viewing is during the winter months from July to September when the dry weather forces animals to congregate around rivers and waterholes. The height and thickness of the vegetation is much less at this time of year making it easier to spot wildlife. The disadvantage of game viewing in winter is that the animals are not in their best condition, while the winter landscape looks harsh and barren. Summer weather, from November to January when rainfall is at its highest, is the best time of year for the animals – they will be in good condition after feeding on the new shoots, and there are chances of seeing breeding displays and young foals. The landscape is green and lush at this time of year and is particularly beautiful but the thick vegetation and the wide availability of water will mean that the wildlife is far more widespread and difficult to spot.

Driving around endlessly searching for animals is not the best way to spot many of these creatures. The optimum speed for game viewing by car is around 15 km per hour. The drives can be broken up by stops at waterholes, picnic sites and hides. Time spent near a waterhole out of your car gives you an opportunity to listen to the sounds of the bush and experience the rhythms of nature as game moves to and from the water. The areas where you are allowed out of your car are quite specifically designated; game reserves are not just large parks and the animals are wild and should not be approached on foot. **Never** get out of the car unless it is at a designated area. Not only are you liable to be prosecuted and thrown out of the park, but you may well be seriously injured or killed.

South Africa's game reserves are very well-organized and following the few simple park rules will ensure an enjoyable stay. The parks are only open to visitors in their own cars during daylight hours; camp leaflets will give you the details of seasonal changes, so it is important to plan your game viewing drive so that you can start at first light and return before the camp gates shut just before dark.

It is forbidden to feed the animals, as they will develop a dependency on humans as a source of food. Once animals such as elephants learn that food is available from humans they can become aggressive and dangerous when looking for more and will eventually have to be shot. Litter is not a serious problem within the parks, but be sure to keep your litter inside the car and dispose of it when you reach a camp.

If your car breaks down while in the park don't leave the car in search of help. Stay inside your car until a park ranger comes to your rescue. Other visitors will be using the same roads as you and you will be able to pass a message on to the park authorities. If the worst happens and night falls before you are rescued, remember that parks keep a record of all the cars that have entered each day. If your car has not returned by nightfall the park rangers will know you are missing and should send out a search party.

The weather can be hot and dusty in the parks, and it is a good idea to take water bottles and fruit juice with you. Some parks have designated picnic spots where you will be able to leave your car and have lunch. Most picnic spots will have braai sites for cooking on. These areas are not fenced off and there is still a possibility of wild animals passing through. The leaflets and maps available from the camp offices will indicate where these sites are.

Travelling around on dusty roads will also mean that the car and you will be covered in dust before the end of the trip. The only sure way of avoiding this is to travel with the windows rolled up and the air conditioning unit on full. Otherwise wear comfortable old clothes, preferably in dull greens or khakis.

One piece of invaluable equipment for game viewing is a good pair of binoculars. The wildlife is not always conveniently close to the car and a pair of binoculars will enhance your enjoyment of the game reserve. It is a good idea to buy your binoculars before you reach South Africa as they are imported here and will be more expensive. When you are buying a pair, don't only consider the strength of magnification – much of the best game viewing is done when light levels are low, so a large aperture (which lets in more light) can be as useful as high magnification.

Once you have reserved accommodation in a game reserve (see page 41), you will be able to move in any time after midday until the camp gates shut at nightfall. The larger public rest camps in Kruger are famous for their supermarkets, laundrettes, post offices, and banks, but most camps in game reserves are rather more basic. Camp reception is usually located with the shop or office, where you can arrange guided walks and game drives (see below). The shops sell a good range of books for identifying game as well as maps, leaflets and food. Most accommodation is self-catering so there will often not be a restaurant to eat at except at the larger camps. The camp shops do sell some food but this tends to be just basic provisions which are not enough for a balanced meal. The quality of food in the camps with restaurants and cafeterias is variable and can be surprisingly bland. Visitors who choose not to stay in self-catering accommodation are left to the mercy of the cooks. Check the times at which the

Essentials

Advice & information

Game reserve camps

restaurants close as South African visitors tend to eat their dinner early and restaurants can be closing by 2030. Petrol is usually available at the camps. Road conditions between camps on game viewing trips are good. There are well-maintained surfaced gravel roads which are quite adequate for a saloon car, a four-wheel drive is not necessary. When you make your reservation you will receive a leaflet detailing all the available facilities at your camp.

Safari companies There are numerous safari companies operating out of Johannesburg, Durban and Cape Town who can arrange accommodation and game viewing trips as part of a tour. The cost of tours varies, there are good budget options as well as more expensive luxury safaris. You must balance the advantages of going on an organized tour where all your needs are taken care of with the option of hiring a car and staying in self-catering accommodation.

Game drives & game walks Short game drives and game walks can be reserved at the camp offices when you arrive. Availability on walks and drives is on a first come first served basis and cannot be booked before you reach the park.

Exploring the wilderness with a park ranger is an excellent way to find out about the wildlife in the park. Game drives and walks depart at dawn and last up to three hours. Some parks also offer night drives where visitors have the chance to see unusual nocturnal animals. There is some doubt about the validity of night drives as once animals are visible in the spotlights of the jeep, they will also be visible to passing predators.

Wilderness trails are one of the most exciting ways to experience a game reserve. Trail walkers stay in an isolated base camp and go on a number of day walks dedicated to game viewing with an armed ranger. Wilderness trails are extremely popular and can be booked up to 12 months in advance (see page 534).

Safari expeditions There are two fascinating undeveloped areas at opposite ends of South Africa, Maputaland and Richtersveld (see pages 442 and 724). If you want to explore these areas you will need a four-wheel drive as the road network is still unfinished. There are car hire companies based in Johannesburg who rent out specially equipped four-wheel drive safari vehicles. These can be used either in South Africa or on expeditions into Botswana, Namibia or Zimbabwe.

Useful addresses *South African National Parks (SANPARKS)*, Head Office, PO Box 787, Pretoria 0001, T012-3431991, F012-3430905; Tourist Junction, 160 Pine St, Durban, T031-3044934, F3043868; V&A Waterfront Office, Clocktower Centre, Cape Town, T021-4222810, F021-4222816. They also have an office at the main Cape Town Tourism Centre. reservations@parks-sa.co.za, www.parks-sa.co.za *Western Cape Nature Conservation*, Private Bag X9086, Cape Town 8000, T021-2102269, www.cnc.org.za *KZN Wildlife*, PO Box 13053, Cascades, 3202, Pietermaritzburg, T033-8451000, F8451001, bookings@kznwildlife.com www.wildlife.com *Mpumalanga Parks Board*, PO Box 1990, Nelspruit 1200, T013-7533931.

Whitewater rafting

The most famous place in Southern Africa for whitewater rafting is at the Victoria Falls in Zimbabwe, but there are a several lesser-known but excellent rapids in South Africa: the **Umzimvubu Falls** in Transkei; along the **Umzimkulu River** in KwaZulu Natal; on the Orange River by the **Augrabies Falls** or near Kimberley; the **Great Usutu River** in Swaziland and the **Sabie**, **Olifants**, and **Blyde** rivers in Mpumalanga.

Whale watching

The **Whale Coast**, around Walker Bay (Hermanus) near Cape Town, claims to have the best land-based whale watching in the world. Between the months of July and November southern right and humpback whales enter the bay to calve. Whales can also be seen during this time in the sheltered bays from **Elands Bay** on the west coast all the way round to **Mossel Bay** and even **Ttsitsikamma** on the south coast. Contact the *Greater Hermanus* Tourism Bureau, Old Station Building, Mitchell St, T3122629, F3130305, www.hermanus.co.za Boat-based whale watching is also becoming popular from many points along the coast of KwaZulu Natal, particularly from June to October when many southern right, mink, and humpback whales travel from the warmer waters of Mozambique to their breeding grounds at the Cape.

Wild flowers

Between mid-August and mid-September the fynbos areas of the West Coast and the semi-desert of Namaqualand explode into blossom as wild flowers bloom after the first rains. This is one of the great natural sights in the country and well worth a detour. Springbok has developed much of its tourist industry around the flowers, and the area gets very busy during the season. Note that where and when the flowers appear is closely related to climatic conditions and it is difficult to predict where and when the best blooms will be. There is a **Flower Hotline** with information on where the best flowers are T083-9101028 (mob). The number closes at the end of October. Other local numbers worth calling are **Namaqua National Park**, T027-6721948; **Goegap Nature Reserve**, T027-7121880; and the **regional tourist office in Springbok**, T027-7182985, www.northerncape.org.za

Throughout the flowering season many of the local towns put on flower shows, usually lasting a long weekend. The following list includes a few of the popular flower reserves and botanical gardens to be found in the Western Cape. In total there are almost 60 such reserves in the region: **Harold Porter Botanical Garden**, **Yzerfontein Nature Garden**, **Ceres Mountain Fynbos Reserve**, **Southern Cape Herbarium** and **Featherbed Nature Reserve**.

Health

South Africa is a beautiful country left with a post-apartheid legacy of illiteracy, gun crime and epidemic HIV. But the country that gave us the late Professor Christiaan Bernard cannot be all bad as far as medicine is concerned and for those who can afford it, medical facilities rival those in any other Westernized nation. Obviously there are under-developed areas, where infectious diseases thrive in much the same way as they did in the West some decades ago but for a tourist or business traveller who keeps to the major cities, the risk of serious illness is minimal. As for all countries, if a hospital is grubby and staff wear grey coats instead of white ones, then be wary of the general standard of medicine and hygiene. It's worth contacting your embassy or consulate on arrival and asking where the recommended (ie those used by diplomats) clinics are. Providing embassies with information of your whereabouts can be also useful if a friend/relative gets ill at home and there is a desperate search for you around the globe. You can also ask them about locally recommended medical do's and don'ts. If you do get ill, and you have the opportunity, you should also ask your medical insurer whether they are satisfied that the medical centre or hospital that you have been referred to is of a suitable standard.

However, before discussing the disease-related health risks involved in travel within South Africa, remember to try to avoid road accidents and gun-crime. You can reduce the likelihood of accidents by not drinking and driving, wearing a seatbelt in cars and a helmet on motorbikes, but you should be aware that others on the road may think that they are in the remake of Death Race 2000 (reviewers tell me it is an awful film). The best way to avoid gun-crime may be to avoid looking rich, see the safety section, page 37 for more on security within he country.

Before you go

Ideally, you should see your GP or travel clinic at least 6 weeks before your departure for general advice on travel risks, malaria and vaccinations. Make sure you have travel insurance, get a dental check (especially if you are going to be away for more than a month), know your own blood group and if you suffer a long-term condition such as diabetes or epilepsy make sure someone knows or that you have a Medic Alert bracelet/necklace with this information on it.

Vaccinations	Vaccination	Obligatory/Recommended
for your South	Polio	Yes if nil in last 10 years
Africa trip	Tetanus	Yes if nil in last 10 years (but after 5 doses you have had enough for life)
	Typhoid	Yes if nil in last 3 years
	Rabies	Yes for most areas
	Hepatitis A	Yes - the disease can be caught easily from food/water
	BCG	Yes if staying for more than 1 month

A special note re Yellow Fever: South Africa is not regarded as a risk area for this disease but other African countries north of it are. If you are likely to use South Africa as a base for more extensive African travel then cut your loses and get vaccinated.

Malaria in South Africa
Always check with your doctor or travel clinic for the most up to date advice

The malaria situation in South Africa is best described as fluid. Just when someone assures you that an area is free of the disease there will be a death from malaria. The problems are increasing with immigration of infected workers from elsewhere in Africa and the environmental problems of the flood-stricken neighbour, Mozambique. In Durban a phenomenon known as 'taxi malaria' is described, in which the infected mosquito hitches a ride with you and infects you in the taxi. Malaria occurs in northern and eastern Mpumalanga, eastern Limpopo Province, northern KwaZulu Natal and Swaziland, particularly in the Lowveld region in and around Kruger National Park (no matter what anyone else tells you). If you look at a map of South Africa and draw a line from the border between Botswana and Zimbabwe in the north, and the Tugela river mouth in northern KwaZulu Natal to the south, all the regions to the east of this line, lie within a malarial area.

Items to take with you

Anti-malarials. Important to take for the key areas. Specialist advice is required as to which type to take. General principles are that all except Malarone should be continued for four weeks after leaving the malarial area. Malarone needs to be continued for only seven days afterwards (if a tablet is missed or vomited seek specialist advice). The start times for the anti-malarials vary in that if you have never taken Lariam (Mefloquine) before it is advised to start it at least 2-3 weeks before the entry to a malarial zone (this is to help identify serious side-effects early). Chloroquine and Paludrine are often started a week before the trip to establish a pattern but Doxycycline and Malarone can be started only 1-2 days before entry to the malarial area. NB It is risky to buy medicinal tablets abroad because the doses may differ and there may be a trade in false drugs. **Mosquito repellents.** DEET (Di-ethyltoluamide) is the gold standard. Apply the repellent every 4-6 hours but more often if you are sweating heavily. If you want to use a non-DEET product, check who tested it. Validated products (tested at the London School of Hygiene and Tropical Medicine) include Mosiguard, Non-DEET Jungle formula and non-DEET Autan. If you want to use citronella remember that it must be applied very frequently (ie hourly) to be effective. If you are popular target for insect bites or develop lumps quite soon after being bitten, carry an Aspivenin kit. This syringe suction device is available from many chemists and draws out some of the allergic materials and provides quick relief. **Sun Block.** The Australians have a great campaign, which has reduced skin cancer. It is called Slip, Slap, Slop. Slip on a shirt, Slap on a hat, Slop on sun screen. **Pain killers.** Paracetomol or a suitable painkiller can have multiple uses for symptoms but remember that more than eight paractemol a day can lead to liver failure. **Ciproxin (Ciprofloxacin).** A useful antibiotic for some forms of travellers diarrhoea (see below). **Immodium.** A great standby for those diarrhoeas that occur at awkward times (ie before a long coach/train journey or on a trek). It helps stop the flow of diarrhoea and in my view is of more benefit than harm. (It was believed that letting the bacteria or viruses flow out had to be more beneficial. However, with Immodium they still come out, just in a more solid form.) **Pepto-Bismol.** Used a lot by Americans for diarrhoea. It certainly relieves symptoms but like Immodium it is not a cure for underlying disease. Be aware that it turns the stool black as well as making it more solid. **MedicAlert.** These simple bracelets, or an equivalent, should be carried or worn by anyone with a significant medical condition. For longer trips involving jungle treks taking a clean **needle pack**, clean **dental pack** and **water filtration devices** are common-sense measures.

Further Information

Foreign and Commonwealth Office (FCO) (UK), www.fco.gov.uk This is a key travel advice Websites site, with useful information on the country, people, climate and lists the UK embassies/consulates. The site also promotes the concept of 'Know Before You Go'. And encourages travel insurance and appropriate travel health advice. It has links to the Department of Health travel advice site, see below.

Department of Health Travel Advice (UK), www.doh.gov.uk/traveladvice This excellent site is also available as a free booklet, the T6, from Post Offices. It lists advice on vaccines and requirements for each country.

Medic Alert (UK), www.medicalalert.co.uk This is the website of the foundation that produces bracelets and necklaces for those with existing medical problems. Once you have ordered your bracelet/necklace you write your key medical details on paper inside it, so that if you collapse, a medical person can identify you as someone with epilepsy or an allergy to peanuts etc.

Blood Care Foundation (UK), www.bloodcare.org.uk The Blood Care Foundation is a Kent-based charity "dedicated to the provision of screened blood and resuscitation fluids in countries where these are not readily available." They will dispatch certified non-infected blood of the right type to your hospital/clinic. The blood is flown in from various centres around the world.

Public Health Laboratory Service (UK), www.phls.org.uk This site has up-to-date malaria advice guidelines for travel around the world. It gives specific advice about the right drugs for each location. It also has useful information for those who are pregnant, suffering from epilepsy or planning to travel with children.

Centers for Disease Control and Prevention (USA), www.cdc.gov This site from the US Government gives excellent advice on travel health, has useful disease maps and details of disease outbreaks.

World Health Organisation, www.who.int The WHO site has links to the WHO Blue Book (it was Yellow up until last year) on travel advice. This lists the diseases in different regions of the world. It describes vaccination schedules and makes clear which countries have Yellow Fever Vaccination certificate requirements and malarial risk.

Tropical Medicine Bureau (Ireland), www.tmb.ie This Irish based site has a good collection of general travel health information and disease risks.

Fit for Travel (UK), www.fitfortravel.scot.nhs.uk This site from Scotland provides a quick A-Z of vaccine and travel health advice requirements for each country.

British Travel Health Association (UK), www.btha.org This is the official website of an organization of travel health professionals.

NetDoctor (UK), www.Netdoctor.co.uk This general health advice site has a useful section on travel and has an "ask the expert", interactive chat forum.

Travel Screening Services (UK), www.travelscreening.co.uk This is the author's website. A private clinic dedicated to integrated travel health. The clinic gives vaccine, travel health advice, email and SMS text vaccine reminders and screens returned travellers for tropical diseases.

Travellers' Health: How to Stay Healthy Abroad, by Dr Richard Dawood ISBN Books & leaflets 0-19-262947-6. An excellent book and has at last been updated in 2002. *The Travellers Good Health Guide*, by Dr Ted Lankester by ISBN 0-85969-827-0. *Expedition Medicine*, (The Royal Geographic Society) editors David Warrell and Sarah Anderson ISBN 1 86197 040-4. *International Travel and Health*, World Health Organisation Geneva ISBN 92 4 158026 7. *The World's Most Dangerous Places* by Robert Young Pelton, Coskun Aral and Wink Dulles ISBN 1-566952-140-9.

The Travellers Guide to Health (T6), can be obtained by calling the Health Literature Line on T0800-555777. *Advice for Travellers on Avoiding the Risks of HIV and AIDS (Travel Safe)*, available from Department of Health, PO Box 777, London SE1 6XH. The *Blood Care Foundation order form*, PO Box 7, Sevenoaks, Kent TN13 2SZ T01732-742427.

On the road

The greater disease risk in South Africa is caused by the greater volume of disease carriers, in the shape of mosquitoes and sandflies. The key viral disease is Dengue fever, which is transmitted by a mosquito that bites during the day. The disease is like a very nasty form of the 'flu with 2 -3 days of illness, followed by a short period of recovery, then a second attack of illness. Westerners very rarely get the worst haemorrhagic form of the disease. Bacterial diseases include tuberculosis (TB) and some causes of the more common traveller's diarrhoea. The main parasitic disease is malaria.

Diarrhoea & intestinal upset

This is almost inevitable. One study showed that up to 70% of all travellers may suffer during their trip

Symptoms Diarrhoea can refer either to loose stools or an increased frequency; both of these can be a nuisance. It should be short lasting but persistence beyond two weeks, with blood or pain, require specialist medical attention.

Cures Ciproxin (Ciprofloxacin) is a useful antibiotic for bacterial traveller's diarrhoea. It can be obtained by private prescription in the UK. (**NB** Do not take any antiboitics before consulting a doctor, and always finish the course.) You need to take one 500mg tablet when the diarrhoea starts and if you do not feel better in 24 hours, the diarrhoea is likely to have a non-bacterial cause and may be viral (in which case there is little you can do apart from keep yourself rehydrated and wait for it to settle on its own). The key treatment with all diarrhoeas is **rehydration**. Try to keep hydrated by taking the right mixture of salt and water. This is available as Oral Rehydration Salts (ORS) in ready-made sachets or can be made up by adding a teaspoon of sugar and a half-teaspoon of salt to a litre of clean water. Drink at least one large cup of this drink for each loose stool you pass. You can also use flat carbonated drinks as an alternative. **Immodium** and **Pepto-Bismol** provide symptomatic relief.

Prevention The standard advice is to be careful with water and ice for drinking. Ask yourself where the water came from. If you have any doubts then boil it or filter it and treat it. There are many filter/treatment devices now available on the market. Food can also transmit disease. Be wary of salads (what were they washed in, who handled them?), re-heated foods or food that has been left out in the sun having been cooked earlier in the day. There is a simple adage that says 'wash it, peel it, boil it or forget it'. Also be wary of unpasteurised dairy products, these can transmit a range of diseases from brucellosis (fevers and constipation), to listeria (meningitis) and tuberculosis of the gut (obstruction, constipation, fevers and weight loss).

Malaria & insect bite prevention

Symptoms Malaria can cause death within 24 hours. It can start as something just resembling an attack of flu. You may feel tired, lethargic, headachy, feverish; or more seriously, develop fits, followed by coma and then death. Have a low index of suspicion because it is very easy to write off vague symptoms, which may actually be malaria. If you have a temperature, go to a doctor as soon as you can and ask for a malaria test. On your return home if you suffer any of these symptoms, get tested as soon as possible, even if any previous test proved negative, the test could save your life.

Cures Treatment is with drugs and may be oral or into a vein depending on the seriousness of the infection. Remember **ABCD**: Awareness (of whether the disease is present in the area you are travelling in), Bite avoidance, Chemoprohylaxis, Diagnosis.

Prevention This is best summarized by the B and C of the ABCD: bite avoidance and chemoprophylaxis. Wear clothes that cover arms and legs and use effective insect repellents in areas with known risks of insect-spread disease. Use a mosquito net dipped in permethrin as both a physical and chemical barrier at night in the same areas. Guard against the contraction of malaria with the correct anti-malarials (see above). Some would prefer to take test kits for malaria with them and have standby treatment available. However, the field tests of the blood kits have had poor results: when you have malaria you are usually too ill to be able to do the tests correctly enough to make the right diagnosis. Standby treatment (treatment that you carry and take yourself for malaria) should still ideally be supervised by a doctor since the drugs themselves can be toxic if taken incorrectly. **NB** The Royal Homeopathic Hospital in the UK does not advocate homeopathic options for malaria prevention or treatment.

Symptoms If you go diving make sure that you are fit do so. The *British Scuba Association (BSAC)*, Telford's Quay, South Pier Road, Ellesmere Port, Cheshire CH65 4FL, United Kingdom, T01513-506200, F506215, www.bsac.com, can put you in touch with doctors who do medical examinations. Protect your feet from cuts, beach dog parasites (larva migrans) and sea urchins. The latter are almost impossible to remove but can be dissolved with lime or vinegar. Keep an eye out for secondary infection.

Cures Antibiotics for secondary infections. Serious diving injuries may need time in a de-compression chamber.

Prevention Check that the dive company know what they are doing, have appropriate cer-tification from *BSAC* or *Professional Association of Diving Instructors (PADI)*, Unit 7, St Philips Central, Albert Rd, St Philips, Bristol, BS2 0TD, T0117-3007234, www.padi.com, and that the equipment is well-maintained.

Essentials

Sun protection

Symptoms White Britons are notorious for becoming red in hot countries because they like to stay out longer than everyone else and do not use adequate sun protection. This can lead to sunburn, which is painful and followed by flaking of skin. Aloe vera gel is a good pain reliever for sunburn. Long-term sun damage leads to a loss of elasticity of skin and the development of pre-cancerous lesions. Many years later, a mild or a very malignant form of cancer may develop. The milder basal cell carcinoma, if detected early, can be treated by cutting it out or freezing it. The much nastier malignant melanoma may have already spread to bone and brain by the time that it is first noticed.

Prevention Sun screen. SPF stands for Sun Protection Factor. It is measured by deter-mining how long a given person takes to "burn" with and without the sunscreen product on. So, if it takes 10 times longer to burn with the sunscreen product applied, then that product has an SPF of 10. If it only takes twice as long then the SPF is 2. The higher the SPF the greater the protection. However, do not just use higher factors just to stay out in the sun longer. 'Flash frying' (desperate bursts of excessive exposure), as it is called, is known to increase the risks of skin cancer. Follow the Australians' with their Slip, Slap, Slop campaign.

Altitude

There is only one area in southern Africa where the peaks and highest trails are over 3,000 m – between Sani Pass and Mont-aux-Sources, where the Drakensberg mountains straddle the border between South Africa and Lesotho. Health problems related to altitude are rare.

Symptoms Acute mountain sickness can strike from about 3,000 m upwards and in general is more likely to affect those who ascend rapidly (for example by plane) and those who over-exert themselves. Teenagers are particularly prone. On reaching heights above 3,000 m, heart pounding and shortness of breath, especially on exertion, are almost universal and a normal response to the lack of oxygen in the air. Acute mountain sickness takes a few hours or days to come on and presents with heachache, lassitude, dizziness, loss of appetite, nausea and vomiting. Insomnia is common and often associated with a suffocating feeling when lying down in bed. You may notice that your breathing tends to wax and wane at night and your face is puffy in the mornings – this is all part of the syndrome.

Cures If the symptoms are mild, the treatment is rest, painkillers (preferably not aspi-rin-based) for the headaches and anti-sickness pills for vomiting. Should the symptoms be severe and prolonged it is best to descend to a lower altitude immediately and reascend, if necessary, slowly and in stages. The symptoms disappear very quickly with even a few 100 m of descent.

Prevention The best way of preventing acute mountain sickness is a relatively slow ascent. When trekking to high altitude, some time spent walking at medium altitude, getting fit and getting adapted, is beneficial. On arrival at places over 3,000 m a few hours' rest and the avoidance of alcohol, cigarettes and heavy food will go a long way towards preventing acute mountain sickness.

Other problems experienced at high altitude are sunburn, excessively dry air causing skin cracking, sore eyes (it may be wise to leave your contact lenses out) and sore nostrils. Treat the latter with Vaseline.

Do not ascend to high altitude if you are suffering from a bad cold or chest infection and certainly not within 24 hours following scuba diving.

Dengue fever **Symptoms** This disease can be contracted throughout South Africa and is an increasing problem. In travellers this can cause a severe 'flu-like illness which includes symptoms of fever, lethargy, enlarged lymph glands and muscle pains. It starts suddenly, lasts for 2-3 days, seems to get better for 2-3 days and then kicks in again for another 2-3 days. It is usually all over in an unpleasant week. The local children are prone to the much nastier haemorrhagic form of the disease, which causes them to bleed from internal organs, mucous membranes and often leads to their death.
Cures The traveller's version of the disease is self-limiting and forces rest and recuperation on the sufferer.
Prevention The mosquitoes that carry the Dengue virus bite during the day unlike the malaria mosquitoes. Which sadly means that repellent application and covered limbs are a 24 hour issue. Check your accommodation for flower pots and shallow pools of water since these are where the dengue-carrying mosquitoes breed.

Hepatitis **Symptoms** Hepatitis means inflammation of the liver. Viral causes of the disease can be acquired anywhere in South Africa. The most obvious symptom is a yellowing of your skin or the whites of your eyes. However, prior to this all that you may notice is itching and tiredness.
Cures Early on, depending on the type of hepatitis, a vaccine or immunoglobulin may reduce the duration of the illness.
Prevention Pre-travel hepatitis A vaccine is the best bet. Hepatitis B (for which there is a vaccine) is spread through blood and unprotected sexual intercourse, both of these can be avoided. Unfortunately there is no vaccine for hepatitis C or the increasing alphabetical list of other Hepatitis viruses.

Tuberculosis **Symptoms** Cough, blood in spit, weight loss, fever, night sweats. If you drink unpasteurised
(TB) milk you can get gut or pelvic TB which can lead to intestinal obstruction and infertility.
Cures At least three drugs are required and the total treatment period is at least 6 months.
Prevention If staying for over 1 month have a skin test for TB followed by the BCG vaccine. Try to avoid people coughing on your face and if you have an unexplained illness on your return ask your doctor to think about TB.

Rabies **Symptoms** Most of you will know when you have been bitten. It may take days or weeks before odd tingling sensations occur in the affected part, followed by a fear of drinking water and spasms which lead to death.
Cures There is no cure for rabies once it has hold of the Central Nervous System.
Prevention Avoid getting bitten. Dog lovers have to remember that this is a whole new ball game and you are the ball. A full course of rabies vaccine is 100% effective. If you get bitten you will need more vaccine and if you had no pre-exposure vaccine or an inadequate amount you will also need to be injected with something called immunoglobulin. It is always wise to wash the wound but animal bites should ideally not be stitched up in the early stages.

Sexual Health Sex is part of travel and many see it as adding spice to a good trip but spices can be uncomfortable. Think about the sexual souvenirs any potential new partner may have picked up or live with. The range of visible and invisible diseases is awesome. Unprotected sex can spread HIV, Hepatitis B and C, Gonorrhea (green discharge), chlamydia (nothing to see but may cause painful urination and later female infertility), painful recurrent herpes, syphilis and warts, just to name a few. You can cut down the risk by using condoms, a femidom or avoiding sex altogether. If you do stray, consider getting a sexual health check on your return home, since these diseases are not the sort of gift people thank you for.

Cape Town

3

Cape Town

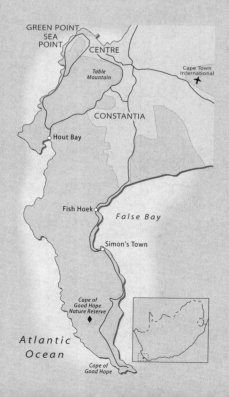

South Africa's 'Mother City', dominated by the soaring Table Mountain and surrounded by the wild Atlantic, has one of the most beautiful backdrops in the world. A mountainous spine stretches between two seaboards and is edged by rugged coast and dramatic beaches. Lush forests and verdant vineyards sit hard by rugged hillsides and barren flatlands.

The city itself is similarly diverse, with grandiose colonial buildings and beautiful public gardens standing cheek by jowl with 1960s eyesores. Atmospheric Victorian suburbs stretch around the lower slopes of the mountain, while further out lie the Cape Flats, their sprawling townships a lasting testimony of the apartheid era.

As if mirroring these surroundings, Cape Town's population is the most cosmopolitan in the country, a unique mix of cultures that seems to drive the very pulse of the city. It has a comparatively small black African population – about a quarter of the total – while the distinctive 'Cape Coloured' community makes up over half of the population. These are descendents of slaves brought from the Far East and West Africa who interacted with European and local indigenous people. The remaining quarter is made up of white descendents of Dutch and British settlers. The result of this mishmash is a vibrant cultural scene – music, and particularly Cape Jazz, lies at the very core of city life.

It is this mix of environments and communities that makes Cape Town such an instantly likeable and captivating place. Few places in the world can offer mountain hiking and lazing on a beach in just one morning, or tasting world-class wines and drinking beer in a township shebeen in one afternoon. It would take months to appreciate fully Cape Town's different sides, but just a few days is enough to understand why visitors keep coming back to the Mother City.

★

Things to do in Cape Town

- Climb **Lion's Head** and watch sunset over the city and ocean, then descend in the bright glare of a full moon.
- Do the adrenaline thing and **bungee jump** from the Table Mountain cable car.
- Try a glass of the famous **Vin de Constance** while overlooking the historical estates and rolling vineyards of Constantia.
- Listen to **live Cape Jazz** and try home-brewed beer on a **township shebeen tour**.
- Learn about the country's turbulent past at the **District Six Museum**, **Slave Lodge**, the **Nelson Mandela Gateway** and the **Robben Island Museum**.
- Experience alternative Cape Town and its vibrant comedy, dance and rock scene at the **Obs Festival** in December.
- Spend a day star-spotting and sun-worshipping with the beautiful people on **Clifton Beach**.

Ins and outs

Getting there

Postal code: 8000
Phone code: 021
(NB Always use 3-figure prefix)
Colour map 4, grid C1 & 2

For more detailed information, see Transport, page 124

Cape Town International Airport, formerly known as DF Malan, has a large number of international and national flights arriving there every day. A large proportion of which are from Europe. This is good news for overseas visitors, and if you have the option, Cape Town is a far preferable entry point to South Africa than Johannesburg. International and domestic terminals are 20 mins' drive, 22 km, from the city centre. Airport enquiries, T9371200, www.airports.co.za

The main **railway station** is in the centre of town. Next to the railway station, at Adderley St, is where the *Greyhound*, *Intercape* and *Translux* **long distance bus** services arrive.

The *Cape Town Tourism* office is located a 5-min walk away, on the corner of Burg and Castle streets (see below). If possible we suggest you organize a place to stay in advance, and then on arrival head straight for the taxi rank. If you are staying at a backpackers' hostel call ahead to arrange collection. You do not want to start walking the streets of Cape Town with a rucksack on your back if you can help it.

Getting around

As with many major cities, Cape Town may at first sight seem large and difficult to navigate around, but fortunately this is not so. Most of Cape Town's oldest buildings, museums, galleries and the commercial centre are concentrated in a relatively small area and best explored on foot. However, to explore more of the city, and to visit Table Mountain, the suburbs or the beaches, it's a good idea to rent a car. Otherwise the local commuter train network is worth using for some sights and taxis are affordable.

To get the best idea of Cape Town's layout, head to the top of **Table Mountain**. From its summit, the city stretches below in a horseshoe formed by the mountains: Table Mountain is in the centre, with **Devil's Peak** to the east and **Lion's Head** and **Signal Hill** to the west. Straight ahead lies the **City Bowl**, the central business district backed by leafy suburbs. This is also the site of Cape Town's historical heart and where all the major museums, historical buildings and sights are. Further down is the **Victoria and Alfred Waterfront**, a slick development of shopping malls and restaurants. Following the coast around to the west, you come to the modern residential districts of **Green Point** and **Sea Point**, and further around are the beautiful Atlantic beaches of **Clifton** and **Camps Bay**. In the opposite direction lie the **Southern Suburbs** which stretch west and south, dipping from the mountain's slopes. These are some of Cape Town's most attractive areas, and have a number of interesting sights too. The suburbs finally lead to **False Bay**, a huge bay of seaside villages and long beaches.

Tourist offices

Cape Town Tourism, The Pinnacle, corner of Burg and Castle streets, T4264260, F4264266, www.cape-town.org Open Mon-Fri 0800-1900, Sat 0830-1400, Sun 0900-1300. This is the official city tourist office and can help with bookings and tours throughout the Western Cape. It is an excellent source of information and a good first stop in the city. In addition to providing practical information about Cape Town, it can help with accommodation book-ings and visiting other provinces, and has a good café and internet access.

Western Cape Tourism Board, PO Box 3878, Tyger Valley, 7536, T021-9144613, F9144610, wctbcape@iafrica.com, www.wcapetourism.co.za This office provides tourist information on the Cape outside of Cape Town (see Western Cape chapter, page 145).

Cape Peninsula

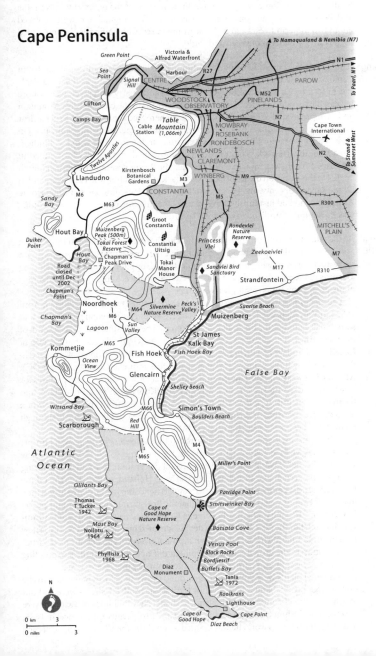

Cape Town

History

First people The first evidence of human inhabitants in the Cape has been dated back to nearly 30,000 years ago. Rock art found in the area was created by nomadic San people (also known as Bushmen), a hunter-gatherer group which roamed across much of Southern Africa. Some San groups continue to survive today, mostly in Namibia and Botswana, despite continuing persecution. The original San were replaced about two thousand years ago by Khoi groups, a semi-nomadic people who settled in the Cape with herds of sheep and cattle.

First landing **António de Saldanha**, a Portuguese admiral who lost his way going east, landed in Table Bay in 1503. They called the bay Aguada da Saldanha (it was renamed Table Bay in 1601 by **Joris van Spilbergen**). Saldanha and a party of the crew went ashore in search of drinking water. They followed a stream to the base of Table Mountain and then proceeded to climb to the top. From here Saldanha was able to get a clear view of the surrounding coastline and the confusion caused by the peninsula. On their return they found the crew unsuccessfully trying to barter with local indigenous Khoi for livestock. The trade quickly developed into a row which ended in bloodshed. There was another battle between the Portuguese and the Khoi in March 1510. On this occasion the Khoi had struck back after children and cattle were stolen by the sailors. Seventy five Portuguese were killed, including **Dom Francisco de Almeida**, who had just finished five years as the first Portuguese Viceroy to India. Few Portuguese ships landed in Table Bay after this.

The Dutch & the VOC By the end of the 16th century British and Dutch mariners had caught up with the Portuguese and they quickly came to appreciate the importance of the Cape as a base for restocking ships with drinking water and fresh supplies as they made their long journeys to the east. Indeed, seafarers found that they were able to exchange scraps of metal for provisions to supply a whole fleet.

The first moves to settle in the Cape were made by the Dutch, and on the 6th April 1652 **Jan Van Riebeeck** landed in Table Bay. His ships carried wood for building and some small cannons, the first building to be erected being a small fort at the mouth of the Fresh River. The site of the original fort is where Grand Parade in the centre of Cape Town is today. Van Riebeeck was in charge of the supply station that belonged to the Dutch East India Company (Vereenigde Oost-Indische Compagnie or VOC). After the fort was built, gardens for fruit and vegetables were laid out and pastures for cattle acquired. As the settlement slowly grew, the Khoi people were driven back into the interior. Surprisingly, the early settlers were forbidden from enslaving the Khoi; instead, slaves were imported by the VOC from Indonesia and West Africa. Although many died, these slaves were the origin of the Cape Malay community.

In 1662 Jan van Riebeeck was transferred to India. Because of rivalries in Europe, the VOC was worried about enemy ships visiting the Cape, so work started on a new stone fort in 1666. Over the next 13 years several Governors came and went. During this time the French and British went to war with Holland, but the British and the Dutch East India companies joined in a treaty of friendship in March 1674, and then in July 1674 a ship arrived with the news that the British and Dutch had made peace. In October 1679 one of the most energetic Governors arrived in the Cape, **Simon van der Stel**. For the next 20 years van der Stel devoted his energies to creating a new Holland in southern Africa. During his period as Governor, van der Stel paid particular attention to the growth and development of Cape Town and the surrounding farmlands. The company garden was replanted, nursery plots were created and new experimental plants were collected from around the world. North of the gardens he built a large hospital and a lodge to house VOC slaves. New streets were laid out which were straight and wide with plenty of shade. New buildings in the town were covered in white limewash, producing a smart and prosperous appearance. In 1685, in appreciation for his work, he was granted an estate by the VOC, which he named

Constantia. During his life he used the estate as an experimental agricultural farm and to grow oak trees which were then planted throughout the Cape.

One of his more significant contributions was the founding of the settlement at Stellenbosch. He directed the design and construction of many of the town's public buildings, and then introduced a number of the crops to be grown on the new farms. For many years he experimented with vines in an effort to produce wines as good as those in Europe. He was particularly pleased when in 1688 French Protestant Huguenot refugees arrived in the Cape. He saw to it that they were all settled on excellent farmlands in what became to be known as **Franschhoek** (French glen), the upper valley of the Berg River. In 1693 he had the foresight to appoint the town's first engineer to tackle problems of a clean water supply, and the removal of rubbish. Van der Stel died in June 1712 at Constantia.

The next period of Cape Town's history was closely related to events in Europe, particularly the French Revolution. The ideas put forward by the revolution of liberty, fraternity and equality were not welcome in colonies such as the Cape. The Dutch East India Company was seen to be a corrupt organization and a supporter of the aristocracy. When the French invaded Holland, the British decided to seize the Cape to stop it from falling into French hands. After the Battle of Muizenberg in 1795, Britain took over the Cape from the representatives of the Dutch East India Company, which was bankrupt. In the Treaty of Amiens (1803) the Cape was restored to the Batavian Republic of the Netherlands. In 1806 the British took control again at the resumption of the Anglo-French wars.

Under the British

When the British took over power it was inevitable that they inherited many of the problems associated with the colony. The principal issue was how to manage European settlement. The Dutch East India Company had only encouraged settlement as a cheap and efficient means of supplying their base in Cape Town. Thereafter they were only interested in controlling the Indian Ocean and supplying ships. By the time the British arrived, the Dutch settler farmers (the Boer) had become so successful that they were producing a surplus. The only problem was high production costs due to a shortage of labour. To alleviate the situation, a policy of importing slaves was implemented. This in turn led to decreased work opportunities for the settler families. Gradually the mood changed and the Boer looked to the interior for land and work. They were not impressed by the British administration and in 1836 the Great Trek was under way.

Industrialization in Europe brought great change, especially when the first steamship, the *Enterprise*, arrived in Table Bay in October 1825. After considerable delay and continual loss of life and cargoes, work began on two basins and two breakwater piers. The first truckload of construction rocks was tipped by Prince Alfred, the 16-year-old son of Queen Victoria, on 17 September 1860. The Alfred Basin was completed in 1870 and a dry dock was added in 1881.

The growth of the city & the port

No sooner had the first basin been completed than diamonds and gold were discovered in South Africa. Over the next 40 years Cape Town and the docks were to change beyond recognition. In 1900 work began on a new breakwater which would protect an area of 27 km. After five years' work the **Victoria Basin** was opened. This new basin was able to shelter the new generation of ships using Table Bay but was unable to cope with the increase in numbers during the **Anglo-Boer War**. A third basin was created to the east of Victoria Basin in 1932 and for a while this seemed to have solved the problem, but fate was against Cape Town. In January 1936 the largest ship to visit South Africa docked with ease at B berth in the new basin. The boat, which was being used to help promote tourism in South Africa, was filled with wealthy and famous visitors. The morning on which she was due to sail, a strong southeasterly wind blew up and pressed the liner so firmly against the quay that she couldn't sail. In one morning all of the new basin's weaknesses had been exposed.

The next phase of growth was an ambitious one, and it was only completed in 1945. The project involved the dredging of Table Bay and the reclaiming of land. The spoil from the dredging provided 140 km of landfill, known as Foreshore. This new land extends from the present day railway station to **Duncan Dock**. As you walk or drive around Cape Town today, remember that just over 50 years ago the sea came up to the main railway station.

Impact of the apartheid years
For the best record of the vibrant community that once thrived here, visit the excellent District Six Museum (see page 85)

The descendants of the large and diverse slave population have given Cape Town a particularly cosmopolitan atmosphere. Unfortunately Apartheid urban planning meant that many of the more vibrant areas of the city in the earlier part of this century were destroyed. The most notorious case is that of District Six, a racially mixed, low income housing area on the edge of the City Bowl. The Apartheid government could not tolerate such an area, especially so close to the centre of the city, and the residents, most of whom were classified as 'Coloured', were moved out to the soulless townships of the Cape Flats, such as Mitchell's Plain. The area was bulldozed but few new developments have taken place on the site: this accounts for the large areas of open ground in the area between the City Bowl and the suburb of Woodstock. Happily, the government recently announced that much of the land is going to be re-developed and given back to the ex-residents of District Six and their descendants. What the area will become remains to be seen.

Other reminders of the cosmopolitan history of Cape Town can be experienced in the area to the west of Buitengracht Street. This district, known as **Bo-Kaap**, is still home to a small Cape Malay community that somehow managed to survive the onslaught of Apartheid urban planning. The coloured population of Cape Town has historically outweighed both the white and African populations: hence the widespread use of Afrikaans in the city. This balance was maintained by Apartheid policies that prevented Africans from migrating into the Western Cape from the Eastern Cape and elsewhere. This policy was not, however, able to withstand the pressure of the poor rural African's desire to find opportunities in the urban economy. Over the past couple of decades there has been an enormous growth in the African population of Cape Town. Many of these new migrants have been forced to settle in squatter areas, such as the notorious Crossroads Camp next to the N2 highway. During the Apartheid era these squatter camps were frequently bulldozed and the residents evicted but as soon as they were cleared they sprang up again. Crossroads was a hotbed of resistance to the Apartheid state and much of the Cape Flats area existed in a state of near civil war throughout much of the 1980s.

Today, Cape Town remains the most cosmopolitan city in South Africa. The official colour barriers have long since disappeared and residential boundaries are shifting. The economic balance, too, is beginning to change: a black middle class has emerged in recent years, and the coloured middle class is strengthening.

Sights

Table Mountain

Cape Town is defined, first and foremost, by Table Mountain. Rising a sheer 1073m from the coastal plain, it dominates almost every view of the city, its sharp slopes and level top making it one of the world's best-known city backdrops. For centuries, it was the first sight of Cape Town afforded to seafarers, it's looming presence visible for hundreds of kilometres. Certainly, its size continues to astonish visitors today, but it is the mountain's wilderness, bang in the middle of a bustling conurbation, that makes the biggest impression. Table Mountain sustains over 1,400 species of flora, as well as baboons, dassies (large rodents) and countless birds.

Between September and March you have the additional pleasure of seeing the mountain covered in wild flowers. The most common vegetation is fynbos, of which there is an extraordinary variety, but you'll also see proteas plus the rare silver tree, *Leucadendron argenteum*.

Much of the area is a nature reserve, and the mountain itself is protected as a national monument. For many years there were only a few known paths to the top, but today there are an estimated 500. One of the easier popular routes starts from Kirstenbosch Botanical Gardens and takes about three hours to the top. However, even busy routes should not be taken lightly. Given Table Mountain's size and location, conditions can change alarmingly quickly. The weather may seem clear and calm when you set out, but fog (the famous 'Table Cloth' which flows from the top) and rain can descend without warning. Numerous people have been caught out and the mountain has claimed its fair share of lives.

Before venturing out, ensure that you have suitable clothing, food and water. Take warm clothing, a windbreaker, a waterproof jacket, a hat, sunscreen, sunglasses, plenty of water (2 litres per person) and energy foods. Never climb alone and inform someone of which route you're taking and what time you should be back. A detailed map is essential – these can be purchased at the main tourist office. It's also a good idea to invest in *Approved Paths on Table Mountain*, published by the Mountain Club of South Africa. Inexperienced hikers, or those interested in learning more about the mountain's flora and fauna, should take a guide or a walking tour (see Sports on page 120).

The dizzying trip to the top in the new Aerial Cableway, which started running in October 1997, is one of Cape Town's highlights. There are now two cars, each carrying up to 65 passengers, and as you ride up the floor rotates, allowing a full 360 degree view. The average journey time is just three minutes. There is a bistro restaurant at the top station, as well as a cheaper café which gets busy when the Cableway queues are long. A souvenir shop has been added to the complex.

It is a long walk from the city centre to the Lower Cableway. Normal city buses run a service which goes via Kloof Nek, the closest you can get to the cableway by public transport. More expensive but much more convenient is the shuttle service provided by the tourist office, which leaves every half hour or so from the main office on Burg Street. If you have your own car, drive up Buitengracht St from the centre of town and follow the signs. If you go by taxi, expect to pay in the region of R50-60 from the City Centre to the Lower Cableway, and R50-70, from mid-Sea Point.

■ *0830-2100/2200 (1930 in winter). R85 adult return, discounts for children. Bookings T424818, www.tablemountain.co.za*

Signal Hill's summit offers spectacular views of the city, the Twelve Apostles (the mountainous spine stretching south from Table Mountain) and the ocean. Visit at sunset if possible. An added bonus, depening on your viewpoint, is the fact that it is possible to drive to the 350 m summit, although this obviously means that it can get crowded with tour groups enjoying sundowners. From the town centre, follow signs for the Lower Cableway Station and take a right opposite the turning for the cableway station. The hill is home to the Noon Gun which is fired electronically at noon every day, except Sunday. There is also a *karamat* (Islamic tomb) on the hill.

Halfway along the road up Signal Hill you pass Lion's Head, a popular hiking spot. The climb to the peak is fairly easy going, and takes about two hours, and the 360° views from the top are incredible. There are two routes to the top: the easier of the two winds around the mountain; the quicker one involves climbing up a couple of drops with the aid of chains. Both are signposted. This hike is especially popular at full moon, when Capetonians watch the sunset from the peak and then descend by the light of the moon. Take plenty of water and a torch, and always climb in a group.

The City Bowl

From the Lower Cableway Station, you look out over the central residential suburbs of Tamboerskloof (Drummers' Ravine), Gardens, Oranjezicht (Orange View), and Vredehoek (Peaceful Corner), and beyond here lie the high-rise blocks of the business

Climbing Table Mountain
Mountain Rescue: T10111
Latest mountain weather reports: T4245148

Cape Town

Aerial Cableway

Signal Hill

Lion's Head

City centre

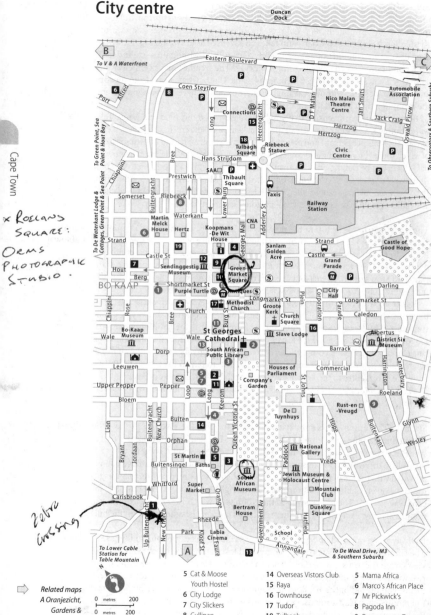

Cape Town

Related maps
*A Oranjezicht,
Gardens &
Tamboerskloof,
page 103*
*B Green Point &
Waterfront,
page 104*
*C Southern suburbs,
page 93*

0 metres 200
0 metres 200

■ Sleeping
1 Backpack & African
 Travel Centre
2 Bob's Backpack & Bistro
3 Cape Gardens Lodge
4 Cape Sun
 Intercontinental

5 Cat & Moose
 Youth Hostel
6 City Lodge
7 City Slickers
8 Cullinan
9 Elephant On Castle
 Backpackers
10 Holiday Inn
 Greenmarket Square
11 Long St Backpackers
12 Metropole
13 Mount Nelson

14 Overseas Vistors Club
15 Raya
16 Townhouse
17 Tudor
18 Tulbagh
19 Tulip Inn

● Eating & Drinking
1 Africa Café
2 Crypt
3 Five Flies
4 Kennedys Bar

5 Mama Africa
6 Marco's African Place
7 Mr Pickwick's
8 Pagoda Inn
9 Perseverance Tavern
10 Primi Piatti
11 Shambhala
12 Star
13 Yellow Pepper Deli

district. Together these form the City Bowl, a term inspired by the surrounding mountains. Closest to the mountain is Oranjezicht, a quiet district with a good selection of guesthouses and B&B accommodation. Up until 1900 the area was a farm of the same name. On the boundary with Gardens is the **De Waal Park** and **Molteno Reservoir**. Originally built as a main storage facility for the city in 1881, the reservoir now provides a peaceful wooded spot from where you can enjoy a view of the city. Close by, on the corner of Prince St and Sir George Grey St, is an **old iron pump**. Such pumps were once dotted about the city for people to draw water for domestic use.

There is nothing peaceful about **Vredehoek** today, as the De Waal Drive (M3) brings rush hour traffic into the top end of town from the southern suburbs and beyond. Most of the area has been given over to ugly high-rise apartments, though the residents benefit from some excellent views. This was the area in which many Jewish immigrants from Eastern Europe settled, and have to a large part remained.

Gardens is a lively neighbourhood with a choice of quality restaurants and comfortable guesthouses. Cape Town's smartest hotel, the *Mount Nelson*, is situated here in its own landscaped gardens. The grand gateway to the hotel was built in 1924 to welcome the Prince of Wales from England. From here the land slopes gently towards the Waterfront, with the commercial heart of the city laid out in between. This was the area where the Dutch East India Company first created fruit and vegetable gardens to supply the ships' crews who suffered greatly from scurvy. Across Orange Street from the entrance to the *Mount Nelson Hotel* is the top end of **Government Avenue**, a delightful pedestrian route past Company's Garden and many of the city's main museums. Originally sheltered by lemon trees, it is now lined with oaks and myrtle hedges, and is one of Cape Town's most popular walks. It was declared a national monument in 1937.

Bertram House

This early 19th-century red brick Georgian House has a distinctly English feel to it. The building houses a collection of porcelain, jewellery, silver and English furniture, the majority of which was bequeathed by Ann Lidderdale. Winifred Ann Lidderdale was an important civic figure in Cape Town in the 1950s. After her marriage to Henry Maxwell Lidderdale, she lived in England and the USA, but in 1951 the couple returned to Cape Town for their retirement. It was her desire to establish a home museum to commemorate the British contribution to life at the Cape - this was made possible by her bequest to the nation, and Bertram House was opened as a Georgian town house in 1984. Downstairs the two drawing rooms contain all the trappings of a bygone elegant age – card tables, a Hepplewhite settee, a square piano and a fine harp. Three rooms have wallpaper from London, a very expensive luxury for the period. Upstairs the Doris Tothill silver tea set and the hair jewellery are particularly fine. There is a café set in the gardens. ■ *Tue-Sat, 0930-1630, R5. On corner of Government Av and Orange St. T4249381.*

South Africa Museum & Planetarium

This is one of the city's most established museums, specializing in natural history, ethnography and archaeology and is a good place to take children. The first part of the collection, to the left of the entrance hall, has some interesting displays depicting the pre-European history of southern Africa. In the Stone Age room is the Linton panel, a beautifully preserved example of San rock art representing what has been interpreted as trance experiments. The ethnographic galleries offer excellent displays on the San, Khoi and Xhosa, amongst others, as well as the original Lydenburg Heads (see page 620). There is also a small display of pieces recovered from Great Zimbabwe which illustrate what an important trade centre it was: cornelian beads from Cambay, India; Chinese Celadon ware; 13th-century Persian pottery and Syrian glass from the 14th century. The shop has an above average selection of trinkets and the café serves good coffee and snack lunches. ■ *Daily 1000-1700. R8, free on Wed. 25 Queen Victoria St, at the top end of Company's Garden.* At the **Planetarium** next door presentations change every few months, but a view of the current night sky is shown on the first weekend of each month. Shows last an hour and are quite fascinating. ■ *Show times, Mon-Fri 1400, Sat and Sun, 1300, 1430, late showing on Tue 2000, R10. T4243330.*

Jewish Museum In 1841 a congregation of 17 men assembled for the first time in Cape Town to celebrate Yom Kippur. At the meeting they set about the task of raising funds to build a synagogue, and in 1862 the foundation stone was laid for the first synagogue in Southern Africa. The following year the building was completed and furnished – quite a feat for such a small community at the time. Inside the newly renovated museum is a rich and rare collection of items depicting the history of the Cape Town Hebrew Congregation and other congregations in the Cape Province. On display upstairs are bronze Sabbath oil lamps, *Chanukkah* lamps, *Bessamin* spice containers, *Torah* scrolls, *Kiddush* cups and candlesticks. There is a beautiful stained-glass window depicting the Ten Commandments in Hebrew. From here a glass corridor leads you to a new section of the museum which is devoted to the history of Jewish immigration to the Cape, mainly from Lithuania. A lot of thought has been put into the displays, which include photographs, immigration certificates, videos and a full reconstruction of a Lithuanian *shetl*, or village. The museum complex also houses a library, café and bookshop. ■ *Sun-Thu 1000-1700, Fri 1000-1400. Closed on Jewish and public holidays. 88 Hatfield St. T4651546, F4650284, www.sajewishmuseum.co.za*

Holocaust Centre Cape Town's newest museum is also one of its best, comprising an intelligent and shocking examination of the Holocaust. Exhibits follow a historical route, starting with a look at anti-Semitism in Europe in previous centuries, and then leading to the rise of Nazism in Germany, the creation of ghettos, death camps and the Final Solution, and liberation at the end of the war. Video footage, photography, examples of Nazi propaganda and personal accounts of the Holocaust produce a vividly haunting and shocking display. The exhibits cleverly acknowledge South Africa's recent emergence from Apartheid and draw parallels between both injustices, as well as looking at the link between South Africa's Greyshirts (who were later assimilated into the National Party) and the Nazis. The local context is highlighted further at the end of the exhibition, with video accounts of Jews who survived the Holocaust and moved to Cape Town. ■ *Sun-Thu 1000-1700, Fri 1000-1300, entry by donation. 88 Hatfield St. T4625554, F4625554, www.museums.org.za/ctholocaust*

National Gallery The National Gallery houses a permanent collection of local and international art, as well as some interesting temporary exhibitions. The original collection was bequeathed to the nation in 1871 by Thomas Butterworth Bailey. Of particular interest is the collection of 18th- and 19th-century British sporting paintings donated by Sir Abe Bailey. Most of South Africa's best known artists are also represented, and the Hyman Liberman Hall is devoted to exhibiting new South African art. Snacks and light lunches are available at the Gallery Café. ■ *Mon 1300-1700, Tue-Sun 1000-1700. Entry by donation. T4651628.*

Rust en Vreugd A few hundred metres east of the National Gallery, at 78 Buitenkant Street, hidden behind a high whitewashed wall, is this 18th century mansion. It was declared a historical monument in 1940, and subsequently restored to its best period. Today it houses six galleries displaying a unique collection of watercolours, engravings and lithographs depicting the history of the Cape. Of particular note are Schouten's watercolour of Van Riebeeck's earth fort (1658), watercolours by Thomas Baines (a British artist who travelled extensively in SA and Australia) of climbing Table Mountain, lithographs by Angas of Khoi and Zulus and a collection of cartoons by Cruikshank depicting the first British settlers arriving in the Cape. These are all part of the **William Fehr** collection. Commercial exhibitions are held in the galleries upstairs. The grounds have been laid out to recreate an 18th century Dutch garden; of particular note is the herb garden. ■ *Mon-Sat 0900-1600. Free if you have earlier visited the Castle of Good Hope (see page 86) and kept your ticket. T4653628.*

Company's Garden

Running alongside Government Avenue is the peaceful Company's Garden, situated on the site of **Jan van Riebeeck's** original vegetable garden, which was created in 1652 to grow produce for settlers and ships bound for the East. Governor Simon van der Stel added an irrigation canal, and so the gardens developed into the oasis people enjoy today. It is now a small botanical garden, with lawns, a variety of labelled trees and ponds filled with Japanese Koi. The grey squirrels living amongst the oak trees were introduced by Cecil Rhodes from America. There are also a couple of statues here: opposite the South African Public Library at the lower end of the garden, is the oldest statue in Cape Town, that of Sir George Grey, Governor of the Cape from 1854 to 1862. Close by is a statue of Cecil Rhodes, pointing northwards, with an inscription reading, "Your hinterland is there," a reminder of his ambition to paint the map pink from the Cape to Cairo. There is a pleasant café in the garden, serving drinks and snacks beneath the trees.

South African Public Library

Adjoining the gardens is the South African Public Library, on Queen Victoria St, behind St Georges Cathedral. Opened in 1818, it is the country's oldest national reference library and was one of the first free libraries in the world. Today it houses an important collection of books covering South Africa's history. The building also has a bookshop and an internet café. ■ *Mon-Fri 0900-1700. T4246320.*

Houses of Parliament

On the other side of the avenue are the Houses of Parliament. The building was completed in 1885, and when the Union was formed in 1910 it became the seat for the national parliament. In front of the building is a marble statue of Queen Victoria, erected by public subscription in honour of her Golden Jubilee. It was unveiled in 1890. ■ *While parliament is sitting (Jan-Jun) it is possible to watch from the visitors' gallery, Mon-Fri. Overseas visitors must show their passports and call in advance to watch debates. Guided tours of the chambers and Constitutional Assembly are given Mon and Fri at 0900, 1000, 1100 and 1200. T4032460.*

St George's Cathedral

The cathedral has figured in the news a little more than one might expect: up until June 1996, this was where Archbishop Desmond Tutu gave many of his famous sermons (see page 84)

The last building on Government Avenue is St George's Cathedral. The building you see today is comparatively new: it was built at the beginning of the 20th century, after the first design, based upon St Pancras' Church in London, was turned down. The present cathedral was designed by Sir Herbert Baker. Inside, some of the early memorial tablets have been preserved, while over the top of the stairs leading to the crypt is a memorial to Lady D'Urban, wife of Sir Benjamin D'Urban, the Governor of the Cape from 1834 to 1838. Under the archway between the choir and St John's Chapel is a bronze recumbent statue of Archbishop West Jones, the second Archbishop of Cape Town, 1874-1908. The Great North window is a fine piece of stained glass depicting the pioneers of the Anglican church. There is a small café, The Crypt, open during the day for light snacks and breakfasts

Bo-Kaap Museum

About 600 m west along Wale Street is the Bo-Kaap, Cape Town's historical Islamic quarter and one of the city's most interesting residential areas. The Bo-Kaap museum, housed in an attractive 18th-century house, is dedicated to the Cape's Malay community and contains the furnishings of a wealthy 19th-century Muslim family. In the front room there is one item of original furniture, a table inlaid with mother of pearl. In the prayer room, *langgar*, is an old Koran and *tasbeh* beads set in front of the mihrab alcove, while the courtyard holds a collection of coaches and early carts. The house itself is one of the oldest buildings in Cape Town surviving in its original form. It was built by Jan de Waal for artisans in 1763 and it was here that Abu Bakr Effendi started the first Arabic school and wrote some important articles on Islamic Law. He originally came to Cape Town as a guest of the British government to try and settle religious differences amongst the Cape Muslims. ■ *Tue-Sat 0930-1630. Small entrance fee. T4243846.*

Desmond Tutu

Like Nelson Mandela, Desmond Tutu is accepted as an influential and respected figure far beyond the borders of South Africa. His powerful oration and his simple but brave defiance of the Apartheid state has impressed the world. Tutu first caught the international headlines as an outspoken secretary general of the South African Council of Churches in the late 1970s, especially with his call for the international community to stop buying South African goods. But it was the award of the Nobel Peace Prize in 1984 that really established him as an international figure.

Desmond Tutu was born on 7 October 1931 in Klerksdrop and was educated in local mission schools and the Johannesburg Bantu High School in the Western Native township. After obtaining a BA and teaching diploma he taught at a high school in Krugersdorp before going to St Peter's Theological College to train as an Anglican priest. After being ordained he moved to London with his wife and young family, living in Golders Green, whilst he studied for both a BA and MA in Theology. In 1966 he returned to South Africa.

After a spell teaching in the Eastern Cape Tutu became a lecturer at the National University of Lesotho. He was in England again for three years in the early 1970s, before taking an appointment as the Anglican Dean of Johannesburg, but then quickly moved back to Lesotho to become Bishop. In 1978 he moved to Johannesburg once again, now as the secretary general of the South African Council of Churches. It was at about this time that the press began to take notice of Tutu's forceful anti-Apartheid statements.

In response to Tutu's comments about Apartheid the South African government took away his passport to prevent him speaking at international conferences, though he was occasionally allowed temporary travel documents and was able to address some important meetings and hold discussions with other religious leaders. Tutu made it clear that he believed that economic sanctions on South Africa were essential to make the Apartheid state introduce reforms at a faster pace. These comments obviously annoyed the South

African government and they regarded Tutu as a dangerous opponent. They were, however, always wary of treating him as cruelly as they treated many of their other opponents. They were aware that any mistreatment would lead to an enormous international outcry. This was especially so after 1984, when he was awarded the Nobel Peace Prize.

In February 1985 Tutu was made Bishop of Johannesburg and finally in April 1986 he was elected Anglican Archbishop of Cape Town. His election was not popular with many white rank and file members of the Anglican Church who believed his calls for economic sanctions were harming their economic interests. The Anglican Church's white congregation have tended to come from the English-speaking sections of the community who regard themselves as more liberal than the Afrikaners. They did not want to be seen to oppose Tutu on grounds of race. Furthermore, it would have appeared unchristian to complain too vocally about how their privileged pockets had been affected by his stance on sanctions. Opposition was, therefore, most commonly expressed through the criticism that he was mixing religion with politics. This claim was not easy to sustain, however, as Tutu always brought a strictly moral and Christian approach to all his 'political' interventions. He often headed protest marches dressed in his Archbishop's robes, though this did not stop him being arrested on a couple of occasions and even teargassed.

Since the arrival of democracy in South Africa Tutu has continued to play a prominent though not quite as central a public role. During 1996 he chaired the hearings of the Truth and Reconciliation Committee and argued forcibly that the policy of granting amnesty to all who admitted their crimes was an important step in healing the nation's scars. His continued espousal of a Christian philosophy of forgiveness has at times angered some of the families of the victims of Apartheid, who emphasize instead the need for justice, but few could deny the sincerity of Tutu's belief in what he sees as a healing process.

On the corner of Adderley and Wale Streets is Slave Lodge, previously known as the **Slave Lodge**
Cultural History Museum. This, the second oldest building in Cape Town, has had a
varied history, starting life as a lodge for slaves, and then becoming a library, a post
office, the Cape Supreme Court, and finally a museum in 1966. Its most significant
role, however, was as a slave lodge for the VOC. Between 1679 and 1811 the building
housed up to 1000 slaves. Local indigenous groups were protected by the VOC from
being enslaved; most slaves were consequently imported from Madagascar, India
and Indonesia, creating the most culturally varied slave society in the world. Conditions at the lodge were terrible and up to 20% of the slaves died every year. Sadly only
a glimpse of this history is displayed by the museum. Instead, much of the collection
celebrates colonialism and includes rambling displays of British and VOC weapons,
household goods, furniture and money, as well as relics from Japan and ancient
Rome, Greece and Egypt. There is also a room on the 'Cape Kaleidoscope', representing the history of Cape Town, and a display explaining some of the history of
slavery. Perhaps the most interesting feature of the museum is a series of plaques
describing the function of each room within the slave lodge. The museum's planners
are now in the process of restructuring much of the museum – many of the colonial
collections will be replaced with displays depicting slavery in the Cape and the lasting effects it has had on South African society. ■ *Mon-Sat 0930-1630. R5. Guides are
available on request. T4618280.*

Nearby is one of Cape Town's older corners, **Church Square**, site of the Groote Kerk. **Groote Kerk**
Up until 1834 the square was used as a venue for the **auctioning of slaves** from the *Look out for the special*
Slave Lodge, which faced onto the square. All transactions took place under a tree – a *pews with their own*
concrete plaque marks the old tree's position. *locked doors. These*
   The Groote Kerk was the first church of the **Dutch Reformed** faith to be built in *belonged to wealthy*
South Africa (building started in 1678 and it was consecrated in 1704). The chiming *families who didn't*
bell dates from 1726 and was cast in Amsterdam. The present church, built between *want to pray with the*
1836 and 1841, is a somewhat dull, grey building designed and built by Hermann *common people*
Schutte after a fire had destroyed most of the original building. Many of the old gravestones were built into the base of the church walls, the most elaborate of which is the
tombstone of Baron van Rheede van Oudtshoorn. Inside, more early tombstones and
family vaults are set into the floor, while on the walls are the coats of arms of early Cape
families. Two of the Cape's early governors are buried here – Simon van der Stel
(1679-99), and Ryk Tulbagh (1751-71). Of particular note is the beautiful pulpit
carved by **Anton Anreith**, whose work can also be seen at **Groot Constantia**. The two
baroque heraldic lions which support the pulpit are said to represent the power of
faith. ■ *1030-1200, 1400-1500, weekdays. Free guided tours available on request.*

This small museum, housed in the Methodist Church at 25a Buitekant Street, is one **District Six**
of Cape Town's most powerful and gives a fascinating glimpse of the stupidity and **Museum**
horror of Apartheid. District Six was once the vibrant, cosmopolitan heart of Cape
Town, a largely coloured inner city suburb renowned for its jazz scene. In February
1966, P W Botha, then Minister of Community Development, formally proclaimed
District Six a "white" group area. Over the next 15 years, an estimated 60,000 people
were given notice to give up their homes and moved to the new townships on the
Cape Flats. The area was razed, and to this day remains largely undeveloped.
   The museum contains a collection of photographs, articles and personal accounts
depicting life before and after the removals. Highlights include a large map covering
most of the ground floor, upon which ex-residents have been encouraged to mark
their homes and local sights. The "Namecloth" is particularly poignant: a 1.5 m-wide
length of cloth has been provided for ex-residents to write down their comments, part
of which hangs by the entrance. It has grown to over 1km in the last eight years, and
features some moving and insightful thoughts. ■ *Mon-Sat 0900-1600. Entry by donation. T4618745. There is a small café serving cakes and sandwiches at the back.*

Cape Town

City Hall & Grand Parade

From Adderley Street, a short walk down Darling Street will take you to the City Hall and the Grand Parade. The latter is the largest open space in Cape Town and was originally used for garrison parades before the Castle was completed. Today the oak-lined parade is used as a car park and twice a week it is taken over by a colourful market (see page 120). The neo-classical City Hall, built to celebrate Queen Victoria's golden jubilee, overlooks the parade. Its clock tower is a half size replica of Big Ben in London. In 1979 the municipal government moved to a new Civic Centre on the Foreshore, a dominant tower block which straddles Hertzog Boulevard. The hall is now headquarters of the Cape Town Symphony Orchestra and houses the **City Library**. The library reading room has local, national and international newspapers – visitors can get a Holiday Visitors' Card valid for three months for a small fee. After his release from prison, **Nelson Mandela** made his first speech to over 100,000 people on the Grand Parade from the City Hall on 9 May 1994.

Castle of Good Hope

Beyond the Grand Parade, on Darling Street, is the main entrance of South Africa's oldest colonial building, the Castle of Good Hope. Work was started in 1666 by Commander Zacharias Wagenaer and completed in 1679. Its original purpose was for the Dutch East India Company to defend the Cape from rival European powers, and today it is an imposing sight, albeit a rather gloomy one. Under the British, the Castle served as government headquarters and since 1917 it has been the headquarters of the South African Defence Force, Western Cape.

Today the castle is home to three museums. The **William Fehr Collection** is one of South Africa's finest displays of furnishings reflecting the social and political history of the Cape. There are landscapes by John Thomas Baines and William Huggins, 17th-century Japanese porcelain and 18th-century Indonesian furniture. Upstairs is an absurdly huge dining table which seats 104, in a room still used for state dinners.

To the left of the Fehr Collection is the **Secunde's House**. The Secunde was second in charge of the settlement at the Cape, responsible for administrative duties for the Dutch East India Company. None of the three rooms contain original furniture from the Castle, but they do recreate the conditions under which an official for the Dutch East India Company would have lived in the 17th, 18th and early 19th centuries. The third museum is the **Military Museum**, a rather indifferent collection depicting the conflicts of early settlers. More absorbing are the regimental displays of uniforms and medals.

There are free **guided tours** at 1100, 1200 and 1400. These are informative and fun, although a little short. Tour highlights include the torture chambers, cells, views from the battlements and Dolphin Court, where Lady Anne Barnard was supposedly seen bathing in the nude by the sentries. ■ *0900-1600. R15 entrance, fee includes a guided tour and entry to Rust en Vreugd, see page 82. Entry from the Grand Parade side. T4691249, www.castleofgoodhope.co.za Expect to have any bags checked since the castle is still used as the regional offices for the National Defence Force. While waiting for a tour you can enjoy coffee and cakes at a small café, or explore van der Stel's restored wine cellars, where you can taste and buy wines. Audio tapes can also be hired for R25 and provide a 45 min tour. There is full ceremonial Changing of the Guard at noon.*

Adderley Street & Heerengracht

Adderley Street is one of the city's busiest shopping areas, and is sadly marred by a number of 1960s and 70s eyesores, but it does still boast some impressive bank buildings. On the corner of Darling Street is the **Standard Bank Building** (1880), a grand structure built shortly after the diamond wealth from Kimberley began to reach Cape Town. The exterior has a central dome surmounted by the figure Britannia, but it is the main banking hall which is of most interest, with all the original Victorian features remaining largely intact. Diagonally across Adderley Street is the equally impressive **Barclays Bank Building** (1933), a fine Ceres sandstone building which was the last major work by Sir Herbert Baker in South Africa. Though built 50 years after the Standard Bank, its interior is just as detailed in design. The windows with half shutters are made from teak, while the main banking hall is resplendent with travertine and marble finishes. Baker even designed the chairs and the pewter inkwells.

Karamats

Karamats *are the tombs of Imams who lived and worked with the Muslim community of Cape Town. They are dotted around Cape Town in a circle that is believed to provide the city with a protective spiritual boundary, preventing natural disasters. Surprisingly little is made of the Karamats in tourist literature, but for devout Cape Muslims they are very important. For an overseas visitor they are worth visiting for their pleasing architecture and peaceful locations. Before embarking upon haj a local muslim will visit each Karamat in turn. Sheik Yussuf's Karamat is the first and most important. The memorial was only built in 1925 by Hadji Sullaiman Shah. It is situated on a hillock close to the Eerste River, Macassar. Take the Firgrove turning off the N2 just before Somerset West. Five other*

Karamats *complete the magic circle – off the road to the Signal Hill viewpoint, Sayed Muhammad Hassan Gaibi Shah is buried here; at the top end of Strand Street, on the slopes of Signal Hill, the bodies of four holy men entombed here including that of Tuan Guru, the first Imam in the Cape, and founder of the first mosque; on Robben Island, the tomb of Sayed Abdurahman Matura, Prince of Ternate; Oudekraal, off the Victoria Road, near Bakoven Beach, a concrete stairway leads up to the tomb hidden in the trees, Nureel Mobeen buried here; and Constantia Valley, on the slopes of Islam Hill, is the tomb of Abdumaah Shah, by the gate to the farm Klein Constantia.*

Special tours*: organized by Sulayman Habib, a registered guide, T235579.*

At the corner of Adderley Street and Strand Street stands a modern shopping mall complex, the **Golden Acre**. On the lower level of the complex the remains of an aqueduct and a reservoir dating from 1663 can be viewed. The line of black floor tiles close to the escalator which links the centre with the railway station mark the position of the original shoreline before any reclamation work began in Table Bay. Continuing down towards the docks, Adderley Street passes Cape Town Railway Station. At the junction with Hans Strijdom Street is a large roundabout with a central fountain and a bronze statue of **Jan van Riebeeck**, given to the city by Cecil Rhodes in 1899. At the bottom end of Adderley Street on the foreshore are statues of Bartholomew Dias and Maria van Riebeeck, donated respectively by the Portuguese and Dutch Governments in 1952 for Cape Town's tercentenary celebrations.

In front of the Medical Centre on Heerengracht is the **Scott Memorial**. What is on show is in fact a bronze replica; the original, a stone argosy, was smashed by vandals. Its location has barely changed, but when it was unveiled in 1916 it was on the approach to a pier at the foot of Adderley Street, a further indication of how much additional land has been reclaimed from Table Bay over the years. The palm trees once graced a marine promenade in this area. Up until the 1850s there was a canal running the full length of Heerengracht and Adderley streets. This was covered over as the city prospered and traffic congestion became a problem.

Just off **St George's Mall**, a pedestrianized road lined with shops and cafés is the delightfully peaceful Koopmans-De Wet House on Strand Street. Surviving in the midst of ugly modern buildings and the bustle of central Cape Town, it is one of the more interesting museums in town. The house is named in memory of Marie Koopmans-De Wet, a prominent figure in cultured Cape Society who lived here between 1834 and 1906. The inside has been restored to reflect the period of her grandparents who lived here in the late 18th century. All of the pieces are numbered and a small catalogue gives a brief description. Though not too cluttered, there is a fascinating collection of furnishings which gives the house a special tranquil feel. In the front left room is a fine gabled bureau bookcase (# 4 in the catalogue) made from stinkwood with silver and brass mounts. In the music room is a square piano (# 93), made by W Stoddart of London in 1802. Upstairs there is a spacious upper hall leading to a couple of bedrooms and a small library. Note the linen in the main bedroom,

Koopmans-De Wet House

Cape Town

neatly wrapped and tied with red bows in a gabled cabinet made from satinwood and stinkwood (# 230). At the head of the stairs is an early map of the Cape coastline dating from 1730 – Saldanha Bay and Cape Agulhas are clearly visible (# 286). At the back of the house is a shaded courtyard and the original stables with the slave quarters above. ■ *Tue-Sat 0930-1630. Small entrance fee. T4242473.*

Lutheran Church & Martin Melck House

A few blocks west of Koopman's-De Wit House, at 96 Strand Street, is the Lutheran Church and Martin Melck House. For 130 years after the establishment of the settlement at the Cape, the Dutch authorities refused to tolerate any churches other than those belonging to the established religion, the Dutch Reformed Church. From 1742 the Lutheran community tried unsuccessfully to gain permission to build a church. In 1774 **Martin Melck**, a wealthy burgher, funded the building of a 'wine store', 28x20 m, on Strand Street. It was designed with easy conversion to church in mind, and services were held here from 1776 onwards. In 1787 the adjoining house was built as the parsonage. In 1818, not long after the Dutch rule had been replaced by the British, the Church was partially rebuilt, and it finally got a tower. The bell tower and canopied pulpit were designed by **Anton Anreith**. The house, built by **Thibault**, is one of the few remaining typical Cape town houses of the 18th century. Both buildings are national monuments. ■ *Tue-Sat 0930-1630. T4242473.*

Greenmarket Square

A couple of blocks south of the junction of Strand Street and St George's Mall is Greenmarket Square, the old heart of Cape Town and the second oldest square in the city. It has long been a meeting place, and during the 19th century it became a vegetable market. In 1834 it took on the significant role of being the site where the declaration of freeing all slaves was made. Today it remains a popular meeting place and is lined with outdoor cafés and restaurants. A busy daily market sprawls across the cobbles, with stalls selling African crafts, jewellery and clothes.

Most of the buildings around the square reflect the city's history. Dominating one side is a *Holiday Inn* hotel, housed in what was once the headquarters of *Shell Oil* – note the shell motifs on its exterior. Diagonally opposite is the **Old Town House** (1751), originally built to house the town guard. It became the first town hall in 1840 when Cape Town became a municipality. Much of the exterior remains unchanged, and with its decorative plaster mouldings and fine curved fanlights is one of the best preserved Cape Baroque exteriors in the city. The first electric light in Cape Town was switched on in the Old House on 13 April 1895. Today the white double-storeyed building houses the **Michaelis collection** of Flemish and Dutch paintings. ■ *Viewing daily 1000-1700.* At the entrance to the house is a circle set into the floor which marks the spot from which all distances to and from Cape Town are measured. Next to the *Tudor Hotel* is the second oldest building in the square – the **Metropolitan Methodist Church** (1876). This is the only high Victorian church in Cape Town and has a tall spire with a unique series of miniature grotesques decorating its exterior. The church was designed by Charles Freeman and is regarded as one of the finest in the country.

If you are interested in antiques, walk out of the square past the Methodist church to Church St. The area between Burg and Long streets is the venue for an antique street market

Long Street

This stretch is one of the trendiest in Cape Town, and gets particularly lively at night. Lined with street cafés, fashionable shops, bars, clubs and backpacker lodges, it has a distinctly young feel about it, but is also home to some fine old city buildings. One of Cape Town's late Victorian gems is at number 117, now an antique shop. On the outside is an unusual cylindrical turret with curved windows; inside is a fine cast iron spiral staircase leading to a balustraded gallery.

South African Missionary Meeting-House Museum

One of the more interesting buildings on Long Street is the Sendinggestig Museum, or South African Missionary Meeting House Museum at number 40. It is the oldest mission church in South Africa, built between 1802-4 as the mother church for missionary work carried out in rural areas. Fortunately the building was saved from demolition in 1977 and restored to its present fine form. Though utilized by directors and members of the South African Missionary Society, it was more commonly used for religious and literacy instruction of slaves in Cape Town. By 1960 most of its congregation had been moved to the Cape Flats or died. Before having a look inside, cross the street and admire the façade of Corinthian pilasters carrying four urns. Inside, the wooden arch ceiling and balcony are particularly fine, while the pulpit, made by Kannemeyer, has stairs either side of the lectern and a canopy. Also of note is the German organ decorated with flowers. There is a permanent display of missionary work throughout the Cape, and behind the pulpit are display cabinets showing early cash accounts and receipts for transactions such as the transfer of slaves. ■ *Mon-Fri 0900-1600, Sat 0900-1200. T4236755.*

Victoria and Alfred Waterfront

The V & A Waterfront, Cape Town's original Victorian harbour, is the city's most popular attraction. The whole area was completely restored in the early 1990s, and today it is a lively district packed with restaurants, bars and shops. Original buildings stand shoulder to shoulder with mock-Victorian shopping centres, museums and cinemas, all crowding along a waterside walkway with Table Mountain towering beyond. Prices are a little higher in restaurants and bars here and many have argued that the area is over-sanitized and artificial. But despite being geared towards tourists it remains a working harbour, which provides much of the area's real charm. Even if it's not to your taste, the choice of shops, restaurants and entertainment is unrivalled, all accessible in a clean and safe environment.

Getting there A Waterfront bus, with a distinctive blue wave pattern on the side, runs **Ins & outs** every 15 mins between Cape Town railway station and the Waterfront. There is also a service between the Waterfront and Sea Point. Avoid walking as you have to follow an unpleasant stretch along a car-exhaust-chocked highway.

Tourist information There is a brand new tourist information centre in the Clock Tower centre, across the swing bridge from the main development. As well as handing out maps and leaflets on the area, you can also book flights, tours, car rental, check your email and have a coffee overlooking the harbour. Open 0900-1800. T4054500, www.waterfront.co.za

There are also several kiosks on the ground floor inside Victoria Wharf shopping centre. The staff at the centre are also happy to explain how the whole development will look when completed in 2003, including a canal linking the Waterfront to the Strand in the town centre. (Considering the Waterfront is at present virtually cut off from the city centre, it should prove useful.) The staff in the centre are very helpful and enthusiastic about the whole development – little surprise as it probably represents the most successful tourist development in South Africa.

The Victoria and Alfred Waterfront derives its name from the two harbour basins **History** around which it is developed. Construction began in 1860, when Prince Alfred, Queen Victoria's second son, tipped the first load of stone to start the building of the breakwater for Cape Town's harbour. Alfred Basin could not handle the increased shipping volumes and subsequently a larger basin, the Victoria Basin, was built. A number of original buildings remain around the basins and are an interesting diversion from the razzmatazz of the shops and restaurants.

At the narrow entrance to the Alfred Basin, on the Berties Landing side, is the origi- **Clock tower** nal Clock Tower, built in 1882 to house the Port Captain's office. This is in the form of a red octagonal Gothic-style tower and stands just in front of the Clock Tower Centre, the newest collection of shops, offices and restaurants on the Waterfront. The ground floor of the Clock Tower houses an information kiosk and the original tide gauge mechanism which enabled the exact depths in the basin to be checked. Sadly the other rooms are now closed to the public, although it is sometimes possible

Cape Town

to climb to the roof, which allows fine views of the surroundings. The Clock Tower centre opposite houses the new Nelson Mandela Gateway to Robben Island, from where you catch the main ferry to the island.

Union Castle Building

Walking across the swing bridge from the Clock Tower (look out for the Cape Fur seals as you cross), you come to the *Victoria and Alfred Hotel*. Opposite here is a stocky square building known as Union Castle Building (1919), designed by the firm of architects owned by Sir Herbert Baker. The Union Steamship Company and the Castle Line both ran monthly mail ships between Britain and South Africa, in the late 19th century. In 1900 they amalgamated and from then on mail was delivered every week. The last Union Castle ship to sail to England with the mail was the *Windsor Castle* in 1977. The building now houses *Telekom Exploratorium*, a small museum focussing on technology and communication, aimed primarily at children. ■ *Tue-Sun 0900-1800. R10. T4195957.*

Victoria & Alfred Waterfront

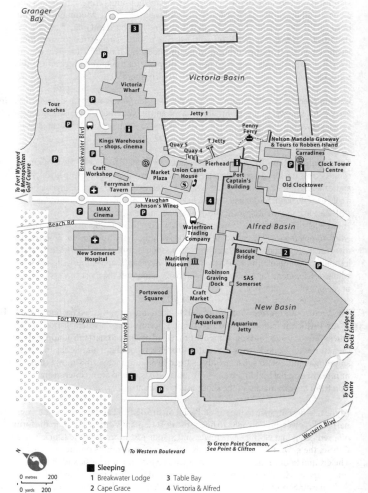

Sleeping

1 Breakwater Lodge
2 Cape Grace
3 Table Bay
4 Victoria & Alfred

Behind the Union Castle Building is the *Victoria and Alfred Hotel*. Now a luxury four-star hotel, this building was originally built as a coal store before being converted into Union Castle's warehouse and customs baggage store. It originally had a third floor but this was destroyed in a fire in 1939. This building is a perfect example of how effective restoration can be, and how with a bit of imagination a whole area can be given a new lease of life. This was the first hotel to be opened at the Waterfront and it is an important part of the success of the whole venture.

Time Ball Tower

Heading west from there, on the other side of Dock Road above the car park, is the **Time Ball Tower**. This dates from 1894; its purpose was to act as an accurate reference for ships' navigators to set their clocks as the ball on the roof fell. Correct time was vital for the navigator to be able to determine precise longitude before the development of more modern equipment. Beside the tower is a 100-year-old Dragon Tree, *Dracaeno draco*, from the Canary Islands, and next to the tree is the original Harbour Master's Residence, 1860.

Two Oceans Aquarium

The top attraction on the Waterfront is this aquarium on Dock Road, focussing on the unique Cape marine environment created by the meeting of the **Atlantic and Indian Oceans**. The display begins with a walk through the Indian Ocean, where visitors follow a route past tanks filled with a multitude of colourful fish, turtles, seahorses and octopi. Highlights here include giant spider crabs and phosphorescent jellyfish, floating in a mesmerizing circular current. From here you walk past touch pools, where children can pick up spiky starfish and slimy sea slugs. The basement holds the Alpha Activity Centre, where free puppet shows and face painting keep children busy. The main wall here is part of the Diving Animals pool, where you can watch Cape fur seals dart and dive before the glass. On the first floor is the Story of Water exhibit, an interesting enough display although the resident African penguins seem rather confined in their enclosure. Next is the Kelp Forest, an extraordinary tangle of giant kelp which sways drunkenly in the artificial tides. The highlight is the Predators exhibit, an enormous tank complete with glass tunnel, holding ragged-tooth sharks, eagle rays, turtles, and some impressively large hunting fish. There are daily feeds at 1530. ■ *Daily 0930-1800. R45. Entrance is on Dock Road next to the Maritime Museum, by the Waterfront Craft Market. T4183823, www.aquarium.co.za*

Maritime Museum

This museum houses a collection of shipwreck salvage models and figureheads. Outside in front of the *Victoria and Alfred Hotel*, alongside the North Quay of the Alfred Basin, is the museum ship, the *SAS Somerset*. The tug which was kept here is now used for harbour cruises. ■ *Daily 1000-1700. Small entrance fee. T4192556.*

Cape Medical Museum

Close by the Waterfront, at the City Hospital Complex on Portwood Road, Green Point, the medical achievements of South Africa's doctors are celebrated in this interesting display, a must for any medical students doing their elective in Cape Town. ■ *Mon-Fri 0900-1600. T4185663.*

Robben Island

Lying 13 km off Green Point's shores, Robben Island is best known as the notorious prison that held many of the ANC's most prominent members, including Nelson Mandela and Walter Sisulu. It was originally named by the Dutch, after the term for seals, '*rob*' – actually a misnomer as none are found here. The island's history of occupation started in 1806, when John Murray was granted permission by the British to conduct whaling from the island. During this period the authorities started to use the island as a dumping ground for common convicts; these were brought back to the mainland in 1843, and their accommodation was deemed suitable for lepers and the mentally ill. These were in turn moved to the mainland between 1913 and

1931, and the island entered a new era as a military base during the Second World War. In 1960 the military passed control of the island over to the Department of Prisons, and it remained a prison until 1996. On 1 December 1999 the island was declared as a World Heritage Site by UNESCO.

Robben Island's effectiveness as a prison did not rest simply with the fact that escape was virtually impossible. The authorities anticipated that the idea of "out of sight, out of mind" would be particularly applicable here, and to a certain extent they were correct. Certainly, its isolation did much to break the spirit of political prisoners, not least Robert Sobukwe's. Sobukwe was the leader of the Pan African Congress, and was kept in solitary confinement for nine years. Other political prisoners were spared that at least, although in 1971 they were separated from common law prisoners, as they were deemed a "bad" influence. Conditions were harsh, with forced hard labour and routine beatings. Much of the daily running of the maximum security prison was designed to reinforce racial divisions: all the wardens, and none of the prisoners, were white; black prisoners, unlike those deemed coloured, had to wear short trousers and were given smaller food rations. Contact with the outside world was virtually non-existent – visitors had to apply for permission six months in advance and were allowed to stay for just half an hour. Newspapers were banned and letters were limited to one every six months.

Yet despite these measures, the B-Section, which housed Mandela and other major political prisoners, became the international focus of the fight against Apartheid. The last political prisoners left the island in 1991.

It is also possible to view **wildlife** on the island – as a prison, the area was strictly protected allowing the fish and bird populations to flourish. There are over 100 species of bird on the island, and it is an important breeding site for African Penguins.

Robben Island Tours
You must remain with your guide during the tour. Do not drink any tap water on the island

Tours to the island are run by the *Robben Island Museum*, T4191300, F4191057, www.robben-island.org.za The Nelson Mandela Gateway at the Clock Tower Centre is the embarkation and disembarkation point for the tours. The Gateway also holds a shop, the ticket office and a museum (not yet opened at time of writing), open 0900-1800. An air-conditioned, fully licensed catamaran completes the half-hour journey. Tickets cost R100 for adults, R50 for children under 17. Tours begin with a drive around the key sites on the island, including Sobukwe's house, the lime quarry where Mandela was forced to work, the leper cemetery, and the houses of former warders. Tours around the prison are conducted by ex-political prisoners, who paint a vivid picture of prison life here. Departures are on the hour between 0900 and 1500, and tours allow two and a half hours on the island. Be sure to book a day ahead as tickets sell out quickly. There is an extra 1700 "sunset" departure in summer, although rates are higher and don't include the usual prison tour.

Southern suburbs

Primarily encompassing the more affluent residential areas of Cape Town, the suburbs, stretching southeast from the city centre, are an interesting diversion to the usual tourist spots.

Ins & outs   **Getting there**   Although a car is the best way to visit, it is possible to reach all by train – the Metro service between the city centre and Simon's Town runs through all the suburbs. Keep in mind that it's best to avoid the trains when it's not busy.

Woodstock & Observatory   The first suburb, Woodstock, is a mixed commercial and residential area, historically a working class coloured district. In the 19th century it was a thriving community, when it was known as Papendorp. It became a municipality in 1881 and the local residents were invited to choose a new name. The most popular drinking haunt at the time was the *Woodstock Hotel*, and so the suburb got its new name. Today it seems a little run down and depressing, although the back streets are an attractive mesh of Victorian bungalows, some of which are being snapped up by a new yuppie class.

Observatory is an attractive area of tightly packed houses, narrow streets and student hangouts. In recent years, it has managed to create its own special ambience, and once settled here you can quickly forget about the town centre or Waterfront. Being close to the university, there is a wide range of trendy bars, cafés and restaurants catering for a mixed scene of students, bohemian types and budget backpackers. This is a good area to stay in and has an enjoyably liberal atmosphere not so easily found in some of the other suburbs. The observatory after which the suburb is named is where Station Road intersects Liesbeeck Parkway. The first Astronomer Royal to work at the Royal Observatory was also a clergyman, the Rev Fearon Fellowes. Aside from making astronomical observations the observatory was responsible for accurate standard time in South Africa. It has also been an important meteorological centre and has a seismograph which records earthquakes around the world. Observatory is also where you'll find the **Groot Schuur Hospital** on Main Road, the site of the world's first heart transplant. A small museum in the hospital commemorates this.

Southern suburbs

The next suburbs of Mowbray, Rosebank and Rondebosch lie just below the **University of Cape Town**. Again, they are popular with students and have a good selection of restaurants and shops. Mowbray was originally known as Driekoppen, or three heads, after the murder by three slaves of a European foreman and his wife in 1724. On their capture they were beheaded and their heads impaled on stakes at the farm entrance to act as a deterrent. Rondebosch, conversely, has for some time been associated with education. Aside from the university, several important schools were founded in the district: the Diocesan College, Rustenberg Girls' High School, Rondebosch Boys' High School and the Marist Brothers' College. The area was also important from a practical point of view: in 1656 Van Riebeeck realized that Company's Garden was exposed to a damaging southeast wind. His first choice of a more sheltered spot was Rondebosch. This proved a success and a grain storage barn was built. Early written accounts describe the area as wild country, with the farmers frequently losing livestock to hyenas, lion and leopards – an image that is hard to imagine as you sit in the evening rush hour traffic jam on Rhodes Drive. Also in Rondebosch is **Groot Schuur**, the

Mowbray, Rosebank & Rondesbosch

Prime Minister's official residence; **Westbrooke**, home of the State President; and the original residence of the Cape Governor over 200 years ago, **Rustenburg**.

Irma Stern Museum A lesser-known but fascinating tourist attraction in the area is this museum, on Cecil Road. Irma Stern was one of South Africa's pioneering artists and her lovely house displays a mixture of her own works, a collection of artefacts from across Africa, and some fine pieces of antique furniture from overseas – 17th-century Spanish chairs, 19th-century German oak furniture and Swiss *mardi gras* masks. Her portraits are particularly poignant and those of her close friends are superb, while her religious art is rather more disturbing. Stern's studio, complete with paint brushes and palettes, has been left as it was when she died. The most important African items were collected in the Congo and Zanzibar. Of particular note is the Buli Stool, one of only 20 known carvings by a master carver from southeast Zaire. The kitchen houses a collection of Chinese ceramics including two fine Ming celadon dishes. ■ *Tue-Sat 1000-1700. R8. T6855686.*

Rhodes Memorial The best-known attraction in the area is the Rhodes Memorial, off Rhodes Drive, by the Rondesbosch turning. The imposing granite memorial to Cecil John Rhodes (Cape Prime Minister from 1890-96) was designed by Francis Masey and Sir Herbert Baker. Four bronze lions flank a wide flight of steps which lead up to a Greek Temple. The temple houses an immense bronze head of Rhodes, wrought by JM Swan. Above the head are the words "slave to the spirit and life work of Cecil John Rhodes who loved and served South Africa". At the base of the steps is an immense bronze mounted figure of Physical Energy given to South Africa by GF Watts, a well regarded sculptor of the time; the original stands in Hyde Park, London. Other than the memorial, the great attraction here is the magnificent view of the Cape Flats and the Southern Suburbs. Behind the memorial are a number of popular trails leading up the slopes of Devil's Peak. Also tucked away here is an excellent little tea house set in a garden of blue hydrangeas which serves good cheesecake, sandwiches and cream teas – it's very popular spot, especially for lunch at weekends. ■ *0930-1700 Tue-Sat, 1300-1700 Sun.*

South of Rondesbosch By this point the southern suburbs have reached right around Devil's Peak and the shadowy peaks now dominating the views represent an unfamiliar view of Table Mountain. **Newlands** backs right up to the slopes of the mountain and is probably best known for being the home to Western Province Rugby Union and the beautiful Newlands cricket test ground. Sports fans shouldn't miss the chance of seeing a game here. There are several good hotels and guesthouses in the area.

Also in Newlands is the **Rugby Museum**, on Boundary Road, housed in the Sports Medical Research Institute Building. The collection commemorates the history of the sport in the country and is also home to the Currie Cup, the premier domestic competition trophy. ■ *Mon-Fri 0830-1700. Small entrance fee. T6596700.*

Also on Boundary Road is **Josephine Mill**, the only surviving watermill in Cape Town, which has been restored as a working flour mill. Of particular note is the massive 1840 water-wheel. The building is in the style of a Cornish red-brick mill, built by a Swede, Jacob Letterstedt, and named in honour of his Crown Princess, Josephine. There is also an interesting reconstruction of a mid-20th-century blacksmith's, with authentic tools. The mill is tucked away between the Newlands Rugby Stadium and has a brewery and a peaceful tea garden. During the summer months, concerts, as part of the Nedbank Sunday Summer Concert Season, are held in the grounds on the banks of the tree-fringed Liesbeek River. ■ *Mon-Fri 0900-1600. R5. T6864939.*

Claremont offers little of interest. On the main road is the upmarket Cavendish Square Complex, another of South Africa's shopping malls. There are two good cinema complexes here – the Ster-Kinekor Commercial, on the second floor, shows big releases, while the Ster-Kinekor Nouveau specializes in alternative and foreign-language films.

Nearby are **Ardene Gardens**, a Victorian park which has escaped the developer. These were first planted in 1845 by Ralph Arderne, who was so charmed by the Cape while en route for Australia that he decided to settle here instead. He succeeded in creating a garden that would represent the flora of the world. When his son died the estate was split up but fortunately in 1927 the Cape Town Municipality bought 11 acres of the garden. Today the arboretum with specimens from all over the world is probably the best collection of trees in South Africa. There are Indian rubber trees, Norfolk pines, Himalayan cypress, Java plum trees and some fine Australian Kauri pine, to name but a few species. The gardens were declared a historical monument in 1962. There is an obelisk which marks the site from which the famous astronomer, Sir John Herschel, carried out his research from 1834-38. ■ *0800-sunset.*

A little further along the main road takes you to **Wynberg**. Apart from a few curio shops, the main attraction here is the district known as **Little Chelsea**. This is a group of well-preserved 19th-century homes which have infinitely more character than most new buildings in Cape Town. By this point the city centre seems miles away, and yet as the crow flies it is just on the other side of Table Mountain. South of Wynberg the countryside opens up. To the west lie the fertile and prosperous valleys of Constantia and Tokai; due south the road quickly brings False Bay (see page 131) into view and the coastal resort of Muizenberg. To the east lie the exposed high density suburbs on the Cape Flats – Crossroads, Guguletu, Khayelitsha, Langa and Mitchells Plain.

Five kilometres south of Rondesbosch is Kirstenbosch, South Africa's oldest, largest and most exquisite botanical garden. It is one of the finest in the world, and its setting alone is incomparable. The gardens stretch up the eastern slopes of Table Mountain, merging seamlessly with the fynbos of the steep slopes above. Cecil Rhodes bought Kirstenbosch farm in 1895 and promptly presented the site to the people of South Africa with the intention that it become a botanical garden. It was not until 1913 that Kirstenbosch was proclaimed a National Botanical Garden – the

Kirstenbosch Botanical Gardens

Cape Town

Kirstenbosch Botanical Gardens

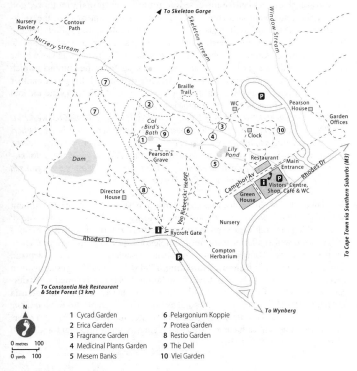

1 Cycad Garden	6 Pelargonium Koppie
2 Erica Garden	7 Protea Garden
3 Fragrance Garden	8 Restio Garden
4 Medicinal Plants Garden	9 The Dell
5 Mesem Banks	10 Vlei Garden

Cape Town

Anglo-Boer War had caused the delay. The first director of the gardens was Professor Harold Pearson, who sadly only lived for a further three years after the garden's creation. A granite Celtic Cross marks his grave in the Cycad garden. There is a fitting epitaph on the grave, "if ye seek his monument, look around you". The real development of the gardens was under Professor RH Compton, who cared for the gardens for 34 years. The herbarium is named after Compton – it houses over 250,000 specimens, including many rare plants.

A great deal of time and effort has been made to make the gardens accessible to the general public, making them a pleasure for both serious botanists and families enjoying a day out on the slopes of Table Mountain. As with all botanical gardens they are divided into smaller specialist gardens. Of particular note are the Fragrance garden, the Dell, the Medicinal Plants garden and Van Riebeeck's Hedge.

The **Fragrance garden** features herbs and flowers set out to make appreciating their scents effortless. On a warm day, when the volatile oils are released by the plants, there are some rather overpowering aromas; the plaques are also in Braille. The **Dell** follows a beautifully shaded path snaking beneath ferns and along a stream. Indigenous South African herbs can be inspected in the **Medicinal Plants garden**, each one identified and used by the Khoi and San peoples in the treatment of a variety of ailments. The plants' uses are identified on plaques, and it seems that most ailments are covered – kidney trouble, rheumatics, coughs, cancer, piles and bronchitis. For a sense of the past, it is worth visiting what is known as **Van Riebeeck's Hedge**. Back in 1660 a hedge of wild almond trees (*Brabejum stellatifolium*) was planted by Van Riebeeck as part of a physical boundary to try and prevent cattle rustling. Segments still remain today within the garden.

The **Skeleton Path** can be followed all the way to the summit of Table Mountain. It starts off as a stepped path, but becomes fairly steep near the top. It involves a climb up a rocky waterfall – take special care in the wet season.

Also available for a small fee are eco-adventure tours, and tours by motorized golf cart. Just beyond the entrance concourse is an excellent shop and a café on the courtyard terrace. The shop has the usual collection of curios, along with a good choice of books on South Africa and a selection of indigenous plants for your garden. The café serves over-priced sandwiches and cakes; better value and with far nicer views is the restaurant inside the gardens, just around the corner from the entrance, which serves good meals and is open until 2200. Another alternative is the picnic hamper service. For a reasonable price you can have a ready-made picnic with wine and join the Capetonians for a picnic lunch on the lush lawns.

■ *Sep-Mar 0800-1900, Apr-Aug 0800-1800. R15. Enquiries T7998783, weekends T7998620, www.nbi.ac.za By far the easiest way of getting here is by hire car. Otherwise there are trains to the nearest station at Mowbray, 10 mins from the city centre. From here there is an erratic bus service or a long walk. Alternatively, take a Rikki – they will pick up and drop off at any time other than rush hour. Most of the organized city tours also include the gardens on their itinerary.*

Constantia   South of the Botanical Gardens lies Cape Town's most elegant suburb, the verdant area of Constantia and its winelands. This historical district was the first site of wine-making in South Africa and today it is an attractive introduction to the country's wines as well as offering some fine examples of Cape Dutch architecture. There are five estates here, of which **Groot Costantia** (see below) is the best known and definitely worth a visit. **Buitenverwatchting**, T7945191, is a working estate with an excellent restaurant (see below). **Klein Constantia**, T7945188, is famed for its dessert wine, Vin de Constance, allegedly Napoleon's favourite wine. **Constantia Uitsig**, T7941810, has excellent wines and two superb restaurants, *Constantia Uitsig* (see page 109) and *La Colombe* (see page 114). **Steenberg**, T7132211, also offers superb wines as well as having luxurious lodgings, a good restaurant and a golf course (see pages 109 and 114).

This old wine estate, which gave its name to one of the smartest inland residential **Groot** districts around Cape Town, encapsulates everything that is the old Dutch Cape. **Constantia** The house, outbuildings, museum and vineyards mirror a life and time that were the formative years of Cape Town and South Africa.

The Cape Governor Simon van der Stel lived here between 1699 and 1712. He named the estate after Constantia, the daughter of the company official who had granted the land to him. Keen to build a home worthy of the Governor, he checked on every corner and curve with his builders. Before his death, van der Stel planted most of the vines, but it was not until 1778 that the estate became famous for its wines. During this period the estate was unable to meet the demands from Europe, especially France. The magnificent wine cellar behind the main house was designed by the renowned French architect, Louis Thibault.

The main house is now a museum full of period furniture. A booklet is available giving a brief description of all the objects. Behind the house is a shady garden and pool overlooked by the wine cellar. This has also been converted into a museum, with displays on brandy and wine making. There are two impressive giant oak vats each with a capacity of over 4,000 litres. ■ *An entrance fee is payable at the gate plus a further charge to visit the manor house and the old wine cellar. T7945128. When you arrive, follow the road up past the wine sales room to a couple of car parks set amongst the vines. The entrance office is clearly signposted, at the far end of the lower car park. Behind the ticket office is an interesting display of the restoration work which has been carried out on some of the outbuildings, including the one you are standing in.*

Rondevlei Nature Reserve

This 120-km reserve was originally established to protect the birdlife and the coastal *Despite being* fynbos vegetation. Today it is an important environmental education centre for *surrounded by* local schools. Only the northern shore of the lake is open to the public. There is a *suburban sprawl* path which follows the vlei's edge, along which there are two lookout towers *the sanctuary is one* equipped with telescopes. There are several hides along the water's edge, and cuts *of the best bird-* within the reeds allow views across the water. The best time to visit the reserve is Jan- *watching spots close* uary-March when many European migrants can be seen. Over 200 bird species have *to Cape Town* been recorded, this figure includes rare visitors, on a good day the visitor should be able to see more than 65 species. There are a few small shy mammals in the reserve, plus a small population of hippopotamus. ■ *Daily, 0800-1700. Small entrance fee. Enquiries T7062404. There is a picnic site near the entrance gate. Getting there: coming from Cape Town take the M5, Prince George Dr, turn left into Victoria Rd in Grassy Park, and then right into Fisherman's Walk, about 17 km from the town centre, 6 km from Muizenberg.* Inside the reserve is the **Leonard Gill Museum** with displays of mounted birds and local mammals.

This is 20 km of protected coastal marshland. There are a few bird hides, but viewing **Sandvlei** it is not as good as at Rondevlei. A large caravan and campsite has been built on the **Sanctuary** eastern shore. The City Council Parks and Forests Officer issues access permits. **Nature Reserve** ■ *To get there, it's a short walk signposted from Steenberg Railway Station on the Metro line to Simon's Town. By car follow the M4 from Cape to Muizenberg, take a left turning just before the road reaches False Bay.*

Tokai Forest

Tokai was set up as a forest nursery in 1883 to try and stem the destruction of forest reserves, and start a programme of conservation and reforestation. It is within the lands of an old wine estate, Tokai Homestead (1795), named after a wine region of Hungary. This is one of the few areas where the region's indigenous forest and some wildlife have been fully protected and preserved. The arboretum contains 40 tree species – there are two walking trails in the forest, and horse riding and picnicking are possible in the low-lying section of the forest. One of the designated walks is marked by white 'elephants', a trail which leads you up the mountain through the forest to Elephant's Eye cave. Allow at least two hours. You need good weather to fully appreciate the scenery. ■ *Open daily during daylight hours, entry to arboretum by donation; picnic area entrance R5 per person and R2 per car. Contact Chris Bota, T7127471. Bikeabout Cycle Tours, T5313274, organizes cycle tours in the forest. To get there take the M3 out of town towards the Southern Suburbs. Just before Muizenberg, turn right into Tokai Street and follow the signs for Tokai Manor House.*

Atlantic Seaboard

The Atlantic Seaboard stretches from Green Point to the Cape of Good Hope. It is the area's most spectacular coastline, at times clinging dramatically to the Twelve Apostles, the spine of mountains stretching south. This is where the most immediately attractive beaches are, although the water on this side of the peninsula is far colder that on the False Bay side – swimming is often not an option. Nevertheless, the area is hugely popular, both with day-trippers soaking up the sun and with domestic tourists renting beachside apartments for the summer. Although Green Point is close to the Waterfront, the rest of the coast is a drive away.

Ins & outs   **Getting there**   Public transport is limited to a regular bus which departs from in front of OK bazaars on Adderley St and runs along the Atlantic coast road s far as Hout Bay. Alternatively, take a Rikki taxi.

Green Point   These suburbs are the closest seaside residential areas to the city, but they lack much
& Sea Point   of the charm and character found in the rest of Cape Town. Both are a mixture of high-rise apartment blocks lining the rocky seafront, and more attractive houses that creep up the mountain. Green Point has become the focus of Cape Town's gay scene, and has a correspondingly lively nightlife. Sea Point has an excellent selection of accommodation, as well as bars, shops and restaurants. The beach is unsafe for swimming, although there are a couple of rock pools, including Graaf's Pool (men only) and Milton's Pool.

Clifton Beach   Cape Town's best-known beaches stretch along Clifton, and are renowned as the
Each has a distinct   playground of the young and wealthy – this is *the* place to see and be seen. Other
character – if you're   than being hotpots of high society, Clifton's four sheltered beaches are stunning,
bronzed and beautiful,   perfect arches of powder-soft white sand sloping gently into turquoise water. The
head to First beach.   beaches are divided by rocky outcrops and are imaginatively numbered: First,
More demure visitors   Second, Third and Fourth. The sunbathing and surfing are good on all the
may feel more   beaches, but the water is cold. Most of the relatively small-scale development has
comfortable on Fourth,   been behind the beaches against the cliff face (some impressive houses can be
it's popular with   glimpsed through the greenery). Be warned that there is limited parking and it's a
families   steep climb down footpaths to the beach.

Camps Bay   Following the coast south, you soon skirt around a hill and come out over Camps Bay, a long arch of sand backed by the Twelve Apostles. This is one of the most beautiful (and most photographed) beaches in the world, but the calm cobalt water belies its chilliness. The sand is also less sheltered than at Clifton, and sunbathing here on a windy day can be quite painful. But there are other distractions; the beachfront is lined with a number of excellent seafood restaurants, and having a sundowner followed by a superb meal is quite the perfect ending to a day in Cape Town.

The drive between Camps Bay and Hout Bay runs along the slopes of the Twelve Apostles and is quite beautiful. Apart from the turning to Llandudno, there is no easy access to the coast until you reach Hout Bay. **Llandudno** itself is a small, exclusive settlement with a fine beach and excellent surf.

Cape Town

Hout Bay may seem strangely familiar – little surprise considering how often it is featured on postcards and coffee table books. The view from Chapman's Peak Drive is frequently photographed, and deservedly so. Hout Bay is a perfect cove with a white sandy beach, clear blue waters and a busy fishing harbour. It is from here that the famous Chapman's Peak Drive begins, and as the sun sets in the summer months every pullover along the road gets occupied by groups watching the sun go down, drink in hand.

Unless you're planning on taking a boat trip from the harbour, the best place to leave your car is in the car park opposite *Chapman's Peak Hotel*. From here you can easily walk to all the shops or down to the beach. Before Cape Town had established itself as the foremost port in the district, Hout Bay was an important natural sheltered anchorage. Today, activity centres around two locations: at the western end of the bay is the fishing harbour; at the other end is a collection of shops and popular restaurants. By the harbour is a commercial complex known as **Mariners Wharf**, the first of its kind in South Africa and a very popular attraction. It is based upon Fisherman's Wharf in San Francisco, and a lot of thought has gone into the building. The restaurant serves a wide selection of fresh seafood and has a wine list to match. Another attraction is **Snoekies Fresh Fish Market**, close to the harbour gates. Even if you're not intending to buy anything it is well worth the visit to see the huge variety of fish that are caught off this coast. **Hout Bay Museum**, housed in a small former school principal's house at 4 Andrews Road, has displays on the natural and cultural history of the area, with local tourist information. ■ *Tue-Sat 1000-1230, 1400-1630. T7903270. Drumbeat Charters*, Harbour, T7904859, organize tours to see seals on **Duiker Island** (1 hour). Trips depart at 1130, 1330 and 1530 and cost R35. Bring warm clothing in case the wind picks up in the evening. Recommended as an opportunity to admire the Cape peninsula from the sea. No trips between May and August.

World of Birds, at Valley Road, is set in 4 km of open land in walk-through aviaries, with over 400 species of birds. A popular attraction, but perhaps a little strange for an overseas visitor when the birds you see strolling around the mountains or at Zandvlei are more exotic than anything they are likely to have ever seen at home in the wild. The fact remains you can see hundreds of birds in South Africa without having to look too hard. ■ *Daily 0900-1700. T7902730, www.worldofbirds.org.za*

It is worth hiring a car for a day just to drive along Chapman's Peak Drive, a breathtaking 15 km route carved into the cliffs 600 m above the sea. The views of the coast and ocean are outstanding and one of the Cape's highlights. The best time to drive along here is close to sunset in the summer, but the views of Hout Bay are recommended at any time. The original road was built between 1915 and 1922. **NB** Early in 2000, Chapman's Peak Drive was closed after a series of major rock falls. Much of the road remains closed, although it should be open by the end of 2002. It is still possible to drive up to the highest viewpoints from the Hout Bay side. Check with Cape Town tourism for the latest news.

The greatest attraction here is the 8 km long deserted beach with a couple of tidal lagoons behind it which offer excellent bird watching. The *Chapman's Peak Trading Centre* on Beach Road is a good shopping spot, including a Kakapo farm stall and bakery, Milkwood Craft Co-op, curios and clothes. This is also a popular setting for **horse riding** along the shore. Contact *Nordhoek Beach Horse Rides*, T082-7741191 (mob), www.horseriding.co.za, or *Sleepy Hollow Horse Riding*, T7892341, T083-2610104 (mob).

Driving along the Atlantic side of the peninsula, you could miss Kommetjie altogether if you were to follow the signs for Ocean View. Kommetjie means 'little basin', a reference to the natural inlet in the rocks which has been developed into a tidal pool. The settlement is small with a pub, restaurant, caravan park and little else. It is, however, a major surfing spot and Long Beach to the north is always busy with surfers, even in winter. There is also an interesting walk along Long Beach to the wreck of

Hout Bay
Phone code: 021
(NB Always use
3-figure prefix)
Colour map 4, grid C1

Cape Town

Chapman's Peak Drive

Noordhoek

Kommetjie
Phone code: 021
(NB Always use
3-figure prefix)
Colour map 4, grid C2

the *Kakapo*, offering a rare opportunity to examine a wreck at close quarters without having to don full scuba equipment. The *Kakapo* is a steamship which was beached here in May 1900 on her maiden voyage when the captain apparently mistook Chapman's Peak for Cape Point during a storm. The boiler and shell are still intact about 100 m above the high tide mark.

Scarborough This is a scattering of weekend and holiday homes on the hillside overlooking the Atlantic. There is a broad and long beach but swimming is not a good idea as the water is cold and there are strong currents. Just outside of Scarborough, close to the entrance to Cape of Good Hope Nature Reserve, is the **Cape Point Ostrich Farm**. The farm is open daily, 0930-1730 and worth a visit if your holiday does not include a visit to similar ostrich farms in the Little Karoo.

Essentials

Sleeping

■ on maps
Price codes:
see inside front cover

If visting during Dec and Jan, book 5-6 months in advance. Even the cheapest hostel gets booked up

NB During peak season, Cape Town simply does not have enough rooms. While it is always wise to book accommodation well in advance, be sure to call several months ahead if you're visiting during the summer months. Visitors who have a hire car or their own overland four-wheel drive vehicle should note that the majority of backpacker hostels and cheaper guesthouses do not have secure off-street parking. While car theft is not a major problem in Cape Town, you should nevertheless enquire about parking conditions before you confirm a room. Secure parking has been mentioned in the text wherever we had the information.

City centre
See map, page 80

AL *Cape Sun Intercontinental*, Strand St, T4885100, F4238875. 368 rooms in an ugly, modern tower dominating the centre of town. All the rooms benefit from panoramic views of the city, some non-smoking rooms, plenty of marble and chrome in the public areas, a choice of 3 excellent restaurants – *Riempies* serves delicious Cape Malay food – curio shop, hairdresser, gym, sauna, swimming pool, but suffers from not having any gardens. There are plenty of other hotels in Cape Town with much more character and relaxing surrounds; nevertheless the service and facilities are excellent.

A *The Cullinan*, 1 Cullinan St, T4186920, F4183559, www.thecullinan.co.za Smart upmarket hotel a short walk from the city centre and the Waterfront. Very comfortable rooms, large hotel popular with businessmen, restaurant, bar and nightclub. **A** *Holiday Inn Greenmarket Square*, 10 Greenmarket Sq, T4232040, F4233664, www.basshotels.com Solid building built in 1929 as the headquarters for Shell Oil (look out for the shell motifs on the outside), 168 blandly decorated rooms, some non-smoking rooms, large restaurant, terrace café overlooking the lively daily market, *McGinty's* themed pub serving pub food, perfect central location, airport transfer service, secure parking, but rather characterless and indifferent service. **A-B** *De Waterkant Lodge & Cottages*, 20 Loader St, T/F4191097, waterknt@iafrica.com One of the more unusual places to stay at in the Cape. This complex is on the edge of Bo-Kaap suburb. Two streets, Loader and Waterkant, have been cordoned off and 16 cottages luxuriously restored as self-catering units. Each house is unique, all have 2 double rooms, modern kitchens, TV, a/c, telephone, are serviced daily and are close to the shops and restaurants. The Lodge is over 150 years old and has been restored and furnished in style. All guests also have access to a swimming pool, jacuzzi and sauna. Good value. Airport transfer easily organized.

B *Cape Gardens Lodge*, 88 Queen Victoria St, T4231260, F4232088, lodge@dockside.co.za 57 rooms, those at front have views across Company's Garden and Table Mountain, breakfast lounge but no restaurant. **B** *Tulip Inn*, corner of Bree and Strand St, T4235116, F4242720, tulipinn@netactive.co.za 77 rooms, en suite bathrooms, TV, spacious restaurant, Tavern Bar, a busy functional hotel used a lot for conferences, central but noisy location. **B** *Raya Hotel*, Pier Place, Heerengracht, T6921260, F6917079. 169 rooms, some triples, non-smoking room, nothing special for the price, swimming pool, guests have free membership to a neighbouring Health and Racquet Club, poor reports on the restaurant. **B** *Townhouse Hotel*, 60

Corporation St, T4657050, F4653891. 104 rooms, some non-smoking, restaurant, bar, friendly service, delicious snacks served in the lounge, swimming pool, sauna, gym, not very well sound-insulated, could be disturbed by traffic during the night, secure parking. **B** *Tudor Hotel*, Green Market Sq, T4241335, F4231198, www.tudorhotel@iafrica.co.za 30 rooms, a small, welcoming hotel which hasn't lost its character through redevelopment, all the rooms have a worn but homely feel. The restaurant, bar and café have a continental atmosphere and serve good food. Watch Cape Town go by through the large windows. Taxi rank next door in front of the Methodist church, ideal location for exploring the city centre, covered parking, good value, booking advised. Recommended. **B** *Tulbagh Hotel*, 9 Tulbagh Sq, T4215140, F4214648. 55 rooms, restaurant, bar, secure parking.

C-D *Metropole*, 38 Long St, T4236363, F4265312. 45 double rooms, a/c, MNet TV, ensuite shower and toilet. Old-fashioned town hotel with appealing air of faded grandeur. The better rooms are large with marble bathrooms and brass fittings, lovely old teak lift, popular café overlooking Long St, private bar, conveniently situated, a bit noisy, good value. Recommended.

Backpacker hostels in the centre This is one of the major growth industries in Cape Town, and the choice is impressive compared to any other South African town. All are of a similar price and most are a good source of information on what is going on in Cape Town, as well as the rest of southern Africa. Many people travelling overland from Nairobi or Harare end their journey here, so the hostels are often good places to meet people and swap travelling information. A lot of hostels also offer non-dormitory rooms at very reasonable rates – usually less than R100 per person. Rates for dorms may be R60 per person during the peak season, although if you are looking for a long-term room or bed you should be able to negotiate a discount. During peak periods, be sure to call in advance to check availability, especially around Christmas and the New Year. Thanks to the stiff competition, Cape Town's hostels tend to be of a higher quality and offer better service than elsewhere in South Africa, and places with a bad reputation get found out quickly.

If you are returning to Cape Town you will be interested to know that security on Long St has improved dramatically in recent years, and it is now much safer to wander along here after dark. Do, however, always keep your wits about you, and take special care if you're venturing off Long St

F *Overseas Visitors Club*, 230 Long St, T4234477, F4234870, www.ovc.co.za You'll get a warm welcome from Wilmot the manager in this unlikely looking place above the *Maharaja* Indian restaurant. It's a great little hostel with 18 beds, pleasant single-sex dorms, great balcony with braai overlooking Long St and views of Table Mountain, bar, excellent travel centre upstairs specializing in youth travel. One of the friendliest on Long St. **F** *Bob's Backpack & Bistro*, 187 Long St, T4248223, reservations@backpackerlodge.co.za Above a fully licensed bar which serves decent meals. 5 dorms (with 8 beds) and 5 doubles spread across a couple of floors of an apartment building, each with own bathroom and kitchen, run down and grubby with stained carpets, musty bar, not much of an atmosphere, a last resort on Long St. **F** *Cat & Moose Youth Hostel*, 305 Long St, T423 7638, F4239933, catandmoose@hotmail.com Bright set-up, central location in an atmospheric old town house. Dorms and doubles are nicely furnished but a bit dark, those at front can be noisy, some have balconies overlooking Long St, lovely courtyard with sun deck and braai, good bar, small travel centre, TV/video lounge. Laid-back, friendly atmosphere. **F** *City Slickers*, 25 Rose St, corner Hout St, T4222357, F4222355, cityslickers@hotmail.com A professionally run backpacker hostel, but lacks the casual feel of smaller hostels. Large purpose built ochre breezeblock building, no dorms, all private rooms with bunks or doubles, spacious organized kitchen, good hot showers, TV lounge-cum-reception, rooftop bar with views of Table Mountain, central location, pool table, laundry, secure. Please note that we've had reports of problems of safety on the streets in the neighbourhood from late afternoon onwards. **F** *Elephant on Castle Backpackers*, 57 Castle St, T/F4247524, castle@iafrica.com Small, friendly place around the corner from the tourist office, musty dorms and doubles, only 20 beds, could do with a clean, TV lounge, free cooked dinner on Sundays, sunny balcony with braai, good place to meet people, not good for early nights. **F** *Long St Backpackers*, 209 Long St, T4230615, F4231842, longstbp@mweb.co.za Sociable hostel spread around leafy courtyard, small clean dorms and doubles, some with own bathrooms and balconies overlooking Long St, fully equipped kitchen, TV/video lounge, pool room, internet access, travel centre, free pickup. Good security with 24-hr police camera opposite. Lively atmosphere, occasional parties organized and weekly communal braais, can be noisy.

Oranjezicht, Gardens & Tamboerskloof
See map, page 103

AL *Mount Nelson*, 76 Orange St, Gardens, T4231000, F4247472. 131 rooms, 28 suites, 8 garden cottage suites, this is *the* luxury hotel in Cape Town, set in 7 km of its own landscaped parkland, heated swimming pool, tennis courts, squash court, beauty centre, excellent restaurant serving Cape specialities – don't miss the cream teas on the veranda.

A *Kensington Place*, 38 Kensington Gardens, Higgovale, T4244744, F4241810, www.kensingtonplace.co.za Stylish boutique hotel in a quiet, leafy area. Small and well run with excellent service. Beautiful rooms, individually styled with views over the city, bar, small pool and deck, excellent restaurant. Recommended. **A** *No 1 Chesterfield*, 1 Chesterfield Rd, Oranjezicht, T4617383, F4614688. 8 rooms, each decorated in a different theme: Cape Dutch, French, Zulu and West African. Swimming pool, quiet setting, evening meals on request, secure off-street parking. **A-B** *Hilltop House*, 30 Forest Rd, Oranjezicht, T4613093, F4614069. Elegant, upmarket guesthouse with 7 rooms, each with en suite bathroom and TV, non-smoking room, swimming pool, laundry service. **A** *Villa Belmonte*, 33 Belmont Av, Oranjezicht, T4621576, F4621579. 8 rooms, TV, an award-winning luxury Italian-style villa. Relax on a large shady veranda with views of Table Mountain, breakfast will keep you going all day, lunch and dinner by arrangement, swimming pool, very smart and elegant, German and French spoken.

B *Cape Swiss*, Nicol St, Gardens, T4238190, F4261795. 44 rooms, smart middle market hotel close to Kloof St, restaurant, bar, some rooms with views of Table Mountain, secure parking. **B** *Holiday Inn Garden Court De Waal*, Mill St, T4651311, F4616648. Large, modern hotel with gardens at foot of Table Mountain. 130 rooms, some non-smoking, restaurant, bar, swimming pool, airport transfer service. **B** *Ikhaya Guest Lodge*, Dunkley Sq, Gardens, T4618880, F4618889, www.ikhayalodge.co.za A smart, tasteful development just a short distance from the city centre. 11 double rooms, 5 apartments for self-catering guests, conference centre. Full of character thanks to the natural woods, African fabrics and recycled products (the bedside lamps are made from old ginger beer bottles) used to decorate the rooms. Secure parking. Recommended. **B-C** *Longwood Guest House*, 5 Montrose Av, T4615988, F4615953. Executive-style, good location, 6 double rooms, swimming pool. **B** *Underberg Guest House*, 6 Tamboerskloof Rd, T4262262, F4244059, underbrg@netactive.co.za Smart old corner house with decorative iron balconies, 9 spacious rooms with en suite bathrooms, TV and mini bar, full English breakfast, laundry service, secure parking, convenient for city centre, friendly and helpful owners. Highly recommended.

C *Ambleside Guest House*, 11 Forest Rd, Oranjezicht, T4652503, F4653814, guest T4655281. 8 rooms, breakfast served in your room, fully equipped kitchen available for guests' use. An excellent, peaceful guesthouse which enjoys good views of Table Mountain. Good value. Recommended. Ask for John or Leonora. **C** *Bergzicht*, 5 Devonport Rd, Tamboerskloof, T4238513, F4245244. 6 rooms, some non-smoking, hearty breakfasts, tidy gardens with swimming pool, excellent views, helpful owners. **C-D** *The Cape Colonial*, 13 Union St, Gardens, T4237382, F4237383. Small B&B a short walk from a shopping centre, en suite bathroom, TV, fans, French and German spoken. **C** *Glynnville Lodge*, 15 Glynnville Terrace Gardens, T4611784, F4611668. A fine restored Victorian house with a mix of double rooms, some with en suite bathroom, TV, central lounge and bar area. **C** *Inn with a View*, 127a Kloofnek Rd, Gardens, T4245220, F4245293. Good location just before the Lower Cableway Station turn off. Comfortable double rooms with en suite bathrooms, excellent food and service, good views of Table Mountain. Highly recommended. **C** *Leeuwenvoet House*, 93 New Church St, Tamboerskloof, T4241133, F4240495, stay@leeuwenvoet.co.za 10 rooms, comfortable homely décor, some a/c, TV, telephone, excellent breakfasts, swimming pool, off-street secure parking, close to shops and restaurants but retains a peaceful atmosphere. Recommended. **C-D** *Parker Cottage*, 3 Carstens St, Tamboerskloof, T4246445, www.parkercottage.co.za Stylish guesthouse in a restored Victorian cottage, 8 en suite bedrooms, tasteful décor, flamboyant colours with a Victorian touch, good breakfasts, friendly service, gay-friendly. **C** *Table* Mountain Lodge, 10A Tamboerskloof Rd, Tamboerskloof, T4230042, F4234983, tml@iafrica.com This house was originally a lodge on a large private estate at the foot of Table Mountain. It now has 6 spacious rooms with en suite bathroom, TV, telephone, mature gardens and a pub for residents. Recommended.

D *Flower Street Villa*, 3 Flower St, Oranjezicht, T/F4657517. Medium-sized whitewashed house set in quiet suburb. 20 spacious rooms, fully equipped kitchens, dining rooms and lounge, daily maid service, short walk to shops, secure parking, good value, advance booking recommended, served by the Airport Shuttle Bus.

Backpacker hostels F *Ashanti Lodge*, 11 Hof St, Gardens, T4238721, F4238790, www.ashanti.co.za This has become one of the city's best-known hostels, not least for its party atmosphere. Medium size dorms and small doubles in huge old house with polished

Oranjezicht, Gardens & Tamboerskloof

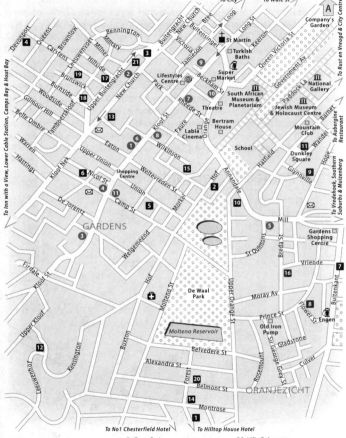

N	
0 metres 200	
0 yards 200	

■ Sleeping
1 Ambleside Guest House
2 Ashanti Lodge
3 Backpack & Africa Travel Centre
4 Bergzicht
5 Cape Colonial
6 Cape Swiss
7 Cloudbreak Backpackers
8 Flower Street Villa
9 Glynnville Lodge
10 Holiday Inn Garden Court De Waal
11 Ikhaya Guest Lodge
12 Kensington Place
13 Leeuwenvoet House
14 Longwood
15 Mount Nelson
16 Oak Lodge
17 Parker Cottage
18 Table Mountain Lodge
19 Underberg Guest House
20 Villa Belmonte
21 Zebra Crossing

● Eating
1 Arnold's
2 Blue Danube
3 Café Paradiso
4 Keg & Squirrel Pub & Saigon
5 Kotobuki
6 Maeströs (Maeströs)
7 Naked on Kloof
8 Ocean Basket
9 Rozenhof
10 Sukhothai
11 Yindee's

Related map ⇨
A City centre,
page 80

wooden floors, large windows and communal balconies. Some rooms surround a courtyard and small pool. Lively bar serving good snacks, with pool table and MNet TV. Free airport and station pickup, plus excellent booking centre, internet access and video room. Not to every-one's liking as it is firmly on the busy overland truck route and can be very noisy (and the bathrooms get rather messy), although it's perfect if you're looking for people to travel or party with. One of our top-5 hostels. **F** *The Backpack*, 74 New Church St, T4234530, F4230065, www.backpackers.co.za One of the original Cape Town hostels, this has now developed into one of the biggest and best-run. Toni and Lee have put money back into the place and there are now 6 dorms and 10 double rooms, non-smoking room, restaurant, lively bar, swimming pool and terrace, games room, laundry service, reliable information, one of the most expensive hostels, often full. Their experience shows, but we have had reports of an "attitude problem". **F** *Cloudbreak Backpackers*, 219 Upper Buitenkant St, T4616892, F4611458, www.cloudbreakbackpackers.co.za Friendly and lively set-up with dorms and double rooms, internet facilities, secure parking. 15 min stroll to the centre. We've had excel-lent reports of this place. One of our recommended top-10 hostels. **F** *Oak Lodge*, 21 Breda St, T4656182, F4656308, lodge@intekom.co.za Beautiful Victorian house which started out as a commune and was developed into a hostel several years ago. The hippie vibe continues throughout. Large, attractive dorms, comfortable doubles (some in bungalow next door), great showers, relaxed bar, chill-out room, two video rooms and a homely kitchen. Décor is an interesting mix of African masks, ethnic fabrics and medieval wall murals. Recommended. **F** *Zebra Crossing Backpackers*, 82 New Church St, T/F4221265, guest phone T4239841,

Green Point & Waterfront

zebracross@intekom.co.za Started life as a relatively small place, now expanded into house next door with more spacious rooms. Several spotless dorms plus double rooms, good views of Table Mountain, internet access and travel centre, café and bar serving great breakfasts, snacks and meals, helpful management, but can be a bit too quiet.

AL *Cape Grace*, Waterfront, T4107100, F4197622, www.capegrace.com This has become one of the most luxuriant hotels in Cape Town. Large development, just a short walk from the main Waterfront shops and restaurants. Very comfortable rooms with all the mod cons, traditional décor, balconies have views of the Waterfront, service and food is excellent, 2 bars and the Quay West restaurant, swimming pool and deck with bar opens out from the restaurant. **AL** *Table Bay Hotel*, Quay 6, Waterfront, T4065000, F4180495. The latest luxury offering from the Sun International Group, 329 rooms all the facilities one would expect for the price, good location with views.

A-B *Hotel Graeme*, 107 Main Rd, Green Point, T4349282, F4340605, hotel@mweb.co.za 20 rooms, all en suite, and 4 self-catering suites. Secure off-street parking, laundry, business centre. A very comfortable, good value set-up without too many extras. **A** *Victoria & Alfred*, Pierhead, Waterfront, T4196677, F4198955. 68 luxuriant and spacious a/c rooms with king size beds, modern furnishings, bath and separate shower, mini bar. The rooms overlook either Table Mountain or the Piazza; the mountain side is quieter in the evenings. Breakfast is extra but the *Waterfront Café* is a perfect setting for morning treats. A smart development with high standards in the heart of the Waterfront development.

**Waterfront &
Green Point**
*See maps, pages 90
and opposite*

Cape Town

B *Cape Victoria*, 13 Torbay Rd, Green Point, T/F4397721. A mix of exclusive hotel service and the privacy of a guesthouse, 10 tastefully furnished rooms with antiques, en suite bathrooms, TV, mini bar and views of the sea or Table Mountain, swimming pool, booking essential. Recommended. **B-C** *City Lodge*, corner of Alfred and Dock Rd, Waterfront, T4199450, F4190460. 164 rooms, majority are single, some non-smoking, bar, no restaurant, swimming pool, simple, good value. **B-D** *Breakwater Lodge*, Portswood Rd, Waterfront, T4061911, F4061070, www.breakwaterlodge.co.za An early part of the Waterfront development, this hotel stands on the site of the notorious Breakwater Prison (1859). The 330 rooms are fairly small but comfortable. *Stonebreakers* restaurant, swimming pool, ideal if you want to be close to the Waterfront. Next door is the Graduate School of Business – many of the MBA students seem to live in the lodge during term time.

C *Brenwin & Chamel Guest House*, 1 Thornhill Rd, Green Point, T4340220, F4393465, brenwin@netactive.co.za 14 large rooms with en suite bathrooms, shady patio overlooking tidy tropical garden with swimming pool, within easy walking distance of the Waterfront. Very helpful owner who enjoys helping and advising guests with their travel plans. **C** *Dale Court*, Exhibition Terrace Rd, Green Point, T4398774, F4345597, www.dalecourt.co.za A very smart guesthouse with spacious rooms, outside bathroom, TV, telephone, breakfast

13 Waterfront Suites   3 The Restaurant

● **Eating**
1 Buena Vista Social Café
  & News Café
2 Chariots

served in a central room with glass roof, clean but lacking in character, good value, ideal for a family, book in advance. **C** *Forty Winks Guest House*, 2 Ravenscraig Rd, Green Point, T4347936, F4347988. A luxury guesthouse with 3 double rooms, en suite bathroom, mini bar, garden, swimming pool, lounge and bar. Comfortable house but the colour scheme may put you off. Friendly, good value. **C** *Waterfront Suites*, 153 Main Rd, Green Point, T4395020, F4395031. A selection of 27 'executive' apartments which can sleep up to 6 people, fully equipped kitchens (continental breakfasts can be delivered to your room), laundry service, TV, telephone, plunge pool, 24-hr reception, secure parking. A small, modern block on a busy road midway between the town centre and Sea Point, ideal for business people or someone working for a few months in Cape Town.

D *Altona Lodge*, 19 Croxteth Rd, Green Point,T4342572, F4348075. Comfortable B&B in a central location. Guests have use of a TV lounge and there is space to park your car. Call in advance to confirm availability. You may be asked for a deposit. **D** *Claridges B&B Hotel*, 47 Main Rd, Green Point, T4341171, F4346650. Good value en suite rooms, nothing fancy, easy access to Waterfront and Sea Point.

Backpacker hostels F *Brown Sugar*, 1 Main Rd, Green Point, T4330413, F0860102291, www.brownsugar.get.to Busy but laid-back hostel near the Waterfront, on noisy Main Rd, dorms, doubles and some camping space, shared bathrooms, popular bar with party atmosphere, Ganeshi restaurant with chill-out Goa lounge, good place to meet people. **F** *St John's Waterfront Lodge*, 6 Braemar Rd, Green Point, T4391404, F4391424, www.stjohns.co.za Closest hostel to the Waterfront. Dorms and doubles spread across two houses, sundeck, two pools, bar, braai, friendly and helpful staff, travel centre.

Sea Point
See map, page 107
This area has a holiday resort feel about it and has far less character than other areas in town. It does have an excellent range of accommodation though, and there is some good nightlife towards Green Point.

AL *Le Vendôme*, 20 London Rd, T4301200, F4301500, www.le-vendome.co.za A large, well-designed luxury hotel. All rooms a/c, satellite TV, internet facilities, private fax, room safe, 2 restaurants, swimming pool, secure parking. **AL** *Peninsula*, 313 Beach Rd, T4398888, F4398886, www.peninsula.co.za 'Timeshare Hotel' with 110 suites including kitchen facilities. Friendly service, bar, restaurant and swimming pool. Perfect location in Sea Point right on one of the few sandy stretches of seafront, a short walk from all the shops and restaurants in Sea Point. The rooms in the newer part are better.

A-B *The Clarendon*, 67 Kloof Rd, T4393224, F4346855, www.clarendon.co.za Pleasant guesthouse with 7 spacious rooms, some with mountain views, all with en suite bathroom, TV and safe. Peaceful location and only a short walk to the shops in Sea Point, there is secure parking. **A** *Protea Hotel Sea Point*, Arthur's Rd, T4305000, F4305320, www.proteahotels.com One of the Protea chain hotels, 123 a/c rooms with balconies overlooking the sea. The garden terrace serves light meals around a plunge pool, excellent buffets laid on in the restaurant, English-style pub plus a cocktail bar, easy walk to sandy beach, short drive to city centre.

B-C *Blackheath Lodge*, 6 Blackheath Rd, T4392541, F4399776, www.blackheathlodge. co.za 5 smart double rooms in a converted Victorian mansion. Off-street parking, TV, mini bar, palm fringed patio, good size swimming pool, but no children under 14. Recommended for couples. **B** *Cape Manor*, 1 Marais Rd, T4349559, F4396896. 101 a/c rooms, restaurant, bar, a friendly seafront hotel, 3-stars. **B-C** *Cape Town Ritz Hotel*, Main Rd, T4396010, F4391848. 222 functional a/c rooms. The main feature of the hotel is the bar and restaurant on the 21st floor which, not surprisingly, has unique views of Cape Town and Table Bay. Swimming pool, jacuzzi. **B** *The Glen Guest House*, 3 Glen Rd, T4390072. Italian-style villa with views of Signal Hill and tropical garden with palm trees and shaded seating areas. 11 rooms, each decorated with fine pieces of furniture and art, TV, bar, fridge, telephone, swimming pool, restaurant. **B-C** *'t Huijs Haerlem*, 25 Main Drive, T4346434, F4392506. 5 rooms with en suite facilities, friendly relaxed atmosphere, comfortable and homely furnishings, magnificent views towards the Atlantic, solar heated salt water swimming pool, German and Dutch spoken, good value.

Recommended. **B** *Palm Garden Hotel*, 75 Regent Rd, T4391171, F4341662, palmgard@iafrica.com A modern block close to the trendy beaches at Clifton, this is part of the Protea chain and is quieter than hotels closer to the centre of town. 83 recently refurbished a/c rooms, 2 restaurants, 2 bars, swimming pool, conference facilities. **B-C** *Winchester Mansions*, 221 Beach Rd, T4342351, F4340215, www.winchester.co.za A well-run family hotel that has managed to retain plenty of old charm despite its size. 35 stylish double rooms, each with TV, en suite bathroom, and 18 suites. All rooms overlook a large, tranquil courtyard were meals

Cape Town

Sea Point

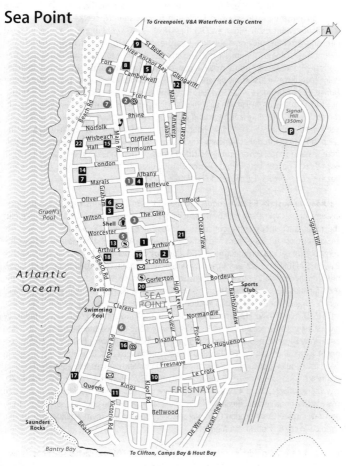

Related map
A *Green Point &*
Waterfront, page 104

are served beneath the palms. Harvey's, a new sea-facing restaurant, offers innovative meals and Sunday jazz brunches.

C *Ascot Manor*, 369 Main Rd, T4393885, F4392865. A large guesthouse (35 rooms) which lacks the friendly atmosphere of smaller establishments. Restaurant, close to shops, efficient service. **C** *Olaf's Guest House*, 24 Wisbeach Rd, T4398943, F4395057. 6 rooms with en suite shower, telephone and TV in each room, well-run B&B in a very convenient location, swimming pool, German spoken. **C** *Villa Rosa*, 277 High Level Rd, T4342768, F4343526, www.villa-rosa.com 2 'flatlets', 6 rooms with en suite bathrooms, TV, mini safe. A red brick Victorian house in a quiet side road, family-run, friendly attentive service.

D *Ashby Manor*, 242 High Level Rd, T4341879, F4393572. 9 rooms in a medium-sized rambling Victorian house on a quiet road. Secure and clean rooms with fridge, shared bathrooms, large communal lounge and dining area, ideal kitchen for those wishing to self-cater, card telephones, limited off-road parking, an easy walk from the shops and restaurants in Sea Point, friendly service, sensibly priced, popular with visitors from Europe. **D** *Bellevue Manor House*, 5 Bellevue Rd, T4340375, F4391511, www.bellevue.co.za 9 rooms in beautiful Victorian town house with stylish iron balconies and fine palm trees, all rooms have en suite bathrooms, TV, non-smoking, laundry, friendly service. **D** *Kinneret Guest House*, 11 Arthur's Rd, Sea Point, T4399237, F4348998. 10 light and airy rooms, private bathroom, fridge, TV and telephones. A comfortable, lemon yellow 2-storey house with 1st floor balcony, short walk from sea and shops. **D** *Norman Road Guest House*, 5 Norman Rd, Green Point, T4347055, F4347066. A peaceful guesthouse within walking distance of the Waterfront. All the rooms have en suite shower, TV, fridge and kettle.

Backpacker hostels **F** *Beach Lodge*, 7a Milton Rd, T4341605. Dorms, kitchen, laundry, lockers, email, pool table and bar. Convenient location off the main street ,close to the beach plus the restaurants, shops and nightlife of Sea Point. **F** *Bunkers*, 15 Graham Rd, Sea Point, T4340549. Close to all the shops and restaurants, call for pick up, garden, close to seafront, not very good on backpacking information. **E-F** *Carnaby Backpacker*, 219 Main Rd, Three Anchor Bay, T4397410, F4391222, www.carnabybackpacker.co.za Building used to be a hotel, now offers great value double rooms with ensuite facilities, as well as spacious dorms, and all the usual facilities expected in a well managed backpacker hostel. Bar, swimming pool, good travel service. One of our top-10 hostels in Cape Town. **F** *Globe Trotter*, 17 Queens Rd, Sea Point, T4341539, guest T4397113. Small town house on the fringe of Sea Point with 3 dorms, TV lounge, dining area, secure lockers. It's an easy walk along the coast to the beaches of Clifton and Bantry Bay, easy public transport to city centre, cheapest in town. **F** *St John's Lodge*, corner St John's and Main Rd, T4399028, stjohnslodge@mweb.co.za One of the first hostels in Cape Town, quiet spot compared to many others, dorms and doubles, fully equipped kitchens, restaurant and sea views. **F** *Sunflower Stop*, 179 Main Rd, T4346535, F4346501, www.sunflowerstop.co.za Dorms with a bit more room than most, doubles, excellent clean place with a huge kitchen, meals available for the lazy. Swimming pool, bar, satellite TV, tours and travel advice. Great location. Currently one of the best in Cape Town, a definite top-10. Free airport and city pick up. Recommended.

Southern suburbs

This suburbs extend east of the city, along the Eastern Blvd and around Devil's Peak towards Constantia, in the following order: Woodstock, Observatory, Mowbray, Rosebank, Rondebosch, Newlands, Claremont and Wynberg

All suburbs are a short drive or train journey from the city centre. Each district has its own character and plenty of shops and restaurants close by.

A *Andros*, Newlands Av, Upper Claremont, T7979777, F7970300. Grand town house with a peaceful, homely ambience. 8 rooms with TV, under-floor heating, swimming pool. Lunch and dinner served on request. **A** *The Vineyard Hotel*, Protea Rd, Newlands, T6833044, F6833365. 155 a/c rooms in an 18th-century house; the décor is early Cape Dutch with plenty of yellowwood furniture. The oldest part was originally built as a country house for Lady Anne Barnard in 1799. Coffee shop and pâtisserie, elegant restaurant, swimming pool and old gardens. One of the best value upmarket hotels in Cape Town. Recommended.

B *Harfield Cottage* , 26 1st Avenue, Claremont, T6837376, F6716715, harfield@grm.co.za A comfortable, smart B&B where attention to detail makes all the difference. Spacious, en suite rooms with TV, mini bar and views of Table Mountain. Lounge/bar, sundeck and swimming pool, bicycle hire, secure off-street parking. Relaxing ambience during the winter months when log fires help to keep you warm. Strongly recommended. Ask for Jenni or Graham.

C *Baker House*, 18 Goldbourne Rd, Kenilworth, T7624912, F7973769. A solid Edwardian town house with 5 luxury suites and excellent service. Good value. Recommended. **C** *City Lodge Pinelands*, Mowbray Golf Park, off Raapenberg Rd, Mowbray, T6857944, F6857997. 134 a/c rooms, some non-smoking, restaurant, swimming pool. **C** *Devonshire House*, 6 Lovers Walk, Rondebosch, T/F6861519. Homely restored house with 5 double rooms, all with en suite bathroom, TV, friendly service. The old wooden floors greatly add to the atmosphere. Recommended. **C** *Koornhoop Manor House*, 24 London Rd, Observatory, T4480595, F4470956. Victorian house in a large, peaceful garden, with 9 rooms, all en suite, secure parking, good value. **C** *Little Scotia*, 5 Rostenberg Av, Rondebosch, T6894852, scotia@new.co.za Friendly guesthouse with 9 rooms, some non-smoking, B&B, well-tended garden and swimming pool.

Backpacker hostels F *The Green Elephant*, 57 Milton Rd, Observatory, T0800-222722/ 4486539, guest telephone T4475842, greenelephant@iafrica.com A full-on backpacker joint, not to everyone's taste but helpful and knowledgeable staff, plenty going on in the area away from the city centre, old house hidden behind high walls in compact suburb, dorms plus a couple of double rooms with four-poster beds, happy to organize trips to the regional sights, free collection, have a second house with 5 double rooms which is very popular. **F** *SA's The Alternative Place*, 64 St Michaels Rd, Claremont, T/F6742396, alternative_place@mweb.co.za Clean dorms sleeping 4, 2 double rooms, kitchen, garden with pool, bar and braai. A small homely setup run by Susan and Alun who have excellent southern and east African travel experience. A bit far from the town centre, but worth checking out. Free airport pickup.

Constantia is best-known for its celebrated wine estate, founded in the 18th century by the **Constantia** governor of the Cape, Simon van der Stel. In its heyday the estate produced some of the finest wines in South Africa, their demand spreading as far as Europe. This fine Cape Dutch homestead and vineyard is now surrounded by one of Cape Town's most exclusive suburbs. Close by in forested Constantia Valley are elegant hotels and peaceful guesthouses, all a short drive from the busy city centre or Atlantic beaches.

AL *The Cellars-Hohenhort*, 93 Brommersulei Rd, 15 mins from Cape Town city centre, T7942137, F7942149. Luxury hotel in 2 converted manor houses and a wine estate, with 15 spacious suites and 38 individually decorated rooms. Thoughtfully renovated with plenty of mock antiques, 2 excellent restaurants, one has a good reputation for French and English meals, the other for Cape Malay dishes. Conference facilities, 2 swimming pools, tennis court, single golf hole, set in 9 acres of mature gardens which overlook False Bay, not to everyone's taste. **AL-A** *Constantia Uitsig*, Spaanschemat, River Rd, Constantia, T7946500, F7947605. This is the perfect hotel to start or finish a holiday in the Cape. It has spacious, cool cottages set in neat gardens with views across vineyards to the mountains, but is only a short drive to the city centre. There are 2 restaurants, one by the swimming pool where breakfast is served when the weather permits. The food is excellent and it is advisable to reserve a table for evening meals, as both dining rooms are very popular with non-residents. **AL-A** *Steenberg Country Hotel*, 20 km from Cape Town in the Constantia Valley, T7132222, F7132221, www.steenberghotel.com Luxurious country hotel with tasteful rooms, some in converted farm buildings. Enjoy breakfast overlooking neat gardens and the working vineyards. Swimming pool, horse riding and golf all available to guests. Relaxed and friendly atmosphere.

A *Alphen Hotel*, Alphen Drive, 20 mins' drive from the city centre, located at the head of Constantia Valley, T7945011, F7945710. 26 spacious rooms in one of the most elegant 18th-century Cape Dutch estates. Suites and rooms are decorated with fine antiques, beautiful rugs on polished floors and log fires during winter months. Lunches are served in a pub or in the gardens during the summer, and in the evening there is a popular restaurant in the Manor House which attracts many non-residents. Swimming pool and free use of a nearby sports centre.

Cape Town

B-C *Houtkapperspoort*, Hout Bay Rd, Constantia Nek, T7945216, F7942907, www.houtkapperspoort.co.za Broad selection of self-catering cottages set in mature gardens with mountain views. Tennis courts, swimming pool, local hiking trails. Largest cottage is suitable for 8 people. Each has TV, lounge, telephone and fully equipped kitchens. Daily maid service and laundry. Home cooked frozen meals available. Recommended. **B-C** *Little Ruo*, 11 Willow Rd, T7942052, F7941981. Peaceful B&B in a central location with 3 double rooms, 2 suites, with en suite bathroom, TV, garden, swimming pool.

Atlantic **NB** Much of the accommodation along the Atlantic Seaboard and False Bay (see page 131)
Seaboard is aimed at the domestic self-catering market, where families rent houses or flats for a minimum of one week. Most places will be booked up months in advance for the school holidays and Christmas periods. The quiet season is from 1 May until 30 September, during which you should be able to negotiate very reasonable rates. There are only a few hotels and these are all small, family-run establishments. Keep in mind that out of season quite a few restaurants and shops may be closed for the winter.

Camps Bay AL-A *The Bay Hotel*, Victoria Rd, Camps Bay, T4384444, F4384455, www.www.thebay.co.za 70 luxurious a/c rooms all with views across the bay. Restaurant, swimming pool, excellent service, a well known place for the rich and famous. **C** *Bay Atlantic*, 3 Berkley Rd, Camps Bay, T4384341, T082-7778007 (mob). A few rooms in a luxury villa, plus a beachside villa only 150 m from the sea. All rooms with TV, set in mature gardens with swimming pool. Evening meals available. Book well in advance for visits during the peak season. Recommended by some readers. **C** *Whale Cottage Guesthouse*, 57 Camps Bay Drive, Camps Bay, T4383840, F4384388, www.whalecottage.com 4 double rooms with ensuite bathrooms, small tasteful place with marine décor, breakfast deck overlooking the beach, good views of the Twelve Apostles, satellite TV and internet access. **F** *Stans Halt Youth Hostel*, The Glen, Camps Bay, T4389037. A great, cheap alternative amongst the super-wealthy. 5 dorms with 6 beds in each, set in a wooded garden, with kitchen, breakfasts and dinner to order. Member of Hostelling International, bicycle hire, very popular in season, call in advance to check for space.

Llandudno B-C *Llandudno Heights*, 19 Llandudno Rd, Llandudno, T/F4382305. 5 rooms, 3 self-catering apartments and a swimming pool.

Hout Bay C *Beach House*, Royal Av, midway between the fishing harbour in Hout Bay and the road to Noordhoek, T7904228. 11 double rooms, typical seaside family home which had been enlarged into a guesthouse, clean neat gardens with palm trees and colour. **C** *Black Rock*, Blackwood Drive, Hout Bay, T7905985. Self-catering lodge, sensible furnishings, ideal for a short break. **C** *Sorgh Vliet Lodge*, Valley Rd, Hout Bay, T7902767, F7903861. 2 suites with TV, bathroom with shower, kitchen corner with microwave, sitting area, swimming pool. Roona and Rainer have recently taken over the lodge and are excellent hosts. Recommended. **C-D** *Dune Lodge*, 8 Edward St, Hout Bay, T7905847, T082-3383188 (mob), www.dunelodge.co.za 6 double rooms with en suite bathrooms, TV lounge, overlooking port, pleasant glassed-in veranda, popular holiday guesthouse. **C-D** *Froggs Leap*, 15 Baviaanskloof Rd, Hout Bay, T/F7902590. 3 double rooms with en suite bathroom, TV, mini bars and relaxing décor with a seaside feel. Transfers to airport by prior arrangement. **D** *Harbour Master*, PO Box 26826, Hout Bay, T7906910, F7907255, ronassoc@iafrica.com New B&B, small with cosy and clean rooms, fridge, good value. **D** *Forest Lodge*, Stirrup Lane, Hout Bay, T7904706, F7906827, www.forestlodge.co.za Small friendly place with 3 self-catering and 1 B&B room, arranged around a swimming pool with peaceful shady veranda, beautiful gardens are full of colour during the summer, good views. **E-F** *Chapman's Peak Caravan Farm*, Dassenheuwel, T7891225. 5 caravans with hot water and power points, camping allowed, swimming pool, peaceful rural setting. Recommended.

Noordhoek B *Monkey Valley*, Mountain Rd, Noordhoek, T7891391, F7891143. Luxurious self-catering thatched log cottages set in woodland overlooking Noordhoek Bay. Each has a secluded veranda with superb views, ideal for a sun downer or lazy breakfast. **B-C** *Tabankulu Lodge*, overlooking Noordhoek Beach, T7851432, F7852828. 4 double rooms in a delightful thatched house, plus 2 self-catering cottages in secluded corners of the mature gardens. Swimming pool, sauna, bar, superb location. **C** *Goose Green Lodge*, Briony Close, Noordhoek, T/F7892933, www.goosegreen.co.za B&B with 5 cosy rooms, swimming pool, easy access to Chapman's Peak and the beach.

Kommetjie E-F *Imhoff Caravan Park*, Wireless Rd, Kommetjie, T7831643, F7832871, www.imhoff.co.za Large site with self-catering chalets, all grass, electric points, well lit, laundry, games room, TV lounge, 500 m from beach. An ordered upmarket park with all the facilities for a family holiday.

There are several agencies which specialize in medium and long-term holiday lets of private homes, self-catering flats or home swaps. These are good value for families or groups; bring reliable references with you. *Apartments and Homes*, 154 Main Rd, Sea Point, T4394126, F4399621, www.capeholidays.co.za Apartments, family homes, furnished or unfurnished. *Cape Holiday Homes*, 179 Loop St, Box 16241, T4220335, F4220353. Private homes in the Peninsula and coastal area. *Holiday Booking Service*, Box 6598, T4194313, F4194319. Luxury furnished flats. *International Home Exchange*, Box 23188, Claremont, T/F7943433. Affiliated to *HomeLink International* in the UK. A directory is available for home swaps in over 40 countries.

Long-term stays

Eating

Unlike the rest of South Africa, Cape Town likes to eat out, a fact which is reflected in its multitude of restaurants – and the extent to which they get packed out. Summer is the most popular time for eating out, and the Waterfront, perhaps the city's most popular eating area, gets very busy out. Booking ahead is often a good idea. A good starting point for choosing a restaurant is buying the latest edition of *Eat Out*, a magazine guide edited by Lannice Synman, which features South Africa's best choice of restaurants. The magazine costs R24.95 and is available in newsagents and tourist offices.

● *on maps*

The Africa Café, Heritage Sq, 108 Shortmarket St, T4220221. The original in Observatory moved here recently, but despite becoming more upmarket, the food remains an excellent introduction to the continent's cuisines. The menu is a set 'feast' and includes 10 dishes that rove around the continent, from Malawian Mbatata balls and Kenyan patties, to Cape Malay mango chicken curry and Egyptian dips. The price includes the chance to order more of the dishes you like, as well as coffee and desert. Good value and excellent service, although it's very touristy. *Biesmiellah*, 2 Upper Wale St, T4230850. Closed Sun, one of the better known and well established Malay restaurants, serving a delicious mix of Indian and Cape Malay dishes. If you like your curry hot then this is the place to come, a real treat for any fan of spicy food. No alcohol. Recommended. *The Crypt*, 1 Wale St, below St George's Cathedral, T4249426. Despite its suspect location, this restaurant has lovely sunny tables set out on Wale St and serves the usual sandwiches and salads plus excellent daily pasta specials. Perfect for people-watching in the summer, or huddling in the vaulted interior in winter. *Five Flies*, 14 Keerom St, T4231048. Preferred haunt of lawyers and judges, attractive restaurant and old-fashioned bar. *Mama Africa*, 178 Long St, T4248634. Popular restaurant and bar serving 'traditional' African dishes often with great live music. Popular with tourists, tasty food if overpriced, excellent service. Centrepiece is a bright green carved Mamba-shaped bar. Slightly tacky but a fun place nevertheless. *Marco's African Place*, 15 Rose St, T4235412, African menu, live music, huge place with a friendly atmosphere, excellent starters but main courses are disappointing. *Pagoda Inn*, 29 Bree St, T4252033. Chinese restaurant with a good selection of dishes, choice of small or large portions. *Primi Piatti*, Greenmarket Sq, T4247466. Lively spot for lunch overlooking the square from the huge open windows. Superb pizzas, good pasta and salads, huge portions at reasonable prices, popular with a young fashionable crowd. *Shambhala*, 134 Long St, T4265452, www.shambhala.co.za Relaxed vegetarian restaurant serving salads, sandwiches and good daily specials. Calm Buddhism-inspired décor, friendly service, great spot for lunch. *Star**, 273 Long St, T4246576. Trendy establishment serving good seafood, salads and a couple of Portuguese dishes. Friendly service and getting popular with a well-heeled young crowd. Turns into a fiercely fashionable bar from about 2300. Only 7 tables, so come early or book.

City centre
See map, page 80

Cape Town

Oranjezicht, Gardens & Tamboerskloof
See map, page 103

Arnold's, 60 Kloof St, Gardens, T4244344, www.arnolds.co.za Good value lunch spot on busy Kloof St, good salads, pasta and more substantial meals like ostrich steak. Fast, friendly service. **Aubergine**, 39 Barnet St, Gardens, T4654909. Sophisticated and award-winning menu, modern slants on classical European dishes, excellent wine list. One of the best in town. Stylish shaded courtyard, lounge/bar, good service. Recommended. **Blue Danube**, 102 New Church St, Tamboerskloof, T4233624. Closed Sun and Mon lunch. Chef Thomas Sinn combines traditional Austrian dishes with an international fusion menu, served in a fine old building with spacious rooms and mountain views. Recommended. **Café Paradiso**, 110 Kloof St, Gardens, T4238653. Tuscan setting for this relaxed Italian restaurant. Some fine local dishes, but the best options are the Italian dishes. Recommended. **Cape Colony**, *Mount Nelson Hotel*, 76 Orange St, T4831000. One of Cape Town's finest restaurants in the impressive setting of the Mount Nelson. Dishes are classical Cape Cuisine plus a couple of Thai and African dishes. Impeccable service. Expensive. **Kotobuki**, 3 Mill St, Gardens, T4623675. Japanese, no-frills top-class menu, expensive for Cape Town, but a favourite amongst the Japanese community, closed Mon. **Maeströs**, Kloof St, T4243015, restaurant and pub, food of a high standard. **Ocean Basket**, 75 Kloof St, Gardens, T4220322. A successful franchise serving seafood and salads, pleasant setting with a large courtyard at the back. Open only in the evening at weekends. No bookings, expect to queue outside on the street. **Rozenhof**, 18 Kloof St, T4241968. Closed Sun, smart restaurant set in an attractive 18th-century town house, decorated with local artwork and chandeliers, food to match the surrounds, sensible light dishes full of flavour, look out for seasonal dishes such as asparagus and salads, good choice for vegetarians. Recommended. **Saigon**, corner Camp and Kloof Sts, T4247670, zenasia@iafrica.com Superb Vietnamese cuisine, very popular place overlooking busy Kloof St, brilliant crystal spring rolls, barbequed duck and caramelised pork with black pepper. Book ahead. Recommended. **Sukhothai**, 12 Mill St, T4655846. Good Thai cuisine, set menus for the confused, advisable to book at the weekend, authentically Thai, hot and spicy. **Yindee's**, 22 Camp St, Tamboerskloof, T4221012. Closed for lunch on Sat and all day Sun. An excellent Thai restaurant serving authentic spicy curries and soups. Served in a sprawling Victorian house with traditional low tables. Service can be very slow, but the place is always popular, so book ahead. **yum**, 2 Deer Park Drive, Vredehoek, T4617607. Stylish deli and restaurant serving excellent sandwiches, salads and original pasta dishes, such as roast lamb tortellini or goat's cheese and roasted pepper lasagne. Good service, relaxed young crowd, delicious pickles and chutneys on sale. Recommended.

Victoria & Alfred Waterfront
The Waterfront is one of the most popular districts in Cape Town to come for a meal and gets very busy

There are too many restaurants, bars and cafés to list them all here; the following are just a sample of what is on offer. The area is still under development, so new places open every few months. Competition is tough, but prices remain higher here than elsewhere.

Aldo's, ground floor, Victoria Wharf, T4217846. One of the better Italian restaurants in town, reflected in the imaginative range of dishes on offer. **Arlindo's**, ground floor, Victoria Wharf. Mouth watering selection of game and seafood dishes, excellent calamari, reasonable wines, polite and attentive service, outside terrace gets a bit crowded. Recommended. **Baia**, top floor, Victoria Wharf, T4210935. Newest addition to Cape Town's fine restaurants. Very smart (and expensive) venue specializing in seafood. Delicious rich dishes following a Mozambique theme – try the beer baked prawns. Very stylish interior with views of Table Mountain, slightly erratic service. Book ahead. **Cantina Tequila**, Quay 5, Victoria Wharf, T4190207. Full range of Mexican dishes, good cocktails, live music Wed-Sun, outside terrace, touristy, indifferent service and erratic food. **Cape Town Fish Market**, ground floor, Victoria Wharf, T4135977. Popular fish restaurant, but the reason to come here is the revolving sushi bar, serving excellent sushi and sashimi. Dishes on offer are limited but very fresh and good value. **Café Balducci**, Victoria Wharf, T4216002. Mix of Italian and South African food, popular, book ahead. **Den Anker**, Pierhead, T4190249. Popular Belgian (Flemish) restaurant and bar, continental feel, high ceiling flying the various duchy flags, newspaper plastered pillars, airy leafy bar, views across Alfred Basin of Table Mountain, civilized atmosphere. Plenty of Belgian dishes to sample plus an amazing selection of imported bottle beers. **The Edge**, Pierhead, T4212583. Terrace tables on a first-come basis, spicy mix of Cape cuisine with an emphasis on seafood dishes, a good mix of South African meals. *Emily's*, Clock Tower centre, T4211133. The old Woodstock favourite recently moved to the top floor of the new Clock Tower centre. Very smart restaurant serving excellent French-style cuisine, great views from balcony overlooking the Waterfront, polite service, popular, book ahead. *Hildebrand*, Pierhead, T4253385. Well-established Italian seafood place, excellent pasta, good reputation, touristy given the location. *Morton's on the Wharf*, upstairs, Victoria Wharf, T4183633. A busy New Orleans-style restaurant and bar, Creole fish dishes or spicy Cajun country food, a playful and fun evening with live music, Jazz, Mardi Gras and Blues, check out the Sunday Jazz brunch. *The Musselcracker*, upstairs, Victoria Wharf, T4194300. Popular seafood restaurant and oyster bar, lunchtime buffets, some bad reports but remains popular. *Teacher's*, T4193122. A floating restaurant and popular venue for functions. Busy in the evening.

Avanti, 341 Main Rd, Sea Point, T4391857. Full range of Italian meals, good value. *Buena Vista Social Café*, Main Rd, Green Point, T4330611. Cuban-themed bar and restaurant. Live Latin music at weekend, very fashionable, excellent but pricey food. *Chariots*, 107 Main Rd, Green Point, T4345427. Excellent local Italian restaurant serving traditional and innovative pasta dishes (try the curried butternut ravioli), superb risotto, salads and meat dishes. Low-key and relaxed, good service, tables overlooking Main Rd, popular with young professionals. Excellent value for money. Recommended. *Golden Dragon*, 359 Main Rd, Sea Point, T4345391. Full range of Chinese dishes, 'Early Bird' specials. *L'Orient*, 50 Main Rd, Sea Point, T4396572. Indonesian and Malaysian, evening only, 1900-2300, a popular and authentic restaurant serving a wide range of exotic dishes. The Rijsttafel has 17 individual dishes. Recommended. *Mr Chan*, 178a Main Rd, Sea Point, T4392239. Smart upmarket restaurant serving Peking, Cantonese and Szechuan meals. Expensive but some top-quality dishes. Recommended for a treat. *News Café*, corner Main and Ashtead Rds, Green Point, popular café and bar serving sandwiches, salads, pub meals, stylish decor, gets busy in the evenings. *The Restaurant*, 51a Somerset Rd, Green Point, T4192921. One of Cape Town's finest, serving superb seafood and meat dishes in a stylish and understated setting. Brilliant deserts and attentive service. Very popular so booking essential. *San Marco*, 92 Main Rd, Sea Point, T4392758. A long-term favourite. Extensive Italian menu specializing in seafood. Excellent anitpasto, plenty of vegetarian options, wonderful desserts. Up-market and expensive, but worth it. *Wangthai*, 105 Paramount Pl, T4396164. Great Thai restaurant serving mouth-watering stir fries, curries with coconut milk and plenty of lemon grass. Reservations advised.

Green Point & Sea Point
See maps, pages 104 and 107

Cape Town

Au Jardin, Vineyard Hotel, Colinton Rd, Newlands, T6831520. A very smart hotel restaurant with one of the best French menus in Cape Town. Six course meals or a quick plat du jour served in a stylish setting with views of the mountain. Polite service, excellent presentation. The best local ingredients turned into the best European recipes. Recommended. Booking always advised. Closed Sun, Mon and Jul. *Barrister's Grill*, corner of Kildare and Main St, Newlands, T6741792. Open daily from breakfast through to late evening. A popular steakhouse that has expanded into a trendy bistro/café during the day with plenty of alfresco tables. Still retains the Mock-Tudor timber décor of the steakhouse. Plenty for vegetarians. *Don Pedro's*, 113 Roodebloem Rd, Woodstock, T4474493, info@donpedro.co.za Informal, bustling restaurant serving huge portions of South African food, pasta and pizza at cheap prices. Very popular, focal point of the community, great mixed crowd, book ahead. Recommended. *Fiamma's*, 23-25 Wolf St, Wynberg, T7616175. Closed Sun. Smart new Italian restaurant serving fine traditional dishes with a South African twist. Friendly service, attractive surrounds. *Fratelli*, Cavendish Sq, Claremont, cheerful good-value pasta and steaks. *Mango*, Cavendish Sq, Claremont. Friendly place serving a mix of South African and US-style food, ribs, stews, seafood, burgers. Good spot to fill up before seeing a film upstairs. *Pancho's*, Lower Main Rd, Observatory. Mexican dishes in a lively atmosphere, all the usual tacos and fajitas, good home made nachos, nothing fancy but a fun place. Tasty cocktails. *Rory's*, Lower Main Rd, Observatory, T4488301. Stylish and homely restaurant run by chef Rory, menu changes daily, excellent fresh ingredients with a fusion twist, relaxed setting and trendy crowd.

Southern suburbs

Constantia *Buitenverwachting*, Klein Constantia Rd, Constantia, T7943522. One of the best restaurants in Cape Town, flawless Italian and French cuisine, good service, upmarket, prices reflect the quality of the food. *The Cellars*, The *Cellars-Hohenort Hotel*, 93 Brommersvlei Rd, Constantia, T7942137. A highly praised menu which might be too trendy for some palates. The restaurant is in an exclusive 5-star hotel. A little too formal for a fun night out, but still one of the best hotel-based restaurants in the area. *La Colombe*, Constantia Uitsig, Constantia, T7942390. Closed Tue and Sun evening, Jul and Aug. Excellent French menu with strong Provençal flavours. Delicious fresh fish and a range of meat and duck dishes, with an emphasis on rich sauces. During fine weather you can sit outside and look over the gardens and a pool. *Parks*, 114 Constantia Rd, Constantia, T7978202. Closed Mon. Enjoy a drink in the lounge before moving into one of the two dining areas overlooking a colourful garden. Broad range of well-presented dishes, making good use of fresh local produce. Mostly traditional dishes, plenty for vegetarians, excellent service. Recommended. *Steenberg*, *Steenberg Country Hotel*, Spaanschemat River Rd, Constantia, T7132222. The principal restaurant in a 5-star hotel. Tables are set in cosy alcoves created from old wine vats. An expensive and smart place to dine out, but like many hotel restaurants lacks a spontaneous character. International menu designed to satisfy the tastes of hotel guests from all over the world.

Atlantic Seaboard **Clifton** *Clifton Beach House*, 4th Beach, Clifton, T4381955. Breakfast, lunch and dinner overlooking Clifton's beautiful beach, good seafood plus some Thai dishes, relaxed during the day but more elegant at night.

Camps Bay *Blues*, Victoria Rd, Camps Bay, T4382040. Popular and well-known seafood place with superb views, Californian-style menu served to a beautiful crowd. Good, stylish food, although you pay for the restaurant's reputation. *The Codfather*, corner Geneva Drive and The Drive, T4380782. One of the best seafood restaurants in Cape Town, stylish laid-back place offering a range of superbly fresh seafood. No menu – the waiter takes you to a counter and you pick and choose whatever you like the look of. Also has an excellent sushi bar. Highly recommended. *Ocean Blue*, Victoria Rd, Camps Bay, T4389838. Friendly seafood restaurant on road overlooking the beach. Excellent fresh seafood, especially daily specials, superb grilled prawns and butterfish kebabs. Less pretentious than many of the restaurants in the area. Recommended.

Hout Bay *Chapman's Peak Hotel*, Hout Bay, T7901036, opposite end of town to harbour. Book in the evenings, a lively restaurant and bar. *Dirty Dick's Tavern*, Harbour Rd, Hout Bay, T7905609. Beer garden and restaurant with open-air terrace overlooking the Marina. Steaks, fish and salads. *Dunes*, Hout Bay Beach, T7901876. Sprawling restaurant overlooking the dunes behind the beach, very popular with families, large menu, quick service but the food can disappoint – stick to the tasty fish and chips. *Fish on the Rocks*, Harbour Rd (beyond Snoekies Market), Hout Bay, T7901153, simple and delicious fresh fish and chips, no frills. Recommended. *Oven Door*, Main Rd, Hout Bay. A very popular street café next to some curio shops and the information centre, unfortunately because of location on the main road, it suffers from fumes during holiday months when traffic is non-stop. *Rumblin' Tum*, Shoreline Centre, Hout Bay. Family coffee shop and restaurant serving good breakfasts (delicious muesli and yoghurt), but small portions. Mix of light lunches, outside terrace and small patio, sluggish service. *Red Herring*, Chapman's Bay Trading Centre, Beach Rd, T7891783. Excellent country cuisine, attached *Sunset* pub, but distracting sunlight from the stained glass windows. Closed Mon.

Scarborough *Camel Rock*, Scarborough, T7801122, open 1200-1700, 1900-2300. A Mediterranean-style seafood restaurant. Sit out on the balcony and enjoy the oysters or excellent calamari, bring your own wines, good stop for lunches. Recommended.

Vegetarian, coffee shops & delis *Café Erté*, 265 Main Rd, Sea Point, T4346624. Trendy café playing loud trance and techno, good breakfasts and snacks, internet access. *Charly's Bakery*, 20 Roeland St, T4615181. Tiny café serving brilliant cakes, pastries and pies – don't miss the spinach and feta pie. *Charters Coffee Shop*, Pierhead, T4193103. In the restored grey and white Old Port Captain's Building, also home to *Waterfront Charters Boat Trips*. Sandwiches and light lunches. *Juicy Lucy*, Link Centre, Claremont, T6717407. Coffee shop and juice bar, good toasted sandwiches, fresh juices and milkshakes. *Marigolds*, 5 Grove Av, Claremont, T6744670. One of the few vegetarian restaurants in town, usual selection of quiche, soups and salads, closed evenings, no smoking. *Mugg & Bean*, Victoria Wharf, T4196451, also branch in Cavendish Sq, Claremont, and the Lifestyles centre on Kloof St. Café serving mouth-watering muffins, cakes and sandwiches and good coffee. *Naked on Kloof*, 47 Kloof St, Gardens, T4244748. Healthy fast-food joint selling wraps, sandwiches and juices, open late so good for a mid-Saturday night snack. *Obz Café*, 115 Lower Main Rd, Observatory, T4485555. Popular place open all day for light meals, coffee or cocktails, great salads and sandwiches, some tables on pavement outside. *Olympia Café*, 138 Main Rd, Kalk Bay. Hugely popular café and deli serving up breakfast, soups, sandwiches and more substantial meals at lunchtime. *Marc's Deli Bar*, Shop 16, The Promenade, Camps Bay, T4382322. Smart first-floor deli and café overlooking Camps Bay beach, serving wonderful pastries, muffins and cakes as well as selling a fine selection of breads and cheeses. *Mr Pickwicks*, 158 Long St. Trendy spot serving the best milkshakes in town, excellent French loaf sandwiches, healthy salads, large pasta portions, licensed, gets very busy with an after-work crowd, open late. Also sells tickets to Cape Town's major club nights and gigs. *New York Bagels*, 51 Regent Rd, Sea Point, T4397523. Cafeteria-style deli serving a good range of food, from hearty American breakfasts and smoked salmon bagels through to salads, hotdogs and fish and chips. Attached deli shop next door sells bagels to take away. *Nino's*, Cavendish Sq, Claremont, T6837288. Popular haunt for shoppers to rest up and try one of *Nino's* delicious toasted paninis, salads or pasta dishes. *Sunflower Health Café*, 161 Longmarket St. Closed evening, good value vegetarian meals, drinks, plus health shop. *Yellow Pepper Deli*, 138 Long St. Open Fri and Sat evenings, closed Sun, good breakfast, exciting and unusual range of home-cooked European dishes, trendy and very popular. *We Live Like This*, Main Rd, Kalk Bay. Stylish deli and kitchen shop selling sandwiches and healthy snacks.

Bars and nightclubs

169, 169 Long St. R&B club with a lively, mixed crowd. Gets packed on Fri. *Club More*, 74 Loop St, T4220544. Popular dance venue playing garage, house and techno Wed-Sat. *D-lite*, Loop St. Late starter, house sounds with a factory interior. *The Fez*, 38 Hout St, www.fez.co.za Moroccan-themed interior, young and well-heeled crowd, funky house and themed parties. *The Lounge*, 194 Long St. Fashionable bar and club with several small rooms, big sofas, house music most nights, drum 'n' bass on Wed, great balcony overlooking Long St. Closes at 0200, but don't bother turning up before midnight, closed Sun. *Jo'burg*, 218 Long St. Trendy bar serving pints and cocktails to a mixed crowd, gay-friendly, relaxed during the week but gets very busy at weekends when DJs spin funky house and drum 'n' bass. Recommended. *Kennedy's Cigar Bar*, 251 Long St, T4241212. Up-market cigar and cocktail lounge with daily live jazz. *Mama Africa*, 178 Long St, T4248634. Great live music every night, usually Marimba. *Perseverance Tavern*, 83 Buitenkant St. Cape Town's oldest pub, pub food available in two dining rooms, beer garden, plenty of drinking corners, full on at the weekend, good Sun roast lunch, live music. *Poo Na Na Souk Bar*, Heritage Sq, 100 Shortmarket St, T4234889. Ultra-trendy bar decked out in Moroccan lanterns and expensive fabrics, lovely balconies overlooking the even trendier *Strega* restaurant, usually relaxed atmosphere but sometimes host to big-name international DJs. *Purple Turtle Pub*, Long St. Grotty, grungy pub which remains very popular, pub lunches, pool tables, live bands on Sat, bank of TV video screens. *Virtual Turtle* is their internet café spin-off, found upstairs and around the city. *Vacca Matta*, Seeff House, Foreshore, T4195550. Full-on drinking haunt and club with waitresses dancing on the bar, 'ladies' get in for very little and often get free cocktails, tacky but resolutely popular.

City centre
The Cape Times and Argus have good listings sections, as does the Cape Review magazine. Otherwise, check out www.clubbersguide. co.za, a good guide to South Africa's nightlife

See also Gay and lesbian Cape Town, page 117

Cool Runnings, 108 Kloof St, T4248388. One of Kloof Street's most popular drinking holes, with a beach-bar themed deck overlooking the street, pub meals, always gets packed at weekends with a lively throng. *Dharma Club*, 68 Kloof St, T4220909, www.thedharmaclub.com Small,

Oranjezicht, Gardens & Tamboerskloof

Cape Town

trendy with vaguely Asian décor. Intimate setting and excellent music mixed by a live DJ, good fusion meals, but an over-dressed, pretentious crowd. *Dros*, Kloof St, T4236800. Busy pub and bar serving standard pub fare, nice tables overlooking Kloof St. *Drum Café*, 32 Glyn St, Gardens, T4611305, www.drumcafe.co.za Popular bar serving light meals and featuring communal drumming sessions. Grab a drum and join in, or watch the professionals on Fri and Sat nights. *Keg & Squirrel*, Kloof St, Gardens. Part of a popular English-style chain, pub atmosphere plus good value dining area. *Maeströs*, 60 Kloof St, T4243014. Large range of beers, lively place, pub meals, steaks, burgers, pasta.

Waterfront *Den Anker*, Victoria & Alfred Pierhead. Belgium restaurant and bar specializing in a range of Belgium draught and bottled beers. *Cantina Tequila*, Quay 5, Victoria Wharf, T4190207. This Mexican restaurant transforms into a packed nightclub after about 2300, mostly chart music, popular with tourists. *Quay Four*, T4192008. Large shady deck overlooking the water, popular with well-heeled locals and tourists, good meals and great draught beer, one of the more pleasant pubs on the Waterfront. *Ferryman's Tavern*, Waterfront. A popular haunt with restaurant upstairs, outside seating, TV continually showing sports action, the olives and feta go well with the Mitchell's Beer brewed on site, a lively mixed crowd. *Sports Café*, Victoria Wharf. Large sports bar showing matches on big screens.

Green Point *Bosa Nova*, Somerset Rd, Green Point. Large bar with seats overlooking the street, dance
& Sea Point floor at the back, pop and house music. *Bronx*, 35 Somerset Rd corner Napier St, Green
The area between De Point, www.bronx.co.za Very popular gay bar and club, gets packed out at weekends,
Waterkant and Green mostly men but women welcome, live DJs spin out thumping techno every night. *Buena*
Point is the focus of *Vista Social Café*, Main Rd, Green Point, T4330611. Cuban-themed bar and restaurant
Cape Town's gay and catering to a well-heeled crowd. Latin music, live bands at weekend, tasteful décor and a
lesbian scene, with a relaxed atmosphere, nice balcony overlooking Main Rd, great spot for sophisticated cock-
number of trendy bars, tails on a hot evening. *Chilli n' Lime*, 23 Somerset Rd, Green Point. Trendy bar and club,
clubs and cabaret pretentious, over-priced and very young, but playing excellent hip-hop on Sat nights. *Club*
venues. For more *55*, Somerset Rd, Green Point, T4251849, www.55.co.za Popular gay club, seats on pave-
details, see Gay and ment lead to busy dance floor inside, well-known DJs spin trance and progressive house
Lesbian Cape Town on Fri and Sat, cabaret on Tue, Thu and Sun.
below, page 117

Southern *Bijou*, Lower Main Rd, Observatory. New ultra-trendy bar/club/theatre very popular with an
Suburbs arty pack, weekly fashion shows, plays, gigs and parties held in a huge open-air concrete
Observatory is the city's theatre on the roof, dancing area on 2nd floor, groovy bar on ground floor, great cocktails,
alternative nightlife expect to pay an entry fee after 10pm or have a personal invite. *Café Ganesh*, Trill Rd, Obser-
centre and the place vatory. Lively little café and bar serving hearty Cape dishes and ice-cold beers in a leafy court-
to head for laid-back yard leading to a characterful interior. Very friendly, great place to meet local Obs characters.
bars and clubs with a *Forester's Arms*, Newlands Av. A favourite with students, especially the sports jocks, a
bohemian feel, while fun-loving, boozy scene. *The Green Man*, Main Rd, Claremont. Most popular bar in Clare-
Rondebosch and mont, very young boozy crowd, small dancing area, mostly rock music, often frequented by
Claremont have plenty Springbok players. *Independent Armchair Theatre*, 135 Lower Main Rd, Observatory. Popu-
of sports bars popular lar venue with huge sofas to lounge in, featuring films on Mon, jazz on Thu, live bands most
with, er, sporty types nights, excellent stand-up comedy from the Cape Comedy Collective on Sun. Recommended. *Keg & Grouse*, Riverside Centre, Rondebosch. English-style pub serving bar meals.
Sports Café, Atrium Centre, Claremont. Popular bar showing all the important games on big
screen TVs, busy balcony overlooking Main Rd. *A Touch of Madness*, Pepper Tree Sq, Nuttal
Rd, Observatory. Flamboyant bar with series of rooms decked out with tongue-in-cheek
opulence, eccentric regulars, great atmosphere, good light meals. Recommended.

Atlantic *Café Caprice*, Victoria Rd, Camps Bay. Popular café and bar with outdoor seats, great
Seaboard fresh-fruit cocktails. *Dizzy Jazz Café*, 41 The Drive, Camps Bay, T4382686. Busy bar and live
music venue, popular jazz nights at the weekend. *La Med*, Glen Country Club, Victoria Rd,
Clifton, T4385600, www.lamed.co.za Popular meeting place for Cape Town's rich and beautiful, busy bar overlooking the sea, good pub food, great for a sundowner, turns into a rau-
cous club later on. *Sandbar*, Victoria Rd, Camps Bay. Popular for sundowners at one of the

shady tables on the pavement. *Skebanga's*, Red Herring, Nordhoek, T7891783. Outdoor deck overlooking the beach, sports events screened. *Tuscany Beach Café*, Victoria Rd, Camps Bay. Minimalist interior, good bar snacks, laid-back and trendy.

Café Camissa, Kloof St, Gardens, T4242289. Pleasant spot with outdoor seating, live music Wed and Sun nights. *Dizzy Jazz Café*, 41 The Drive, Camps Bay, T4382686. Busy bar and live music venue, popular jazz nights at the weekend. *Drum Café*, 32 Glyn St, Gardens, T4611305, www.drumcafe.co.za Popular bar featuring communal drumming sessions, grab a drum and join in, or watch the professionals on Fri and Sat nights. *Green Dolphin*, V & A Waterfront, T4217471. Top local jazz groups. *Independent Armchair Theatre*, 135 Lower Main Rd, Observatory. Popular venue with huge sofas to lounge in, jazz on Thu, live bands most nights. *Kirstenbosch Summer Concerts*, www.nbi.ac.za Every Sun at 1700 Nov-Mar, idyllic setting, picnics on the lawns, concerts varying from folk and jazz to classical and opera. Recommended. *Mama Africa*, 178 Long St, T4248634. Great live music every night, usually Marimba. *V & A Waterfront Amphitheatre*, outdoor venue on the Waterfront with daily concerts, live performances, mainly jazz.

Live Music

Entertainment

Cape Town's outdoor-friendly character makes it a great place to take the kids, with plenty of sights that interest adults while keeping children busy. An added bonus is that many attractions offer free entrance or substantial reductions to children (usually under 16). Take the new **Aerial Cableway** to the top of Table Mountain, see page 79. **Ratanga Junction**, South Africa's largest theme park is a recreation of a 19th-century mining town, crammed with impressive thrill rides, roller coasters and family rides. Your ticket allows you to go on as many rides as often as you like, but some rides have a height restriction. Wed-Fri and Sun 1000-1700, Sat 1000-1800 (extended days and hours during school holidays), entrance R75, children R39. Follow the N1 to Belville and take exit 10 for Century City, T5508500. **South Africa Museum and Planetarium**, see page 81. **Telekom Exploratorium**, see page 90. **Two Oceans Aquarium**, see page 91.

Cape Town for kids

The 2 major cinema groups are Nu Metro and Ster-Kinekor. New films are released on Fri. Evening shows are very popular, booking advised. Daily newspapers and the monthly *Cape Review* have full listings. *Nu Metro*, V&A Waterfront, T4199700; Century City, T5552510; Claremont, T6831122. 11 screens. *Ster-Kinekor*, Golden Acre, Adderley St, T9395126; Cavendish Square, T6836238; Kenilworth, T6831208/9.
    Cape Town has an annual film festival in Apr. Most of the festival films are shown at the University of Cape Town campus, the Baxter cinema and the Labia. *Baxter*, Main Rd, Rondebosch, T6891069. 2 screens, part of the theatre complex. *Labia*, 68 Orange St, Gardens, T4245927, labia@new.co.za 2 screens, International Art House films. The *Imax* cinema, T4197365, in the BMW Pavilion at the Victoria and Alfred Waterfront shows special format films on a giant screen with 'six-channel wrap-around digital sound'. Check the papers for listings of what's on. Tickets cost approximately R50 for adults and each film lasts for 1 hr.

Cinemas

Cape Town is rated, along with Sydney and San Francisco, as one of the 'Gay Capitals' of the world. Certainly, it is the most gay- and lesbian-friendly city in Africa and is drawing increasing numbers of gay travellers from across the country and continent. The scene is correspondingly vibrant, with plenty of bars, clubs and events aimed specifically at a gay crowd. Predictably, these venues tend to be the trendiest in town, so nights are generally very popular and more mixed than you might expect. The area around Green Point is the focus of Cape Town's gay and lesbian scene, and all the main bars and clubs are found along Somerset and Main Rd. The main gay event and one of the best parties of the year is the *Mother City Queer Project*, www.mcqp.co.za, a fantastically extravagant costume party and rave – not to be missed if you're in town in Dec.

Gay & lesbian Cape Town

Information An excellent guide to the gay scene is the free *Pink Map*, available at tourist offices and a number of trendy shops and bars around town. It has useful listings and up-to-date details of everything from bars and clubs to accommodation and steam baths.

Gay & Lesbian Helpline, T4222250. Daily 1300-2100. *GALACTTIC*, T4246445, www.galactic.co.za Association of gay-related businesses promoting gay commerce. *Out in Africa*, T0214659289, www.oia.co.za Organize annual gay film festival, last 2 week of Feb. *Life Line Aids*, T0800012322. 24 hrs. *Triangle Project*, T4483812/3. HIV testing, counselling and a library. *Cape Organization of Gay Sport*, T5577195. Ask for Sarel. *q on line*, www.q.co.za South Africa's main gay and lesbian website with email access, chat rooms and a dating service. *Cedarberg Southern African Travel*, T4822444, info@pinkroute.co.za Tour operator using gay-owned and gay-friendly accommodation, organizes trips along the 'Pink Route'. *Strata Tours*, T083-3024492 (mob), stratatours@freemail.abxa.co.za Owned by two women, tours around Cape Town and South African, aimed at lesbian market. *Way Out Tours*, michele@oia.co.za City and nationwide tours, mainly focussing on gay events and associated with the *Out in Africa* film festival.

Bars and clubs *Angels*, 27 Somerset Rd, Green Point, T4198547. Courtyard with outside bar leading onto huge dance floor, unpretentious crowd up for a good time, house and techno plus some cheesy tunes, open from 2200 on Wed, Fri and Sat. *Bronx*, corner Somerset Rd and Napier St, Green Point, www.bronx.co.za Very popular gay bar, live DJs spin out thumping techno every night, gets packed out at weekends with crowds spilling onto the pavements, mostly men but women welcome. *Club 55*, Somerset Rd, Green Point, T4251849, www.55.co.za Popular gay club, seats on pavement lead to busy dance floor inside, well-known DJs spin trance and progressive house on Fri and Sat, cabaret on Tue, Thu and Sun. *Evita se Perron*, Darling Station, Darling, 55 mins from Cape Town, T0224922831, www.evita.co.za Evita is a South African gay institution, a sort of Afrikaans Dame Edna, hosting lively events at her café-theatre, including Bambi's Berlin Bar, a shop, restaurant and gallery. *S.K.Y*, Napier St, Green Point, T4198547. Fashionable dance complex, industrial interior, 2 dance floors, 4 bars, courtyard with outside bar, mixed crowd, mostly techno and progressive house, open from 2300, Fri and Sat.

Outdoors Boulders Beach is one of the most attractive beaches on the False Bay Seaboard and is also the best place for spotting African penguinse, see page 139. **Fish Hoek** has a pleasant beach with small waves and a playground, see page 136. On the Atlantic side, **Camps Bay** has a tidal pool and shady, grassy areas, see page 98. **Nordhoek** is too rough for swimming, but is a great place for kite-flying or a horse ride, see page 99. **Kirstenbosch Botanical Gardens**, South Africa's oldest, largest and most exquisite botanical garden is the perfect spot for a family picnic, see page 95. **World of Birds** bird park has over 330 species of birds and a children's touch park, see page 99. **Cape of Good Hope Nature Reserve**, is a wonderful area to spend a day wandering and picnicking, see page 129. Alternatively, the more developed seaboard (on the False Bay side) has braai areas, a pleasant way of spending a quiet afternoon by the sea.

Theatre *Artscape*, DF Malan St, Foreshore, T4109800. Major complex offering opera, theatre and music. *Baxter*, Main Rd, Rondebosch, T6857880, www.baxter.co.za Long term involvement in black theatre, good reputation for supporting community theatre, international productions and musicals. *Long St Theatre*, St Johns Arcade, T4183496. Drama and dance plus a small cabaret venue. *Nico Theatre Centre*, DF Malan St, T4215470. Three theatre complex – Main Theatre, Arena and the Opera House, musicals, dance and new experimental theatre; opera is rarely staged because of production costs. *V&A Theatre*, Victoria Wharf, T4194767.

Festivals

See The Cape Times or www.capetownevents. co.za for more listings Celebrations are a serious business in Cape Town, and during the summer months you'll be hard pressed to find a free weekend. Street carnivals and festivals compete with cultural and sporting events, although publicity is often limited.

January *Karnaval*, **2nd Jan**, begins in the Bo-Kaap district and ends up in the Green Point Stadium, this is city's most popular festival, includes procession of competing minstrel bands, complete with painted faces, straw boaters and bright satin suits, www.espafrika.com *Cape to Rio* yacht race, every 2 years, next race is in 2004, starts first weekend Jan. *J&B Metropolitan Handicap*, **last Sat in Jan**, South Africa's major horse-racing meet at Kenilworth Race Course, www.jbmet.co.za **March** *Test Match*, Newlands throughout **Mar**. *African Harvest North Sea Jazz Festival*, Good Hope Centre, second leg of the North Sea festival, four stages with local and international jazz artists, **last weekend**, www.nsjfcapetown.com *Cape Argus Pick 'n' Pay Cycle Tour*, world's largest timed cycling event, www.cylcetour.co.za *Two Oceans Marathon*, 56 km race with over 9000 competitors, **last weekend**, www.twooceansmarathon.org.za **April** Start of *Rugby season* at Newlands and the *Film festival*, see Cinemas above. **August** Start of *wild flower season*, a Flower Hotline keeps you up to date, T4183705. *Cape Times Wine Festival*, V & A Waterfront, taste 300 wines from 85 estates, plus cheese hall, **last weekend**. **September** *Hermanus Whale Festival*, marks beginning of calving season of southern right whales, excellent viewing, **last week**, www.whalefestival.co.za **October** *Cape Times/FNB Big Walk*, world's largest timed walk started in 1903, www.bigwalk.co.za *Smirnoff International Comedy Festival*, Baxter Theatre, week-long festival featuring local and international talent. **November** *Nedbank Summer Concerts*, musical performances, classical, jazz, folk, swing and choral, held at the Josephine Mill, Newlands, **every Sun through to Feb**. **December** *Obz Festival*, Observatory, huge street party with stalls, live music and all-nights parties. *Long Street Carnival*, street party with several stages of live music and comedy, plus stalls and fairground rides. *Mother City Queer Project costume party*, biggest gay event in town and one of best parties of the year, www.mcqp.co.za *Clifton Challenge*, Clifton Beach 4, fitness challenge between Springbok rugby team and Clifton lifesavers, the event for beautiful people. *Kirstenbosch Summer Concerts*, **every Sun until Mar**, picnics on the lawns, concerts varying from folk and jazz to classical and opera, www.nbi.ac.za

Shopping

African Image, 52 Burg St, T4238385. Not your everyday curio shop, the tribal art and crafts here are of a superior quality and could well be an investment. *Art Etc*, 149 Kloof St, T4240567. Unusual collection of art and ceramics by local artists. *Constantia Craft Market*, Constantia Centre, T5312653. First and last Sat and first Sun of every month, known for its wooden furniture, glass and pottery. *Indaba*, Pierhead, V&A Waterfront, T4253639. Plenty of choice, both in price and size of curio. *Red Shed*, part of Victoria Wharf shopping centre. Handful of local craftsmen, glass blowers, goods are of suspect taste. *The Collector*, 52 Church St, T4231483. Top dealer in authentic African tribal art, quality collection of pieces from all over Africa, the prices reflect the uniqueness of the stock. *Greenmarket Square Market*, lively market selling crafts, textiles and clothes from across the country. *The Pan African Market*, Long St, T4242957. Centre selling crafts from across the continent, good local crafts made from recycled material, beadwork, ceramics. Café specializing in African food. *Waterfront Craft Market*, Dock St, T4182850. Stalls selling selection of arts and crafts from around Africa.

Arts, crafts & curios

CNA (Central News Agencies), city-wide chain of shops carrying a reasonable stock of guide books, glossy coffee table publications, some colourful maps, foreign newspapers and magazines. *Exclusive Books* is a more upmarket chain with branches in most shopping centres. *Clarke's Bookshop*, 211 Long St, T4235739. A mass of antiquarian, second-hand and new books, a must for any book lover. *Jeffrey Sharpe*, Alfred Mall, Victoria Wharf, T4254641. Africana and antiquarian maps. *AA of South Africa*, T0861111994. *The Map Studio*, Struik House, 80 McKenzie Rd, Gardens, T4624360. Tourist maps of towns and regions as well as official survey maps.

Books & maps

Most of the better clothes chains and small boutiques are in Cape Town's shopping malls. Particularly popular with the young and well-heeled are the units in Victoria Wharf, at the

Clothes

Waterfront, T4182369, and Cavendish Square, in Claremont, T6743050. Prices here are marginally cheaper than back home. Long St and Kloof St are good bets for more alternative clothes – notables include *Scar*, on Long St, *the* place to head for quirky one-off designs and *Colour Kissis*, next to the Lifestyles centre at the bottom of Kloof St, T4265223, has trendy accessories, T-shirts and bags. *Second Time Around*, 196 Long St, T4231674, is great for 1950s and 60s clothes, and *The Stock Exchange*, 116 Kloof St, T4245971, is good for second-hand designer labels.

Markets   *Church St Market*, antiques, between Long and Burg Sts, Mon-Sat, most interesting pieces shown on Fri and Sat. *Grand Parade Market*, a general market selling clothes, fabrics and flowers, which takes over the large parade ground in front of the old City Hall, 0800-1400, Wed and Sat. *Greenmarket Square*, a lively flea market on a picturesque cobbled square, formerly a fruit and vegetable market, flanked by several terrace cafés, Mon-Fri 0800-1700, Sat 0800-1400. *Green Point Market*, beside Green Point stadium, 0800-1700 Sun only, good mixture of curios, plenty of buskers. *Waterfront Explorers Market*, The Red Shed, not as interesting as other markets, weekends only.

Health   *The Sunflower*, 161 Long St, T4246560, health café serving wholesome snacks, herbal reme-
foods   dies and vitamins. *Vitamin Express*, King's Warehouse, Waterfront, T4252819, also in Caven-
dish Sq in Claremont, herbal remedies, fruit drinks and herb teas. *Wholefood Store*, 73 Lower Main Rd, Observatory, mainly nuts and dried fruit, plus aromatherapy oils.

Music   *Musica* is the biggest music shop chain, selling all the latest CDs, videos and DVDs, and can be found in every shopping centre and along high streets. For African music, head to *The African Music Store*, 90a Long St, T4260857, africanmusic@sybaweb.co.za The shop stocks an excellent choice of albums by major Southern African artists as well as compilations and reggae. The staff are incredibly helpful and are happy to let you listen to any number of CDs before purchasing. Recommended.

Supermarkets   Each of the suburbs has its own shopping complex with a branch of one of the major supermarket chains – *Pick 'n' Pay*, *Chequers*, *Shoprite*, *OK Bazaar* and *Spar*. For high-quality groceries try the *Woolworths Stores*, which are much the same as *Marks & Spencer's* in Britain, with the equivalent price premium.

Sports

With its equitable climate and outdoor lifestyle, Cape Town is a great place to try a wide vari-
ety of adventure sports and activities. Most of the backpacker hostels promote a huge choice of activities, particularly the more strenuous and action-packed such as kloofing, abseiling, paragliding and the ubiquitous bungee. One of the best places to visit and find out about all the options on offer is a store called *Adventure Village*, 229 Long St, T4241580, www.adven-
ture-village.co.za By all accounts this is a very friendly and helpful outfit which can organize courses and transportation. Most of what is on offer here is the same as what's available through a backpackers, but the advice and knowledge on hand is superior.

Abseiling   *Abseil Africa*, T4241580. Operates the world's highest and longest commercial abseil –
112 m down Table Mountain.

Bungee   Most of the area's bungee jumps are along the Garden Route, but true adrenaline junkies can
jumping   jump from the Table Mountain Cable Car. Call T4245148 for more information.

Cricket   In the southern suburb of Newlands is the famous Cape Town test match ground named after the suburb. Despite considerable redevelopment, a few of the famous old oak trees remain and it is still possible to watch a game from a grassy bank with Table Mountain as a backdrop. Don't be too put off by the brewery chimneys in the foreground. Some of the public seats are very exposed – if you are fair skhinned, wear a hat and have plenty of suncream

to hand. *Newlands*, PO Box 23401, Claremont 7735, 161 Camp Ground Rd, Newlands. Ticket enquiries: T6836420, F6834934, www.wpca.cricket.org The opening match of the 2003 Cricket World Cup will be held in Cape Town.

The most common catches are mako shark, long fin tuna and yellowtail, but there are strict rules governing all types of fishing. The simplest way of dealing with permits and regulations is by booking through a charter company. *Big Game Fishing Safaris*, T6742203, skipper@gamefish.co.za 12 m catamaran, daily excursions including crayfish lunch, specializes in tuna and swordfish fishing. *Nauticat Chaters*, T7907278, nauticat@mweb.co.za Game fishing and boat charters. *Waterfront Charters*, T4180134, www.waterfrontcharters.co.za Based on the V & A Waterfront. **Fishing**

Expect to pay green fees of around R120-200 for 18 holes. The following is a selection of the golf clubs which are open to overseas visitors. *Metropolitan Golf Club*, Mouille Point, T4347808. 9-holes. *Milnerton Golf Club*, Bridge Rd, Milnerton, T5521047, F5515897. Length: 6,011 m, par 72. Green fees about R120. This is a true links course in the shadow of Table Mountain, watch your par when the wind blows. A popular course set between the Atlantic Ocean and a river. *Mowbray Golf Club*, Ratenberg Rd, Mowbray, T6853018, www.moybraygolfclub.co.za One of the oldest clubs, hosts national championships, a par 74 course with plenty of trees, bunkers and water holes. *Rondebosch Golf Club*, Klipfontein, Rondebosch, T6894176, rgc@mweb.co.za A tidy course with the Black River flowing through it. *Royal Cape Golf Club*, 174 Ottery Rd, Wynberg, T7616551, F7975246. Length: 6,174 m, par 74. Expect to pay about R200 for green fees. An old course which has been the venue for major professional tournaments. **Golf**
For further details contact the Western Province Golf Union, T6861668, F6861669

There are 29 flying sites close to the city. For details contact the *Cape Albatross Hang-gliding Club*, PO Box 342, Sea Point, 8000, T4239021; *Two Oceans Paragliding Club*, T4248967, T083-4637113 (mob). **Hang-gliding & paragliding**

SA Mountain Guides Association, T4478036. Can organize personal guides. *Due South*, T083-2584824 (mob), www.hikesandtours.co.za Ask for John Shardlow. Organize half- and full-day walking trips up Table Mountain. Rates include transport to/from the start point for your hike, snacks and water, and a packed lunch on full-day hikes. Take note of advice given for hiking on the mountain; bad preparation can spoil a walk for yourself as well as others in your group. Expect to pay upwards of R175 per person. *Peninsula Ramblers*, T7154434, www.ramblers.co.za. Organizes variety of hikes around the peninsula, mix of relaxed rambles with picnics and strenuous hikes. **Hiking**

There are plenty of interesting riding trails around the city, and Nordhoek Beach is especially popular at sundown. *Horse Trails Safaris*, T7034396, F7031417. *Nordhoek Beach Horse Rides*, T082-7741191 (mob), www.horseriding.co.za *Sleepy Hollow Horse Riding*, T7892341, T083-2610104 (mob). **Horse riding**

The Cape's strong winds have made it a very popular site for kitesurfing. The best spot is Dolphin Beach at Table View, north of the city centre where winds are strong and waves perfect for jumping. If you're new to the sport, contact the *Cape Sports Centre*, T0227221114, www.capesports.co.za, in Langebaan for advice on equipment and tuition. **Kitesurfing**

Kloofing (canyoning) involves hiking, boulder-hopping and swimming along mountain rivers. It is very popular on and around Table Mountain; many of the tour companies listed below (page 124) organize daily excursions. **Kloofing**

Bikeabout, T5547763. For equipment hire and route advice. *Downhill Adventures*, T4220388, downhill@mweb.co.za Rent out bikes and organize tours on Table Mountain, Cape Point Nature Reserve and the Winelands. *Pedal Power Association*, T6898420. **Mountain biking**

Cape Town

Mountain climbing *Mountain Club of South Africa*, 97 Hatfield St (close to the Jewish museum), T4653412, F4618456. Good source of information on climbing here and throughout South Africa.

Rugby International games are played at the *Western Province Rugby Football Union* ground, Boundary Rd, Newlands, T6894921. Tickets for major games can be bought through *Computicket*, T9188910.

Sailing Regattas are regularly held in Table Bay. The following clubs are for members only, but they do accommodate visitors if they are a member of an affiliated international club: *Royal Cape Yacht Club*, T4211354, *False Bay Yacht Club*, T7861703 and *Hout Bay Yacht Club*, T7903110.

Sandboarding Try the latest addition to board sports on sand dunes. It is not a very fast sport and can be frustrating if you're used to snow, but it can be a fun day out. *Downhill Adventures*, T4220388, downhill@mweb.co.za Organize day trips to dunes about an hour from Cape Town.

Scuba diving The Cape waters are cold but are often very clear and good for wreck and reef diving. A number of dive operators also specialize in great white shark cage dives along the coast. Daily dive report: T082-2346320 (mob). *Dusky Dive Academy*, T4261622. Beginner's instruction. *Two Ocean Divers International*, 1 Central Parade, Victoria Rd, Camps Bay, T/F7908833, www.two-oceans.co.za Full range of PADI-recognized instruction and equipment hire, as well as organized tours to the best dive sites and great white shark cage dives. *Table Bay Diving*, V & A Waterfront, T4198822, spero@netactive.co.za Organizes night diving, wreck dives and seal dives and sell scuba gear.

Skydiving *Cape Parachute Club*, T5588514. Offers tandem jumps on the West Coast. *Citrusdal Parachute Club*, T4625666. Organizes jumps and offers static line courses in Citrusdal.

Snooker & pool *Rolling Stones*, popular pool bar chain with branches on Long St, Observatory and Claremont, plenty of tables, loud music, good atmosphere, open till late.

Surfing Surfing is a serious business in Cape Town, and there are excellent breaks catering for learners right through to experienced surf rats. Some of the best breaks are on Long Beach, Kommetjie, Noordhoek, Llandudno, Kalk Bay, Muizenberg and Bloubergstrand. Daily surf report: T7881350. *Downhill Adventures*, T4220388, downhill@mweb.co.za Organize day and multi-day courses as well as "Secret Surf Spots" tours. *Adventure Village*, T4241580, www.adventure-village.co.za Offer good surfing advice. Otherwise, the best people to ask are local surfers or at surf shops.

Swimming The beaches on the Atlantic Seaboard are almost always too cold to swim in – even during the hottest months, the water temperatures rarely creep above 16°C. False Bay, however, is always a good 5°C warmer, and is perfectly pleasant for a dip during summer. Additionally, a number of beaches have artificial rock pools built by the water, which although rather murky can be perfect for paddling children. There are some very good municipal swimming pools in Cape Town, in Newlands, Sea Point and Woodstock. All are open air and with views of the mountain.

Tennis *Green Point Lawn Tennis Club*, Vlaenberg St, T4349527. Casual popular courts. *River Club Centre*, Liesbeek Parkway, Observatory, T4486117. Friendly club, no equipment hire, book in advance. The *Western Province Tennis Association*, T6863055. Can provide details of clubs and competitions.

Windsurfing Langebaan has the best reputation for surfable winds on the Cape; the southeasterly roars between Sep and Apr. In Mar there is a Boardsailing Marathon in False Bay, while Big Bay at Blouberg is a good spot for wave-jumping. Daily windsurf report: T082-2346324 (mob). Contact *Windsurfari*, Blouberg, T082-4499819 (mob); *Cape Sports Centre*, Langebaan Lagoon, T0227721114, www.capesports.co.za; *International Windsurfer Sailing Schools*, T7972824.

Tours and tour operators

Cape Town's layout can be quite confusing, especially if you're staying in the suburbs or along one of the seaboards. When you first arrive, it's a good idea to join a city tour in an open top bus to get a feel for the city's layout and what each district has to offer. Cape Town Tourism owns the **Explorer Bus**, a double-decker topless bus which follows a 2-hr route around the city. Contact the main tourist office for details, T4264260. *Elwierda Topless Tours*, T4185888, also organizes a 2-hr city tour. Buses depart hourly between 0940 and 1440, starting from the Waterfront.

City Centre tours

Grassroute Tours, T7061006, F7050798, www.grassroutetours.com Specializes in township tours beginning in District Six and continuing to Langa and Khayelitsha, also History of Cape Muslims tour. This company works with the communities it visits, putting back some of the proceeds. Half day tours cost around R225. Recommended. *Western Cape Action Tours*, T4611371, F4614387, wcat@iafrica.com Township tours with a strong focus on political issues, with visits to historically significant sights, discussions are encouraged, tours are led by people who took part in the liberation struggle. More thought-provoking and less voyeuristic than most other tours. Half-day tours R180. Recommended. *Tana-Baru Tours*, T4240719. Specialist tours of the Cape Malay Quarter lasting 2 hours led by Shereen Habib, interesting and good value, expect to pay about R80 per person. Also township tours which last 3 hrs and cost from R250. *Thuthuka Tours*, T4392061, www.townshipcrawling.com Specializes in township tours, half-day walking tours, music tours in the evening, Xhosa folklore tours. *Roots Africa Tours*, T9878330, F9885641, www.rootsafrica.co.za Khayelitsha township tours, Winelands, Robben Island trips.

Cultural tours

Condor Charters, T4191780. Harbour tours in a luxury motor yacht, fully equipped for private parties, leaves from in front of Quay Four. *Hylton Ross*, T5111784, F5112401, www.hyltonross.co.za 30 mins and 1 hr Waterfront cruises. *'Spirit of Victoria'*, T4191780. A 58-ft Graff rigged Schooner, a stylish way to explore the harbour and the bay, German and French spoken. *Tigresse Cruises*, T4241455. Daily departures from the Waterfront, sunset cruises and day trips in a fine modern sailing boat, booking advised during peak periods. *Waterfront Charters*, Quay 5, V&A Waterfront, T4180134, sales@waterfrontcharters.co.za Offers a variety of boat trips in and around the harbour. Champagne Sunset cruise every evening, duration 90 mins. Harbour Tour, 1400, a chance to see the city from the water, plus the operational International Docks.

Boat tours
Also see page 92 for Robben Island Tours

Chilwans, T9344786, F9344868. *Elwierda Tours*, T4185888. Full-day tours to Cape Point and Peninsula. *Hylton Ross*, T5111784, F5112401, www.hyltonross.co.za Full and half day tours to Cape Point, historic city tours, Winelands tours. *Intercape Travel Tours*, T3864444, F3864453. *Mother City Tours*, T4483817, F4483844. Full and half day Peninsula tours. *Springbok Atlas*, T4604700, F4480003.

Coach tours

Other tour operators

See also tour operators listed in the Gay and lesbian section, page 117

Bikeabout, T5547763, mountain biking along some of the most beautiful coast in the Cape, tours organized to Cape Point, Chapman's Peak and Stellenbosch, bicycle and helmets provided, involves on average 25 km of riding. **Day Trippers**, 8 Pineway, Pinelands, T5313274, T082-8079522 (mob), www.daytrippers.co.za Active tours popular with backpackers, good value day trips as well as longer tours to the Cedarberg and the Karoo. Recommended. **Downhill Adventures**, T4220388, downhill@mweb.co.za Rent out bikes and organize tours on Table Mountain, Cape Point Nature Reserve and the Winelands. **Elwierda Tours**, T4185888. Town tours in an open top bus, plus longer trips to the Winelands and Cape of Good Hope. **Felix Unite**, 141 Lansdowne Rd, Claremont, T6836433, F6836486. Tours use 10-seater a/c minibuses, full and half day tours to Winelands and Cape Point, expert guides who are essential when exploring the unique plant life of the Cape. Recommended. **Greencape Tours**, T/F7970166, greencap@gem.co.za Specialist Natural History trips run by Bruce Terlien who has a keen interest in the flora and fauna of the Cape, maximum group size is 7. **Legend Tours**, T6974056, F6974090, www.legendtourism Usual selection of trips around Cape Town – Winelands, Cape Flats, Peninsula, Table Mountain, Cape Point and Waterfront, free collection from your accommodation. **Mother City Tours**, T4483817, F4483844. Good selection of different trips, price includes entrances and wine tastings, full and half day options. **Namibian Tourist Office**, Main Tower, Standard Bank Building, Hertzog Blvd, T4193190, F4215840. If you are planning a trip to Namibia it is well worth picking up a copy of the government guide to hotels and national parks accommodation. (See Footprint's *Namibia Handbook*). **One World Travellers Space**, 309 Long St, T/F4230777. Excellent travel shop which can organize good value township tours, car hire and any other adventures you might have in mind, helpful and friendly, the shop also has a great African music selection, recommended by several readers. **Protea Travels**, T9351427, proteaaf@iafrica.com City centre and regional tours. **Quagga Tours**, T4612231. A privately run tour company which will create itineraries to suit your interests. **SATOUR**, Tijgerpark, Willie Van Schoor Av, Durbanville, T9487830, F9487809. **NB** This office is not in Cape Town. Durbanville is a suburb off the N1 heading towards Paarl. **Union Limited Steam Rail Tours**, Spoornet Building, 1 Adderley St, T4494391, F4494395. Luxury travel on beautifully restored steam trains, most popular route is to Knysna via the Winelands (6 days from US$600 fully inclusive), longer tours are also organized to Pretoria, good standards of service and food, the ultimate treat. **Vineyard Ventures**, 5 Hanover Rd, Fresnaye, T4348888, F4349999.

Transport

Local

See also Ins and outs on page 74

See page 43 for further advice on car hire and driving in South Africa

Car hire Cape Town and the surrounding Winelands are best explored in a hired car. The list below should be treated as a guide and starting point to arranging hire. At quiet times prices should be considerably cheaper than around Dec and Jan. The cheapest local car hire companies change frequently – it's a good idea to check at backpacker hostels to see which ones they recommend. Two important points to note is where you plan on driving and where you want to drop off the car. It makes sense to deal with a large nationwide company if you intend to drive across the country and end your journey in Johannesburg. All of the large firms now have toll free phone numbers which can be dialled from anywhere within South Africa.

Adelphi Car Rental, 94 Main Rd, Sea Point, T4396144, F4395093, adelphi@intekom.co.za **Atlantic Car Hire**, T9344600, F9344549, T082-9004278 (mob). **Avis**, 123 Strand St, T4241177, F4233601, T0800-021111, www.avis.com **Best Boland Motors**, T9814113, original VW Beetles. **Brights**, 13 Foregate Sq, T4252687, Foreshore. Good value small company. **Budget**, 63 Strand St, T0860-016622, www.budget.com **Cape Car Hire**, 217 Lansdowne Rd, Claremont, T6832441, F6832443, www.capecarhire.co.za **Europcar**, 33 Heerengracht, Foreshore, T4180670, F4180609. **Hertz**, 371 Main Rd, Sea Point, T4391144, F4394031, T0800-600136, www.hertz.com **Imperial**, Strand St, T4215190, F4252382, T0800-131000. **Tempest**, Wale & Buitengracht streets, T4245000, F4244190.

The following companies have a kiosk in one of the airport terminals. Their main offices and depot are to the left when you exit the arrivals building. *Avis*, T9340330, T0800-021111, www.avis.com *Budget*, T9340216, F9340151. *Europcar*, T9342263, F9346620. *Hertz*, T4221515, F4221703. *Imperial*, T3863239, F3863240. *Tempest*, T9343845, F9343853.

Camper van and motor home hire   Almost every town in South Africa has a private or municipal campsite and caravan park. During the local school holidays the popular parks are fully
booked, including the sites reserved for tents only. To take advantage of these excellent value
facilities, you can hire a Camper van or Motor home. The daily hire rates are on average double the
rate for a family saloon car. The hire price should include all bedding, cooking utensils and crockery. If you plan ahead, this can work out as a cheap and enjoyable way of seeing rural South Africa.
Britz Africa, Old Paarl Rd, Brackenfell, T9818947, F9818946. A good choice of 2-5 berth vehicles.
Camper King, T083-4502928 (mob), F5580797, www.camperking.co.za Campers and motor
homes. *Maui Camper Hire*, T9825107. Stocks similar vehicles.

Minibus taxis   These serve all areas of the city on fixed routes, and leave from the minibus
terminal accessed from the top floor of the Sanlam Golden Acre shopping centre on
Adderley St. They can also be flagged down from the street. Minibuses to the Atlantic coast
usually leave from outside OK Bazaar's on Adderely St. Most trips cost R2.50-R3. Buses stop
running at 1900. Unlike in many South African cities, these are generally safe to use, although
you'd be advised to do your best not to look like a tourist and leave all valuables at home.

Taxis   There are several ranks dotted around town – the most useful ones are outside the
train station at Adderley St, by the *Holiday Inn* on Greenmarket Sq, and on Long St. You can
also flag down any that you see cruising around. If you are outside the city centre, you will
have to call one in advance. Be sure to get a quote as prices can vary a lot. See also Airport
information below. *Dalhouzie Taxis*, T9194659/9192834, *Marine Taxis*, T4340434, *Unicab*,
T4481720. **Rikki taxis**   These small shared people-carriers are a cheaper alternative to getting around the city. You need to call one, but they pick up several people along the route,
bringing down costs. T4234888.

Metro trains   *Metrorail*, T0800-656463, serve the suburbs. Services run as far as Simon's
Town, but also go out as far as Worcester. Unfortunately, they do not allow bicycles on trains.
We have received conflicting reports as to how safe these trains are; one reader wrote that "it
is essential to travel only in first class carriages". We do not agree with this, but if you are concerned for your safety it is worth noting that each station has signs as to where the first class
carriage will be when the train comes in. It is probably safest to only use the trains at peak
times when all carriages and classes are busy.
  To **Simon's Town**, Mon-Fri: first train departs **Cape Town** at 0529, then approx every 15
mins until 1930. Sat: first train departs at 0529 then approx every 20 mins until 1824.
  To **Cape Town**, Mon-Fri: first train departs **Simon's Town** at 0533, then approx every 25
mins until 1958. Sat: first train departs at 0633 then approx every 35 mins until 1858. Check
times as these change frequently.

Air   Cape Town International Airport, formerly known as DF Malan, has both international and domestic terminals. These are 20 mins' drive from the city centre, 22 km. Within
the terminal building, **Western Cape Tourism** can help with finding any type of accommodation (hotel, guesthouse, self-catering, backpackers), open 0700-1700. The Trust Bank
exchange counter remains open for international arrivals. You can also hire mobile phones at
several outlets here. Look out for joint deals between car hire companies and mobile phone
companies. **Transport to/from airport** *Airport Shuttle Service*, T082-3509956 (mob).
Good value for more than one, rates vary according to number of people and suburb – service extends as far as Simon's Town and Kommetjie, minimum charge of R40, only use for
travel to or from the airport. *Backpackers Shuttle*, T4260294, T083-2656661 (mob),
www.extremeadventures.co.za 24-hr, collects from central hostels, expect to pay between
R35-R90 to the airport, depending on time and number of passengers. *Intercape Shuttle*,
T9340802. Every 30 mins to the train station on Adderley St, or any hotel in the Cape Peninsula. *Mayfly*, T4261641. Private passenger service which does airport runs along with tours
around Cape Town. Any **taxis** running between the airport and town centre should have a
special airport licence and they must use their meter by law. Expect to pay up to R250 to
hotels in the centre of town by taxi.

Long distance

Airport enquiries:
T9340407,
www.airports.co.za
Airport departure tax
is normally included
in the ticket price

Cape Town

Domestic routes *Comair*, T08600-11747, and *British Airways*, T080600-11747, 8 flights/day to **Johannesburg**, slightly fewer at the weekend. *National Airlines*, T9340350, F9343373, have 3 weekly flights to **Springbok**, a useful service if you wish to view the wild flowers in spring but are short of time. *Sabena Nationwide*, T9348101, F9348106, daily flights to **Johannesburg**, check for competitive rates.

The following details are a brief summary of the routes operated by *South Africa Airways*, *SA Express* and *SA Airlink*. For enquiries and reservations, T9361111. **Bloemfontein** (2 hrs): Mon-Fri, 1-3 flights/day; **Durban** (2 hrs non-stop): 5-8 flights/day; **East London** (2 hrs): 4 flights a week; **George** (1 hr): Mon-Fri 5 flights/day, Sat and Sun 2-4 flights/day; **Johannesburg** (2 hrs): up to 25 flights a day; **Kimberley** (2 hrs): Mon-Fri 2 flights/day, Sun 1 flight; **Plettenberg Bay** (1 hr): 1 flight/week (Sun); **Port Elizabeth** (1 hr): Mon-Fri 4 flights/day, Sat & Sun 3 flights/day.

International routes (*South African Airways*) Most of these stop in Johannesburg. **Amsterdam**: daily except Sun; **Bangkok**: Mon, Thu, Sat; **Copenhagen**: Wed and Sun; **Frankfurt**: 2 daily; **London**: daily; **New York**: daily except Sun, links to all other major cities in US; **Paris**: 4 weekly; **Walvis Bay**: daily; **Windhoek**: twice daily.

Rail Cape Town has one main railway station in the centre of town. Both long distance and suburban services leave from here. Leaflets with train times and fare structure are available in the concourse. The rail network is known as *Spoornet*, www.spoornet.co.za Always check for seasonal discounts, especially for students around local holiday times. **Sales & Ticket Offices**: Cape Town, T086-0008888; Pretoria, T012-3348470; Johannesburg, T011-7732944; Nelspruit, T013-7529257; Kimberley, T053-8382631; Port Elizabeth, T041-5072400. Left luggage on platform 24, T4052611. Open Mon 0800-1900, Tue-Thu 0800-1600, Fri 0600-1800. Lost property, T4052887.

Principal destinations are served by the services known as 'Name Trains'. On these services all 1st and 2nd class tickets must be pre-booked. This can be done up to 3 months in advance. At the time of booking you can specify whether you want non-smoking berths and upper or lower bunks. No advance reservations necessary for 3rd Class. It is also possible to book via the internet at www.spoornet.co.za There are also several 'luxury' train services which operate between Cape Town and a few popular tourist sights along with Johannesburg / Pretoria (see Gauteng chapter for details). The distances involved are vast: 1,004 km to Bloemfontein; 1,753 km to Durban; 1,122 km to East London; 640 km to Graaff-Reinet; 1,402 km to Johannesburg; 962 km to Kimberley; 656 km to Namibian border (*Vioolsdrif*); 769 km to Port Elizabeth; 1,948 km to Zimbabwe border (*Beitbridge*).

The *Blue Train* is South Africa's premier luxury train, with trips to **Pretoria** which run approx 3 times a week. They also have monthly trips to **Port Elizabeth**. T4494020, www.bluetrain.co.za

The *Southern Cross* service departs Fri at 1815 for **Oudtshoorn** (15 hrs), via **Robertson** (4 hrs), **Swellendam** (6 hrs), and **George** (9 hrs). The return service departs Oudtshoorn on Suns and arrives back in Cape Town on Mon morning. T086-0008888, www.spoornet.co.za

The *Trans Oranje* service departs Mon at 1850 for **Durban** (36 hrs), via **Beaufort West** (7½ hrs), **Ladysmith** (31 hrs), and **Pietermaritzburg** (34 hrs). The return service departs Durban on Weds at 1730 and arrives back in Cape Town on Fri morning. T086-0008888, www.spoornet.co.za

The *Trans Karoo* service departs daily at 0920 for **Johannesburg** (28 hrs) and **Pretoria** (26½ hrs) via **Kimberley** (10½ hrs). T086-0008888, www.spoornet.co.za

If the only bus journey you plan on making is between Cape Town and Durban, with no stops, the Greyhound ticket is half the price of the Baz Bus

Road Bus: *Greyhound*, *Intercape* and *Translux* all depart/arrive from Adderley St, next to Cape Town railway station. Booking offices are also here. There is a taxi rank outside the train station on Adderley St.

Greyhound, 1 Adderley St, T5056363, www.greyhound.co.za Online booking available. **Bloemfontein** (9 hrs): daily, 1745; **Durban** (26 hrs): daily, 1945, via coastal route; **East London** (17 hrs): daily, 1945; **George** (7 hrs): daily, 0645, 1945; **Johannesburg** and **Pretoria** (18 hrs): daily, 1745, 2000; **Kimberley** (13 hrs): daily, 2000; **Knysna** (7 hrs): daily, 0645, 1945; **Port Elizabeth** (11 hrs): daily, 0645, 1945.

Intercape, T3804400, F3862488, www.intercape.co.za Reservations must be made 72 hrs before any departure. Online reservations available. **Port Elizabeth** (10 hrs): daily 0700, 1830, via the N2 stopping at most Garden Route towns. **Johannesburg** and **Pretoria** (15½ hrs): daily, 1730, via the N1. The service on Mon and Sat is via **Kimberley**, not Bloemfontein. There is also a day service twice a week, this is convenient if travelling as far as Bloemfontein or Kimberley, but it arrives at 2300 in Johannesburg. Unless you have arranged to be picked up from the bus station we recommend taking an alternative service arriving at a more convenient time. **Bloemfontein** (12 hrs): Sun, 0700; **Kimberley** (11 hrs): Thu, 0700; **Johannesburg** and **Pretoria** (17 hrs): Thu and Sun, 0700. **Upington** (10½ hrs): Mon, Wed, Fri, Sun, 1900. **Windhoek** (16½ hrs): Tue, Thu, Fri, Sun, 1230, via the N7 at the following West Coast towns, (journey time from Cape Town): **Citrusdal**, (2½ hrs), **Clanwilliam** (3 hrs), **Vanrhynsdorp** (4 hrs), **Springbok** (7 hrs), **Noordoewer** – Namibian border (8 hrs). Coach also stops at **Keetmanshoop** and several smaller towns in Namibia before arriving in Windhoek at 0645 the next morning. **NB** It is your responsibility to have all the correct visas and passport necessary to enter Namibia.

Translux, T4493333, T0117743333, www.translux.co.za Online reservations available. **Beaufort West** (6 hrs): daily, 1000, 1300. **Bloemfontein** (13 hrs): daily, 1000, 1300. **Durban** (20 hrs): daily, 1000, 1800. **East London** (15½ hrs): daily, 1730, 1800; **Johannesburg** and **Pretoria** (19 hrs): daily, 1400, 1730. **Kimberley** (12 hrs): daily, 1730. **Knysna** (7½ hrs): daily, 0155, 0645. **Port Elizabeth** (12 hrs): daily, 0645, 1800 via Garden Route towns.

Budget buses: a good service for backpackers is the *Baz Bus*, 8 Rosedene Rd, Sea Point, T4392323, info@bazbus.com, www.bazbus.com This is a company that has seen off the competition – the *Walkabout Bus*, *Route 49* and *The Hopper Bus* – and continues to grow. They run between backpacker hostels, thus saving you the hassle of getting to a base at the end of your journey, plus they are a great way of meeting other travellers. There is no time limit to the tickets, and you are free to 'hop-on' and 'hop-off' as many times as you like. Daily service from Cape Town to Port Elizabeth. Service continues from Port Elizabeth to Lesotho, Durban, Swaziland, Johannesburg and Pretoria. The bus picks up from most hostels in town, so it can take a while before you are on the road. Note that if you plan on going straight through to Durban with a minimum of stops, it is cheaper to travel by the Greyhound coach service. See above for details. This is an excellent service, with a flexible price system, and for first time travellers or those on a tight budget and schedule probably the best way to see South Africa.

Directory

Air Namibia, T9362755. *Air Zimbabwe*, T9361186. *British Airways*, T T080600-11747. *Comair*, T9369000. *Egypt Air*, T4618056. *KLM*, Main Tower, Standard Bank Centre, T4211870, T9343495, F4182712. *Lufthansa*, T4153535, T9348534, F9345063. *Malaysia Airlines*, Safmarine House, 22 Riebeeck St, T4198010. *National Airlines*, T9340350, F9343373. *Olympic Airways*, 22 Riebeeck St, T4192502, F4211199. *Singapore Airlines*, 21 Dreyer St, Claremont, T6740601, F6740710. *South African Airways*, Southern Life Centre, 8 Riebeeck St, reservations: T9361111, F4055944. *Swissair*, T9348101. **Airline offices**

There are plenty of 24-hr cash machines (ATMs) throughout the city, making it easy to remain cash rich. There are also a number of banks where you can cash traveller's cheques. All the main branches are open weekdays 0830-1530 and Sat 0800-1100. The following telephone numbers are for the principal branches in Cape Town city centre (Adderley St). *ABSA*, T4801911; *First National Bank*, T4232202; *Standard Bank*, T4017500; *Trust Bank*, T4234080. **Banks** *Only change money in hotels as a last resort: their exchange rates are unbelievably poor*

There are two main bureaux de change. *Amex*, Thibault House, Thibault Square, T4089700, who will receive and hold mail for card holders, open Mon-Fri 0830-1700, Sat 0900-1200. They have a second office at the Victoria and Alfred Waterfront in Alfred Mall, T4193917, open until 1900 on weekdays and 1700 weekends. *Rennies Travel* (Thomas Cook representatives), Southern Life Centre, 2 St Georges Mall, T4181206, open Mon-Fri, 0830-1700, Sat, 0900-1200, also have a branch at the Waterfront, on the upper level of Victoria Wharf, T4183744. *Rennies Travel* also provides all the usual services of a travel agent.

Communica- Internet access is available at backpacker hostels, Postnet branches (see below) and at the main
tions tourist office. *Virtual Turtle* is a popular chain of 24-hr internet cafés, with branches at 303a Long St,
T4237508, 12 Mill St, Gardens, T4260470 and 1st floor Purple Turtle building, Short Market St,
T4241037. *M@in Online*, in the Lifestyles centre at the bottom of Kloof St, Gardens, has plenty of
computers and is fairly new so has low rates. There are also internet cafés in all the shopping centres,
including Victoria Wharf at the Waterfront. **Post** The *General Post Office* is between Parliament and
Plein Sts by the Golden Acre shopping centre. *Post Restante* is in the main hall, open 0800-1630, Sat
0800-1200. There is a separate entrance for parcels in Plein St. Regional Office, T5905400. Post offices
are found in all the suburbs close to the principal shopping centres. **Courier Service**: *Citi-Sprint*, 105
Strand St, T4247131. **Telephone** International Enquiries, T0903; Local Enquiries, T1023; Weather
Enquiries, T082162. *Postnet* is a useful chain found throughout the city, usually in shopping malls. The
main branch is in the Union Castle Building, 6 Hout St, T4260179, F4260078. Services include sending
parcels, internet access, fax sending and receiving, phonecards, passport photos, open Mon-Fri
0830-1700, Sat 0830-1300.

Embassies & Most foreign representatives have their head offices in either Pretoria or Johannesburg, but many
consulates countries also have representatives in Cape Town and Port Elizabeth. *Australia*, 14th Floor, BP Centre,
Thibault Square, T4195425. *Belgium*, Vogue House, Thibault Square, T4194690. *Canada*, Reserve Bank
Building, 30 Hout St, T4235240. *Denmark*, Southern Life Centre, Riebeeck St, T4196936. *Finland*,
Lincoln Rd, Oranjezicht, T4614732. *France*, 2 Dean St Gardens, T4231575. *Germany*, 825 St Martini
Gardens, Queen Victoria St, T4242410. *India*, The Terraces, 34 Bree St, T4198110. *Israel*, Church Square
House, Plein St, T4657205. *Italy*, 2 Greys Pass, Gardens, T4241256. *Japan*, Main Tower, Standard Bank
Centre, Heerenracht, T4251695. *Mozambique*, 45 Castle St, T4262944, visas issued within 24 hrs.
Namibia, Main Tower, Standard Bank Building, corner of Adderley St and Hertzog Blvd, T4193190.
Netherlands, 100 Strand St, T4215660. *Portugal*, Standard Bank Centre, Herzog Blvd, T4180080.
Russian Federation, Southern Live Centre, Hertzog Blvd, T4183656. *Spain*, 37 Short Market St,
T4222415. *Sweden*, 10th Floor, Southern Life Centre, 8 Riebeeck St, T4253988. *Switzerland*, 1 Thibault
St, Long St, T4183669. *UK*, Southern Life Centre, 8 Riebeeck St, T4617220. *USA*, 4th Floor, Broadway Ind
Centre, Heerengracht, T4214280. *Zimbabwe*, 55c Kuyper St, T4614710.

Media Cape Town has an English morning paper, the *Cape Times*, and an evening paper, the *Argus*. Both are
good sources of what's going on in the city, with daily listings and entertainment sections. There is also
a daily paper in Afrikaans, *Die Burger* and Xhosa. **Radio**: *Radio KFM*: 94.5 FM, contemporary music, mix
of old classics and new hits. *Radio Good Hope FM*: 94-97 FM, teenage pop music, current hits. *Radio
Lotus*: 97.8 FM, general Indian affairs and music.

Medical Ambulance: T10177. **Dentists and doctors**: these are listed in the telephone directory under 'Dental
Services Practitioners' and 'Medical Practitioners'. Also ask at your hotel reception. **Emergency pharmacies**:
Cape Town Station, Glengariff, Sea Point; *Southern Suburbs Pharmacy*, Belvedere Rd, Claremont;
Waterfront Pharmacy. **Hospitals**: casualty facilities available at: *Groote Schuur*, Observatory,
T4049111, 24 hrs; *Somerset*, Green Point, T4026911; *Tygerberg*, Bellville, T9384911; *Victoria*, Wynberg,
T7991111. **Mountain rescue**: T10111. **Opticians**: *Eyelights* and *Frames Unlimited* have branches
throughout the town. **Sea rescue**: T4493500.

Places of *Anglican*, St George's Cathedral, T424 7360; *Buddhist*, information line T6853371; *Dutch Reformed*,
worship information line T4249131; *Jewish*, Cape Town Hebrew Congregation, T4651405; *Muslim*, Muslim
Judicial Council (0830-1300), T6965150; *Roman Catholic*, St Mary's Cathedral, T4611167.

Useful services AIDS Counselling: T4003400. **Citizen's Advice Bureau**: T4617218. **Computicket**: T9188910 for
Police: T10111 nationwide theatre, concerts and sport events. **Crimestop**: T0800-111213. **South African National
Ambulance: T10177 Parks (SANPARKS)**: V&A Waterfront Office, Clock Tower Pier, (Old Bertie's Landing), Fish Quay.
Tourist Assistance T4222810, F4222816, reservations@parks-sa.co.za Open Mon-Fri, 0900-1645. Also have a desk at the
Police Unit: main tourist office and the V & A Waterfront tourist office. **Police**: T10111. **Stolen credit cards**: T080
T4182852/3 9534300. **Tourist Assistance Police Unit**: T4182853, based at the Tulbagh Centre, will help contact
Stolen credit cards: your consulate or embassy and can locate translators when required.
T080 9534300

Cape of Good Hope Nature Reserve

The Cape of Good Hope Nature Reserve was established to protect the unique flora and fauna of this stretch of coast. In 1928 the area was under threat from developers who were looking to build more seaside resorts. Fortunately the Smith family, who owned the farm which extended across the peninsula from Buffels Bay, were persuaded to sell their land to those in favour of a reserve. Shortly after, the Hare family who owned the farm Bloubergvlei also agreed to sell their land for a reserve. For a while Cape Town city council remained opposed to the idea despite the fact that it was clearly very popular amongst the majority of the population. On 11 April 1939 they finally saw the wisdom of the project and the reserve came into existence. Some game animals were introduced and the land has since been left to its own devices.

Colour map 4, grid C2

During the summer, Nov-Mar, conditions are often windy. Spring, Sep-Oct, is the best time to visit, when the wild flowers are in bloom

Cape Town

Ins and outs

Given the reserve's location at the southern tip of the peninsula, you can approach it in two directions: along the False Bay shoreline via Muizenberg and Simon's Town; or by the quieter M65 via Kommetjie and Scarborough. It is about 70 km from Cape Town centre to the reserve gates. There is no public transport to the reserve, although you can take a Rikki from Simon's Town (accessible by train). Ask on your outward journey about arrangements for the return leg.

Getting there
Emergency T4233210
(Kloof Nek Control)

From the entrance to the reserve take a left and follow the M65 along the edge of the reserve. After 8 km the road divides; the right turn winds over the Swartkopberge to Long Beach and Simon's Town. Known as Red Hill (M66), this is a quicker route back to Cape Town if your time is short. There are two picnic spots with braai facilities along here. The road to the left leads down to Scarborough, and then along the coast to Kommetjie, 18 km from the reserve gates. There is a pottery craft centre just after the junction, on the right.

Getting away

The park is open 0600-1800 Oct-Mar, 0700-1700 Apr-Sep. Entrance fee R25, T7018692, www.cpnp.co.za We strongly recommend you come with your own transport to see the reserve; alternatively, there are several companies that organize good day trips from the city. A funicular railway takes visitors up from the main car park to the original lighthouse where there are a series of paved footpaths and viewpoints: open 0800-1700; R12 adult return, R8 single, R4 child return. The walk is fairly steep and takes about 20 mins, depending on how fit you are. Next to the car park is the *Two Oceans Restaurant*, T7809010, www.two-oceans.co.za The menu is mainly seafood but there are also steaks, chicken dishes and salads. Between Dec-Mar it is advisable to book a table. There is also a takeaway cafeteria which sells hamburgers, sandwiches, cold drinks, tea and coffee, as well as an information centre, curio shop, toilets and telephones (card and coins).

Getting around
Several travellers have written in complaining about the lack of parking space and long delays on the railway. Try to avoid weekends during school holidays

Around the reserve

The Cape of Good Hope is an integral part of the Cape Floristic Kingdom, the smallest but richest of the world's six floral kingdoms. A frequently quoted statistic is that within the 7,750 ha of the reserve there are as many different plant species as there are in the whole of the British Isles. In addition to all this there are several different species of antelope: eland, bontebok, springbok, cape grysbok, red hartebeest and grey rhebok, as well as the elusive cape mountain zebra, snakes, tortoises and pesky baboons.

Flora & fauna

Although the strong winds and the low lying vegetation are not ideal for birds, over 250 species have been recorded here, of which about 100 are known to breed within the reserve. There are plenty of vantage points where you can watch open sea birds – you should expect to see the Cape gannet, shy albatross, sooty shearwater, white-chinned petrel, Sabine's gull and Cory's shearwater. In the Strandveld vegetation along the coast you can expect to see many fruit eating birds such as the southern boubou, Cape robin and bully canary. Around Sirkels Vlei

Cape Town

you will find some freshwater birds. Finally there are a couple of rarities: the white-rumped sandpiper from South America, macaroni penguins from Antarctica, and the purple gallinule from the US have all been seen within the reserve. The Vlei Museum issues a check list of 100 birds. Alongside each name is a code telling you the typical habitat and the bird's resident status. More information is available from the Cape Bird Club, T5590726.

Cape Point **Cape Point Lighthouse** is nothing special in itself, and is adorned with a fair amount of graffiti, but the climb up here is well worth it for the best view of Cape Point. On a clear day the ocean views stretching all around are very special. You can take the funicular to the top, but the 20 minute walk allows better views of the coast. There are plenty of viewpoints, linked up by a jumble of footpaths.

Cape of Good Hope Nature Reserve

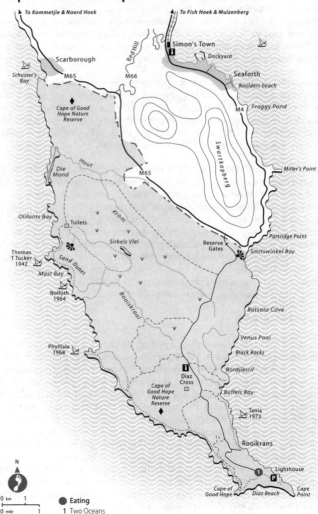

N

0 km 1
0 mile 1

● Eating
1 Two Oceans

The first lighthouse came into service in May 1860, but it quickly became apparent that the most prominent point on a clear day was far from ideal in poor weather. It was quite often shrouded in cloud while at sea level all was clear. In 1872 the Lighthouse Commission decided on a lower site, but it was only after the Portuguese ship, the *Lusitania*, struck Bellows Rock in April 1911, that work started on a new lighthouse. This was built just 87 m above sea level, close to Diaz Rock and remains the Cape's most important lighthouse today. The current beam can be seen up to 63 km out to sea, and 18 km out there is a red lamp which warns ships that they are in the danger zone.

From the top point of the railway there are still approximately 120 steps to the old lighthouse where you get some of the best views. If you are reasonably fit and have a good head for heights, there is a spectacular walk to the modern lighthouse at Diaz Point. From the renovated old lighthouse you can see the path running along the left side of the narrow cliff that makes up the point. The round trip takes about 30 minutes, but do not attempt if it is windy – the winds around the Cape can reach up to 55 knots (100 km per hour).

As you look down from the lighthouse at Cape Point it is easy to see how ships could suffer on a dark night in a storm, especially before the lighthouse was built. There are 23 wrecks in the waters around the Cape, but only five can be seen when walking in the reserve: *Thomas T Tucker*, 1942; *Nolloth*, 1964; *Phyllisia*, 1968; *Shir Yib*, 1970 (at Diaz Beach) and the *Tania*, 1972, the most recent wreck which can be seen at Buffel's Bay. The first wreck was the *Flying Dutchman* in 1680, which has since become famous as a ghost ship. The most famous sighting was by midshipman King George V in 1881.

Cape of Good Hope & Diaz Beach

Apart from visiting Cape Point and the Cape of Good Hope there are a few minor attractions dotted about the reserve as well as three excellent walks, probably the best way of appreciating the splendour of the coastline. You can drive down to the **Cape of Good Hope** and then walk to beautiful **Diaz Beach** via Maclear's Peak, a very steep walk in parts. You can also approach Diaz Beach via a 253-step staircase. **Diaz Cross**, further inland, is a memorial cross, although the original site is not known. Note how it is painted black on one side so that sailors can see it against the horizon.

Hiking

Hiking is encouraged within the reserve. There are several marked paths and maps are available from the Veld Museum. One of the most spectacular walks is along the coast from **Rooikrans** towards Buffels Bay. Look out for the wreck of *Tania*, 1972. On the west side close to **Olifants Bay** there are a couple of walks; one to the inland lake, **Sirkels Vlei**, the other along the coast where you can see the wrecks of the *Thomas Tucker*, 1942 and *Nolloth*, 1964. You can light a braai at one of the designated areas at Buffels Bay and Bordjiesrif.

False Bay

On the other side of the peninsula lies False Bay, a more popular stretch of coast thanks to the warmer waters – temperatures can be as much as 8°C higher. The area is also more sheltered and better developed for tourism, although certainly some of the landscape seems almost dull after the Atlantic Seaboard. Nevertheless, the area has some excellent beaches and is very popular with domestic tourists in summer. In spring, False Bay is the favoured haunt of calving whales, offering excellent opportunities of seeing southern right, humpback and bryde whales. There are also some interesting fishing villages which are well worth a visit.

Colour map 4, grid C2

Cape Town

Ins and outs

Getting there False Bay is easily accessed from the city centre by the M3. Alternatively, the Metro train line
& around continues through the southern suburbs to Simon's Town – the stretch following False Bay is
spectacular. Trains go as far as Simon's Town and leave approximately every 30 mins; some
have a good private restaurant car (called *Biggsy's*) serving drinks and meals – check with the
tourist office for times. The last train back leaves Mon-Fri at 2029, Sat, 2019, Sun, 2059, but
check as these change frequently. The *Golden Arrow* runs a bus service to and from
Adderely St: information, T9378800. There are only 2 routes across the mountainous spine
linking the roads which hug the coast around the peninsula: you can cross from Noordhoek
to Fish Hoek via the M65 and Sun Valley, or further south take the Red Hill road from
Scarborough to Simon's Town. Each route is convenient if your time is short, but the most
scenic route is to follow the M65 along the coast from the Atlantic Seaboard to False Bay. It is
impossible to get lost as there is only one road along the shoreline.

Muizenberg

Phone code: 021
(NB Always use
3-figure prefix)
Colour map 4, grid C2

Travelling out from the city centre, Muizenberg is the first settlement you reach
on False Bay and as such has always had potential as a local bathing spot. The settlement was first propelled to the forefront of popularity when **Cecil Rhodes**
bought a cottage here in 1899. Many other wealthy and famous people followed,
building some fine Victorian and Edwardian cottages along today's back streets.
Rudyard Kipling, a frequent visitor, wrote about the white sands of Muizenberg
in one of his poems. Today the town and its seafront have become rather rundown and cheesy, but the beach itself is beautiful: a vast stretch of powder-white
sand sloping gently to the water. It is safe for swimming as there is no backwash,
and it is easy for surfers. At low tide you can walk into the shallow sea for more
than 300 m without having to swim.

Beaches **Sunrise Beach**, 2 km to the east, is the most popular today. There are toilets, changing rooms and a snack kiosk here. Behind **West Beach** is a large red and white
striped pavilion built in the 1970s, a fun fair, mini golf, fast food outlets, and a collection of distinctive, colourful private bathing huts, reproductions of those built here
in the 19th century. Unfortunately these are let by the season, not the day or the
weekend. The beachfront extends for the full length of the town, and as you head
towards St James, the railway line runs between the beach and the main road.

Historic Mile The walk along the main street towards St James is known locally as the Historic
Mile and will take you past a number of interesting old buildings. Some of these
are national monuments, but not all are open to the public – a few are still private
homes. The first of note is the **Station building**, a fine example of Art Deco
architecture built in 1912. Further along is the **South African Police Museum**, a
rather dull collection housed in what is thought to be the oldest building on False
Bay, **Het Post Huijs**, built in the late 17th century. ■ *Mon-Fri 0800-1530,*
entrance by donation.

The **Natale Labia Museum**, at 192 Main Road, is part of the National Gallery and
houses a collection of works of art and furniture. It also acts as something of a cultural focal point, and regularly hosts lectures, readings, drawing classes and monthly
exhibitions. There is a café serving snacks and light lunches. Also of interest is the
house itself, built in 1929 as the official residence for Italy's diplomatic representative to South Africa, Prince Natale Labia. Designed in a Venetian style, the fittings
were all imported from Venice. ■ *Tue-Sun 1000-1700, closed Aug, R3; café open*
Tue-Sun 0930-1630. T7884106.

Rhodes Cottage, at number 246, is surprisingly small and austere for someone as
wealthy as Cecil Rhodes. It has been restored and now contains many of his personal
items and is a pleasant place to wander around, with a lovely garden at the front. This is

where he died on 26 March 1902, and his body was transported with great ceremony to the Matobo Hills outside Bulawayo in Zimbabwe, where he was buried in a giant rock outcrop. ■ *Mon-Sat, 0930-1630, Sun 1030-1630, free entrance. T7881816.*

Graceland is one of the largest and most impressive mansions along the coast. It was the home of John Garlick, a well-known merchant at the turn of the century. The house has a Spanish feel to it, with arched balconies and glazed clay roof tiles. Unfortunately the house is not open to the public. Just before you reach St James you pass another grand house, with palm trees in the garden, known as **Stonehenge**. Built in the style of an Italian villa this house once belonged to HP Rudd of De Beers Consolidated Mines.

Hiking

There are several paths leading from the back of the town into the Kalk Bay Mountains and the Silvermine Nature Reserve. If you don't have your own transport, consider doing these walks in reverse – then you can end the day on the beach close to restaurants, bars and most importantly get a train back to Cape Town. However, to get to the main entrances of the nature reserve you will probably have to rely on hitching a lift.

The following walks are written up in detail in Shirley Brossy's book (see page 136). Turn right out of the station onto the main road, then left into Camp Road. There is a short walk up the hill to Boyes Drive which runs along the hillside above Muizenberg. Turn left onto Boyes Drive and look out for some steps over the wall a few metres along the road. This marks the start of two paths; to the right takes you up **Pecks Valley** and on to **Muizenberg Peak** (507 m), a steady climb that should take about two hours. You will pass a couple of small waterfalls on the way up.

If you take the left trail from the wall, the path follows the contours for a while before turning up a stepped footpath along **Mimetes Valley**. At the top of this valley (a two-hour walk) you will meet a jeep track. A right turn at a crossroads takes you to **Nellie's Pool** and **Muizenberg Cave**, both of which can easily be reached from the entrance to the eastern sector of Silvermine Reserve (see below).

Sleeping
Price codes:
see inside front cover

C *Green's*, 90 Beach Rd, T7881131. 21 rooms, restaurant, swimming pool and gardens. **C** *The Lamp Guesthouse*, 14 Watson Rd, T7881041, F7881070. A fabulous guesthouse run by Roy and Marion, has very comfortable rooms (one is decorated to look like a safari tent), superb breakfasts, small veranda and garden, no smoking. Recommended. **C** *Sonstraal Guest House*, 6 Axminster Rd, T/F7881611. This is in fact 2 guesthouses on either side of the road; the main house has 3 comfortable rooms which are situated around a courtyard full of house plants, TV lounge, swimming pool; the second house has 5 double rooms all with en suite bathrooms, TV lounge, plunge pool, breakfast room, welcoming atmosphere. Guests have use of a private beach hut and paddle boats. German spoken. The ideal place to spend time on the coast. Recommended. **E** *Zandvlei Caravan Park*, 'The Row', T7885215. 12 self-catering cabins, large site with hot water and power points, camping allowed, swimming pool. **E-F** *Wipeout Backpackers*, corner Camp and Main Rd, T7884803, F7883700, wipeout@iafrica.com Relaxed place on busy Main Rd, popular with surfers, TV with Mnet, *Wipeout* surfer bar downstairs, free use of mountain bikes and surf boards.

Eating & drinking

Gaylords, 65 Main Rd, T7885470. Closed Mon and Tue. Excellent Indian meals, recommended for seafood and vegetarian dishes. *Railway House*, Railway Station, T7883251. Closed Sun evening. Newly refurbished restaurant, friendly service, seafood and steaks (including ostrich). *Whalers Tavern*, York Rd. A lively pub serving snack meals, all the usual trappings for a rowdy drinking night, views across False Bay. *Wipeout Bar*, corner Camp and Main Rd, T7884803. Large bar, popular with backpackers and surfers, pub food, cocktails, live music at weekends.

St James

Just beyond Muizenberg lies the more upmarket resort of St James, an appealing village with characteristic brightly coloured bathing huts lined along its shore. The village is named after a Roman Catholic Church which was built here in 1854 to save Catholics having to travel as far as Simon's Town to attend services – interestingly, some of the early settlers were Catholic Filipino fishermen. There is a small sheltered beach and reasonable surf off **Danger Beach**. Several readers have recommended the tidal pool as a safe place for a swim. During the week all is quiet, but at the weekend this is a popular spot and you'll have trouble finding a parking space; it's best to take the metro train.

St James is also a suitable starting point for a hike in the excellent **Silvermine Nature Reserve**. A path starts on Boyes Drive and climbs up through the Spes Bona Forest to Tartarus Cave. The views alone are worth the hike (see page 135 below for further hiking details in the reserve).

Kalk Bay
Phone code: 021
(NB Always use
3-figure prefix)

Kalk Bay is one of the most attractive settlements on False Bay and a great spot to relax for a day or two. The town is named after the **lime kilns** which produced *kalk* from shells in the 17th century. An important local product, the lime created the white-walled appearance of many new houses in the Cape, especially amongst the Bo-Kaap community. Until the arrival of the railway in 1883, the local fishermen hunted whales, seals and small fish. Today it remains a fishing harbour, worked mainly by a coloured community which somehow escaped the Group Areas Act under Apartheid. It is one of the few remaining coloured settlements on the peninsula.

Main Road is an appealing spot, lined with antique shops and art galleries, and the beach is sandy and safe for swimming, with a couple of tidal pools for children to explore. Between June and July the harbour is busy with the season for snoek, one of the most plentiful local fish harvests. Look out for the returning deep sea fishing boats around the middle of the day, as there's a daily impromptu quayside auction. You can buy a variety of fresh fish at the counters and for an extra R3 get them to gut them for you too. Another attraction is **Seal Island**, an important breeding ground for birds and seals, the latter attracting hungry great white sharks. Cruises run from the harbour with *Captain Rob's Tours*, T7885261.

You should also look out for the **Holy Trinity Church** on the Main Road. It has a thatched roof, but its appeal is it's windows, considered to be some of the finest in the Cape. On Quarterdeck Road is a tiny mosque built in the 1800s. If you are interested in local art, a visit to **Kalk Bay Gallery**, 62 Main Road, is recommended. They have a comprehensive collection of watercolours, oils and engravings capturing the beauty of the Cape. However, perhaps the most popular attraction in Kalk Bay is the Brass Bell, a simple seafood restaurant wedged between the railway tracks and the water (see Eating below).

Two of the **footpaths** from the Silvermine Nature Reserve (see next page) start and end on Boyes Drive behind Kalk Bay harbour and railway station. These are the paths along **Echo Valley** and **Spes Bona Valley**. It is in fact possible to make a circular hike by walking up Echo Valley to a natural depression known as the 'amphitheatre'. Cross over to **Kalk Bay Mountain** (516 m), and return down Spes Bona Valley. At the end of the valley you will meet a gravel road; if descending, turn right when you meet this road. Allow at least four hours for the walk. There are some small stands of indigenous forest at the top of the valleys, which at one time covered the whole mountain.

Price codes:
see inside front cover

Sleeping C *Castle Hill*, 37 Gatesville Rd, T7882554, F7883843, www.castlehill.co.za Small *Satour* accredited B&B in a restored Edwardian house, some non-smoking rooms, TV lounge, large veranda with good views of the bay, perfect for whale watching during the season. Secure parking, clean, well-run, friendly. **F** *Harbour Side Backpackers*, 136 Main Rd, T7882943, F7886452, harboursidebackpackers@hotmail.com Hostel above a pub and restaurant, 8-bed dorms, double beds with views across False Bay, good value restaurant serving excellent wholesome meals, plenty of trips and sporting adventures organized, close to the *Brass Bell*, good alternative base to Cape Town.

Eating and drinking *The Brass Bell*, T7885455, by the railway station. A well-known and very popular restaurant, young clientele, gets very busy around sunset. Great location right by the waves, simple set-up serving pub meals and good fresh fish and chips, great for a cool beer outside close to the waves. *Cape to Cuba*, Main Rd, T7883695. Atmospheric Cuban restaurant and cocktail bar serving good-value seafood with a Caribbean edge. Great setting on the water's edge with tables overlooking the harbour, funky décor, enjoyable Cuban music. *Harbourside Pub*, 136 Main Rd. Old-fashioned and pleasant pub on the first floor with a great balcony overlooking Main Rd and the harbour. Good meals, live music – usually jazz – at weekends. *Mykonos*, Main Rd. Authentic Greek food, friendly service. *The Timeless Way*, 106 Main Rd, T/F7885619. An excellent restaurant serving Cape cuisine, steaks and seafood. Ronny and Kelly ensure a high standard of service. Recommended.

Continuing along the main road, the next settlement you reach is Clovelly, tucked between the waters of False Bay and the mountains of the Silvermine Reserve. Along the main street are several shops and places to have a snack. Anyone visiting from the west country in Britain will be interested to know that this community is named after the village in Devon. **Golf** enthusiasts should head a little way inland for the *Clovelly Country Club*, T7821118, F7826853. In order to use the golf course (18 holes) or eat in the delightful restaurant you need to take out temporary membership. The course itself has very narrow fairways and is considered quite difficult.

Clovelly

Silvermine Nature Reserve

This is a popular local reserve, but not often visited by overseas visitors. Table Mountain and Cape Point tend to dominate the open-air attractions, and rightly so, but this reserve is well worth a visit if you enjoy hiking, plus there are some tremendous views across False Bay and the Atlantic Ocean from the high peaks.

Colour map 4, grid C1

The reserve encompasses, like much of the Cape, one of the oldest floral kingdoms in the world. Over 900 species of rare and endangered species have been recorded in the mountains, including many types of *proteas*, *ericas*, and *reeds*. In addition to the plants there are a couple of patches of indigenous forest in the Spes Bona and Echo valleys. Ornithologists should look out for black eagles, ground woodpeckers, orange-breasted sunbirds and rock kestrels. If you're extremely lucky, you may also come across small shy mammals such as lynx, porcupine and various species of mongoose.

Getting there The reserve is split into 2 sections by the Ou Kaapseweg Rd as it crosses the Kalk Bay Mountains – the eastern sector and western sector. There is no public transport along this road. By car you can either approach from the Cape Town side or from Noordhoek and Fish Hoek. Driving out from Cape Town, follow the M3 from Newlands to its very end and then take a right. After 2 km turn left into Ou Kaapseweg Rd, M64. Note that this road has one of Cape Town's highest accident rates, so take care when driving.

Ins & outs
Mountain Rescue:
T9489900
Fire: T5351100
Park Info: T7892455

Getting around A variety of footpaths from Muizenberg, St James, Kalk Bay and Chapman's Peak Drive all lead into the reserve and make a pleasant day trip from Cape Town. Access into the reserve is allowed between sunrise and sunset; 1 Sep-31 Mar, 0800-1900; 1 Apr-31 Aug, 0800-1800. Toilet facilities are found at Silvermine Reservoir, Hennies Pool, Bokkop Peak, and at the car park near Maiden Peak in the eastern sector of the reserve. Braais are only permitted within the Hennies Pool, Silvermine Reservoir and Bokkop picnic areas.

A tarred road leads from the **western sector** gates to the Silvermine Reservoir built in 1898 to supply Kalk Bay and Muizenberg with water until 1912. There is a shady picnic site under some pine trees close to the dam. One of the more popular walks from here is to **Noordhoek Peak** (754 m), a circuit of about 7 km from the dam. The

Around the reserve

path is marked by stone cairns. At the summit there are spectacular views of the Sentinel and Hout Bay. Another interesting walk is from the car park to **Elephant's Eye Cave**, covered with ferns and hanging plants. En route you pass the **Prinz Kasteel waterfall**. Allow about three hours for the round trip. The cave can also be reached from Tokai Manor through the Tokai Forest.

The **eastern sector** of the reserve has plenty of sandstone caves to explore, while the views from the peaks here are across False Bay. One of the popular trails is to **Steenberg Peak** (537 m) via the Wolfkop picnic site. If you have made your way to the top without a car, try an interesting walk which drops down to Muizenberg or St James via the **Spes Bona Valley**. Be careful if exploring any of the caves as there are dangerous deep drops. The Speleological Association in Cape Town regularly organizes trips to the Kalk Bay Mountains. Serious hikers or anyone who is looking for a bit of variety are strongly recommended to buy *A Walking Guide for the Hout Bay to Simon's Town Mountains*, by Shirley Brossy. The trails are well described and the illustrations clear enough to follow while walking.

Fish Hoek

Phone code: 021
(NB Always use 3-figure prefix)
Colour map 4, grid C2

For tourist information contact the Publicity Bureau, T7821115

Fish Hoek is one of the most conservative settlements on the coast, not least as the sale of alcohol is famously prohibited here. It does, however, have a fine beach, perhaps the best for swimming along the coast. It stretches right across the Fish Hoek valley – swimming is safe at the southern end of the bay, but **avoid** the northern end where a small river enters the sea, as there is the danger of quicksand. From mid-August, there is a good chance of catching a glimpse of whales from here. The valley which stretches behind the town joins with Noordhoek beach on the Atlantic

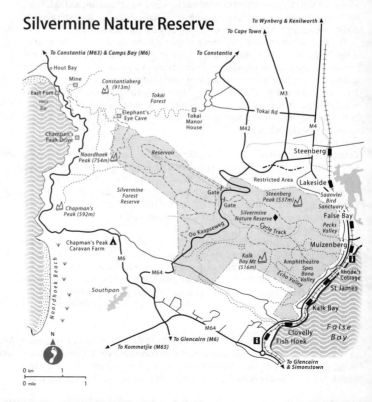

Silvermine Nature Reserve

coast. In recent geological times this was flooded and all the lands towards Cape Point were in fact an island.

Peers Cave, inland from the Country Club, is a well-known rock shelter where six fossilized human skeletons were discovered in 1927, dated at over 10,000 years old. One of the skulls is on display in the South Africa Museum in Cape Town. There are also some paintings on the walls, and it is now a national monument. The shortest route to the cave is to approach along Kommetjie Road from Fish Hoek, turning down 20th Avenue to the police station. From here it is about 45 minutes' walk to the cave, crossing ancient sand dunes, further evidence of the change in sea level.

B Sunny Cove, T7822274. Smart B&B in a solid old Manor house overlooking False Bay. **C** The Avenue Hotel, 1st Av, T/F7826026. Smart double rooms, restaurant, swimming pool, just across road from the beach. One of the few hotels along the coast. **C** Makapa Lodge, 18 Java Close, Capri Village, T7853512, F7853416. 2 self-catering apartments, breakfast available, swimming pool.

Sleeping
Price codes:
see inside frton cover

Bay View Galley, on the beach, T7823354. Serves continental dishes and a good choice of fresh seafood. Recommended.

Eating

It is very easy to drive through this coastal resort without realizing you've actually been here. There is a small beach by the railway station but it is exposed to the southeast winds. Be wary of the cross currents close to the inlet where a small river enters the sea. At low tide you can occasionally see the remains of a steamship, the *Clan Stuart*. She was blown aground on 20 November 1914 while the crew drank in the local hotel.

Glencairn

Sleeping C Glen Adinda, 12 Glen Rd, T7821122. 11 double rooms, en suite bathroom and 1 luxury suite with lounge and dining area, each room has been tastefully decorated with period furnishings. Other facilities include Judy's lounge for afternoon teas, Wilhelmina's restaurant and a lively bar, Victor's. **D** Glenview Cottage, 56 Camilla St, Glencairn Heights, T7821324. Family run B&B, 2 double rooms, en suite bathroom, TV, small fridge, private patio, secure off street parking, separate entrance, braai facilities in the garden.

Simon's Town

This is perhaps the prettiest town on False Bay, with a pleasant atmosphere and numerous old buildings dating from Victorian times along the Main Street. If you want a break from Cape Town, this makes for an excellent alternative base from which to explore the Southern Peninsula.

Phone code: 021
(NB Always use
3-figure prefix)
Colour map 4, grid C2

The town is fairly quiet for most of the year but becomes very busy with families during the summer school holidays. Whenever you visit, take some time to wander up the hill away from the main road – the quiet, bougainvillea-bedecked houses and cobbled streets with their sea views are a lovely retreat from the bustling beaches. The main swimming spot is **Seaforth Beach**, not far from **Boulders**. To get there, turn off St George's Road into Seaforth Road after passing the navy block to the left. The beach is the second on the right, on Kleintuin Road. A little further towards Cape Point are two other popular bathing beaches, **Windmill** and **Fisherman's**. As a popular tourist destination, some thought has gone into the development of Seaforth Beach. There are changing and toilet facilities, snack bars, restaurants and a clean stretch of shady lawn bordering the beach with some picnic spots and bench seats. The swimming is safe, but there is no surf due to offshore rocks which protect the beach. For children there is a water slide and a wooden raft in the water. Look out for some giant pots, a legacy from whaling days, when they were used for melting whale blubber.

For tourist information,
contact the extremely
helpful Publicity
Association, T7862436,
pensimon@yebo.co.za

Simon's Town is named after Simon van der Stel, who decided that an alternative bay was needed for securing ships in the winter months as Table Bay suffered from the prevailing northwesterly. However, because of the difficult overland access, the bay was little used in the early years. It was not until 1743 that the Dutch East India

Cape Town

Company finally built a wooden pier and some barracks here. In 1768 the town transferred into British hands, and following the end of the Napoleonic Wars in Europe, the British decided to turn Simon's Town into a naval base. It remained as such until 1957.

Sights **Heritage Museum**, Amlay House, King George Way, is an excellent place which faithfully charts the history of the Muslim community in Simon's Town. The town was designated a "white" area during the Group Area Act and over 7,000 people classified as coloured were relocated. The Amlay family were the last to be forcibly removed from Simon's Town – today the Muslim community has all but disappeared here, although there is still an attractive working Mosque up behind Main Road. The exhibition in Heritage House consists mainly of pictures and artefacts dating back to the turn of the century. There is a traditional bridal chamber, with wedding clothes and a display in the Hadj room. Zainab Davidson is the co-founder of the Nourul Islam Historical Society and started the museum. There are also Mosque and Karamat tours organized by the museum. ■ *Tue-Fri, 1100-1600, Sat, 1100-1300, R3. T7862302.*

In the Old Residency, Court Road, is **Simon's Town Museum**. This is a collection of local objects, most of which relate to the town's history as a naval base for the British and South African navies. There is also a display of material collected from two local shipwrecks. The building dates from 1777 when it started life as the residency for the Governor of the Dutch East India Company. It was converted into a magistrate's court in 1814; at the back of the building you can view the punishment cells and stocks. The trial cell has some interesting graffiti while the marks on the ceiling of the punishment cell are reputed to be whip marks. The museum also organizes guided walk along the 'Historical Mile' on Tue and Sat, R15. ■ *Daily, 1000-1600. Small donation as an entrance fee. T7863046.*

The **South Africa Naval Museum**, on Court Road, was opened in 1993, and includes a collection of model ships, a modern submarine control room plus relics from the Martello Tower. ■ *Daily 1000-1600. T7874686 for organized tours.*

Cape Town

Glencairn, Simon's Town & Boulders Beach

Worth a quick peek is the **Warrior Toy Museum**, on St George's Street, a tiny museum with an impressive collection of model cars, trains, dolls and toy soldiers. This is a great little place and definitely worth a stop – nostalgic for adults and fun for kids. New and old model cars are also for sale. ■ *Daily 1000-1600. R3. T7861395.*

Mineral World, on Dido Valley Road, is an important gemstone factory where you can watch the different stages of polishing and buy the finished product. There is also the 'Scratch Patch', a large landscaped yard covered with a deep layer of polished stones. You can purchase different sized containers, R10+, and fill them with whatever stones you like. ■ *Mon-Fri 0830-1645, Sat and Sun 0900-1730. T7862020.*

The **Quayside Centre** is a smart development on Wharf Street, next to Jubilee Square in the centre of town, which has greatly enhanced the seafront. Above the shops and restaurants is a comfortable new hotel, the *Quayside Lodge*. Cruises to Cape Point can be booked here.

About 2 km south of Simon's Town is a lovely series of little sandy coves surrounded by huge boulders (hence the name). It is a peaceful spot, safe for swimming and gently shelving, making it good for children.

Boulders Beach
Directory
Police: T7862127
Sea Rescue: T7861624
or contact police

The real attraction here, however, is the colony of African Penguins that live and nest between the boulders. **Boulders Coastal Park** has been created to protect the little creatures, and their numbers have flourished. Bizarrely, they take little notice of their sunbathing neighbours and happily go about their business of swimming, waddling and braying (their characteristic braying was the reason they were, until recently, known as Jackass Penguins). This is one of two colonies on mainland Africa, the other being in **Lambert's Bay** (see page 184). The best time to see large numbers of penguins is just before sunset, when they return from a day's feeding at sea. Now that the beach is a protected area, there is a R10 admission charge (between 0800-1700, T7862329, boulders@parks-sa.co.za), which is well worth it to get close to the penguins – but be sure to avoid the nesting areas. Note that the first cove gets very busy with families at weekends and during school holidays. Walk along the boardwalk or crawl under the rocks on one side of the beach to get to a more peaceful spot.

This is the last easy access to the sea on this side of the peninsula. Beyond **Partridge Point** the main road cuts into the hillside, and access to the beach is via steep footpaths. Miller's Point is one of the few remaining beaches to levy a small entrance fee. Gates close at 2000. There is a large caravan site here plus a picnic area and a restaurant. The road climbs above the sea before rounding the mountains by **Smitswinkel Bay**. On a clear day you can look back to a perfect view of the cliffs plunging into the sea. A short distance from the shore is the Cape of Good Hope Nature Reserve entrance (see page 129).

Miller's Point

There are several easy-going hikes just behind Simon's Town in the mountains. Close to the railway station is a track referred to as **Redhill Path**, which actually leads up over Redhill to the village of Scarborough on the Atlantic Coast. You'll need to make arrangements for someone to drive around and collect you from the far side. Far less ambitious, but still as rewarding with the views on offer, is the path known as **Klawer Steps**. This route starts from the end of Barnard Street, which is off Runciman Drive. At the other end of town, behind the school by Seaforth Beach, you can begin a two-hour walk along an old mule track to a blockhouse which overlooks the harbour. To find it, turn off the main road into Harrington Road and then take a left into Jan Smuts Drive. The mule track is near the far end to the right. For further, detailed notes, consult Mike Lundy's excellent book, *Easy Walks in the Cape Peninsula*. The local *Flora Conservation Group*, T7861620, organizes regular guided walks in to the Silvermine Reserve.

Hiking

Boat trips
For operators, see page 141

A number of boat trips to the **Cape of Good Hope** originate from Simon's Town harbour. Taking a trip from here allows views of the spectacular coastline and its hinterland from a different angle. In addition to straightforward sightseeing tours, there are several options for viewing bird life, seals and whales during the right season. There are advantages in joining a boat tour from Simon's Town as opposed to the V & A Waterfront or Hout Bay: you get a good view of the Hottentots Holland mountains and False Bay; the waters in False Bay are less rough than those on the Atlantic side; and the journey time to the Cape of Good Hope is shorter. Finally, the whole experience is far more relaxed than the large crowds around the V&A Waterfront.

Sleeping
■ *on map, page 138*
Price codes:
see inside front cover

There is a wide choice of accommodation here, and a good starting point is the *Beach & Bay Accommodation*, T/F7863934, a local association formed by B&B owners. Contact Jennie Napier for details.

A *Quayside Hotel*, Quayside Centre, Wharf St, on the seafront in the centre of town, T7863838, F7862241, www.quayside.co.za A very smart new development in a great location with 28 double rooms, all with nice views across the harbour but rather over-priced. Book well in advance for visits during local holidays. **B-D** *Bosky Dell*, 5 Grant Av, near Boulders Beach, T7863906, F7861830. Peaceful complex of self-contained units with choice of one to three bedrooms. Clean and tidy but slightly rundown. Each flat has TV and is serviced daily, plus secure parking and private gardens leading down to beach. Advance booking essential during local holidays. **B-C** *British Hotel Apartments*, 90 St George St, T/F021-7904930, T082-5585689 (mob). 4 elegant self-catering apartments in a fully restored Victorian building. 3 bedrooms in each, sleeping up to 6, smart polished wooden floors, sea views from the magnificent balconies, breakfasts available on request. Highly recommended. **B-C** *Tudor House by the Sea*, 43 Simon's Town Rd, T7826238, F7825027. 6 luxury self-catering apartments, all mod cons, serviced daily, secure parking, secluded gardens, ideal for a longer break for those wishing to explore the area and not be confined to a hotel, very popular in season, advance reservations necessary. **C** *Bayview*, 12 Harington Rd, T082-3791991 (mob). 1 double room, 1 suite, a beautiful old house with views out to sea, garden, non-smoking. Recommended. **C** *Boulders Beach Guest House*, 4 Boulders Place, T7861758, F7861825, www.bouldersbeach.co.za One of the most relaxed places you could stay in the area, just meters from the beach. This friendly, well-run guesthouse is a firm favourite with us. 18 double rooms with en suite bathrooms, most arranged around a paved yard without seaview, good size beds and baths, simple refreshing design. At night you're likely to see penguins exploring the grounds after everyone has gone home. Excellent restaurant (see below). Strongly recommended. **C** *High Gables*, 32 Victory Way, T/F7861226, highgables@iafrica.com A family-run B&B with 2 double rooms, separate entrance. Excellent location high above the town with a grand view of the harbour and False Bay. **C** *Lord Nelson Inn*, 58 St George's St, T7861386, F7861009. A pleasant, small family-run hotel in a classic Victorian building. 10 very comfortable rooms with balconies and sea views, restaurant and 2 bars (see Eating below), peaceful gardens, a good alternative for those not wishing to stay in the bustle of Cape Town. Recommended. **C** *The Outpost*, 28 Nelson Way, T7865594. Lovely B&B set high above Simon's Town, great views of False Bay, comfortable en-suite rooms, quiet and relaxing place. **C** *Rocklands*, 25 Rocklands Rd, Murdoch Valley South, Simon's Town, T7863158, simonstown@mweb.co.za Cool comfortable B&B, airy rooms with balconies, tiled floors, sea views, short walk to the beach. **C** *Roman's Rock*, Main Rd 432, past Simon's Town on way to Cape Point, T7863431, rrock@iafrica.com Comfortable and modern self-catering apartments with balconies overlooking the sea, braai facilities, parking, secluded setting. **C** *Toad Hall*, 9 AB Bull Rd, Froggy Farm, T7863878, F7011682, www.toad-hall.co.za Secluded self-contained apartment, sleeps 4, lounge, en suite bathroom, short walk down to Boulders Beach. **E** *Kijabe*, 32 Disa Rd, T7862433. Small B&B a short drive from town, two rooms, TV lounge, breakfast room, small swimming pool, friendly place. **E-F** *Top Sail House*, 176 St George's St, T7865537. Backpacker's hostel set in an old convent school building, quiet place with dorms, doubles, balcony overlooking St George's

St, bike hire, friendly. **F** *Oatlands Holiday Village*, Froggy Pond, south of Simon's Town centre, T7861410, F7861162, www.caraville.co.za/oatlands.htm A medium-sized holiday resort with apartments, camping and caravans, hot water and power points, limited privacy, swimming pool, part of the Club Caraville group.

Bertha's, Quayside Centre, Wharf Rd, T7862138. A seafood grill and coffee house in the centre of town in a prime location overlooking the yacht harbour. During the day the outside terrace is a good place to enjoy good fresh seafood and watch the goings on in the harbour. Inside is a dining area perfect for large family meals. Great selection of fresh seafood dishes, good value. Recommended. *Black Marlin*, Miller's Point, 2 km from Simon's Town, T7861621. Sea views and a wide range of fresh seafood, excellent crayfish, comprehensive wine list. Recommended, although it can get very busy with tour buses in summer. *Bon Appetit*, 90 St George's St, T7862412. Closed Mon. One of the best restaurants in the area. Excellent French menu, very fresh ingredients, simple seafood and meat dishes, popular, book ahead. *Café Pescado*, 118 St Georges St (opposite Jubilee Square), T7862272. A popular family set-up serving some of the best seafood along the coast. Try the calamari and always check what the catch of the day is. Recommended. *Caribbean Coffee Company*, Quayside, T4480316. Sandwiches, salads and filled pancakes, tables overlooking the harbour, good coffee, nice place for lunch. *Dixies*, 143 Main Rd, T7862105, Indonesian and Dutch meals. *Hardy's* in the *Lord Nelson Inn*, Simon's Town, T7861386, excellent informal lunchtime pub meals. *Horatio's*, also in the *Lord Nelson Inn*, Simon's Town, T7861386. This is the hotel's smarter restaurant, serving good but pricey seafood and roasts. *Mediterraneo*, Quayside Centre. Homemade soups, cakes and deli. Breezy setting, great for afternoon snacks. *Penguin Point Café*, Boulders Bay. Excellent restaurant with bar and sundeck which is always busy with day-trippers. Good English breakfasts, cocktails (including the popular Pickled Penguins) and meals made from fresh ingredients with a slight experimental feel to them. Try the salads during the day and the fresh fish by night. *Plymouth Sound*, T7862993, Runciman's Building, St George's St. Good breakfasts and snacks, check the daily specials, comfortable old-style setting. *Salty Sea Dog*, next to Quayside Centre. Cheap and cheerful place serving fresh fish and chips with seats overlooking the harbour. *The Two and Sixpence*, Main Rd, next to the *British Hotel*. Friendly bar with pool tables, pub food, good beers.

Eating
● *on map, page 138*

Cape Town

Game fishing Several charter companies run trips to the waters off Cape Point. Contact the *Marlin & Tuna Club*, part of the *False Bay Yacht Club*, on T7861703, for further details. **Golf** There is a 9-hole, 18 tee, links course on the seafront, just by the turning for Boulders Beach. This is a narrow course and is a real test for anyone not used to playing in very windy conditions. Contact the *Simon's Town Country Club*, T7861233. **Scuba diving** *Oatlands Holiday Village*, Froggy Pond, T7861410, F7861162, www.caraville.co.za/oatlands.htm A well-run local scuba diving school based at a holiday village. Full range of PADI scuba diving courses are available. The best season for diving here is during the winter months when the weather ensures the sea is flat as the prevailing winds blow offshore. Water temperatures are between 12°C-18°C; visibility is usually between 5-10 m. When the winds change direction in the summer months visibility can be reduced to almost zero. There are a number of interesting wreck dives along the coast and most sites can be reached direct from the shore. If you are already qualified, ask at the tourist office or the adventure diving centre about local dive clubs and opportunities at the weekend.

Sports
Diving is a very popular activity around the Cape Peninsula

Spirit of Just Nuisance, T082-7375263 (mob) or T083-2577760 (mob). Short tours around the harbour area which includes a special visit to the naval dockyard. The boat departs approx every 45 mins from the pier by the Quayside Centre. Expect to pay R20 for adults, R10 for children. Recommended if you only have a limited amount of time to spend in Simon's Town. They also organize trips to Seal Island and fishing trips – call ahead to check times. *S.V. Curlew*, T7861226 or T082-2243909 (mob), highgables:iafrica.com Traditional sailing vessel that can carry up to 25 passengers. Cruises around the bay and sunset cruises by appointment. *Sweet Sunshine*, T082-5755655 (mob). 42-ft motorized sailing catamaran, offering a

Boat tour operators

variety of cruises including a 4-hr trip around Cape Point, trips to Seal Island and sunset cruises. Outing and trips towards whales (during the season, Jul-Nov). Departs from the pier by the Quayside Centre.

Whale watching The whale-watching season starts in Oct. Rules surrounding trips to the see the whales are very stringent, and only one boat a year is given a permit to run whale-watching cruises. These change every year, so it is best to contact the very helpful and informative Publicity Association on St George's Rd for details on which boat is running trips at present. T7862436, pensimon@yebo.co.za

Western Cape

4

Western Cape

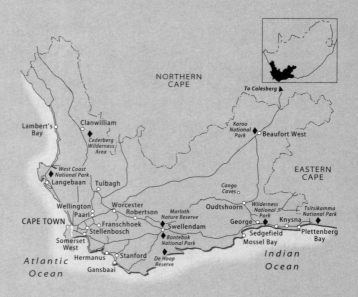

NORTHERN CAPE

To Colesberg

Lambert's Bay

Clanwilliam

Cederberg Wilderness Area

Karoo National Park

Beaufort West

EASTERN CAPE

West Coast National Park

Langebaan

Tulbagh

Cango Caves

Wellington

Worcester

Robertson

Oudtshoorn

Wilderness National Park

Tsitsikamma National Park

Paarl

CAPE TOWN

Franschhoek

Stellenbosch

Marloth Nature Reserve

Swellendam

George

Knysna

Plettenberg Bay

Somerset West

Bontebok National Park

Sedgefield

Mossel Bay

Hermanus

Stanford

De Hoop Reserve

Gansbaai

Atlantic Ocean

Indian Ocean

The Western Cape is arguably the most beautiful and varied of South Africa's nine provinces. It has just about everything that the entire country has to offer, from endless beaches and indigenous forests to historic wine estates and scorched semi-desert. Consequently, it is the most visited area in the country, with a well-developed tourist infrastructure and the inevitable seasonal overcrowding.

The first port of call for most visitors to the Cape is the beautiful **Winelands** region, with the historic towns of **Stellenbosch**, **Franschhoek** and **Paarl** stretching across a range of mountains and surrounded by old wine estates. The **Breede River Valley** is better known for its farming, with isolated settlements tucked away along its river banks. Further east lie the parched plains of the **Karoo**, their endless shimmering horizons peppered with craggy mountains and the odd farm. The southern coast begins with **Walker Bay**, which claims to have the best land based whale watching in the world. Further east stretches the celebrated (or overrated) **Garden Route**, an area of endless sandy beaches, nature reserves, lush forests and tourist-friendly seaside towns.

Far less visited is the **West Coast**, north of Cape Town, a wild coast of fynbos-covered sand dunes, sun-bleached beaches and remote fishing villages. Inland lie the **Cederberg Mountains**, a rugged range riddled with ancient San rock art and offering some of the best hiking in the country.

The Winelands

The Winelands is South Africa's oldest and most beautiful wine-producing area, a fertile series of valleys quite unlike the rest of the Western Cape. Despite producing less than a third of South Africa's wines, it is the Cape's biggest attraction after Cape Town. Its appeal is simple: it offers the chance to sample several hundred different wines in a historical and superbly scenic setting.

This was the first region after Cape Town to be settled, and the towns of Stellenbosch, Paarl and Franschhoek are some of the oldest in South Africa. Today, their streets are lined with beautiful Cape Dutch and Georgian houses, although the real architectural gems are the manor houses on the wine estates. While the wine industry flourished during the 18th and 19th centuries, the farmers built grand homesteads with cool wine cellars. Most of these still exist today and can be visited during a trip to a vineyard – a few have even been converted into luxury hotels.

Ins and outs

Getting there   The N2 highway goes past Cape Town International airport, 22 km, and then continues along the northern fringes of the Cape Flats. To the south are the large sprawling townships on Mitchells Plain, Nyanga and Khayelitsha. The R310 left turning is the quickest route to Stellenbosch, 16 km. At Firgrove junction a right turning leads to Macassar and Sheik Yussuf's Karamat (see box page 87). The N2 continues east splitting the towns of Strand and Somerset West before climbing over the Hottentots Holland Mountains into the Overberg (see page 234) via Sir Lowry's Pass. The **R44** is an alternative route to the heart of the Winelands country – Stellenbosch.

Tourist boards   *Western Cape Tourist Board*, T021-4265674, F4265640, www.wcapetourism.co.za

South African wines

South Africa has become one of the world's major wine producers, and although not yet as successful as those of Australia, standards are increasing rapidly. A number of Cape wines are quite excellent – all are very good value.

A history of wine
It is a little-known fact that the first vineyards of the Cape were planted before those in the Bordeaux region of France

The Cape's wine industry was started in earnest by Simon van der Stel in 1679. Previously, vines had been grown by Van Riebeeck in Company's Garden and in the area known today as the suburb of Wynberg. The first wine was produced in 1652, and not surprisingly there was soon a great demand from the crews of ships when they arrived in Table Bay after several months at sea. As the early settlers moved inland and farms were opened up in the sheltered valleys, more vines were planted. Every farmer had a few plants growing alongside the homestead, and by chance the soils and climate proved to be ideal for grape growing. Van der Stel produced the first quality wines on Constantia estate, with the help of Hendrik Cloete. These were sweet wines made from a blend of white and red Muscadel grapes, known locally as *Hanepoort* grapes.

The industry received a boost in 1806 when the English, at war with France, started to import South African wines. However, under Apartheid sanctions hindered exports and the Kooperatieve Wijnbouwers Vereniging (KWV) controlled prices and production quotas. Since then though sanctions have bene lifted and the KWV has since lost much of its power, allowing the industry to experiment and expand.

The modern wine industry has developed out of the need to find better quality grapes. The Hanepoort grape proved to be too delicate to travel. New varieties were introduced from overseas, and the industry started producing a greater range of wines. These days hundreds of varieties are cultivated in the Cape. The most successful red varieties include: the **Pinotage**, developed in 1928 as a hybrid of

Things to do in the Western Cape

- Sit beneath centuries-old oak trees sipping on some of South Africa's finest wines on the historical estates of **Vergelegen** and **Boschedal** - or try homemade cheeses and watch the goats being milked on **Fairview** estate.
- Have a close encounter with a great white shark off the coast of **Gansbaai**.
- Get a bucket and spade and join the holidaying family throngs on the beautiful soft-sand beaches of **Plettenberg Bay**.
- Slurp down half a dozen Knysna oysters before hiring a canoe and exploring the wide, protected **Kynsna lagoon**.
- Spend a morning sitting on a cliff-top in **Hermanus**, watching dozens of southern right whales flipping their magnificent tales and breaking the surface with their vast, shiny backs.
- Get harnessed up to some forest giants in **Tsitsikamma National Park** and fly above the trees on an exhilarating canopy tour.
- Clamber onto the back of an ostrich and race it round an **ostrich farm** in Oudshoorn, home to 98% of the world's ostrich population – and finish the day with an ostrich omelette, or ostrich steak, or ostrich biltong, or ostrich mince…

Western Cape

Winelands

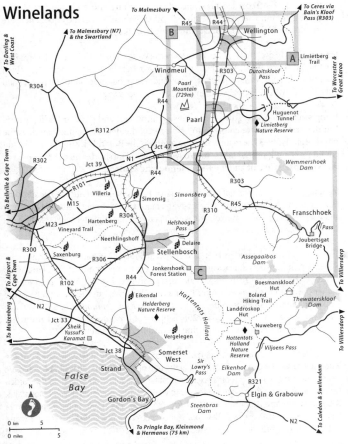

Detailed maps
A *Wellington district,*
page 172
B *Paarl Winelands,*
page 170
C *Franschhoek Valley,*
page 164

Hermitage and Pinot Noir; the **Shiraz**, originally from Iran; the **Red Muscadel**; and the **Muscat Red**. Each river valley produces its own distinct wine, using the grape best suited to the local climatic conditions. Today wine is produced as far north as the Orange River Valley in the Northern Cape.

Around Strand and Somerset West

Phone code: 021
(NB Always use
3-figure prefix)
Colour map 6, grid B5

Although principally an industrial area, Strand is also a seaside resort with an excellent 5-km white sand beach and an important commuter town linked to Cape Town by the Metro Suburban service. It mainly caters for the domestic tourists. Further inland, Somerset West is a prosperous town and again a major commuter centre to Cape Town. It has a beautiful location on the slopes of the Helderberg Mountains, with unimpeded views of False Bay, and occasionally, Cape Point. If you are planning to stay in either town, the range of accommodation is better in Somersest West than in Strand. There is a **tourist information** office on Main Street in Somerset West, opposite the new police station, T8514022.

Hottentots
Holland
Nature
Reserve

The Hottentots Holland Mountains are the southern end of a continuous mountainous chain which extend inland as far as Ceres and beyond, effectively cutting the Cape off from the rest of South Africa. The reserve is set in the mountains overlooking False Bay. Its an important conservation area for mountain fynbos: over 1,300 species have been recorded here, including some rare and endemic plants. The range of birds found here is greater than in other fynbos areas of the Cape. There are also small populations of rhebuck, klipspringer, duiker and grysbok.

Field rangers patrol
the reserve checking
for hiking permits

Ins and outs   To get there from Strand or Somerset West, follow the N2 over Sir Lowry's Pass and turn left at Elgin, R321. After about 10 km, at the bottom of Viljoens Pass past Nuweberg Dam, turn left to the Nuweberg Forest Station and reserve office. **Bookings** for permits and huts: T028-8404826, F8404457, lourens@hottentotsholland.co.za

Due to flooding, all
hiking trails are closed
from July to the
end of August

Being so close to Cape Town makes this an important and popular hiking region. Various restrictions are enforced to help protect the flora and fauna as well as the physical landscape. The main trail in the reserve is the **Boland Hiking Trail**. The full circuit is 50 km long and takes three days to cover. The shorter hikes are known as the **Nuweberg Circuit** and the **Riviersonderend Canyon**.

Sleeping   There are 2 overnight huts in the reserve: **F** *Boesmanskloof Hut* and *Landdroskop Hut*. There is no accommodation at the reserve entrance, Nuweberg, but there are some toilets and shower facilities. Each overnight hut is equipped with bunks, mattresses and water. Fires are only allowed at braai sites as there is a high risk of veld fires.

Helderberg
Nature Reserve

This park was proclaimed in 1960 and covers an area of 245 ha. The slopes are particularly rich in protea species and Cape fynbos, although many of the plants were destroyed by a major fire in 1995. Walking is permitted throughout the reserve. The higher the altitude the more strenuous the trails become, but there are paths to the peaks. ■ *There is a small entrance charge. For reserve information call T8514060. The Duck Inn inside the reserve, T8517256, is open for breakfast, lunch and afternoon tea, and is an excellent spot for viewing the birdlife. Recommended.*

Sleeping in
Somerset West
Price codes:
see inside front cover

A *Lord Charles*, Old Stellenbosch Rd, T8551040, F8551107. Luxury hotel well-suited to those who want to see the Cape without being in the hub of Cape Town. 196 well-appointed a/c rooms, some non-smoking rooms, excellent restaurant, light meals served on the garden terrace, swimming pool, private gardens with views of the Hottentots Holland Mountains.
A-B *Erinvale Estate*, Upper Lourensford Rd, T8471160, F8471196, hotel@erinvale.co.za Smart hotel, part of an exclusive development overlooking a golf course. 57 a/c rooms and suites, most of which are in converted stables with thatched roofs. 2 restaurants with

outdoor tables for light lunches, reliable Cape cuisine, atmospheric bar with large log fires, swimming pool, good service, immaculate gardens. Residents are offered discounted green fees. **B** *Die Ou Pastorie*, 41 Lourens St, T8522120, F8513710. Restored parsonage originally built in 1819, 9 luxurious rooms, TV, en suite bathrooms, all rooms in separate complex from restaurant, mature Victorian gardens, swimming pool. Attached restaurant is popular and has a very good local reputation. **B** *Willowbrook Lodge*, Morgenster Av, T8513759, F8514152. Homely country lodge set in a beautiful garden, 11 large rooms, antiques add to the atmosphere of restaurant and lounge, French and Italian spoken. **B** *Zandberg Guest Cottages*, 96 Winery Rd, just out of town off the Stellenbosch Rd, T/F8422945, www.zandberg.co.za Award winning B&B, 11 luxury cottages set in immaculate gardens, swimming pool, fine restaurant. Recommended. **B-C** *Somerset Lodge*, 200 Main Rd, T8517853, F8517841, somlod@iafrica.com Small pub and restaurant with rooms, good value, clean and comfortable. **C** *Somer Place*, 14 Freesia Av, T8517992. Peaceful B&B in the suburbs, homely atmosphere.

Die Ou Pastorie, 41 Lourens St, T8522120. Excellent smart French restaurant, part of lodge, booking advised at weekends. *Helderberg Winery*, Winery Rd, T8813870. Serves light lunches either in the tasting room or on a fine day outside on the vine covered patio, reasonable prices. Recommended. *Zandberg Wine Estate*, 96 Winery Rd, T8422945. An excellent restaurant in an informal farmhouse setting. Also has luxury overnight cottages on the estate (see above). Highly recommended. **Eating**

Train Daily commuter service to **Cape Town** on the metro train; 31 km from Cape Town International Airport. **Transport**

Vergelegen Estate

This is one of the Cape's finest estates, and you should allow several hours for a visit. The main draw here is the superb manor house, stocked with antiques and historical paintings. The modern cellars are buried on Rondekop Hill, overlooking the estate – there are good views from here of the mountains and False Bay. You have to drive up to the cellar, although lifts are available from the reception. The cellar is arranged into three levels, which allows gravity to be used throughout the wine making process. *Phone code: 021 (NB Always use 3-figure prefix)*

Getting there Take the N2 out of Cape Town past the International Airport, turn off at exit 43, signposted Somerset West, and then turn left on to the R44. Take a right at the traffic lights (by the *Lord Charles Hotel*), and after 1½ km turn left into Lourensford Rd. After 4 km look out for the estate signpost in green and white on the right side of the road. **Ins & outs**

Information Open daily, 0930-1600. T8471344. Entrance: R7, fee includes wine tasting and a cellar tour. The reception area has a shop and contains some interesting books on the early history of the Cape. Across the courtyard is a smart wine tasting room where you can sample the few wines that are currently bottled under the Vergelegen label. Cellar tours: 1030, 1130 and 1430, closed Sun. Lady Phillips Tea Garden, T8526666, open daily, 1000-1600. Enjoy good food in the shade overlooking the croquet lawn, a very popular lunch spot, recommended if you are visiting the house and grounds.

The highlight is a visit to the magnificent manor house filled with beautiful period furniture and historical paintings, similar to the collection at Groot Constantia. At the front of the house are five **Chinese camphor trees** which were planted by Willem van der Stel between 1700 and 1706. They are the oldest living documented trees in South Africa and are a now national monument. Behind the house is a walled octagonal garden – many of the plants were planted here by Lady Phillips (wife of Sir Lionel Phillips, owner for 25 years from 1917), who wished to recreate a typical English garden, complete with herbaceous border. Also look out for the splendid collection of roses next to the main house on the site of a tennis court. Between October and April you can have **Around the estate**

Willem van der Stel

Two of the farms on the banks of the Lourens River, Parelvallei and Vergelegen, belonged to two sons of Governor Simon van der Stel. When Simon van der Stel retired as Governor of the Cape he went to live on his estate of Constantia. The directors of the Dutch East India Company honoured his works in the Cape by appointing his son, Willem Adriaan, as his successor to the governorship. This proved to be a disaster since Willem principally devoted his energies to building up his estate, Vergelegen. Over the next six years he acquired most of the land in the valley and used the Cape's resources to improve the estate. He was not unskilled at farming, and before he was found out Vergelegen was regarded as one of the most gracious and successful country estates in the Cape.

However, in 1707 the Dutch East India Company was made aware of the corrupt nature of Willem's dealings and he was recalled to the Netherlands. Vergelegen was confiscated, divided into four farms and sold. Since Simon van der Stel died at Constantia on 24 June 1712 there have been no van der Stels in the Cape, a sad fact considering what an important role the family had in the foundation of the colony.

an alfresco lunch overlooking them. The final garden of note is the herb and vegetable garden, only recently planted but already supplying the restaurant with some of its produce. After exploring the house and formal gardens you can wander around the open parkland, much of which is very similar to an English country estate.

Verlegen to Stellenbosch The R44 is the direct road to Stellenbosch (16 km). En route you pass a couple of wine estates which are members of the Stellenbosch Wine Route. **Eikendal** is 4 km from Somerset West in the lee of the *Helderberg* as you approach Stellenbosch via the R44. The microclimate on the western slopes of the mountain is ideal for the growing of good wines. The estate is currently Swiss-owned and produces a number of quality wines. ■ *Sales and tasting Mon-Fri 0900-1700; Sat 0900-1600 (closes 1300 May-Sep); Sun 1030-1600. Cellar tours: Mon-Fri (Dec-Feb) 1130 and 1430. T012-8551422, www.eikendal.com Light lunches served in the wine tasting room or the gardens, daily, 1200-1400, closed Sat. Swiss cheese fondues are served on Fri evenings from Jun-Sep. There is a lodge offering luxury accommodation, T021-8553617, F8553862.*

Stellenbosch

Phone code: 021
(NB Always use
3-figure prefix)
Colour map 6, grid B5

Stellenbosch, the centre of the Winelands, is the oldest and most attractive town in the region and, indeed, one of South Africa's finest. The town itself is a pleasing mix of architectural styles – Cape Dutch, Georgian, Regency and Victorian houses line broad streets dappled with shade from centuries-old oak trees, and roadside furrows still carry water to the gardens. It is the most pleasant of the Wineland towns, has several good museums, fun nightlife thanks to the university, and is a perfect base for visiting the wine estates.

Ins and outs

Getting there The town is served by the suburban Metro railway; Cape Town, platform 1. If visiting on a day trip return times are 1545 and 1715. Journey time approximately 1 hr. Enquiries, T4492111. It is 46 km to **Cape Town**, 31 km to **Franschhoek**, 32 km to **Paarl**, 14 km to **Somerset West**.

Getting around Stellenbosch is perfect for exploring on foot as many of the interesting sights are concentrated in a small area along Church, Dorp and Drostdy streets. Guided walks leave from the tourist information office every day. The office also issues a pamphlet, *Discover Stellenbosch on Foot*. Some people will find the whole walk too tiring for a single day, so you may wish to concentrate on the buildings in the centre of town. Bike hire available from: *Village Cycles*, 3 Victoria St, T8870779, route maps provided; *Village Sport*, T8870779; and *Stumble Inn*, 12 Mark St, T8874049, good local route suggestions. *Avis*, T8870492; *Budget*, T8876935; *Imperial*, T8838140; are all represented, but cheaper deals are available from Cape Town. *Pool Taxis*, T8866282 and *Solomon Taxis*, T8813497.

Stellenbosch Tourist Bureau, 36 Market St, T8833584, F8838017, www.istellenbosch.org.za **Tourist office**
Open Mon-Fri 0800-1800, Sat 0900-1700, Sun 0930-1630. Between Jun and Aug the office opens 30 mins later and closes 30 mins earlier. A helpful and professional office supplying maps, guide books and tour information. They also have the menus from several town restaurants, plus good advice on the types of accommodation available in the area. The wine route information office operates from the same address. Guided walks leave from the office every day. Their annual guide to Stellenbosch is a useful introduction to the town and region, but be aware that they only list places which pay and that there are plenty of other excellent restaurants in and around the town which don't get a mention. Ask around – local folk will always be happy to offer an opinion.

History

In November 1679 Simon van der Stel left Cape Town with a party of soldiers in order to explore the hinterland. There was already a great need for additional land to be brought under cultivation to supply both Cape Town and passing ships calling for fresh supplies. On the first night the group camped beside a stream they named the Kuilsrivier. The stream turned out to be a tributary of a much larger river, the Eersterivier. As they followed the Eersterivier towards the mountains they found themselves in a very fertile alluvial valley. There was no sign of human habitation, the waters were cool and clean and everything seemed to grow in abundance – exactly the type of land van der Stel had been sent to discover. Several days after entering the valley the group camped under a large tree on an island formed by two branches of the Eersterivier. The camp was named Van der Stel se Bosch, or Van der Stel's wood.

Six months later, in May 1680, eight families from Cape Town moved into the area, tempted by the offer of as much free land as they could cultivate, and by the summer of 1681 Stellenbosch was a thriving agricultural community. This became the first European settlement in the interior of Southern Africa. By the end of 1683 more than 30 families had settled in the valley, a school had been built and a *landdrost* (magistrate) had been appointed. Throughout his life Simon van der Stel maintained a close interest in the development of the town. One of his greatest legacies was to order the planting of oak trees along the sides of every street. Canals were also built to bring water to the town gardens. Today, a number of the original oaks are still standing and some have been proclaimed national monuments.

It is difficult to picture it today, but at the end of the 17th century this new settlement was a frontier town. For the next 100 years the magistracy had dealings with the explorers, hunters, adventurers and nomadic peoples who lived beyond the Cape, and the authority extended over 250,000 square km. In the meantime, the town prospered as an agricultural centre and also emerged as a place of learning. In 1859 the Dutch Reformed Church started a Seminary which in 1866 became the Stellenbosch Gymnasium, renamed Victoria College in 1887. After the creation of the Union of South Africa in 1910, there was pressure on the new government to establish a single national university. By this stage Victoria College had emerged as a respected Afrikaner school, and Stellenbosch itself was regarded as an important centre of Afrikaner culture. In 1915 a successful local farmer, Johannes Marais died and left £100,000 towards higher education in Stellenbosch. This bequest finally persuaded the government to yield to public pressure and in April 1918 the Victoria College became the University of Stellenbosch.

Sights

Many of the finest buildings are not open to visitors and can only be admired from the outside

Stellenbosch offers two approaches to sightseeing: walking around the town centre viewing public buildings, oak-lined streets and stately homes; or going on a wine tour, visiting one of five co-operative wineries and 23 private cellars. Spend a couple of days in Stellenbosch and you'll get to do both.

Around the centre

No other town in South Africa has such an impressive concentration of early Cape buildings. However, like Swellendam (see page 257), many of the earliest buildings were lost to fires in the 18th and 19th centuries. What you see today is a collection of perfectly restored buildings. Following each fire, the destroyed buildings were recreated with the help of photographs, original plans and sketches, although the technology and materials of the day were used in their building. This is perhaps why they appear to have survived in such good condition. This is not unusual: the town of Tulbagh in the Breede River Valley was completely destroyed by an earthquake in 1969. Today it has the look and feel of an unspoilt quaint Victorian village.

Dorp Street, which runs east-west in the southern part of town, is one of the finest in Stellenbosch. It has all the classic features – an avenue of oak trees, running water in open furrows and carefully restored white-walled buildings. A walk from

Western Cape

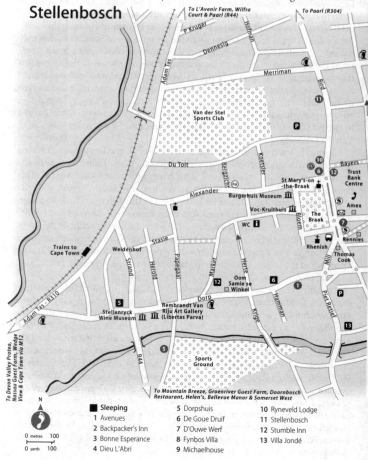

Stellenbosch

Sleeping		
1 Avenues	5 Dorpshuis	10 Ryneveld Lodge
2 Backpacker's Inn	6 De Goue Druif	11 Stellenbosch
3 Bonne Esperance	7 D'Ouwe Werf	12 Stumble Inn
4 Dieu L'Abri	8 Fynbos Villa	13 Villa Jondé
	9 Michaelhouse	

Libertas Parva to the Theological College takes you through the oldest parts of town and past some of the best preserved old buildings. The **Rembrandt van Rijn Art Gallery** is housed in the beautifully restored Libertas Parva, a classic H-shaped manor house built in 1783. It houses a small collection of 20th-century South African art, including paintings by Irma Stern. ■ *31 Dorp St. Mon-Fri 0900-1245, 1400-1700, Sat 1000-1300, 1400-1700. T8864340.*

Next door, on the corner of Dorp Street and Strand, is the **Stellenryck Wine Museum** which houses an assorted collection of old wine-making tools and some furniture. The collection at Groot Constantia is more impressive. Look out for the giant wine press outside. ■ *Mon-Fri 0900-1245, 1400-1700, Sat 1000-1300, 1400-1700. T8863588.*

Heading east along Dorp Street you'll pass the famous **Oom Samie se Winkel**, a Victorian-style general store (see Shopping below). Of particular note are the town houses just past the junction with Helderberg Street. Numbers 153, **Hauptfleisch House**, 155, **Bakker House**, 157, **Loubser House**, and 159, **Saxenhof**, are regarded as the best-preserved street façades in old Stellenbosch.

Branching off from Dorp Street is **Drostdy Street**, dominated by a building with a tall tower known as Utopia. Also in this street is the town church, the **Moederkerk**, actually the fourth incarnation of the town church. The current steeple church was

Western Cape

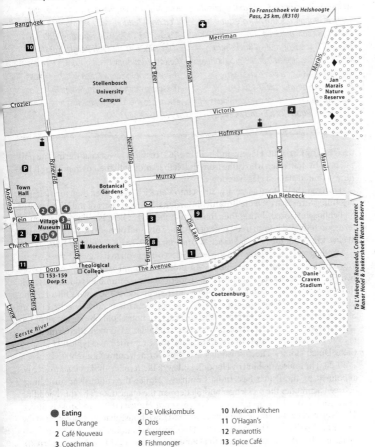

● Eating

1 Blue Orange	5 De Volkskombuis	10 Mexican Kitchen
2 Café Nouveau	6 Dros	11 O'Hagan's
3 Coachman	7 Evergreen	12 Panarottis
4 Decameron	8 Fishmonger	13 Spice Café
	9 Ha! Ha!	

The Brandy Route

*The Brandy Route starts at the **Van Ryn Brandy Cellar** at Vlottenburg, 8 km from Stellenbosch. This is the oldest working cellar in the Cape. You not only view the distillation process but the tour includes a visit to the workshop where the coopers make the maturation barrels from French oak. During the peak season, December and January, tours start at Monday-Friday 1000, 1130, 1500; Saturday 1000, 1130. For the rest of the year there is one morning tour and one afternoon tour, weekdays only. T021-8813875.*

*The route continues to the **Oude Molen Brandy** museum in Stellenbosch, visits by appointment only, T021-8086911. This is where the Frenchman, Rene Santhagens, the "saint of brandy in South Africa", established the first pot stall at the beginning of the 20th century. Next on the route is **Backsberg**, a well-known wine estate between Simondium and Klapmuts. Open weekdays from 0830-1700, Saturday 0800-1300, T021-8755141. The route then continues into Paarl to the **Paarl Rock Brandy Cellar**,*

*founded by the De Villiers family in 1856. Visitors are offered a taste of the only Hanepoot brandy in the world. Closed at weekends, T021-8626159. From Paarl you can either visit a cellar in Franschhoek or continue along the N1 to Rawsonville and Worcester where the route ends at the **KWV Brandy Cellar**. This is the largest brandy cellar in the world – there are 120 copper-pot stalls in use. Tours here are conducted in English (1400) and Afrikaans (1430). Book in advance for tours in French, Portuguese, Spanish, Italian and German, T023-3420255.*

*The **Cabrière Cellar** in Franschhoek is a unique underground cellar. It is known for a 100% Fine de Jourdan Brandy which Achim von Arnim has made from a blend of Pinot Noir and Chardonnay. Open Monday-Friday 1100-1300, 1400-1630, Saturday 1100-1300, T021-8762630. The **Oolf Bergh Brandy Cellar** in Rawsonville is unusual in that it is the only one in South Africa which employs the solera method of maturation. The cellar opened to the public for the first time late in 1997, T023-3493600.*

designed by Carl Otto Hagen, and built in 1862. Inside it is worth admiring the pulpit, built by craftsmen who came from the Netherlands with their own timber. It has nine coloured stained glass windows.

Turn right at the top of Drostdy Street into Van Riebeeck Street, then turn left into Neethling Street to reach the **Botanical Gardens**. These are part of the University of Stellenbosch (closed during the University holidays). There is a fine collection of ferns, orchids and bonsai trees. One of the more unusual plants to look out for is the *Welwitschis* from the Namib Desert. ■ *Mon-Fri 0900-1630, Sat 0900-1100.*

If you only have time to visit one place in Stellenbosch then this museum is the most rewarding

Heading west back along Van Riebeeck Street brings you to Ryneveld Street, where you'll find the entrance to the **Village Museum**. The complex currently spreads over two blocks in the oldest part of town. If you follow the guide numbers you will be taken through four houses, each representing a different period of the town's history. The oldest of these is **Schreuderhuis** (1709), one of the earliest houses to be built in Stellenbosch. The simple furniture and collection of household objects are all of the same period. The house was built by Sebastian Schreuder, a German. **Blettermanhuis** (1789) is a perfect example of what has come to be regarded as a typical H-shaped Cape Dutch home. The furnishings are those of a wealthy household between 1750-80. The house was built by Hendrik Lodewyk Bletterman, the last *landdrost* to be appointed by the Dutch East India Company. Notice the contrast in furnishings between Schreuder the messenger and Bletterman the magistrate. The third building in the museum to have been restored is **Grosvenor House** (1803), in Drostdy Street. This is an excellent example of the two-storeyed town house that once dominated the streets of Cape Town. The home was built by Christian Ludolph Neethling, a successful farmer, in 1782. The fourth and final house is the fussy **OM Bergh House** (1870), which once had a thatched roof. All four houses are set in neat kitchen gardens which have been recreated to reflect the popular (garden) plants of each period. Guides dressed in period clothes are at hand in the houses to answer any questions and point out interesting details. A fifth house is being restored at the corner of Drostdy and Church streets. Here you have the chance of viewing the painstaking work of conservation and restoration. ■ *Mon-Sat 0930-1700, Sun 1400-1700. R10. T8872902.*

Midway along **Church Street** is the *D'Ouwe Werf Hotel* (see Sleeping below), which stands on the site of the first church. The current owners have preserved the foundations and they can now be viewed in the cellar of the garden coffee house. As you look back towards the church, the steeple is perfectly framed by grand old oak trees. Much of the town's activity today seems to take place around the **Braak**, at the western end of Church Street. This is the original village green, and one-time military parade ground. On the western edge by Market Street is the **VOC-Kruithuis**, or Powder House, built in 1777 as a weapons store. Today it is a military museum. ■ *Mon-Fri 0930-1300.* The bell tower was added at a much later date. A short distance north, on the corner of Alexander Street, is the **Burgerhuis Museum**, a classic H-shaped Cape Dutch homestead built by Antonie Fick in 1797. ■ *Mon-Fri 0900-1245, 1400-1700, Sat 1000-1300, 1400-1700.*

Two churches overlook the Braak. The first is **Rhenish Church**, built in 1832 as a training school for coloureds and slaves, which has a very fine pulpit. The other is **St Mary's-on-the-Braak**, an Anglican church completed in 1852.

Jonkershoek Forest

About 12 km out of town, beyond the *Lanzerac Hotel*, is this forestry plantation, open to the public for hiking, fishing and mountain biking. If you don't fancy walking you can follow a 12-km gravel road through the forest. The **Boland Hiking Trail**, a 50-km trail across the Hottentots Holland Mountains to Franschhoek village, can be started from here (see Hottentots Holland Nature Reserve above). ■ *Small entrance fee payable at the gate, depending on your mode of transport. Hiking permits are issued at the gate, 0730-1700. For further details on long hikes contact T8891560.*

Essentials

In addition to the selection of hotels within the town there is a wide choice of accommodation on local farms and vineyards. These tend to cater for an exclusive market, but are strongly recommended if you wish to appreciate fully the beauty of the Winelands.

Sleeping

■ *on map, page 152*
Price codes:
see inside front cover

Hotels and some guesthouses tend to be overpriced when compared to other areas of the Western Cape

Central AL *Lanzerac Manor*, 2 km from town centre towards Jonkershoek Reserve, Jonkershoek Rd, T8871132, F8872310, www.lanzerac.co.za 48 rooms, some around a patio and swimming pool, spacious and well equipped, 3 restaurants. This is a smart hotel based around a luxury 18th century Dutch manor house. The food in the main dining room does not measure up to the status of the hotel; service is slow and the mock French chateau atmosphere doesn't work. *Vinkel en Koljander* restaurant is much better, excellent food, a helpful and efficient manager, closed in the evenings. **A** *D'Ouwe Werf*, 30 Church St, T8871608, F8874626, www.ouwewerf.com Converted Georgian house with 25 a/c rooms all with their own individual collection of antique furnishings. Polished floors, off-street parking, pool, celebrating its 200th year, popular vine-shaded terrace. Recommended as a treat.

B *Bonne Esperance*, 17 Van Riebeeck St, T8870225, F8878328, www.bonneesperance.com Restored Victorian town house, 15 rooms with en suite bathrooms, elegant and spacious dining room, small swimming pool, peaceful garden. Recommended. **B** *De Goue Druif*, 110 Dorp St, T8833555, F8833588, http://gouedruif.hypemart.net. Ultra smart and modern guesthouse, luxury bedrooms, lush garden, gym, sauna and steambath. Secure off-street parking. Ideal location for exploring town on foot. **B** *Dorpshuis*, 22 Dorp St, T8839881, F8839884, www.relaishotels.co.za 15 a/c rooms, marble-clad bathrooms, TV, private patio, antiques adorn each room, tasty large breakfasts with plenty of choice, neat gardens, swimming pool, a very smart Victorian town house. Recommended. **B** *Stellenbosch*, 162 Dorp St, T8873644, F8873673, stb-hotel@mweb.co.za 20 a/c rooms in a gorgeous building which is protected as a National Monument. Seafood restaurant, brasserie and bar. Smart option in the centre of town. **B-C** *Dieu L'Abri*, 71 Victoria St, T8865652, F8871501. 10 luxury rooms with tasteful décor, en suite shower rooms, TV lounge, a fine Victorian house with beautiful wooden floors. Recommended. **B-C** *Fynbos Villa*, 14 Neethling St, T8838670, F8838479, fynbos@iafrica.com 6 a/c rooms, some non-smoking, restaurant, swimming pool and gardens. A smart, well-managed guesthouse which is also a National Monument. German spoken. **B-C** *L'Auberge Rozendal*, Omega St, Rozendal Farm, T8838737, F8838738. A family-run guesthouse with 16 double rooms, small dining room with a fixed menu, pleasant veranda overlooking woods. Swimming pool, shady gardens, a fine old house. Recommended.

C *Avenues*, 32 The Avenue, T8871843, F8872733. 6 rooms, some non-smoking, TV, laundry service, Satour accredited, secluded gardens. Recommended. **C** *Crofters*, 15 Thibault St, T8872237, F8838658, crofters@adept.co.za Family-run B&B on the banks of Eerste River in a quiet suburb close to town. 3 self-catering suites, swimming pool, nice location. **C** *Michaelhouse*, 29 van Riebeeck St, T/F8866343. 4 stylish double rooms, individually decorated, en suite, TV, lovely sunny courtyard, breakfasts included. **C** *Ryneveld Lodge*, 67 Ryneveld St, T8874469, F8839549, www.ryneveldlodge.co.za B&B in a smart Victorian house, plenty of detail to furnishings, enclosed swimming pool, secure parking, but overpriced. **C** *Villa Jondé*, 27 Noordwal West, T/F8833568. Secluded B&B set in shady gardens, 8 en suite rooms. French and German spoken, close to the river. Recommended. **C** *Wilfra Court*, 16 Hine St, T/F8896091, T082-9200085 (mob). 2 double rooms with shared bathroom, all very clean, continental or English breakfasts included, secure parking, approximately 5 km from town centre off the R44 road to Paarl, run by William and Frances, a very friendly couple. Anyone with an interest in South African political affairs should stay here, as this was the first guesthouse in the region run by coloured people. William was an MP for more than 30 years. Strongly recommended. A great experience.

D *The Attic*, T8879037, F8866211. Self-catering flat for 2-4 people, separate entrance. Non-smokers. Excellent value, central location, run by a friendly couple. Recommended. **D-E** *Helen's*, 97 Buitekring Av, T8833942, armandt@kingsley.co.za En suite room, separate entrance, off-street parking, one of the cheaper options in town. For an extra fee you can have breakfast in bed!

F *Backpackers Inn*, de Wet Centre, Church St, T8872020, bacpac1@global.co.za Spotless dorms and double rooms in a modern block in the centre of town. Fairly spacious and with kitchen. Popular with families. **F** *Mountain Breeze*, 6 km south of town on R44, T/F8800200. Caravan and camping site, hot water, electric points, swimming pool. **F** *Stumble Inn*, 12 Market St, T/F8874049, stumble@iafrica.com Popular hostel in two separate old Cape houses. Spacious double rooms and cramped dorms. Original house has attractive garden, bar, TV room, kitchen, hammocks, shady cushion banks; other house has small pool, kitchen. Very relaxed and friendly place, although could do with a clean. Excellent value Easy Rider wine tours (see below), bicycles to hire, remains by far the best budget option in town.

These recommend-ations, all within a short distance of the centre, are a mix of private converted farms, wine estates and country hotels. The emphasis tends to be on luxury and exclusiveness – South African-style

Out of town **B** *L'Avenir Farm Guesthouse*, 5 km north of Stellenbosch off the R44 towards the N1 and Paarl, T021-8895001, F8897313, lavenirguesthouse@freemail.absa.co.za A peaceful setting on a smart wine farm with elegant bedrooms, all with en suite bathrooms. Recommended. **B** *Bellevue Manor*, Strand Rd, T8801086, F8801076, www.bellevuestellenbosch.co.za Purpose-built a/c cottages with TV, fridge, private terrace, a round pool with braai area, close to golf course. **B** *Nassau Guest Farm*, 7 km west of Stellenbosch, T8813818, F8813583. Tastefully furnished self-contained thatched cottages overlooking a neat farm, with swimming pool and tennis court. The friendly owner has a vintage car collection which you may be able to try out. **B** *Wedge View*, The Bonniemile, 5 km south of town, T/F8813525, www.wedgeview.co.za Attractive thatched farmhouse, en suite rooms, snooker room, bar, drawing room, attractive gardens, pool. **B-C** *Devon Valley Protea*, Devon Valley Rd, 6 km south, T8822012, F8822610, www.protea.com 40 plain a/c rooms with pine furniture, complex of flats set in the country, shady terrace overlooking vineyards, neat gardens, restaurant, sheltered swimming pool. **B-C** *Groenrivier Guest Farm*, Annandale Rd, 10 mins south on R44, T8813767, F8813069. Charming late-18th century farmhouse built in 1786. 2 self-contained flats on a beautiful rose farm with views of the Helderberg. Breakfast provided, swimming pool, tennis court, braai area.

Blue Orange, Dorp St. Excellent breakfasts, good value snacks and sandwiches, popular with students. *Café Nouveau*, Plein St, lovely old-fashioned café serving sandwiches, coffee and cakes. *The Coachman*, Ryneveld St next to Village Museum. Beer garden serving light meals and snacks, nice setting, popular with tour groups. *Decameron*, 50 Plein St, T8833331. Italian cuisine, decent pasta, relaxing beer garden under vines. *Doornbosch*, Old Strand Rd, T8875079. Closed Sun evening, Italian and French dishes, served in a long thatched cottage set in beautiful gardens, the perfect spot during the summer, popular, booking advisable. Recommended. *Dros*, corner of Bird and Alexander streets. A large bar-cum-restaurant with plenty of outdoor seating in a lively square. Popular chain serving standard pub fare such as burgers, steaks and pizza. Good value, but portions are on the small side. *Evergreen*, 5 Plein St. Closed Sun, breakfasts and light vegetarian meals. *Fishmonger*, Sanlam Bldg, corner of Plein and Ryneveld streets, T8877835. A very popular seafood restaurant, sensibly priced, good service, booking essential. Recommended. *Ha!Ha!*, Ryneveld St, opposite Village Museum. Good place to stop for a cool drink or coffee and cake after visiting the museum. *Mamma Roma*, Stelmark Centre, Merriman Av. Essentially Italian plus seafood from the Cape. *Mexican Kitchen*, 25 Bird St, T8829997. Great new cantina-style restaurant serving huge portions of nachos, bean soup, fajitas, tacos and steaks. Relaxed setting with inventive décor – some of the seats are swings. Recommended. *Midnite Grill*, 59 Plein St. Late night venue. *Panarottis*, Bird St. Pizza, pasta and juice bar, take-aways, good value and popular high street chain. *Spice Café*, 34 Kerkstraat. Cosy eccentric place with a garden, serving simple tasty meals. *Vinkel & Koljander*, in the *Lanzerac Hotel*. Light lunches and country dishes, with an open terrace. *De Volkskombuis*, Old Strand Rd, T8872121. Closed Sun evening, a high standard of food and service, specialities are Cape dishes with strong European influences. Try the home-made oxtail or springbok pies. The atmosphere is enhanced by the character of the building, a restored Herbert Baker Cape Dutch homestead, with views across the Eerste River. A sensibly priced treat.

Eating

● *on map, page 152*

Thanks to the university, Stellenbosch has an unusually large number of bars and good value restaurants to choose from. But the best place for lunch is at one of the Wine Estates. Out of term time some of the smaller student haunts close

Bohemia Pub, Ryneveld St. One of the main student haunts, serves snacks, relaxed atmosphere. *Dros*, corner of Bird and Alexander streets. The restaurant turns into a noisy bar later at night. Seats spill out on to the square at 25 Bird St. Popular with backpackers and students. *Elle 51*, 51 Plein St, T8839525. Breezy and stylish bar serving snacks and drinks to yuppies and trendy students. *Fandango*, 25 Bird St. Café and bar offering internet access, tables on square. *Finlay's Wine Bar*, Plein St. A lively long bar with a few tables for quick meals served from the back, buzzing at lunch and after work, large selection of wines, popular with the yuppie crowd, prices above average, friendly service. *Live*, Adringa St. Popular student hangout, bar and club. *Mavericks*, corner of Bird and Plein streets. Bar and club, another popular student haunt. *O'Hagans*, 43 Bird St. Irish theme pub, part of a chain which serves generous pub meals, good range of beers including imported (check sell by dates – they don't move fast on account of the price), popular most nights, a serious drinking haunt with food. *Stones*, Bird St. Lively bar and pool hall, plenty of tables, seats on outdoor balcony overlooking the street, very popular, gets packed and noisy later in the night. *The Terrace*, Alexander St. Busy pub with outdoor tables overlooking the Braak, live music most nights.

Bars & pubs

Computicket have an office in the Eikestad Mall, T4214715. Tickets for all local and national events can be reserved and bought from here. **Cinemas** *Ster Kinekor Eikestad Mall*, Andringa St, T8864464. 6 screens, all new releases. **Theatre** *Endler Hall*, T8082334. Musical concerts. *Oude Libertas Amphitheatre*, T8087474. Outdoor events from Nov-Mar. For all details check at the Publicity Association.

Entertainment

Stellenbosch Festival, held in **Sep**, is a musical and arts event concentrating on chamber music and art exhibitions, T8833891. *Simon van der Stel Festival*, in the middle of **Oct**, held every year on the Fri and Sat nearest to the 14 Oct, Simon van der Stel's birthday. Horsemen parade in traditional dress and target shooting and other activities depicting the era are acted out on the *Braak*, T8833584. *Food and Wine Festival*, in the last week of **Oct**, is an annual event to promote local award-winning wines along with traditional rural cuisine, T8864867.

Festivals

Western Cape

Shopping The most famous shop in Stellenbosch is as much a tourist attraction as an ongoing business. *Oom Samie se Winkel* (Uncle Sammy's Shop), 84 Dorp St, has been trading since 1791. The first owner, Pieter Gerhard Wium, traded in meat, but the shop became famous between 1904 and 1944 when the store was owned and run by Samuel Johannes Volsteedt. He stocked virtually everything you could need, and was known throughout the town. Today the shop still sells a wide range of goods and it has retained its pre-war character with items hanging from all corners and old cabinets full of bits and pieces. It has all the makings of a tourist trap, and so it is, but unlike many others, it is genuine. Next door is a restaurant and wine shop.

Sports **Horse riding** *Amoi Horse Trails*, T8871623. *Little Creek Horse Trails*, T082-4855513 (mob). *Spier Horse Trails*, T091100.

Tour operators *Easy Rider Wine Tours*, T8864651, stumble@iafrica.com Hugely popular wine tour organized by the *Stumble Inn* (see above). Tours take in 5 estates, with 5 tastings in each, restaurant, lunch and cheese tasting included, good value although they seem to take too many people making it rather chaotic. Alternatively, there are a number of private registered tour guides. A few are listed here but it is best to check with the *Tourist Bureau* about prices and whether they are still registered or recognized by the local authorities. *Antoinette du Toit*, T8833370; *Hildegard Kidd*, T8875727; *Judith Krohn*, T/F8514205.

Directory **Banks** All the main South African banks are found here. The following **Bureaux de Change** are open for longer hours. *Rennies Foreign Exchange* (local representatives of Thomas Cook), Mill St, T8865259. Open Mon-Fri 0830-1700, Sat 0900-1200. *American Express*, 4 Plein St, T8870818. Open Mon-Fri 0830-1700, Sat 0900-1200. **Communications** *Fandango* 25 Bird St. Café and bar offering internet access. You can also check your email at the *Tourist Office* on Market St. **Main Post Office**: Plein St. A Post Restante service is available. *PostNet*, Trust Bank Centre, T8865761. Open Mon-Fri 0830-1700, Sat 0900-1230. International postal and telephone service, photocopies, passport photos and courier services. **Useful services** Ambulance: T10177. Fire Brigade: T8088888. Hospital: T8870310. **24-hr** Medi-Clinic: T8838571. Police: T10111.

Stellenbosch Wine Route

Remember the drink drive laws in South Africa. When wine tasting, you may be offered up to 25 different wines to sample at each estate, so make sure one of you stays off the booze

This was the first wine route to open in South Africa, in April 1971. It was the idea of three local farmers: Neil Joubert, Frans Malan and Spatz Sperling. It has been hugely successful, attracting tens of thousands of visitors every year, and today the membership is comprised of 42 private cellars. It is possible to taste and buy wines at all of them, and the cellars can arrange for your purchases to be delivered internationally. Many of the estates have developed excellent restaurants as well as providing very popular picnic lunches – at weekends it is advisable to book if you wish to eat at a particular place. ■ *Further information: Wine Route Office, T8864310, F8864330, www.wineroute.co.za Open Mon-Fri 0830-1300, 1400-1700. Exporters: Stellenbosch Wines Direct, T8839315. Steven Rom, T4346023, www.stevenrom.co.za Vineyard Connection, T8844360, info@vineyardconnection.co.za*

Delaire This is a small estate which has managed to produce some very high-standard wines. During the last five years their **Chardonnay** has been a popular export label. The estate is on the right at the head of Helshoogte Pass, on the R310, as you drive towards Franschhoek. On a clear day visitors are rewarded with views of the Simonsberg Mountains. ■ *Sales and tastings: Mon-Sat 1000-1700, Sun 1000-1600. Cellar tours by appointment only. Light lunches served Tue-Sun, 1200-1500. Also open for evening meals. Booking advised. Between Oct and Apr picnic hampers are also available. The estate offers accommodation in the form of 2 self-catering mountain lodges, each of which can sleep up to 6 people. T8851756, www.delairewinery.co.za*

Delheim This is one of the more commercially orientated estates and may seem a little too impersonal. However, the *Vinter's Platter Garden Restaurant* has a beautiful setting

Vineyard Hiking Trail

An energetic way to get a feel for the Winelands is to walk along part or all of the Vineyard Trail. The full hike which runs between Stellenbosch and Kuils River is 24 km long. The trail passes through vineyards, olive groves, and a few patches of indigenous vegetation. There are two

shorter options but these are still 12 km and 16 km long. The Tourist Bureau issues an excellent map showing all the alternative trails. All the trails start at the Oude Libertas Amphitheatre complex of Stellenbosch Farmers' Winery, close to the old cemetery.

with views towards Cape Town and Table Mountain. Tastings are conducted in a cool downstairs cellar. ■ *Sales and tastings: Mon-Fri 0830-1700, Sat 0900-1500, Sun 1100-1500 (Oct-Apr only). Cellar tours: Mon-Fri 1030 and 1430, Sat 1030. Lunches: Mon-Sat 1230-1500, Sun (Oct-Apr only). T8822033, www.delheim.com*

This privately owned old estate, founded in 1692, is off the Bottelary Road, 10 km north of Stellenbosch. The first owners, Coenraad Boom and Christoffel L'Estreux planted 2,000 vines, grew wheat and kept sheep. A wide variety of red and white wines are produced from 16 different grape varieties. During the summer, lunches are served in the shade and peace of the gardens; come winter the tasting room doubles up as a restaurant with warming log fires. Their **Semillon** blended white has been well received. ■ *Sales and tastings: Mon-Fri 0900-1700, Sat 0900-1500. Lunches: Mon-Sat, 1200-1400, closed Sun. T8652541, www.hartenbergestate.com*

Hartenberg
The underground cellar is decorated with some beautiful stained glass by Karel Hans Wilhelm

The first vines were planted on this estate in 1692 by a German, Barend Lubbe, and the manor house was built in 1814 in traditional Cape Dutch H-style. Today this has been converted into the *Lord Neethling* restaurant, and is 4 km west of Stellenbosch, off the M12 (look out for the flag poles). The new owners have invested in the latest cellar technology and replanted the vineyards – the results have won awards throughout the last decade. Ones to look out for include the **Cabernet Sauvignon '95** and the **Lord Neethling Pinotage '97**. ■ *Sales and tastings: Mon-Fri 0900-1700/1900; Sat and Sun 1000-1600/1800. Cellar tours: by appointment. Vineyard tours: daily, 1100, 1200 and 1300 (Nov-Apr only). Lunches: choice of the Lord Neethling restaurant, which is divided into rooms of different character, or Palm Terrace, a popular outdoor lunch venue. T8838988, www.neethlingshof.co.za*

Neethlingshof
The approach to the manor house is via a strange stone pine avenue. Just over 1 km long, the avenue now features on the labels of the estate wines

This estate lies 14 km from Stellenbosch, off the M12, close to Kuils River. In 1693 Simon van der Stel granted land to a freeburgher, Jochem Sax. Sax planted the first vines and built the manor house in 1701, but four years later the farm was bought by two Swedish soldiers who had retired from the Dutch East India Company. The estate's name is a mix of the names of the first three owners. It is only in the last decade that the estate has been developed into a showpiece on the Wine Route. The estate only produces a small number of cases each year, but some of the Private Collection is very good. The *Guinea Fowl* restaurant attracts most of the visitors. ■ *Sales and tastings: Mon-Fri 0900-1700, Sat 0900-1600, Sun 1100-1700 (Sep-Oct only). No cellar tours. Guinea Fowl (T9065232) is a popular restaurant open daily for lunch and dinner. T9036113, www.saxenburg.co.za*

Saxenburg

This large estate has in recent years produced some exceptionally fine wines. Simonsig was voted top estate at Veritas in 1999, and the **Tiara**, a cabernet blend, has won several awards. Their **Chardonnay** is consistently very good. ■ *Sales and tastings: Mon-Fri 0830-1700, Sat 0830-1600. Cellar tours: Mon-Fri 1000 and 1500, Sat 1000. T8884900, www.simonsig.co.za*

Simonsig

Western Cape

Uittyk Off the R44 between the N1 and Stellenbosch, this excellent estate does not appear as a member of the Stellenbosch Wine Route. A fine Georgian-style manor house dating from 1712 is the centre piece of this beautiful estate. Wine tastings are conducted in a relaxed and friendly atmosphere. Highly recommended. Two of the best wines on offer are their **Sauvignon Blanc '97/98** and **Cabernet/Shiraz '94**. ■ *Sales and tastings: Mon-Fri 0900-1700, Sat 0090-1230, closed Sun. T8844416, F8844717.*

Franschhoek

Phone code: 021
(NB Always use
3-figure prefix)
Colour map 6, grid B5

This is undoubtedly one of the most pleasant Wineland villages, but the reality is that most of the attractions here have been created to serve the tourist industry. The outlying wine estates all have their individual appeal, but the village itself is mostly restaurants and touristy shops. However, many of the restaurants are very good and a visit to Franschhoek should always include a good meal.

Ins & outs Franschoek is 71 km from **Cape Town** (via N1), 26 km from **Paarl**, 31 km from **Stellenbosch**. There is no regular public transport to Paarl. If you are on a budget consider a hired car for a day, between 4 this could cost as little as 100 Rand each, and on a long day you could visit all the Wineland towns and still catch the sunset at Cape Point.

Tourist office 68 Huguenot Rd, T8763603, www.franschhoek.org.za Open daily. Helpful staff, a useful set of restaurant menus are on display, a chance to check out prices and choice without walking all over town. For information on hiking in Jonkershoek, T8866543.

History Although the first Huguenots arrived at the Cape in 1688, the village of Franschhoek only took shape in 1837 after the church and the manse had been built. The first immigrants settled on farms granted to them by Simon van der Stel along the Drakenstein Valley at Oliphantshoek in 1694. Franschhoek is built on parts of *La Cotte* and *Cabrière* farms. The village became the focal point of the valley but the oldest and most interesting buildings are to be found on the original Huguenot farms and wine estates.

Sights The **Huguenot Memorial Museum** and Monument collection is housed in two buildings either side of Lambrecht Street. The main building, to the left of the Huguenot Monument, is modelled on a house designed by the French architect, Louis Michel Thibault, built in 1791 at Kloof Street, Cape Town. The displays inside trace the history of the Huguenots in South Africa. There are some fine collections of furniture, silverware and family bibles, but little to hold one's attention for very long. Perhaps the most interesting displays are the family trees providing a record of families over the past 250 years. One of the roles of the museum today is to maintain an up-to-date register of families and their children, so that future generations will be able to trace their ancestors. ■ *Mon-Fri 0900-1700, Sat 0900-1300, 1400-1700, Sun 1400-1700. Small admission fee. If you wish to have a guided tour ask at reception.*

Next door to the museum is the unattractive **Huguenot Monument**, a highly symbolic memorial built to mark 250 years since the first Huguenots settled in the Cape. It is set in a peaceful rose garden with the rugged Franschhoek Mountains providing a contrasting background. The architect was JC Jongens and the central female figure is the work of C Steynberg. The three arches represent the Trinity, and the golden sun and cross on top are the Sun of Righteousness and the Cross of Christian Faith. In front of the arches is a statue of a woman with a bible in her right hand and a broken chain in her left, symbolizing freedom from religious oppression. If you look closely at the globe you can see several objects carved into the southern tip of Africa: a bible, harp, spinning wheel and a sheaf of corn and the vine. These represent different aspects of the Huguenots' life, respectively their faith, their art and culture, their industry and their agriculture. The final piece of the memorial, the curved colonnade, represents tranquillity and spiritual peace after the problems they had faced in France.

Western Cape

The Huguenots

The Huguenots were French Calvinists who during the 16th century became an influential force under the leadership of the Prince de Condé, Gaspard de Coligny and Prince Henry of Navarre. After the death of King Henry IV, the Catholics at the royal court started to pursue a policy of persecution. In 1685 the rights of all Protestants were revoked in the Edict of Nantes. Soon afterwards thousands were forced to flee France to Britain, Germany and the Netherlands. This coincided with the Dutch looking for additional settlers in their new Cape colony to help provide sufficient supplies for passing ships. Between 1688 and 1720 about 270 Huguenots settled at the Cape. Within two generations the only reminder of their French past was their family and farm names. From the outset Governor Simon van der Stel had forced the use of Dutch in schools and at church.

The **'Cat Se Pad' Hiking Trail** follows the original alignment of one of the first passes to be built over the mountains in the Cape. The first stage of this hike is a 2-km climb from the village to the top of Franschhoek Pass, offering stunning views over the valley. The path then continues for a further 10 km down towards Villiersdorp.

AL-A *Auberge du Quartier Français*, corner of Wilhelmina and Berg streets, T8762151, F8763105, res@lqf.co.za An elegant country house with 14 large en suite rooms all with fire-places and views over the gardens. There is a small central swimming pool and peaceful court-yard. The attached restaurant is rated as one of the best in the Western Cape, but the food can be fussy and disappointing – 'pretentious', as one reader put it. Nevertheless, a good hotel for a treat. **A** *Plumwood Inn*, 11 Cabriere St, T8763883, F8763803, www.plumwoodinn.com A small, exclusive guesthouse, but slightly over-priced. 4 a/c spacious double rooms, furnished with antiques and decorated in soft pastel colours. The lounge has a high ceiling and tiled floor which helps keep the room cool in the summer. Swimming pool. No children.

B-C *Auberge Bligny*, 28 Van Wijk St, T8763767, F8763483, bligny@mweb.co.za A beauti-fully restored house dating from 1860, with 7 double rooms with en suite bathroom, includ-ing a special honeymoon suite which opens on to a shaded veranda. TV, lounge with a small library and fireplace in winter, neat gardens, swimming pool, central location, run by Gill and Jack. Recommended. **B** *Auberge Chanteclair*, 500 m behind the Huguenot Monument, T8763685, F8762709, chanteclair@mweb.co.za Beautiful, spacious rooms with en suite bathrooms and old-fashioned décor, in a Victorian farmhouse, comfortable lounge, swim-ming pool, secluded gardens set amongst orchards and vineyards, a superior B&B with attentive service to match, convenient location. Recommended. **B** *Auberge La Dauphine*, PO Box 384, T/F8762606, moates@ct.lia.net One of the most peaceful locations in the valley. 5 luxury rooms each with a spacious lounge in a carefully restored and converted wine cellar. Surrounded by beautiful gardens and vineyards. There is a large swimming pool, guided tours of the farm, plus mountain bike trails and horse-riding in the nearby mountains. Miles and Lianne successfully offer the best of Franschhoek with its original French heritage. Rec-ommended. **B** *La Cabriere*, Middagkrans Rd, T8764780, lacabriere@icon.co.za Small luxuri-ous guesthouse, 4 a/c en suite rooms with Provençal décor, fireplaces and views of vineyards and mountains. Understated and stylish spot. **B-C** *Résidence Klein Oliphants Hoek*, 14 Akademie St, T/F8762566, www.kleinoliphantshoek.com A very fine guesthouse in the cen-tre of the village which was built originally as a missionary hall in the 1888. There are 6 cosy and comfortable a/c double rooms with en suite bathrooms and TV (M-Net). The breakfast room-cum-lounge is the original meeting hall. To one end is a fireplace which warms the room during winter months; at the other is a fine balcony. Here you can choose to read up on the Huguenots from the extensive library or just pass the day on the terrace by the swim-ming pool. Recommended. **B** *Dartrey Lodge*, 5 D Uys St, T8763530. 5 homely rooms (3 in garden), elegant lounge, TV room, neat gardens, swimming pool, run by May and Les. **B-C** *Huguenot*, 34 Huguenot Rd, T8762092, F8763038. 12 rooms, restaurant, bar, swimming

Sleeping
■ *on maps, pages 162 and 164 Price codes: see inside front cover*

Some of the places recommended here are not in the centre of the village, but are along the Franschhoek Valley (see map)

pool, mountain views, simple town hotel, good value. **B** *La Fontaine*, 21 Dirkie Uys St, T/F8762112. This is a fine double-storey house with a swimming pool in the relaxing garden, 3 double rooms with en suite bathrooms, plus a family suite and a garden cottage. All rooms have views of the valley and surrounding mountains. Breakfast can be enjoyed on the vine shaded veranda during the summer months. It is also within easy walking distance of the many excellent restaurants in the village. Recommended. **B** *Franschhoek Country House*, Main Rd, T8763386, www.fch.co.za Smart, restored country house with 6 neat and spacious rooms, four-poster beds, excellent service, mature gardens, swimming pool.

C *La Gileppe*, 47 Huguenot Rd, T8762146, lagileppe@lagileppe.co.za Beautifully restored Victorian town house with a few braai spots dotted about the neat garden. Double rooms with en suite bathrooms, honeymoon suite. Advance booking advised. Central, just a brief walk from the shops and restaurants. **C** *Le Ballon Rouge*, 7 Reservoir St, T8762651, F8783743, www. ballon-rouge.co.za 7 double rooms, popular guesthouse with attached restaurant. **C** *Le Jardinet*, 3 Klein Cabriere St, T/F8762186, regeorge@mweb.co.za Peaceful B&B in a quiet side street just a few mins' walk from the restaurants and shops. Double rooms with en suite bathroom, each overlooking the garden. Guest lounge has a library, fridge, TV and video player. One of our favourites in the village. **C** *Lekkerwijn*, T8741122, lekkerwijn@new.co.za 10 mins' drive from the centre of Franschhoek, heading towards Paarl. Look out for the signs to your right just before the junction with the R310 to Stellenbosch. A fine B&B in an old family home full of character. 3 double rooms and 1 single room, each with an en suite bathroom. The four rooms are arranged around a private courtyard and have their own separate access. Guests have use of a tastefully furnished lounge and the swimming pool. Well run. Recommended. **C** *Bo La Motte*, Middegkrans Rd, T8763067, F8763498, www.bolamotte.com 3 fully equipped cottages with fireplaces, shared pool, good views. Peaceful spot just outside the village. **C** *Stonehedge Cottages*, T8763760, stonehedge@mweb.co.za Self-catering farm cottage at the head of the valley, sleeps 4, TV, fireplace, plunge pool, superb views, a perfect retreat, ask for Diane.

D-F *La Bri Holiday Farm*, Robertsvlei Rd, T8763133. Choice of self-catering cottages which can sleep up to 6, or dormitory, peaceful rural location, swim in the farm dam, must have your own transport to get here.

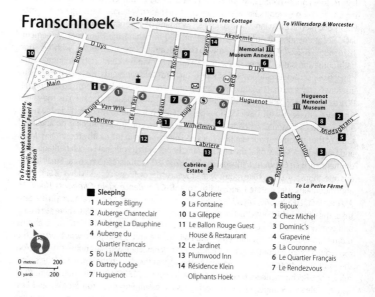

Franschhoek

0 metres   200
0 yards   200

At the weekend, especially Sun, most places will be full of people from Cape Town spending a day in the country. Arrive early, or book in advance. Most establishments have a French flavour, but be prepared for a South African twist. Surprisingly, many restaurants cater well for vegetarians, very rare in South Africa generally. *Le Ballon Rouge*, 12 Reservoir St, T8762651. Next to the guesthouse, sensibly priced meals made from fresh, local produce, not your typical South African fare. Its deserved success has made this a popular restaurant, but when full it lacks the intimate and peaceful ambience of elsewhere in the village. *Bijoux*, 58 Huguenot St, T8763474. Relaxed bistro serving grills, seafood, good oysters, outdoor terrace, very popular. *Chez Michel*, Huguenot Rd, T8762671. A small easy-paced restaurant, good selection of imaginative dishes, rather over-the-top décor. *La Couronne*, Robertsvlei Rd, T8762770. Small, formal restaurant in a perfect setting among vines. Light lunches, 5-course dinners, good local and international dishes. *Dominic's*, 66 Huguenot Rd, next to the information office, T8762255. Easy-going country pub serving hearty meals, enjoy the shady gardens in the summer and the log fire in the winter. *The Grapevine*, Huguenot Rd, T8762520. Recommended for fish and game braais. *La Maison de Chamonix*, 1 Uitkyk St, T8762393. Closed Mon, upmarket country-style on the wine estate (see below), good vegetarian menu. *Monneaux*, Main Rd, T8763386. Contemporary fusion cuisine, more up-to-date than many restaurants in Franschoek, attractive outdoor terrace and cosy dining room. *Mountain View*, Excelsior Rd, T8762071. Large restaurant in *Franschhoek Country Manor*, plenty of tables in the garden, vegetarian menu, popular for Sun lunch, booking advised during holiday season. *La Petite Fêrme*, Pass Rd, 2 km out of town, T8763016. Local trout and lamb, vegetarian menu, good views of the valley, especially in the autumn. Recommended. *Le Quartier Français*, 16 Huguenot Rd, T8762151. Rated as one of the best restaurants in the Western Cape. Expensive French and South Arican dishes, rather fussy and over-rated, but nevertheless a place for a treat. *Le Rendezvous*, Huguenot Rd. Restaurant and coffee shop in the Oude Stallen Centre, peaceful outdoor terrace, light meals and traditional dishes.

L'Afrique, local art and crafts. *Pippin Farm Stall*, Huguenot Rd. Fresh produce such as jams and smoked salmon trout. *Bordeaux*, Huguenot Rd. Selection of antique Cape furniture and china.

Horse riding *Paradise Stables*, T8762160. Guided trails throughout the vineyards, wine tasting tours with lunch, run by Pieter Hugo, no rides on Sun. *Mont Rochelle Stables*, T083-3004368 (mob). 1-3-hr tours, wine tasting rides.

All-Over, 17 Dirkie Uys St, T083-4505273 (mob), www.aotours.co.za Mon-Fri, essentially the local travel agent but could be of service if you need to confirm a flight or need more information about travel in South Africa.

Eating
● on maps, pages 162 and 164

Franschhoek has a reputation for being the culinary capital of the Western Cape

Shopping

Sports

Tour operators

Western Cape

Franschhoek Wine Route

All the vineyards lie along the Franschhoek Valley, making it one of the most compact wine routes in the region. What makes this such a rewarding route is that several estates have opened their own excellent restaurants and five also offer luxury accommodation. All the valley's wine can be tasted at the **Franschhoek Vineyards Co-operative**, located on the right just before you enter the village when approaching from Stellenbosch. There is a restaurant, and information on all the estates is available here. ■ *Mon-Fri 0930-1700, Sat 1000-1600, Sun 1100-1500. T8762086.*

Opening hours at some estates are longer between Nov and Apr. Most close on Sun

Boschendal estate has been growing wine for 300 years and is today one of the most popular estates in the region. The estate started life as two farms in 1687. In 1715 the land was bought by Abraham de Villiers and today the house is regarded as the seat of the De Villiers family. Most of the wine produced on the estate is white; their sparkling wines are highly regarded. ■ *Sales and tastings: Mon-Sat 0830-1630; Nov-Apr, Sun 0930-1230. Vineyard tours: 1030 and 1130, by appointment. The wine cellar has been converted into the excellent Boschendal restaurant which serves a superb buffet lunch; between Nov-Apr a second restaurant, Le Pique Nique, offers picnic hampers in*

Boschendal
The restored H-shaped manor house is one of the finest in South Africa

the gardens (booking essential). Le Café is open daily for snacks and afternoon teas. Booking essential for lunches during the holidays. T8704203, www.boschedalwines.co.za

Chamonix This is one of the largest farms in the valley. The underground cellar is a welcome cool tour at the height of summer. There are two smart self-catering cottages on the estate for overnight stays, T8762494. Many of the vines have been recently replanted, it will be a while before their true potential is realized. Their **Chardonnay** is highly rated. ■ *Sales and tastings: daily, 0930-1700. Cellar tours: by appointment. La Maison de Chamonix, closed Mon, an excellent French-style restaurant, outside tables in the summer, popular buffet lunch on Sun. T8763241, www.chamonix.co.za*

Mont Rochelle This estate has one of the most attractive settings in the region with beautiful views of the valley. Graham and Lyn de Villiers, eighth generation descendants of the original Huguenot Jacques de Villers, have redeveloped this estate and re-fitted the 150-year-old Victorian cellar, an usual sight in this area. Wine tasting and cellar tours are conducted 6 days a week and there is small restaurant on site open for lunch. ■ *Sales and tastings: Mon-Sat 1100-1700, Sun 1100-1300. Cellar tours: Mon-Fri 1100, 1230, 1500. T8763000, montrochelle@wine.co.za*

La Motte The original manor house and cellars were built in 1752 and the grand old cellars, alone worth a visit, are now used for wine tasting. All the wines are made and bottled

Franschhoek Valley

on the estate. As a relatively small producer, only 15,000 cases per annum, the estate has managed to create some excellent wines. Look out for their **Millennium '97**. ■ *Sales and tastings: Mon-Fri 0900-1630, Sat 0900-1200. Cellar tours: by appointment. T8763119, www.la-motte.co.za*

This vineyard has a beautiful setting on the slopes of the Drakensteinberge, above the Bellingham estate (an excellent estate, but no longer open to visitors). In 1969 the estate was bought by Anton Rupert who immediately set about renovating the farm buildings and redeveloping the vineyard. The present homestead was built in 1811 – from its grand marble halls and staircases you look out across an ornamental pond and neat mature gardens. The other notable attraction is the original wine cellar; this has been carefully restored and now houses a set of giant wine vats. The new cellars have been described as a "winemaker's dream", as their design incorporates all the latest ideas in cellar technology. It is therefore not surprising to learn that the estate has won a large number of medals and trophies over the last 25 years. ■ *Sales and tastings by appointment only: Mon-Fri 0900-1630, Sat 0900-1200. Cellar tours: by appointment. T8741026, montrochelle@wine.co.za*

L'Ormarins
The original lands were granted to the Huguenot, Jean Roi, in 1694, who named the farm after his village in the South of France

Four Passes route

One of the popular recommended day drives from Cape Town is known as the **Four Passes** route. This takes you through the heart of the Winelands, and, as the title suggests, over four mountain passes. The first stop on the drive is Stellenbosch. From here you take the R310 towards Franschhoek. Driving up out of Stellenbosch you cross the first pass – **Helshoogte Pass**. After 17 km you reach a T-junction with the R45; a left turn would take you to Paarl, 12 km, but the route continues to the right. This is a very pleasant drive up into the Franschhoek Valley. The road follows a railway line and for a part the Berg River. After passing through Franschoek, take a left in front of the Huguenot Monument and climb out of the valley via the **Franschhoek Pass**. This pass was built along the tracks formed by migrating herds of game centuries earlier, and was originally known as the Olifantspad (elephant's path). One of the more surprising aspects of this drive is the change in vegetation once you cross the lip of the pass, 520 m above the level of Franschhoek. As the road winds down towards Theewaterskloof Dam you pass through a dry valley full of scrub vegetation and fynbos – gone are the fertile fruit farms and vineyards.

Take a right across the dam on the R321 towards Grabouw and Elgin. An alternative route back to Cape Town, but much longer in distance, is to take a left here, R43. This is the road to Worcester, 50 km, the principal town in the Breede River Valley (see page 198). From Worcester follow the N1 back to Cape Town.

The Four Passes Route continues across the Theewaterskloof Dam and then climbs **Viljoens Pass**, the third of four. To the right lies the Hottentots Holland Nature Reserve (see page 148), a popular hiking region. The country around here is an important apple growing region. At the N2 highway turn right and follow the road back into Cape Town. The fourth and the most spectacular pass is **Sir Lowry's Pass**, which crosses the Hottentots Holland Mountains.

Paarl

While Paarl is home to two of South Africa's better known wine estates, KWV and Nederburg (see page 170), the town itself is not as interesting as Stellenbosch or as fashionable as Franschoek. All of the attractions and restaurants are strung out along Main Street at the base of Paarl Mountain. When the first European, Abraham Gabbema, saw the mountain in October 1657 it had just rained; the granite domes sparkled in the sunlight and he named the mountains *paarl* (pearl) and *diamandt* (diamond). The first settlers arrived in *Paarlvallei* in 1687, and shortly afterwards the French Huguenots settled on four farms, *Laborie, Goede Hoop, La Concorde* and

Phone code: 021 (NB Always use 3-figure prefix) Colour map 6, grid B5

Picardie. The town grew in a random fashion along an important wagon route to Cape Town. Several old buildings survive, but they are spread out rather than concentrated in a few blocks like Stellenbosch. The helpful **tourist office** is at 216 Main St, entrance is in Auret St, T8723829, F8729376, www.paarlonline.com Open 7 days a week.

Sights

Nelson Mandela spent his final years in prison near Paarl. His first steps of freedom were from Victor Verster Prison, 9 km south of town

The 1-km walk along **Main Street** will take you past most of the finest buildings in Paarl. Here you'll find one of the oldest buildings, the **Paarl Museum**, at 303 Main Street. This houses a reasonably diverting collection of Cape Dutch furniture, kitchen copperware plus some more delicate silver. There is also a small section outlining Paarl during Apartheid, although the fact that **Nelson Mandela** spent his final years in prison in Paarl is barely mentioned. ■ *Mon-Fri 0800-1700, T8762651.* Only a few hundred metres away, in Gideon Malherbe House, on Pastorie Street, the **Afrikaans Language Museum** gives a detailed chronicle of the development of the Afrikaans language and the people involved. ■ *Mon-Fri 0900-1300, 1400-1700, T8723441.* Near Lady Grey Street is **Zeederberg Square**, a 19th-century square with a fine mix of restored buildings and lively restaurants. Further south on Main Street is the **Strooidakkerk**, a thatched roof church, consecrated in 1805, and still in use. It was designed by George Küchler – note the gables, a sounding-board to amplify sermons, and the fine pulpit. You may have to ask for a key from the church office.

On the east bank of the Berg River is a 31-ha **Arboretum**. From the Publicity Office go down Market Street and cross the river; the arboretum is on the right. It was created in 1957 to mark the tercentenary of the discovery of the Berg River Valley. To help establish the parkland the town treasurer, Mr AE Short, asked other municipalities in South Africa to contribute trees and shrubs from their region. The response was excellent and when Professor HB Rycroft (Director of the National Botanic Gardens of South Africa) inaugurated the Paarl arboretum there were trees from 61 different regions. Today there are over 700 different species in a total of 4,000 trees. The grounds have been divided into six sections, each containing species from different continents. ■ *Open during daylight hours.*

The best views of the surrounding countryside are from Bretagne Rock; on a clear day you can see False Bay, Table Mountain and all the vineyards

Paarl town runs along the eastern base of Paarl Mountain, a giant granite massif, which, in 1970, was declared the **Paarl Mountain Nature Reserve**. Within the 1,900-ha reserve are a network of footpaths, a circular drive and a couple of dams. The vegetation differs from the surrounding countryside because of the different bedrock – the granite mass is not so susceptible to veld fires and many of the fynbos species grow exceptionally tall.

The domed summit is easy to climb, and near the top you will see an old cannon dating from the early days of the Cape Colony. On the summit are three giant granite rocks. The highest point is 729 m and there is a chain to help you up the last steep incline. Nearby is **Gordon's Rock**, named after Colonel Robert Jacob Gordon who commanded the British troops at the Cape from 1780 to 1795. This rock is dangerous and should only be climbed by experienced rock climbers. The third rock is known as **Paarl Rock**. Just below the rocks a mountain stream flows through the **Meulwater Wild Flower Reserve**. This garden was created in 1931, and contains the majority of flowers found around Paarl Mountain.

There is a small entrance fee to the reserve, but you do not need to obtain further permits for hiking. The publicity office should be able to give you a clear colour map which has details of access, roads and footpaths. There are several car parks with toilets and braai spots. You can purchase firewood in the reserve for your braai. If you wish to fish in one of the dams you need to go to the municipality for a permit.

Set high on the slopes of Paarl Mountain amongst granite boulders and indigenous trees stands the **Taal Monument** – three concrete columns linked by a low curved wall. This is the Afrikaans language monument, inaugurated in October 1975 and designed by Jan van Wijk. Each column represents different influences in the language. The relative heights of each column and the negative connotations associated with them have been the subject of criticism in recent years. From here you have an excellent view across the Berg River Valley. ■ *Small entrance fee.*

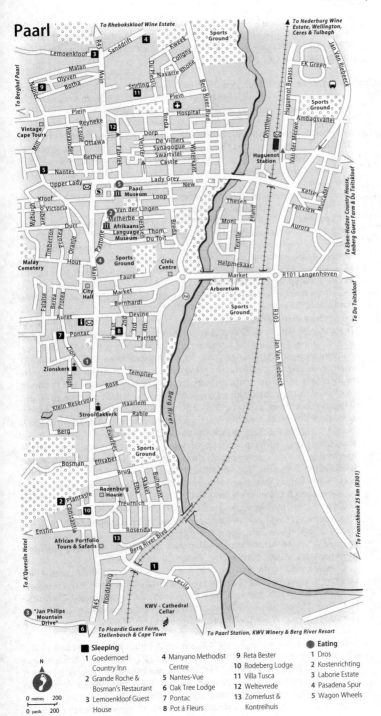

Paarl

N

0 metres 200
0 yards 200

■ **Sleeping**
1 Goedemoed
  Country Inn
2 Grande Roche &
  Bosman's Restaurant
3 Lemoenkloof Guest
  House

4 Manyano Methodist
  Centre
5 Nantes-Vue
6 Oak Tree Lodge
7 Pontac
8 Pot á Fleurs

9 Reta Bester
10 Rodeberg Lodge
11 Villa Tusca
12 Weltevrede
13 Zomerlust &
  Kontreihuis

● **Eating**
1 Dros
2 Kostenrichting
3 Laborie Estate
4 Pasadena Spur
5 Wagon Wheels

Those with kids in tow may wish to visit **Butterfly World**, the largest such park in South Africa, with butterflies flying freely in colourful landscaped gardens. Craft shop and tea garden. ■ *Klapmuts, T8755628. R15 per person. Open daily, 0900-1700; Jun-Aug, 1000-1600.*

Sleeping

■ *on map, page 167*
Price codes:
see inside front cover

Paarl has yet really to cater for budget travellers – most of the accommodation is aimed at the top end of the market. Stellenbosch is a far better choice for backpackers, for accommodation and nightlife

AL *Grande Roche*, Plantasie St, T8632727, F8632220, www.grandroche.com An 18th century manor which has quickly established itself as one of the top hotels in South Africa. A collection of restored farm buildings stand in peaceful gardens, surrounded by vineyards. 35 luxury a/c suites, non-smoking rooms, 2 floodlit tennis courts, swimming pool, gym. *Bosman's* restaurant was voted the best in South Africa in 1993, and is still regarded as one of the best in the Cape. The food and surroundings match such a billing – the crystal chandeliers say it all. Meals are rich and made from the finest ingredients the Cape can offer, friendly service. Will collect from Cape Town airport. **AL-A** *Zomerlust*, 193 Main St, T8722117, F8728312, www.zomerlust.co.za 14 rooms in a restored country house in the centre of town. Some rooms are in converted stables. Courtyard, terrace, cellar pub and popular attached restaurant – *Kontreihuis*, check for winter discounts, swimming pool. Recommended.

B *Lemoenkloof Guest House*, 396a Main St, T8723782, F8727532. Luxurious country house with plenty of character and atmosphere. 14 a/c rooms with TV and mini bar. Shady gardens, healthy large breakfasts, evening meals on request, swimming pool. Recommended. **B** *Mooikelder*, 2 km north of Paarl off the road to Windmeul, T8638491, F8638361, moikel@mweb.co.za A smart Cape Dutch homestead with relaxing gardens. Each room has its own character, although some are a bit small. The lounge has teak panelled walls, and there is a swimming pool, evening meals on request. A good base from which to explore the region. **B-C** *Nantes-Vue*, 56 Mill St, T/F8727311. Elegant B&B set in a Victorian house in the centre of town. All rooms have en suite bathrooms and a private entrance. **B-C** *Oak Tree Lodge*, 32 Main St, T8632631, F8632607, www.oaktreelodge.co.za 12 rooms with en suite bathrooms, restaurant, non-smoking room, secure parking, guest TV lounge, spacious garden, swimming pool, central location. **B** *Palmiet Valley*, T8627741, F8626891, www.palmeit.co.za A restored historic homestead, located on an estate to the east of the town centre. 6 spacious double rooms with en suite bathrooms, satellite TV in each room, room safes, each decorated with antiques, neat garden, swimming pool. Recommended. **B** *Picardie Guest Farm*, Laborie St, T8633357. A friendly B&B located on the southern edge of town. The nearby *Laborie Estate* can be recommended for meals. **B** *Rodeberg Lodge*, 74 Main St, T8633202, F8633203, roderberg@ctm-web.co.za Peaceful small B&B in centre of town. 6 a/c rooms, 1 loft room with plenty of character, non-smoking, TV lounge, 4 bed garden cottage is a self-catering option, German spoken. **B** *Roggeland Country House*, Roggeland Rd, Dal Josafat, T8682501, F8682113, rog@iafrica.com A fine Cape Dutch farmhouse with 11 luxury rooms, with en suite bathroom, mature gardens, swimming pool, excellent cuisine. **B-C** *Weltevrede*, 40 Fabriek St, T082-5769575 (mob). A smart self-catering house in the centre of town, sleeps up to 6, equipped with all mod cons, an ideal base for 4 or more wishing to spend time in the area. **B-C** *Eben-Haëzer Country House*, T8627420, F8623829. Original Cape Dutch homestead, rooms are individually decorated with antiques and have Victorian-style bathrooms, breakfast under oak trees or in the 18th century dining room. Louise is a SATOUR guide and is available for Winelands tours.

C *Goedemoed Country Inn*, Cecilia St, T8631102, wsteenkamp@hixnet.co.za A fine Cape Dutch family home with large reception rooms, relaxed atmosphere, 9 en suite rooms, swimming pool, set in the middle of a wine estate, good value. Recommended. **C** *Reta Bester*, 29 Olyven St, T8723368. Small B&B with 2 double rooms, shared bathroom, use of kitchen, swimming pool, good value. **C** *Villa Tusca*, 8 Sterling St, T/F8728222, vtusca@mweb.co.za A smart villa with double rooms or self-catering option.

D *A'Queeslin*, 2 Queen St, T/F8631160. Small B&B with comfortable en suite rooms, self-catering option, separate entrance, pool, patio, braai, central location between vineyards. **D** *Pot á Fleurs*, 8 Second Av, T8724387. Central B&B or self-catering. Swimming pool, private gardens, secure off-street parking. **D-E** *Amberg Guest Farm*, Klein Drakenstein, T8630982, amberg@mweb.co.za One of the few budget options here, great setting with mountain views, mix of cottages and dorm accommodation, self-catering or

B&B, large pool, indigenous garden, braai. **E-F** *Berg River Resort*, 5 km out of town towards Franschhoek (R45), south side of the N1, T8631650. Chalets, caravan and camping park, hot water, electric points, swimming pool, mini-golf, restaurant, helpful staff, will collect from railway station. **E** *Manyano Methodist Centre*, Sanddrift St, T8722537. Large budget set up (can sleep up to 140), used by groups, so you will find it either overrun or all to yourself. One of the few central budget options.

Boschendal, Pniel Rd, T8704211. Picnic hampers in a lovely rural setting from Nov-Apr. Also a café and restaurant serving a cellar buffet. The vegetarian menu is exceptionally good for the country. The manor house was once the home of Cecil Rhodes. *Bosman's*, at *Grande Roche Hotel*, Plantasie St, T8632727. International cuisine of the highest standard, imaginative vegetarian menu, huge selection of wines, all the trappings of a luxury hotel. *Dros*, Main Rd. Outlet of successful chain serving steaks, ribs and pasta dishes in a cellar atmosphere. Also has a good choice of beers at the bar. *Kontreihuis*, in *Zomerlust guesthouse*, 193 Main St, T8722808. Traditional Cape meals served in an attractive dining room, the sort of place you are liable to linger in after your meal. *Kostenrighting*, 19 Pastorie Av. Coffee shop serving light meals, sandwiches and coffee and cakes, tables in the dappled shade of oak trees. *Laborie*, Taillefert St, T8073095. Restaurant in the wine estate, Cape and Mediterranean dishes, quite smart but relaxed atmosphere, good service. *Pasadena Spur*, Main St. Good value steakhouse, salad bars, lively, part of a very popular chain. *Pontac*, in *Pontac Guesthouse*, 16 Zion St, T8720445. Informal and friendly restaurant serving traditional dishes with a 'New World flair'. *Rhebokskloof*, Rhebokskloof Estate, T8638606, restaurant@rhebokskloof Excellent restaurant serving simple traditional fare as well as more fancy international dishes, excellent wine list. *Spring Fontein*, Boland Dal Kosafat Estate, T8682808. Traditional South African dishes served on a veranda with pretty views. *Wagon Wheels*, 57 Lady Grey St, T8725265. Popular upmarket steakhouse serving excellent steaks and a small selection of fish dishes and salads. *Wilderer's*, Wilderer's distillery, 3 km outside Paarl on R45, T8633555. Lunch only. Relaxed French restaurant in a schnapps distillery, speciality is *Flammkuchen*, a type of pizza from Strasbourg. Finish off with a shot of their pear or fynbos schnapps.

Eating
● *on map, page 167*

Cricket This is a delightful place to watch an international cricket match in a peaceful rural setting. A good braai and some fine local wines make for a perfect day out. Paarl is the home of the Boland Cricket Board. Boland cricket team is similar to Border and Griqualand in as much as it competes in all the domestic competitions, but is not associated with a province, but a region within a province.

    Boland Bank Park, PO Box 2969, Langenhoven St, Paarl 7620. Ticket enquiries: T8624580, F8621298, bolcrick@mweb.co.za The following international matches will be played here in the 2002-03 season: India v Holland, World Cup, 12 Feb 2003; Pakistan v Holland, 25 Feb 2003.

Sports

African Portfolio Tours, T8631378, F8632231, portfolio@iafrica.com *Vintage Cape Tours*, Main St, PO Box 162, T/F8721484, vctours@adept.co.za *Paarl Vintners*, 216 Main St, T8723605, F8723841, paarl@wine.co.za

Tour operators

Local Bicycle hire: *Bike Point*, T8633901, T083-2353260 (mob). Organize fun rides in the regions, as well as renting out bikes and providing route maps. **Car hire**: if you want to save money consider taking the train from Cape Town to Paarl, and then hiring a car for the weekend. *Wine Route Rent-a-Car*, 145 Main St, T8728513. **Taxis**: a service is available from Huguenot railway station. *Paarl Radio Taxis*, T8725671.

Transport

Rail There are 2 train stations in town: Paarl station is at the southern outskirts (convenient for the campsite); Huguenot station is across the river from Lady Grey St. **Metro service**: **Cape Town**, platform 1. If visiting on a day trip return times as follows: 1545 and 1715. Journey time to Cape Town, approximately 1 hr. For **Stellenbosch**, platform 1, take a Cape Town train and change at **Muldersvlei**.

Western Cape

Western Cape

Do not use these buses for journey from Paarl to Cape Town as the price structure makes them very expensive

Road 55 km to **Cape Town**, 32 km to **Stellenbosch**, 26 km to **Franschhoek**, 45 km to **Worcester** (via tunnel). **Bus**: *Translux*, depart from outside the railway station. **Beaufort West** (5½ hrs): daily, 1350, 1500, 1830. **Bloemfontein** (11 hrs): daily, 1350, 1830. **Durban** (17 hrs): daily, 1350, via **Bloemfontein**, 2025, via **Port Elizabeth**. **Johannesburg** and **Pretoria** (18 hrs): daily, 1830. **Kimberley** (11 hrs): daily, 1500. **Port Elizabeth** (10 hrs): daily, 2025. **Worcester** (40 mins): daily 1350, 1500, 1830. *Greyhound*, depart from the *International Hotel* in Tabac St. **Bloemfontein** (10½ hrs): daily, 1845. **Johannesburg** and **Pretoria** (17 hrs): daily, 1845, 2100. **Kimberley** (11 hrs): daily, 2100.

Paarl Wine Route

The wine route information office is in the same building as the Paarl Publicity Office, T8723605, www.paarlwine.co.za

The route was set up in 1984 by local producers to help promote their wines and attract tourists into the area. The programme has been a great success and some of the estates have opened their own restaurants. These are usually very good, but don't expect huge discounts on the wine with your meal. All of the estates have tastings and wine sales on a daily basis. Today there are 23 members, but only the largest estates conduct regular cellar tours.

Boland Kelder

The estate has an excellent wine cellar, and offers one of the most interesting cellar tours. One of their best wines is the **Noble Late Harvest '92**, made from the chenin blanc grape. ■ *Sales and tastings: Mon-Fri 0800-1700, Sat 0830-1300. Cellar tours: by appointment. Follow the R45 towards Wellington and look out for the sign to the left a short distance out of town. T8726190, boland@wine.co.za*

Fairview Wine Estate

This popular estate has a rather unusual attraction in the form of a goat tower, a spiral structure home to two pairs of goats. In addition to a variety of very good wines (look out for the popular **Goats do Roam** and their **2000 Chardonnay**) visitors can taste goat and Jersey milk cheeses. The goats are milked each afternoon from 1530 onwards. ■ *Wine and cheese sales and tastings: Mon-Fri 0800-1700, Sat 0800-1700, R10 for cheese tastings. From the town centre head south on the R45, pass under the N1 and turn right on to the R101. Take the first right which crosses over the N1; the estate is 2 km on the right. T8632450, F8632591, fairback@iafrica.com*

Laborie & KWV

This is the easiest cellar to visit as it is close to the centre of town

The Laborie vineyard has been developed with tourism in mind. The original Cape Dutch homestead, surrounded by rose bushes, has been turned into a restaurant serving good value buffets or a more fancy à la carte menu. There is a lovely tasting terrace, and rolling lawns overlooking the vineyards. ■ *Sales and tastings: daily, 0900-1700. Closed Sun and Mon evening. Cellar tours: by appointment. Almost in the town, close to Paarl railway station. T8073390, F8071955, grovelj@kwv.co.za*

KWV

A short distance from the Laborie estate is the famous **KWV Cellar Complex** which contains the five largest vats in the world. The Ko-operatieve Wijnbouwers Vereniging van Zuid-Afrika (Co-operative Wine Growers' Association) was established in Paarl in 1918 and is responsible for exporting many of South

Paarl Winelands

■ **Sleeping**
1 Berg River Resort
2 Mooikelder
3 Palmiet Valley
4 Roggeland

Africa's wines. Their flagship range is the Cathedral Cellar label. ■ *Tours: Mon-Fri 0900-1600, Sat 0900-1400. T8073008, www.kwv.co.za*

This is one of the largest and best known estates in South Africa. Their annual production is in excess of 650,000 cases – the small Paarl estates produce in the region of 3,000 cases. As such a large concern they are involved in much of the research in South Africa to improve the quality of the grape and the vine. Every April the annual Nederburg Auction attracts buyers from all over the world. The homestead was built in 1800, but throughout the 19th century the wines weren't considered to be anything special. This all changed in 1937 when Johann George Graue bought the estate. New vines, Riesling and Cabernet Sauvignon varieties were planted, and the cellars completely modernized. By the 1980s the wines had won more than 900 international awards. The best wines compare favourably worldwide; the **Cabernet Sauvignon '91** is rated by John Platter as a classic wine. ■ *Sales and tastings: Mon-Fri 0830-1700, Sat 0900-1300 (Nov-Feb). Cellar tours: Mon-Fri, appointment only, also conducted in German, French and Spanish. The restaurant is open for light lunches and snacks. From the centre of Paarl, cross the Berg River and take the R303 towards Wellington. As you leave town the estate is signposted to the right. T8623104, www.nederburg.co.za*

Nederburg

This is a very pleasant estate to spend the afternoon exploring. Their **Cabernet Sauvignon** has won several local awards. ■ *Sales and tastings: Mon-Fri 0800-1800, Sat 0900-1400. Restaurant is open during the summer months, picnic baskets also available for lunches on the estate. From Paarl centre follow the R45 north towards Malmesbury. Take a left at the crossroads 5 km out of town; the estate is on the right, past the Klein Rheebokskloof guesthouse. T8638453, F8638424, www.nelsonscreek@wine.co.za*

Nelson's Creek

This old estate is now a thoroughly modern outfit. A good reason to visit on a Sunday is their restaurant, though booking is advised during local holidays. The terrace café is popular with tour groups. One of their best wines is a **Cabernet Sauvignon**. ■ *Sales and tastings: daily, 0900-1700. Cellar tours: by appointment. Restaurant is closed on Wed. Follow the R45 towards Wellington, take a left signposted Windmeul, and the estate is on the left after 2 km. T8638386, rhebok@iafrica.com*

Rhebokskloof

This winery is fundamentally different from most in the Winelands as it is community-driven, where the farm workers have a direct input in the running of the business. One of the better wines produced here is **Winds of Change**, an organic Semillon chardonnay blend. ■ *They have only recently started tastings, so be sure to phone ahead to check that it's possible. Head north out of Paarl on the R45, then turn left at the WR8 junction. Sonop is 4 km on the right. T8872475, sonop@iafrica.com*

Sonop Winery
Proceeds go towards local community projects and schools

Villeria is highly regarded and produces some of the best wines in the Cape. There are plenty of classic wines to choose from, including the **Cru Monro**, the **Merlot '89** and their **Sauvignon Blanc**. They no longer conduct cellar tours, but allow 'self-guided' tours. ■ *Sales and tastings: Mon-Fri 0830-1700, Sat 0830-1300. Cellar tours: by appointment. Although a member of the Paarl wine route, this estate is closer to Stellenbosch. From Paarl take the N1 towards Cape Town, turn off at junction 39 (R304, Stellenbosch), and take the first right, R101. T8822002, villiera@mweb.co.za*

Villeria

Wellington

Like the other Wineland towns not only is Wellington surrounded by beautiful countryside, but the town itself is also a pleasant place to visit, with a number of fine historical buildings and far fewer tourists than in nearby towns. Although it produces wines, it is best known for its dried fruit. (The other important fruit centres, Ceres and Tulbagh, are on the eastern side of the Limietberg. They can be visited via the

Phone code: 021
(NB Always use 3-figure prefix)
Colour map 6, grid B5

Western Cape

magnificent Bain's Kloof Pass, see page 174.) To the north, the countryside quickly opens up into the rolling Swartland, an important wheat region (see page 189). A short drive to the south reveals steep hills where all the farmland is given over to vines.

There is a good selection of local wines on sale here

Wellington Tourism Bureau, Main Rd, housed in the Old Market Building next to the Dutch Reform Church, T8734604, F8734607, www.visitwellington.com, is closed Saturday afternoon and Sunday. The staff are helpful and organized.

Sights

Several buildings are listed by the local information centre as being of historical interest, most are typical Victorian townhouses

The Murray Jubilee Hall and Samuel House were once an institute for training Dutch Reformed Church missionaries; they are now part of **Huguenot College**. The shady **Victoria Park** in Church Street is notable for its roses. Look out for the archway which was built to commemorate the coronation of King Edward VII in 1902. The fountain in **Joubert Square** was unveiled in 1939 as a memorial to the Huguenot settlers in the valley. The **Wellington Museum** on Church Street has a small collection on the history of the town and the Huguenot farms in the district. The archives of the Huguenot Seminary are kept here. ■ *Mon-Fri 0800-1700, free entrance.*

North of town, on the Porterville road (R44), is the **Wellington Blockhouse**. This is the most southerly relic from the Anglo-Boer War. About 8,000 of these forts were built by General Kitchener to protect the British lines of communication. Many are found alongside the railways. At first they were built every 3 km, but then additional ones were built every kilometre along a route. Each was garrisoned by seven men of the South Africa Constabulary. Most of the forts were built from corrugated iron and have long since disappeared, but the Wellington Blockhouse is double storey and built from stone. The only access was by ladder.

Limietberg Nature Reserve

This large reserve protects the mountains which form the catchment area for the Breede and Berg rivers. It is the first range of mountains one encounters when travelling east from the Cape towards the Great Karoo. The reserve covers an area of 117,000 ha, stretching from Jonkershoek (between Stellenbosch and **Franschhoek**) in the south, to the *Voëlvlei Dam*, in the north (where the R46 cuts through Nuwekloof Pass to Tulbagh).

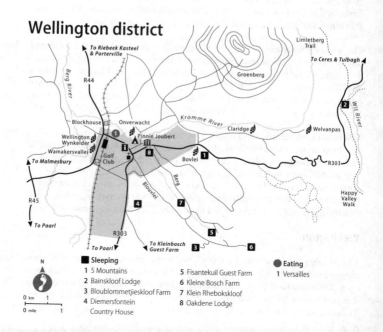

Wellington district

Sleeping
1 5 Mountains
2 Bainskloof Lodge
3 Bloublommetjieskloof Farm
4 Diemersfontein Country House
5 Fisantekuil Guest Farm
6 Kleine Bosch Farm
7 Klein Rhebokskloof
8 Oakdene Lodge

Eating
1 Versailles

Ins and outs The reserve can be accessed from several different roads. From Wellington, drive east along the R303, signposted for Wolseley and Ceres. There is a car park at Tweede Tol. If you stay at the *Bainskloof Lodge* you are well-placed to start walking early.

All trails need to be booked, on T021-9454570, or T021-9454571. During the school holidays you may have to book a few weeks in advance. If you are planning a long hike, consider buying the following maps: 1:50,000 Franschhoek (3319 CC) and 1:50,000 Bainskloof (3319 CA).

This is a popular hiking region and two of the Cape's more famous passes dissect the mountains – Bain's Kloof and Dutoitskloof. The Huguenot tunnel is a third route through the mountains and the reserve. During the winter months snow often falls on the high ground and there can be heavy rainfall. There is little shelter as only a few stands of forest remain in the deep valleys. Most of the vegetation is mountain fynbos, and the highest point is Du Toits Peak at 2,182 m.

As noted above the weather can quickly change. Always carry waterproofs and drinking water

Day walks can be started from Bain's Kloof Pass and from Dutoitskloof Pass. Only the former are mentioned here. Two walks start from the R303 at Eerste Tol. **Happy Valley**, about 5 km long, follows the Wit River to a popular bathing spot known as **Junction Pool**. From here you follow your route back. This walk forms part of the much longer **Limietberg Trail** (formerly known as Hawequas), a two-day trail across the middle of the reserve. Another route is following **Bobbejaans River** for approximately 4 km to a small waterfall. The path is steep in places but it goes through some beautiful forest. A third option is to walk the last section of the Limietberg trail from Eerste Tol to the reserve campsite at Tweede Tol. The camp is further down Bain's Kloof Pass towards Ceres.

Western Cape

B *Diemersfontein Country House*, coming from Paarl turn right off the R303, T8732671, F8642095. A classic luxury country house set in beautiful mature gardens. 16 rooms, elegant teak panelled lounge, relax on the grand veranda, swimming pool. Recommended. **B-D** *Fisantekuil Guest Farm*, Horseshoe Rd, 4 km out of town – turn down Berg Rd by the museum, T8641184. 2 self-contained cottages, private garden, wood stove for winter months, swimming pool, plus a 2-bedroom cottage in the forest, all on a working organic fruit and nut farm, swimming pool, earth dam for fishing, a peaceful rural retreat just a short drive from Cape Town.

Sleeping
■ *on map*
Price codes:
see inside front cover

Because of its popularity, places in Paarl tend to be more expensive – there is an excellent choice of guest farms and self-catering cottages near Wellington

C *The 5 Mountains*, east of town on the R301 towards Bain's Kloof, T8643409, F8736471, www.the5mountains.com 5 luxurious garden cottages, stylish bedrooms, very comfortable with en suite bathrooms, private deck with beautiful views, breakfast served by the pool or in an attractive dining room, meals on request. Very friendly and family-run, excellent choice for a relaxing night. Recommended. **C** *Bainskloof Lodge*, out of town on the Tulbagh Rd (R303), T8641159, F8641274. Smart, small lodge in a beautiful location by the Wit River, large rooms with en suite bathroom, restaurant, open log fires in the lounge, several hikes in the Limietberg Nature Reserve start from here including the Limietberg Trail and the Happy Valley Walk (see above), full board is good value in this peaceful lodge. **C** *Klein Rhebokskloof*, 4 km out of town, off Berg St, T/F8734115. 4 rooms, en suite bathroom, plus 2 luxury suites which are suitable for self-catering, old country guesthouse, shared lounge, swimming pool with sun deck. All set in a beautiful garden with plenty of colour and trees. **C-D** *Bloublommetjieskloof Farm*, Olyvenbosch Rd, off Blouvlei Rd, T/F8733696. 4 self-contained apartments, 6 rooms, non-smoking rooms, swimming pool, an interesting 'bio-dynamic' farm, enjoy their healthy produce – vegetables, nuts, and juices, excellent vegetarian meals provided, a rare treat in South Africa, also runs courses on the farming methods. Recommended. **C-D** *Kleinbosch Guest Farm*, south of the town off the R303, T8682481. A fine converted Cape Dutch homestead set in orchards, rooms with en suite bedrooms, à la carte restaurant next door. Self-catering available, swimming pool, mountain walks. **C-D** *'t Soete Huys*, 1 Stadsig, T8643442, F8732299, info@soetehuys.com Beautiful converted family house, en suite rooms, pleasant furnishings with wrought iron beds, terracotta tiled floors, good breakfasts served, quiet location on the outskirts of town.

D *Kleine Bosch Farm*, follow the signs off the Bloulei Rd, a short distance from the information centre, T4615417, F4616642, kleinebosch@freemail.absa.co.za An isolated country house suitable for a self-catering holiday in the mountains.

Bain's Kloof Pass

No matter which direction you take when leaving the Cape by road you will at some stage have to pass through the mountains via a spectacular pass. Bain's Kloof Pass is regarded as one of the great passes – as you drive along enjoy the views but also take note of its construction history. The route has not changed since the pass was first built, the only change made in 144 years of use has been to tar the road in 1934. This really was a great engineering feat.

In 1846 **Andrew Geddes Bain**, the Inspector of Roads, while working in the Breede River Valley noticed a 'gap' in the mountain range in the direction of Wellington. A few months later, he traversed the mountains via the 'gap' and put forward a proposal for a new pass. John Montagu, the Colonial Secretary, gave his full backing to the project, but work did not start until 1849.

This was the greatest period of road building in the Cape, but these ambitious projects could only be afforded by using convict labour. On his arrival in the Cape, John Montagu had been shocked by the conditions on Robben Island, where convicts were incarcerated. In 1847, Ordinance 7, for the Discipline and Safe Custody of Convicts Employed on Public Roads, was promulgated. This was Montagu's plan to reform conditions and the system of punishment. The first pass to be constructed under the new system was Mitchell's Pass in 1846. Up until 1888 all the major roads and passes were built using the convict system. It was considered a great success, but the labour was hard and the prisoners wore chains. The only tools available were picks, shovels, sledgehammers, rock drills and gunpowder.

Before work could start at Bain's Kloof neat stone barracks were built to house over 200 convicts. Conditions were better than in prison and local farmers were contracted to supply fresh straw for palliasses on a weekly basis. The total cost of Bain's Kloof Pass was £50,000; the convicts were paid 60 pence per month, but the cost of their daily rations, seven pence, was deducted from this; Bains was paid an annual salary of £300; the Head Warders and the Chaplains were paid £100 per annum, while the ordinary warders received £12 per annum plus rations. The cost of gunpowder used was £1,223. And over 10 km of rock had to be blasted out.

The pass took 1,608 days to complete, a considerable achievement considering the terrain and the tools available. Most of the labour was unskilled (at the outset) and yet retaining walls were built, culverts, aqueducts, and drains – all using drystone masonry techniques. What's more, all these features are still in place and use today. The pass was opened by Petrus Borchardus Borcherds, Chairman of the Central Roads Board, Cape Town, on 14 September 1853. There were great celebrations. The new route between Cape Town and Worcester was 57 km shorter and it saved two days' travel.

E-F Wellington Resort, Addey St, T8732603. Large caravan park, camping allowed, grassy and shady, swimming pool, close to all amenities, electric points, busy in holidays.

Eating
● on map

Capon's, 60 Church St, T8641422. Good family restaurant serving the usual choice of steak, pizza and pasta. **The Oasis**, Bain's Kloof Rd, T8734231. Closed Mon, closes at 1800. Well-placed tea garden serving light lunches, home-made cakes and a popular carvery on Sun, good fresh home cooking, refresh here after a hike. **The Bell Inn**, 96 Church St, T8731749. Busy local pub serving pub lunches and steak dinners. *Kontiki*, Church St, T8732748. Popular local steakhouse. **Versailles**, Main Rd, T8731276. Popular family restaurant in town centre, steaks and country cooking, a classic Cape Dutch building.

Shopping
The *South African Dried Fruit Co-operative Ltd* (S.A.D.) has its main office here. They have a shop selling a wide range of dried fruits and sugary fruit dainties, as well as condiments and wines at 21 Main Rd, T8648600.

Rail The *Southern Cross*, a weekly service between **Cape Town** and Outdshoorn. Cape Town (80 mins), Sun 0719. **Outdshoorn** (22 hrs), Fri 1939, via **Swellendam** and **George**.

The *Trans Oranje*, a weekly service between **Cape Town** and **Durban**. Cape Town (80 mins), Wed 0442. **Durban** (35 hrs), Mon 2014, via **Bloemfontein** and **Harrismith**. The *Trans Karoo*, a daily service between **Cape Town** and **Pretoria**. This is the best option if you wish to go to Cape Town. **Cape Town** (80 mins), daily 1251. **Pretoria** (25 hrs), daily 1048, via **Beaufort West** and **Kimberley**.

Road 72 km to **Cape Town**, 131 km to **Saldanha**, 49 km to **Stellenbosch**. **Bus**: connections are poor. You'll have to make your own way to Paarl if you intend on travelling by the long distance coach services. Neither *Translux* nor *Greyhound* stop in Wellington. **Driving**: to return to Cape Town take the R44 around Paarl Mountain, and turn right after 20 km onto the N1. The R45 to Malmesbury continues west towards Saldanha Bay and the Atlantic. A third option is to travel north on the R44 to Porterville and join with the N7 before it starts to climb Grey's Pass. From the top of the pass you descend into the **Olifants River Valley**.

Much of the farmland in the district is devoted to the production of wheat and dried fruit. The following is a selection of winemakers who open their doors to the public.

Wellington Wine Route
One of the smallest routes in the area, with only nine members all within a short drive of each other and the town centre

Bovlei was established in 1907 and has a completely modernized cellar. They produce mainly white wines and offer tastings and sales, but no tours. ■ *Sales and tastings: Mon-Fri 0830-1230, 1330-1700, Sat 0830-1230. Out of town on the R301 towards Bain's Kloof Pass. T8731567, www.bovlei.co.za*

Wamakersvallei Wine Cellar is one of the largest wine producers on the Wellington route. Its white and fortified wines have won several awards, and are exported in bulk to the UK. They offer tastings and sales, but no tours. ■ *Sales and tastings: Mon-Fri 0830-1300, 14300-1700, Sat 0830-1230. North of town on the R44. T8731582, www.wamakersvallei.co.za*

Wellington Wynkelde was voted as champion winery of South Africa at the 1992 Paarl Show. It's worth a visit to see some of the most advanced wine-making technology in the region ■ *Sales and tastings: Mon-Fri 0800—1700. Cellar tours: by appointment. Close to the railway station. T8731163, F8732423, wellwyn@iafrica.com*

West Coast

The West Coast is vastly different from the more visited Garden Route – a wild, bleak stretch lashed by the icy Atlantic and backed by rolling dunes covered in coastal fynbos far removed from the lush green landscape full of rivers and waterfalls found in the south. It has only recently become a standard fixture on tourist routes, who are attracted by both the sun-bleached coast and the spectacular flowers that blanket the area in spring. The cold Benguella of the Atlantic also brings with it some of the most nutrient-rich waters found on the planet. This fertile sea supports an enormous wealth of marine life. The fishing is superb, and the coast is famous for its excellent seafood. The crayfish industry alone earns about R150 million each year. Inland lies a fertile farming region known as the Swartland. Further north, the N7 highway passes along the magnificent Cederberg, a wilderness area with some of the best hiking in South Africa.

Ins and outs

Driving out of Cape Town, follow the signs for the N1 and Durbanville for the West Coast. If time is not an issue, turn off the N1 at the Maitland junction, signposted, Milnerton, M5, and follow the signs for the R27. This is the old coast road which runs all the way north to Vanrhynsdorp. If you are pressed for time, take a left at Acacia Park and follow signs for the N7. This is the main highway from Cape Town to Namibia running up the West Coast.

Western Cape

Climate While the sea may be too cold for swimming, the region's climate is very favourable. As you travel north from Cape Town the summer temperatures are higher, and the rainfall is less. The air is dry and even in winter, providing the winds aren't blowing, it can be very warm. Most of the rain falls between June and September.

Cape Town to Vanrhynsdorp via the coast

Blouberg-strand
Colour map 6, grid B4

Only 25 km from Cape Town, this is a popular spot for taking the classic photo of Cape Town, backed by Table Mountain. The area has proved to be popular with modern developers, and what was once a small fishing village has now become engulfed in sprawling residential suburbs. Despite the cold water this is a popular spot, especially amongst surfers – great rollers sweep into the bay. There is a sandy beach with safe swimming, frequented by families. If you've had enough of the beautiful people on Cape Town's city beaches, head here.

Most of the eating options are fast food joints

Sleeping and eating B-C *Blue Peter*, Popham Rd, T5541956, www.bluepeter.co.za A well-known hotel and hugely popular meeting point right by the beach, restaurant, seats spill out onto the lawn overlooking the beach, hard to get served in peak season. *Ons Huisie*, an old fisherman's cottage now an excellent seafood restaurant on the beach front. Recommended.

Mamre
Colour map 6, grid B4
Tourist information, T022-661073

North of Melkbosstrand, the R307 branches off the coast road to this small settlement, which comes to life at the weekend when a large proportion of the coloured residents return from their jobs in Cape Town. The settlement began in 1808 when the Moravian Missionary Society was given three farms by the governor of the Cape, the Earl of Clarendon. The mission's objective was to try and convert the remaining Khoi in the area and the church was completed in 1816. Today, many of the old buildings have been restored, and an old water mill has been turned into an interesting local museum. A number of the whitewashed homes have brightly coloured doors, a common and picturesque feature of the West Coast. To add to this, the thatch on some of the cottages has sprung up with wild flowers.

Darling
Phone code: 022
(NB Always use 3-figure prefix)
Colour map 6, grid B6

Darling was named after a Lieutenant Governor of the Cape, Sir Charles Henry Darling; previously it had been known as Groene Kloof

This small, thriving town reflects the prosperity of the surrounding area. It is in typical **Swartland** country, surrounded by vast expanses of wheat fields and lush irrigated pastures for dairy herds. Few visitors will spend much time here, except during the spring months of August and September, when the wild flowers on the veld are blooming – a **Wild Flower Show** has been held here during the third weekend of September since 1917. The most common flowers found here include daisies, nemesias, vygies and lilies. The **tourist information** office, on Pastorie Street, T4923361, F4922935, is a good source of local information when the wild flowers are in bloom.

More recently, Darling has become well-known as the home of Evita Bezuidenhout, a sort of Afrikaans Dame Edna created by comedian Pieter Dirk-Uys. Evita is something of a South African gay institution, and hosts lively cabaret shows at her **Evita se Perron** café-theatre in the tiny old railway station. For information and bookings, T4922831, www.evita.co.za

In the old City Hall, Pastorie Street, is a **museum** with a typical small town collection devoted to depicting the region's history. The slightly unusual display traces the history of the butter industry in Darling. ■ *Mon-Sat 0900-1200, TT4922831. Staff at the museum will direct you to local private farms which are open for viewing wild flowers during the flowering season.*

At Kraalbosdam farm, 6 km to the north, stands the **Hildebrand Memorial**. This commemorates the southernmost confrontation of the Anglo-Boer War (1899-1902). There is a memorial and the gravestone of Hildebrand, a Boer Commando who was killed here. The local farm, Oudepost, is famous for its orchid nursery, the largest in South Africa. These amazing blooms are available locally, but the majority are for the export market.

Sleeping and eating **C** *Nemesia*, Main Rd, T4922263. 12 rooms, restaurant, bar. **C** *Trinity*, 19 Long St, T4923430, mclaughlin@worlonline.co.za Beautifully converted family home, with stylish, understated bedrooms, old-fashioned bathrooms, lovely bright breakfast room, friendly owners Shaun and Debbie. Recommended. **C-D** *Darling Guest House*, 22 Pastorie St, T4923062. A comfortable, restored 19th-century townhouse with a stream running through the garden. 3 double rooms with shared lounge and fridge. Recommended. *Café Mosaic*, T4922307. Breakfasts, snacks and coffee and cakes in the afternoons. *Evita se Perron*, in the old railway station, T4922831, www.evita.co.za A range of entertainments set in the old railway building, including a restaurant, coffee shop and famous cabaret shows performed by Evita Bezuidenhout (see above). Good food and excellent entertainment.

Driving north from Cape Town (79 km) on the R27, Yzerfontein is the first settlement of any size along the West Coast. It is named after a local spring rising from an ironstone formation. The village sits on the edge of an exposed rocky headland which in turn forms a sheltered bay. The harbour has a slipway suitable for the launching of small fishing boats, popular for the abundant shoaling snoek found off the coast. To the south of the village is an excellent sandy beach which is safe for swimming, although the water is always cold. A further attraction is the strong swell in the bay which makes it great for **surfing**. For **tourist information**, contact the *Yzerfontein Tourism Bureau*, 46 Main Road, T4512366.

If you have access to a boat, **Dassen Island**, 9 km to the southwest, makes for an interesting daytrip. The island, the largest along the West Coast, is in fact the peak of an underwater mountain. When Jan van Riebeeck first visited here in 1654, the island was home to hundreds of seals. These have long since been hunted out, but there remain large **cormorant** and **African penguin** breeding populations. A caretaker lives on the island to monitor and protect the only breeding ground in the Cape for the **great white pelican**. Closer to the shore is a smaller island, **Meeurots**, which has become home for cormorants and gulls.

Just before the village you drive past a couple of **lime kilns**, shaped like giant beehives. Although they only date from 1940, they are national monuments. The process used to create lime for building was exactly the same as that employed by Jan van Riebeeck way back in 1653. The shells of black mussels collected along the coast were used to produce 300 bags a day.

Sleeping and eating **C** *Cashel Bed & Breakfast*, 26 Lutie Catz Rd, T/F4512475. White-washed villa overlooking beach. 4 attractive rooms with perfect sea views, self-catering available, heated pool. Recommended. **C** *Kaijaiki*, PO Box 305, T/F4512858. Comfortable, homely guesthouse. Each room has its own fireplace, decorated with old photos and antiques, good restaurant attached. Recommended. **C** *Emmaus on Sea*, 30 Versveld St, T/F4512650. B&B or self-catering, enclosed terrace offers sea views without the wind. **E-F** *Caravan Park*, Park St, T4512211. Good facilities, next to the dunes on the main beach, bungalows and caravans for hire, but camping not allowed. *Beaches*, T4512200. À la carte restaurant specializing in seafood, also serves steaks and some vegetarian dishes. *Cashel*, light meals, sandwiches and coffee. *Die Strandkombuis*, T4512206. Open-air seafood braai.

Langebaan

A little more than an hour by road from Cape Town (125 km), this is a very popular family resort which has been all but spoilt by heavy development. Situated on the sheltered waters of the beautiful **Langebaan Lagoon**, it is an ideal centre for watersports – sailing conditions are reputedly the best along the Western Cape coastline. Today it is impossible to picture the town's origins as a small fishing village in the 1880s. The hillside is a mosaic of new houses and vacant plots waiting for the next building to obstruct the view of an earlier speculator.

The first Europeans to visit the region were French seal hunters in the 17th century who stored their booty – whale-oil and seal skins – on an island in the lagoon

Yzerfontein
Phone code: 022
(NB Always use 3-figure prefix)
Colour map 6, grid B4

At times it may be possible to see whales sheltering in the bay, although there are better spots along this coast for whale watching

Western Cape

Many of the local holiday homes stand empty and the town can be very quiet out of season. Most of the local amenities are concentrated around the garage

Phone code: 022
(NB Always use 3-figure prefix)
Colour map 6, grid B4

known as Isle la Biche. This was renamed by the first Dutch settlers as **Schaapen Island**. It was not until 1870 that a village began to take shape. Prior to this, Langebaan was put on the map by Lord Charles Somerset, Governor of the Cape in the 1820s, who built a hunting lodge on a private farm overlooking the lagoon. The growth of the village was slow due to a shortage of fresh water, a problem which was only solved after the Second World War when a pipeline was built to bring water from the Berg River to the northeast.

The lagoon is an important feature of the region. The northern part, opening onto the Atlantic Ocean, is known as **Saldanha Bay** and is the deepest and safest natural harbour in South Africa. Not surprisingly, it has been fully utilized by the South African navy. More recently, mining interests have built a large iron ore wharf on the bay, a true eyesore which is visible from angles. In contrast, the southern shores and waters are part of the fascinating **West Coast National Park** (see page 179) – a rather precarious situation, as heavy ore carriers and naval boats frequenting the lagoon threaten the fragile marine environment.

The **Langebaan Information Office** is in the municipality, corner of Breë and Oostewal streets, T7721515, F7721531, www.langebaaninfo.com It's open Monday-Friday, 0900-1630, Saturday 0900-1200.

Sleeping
Price codes:
see inside front cover

There are plenty of options given the town's popularity on the domestic holiday front, but many of these choices are for a minimum period of a week and close in the winter. Nevertheless, visitors have considerable bargaining power in the winter months. As with all South African coastal resorts advance booking is necessary during the school holidays, especially Dec-Jan

B *The Farmhouse*, 5 Egret St, T7722062, F7721980, farmhouse@mweb.co.za A smart and cosy converted Cape Dutch farmhouse. 10 rooms with fireplaces, en suite bathroom or shower, TV, good restaurant with pine furnishings, swimming pool, overlooks Langebaan lagoon, library, always check room availability, no young children. Recommended. **B** *Langebaan Country Club*, T7722498. Comfortable and private lodges, restaurant, bar, surrounded by golf course, tennis, bowls. **C** *Falcon's Rest*, PO box 6, 21a Zeeland St, T/F7721112, falcon@imaginet.co.za Large converted family home with 12 double rooms with en suite bathroom, TV, several lounges, panoramic views from the garden, pool, sundeck. Attentive service. Ask for Jenny. **C-F** *Oliphantskop Farm Inn*, opposite turning for *Club Mykonos*, T7722326. Set of tastefully converted farm buildings, 17 en suite rooms plus some self-contained chalets, TV, comfortable with pleasing décor. Also has a backpacker section – off-season, backpackers are put in main rooms for budget rates, making it extraordinarily good value. Stables on the farm, specializes in horse trails. Candlelit restaurant set in long barn with log fires, choice of good-value seafood and steaks, beer garden, very friendly service. Highly recommended. **D** *Langebaan Beach House*, 44 Beach Rd, T7722625, lbh@intekom.co.za Small guesthouse in idyllic setting right on beach overlooking the lagoon. Tastefully furnished rooms, understated with terracotta-tiled floors, white linen, en suite, TV, some have private lounge and veranda overlooking beach, cooked breakfasts served on terrace, neat gardens and pool. Recommended. **E-F** *Sea Winds Backpackers*, just before you get to town on Main Rd, T7221612, T083-6277421 (mob). More of a budget B&B, with rooms sleeping up to 4, no bunks, shared bathroom, TV lounge, breakfast included. **E-F** *Seebries Caravan Park*, T7722442. Chalets and caravan park, more peaceful, out of town off the road to *Club Mykonos*.

Eating

Farmhouse, 5 Egret St, T7722062. Good lamb steaks, fresh seafood, quality food, vegetarian menu, views across the bay. *Flamingo's*, T7721915. Lively bar with dancing. *Hot Spot*, Breë St, T7721073. Trendy bar and restaurant, light lunches and usual steak dinners, outdoor seating area, has attached internet café. *La Taverna*, 1 Breë St, T7722870. Closed Mon and Tue out of season, good value seafood, pizza and pasta, very popular during holiday season. *Lagoon Fisheries*, Breë St. Fast food joint dishing out tasty fish and chips. *Pearlie's*, 46 Beach Rd, T7722734. Fresh seafood and spare ribs, very popular, be prepared to wait during busy periods since all the dishes are freshly prepared, relaxing views across the lagoon. Recommended. *Strandloper*, T7722490. Follow signs for *Club Mykonos*, on the beach, casual, romantic surroundings serving excellent seafood buffets, award winning, booking advised during peak periods, light guitar music in the evenings. Expect to pay approximately R100 per head for an all-you-eat-manage meal. Recommended.

Freeport is a large shopping and accommodation development with a supermarket, bakery, bottle shop and café. All other shops and restaurants are in Brë St, close to the Town Hall. Here you will find a bookshop, laundrette, Standard Bank and curio shops. **Shopping**

Boating: contact *Lagoon Sports* for water skiing and parasailing, T7722380. **Golf and tennis**: *Langebaan Country Club*, T7722112. **Mountain bikes**: available for hire from *Cape Sports*, T7721114. Also organize **windsurfing**, **kitesurfing** and **watersports**. *Bumpheadz*, T7722997, bumpheadz@mweb.co.za. Also organizes windsurfing and kitesurfing, plus **sandboarding** and **sea kayaking**. **Sports**

Useful services **Ambulance**: T10177. **Doctor**: T7722183. **Pharmacy**: T7722470. **Police**: Oostewal St, T7722111. **Directory**

Western Cape

West Coast National Park

Although it may not seem very remarkable at first sight, this park remains unmatched in South Africa. Covering 30,000 ha, it was established in 1985 to protect the rich marine life in the lagoon and the rare coastal wetlands. It extends from just north of Yzerfontein to Saldanha Bay, and includes the Postberg Nature Reserve, Langebaan lagoon and the islands – Malgas, Jutten, Marcus and Schaapen. The diversity of species here is impressive, but the main attraction is the excellent variety of birdlife. *Colour map 6, grid B4*

Getting there You can enter the park from two directions: from the south (look out for the signs along the R27); or by driving south out of Langebaan town. If you don't mind paying the small entrance fee, it is a pleasant alternative to drive through the park when travelling between Langebaan and Cape Town. All the roads are surfaced. **Ins & outs**

Information Open Apr-Sep 0700-1930; Oct-Mar 0600-2000. Entrance fee: R8 per adult. In season (Aug-Sep, Dec-Jan, Easter) the price doubles to R16 per person. The main information centre is housed just before the entrance to the park (follow the signs from Langebaan centre), and has maps and information on the area. Within the park, a beautiful farmstead dating from 1860 has been fully restored and turned into an environmental centre and tea rooms. This is found at the southern end of the lagoon and is known as the Geelbek homestead. Most visitors to the park, including tour groups, stop here. Apart from the attraction of a pot of tea or toasted sandwich, there are some interesting displays on the different ecosystems found in the park. Several walks start from here, leading to simple hides in amongst the reed beds and the mud flats.

The Parks Board runs 2 daily **boat trips**. The first is to Malgas Island and lasts 3 hrs. The trip leaves at 0900, depending on demand (must be a minimum of 4 people), and costs R120 per person, including a cool drink. The other trip is around the lagoon, lasts 1-2 hrs and costs R90 per person. Both are guided. Reservations are necessary, T022-7722144.

The main attraction in the park is the varied and impressive birdlife, and there are a number of hides allowing good viewing. Almost 250 species of bird have been recorded here, and the variety is quite remarkable: **flamingos** from the Etosha Pan in Namibia are found here; an estimated 50 per cent of the world's population of **swift terns** live here during season; 25 per cent of the world's **Cape gannets** are also found here, as are a sizeable number of rare African **black oystercatchers**. Other rare birds to look out for are the black harrier, great crested grebe and the silver gull. Each year over 65,000 waders visit the lagoon – many of these birds started life in the Siberian marshlands. The greatest influx of birds occurs between September and April. It takes the birds about six weeks to complete the 15,000 km journey from Siberia to Langebaan. Without the protected environment of the lagoon, it is **Birdlife** uncertain where these birds could or would migrate to. For this reason alone it is vital that the habitat is protected as far as possible.

The best time for flowers is Sep

The other major attraction of the reserve is its wild flowers which bloom after the first spring rains. Because of the variety of soil types, you can see many different flowers within a small area. The most colourful spreads are frequently found in **Postberg**.

Postberg Nature Reserve

Allow sufficient time to exit the park at the end of the day as it is a long drive all the way round the lagoon

Since August 1987, this private nature reserve has been administered by the National Park, while the actual lands remain the property of farmers. Three farms make up the reserve: Nieuwland, Kreeftebaai and Oude Post. Between 1838 and 1966 the land was used as winter grazing for cattle. In February 1969 it was declared as a private nature reserve which would be open during the flower season. It is found at the tip of the peninsula which forms the western shore of the lagoon. It is still only open from August to September, but during the spring it is one of the best places to see wild flowers. The land has also been stocked with eland, zebra, hartebeest, kudu and wildebeest. There are three picnic sites with toilets.

Saldanha Bay & West Coast National Park

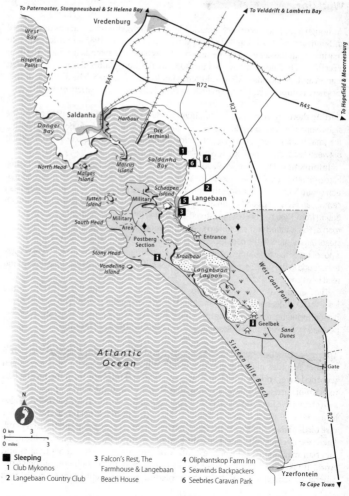

■ Sleeping	3 Falcon's Rest, The	4 Oliphantskop Farm Inn
1 Club Mykonos	Farmhouse & Langebaan	5 Seawinds Backpackers
2 Langebaan Country Club	Beach House	6 Seebries Caravan Park

Western Cape

Sishen-Saldanha Railway

For anyone driving north from Saldanha Bay you are likely to follow a route close to the Sishen-Saldanha railway. This was purpose-built between 1973 and 1976 to transport high grade iron ore from the Northern Cape to a new deep water harbour in Saldanha Bay. The line is 861 km long and only has three bends. It has earnt a place in the Guinness Book of Records. *In 1989 a world record was set when the longest and heaviest train covered the route. The train was 7.3 km long, there were 660 loaded trucks weighing 71,210 metric tonnes and it was pulled by 16 locomotives. You can see long segments of a train in the marshalling yards just outside the harbour, when there is a waiting train the road to Langebaan is diverted. Organized tours of the harbour, bookings essential, T022-7157295.*

The beautiful lagoon, a wide expanse of sparkling turquoise water, is an important **Langebaan** and integral part of the park. It is rich in nutrients – twice a day the tides replenish the **Lagoon** lagoon with cold plankton-rich water – and home to thousands of birds. Looking down from a high vantage point helps one appreciate how exceptionally clear the waters are. This has been attributed to colonies of mussels which filter the microscopic particles brought in by the tide. The water is also much shallower here than in Saldanha Bay, making the water slightly warmer than the ocean. It still rarely reaches above 15°C, too cool for swimming but fine for scuba diving in a wetsuit.

At the northern end of Langebaan lagoon, Saldanha is the largest town in the area **Saldanha** and certainly at the less appealing end of the lagoon. Large numbers of fishing *Phone code: 022* vessels offload their harvests here to be processed in one of three factories. The *(NB Always use* greatest blight in the area, however, is the long iron ore jetty and the bulk ships *3-figure prefix)* which sit complacently in the bay waiting to transport the ore. Following the *Colour map 6, grid B4* completion of the jetty in 1976, the new venture of aquaculture was started in the lagoon. At first this was somewhat derided by locals and the government, but today it has grown into a very important local industry. The first harvest was in 1984, and the quality was exceptional – suprising perhaps, considering the vicinity of the jetty. The main crop is the Mediterranean blue mussel, along with Japanese oysters and local clams.

Saldanha is also an important tourist centre for the thousands of South Africans who descend on the lagoon every summer. Conditions are safe and ideal for watersports, which means that the lagoon gets its fair share of boats and jet skis zipping up and down the otherwise peaceful waters. There is a **tourist office** on Van Riebeck St, T7142088, bureau@kingsley.co.za Open Mon-Fri 0830-1630, Sat 0900-1200.

Sleeping **B** *Saldanha Bay Protea*, 51 Main Rd, T7141264, F7144093. Standard chain hotel in *Price codes:* centre of town, 58 rooms, some non-smoking, TV, restaurant, swimming pool, secure parking. *see inside front cover* **B-C** *Jane's Guest House*, 8 Beach Rd, T7143605, F7141522. Pleasant seafront house. 5 rooms with en suite bathroom. **C** *Avondrust*, 16 Salamander St, T7142369, F7142360. Smart guesthouse run by a Belgian family. 4 double rooms, 1 family room, swimming pool, sauna, meals available on request. **C** *The Moorings Guest House*, Po Box 368, Vondeling St, T/F7144087. A very smart guesthouse, newish building designed in a traditional Cape Dutch style. All the rooms have sea views, most have en suite bathrooms. The rooms at the top of the house are built into the slope of the roof and have reeded ceilings. The breakfast room has a panoramic view of the lagoon. Good location, well-run, with lots of attention to detail. **C** *Hoedjies Bay*, Main Rd, T7143077. 32 rooms, a modern seafront hotel, popular with families, restaurant, bar. **C** *Oranjevlei Guest Farm*, T7142261, F7142262. Converted historic farm buildings, hiking trails on a working wheat and cattle farm, pub lunches, swimming pool, tennis courts, a well-run rural setup. **C-D** *Bluewater Bay Holiday Resort*, Camp St, T7141177. Self-catering cottages, swimming pool, tennis, windsurfing, overlooking Saldanha lagoon. **E** *Saldanha Holiday*

Western Cape

Resort, Camp St, T7142247. Camping and caravan site, gest very busy over Christmas. **E-F** *Tabak Bay Resort*, Diaz Rd, T7142248. Caravan and camping park.

Eating *Pedro's*, T7143243. Part of *Galley Pub*, popular seafood restaurant, also serves steaks and pub lunches. *Musselcracker*, 51 Main Rd, T7141264. Part of *Protea Hotel*, smart seafood restaurant with views across bay, good fresh fish, crayfish and mussles. *Slipway*, Main Harbour, T7144235. Evenings only. Seafood, braais, steaks and pasta dishes. Recommended.

Directory **Useful services** Police: T7141414.

Coastal fishing villages

Phone code: 022
(NB Always use 3-figure prefix)
Colour map 6, grid B4

Running in a clockwise direction to the north of Vredenburg are the small fishing communities of Paternoster, Stompneusbaai, St Helena Bay, Laaiplek and Dwarskersbos. None of these have much to keep visitors in the area for long, but all are within a day's drive of Cape Town and offer a view of quiet coastal life.

Paternoster Paternoster is a typical fishing village 15 km northeast of Vredenburg along a gravel road. The coloured fishing community is supported by a thriving Cape lobster export business. At the south end of Paternoster Bay is a lighthouse marking the treacherous Cape Columbine which has wrecked many ships. Columbine was in fact a wrecked barque in 1829. The lands around here make up the **Columbine Nature Reserve**. This area of protected coastline has a rich mix of wild flowers in the spring, Karoo succulents and nesting seabirds. The reserve is open daily during daylight hours, minimal entrance charge, T7522718.

Stompneusbaai Stompneusbaai is a similar coastal village, although it does have a fish processing factory. While its appearance and smell may rather detract from the attractive local fishermen's cottages, it is an important source of income for the village. This is also the area where **Vasco da Gama** landed in 1497 after three months at sea, the first voyage he had made this far south. The modern monument commemorating this is hardly worthy of his feat.

St Helena Bay A surfaced road links Stompneusbaai with St Helena Bay, an important centre of South Africa's commercial fishing industry. The bay was named by Vasco da Gama who anchored here with four vessels on 7 November 1497, St Helena Day. Fortunately for the crews they found plenty of fresh spring water. For **tourist information** contact the *St Helena's Bay Tourism Bureau*, T/F7151142.

Sleeping **C-D** *St Helena's Hotel*, Main Rd, T7361160, F7361560. Has a mix of 20 en suite double rooms, 10 cottages, four self-catering chalets and a caravan park. There is a restaurant, bar, TV lounge, swimming pool and a conference centre. All the rooms have panoramic views of the bay. Good base for exploring the region. **E** *Laingville Caravan Park*, Strand St, T7361685. Is quiet until the school holidays, when it gets far too crowded.

Rocher Pan Twelve kilometres beyond Dwarskersbos is this important and rarely visited bird
Colour map 6, grid A4 sanctuary. More often than not, you'll have the reserve to yourself with only the sound of thousands of birds feeding. This 914-ha reserve was established in 1967 around a seasonal vlei. In 1988 the boundaries were extended to include all the area up to the shore of the Atlantic Ocean. When fully flooded the vlei, fed by the Papkuils River, is nearly 3 km long, although it is unable to drain into the sea because of the sand dunes. This mix of protected habitats provides excellent breeding and feeding conditions for over 180 varieties of bird species. Nearly 70 different waterbirds have been recorded here, including some endangered species. If you are lucky you might spot the African black oystercatcher, one of the rarest endemic breeding coastal birds in South Africa. During its breeding season, between November and March,

The Jackass Penguin

This flightless sea bird is only found on the coast of southern Africa. Once they nested in guano burrows, today on Bird Island concrete piping provide the necessary shelter. In the 1930s estimates put their population at over one million birds, today less than 110,000 penguins are left. This considerable decline in the population has been put down to commercial fishing competing with their food

stocks and the collection of their eggs for food. They eat sardines, maasbanker, anchovy and squid. Along with Boulders Beach just outside Simon's Town in the Cape Peninsula, this is the only place where they can be seen nesting on the mainland. These are some of the smaller penguins, but you won't get a better view unless you go to Antarctica or the Falkland Islands.

Western Cape

listen out for its high-pitched call, designed to startle intruders. It usually feeds at low tide looking for mussels and limpets. White pelicans, Cape shovellers and flamingos are often seen here. There is also the chance of seeing a few of the resident small mammals such as steenbok, duiker and the water mongoose, as well as the shy **African wild cat**. ■ *Open daily, Sep-Apr 0700-1800, May-Aug 0800-1700. T022-9521727. There is no admission fee, but visitors should sign in at the office where you can collect an excellent bird checklist with map. There are two sturdy bird hides beside the freshwater lake. Close to the first hide are some braai facilities and toilets. Behind the car park a footpath leads across the dunes to the desolate beach.*

This small and isolated coastal community has three very good reasons for visiting, which makes it all the more surprising to find that tourism has barely made its mark. Firstly, the bay is a good location for **whale viewing** – this is about the furthest north southern right and humpback whales can be seen from the shore. Secondly, the bay is well known for its good **surfing** conditions. Finally, it lies at the mouth of **Verlorenvlei**, a stream with many marshlands which creates an important environment for a large and varied aquatic bird population. Over 230 bird species have been recorded in the area. There is also an interesting walk out to Baboon Point with good views of the bay. Ask for directions to the cave which has some San paintings. All activities are concentrated around an open square by the *Eland Hotel*. There is a Post Office, bottle shop, supermarket and a cheap café. The *Eland Hotel* also acts as the local **tourist information** office, T9721640.

Elands Bay
Phone code: 022
(NB Always use 3-figure prefix)
Colour map 6, grid A4

Sleeping A-B *Verlorenvlei Country Inn*, 6 km out of Elands Bay on the Redelinghuys Rd, T724, F681. Small, exclusive lodge, 5 comfortable rooms, lounge with open fireplace, excellent restaurant in a converted barn (try the crayfish pie), popular for serious birdwatchers as the grounds overlook Verlorenvlei and its reed beds, swimming pool, picnic lunches available, no young children. Recommended. **B-C** *Eland*, Beach front, T/F9721640. Sea views from a large and airy restaurant, TV lounge, braai facilities, the principal building in the village, cheaper rooms in annexe, prices are for full board. **C** *Villa Almaré*, 59 Duine St, T9721762. Small guesthouse a short walk from the beach. 4 double rooms with en suite bathrooms, good value. **F** *Elands Bay Caravan Park*, T9721745. Small municipal site right on beach front in the village centre, windy but low thick hedges provide some shelter, ideal for surfing, short walk from shops and the *Eland Hotel*.

Price codes: see inside front cover

Nearby, on the way to Lambert's Bay, is Wadrif Salt Pan. After rains there are a couple of shallow ponds here, providing an excellent chance of seeing **flamingos**. Take a left by the railway bridge and follow the railway line to Lambert's Bay. One short stretch belongs to the railways and you may have to pay a small toll fee. Wadrif Salt Pan is by the railway line. Before you reach Lambert's Bay you will pass the original beach restaurant, *Muisbosskerm*, which has become famous along the West Coast and is responsible for putting Lambert's Bay on the map (see below).

Wadrif Salt Pan

Lambert's Bay

Phone code: 027
(NB Always use
3-figure prefix)
Colour map 6, grid A4

Once just a small fishing village, Lambert's Bay has become a popular holiday town and gets very busy during summer. As noted above, the excellent *Muisbosskerm* restaurant played an important role in drawing visitors to the region, but the bay has in fact appeared on maps for many years – this was the last point at which Bartholomeu Dias went ashore, before sailing around the Cape for the first time in 1487. The village is named after the British admiral, Sir Robert Lambert, who produced detailed charts of this coastline between 1826-40. In 1918 Axel Lindstrom established the *Lambert's Bay Canning Co* and the future of the small fishing community was assured. The **tourist office** is on Church Street, T4321000, F4322335, www.lambertsbayinfo/lambert.co.za Open Mon-Fri, 0900-1300, 1400-1700, Sat 0900-1230.

Between Jul and Nov you have a good chance of seeing the southern right whale migrating north

The town itself is modern and rather unattractive, although it has one absorbing, if pungent, attraction: **Bird Island**. No longer an island, this rock outcrop is now joined to the land by a concrete jetty. It is an important breeding ground for African penguins, Cape gannets and cormorants. Most of the island is fenced off, but there is a rather dilapidated viewing tower (R10). Early morning and evening are the best time to see the birds, as during the day they are at sea looking for food. Although the birds make for interesting viewing, their cantankerous screeching and overpowering smell leaves a rather longer-lasting impression. If you have the time, walk to the end of the jetty where there are good views of the fishing fleet and plenty of sea birds. **NB** Around high tide, breakers crash across the jetty as you walk out to the island. Wear shoes with grip, as the surface is very slippery and uneven. The **Sandveld Museum** on Church Street, depicts the history of the region since the first settlers from the Cape moved north. There is a **Crayfish Festival** held in town every March.

Sleeping
*Price codes:
see inside front cover*

C *Lambert's Bay Hotel*, Voortrekker St, T4321126, F4321036, marinelb@kingsley.co.za 47 large rooms with marine décor, front upstairs rooms have a mixed view of the scenic harbour and ugly fish processing factory – do NOT open your windows when the factory is working! Popular *Waves* restaurant specializes in fresh, quality seafood, lively bar, within walking distance of all shops, plus Bird Island, ask about boat trips. **C-E** *Eureka Apartments*, 5 Seekant St, PO Box 88, T4321211, F4322627. A series of modern blocks of self-catering apartments owned and run by Jan (a keen rugby and sports fan) and Soljé, a friendly couple who know everything about this area of the coast. The apartments are immaculate and have been sensibly planned and decorated, everything you need for a few quiet days by the sea, prices vary according to the season: excellent value in quiet periods, very busy over Christmas. Recommended. **D-E** *Maki-Tuis Woonstelle*, 46 Korporasie, T/F4321240. 7 self-catering units for up to 3 people/room, TV, set back from the beach front, good value out of season. **E-F** *Lambert's Bay Caravan Park* , T4322238. Overlooks the main beach, a bit exposed, very busy in peak season.

Eating

Several years ago a new style of restaurant evolved on the outskirts of Lambert's Bay – an open air, no-frills seafood braai. Today there are several such places along the coast, but the first was the *Muisbosskerm*. The only evidence of its existence was a thorn hedge to shield guests from the wind, and lines of parked cars plus the occasional helicopter. Guests sit around long tables as if at Scout Camp.

Bosduifklip, 4 km out of town towards Clanwilliam, T4322735. Set amongst some rock formations on Albina farm. A popular open air restaurant serving meals in West Coast style, bring your own drink, booking essential at weekends and in holidays. Enjoy a tasty selection of seafood dishes including mussels, crayfish, smoked snoek and pickled fish. The salads are slightly unusual, but go well with the homemade breads and butter. *Die Kreef Huis*, T4322235. Closed Sun evening, an excellent seafood restaurant opposite the entrance to Bird Island. Treat yourself to some quality shellfish – you can select your own lobster from the tank. Good selection of wines, light easy going atmosphere, high standard of service, a must if you are in the area, booking advised during peak seasons. Acts as a coffee shop in the mornings and after lunch when homemade cakes and breads are served. *Muisbosskerm*, 5 km towards Elands Bay, T4321017. Extremely successful and popular open air restaurant, for a

Western Cape

fixed price (approximately R100) you have a wide choice of seafood and meat dishes cooked over a braai, baked and smoked, eat as much as you like, meals last about 3 hrs, bring your own drink, small corkage fee, book even out of season, the tourist office in town will help out. During peak periods there can be more than 150 people eating here – it can become a bit of a scrum around the braais. *Bay Breeze*, T4322911. Next to the police station, medium priced steakhouse. *Plaaskombuis*, 9 km south of town on Steenbokfontein Farm, T4322720. A traditional Sandveld farm menu with plenty of fresh produce straight off the farm. Large meals which should not be rushed. Try the homemade sausages plus the pot roast lamb. Breakfast is also recommended. Dinner by reservation only. Recommended. *Villa Romana*, Voortrekker St, T4322835. The local Italian option, above average pasta dishes.

Shopping There are several **souvenir** shops within walking distance of the *Lambert's Bay Hotel*, including *Driftwood Den* and *Isabella's*.

Sports **Fishing** Game fishing is very popular along this stretch of coast, as is collecting crayfish. Crayfish permits are issued by the Department of Sea Fisheries in the harbour area, T4321631. **Golf** There is a 9-hole golf course amongst the old dunes, T4321167. **Horse riding** Available at *Panorama Park*, 5 km out of town on Clanwilliam Road, T4321722. Small game reserve, daily horse trails.

Tour operators *Lambert's Bay Boat Charters*, Waterfront, T082-9224334 (mob). A knowledgeable local company which can organize trips to suit you to the smaller places of interest overlooked by the major players based in Cape Town. Strongly recommend boat trip to see dolphins, seals, whales (and sharks if you're lucky), expect to pay around US$25 per person.

Directory **Banks** *Standard Bank* in Church St is the best place to change money, there is also a branch of the *Boland Bank*. A 24-hr ATM is available. **Internet** *Trawler's*, erratic internet access, opposite *Lambert's Bay Hotel*. **Useful services** **Doctor**: T4321136. **Police**: T4321122.

Lambert's Bay to Vredendal

Doring Bay is a small fishing village based around a crayfish factory. The rocky coastline and deep coastal waters make this an ideal spot for crayfish to live in. The **Doring Bay Tourism Bureau**, on Main Street, T/F027-2151321, waves@kingsley.co.za, can provide advice on several of the local villages. There is a fish restaurant on the edge of the village, *The Cabin*, T027-2151016, run by a family team.

About 8 km further on is the northernmost village on the coast, **Strandfontein**. This is a delightful settlement built on the slopes of a small basin. The coastline is quite rocky and mountainous along here with a clean white sand beach with excellent surfing conditions. Although usually quiet, the village is very popular during the school holidays when there are full-time lifeguards present on the beach. There are strong cross currents so only swim in front of the town.

Sleeping **D** *Die Anker*, T027-2151016. Main local hotel, mix of accommodation including B&B, self-catering and some camping space. Meals on request. **E-F** *Strandfontein Resort*, Kreef Rd, T027-2151169. A well-equipped park which is a bit hectic when all 150 stands are occupied during the holidays. At quieter times of the year this is a relaxing spot to have a break. It is situated next to the beach, with self-catering chalets, power points, tidal swimming pool, café open all year plus a small kiosk (open in peak season).

Price codes: see inside front cover

Papendorp, close to the estuary of the Olifants River, is more of a cluster of cottages than a village. There is a small island in the middle of the river mouth, and at low tide there are thousands of water birds on the mud flats. From this point the road turns inland towards Lutzville (20 km from Strandfontein) and Vredendal. Previously known as Fleermuisklip, **Lutzville** is a small farming village surrounded by irrigated vineyards and vegetable farms. Johan Lutz was one of the engineers responsible for developing the irrigated lands along the Olifants River. The first house was built here as recently as 1947 – prior to the development of irrigated agriculture there was no viable means of making a living in this arid region. Tourist information is available on Du Toit Street; T/F027-2133678, or T082-5496035 (mob).

Sleeping There is a good hotel in town, **C** *Lutzville*, T027-2171513, plus an 18-hole golf course. Try eating at *St Geran*, Kant St, T027-2171840, fully licensed (there's another branch in Vredendal). Another good restaurant, in an open setting under an overhang which features some San rock art, is *Die Kliphuis*, T027-2171790. The place is well-known for its braais and booking is essential. Recommended.

Vredendal
Phone code: 027
*(NB Always use
3-figure prefix)*
Colour map 6, grid A4

Despite the fact that it is some distance west of the main N7, Vredendal is the principal commercial centre in the northwestern Cape. It is a modern town which owes its existence entirely to the Olifants River irrigation scheme. The first settlers came to the region as early as 1732 when the Dutch East India Company granted a farm to Pieter van Zyl, but it was only when the Bulshoek Dam was built that new farmers were attracted to the area. In 1925 a bridge was built across the Olifants River and the town grew rapidly into its present form. There are few sights in town, although one of the more unusual local industries open to the public is a seaweed-drying factory just outside the town. (It's used as a binding agent in ice cream, to make jelly sweets and as pet food.) The region is also home to several mines which produce dolomite and limestone. Anyone interested in visiting a mine should contact *Industrial Minerals*, T027-2133090. For **tourist information** contact the *Vredendal Information Office*, 11 Voortrekker Street, T/F2133678, vredilibrary@matzikama.co.za

*Price codes:
see inside front cover*

Sleeping and eating **C-D** *Vredendal Hotel*, 11 Voortrekker St, T2131064, F2131003. Main hotel in town, 2-storey brick building with 51 a/c rooms, restaurant, bar, swimming pool. **C-D** *Maskam*, T2131336, F2132715. Simple small hotel, some a/c rooms, not all rooms have bathroom, no restaurant, steakhouse next door. **D** *Tharrakamma Guesthouse*, 18 Tuin St, T/F2135709. 3 double rooms, 2 family rooms, a/c, TV, non-smoking available, garden. Recommended. *Oaisi*, Shoprite Centre, Voortrekker St. Coffee shop and ice cream parlour. *Saddles*, Voortrekker St , T2134629. Reliable steakhouse, always busy with families. *St Geran*, 31 Matsikama St, T2131626. Popular local family outlet.

There are also a couple of guesthouses on nearby farms and vineyards, no more than 10 mins' drive from the centre. The cottages are designed for long stay, self-catering family groups, although most will also take B&B guests. **C** *Voorsorg*, 1 km to the south of the town centre, off the R363, PO Box 5, T2132243. 3 cottages with 2, 3, or 5 bedrooms. Each house has a fully equipped kitchen, en suite bathrooms, a/c in the bedrooms and access to a swimming pool. **C** *Houmoed*, 7 km out of town off the R363 towards Klawes, PO Box 238, T/F2132377. 2 fully equipped guesthouses, 2 or 3 bedroom, a/c, carport, breakfast can be provided. **C-D** *Kerndolsie*, 9 km from the centre, off the Klawer road, PO Box 278, T/F2132370. 2 cottages for either 2 or 4 guests. Kitchen, lounge with TV, a breakfast pack is provided to cook yourself.

Karoo to Breede River Valley

If your time is short or you want to get to the Northern Cape, the quickest way out of Cape Town is to take the N7 highway. The first part of the route passes through rolling wheat country known as the Swartland, or 'Black Country', named after the dark hue of rhinoceros bush which once covered the area. Most of the towns in the region are small, prosperous farming communities, with little in terms of sights, despite their long history. The principal centres of the wheat industry are Malmesbury and Moorreesburg. The eastern boundary of the Olifants River valley is made up of the spectacular Cederberg Mountains, a striking wilderness area offering some of the best hiking in South Africa. Both Citrusdal and Clanwilliam make good bases for exploring the area, their irrigated valleys providing a powerful contrast to the seemingly barren Cederberg.

About 50 km from Cape Town the N7 passes Malmesbury, the centre of the surrounding wheat industry and the principal town in the Swartland. The town lies in a shallow valley close to the Diep River. It was founded in 1743 around what was then a well-known warm sulphur chloride mineral spring. The spring is currently in disuse, but given modern trends it may yet be developed into a health spa.

Malmesbury
Phone code: 022
(NB Always use
3-figure prefix)
Colour map 6, grid B5

The town was given its current name in 1829 when the British Governor, Sir Lowry Cole, visited and renamed it in honour of his father-in-law, the Earl of Malmesbury. Today the skyline is dominated by the unsightly grain silos and huge flour mills. The **Swartland Cellars** winery, 4 km out side town, produces a full-bodied red wine and the famous Hanepoot, a strong honey-flavoured wine popular as a dessert wine. These wines have won a number of awards, despite the fact that experts claim local climatic conditions are far from ideal. The cellars are worth a visit if you have missed out on the Winelands vineyards around Stellenbosch. For **tourist information**, visit the *Malmesbury Tourism Bureau*, 131 Voortrekker Road, T4871133, F4872063, swartlandinfo@westc.co.za

One of the grandest buildings in town is the **Dutch Reformed Church** on Church Street, opposite the City Hall. Although the original building was completed in 1751, the present form dates from around 1899 when the church was enlarged by building the existing wings. In the intervening period it had a chequered history: it was extended in 1831, rebuilt in 1860, and was washed away by rains in 1862. In 1877 the steeple of the new church collapsed, and in 1880 the building was completely renovated. The impressive original pulpit somehow survived, and in July 1979 the church was declared a national monument.

The magnificent heavy church bell isn't rung for fear of the vibrations damaging the structure – instead, a recording is played at services!

The early history and growth of the town is displayed in an old synagogue, now known as the **Cultural History museum**, T4822332. The original building was constructed in 1911, but most of the Jewish community had moved away within 30 years. The building was donated to the community by Dr Goldman, to be used solely as a museum. One other building of note is a 19th-century manor house which was brought out to South Africa in kit form from England in the 1880s. Known as **Gerrie Thiart House** after the current owner who saved it from demolition, it can be viewed by appointment, ask at the Tourism Bureau.

Sleeping and eating C *Swartland Guest Lodge*, corner of Voortrekker and Ludolf streets, T4871771. 12 rooms, most with bathroom, restaurant and bar. **C-D** *Almond Bridge*, T4823590. Guesthouse and B&B option. **E-F** *Caravan Park*, Piketberg Rd, T4873266. Chalets and shady caravan stands, laundry, public telephone, swimming pool, a small, well-run site. *The Manor House*, 1 Loedolf St, T4871771. Closed Sun evening. Open for breakfasts and afternoon teas. Enormous choice on the à la carte menu, set menu on Sun includes a local roast with fresh vegetables. Friendly service, garden setting. Recommended.

Price codes:
see inside front cover

Transport Bus: *Intercape*, T021-3804400. Coaches depart from outside *Malmesbury Motors*. **Cape Town** (45 mins): daily, 1245, 0400. **Clanwilliam** (5 hrs): daily, 1145, 2045. **Springbok** and **Namibia**: daily, 1145. **Upington** (9 hrs): daily, 2045.

The small rural village of Riebeek West was the birthplace of two of South Africa's prime ministers: **DF Malan** was born on *Allesverloren* farm; **Jan Smuts** was born at *Ongegund*. Smuts's cottage is open to the public. In the village, the **Wamakers' Museum** has some good displays on the old craft of wagon making. One other building of note is a 100-year-old **Trading Store**. The original serving counter and storage containers are still in place, and part of the shop has been turned into a restaurant.

Riebeck West & Riebeck-Kasteel
Phone code: 022
(NB always use
3-figure prefix)
Colour map 6, grid B5

Sleeping B *Riebeek Valley Hotel*, 4 Dennehof St, T4612672, F4612692. An elegant house from the 1920s, with 10 large double rooms, a/c, luxury en suite bathrooms, indoor heated swimming pool, billiard room and a relaxing conservatory. Attached *Bishops* restaurant. Recommended. **B-C** *Dalmar Country House*, 10 Long St, T4612245. 5 rooms with en suite

Western Cape

bathroom, long shady veranda, library, swimming pool, good country cooking in restaurant, cosy bar, attached art gallery and secure parking; a surprise package for a small village. Booking for restaurant is advised at weekends.

Beaverlac Private Nature Reserve

As the R44 continues north, the **Olifants River Mountains** dominate the eastern horizon. Between the road and the mountains are rippling expanses of wheat fields, picturesque despite their lack of trees, especially at sunset. Tucked away in the mountains is the seldom visited Beaverlac Private Nature Reserve. The principal attraction of the area is hiking past strange rock formations, sculptured by water through time. The actual reserve is part of four farms at the top of Dasklip Pass. At the highest point, 815 m, you can see the Atlantic Ocean to the west, while to the northeast is a narrow valley through which the young Olifants River flows north. Visitors can walk freely within the reserve – look out for small antelope such as duiker, klipspringer, steenbok and grysbok. Fishing is possible if you walk down to the Olifants or Ratel rivers to the east.

Moorreesburg

Phone code: 022
(NB Always use 3-figure prefix)
Colour map 6, grid B5

Back on the main N7, 102 km north of Cape Town, is this important farming and railway centre in the heart of the Swartland. Like Malmesbury, the surrounding area is devoted to wheat fields and sheep farming. Close to the railway are enormous grain silos and flour mills – wheat has been grown in the area since 1752. The settlement was founded in 1879 on a farm called *Hooikraal*, as a church centre. The town was named after the Rev HA Moorrees. The **tourist office** is in the Municipality building, corner of Plein and Retief streets, T/F4331072, mooresburg@westc.co.za

The **Wheat Industry Museum** (proudly proclaiming that it is one of only three in the world) is on the Main Road and has a fairly diverting collection which traces the history of the crop. Before the cultivation of the area, the dominant vegetation was rhinoceros bush, a dark shrub found throughout the Swartland which first gave it its name. Some of the early harvesting and threshing machines are well worth a look; they remind one of kit models, which in many ways is what they are, having been shipped out from England in pieces. ■ *Mon-Thu 0900-1700, Fri 0800-1600. Small entrance fee. T4331093.* There is a small art collection on show in the **Dirkie Uys Art Gallery**, housed in the high school, T4331072. Most of the works are by older South African artists, including Laubscher, Boonzaaier and Pierneef.

Price codes:
see inside front cover

Sleeping and eating **C** *Samoa*, Central St, T4331201, F4332031. Friendly rural hotel with comfortable a/c rooms, popular *De Kraal* restaurant, bar, swimming pool, secure parking. **C** *Klipvlei Guest House*, PO Box 115, T4332401. A smart farm with 6 en suite double rooms. Evening meals available on request. Swimming pool, games rooms. Recommended. **C-E** *Kolskoot Safaris and Guest Farm*, 10 km from the town centre, T/F4332528. This building has an odd history – it was built during World War II by Italian POW's as a chicken coop. Today it has 6 en suite double rooms, 1 family room, each decorated with rustic furniture and paintings by a young local artist. Also organize a range of activities including mountain biking, horse riding safaris, clay pigeon shooting and hunting. Also has some good value backpacker accommodation. Recommended. Booking is essential. **F** *Caravan Park*, Hoofweg, T4332597. On the outskirts of town, small site, shady but not grassy, fully serviced tents available, short walk to shops and town swimming pool. *Ou Stasie*, Railway St, T4331185. Closed Mon and Sun evening. Continental-style menu with some fresh seafood and pasta dishes. The restaurant is in a restored railway station and guests can dine outside on the platform during the summer months. Good value, one of the better places to eat in the area.

Transport **Bus**: *Intercape*, T021-3804400. Coaches stop outside Swartland Motors. **Cape Town** (45 mins), daily 1245, 0400. **Clanwilliam** (5 hrs), daily 1145, 2045. **Springbok** and **Namibia**, daily 1145. **Upington** (9 hrs), daily 2045.

Piekenierskloof Pass

After 31 km the N7 passes the turning for Velddrif and the village of Piketberg. The **Piketberg hills** rise as a large massif to the east as the road heads across the

Swartland: green plus yellow equals black

The name Swartland means 'black country', a term used by Jan van Riebeeck when he first visited the region. He was referring to the black colour of the original vegetation, renosterveld, and not the soil itself, as is sometimes suggested. Black country is something of a misnomer, this is the most important wheat growing region in South Africa. During the season the region starts as lush green wheatfields which gradually turn yellow by harvest time. Along the roadside there is a mass of colour in spring as the wild flowers come

into bloom. It is perhaps only the few weeks after the harvest that the landscape looks somewhat barren and dark.

The climate of the Swartland is characterized by warm to hot summers, with winter rainfall. In the summer temperatures can reach 28°C, but at times it can feel cooler if the breeze is blowing off the Atlantic. The spring months, September-October, are when the countryside looks its best. The rains have finished, marshes and dams are full, and the wild flowers are usually in full bloom.

Western Cape

plains to the **Olifants River Mountains**. Before the road starts to climb, you pass the turning on the right for Porterville. This is the R44 and takes you back towards Paarl and Cape Town. Climbing the Piekenierskloof or Grey's Pass there are superb views across the flat Swartland. From the top of the pass the views change – no longer is the country flat, and you have your first view of the magnificent **Cederberg**. At sunset, the mountains take on a striking purple hue. To the right, at the summit of the Piekenierskloof Pass, you pass the **Piekenaar's Kloof resort** (see below). The road then descends into the Olifants River Valley and the town of Citrusdal, the landscape changing again with the arrival of the startling green citrus groves.

Piketberg is another typical agricultural town, with a few old buildings and churches in the centre surrounded by modern suburbs, which in turn give way to the ubiquitous rolling wheat fields. The town was one of the locations where cannons were fired to let farmers know when a new ship was arriving in Table Bay to take on board fresh supplies. The cannon was also used to warn of the approach of Khoi-San people – it can be seen in the grounds of the high school. The name of the town dates back to 1792 when a lookout post was set up on Honigberg Farm to protect the local farmers from being looted by the Khoi-San. The actual word is derived from the French word *picquet*, referring to a small group of soldiers on the lookout. For **tourist information**, contact the local bureau, T9132063.

Piketberg
Phone code: 022
(NB Always use
3-figure prefix)
Colour map 6, grid B5

Like most of the small towns in the region, the dominant building is the **Dutch Reformed Church**, built between 1880-82. It is a striking building, neo-gothic in style with plenty of turrets and plastered panels. There is an obelisk in its grounds commemorating the 1838 Great Trek. In 1938 the building was declared a national monument. There is a small **museum** housing antiques donated by the community.

Sleeping B-C *Noupoort Farm*, PO Box 101, T9145754. A magnificent mountain retreat with a mix of self-catering and B&B accommodation, full board rates also available, 10 fully equipped cottages with kitchens and braai area, mix of doubles and twins, meals available on request, 9 newer units with magnificent views of the West Coast, split level with mini-bar. The farm is about 90 mins' drive from Cape Town, excellent base from which to explore the West Coast and the Cederberg Region. To get there, turn off the N7 at Piketberg and follow Langstraat into the town. At the T-junction turn right on to the Elands Bay Road. Take a left turn after 1 km, signposted 'Versfeldpas Drive'. Follow this road for approximately 13 km up the pass to the top of the mountains, and look out for a left turning marked 'Langeberg Afdelings pad'; the turning for the farm is 5 km along this road.

Price codes:
see inside front cover

Olifants River Valley

The area was once home to huge elephant herds, giving the river its name, but these are sadly long gone

As you drop down from the Piekenierskloof Pass, the scenery changes significantly with the arrival of the Olifants River. Although not one of South Africa's largest rivers, it is of vital importance to the region, irrigating over 12,000 ha of farmland. This is most immediately obvious in the brilliant green citrus farms interspersed with vineyards. Marking the east of the valley are the stark and magnificent Cederberg Mountains.

Citrusdal

Phone code: 022 (NB Always use 3-figure prefix) Colour map 6, grid A5

As the name implies, this modern rural town is the centre of the local citrus industry, nestling in a valley filled with verdant citrus farms. During spring, the air is heavy with the scent of orange blossom, and from May hundreds of thousands of oranges are packed up and sent around the world. Even more impressive is the town's striking setting at the southern edge of the Cederberg Mountains. Along with Clanwilliam, Citrusdal makes an ideal base for exploring the wilderness of the mountains. The **tourist office**, *CITOUR*, is on Vortrekker Street, T/F9213210, www.citrusdaltourism.co.za, housed in a recently built example of a typical Sandveld dwelling. ■ *Open, Mon-Fri 0830-1630, Sat 0900-1300.*

The town **museum** is in an old stone building which started life as the first church in the settlement. The display covers most aspects of local history including the life of the San and their works of art. There is also a life-size model of an early pioneer dwelling. Look out for an old cannon in the grounds of the high school. This was used to communicate with Cape Town – there were a series of cannons along the mountain slopes, all the way to the Cape. ■ *T9212181.*

There are some interesting San paintings on the **Hexrivier** farm, 20 km north from town, also home to *Gekko Backpackers*. You need to call ahead, T9213353, to arrange a tour; otherwise if you choose to stay here, Reinhard will drive you to them.

Many of the surrounding farms are now growing grapes, and the region is known for its excellent **Goue Valley Wines**. There is a Goue Valley shop on Vortrekker Street, near the tourist office, with sales and tastings, T9212235. Tours can also be arranged to the **Goede Hoop Citrus Co-op** to see the packing of fruit, T9212211.

Just out of town, by the turning for *The Baths*, is **Craig Royston**, a historic building and one of the first built in the area. It houses a small country **museum** outlining local history, but its main appeal is as a farm stall offering good light meals and wine tasting, T9212181.

Sleeping

Price codes: see inside front cover

Plenty of farms in the region provide accommodation, convenient for hiking. Full lists are available from the tourist office

B-C *Piekenaarskloof Mountain Lodge*, Piekenierskloof Pass, T9212569. Tremendous views across the Cederberg Mountains. A large complex, great base in season (but reminds me a little of *The Shining* when there are only a few guests!). A mix of thatched chalets plus a cheaper lodge for hikers, restaurant, swimming pool, large comfortable lounge with log fires. **C** *Cederberg Lodge*, 67 Voortrekker St, T9212221, F9212704, www.cederberglodge.co.za Family-run town hotel with 26 a/c rooms, TV with M-Net, swimming pool, full-size billiard table, gardens, *Tangelo's* restaurant has a good reputation, pub with big-screen TV showing sports. **C-D** *Wolfkop*, 7 km south of Citrusdal, T082-5675816 (mob), wolfkop@apteker.co.za 2 well-equipped cottages with views of valley. Each cottage sleeps 4, a/c, TV, fridge, cooking facilities including microwave, fireplace, braai area and veranda. **C-D** *Olifantsrus Guest House*, T9213528, elephant@kingsley.co.za Small guesthouse set on citrus farm, 4 en suite bedrooms, B&B. Also own the **D-E** *Elephants Leisure Resort*, T9212884, elephant@kingsley.co.za Self-catering chalets, heated swimming pool, TV, bathrooms with jacuzzi, 4-wheel drive trips organized. **D** *Tree Tops*, 25 km south of Citrusdal, follow signs from turning to *The Baths*, T9213626. Innovative guesthouse with double rooms set in treehouses, comfortable, fun place to stay. Good value.

B-E *The Baths*, 18 km to the south of Citrusdal, T9213609, baths@kingsley.co.za A popular and long established natural hot water spring surrounded by citrus groves, the first resort was established here in 1739 and the main Victorian stone buildings survive. Accommodation is in 5 well-equipped chalets, 12 flats and campsite, all self-catering, shop on site but it's best to buy fresh groceries in Citrusdal, hot swimming pool, tennis courts, mountain biking, variety of hiking trails, recommended if you enjoy health spas. **F** *Gekko Backpackers*, 20 km north of Citrusdal on the N7, turning to left is signposted, T9313353, vism@mweb.co.za Excellent backpacker lodge set amid orange trees on a citrus farm. 2 double rooms, 2 dorms, still fairly new so everything is in good condition, brightly painted bathrooms, large kitchen, bar, table-tennis room, small lounge, hammocks strung underneath trees. Idyllic setting, perfect for relaxing on the lawns or wondering through citrus groves. Access to swimming holes in river and added bonus of San rock art on the farm – Rienhard will take you there. Popular with overlanders, so can get rowdy, but usually very peaceful. Highly recommended.

Dankert's Grill, De Klerk St, T9213783. Steak house, serving steaks, burgers, ribs, some pasta dishes. *Patrick's*, Voortrekker St, T9213062. Good restaurant with an Irish theme, although the meals are rather more local – excellent ostrich steak, also good grilled linefish and wide range of steaks, good value and friendly. *Tangelo's*, in *Cederberg Lodge*, 67 Voortrekker St, T9212221. Popular family restaurant with a good reputation, mix of usual steaks with country cooking.

Eating

Mountain biking *Goede Hoop Cooperative* have plotted 11 trails in the district – the longest is 60 km, and the shortest 6 km. Some have very steep sections while others are all down hill. Collect a leaflet from the tourist office which has a simple map and a brief description of each route. There is an annual Citrus festival mountain bike rally each Sep.

Sports
Respect the conditions of the owners who have agreed to allow cycling on their farms

Bus *Intercape*, T021-3804400. Coaches depart from outside Sonop Motors. **Cape Town** (3 hrs): daily, 1245, 0400. **Clanwilliam** (1-2 hrs): daily, 1145, 2045. **Springbok** and **Namibia**: daily, 1145. **Upington** (9 hrs): daily, 2045.

Transport

Western Cape

Clanwilliam

Clanwilliam, lying at the northern edges of the Cederburg, is a peaceful agricultural centre and one of the oldest towns in South Africa. During the spring, the profusion of wild flowers that blanket the area attract a large number of visitors, many of whom travel up from Cape Town. Just off the N7, Clanwilliam is a good base for exploring the Cederberg, and more peaceful and picturesque than Citrusdal. **Clanwilliam Tourism Bureau**, is on Main St, just to the left of the Old Jail, T4822024, F4822361, cederberg@lando.co.za It a very helpful and friendly office. Open Mon-Fri 0800-1630, Sat and Sun 0900-1300. Worth a visit, although for more detailed advice on hiking in the area, you'll have to go to the office in Algeria (see below).

Phone code: 027
(NB Always use 3-figure prefix)
Colour map 6, grid A5

The entire area of the Cederberg was populated by nomadic San people for over 20,000 years, and a profusion of rock art lies testament to their presence and displacement from the area. The area was first settled by white farmers in 1726; Jan Dissels started one of the first farms here, building a homestead close to the wagon track route from Table Bay. At the time, this spot was referred to as *Aan de Renoster Hoek*, literally, 'by the rhinoceros corner'. Similar names in the region refer to *olifant* and *seekoei*, elephant and hippopotamus, providing further evidence of the wildlife that once roamed the area.

History

In 1808 a garrison was constructed to try and deal with the problem of cattle rustling by Khoi people. The hot and arid farming conditions further dissuaded families from settling here, and the first British settlers were in fact brought here by the British Government to create a human buffer in a grand scheme to stabilize the border from further tribal incursions. Only six families remained, and when the village was renamed in 1814 there were only 16 families living in the area. The new name was given by Sir John Cradock, the Governor of the Cape, in honour of his father-in-law, the Earl of Clanwilliam. Despite being a strong Afrikaner region, the name has stuck.

Western Cape

Sights

For tours of the jail or tea factory, contact the tourist office, T4822155, cederberg@lando.co.za

The majority of South Africans come to Clanwilliam to make use of the sporting facilities on and around the beautifully situated **Clanwilliam Dam**. But in town there are a couple of sights worth seeing. The **Old Jail**, built in 1808, is a stocky white fort-like building overlooking the main street. The first part of the museum is devoted to the works of Clanwilliam's two famous residents: Dr P le Fras Nortier, who worked on citrus and the rooibos bush; and Louis Leipoldt, a well-known nature poet. There are also some displays on the rooibos and cedar industries. At the back of the museum is an incredible giant threshing machine which was shipped out to South Africa in parts from Ipswich, England. ■ *Mon-Fri 0800-1300, R5.*

Following the road to the right of the old jail leads to the **Rooibos Tea Factory**. The industry originally flourished during the World War II when teas from the Far East were difficult to obtain in Europe. After the war the market collapsed, but in recent times it has grown in popularity since it is caffeine-free and low in tannin. Today it is the biggest industry in the area and is a refreshing, if acquired, taste. Further along the same road is the **Clanwilliam Dam Resort**, part of which is the **Ramskop Nature Reserve**, T027-4822133. Open between July and October, it is worth visiting to view its magnificent wild flowers in bloom.

Sleeping

Price codes: see inside front cover

C-D *Cedar Inn*, N7 highway, 7 km from town, T/F4822185. A characterless motel with basic rooms, restaurant, close to the dam. **C** *Strassberger's Hotel Clanwilliam*, Main St, T4821101, F4822678, strassberger@lando.co.za Friendly and homely family-run hotel, excellent place to use as a base. Large comfortable rooms, en suite, a/c, TV, good restaurant, swimming pool, sauna, good value. Recommended. **C** *The Rectory*, Main St, T4821629. Appealing guesthouse set in a historical Cape Dutch home with thatched roof. Cosy rooms, attractive breakfast room, gardens with pool. **D** *Brannewijnkop*, 5 km out of town, T4822882. An excellent B&B run by a young couple who are very enthusiastic and knowledgeable about the area. Modern house in a peaceful setting, good breakfasts, evening meals by arrangement. Recommended. **D** *Marg-Will*, 4 km out of town on Fish Eagle estate, T/F4822537. Farm-style B&B, 2 rooms each with 3 beds and en suite bathroom, no smoking, swimming pool, excellent spot for bird watching. **D** *Blommenberg*, 1 Graafwater Rd, T4821851, F4821515. Comfortable set of self-catering units, en suite, TV, breakfasts served, garden, pool, hard to miss on the right hand side just before town. **F** *Clanwilliam Dam Public Resort*, 1 km out of town beside the dam, T4822133. Huge resort with 180 grassy caravan and tent stands, self-catering chalets, plenty of trees offering shade, electric and gas points, gets very busy and noisy in season.

Eating

L'Andru, next to petrol garage just before town, T4821037. Sports café and bar, burgers and steaks. *Nancy Tearoom*, Main St, T4821101. Coffee shop set in beautiful gardens, serves good sandwiches and excellent cakes. *Olifantshuis*, Main St, T9822301, popular bar serving steaks and pizzas. *Reinhold's*, smart à la carte opposite *Strassberger's Hotel*, closed Sun-Tue, evening only, small bar and cosy atmosphere, the best option in the area. *Strassberger's*, hotel dining room serves excellent value 4-course meals, their breakfast will keep you going all day. Recommended.

Tour operators

Blue Yonder, T083-2324306 (mob). Adventure trips using 4-wheel drive and 'Xumbugs', small 4X4 go-carts. *Cederberg Tours*, T4822444, info@cederberg.co.za Day tours in the mountains, adventure trips, hikes, also organize trips from Cape Town.

Transport

Road Clanwilliam is 240 km from **Cape Town** and 230 km from **Springbok**. **Bus:** *Intercape*, T021-3804400. Buses depart from *Cedar Inn*. **Cape Town** (4 hrs): daily, 1245, 0400. **Citrusdal** (1-2 hrs): daily, 1145, 2045. **Springbok** and **Namibia**: daily, 1145. **Upington** (9 hrs): daily, 2045.

Wuppertal

Colour map 6, grid A5

Originally a Rhenish mission founded in 1830, this remote settlement lies on the eastern edge of the Cederberg Mountains in the Tra-Tra Valley, accessible only by dirt road. After the emancipation of slaves in 1838, the mission grew considerably and today it is renowned for its vernacular architecture. It is a beautiful spot to visit, but it remains remote and you should allow plenty of time to get there given the poor road.

Nollace Salomo, a local guide and the tourism official (T027-4823410), can show you around. At the end of the tour, guests are usually treated to a traditional meal at the *Lekkerbekkie Restaurant*, Church Square. This also acts as the local tourism bureau.

Cederberg Wilderness Area

The Cederberg is famous for its rugged scenery, stunning rock formations and ancient rock art, all of which make it fantastic walking country. There are over 250 km of paths in the mountains, passing streams, waterfalls and bizarre mountain flora. The highest peaks are Snow Peak, 2,028 m and Table Peak, 1,969 m, while the most notable sandstone features include the **Wolfberg Arch**, the **Maltese Cross**, the **Wolfberg Cracks**, **Lot's Wife**, the **Town Hall** and the **Valley of the Red Gods**. All these lie along the most popular hiking trails. Other trails focus on San rock art, usually found in caves or under overhangs.

*Phone code: 027
(NB always use
3-figure prefix)
Colour map 6, grid A5*

Getting around All of the roads into the Cederberg Mountains are gravel, with steep and twisting sections, although some of these have been covered with tarmac. The principal administrative centre for the wilderness is Algeria. There are 2 roads from which you can access the main trails and sights. The most popular runs south from Clanwilliam along the Rondegat River Valley to Algeria, and then on to the small centres of Cederberg and Uitsig. This road runs along the western side of the mountains. Approaching from Citrusdal, the quickest route to Algeria is north along the N7; after 27 km take a right, signposted Kriedouwkrans and Algeria. You will cross the Olifants River via a low level bridge and then descend into Algeria via Nieuwoudt Pass.

Ins & outs

The second road into the mountains is the route serving the remote mission station at Wuppertal. This is a much longer route and in parts requires 4-wheel drive vehicles. Follow the Calvinia road east from Clanwilliam and take a right by the 'Englishman's grave'. Wuppertal is 75 km from Clanwilliam.

Tourist offices The best regional information is available from the office in Algeria. *Cederberg Tourist Information*, T4822812, F4822406, cederberg@cnc.org.za

Best time to visit Climate is an important factor to bear in mind when planning a hike. During the summer months daytime temperatures are high, most streams and pools are dry, and you will need to carry plenty of water. Conversely, in the winter there can be heavy snowfalls, so you must carry the appropriate equipment. The best months for hiking are Mar-Apr and Sep-Dec. Jan and Feb are very hot and few people walk during these months; between Jun and Aug you can expect to encounter snow on the high ground.

As an officially declared wilderness, you are allowed to walk and camp anywhere in the mountains. There are, however, important rules to observe. No fires are allowed, so gas or paraffin stoves must be carried on overnight hikes. All waste material must be carried out – if you come across other people's rubbish, don't ignore it but carry it with you. Finally, while you are allowed to swim in the streams and pools, **do not wash with any form of soap** in the waters. The idea behind a wilderness is that the entire watershed is left to its own devices with the minimal interference from man. There are few areas, even in South Africa, where you can wander so freely, so enjoy it and respect the rules. While there are recognized trails, these are not always easy to follow. Anyone planning a hike of more than one day should buy the excellent Cederberg map issued by the Forestry Department, and always carry a compass.

Hiking

There is a limit on the number of visitors who can enter the wilderness each day. The region is divided into three blocks and 50 people are allowed in each block per day – you shouldn't have to book permits in advance, even in peak season. Permits are issued from the Algeria office, and from some of the private farms by the trails.

Warning There are 16 species of **snake** found in the mountains. Though not aggressive, hikers may encounter a snake sunning itself on a path. Wear strong

Western Cape

Western Cape

Cedar trees – long term conservation

*The Cederberg mountains owe their name to the large stands of cedar trees that once covered the slopes. In a very short time this magnificent tree, **Widdringtonia cedarbergensis**, once found throughout the surrounding mountains, has almost completely disappeared. These slow growing trees were ruthlessly felled for telegraph poles and beams in houses. Records show that 7,200 young trees were felled for telegraph poles between Piketberg and Calvinia. In 1967 the removal of dead trees was halted, other forms of exploitation ended in 1973. This is despite the fact that the first forester to oversee the region was appointed in 1876. Sadly, it looks as if the lessons have been learnt too late.*

These days it is an important target of conservationists. It will be difficult to restore the hills to their former forested glory as this slow growing tree can live for over 800 years. The few cedar trees that remain are found above 1,000 m, against cliffs and overhangs. Despite conservation efforts their numbers are still in decline. Unfortunately nature's way in the mountains results in hot fires, which now cause more damage than good, given the limited number of trees. Currently there is a programme of planting young trees in suitable places within the reserve, but it will take years before the success of such a project can be measured .

hiking boots and check your camp at night. The most harmful species are the puff adder and berg adder, both of which can be sluggish but are highly venomous.

Flora & fauna
Beware of baboons stealing food at night from your camp

Although once covered in cedar trees, the vegetation that remains is predominantly mountain fynbos. There are few trees found along the major hikes – shade and shelter is usually provided by rock overhangs. In the wetter gullies and valleys you will find yellowwoods, hard pears and the Cape beech. The rare endemic snow protea, *Protea cryophila*, grows above the snowline. It is only found in a few locations but these are kept a secret. There are some photos of the flowers in the Clanwilliam museum.

The most common antelope found here include klipspringers, duiker and grey rhebok, but it is unlikely that you'll see any of these during a hike. Since 1988 there has been a programme to protect the leopard population, and apparently there are plenty in the mountains, although it is virtually impossible to see them. Given the lack of vegetation at higher altitudes, the birdlife is not very varied, but look out for grey-wing francolin, cape siskin, cape sugarbird and victorin's warbler.

Rock art
The Cederberg is literally littered with ancient San rock art, and peeking underneath a rocky ledge or in a cave will often reveal the faint markings of worn away images. Some of the better-preserved sites have become major tourist attractions, and seeing these old paintings in such a stunning setting is a real highlight.

One of the best ways of seeing a good selection of San art is by walking the **Sevilla Trail**, a 8 km hike on private land. The walk is fairly easy-going and crosses a rocky plain, passing along a 4-km-long stretch of rocky overhangs, outcrops and caves. There are 10 sites in total, ranging from simple hand prints to extraordinary images of hunters, processions of women, running antelope and elephants. The highlight of the hike is Site Five, a rocky overhang covered with images in various stages of corrosion, with a beautifully clear hunter carrying a bow, and a painting of a zebra foal, perfectly embodying its first uncertain steps. Even those with just a passing interest in San art will find this walk thoroughly absorbing and quite fascinating. The stunning rock formations, silent bush and shimmering mountains add to the awe-inspiring atmosphere. If your interest isn't satiated and you've got plenty of cash to spend, spend a day or two at *Bushman's Kloof* (see below). The trail begins at *Traveller's Rest Farm*, 34 km from Clanwilliam on the Wupperthal Road, over the Pakhuis Pass. Permits are issued from the farm, which also has 2 self-catering **E** *Cottages*, T4821824, as well as the *Khoisan Kitchen* restaurant, only open for groups.

Outside Citrusdal and Clanwilliam there are a host of private farms offering accommodation in the Cederberg region. The list below only includes the options closest to the mountains. Bookings and general enquiries are handled by the Algeria office: *Cape Nature Conservation*, T4822812, F4822406, cederberg@cnc.org.za

Self-catering There are several excellent self-catering options, all within walking distance of the mountains: **E-D** *Sanddrif*, T4822825. 15 chalets, a choice of plain self-catering chalets, luxury chalets or a grassy and shady campsite. The plain chalets have no shade but views of the mountains, and all are close to the river. 20 mins' walk downstream is Maalgat, an 8-m-deep pool popular with divers. There are powerpoints at the campsite, and campers can use the deep freeze in the office at Dwarsriver. The farm sells fresh milk, butter and their own wine, a well-run set-up. Recommended. The advantage of staying here is that you can easily visit the Maltese Cross, Wolfberg Cracks and the Wolfberg Arch on a day's walk from

Sleeping
Price codes:
see inside front cover

Park and campsite administration office is open 0800-1630 If you are self-catering, stock up in advance at Clanwilliam or Citrusdal. Basic groceries can be bought at Cederberg

Western Cape

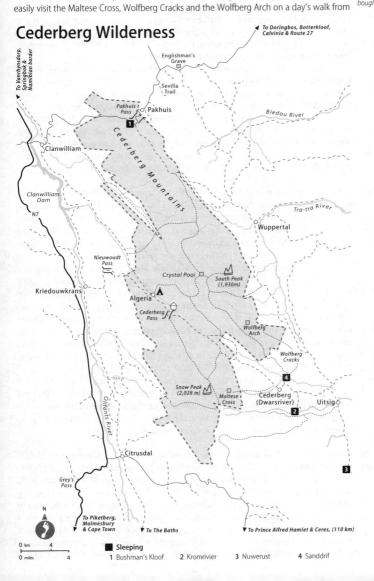

Cederberg Wilderness

■ Sleeping
1 Bushman's Kloof   2 Kromrivier   3 Nuwerust   4 Sanddrif

the camp without having to drive anywhere. **E** *Kromrivier*, T4822807. Self-catering chalets overlooking a dam and the Krom River, campsite, a well-appointed, convenient base for exploring the southern end of the wilderness. **E** *Nuwerust*, T4822813. Self-catering furnished cottages, camping, swimming pool, all you need but on the fringe of the mountains, perfect if you like walking! **E** *Cederberg Oasis*, T4822819, cederbergoasis@hotmail.com From Citrusdal, take the Algeria/Cederberg turn-off from the N7 heading north. This backpackers is 59 km on a gravel road, but well-placed for many of the major hikes. It has a range of good value cottages, self-catering, also serves breakfasts and meals on request.

Camping F *Algeria Campsite*, T4822812. A beautiful setting on the edge of a pine forest plantation by a cool mountain stream. Well-shaded level grass stands, no electricity, firewood sold, exceptionally clean and well-run, very popular, telephone in advance especially during school holidays, helpful office from which permits are issued. Some of the longer hiking trails in the Cederberg Mountains can be started from the camp. If you are unfamiliar with the region there is an informative centre next door to the office. The closest shop is at Cederberg. 5 km to the south of Algeria are 4 **E-F** *Cottages* at the foot of Uitkyk Pass, T4822812. These are very basic, no bedding or electricity, although there is a gas-run fridge and stove.

A luxurious option within the Cederberg is **A-B** *Bushman's Kloof*, on the Wupperthal Road over the Pakhuis Pass. This private reserve claims to have the 'world's largest open air art gallery', and it certainly is one of the best San art sites in South Africa. Activities on offer include 4-wheel game drives, mountain biking and abseiling, but the highlight is the superb rock art. There are over 125 sites, dating back as far as 10,000 years. Daily guided tours. Accommodation is in luxurious cottages and in the main building. All rooms are a/c, with en suite bathrooms, 4-poster beds, tasteful decorations, log fires, wooden decks overlooking a lake, excellent restaurant with outdoor *boma*. Prices include all meals, game drives and tours. **Reservations**, T021-7970990 (Cape Town), T027-4822627 (lodge), www.bushmanskloof.co.za

Calvinia

Phone code: 027
(NB Always use 3-figure prefix)
Colour map 6, grid A5

Although Calvinia is actually in the Northern Cape, it is relatively far from most sights in the north, and therefore usually visited as part of the Western Cape. It is a typical hot, sleepy Karoo town that most people just pass through, perhaps stopping for petrol and a cool drink. It has a beautiful setting though, at the foot of the Hantams Mountains. It's also an important sheep farming centre, though given the size of the farms, chances are you won't see any sheep.

Your first port of call should be the **Calvinia Museum** on Church Street (the **tourist office** is also here, T3411712). The building was in fact a synagogue dating from 1920. As in many rural towns, the Jewish community has almost disappeared as Jewish families have moved to urban centres. The collection in the museum relates to the early history of the region, made up of photographs, farming implements and displays on sheep. It is worth a look if you're keen to learn more about the history and farming of region. In the garden is a Class 24 steam locomotive from England which used to work on the branch line linking Calvinia with Hutchinson. ■ *Mon-Fri 0800-1300, 1400-1700, Sat 0800-1200, T3411011.*

In the centre of the town is a rockery filled with a fine collection of aloes. Look out for the **giant post box** in Hoop Street; it is 6.17 m high. On the other side of the road is **Hantem House**, the oldest surviving building in town. It started life as a homestead in 1853 and today is a smart café and gift shop. Another fine old building can be seen at 29 Water Street, which you can only view from the outside.

Akkerendam Nature Reserve

About 4 km north of town, close to the mountains, is the Akkerendam Nature Reserve. This reserve was created to help preserve the typical karoo flora and birdlife of the area. The Karee dam is an oasis attracting migrating birds. Two hiking trails have been created to suit different levels of fitness. The Sterboom path is 12 km long and involves a steep climb up the eastern face of the Hantamsberg to the plateau summit. Allow a minimum of six hours. The Kareeboom route is a straightforward 2-km circuit with no strenuous sections. The main point to bear in mind is the lack of water in the reserve – you must carry several litres per person. During the summer, the daytime temperatures are very high and there is minimal shade. You can expect some rain showers between April and September. Permits and further information are available from the tourist office, T3411712.

Sleeping and eating **B** *Die Dorphuis*, 63 Water St, T/F3411606. Set of 3 converted Victorian houses, with luxury en suite rooms, antique furniture, overall very smart and of a high standard. Recommended. **C** *Hantam Hotel*, Kerk St, T3411512. A large solid building with great shady verandas, a/c rooms or fans, restaurant, bar, the principal town hotel. **D** *Commercial*, 19 Water St, T3411020. A/c rooms with en suite bathroom, small steakhouse and pub. **D** *Nel's Guesthosue*, T2681277. Guesthouse and B&B. **F** *Steenkamp*, Tuin St, T3411011. Medium size, well-shaded but little grass, electric points, tents allowed, swimming pool. *Busibee*, Kerk St, fully licensed steakhouse in the *Hantam Hotel*. *Die Hantam Huis*, 44 Hoop St, T341106. Restored 19th-century homestead, the best place to try traditional Karoo cuisine, excellent breakfasts. Recommended.

Price codes:
see inside front cover

Transport **Bus**: *Intercape*, T021-3804400. Buses depart from *Trokkies Service Inn*. **Cape Town** (6 hrs), daily 1245, 0400. **Upington** (6 hrs), daily 2045.

Directory **Banks** *Standard*, 21 Hoop St. *ABSA*, 25 Hoop St.

This town is known as the gateway to arid Namaqualand. North from here the countryside seems to be a thousand miles from the fertile Cape. The town is named after Petrus Benjamin van Rhyn, the first representative for Namaqualand to sit in the old Cape Legislative Council. Although the region was first visited by Pieter Crythoff in 1662 it was only settled in the 1740s. The town itself first took shape in 1887 with the building of a church. The **tourist office** is in the museum on Van Riebeeck Street, near the **Old Jail**, T/F2191552, www.vanrhynsdorp.co.za

The green-fingered may want to visit the **Kern Succulent Nursery** on the outskirts of town. Gardeners come here from afar, and it's worth a visit if you're here out of the flower season. It claims to be the largest such nursery in South Africa. ■ *Mon-Fri 0800-1700, small entrance charge, T2191062.* **Latsky Radio Museum** is a small private collection of home radios covering the period 1915-65, close to the Post Office, on Kerk Street. ■ *Mon-Sat 0900-1200, 1400-1700, T2091032.*

Vanrhynsdorp
Phone code: 027
(NB Always use 3-figure prefix)
Colour map 6, grid A4

Sleeping **C-D** *Namaqualand Country Lodge*, Voortrekker St, T2191633. Some old rooms plus new rooms in block at back, comfortable TV lounge and open central courtyard decorated with wood carvings, used by tour groups, set menu in restaurant, small bar, smart external appearance let down by rooms. **D** *Lombards Guest House*, 15 Commercial St, T/F2191424. 3 double rooms, 2 family rooms, all with en suite bathrooms, TV, non-smoking room available, lunch and dinner also available, nice old house, comfortable gardens, central. Recommended. **D** *Vanrhyn Guest House*, T2191429. 9 rooms, non-smoking rooms, gardens set back from road.

Price codes:
see inside front cover

Transport **Bus**: *Intercape* buses stop outside *Turck's Garage*. **Cape Town** (4 hrs), daily 0930. **Springbok** and **Namibia**, daily 1530.

Directory **Useful services** Ambulance: T2191090. Police: T2191001.

Breede River Valley

Only 310 km long, the Breede River (also known as the Breë, meaning 'broad') is one of the most important rivers in the Cape, and its valley is a beautiful boundary zone. Fed by streams from the mountains, the river is a major source of water for a large number of orchards and vineyards. Leaving the mountains behind at Swellendam, the river

Western Cape

passes through the Bontebok National Park and then flows across an undulating coastal terrace, meandering through the wheat fields of the Overberg before entering the Indian Ocean at St Sebastian Bay.

Worcester is the principal town of the region. Along the broad valley are important farming centres such as Ceres, Prince Alfred Hamlet, Ashton and Bonnievale and the picturesque villages of Tulbagh, McGregor and Montagu. These old settlements are surrounded by vineyards and fruit farms which undergo beautiful colour changes through the seasons. Behind the farms are mountains rising to 2,000 m with challenging hiking trails and hidden valleys, their peaks capped with snow in the winter. The valley acts very much as the dividing line between two contrasting regions of South Africa. To the southwest are the verdant Winelands and populous Cape Town, both very fertile and prosperous districts. To the northeast is the start of the Karoo, a vast expanse of semi-desert, dotted with the odd sheep farm or isolated Victorian town.

Ins and outs

Getting there & around Since the opening of the Huguenot Toll Tunnel it has been possible to drive to Worcester from Cape Town in less than an hour. Worcester lies just to the south of the N1, and is the largest town in the Breede Valley. From Worcester you have the choice of continuing your journey in three different directions. Firstly, the main N1 highway continues for another 1,300 km to Johannesburg. South Africans tend to regard this road as dull and something to be got over with as quickly as possible. The road passes through the southern margin of the Great Karoo, known as the Koup. While most people only pause here to refuel or stay overnight, this is a wonderful region to explore with a couple of beautiful Victorian towns as well as the superb Karoo National Park outside Beaufort West.

Heading north from Worcester along the R43, you quickly reach the N7 highway. The N7 is the main road between Cape Town and Namibia, running up the West Coast. This route will take you to the upper reaches of the Breede River Valley and the agricultural centres of Tulbagh and Ceres.

The final direction you could take when leaving Worcester is to follow the R60 along the Breede River Valley as far as Swellendam in the Overberg and then head east along the N2 highway to the Garden Route and Port Elizabeth.

The 3.9-km-long Huguenot tunnel reduces the journey through the mountains by 11 km. As you emerge on the Cape Town side, the road is perched high on a viaduct with superb views of the Paarl mountain, its hillsides covered with ordered vineyards – a sharp contrast to the countryside at the other end of the tunnel. The tunnel was opened in 1988 and has greatly improved speed of access to Cape Town for towns such as Worcester.

Worcester

Phone code: 023
(NB Always use 3-figure prefix)
Colour map 4, grid B3
Altitude: 242 m

A drive around the quiet suburbs reveals some perfect 19th-century homes

This medium-sized farming centre is the capital of the Breede River Valley, a prosperous town with a large number of historical buildings and museums. The first European inhabitants to settle in the region were farmers, and when it became necessary to build a settlement, their land had to be acquired. Two farms, Langerug and Roodedraai, were bought from the Du Toit family. As the streets were laid out so the first plots were sold on 28 February 1820. The new settlement was named after the **Marquess of Worcester**, the eldest brother of the Governor of the Cape, **Lord Charles Somerset**. One of the first buildings to emerge was the local magistracy (*drostdy*), which was also the home for the local magistrate (*landdros*). Lord Charles Somerset let it be known that he would be using the *drostdy* as his residence during official visits to inland areas. The grand building that was built as a result has turned out to be one of the finest Cape buildings in South Africa. Today it is part of the Drostdy Technical High School.

The growth of Worcester was stimulated by the arrival of the railway in 1877. The wealth in the region is almost entirely derived from agriculture, a fact which is easy to appreciate while travelling past the numerous vineyards and orchards of the valley. Much of the area around Worcester is dry and many of the neat farms visible from the roadside depend upon irrigated waters. The principal source is **Lake Marais**, which was created when a dam was built over marshlands fed by the Breede River. The highly fertile neighbouring **Hex River Valley** is in effect the last of the productive Cape farmlands. In contrast, driving east from the valley one quickly comes to the dry and arid **Karoo**.

For a small rural town, Worcester has a fine collection of museums, interesting old buildings and a good selection of outdoor pursuits including the excellent Karoo National Botanical Garden. **Worcester Tourism Bureau**, at 75 Church St, T3482795, F3474678, jdamens@breedevallei.gov.za, is open Mon-Fri 0800-1700, Sat 0830-1230. For general information on the Breede River Valley, contact **Breede Valley Bureau**, PO Box 91, Worcester 6849, T3476411, www.breederivervalley.co.za

Sights
The main sights are central and close together, and the grid street pattern makes it easy to find your way about

If time permits, a short walk around the centre is very pleasant. There are some fine Victorian town buildings, although the main road is made up of mostly modern shops and fast food outlets. Many of the old buildings are along **Church Street**, most of which were built between 1840 and 1855. Also in Church Street is the **Congregational Church**, housing some fine original examples of wooden church furnishings and standing in a well-kept garden. The **Dutch Reformed Church** dates from 1832, a Gothic-style building which dominates the town skyline. Its spire has an interesting history: the original was considered to be too squat and was replaced by a cheap tin version in 1899. The current spire was built in 1927 after the tin one had twice been blown down by the summer gales from the southeast.

Next to **Church Square** is a Garden of Remembrance which contains some monuments commemorating local residents. It was designed by one of the town's more famous citizens, the artist Hugo Naudé. Each Saturday morning a **Flea Market** is held on Church Square. An interesting **Arts and Crafts Market** is also held once a month at 43 Russell Street, with some more unusual items on sale. Worcester is well-known throughout South Africa as being the home of two important institutes for the disabled set up by the Dutch Reformed church. In 1881 an **Institute for the**

Western Cape

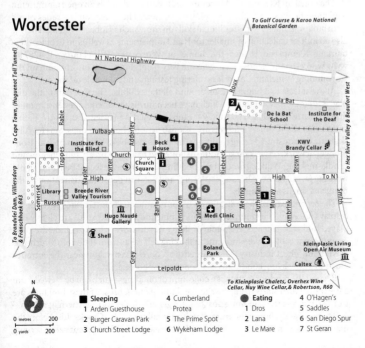

Worcester

To Golf Course & Karoo National Botanical Garden

N1 National Highway

To Cape Town, (Huguenot Toll Tunnel)

De la Bat

De la Bat School

Institute for the Deaf

Rabie

Tulbagh

Institute for the Blind

Beck House

Church

Church Square

KWV Brandy Cellar

To Hex River Valley & Beaufort West

Adderley

High

Napier

Porter

Trappes

Library

Breede River Valley Tourism

Russell

Somerset

Hugo Naudé Gallery

Shell

Baring

Stockenstroom

Fairbairn

Medi Clinic

Durban

Riebeeck

Brown

High

Meling

Sutherland

Murray

Combrink

Smith

To N1

Boland Park

Kleinplasie Living Open Air Museum

Grey

Leipoldt

Caltex

To Brandvlei Dam, Villiersdorp & Franschhoek R43

To Kleinplasie Chalets, Overhex Wine Cellar, Nuy Wine Cellar,& Robertson, R60

N

0 metres 200
0 yards 200

■ **Sleeping**
1 Arden Guesthouse
2 Burger Caravan Park
3 Church Street Lodge
4 Cumberland Protea
5 The Prime Spot
6 Wykeham Lodge

● **Eating**
1 Dros
2 Lana
3 Le Mare
4 O'Hagen's
5 Saddles
6 San Diego Spur
7 St Geran

Blind was opened, and a few years later a similar **Institute for the Deaf** was founded in De la Bat Street. Each institute has opened a shop in the town centre selling crafts made by members (see Shopping below). The institutes are also open to visitors who wish to learn more about the pioneering work undertaken with blind and deaf people. You will notice that, unlike in most South African towns, the pedestrian crossings here emit sounds for the blind.

On the corner of Baring and Church streets is **Beck House**, built in 1841 in typical Cape Dutch style. It has an interesting display depicting the town life of an important Worcester citizen, Cornelius Beck. There are some excellent examples of late 19th-century townhouse furnishings – the quality of the yellowwood and stinkwood furniture is regarded as some of the best in South Africa. Several outbuildings have also been restored. Look out for the Cape cart in the old coach house, the bath house and the delightful herb garden awash with fragrances. ■ *Mon-Fri 0800-1230, 1400-1630, small entrance fee, T3422225.*

Another interesting house found nearby, at 23 Baring Street, is **Stofberg House**, now housing the tourist office. It is a slightly newer town house dating from 1920, with a full length veranda at the front. For many years this was the practice and home of a popular town dentist, Dr Stofberg.

The interesting **Hugo Naudé Gallery** is at 113 Russell Street, and is home to a mixed collection of works by prominent South African artists. The first collection is of sculptures by Bill Davis, displayed in the garden. Inside are paintings by Jean Welz, Paul de Toit and Hugo Naudé. Hugo Naudé was a pioneer painter who also designed this large double-storey building and had it built as his home in 1904. He lived and worked here until his death in 1941. The gallery also occasionally puts on temporary exhibitions. ■ *Mon-Fri 0830-1630, Sat 0900-1200.*

The giant **KWV brandy cellar** on Church Street is the largest in the world under a single roof. There are 120 copper pot stills producing 10 and 20-year-old brandies. ■ *Mon-Fri 0800-1630. Guided tours of the distillery are conducted on weekdays in English and Afrikaans. English: Mon-Fri 1400; Afrikaans: Mon-Fri 1000. T3470785.*

The excellent **Kleinplasie Museum**, on Robertson Road, is an open air museum depicting the lifestyle of the early pioneer farmers. The collection is a series of old farm buildings, many with traditional skills on show such as tobacco rolling. There is also an indoor collection of smaller tools and implements as well as an excellent restaurant. Kleinplasie is also the home of **Worcester Winelands**, T3428710, www.worcesterwinelands.co.za, who are very helpful in giving information on the surrounding Winelands, as well as offering tastings and sales of local wines.

Allow at least two hours to look around all the exhibits. The first part of the display is a series of 26 buildings which have been furnished or equipped in a manner fitting the period 1690 to 1900. Only the tobacco shed is an original structure, dating from 1900; all the other buildings are reconstructions, but good ones. Several rural skills are demonstrated using traditional methods and tools. You can watch an ironmonger at work, or view the grinding of flour and baking of bread, plus cheese- and candle-making. Walking around the buildings gives one the feel of being on an old working farm: there are horses, cattle, pigs and geese in pens, not to mention all the farmyard smells and sounds.

The second part of the collection is indoors and equally interesting. Most of the displays are of old farm implements and home industry pieces. All are clearly displayed and well-labelled. A couple of items worth a closer look include the early example of a fruit grader, and a mean looking self raker from the 1860s which was used in the wheat industry. The painted-up Voortrekker wagon near the entrance illustrates how living conditions were on these wagons.

Beyond the outdoor section is a collection of buildings which can be viewed from a toy train which starts from close to the dipping *kraal*. Most of these buildings are from a rural village, including a post office, a general dealer and a cartwright's shop.

There is a craft shop at the entrance with a small selection of books. Just before the main entrance on the right is the *Kleinplasie* restaurant. It is excellent value, serving fresh healthy meals. This is also a good place to sample local wines served from small containers. There is a cheaper cafeteria inside the main building where snacks and cool drinks are sold. Behind the farm buildings is a picnic site. ■ *Restaurant open Mon-Sat 0830-1630, Sunday 1030-1630; museum open Mon-Sat 0900-1630, Sun 1030-1630. Entrance R12 per person. T3422225.*

Next to the Open Air Museum (take a right at the entrance gates) is the attached **Reptile Park**. You can park the car by the ticket office. The park has a fairly interesting collection of snakes along with a few crocodiles in pits and behind glass. Most interesting are the daily demonstrations of venom milking and feeding. ■ *Open daily 0900-1700, small entrance charge. T3426480.*

This garden, hidden away from the commercial centre of town, off Roux Street beyond the golf club on the north side of the N1, combines 144 ha of natural semi-desert plants and 10 ha of landscaped gardens filled with plants from similar arid regions within South Africa. The collection was originally started at Whitehill near Matjiesfontein in 1921, but moved to Worcester in 1946 after the National Botanical Garden approached the municipality with the idea of making the gardens more accessible to visitors from Cape Town.

Karoo National Botanical Garden

Visiting during a time of year when many the species are in flower allows you to appreciate how colourful deserts can be when it rains. August, September and October are good months to go, assuming the rains have been good. Stapelias bloom from the New Year through to mid-March, and June is the ideal period to see the exotic aloes in flower. In the formal gardens there are a few greenhouses which display a collection, world-famous among botanists, of **stone plants**, *conophytums*. Two common plants of the region to look out for are the Namibian wild grape, *cyphostemma juttae*, and the Karoo bush, *Pteronia paniculata*. Given that the collection comprises over 400 species of flowering plants (*aloes, lampranthus, lithops, conophytum*) it is not surprising to find that the local birdlife is exceptionally rich. Over 70 species have been recorded in the gardens. There are also several short trails in the gardens, including an excellent 1 km long Braille Trail. Children will especially enjoy the porkwood plant maze. ■ *Open daily, daylight hours. Free entrance, except during the three flowering months (Aug-Oct), R9 at weekends. There is a plant shop, open Mon-Fri 0800-1800. T3470785.*

Essentials

While there is a wide selection of accommodation in Worcester you could easily find yourself staying at least 10 km from the commercial centre. There are few places in the town itself, most of the private accommodation is on farms in the surrounding valleys. These are all very pleasant and in most cases good value.

Sleeping
■ *on maps, pages 199 and 204*
Price codes:
see inside front cover

In town centre B *Cumberland Protea*, 2 Stockenstroom St, T3472641, F3473613, www.cumberland.co.za 55 comfortable a/c rooms, non-smoking room available, breakfast extra, two restaurants, 1 smart à la carte plus a daytime coffee shop, immaculate swimming pool in the centre, health complex including a gym, sauna, spa bath, squash courts and a tennis court, conference facilities. Check for special offers and discounts. **B-C** *Church Street Lodge*, 36 Church St, T3425194, F3428859, manager@churchst.co.za 21 clean bedrooms with all the little extras such as coffee facilities, fridge, satellite TV. A modern medium-sized guesthouse which in effect is a small hotel but still retains the personal charm of a B&B. Swimming pool set in peaceful grounds, all meals available from an attached café, the *Table Talk*. Self-catering also possible. Recommended. **C** *The Prime Spot*, 54 Church St, T/F3472391. A popular B&B close to the shops and museums. 2 double rooms and 1 single room each with an en suite bathroom, TV lounge, attached bar and restaurant. Recommended. **D** *Arden Guesthouse*, 57 Sutherland St, T3477899. Pleasant family home with 4 comfortable rooms, English breakfasts served, meals on request, short walk to town. **D** *Wykeham Lodge*, 168 Church St, T/F3473467, wykehamlodge@telkomsa.net A pleasant

Western Cape

B&B on the edge of town overlooking open parkland. 2 double rooms with en suite bathroom, TV, secure off-street parking. **E** *Burger Caravan Park*, De La Bat St, T3423461, F3473671. A cheap option close to the town centre run by the municipality. Electric points, good shade, within walking distance of the KWV Brandy Cellar and swimming baths.

The Worcester district map shows where all the recommended options listed here are in relation to the town centre

Out of town B *Merwida Country Lodge*, 3 km from Rawsonville, 13 km from Worcester, PO Box 625, Worcester, T/F3491435. An elegant luxury lodge built in the style of an American colonial mansion, set on a wine estate. The façade is dominated by tall columns and a balcony. Inside, the reception hall contains a giant marble staircase that leads up to the bedrooms. Some suites have private balconies overlooking the mountains. Downstairs are two spacious lounges with open log fireplaces, a billiard room, restaurant, breakfast room and a pub. The back of the house opens onto a shaded terrace and crystal clear swimming pool. The grounds are surrounded by vineyards and mountains. Booking essential. Recommended. **B-C** *Nekkies Lake Resorts*, 51 Trappe St, T3432909, F3432911. 14 double chalets overlooking Lake Marais, self-catering only. **D** *Nooitgedacht*, 8 km from town on the R60 towards Robertson, T3421284, F3422046. B&B, 2 bedrooms with 4-poster beds in a neat Boland farmhouse, fully self-contained, lounge, enjoy walking around the vineyards or fishing in the farm dam. **C** *Nuy Valley*, 19 km from town off the R60 towards Robertson, T3421258, F3471356. A large, well kept B&B close to the river in the quiet countryside on a wine estate. Swimming pool, neat gardens with rose trees and ornamental ponds. A local walk will take you to a refreshing waterfall. There are 50 beds here, which if full can detract from the peace – call ahead to check if a wedding or conference is on. The wine cellar is nearby on the other side of the main road. **C-D** *Grietjiesdrif*, Slanghoek Valley, 24 km from Worcester, T3493161, F3493126. Rural guesthouse on a farm with 4 double rooms all with private access. Ask for Johan or Louella, meals available, fully licensed, shared lounge with books on the region. **C-D** *Kleinplasie Chalets*, Kleinplasie, off Robertson Rd, T/F3470091. 18 rooms and 9 chalets, restaurant, swimming pool, the house is a National monument, secluded in its own gardens. **D** *Damas B&B*, T/F3421477, damas@mweb.co.za 5 modern brick chalets, en suite facilities, TV, kitchenette, vine shaded veranda, restaurant. **D-E** *Rustig Holiday Resort*, off the N1 close to the Brandwacht Mountains, T/F3427245. Self-catering chalets in 3 categories with shaded timber balconies, camping and caravan sites which have braai area and water, some electric points, laundry, swimming pool, shop, café.

Goudini Spa, 22 km from the town centre, T3493013, F3493148. A very popular warm mineral water spa. It has 154 self-catering rondavels and duplex flats, plus excellent facilities, outdoor pools, tennis courts, mini golf and jacuzzis, in beautiful setting in the lee of Slanghoek Mountains, surrounded by vineyards.

Eating
● *on map, page 199*

Cumberland, main restaurant in the *Cumberland Hotel*, smart dining room with rough plaster arches, good selection of meals to suit all palates, open later than most. *Dros*, 29 Baring St, T3475131. Popular pub, part of a successful chain serving solid but unimaginative meals. *Damas*, 5 km out of town towards the Brandwacht Mountains, T/F3421477. Large à la carte restaurant with accommodation also available. Closed Mon. *St Geran*, Church St, T3422800. Grill and seafood restaurant, good steaks, pasta and salads. *O'Hagen's*, Church St, T3471698. A Irish-themed pub serving generous meals, steaks, pasta and hot stews. The bar serves a funny sort of Guinness. *Kleinplasie*, in the museum complex, T3475118. Great setting in the museum grounds, good Cape cuisine, healthy meals using fresh local produce. Recommended. *Lana*, Fairbairn St, New Thai restaurant, good range of aromatic dishes, makes a great change from the standard South African fare. *Le Mare*, 47 Fairbairn St, T3477498. Portuguese restaurant serving good peri-peri chicken, prawn dishes and steak rolls. *Saddles*, High St, T3427779. Good value steakhouse, fast service, popular with family groups. *San Diego Spur*, 39 High St, T3423540. Part of the large chain, overly cheerful décor, good value meals, popular with families.

Entertainment

Theatre The regional *Hugo Naudé Theatre*, Russell St, T3425802, is over 50 years old, and one of the finest of its type in South Africa. It is run by 2 sisters dedicated to the arts and the quality of the productions is such that it remains one of the only groups to tour the country.

Curios *Barn Art Gallery*, 170 Church St. An interesting collection of hand blown glass **Shopping**
objects, with demonstrations by the master glass blower, David Reede. The shop is situated in a renovated wine cellar. *Blind Shop*, 126 Church St. Furniture, woodwork and
woven products made by the visually impaired and are sold from this outlet. Visits to the
workshop are possible. *Deaf Shop*, De la Bat St. Handicrafts such as ceramics, cane work
and art curios – with some excellent pieces at very reasonable prices. Again, it is possible
to visit the workshop.

Canoeing *African Water Wanderers*, based in nearby Rawsonville, T082-3456878 (mob), **Sports**
africanww@xsinet.co.za Organize full-day river rafting trips on the Breede River (Oct-Mar).
   Cycling Contact T3491437 for details of mountain bike trails and bike hire.
   Flying Worcester is home to the *Cape Gliding Club*, T3432904. Local conditions are
ideal and it is not uncommon to record flights of up to 6 hrs. This is the most stunning way to
appreciate the mountains and valleys which surround Cape Town.
   Golf *Worcester Golf Club*, 3 km north of town across the N1. Enquiries about guest rounds
and rates, Pro Shop, T3472542. The club was founded in 1895. The present 18-hole course
designed by the Gary Player Group is 10 years old and has some large greens of tournament
standard. The mountains are a perfect backdrop. The large modern club house has good restaurant facilities. *Riverside Club*, T3425049. A 9-hole course on the south side of town.
   Swimming The *Cumberland Hotel* has a pool open to non-residents. The *Municipal
Baths* are Olympic size. There is a long distance swimming club based at Brandvlei Dam on
the outskirts of town.
   Tennis *Worcester Tennis Club*, Boland Park, Fischer St, T3470725. There are also courts
at the *Cumberland Hotel*.

Rail Take the *Southern Cross* for destinations in the Breede River Valley and along the **Transport**
Garden Route. The *Trans Karoo* is the main service to Johannesburg and Pretoria and is a
good service for Kimberley. The *Trans Oranje* is a slow, roundabout route from the Cape to
Durban. This is useful for Bloemfontein and smaller towns in the Karoo or KwaZulu Natal.
The *Southern Cross*, a weekly service between **Cape Town** and **Outdshoorn**. **Cape
Town** (3 hrs), Sun 0547, via **Wellington**. **Outdshoorn** (18 hrs), Fri 2127, via **Swellendam**,
George and **Oudtshoorn**. The *Trans Oranje*, a weekly service between **Cape Town** and
Durban. **Cape Town** (3 hrs), Wed 0306. **Durban** (33 hrs), Mon 2205, via **Bloemfontein**
and **Harrismith**. The *Trans Karoo*, a daily service between **Cape Town** and **Pretoria**. This
is the best option if you wish to go to Cape Town. **Cape Town** (3 hrs), daily 1102. **Pretoria**
(14 hrs), daily 1245, via **Kimberley**.

Road Worcester is 112 km from **Cape Town**; 60 km from **Ceres**; 50 km from **Paarl**; and 117
km from **Swellendam**. **Bus**: all services arrive/depart from the Breede Valley Shell Ultra City
and the railway station. Each of the major long distance luxury bus services stop here as they
head inland from the Cape, but they do not offer good value for the 2-hr journey to/from
Cape Town. *Greyhound*, T011-2498900: **Beaufort West** (4 hrs), daily 1555, 2005. **Cape
Town** (2 hrs), daily 0530, 0755. **Johannesburg** and **Pretoria** (16 hrs), daily 1555, 2005.
Kimberley (11 hrs), daily 1555, 2005. *Intercape*, 24-hr information, T021-3804400: **Beau-
fort West** (3 hrs), daily 1915. **Bloemfontein** (9 hrs), daily 1915. **Cape Town** (2 hrs), daily
1045, 0415, 1400. **Johannesburg** and **Pretoria** (14 hrs), daily 1545, 1915. *Translux*,
T021-4493333: **Beaufort West** (4 hrs), daily 1440, 1540. **Bloemfontein** (11 hrs), daily 1445.
Cape Town (2 hrs), daily 1445, 1555, 0520. **Durban** (18 hrs), daily 1440. **Johannesburg** and
Pretoria (17 hrs), daily 1415, 1445, 1915. **Kimberley** (10 hrs), daily 1415. **Port Elizabeth** (8
hrs), daily 0855, via **Garden Route**.

Medical Services Hospitals: *Eben Dönges*, Durban St, T3481100. This is the local provincial hospital. **Directory**
There is a private hospital in Fairbairn St which runs a day clinic, *Medi-Clinic*, T3481500. **Pharmacy**: 26a
Hoog St, after hours T3471143. **Useful services** Ambulance: T10177. **Police**: T3471444.

Western Cape

Worcester Wine Route

There are 21 estates listed as part of the Worcester Wine Route. All are fairly local, and some of them offer tastings, tours and sales to visitors. Note that unlike many of the more visited wineries around Stellenbosch, the oldest cellar here was founded in 1946 – the farm buildings therefore lack much of the history and beauty found elsewhere. Furthermore, the countryside is not as dramatic as that around Paarl, and none of the cellars yet offers the excellent meals available on the Franschhoek Valley estates. That's not to say that the route is not worth visiting – one major advantage it has is that it is far less commercial and fairly tourist-free compared to the Winelands.

The list below is a selection of some of the more interesting cellars and their opening times. The **Worcester Winelands** office is in the Kleinplasie Musuem and is a good starting, T3428710, www.worcesterwinelands.co.za They can provide you with additional information on other members of the wine route and also offer tastings and sales of many of the best wines produced in the area.

Botha Winery This is a pleasant co-operative with a neat tasting centre beside a colourful rose garden. The cellar is known for its **chardonnay**, **Hanepoort jerepiko** and **port**. Several varieties are on sale including some dessert wines and very good grape juice. ■ *Sales and tastings: Mon-Fri 0830-1730, Sat 1000-1300. Cellar tours: by prior arrangement, T023-3551740. 20 km along the R43 towards Ceres.*

Bergsig Estate Bergsig has belonged to the Lategan family for six generations. It is a friendly estate with some good off-dry and semi-sweet whites. ■ *Sales and tastings: Mon-Fri 0800-1700, Sat 0900-1300, no charge. Cellar tours and lunches: by prior arrangement, T023-3551603, wine@bergsig.co.za 40 km along the R43 towards Ceres.*

De Wet Wine Cellar This is the oldest wine cellar in the Worcester region, founded in April 1946. Recently modernized, the cellar has produced the local champion wine for the past few years. They also produce a '**Heart Mark**' wine, which is low in alcohol and calories. Most of

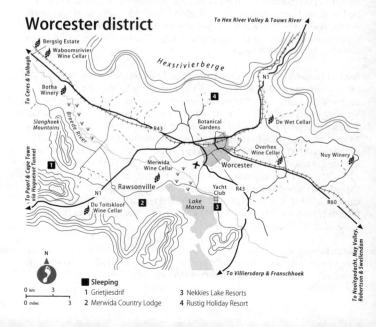

Worcester district

To Hex River Valley & Touws River

Bergsig Estate
Waboomsrivier Wine Cellar
Hexsrivierberge
To Ceres & Tulbagh
Botha Winery
N1
Slanghoek Mountains
Breede River
R43
Botanical Gardens
De Wet Cellar
To Paarl & Cape Town via Huguenot Tunnel
1
Overhex Wine Cellar
Nuy Winery
Merwida Wine Cellar
Worcester
N1
Rawsonville
Yacht Club
R43
R60
Du Toitskloof Wine Cellar
2
Lake Marais
3
To Nooitgedacht, Nuy Valley, Robertson & Swellendam
4

N

0 km   3
0 miles   3

■ **Sleeping**
1 Grietjiesdrif
2 Merwida Country Lodge
3 Nekkies Lake Resorts
4 Rustig Holiday Resort

To Villiersdorp & Franschhoek

their production is sent to wholesalers, but some of their semi-sweet whites, sweet **muscadets** and **Hanepoort** wines are available from the cellar. ■ *Sales and tastings: Mon-Fri 0800-1700, Sat 0900-1200. Cellar tours: Wed and Fri during the harvesting season, and by advance appointment, T023-3412710, dewetwynkelder@mweb.co.za 8 km north from Worcester along the N1 towards the Hex River Valley.*

Some of the best award-winning local wines are produced here. The cellar claims to be one of the most progressive estates in the country. It has a mixture of red wines, semi-sweet whites, dessert wines and grape juices. ■ *Sales and tastings*: *Mon-Fri 0830-1730, Sat 0830-1200. Cellar tours: weekdays by appointment, T023-3491601, www.dutoitskloof.com 20 km from Worcester along the N1 towards Cape Town.*

Du Toitskloof Wine Cellar

Despite being a small and relatively young cellar, Merwida produces some excellent wines, including an award-winning ruby cabernet and an excellent white. Also has a luxurious guesthouse. ■ *Sales and tastings: Mon-Fri 0830-1200, 1330-1730. Cellar tours: by appointment, T023-3491144, wines@merwida.com 10 km from Worcester off the road to Rawsonville.*

Merwida Wine Cellar

This excellent small cellar is well-known for its award-winning dessert wines and is situated in the lee of the Langeberg Mountains. The office and shop are welcoming and there is a restaurant and guesthouse. ■ *Sales and tastings*: *Mon-Fri, 0830-1630, Sat, 0830-1230. No cellar tours, T023-3470272, wines@nuywinery.co.za 22 km from Worcester along the R60 towards Robertson.*

Nuy Winery

Overhex Wine Cellar A smart, modern cellar, Overhex offers a range of wines from muscadets to sparkling whites plus some sweet grape juices. ■ *Sales and tastings: Mon-Fri 0830-1700, Sat 0900-1200. Cellar tours: by appointment, T023-3471057. 6 km from Worcester along the Robertson Rd.*

Waboomsrivier Wine Cellar This cellar has a good tradition of wine makers. There are 47 members who farm from the banks of the Breede River to the slopes of the Mostertskop. Their whites include a chenin blanc, riesling, and Perlé. The reds on sale are a ruby cabernet, pinotage and cinsaut. ■ *Sales and tastings: Mon-Fri 0800-1700, Sat 0800-1000. Cellar tours: Mon-Fri, only by appointment, T023-3551730. Close to Bergsig along the Ceres road.*

The Hex River Valley

Approaching from the arid landscapes of the east, this is the first glimpse one gets of the fertility and splendour of the Cape. The soils are naturally productive and this has for a long time been an important **grape growing** region. Over 60 of the table wines grown for export originate from here, and there are an estimated eight million vines growing in the valley and on the mountain slopes. This multitude of vines provides a colourful backdrop: verdant green in summer, rich bronzes and reds in autumn, beautiful snow-capped peaks against the leafless plants in winter.

Colour map 6, grid B5

No matter what the time of year you visit, this is one of the most beautiful valleys in South Africa

A **festival** is held every May to celebrate the harvest of a late grape known as Baarlinka 'natrossies'. They are exceptionally sweet and ripen on the vine. In addition to producing fruit, the climate has proved perfect for the commercial cultivation of roses. Close to **De Doorns** is a large nursery growing rose trees for national and export markets.

Aside from the natural beauty of the valley, the long history of farming here has left many fine examples of early **Cape Dutch homesteads**, built between 1768 and 1815. Some of these have been restored and turned into superior guesthouses, while others can be visited on tours – look out for *The Pines*, *Clovelly* and *Buffelskraal*. A one-time coach house known as *Die Monitor* has been turned into *Die Vlei Country Inn*, a popular overnight or lunch stop. For **tourist information** on the area, contact *Hex River Tourism*, T021-3562041, www.grapeescape.co.za

Western Cape

Western Cape

Hex Valley four-wheel drive trail

A somewhat bizarre offering in an area of outstanding natural beauty, this appears to be an opportunity to run amok in your clean four-wheel drive on a weekend trip from the city. An old ox wagon trail has been cleared and opened to four-wheel drive vehicles only. There are two sections to a 47 km long route which can be completed in 6-7 hours depending on your driving skills and perhaps how often you pause to admire the views. Don't expect to see too much wildlife!

*The first section, known as the **Karoo route**, starts from Keurbosch farm 8 km out of De Doorns, at the foot of the Quado*

*mountains. It is 27 km long, climbs to 1,300 m and offers superb views of the Hex and Koo valleys. The second section, the **Fynbos route**, is 20 km long. This ends at an overnight hut on a farm run by Mr Hugo near Touws River. Full details and permit payments should be carried out in advance at the Sentrale Garage in De Doorns, T/F023-3562114, a map is provided. When you stop and turn your engine off, high up and alone in the hills, you have the opportunity to see the valley in all its colourful glory, but I'd recommend you go walking any day in preference to this.*

De Doorns
Phone code: 023
(NB Always use 3-figure prefix)
Colour map 6, grid B5

Heading towards the interior, 32 km along the N1 from Worcester, is this small settlement lying in the centre of a major grape producing region. The name is derived from a local thorn bush.

Sonskyn Rose Garden, essentially a nursery, is nonetheless a beautiful garden worth looking around and marvelling at for the variety of rose trees it holds, especially between October and May when the blooms are at their best. Every year 400 varieties make up the total sales of over 150,000 plants. The tea garden serves fresh cheesecake, scones and pots of rose tea. ■ *Information, T3568632.*

De Doorns Wine Cellar, next to the N1, is a large co-op in an old Cape Dutch building. In addition to producing a popular **Hanepoort Jerepigo**, you can buy refreshing red or white grape juices plus sherries and an alcohol-free sparkling wine. ■ *Mon-Fri 0800-1300, 1400-1800, Sat 0800-1200. Tours are only available from Feb-May. Tastings and tours, T3562100.* Nearby are a couple of **farm stalls** selling a good range of fresh local produce – look out for *Veldskoen Fruit Stall* and *Pit's*.

Given the excellent choice of places to stay in the valley, De Doorns is usually only visited by day visitors

Sleeping B-C *De Vlei Country Inn*, 5 km out of town, T/F3563281. A well-restored Cape Dutch coach house, peaceful location, 5 well-appointed double chalets, good restaurant, always worth stopping for a meal here. **C** *Hex Valley*, Station Rd, T/F3563304. A simple hotel with 20 rooms where the valley views make the stay worth it. **D-E** *Karbonaatjeskrael*, on the road between De Doorns and Touws River, T3582134, F3582133. A peaceful overnight B&B on the edge of the Karoo. It has 4 large rooms sleeping up to 3, en suite bathroom, TV lounge, swimming pool and horse riding. Also some cheaper rooms with outside bathroom.

North from Worcester

The R43 follows the Breede River Valley to Wolseley and the major fruit producing regions. Most of the farms can be visited on a day visit from Worcester, but there is a greater variety of choice in places to stay on the farms around Tulbagh and Ceres. The Breede River flows amongst the vineyards following the road towards its source.

Wolseley
Phone code: 023
(NB Always use 3-figure prefix)
Colour map 6, grid B5

This small town is in a unique position on the watershed of two rivers, one flowing into the Atlantic Ocean, the other into the Indian Ocean. The town is named after Field Marshal Sir Garnet Wolseley and was developed as a railhead for the surrounding fruit farms. The fruit industry built its first fruit-canning factory here in 1936. Given the beauty of the surrounding countryside and the variety of tourist sights in Tulbagh and

Worcester, there is no reason to spend much time here aside from a lunchtime meal. The few interesting old buildings that had survived through time were destroyed in the same earthquake that caused much of the damage in Tulbagh in 1969. To the south on the R43 are two well-preserved **blockhouses**. These date from the Anglo-Boer War and were built to guard the bridge across the Breede River.

Sleeping and eating C *Mill & Oaks*, 7 km from Tulbagh, T2310860. Double rooms with bathroom, a peaceful country inn, restaurant, bar. *Traders* is an old-fashioned general store and coffee shop on the main road, selling local produce and serving good home-cooked meals.

Tulbagh

Tucked away in the Tulbagh Valley, surrounded by the Winterhoekberg, Witsenberg and Saronsberg Mountains, is this small village with a beautifully preserved centre of traditional Cape buildings. Along with Swellendam in the Overberg, it rates as one of the best examples of a rural Victorian settlement in South Africa. Like Swellendam, however, the state of the buildings is somewhat artificial because much of the settlement was destroyed by a sudden earthquake on 29 September 1969. This was a significant local tragedy: nine people died and considerable damage was done to property. However, the earthquake gave way to the largest restoration project in South Africa's history. Many of the old buildings had been in a bad state of repair and some were practically derelict, but the village underwent heavy restoration and became the fine settlement you see today.

Phone code: 023
(NB Always use 3-figure prefix)
Colour map 6, grid B5

Western Cape

The original name of the valley was *Land van Waveren,* an outpost of the Dutch East India Company dating from 1699. In the early days of Dutch rule the western hinterland, stretching as far north as present day Piketberg and Porterville, was known as *Waveren*. The first settlers arrived in the valley on 31 July 1700 but it was another 40 years before permanent structures appeared and a village took shape. As with many settlements in the Cape, Tulbagh is named after a former Governor of the Cape (1751-71), **Ryk Tulbagh**. Present day Tulbagh is a prosperous and peaceful settlement, isolated from Cape Town by several intervening mountain ranges. North of the town, the upper valley of the Little Berg River is a centre for some small wine estates and fruit farms. Sheep and wheat farming are also important to the local economy.

The **tourist information office** is at 14 Church Street, T2301348, www.tulbagh.com It is open Monday-Friday 0900-1700; Saturday 1000-1600; Sunday 1100-1600. A very enthusiastic and friendly office, with some interesting and useful leaflets covering the area. There is an attached restaurant and coffee shop with outdoor seating overlooking beautiful Church St. The office is in one of the houses which is part of the museum, entry tickets for all the museum buildings are sold here.

The main attraction is the delightful tree-lined **Church Street**; 32 of its original buildings were restored after the earthquake, and the whole street feels like a living museum. The majority of the buildings are in private ownership, but three are part of the town museum (see below) and a couple have been converted into B&Bs. The old slave lodge is now the *Paddagang* ('frog passage') *Restaurant,* set back from the street overlooking lush lawns. In complete contrast, the main commercial centre, Van der Stel Street, is a straight line of dull modern buildings saved by a colourful municipal garden.

Sights in the town

At 2 Church Street is the **Oude Kerk Volksmuseum**, one of the most interesting collections of Victorian furniture and objects in the Cape. The high ceiling and good light of the church makes it an ideal display case. ■ *Mon-Fri 0900-1700, Sat 0900-1600, Sun 1100-1600, small entrance charge, T2301041.*

If your time is short then this is the one place to visit in Tulbagh

The **Town Museum** is housed in three different buildings in Church Street – numbers 4, 14 and 22. All are within walking distance of each other. At number 4 is an excellent photo display tracing the history of the houses in Tulbagh. There are pictures showing buildings before restoration and the earthquake damage, and the accompanying text lists the different families who lived there. Number 22 has been furnished with 19th century items, while number 14 is now a guesthouse, restaurant and museum shop. ■ *Mon-Fri 0900-1300, 1400-1700. Sat, during the school holidays.*

Sights outside the town

Four kilometres out of town is the **Old Drostdy Museum**, built on one of the early settler farms, *Rietvlei*. Designed by Louis Thibault, it has been restored and now houses a fine collection of sherry vats in the cellars, plus a museum devoted to antique furniture upstairs. ■ *Mon-Sat 1000-1230, 1400-1630, Sun 1430-1630. Small entrance charge, T2300203.* Nearby are the **Drostdy** wine cellars where local wines and sherries are made (see below). The old Drostdy building appears on their wine labels. Their sherries can be tasted in the atmospheric, candle-lit cellars.

The **Upper Valley** of the **Little Berg River** is worth a detour if you're in the area for more than a day. Just to the north of town the road splits in two: one route heads towards the **Old Drostdy** (see above) and **Vrolikheid Farm**; the other heads towards the **Twee Jonge Gezellen Wine Estate**. Along each route are a couple of **wine estates** open for wine tastings. While the buildings are modern and characterless, the local wines are excellent. The hills at the head of the valley are known as the **Groot Winterhoekberg** and offer some excellent hiking opportunities. Access to this mountainous region is via the Groot Winterhoek Forest Station off the Porterville road, R44.

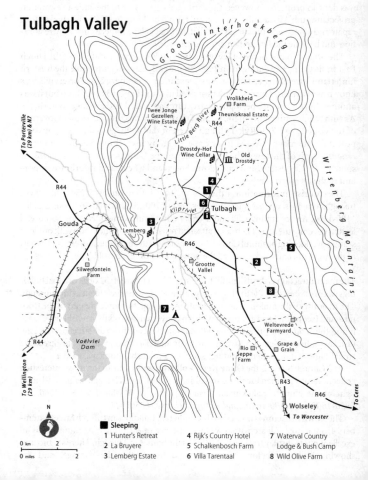

Tulbagh Valley

■ Sleeping
1 Hunter's Retreat
2 La Bruyere
3 Lemberg Estate
4 Rijk's Country Hotel
5 Schalkenbosch Farm
6 Villa Tarentaal
7 Waterval Country Lodge & Bush Camp
8 Wild Olive Farm

At the top end of the valley are some orchards, beautiful in spring when they are in full blossom, and autumn when the leaves turn golden brown. Early winter snowfalls on the mountains complete the peacefulness of the area.

This area is in fact better known for its fruit production – Ceres, the centre of the fruit industry, is only 35 km away. **Drostdy Wine Cellar** (see above) is due north of the village, beyond the signs for Kliprivier Park. ■ *Sales and tastings: Mon-Fri 0830-1200, 1315-1700, Sat 0830-1200. Cellar tours: Mon-Fri 1100 and 1500, T2301086.* North of Tulbagh is **Theuniskraal Estate**, which has been in the hands of the Jordaan family since 1927. Their white wines have won several awards. Their **Riesling**, with John Platter's seal of approval is highly acclaimed. ■ *Tastings and sales: Mon-Fri 0900-1700, Sat 1000-1200. Tours by appointment only, T2300688.* **Twee Jonge Gezellen** has the only underground champagne cellar in South Africa and there's a restaurant open during peak season. ■ *Sales and tastings: Mon-Fri, 0900-1600, Sat, 0900-1400. Cellar tours: Mon-Fri 1100 and 1500, Sat 1100, T2300680. To get there, take a left turn at the north end of Church Street.*

Wine Route

Just a couple of the cellars close to the town have been listed here. The tourist office can provide all the details of other estates in the valley

B *De Oude Herberg Guest House*, 6 Church St, T/F2300260. 5 rooms, TV, no smoking policy, ideally for walking to main town attractions, restaurant (closed Mon), sheltered sunny courtyard, swimming pool, laundry service. **C-D** *Tulbagh*, 22 Van der Stel St, T2300071, F2301411. Simple town hotel, 13 rooms some without bathroom, within walking distance of all the town sights. **D** *Tulbagh Country House*, 24 Church St, T2301171, tulbaghguesthse@mweb.co.za Delightful renovated Cape Dutch house, complete with thatched roof and neat flower garden. Attractive, comfortable rooms with polished wood floors and antique furnishings. Ginny serves up huge breakfasts in an appealing dining room. Also acts as an art gallery. Perfect for a night in a historical Tulbagh home. Recommended. **D-F** *Klipriver Park*, Van der Stel St, T2300506, F2301250. Large caravan park with excellent amenities, also has 10 self-catering chalets with 2 bedrooms, hot water, electric points, shop, restaurant, swimming pool, set amongst trees close to river dam, chalet prices lower out of season.

Sleeping
■ *on map*
Price codes:
see inside front cover

Farm cottages B *Rijk's Country Hotel*, PO Box 340, Tulbagh, T2301006, F2301125. Luxury development on a wine estate on the outskirts of town. 12 suites, 3 self-catering cottages. Swimming pool, excellent restaurant, bar, extensive gardens. Recommended. **B** *Waterval Country Lodge*, T2300807, F2300757, waterval@gem.co.za 8 km from Tulbagh, follow the R46 towards Wellington. A restored homestead on the edge of the Watervalsberg Hills, 5 smart double rooms with en suite bathrooms, communal lounge with a cosy log fire during winter months, 6 log cabins with en suite bathrooms, self-catering. Very comfortable, spring-fed swimming pool, dinner on request, peaceful location, no children, walk in the gardens and forested hills immediately behind the house, a high standard set-up, run by John and Jenny. Recommended. Within the grounds is the **B-C** *Waterval Bush Camp*, T2300807, F2300757, waterval@gem.co.za Luxury tents of the highest standard, each with tiled floors, immaculate bathrooms, self-catering option or take your meals at the nearby Country Lodge, unimpeded views of Witsenberg Mountains, an exciting change from your average hotel room or guesthouse. **C** *Hunter's Retreat*, 2 km from Tulbagh, T2300582, F2300101. On *Ruimte* farm, 2 en suite double rooms in an original labourer's cottage, shared lounge, plus 2 luxury suites with Victorian bathrooms, B&B. Ask about the aromatherapy, sauna and steam room. Clean and well-managed. **B-C** *Schalkenbosch Farm*, 8 km east of Tulbagh in the lee of the Witsenberg Mountains, T/F2300654. A historic manor house dating back to 1792, declared National Monument, 3 luxury self-contained cottages, swimming pool, billiard room, views across Tulbagh Valley, no young children. **B-C** *Lemberg Estate*, T2300659. Private self-contained cottage on a wine estate, can sleep 3, German spoken, extra charge for breakfast which is not usually the case, evening meals by prior arrangement. **C** *Villa Tarentaal*, PO Box 102, Tulbagh 6820, T2300868, mhunter@intekom.co.za Attractive self-contained cottage set on farm, open-plan kitchen, lounge, bathroom, veranda with beautiful mountain views, braai area. Aromatherapy massages, reflexology and facial treatments on offer. **C** *Wild Olive Farm*, 7 km south of Tulbagh turn off on the R46, T2301160. 6

Some of the rates are per cottage – if there are 4 or more of you staying, they are very good value

Western Cape

self-contained cottages, each with a different configuration, ranging from a basic room with hot plate to 2-bedroom cottage with kitchen, lounge, TV. Each comes with fresh farm produce for breakfasts. **C-D** *La Bruyere*, T2300808. Small self-contained cottage, sleeps 2, good value rate charged per person.

Eating *De Oude Herberg*, 6 Church St, T2300260. Closed Tue. Fresh country cooking, popular Sun lunch, evening meals by appointment only. *Forty's*, 40 Church St, T2300567. Evenings only. Jovial pub and restaurant set on beautiful Church St, some tables overlooking the street, good home-cooked meals, popular local drinking hole. *Grain & Grape*, off the R46 to Wolseley. Open daily for lunch and afternoon snacks. Farmhouse cooking. *Gouda*, 12 km from Tulbagh on the R44, T2320212. Old country hotel with excellent family restaurant, good steaks and *bobotie*, quirky décor – the walls are plastered with rugby mementos. *Paddagang*, 23 Church St, T2300342. Daily for lunch, evenings Wed and Fri. Good for late breakfasts, quality fresh Cape cuisine, selection of Tulbagh wines, set in well kept tranquil gardens, very popular, well worth a visit, also conduct wine tastings of all the local wines, daily, 1030-1600. Recommended. *Pieter Potter*, Van der Stel St, T2301626. Closed Mon. Choice of steak, pasta or seafood, nothing very special. *Readers*, Church St, T2300087. Closed Tue. Quality home cooking in a pleasant old dining room. *Rijk's*, south of the town, T2301006, bookings@rijks.co.za Very smart country hotel set on wine estate, excellent restaurant and wine cellar, delicious food in a stylish environment. Recommended.

Festivals Each **Sep** the local *Agricultural Show* is held on the banks of the Kliprivier. This is the oldest of its kind in South Africa. There is also a *Visual Arts Show* held in **Oct** where many of the historical houses on Church St open up as art and crafts galleries.

Sports While some farms have converted outbuildings into self-contained holiday cottages, others have opened up their land for outdoor sports such as fishing, mountain biking and horse riding. The following farms are all within a short drive of Tulbagh. *Grootte Vallei*, T2300660. Organized horse trails. Also has trout fishing in the mountain streams which run through the farm. *Silwerfontein Farm*, T2320531, ask for Bernd. Mountain bikes, horse riding, 1 or 2-day organized hikes or a peaceful day fishing on *Voëlvlei Dam*. When conditions are right you can windsurf on the dam. Also has self-contained cottage for 2 (**D**). *Vrolikheid Farm*, 8 km from the centre of Tulbagh, turn right off the Winterhoek Rd, T2300615, run by Antoinette; horse trails must be booked in advance, outings last for up to 2 hrs; when the conditions are right, moonlight and sunset rides are run.

Tour operators *Frans Hackl*, T2300031. Informative Church St tours, as well as wine valley tours and tastings.

Transport There is no public transport to Tulbagh. **Bicycle hire** *Tulbagh Country House*, T2301171. Guesthouse rents out mountain bikes and can organize trails on farms.

Ceres

Phone code: 023
(NB Always use 3-figure prefix)
Colour map 6, grid B5

Of the many fruits that are grown here the most abundant include apples, pears, peaches, plums, cherries, apricots and nectarines

Anyone travelling for some time in South Africa will undoubtedly try one of two brands of fruit juice – **Liquifruit** or **Ceres**, both of which are packed in Ceres. This is the most important fruit-growing centre in the country, and all types of soft fruits are grown and processed in the valley. Surrounded by the harsh and rugged Skurweberg Mountains, this attractive farming centre was founded in 1854 and aptly named after the Roman goddess of agriculture. During the winter months there can be heavy **snowfalls** in the mountains, enough at times for some limited winter sports. When the snows melt, the Dwars, Koekedouw and Titus rivers become the perfect environment for trout fishing.

One of the town's first magistrates, **JA Munnik**, was responsible for planting numerous trees around the town to provide shade. Fortunately, this tradition has been maintained throughout the town's history. As a result, there are plenty of mature trees lining the roads and the banks of the Dwars River, which flows through the town centre and the gardens of the *Belmont Hotel*. Until recently, visitors were encouraged to view the river and its tree-lined banks from a bridge known as **Lovers' Bridge**. The bridge is now closed due to sections of the bridge being stolen for use as firewood. The view, however, remains intact. For **tourist information**, visit *Ceres Tourism* in the town library on Owen Street, T/F3161287, www.ceres.org.za

Togryers' Museum (Transport Rider's Museum), at 8 Oranje Street, houses a fine collection of horse-drawn vehicles. All types of wagons and carriages are on show, celebrating the town's past importance as a centre for making these vehicles. Before the railways arrived, the fruit produced here had to be transported to the Cape in such wagons. Some excellent photographs capture the spirit of the time. ■ *Mon-Fri 0900-1300, 1400-1700, small entrance charge.*

Sights

The following fruit packhouses and factories allow visitors to look around on tours – a sort of **fruit route**, if you like. It is surprisingly interesting to see how life starts for a peach or a potato which is going to end up on a local supermarket shelf in a few months. Tours are free and usually run twice a week but they must be booked in advance. Note that most of the factories insist on visitors wearing closed shoes and long trousers or skirts for hygiene purposes. **Ceres Fruit Growers (CFG)** is worth visiting to see its cold storage facilities. This is one of the larger co-operatives specializing in deciduous fruits. ■ *Tours are on Tue and Thu, 1000. T3123121. The tourist office also runs daily tours (depending on demand) to CFG at 1400, costing R20 and lasting about an hour.* **Ceres Fruit Juices (CFJ)** is home to the award-winning juices found on supermarket shelves around South Africa. ■ *Tours run on Thu, depending on demand. T3169100.* **Ceres Potatoes** is a similar operation but with a crop of onions and potatoes. ■ *Tours run twice a week from Feb-May; trips to the growing farms can also be organized. T3133100.* Continuing on the fruit theme, you can visit the **Klondyke Cherry Farm** from mid-November to early January to pick cherries, T3122085.

Ceres

Sleeping		7 Village Guest House	2 La Scala
1 Belmont	4 Herberg Guest		3 Rocky River Spur
2 Beyerhof	House & Restaurant	
Guest House	5 Hindenberg	**Eating**
3 Chantilly Guest House	6 Pine Forest	1 Barumba Pub &
	Caravan Park	Coffee Shop

Western Cape

Sleeping

■ *on maps, pages 211 and 213*
Price codes: see inside front cover

There is a surprisingly small choice of accommodation within the town, but there are several excellent places in the surrounding countryside

Town centre **C** *Belmont Hotel*, Porter St, T/F3121150, www.belmonthotel.co.za Principal hotel in the district, old-fashioned regional hotel set in large grounds, characterful during season but distinctly spooky when quiet. 45 a/c rooms plus individual rondavels with 2 bedrooms and bathrooms. Neat, mature gardens, large outdoor pool, indoor pool with jacuzzi, tennis court, 2 restaurants, bar. **C-D** *Chantilly Guest House*, 18 Alheit St, T3161885, F3161885. Friendly B&B set in quiet residential area, short walk to town centre. Comfortable a/c rooms, TV, lounge area with fireplace, garden with pool, secure parking. Also has 1 garden suite. Recommended. **C-D** *Herberg Guest House*, 125 Voortrekker Rd, T/F3122325, herbergceres@lando.co.za Modern house with 15 rooms, TV, 7 apartments, restaurant, meals served in large garden, swimming pool, good value and popular. **D** *Beyerhof Guest House*, 1 Umzumaai Av, T3122863. Modern B&B, neat gardens. **D** *Village Guest House*, 64 Vos St, T/F3162035. En suite rooms with separate entrances, all facing a central courtyard. Attached restaurant, bar, shady gardens, swimming pool, off-street parking. **D** *Hindenberg*, 35 Owen St, T3121930. B&B guesthouse, plus a self-catering cottage, convenient location next to the tourist office. **F** *Pine Forest*, Carson St, 1 km from town centre, T3161882. Large caravan park with some self-catering rondavels, camping permitted on request. A well-organized municipal site in a great setting beneath towering pine trees, swimming pool, squash courts, mini golf, table tennis and pool table, boats can be hired on nearby dam, trout fishing. Book ahead during the school holidays.

Country areas **B-C** *Kagga Kamma*, T021-8638334, F8638383, www.kaggakamma.co.za A nature reserve focusing on the traditions of the San, luxurious chalets built into caves in the rock, superb views of stunning countryside, open-air restaurant, swimming pool, curio shop, see below for further details. **C** *Inverdoorn Game Reserve*, T3161264, www.inverdoorn.com Private game reserve with excellent range of wildlife including rhino. 5 luxury chalets plus a/c guest rooms, excellent restaurant on site, pool and deck, library, curio shop, see above for further details. **C** *Long Acre Guest House*, follow the R303 out of Ceres for Citrusdal. Pass through Prince Alfred's Hamlet and climb to the top of Gydo Pass, look out for signs on the right hand side, 30 km from Ceres. T3133367, F3133684. Self-catering or B&B option. Suitable for 4 people. **C** *Rhodene Farm Cottage*, 10 km from Ceres, just off the road to Prince Alfred's Hamlet, T3133607. Self-catering in a neatly restored farm cottage, sleeps 4, fully equipped kitchen, all bedding provided, underfloor heating. A relaxing location in the shadow of the Skurweberg mountains. **D** *Houdenbek Guest House*, 55 km from Ceres centre, follow the R303 towards Citrusdal up the Gydo Pass, take a right turn in the village of Op-Die-Berg (the road is surfaced as far as Sand River, but the last few kilometres are gravel), T3170748, F3170757. Choice of self-catering or B&B. A beautiful and remote spot on the Môrester Estate. Worth spending a few days here walking in the mountains. **D** *Klondyke Cherry Farm*, T3122085. 2 homely cottages on farm with superb views of the mountains, camping also possible. Ideal for keen walkers. Also has cherry-picking between mid-Nov and early Jan. **D** *River Siding at Outdasie*, 9 km from Ceres on the R46 towards Tulbagh, T023-2310726, lidiag@mweb.co.za Self-catering rondavel in beautiful riverside setting, sleeps 4, kitchen, bedding and towels provided, fireplace, 2 bathrooms, 2 campsites. Recommended. **D-E** *Kunje Guest House*, PO Box 66, Koue Bokkeveld, 85 km from Ceres, T022-9213536, F9213662. Self-catering or B&B option, guesthouse with 5 bedrooms, 1 self-catering flat plus mountain cottage for backpackers. An isolated farm with plenty of outdoor activities. There is a strenuous 4-hr walk to the top of the Geelberg Mountain and back again. A sturdy pair of hiking boots is essential during the winter months. **E** *Bergstroom Farm Cottage*, 60 km from Ceres, off the Citrusdal Rd (R303), T3173070, F3133682. Self-catering cottage in the mountains of the Koue Bokkeveld. Sleeps 6, kitchen, lounge, large fireplace, pleasant touch in that breakfast provisions provided. Good base for hiking trails, also possible to water-ski in summer. Be prepared for snow in winter.

Eating

● *on map, page 211*

Barumba Bar, De Keur centre, Voortrekker St, T3162770. Local bar serving pub lunches and afternoon coffee, snacks and music in the evening. *Lona's Tea Garden*, Ceres Nursery, teas, home-baked cakes and light lunches served amid the plants of the nursery. *Herberg*, 125 Voortrekker Rd, T/F3122325. Part of *Herberg* guesthouse, relaxed local cuisine, steaks, pasta, fish 'n' chips, served under trees in summer. *La Scala*, Voortrekker St. Coffee shop, takeaway snacks. *Oom Ben se Vat*, *Belmont Hotel*, Porter St, T3121150. Full range of South African dishes, vegetarian menu. *Pizza Nostra*, *Belmont Hotel*, Porter St, T3121150. Pasta and pizza, closed Sun and Mon evening. *Rocky River Spur*, 140 Voortrekker St, T3161151. Family steakhouse, salad bar, spare ribs, busiest restaurant in town.

Prince Alfred Hamlet

Phone code: 023
(NB Always use 3-figure prefix)
Colour map 6, grid B5

This small village is the second most important farming centre in the Warm Bokkeveld Valley. It was named after the second son of Queen Victoria, who was the first member of the British royal family to visit South Africa. In 1865 he went on a hunting expedition in this region. North from here the road skirts along the western fringes of the arid Karoo for over 100 km, without passing through any settlements of note. The farmlands in this area are very productive, so much so that a rail link was specially built from Ceres to transport out fruits and vegetables. Apples, peaches, plums, nectarines and pears are grown in the valley, and the short drive north from Ceres (R303) is particularly enjoyable during the spring when the orchards are in full blossom. (Popular activities include fruit tours and trout fishing.) Continuing north towards the **Cederberg Mountains** and **Citrusdal**, the road leaves the valley through **Gydo Pass**, R303. This is yet another pass built by Andrew Bain, this time while he was also working on the more important Michell's Pass. It was completed in 1848, and remained as a gravel road until the 1950s. For local **tourist information** you're best off contacting the Ceres office, as Prince Alfred falls under their control, T3161287.

Western Cape

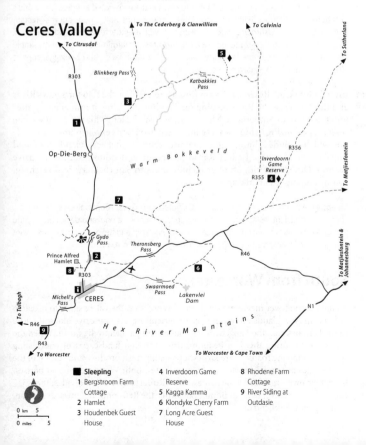

Ceres Valley

Sleeping
1 Bergstroom Farm Cottage
2 Hamlet
3 Houdenbek Guest House
4 Inverdoorn Game Reserve
5 Kagga Kamma
6 Klondyke Cherry Farm
7 Long Acre Guest House
8 Rhodene Farm Cottage
9 River Siding at Outdasie

Sleeping There is only one hotel here, but there are several farms between here and Ceres which offer accommodation. See above for details. **C-D** *Hamlet Hotel*, Voortrekker St, T3133070, F3133682. Typical old town hotel, spacious old-fashioned rooms, bar and *Taylor's Grill* restaurant, permits and gate keys issued from the hotel to those wishing to go trout fishing on Lakenvlei Dam.

Kagga Kamma Nature Reserve

Kagga Kamma Nature Reserve is 90 minutes' drive from Ceres, and is stiuated on the fringe of the Cederberg Mountains. It is a nature reserve which is devoted to the history of the San people who lived here, the remarkable rocky landscape dotted with their ancient rock art. The reserve did have a resident San village within its boundaries, but these have recently moved back to their ancestral lands in the Kalahari. Some San do periodically drop in to sell some 'traditional' wares. The area is one of outstanding natural beauty and the best way of exploring it is on foot. Resident anthropologists accompany visitors to rock art sites to explain their meaning, and are also very knowledgeable about the traditions, lifestyle and beliefs of the San.

It is possible to go on game drives with the reserve, with a good variety of antelope including eland, gemsbok, bontebok, springbok, and kudu. There are also lynx, caracal and leopard, but these are very elusive. If you're in a hurry and have plenty of spare cash, you can fly the 260 km from Cape Town in just 40 minutes.

Price codes: see inside front cover

Sleeping Accommodation in the reserve comes in 2 variations depending on your budget: the **B** *Rest Camp* has luxury chalets built into caves in the rock, voted as one of the world's best honeymoon lodges, with stunning views over the landscape, a pool, open-air restaurant and bar. The **C** *Bushmen Lodge* has luxury huts with a central restaurant and curio shop. They have also recently introduced 2 **E** *Camping sites*, set within the reserve with simple ablution facilities, accessible by four-wheel drive. For information and bookings, contact T021-8724343, www.kaggakamma.co.za

Inverdoorn Game Reserve

The reserve is not open to day visitors

Inverdoorn Game Reserve is 55 km from Ceres. Follow the R46 for Touws River and the N1. Take the R355 turning for Calvinia and almost immediately after join the R356 for Sutherland. The entrance is on the left. This is a private game reserve specializing in four-wheel game drives to view its excellent range of wildlife, which includes rhino, buffalo, giraffe, zebra, wildebeest, eland, kudu and impala. The area is a typical Karoo landscape and quite beautiful to drive around. Other activities on offer include hikes to San rock art, birdwatching, fishing and mountain biking.

Price codes: see inside front cover

Sleeping Accommodation is in 5 luxury **C** *Chalets* or **D** *Guest rooms*, all en suite and a/c. There is an excellent restaurant on site, plus several lounges, a pool and deck, library, curio shop. Day visitors are welcome, and there is a landing strip and helipad for those who want to arrive in style. Reservations, T023-3161264, www.inverdoorn.com

South from Worcester

As the Breede River meanders south from Worcester, the valley starts to broaden out and the level lands are given over to agriculture. As you drive along the R60 towards Robertson, the Langeberg mountains run parallel to the north. When the crops are maturing this is a beautiful drive through landscapes of contrasting colours. Along the roadside are farm shops selling fresh produce and several of the wine estates are open for wine tastings and sales. Both Worcester and Robertson have their own organized wine routes. After **Robertson** the R60 divides; the R317 runs close to the river as far as Bonnievale, while the R60 continues towards Ashton, Montagu and Swellendam.

Robertson

This small, prosperous town has a vaguely time-warped feel to it, with tidy jaca-randa-lined streets, orderly church squares and neat rose gardens. It is the centre of the largest area of **irrigated vineyards** in the Cape with over 20 wineries, many of which have won awards. The high quality dessert wines and liqueurs produced here have ensured the town's continued prosperity, as has the large brandy distillery in town. The town itself was founded in 1852 as a new parish to cope with the growing popula-tion of Swellendam further down the Breede River valley. Conditions are ideal for agri-culture as there is an abundant water supply from the Langeberg mountains to the north and the Riviersonderend hills to the south. While there isn't a great deal to see in town, it is a pleasant enough place to spend a day or two exploring the sleepy centre and nearby vineyards. **Robertson Tourism Bureau**, is on Kromhout St, T6264437, F6264290, www.robertson.org.za Open Mon-Fri 0900-1700, Sat 0900-1300.

Phone code: 023
(NB Always use 3-figure prefix)
Colour map 6, grid B5

Ask about the Food and Wine festival held every Oct, worth stopping in for and an excellent chance to sample the region's varied fresh produce

Robertson Museum, or Druids Lodge, at 50 Paul Kruger Street, remained in the hands of the same family for nearly 100 years. The original house was built circa 1860, only a few years after the grid pattern for the town had been first laid out. In 1883 the resident magistrate, Mr WHD English, bought the house and it remained the property of the family until 1976, when the last living member, Miss Violet Eng-lish, died. The municipality bought the house and set about establishing a museum. Most of the collection is devoted to the lives of William Henry Dutton English and his offspring, as well as the history of Robertson and the area. Of particular note is a beautiful collection of lace. ■ *Mon-Sat, 0900-1200, free entrance.*

Sights

Western Cape

This wine route follows the Breede River Valley and embraces the districts of Robert-son, McGregor, Bonnievale and Ashton. In total there are 32 co-operatives and estates which are open to the public. The greatest concentration of vineyards is found along the R317 as it follows the Breede River between Robertson and Bonnievale.

The region produces an excellent chardonnay and several good muscadets. Unlike the Stellenbosch and Franschhoek Wine Routes only a couple of the cellars have restaurants: **Fraai Uitzicht** in Klaasvoods East, and **Weltevrede Wine Estate**, off the R317 near Bonnievale. The latter also happens to be the only estate which offers accommodation (see page 217). Further details about the various members

Robertson Valley Wine Route
Appointments are necessary for all cellar tours. None of the co-operatives are open for tastings or sales on Sun

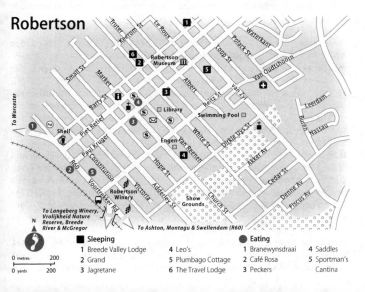

Robertson

Sleeping		Eating	
1 Breede Valley Lodge	4 Leo's	1 Branewynsdraai	4 Saddles
2 Grand	5 Plumbago Cottage	2 Café Rosa	5 Sportman's
3 Jagretane	6 The Travel Lodge	3 Peckers	Cantina

To Worcester

To Langeberg Winery,
Vrolijkheid Nature
Reserve, Breede
River & McGregor

To Ashton, Montagu & Swellendam (R60)

0 metres   200
0 yards   200

and the purchase of wines can be obtained from the *Robertson Valley Wine Route*, PO Box 550, Robertson, T6263167, F6261054, www.robertsonwinevalley.co.za

One of the most welcoming estates along the wine route is **Van Loveren**. Try their **Blanc de Noir** wines. Tastings are conducted in a restored rondavel set in the middle of a colourful garden. Guests are allowed to taste the full range and someone is always close at hand to assist with any queries. ■ *Mon-Fri 0830-1700, Sat 0930-1530. T6162141.*

There are also some wine cellars closer to Robertson. **Langeberg** is a neat complex surrounded by vineyards with a few large shady trees between Robertson and the bridge over the Breede River on the McGregor road. This cellar is worth visiting if you are interested in tasting some local port and sherry. ■ *Mon-Fri 0830-1800, Sat 0830-1300. T6262212.* **Robertson** is the oldest winery in the area. The shop and processing plant are located on Voortrekker road. During the harvest time you can see tractor loads of grapes being delivered to the centre of town. ■ *Mon-Thu 0800-1700, Fri 0800-1630, Sat 0900-1300. T6263059, www.robertsonwine.co.za*

Nature reserves

Dassieshoek Nature Reserve is 8 km from Robertson; follow Voortrekker Road from the town centre towards Worcester. This is essentially a sanctuary to protect fynbos plants; the best way to appreciate the varied plant life is to follow one of the many footpaths. There is a dam which is frequented by water birds, plus a couple of waterfalls – be on the lookout for bushbuck. Permits and a map are issued at the entrance and there is a toilet block by the park office. The reserve is open during daylight hours and the number of visitors is limited to 100 per day, which should not be a problem if you arrive unannounced. A basic overnight shelter is located near the entrance for hikers walking the 23-km **Dassieshoek Hiking Trail**. For hiking trail details and bookings, contact the reserve, T6263112.

Vrolijkheid Nature Reserve is a small nature reserve just off the recently surfaced road between Robertson and McGregor. The landscape is rugged and strikingly scenic, with sandstone and underlying shale formations.

Pat Busch Private Nature Reserve is 15 km from Robertson, off the R60 heading towards Ashton. The reserve encompasses 2,000 ha of spectacular scenery in the foothills of the Langeberg Mountains. There are a series of circular paths which follow the kloofs between the hills. The highest point is Tafelberg at 742 m – a 2 km path leads to the summit. The vegetation consists of a mix of proteas and ericas, with lilies and ferns along the streams. This is an excellent spot to come for birdwatching. A few small antelope have been introduced, and four-wheel drive trails are available for game watching. For accommodation see below.

Sleeping

■ *on maps, pages 215 and 220 Price codes: see inside front cover*

Town centre **C** *Breede Valley Guest House*, 29 Loop St, T6265656, breedel@mweb.co.za A peaceful, restored Edwardian home with 6 double rooms with en suite bathrooms, TV, mini-bar, evening meals available on request. The rooms all have balconies with mountain views. Recommended. **C** *The Grand*, corner of White and Barry streets, T6263272, F6261158. Reasonable old-style town hotel on a corner of leafy White St. 9 double rooms with en suite bathrooms and TV. *Simone's Grill* restaurant, bar, swimming pool, helpful staff. **D** *Leo's*, 8 Church St, T6263911, T082-8908828 (mob). Friendly guesthouse with 4 en suite rooms, traditional furnishings, brass beds, big old-style baths, TV, kettle, good breakfasts served, street can be a bit noisy but it is a good location for the town's sights. **D** *Jagretane*, 47 Paul Kruger St, T6264094. Victorian town house with 1 double room, 3 single rooms, all with en suite bathrooms, TV lounge, gardens, run by Jan and Greta. **D** *Plumbago Cottage*, 15 Van Zyl St, T6262391, T082-8081153 (mob). 4 double rooms, 2 bathrooms, lounge with TV, choice of self-catering or B&B, maximum of 8 people. **D** *The Travel Lodge*, 30 White St, T6261158. Attractive B&B on a quiet, tree-lined street, with 3 double rooms, en suite bathrooms, TV, telephone, swimming pool.

Outside the town **C** *Little France*, 5 km from Robertson on the Worcester Rd, T6264174, ida@intekom.co.za Attractive modern building with stylish furnishings, 5 en suite rooms, tasteful and comfortable with polished wooden floors, brass beds. Dining room, lounge, large pool and deck, good breakfasts served by pool or log fire in dining room, dinner on request. **D** *Goedereede*, PO Box 467, T/F6264173. *Satour* accredited converted farm buildings just out of town. 5 double rooms, 2 bathrooms, TV lounge, self-catering, swimming, hiking, birdwatching. **D** *Hanepoot Huisie*, PO Box 60, T/F6264139, T082-2722207 (mob). Restored old farm cottage set on a 150 ha farm, hidden away amongst vines and fruit trees. Self-catering cottage, sleeps 5. Plenty of activities can be organized including boat trips and fishing. Recommended. **D-E** *Weltevrede Guest Farm*, T6262073, roela@intekom.co.za A beautiful and peaceful location on the wine estate to the west of the town; follow signs for Eilandia. 5 self-catering cottages between the vines, fully equipped, sleeps 4, pool, rose gardens, excellent value, meals on request. **F** *Pat Busch Nature Reserve*, T/F6262033, patbusch@intekom.co.za 3 cottages, *Peach*, *Fig* and *Oak*, plus 2 houses, *House Protea* and *House Erika*. **E-F** *Silverstrand*, 3 km out of town on the sandy banks of the Breede River, T6263321. Only budget option in Robertson area. A large municipal caravan park in a lovely river-side location, with over-priced self-catering chalets, grassy stands, electric points, swimming pool, mini golf, laundry, café. Boating and water-skiing on the river is possible, and the *Dassieshoek Hiking Trail* can be started from here. Gets very busy during school holidays.

Eating
● *on map, page 215*

The town lacks a good choice of restaurants – only a handful are worth trying

Branewynsdraai, 1 Kromhout St, T6263202, F6261031. Closed afternoons and Sun. Light meals during the day and good Cape cuisine in the evenings. Try *skaapsnek* (sheep's neck) for something unusual. During the summer months you can sit outside in the neat gardens as long as the traffic is not too heavy – the restaurant is right next to the main road passing to Worcester. In the winter months a blazing log fire greatly adds to the atmosphere inside. Good meals though, and one of the best restaurants in Robertson. *Café Rosa*, *Robertson Nursery* on Voortrekker Rd, T6262584. Nice setting amongst the plants in the nursery, open all day serving tea, coffee, light lunch and home made cakes, friendly service. *Fraai Uitzicht*, Klaasvoods East, T6266156. Closed Mon and Tue. Restaurant set on the historic wine estate. Standard Cape fare, good service. *Peckers*, Paul Kruger St, T6264495. Close to the tourist office, just opposite the church. Colourful coffee shop serving snacks, light meals, coffee and cakes, also relies upon curios and local crafts for its trade. *Saddles*, Paul Kruger St, T6264982, close to the church. Quality steakhouse chain, nothing fancy, quick efficient service, family atmosphere and good value steaks. *Simone's Grill*, in the *Grand Hotel*, 68 Barry St, T6263272. Exceptionally good food, popular carvery on Sun when all the townsfolk seem to eat out after church, good value set menu lunches, one of the best choices in town. *Sportman's Cantina*, Voortrekker Rd, T6263499. Ugly modern building set on the busy Worcester road, popular pub, the town's main hangout, serves pub lunches and evening meals, steaks and burgers, TVs screen the latest match.

Tour operators

Wine Valley Tours, T6251682. Run daily wine tasting tours from Robertson, also pick up in McGregor. Tours begin at 0900 and return at 1630. Usually take in up to 7 wine estates, on some days also visit the hot springs at Montagu, plus cruises on the Breede River. *Viljoensdrift*, T6151901, viljoensdrift@lando.co.za Wine estate based 12 km from Robertson on the banks of the Breede River, organize relaxed cruises on 'Uncle Ben', their river boat.

Transport

Road 48 km to **Worcester**, 67 km to **Swellendam**. Robertson has surprisingly poor transports connections and at time of writing was only accessible by *Translux* bus. There are no car hire companies in town, and the closest passenger train station is in Worcester. Check with the tourist office if the train station has re-opened for passengers. **Bus**: *Translux*, T021-4493333. **Cape Town** (3 hrs), daily 1510. **Port Elizabeth**, (9 hrs), daily 0940, via **Swellendam** and the **Garden Route**. **Worcester** (45 mins), daily 1510.

McGregor

This picturesque village lies off the beaten track in the lee of the Riviersonderend Mountains. The village is made up of a collection of perfectly preserved, white-washed thatched cottages which radiate out from a Dutch Reformed Church which is in turn surrounded by a neat, colourful garden.

Phone code: 023
(NB Always use 3-figure prefix)
Colour map 6, grid B5

Western Cape

Dr Mary Cooke, a local historian, described McGregor as "easily the best-preserved and most complete example of mid-19th-century townscape in the Cape Province"

Originally, McGregor was known as Lady Grey, after the wife of Sir George Grey, a former governor of the Cape Colony. In 1903 it was renamed, as there was another town in the province with the same name. The new name came from the Rev Andrew McGregor, a Scottish priest who had worked hard in the district during the formative years of the village.

The road from Robertson to McGregor has been surfaced for several years now, which has encouraged more and more visitors to come here. Today the village has a good choice of accommodation, as well as a range of shops and a couple of restaurants. In recent years, McGregor has attracted an increasingly creative population and there are a number of artists, potters and craftsmen living in the small cottages. The village remains far from spoilt, however, and is a beautiful, peaceful spot to explore the Breede River Valley from. For **tourist information** visit the *McGregor Information Bureau*, which is housed between the library and the *Overdraught* pub on Voortrekker Street, T6251954, F6251738, www.mcgregor.org.za ■ *Mon-Fri 1000-1700, Sat 0900-1200.*

Hiking

In the spring this area is covered with a beautiful display of wild flowers

The village was originally going to be built at one end of a mountain pass, which would have brought a road across the Riviersonderend Mountains linking Robertson with Caledon and Cape Town. This would have provided another route for moving goods from the Cape across the mountains into the interior. However, this project was cancelled at an early stage due to a lack of funds. These days a section of the road that was built marks the start of the well-known **Boesmanskloof hiking trail**. Some visitors visit McGregor on foot having crossed the mountains from **Greyton** via this trail (see page 256). The actual trail ends 16 km from McGregor at a spot known as *Die Galg*. From here, hikers follow the course of the road which was never completed across the Riviersonderend Mountains. It is common practice amongst hikers to leave their car in **Greyton**, walk across the mountains, overnight in McGregor and then walk back to Greyton the next day via the same route.

Sleeping

Price codes: see inside frton cover

B *Old Mill Lodge*, PO Box 25, Mill St, T6251841, F6251941. This beautifully restored cottage dates from the 1860s. It is at the far end of the village amongst the vineyards and fruit orchards. Accommodation consists of 4 cottages, each with 2 bedrooms and en suite bathrooms. The central building has a comfortable lounge with an open fireplace, much needed during the winter, and a bar and dining room looking out over the vineyard. Tucked away in a sheltered corner is a swimming pool. Full board is excellent value given the quality of the evening meals. There's an old watermill in the grounds which you can look around. Recommended.

C *Green Gables Country Inn*, PO Box 158, Voortrekker St, T/F6251626. A delightful old town house that was once a trading store. 5 double rooms with en suite bathrooms and separate entrances. Also has a small lounge and good restaurant (see below). Recommended. **C** *McGregor B&B*, PO Box 24, Voortrekker St, T6251656, F6251617. 3 double rooms with en suite facilities, shared lounge. Located in the same building as the local pub – '*The Overdraught*'. Ask for Rob or Maria, good value. **C-D** *McGregor Country Cottages*, Voortrekker St, T6251816, F6251860. A series of restored self-catering thatched cottages, restaurant, swimming pool. Set in a mature garden with lush lawns and shady trees, just to the right as you enter the village. **C** *Whipstock Guest Farm*, PO Box 79, T/F6251733. 8 km from the village on the far side from the Robertson Rd. Choice of 4 cottages, each with a different style. *Rietvlei* cottage is the oldest building, sleeping 4. There is no electricity, but oil lamps and candles help create a peaceful atmosphere in the evenings. Hot water for the bathroom comes from a gas geyser. *Longlands* is a Cape Georgian house tastefully furnished with rural antiques, sleeping 6. *The Barn* sleeps 4, and *Winterfield Cottage* can sleep 6, with en suite bathrooms. Self-catering, but excellent meals are available on request – don't miss the homemade bread. This is a good place to bring children as this is a working farm with plenty to see and do each day.

D *McGregor House*, Voortrekker St, T/F6251925. 8 rooms, pub restaurant (closed Sun evening), swimming pool in a large garden. 2 cottages with double rooms, fireplaces and fully equipped kitchens. The grounds are surrounded by fruit orchards.

E-F *McGregor Camp Ground*, far end of Kerk Street, T6251754. The old school building has been converted into a dorm aimed at school groups, but also open to backpackers. Also space for camping around the building. Enquire at the information office for details of further budget accommodation in the area. There is a selection of hikers' huts along the designated trails.

The popularity of the village as a day trip destination is reflected in the choice of a few good places to grab a meal or have afternoon teas in. Most overnight guests will take their evening meal at their guesthouse or self-cater. *Café Temenos*, T6251871. Open Wed-Sun for lunches and afternoon tea only, closes 1700. Expresso and pasta, all things Italian. *Overdraught Pub*, Voortrekker St, T6251656. An old-fashioned bar, has an English country pub feel to it. Serves a selection of draught beers and good value lunches. Also serves evening meals on Fri and Sat only. *Wine Stop*, at *Green Gables Country Inn*, T6251626. Popular local restaurant serving light lunches and good country fare in the evenings. Recommended. *Villagers*, corner of Breë and Voortrekker streets, T6251951. A typical all-purpose village shop selling curios and local crafts, as well as serving light lunches and good cups of coffee all day long in the garden or on the terrace.

Eating

Vorlijkheid Nature Reserve lies 15 km towards McGregor. The landscape is rugged and strikingly scenic, with sandstone and underlying shale formations. Small mammals such as klipspringer, grysbok and springbok are fairly common, and if you are very lucky you may see a caracal, a type of wildcat. The terrain lends itself to raptors and there are often buzzards or goshawks circling the arid landscape during the summer months. Despite the fact that the reserve lies in an area a good distance to the west of the Karoo, many of the plants and trees are identical to those growing there. Grasses are scarce on the rocky lands, but there are plenty of succulents, and during September the land is covered with a colourful blanket of wild flowers, assuming the spring rains have been good enough.

Vorlijkheid Nature Reserve

Two hiking trails have been clearly marked out, known as the **Heron Trail** and the **Rooikat Trail**. The Heron trail is a simple 3-km walk to a couple of dams where there are some bird hides. Waterbirds can always be seen on the lakes. A rare attraction for enthusiastic herpetologists is the Robertson dwarf chameleon. The office at the gate has species lists and can help you with suggestions of what to look out for, and where. The Rooikat Trail is a much more strenuous 19 km and requires you to carry at least two litres of water per person (none is available en route). The terrain is rocky in parts and proper hiking boots should be worn. This is a circular walk through the Elandsberg Mountains, taking in a few peaks of over 500 m with views of the Langeberg and Riviersonderend Mountains. Allow at least eight hours. From November to March temperatures are high and precautions should be taken against sunstroke. Wear a hat and drink plenty of fluids before and during the walk. A pamphlet available at the gate contains a good scale map with contours shown. This will help you judge how far you are along the Rooikat Trail should you start to worry about time.

Bonnievale

This small town is known for its wines and cheese, and is the site of the main Parmalat factory, a brand that becomes very familiar to visitors in South Africa. The settlement was founded by one of the first farmers fully to appreciate the agricultural potential of the area, **Christopher Rigg**, who arrived in the valley and immediately set about building an ingenious system of canals to irrigate the valley. Most of the land today is devoted to grape and wine production, but you will also find several fruit orchards, including peaches, navel oranges, clementines and apricots. The **Bonnievale Tourism Bureau**, Main Road, T6162105, is in the town museum and is a well-organized and helpful office. ■ *Mon-Fri 0900-1700, Sat 0900-1300*.

Phone code: 023
(NB Always use 3-figure prefix)
Colour map 6, grid B6

In the town itself the only real tourist attraction is the **Myrtle Rigg Memorial Church**, the keys for which are kept at the tourist office. This church has a rather sad story behind it. Two of the Riggs' children died when they were still very young, and

Sights

their third child, Myrtle, died at the age of seven, in 1911. Before her untimely death, Myrtle asked that her parents build a small church to remember her by. This small Gothic style building was constructed using the finest materials from around the world, including roof tiles from Italy, and a fine carved door from Zanzibar. It was consecrated in 1921, but fell quickly into disrepair after the Riggs' death. Fortunately the municipality saw fit to restore it in 1977, and today it is a museum. ■ *The church is kept locked but keys can be obtained from the tourist office during working hours. Guided tours by prior appointment with Piet Coetze, T6162251.* The **Parmalat cheese factory** is another legacy of Mr Rigg. ■ *Factory tours are conducted hourly on the hour, Mon-Fri only, T6162100.*

Bonnievale Wine Cellars
The following is a small selection of wine estates close to Bonnievale, open for tastings and purchases. They are all members of the *Robertson Valley Wine Route*, PO Box 550, Robertson, T6263167, F6261054, www.robertsonwinevalley.co.za The route embraces the districts of Robertson, McGregor, Bonnievale and Ashton. In total there are 32 co-operatives and estates which are open to the public.

De Wetshof, a well-known export label, is a short drive from the town on the far side of the Breede River. The estate was the first registered wine estate in the region and is known for its excellent white wines, especially its award-winning chardonnay. ■ *Mon-Fri 0900-1700, cellar tours by prior arrangement, T6151853, www.dewetshof.co.za* **Langverwacht** has good riesling and colombard. ■ *Mon-Fri 0800-1230, 1330-1700, T6162815.* **Viljoensdrift** is a relatively new member of the wine route which started to produce wine four years ago after a 30-year gap. In addition to wine tastings you can enjoy a one-hour cruise on the raft 'Uncle Ben'. ■ *Mon-Sat 1000-1400, T6151901.* **Weltevrede** Estate with a restaurant and self-catering cottages for overnight stays. ■ *Mon-Fri 0830-1700, Sat 0900-1530, T6162141.* Finally, if you do not have the time to go tasting at the different wineries you can buy all of the region's wines direct from **Mooiuitsig Wholesalers**, off the Robertson Road, T6162143.

Robertson & Bonnievale Wine Route

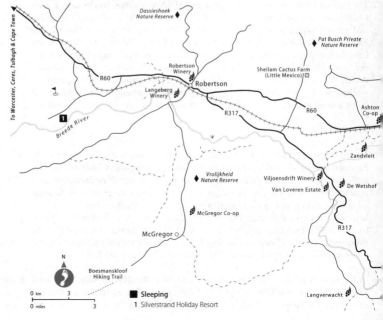

On most farms the river flows through the property, and there are often boats available for hire to explore this beautiful stretch as it winds its way through vineyards, orchards and stud farms.

C *Bonnievale Country Inn*, Main Rd, T6162155, F6163046. 5 double rooms with en suite bathroom, 7 double rooms with shared bathroom, huge breakfasts served. Very popular steakhouse restaurant, and bar which serves pub lunches, large gardens, swimming pool, laundry service. **C** *Kingfisher Cottages*, T/F6162636, T082-5530415 (mob). Choice of 3 self-contained cottages on the banks of the Breede River. Each cottage has its own private garden, a jetty and the free use of a boat. Lisa and Glenys is to provide a free bottle of wine on arrival! All meals available on request. Good value. Recommended. **C** *Merwenstein*, 9 km from town centre off the Swellendam Rd, T6162806, F6162734, merwenstein@lando.co.za An old fruit and vegetable farm offering hearty home-made meals. 3 double rooms with en suite bathrooms, smart restaurant, swimming pool, birdwatching trips on the river. Recommended.

D *Bonnies B&B*, Van Zyl St, T/F6162251. 3 rooms with en suite bathrooms, M-Net TV, 2 of the rooms have patios leading into the garden. Evening meals available on request, healthy breakfasts served with freshly baked bread. Bicycles for hire, braai facilities. Good value. Run by Piet and Irena. **D** *Highlands Cottage*, close to the town centre, T6162378. 3-bedroom cottage, sleeps up to 8 people, TV, evening meals available, braai facilities. Unlike most accommodation in the area this cottage is not on the river but on the side of the valley overlooking the river. The Mooivallei hiking trail passes close by. **D** *Toy Cottages*, 6 km from town centre, T/F6162735. 3 self-catering cottages, each can sleep up to 5 people, TV, fishing, canoe hire, right on the banks of the Breede River. **D-E** *Weltevrede Guest Farm*, T6262073, roela@intekom.co.za A beautiful and peaceful location on the wine estate to the west of the town; follow signs for Eilandia. 5 self-catering cottages between the vines, fully equipped, sleeps up to 4, pool, rose gardens, excellent value, meals on request. Recommended.

Bonnievale Country Inn, at the hotel, T6162155. One of the most popular restaurants in the area, steakhouse and à la carte, plus a pub serving hearty lunches (1200-1400). Set menu in the evenings. *Ca-Ro*, T6162446. Open daily, 0900-1700. Serves healthy breakfasts, light lunches and afternoon teas. The other half of this converted house is a curio shop with an odd cross section of items. *Lys se Kombuis*, T6162806. A popular coffee shop serving light snacks, coffee, tea and cakes in the garden - if the weather permits. *Weltevrede Restaurant*, T6162141. Open Mon-Sat, 1200-1400. One of the few restaurants in the district located on a vineyard. The estate is to the left as you drive out of town towards Robertson. Recommended.

Boat trips The *Breede River Goose* runs daily trips on the river, T6142175. *Viljoensdrift*, T023-6151901, viljoensdrift@lando.co.za Wine estate which organizes relaxed cruises on 'Uncle Ben', their river boat. **Mountain biking** Contact Piet Coetzee, T6162251, for the hire of bikes. There is a recognized trail which runs from Bonnievale to McGregor and back. The complete return route is 40 km long (24 km of which is on gravel tracks). It can be covered in about 3 hrs. Make sure you carry sufficient drinking water and keep an eye on the weather, as conditions can change quickly along the Breede valley. If you are a keen mountain biker look out for the *Leisure Mountain Biking Guide* by the *Breede River Valley District Council*. **Fishing** Possible on the dams and river banks, contact Francois, T6162444.

Sleeping

Price codes:
see inside front cover

There are several places to stay within the town centre, although staying on one of the many farms dotted along the banks of the Breede River is more enjoyable

Eating

Sports

Western Cape

Ashton and around

Western Cape

The small settlement of Ashton is rather an odd place, dominated as it is by two major canning factories. Pass through here on a weekday, and it seems that the entire population of the town is dressed in either green or blue uniforms, depending upon which factory they work in. There is little of interest in town, although there are a couple of wine co-ops. The **Tourism Bureau** is at Main Road, T6151500, F6151563, and is open Monday-Friday 0800-1300, 1400-1700. Next door is a finely preserved steam locomotive built in 1919. For keen **mountain bikers** there is a 29 km trail which starts from just outside the Tourism Bureau. The majority of the trail is off-road, and it should take no more than two hours to complete. The trail passes by close to a dam where there is plenty of birdlife.

A large proportion of local wine production is handled by the **Ashton Wine Co-operative Wine Cellar**, who are also well-known for their excellent grape juice. ■ *Sales and tastings: Mon-Fri 0800-1230, 1330-1700. Guided tours by prior arrangement, T6151135.* If you are keen on your wines, the pleasant **Zandvleit Estate** on the banks of Cogmans River is well worth a visit. Although the cellar's first wine, a shiraz, was first produced as recently as 1975 it has won many prizes and is highly regarded in wine producing circles. The estate has invested heavily in the latest techniques to help grow and produce quality wines. The estate house is a fine example of a traditional thatched Cape Dutch homestead. ■ *Mon-Fri 0900-1700, Sat 0930-1300. T6151146.*

If you have taken the main road, the R60, between Robertson and Ashton you will pass **Sheilam Cactus Farm/Nursery**, or **Little Mexico**, as it is now known. Over the past few years the collection has grown to such an extent that you can call in just to admire some of the 3,000 cactus plants and succulents. Plants and seeds can be bought here and sent back home. ■ *T6264133.*

The 6 km long **Cogman's Kloof** has always been an important route through the mountains and remains a spectacular drive between Ashton and Montagu. The Khoi used to herd their sheep through here to take advantage of pastures on the other side. In the early 18th century a rough wagon track began to take shape, but this was continually hampered by the flooding of Cogman's River. In 1873 Thomas Bain started work on a new road which was completed four years later at a cost of £12,000. You still pass through the **rock tunnel**, 5 m high and 15 m long, on the way to Montagu. Four kilometres from Montagu, on top of the tunnel, are the ruins of a fort built during the Anglo-Boer War to keep the pass closed to the Boer forces. **Sidney Fort** was named after the commander in charge of Montagu during martial law. A plaque in honour of Bain can be seen at the Montagu end of the rock tunnel.

Montagu and around

Although Montagu is very much a Karoo town, it is usually visited by people exploring the Breede River valley. It is 245 km from Oudtshoorn, the administrative centre for the Little Karoo, and only 15 minutes' drive from Ashton and the Breede River. It is a delightful place in a stunning setting, its long oak-lined streets lined with white-washed Cape Dutch houses, sitting humbly beneath jagged mountain peaks. Founded in 1851, the settlement was named after John Montagu who, as the colonial secretary from 1843-53, had been responsible for the first major road-building programme in the Cape. The greatly improved road network enabled previously remote settlements such as Montagu to thrive and grow. From its early days the region was recognized as ideal for fruit and wine production. The valley was fertile and the climate ideal for vines. In 1940 the Langeberg Co-op was formed, which proved to be the necessary boost for the local economy. Within 10 years, local production of apples and pears had doubled, while over a period of 16 years the wine produced increased by fivefold.

The exceptionally helpful and enthusiastic **Montagu Tourism Bureau** at 24 Bath Street, T6142471, www.montagu.org.za, is open Mon-Fri 0845-1645, Sat 0900-1700, Sun 0930-1230. They produce several useful leaflets.

Joubert House, the oldest building in the town, is now part of the **museum** (housed further along Long Street). The house has a collection of late 19th-century furnishings and ornaments and part of the garden has been turned into an indigenous medicinal plant collection. ■ *Long St. Museum: Mon-Fri 0900-1300, 1400-1630, Sat 1030-1230. Garden: Mon-Fri 0900-1300, 1400-1700. Small entrance fee.*

Sights

Long Street is a popular attraction, with 14 national monuments along its length. With so many well-preserved buildings, it is easy to get a vivid impression of how the settlement would have looked in its early days. There are another eight buildings around the town which are national monuments.

The tourist office produces an interesting leaflet outlining the historic homes in the area (R10)

The **Centenary Nature Garden**, on the south side of the Kinga River off Van Riebeeck Street, has the largest collection of *mesembryanthemums* in the country. ■ *Open daily. Small entrance fee. Teas served every Tue and the first Sat of the month, 1000-1130, from May till end Nov. The best time to visit is spring (Aug-Oct).*

Just 3 km from the town centre are the **hot mineral springs**, which have been used for over 200 years for their healing powers. The waters are radioactive and have a steady temperature of 43°C. In January 1980 Montagu suffered a great set-back when continued heavy rains in the Langeberg resulted in a flash flood down the Keissies River. The resort complex built around the hot springs was hit full-on and all the caravans were washed away. The hotel was filled with several metres of sand and debris and the hot springs were covered with mud. Fortunately, the town was barely touched, but all the trees and benches along **Lovers' Lane** were washed away. It was a local catastrophe and 13 people were killed but today all is well again. *Avalon Springs* has two indoor pools and five outdoor pools, which are all at different temperatures. ■ *There is a small entrance fee*

For details of Montagu Springs Resort and Avalon Springs Hotel see Sleeping below

Western Cape

Montagu

To Drie Berge Cellar, Koo Valley & Touwsrivier

charged per person and per car; extra is charged over the weekend and on public holidays. There are two holiday resorts based around the springs.

Tractor rides to the top of the Langeberg mountains are on offer from Niel Burger, a local farmer. The trip judders to the top of the mountains from his farm in the **Koo Valley**. There are impressive views across the Karoo and down into the Breede River Valley from the summit. The round trip lasts about three hours and costs R45 per adult. For an extra R40 you get an excellent meal of potjie, home-baked bread and a drink. There are also 4 self-catering cottages, **C-D** *Protea Cottages*, T6143012, suitable for hikers. It is also possible to do a four-wheel drive trip around the farm. ■ *Tractor trips usually run on Wed at 1000 and Sat at 1000 and 1400, depending upon demand. Contact the tourist office for details and reservations, T6142471. Be sure to wear warm clothes. To get there from Montagu, take the R318 towards Matroosberg. After 30 km the road descends the Burger Pass into the Koo Valley.*

Montagu Wine Route

There are 5 wineries in the district which can be visited for tastings and sales. Cellar tours are by appointment only

The Montagu cellars are best-known for producing white wines with the muscadel grape, and tend to be fairly sweet, fortified dessert wines.

Drie Berge Farm Cellar is 2 km from the town centre past the hot springs on the Touws River road (R318); T6141305, F6142814. ■ *Sales: Mon-Fri 0900-1230, 1330-1830, Sat 0900-1300.* **Montagu Co-op Wine Cellar** is next to the golf course, heading out of town via Bath street. ■ *Sales: Mon-Fri 0830-1230, 1330-1700, Sat 0900-1200.* T6141125, F6141793. **Rietrivier Wine Cellar** is 20 km east of Montagu on the Barrydale road. ■ *Sales: Mon-Thu 0800-1300, 1400-1700, Fri 0800-1500.* T/F6141705. **Uitvlucht Winery**, just off the main road near the police station. ■ *Sales: Mon-Fri 0830-1700, Sat 0830-1330.* T6141340, F6142113. There is also a private winery in the centre of town, at 12 Long Street, called the **Bloupunt Winery**. It is known for its Chardonnay and is the only wine cellar open on a Saturday afternoon. ■ *Mon-Fri 0900-1230, 1400-1700, Sat 0930-1230, 1400-1600. T6142385.*

Montagu Mountain Reserve

Make sure you have enough water and warm clothes for the sudden drop in temperature at night

Starting from the Old Mill at the end of Tanner Street are three hiking trails in the mountains overlooking the town. The most popular of these is **Lover's Walk**, an easy stroll through Badkloof along the Keissies River to the *Avalon Springs* resort. This should take no more than one hour. The other two trails are longer and more strenuous. Permits are not needed, but you must book **overnight stays** in the huts or camping site in the reserve in advance, at Montagu Tourism, Bath Street, T6142471.

The **Bloupunt Trail**, marked with white footprints, is almost 16 km long. The trail climbs up towards *Bloupunt* (1,000 m) along the Riet River valley. The view at the summit is well worth the rough going. On a clear day you can see many of the towns in the Breede River Valley, including Robertson, McGregor, Bonnievale, Ashton and Montagu itself. The path returns via another valley, Donkerkloof. Look out for the turnings to three small waterfalls. The streams flow all year round and the pools are always surrounded by wild flowers and birdlife. The overnight hut, **F** *Klipspringer*, can sleep a large group and has showers and cooking facilities.

The **Cogman's Kloof Trail**, marked with yellow footprints, is slightly easier once the initial 2 km steep stretch has been negotiated. The full trail is 12 km long, and overnight stays are again in the *Klipspringer* hut; camping is also allowed here, but nowhere else in the reserve. All bookings are handled by Montagu Tourism in Bath Street, who also have maps.

MontEco Nature Reserve

As the name suggests, this reserve has an emphasis on eco-tourism and is popular for hiking, bird watching and mountain biking. The reserve is mountainous and spreads over 6,600 ha, covered with a range of fynbos and Karoo succulents, both of which flower spectacularly in spring. The reserve also has a good range of **fauna**, with a chance of glimpsing springbok, gemsbock, klipspringer and kudu. More elusive are the leopards, caracals and bat-eared foxes also found here.

Most visitors come here to **hike**, **mountain bike**, or take a **four-wheel 'eco-drive'**, in over 80 km of maintained trails. There are 10 hiking trails, ranging in length and difficulty, some of which pass examples of ancient Khoisan **rock art**. Accommodation in the reserve is in self-catering chalets, **E**, and camping, **F**. Contact Montagu Tourism, T6142471. For reserve information, visit www.monteco-nature-reserve.com

A *Mimosa Lodge*, Church St, T6142351, F6142418. Excellent local hotel with 9 rooms (those upstairs have balconies), 3 suites including the special Orchard Suite, 3 guest lounges, library, neat walled gardens, restaurant, bar, swimming pool. The restaurant menu reflects the wide variety of locally grown fresh produce and should be booked ahead. Look forward to a warm welcome from Yvette and Andreas. Recommended.

 B *Avalon Springs*, 3 km from town centre, Uitvlucht St, T6141150, F6141906. A well-developed resort including 30 timeshare apartments, conference facilities and a health spa. The hotel has 14 double rooms with en suite bathrooms, 3 restaurants – *Da Vinci's* serves good pasta – bar, shops, swimming pool, gym and sauna, tennis courts. Comfortable and in a peaceful spot, but inconvenient for those wishing to explore the town. **B** *Kingna Lodge*, 11 Bath St, T6141066, F6142405. 8 rooms, some with private patio, TV, non-smoking lounge with collection of art and books, 5 course dinners on request, swimming pool and jacuzzi in private gardens. Mandela and de Klerk both once stayed here. Recommended for both its service and food. **B** *Montagu Country Hotel*, 27 Bath St, T6143125, F6141905. A well-established private hotel in the centre, with 23 large rooms, a/c, TV, a smart dining room with open log fires during the winter months, swimming pool, secure parking. Recommended.

 C *7 Church St*, T6141186, mwjones@yebo.co.za Beautiful views from this stylish, friendly guesthouse, large en suite family room, garden suite with exceptional views, large lounge, good English breakfast, rose and herb garden, off-road parking. Recommended. **C** *Cynthia's*, 3 Krom St, T6142760, F6141326. Delightful restored country cottage with thatched roof. Brass beds add to the homely atmosphere. Suitable for 2-6 people, self-catering. **C** *The John Montagu*, 30 Joubert St, T6141331, F6143981, info@johnmontagu.co.za 5 tastefully decorated rooms, antique furnishings, small beach pool and bar in the gardens at the back, off-street parking. The perfect place to relax after exploring the area. Good value. Recommended. **C** *Montagu Rose*, 19 Kohler St, T6142681, F6142780. A very friendly and well-run B&B. 5 double rooms of varying size, each with en suite bathroom, TV lounge with an open fire in winter. If you enjoy your stay here send a postcard to add to the collection on the walls; the cards provide an interesting insight into the variety of travellers visiting South Africa.

 D-C *The Oaks*, 35 km out of town in the Koo valley off the Touwsrivier road, T6142194, F6142800. 20 self-catering farm cottages surrounded by apple and pear orchards, ideal for exploring the Langeberg mountains. Cottages have shady verandas, open log fires in winter, swimming pool, close to local golf course. Fresh fruit is available in season from the farm. **D** *Montagu Manor*, 28 Piet Retief St, T6141177. 4 double rooms with en suite bathrooms, private lounge with TV, free entry for guests to the hot mineral springs, the *Grill Room* restaurant is in the same complex. **D** *Swiss Inn*, 25 Church St, T/F6142308. 5 double rooms with en suite bathrooms, TV lounge, veranda, gardens with mountain views. Well-managed by Rosy and Franz from Switzerland. **D-F** *De Bos*, follow Bath St west out of town, the entrance to the farm is on the left side just after fording the stream, PO Box 103, T/F6142532. You can choose between private rooms with en suite bathroom, a self-catering flat for long-stay visitors or a backpackers' barn for budget travellers. The farm is no more than 10 mins' walk from the town centre. Also organize long distance trails, rock climbing, mountain biking and guided tours to surrounding villages and beauty spots.

 E-F *Caravan Park*, west end of Bath St, across the Keissies River, T082-9207863 (mob), F6143034. Camping, 4-bed cabins, swimming pool, boating and fishing on the dam. Short walk into the town centre.

Montagu has a surprisingly large number of good restaurants, with a fine variation of cuisines – not just the usual steaks and pizzas. Opinions are divided over whether *Jessica's* or *Prestons* is the best place to eat. Both are excellent value.

 Bella Monta, Market St, T6142941. Friendly restaurant serving excellent value game, steaks and ribs. Popular with families. *Four Oaks*, 46 Long St, T6142778. Closed Mon. Good Italian cuisine that is almost overshadowed by the character of the historic setting, B&B next

Sleeping
■ *on map, page 223*
Price codes:
see inside front cover

Ask at the tourist office for details of budget accommodation suitable for hikers on surrounding farms

Eating
● *on map*

Western Cape

door. *Jessica's*, 47 Bath St, T6141805. A slightly off-beat place serving meals of the highest quality. A good opportunity to sample the best of South African ingredients washed down with good wines. Recommended. *Prestons*, 17 Bath St, T6143013. Open daily. Popular à la carte menu, tasteful décor with a small outside courtyard, friendly hosts. Try the 'Prestons Platter' or the Karoo lamb, all served with excellent salads. Recommended. *Romano's*, 20 Church St, T6142398. Tasty Italian dishes, good value. Closed Sun. *20 Bath Street*, 20 Bath St, T6143108. New bistro and café, serving good snacks, sandwiches and salads. Also has internet access. *Thomas Bain*, 17 Bath St. Pub attached to *Prestons*. Cosy wood bar and tables, outside terrace for warm days, a good option for a light lunch and cold beer.

Sports **Golf** Out of town, just before turning for the hot springs, T6141860. **Hang Gliding** Neil Burger can organize hang gliding and paragliding from his farm in the Koo Valley, T6143012. **Horse Trails** There is a farm about 11 km on the Barrydale Rd which organizes regular horse trails, T6142255, T082-9355193 (mob). There is a more unusual farm 12 km from Montagu which has not just horses but camels to ride, T023-6151869. **Mountain bikes** *Ron Brunings*, T6141932, has 2 bicycles for hire.

Transport **Bus** *Translux*, now runs daily buses to **Cape Town** and **Port Elizabeth**. Contact tourist office for times.

Directory **Banks** *Standard*, Bath St, T6141117. *ABSA*, 25 Bath St, T6141142, outside ATM's. **Medical Services** Hospital: Church St, T6141133. Doctors: Dr Alston, T6141102; Dr Scholtz, T6141780. Dentist: Dr Nolan, T6141281. Pharmacy: 57 Bath St, T6141370. **Useful addresses** Police: Bath St, T6141230. **Post Office**: Bath St. **Public Library**: Piet Retief St.

The Great Karoo

The Great Karoo is a vast, ancient plateau making up nearly a third of the total area of the country. It is a beautiful and extraordinary region, as much for its history as its remarkable emptiness. Today, the landscape is a parched expanse of baked red earth inhabited by tough merino sheep and their even tougher owners. Endless plains stretch between stark mountain ranges, with little but the characteristic steel windmills peppering the horizons. Hundreds of millions of years ago, however, this was an enormous swamp inhabited by dinosaurs, making it a key palaeontological site. More recently, the region has played a significant historical role, evidence of which can be seen in a handful of perfectly preserved Victorian settlements.

The Koup

The 'Koup' refers to the southern districts of the Great Karoo, traversed by the N1 highway between Cape Town and Johannesburg. Travelling east from the Hex River Valley, the countryside quickly becomes arid and seemingly barren, with vast stretches of uninhabited semi-desert stretching to all horizons. Despite the area's arid appearance there is a surprisingly abundant supply of underground water, brought to the surface by characteristic metal windmills which dot the plains. The most common vegetation is the Karoo bush which forms the staple diet of the merino sheep bred here. Most of the farms are for sheep, although more and more are being converted into game farms for game viewing and hunting. The sheer scale of the area is remarkable – the average farm size of over 20,000 ha, which makes popping round to the neighbours' an arduous task.

The isolated Karoo towns have a great sense of history, with many preserved 19th-century buildings, as well as a delightfully slow pace of life. Although rather off the beaten track, visitors often end up spending the night in one of them while en

Karoo: the world's largest graveyard

About 300 million years ago the region was a swamp fed by numerous rivers flowing from the south. Living in and around this huge inland lake were thousands of dinosaurs. Scientists now believe that as the earth started to warm, glaciers melted and slowly the lake was silted up. As the region became more arid many of the animals were trapped in the mud and today you have a region rich in dinosaur footprints and fossils. Such evidence has been found on many farms and

there are several excellent fossil collections.
The Karoo is in fact a palaeontologist's paradise. Scientists regard it as the world's largest graveyard. Most of the fossils found here belong to the order Therapsida. *But it is not the numbers or the type of fossils which so excite the experts, rather the fact that the rock strata contains a virtually unbroken record of species over 50 million years – from 240 to 190 million years ago. It was during this era that the first mammals evolved.*

route to Cape Town or Johannesburg. They are well worth more than a night though, especially after the first rains when the surrounding countryside transforms into a colourful blanket of wild flowers and grasses.

The dry summer months are oppressively hot. During and after the rains, however, the countryside takes on an entirely different appearance. The first rains arrive in the winter months, although centres such as Graaff-Reinet and Colesberg receive their rains in late summer. If you plan on hiking in the region remember that summer daytime temperatures frequently exceed 40°C, while in the winter the nights get very cold and snow can fall on the mountain peaks.

Climate

As the railways moved further inland from Cape Town, this became an important depot for locomotives, bringing about the growth of the town in the 1870s. However, since electrification its importance as a railway centre has all but gone. Given the large number of sidings, the area has become a 'graveyard' for **old steam engines** – an impressive if somewhat eerie open-air museum.

In its early days the station was known as Montagu Road; its present name was taken up in 1883. Other than the steam engines, look out for a pair of concrete pillars behind the town hotel, the *Loganda*. They were used to mount astronomical instruments to view the transit of **Venus**. On 6 December 1882 the British astronomer **A Marth** took readings to help calculate the distance between the sun and earth.

Touws River
Phone code: 023
(NB Always use 3-figure prefix)
Colour map 6, grid B6

Sleeping C-D *Loganda*, T3851130, is the main town hotel, with fairly comfortable rooms, some with a/c, a restaurant and swimming pool

In 1975 the entire village of Matjiesfontein was declared a national monument – small surprise considering the excellent state of repair of its Victorian houses. There is little to the town itself, other than a couple of dusty streets lined with perfectly preserved period houses, the highlight of which is the famous **Lord Milner Hotel**, resplendent with turrets and adorned balconies. The history of the settlement is a reflection of the life of a young Scot, Jimmy Logan, an official on the Cape Government Railways in the 1890s. He originally came here hoping that the dry air would cure a chest complaint. He found the climate so beneficial that he decided to settle permanently. As an ex-railway man he quickly saw the opportunity to supply water to steam trains from his farm. While the engines took on water, he served the passengers cool drinks and meals. So successful was his business that he built the fashionable *Lord Milner Hotel*, attracting rich and influential guests who suffered from lung complaints. During the Anglo-Boer War the town became a military headquarters and a marshalling ground for troops. Logan financed a regiment and served in the war – the hotel's turrets were used as lookout posts. Jimmy Logan lived here until his death in July 1920.

Matjiesfontein
Phone code: 023
(NB Always use 3-figure prefix)
Colour map 6, grid B6

Today the town is a popular stopover for travellers between the Cape and Johannesburg. There is a small town museum, the **Marie Rawdon Museum**, in the old jail under the railway station. The **cemetery**, 11 km to the west, has some interesting monuments and tombstones dating from the 1900s. Visitors travelling on the luxury **Rovos Rail** train and the famous **Blue Train** between Cape Town and Pretoria disembark here for a tour of some of the finest old Victorian buildings. The train normally stops for two to three hours.

Sleeping The original old Victorian town hotel, the **B** *Lord Milner*, T5513011, F5513020, milner2@mweb.co.za, is very much part of the town's history. The large, old rooms in the hotel are filled with antiques, as is the lounge and entertainingly old-fashioned dining room, which serves good value meals. There are cheaper rooms in the garden. Don't miss the wonderfully atmospheric old bar. Recommended.

Western Cape

Laingsburg
Phone code: 023
(NB Always use 3-figure prefix)
Colour map 6, grid B6

Laingsburg, a small town on the main road, started life as a staging post for coaches on a farm belonging to Stephanus Greeff. When the railway arrived, plans for a town were drawn up. It was first called Buffels River, then Nassau, and finally in 1879 it was named Laingsburg. Sadly, little of the original centre remains after a huge flood in 1981 washed away most of the town. The magistrate's court and the old post office have survived. The library contains a collection of photographs taken after the flood. For **tourist information**, contact the Municipality offices, T5511019.

N1 Northeast

After crossing the Dwyka river, you reach the small settlement of **Prince Albert Road**. Turning south on the R328 takes you to Prince Albert (45 km), and **Gamkaskloof**, a secluded valley known as 'The Hell' which is now part of the Gamkapoort Nature Reserve. The next settlement of note along the N1 is **Leeu-Gamka**. The name means 'lion', a sad reminder that the last Cape Lion was shot here in 1857, making the species extinct.

Beaufort West

Phone code: 023
(NB Always use 3-figure prefix)
Colour map 7, grid A2
Altitude: 850 m

This is the largest and oldest of the Central Karoo towns, but despite its history it is an unattractive place. Most of its energies seem devoted to servicing those travelling from Johannesburg to Cape Town – the N1 passes right through town, lined with petrol stations and fast-food joints. It is known as the 'oasis' town, hard to believe when you see hot, dusty streets but, thanks to the presence of the Nuweveld Mountains to the north, its 150 mm annual rainfall is far higher than other towns in the Karoo. Beaufort West was named after the fifth Duke of Beaufort, father of the Cape governor, Lord Charles Somerset. It was established in 1818 to try and control the smuggling of guns and general lawlessness in the region. In 1837 it became South Africa's first municipality. Before the railway reached the town in 1880, all of the locally produced merino wool had to be transported to the coast by wagon across the Swartberg Mountains. The earliest route was via Meiringspoort Pass (see page 278), one of several magnificent passes which link the Great Karoo with the Little Karoo.

The country around Beaufort West is home to the largest variety of succulents in the world. In the town itself, there are more different species than in all of Great Britain. Pear trees provide welcome shade as you walk along the pavements, some of which date back to the 1830s. The **Great Karoo Tourist Office** is at 63 Donkin St, T4151160, F4153675. It's an efficient, well-run office and they have prepared some useful material on the region and its major sights. Visit this office for further advice if you wish to explore the Great Karoo.

Sights
The greatest attraction is the nearby Karoo National Park, see page 230

A short walk around town will take you to the main sights. The old **Town Hall** (1867) on Donkin Street houses the town museum, with a couple of above-average collections relating to two of the town's most famous past residents – **Dr Christiaan Barnard** and **Dr Eric Louw**. Dr Louw was the MP for Beaufort West for many years and rose through the government's ranks to become South Africa's Foreign Minister between 1957 and 1963. Dr Barnard is known throughout the world for his pioneering work with heart transplants. He performed the world's first at Groot Schuur hospital in Cape Town in 1967. The displays include awards and trophies given to each, along with some of their personal effects. Next door is the **Dutch Reformed Mission Church** and the **parsonage** in which Dr Barnard spent his childhood. In the next street are some fine examples of Karoo Victorian single storey homes. These are all private homes; similar buildings can be seen in Matjiesfontein and other Karoo towns. In the **cemetery** is the grave of Stefanus Marais, a member of a group of Voortrekkers from Beaufort West who fought in the Battle of Blood River in Natal in 1838, as well as several British soldiers killed during the Anglo-Boer War.

All the best value lodges and hotels are fully booked months in advance for the start/end of the long Christmas holidays. For the rest of the year trade is much quieter, although there is the continual flow of people driving between the Cape and Gauteng.

Sleeping
Price codes:
see inside front cover

Most room rates are increased during the school holidays

Western Cape

B *Lemoenfontein Game Lodge*, 8 km from town, T4152847, www.lemoenfontein.co.za A luxury lodge, popular amongst the hunting fraternity, 6 rooms, game drives on the farm, horse riding and hiking also available. **B** *Matoppo Inn*, corner of Meintjies and Bird streets, T4151055, F4151080. Set in a quiet residential street, this was originally the Drostdy (magistrate's house). It has been converted into a luxury guesthouse, with high ceilings, beautiful yellowwood floors, comfortable rooms furnished with antiques, evening meals on request, neat garden with swimming pool. Recommended. **B-C** *Ye Olde Thatch*, 155 Donkin St, T/F4142209, T082-5611280 (mob). A lovely old Cape building with thatched roof. 6 rooms with above-average thought gone into the décor, swimming pool, good value restaurant and pub.

C *Clyde House*, 25 Donkin St, T/F4144083. An elegant double storey guesthouse that was originally the doctor's house. 6 rooms, comfortable lounge, B&B, gift shop and art gallery. **C** *Oasis*, 66 Donkin St, T/F4143221. Large, busy hotel with 46 a/c rooms, M-Net TV, restaurant, swimming pool, laundry service, acts as the *Translux Coach* agent, most of the long distance buses stop out front, central location. **C** *Royal Lodge*, Donkin St, T4143241, royallodge@intekom.co.za Standard town hotel, 30 medium sized a/c rooms, some single rooms, clean, restaurant, swimming pool, price includes breakfast. **C-D** *Young's Halfway House*, 143 Donkin St, T4143878. Range of rooms, singles, doubles, trips and family rooms, with or without bathroom, disabled facilities, restaurant, swimming pool, secure parking.

D-F *Donkin House*, 14 Donkin St, T/F4144287. 27 good-value rooms for up to 3 people, cheaper rooms with shared bath, communal TV lounge, swimming pool, good facilities for children. **D** *Safari Rooms*, T4152591. Simple rooms, some with en suite bathroom, kitchen facilities, good for groups, quiet setting. **D** *Wagon Wheel Country Lodge*, 500 m north of town centre on the N1, T4142145, T082-5566361 (mob). Country motel with simple rooms to suit most groups, TV, restaurant, swimming pool, disabled facilities, laundry service.

E *Formule 1*, 144 Donkin St, T4152421, F4152358. Clean, cheap option, characterless, small rooms, but still good value. Best of the cheap options. **Camping** There's an unappealing caravan park on Donkin St as you enter town, but it gets horribly busy and is best avoided. If you want to camp, head instead to the Karoo National Park (see below).

Mac Young's, 156 Donkin St, T4144068. Bustling restaurant serving steaks from a charcoal grill, plus pizza, pasta and seafood. One of their more unusual dishes is haggis, the last dish you'd expect to find in the middle of the Karoo. *Oasis Hotel*, 66 Donkin St, T4143221. Light lunches, bar snacks and quality à la carte evening meals. *Saddles*, 144 Donkin St, T4152491, close to the *Formule I*. Middle of the road steak house, part of a chain throughout the country, good value burgers and steaks, plus standard baked potatoes for vegetarians. *Ye Olde Thatch*, 155 Donkin St, T4142209. Fine home-style cooking in a cosy atmosphere, attached pub frequented by the local residents. Recommended.

Eating
Town hotels have restaurants and most guesthouses also welcome non-residents for evening meals, given sufficient notice

Train The *Trans Oranje*, a weekly service between **Cape Town** and **Durban**. **Cape Town** (9 hrs), Wed 2105. **Durban** (27 hrs), Mon 0400, via Bloemfontein and Harrismith. The *Trans Karoo*, a daily service between **Cape Town** and **Pretoria** via Kimberley. Both the north and

Transport

the southbound trains stop here for almost 30 mins. **Cape Town** (9 hrs), daily 0455. **Pretoria** (17 hrs), daily 1825, via Kimberley (7½ hrs).

Road 465 km to Cape Town, 544 km to Bloemfontein, 950 km to Johannesburg, 199 km to Oudtshoorn. **Bus**: *Greyhound*, T011-2498900. **Bloemfontein** (6 hrs), daily 2400; **Cape Town** (6 hrs), daily 0200, 0730; **Johannesburg** and **Pretoria** (12 hrs), daily 2400, 0230; **Kimberley** (6 hrs), daily 0230; **Worcester** (4 hrs), daily 0200, 0730.

Intercape, 24-hr information, T021-3804400; **Bloemfontein** (5 hrs), daily 2345; **Cape Town** (5 hrs), daily 0645, 0930; **Durban** (17 hrs), daily 2345; **Johannesburg** and **Pretoria** (10 hrs), daily 2345.

Translux, T012-3848000. **Bloemfontein** (6 hrs), daily 1910, 2335; **Cape Town** (6 hrs), daily 0055, 0240, 2105; **Durban** (14 hrs) via **Bethlehem**, daily, 1610; **Johannesburg** and **Pretoria** (13 hrs), daily 1840, 1910, 2335; Tue, Wed, Fri, Sun, 2125; **Kimberley** (6 hrs), daily 1840; Tue, Wed, Fri, Sun, 2125; **Knysna** via **Oudtshoorn** and **Mossel Bay**: Tue, Wed, Fri, Sun, 0620.

NB In the majority of cases you will board the bus services during the night or early hours of the morning – make sure you reserve a seat. The town is surprisingly quiet from as early as 2100, it is unlikely anyone will be around to help you have a problem getting a seat.

Karoo National Park

Colour map 7, grid A2 Only 5 km from Beaufort West, this National Park was created to conserve a representative area of the unique Karoo environment. There are three other conservation areas dotted across the Karoo, each preserving a slightly different eco-system: the Tankwa-Karoo National Park; the Karoo Nature Reserve near Graaff-Reinet; and the Karoo Mountain Zebra Park at Cradock. Despite limited human presence the environment of the Great Karoo has undergone radical change during the past 150 years and the protected areas are now recognized as important conservation centres as well as popular tourist destinations.

Ins & outs   **Getting there**   The main entrance is signposted off the N1 highway 5 km southwest of Beaufort West. The entrance gate is beside the highway and the road takes visitors straight to the park office and accommodation facilities. There is also a campsite in the mountainous area of the park, reached via a route off the R381, Loxton road, to the north of Beaufort West. Bookings for this camp are made at the main camp.

Park information   The gates are open from 0500-2200. It is 7 km from the main entrance to the park office, which is open 0730-2000. Entrance fee for day visitors, R20/vehicle. Next to the office is a shop selling basic groceries, a restaurant, laundry and a swimming pool for overnight residents' use only. This complex is known as *Stolshoek Rest Camp*. The office has trail and park maps as well as pamphlets detailing the main attractions within the park. Local booking and general enquiries, T023-4152828. **Reservations**, Mon-Fri; Pretoria, T012-3431991, F3430905 or via email at, reservations@parks-sa.co.za Bookings can also be made in person at 2 offices in Cape Town, either the Clocktower Centre, V&A Waterfront, or at the Cape Town Tourism Centre situated at the corner of Castle and Burg streets.

Climate   The Karoo is semi-desert, which means extremes – very hot days in summer (average for Jan is 32°C) with temperatures often reaching over 35°C, and warm days in winter but very cold nights (from Jun-Aug frost is common, and snow falls on the mountain peaks). Mar and Apr are regarded as the wet months, although the rainfall only averages 250 mm annually.

History   The 60,000-ha National Park was proclaimed in September 1979 after a long concerted effort by local residents to conserve the Karoo environment before farming practices totally destroyed it. The success of the campaign was primarily due to the efforts of a local farmer, William Quinton. The municipality donated over 7,000 ha, and funds raised by the Nature Foundation were used to purchase two farms, *Stolshoek* and *Puttersvlei*. The success of the park is attributed to the efforts of the first warden, Bruce Bryden and his wife Helena. Between 1977 and 1980 they saw to the removal of all the old farm fences and ripped out as much alien vegetation as possible. This was not without opposition; local farmers feared the reserve would become a protected breeding ground for predators which would then prey upon their sheep. The numbers of caracal and jackal have increased, but so too have the smaller mammals they traditionally prey on, so they now have less need to hunt the farmers' sheep. The Park has modern chalets in a scenically situated camp as well as two stone overnight huts on the Springbok Trail.

The current boundaries of the park encompass an area of Karoo plains, which merge into mountain slopes and a high-lying plateau. The **Nuweveld Mountains** in the north of the park are nearly 2,000 m high. The vegetation in the low-lying areas is a mixture of grasses and shrubs such as honey-thorn and the common *Acacia karroo*. On the steep slopes a sourgrass known as renosterbos (*Elytropappus rhinocerotis*), and harpuis flourish. The flora can be studied along a specially laid out Bossie Trail. Note the difference in vegetation cover between areas within the park and the neighbouring farms. The over-grazed farms have little grass cover and small, unpalatable shrubs.

There is a surprisingly diverse range of game and smaller wildlife in the park. Records list 174 species of birdlife, 38 species of reptiles, 37 types of gecko and lizard, and five different species of tortoise (this is the largest number in a conservation area in the world). In another effort to help restore the area to its previous state, antelope such as eland, black wildebeest, gemsbok, Cape mountain zebra, springbok and red hartebeest have been translocated into the park. The reserve is also home to two endangered species: the black rhino and the riverine rabbit. While the statistics are impressive, actually spotting most of these animals requires a degree of patience, effort and, of course, luck.

Wildlife
Look out for the tent tortoise; it is well-camouflaged and looks like an inverted egg box

The park is home to one of the more interesting hikes in the Karoo region, the **Springbok Hiking Trail**. This is a three-day, 27 km-long circular trail, which starts from the park rest camp. It is fairly tough considering the weather conditions and the rough terrain. A minimum of four people should walk together for safety reasons, and children under the age of 16 are not allowed on the trail. The more moderate spring and autumn months are the most popular period for hikers. Given that there are restrictions on the number of people allowed on the trail, it's a good idea to phone ahead and book.

Hiking in the park
Drinking water is only available at the two overnight huts. Carry a minimum of 2 litres per person during the day

The trail starts by crossing the plains before steadily climbing up into the **Nuweveld Mountains**. The first part of the hike from the park office to *Kortkloof Hut* is a gentle climb but only 5 km long. The second day's route is 14 km long and is a steady climb to the highest point of the trail, 1,890 m, a climb of over 1,000 m from the *Stolshoek Rest Camp*. As you'd expect, the views across the Karoo make the hot, steep climb worth it. The second night's accommodation is at the *Mountain View* camp. On the third day 17 km is covered, but it is all downhill. Take care on the steep sectors.

If long walks or a couple of nights roughing it are not your scene, there are also three short day walks known as the *Fossil Trail*, the *Fonteintjies Kloof Trail*, and the *Bossie Trail*. Each of these explores a different aspect of the park. The most interesting is the the *Fossil Trail* along which you can see fossils *in situ*. The trail has been adapted for the blind as well as people in wheelchairs. The trails all start from near the environmental educational centre where further information about the park is on display.

Visitors in **four-wheel drive** vehicles are allowed to drive on certain short tracks in the park. The park also has its own vehicle for hire and day trips with a nature guide and lunch included can be organized. Other trips on offer include night drives and overnight tours. The trails are rough, slippery and steep in parts and previous experience with a four-wheel drive is essential. There are a few rough roads open for game viewing, but given the mountainous conditions you cannot go too far. Walking remains the best way to enjoy this national park.

Driving in the park

Western Cape

Sleeping
Price codes:
see inside front cover

All the camping sites
have power points,
maximum of 6 people
per site. T023-4152828
for reservations

Next to the park office are the following park facilities: **B-C** *Stolshoek Rest Camp*, 20 self-contained thatched chalets (Cape Dutch style), kitchen, lounge, grouped around the swimming pool, a mix of 6-bed cottages and 3-bed bungalows, tariff includes breakfast and bed linen; **F** *Caravan park & campsite*, caravan stands have grass, good clean washblocks.

Hiking Huts First night: **E** *Kortkloof*, 2 rooms, 6 bunks in each with mattresses, kitchen and fireplace, showers and baths with limited hot water, chemical toilet. Second night: **E** *Mountain View*, rondavels, each with 4 bunks and mattresses, kitchen, living room, braai area. In addition to your food and clothing you must also carry a cooking stove, pots and pans, crockery, cutlery and sleeping bag.

East to Colesberg

The midway point between Cape Town and Johannesburg is the town of **Hanover**. At the end of a long day on the road another 700 km in any direction is too much to consider. Fortunately there is an excellent family run hotel and a guesthouse in Darling Street: **C** *Hanover Lodge*, Queen and Mark Street, T053-64219, has good size clean rooms, secure parking, children under 15 free, restaurant serves good hot meals even for late arrivals, swimming pool, ask about discounts.

Colesberg

Phone code: 051
(NB Always use
3-figure prefix)
Colour map 4, grid B2

Colesberg lies at the base of a distinctive landmark, **Cole's Kop**, visible from 40 km away. This rounded rock outcrop is 1,700 m high and was a very important landmark for early settlers, who moved inland across a largely featureless region. In those days it was called *Toringberg* – Towering Mountain – although some insist it meant Magic Mountain. The town was then named after Sir Lowry Cole, Cape Governor in 1830.

The town is an important junction between the Port Elizabeth road and the busy Cape road (N1), which cuts right through the centre of town. Many of the town's oldest buildings are found along here, and turning off the N1 takes you to further collections of Victorian houses tucked amongst a couple of picturesque hills. In its early days, this was a classic frontier town with illicit trade in a wide range of commodities, especially gunpowder and liquor. During the **Anglo-Boer War** it was close to the front and several battles were fought in the vicinity. The surrounding hills are named after the British regiments who held them: Suffolk, New Zealand, Worcester and Gibraltar. The town itself was captured by the Boers and for four months was part of the Free State territory.

Today Colesberg is the centre of two very successful businesses: horse breeding and sheep farming. Many champion racehorses have been bred around the town, due mainly to the soil type which yields high quality grasses and other fodder. The majority of visitors are just passing through, en route to somewhere else – the town springs to life in the early evening as people start to arrive, there is a burst of action as bills are settled and fuel tanks filled in the morning, and then peace for the rest of the day.

For **tourist information**, go to the information centre, which is part of the municipality, on Murry St, T7530678, F7530574. It's a helpful office, but closed at the weekend.

Sights
The easiest and most
pleasant way to see
the sights is to go on
a walkabout

Most of the historical buildings are within walking distance of the municipality, mainly along **Bell Street**. The flat-roofed cottages which line the street were built between 1860 and 1870, and have today been attractively restored. There is also a working flour mill which is operated by horses. The street is named after Charles Bell, a surveyor who is known in philatelic circles for designing a rare Cape Triangular stamp issued in September 1853.

The **Colesberg Kemper Museum** on Bank Square is a short walk from the *Central Hotel*, and contains an interesting photo collection, objects relating to the Anglo-Boer War and a 19th-century toy collection. It is a fine, solid double storey structure built in 1862 to house the Colesberg District Bank, later absorbed by the Standard Bank. Look out for the pane of glass in the museum on which the letters 'DP' have been scratched. In **1866** John O'Reilly, a diamond trader and transport rider from the Northern Cape diamond fields, brought a stone to the Colesberg magistrate, Lorenzo Boyes, who told O'Reilly that the scratching seemed to confirm that the stone was indeed a diamond. This was the first recognized stone to be found in South Africa. The diamond was 21.25 carats, and was bought for £500 by the Cape's governor, Sir Philip Wodehouse.

There are four churches around town. The most interesting is the **Church of the Province** (1848), designed by the wife of the first Bishop of Cape Town, Lady Grey. She had intended it to be a cathedral, but only the chancel was built. One of the more pleasing aspects of its design is an east-facing stained glass window. The **Dutch Reformed Church** (1866) is a characteristically grand, whitewashed building. Look out for the monument to Queen Victoria's jubilee across the road from this church, made from wrought iron and looking like a fancy gate post with three lanterns on top. The gardens behind add to the neatness of the area.

About 20 km out of town to the northwest is the seldom-visited Doornkloof Nature Reserve on the banks of the Seekoei River. This was once overgrazed farmland which was bought by the Department of Water Affairs in the 1960s, as the valley began to flood following the construction of the Vanderkloof Dam on the Orange River. The higher ground was eventually turned over to the Cape Conservation Department and restocked with kudu, steenbok, grey duiker, brown hyena, bat-eared fox and aardvark. There are several hiking trails, an overnight hut and horse riding available. ■ *Call T051-7531315 for information.*

Doornkloof Nature Reserve

Western Cape

Colesberg is an important overnight stop, especially for families travelling with children. Be sure to book ahead, especially during the school holidays. **B** *Merino Inn*, N1, Cape Town side, T7530781. A dull, soulless roadside motel, comfortable rooms with bathroom, M-Net, restaurant, bar, pool. **B-C** *Central*, Church St, T7530734. A large old town hotel, cheaper rooms have no bath, restaurant. **C** *Donald's Guest House*, 5 Stockenstroom Sq, T7531234. Simple town house, B&B or self-catering facilities, communal lounge where you can swap driving tales, secure parking, ideal as a stopover. **C** *Gordon's Cottage*, 4 Stockenstroom Sq, T7530390. 2-bedroom single storey restored Karoo cottage, self-catering, more than adequate for a short stop, central location for exploring the town. **C-E** *Van Zylsvlei*, on the Philippolis road, T7530589. Roadside motel with range of rooms plus 4 stands for caravans or tents, grassy and shady, electric points, shops at nearby petrol station. **D** *The Lighthouse*, 40 Church St, T7530043. Popular good-value guesthouse, good reports. **E** *Caravan Park*, Church St, T7530797. Not very shady, quite a lot of sand, reservations for holiday period, good washblocks, easy walk to all shops and services. **F** *Colesberg Backpackers*, PO Box 169, 39 Church St, T7530582, F7530642. Friendly backpackers with dorms and doubles plus camping space. Kitchen, laundry, splash pool, veranda perfect for a cold beer at the end of a hot day's driving. A welcome budget stopover on the long road from Johannesburg to Cape Town.

Bordeaux Coffee Shop, T7531582. Simple café serving light lunches, snacks and cakes. An all night eating option is the *Golden Egg* at the Shell Ultra City on the outskirts of town serving the usual array of greasy burgers and *wors*. The town hotels have the best restaurants. *International*, 1 Slater Rd. Family restaurant serving a mix of steaks, pasta and burgers.

Sleeping & eating
The local information centre is well-run and issues a comprehensive list of B&B

Rail The *Algoa* is a daily service between **Johannesburg** and **Port Elizabeth**. Change at Bloemfontein for other train services to Durban, Kimberley and Cape Town. **Johannesburg** (10 hrs), daily 2229, via Bloemfontein; **Port Elizabeth** (7 hrs), daily 0137.

Transport

Road 778 km to Cape Town, 226 km to Bloemfontein, 625 km to Johannesburg. **Bus**: many services depart at awkward times in the middle of the night. Buses use the Shell Ultra City as a terminal, the rest stop generally lasts for around 20 mins to allow passengers to buy refreshments and the drivers to change over.

Greyhound, T011-2498900. **Bloemfontein** (2 hrs), daily 2100, 2325; **Cape Town** (10 hrs), daily, 2355, 0245; **Durban** (12 hrs), daily 2100; **Johannesburg** and **Pretoria** (9 hrs), daily 0320. **Port Elizabeth** (6 hrs): daily, 0200.

Intercape, T021-3804400. **Cape Town** (9 hrs), daily 0215, 0530; **Durban** (12 hrs), daily 0345; **Johannesburg** and **Pretoria** (8 hrs), daily 0010, 0130, 0345; **Port Elizabeth** (6 hrs), daily 0215; Wed, Sat, 0045; **Plettenberg Bay** (9 hrs), daily 0215.

Translux, T011-7743333. **Bloemfontein** (2½ hrs), daily 2000, 2300; **Cape Town** (9 hrs), daily 2305, 0235; **Durban** (10 hrs) via **Bethlehem**, daily 2000; **Johannesberg** and **Pretoria** (9 hrs), daily 2300; **Knysna** (9 hrs) via **Oudtshoorn** and **Mossel Bay**, Mon, Thu, Sat 0155; **Port Elizabeth** (6 hrs) via **Graaff-Reinet**, Tue, Wed, Thu, Fri, Sun 0135.

Car The N1 leaves the Northern Cape and Karoo and enters the Free State. There is the option of leaving at Colesberg via the R58, R56 and N6 to Queenstown and going around the south side of Lesotho to the coast and Durban. Alternatively, follow the R369 towards Kimberley and return to the Cape via the Orange River Valley and Namaqualand.

The Overberg

Overberg Tourism,
T028-2141466,
F028-2121380

While most South Africans can tell you where the Overberg is, they might have difficulty defining its limits. It is a vague term which generally refers to the lands to the east of the Hottentots Holland Mountains extending as far as Mossel Bay. To the north are the Langeberg mountains and to the south the ocean. In the early days of settlement, people would refer to the area beyond the Hottentots Holland as 'over the berg'. It was not until the construction of Sir Lowry's Pass that the region began to be cultivated.

The Overberg area is understandably overshadowed by its neighbours: Cape Town and the Winelands lie to the west, and the much-hyped Garden Route begins in the east. Indeed, many visitors pass through the Overberg without ever realizing they were there. The first stop on most visitors' itineraries is Hermanus, at the right time of year one of the best places in the world for whale watching. During the months of August and September you are guaranteed daily sightings. Elsewhere along the coast there is a chance to see the fearsome great white shark. There are seaside towns with miles of sandy beaches, rock pools, snorkelling and wrecks to scuba dive, plus the southernmost point in Africa – Cape Agulhas.

Further inland are a number of nature reserves. The Marloth Nature Reserve has a six-day hiking trail plus some minor mountain peaks to climb. The De Hoop Nature Reserve has over 50 km of mountain bike trails in the mountains along the coast. Then there is the Bontebok National Park, originally created to save this rare antelope from extinction. At a more sedate level the Harold Porter Botanic Garden is the perfect introduction to the many rare and beautiful wild flowers and fynbos of the region.

If you tire of the great outdoors, Swellendam, Caledon, Bredasdorp and Greyton all have fine examples of early Cape Dutch buildings. The 18th-century drostdy in Swellendam is considered to be the finest in South Africa.

Climate The region's climate features warm, dry summers and cool, wet winters. During the summer there can be strong southeasterly winds which lower the temperature, but the sun remains as dangerous as at any other time. The average daily maximum temperature is over 23°C in December. In winter the daily maximum is closer to 16°C. At this time of the year the coast is not a very pleasant place to be – it is cold and wet, and plenty of storms roll in off the sea.

The Whale Coast

The evocatively named Whale Coast lives up to its title from July to November, when large numbers of whales seek out the sheltered bays along the coast for breeding. Whales can be seen close to the shore from False Bay all the way east to Mossel Bay, but by far the best place for whale spotting is Hermanus.

The most beautiful and exhilarating stretch of the coast is between Gordon's Bay and Hermanus, where the mountains plunge straight into the ocean forming a coastline of steep cliffs, sandy coves, dangerous headlands and natural harbours. This route is often compared to the spectacular Chapman's Peak Drive on the Cape Peninsular, and rightly so. More than 120 ships have been wrecked along this coast (the first recorded wreck dates from 1673) – there are hazardous reefs, headlands and rocks all the way to Cape Infanta and the Breede River estuary. A museum in Bredasdorp traces the misfortunes of the wrecked ships. When not looking out for whales, this coast offers some of the best fishing in South Africa and an opportunity to dive historic shipwrecks.

Gordon's Bay to Hermanus

Set in the lee of the Hottentots Holland Mountains at the eastern end of False Bay, away from the more glamorous beaches of Cape Town, this popular family seaside resort. There are two sandy beaches, Bikini and Main, both of which are safe for swimmers. The rocky shoreline, a short walk from the seafront, is popular for fishing. The most likely catch include mackerel, steenbras and kabeljou.

    The Danie Miller hiking trail starts at the end of Aurora Drive and winds its way up to the anchor. It's 7 km long; no permit required.

Gordon's Bay
Phone code: 021
(NB Always use 3-figure prefix)
Colour map 4, grid C2

C *Van Riebeeck*, Main Beach, T8561441, F8561572, www.vrh.co.za. Functional hotel run by the Protea group, restaurant and bar offer a sheltered view of the sea, a few rooms are sea-facing with a balcony. **C-D** *Polmesarie*, 61 Miller St, T/F8562422. Local guesthouse, range of rooms with en suite bathroom, short walk to beach.

Sleeping
Price codes:
see inside front cover

Bertie's Moorings, Harbour Island, T8563343. Lively pub serving light meals on the waterfront. *Harbour Lights*, Gordon's Bay Harbour, T8561830. Excellent seafood and good views of the yacht basin at night. Recommended. *Neptune's*, 7 Bay Crescent, T8561511. A/c, steaks and local seafood, busy in the holidays. *Old Cape*, 33 Beach Rd, T8560248. Breakfasts, light lunches and evening meals, standard Cape fare. *Port Gordon*, 157 Beach Rd, T8562299. Cosy, bright room with views of the old harbour, seafood and steaks.

Eating

The first small coastal resort after Gordon's Bay is Rooiels (19 km), a cluster of cottages at the mouth of a small river. The beach has a strong backwash, so be wary if children are swimming. Continuing towards Hermanus, the road leaves its precipitous course and climbs the hills inland. After 5 km turn right to Pringle Bay.

    Pringle Bay is dominated by a large rock outcrop known as the Hangklip, 454 m. This is the rock you see when standing by the lighthouse at Cape Point looking across False Bay. There are a few holiday cottages and the Hangklip Hotel, T028-27384489. If you're in no hurry, the gravel loop road around **Cape Hangklip** is a scenic distraction. There is another track leading to Hangklip. The road rejoins the R44 just before Silver Sands.

Rooiels & Pringle Bay

This small holiday village, midway between Strand and Hermanus, is a local gem. The community was named after Betty Youlden, the daughter of a local businessman who had plans to develop the Cape Hangklip area in the 1930s. Fortunately little came of the idea and today the village remains an untidy collection of holiday homes in a beautiful location. At **Stoney Point** there is a reserve to protect a small breeding colony of **African penguins**, one of the few places where you are guaranteed to see these birds breeding on the mainland. Also here are the remains of a whaling station plus the hulk of a whaler, the *Balena*. Behind the village are the well-known **Harold Porter Botanic Gardens**, worth a visit if time permits. Along the main beach is another area of protected land, the **HF Verwoerd Coastal Reserve**. There is safe swimming close to the kelp beds.

Betty's Bay
Phone code: 028
(NB Always use 3-figure prefix)
Colour map 6, grid B5

Rare shells are occasionally washed ashore here

Western Cape

Sleeping **C** *Buçaco Sud*, Clarence Drive, T2729750, www.bucacosud.co.za Stylish Spanish-style villa with tastefully decorated rooms, terracotta tiles, fireplaces in public areas, all rooms have either mountain or coastal views, breakfast served in attractive courtyard with pool. Recommended. **C** *Drummond Arms Tavern Inn*, 38 Main Rd, T2738458. Village pub and restaurant with accommodation, good for pub lunches. **D** *Peter's Place*, 4400 Wallers Way, T2729527, T082-7845084 (mob). 3 rooms with en suite bath or shower, a quiet B&B well-situated for hiking or passing the day on the beach, meals on request.

Western Cape

Harold Porter Botanic Gardens

The best time to visit is from Sep to Nov, but it can still be cool and windy at this time

This garden, lying between mountains and coast, was originally acquired in 1938 by Harold Porter, a keen conservationist. In his will he bequeathed the grounds to the nation. There are 10 ha of cultivated fynbos garden and a further 191 ha of natural fynbos which has been allowed to flourish undisturbed. The reserve is unique in that it incorporates the whole catchment area of the Dawidskraal River. The garden has many fynbos species, including proteas, ericas, legumes, buchus and brunias. Another draw is the chance of seeing red disa flowering in its natural habitat. This usually occurs from late December through to late January. If you have not managed to visit Kirstenbosch Botanical Garden in Cape Town, a couple of hours spent here will be very rewarding. The gardens encompass mountains, waterfalls, forested gorges, marshes and coastal dunes and with such a diverse environment one can expect to see a large selection of birds. More than 88 species have been identified; of special interest are the Orange breasted sunbird and the rare Protea canary, which is only seen in fynbos environments.

There are three longer paths which lead from the formal grounds into the surrounding mountains. Disa Kloof has a small dam and a waterfall; Leopard's Kloof takes you several kilometres into the Kogelberg; and a contour path starts by the Harold Porter memorial stone, from which you have excellent views of the ocean and the gardens. **NB** Fire prevention is an important issue, especially between January and March when the terrain is dry and the prevailing wind from the southeast. The fynbos plant contains resin and oils which are highly flammable. ■ *Daily, 0800-1630. Small entrance fee, free for Botanical Society members. There is a pleasant restaurant and garden shop by the entrance gate. To the left of the entrance is a picnic site and toilets. Guided tours can be arranged in advance, T028-2729311, www.mbi.ac.za*

Kleinmond

Phone code: 028 (NB Always use 3-figure prefix) Colour map 6, grid B5

Exercise caution when swimming in the sea as the sandy beach is steep; children should be watched at all times

This popular summer resort in Sandown Bay has been frequented by the wheat farmers of the interior since 1861. The name Kleinmond refers to the 'small mouth' of the Bot River lagoon. The settlement is overlooked by the magnificent Kogelberg Mountains which in the spring are full of flowering proteas. Local **tourist information** is available from the Kleinmond Bureau, T2715657, F2714742, info@hangklip-kleinmondtourism.co.za

To the east of the village is the **Bot River Lagoon**, a popular sailing and canoeing area. Where the Bot River meets the sea is a large marsh which is home to thousands of water fowl. This is a birdwatchers' paradise, especially at low tide. The more common species are spoonbills, herons, pelicans, gulls, terns, kingfishers and geese. There is also small herd of **wild horses** that roam the marshlands. Their origin is uncertain but after several attempts to cull them in the 1950s they are now protected. Permits are required to see them – it is thought that fewer than 12 exist.

In Mar and Apr the inland valleys are a carpet of red wild flowers, erica pillansii

The **Kleinmond Coastal Nature Reserve** stretches from the Palmiet River to the Bot River, protecting an area of unique coastal and mountain fynbos. The official hiking trail is 18.5 km long. There are reputedly over 1,500 species of plants in the reserve. You can walk along the coast exploring tidal rock pools, or walk inland and climb the peaks known as the **Perde Berg**. A lagoon formed by the Palmiet River is home to swimmers, canoes and boardsailing.

Sleeping **B** *The Beach House*, 13 Beach Rd, Sandown Bay, T2713130, F2714022, beachhouse@relais.co.za Luxurious guesthouse right by the sea, comfortable en suite rooms, some with ocean views, non-smoking room available, *Tides* seafood restaurant,

The crucial whale lexicon

A couple of days along the cliffs of Hermanus is enough to persuade anyone to help save the whale. Here are some useful words to help you convince people of your dedication to the cause.

Breaching Probably the most spectacular sight, this is when whales lift their entire body out of the water in an effortless arc, creating a huge splash as they fall back into the sea. Not an isolated event, a whale will often leap several times so keep your binoculars trained. The experts have yet to agree on why the whale does this, and the whales aren't giving much away.

Blowing This is the sight we are all familiar with, the spout of water vapour accompanied by an echoing sound as air is expelled from their lungs through the blowhole. The seasoned whale watcher will be able to identify the species from the shape of the spout. The vapour is created by condensation when the warm breath comes in contact with the cooler outside air.

Grunting Just a loud grunting sound which carries a long way over water, a moving noise when heard on a calm moonlit night. No translations yet available.

Lobtailing The action of the whale slapping the surface with their tails producing a loud clap. This can be seen repeatedly and over a long time period. Interpreted as some form of warning or social communication.

Sailing Whales lift their tail clear of the water for long periods. There are several theories behind this action; to use the wind to 'sail' through the water (I think not!), to feed on the sea-floor, or as a means of temperature control. The diehard watchers reckon the whales are just showing off.

Spyhopping When the whale lifts its head and part of its body above the water vertically. This gives the whale a 360 degree view of the seas.

See also Whale watching box, page 240

Western Cape

---

peaceful location on the beach, swimming pool, recently taken over by Relais Hotels. **D** *Ceilidh Cottage*, 112 10th Av, T2713965. Self-catering cottage set in tranquil gardens, ideal for hiking and bird watching. **D** *Villa le Roc*, corner of 1st Av and 5th St. Comfortable, T2714550. Spacious self-catering units, sleep 8, open-plan kitchen, some have sea views. **E-F** *Palmiet Caravan Park*, T2714050. Large holiday park, grass, some shade, electric points, quiet out of season, kiosk on the site.

Onrus, meaning 'restless', lying on the east bank of the mouth of the Onrus River, was named by the first European settlers because of the perpetual noise made by the waves along the rocky coastline. The Onrus River forms a small lagoon with a short sandy beach which is safe for children to swim from. The beach is also popular with surfers. There are washroom facilities, a restaurant serving cool drinks and simple meals throughout the day and a post office. Vermont, named after the American state, was founded by CJ Krige who became the first Speaker of the South African parliament. The beach here is sheltered by high dunes and is also safe for children. The area has become a popular retreat for painters, sculptors, poets and Afrikaans authors. West from Vermont is the **Frans Senekal Nature Reserve**. There is a walk along the coast to Hawston harbour – allow two hours.

Onrus & Vermont

Phone code: 028 (NB Always use 3-figure prefix) Colour map 6, grid B5

The villages of Vermont and Onrus seem like ghost settlements outside holiday season

Sleeping and eating **C** *Otters Country House*, 28 Marine Dr, Vermont, T3163167, F3163764, otters@hermanus.co.za Modern family guesthouse overlooking the ocean, with 2 double rooms with en suite bathroom, TV, and 2 suites with en suite bathroom, table d'hôte meals, non-smoking room, laundry, airport transfer available. **D** *Onrus B&B Lodge*, 5 Beach Rd, Onrus, T3163618. Country-style guesthouse, en suite rooms, close to beach, good breakfasts served. **C-D** *Flick's Place*, 8 Beach Rd, Onrus, T3162998, flicksplace@hotmail.com B&B, en suite doubles, modern and comfortable, all with private entrances, satellite TV, meals on request, good breakfasts. **D** *Windswael*, 36 Marine Dr, Vermont, T3161853, T082-5589834 (mob). Seafront B&B with sea views, contact Thea. **E-F** *Paradise Park*, Vermont, off the R43, T3163402. A small

Price codes: see inside front cover

site with 16 self-catering chalets and camping, plenty of grass and shade, electric points, swimming pool, mini golf, shops nearby, snack shop open during holiday season.

Milkwood, Atlantic Dr, Onrus, T3161516. Closed Mon and Sun afternoon, standard choice of fish and meat dishes, open fire in the winter. *What the Dickens*, Onrus Trading Post, Main St, T3163946. Well-known and good value pub lunches with a full menu in the evenings.

Hermanus

Phone code: 028
(NB Always use
3-figure prefix)
Colour map 6, grid B5

Hermanus has grown from a rustic fishing village to a well-known town famous for its superb whale watching. Today it is marketed as the world's best land-based whale watching site, and indeed Walker Bay is host to impressive numbers during calving season (July to November). However, don't expect any private viewings – Hermanus is very popular and has a steady flow of visitors throughout the year. While this means it can get very busy, there is also a good range of accommodation and restaurants, making it a great base for exploring the quieter reaches of the Overberg and while you may find it far too crowded at Christmas, at other times it is a town worth spending a couple of days in. Alternatively, Hermanus is only a few hours from Cape Town, making it an easy day trip from the city.

The Hermanus web
site is one of the best
and well worth a visit

The **Greater Hermanus Tourism Bureau**, Old Station Building, Mitchell St, T3122629, F3130305, www.hermanus.co.za is open, Mon-Sat 0900-1700; Sun, 0900-1200 (May to Jul), 0900-1400 (Aug-Apr). Aside from helping you find suitable accommodation, the office can arrange **guided walks** in and around town. These are run by members of the local Botanical Society who are extremely knowledgeable about whales, local birdlife and fynbos vegetation. ■ *Walks last about 1 hr and cost in the region of R30 per person, minimum groups of 5. One of the easiest ways to find out all there is to know about Hermanus and the immediate region.*

History   The town is named after Hermanus Pieters, an old soldier who set up camp in the bay while looking for better pastures for his animals during the hot summer months.

Hermanus

To Hamewith, Livesey Lodge, Zoete Inval B&B,
Marimba Café & coastal road to Cape Town
To Hardy's Guesthouse

Walker Bay

Sleeping
1 Auberge Burgundy
2 Cottage
3 Hermanus Esplanade
4 Hill St Blues
5 Hortensia
6 Kenjockity
7 Marine
8 Moby Backpackers
9 Whale Rock Lodge
10 Windsor

Eating
1 Bientang's Cave
2 The Burgundy

0 metres 200
0 yards 200

Western Cape (side margin)

The presence of a fresh water spring persuaded him to spend the whole summer here. Soon other farmers arrived with their families from the interior. Almost by accident it became a holiday destination – the herds required little attention, so the men turned their attention to fishing while the women and children set about enjoying themselves on the sandy beaches. When the farmers returned inland to the winter pastures, it was the fishermen who remained and settled here.

In the 1920s the town gained a reputation as an excellent location for convalescing, and even doctors from Harley Street in London were recommending the 'champagne air' of Hermanus. As it became popular with the gentry, so suitably smart hotels were built to accommodate them. After the Second World War the construction of a new harbour stimulated the expansion of the fishing industry and there are now three canning factories in Walker Bay.

The Old Harbour is a national monument and a focal point of tourist activities. A **Sights** ramp leads down the cliff to the old jetty and a group of restored fishermen's cottages, including the **museum**. The displays are based on the local fishing industry and include models of fish, a whale skeleton, some shark jaws, fish tanks and early pieces of equipment. One of the most interesting features is the recordings of calls between whales. There is also a telescope to watch the whales further out. An information plaque helps identify what you see. Outside the museum on the harbour ramp is a collection of small restored fishing boats, the earliest dating from 1855. Also on show are the drying racks for small fish and cement tables which were once used for gutting fish. ■ *T3121475. Mon-Sat, 0900-1300, 1400-1700, Sun 1200-1600. Small entrance charge.*

The **De Wet's Huis Photo Museum**, on Market Square, houses an interesting collection of photography depicting the historical development of Hermanus. ■ *Mon-Fri, 0900-1300, 1400-1700, Sat 0800-1300, 1400-1600, T3130418, small entrance charge.*

Outside the old harbour is a **memorial** to those who died in the First World War. Set in the stonework is a barometer and the words "to help to protect the lives of present and future fishermen". Either side of the beehive-shaped monument are two ship's cannon. The new harbour, to the west of the old harbour in Westcliff, is still a busy fishing port. It's a great idea to head down to the dockside to buy fresh crayfish, mussels or line fish from the fish shop. The staff will be happy to advise you on how best to cook your selection.

The excellent **Cliff Path** starts at the new **Walks around** harbour in Westcliff and follows the **Hermanus** shore all the way round Walker Bay to *On a calm, clear day* Grotto Beach, a distance of just over 15 *this is the perfect way* km. Between cliffs the path goes through *to whale watch* stands of milkwood trees and takes you around the sandy beaches. Walking in a direction away from the new harbour, these are the most popular view points: Dreunkrans, Fick's Pool, Gearing's Point, the Old Harbour, Die Gang, Siever's Punt, Kwaaiwater and Platbank (see the town map). On an ideal day allow at least a morning for the walk. Bench seats are provided at the prime view points, which make them good spots for a picnic.

To Voëlklip, Kammabaai & Grotto Beaches

To Stanford, Bredasdorp & De Hoop Nature Reserve

To Fernkloof Nature Reserve

Golf Club

Fairways

Theron

Main Rd

3 Charlie's Tapas
4 Fisherman's Cottage
5 Fish Shoppe
6 Mallards
7 Ocean Basket
8 Ouzeri
9 Prince of Whales
10 Rossi's
11 San Remo Spur

Western Cape

Western Cape

 Whale watching

The World Wildlife Foundation acknowledges Hermanus as one of the 12 best places in the world to view whales. Hermanus is the ideal destination to head for if you wish to see whales without having to bob around in a boat. The town promotes itself as the 'Heart of the Whale Coast', and during the season most visitors should not be disappointed. The town's specific advantage is that whales can come very close to the shore. The combination of low cliffs and deep water at the base of the cliffs means that from the cliff path (see page 239), you are able to look down into clear water and see the outline of whales from as close as 10 m. A **whale watching hotline***, T028-3122629, provides visitors with the most recent information on the location of whales. This covers the coastline from Betty's Bay to Gansbaai. There is also a special number for reporting any* **strandings***, T0800-228222, this applies to dolphins as well as whales.*

To add to the excitement there is a **Whale Crier** *who between 1000-1600 during September and October strolls around the town centre blowing a kelp horn to announce the arrival of each whale in Walker Bay. The Whale Crier is easily identified by his appearance. He wears a giant Bavarian-style hat and carries a sandwich board which records the daily sightings of whales from different vantage points around Walker Bay.*

The **best months** *are* **September** *and* **October** *when daily sightings are guaranteed. You would be unlucky not to see some sign of a whale during this period, though of course they are just as likely to be in the middle of the bay as up close to one of the*

vantage points along the cliff path. The first southern right whales start to appear in Walker Bay from June onwards. By the end of December most have returned to the southern oceans. The whales migrate north to escape heavy winter storms in the oceans around Antarctica. In August and September most of the calves are born in the calm sheltered bays, the cows then stay with their young for a further two months in the bays. Out of an estimated world population of only 6,000 southern right whales, up to 80 have been recorded seeking refuge in Walker Bay to mate and calve.

The **southern right whale** *(Eubalaena Australis) is distinguished from other whales by its V-shaped 'blow', produced by a pair of blowholes, and callosities which appear randomly on and around the oval head. The callosities are growths of tough skin which grow in unique patterns helping to identify individual whales. They are basically black with occasional streaks of grey or white on the back. Their flippers are short, broad and almost square. They are thought to live for up to 100 years, and a fully grown adult can weigh as much as 80 metric tonnes.*

They are so-named because they were regarded as the 'right' whale to catch. The carcass yielded large quantities of oil and baleen, and the task of collecting the booty was made all the more easy by the fact that the whale floated in the water when killed. The northern right whale is virtually extinct, and the southern right has shown only a slight increase in numbers since international legislation was introduced to protect the species. The South African coastline is the most likely place in the world to see them in coastal waters.

Beaches There are some good beaches just a short distance in either direction from the town centre. The best beaches to the west are found at Onrus and Vermont (see above). Heading east towards Stanford and Gansbaai are long, open beaches or secluded coves with patches of sand and plenty of rock pools. **Grotto Beach** is the largest, best developed and most popular for swimming. The fine white sands stretch beyond the Klein River Lagoon, and there are changing facilities, a restaurant and a beach shop. Slightly closer to the town centre is **Voëlklip Beach**, a little rundown, but with well-kept lawns behind the sand. Conditions are good for swimming and surfing. The most popular spot for surfers is **Kammabaai** next

What to fish and when to fish

Don't forget to buy your permit before going fishing and please observe the rules, which may verge on the pedantic, but are designed to protect the stocks, like so many popular fishing grounds around the world.

The closed seasons

Rock Lobster/Crayfish	*1 June – 15 November*
Perlemoen/Abalone	*1 August – 31 October*
Shad or Elf	*1 September – 30 November*
Galjoen	*15 October – 28 February*

How big and how many shellfish?

Crayfish/Rock Lobster	*minimum size of 80 mm measured along the middle dorsal line of the carapace from the posterior edge to the middle anterior spine*
Oysters	*maximum of 25 per day, plus they must be 51 mm in size*
Perlemoen	*maximum of 4 per day, plus they must be 114 mm in size*
Prawn	*a maximum of 50 per day*
Sea Crab	*a maximum of 15 per day*

Not forgetting the bait

Alikreukel	*5 per day, they must be 63.5 mm in size*
Bloodworms	*5 per day, no size restrictions*
Limpets	*15 per day*
Venus Ear	*10 per day, with a minimum size of 32 mm*

See also Fishing section, page 243

Western Cape

door to Voëlklip beach. There are braai facilities amongst the shade of some milkwood trees, an ideal setting for beach parties.

Fernkloof Nature Reserve

Set in the hills behind the town, the reserve has 4 km of walks through an area rich in protea and coastal fynbos, with three colour-coded self-guided trails. Access is from the east end of Hermanus – just before the Main Road crosses Mossel River, turn up Fir Street. The reserve gates are just beyond the botanical society buildings.

The diversity of plants in this reserve is due to the long period it has been under protection, plus its range of elevation from 60 to 850 m. With such a diverse plant population, there is a wide range of bird and animal species. Higher up in the mountains, look out for breeding black eagles. Small patches of indigenous forest remain in some of the moist ravines. ■ *Open at all times, no entrance fee. Hiking permits are issued by the Municipality, T3138000, along with reservations for the 4-man overnight mountain hut. A visitors' centre, 500 m from the entrance, has a display of the most common plants you are likely to see when walking in the reserve. All the hiking trails start from this centre.*

Hermanus Wine Route

Hidden away in the **Hemel-en-Aarde Valley** behind Hermanus is a small collection of vineyards producing some surprisingly good wines, mostly Burgundy varieties based around pinot noir and chardonnay grapes. These smaller and lesser-known wineries are very pleasant to visit since they are rarely crowded and the owners are enthusiastic about their venture. There are three vineyards which are open to the public and have tastings in their cellars. **Hamilton Russell Vineyards** is one of the more picturesque estates. The cellar and tasting room are set beside a small trout lake. Follow the R43 out of Hermanus towards Cape Town, after 2 km take a right turn marked Caledon, R320; there is a signpost and right turn 5 km along this gravel road. ■ *Tastings: Mon-Fri, 0900-1700, Sat 0900-1300, closed Sun. A chardonnay, a sauvignon blanc and a pinot noir are usually offered for tasting, T3123595.*

If you do choose to visit one of the vineyards, an excellent place for lunch is Country Cookhouse, T028-3124321. See under Eating below for further details

Whalehaven Wines is the newest vineyard in the valley, so all their wines are quite young. The cellars and the production rooms are open to visitors. Take the R320 turning for Caledon as described above. The winery is almost immediately on the right after turning off the R43. ■ *Tastings: Mon-Fri, 0930-1700, Sat 1030-1300, closed Sun. A chardonnay, a sauvignon blanc, a cabernet sauvignon, a merlot, a pinot noir and a Beaujolais blend are usually offered for tasting, T3161633.*

Bouchard Finlayson wines, on the Caledon road 1 km beyond the Hamilton Russell Vineyard, have already won several awards. ■ *Tastings: Mon-Fri, 0900-1700, Sat, 1030-1230, closed Sun. A dry white blend titled Blanc de Mer, a pinot noir, a sauvignon blanc and a chardonnay are usually offered for tasting, T3123515.*

Sleeping

■ *on map*
Price codes:
see inside front cover

If you visit Hermanus during the school holidays or whale season, telephone in advance to guarantee a room

There is a private accommodation agency catering for domestic family holidays. Most of their properties are self-catering and are let for at least a week. Out of season they sometimes offer bargains as owners look to rent out an otherwise empty flat for a couple of nights. **Hermanus Accommodation Centre**, 9 Myrtle Lane, corner of Church St, T/F3130004, hermanus@adept.co.za There is also a notice board on the excellent town website where people post requests for self-catering accommodation during the peak holiday periods.

A *The Marine*, Marine Dr, T3131000, F3130160, www.marine-hermanus.co.za Large, luxurious hotel dominating the waterfront. This is probably the best hotel in town, with facilities to match. Stylish décor, great views, heated swimming pool, jacuzzi, billiard room, art gallery, restaurant – some indifferent reports on food quality. Steps from the garden lead down to the municipal tidal pool amongst the rocks (see Swimming, below).

B *Auberge Burgundy*, 16 Harbour Rd, T3131201, F3131204. 14 rooms, a mix of luxury doubles and suites, the penthouse can sleep 6, all set in an immaculate garden full of herbs and mature trees. Has a luxurious inner courtyard plus a swimming pool with a fine view across Walker Bay. Opposite the *Burgundy* restaurant. Recommended by a couple of readers.

B *Hortensia Lodge*, 66 Mitchell St, T3124358, F3121956. Small comfortable guest house set in gardens with swimming pool. Rooms are en suite with TV and views of the neat garden.

B *Windsor Hotel*, 49 Marine Dr, T3123727, F3122181, www.windsor-hotel.com Large and popular hotel set on cliffs overlooking the ocean. En suite rooms with TV, some have sea views. Excellent views across Walker Bay from the glassed-in lounge. Slightly plain restaurant. Frequently used by tour groups, small boat hire service.

C *Hamewith*, 130 Main Rd, T/F3121236. 3 fully equipped self-catering suites, with superb views of the bay and the old harbour. Recommended for its location alone.

C *Kenjockity*, 15 Church St, T3121772. A typical old Hermanus house which started life as a boarding house in the 1920s. Thoughtfully restored with 11 rooms, some with en suite bathroom, friendly and helpful owners, small breakfasts, within walking distance of the bay and shops. **C** *Livesey Lodge*, 13 Main Rd, T/F3130026, www.liveseylodge.co.za 6 double rooms with separate entrances, en suite bathrooms, TV, mini-bar, small swimming pool in walled garden, self-catering possible. **C** *Whale Rock Lodge*, 26 Springfield Av, T3130014, F3122932. Comfortable B&B with 10 double rooms, en suite shower or bath, TV, laundry, bar. Look out for a white building with a thatch roof, close to the New Harbour and a short walk from the popular cliff path which is an ideal place for viewing whales.

C-D *Hermanus Esplanade*, Marine Dr, T3123610, F3122181. 22 self-catering apartments in a variety of formats, TV, secure parking, complex laundrette, good value for 4 or more, on the seafront. Recommended.

D *Hill Street Blues*, 3 Hill St, T/F3123530. Straightforward B&B with a fondness for the American TV police show, 2 double rooms with en suite bathrooms, central location.

D-F *Zoete Inval*, 23 Main Rd, T/F3121242. 7 double rooms, TV lounge, small library, kitchen facilities available, bicycle hire, laundry service, secure parking. Dorm beds available for backpackers, will meet the Baz Bus at *Bot River Hotel*, but then expect a minimum stay of 2 nights.

E *The Cottage*, 6 Stemmet St, T3123591, 6stemmet@netactive.co.za Simple, good-value cottage sleeping 4, self-catering, close to village and seafront.

F *Moby's Backpackers*, 9 Mitchell St, T3132361, F3123519, www.mobys.co.za Great backpackers offering a good range of rooms: doubles, dorms sleeping 6-8, family rooms, all are en suite. 2 bars, one for residents only, large garden with pool, daily braais, internet access, TV lounge, fully equipped kitchen. Friendly and laid-back place, do Baz Bus pickups. Also orga-nizes very cheap shark dives, as well as wine tasting, sandboarding and the usual excursions.

Eating
● *on map*

Bientang's Cave, T3123454. Closed Wed out of season. The name doesn't lie – the venue is an actual cave. Excellent seafood buffets, simple wood benches and long tables, very popular, book ahead. Access is via steps from the carpark on Marine Drive between the village square and *Marine Hotel*. **The Burgundy**, 16 Harbour Rd, T3122800. Closed Mon. Restored rural cot-tage by the sea. One of the top restaurants in town but very relaxed and good value, with tables spilling onto a shady terrace outside. Excellent seafood including superb grilled crayfish. **Char-lie's Tapas**, Market Sq, T3130110. Light meals, and tapas-type snacks in a lively pub atmo-sphere. **Fisherman's Cottage**, Old Harbour, T3123642. Closed Sun. Tiny place serving excellent seafood, simple dishes such as seafood potjie, charming setting. Choose a veranda table in good weather. Known as the smallest pub in town. **The Fish Shoppe**, Market Sq, T3121819, small seafood restaurant, good value meals. **Flavour of Italy**, Main Rd, opposite *Marine Hotel*, T3122137. Coffee shop and deli, also serving light pasta lunches. **Marimba Café**, 108d Main Rd, T3122148, dinner daily. Fun 'African' restaurant with dishes from across the continent, includ-ing good Mozambique *fejoada*, Moroccan lamb and Cape Malay curries.

Mogg's Country Cookhouse, in the Hemel-en-Aarde Valley, 12 km from Hermanus cen-tre, take the R43 out of town for Cape Town, after 2 km turn on to the R320 for Caledon, T3124321. Meals by appointment only. Limited opening times: lunches from Wed-Sun, eve-ning meals on Fri and Sat only. The restaurant is run by Jenny and her daughter Julia who prepare a seasonal menu. Every dish is freshly prepared and served in a lovely rustic setting. Recommended. **Ocean Basket**, Fashion Sq, Main Rd, T3121529, the usual good, fresh sea-food you can expect from this chain. Good value, quick meals. **Ouzeri**, 60 St Peter's Lane, T3130532. Closed Sun afternoon and Mon. Greek taverna, lively atmosphere, tasty vegetar-ian dishes plus the usual Greek fare, fully licensed. **Prince of Whales**, Astoria Village, T3130725. Excellent breakfasts, pancakes and fresh croissants. **Rossi's**, 10 High St, T3122848. Open daily, evening takeaway service, Italian dishes, good value steaks. **San Remo Spur**, 38 Main Rd, T3121915. Good value steak meals, popular as all outlets are in this chain.

Festivals

Perlemoen Extravaganza in **Jul** is a good time to be eating out in Hermanus, local restau-rants prepare perlemoen in as many different ways as they can come up with. *Whale Festi-val*, www.whalefestival.co.za, in **Sep**, is primarily an arts festival which attracts theatre and singing acts along with children's events and a craft market. A *Wild Flower Show* is held in Fernkloof Nature Reserve.

Shopping
Most shops are concentrated around Long, Aberdeen and Mitchell Streets

As befits a popular tourist town there are plenty of curio shops and speciality boutiques. A popular shopping mall is the *Village Square*. To the west of the town centre, an even larger shopping complex, the *Gateway Centre*, was recently completed. This has all the high street shops as well as a selection of restaurants and amusements for children. **Photography**: *Foto First*, 102 Main Rd, T3130311, 1-hr processing.

Sports
For local fishing regulations, see box page 241

Fishing For many local visitors the principal reason for coming to Hermanus is the excellent sea fishing. There are strict regulations concerning what you can catch, the bait you use and the actual season. Permits where necessary are issued by the local magistrates' office. Most of the coastline in front of the town centre is a Marine Reserve, nothing may be removed from the sea in this area. Chartered fishing trips start from the new harbour; check with the tourist offices for which charters are operating. Always ensure you are protected from the sun.

Because fishing is so popular, anglers are restricted to 10 fish a day in total, but no more than 5 of any of the following may be caught; garrick, bream, white stumpnose, shad, cob and white steenbras. Permits are also required for elf and leervis. Other fish frequently caught from the shore as well as boats are galjoen, john brown, silver fish, red roman, red stumpnose, yellowtail, snoek, tunny and Cape salmon. Crayfish/Rock Lobster (*Jasus Lalandii*) and Perlemoen/Abalone (*Haliotis midae*) are popular amongst divers, but are also subject to stringent regulations. All the details are printed on the reverse side of permits. Phone the Sea Fisheries for more info, T3122609.

Western Cape

Golf *Hermanus Golf Club*, Main Rd, T3121954, F3122333, golfclub@hermanus.co.za Length: 5,798 m, standard 71, par 73. This is a beautiful course in the lee of the mountains with heather-lined fairways, some holes have sea views, visitors welcome. Green fees in the region of R75.

Hiking There is a 10 km cliff path marked around Walker Bay, with plenty of potential whale viewing spots, see page 239.

Horse riding *Klein Paradys*, Main Rd, Bot River, 15 min drive from Hermanus, T021-8597000. Trail, picnic and beach rides.

Paragliding From Rotary Way at the west end of town.

Sailing Kleinrivier Lagoon is a safe and popular venue, *Hermanus Yacht Club*, T3141420, is based here. Crowded in season. For the fit, a special way to spend the day is to take a rowing boat up the Klein River and enjoy the varied birdlife in the sanctuary.

Scuba diving *Scuba Africa*, New Harbour, T3162362, T083-7318235 (mob), scubaafrica@hotmail.com Equipment hire, dive courses and daily organized dives.

In addition to some coral reef and kelp forest dives, there are 3 stimulating wreck dives between here and Arniston. In the Walker Bay, the most rewarding dives close to the shore are at *Tamatiebank*, which is also recommended for snorkelling and *The Haksteen*, a pinnacle with steep drop-offs, 26 m. A short boat trip from the new harbour is *Whale Rock*, or *Table Top*. Conditions are quite calm, maximum depth is 40 m. Expect to see seafans and corals. There are also a few companies offering great white shark cave dives. These are based in Gansbaai. *Shark Lady*, T028-3123287, T083-7468985 (mob); *White Shark Adventures*, 13 Main Rd, Gansbaai, T028-3841380, www.whitesharkdiving.com **NB** From the high-tide mark to 500 m out to sea is a Marine Reserve. No marine animals may be collected or disturbed. **Warning** Do not attempt to dive when whales are in the bay. If you come within 300 m of a whale, either in a boat or the water, there are heavy fines, and overseas visitors will be deported. Enjoy them from the cliff vantage points.

Swimming On a calm summer day Walker Bay looks cool and inviting from the cliff paths, however, it has its dangers. There are strong undercurrents, look out for warnings and advice, especially at the neap and spring tides. During the holidays all the popular swimming beaches have life guards on duty, don't swim alone in isolated coves. There are several **tidal pools** which offer safe bathing for children and a fun place to snorkel for the first time. Below the *Marine Hotel* is the **Marine Tidal Pool** (*Bietang se Baaigat*), this always has plenty of sealife and fish. Along Westcliff Rd is a smaller pool known as **Fick's Pool**. This is a sheltered spot and has the bonus of a sandy bottom. There are toilets and changing rooms close by. Out of town there is a tidal pool at the **Onrus River** campsite which is open to day visitors.

Tour operators *Coastal Kayak Trails*, T341-0405, various routes available, guided kayak tours. *Dyer Island Cruises*, T3841266, boat trips to Dyer Island. *Southern Right Charters*, T082-3530550 (mob), boat-based whale watching. *Walker Bay Adventures*, just out of town towards Gansbaai at Prawn Flats, T3140925, kwanzyl@netdial.co.za All types of boats for hire, canoes, rowing boats, pedaloes, plus fishing equipment. Daily cruises on the lagoon, weather permitting, for larger groups. The ever-popular sundowner cruise is also on offer.

Transport **Local Bicycle hire**: *Hermanus Cycles*, T3132052. **Car hire**: Avis, Eastcliff Service Station, 251 Main Rd, T3123704. **Taxi**: Grab-a-Cab, 17 Long St, T3121388.

Road 120 km from Cape Town (via N2). **Bus**: Despite being a very popular destination, none of the three major coach companies runs a service via Hermanus. One of the easiest ways to visit, if you don't have a car, is to travel on the *Baz Bus* from Cape Town to the *Bot River Hotel* on the N2. From here you can arrange to be collected by your hosts for the nights. Some B&Bs and guesthouses may expect you to stay for a minimum of 2 nights if you have been collected privately, discuss in advance to avoid any misunderstandings. *Splash*, T3164004, Mon-Fri twice daily car service to **Cape Town**.

Directory **Banks** *Boland Bank*, 52 Main Rd, T3121156; *Standard Bank*, 99 Main Rd, T3123630; *ABSA*, 67 Main Rd, T3122180. **Internet** *Hermanus Internet Café*, Waterkant Centre, T3130277. **Medical**

services Chemist: *Alex Grant Pharmacy*, 66 Main Rd, T3121229 and 145 Main Rd, after hours: T3124039, emergency hours and Sun 1000-1200, 1830-1930. **Private Hospital**: T3130168.

East from Hermanus

Follow the R43 east out of town for Stanford and the **Walker Bay Nature Reserve**. Driving out of Hermanus to the east you pass through the suburb known as **Voëlklip**. Be wary of traffic police along the straight stretch, this is a favourite spot for speeding. If you are planning on visiting the Walker Bay Nature Reserve you must collect your entry permit here in Voëlklip. The office is on the corner of 7th Street and 17th Avenue. ■ *Mon-Fri between 0800-1600 only, T3140062.*

Green's on the Square, T3141048, is a good restaurant overlooking the lagoon. It is very popular in the evenings and you should book a table during school holidays.

When the road reaches a T-junction the route to the left leads back up to **Caledon** via the **Akkedisberg Pass**. This is also the quickest route, by surfaced road, to cut across the Overberg region to **Bredasdorp**, **Cape Agulhas** and the **De Hoop Nature Reserve**. Take a right turn for **Stanford** and **Gansbaai**.

Stanford

Western Cape

Stanford, a peaceful Victorian village set inland from the Atlantic, has in recent years become a popular centre with artists and craftsmen. It is an attractive spot, with some well-restored Victorian thatched cottages and a beautiful setting right on the Klein River. This is also the nearest village to the small **Salmonsdam Nature Reserve** (see next page).

Phone code: 028
(NB Always use 3-figure prefix)
Colour map 6, grid B5

The **Stanford Tourism Bureau** is next to the library in Queen Victoria Street. T/F3410340, stanfordinfo@overberg.co.za It is a helpful office which may well encourage you to spend a few extra days in the area. For information on the **Agulhas National Park** (see page 252), contact the park manager, T4356225, F4356225.

Sights

The **Birkenhead Micro-Brewery** is just out of the village off the R326 to Caledon. The first beer was served here in September 1998, and already there is tremendous local demand. The Birkenhead Premium Lager can only be bought from a few outlets in the Stanford area. It is a delicious slow-brewed beer using rich malted two-rowed barley and aromatic Hallertau and Saaz hop cones. Many of the ingredients are grown on the site and you can take a tour of the hop garden before going inside the modern buildings. There is also a fine restaurant on the site. ■ *Daily tours, 1000-1600. Lunches served, 1100-1500. Pub open, daily 1100-1900, T3410183.*

Sleeping
Price codes: see inside front cover

Be wary of baboons around the village accommodation

B *Stanford House*, 20 Queen Victoria St, T3410300, F3410522, www.stanfordhouse.co.za 20 double rooms housed in beautiful restored Victorian cottages, restaurant, bar serves pub lunches, pleasant garden with swimming pool, conference centre. **B-C** *Springfontein*, T/F3410651. 3 comfortable self-catering cottages on a working farm 3 km from Stanford. *Slope Cottage*, access by 4-wheel drive, is a private luxury cottage hidden away in the limestone fynbos, sleeps up to 6, 1 bathroom, gas cooker, no electricity, braai; *Milkwood Cottage*, 2 bedrooms, bathroom, lounge, open plan kitchen, private veranda, log fireplace; *Fisherman's Cottage*, a secluded thatched cottage, single bedroom, original beamed ceiling, bathroom, kitchen. **C** *Old Stanford Inn*, Queen Victoria St, T3410710, F3410218, carson@netactive.co.za County hotel, 8 double rooms with en suite bathrooms, satellite TV, lounge, good restaurant, popular pub, garden terrace with shade provided by an old willow tree. **C** *Fairhill*, off the R43 to Gansbaai, T/F3410230. A private country house converted into a fine guesthouse. 5 double rooms, en suite bathrooms. Bookings need to be made in advance, rates include breakfast. Good service and helpful advice about the sights of the area. **C** *Galashiels*, 10 King St, T3410181, F3410182. A family run guesthouse and conference centre, 5 double rooms, en suite bathrooms, bar, evening meals on request, peaceful mature garden. Recommended, although pricey when compared with similar B&Bs. Self-catering option represents much better value. **C-D** *River Cottages*, 5 Shortmarket St, T3410001, lawsonl@netactive.co.za Set of cottages on Klein river, range of 2-5 bedrooms, fireplaces, leafy gardens, great views.

Eating *Blue Gum Estate*, on R326, T3410116, www.bluegum.co.za Smart restaurant open for lunch, plus evening meals on Fri and Sat, meals served on terrace, cosy pub, set in ground of luxurious country estate. *Old Cowshed*, just outside Stanford off the Hermanus road, T3410287. The best restaurant in the area away from Hermanus. Open for lunch and dinner daily except Sun. Probably your best option for an evening meal if you are staying at a B&B. *Stanhope Pub*, Matilda May St, follow the R43 towards Gansbaai, T3410536. Well worth a visit to sample the locally brewed beer in the surroundings of a proper pub. Pub lunches and a takeaway menu are available. *Stanford House*, corner of Church and Queen Victoria streets, T3410300. Local family restaurant, check out the buffet on Fri evenings for an excellent value feast, good reports from travellers. *Stanford Tea Garden*, off the R43 to Gansbaai, T3410400. Light lunches, tea, coffee and snacks throughout the day. Served in a nice garden when the weather is fine.

Salmonsdam Nature Reserve This small reserve was established in 1962 and covers an area of 834 ha of the mountains which form part of the catchment area for the Paardenberg River. The main attraction here is the opportunity to view how the Overberg region would have appeared before much of the region was cleared by farmers. As you either drive or walk up to the main viewpoint, Ravenshill, you pass by several deep, lush valleys which retain a number of indigenous trees. An added attraction is several waterfalls, best viewed after the rains.

Ins and outs The reserve is 33 km from Hermanus and 16 km from Stanford. It can easily be visited as a day trip from either of these towns. From Hermanus, follow the R43 to Stanford. On reaching Stanford, turn right on to the R326. A few km up this road turn right on to a gravel road. The reserve is clearly signposted.

Reserve information Open to day visitors from 0700-1800. The reserve is managed by Cape Nature Conservation. There are 3 basic cabins and a campsite with 6 stands. The cabins are only fitted out with mattresses, a gas stove and a fridge. You must provide all your own bedding, cooking utensils and food. The nearest shop is in Stanford. The wash block has hot water, but there is no electricity. For further information contact: The Manager, Walker Bay Nature Reserve, Private Bag X13, Hermanus 7200. T028-3140062, F3141814.

Landscape and wildlife There are three distinct vegetation zones to look out for, each of which hosts different bird species. The high areas are covered with mountain fynbos – disas, waboom and ground proteas. Around the campsite and in the low-lying, flooded vleis are reeds, water heath and fountain bush. Between the high and low areas, stands of lush indigenous forest fill the kloofs formed by streams running off the mountains. These forested areas are the most rewarding parts to walk in – three short trails start behind the camping area. Look out for small antelope such as steenbok, grey duiker, grey rhebuck, klipspringer and bontebok.

Gansbaai

Phone code: 028
(NB Always use 3-figure prefix)
Colour map 6, grid C5

The history of this popular fishing centre dates back to 120 years ago when a local youth from Hermanus decided to make his home here. The story goes that in 1881 Johannes Cornelis Wessels walked across the sand dunes between Stanford and Gansgat. He found the fishing to be very good and the natural cove provided a safe and sheltered landing spot for the small fishing vessels in use at the time.

The bay was named by fishermen who used the bay to protect themselves against large storms. The name *gansgat* refers to the colony of Egyptian geese, *kolganse*, which used to nest in the reeds which surrounded a natural spring in the bay. These days the village is a prosperous fishing harbour with a modern deep water wharf and several fish canning factories. It has, however, managed to retain the character of a small community with strong ties with the tourist industry. A number of Capetonians have second houses along this coast, and although they are not used that much they do provide seasonal employment.

Gansbaai Tourism Bureau is on the corner of Berg and Main streets, T3841439, F3840955, gansbaaiinfo@telkomsa.net Ask here for details of a couple of good value guest farms just out of town. The office also produces some good maps of the coastline showing the routes of all the walks in the area.

The **fishing harbour** is still very active, with trawlers unloading their catch at the sardine and fish meal factory. There are a number of shops selling fresh seafood in the centre of town.

Sights

Like Hermanus, at the other end of Walker Bay, there are some excellent vantage points for **whale watching**. A couple of kilometres up the coast at De Kelders (see below) are some tall cliffs which quickly give way to a large white sand beach.

The southern right whales come close inshore to the sheltered deep waters to calve between June and November each year

The local lighthouse is 9 km away at **Danger Point**. In May 1852 the **HMS Birkenhead** sunk here with the loss of 443 lives, an event which is reconstructed every year by local actors. It took the sinking of a further 20 ships before a lighthouse came into operation in 1895.

Starting from the Gansbaai camping site is a 7-km **Coastal Walk**, reaching as far as Klipgat at the southern end of the Walker Bay Nature Reserve. This walk is known as the *Duiwelsgat Trail*, and can be completed in three hours. Along the route you will pass **Stanford's Cove**, a popular picnic spot which is also safe for swimming. A little further on is the **De Kelders** cave complex, and a blow hole known locally as **Duiwelsgat**. A small wall surrounds Duiwelsgat to stop animals from falling to a certain death. The trail ends by more caves which were recently explored by the archaeological unit of the Cape Town Museum, which found considerable evidence of ancient human habitation. The De Kelders sea cave is linked to a maze of limestone tunnels, but take care as it's easy to get lost. Follow local advice and take a guide if you are in doubt.

Dyer Island is named after Samson Dyer, a black American who lived on the island collecting guano around 1806. Today the island is an important breeding spot for **African penguins**. On nearby **Geyser Island** there is a breeding seal population. The presence of the seals attract the endangered **great white shark**.

One of the most popular activities here is cage diving to view **great white sharks**. In the last few years, several companies have sprung up offering trips to view the sharks, and those with a diving certificate can view them from an underwater cage. This has become one of South Africa's booming tourist industries and viewing a great white at such close quarters is certainly an amazing experience. However, more recently **conservationists** have pointed out that these trips can be harmful to the sharks. Firstly, the tour companies feed the sharks and dropping meat and blood into the water to attract them clearly interferes with their natural feeding patterns. Secondly, great whites are thought to be starting to equate humans with food (contrary to popular belief, we do not feature on their usual menu), thus increasing the risk of attacks. If you are considering viewing the sharks off Dyer Island (see below), check which is currently the best company running trips with the tourist office – try to choose one which is partaking in conservation and research into the species.

Great white shark viewing

There are two seasons for viewing: the low season, from October through to mid-January; and the high season. During the low season, operators reckon the probability of viewing a shark is about eight days out of ten. The boats used are 8 m by 3 m motorized catamarans. Trips depart at dawn and last for about 7 hours. At the end of the trip a video of the outing is shown at a guesthouse while a home cooked lunch is served. The total cost is in the region of R1000 per person, including use of all diving equipment.

Recommended operator *White Shark Adventures*, member WHISPRA (White Shark Preservation Association), Gansbaai, T3841380, T082-8226920 (mob), www.whitesharkdiving.com Supports marine research at Stellenbosch University. Their boat, *Master of Happiness*, looks

Western Cape

small and the cage even smaller, but both are within safety standards and adequate for shark viewing. Jackie is full of entertaining shark tales, has an obvious passion for these creatures and takes great pleasure in educating others. An enlightening and thrilling day out for divers and non-divers. Also own *Great White Backpackers* (see below).

Sleeping
Price codes:
see inside front cover

B-C *Klein Paradijs Guest Farm*, follow the main road south out of Gansbaai, direction Pearly Beach, 21 km, T3819760, F3819803, www.kleinparadijs.co.za A pleasant farm just inland from the beautiful white sand beach. There is also a small restaurant popular with people staying at the caravan site. **C** *Marine Guest House*, Kleinbaai, 4 km south of Gansbaai off the road to Pearly Beach, T3840641. 2 double rooms with en suite bathrooms, close to the harbour, B&B or self-catering, popular during holidays. **C** *Sea View*, 12 Market St, Gansbaai, T3840211. Small hotel in the centre of the village, 12 rooms, restaurant, bar, good value rate for double, B&B. **D** *Birkenhead Lodge*, Kleinbaai, 4 km south of Gansbaai on the other side of the headland, T3840253. Family run B&B, close to the golf course and tidal pool. **D** *De Kelders*, De Kelders, T3840045, T082-8084588 (mob), 3 km up Walker Bay from Gansbaai. B&B only, 7 rooms, some with en suite bathroom, swimming pool. The house is perched high up on the cliff, this is the perfect location for whale watching in the bay between Jun and Nov. **E-F** *Uilenkraalsmond Caravan Park*, T3880200, 5 km along the coast, south towards Pearly Beach. A large, modern campsite with 40 self-catering family chalets, wash blocks, grassy, limited shade, sea breeze can be a problem at times. Plenty of facilities for children, supertube, trampoline, crazy golf, swimming in the lagoon. Very busy during local school holidays, but for the rest of the year it is quiet. **F** *Great White Backpackers*, 124 Cliff St, De Kelders, T3841380, www.whitesharkdiving.com Main selling point is the good-value great white cage dives organized here. Comfortable backpackers with dorms, double rooms and camping, kitchen, free breakfast, meals on request. Package deals include transport to and from Cape Town, all meals, 1 night's accommodation and a shark dive.

Eating *Ciro's*, Franken St, T3841106. Popular pub in a historic cottage, great seafood and steaks. Recommended. *Grootbos*, on private nature reserve just outside Gansbaai (see below), T3840381. Excellent restaurant, set menu, specializes in seafood, you can taste 3 wines before your meal. Good service. In fine weather meals are served on terrace overlooking the bay. Recommended. Booking essential. *Klein Paradjis*, 21 km from Gansbaai at Pearly Beach, T3819760. Good quality home cooking made with fresh ingredients grown on the farm. Can get quite busy when the accommodation is full. *Tolbos Bistro*, 34 Main Rd, T3841560. Local coffee shop serving light lunches, with delicious breads. Also acts as an art gallery and curio shop.

Grootbos
Nature Reserve

This is a private nature reserve and luxury camp, covering over 1000 ha of fynbos-clad hills. The reserve lies inland from Gansbaai, with superb views of Walker Bay and the surrounding countryside. It is a beautiful area, and a great chance to spend some time in relative wilderness. As well as fynbos, there are milkwood forests and a few ponds which attract plenty of birdlife. Activities available include horse riding and mountain biking trails through the hills, 3-hour walks with nature guides, boat trips to Deyer Island, again with a nature guide, self-guided walks and trips to the De Kelders caves. There is also a pool and gardens, and special bonuses such as a telescope that is brought out on clear nights; guides point out different constellations and planets. The reserve is highly recommended for an interesting and relaxing few days in fynbos country.

Ins and outs The reserve is 12 km from Stanford. From Hermanus, follow the R43 through Stanford and continue for 13 km. Grootbos is clearly signposted on the left.

Sleeping and eating Accommodation (L1) is in individual luxury cottages, either 1 or 2 bedrooms, en suite bathrooms, open plan kitchen, TV with M-Net, terrace overlooking the bay. There is an excellent restaurant, bar and pool. Friendly and impeccable service. Highly recommended. For more information, contact Michael and Tertius Lutzeyer, T028-3840381, www.grootbos.com

From Gansbaai a minor road continues southeast along the coast, passing through the small resorts of Kleinbaai, Franskraal, Pearly Beach and on to the Die Dam at Sandbaai. Few visitors venture this far into the Overberg – it is the area's relative isolation that is much of its appeal. From Sandbaai, the road turns inland and cuts across wild countryside that remains virtually untouched. During the spring months the fields are full of wild flowers, and throughout the year the area is rich in varieties of fynbos. Follow the signs for Wolvengat, formerly known as Viljoenshof, and continue on to Elim.

South from Gansbaai

Founded by German missionaries in 1824, this is one of the best-known Moravian mission stations in South Africa. The settlement is named from Exodus 15:27, after the spot where the Israelites rested after crossing the Red Sea. To live here you must be a member of the local Moravian church and your livelihood must come from the earth. A new industry has emerged in recent years, based upon two long-lasting species of wild flower – helipterum and helichrysum – which are now successful export crops. Once dried, they are very popular for wreaths in Germany, keeping the historical connections alive today.

Elim
Phone code: 028
(NB Always use 3-figure prefix)
Colour map 6, grid B5

The whole village has been declared a National Monument, so it is not surprising that there is a variety of quaint old buildings still standing and in use. One attraction is a restored **watermill** dating from 1833. It has a huge Burmese teak wheel, which replaced the stone wheels. It was reopened in 1990 to produce wholewheat flour. Two other old buildings worth looking out for are the **parsonage**, and the original **mission church**, which has a thatched roof. If you are in the area in August, a 'love' feast is held at the church.

Although Elim is an important centre, it has not been developed as a tourist destination, and some visitors are disappointed after their steady drive along empty gravel roads. To get the most out of a visit, it is advisable to contact the tourist bureau (see below) in advance and arrange to have a guide meet you and show you around the village. The only accommodation available is in the area in private homes. During the day the *Old Mill Tea Room* serves breakfast and light lunches. Take care when on the gravel roads after the rains. **Tourist information** is available at the *Elim Tourist Bureau*, in the Old Mill behind the church at the top end of the main street; T4821806, F4821750. The office is open Monday-Friday, 0800-1630 and Saturday, 0800-1200.

Bredasdorp

This is South Africa's first *dorp*, founded in 1837 by Michiel van Breda, an important local figure. From his farm, Zoetendalsvlei, he played an active role in the development of the Merino sheep industry throughout South Africa and was the first Mayor of Cape Town in 1840. The old farmstead can be visited by prior arrangement.

Phone code: 028
(NB Always use 3-figure prefix)
Colour map 6, grid B6

There are two **tourist offices** in town, the local publicity association as well as the very helpful, regional tourist office, *Suidpunt Tourism Bureau*, on Dr Jansen Street, T4242584, F4242731, suidpunt@brd.dorea.co.za Open Monday-Friday 0800-1700, Saturday 0900-1300. Internet access is available during office hours. Ask here about the opportunities to visit local sheep farms between April and October.

Despite its age, there is little to keep you in town for long. Worth a peek is the **Shipwreck Museum** on Independent Street. It houses a collection of odd bits and pieces salvaged from along the coast, 24 km away. The whole display is greatly enhanced by the sound effects. In the Shipwreck Hall you hear the distinct shrieks of seagulls and the thunderous sound of waves on a stormy night. Four wrecks are featured: the *Queen of the Thames*, *HMS Birkenhead*, the *Oriental Pioneer* and *HMS Arniston*. In the Coach House is a collection of items relating to the sea, including some unusual pieces of ship's furniture. ■ *Mon-Fri 0900-1645, Sat 0900-1445.*

On the outskirts of town at the very end of the Van Riebeeck Road is the **Bredasdorp Mountain Reserve**. This is a mix of 800 ha of fynbos vegetation plus

Sights

Western Cape

a small cultivated wildflower garden. There are plenty of footpaths criss-crossing the reserve with a number of rest shelters. The best time to visit is from mid-September onwards when the wild flowers are in bloom. A little further out of town on the road to Cape Agulhas is a segment of fence erected in 1837 as part of the earliest attempts to save the Bontebok from extinction.

Sleeping & eating **C** *Anlou*, 32 Unie St, T4242528. Self-catering garden flat with 4 beds, TV. **C** *Firlane Guesthouse*, 5 Fir Lane, T/F4242808. 4 double rooms, 2 with en suite bathroom, comfortable restored family home, evening meals available. Also has a 'wellness centre' on site. **C** *Standard*, 31 Long St, T/F4241140. 30 rooms, restaurant, old town hotel, usually very busy, can get noisy especially when it holds discos. **C** *Victoria*, 10 Church St, T4241159. 30 rooms, en suite bathroom, TV, restaurant, bar, friendly staff, nice rooms, breakfast but no other meals. **C-D** *Prinskraal*, T4242076. Farmhouse rooms, self-catering or B&B. **D** *Earl of Clarendon*, corner of Dirkie Uys and Clarendon streets, T4251420. Historical building with excellent rooms, antiques and Victorian-style claw-foot bath. Also has a restaurant and curio shop. Recommended. **E** *Suikerbossie Caravan Park*, T4251919. Camping ground with good value self-catering chalets. For meals, try the *Blue Parrot*, on Clarendon St. Reliable food and convenient setting. *Lemon Tree*, Dirkie Uys St, opposite Tourist Information, superb homemade cheesecake. Recommended. *Sports Bar*, Dirkie Uys St, opposite. Steaks and burgers, range of beers, sports screened on TVs.

South from Bredasdorp Driving south on the R319 for a further 36 km takes you to the southernmost tip of Africa, **Cape Agulhas**. Before the coast, the road runs close to some large marshes (*vleis*): Karsrivier and Soetendals. These are important breeding grounds for aquatic birds, and there is a good chance of seeing flamingos. At the coast the road passes through **Struisbaai** before ending at a lighthouse and some retirement homes. A second road going south from Bredasdorp, the R316, ends at Waenhuiskrans.

De Hoop Nature Reserve

Colour map 6, grid B6 This is an important coastal reserve which extends 5 km out to sea protecting the shoreline and marine life. It is divided into two sectors. The **western region** is for hiking, game viewing and birdwatching while the **eastern section** is for mountain biking.

The reserve covers an exceptionally varied and rich environment – seven different ecosystems are found within the 36,000-ha reserve. De Hoop is a large freshwater vlei surrounded by marshlands which stretch for 15 km. The coastline is a mix of sandy beaches and rocky headlands and cliffs with wave-cut platforms. A little further inland are giant sand dunes, some as high as 90 m, and behind these are limestone hills and the Potberg Mountains. The higher ground is clearly divided by kloofs covered with indigenous vegetation. It has been estimated that over 1,500 plant species grow here, of which 34 are endemic to the reserve, including rare lowland fynbos species. Details of the rarer plants are displayed at the environmental education centres and the reserve offices at De Hoop and Potberg.

Ins & outs **Getting there** Coming from Bredasdorp, follow the R319 towards Swellendam. After 8 km is a signposted right turn on to a gravel road. After 40 km you reach Ouplaas – take a right for the western section or continue straight on for another 10 km for the entrance to the eastern section. The office and car park are at Potberg. Approaching from the N2, the quickest route is to take the Witsand (see also page 263) turning 12 km east of Swellendam. After 23 km turn right for Malgas and then follow the signs. Both entrances are about 20 km from Malgas.

Information The reserve gates are open from 0700-1800 (1900 on Fri). Overnight visitors must check in at the De Hoop office before it closes at 1600. At the weekend it is only open between 1300-1400. There is a small entrance fee per person/vehicle. An additional cycling fee per person/day applies if you intend to use the five mountain bike trails in the eastern sector. Cycling on the service tracks within the western sector is free. In the eastern sector cars are left at the Potberg Environmental Education Centre. It is 11 km from here to the accommodation at

Cupidoskraal. Allow about 1 hr with a loaded bike. There are information displays at De Hoop and Potberg offices introducing the visitor to the environment and the diversity of species to be found in the reserve. The closest shops and petrol are in Ouplaas, 15 km from the De Hoop office. All advance enquiries are dealt with by The Manager, De Hoop Nature Reserve, Private Bag X16, 7280, Bredasdorp, T028-5421126, F5421247, dehoopinfo@sdm.dorea.co.za

Climate The region enjoys a Mediterranean climate with mild winters and warm summers. Aug is the wettest month, with some morning fogs.

Wildlife

With such a variety of terrain crammed into a relatively small area, the region supports a diverse range of wildlife. Over 250 species of birds have been recorded here, while elusive leopard, bontebok and Cape mountain zebra roam around, along with the more common eland, grey rhebok, baboon and klipspringer. The last known breeding colony of the Cape vulture in the southwestern Cape is close to Potberg, and you may glimpse them circling high in the skies. The **Windheok Cave** is home to a large colony of bats which have attracted their fare share of research interest. Other rare species that you might see include black oystercatchers, which forage amongst the dunes. Finally, there is a chance of seeing **southern right whales**, which calve in the shallow waters and can be seen between July and December (see page 240). Although the whales found here are often in larger concentrations than elsewhere, they are difficult to see since they remain beyond the breakers.

Hiking & mountain biking

The most exciting aspect of the De Hoop Nature Reserve is the series of mountain bike trails within the eastern sector of the reserve. The remainder of the reserve is open for self guided hiking and there is a 20 km circular drive for vehicles. Driving gives you the opportunity to appreciate quickly the diversity of the landscape and explore all corners, although it can detract from viewing wildlife – a quieter approach on foot is more rewarding.

Hiking Trails have been designed for all levels of fitness and with different interests in mind. There are several one-day walks close to the camps and car parks and a much longer five-day circuit along the coast. Simple overnight huts are found at suitable intervals. This trail needs to be booked at the office. The **Vlei Trail** follows the banks of the De Hoop Vlei where you'll find masses of waterbirds.

Mountain Biking The trails vary in difficulty – the toughest are both rough and undulating and are sufficient to satisfy the challenge of experienced cyclists. The trails are limited to 12 cyclists per day. There are five named routes, none of which are circular. All take you across the dunes to a different point along the coast. There are a few rock pools at the end of each trail which are fun to explore. The figures quoted here after the trail name refers to the furthest point from the overnight hut: Cupidoskraal. Hamerkop (6 km), Lekkerwater (7 km), Noetzie (13 km), Stilgat (12 km) and Vaalkrans (12 km). The Stilgat route is probably the most difficult and is very rocky and steep in parts. The only drinking water available is by the overnight hut, so make sure you carry enough for each day. Beware of dehydration and cramp when cycling in the heat. Always carry a rudimentary first aid kit; you will quickly appreciate how isolated you are in the reserve.

The sea, with its strong currents, is very dangerous to swim in. Consult the reserve office for advice on relatively safe spots

Sleeping

Price codes: see inside front cover

Western sector E-F *Cottages and camping*, 11 self-catering cottages with fridge and stove. Some have bedding, but it's a good idea to bring your own, as well as kitchen utensils. The setting is perfect, right on the edge of the vlei. The campsite has basic facilities, also with views over the vlei and set under some milkwood trees. There are no electric points. Firewood is available from the De Hoop office. The *Vlei Trail* starts in the camp and two paths plot a route around the freshwater lake.

A variety of accommodation is available at different sites within the reserve. All are managed by Cape Nature Conservation

Eastern sector E *Cupidoskraal*, a restored farmhouse now acts as the trail hut. 12 beds, storage space for bikes, gas stove, electric light, fireplace, pots and pans provided, but bring food and bedding. Firewood is available. Drinking water is collected in rain tanks. There is a dam 300 m away which is suitable for swimming. Be careful not to pollute the water since it is also a drinking source.

Western Cape

Western Cape

Malgas
Colour map 6, grid B6

This small settlement on the banks of the Breede River was a vital point in the transport route in the mid-19th century of the famous Overberg tycoon, **Joseph Barry**. Until the roads east from Cape Town were improved and the many mountain passes negotiated, the majority of goods were brought into the Overberg region through Malgas. The Barry family had a 158 ton vessel, *Kadie*, especially built to transfer goods from Cape Town to Port Beaufort. From here the cargo was transferred to river boats and taken upstream as far as Malgas, before the final stage of transportation was completed by ox wagon. Today the settlement is famous for being the last manually operated pont in South Africa. Cars are carried across the river during daylight hours. Allow a few extra minutes to look around the fine church on the west bank built in 1856 by the Barry family.

Struisbaai
Phone code: 028
(NB Always use 3-figure prefix)
Colour map 6, grid C6

This small, attractive fishing village has good spear-fishing and safe swimming in the bay, and a 14 km long white sand beach. The principal attraction is nearby **Cape Agulhas**. This is the **southernmost point in Africa**, but it is rather disappointing and lacks the grandeur one might hope for. Aside from the lighthouse, the surroundings are rather dull, although quite a bit of money seems to be flooding in with a number of new holiday homes. The beach is very rocky, but excellent for fishing.

The **lighthouse** was originally built in 1848 and lies 1 km east of the tip of Africa. It was modelled on the Egyptian Pharaoh's light in Alexandria. It now houses a tearoom and a small museum. If you climb up the stairs there are good views over the unforgiving ocean which has claimed many ships and lives. ■ *Tue-Fri, 0900-1645, Sat and Sun, 1000-1300, closed Mon.* In theory this is where the warm waters of the Indian Ocean meet the cooler waters of the Atlantic Ocean. Research has shown the warm waters to reach as far west as Cape Point.

Price codes:
see inside front cover

Sleeping and eating **B-C** *Struisbaai*, 4 Minnetoka, T4356625. Comfortable small hotel with 21 rondavels, restaurant. **D** *St Mungo B&B*, 155 Marine Drive, T4356136. Small B&B, pleasant furnishings, 2 rooms with en suite bathroom, TV with M-Net, non-smoking. Evening meals available on request. Views of the ocean. **E-F** *Agulhas Caravan Park*, Main Rd, T4356820. 16 self-catering chalets and camping, good shade, laundry, shop and café in walking distance, overlooks the sea, short walk to lighthouse. All ablution facilities were modernized recently. In Struisbaai itself there is a small hotel plus a few guesthouses. For meals, try the restaurant in the *Struisbaai Hotel*, or the *Beachcomber*, on Minnetokka St. The latter has the usual menu of fresh seafood and steaks.

Agulhas National Park
Colour map 6, grid C6

This is one of South Africa's newest national parks, encompassing a large area of coastland centred around Cape Agulhas. It was proclaimed to help protect the rugged coastline and the immediate hinterland, known as the Agulhas Plain, which forms the southernmost area of Africa. The Agulhas Plain is home to almost 2,000 species of indigenous plants, of which 100 are endemic to the area. A large part of the area is taken up by a variety of wetlands which attract more than 21,000 migrant and resident birds annually. The park also protects a couple of islands found just off shore which are home to seals and seabirds, as well as the whales which frequent this part of the coastline in spring and early summer. Finally, the area is regarded important in archaeological terms, with several ancient habitation sites already having been discovered. At present, there are limited tourist facilities in the park (a couple of toilets and little else), but there are plans to build a museum and layout nature trails along the coastline.

Ins and outs The quickest route from Cape Town (230 km) is to take the N2 highway as far as Caledon and then turn off on to the R406 for Bredasdorp. From Bredasdorp follow the signs for either Struisbaai or L'Agulhas. At present these are the 2 closest settlements to the park with accommodation facilities. For information on the latest developments, contact the Manager, PO Box 120, L'Agulhas, T/F028-4356222.

This tranquil fishing village, which is rather oddly known by two names – Waenhuiskrans and Arniston – is made up of a jumble of attractive whitewashed, thatched cottages. What were once the homes of poor fishermen are today smart, renovated holiday homes. Just to the west of the village is **Waenhuiskrans Cave**, a huge cavern overlooking the sea which can be explored at low tide. The cavern goes back into the cliffs and is named after the ox wagons which it once held.

The town's other name is derived from the wreck of the *Arniston* (1815), which lies about 1 km from the slipway. Items salvaged from the wreck are on display in the Bredasdorp Shipwreck museum. The wreck can be dived, but there is a heavy swell. There is a monument to the deceased in the town's campsite; only six of the 378 passengers survived. There are two beaches, **Slipway** in front of the *Arniston Hotel*, and **Bikini Beach**. The waters are warm and startlingly blue, with some good snorkelling. At low tide a couple of rock pools are exposed on Bikini beach, fun for children to explore. A few shops in the village stock the basics for self-catering. You can only reach here in your own vehicle or by hitching; there is no public transport.

Waenhuiskrans (Arniston)
Phone code: 028
(NB Always use 3-figure prefix)
Colour map 6, grid C6

This pleasant small reserve is centred around the mouth of the Heuningnes River, 26 km south of Bredasdorp. Two former farms were proclaimed as a nature reserve in 1986. About 10 km of the shoreline is also protected, although most of the land remains inaccessible to the public. A 6.7 km hike known as the Sterna Trail starts from the office, following the beach for several kilometres. Close to the river mouth you may see the shipwreck *Die-Maggie*. This can only be seen during the winter months when storms wash away all the debris. The main attraction for birdwatchers is the chance to see the rare damara tern (*Sterna balaenarum*), easily confused with the little tern which has a yellow tip to the bill, as well as the chance of viewing one of South Africa's most threatened coastal birds, the African black oystercatcher.

De Mond Nature Reserve
Colour map 6, grid C6
The best time to visit is Oct-Mar

Ins and outs The gates are open daily from 0700 to 1600. Vehicles are not allowed in the reserve. There is a car park next to the office by the main gate from where the Sterna trail begins. This is an easy path to follow and winds through a range of different coastal habitats, including dune forest, stabilized dunes, riverine vegetation and some salt marshes. Further information can be obtained from: The Manager, De Mond Nature Reserve, Private Bag X16, Bredasdorp 7280, T028-4242170, F4253708. Entry permits are issued in Bredasdorp; check at the local information office.

Sleeping **A-B** *Arniston*, Beach Rd, T4459000, F4459633, www.arnistonhotel.co.za An elegant seaside hotel, 30 rooms, thoughtfully decorated, but have small bathrooms, TV, sea-facing rooms more expensive, reception rooms have fireplaces and provide a restful contrast to the beach on blustery days. Good food served in a smart restaurant, swimming pool, sheltered garden. Recommended. **B** *Arniston Lodge*, 23 Main Rd, T4459175, lodge@arniston.co.za An appealing thatched cottage which blends in well with the traditional fishermen's cottages. 6 double rooms, 1 single room, upstairs rooms have plenty of character with thatch ceiling and views across the beach, sheltered swimming pool, lounge with log fireplace, B&B but evening meals can be arranged in advance, a welcome peaceful retreat, German spoken. Recommended. **B-C** *Arniston Seaside Cottages*, Huxham St, T4459772, F4459125, cottages@arniston-online.co.za 20 whitewashed thatched cottages, self-contained, log fireplaces, reed ceilings, pine furnishings, some with sea views from private balcony, compact luxury development set amongst the dunes, ideal for a long stay, cottages are serviced every day, all facilities close by, includes the chance to buy fresh fish from the boats as they land, these come highly recommended. **E** *Waenhuiskrans*, du Preez St, T4459620. Municipal caravan park, camping as well as 23 self-catering bungalows, all stands have electric points, limited privacy provided by hedges, tents not permitted during peak Christmas period, firewood sold at the camp. **E** *South of Africa Backpackers Resort*, T4459240, www.southofafrica.co.za A smart backpackers set in the wing of *Die Herberg Hotel*. More expensive than most backpackers, but correspondingly more comfortable. No dorms – singles, doubles and triples, some with own TV, kitchen, chill-out room, TV room,

Price codes: see inside front cover

Western Cape

breakfasts served in hotel restaurant and included in price, full access to hotel's facilities including indoor pool, gym, squash courts.

Eating *Die Waenhuis*, Arniston Centre, T4459797. A small restaurant with timber ceiling and a seaside theme. Good seafood dishes plus a selection of salads and steaks. *Herberg Restaurant*, Waenhuiskrans Rd, T4459240. Country cuisine, vegetarian menu.

The Overberg interior

Having climbed the spectacular **Sir Lowry's Pass**, the N2 highway cuts east across the interior of the Overberg towards Mossel Bay and George. The landscape is immediately very different on this side of the mountains – the road passes through serene forested hills before opening on to the endless dry, orange plains of the Overberg. To the north lie the Langeberg Mountains, their smooth foothills and sharp peaks providing a serene backdrop to the route. Most of the towns en route are quiet farming centres, and were some of the first areas settled by white farmers as they ventured east of Cape Town in search of new farmlands.

Most visitors choose to stick to the main road, and it is easy to pass quickly through the region without taking much in. If you are keen to get to the Garden Route, George can be reached in three hours, but there are several sights worth lingering over on the way. One centre worth a stopover is **Swellendam**, the third oldest town in the Cape. Nearby are a couple of nature reserves, and the town has some well-preserved examples of early Cape architecture.

Ten kilometres from Sir Lowry's Pass is a turning signposted Villersdorp, R321. This takes you back into the heart of the Winelands, or north to the Breede River Valley. A short loop takes you to the undistinguished twin towns of **Grabouw** and **Elgin**. Continuing east, the N2 crosses the Houhoek Pass where there is a famous watering hole, the *Houw Hoek Inn*, always worth a stop (see below). Also a short distance from Grabouw is a small flower reserve known as the **Kathleen Murray Reserve**. At Bot River is the turn-off for **Hermanus**. It is a further 23 km to the regional capital of the Overberg, **Caledon**.

Further local information is available from Elgin Valley Tourism, T021-8599030, F8599723

Sleeping & eating

B *Houw Hoek Inn*, off N2, T2849546, www.houwhoekinn.co.za The oldest licensed hotel in the country. 33 a/c rooms in an elegant country hotel, the oldest section of the ground floor dates from 1779, the upstairs was built in 1860. All the rooms have en suite bathrooms, the dining room is in a converted farm building, it is very popular at weekends when dinner dances are held. The gardens are dominated by large old oak and blue gum trees, swimming pool. **B** *Wildekrans Country House*, Houw Hoek Farm, T2849827. 6 rooms, 4 apartments, TV, non-smoking room, restaurant, swimming pool, wild farm gardens, national monument, quiet setting on a working farm. **C-D** *Mountain View*, T3593952. Family-run B&B. *Orchard Farm Stall*, Oudebrug Rd. Good quality simple light lunches and home cooking, also do breakfast. Several local farms have small stalls selling a variety of fresh fruit juices and other fruit products.

Caledon

*Phone code: 028
(NB Always use
3-figure prefix)
120 km from
Cape Town via N2
Colour map 6, grid B5*

The regional capital of the Overberg lies just off the N2 at the foot of the Swartberg Mountains. It is a typical rural town – small and quiet, with a couple of sights, but only really worth a couple of hours; it's best to press on to Swellendam for an overnight stay. The town is famous for its six naturally occurring **hot springs** which produce 800,000 litres per day. The water has a high ferrous carbonate content. Not surprisingly the first European settler, Ferdinandus Appel, sought to develop the springs. He was granted an 18-ha freehold, on the condition that he built baths and accommodation. Word of their healing powers spread quickly, and distinguished guests from the Dutch East India Company frequented the springs. At the turn of the century the Caledon Mineral Baths and Sanatorium was built to cash in fully on their popularity.

For 40 years they continued to be a popular draw until a fire destroyed the complex in 1946. It was only in 1990 that a new hotel, *The Caledon* (see Sleeping below), was built.

Today the prosperity of the town, and the region as a whole, is based on agriculture. Caledon was the centre of a major development in wool production with a new breed of sheep, the Merino.

For **tourist information** visit the *Caledon Tourist Bureau*, at 16 Constitution St, T2121511, T2141427. Open Monday-Friday, 0800-1300, 1400-1630; Saturday, 0900-1300. Ask here about tours open to local historic farms. The **regional tourist office**, *Cape Overberg Tourism Association*, on Church St, is worth visiting if you plan on staying in the area for a while. Open Monday-Friday 0800- 1630, T2141466, www.capeoverberg.org

Sights

Guided tours of the town start from the **museum**, at 14 Constitution Street. The displays are of local history and crafts. Across the road is a typical Victorian house with a working kitchen where bread is baked every few days. The main building was originally the Freemasons' Lodge. ■ *Mon-Fri 0800-1700, Sat 0900-1300. Small entrance fee. T2121511.* There is a **museum shop** in Donkin Square full of local farm produce and curios. ■ *Mon-Fri 0900-1300, 1400-1630, Sat 0900-1300.* **Mill Street** has a collection of historical buildings which have been declared national monuments – the walking tour introduces you to the more interesting ones. **Holy Trinity Church** on Prince Alfred Drive is a small, neat church dating from 1855. One other attraction in the town is the **Southern Associated Maltsters**, a large independent malt producer. Outings to local **wetlands** and the nearby **nature reserves** can be arranged for bird enthusiasts; contact the tourist office for details, T2121511. Look out for the endangered blue crane which is found in the area on open farmland. Due to their vulnerable status, an Overberg Crane Group was created in 1991 by Cape Nature Conservation to devise a protection programme.

Caledon Nature Reserve

This small reserve, 214 ha, is just on the edge of town. Since 1892 the annual wild flower show has been held in the grounds. Part of the reserve was turned into the **Victoria Wild Flower Garden** by Cecil Young and CW Meiring in 1927, local enthusiasts who had the foresight to protect the amazingly rich local flora. Of the 630 known species of *erica* in the world, over 200 grow in the Caledon district. This may not be everyone's cup of tea (56 ha of the reserve were converted into formal gardens with ponds, shaded paths and picnic spots) but for the botanist it is a unique attraction. Within the reserve there is a 10-km walk, the **Meiring Trail**, a good chance to appreciate the many species of fynbos and birds of the area. There is no shelter and hikers must bring all their drinking water. Allow up to five hours for the full circuit. A leaflet handed out at the publicity office has a simple map of the hiking trail. ■ *0700-1700.*

Sleeping & eating
Price codes:
see inside front cover

B *The Caledon Hotel & Spa*, Nerina St, 1 km out of town just off the N2, T2141271, F2141270, www.caledoncasino.co.za Unattractive modern complex based at the historical springs, with a flashy casino, 95 a/c rooms and a couple of restaurants, including *Ouma's Country Kitchen* restaurant and *Wheatlands* garden terrace for light meals. There is a pub with log fires, extensive gardens, 3 pools, a beauty clinic, mountain bikes for hire, full size snooker tables, 18-hole putting golf and the excellent Victorian hot spring baths enclosed by a pavilion. Most people come here for the brash casino. **D** *Painted Lady*, 3 Donkin St, T2122093. Old-style, homely guesthouse with 5 rooms, 1 with en suite bathroom, breakfast included, can be self-catering. **C-D** *Die Hoek Huys*, corner of Plein and Mill streets, T2121089. Attractive 2-storey building overlooking the main street, 9 en suite rooms, simple and comfortable, popular restaurant downstairs. Can be closed out of season so be sure to call ahead. **D** *Parklands*, 7 Mill St, T2122505, www.parklands.co.za Old-fashioned town hotel, en suite rooms, décor in slightly dubious taste, friendly staff, attached restaurant. *The Barn*, Plein St. Simple family restaurant on the main street, range of steaks plus pizza and pasta. *The Coffee Nook*, 16 Donkin St, T2122744. The oldest coffee shop in town, closed evenings. Local crafts also sold from here. *Die Hoek Huys*, in hotel of same name, popular local restaurant serving standard South African fare, some tables on the veranda outside.

Western Cape

Festivals To coincide with the annual bloom of wild flowers each spring, Caledon holds a festival which celebrates the diversity of the flowers and promotes further research and conservation. The *Wild Flower Festival* runs over the second weekend of **Sep**. It is worth a visit if you happen to be in the area, and is an excellent opportunity to see many of the plants which make up the Cape fynbos, including *protea*, *erica*, *gladioli* and *iridaceae*. Much of the region has been ploughed up, but most of these species can still be found in the valleys and higher up in the Riviersonderend Mountains and Kleinrivier Mountains. The principal display hall is in Hope Street, a short walk from the town museum. Rather more unusual is the *Beer and Bread Festival* held in **Mar**. A large marquee is put up near the Wild Flower garden and live music is laid on in the evenings. Plenty of good local farm produce.

Sports There is a 9-hole **golf** course open to visitors, T2121931. The Klein Swartberg is a popular venue for **mountain biking** and an annual rally is held here. Contact the tourist office for details.

Transport **Road Bus**: *Greyhound*, T021-4184312. Services depart from The Caledon Hotel and Spa. **Cape Town** (2 hrs): daily, 0725; **Durban** (24 hrs): daily, 2115; **Port Elizabeth** (9 hrs): daily, 2115. **Car**: continuing east from Caledon, the N2 passes through rolling wheat fields towards **Mossel Bay**. From Caledon you can also deviate inland to the villages of **Genadendal** and **McGregor**; the R406 makes a convenient loop. Alternatively take the R316 south towards **Bredasdorp** into the heart of Overberg country. The R319 rejoins the N2 just before **Swellendam**.

Genadendal

Phone code: 028
(NB Always use 3-figure prefix)
Colour map 6, grid B5

Genadendal is one of the oldest Protestant missions in Africa. The first buildings were built by Moravian missionaries in 1738, and the school and church buildings remain today – they have been declared National Monuments. The **Mission Museum** is open Monday-Friday, and Saturday mornings. Look out for the old bell tower next to a trading store. Ask at the **Genadendal Tourist Information** on Church Square, T2518291, to see a version of the New Testament printed in 1694 in Amsterdam, a true relic from the early settler days.

The **Genadendal Hiking Trail** starts by the Moravian Church. This is a pleasant hike through the Riviersonderend Mountains that is gradually becoming more popular. Bookings and information from the Vrolijkheid Nature Reserve, T023-6251621.

Greyton

Phone code: 028
(NB Always use 3-figure prefix)
Colour map 6, grid B5

The 5-km road between Genadendal and Greyton is now tarred

Just a short drive north of the main N2 highway, the quiet village of Greyton has attracted an assortment of retired folk and artists. The mixture of restored old buildings and oak lined streets have helped create a low key and peaceful atmosphere. When the first streets were laid out in 1854, the settlement was named after Sir George Grey, who had served two periods as governor of the Cape Colony. To the north lie the Riviersonderend Mountains, which in winter often have snow on their peaks – Kanonberg (1,466 m) is the tallest peak overlooking the village. The **Greyton Nature Reserve** is at the edge of town on the southern slopes of the Sonderend Mountains. The best time to visit is from September to November. The popular and well-known **Boesmanskloof Trail** starts from here. There is a much shorter 20 minutes' walk to the **Noupoort Gorge**, which can be followed close to the Kanonberg summit. There are a number of streams running off the hills through forested valleys, with the occasional waterfall which can be reached by paths. For **tourist information**, contact *Greyton Tourism*, Library Building, Main Street, T2549414, www.greyton.net Tuesday-Friday, 1000-1630, Saturday, 1000-1600, Sunday, 1000-1200.

Boesmanskloof Trail
There is no official accommodation along the trail, and camping is not allowed. Follow the yellow footprints

This 16-km hiking trail links the village of Greyton with McGregor on the northern side of the **Riviersonderend Mountains**. The northern end of the path in fact starts at a spot known as *Die Galg*, or the gallows, at the top of the mountains. At this point the path becomes an old road which was never completed, having reached the summit of the pass. The remaining 14 km to McGregor follows this pass which was built by vagrants who had been forcibly rounded up in the Cape Town area. Work stopped at the summit because the allocated funds were lost through embezzlement. The path requires a reasonable level of fitness. In summer it's hot and you should carry drinking water. In winter, conditions are cold and wet. The trail follows well-forested valleys which are rich in protea and erica species. Antelope can be seen in the forest.

Each direction can easily be completed in a day – the problem lies with transport. There is no easy way to travel quickly between the two towns. Most hikers tend to walk in one direction, overnight in the end town, and then walk back to the start on the next day.

There are private overnight rooms at *Die Galg*. Arrangements can be made through the manager, **Vrolijkheid Nature Reserve**, in Robertson; T023-6251621, F6251674. A very useful map is available when you get your permit. This is a popular trail and numbers are restricted to 50 people per day. It is advisable to book in advance during the local holidays. Rangers do patrol and check for permits.

B *The Post House*, 42 Main Rd, T2549995, F2549920. A high quality country guesthouse, 13 rooms with a Beatrix Potter theme, each with an open fire in the winter and a private veranda. The oldest parts of the building date back to 1860. Good food and service, picnic baskets prepared to order, colourful gardens, swimming pool, quiet setting, easy access to the village, Satour accredited. Recommended. **B** *Greyton Lodge*, 46 Main Rd, T2549876, F2549672. 18 rooms in renovated cottages, restaurant, swimming pool, gardens, Satour accredited, comfortable country lodge feel, a neat whitewashed building with a corrugated iron roof and small veranda. **C** *Guinea Fowl*, corner of Oak and DS Botha streets, T2549550, F2549653. 6 double rooms with en suite bathroom, swimming pool. Meals available from the attached coffee shop. **C** *Blue Crane B&B*, 58 Main Rd, T/F2549839. 5 double rooms with en suite bathroom, each has a spectacular view of the mountains. Comfortable lounge and TV room with open log fire, ideal hideaway during a wet winter's day. Run by Patrick and Simone. **E** *Municipal Campsite*, Krige Rd, 2 km from village centre, T2549620. Simple site with clean washblocks, swimming possible downstream from the site on the Riviersonderend River. **E-F** *Hikers'*, 81 Main St, T2549677. No frills, ideal for those with muddy boots.

Abbey Rose, 19 Main St, T2549771. Coffee shop selling good meals and curios. *Greyton Coffee Shop*, 35 Main St. Closed Sun, serves a good selection of salad lunches, quiche, and homemade pies, popular.

Sleeping & eating (margin)

Swellendam

Founded in 1745, Swellendam is the third oldest European town in South Africa, and is also one of its most picturesque. The main centre bears testament to its age with an avenue of mature oak trees and whitewashed Cape Dutch homesteads. Unfortunately, before the town fully appreciated their inherent charm and tourist potential, many of the trees and older buildings were knocked down in 1974 to widen the main street. Nevertheless, the town is very pretty and has an appealing, quiet atmosphere, which combined with the rural setting and beautiful views, makes it a very pleasant spot to spend a day or two. Swellendam also acts as an important base for exploring the region, with the Breede River Valley, the Little Karoo and the coast all within easy reach.

Phone code: 028
(NB Always use 3-figure prefix)
Colour map 6, grid B6

Tourist information is available at *Swellendam Tourism*, Oefeningshuis, Voortrek St, T/F5142770, www.swellendam.org.za Open Mon-Fri 0900-1300, 1400-1700, Sat 0900-1200. This office is less helpful than most, although it produces a leaflet called 'Swellendam Treasures' which outlines the interesting Cape Dutch buildings still standing today.

Swellendam started as a trading outpost for the Dutch East India Company. The new settlement was named after Governor Hendrik Swellengrebel and his wife, Ten Damme. Once established, all sorts of characters passed through looking for their fortunes or more land. One of the most successful characters was **Joseph Barry** who in the 1800s had a virtual monopoly on all trade between Cape Town and the new settlements in the Overberg and Little Karoo.

History (margin)

In 1795 a particularly strange event took place. Just at the point when British soldiers were bringing an end to Dutch rule in the Cape, the burghers of Swellendam declared themselves to be an independent republic, in a reaction to the misadministration and corruption of the Dutch East India Company. Hermanus Steyn was president from 17 June to 4 November 1795 – once the British had set up a new regime in Cape Town, the republic was quietly forgotten about. During the 19th century the town prospered and grew as the agricultural sector gradually expanded. This came to an abrupt halt in May 1865, when a fire started in a baker's destroyed 40 of the town's finest old buildings. Even greater harm was caused by a prolonged drought, and when in 1866 the influential Barry Empire was declared bankrupt the whole region's fortunes declined. Today the town is a prosperous rural community, and there are enough old buildings still standing (many have been restored) to give you a clear picture of how life once was.

Sights Of all the old Cape buildings in town, the **Drostdy Museum** on Swellengrebel Street is the most impressive and is often described as one of the country's great architectural treasures. The main building dates from 1747, built as the official residence and seat for the local magistrate, the '*landdrost*'. The building itself is as interesting as the collection it houses. Originally built in the shape of a T, the addition of two wings changed the form to an H. Inside, some of the floors have been preserved in their original form; what was the lounge has a lime-sand floor, while the kitchen floor is made from cow dung, which helps keep the room cool. The museum displays concentrate on local history, with a well-preserved collection of 18th- and 19th-century furniture. Other early buildings, both official and private, are now all part of the museum. Within the grounds is a restored Victorian cottage, **Mayville**, which has an antique rose garden plus the original gazebo. ■ *Mon-Fri 0900-1645, Sat and Sun 1000-1545. R10. There is an interesting booklet for sale (R3) entitled 'The Drostdy at Swellendam', which guides visitors to the most interesting objects. T5141138.*

Close by there is an open air display, on the **Crafts Green**, of many of the early farm tools, charcoal burners, wagons and a horse driven mill complete with threshing floor. Opposite the museum is the **Old Gaol** building, which housed both prisoners and local government officials, including the jailer who was also the postmaster. In the middle of all the cells was one without windows, known as the 'black hole'. Today, this is a local arts and crafts centre, with a good café.

Just on the outskirts of town is **Die Stroom (The Stream)**, a popular fishing and canoeing spot on the Breede River. Towards Ashton, 3 km out of town, is **Rheenendal Mill**, a restored watermill originally built in 1864.

Closer to the town centre are more restored buildings from the town's early days. The **Oefeningshuis** (1838) first served as a place for the religious instruction of freed slaves; it now houses the tourist office. Note the painted plaster clock face, which reads 1215, set above a working clock. This was designed for illiterate church-goers – if the painted face was the same as the clock's, it was time for service. Worth a look is the fine, domineering **Dutch Reform Church**. This large whitewashed building has a tall central clock tower and a mix of architectural styles. Just next to the church, on **Church Square**, are some fine examples of early double-storey town houses built by wealthy farmers who used to visit the town for holy communion, but lived out on their farms. The square had to be large enough to hold their ox wagons. Another grand town house is the **Auld House** dating from 1802 which for many years was the family home for the Overberg trader, Joseph Barry. Inside is some furniture, originally fitted on a steamer which used to sail between Cape Town and Port Beaufort. Also worth a visit is the small church of **St Luke** built in 1865. Finally, look out for the double-storey shop, **Buirski & Co**, built in 1880. It has one of the finest examples of Victorian wrought-iron balconies and fittings in the town.

Excursions Swellendam is an ideal base for exploring this part of the Overberg. Close by is the small **Bontebok National Park** (see page 260), and the larger **Marloth Nature**

Reserve. They have only simple accommodation and both can easily be visited on a day trip. **Suurbraak**, 25 km towards Tradouw Pass, is a small village established by the London Missionary Society in 1812. Many of the buildings have been restored to their original forms, and it is very much a living museum. The village is well-known for its hand-made wooden chairs.

B *Klippe Rivier Country House*, from the N2 take the R60, left at crossroads, 2 km, T5143341, F5143337. 6 double rooms in a restored Cape Dutch homestead (1825), declared a national monument. Large rooms with brass beds and cosy fireplaces, private balconies, restaurant, swimming pool, a peaceful and superior location, family owned and managed. Recommended. **B-C** *Swellengrebel*, 91 Voortrek St, T5141144, F5142453. Large bland and modern hotel set on the main road, with 50 rooms, some mountain-facing, restaurant, swimming pool, pool room, jacuzzi, sauna and gym, noisy public bar. Comfortable, but seems a shame to stay somewhere so characterless compared to most of the B&Bs in town.

C *Adin & Sharon's Hideaway*, 10 Hermanus Steyn St, T/F5143316. Award winning B&B in the centre of town. Spacious, comfortable rooms, en suite, overlooking a neat, shady garden. Excellent breakfasts, very friendly hosts. Recommended. **C** *Coachman Guesthouse*, 14 Drostdy St, T5142294, www.coachman.co.za Converted historic homestead with 3 double rooms with en suite bathrooms, plus thatched garden cottages with log fires. TV lounge, laundry, evening meals available, swimming pool. **C** *De Kloof*, Weltevreden St, T5141303. Elegant thatched house set in a neat garden, 2 double rooms with en suite bathroom, non-smoking, TV lounge, garden, evening meals available, very friendly. Recommended. **C** *Klein Drostdy*, 12 Drostdy St, T5141542. 2 rooms with en suite bathroom in an old home full of beautiful antiques. Good breakfasts, swimming pool, billiard room, large leafy gardens, just a short walk from the museum. **C** *Old Mill Cottage*, 243 Voortrek St, T5142790, www.oldmill.co.za Beautiful listed building, 4 double rooms with a rustic theme, TV lounge, superb meals served in the restaurant. Slightly overpriced, but still recommended. **C** *Woodpecker Cottage*, 270 Vortrekker St, T5142924, www.woodpecker.co.za Restored historic thatched cottage, 2 twin rooms with bathrooms, pleasant décor with some antiques, also 1 spacious garden cottage with veranda.

D *Rose Garden*, 19 Andrew Whyte St, T/F5141471. Separate flat with one double bedroom, TV, lounge, laundry, garden. **D** *Mountain View Cottage*, 37 Drostdy St, T5143799. Modern thatched cottage with 1 double room and a loft, can sleep 4, kitchen, TV lounge, fireplace, self-catering only. **D** *Moolmanshof*, 217 Voortrek St, T/F5143258. A 200-year-old home full of character with 2 rooms, en suite bathrooms, swimming pool, mature gardens, ask for John or Allison. Recommended.

E-F *Swellendam Caravan Park*, Glen Barry Rd, T5142705. 20 fully equipped thatched chalets, 4 beds, bring own linen, well-grassed and shady tent stands. A beautiful and peaceful setting within walking distance of town centre, popular during school holidays. **F** *Swellendam Backpackers*, 5 Lichtenstein St, T5142648, F5141249, backpack@dorea.co.za An excellent backpackers' hostel that has succeeded in introducing much of the Overberg region to budget travellers. One small dorm in the main house, plus individual 'Wendy Houses' (no electricity) in secluded corners around the large garden, lots of camping space, email access, well-organized kitchen, meals prepared most evenings. Can arrange local tours, hiking in the mountains and visits to the nearby Bontebok National Park. The *Baz Bus* calls in here twice a day.

Bizzie Bee, 55 Voortrek St. All-day coffee shop selling freshly baked cakes and superb coffee, good for breakfast. *The Connection*, 132 Voortrek St, T5141988. Pleasant restaurant serving a daily menu, mix of hearty soups and Italian cooking, some outdoor tables on terrace. *Goose & Bear*, Voortrek St, T5143101. Popular local pub serving up good, cheap meals. Pool tables and loud music. Lively place at the weekend. *Jorge's*, in the *Swellengrebel Hotel*. Pizza, pasta, steaks, nothing fancy but a reasonable variety, bar in one corner, indifferent, slow service. *Klippe Rivier*, as for guesthouse above, T5143341. Popular restaurant, delicious Cape cuisine, good wine list, open evenings only. Recommended. *La Belle Alliance*, Swellengrebel St, T5142252. Closed evenings. Good place for a lazy lunch in a lovely setting under the trees by the stream. Popular giant breakfasts. *Mattsen's Steak House*, Voortrek St, T5142715.

Sleeping
Price codes:
see inside front cover

Eating
Most local restaurants are closed Sun evening; the Swellengrebel Hotel is the best option, but be prepared to eat by 2100

Western Cape

Rumoured to be one of the best steak houses in the country. Busy restaurant serving excellent, good-value steaks, popular with tour groups. Recommended. Close to the Oefeningshuis (tourist office). *Old Mill*, 241 Voortrek St. Bright pink building, serve good afternoon teas, waffles and pancakes. *Pizza World*, Voortrek St, T5143899. Excellent takeaway pizzas, tasty thin crusts, good value. *Roosjie van de Kaap*, 5 Drostdy St, T5143001. Local word has this down as the best place to eat at in town. Booking essential. Cosy atmosphere in a candle-lit room. Superb pizza plus hearty South African fare. Recommended. *Zanddrift*, Swellengrebel St, next to the museum, T5141789. An old Cape Dutch farmhouse interior, closed in evening, steaks, pasta, salads, a good place to sample a typical large South African breakfast, good value. Recommended.

Sports   **Golf** 9-hole course, Andrew Whyte St, in the lee of the Langeberg Mountains. **Gliding** 4 km to the south of the town is the *Swellengrebel Airfield*. The Langeberg Mountains provide excellent thermals.

Tour   *Bontebok Tours*, 91 Voortrek St, T5143650, bonteboktours@worldonline.co.za, excellent local
operators   travel agent, organizes a range of local tours plus trips to Bontebok and Marloth marks, bird-watching trips and walking tours. Also acts as local information office and has internet access. *Felix Unite River Adventures*, T5141464, www.felixunite.co.za, professional outfit with an office in Cape Town, organize a range of trips on the river, with overnight accommodation in bush camps, restored Trekker ox-wagons and A-frame houses. Recommended. *Breede River Dream Cruises*, T028-5421049. *Two Feathers Horse Trails*, T082-4948279 (mob).

Transport   **Rail**   The station is on the other side of the N2 highway from the old part of town. Station St passes under the N2 and runs straight to Voortrek St. The only train to stop here is the weekly *Southern Cross*, which runs between **Cape Town** and **Oudtshoorn**. The timing of its departure is inconvenient for both directions of travel. **Cape Town** (6 hrs), Sun 0210, via **Bonnievale**, **Robertson** and **Worcester**. **Oudtshoorn**, Fri 0034.

Road   240 km to **Cape Town**, 225 km to **George**, 560 km to **Port Elizabeth**, 270 km to **Knysna**. **Bus**: *The Baz Bus*, T021-4392323, www.bazbus.com, stops daily in Swellendam, can take you as far as Port Elizabeth in a day. *Greyhound*, T021-5066363, coaches depart from outside the Groentemark Café. **Cape Town** (3 hrs), daily 0540; **Durban** (21 hrs), daily 2305; **Knysna** (3½ hrs), daily 2305; **Port Elizabeth** (7 hrs), daily 2305, 2345.
Intercape, T021-3804400, coaches depart from the Groentemark Café. **Cape Town** (3 hrs): daily, 1415, 0330. **Port Elizabeth** (7¼ hrs), daily 1040 2215, via the N2 stopping at main Garden Route towns.
Translux, T021-4493333, coaches depart from the Swellengrebel Hotel. **Cape Town** (3 hrs), daily 0350. **Port Elizabeth** (7 hrs), daily 2145, service calls at main towns along the **Garden Route**.

Directory   **Banks** *Standard Bank*, 32a Voortrek St; *ABSA*, 14 Voortrek St. **Medical Services** Dentist: Dr Joubert, 17 Heemraad St, T5143345. **Doctor's Surgery**: 114 Voortrek St, T5141173 and 31 Veldkornet St, T5141721. Optometrist: 140 Voortrek St. **Pharmacist**: *Swellendam Pharmacy*, 45 Voortrek St, also does 1 hr film developing. **Useful services** Ambulance: T10177; **Fire Brigade**: T5141330; **Hospital**: T5141140; **Laundry**: Nelson St; **Library**: T5141755; **Police**: T10111; **Post Office**: T5141340.

Bontebok National Park

Colour map 6, grid B6

The park is primarily a game reserve with a good range of antelope

Although this is one of South Africa's 17 national parks, it has less of interest than other parks. Nevertheless, this is a good place to spot several species of antelope, and has a pleasant riverside setting. Most of the park is accessible by car, and there are two 2-km self-guided nature trails which you can walk at any time without a permit or booking. **Guided walks** are organized when there is sufficient demand. Swimming and fishing are both possible in the Breede River, but only within the confines of the campsite. An angling licence must be shown.

Getting there The park is 238 km from Cape Town and 6 km from Swellendam. The turning   **Ins & outs**
off the N2 is clearly signposted, on the George side of Swellendam. There are 5 km of gravel
road from the highway to the entrance gate.

   Park information Entrance gate and office are open, Oct-Apr, 0800-1900; May-Sep,
0800-1800. The information centre detailing the history of the park is open for the same hrs.
There is a small shop in the office selling basic groceries, meat, wine and beer; all other supplies can be bought 6 km away in Swellendam. Petrol is available in the park. Electricity is
generated in the park and goes off at 2130. As a National Park, all reservations and enquiries
can be made through the central offices. Accommodation reservations, Pretoria,
T012-3431991, F3430905, reservations@parks-sa.co.za Bookings can also be made in person at two offices in Cape Town, at the V&A Waterfront Office, Clocktower Centre, or at Cape
Town Tourism Centre, corner of Castle and Burg streets. The local office address is PO Box
149, Swellendam, T028-5142735, F5142646.

At the beginning of the 20th century the **bontebok** was the rarest species of antelope   **History**
in Africa. They had been hunted and driven off their natural habitat by the settler
farmers in the Overberg. Fortunately, something even scarcer came to their rescue –
a group of local conservation-minded farmers, who recognized the need to set up a
protected area to save the remaining animals. In 1931 the first reserve was established, but it was not until the herd was moved to a more suitable environment
beside the Breede River in 1960 that the numbers started to recover significantly.
This has proved to be a success, and although no longer endangered there are still
not many places where the bontebok can still be seen in the wild. Today, other antelope indigenous to the Overberg have been introduced to the reserve including red
hartebeest, steenbok and duiker plus the rare Cape mountain zebra. There are some
very fine old trees along the banks of the Breede River.

D *Chalavans*, T5142735. An unappealing option in a 6-berth caravan with a prefab structure   **Sleeping**
on one side which provides more space and headroom. The caravans are a bit run down and   *Always check*
shabby. **F** *Camping*, no electric points, lanterns used, shower blocks. The location on the   *availability in*
Breede River makes up for the tired facilities. Given the park's proximity to Swellendam,   *advance if you*
many visitors choose to stay in town and come to the park as a day visitor.   *plan on staying*
  in the park

Marloth Nature Reserve

This mountain reserve encompasses a number of the peaks and forested valleys of   *Colour map 6, grid B6*
the Langeberg Mountains. Looking at the peaks from the centre of Swellendam,
locals claim to be able to tell the time between 0700 and 1300 by the shadows cast by
seven of the 'Clock Peaks'. There are a variety of hiking trails, including a rewarding
six-day route. Small stands of indigenous forest have been preserved. These are very
important when you consider that the mountains were once forested all the way
along this coast from Cape Town to Port Elizabeth and beyond. Today, only a few
small pockets of forest remain. Some of the more common indigenous trees which
can be seen in the reserve include yellowwood, red alder, hard pear, spoon wood,
Cape beech and cherrywood. The fauna is confined to mountain species – look out
for klipspringer standing on rock outcrops, and if you are lucky you may glimpse
bushbuck in the cooler, darker patches of forest. The colourful Cape sugarbird is a
common sight on the flowering aloes and ericas.

Getting there Follow the signs to the forest station, 3 km to the north of Swellendam. The   **Ins & outs**
ideal time to visit the reserve is in the spring (Sep-Oct) when the flowers are at their best. The
wettest months are Mar and Oct.

   Permits for the six-day walk or climbing the peaks are issued by the reserve manager,
Mon-Fri, 0800-1600, T028-5141410. Check on availability at weekends, as numbers are limited and routes can be reserved by telephone.

Western Cape

Hiking The **Swellendam Trail** is the principal hiking trail in and around Marloth Reserve. The complete circular route is 74 km long and hikers are advised to allow six days for the full circuit. This was the first trail designed in the Cape to return hikers back to their starting point without having to backtrack over terrain. Hiking conditions require a medium level of fitness, as there are strenuous segments when the trail goes around several peaks. Each day's walking passes through montane forest as well as open fynbos terrain. Be wary of the sun and carry plenty of water. There are six basic overnight huts, fitted out with bunks, toilets and drinking water. Do not walk in heavy rains or misty conditions.

It is no longer possible to take the short cut through the forest on this trail as there have been problems with hikers getting lost. Check with the manager, T028-5141410, if there have been any changes. Permits for the hiking trail are also issued by the manager of the reserve. Separate permits are issued for climbing any of the peaks. These should not be attempted by walkers with limited climbing experience.

Shorter day walks are possible in the vicinity of the entrance gate by the forest station. Six trails have been defined, ranging from an easy stroll to the picnic site in a sheltered valley known as the *Hermitage*, to an all day trail taking in two of the peaks closest to Swellendam. The most difficult day walk climbs from the car park to the Tienuurkop (1,195 m) peak, along a joining ridge to Twaalfuurkop (1,428 m), and then zigzags back down to the entrance. The walk is 9 km long and takes at least eight hours. The other day walks are on the lower slopes and most can be completed in less than three hours. Day walks do not require permits or pre-booking.

Sleeping
Price codes:
see inside front cover

The Manager, Marloth Nature Reserve, PO Box 28, Swellendam, T028-5141410, deals with bookings for hiking permits and overnight accommodation within the reserve. The reserve is administered by Cape Nature Conservation. The only accommodation within the reserve are the 6 basic overnight **F** *Hiking huts*, equipped with bunks, toilets and drinking water. Pay for the number of nights use when the permit is issued. If you stay in these huts bring all your provisions, they only provide a roof and a mattress. Even firewood is only provided at 2 of the huts, Koloniesbos and Wolfkloof. Do not light fires elsewhere in the reserve.

Heidelberg
Phone code: 028
(NB Always use
3-figure prefix)
Colour map 6, grid B6

Continuing east from Swellendam along the N2 highway the road bypasses several small agricultural towns which have little of interest to hold up most tourists. One of these is Heidelberg, which is dominated by its Dutch Reformed church on the banks of the Duivenhoks River. The first settlers arrived in the valley in 1725, and in 1855 it was named *Heidelberg* after the city in Germany. To the north in the Langeberg Mountains is the Grootvadersbosch Nature Reserve (see below). The Anglican church, St Barnabas, has some wood sculptures of note and particularly fine rose windows.

Grootvaders-
bosch Nature
Reserve
The 250 ha of
preserved forest is the
finest remaining cover
of indigenous forest in
the southwestern Cape

One of the places worth visiting around here is the Grootvadersbosch Nature Reserve outside Heidelberg. There is an excellent hiking trail (see below) and paths which provide easy access to the forest. The early settlers in the Overberg managed to satisfy the huge demand for hardwoods at the turn of the 19th/20th century throughout South Africa, but in doing so almost totally destroyed the unique forests in the Cape. Grootvadersbosch was established to preserve and restore the area to its former beauty. Between 1896 and 1913 alien trees such as ash, bluegum, Californian redwood, Australian blackwood and camphor were planted on the slopes, cleared of indigenous forest. Efforts are now being made to reclaim these areas to indigenous forest. The wilderness areas remain untouched and this is noticeable from the richness of wildlife and birdlife one encounters while walking here. There is a good chance of seeing the shy bushbuck in the forest.

Ins and outs The reserve is 22 km northwest of Heidelberg on the R322 towards Tradouw Pass. Coming from Swellendam, take the R324 turning for Suurbraak – the left turning for the reserve is 27 km further on. All advance details and reservations are made through the Manager, PO Box 109, Heidelberg, T/F028-7222412. Permits are available in the reserve on arrival, but note that the trails have a limit of 12 people. There is a simple campsite by the entrance gates. Look out for a bird hide 500 m into the reserve. The nearest comfortable accommodation is in Swellendam, 40 km away.

The Bushbuck Trail is a series of paths allowing you to choose a route between 2-10 km without having to backtrack too often. The paths weave between the moist and dry forest of the slopes of the Langeberg Mountains. The best periods for walking are May-July and December-January. There is a limit of 12 people on the trail, but it is very unlikely that you'll be refused a permit.

Just outside Swellendam is the R324 turning to Witsand, a quiet, picturesque seaside town at the mouth of the Breede River. The area is best known for its land based whale watching and its excellent fishing, but there is little other reason to come here. The village is small and peaceful and as such attracts mainly older couples wanting to escape the bustle of larger resorts. The river is popular for small pleasure boats such as canoes and dinghies. It is possible to travel 32 km upstream, recommended if you have a suitable craft. On the opposite bank from Witsand is the small hamlet of **Infanta**. Out in San Sebastian Bay there is some excellent snorkelling. In town, one building of note is the wool store built for the Barry family business. The neighbouring settlement of **Port Beaufort** was built by Joseph Barry, a businessman from Swellendam who for a period dominated all forms of trade in the Overberg (see page 257). Large boats from Cape Town unloaded their cargo here, which were then transferred to river boats and taken upstream as far as Malgas. The Barry family built a church in the village which is now a national monument. For tourist information, contact the Witsand Tourism Bureau, T5371010, www.witsand.com

Witsand
Phone code: 028
(NB Always use 3-figure prefix)
Colour map 6, grid B6

Sleeping B-C *Breede River Lodge*, T5371631, www.breederiver.co.za Comfortable en suite lodges and hotel cabins overlooking the river, well-furnished, great views, restaurant serves fresh seafood, bar, boats and fishing tackle for hire for trips up the river as far as Malgas, ferry service across the Breede River, also part of a timeshare complex. **D** *Big Cob Chalets*, 104 Main Rd, T5371942, bigcob@garndenet.co.za 3-bedroom self-catering chalets, thatched roof, neat gardens, each room has twin beds, fully equipped, braai area, secure parking. **F** *Caravan Park*, T5371627. Comfortable site with plenty of grass and shade, close to Breede River, shops nearby.

Price codes:
see inside front cover

Riversdale is a small farming centre based around wheat, wool and potatoes. There is little in town for visitors other than fuel and food, although there is the small **Julius Gordon Africana Museum**, on Long Street, which outlines the lives of several local characters and is home to some paintings by Thomas Baines and Peter Wenning. ■ *Mon-Fri 0800-1300*. The district is well-known for the growing of Agathosma shrubs which emit a very strong aroma. For anyone with an interest in wild flowers the **Van Riebeeck Garden** has a superb collection of aloes and vygies. The best time to visit is in May and Jun when the flowers are in full bloom. The **Werner Frehse** nature reserve outside the town has a few small antelope. The road to Ladismith in the north crosses the spectacular Garcia Pass before entering the Little Karoo.

Riversdale
Phone code: 028
(NB Always use 3-figure prefix)
Colour map 7, grid B1

Sleeping C *Rusticana Guesthouse*, on Moodie St, T7132154, which has homely en suite rooms set in a converted family home, good breakfasts, meals on request. **C** *Sleeping Beauty*, 3 Long St, T7131651, sleepingbeauty@dorea.co.za A Victorian guesthouse with 5 double rooms, 1 family room, home-made breads served for breakfast, lush gardens.

This small fishing village is in a beautiful spot straddling both sides of the Kafferkuils River. On the west bank is a fishing harbour, while the east bank holds a cluster of holiday cottages and shops. The beach is sandy and safe for swimmers. Surfers speak of good waves here, while the river is ideal for small pleasure boats. The bridge joining the two settlements was opened in 1955, replacing a pontoon which had been in

Still Bay
Phone code: 028
(NB Always use 3-figure prefix)
Colour map 7, grid B1

Western Cape

use since 1930. Like many South African seaside towns, Still Bay remains eerily quiet for much of the year, but during the summer school holidays the place comes alive with holidaying families.

Price codes:
see inside front cover

Sleeping D *Bellevue Inn*, 6 Osler St, T7541505, bellevueinn@telkomsa.net Modern hotel, short walk from the beach. En suite rooms, also self-catering apartments, restaurant, pool, crazy golf, coffee and gift shop. Very popular with families. **D** *Papillon*, corner of Perlemoen and Seebreis streets, T7542771, papillon@telkomsa.net Beachfront cottage, 3 bedrooms, 2 doubles and 1 single, fully equipped kitchen, laundry, gardens rolling down to beach, braai area, TV and video, email facilities.

Albertina
Phone code: 028
(NB Always use
3-figure prefix)
Colour map 7, grid B1

From Albertina it is
only 50 km to Mossel
Bay and the start of
the Garden Route
(see page 279)

Being only a few hours from Cape Town and tantalizingly close to the Garden Route, few people stop here. The predominant business is still wheat and sheep farming, although the local economy was able to diversify following the discovery in the 1920s of large ochre deposits. Another unusual product collected around Albertina is the juice from aloe plants, *Aloe ferox*, which is an important solution in medicine and cosmetics. You can visit the **Alcare Aloe Factory**, just outside town. They conduct free daily tours, T7351454, alcare@garenet.co.za There is a comfortable town hotel with friendly service, the *Albertina*, **C-D**, on Main St, T7351030, albertina-hotel@ gardenet.co.za It has 16 en suite rooms with TV, and a good traditional restaurant.

Little Karoo

Unlike the Great Karoo to the north, the Little Karoo is not a flat, dry and empty landscape; instead, it is made up of a series of parallel fertile valleys, enclosed by the Swartberg Mountains to the north and the Langeberg and Outeniqua Mountains to the south. It is an especially rewarding region to explore and much of it is hardly visited by tourists. The Cango Caves are a big attraction, as are the ostrich farms, but further afield lies spectacular and peaceful countryside, dotted with a multitude of small, historic villages. Here are some of the most dramatic kloofs and passes in South Africa (there are 14 in all) with excellent hiking and the springtime allure of bright patches of flowers in an otherwise barren landscape.

The majority of the passes, built in the late 19th century, were surveyed and built by Thomas Bain, a truly remarkable engineer. Perhaps the greatest testament to his work is that almost every pass he constructed is still in use today along almost identical lines. A fairly new tourist initiative is 'Route 62', a beautiful stretch of road following the R62 from De Rust in the east to Montagu in the west and passing a few wine estates on the way – it is marketed as the 'longest wine route in the world'.

Climate   The climate of the Little Karoo is markedly different from that of the coastal Garden Route, and yet it is no more than 30 km further inland. The principal reason for this is the mountains which act as a barrier to the weather moving inland. In the summer it is hot and dry and daytime temperatures of 40°C are not uncommon. During the winter you can expect to see snow on top of the Swartberg Mountains. Average annual rainfall is about 300 mm; water has to be carefully managed and farmers need to irrigate crops.

Flora and fauna

There are five nature reserves managed by Cape Nature Conservation in the region: Anysberg, Towerkop, Gamkapoort, Gamkaberg and Swartberg. For the botanist, the region is one of the best-suited environments in the world for succulents. There are many fascinating small plants which have adapted to scorching hot sunshine, erratic, limited rainfall, and rocky shallow soils. Aloes, lilies, geraniums and fynbos vegetation dot the landscape. A rare red variety of protea (*Aristata protea*) grows only in the Seweweekspoort Valley. The Ladismith-Klein Karoo Nature Reserve is very good for wild flowers in the spring. The guided tours in Gamka Mountain Reserve are some of the most informative outings, and will leave you with a greater appreciation of the uniqueness of the Karoo landscape.

Around Oudtshoorn, you'll see ostrich peering at you over fences everywhere you turn. When explorers from the Cape first came to the valley, they found it to be teeming with buffalo, elephant, rhino, lion, hippo, kudu, and the now-extinct **quagga**. Today only a few leopard remain in the remote hills; the more common antelope can be found in the reserves. The **Gamka Mountain Reserve** is home to the rare Cape mountain zebra, as well as antelope such as steenbok and klipspringer. Similar antelope can also be seen in the **Gamkapoort Nature Reserve**.

Oudtshoorn

By far the largest settlement in the Little Karoo, this is a pleasant administrative centre which still retains much of the calm of when it was first settled. It is a major tourist centre thanks to the nearby Cango Caves, a highlight of the Western Cape, and the countless ostrich farms surrounding Oudtshoorn. The town itself is also appealing, with broad streets, smart sandstone Victorian houses, many or which are now B&Bs, and a good choice of restaurants.

Phone code: 044
(NB Always use
3-figure prefix)
Colour map 7, grid B2

Oudtshoorn Tourist Bureau, Baron van Reede St, T2792532, F2728226, www.oudtshoorn.com, is open Mon-Fri, 0800-1800, Sat, 0830-1300. A well-informed, enthusiastic and helpful team, worth a visit for details on accommodation and less well-known sights of the Karoo. Behind this office there is a **Cape Nature Conservation**, office that can provide maps and information on the national parks in the region, T2791739, F2728110.

In 1838 a small church was inaugurated on the Hartebeestrivier farm to serve the farmers who had settled along the banks of the Olifants and Grobbelaars rivers. Nine years later the village of Oudtshoorn was founded when land was subdivided and sold by the surveyor J Ford. The town was named after Baron Van Rheede van Oudtshoorn, who died on his way to the Cape to take up the post of Governor in 1773. In 1858 the first group of British immigrants settled in the village.

History

When visiting outside the rainy season it is not difficult to believe that for many years the supply of water to the new settlement restricted its growth. A severe drought in 1865 persuaded many established farmers to move on and most made the long trek to the Transvaal. In its early days, water was brought to the town in barrels and then sold to households at sixpence a bucket. But the local farmers learnt to cope with this handicap and many of South Africa's early irrigation experts came from the region. When you cross the Grobbelaars River in the centre of town during the dry season, all the bridges and culverts seem redundant but they provide ample evidence of how much water can pass through when it rains. If you have time, walk across the Victorian **Suspension Bridge** where St John's Street crosses the river; this is now a protected National Monument.

It was the advent of two ostrich feather booms (1865-70 and 1900-14) that truly established the town, and led to the erection of the fine sandstone buildings and 'ostrich palaces' which now line Oudtshoorn's streets. For a period of almost 40 years it was the most important town east of Cape Town. At the peak of fortunes, ostrich feathers were selling for more than their weight in gold – little wonder that so many birds were bred. The boom attracted a large Jewish community, most of which had emigrated from Lithuania to escape the Tsarist pogroms. But when the good years finished, few chose to remain. While ostrich farming no longer brings in as much wealth, it remains an important business in the Karoo. Today, it is the specialized agricultural seed production which contributes most to the town and the region's wealth.

Sights

The two major reasons for coming here are the ostrich farms and the superb Cango Caves. There are also several nature reserves and scenic drives which are introductions to the diversity of this seemingly arid landscape

Within the town limits there is little to see aside from appreciating the sandstone Victorian buildings. There are several **Ostrich Palaces** in town which unfortunately are not open to the public. They are still worth a look from the outside since their ornate exteriors were very much part of their design. Most examples are in the old part of town on the west bank of the Grobbelaars River. Look out for **Pinehurst**, St John Street, designed by a Dutch architect, and **Gottland House**, built in 1903 with an octagonal tower. Other buildings of note include **Mimosa Lodge, Oakdene,** and **Rus in Urbe**. Unfortunately many fine Victorian buildings were demolished in the 1950s.

The **Catholic Cathedral**, on Baron von Rheede Street, is a fascinating modern building built in cruciform with splendid stained glass windows and a chapel beneath the main altar. The building houses two notable works of art – a painting given by Princess Eugene, in memory of her brother, the last of the Bonapartes who died fighting with the British against the Boers, and was supported by a priest from Oudtshoorn. The other item is a replica of a Polish icon onto which have been incorporated childhood items from refugee children sent to Oudtshoorn during the Second World War and who returned bearing the gift to celebrate the 50th anniversary of their evacuation.

In the centre of town, next to the old *Queen's Hotel* on Baron van Rheede, is the **CP Nel Museum**. This fine sandstone building was originally built as a Boys' High School. The masons who designed the school had been brought to Oudtshoorn by the 'feather barons' to build their grand mansions. The displays include a reconstructed trading store, synagogue and chemist, plus an interesting section on the history of the ostrich boom and the characters involved. The rest of the collection of historical objects was bequeathed to the town by CP Nel, a local businessman. ■ *Mon-Fri 0800-1700, Sat 0900-1300, closed Sun. Small entrance fee.*

Oudtshoorn

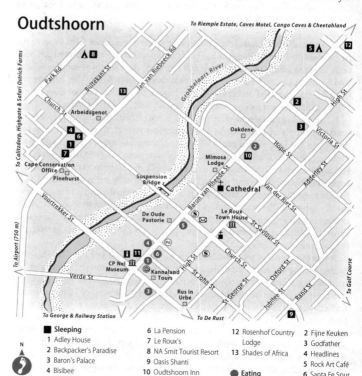

N

Not to scale

■ **Sleeping**	6 La Pension	12 Rosenhof Country Lodge	2 Fijne Keuken
1 Adley House	7 Le Roux's		3 Godfather
2 Backpacker's Paradise	8 NA Smit Tourist Resort	13 Shades of Africa	4 Headlines
3 Baron's Palace	9 Oasis Shanti		5 Rock Art Café
4 Bisibee	10 Oudtshoorn Inn	● **Eating**	6 Santa Fe Spur
5 Kleinplaas Holiday Resort	11 Queens	1 Bernard's Taphuis	

A short walk away is **Le Roux Town House**, 146 High Street, which is part of the CP Nel museum. This classic town house was built in 1908. The interior and furnishings are decorated in art nouveau style. During the summer, teas are served in the garden. ■ *Mon-Fri 0900-1300, 1400-1700.* **Arbeidsgenot**, Jan van Riebeeck Road, is the former home of Senator Cornelius Langenhoven, a leading figure in the history of the Afrikaans language who wrote the old national anthem of South Africa. The museum is based around his belongings but it provides a real feel for how the wealthy lived in the fine houses of Oudtshoorn.

Visiting an ostrich farm in the area can be great fun, although the appeal of riding ostriches, feeding ostriches, buying ostrich eggs and leather, or eating ostrich egg omelette can fade quickly. To keep visitors there for longer, some farms have introduced different species, but opinions also vary as to which farm is the least commercialized. Visiting the farms, or the Cango Caves, without your own transport can be surprisingly tricky. There are no longer any tour companies that organize daily trips, although it is possible to organize a guide through the tourist office. Otherwise, you might want to hire a car for the day. If you're staying in a backpacker lodge, trips are made easier as daily shuttles run from all the hostels.

Excursions
The major attraction in the area are Cango Caves, which are described on page 271

Cango Ostrich Farm, in the Shoemanshoek Valley, is particularly convenient to visit as it is on the way to and from the Cango Caves. The farm attractions are also within walking distance of each other. You can interact directly with the birds – hand-feed an ostrich, be 'kissed' by an ostrich and have a 'group hug' with the birds. After learning about ostriches you can buy local curio items and sample local Karoo wines and cheeses. ■ *Daily, 0800-1700. Entrance: adults R29, children R11. Tours every 15 mins, duration 45 mins. T2724623, www.cangoostrich.co.za*

Wilgewandel Camel Riding is also in the Shoemanshoek Valley on the way to the Cango Caves. This opened fairly recently, and offers you the chance to ride a camel around the farm – a pleasant change from all those ostriches. There are also farmyard animals and a pet area aimed at small children, a restaurant and bumper boats. ■ *Daily, 0800-1500. Entrance: adults R12, children R6, T2720878.*

Highgate Ostrich Farm is 10 km from Oudtshoorn off the R328 towards Mossel Bay. This very popular show farm, named after the London suburb of Highgate, has been owned by the Hooper family since the 1850s. It has won prizes in the last few years for its high standards, and is very well-run and better organized than other farms. You will learn everything there is to know about the bird, and can then try your hand at riding (or even racing!) the birds. Snacks and drinks are served on the porch of the homestead and are included in tour price. Guides speak German and Dutch. ■ *Daily, 0800-1700. Entrance: adults R30, children R12. Tours every 15 mins, duration 1 hr. T2727115, www.highgate.co.za*

Safari Ostrich Farm, 6 km from Oudtshoorn on the Mossel Bay road, has the usual array of ostrich rides, educational exhibits and curio shops. There is also a smart homestead known as *Welgeluk*. The house was built in 1910, and is a perfectly preserved example of an ostrich palace. There are roof tiles from Belgium, teak from Burma and expanses of marble floors, proof of the wealth and influence the short-lived boom brought to Oudtshoorn families. Unfortunately, the house is closed to visitors; the closest you can get is the main gate. ■ *Daily 0800-1630. Adults R30, children R15. Tours every 30 mins, duration 1 hr. T2727311.*

Cango Wildlife Ranch is 3 km along the R328 towards Cango Caves and a popular stop for tour groups. There are mixed opinions on this place since it is in effect a zoo which only stocks the most appealing animals – including pygmy hippos, leopards, cheetahs, and, oddly, a rare white Bengal tiger. It seems a pity to visit here when you have the chance to see animals in the wild in such magnificent parks as Kruger and Umfolozi. After walking safely above the animals, you have the choice of spending a little more to pet a cheetah. You are then led to a bizarre curio shop full of crocodile skin goods and even cheetah skins. ■ *Daily 0800-1700. Adults R25, children R9, over-priced. Tours every 30 mins, duration 1 hr. T2725593, cango@kingsley.co.za*

Western Cape

In keeping with the unusual animal farm theme is **Cango Angoré**, a working Angora Rabbit Show Farm with a restaurant and tea garden. It is especially fun for children, as they can pet the fluffy bunnies, try spinning their wool, and have donkey cart rides. Sadly, the farm is becoming increasingly overpriced. The farm is 15 km from Oudtshoorn on the R328 towards Cango Caves, take the turning by Cango Potteries. ■ *Daily 0900-1700. Adults R33, children R20. Guided tours. T2728842.*

Sleeping

■ *on map, page 266*
Price codes:
see inside front cover

For a town slightly off the main tourist trail, Oudtshoorn has a good and varied choice of accommodation. However, if you plan to stay at either a guesthouse or a B&B, book in advance

Western Cape

B *Oudtshoorn Inn*, Baron van Rheede St, T2722201, F2723003, oudtshoorn.inn@iafrica.com Modern, characterless hotel with 120 a/c rooms, some non-smoking, restaurant, bar, swimming pool, tennis court, miniature golf. **B** *La Pension*, 169 Church St, T/F2792445, lapension@pixie.co.za A well furnished B&B set in large garden with shady fruit trees. 3 rooms, TV, self-catering garden flat, sauna, swimming pool. Ask for Len or Jean. **B** *Queen's*, Baron van Rheede St (next to CP Nel Museum), T2722101, F2722104, queens@xsinte.co.za Historical hotel set in tidy gardens in the centre of town. 60 a/c rooms, en suite, stylish and comfortable. Good restaurant on first floor with balcony, serves a buffet lunch on Sun. Has a swimming pool, tennis courts, curio shop, laundry service and secure parking. A comfortable and friendly hotel which is owned and run by the Barrow family, the care and interest is reflected in the helpful staff, good value with discounts during quiet periods. Recommended. **B** *Rosenhof Country Lodge*, 264 Baron van Rheede St, T2722232, F2723021. 12 a/c rooms, TV, great thought and care has gone into choosing the furnishings of this restored Victorian house. The fabrics and the ornaments create a comfortable homely atmosphere. There is a swimming pool, beautiful rose garden and conference facilities. Not quite small enough for real privacy but still of a very high standard. Recommended. **B-C** *Riempie Estate Protea*, Baron van Rheede St, 3 km from town centre, T2726161, F2726772. Mix of thatched rondavels and double a/c rooms surrounded by farmland. 40 a/c rooms, 2 non-smoking rooms. The restaurant offers tasty country cuisine. Swimming pool, horse riding, mature shady gardens, part of Protea hotel group.

C *Bisibee*, 171 Church St, T2724784, F2792373, bisibee@hotmail.com 4 rooms, all with en suite bathroom, B&B, swimming pool, ask for Issabé – one of the friendliest welcomes you will receive in South Africa. Breakfast will keep you going all day, outstanding evening meals, recommended to us every year by other visitors. **C** *Baron's Palace*, 213 High St, T2791727, F2791747, www.baron.co.za 24 spacious rooms, the grand staircase reflects a bygone era, restaurant, swimming pool, secure parking. **C** *Hlangana Lodge*, 51 North St, T2722299, F2791271, info@hlangana.co.za An excellent lodge with 12 double rooms, a/c, TV, safe, mini bar, salt water pool, mountain bikes for hire, run by Stefan and Ellen, attentive and friendly hosts, good value luxury. Recommended. **C** *Shades of Africa*, 238 Jan van Riebeeck Rd, T/F2726430, shades@pixie.co.za A new building which has been decorated with some fine examples of African art. 5 double rooms with en suite bathroom, 4 in a separate block by a swimming pool. **C** *The Yotclub*, 9 Rudds Lane, T/F2792247. Good value B&B which has been recommended to us. Run by Des and Liz. **C-D** *Adley House*, 209 Jan van Riebeeck Rd, T/F2724533, adley@pixie.co.za A comfortable B&B set in large grounds a short distance from the town centre. 10 rooms, all with en suite bathroom, M-net TV, mini bar, heaters in winter. Excellent evening meals available. Two swimming pools. Well-run by Hilda and Pieter. Recommended. **C-D** *Le Roux's*, 207 Jan van Riebeeck Rd, T/F2725353, lerouxs@lantic.net Modern house with 3 brightly decorated rooms with en suite bathroom, TV with M-net, plus one self-contained flat with kitchen. Gardens with swimming pool, run by Kobus and Gerrida.

D *Best Little Guest House*, 15 Plein St, T2792137, niclubbe@kingsley.co.za A little out of town, attractive old-fashioned farm house with broad verandas, 8 rooms, en suite, ceiling fans, pub, evening meals on request, garden with 'mountain' pool. Friendly and relaxed, the Lubbe family try to make visitors feel at home. **D** *Caves Country Lodge*, off the R328, north out of town, T2722511, caves.motel@pixie.co.za Bland roadside motel, 39 en suite rooms with TV, restaurant, bar, gardens, swimming pool, children's playground.

E-F *Kleinplaas Holiday Resort*, 171 Baron van Rheede St, T2725811, kleinpl@mweb.co.za Caravan and camping with plenty of shade, fully equipped chalets, electric points, swimming pool, shop, laundromat. **E-F** *NA Smit Tourist Resort*, Park Rd, T2724152, F2791915. Large

Everything you ever wanted to know about ostriches

*The Ostrich (*Struthio camelus*) has been around since the Pliocene period, and has changed little in the intervening eight million years. Here are some ostrich-related facts with which to impress your friends.*

■ *A giant feather fan was discovered in Tutankhamen's tomb.*

■ *The Oudtshoorn area has 97 % of the world's population.*

■ *The shell can withstand the weight of a human adult.*

■ *Incubation, 42 days, is carried out by both birds; the male sits at night, the female during the day.*

■ *Each egg can weigh more than one kilogram, they make good omelettes, and can feed 20 people in one go.*

■ *It takes two years for the chick to mature.*

■ *The best quality feathers are produced by birds aged between three and 12 years.*

■ *Plucking occurs every nine months, about one kilogram of feathers is removed.*

■ *Over 80% of the feathers are exported.*

■ *Their skin makes excellent handbags and wallets.*

■ *The meat once used only for biltong is now popular in Europe and America because it is almost fat free.*

■ *The male bird has a vicious kick and a sharp toenail – beware!*

caravan and shady campsite, 150 stands, hot plates and fridges for campers, chalets with TV, gets crowded during holidays. **F** *Oasis Shanti*, 3 Church St, T/F2791163. Clean and quiet back-packers with a good range of rooms, including singles, doubles, triples and uncrowded dorms. Swimming pool with braai area, nightly ostrich braais and also cook vegetarian meals, TV lounge, bicycle hire, good travel advice from Mark the owner.

F *Backpacker's Paradise*, 148 Baron van Rheede St, T2720725, F2720877, jubi-lee@pixie.co.za Spotless lodge set in an old town house, with a mix of dorms and doubles, camping, volleyball court, well-stocked and clean kitchen, pub with pool table, nightly ostrich braais, small swimming pool, email facilities, within walking distance of shops, free town pickup. Plenty of activities can be organized from here, mountain biking, wine tastings and cave trips. Usually quiet although the pub can get rowdy.

Bernard's Taphuis, Baron van Reede St, T2723208. Good place to try a variety of traditional Karoo-style dishes, including Karoo lamb and ostrich steaks on an outside terrace. *Die Kolonie*, *Queen's Hotel*, Baron von Rheede St, T2722101. Good restaurant set in this historical hotel. Menu has an excellent range of local dishes, such as Karoo lamb, springbok steak and ostrich. Balcony overlooking the main street, good atmosphere and service. Recommended. *Fijne Keuken*, Baron van Rheede St, T2726403. A fine menu served in a cosy converted townhouse. Good range of ostrich dishes including good steaks and a more affordable ostrich stroganoff served with pasta. Good service, popular and bustling place. Recommended. *The Godfather*, 61 Voortrek St, T2725404. Open evening only, good game menu with springbok steaks and ostrich plus pizza, tasty meals but a little more expensive than elsewhere. *Headlines*, Baron van Reede St, T2723434. Coffee shop and restaurant specializing in ostrich dishes of all shapes and sizes. *Rock Art Café*, Van Rheede St, T2791927. Good value steaks, pasta and pizza, plus some ostrich dishes including a good pie. Popular with backpackers. *Santa Fe Spur*, Baron van Reede St. Popular chain, steaks, ribs, burgers, salad bar, generous portions, good value but the same menu as anywhere else in the country. *Zidago's*, Cango Rd. Next to *Caves Country Lodge*, thatched building overlooking lake at which animals from the Wildlife Ranch come to drink in the evening. Outside balcony, bar, pizza and burgers served, not surprisingly ostrich and crocodile both appear on the menu; the crocodile gateway may not be to everyone's taste.

Eating
● *on map, page 266*

Most of the hotels have their own bar and restaurant, which tend to stay open a little later than the restaurants in town

Baron van Rheede St is lined with many curio shops selling every ostrich by-product imaginable, from expensive leather purses, to feather dusters and tacky enamelled eggs. One such emporium is *Kuriopik*, on the High St. For arts and crafts, try *De Oude Pastorie*, 43 Baron van Rheede St.

Shopping

Western Cape

Thomas Bain, the man who opened up the Karoo

*In his own unique way **Thomas Bain** probably did more than any other settler to open up South Africa and contribute to the rapid downfall of the indigenous peoples. For 45 years (1848-93), he was employed by the Cape colonial government as an engineer. During this period he built 10 passes through the mountains which in effect had cut Cape Town off from the rest of the country. It may be difficult to appreciate quite what an impact his projects had, but as an example, villages which were only 30 km apart in a straight line took over a month to reach before his routes through the mountains started to open up the interior. Along with his father, Andrew Geddes Bain, they were responsible for most*

road and rail engineering projects in South Africa. The following are the passes he worked on in the vicinity of the Cape. Once you have crossed a few imagine what it was like building these routes with no heavy machinery and only dynamite to help clear the way. In no particular order: Cogman's Kloof, Piekenierskloof, Tulbagh Kloof (Nuwekloof Pass), Prince Alfred's Pass, Robinson Pass, Garcia's Pass, Tradouw Pass, Swartberg Pass, Pakhuis Pass and Van Rhyn's Pass.

In addition to these he built the Victoria Road from Sea Point to Hout Bay in Cape Town, as well as surveying the Orange River for irrigation schemes and extending the railway line beyond Wellington.

Transport　**Air** SM Greeff airport is less than 1 km from the town centre. There are services to **Cape Town** and **Johannesburg**. *Greyhound* services depart and arrive from SM Greeff airport.

Rail The station is south of the town centre, off the road to George. Enquiries T2032203. The *Southern Cross* runs between **Cape Town** and **Oudtshoorn**. Cape Town (15 hrs), Sun 1740, via **Swellendam** and **Worcester**.

Road 172 km to **Beaufort West**, 510 km to **Cape Town**, 60 km to **George**, 245 km to **Montagu**, 93 km to **Mossel Bay**. **Bus**: *Intercape*, T021-3804400, coaches departs from the Queen's Riverside Mall. **Knysna** (2 hrs) and **Plettenberg Bay** (3 hrs), daily 0815, Mon, Tue, Fri, Sat, 0615; **Johannesburg** and **Pretoria** (15 hrs), via **Kimberley** (8 hrs) daily 1900, Sun, Mon, Thu, Fri, 1615.

　　Translux, T021-449333, coaches departs from the Queen's Riverside Mall. **Beaufort West** (2 hrs): Tue, Wed, Fri, Sun, 1920; **Bloemfontein** (8 hrs): Mon, Thu, Sat, 1920; Mon, Tue, Thu, 2010; **George** (2 hrs): daily, 2305; **Knysna** (2 hrs) and **Plettenberg Bay** (3 hrs): Mon, Thu, Sat, 0810; Tue, Wed, Fri, Sun, 1920; **Johannesburg** and **Pretoria** (14 hrs) via **Kimberley** (7 hrs) or **Graaf Reinet** (5 hrs): daily, 1920.

Directory　**Communications** Internet: *Internet Café*, 150 Baron van Rheede St. **Useful services** Ambulance: T10177. **Pharmacy**: *Watson & Brink*, High St, T2722184. **Private Hospital**: T2728921. **Police**: 10111.

North of Oudtshoorn

Following the R328 north, the road passes several ostrich farms and then follows the Grobbelaars River Valley towards the Cango Caves (see below). 15 km from Oudtshoorn is the small village of **Schoemanshoek** in a lush valley with small farms and homesteads.

Price codes:
see inside front cover
Sleeping There is a peaceful but working ostrich farm, **B** *Altes Landhaus*, look for signs by the church, T044-2726112, F2792652. It has 5 double rooms with en suite bathroom/shower, some with air conditioning. Each room has its own special character, evening meals available on request, salt pool in garden, German spoken, recommended. A comfortable B&B is **C** *Oue Werf*, T044-2728712. T082-7102761 (mob). It has 2 self-contained cottages in the grounds of old farmhouse, with swimming pool, plus boating on farm dam,

What's in a drip?

Dripstone *More commonly known and recognized as **stalagmites** (growing from the floor) and **stalactites** (hanging from the ceiling). As the name suggests they are formed by the dripping of water containing calcite. Stalagmites form when there is rapid dripping of water and it falls to the floor. In Cango Caves the growth rate has been estimated at 5-16 mm per 100 years for stalagmites, and 2-5 mm per 100 years for stalactites. Eventually they may meet and join to form columns, which can be vulnerable to any tectonic activity and may cause the gap between ceiling and floor to diminish. Where there are several columns close to each other, they may eventually unite to form a curtain-like formation.*

Rimstone *This formation is a horizontal deposit affixed to the upper rim of a pool. Deposition occurs where water in a cave pool containing calcium bicarbonate in solution meets the cave air.*

Flowstone *Instead of a drip action*

these deposits occur when water containing calcite flows from cracks in the cavern walls, depositing calcite where the film of water meets the cave air. Combined with dripstone these can create some spectacular formations. Look out for the 'Organ Pipes' in Van Zyl's Hall.

Helictites *Little is known about how these weird shapes form. They can grow in all directions with little regard for gravity, it is a drip process and a very slow one.*

Cave Crystals *These are found on the ceilings and against the walls where thin films of saturated moisture accumulate. They can take many shapes, the most common being sharp needles. They are difficult to see high up in the cavern.*

Shelfstone *Very similar to rimstone, but comes about when the saturated water remains at the same level for a much longer period of time. The deposits have a chance to grow inwards across the surface of the lake.*

Western Cape

evening meals on request; an ideal base from which to explore the area. **C-D** *De Opstal*, just off the road to Cango Caves, T/F044-2792954, has 7 double rooms with en suite bathrooms, some of which are converted farm buildings with plenty of character, swimming pool, evening meals available, an ideal local base, recommended. **D-F** *Cango Mountain Resort*, 7 km before Cango Caves is a turning off the R328, the resort is 3 km down the road (the road follows the Oude Murasie Valley and can be followed all the way to De Rust, see below), T044-2724506. A large resort with chalets and a campsite, electric points, a shop and a swimming pool suitable for children. It is close to the Koos Raubenheimer Dam, a peaceful spot which gets busy during local holidays. It is possible to visit the dam on a day trip. There are the usual collection of braai spots amongst the oak trees.

Cango Caves

About 30 km from Oudtshoorn is the turning for Cango Caves. This magnificent network of calcite caves extending into the Swartberg foothills are recognized as among the world's finest dripstone caverns. In 1938 they were proclaimed as a National Monument. Despite being seriously hyped and very touristy, they are well worth a visit. Allow a morning for a round trip if based locally; it is also possible to visit them on a day trip from towns along the Garden Route such as Mossel Bay, George and Wilderness. *Colour map 7, grid B2*

Getting there The caves are 29 km north of Oudtshoorn along the R328, clearly signposted from the centre of town. The road goes straight to the caves; you have to turn left for the Swartberg Pass and Prince Albert. **Ins & outs**

Information Open 0900-1700, daily. You can only enter the caves on a tour (see below) – these run until 1600. A range of facilities has been developed in the middle of this sparsely inhabited wilderness. There is a restaurant with a pleasant balcony overlooking a valley, a crèche, several curio shops and a small money exchange. The caves are usually around 20°C, so a T-shirt and shorts will be fine. Wear shoes with reasonable grip, as after rain the floors can become a little slippery. It is a criminal offence to touch or take anything from inside the caves. Please adhere to these rules and be careful not to touch the rock formations – the acidity of human sweat that is left from our wandering hands has already caused considerable damage. Eating, drinking and smoking are also forbidden inside.

NB During the holidays it gets very crowded and nearly 200,000 people pass through the caves each year. Each tour has a maximum number of people it can take, so you may have to wait an hour or more before seeing the caves. It's a good idea to get here early in the morning to avoid queues.

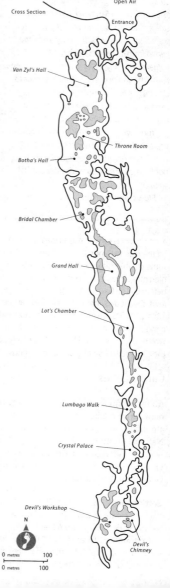

Cango Caves

Cave tours The only access to the caves is on a guided tour: adults R33. These run hourly from 0900, with the last tour at 1600. There are 3 three tour options: lasting 30 mins, 60 mins or 90 mins, depending on how far into the system you wish to venture. The **short tour** takes in two chambers and is really too short a time in which to appreciate the cave complex. The most popular tour takes in six caves, while the 'Adventure tour' follows narrow corridors and involves some crawling (see below). During the tours, each section is lit up and the guide points out interesting formations and their given names. Although one small chamber is still lit up with gaudy coloured lights, the rest are lit with white light to best show off the formations. These are turned off behind you as you progress further into the system as research has shown that continued exposure to light causes damage to the caves.

The caves are not just a beautiful series of bizarre formations, but represent over a million years of slow chemical processes. The Cango cave system is known as a phreatic system, the term given to caves which have been chemically eroded by underground water. Once the caves had been exposed to air, the first deposits started to form – these now make up the incredible stalagmites, stalactites and flowstones visitors can see. The timescale of some of the formations is mind-boggling; many of the pillars took hundreds of thousands of years to form, while the oldest flowstone is over a million years old. The guides who show you around are very knowledgeable and are happy to discuss the formation of these deposits. For **Further reading** see *Kango* by TV Bulpin and Hans Oosthuizen, Struik Publishers, Cape Town, 1983.

Oubaas Johnnie – the cave man

Probably the greatest of Cango guides, Mr JW van Wassenaer, 'Oubaas Johnnie', worked at the caves for 48 years. When he started as a guide in 1880 there was no gate to the complex, nor a road leading up to the cliff face. Anyone found inside the caves without permission had to pay a fine of four guineas. Two years after he retired electric lighting was installed, he had always used magnesium lamps. What is so incredible is the amount of time he spent inside the caves – four nights a week he would explore in the near-dark. He estimated that in his time he had made over 7,000 journeys, alone, and never once got lost. He ventured over 16 miles into the system, and in all probability found chambers which to this day no one else has seen. Sadly, he never found the opening to the underground river which had once flowed through the system. But then again, neither has anyone else yet.

The **standard one hour tour** is a good introduction to the caves and allows you to see the most impressive formations. It is, however, aimed at tour groups, so visitors with a special interest may find it rather simplistic. The **adventure tour** lasts for 1½ hrs, is over 1 km long and there are over 400 stairs. This can be frightening for some people, since it involves crawling along narrow tunnels, and at the very end climbing up the Devil's Chimney, a narrow vertical shaft. It leads up for 3½ m and is only 45 cm wide in parts – definitely not for broad people. If at any stage you feel you can't go on, inform the guide who will arrange for you to be led out. Although strenuous, this tour allows you to see the most of the caves, and gives a real feeling of exploration.

Swartberg Pass
Colour map 7, grid B1

One of the most spectacular passes in South Africa, the Swartberg Pass is a national monument in recognition of the engineering genius of **Thomas Bain** (see box page 270). Following severe floods in 1875 which closed Meiringspoort and Seven Weeks Poort and washed away parts of the road, farmers in the region petitioned the government in Cape Town to build a reliable road across the Swartberg. After the first contractor went bankrupt Bain finished the job. It was built between 1881 and 1888 using convict labourers. The route is 24 km long; the top of the pass is 1,577 m and the summit is often closed in winter due to snow. The road today follows much the same route and care must be taken. It is very steep: the road climbs 1,000 m within 12 km, and there are very sharp, blind hairpins. As you descend towards Prince Albert there are plenty of shaded picnic sites to pause at and enjoy the views.

Gamkapoort Nature Reserve: The Hell

This is one of the more unusual places to visit in South Africa. It is an isolated valley, which is hidden away in the mountains, and whose residents have managed to avoid the change going on all around them. For more than 50 years these European immigrants were the forgotten people. They paid no taxes, had no schoolteachers and made their own clothes. It was only in 1963, 126 years after the first Europeans built their homes here, that a road was built connecting the valley to the outside world. Prior to this all provisions had been brought in by pack donkeys from Prince Albert.

Ins and outs 3 km past the summit of Swartberg Pass, coming from Oudtshoorn, is a gravel road to the left signposted 'The Hell'. The Otto du Plessis road is suitable for a saloon car but be sure to take care driving here. The road is narrow and steep in parts and there are many blind bends. In all, it is 58 km to the start of the valley; allow at least 1½ hours each way. Gamkaskloof is 16 km long with two seasonal rivers criss-crossing the road.

History

It was during the Great Trek that farmers searching for a place free of the influence and interference of British officials decided to settle in the kloof. Amongst the last people to leave the valley were their descendants. The last farmer, Piet Swanepoel, left the valley in 1991. An account written in 1955 in *Karoo*, by L G Green, relates an accurate image of conditions in the valley. "Calitzdorp is the nearest village, but 'The Hell' can be reached in comfort only by helicopter. It has no road, nothing but a track for pack-donkeys. As there are only about 20 families living in the kloof, the road-makers have by-passed this solitude. You must leave your car at Matjiesvlei farm and struggle along the Gamka River banks on foot for two or three hours, sometimes knee-deep in water, to meet white people who have never seen the outside world."

Efforts have been made to conserve and restore some of the houses – you pass several of them on the route, as well as an old watermill. There is also a camping site open to visitors. For information and maps, contact **Cape Nature Conservation**, Oudtshoorn, T044-2791739, F2728110.

Swartberg Nature Reserve
Despite high temperatures during the day it can get very cold at night

Within this reserve is a maze of trails snaking through the mountains behind the Cango Caves. The trails are between 2,000 and 3,000 m high. The longest trail, which is known as the **Swartberg Hiking Trail**, is 60 km long. The main attractions here are the mountain fynbos and a varied birdlife. There are three overnight huts at Ou Tol, Bothashoek and Gouekrans, with bunks, showers and braai facilities. Permits and maps are issued by the Cape Nature Conservation office in Oudtshoorn, T044-2791739, F2728110. **NB** Water has to be carried between huts during the day.

Prince Albert
*Phone code: 023
(NB Always use
3-figure prefix)
Colour map 7, grid B1*

This old village lies on the edge of the Swartberg Mountains. Canals from these hills bring water to the gardens, helping to give an oasis feel to the settlement. There is an old watermill on the edge of town. A few minutes walking about the village quickly gives one an impression of life at the turn of the 19th/20th century during the hot summers of the Karoo. Fortunately, many of the homes from this period have survived in a good state of repair. Reflecting the richness of the landscape is the **Fransie Pienaar** collection of fossils, one of the largest in the world, housed in the local museum. There is also an excellent private mineral collection which can be viewed by appointment. Contact the local tourism bureau at 42 Church St, T5411366, for more information. There is a supermarket, general shops, an excellent farm stall, *Sampie se Plaasstal*, plus a couple of restaurants.

*Price codes:
see inside front cover*

Although there is little choice, this is an ideal base for the many hiking trails in the area

Sleeping C *Saxe-Coburg Lodge*, 60 Church St, T5411267, F5411366. A well-preserved Victorian house with 4 rooms, self-catering or meals on request. The pub lounge is a relaxing place to end the day by the fire. French and German understood. **C** *Swartberg Country Lodge*, 77 Church St, T5411332, F5411383. 17 rooms plus some rondavels, delightful restored Victorian home, over 150 years old, restaurant, swimming pool, sauna. **D** *No 56*, 56 Church St, T5411768. An excellent B&B run by Susan and Herman, comfortable, good value rooms, B&B, plus 1 self-catering cottage which sleeps 4. Very welcoming. Recommended. **D** *Dennehof*, 5 mins from the village on the R328, T5411227, F5411158. Authentic rustic accommodation in 2 self-contained Karoo-style cottages, each with 2 double rooms with bathrooms. Large garden with views of the Swartberg, swimming in the summer months in a country dam. The main house is a well preserved Cape Dutch farmhouse, the oldest in the village. B&B or self-catering, evening meals on request, friendly and helpful hosts. Recommended.

West of Oudtshoorn

The main road through the Little Karoo to the west of Oudtshoorn is the R62, a beautiful stretch which is now marketed as **Route 62**. After 52 km you reach Calitzdorp, a small farming centre. Take the old road which follows the Olifants River to visit the Gamka Mountain Reserve and Calitzdorp Spa. North from Calitzdorp is a gravel road to Groenfontein along the Nels River Valley. This route is narrow and full of tight bends, and should not be travelled after heavy rains in an ordinary road vehicle. Eventually it joins up with the R328, Oudtshoorn-Prince Albert road. A loop back to Oudtshoorn via the Cango Caves is a possible circuit. Continuing west from Calitzdorp, the R62 crosses the Dwyka River. After 24 km is a turning north to Seven Weeks Poort. Soon after this you pass the mission stations of Amalienstein and Zoar. It is another 21 km to Ladismith. The area around Ladismith is good for hiking in the Karoo and the Swartberg Mountains.

The reserve encompasses the Gamka Mountains, a relatively isolated range in the midst of the Karoo. The stimulus behind its foundation in 1974 was to protect the natural habitat of the endangered Cape Mountain Zebra (*equus zebra*). In 1965 it was estimated that less than 100 animals were still living in the wild. Over 9,400 ha is now protected and apart from the zebra you can expect to see eland, grysbok, grey rhebuck and many other smaller mammals. To see leopard and the honey badger, both rare species, would be a special bonus.

Gamka Mountain Nature Reserve
Colour map 7, grid B1

Four types of vegetation can be seen in the reserve: dry mountain fynbos, succulent mountain scrub and renosterveld. Although the Karoo is an arid region, a colourful carpet of wild flowers appears in the reserve after the spring rains. Of particular interest to the botanist is the occurrence of a recently discovered rare protea species, *Mimetes chrysanthus*. Most of the landscape is rough terrain and there are several forested river valleys. **Bakenskop** (1,099 m) in the centre of the reserve is a good view point.

Ins and outs The reserve is midway between Oudtshoorn (33 km), and Calitzdorp (32 km). Coming from Oudtshoorn, take a left turning off the R62, signposted Warmbad, Gamkaberg and Calitzdorp Spa. This is a cement road. After 18 km a dirt track to the left is signposted, Gamkaberg – a further 6 km brings you to the main entrance. From Calitzdorp, follow the signs for Gamka Mountain along Andries Pretorius Road. Shortly after crossing the railway turn left. Ignore the right turning for Calitzdorp Spa and continue until you see the reserve signposted on your right. There is a second gate in the southwest corner of the park; follow the signs for Volmoed, south of Oudtshoorn.

Reserve information The gates are open from 0700-1700. All cars have to be left at the information centre. For hiking or 4-wheel drive enquiries call T044-2791738 in advance, sberg.cnc.karoo@pixie.co.za

Climate One of the best times to visit is in Sep when the wild flowers are out. In Feb temperatures can be as high as 44°C, while in Jul there are frosts. Expect light showers in Jun/Jul, and thundershowers in Dec/Jan. Take note if you are planning on camping.

Hiking and four-wheel drive The most satisfying way to enjoy the scenery is to hike in the area. There are six trails of varied length – the longest is a two-day guided trail, where a local guide introduces you to the terrain and fauna of the Karoo. The shorter trails, Mousebird and Pied Barbet, are suitable for children and can be completed in one to two hours.

An alternative to walking is driving around in a four-wheel drive vehicle. There are 60 km of gravel tracks which end up at three viewpoints. Prior permission is required to bring vehicles into the reserve (note that only four-wheel drive vehicles are admitted). Enquire at the information centre about areas open for mountain biking.

Sleeping There are 2 camps in the reserve at Tierkloof and Oukraal. **F** *Oukraal*, 15 km from the entrance, is no more than a level, cleared area with firewood and a braai. You must bring everything you need for an overnight stay. At **E** *Tierkloof Camp*, 2 km from entrance gates, tents are provided along with a fridge, cooking stove and an ablution block. All bedding and supplies have to be brought with you. More comfortable accommodation is available at **D-E** *Calitzdorp Spa*, 10 km from the reserve entrance towards Calitzdorp (22 km), T/F044-2133371. 42 modern chalets, shady caravan park, electric points, restaurant, swimming pool, sauna, tennis, shop, petrol. The warm waters of the spa are rich in minerals, and as with all such waters are reputed to have healing powers. A 3-km hiking trail along the hills has been marked out.

Price codes: see inside front cover

Western Cape

Calitzdorp

Phone code: 044
(NB Always use
3-figure prefix)
Colour map 7, grid B1
Tourist information:
T2133312, F2133295

Until the branch line from Oudtshoorn arrived in 1924, this settlement remained a small service stop for farmers. The village is now a successful agricultural centre and an important area for **port** production in South Africa. It is possible to visit a couple of port farms, and a **port festival** is held every July (T2133314). At harvest time, fresh fruits are sold along the wide roads of the village. The village is also known for the warm healing waters at *Calitzdorp Spa*, 22 km towards Oudtshoorn on the old cement road (see above). When the first farms were established in the area, the surrounding plains were full of game. Sadly today only the early farm names survive as a reminder.

Price codes:
see inside front cover

Sleeping **C** *Port Wine Guest House*, 7 Queen St, T/F2133131. A smart guesthouse in a historic building built in 1830. 5 double rooms with en suite facilities and four-poster beds. Both the lounge and the dining room have open fires during the winter months. Evening meals available on request. The owners, Chris and Andrea, are excellent hosts and can tell you all you need to know about the region. If you have the time, try to arrange a visit to their ostrich farm. Recommended. **D** *Die Dorpshuis*, Van Riebeeck St, T2133453. B&B with attached restaurant. 2 cottages with double rooms, plus one large en suite room. Breakfasts included. **D** *Welgevonden*, T/F2133642. A peaceful country guesthouse. 4 rooms with en suite bathrooms, communal lounge and kitchenette. Enjoy the comfort of a family home, evening meals by arrangement.

Seven Weeks Poort

A road branches north opposite the Amalienstein turning on to the Seven Weeks Poort, one of the earliest routes farmers used to cross the Swartberg. It follows the valley cut by the Huis River. When it was opened in June 1862 the public refused to accept the contract to levy a toll. The road was considered too vulnerable to flooding, closure and repairs. It is a very beautiful pass, but even today after heavy rains it is closed. At the northern end are the ruins of the first toll house. Midway through the valley is a picnic spot beside the stream. It was in this area that a rare species of protea was rediscovered, *Protea aristata*.

Amalienstein & Zoar

Colour map 7, grid B1

These two mission stations are only 2 km apart and have an interrelated past. The first to be established was Zoar in 1817, by Petrus Joubert, a missionary of the South African Missionary Society. Orchards and vineyards were planted around the mission and the local Khoi were taught sedentary farming techniques. When Joubert left, the Berlin Missionary Society looked after the mission. In order to retain their own position in the area, they built another mission nearby in 1833. The new complex was named after Amalie von Stein, a major benefactor of the society. Both missions have created an oasis of fruit and vegetables in a dry region. There is a fine **Lutheran Church** and similar buildings adding to the atmosphere of the settlements.

Ladismith

Phone code: 028
(NB Always use
3-figure prefix)
Colour map 7, grid B1

Ladismith is a typical sleepy Karoo town, its wide streets lined with historical white-washed houses. The views are dominated by the twin pinnacles of the **Towerkop** or 'Bewitched Peak', of 2,203 m, which according to legend was split by a local witch. The last 100 m of the peak is considered to be one of the toughest climbs in South Africa. If you pass through the town centre, look out for the old white Dutch Reformed church. Built in 1873 it is now used as a warehouse. Other buildings of note are along Church Street and the synagogue in Van Riebeeck Street. The Town Hall has a pleasant façade with a small first floor balcony above the entrance.

Like several Karoo towns, Ladismith enjoyed a period of prosperity during the ostrich feather boom. At the end of the boom the town was bankrupt, and recovery only came about 10 years later in 1925 when the railway arrived, connecting the region to outside markets. The surrounding farms began producing dried fruits and dairy products, and the farmers' fortunes began to improve. Visitors who have missed good cheese on their travels may find it interesting and worthwhile to visit the local *Towerkop Cheese Factory*. There is also a small wine co-operative here. For tastings, contact T5511042. For **tourist information**, contact the *Tourism Office* on T5511023.

There are a couple of reserves around Ladismith (see below) which can be visited on a day trip, depending on how long you wish to walk for. In some cases, simple overnight accommodation is available.

Sleeping C *Albert Manor*, 26 Albert St, T/F5511127. Classic Victorian house with views of the Klein Swartberg. 3 rooms, private bathrooms, TV lounge, B&B, evening meals available on request. Recommended. D *De Oude Herehuis*, 2 South St, T5511769. Homely guest-house with simple rooms, B&B, comfortable furnishings, good breakfasts.

A short distance along the R62 road towards Barrydale is this small, private reserve in the surrounding hills. An area of 2,800 ha has been set aside to protect the variety of plants that have adapted to the hot, arid conditions of the Karoo. Plants and shrubs that can be seen in the reserve include the Karoo num-num, karee, taaibos and the guarri tree. The main feature of the reserve is the circular **Klapperbos Trail**, named after a drought resistant plant whose seed pods are used in decorations because of their rose pink colour. There is little game in the park, although you may glimpse eland and springbok. Allow at least six hours for the walk – it is about 12 km long, but the terrain is hilly, and in summer it gets very hot. Permits and keys for the main gate are available at the Ladismith municipality. There are no facilities here, so make sure you carry plenty of drinking water.

Ladismith-Klein Karoo Nature Reserve

The R62 continues southwest towards Barrydale (see below). About 16 km south of Ladismith is a right turning (R323) for Laingsburg and the N1 highway. This is also the main access route for Anysberg Nature Reserve (see below). Most of this road is dirt, so drive carefully. A left turn on to the R323, to Riversdale via the Garcia Pass, is a seldom used route back into the Overberg. Garcia Pass was commissioned in July 1872. The plan was to use the convict labour which was at the time working on the Tradouw Pass (see below). Although Thomas Bain was working for the railways at this time, he managed to stake out the course of the pass, but was unable to supervise the detailed works. It proved to be a complex job and two foremen were sacked before the road was completed in December 1877. A project that Bain had estimated would cost R3,200 ultimately cost R58,700. At the top of Garcia Pass near the old Toll House are three **hiking trails** in the Garcia forest. This is a small patch of indigenous forest which contains some rare erica species, as well as ironwoods, yellowwoods, kuerboom, rooiels and boekenhout. The **Sleeping Beauty Trail** takes about four hours; if you are fit there is a steep climb at the end to the summit, 1,200 m.

Garcia Pass

This is one of the newer reserves in the region, reflecting the need to protect the Karoo. Created in 1988, the area covers 34,000 ha and has a rich and varied fauna and flora along with some well-preserved Khoisan paintings in the Anysberg hills. The further you explore into the wilderness, the more likely you are to see elusive wildlife such as scrub hare, black-backed jackal and the caracal. There are some spectacular gorges which are home for birds such as the black eagle and the pale chanting goshawk. During dry periods the dams provide a focal point for both wildlife and birds. During the weekend a reserve horseman leads a two-day circular horse trail through the reserve; this is not strenuous and is suitable for inexperienced riders. Walking is allowed but no trails have been marked out.

Anysberg Nature Reserve

Getting there The reserve is on the northern fringe of the Little Karoo. There are two possible routes to the campsite and offices. From the north, travelling along the N1 highway between Touwsriver and Beaufort West, take the turning at Laingsburg. For the first 25 km the road is surfaced. Take a right turning onto a good dirt road (signposted Ladismith), and after another 25 km another right turning takes you into the hills towards the nature reserve. The camp is 23 km from here. From Ladismith it is about the same distance to the camp, but this involves more driving on the R323 dirt road. This is a beautiful drive as the road climbs up into the Swartberg Mountains.

Western Cape

Barrydale

Phone code: 028
(NB Always use
3-figure prefix)
Colour map 6, grid B6

This is the centre of a small farming community set in a fertile valley between the Little Karoo and the Breede River Valley. The surrounding farmland is a colourful mix of vineyards and wild flowers – in the spring the hillsides are covered with *mesembryanthemums*. The area also produces peaches, apricots, apples and brandy. The local wine co-operative has been a great success and any meal eaten in the locality should be accompanied by their *Chardonnay*. For tastings, T5721012. Local information is available from the town clerk, T6162105.

Price codes:
see inside front cover

Sleeping C *Barrydale Country Inn*, T5721226, Van Riebeeck St. Town hotel with double rooms, en suite bathrooms, attached restaurant, swimming pool. **E** *Tradouw Guest House* , 46 Van Riebeeck St, T5721434. Signposted by the Wynkelder off the R62, by the Huis River. B&B, double rooms, plus some shaded campsites with electric points, attached restaurant. An added attraction is the Anna Roux Wild Flower garden which is full of succulents and cacti.

Tradouw Pass

Running parallel to the Langeberg Mountains, the R62, or 'Route 62', continues west along the course of the Kingna River to Montagu, 66 km. To the south, the R324 passes over the spectacular Tradouw Pass through the Langeberg Mountains. When opened in 1873, the pass provided an important trade route for the farmers of the Little Karoo with Port Beaufort at the mouth of the Breede River. As with many civil engineering projects of the time, convict labour was used to build the road, under the direction of Thomas Bain. Halfway up the remains of the prisoners' camp can still be seen. At the northern end **San rock paintings** adorn some caves. Close to these a track leads to the river and a refreshing pool suitable for swimming. The pass was originally named after the magistrate of Swellendam, Robert Southey, who had led the petition for the route to be opened up. But the original name used by the Khoi long before the white settlers arrived has remained in use.

East of Oudtshoorn

Mons Ruber
wine estate

Just before the road crosses over the railway at Le Roux, 27 km east of Oudtshoorn, is a right turning to Mons Ruber wine estate, T044-2516550. An old hotel building has been restored to house a small display and wine tastings. The grapes grown here have a high sugar content and are particularly suitable for **dessert wines**. ■ *Sales and tasting: Mon-Fri, 0830-1700, Sat, 0830-1300.* Close to the winery is a short walk around the **Rooikoppe hills**, a pleasant place to stretch your legs and admire some ancient rock formations. Permits are issued from the winery. The N12 (formerly the R29) reaches De Rust 35 km east of Oudtshoorn.

De Rust

Phone code: 044
(NB Always use
3-figure prefix)
Colour map 7, grid B2

This well-preserved village has a number of classic Karoo homes. Surprisingly it is world renowned for its rare pelargoniums from which geraniums were first grown. If you have time, the wine farm **Domein Doornkraal** has tastings and sales of the local wines. Local information is available from *De Shop in de Rust*, Main St, T083-3651362 (mob), also a curio shop and internet café. The village is named after the farm owned by the farmer who found the first route north through the Swartberg Mountains – his name was Petrus Johannes Meiring.

Every November
a half-marathon
is run in the pass

The road through the **Meiringspoort Pass** in the Swartberg Mountains is worth the petrol; so too is the 60 m high **Meiringspoort waterfall**. This can be reached via a short path from the car park. The road through the mountains was built by AG de Smidt, the son-in-law of the famous road builder Andrew Bain. It was opened in 1857, but because it more or less followed the course of the River Groot, it suffered considerable damage during the rains and by 1885 had been completely washed away. Funds collected at the tollgate were never sufficient to pay for repairs. The tar road still survives today along the base of the gorge, and crosses the river 30 times. The 17 km drive is one to be savoured as the vast sandstone cliffs loom above you. Following the road through the gorge, you eventually end up at **Prince Albert**, a journey of about 90 km. You can then return to Oudtshoorn (72 km), via the Swartberg Pass along the R328.

Sleeping and eating D *Olivier's*, Main St, T2412258. Guesthouse set in a modern bunga-low, garden, pool, braai area, attached Herrie's coffee shop. D *Oulap*, T2412250. B&B. *Die Groen Bliktrommel*, homemade lunches and afternoon teas, also a local craft shop. *Herrie's*, recommended for a hearty breakfast. Try their homemade breads.

Transport Bus: *Greyhound* (Pretoria-Mossel Bay route) and *Intercape* (Pretoria-Knysna route) bus services stop briefly here at the *Maihova Garage*, **Oudtshoorn** 30 mins but hitch-ing is your best option for such a short distance.

Garden Route

The Garden Route is probably South Africa's most celebrated area, a stretch of coast heralded as one of the country's highlights. Its high level of exposure has made it hugely popular, and few visitors to Cape Town miss it. Nevertheless, opinions vary on the area's merits and many maintain that it is hyped and in reality has little to offer. Few, however, can deny that it is a beautiful area, a 200 km stretch of rugged coast backed by lush mountains. The route follows the coast between Heidelberg in the west and Tsitsikamma National Park to the east, separated from the interior by the Tsitsikamma and Outeniqua mountain ranges. In contrast to the dry and treeless area of the Karoo on the interior side of the mountains, rain falls all year round on the Garden Route and the ocean-facing mountain slopes are covered with luxurious forests. It is this dramatic change in landscape, which occurs over a distance of no more than 20 km, that prompted people to refer to the coastal area as the Garden Route.

The attractions along the Garden Route are numerous. The larger towns, such as George and Knysna, are highly developed tourist resorts, while other areas offer untouched wilderness and wonderful hikes, including one of the most famous in the country, the Otter Trail. This runs along the coast in Tsitsikamma National Park, one of the most popular national parks in South Africa. There is a second national park, Wilderness, which is also very popular. If hiking isn't your scene, the beaches are stun-ning, offering a mix of peaceful seaside villages and livelier surfer spots.

Ins & outs
It is quite easy to drive the full length of the Garden Route in a day, but most visitors either choose a base for exploring the area, or spend a day or two in several places of interest along the way. The area's popularity means that good value accommodation is difficult to find, and it gets booked up months in advance, especially during peak season. It is advisable to avoid the area during the two weeks over Christmas and the New Year, and at Easter. For the rest of the school holidays most of the self-catering accommodation will still be fully booked, but bed and breakfasts or hostels should have a free room – call in advance to be sure.

Conservation
Travelling along the coast, the vegetation is markedly lush and green compared to the interior, but this hides the fact that the majority of the Knysna and Tsitsikamma forest was completely destroyed by the early settlers. What remains today is only a small fraction of the indigenous forest, and this is threatened from the encroach-ment of alien species. The recent history of the region is closely linked with the search for timber for the growing population in the Cape. It only took a few years for the small patches of forest in Hout Bay, Rondebosch, Newlands and Kirstenbosch to be depleted, and the first white colonists to reach Mossel Bay in 1711 came looking for wood. During the 1850s the forests around the Humansdorp area were exploited, but it was not until a road was cut through to the Keurbooms River in 1867 that the Tsitsikamma forest came under threat.

In 1880, Comte De Vasselot de Regne, a forestry scientist of international repute from the French Forestry School at Nancy, was appointed Superintendent of Forests for the Cape Colony. He held the post for 12 years and during this period managed

Western Cape

to make people begin to value the indigenous forest and start to think along the lines of proper resource management. When he returned to France, the remaining Cape forests were well-protected by legislation and a start had been made with the planting of exotic pine species. However, it was only as late as 1938 that over-exploitation ceased to be a problem, when all remaining woodcutters were pensioned off. The first exotic species were planted in 1891; red gum and cluster pine were planted near Bloukrans to replace sections of the forest damaged by the great fire. In 1896 a nursery was established at Witfontein. The supply of timber for the industry is now based entirely upon fast growing exotic species such as slash pine, monterey pine, karri gum and Australian blackwood. However, these species are having a negative effect on indigenous species – their fast water absorption has in places starved other trees, in effect suffocating indigenous species. Some areas are beginning removal schemes of exotic aliens to bring the problem under control. Today only 65,000 ha of the original forest remain along the Garden Route, most of which lies within the Tsitsikamma National Park and around Knysna.

Mossel Bay

Phone code: 044
(NB Always use
3-figure prefix)
Colour map 7, grid B2

Built along a rocky peninsula which provides sheltered swimming and mooring in the bay, Mossel Bay is one of the larger and least appealing seaside towns along the Garden Route. During the school holidays the town is packed, but for the rest of the year it is just another dull coastal town. A fact often overlooked in promotional literature is that since the discovery of offshore oil deposits, Mossel Bay is also the home of the ugly *Mossgas* natural gas refinery and a multitude of oil storage tanks.

Interestingly, the town has a number of Portuguese flags and names dotted around, thanks to the first European to anchor in the bay – **Bartolomeu Dias**, who landed in February 1488. His efforts to communicate with local Khoi herdsmen were met with stone throwing, but **Vasco da Gama**, who moored in the bay in 1497, had more luck; he managed to establish trading relations with them. The bay's safe anchorage and its freshwater spring ensured that it became a regular stopping off point for other seafarers. The town's name was given by a Dutch trader, Cornelis de Houtman, who in 1595 found a pile of mussel shells in a cave below the present lighthouse.

Mossel Bay Tourism Bureau, on is the corner of Church and Market streets, T6912202, F6903077, www.gardenroute.net/mby Open Mon-Fri, 0800-1800, Sat & Sun, 0900-1700. It acts as a central reservations office for local accommodation.

Sights

Unsurprisingly, many of the local attractions relate to the sea and reflect the bay's importance to early Portuguese navigators and Dutch explorers. All the museums are on one site known as the **Bartolomeu Dias Museum complex**, T6911067, http://diasmuseum.museum.com The displays in the Maritime Museum are arranged around a full-size replica of Bartolomeu Dias' caravel. A tree with a fascinating past is the **Post Office Tree**, a giant milkwood situated close to the freshwater spring. History relates that in 1500 a letter was left under the tree by a ship's captain. A year later it was retrieved by the commander of the Third East India Fleet en route to India. Messages were also left carved in rocks and left in old boots tied to the branches. The tree has been declared a national monument.

Cage diving is possible
here – check with the
tourist office for
reputable operators

In the middle of the bay is **Seal Island** which can be visited by cruises departing from the harbour. The island is inhabited by colonies of African penguins and Cape fur seals (the best month to see seal pups is November). It's also possible to see **great white sharks** and small hammerhead sharks which prey upon the seals. Between September and November the warm waters of the bay are often visited by southern right, humpback and brydes whales while calving. Another vantage point for viewing whales and dolphins is **The Point** at the end of Marsh Street. Close by is **Street Blaize Lighthouse**, one of only two remaining 24-hour manned lighthouses in South Africa.

The **St Blaize Trail** is a perfect introduction to the spectacular coastline that you are likely to encounter along the Garden Route. This is a 13.5 km walk along the cliffs

The milkwood tree

*Four white milkwood (*Sideroxylon inerme*) trees in South Africa have been proclaimed as national monuments. All milkwoods are protected to such an extent that a permit is required before an individual can even prune a tree on their land. Their name is derived from the milky latex found in the fruit and the bark. The flowers have a very distinctive smell which attracts insects, which in turn attract birds. They also bear fruit which when ripe turns a purple colour and is eaten by birds and baboons. These beautiful shade trees are found all along the Pacific coast in many shapes and sizes. In the harshest of conditions they may only grow into a shrub-like bush, the largest tree is on a farm near Bredasdorp.*

It has a spread of 20 m, a trunk girth of over 3 m, and is thought to be over 1,000 years old. The most famous milkwood is the Post Office Tree in Mossel Bay which must be at least 500 years old. They were one of the species of tree that early settlers singled out for economic use, their wood is hard and durable and was used for building boats, bridges and homes. These days the threat comes from natural causes, alien vegetation in the forests. During a bush fire alien plants burn fiercely and any milkwoods close by may die as a result of the intensity of the heat. Thick alien growth also prevents the germination of milkwood seed and the growth of the saplings.

Western Cape

and rocky coast west from Mossel Bay. The official trail starts from Bats cave, just below the lighthouse; the path is marked by the white image of a bird in flight. As you walk further from the town the scenery becomes more and more spectacular. You can leave the coast at Pinnacle Point, and follow a path inland to Essenhout Street. This cuts about 5 km off the walk. The path ends by a group of houses in Dana Bay. From here you will have to organize your own transport back into town. This should not be too difficult as the road leads up to the junction with the N2 where most traffic turns off the main road to enter Mossel Bay. A helpful map is available from the tourist information centre. You are rightly warned to be careful in places during strong winds, as there are some precipitous and unprotected drops from the cliff tops. Khoi-San articles dating back 80,000 years were recently discovered in Cape St Blaize Cave – they were not open to the public at time of writing, but check at the tourist centre for more information.

B *Old Post Office Tree*, corner of Church and Market streets, T6913738, F6913104, www.oldposttree.co.za Comfortable rooms in a smart manor house which is the third oldest building in Mossel Bay. Outdoor dining area with views across bay, swimming pool, private yacht, popular and always recommended by visitors, check for seasonal discounts. **B** *The Point*, Point Rd, T6913512, F6913513, www.pointhotel.co.za Large, ugly construction but in an unbeatable location, right on the rocks below the lighthouse. All rooms have sea views and private balconies, are en suite and have satellite TV. There is a rock pool just outside which is good for swimming. **B-C** *Allemans Dorpshuis*, 94 Montagu St, T6903621. Lovely old-fashioned hotel in a fine restored Victorian town house with the original iron balcony at the front. Beautifully furnished rooms with en suite showers and polished wooden floors. French and German spoken. **C** *Huijs te Marquette*, 1 Marsh St, T6913182, marquette@pixie.co.za A comfortable house which has been decorated with a lot of thought, 14 en suite rooms, relaxed atmosphere, evening meals on request, swimming pool, secure parking. Recommended. **C** *Mossel Bay Guesthouse*, 61 Bruns Rd, T6912000. Friendly guesthouse with 4 double rooms, with en suite bathrooms and sea views. The house is tucked back from the town centre up the hill. **C-D** *Dolphin Heights*, 7 Sebastian St, T6904421, fritz@lando.co.za Modern, 3-storey house with en suite double rooms, TV, sea views from all rooms, lounge, B&B, fully equipped kitchen, laundry, off-street parking.

E-F *Santos Caravan Park*, on the George road 2 km from town centre, T6912915. Large well-grassed park, limited shade, some self-catering chalets, not the place to stay at when full, but fine at the quiet time of year, right on the beach. **E-F** *Mossel Bay Backpackers*, 1

Sleeping
■ *on map, page 282*
Price codes:
see inside front cover

During busy periods contact the Mossel Bay Tourism Bureau to confirm overnight accommodation. It acts as a central reservations office for registered members, T6912202, F6903077

Marsh St, T/F6913182, marquette@pixie.co.za Part of *Huijs te Marquette*, dorms and double rooms, TV room, convenient location, popular. **F** *Barnacles Backpackers*, 112 High St, head up Church St until you see the large purple Barnacles sign, T/F6904584, barnacles@mweb.co.za Spotlessly clean place with doubles and dorms, 2 kitchens, good breakfasts, TV area, balcony, garden and rooftop braai area. Friendly, quiet place. **F** *Santos Express*, T6911995. santos_express@mweb.co.za Converted train carriage set on Santos beach with tiny rooms and an onboard pub and snack bar.

Eating
● *on map*

Annie's Kitchen, Marsh St, T6903708. One of several nearby cafés serving coffee and breakfast throughout the day. *Camelot*, Market St, T6911000, opposite tourist office. Mixed menu, live bands at weekend. *Fynbos Coffee Shoppe*, Marsh St, T6911366. Combined coffee and gift shop, with freshly baked cakes. *Gannet*, Market St, T6911885. Next to *Old Post Tree Guest House*, a well-established seafood restaurant, popular all year round since the tour buses stop here, seafood grills and pizza from a wood oven, enjoyable bay views from a shady outdoor terrace, mixed reports on quality of the food. *Jazzbury's*, 11 Marsh St, T6911923. A popular restaurant serving good value traditional South African meals. Recommended. *Kingfisher*, The Point. Modern development overlooking the beach, seafood restaurant, good grilled fish served with rice and chips, some meat dishes, indifferent service. There is an attached pizza and pasta restaurant downstairs. *Pavillion*, Santos Beach, T6904567. The ideal spot for lunch, just stroll up straight from the beach on to the old wooden veranda and enjoy a steak or light lunch while watching the boats sailing in the bay. Bustling atmosphere. *Pizza Express*, Marsh St. Cheap and cheerful place for take away pizzas. *The Post Tree*, Powrie St, T6911177. Closed Sun. Pasta and seafood, recommended for line fish, one of the best in town. *Spur Minnesota*, 55 Marsh St, T6911306. Steakhouse with the usual range of trimmings. *Sugar & Spice*, 49 Marsh St. Daytime coffee shop. *Tidals*, The Point. Seafront

Mossel Bay

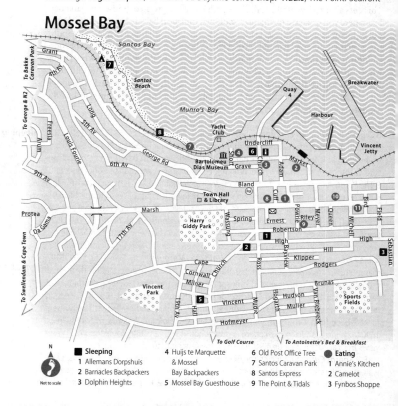

N
Not to scale

■ **Sleeping**		● **Eating**
1 Allemans Dorpshuis	4 Huijs te Marquette	6 Old Post Office Tree	1 Annie's Kitchen
2 Barnacles Backpackers	& Mossel	7 Santos Caravan Park	2 Camelot
3 Dolphin Heights	Bay Backpackers	8 Santos Express	3 Fynbos Coffee Shoppe
	5 Mossel Bay Guesthouse	9 The Point & Tidals	

tavern built on the rocks, cool rooms with a high ceiling and plenty of light, recommended for pub lunches. Lively late nights at the weekend.

Shopping

The *Ocher Barn* has a variety of shops. The *Liberty Shopping Centre* on Bland St contains most of the shops you'll need including chemists, bookshops, a wine store and a *Pick 'n' Pay* supermarket. *Foto First*, Liberty Shopping Centre, Bland St, 1-hr film developing.

Sports

Bungee jumping As you drive along the N2 between Albertina and Mossel Bay you'll see a crowd of people gathered at the Gouritz River bridge, 10 km out of Albertina. This is a popular bungee jump from the road bridge into the 65-m deep river gorge. The jumps are organized by *Face Adrenaline*, T6977001, www.faceadrenaline.com

Scuba diving *Mossel Bay Divers*, *Santos Protea Hotel*, T6911441, on the waterfront, equipment hire and boat charters, also offer PADI courses. *Diving Academy*, T6931179, diving.academy@usa.net Dive trips and courses. The best time for diving is between Dec and the end of Apr. During this period the sea is at its calmest and conditions in the bay are clear and safe. Close to Santos Beach are 4 recognized dive sites but none could be considered spectacular. All can be reached from the shore. For experienced divers, the **Windvogel Reef**, 800 m off Cape St Blaize, is highly recommended. The reef is fully exposed to the ocean and should therefore only be dived when the sea is calm. There are drop-offs and a few caves. Soft corals and colourful sponges are plentiful. The maximum depth is 27 m. (See also Diving section in Essentials, page 51.)

Tour operators

Romonza, T6903101, romonza@mweb.co.za, runs daily pleasure cruises from the harbour off Bland St. The most popular outings are to Seal Island (see above) and the sunset cruise. Romonza also offers the only licensed boat-based whale watching in Mossel Bay. Advance booking necessary during local holidays. At weekends and during the holidays a boat leaves every hr on the hr between 0900 and 1700. The sunset cruise lasts for 2 hrs and for R65 you can enjoy champagne and seafood dishes. Another popular trip is a breakfast cruise. This is an invigorating way to start the day: a full cooked breakfast and fresh fruits is included in the price of R50 per person. Each boat can be chartered for large groups; minimum 2 hrs. Trips leave from the blue tent on the harbour.

Western Cape

Mossel Bay

4 Gannet
5 Jazzbury's
6 Kingfisher & Tidals
7 Pavillion
8 Pizza Express
9 Post Tree
10 Spur Minesota
11 Sugar & Spice

Transport

Rail Trains for Mossel Bay stop at a station called **Hartenbos**, a small seaside village 7 km from Mossel Bay. The weekly *Southern Cross* which runs between **Cape Town** and **Oudtshoorn** stops here. **Cape Town** (11½ hrs), Sun 2102, via Swellendam, Robertson and Worcester. **Oudtshoorn** (6½ hrs), Fri 0547.

Road 365 km to **Cape Town**, 55 km to **George**, 116 km to **Knysna**, 80 km to **Oudtshoorn**, 206 km to **Tsitsikamma**, 375 km to **Port Elizabeth**. The N2 bypasses Mossel Bay, almost halfway between Cape Town and Port Elizabeth. **Bus**: *Baz Bus*, T021-4392323, www.bazbus.com Book a day in advance to continue your journey. Service runs daily in each direction between Cape Town and Port Elizabeth. Towards

Cape Town: expect to be collected between 1200-1600. Towards Port Elizabeth: expect to be collected between 1300-1505. Onward connections from Port Elizabeth to Durban run daily.

Greyhound, T021-5056363, coaches depart from Shell Truck stop, Voorbaai. **Cape Town** (6 hrs), daily 0320, 0730; **Durban** (19 hrs), daily 0125; **East London** (13 hrs), daily 0125; **Port Elizabeth** (5 ½ hrs), daily 0125.

Intercape, T021-3804400, coaches depart from Shell Truck stop, Voorbaai. **Cape Town** (6 hrs): daily, 1200, 0115; **Durban** (19 hrs), daily 1315, 0045; **Johannesburg** and **Pretoria** (16 hrs), daily 1715; Mon, Thu, Fri, Sun, 1430; **Port Elizabeth** (5½ hrs), daily 1315, 0045.

Translux, T021-4493333, coaches depart from Shell Truck stop, Voorbaai. **Cape Town** (6 hrs), daily 0140, 1210; **Durban** (19 hrs), daily 0025; **East London** (13 hrs), daily 0025; **Johannesburg** and **Pretoria** (16 hrs), daily 2000; Mon, Thu, Sat, 1815; **Knysna** (1½ hrs), daily 1440, 0025; Mon, Thu, Sat, 0935; **Port Elizabeth** (5 ½ hrs), daily 0025, 1305.

Directory **Useful services** Ambulance: T10177. **Emergency Pharmacy**: T6930892. **Hospital**: T6912011. **Police**: T10111. **Sea Rescue**: T10177.

George

Phone code: 044
(NB Always use
3-figure prefix)
Colour map 7, grid B2
Altitude: 225 m

Often referred to as the gateway to, or the capital of, the Garden Route, George owes its status to the fact that it has an airport. It is also an important junction between the N2 coastal highway and the N9 passing through the Outeniqua Pass into the Karoo. It lies in the shadow of the Outeniqua Mountains, but unlike the majority of towns along the Garden Route, it is not by the sea. The town itself is a mostly modern grid of streets interspersed with some attractive old buildings and churches. While it is pleasant enough, it has little appeal compared to other towns along the coast; the main reason overseas visitors come here is for the championship golf course (see below).

There's a very helpful **Tourism Bureau**, 124 York St, T8019295, www. georgetourism.co.za, open Mon-Fri, 0800-1630, Sat, 0900-1200, with a wide range of information on the Garden Route. But like many offices along the Garden Route, they only promote accommodation which pays a fee to the office.

History The first settlement appeared here in 1778 as a forestry post to process wood from the surrounding forests. In 1811 it was formally declared a town, and named after King George III. It was at this time that its wide tree-lined streets – Courtenay, York and Meade – were laid out. For the next 80 years the town remained the centre for a voracious timber industry. Much of the indigenous forest was destroyed supplying wood for wagons, railway sleepers and mine props. Some of the trees came to be known as **Stinkwoods** because of their odour when freshly cut. Few remain today; they are slow growing and endemic to South Africa.

Sights Within the town itself there are only a few sights of interest. On the corner of Cathedral and York streets is **St Mark's Cathedral**, consecrated in 1850. The building has an unusually large number of stained glass windows for its size, and gave George its city status. Many of the windows were designed by overseas artists of limited fame. In 1911 a Bible and Royal Prayer Book were given to the church by King George V. The interior of the **Dutch Reformed Mother Church** at the north end of Meade Street reflects the town's early history as a centre for the timber industry. The pulpit is carved out of stinkwood and took over a year to create. The ceiling was built from yellowwood, and six yellowwood trunks were used as pillars.

The mountains
create an impressive
backdrop to the
Dutch Reformed
Mother Church when
viewed from the
corner of Courtenay
and Meade streets

In front of the tourist office, housed in the King Edward VII library, is an ancient oak tree known as the **Slave Tree**. It is one of the original trees planted by Adrianus van Kervel in the early 1800s and has been declared a national monument. The tree is known as the 'slave' tree because of the chain embedded in the trunk with a lock attached to it. The story of the chain can be traced back to when a public tennis court was in use next to the library (now housing the information office), and the court roller was secured to the tree to prevent playful children from rolling it down the street. The **Drostdy Museum**, on Courtenay Street, has displays on the timber industry as well as musical instruments and a collection of old phonographs. In the Sayer's Wing is an exhibition devoted to former President PW Botha, who was a member of parliament for George for 38 years. ■ *Mon-Fri 0800-1700*. There is a fairly new **Railway Museum** on Mission Street (just off Knysna Road), T8018288, with an interesting display outlining the history of steam train travel, and is adjacent to the new platform from which the Outeniqua steam train departs. **George Crocodile** Park, on Pacaltsdorp Road, has the usual collection of reptiles in captivity, with daily feeding at 1500. ■ *0900-1700, T8734302*.

Sleeping
■ *on map*
Price codes:
see inside front cover

A *Fancourt*, 6 km from George Airport, T8040000, F8040700, www.fancourt.com A smart estate built around a 18-hole championship golf course which was designed by Gary Player. There is a mix of double rooms in the Manor House and garden suites, plus 4 restaurants, 3 swimming pools, a gym, mini cinema, crèche and health spa. **B** *King George Protea*, King George Dr, T8747659, F8747664, king.george@pixie.co.za Smart Victorian hotel now under Protea management, close to golf course, 60 comfortable rooms. **B-C** *Oakhurst*, corner of Meade and Cathedral streets, T8747130, F8747131, oakhurst@fortesking-hotels.co.za Luxury town inn in the design of a classic Cape Dutch house with thatched roof, 25 smart en suite rooms, large restaurant, lounge and 'ladies' bar. **C** *Far Hills Country Hotel*, off the N2 towards Wilderness, T8890000, www.farhills.co.za A comfortable country hotel in the lee of the Outeniqua Mountains. 49 rooms, some with superb views across the forest, but a bit cramped. Restaurant with open terrace, lounge, bar and swimming pool. More suited to an overnight stop than a holiday base, short drive from George airport. **C** *Foresters Protea Lodge*, 123 York St, T8744488, F8744428, foman@webonline.co.za Large hotel in an attractive Cape Dutch-style building. Good location on the main road, with 50 standard but comfortable a/c rooms, restaurant and bar. **C** *Hawthorndene*, Langenhoven Rd, T8744160, F8745452. Family-run country inn with 26 rooms, a good restaurant and bar. **C** *Pine Lodge*,

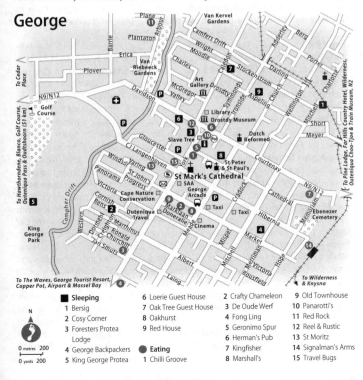

George

■ **Sleeping**	6 Loerie Guest House	2 Crafty Chameleon	9 Old Townhouse
1 Bersig	7 Oak Tree Guest House	3 De Oude Werf	10 Panarotti's
2 Cosy Corner	8 Oakhurst	4 Fong Ling	11 Red Rock
3 Foresters Protea Lodge	9 Red House	5 Geronimo Spur	12 Reel & Rustic
4 George Backpackers	● **Eating**	6 Herman's Pub	13 St Moritz
5 King George Protea	1 Chilli Groove	7 Kingfisher	14 Signalman's Arms
		8 Marshall's	15 Travel Bugs

0 metres 200
0 yards 200

To The Waves, George Tourist Resort, Copper Pot, Airport & Mossel Bay

To Wilderness & Knysna

Western Cape

Knysna Rd, close to Pick 'n' Pay, T8711974, pingeo@mweb.co.za Large resort close to Victoria Bay with 48 self-catering chalets, each with M-Net TV, telephone, braai area. There is also a restaurant, bar, tennis courts and a swimming pool. **C-D** *Loerie Guest House*, 91 Davidson Rd, T/F8744740. Modern buildings with 22 large and comfortable rooms, a neat garden with a swimming pool. However, breakfast is small and the service lacks the friendliness you would expect in such an establishment. **C** *The Waves*, 6 Beach Rd, Victoria Bay, T/F8890166, thewaves@intekom.co.za Family-run B&B on the beachfront in nearby Victoria Bay. Comfortable en suite rooms with balconies and sea views, friendly, low-key place, a more pleasant location than the centre of George.

D *Bergsig*, 49 Stander St, T8715170, cug@mweb.co.za B&B with 4 en suite rooms, 1 self-catering unit, buffet breakfasts, sun deck, mountain views, ask for Suzelna. **D** *Cedar Place*, 3 Cedar Av, T8745742, www.cedarplace.co.za Cottage in the garden of a Cape Dutch home, 2 en suite bedrooms, kitchen, TV, fireplace, wheelchair-friendly, superb views of the mountains, good value. **D** *The Red House*, 28 Aspeling St, T8841577, theredhouse@intekom.co.za Small guesthouse with 2 en suite rooms and 1 self-catering apartment, private entrances, neat garden, off-street parking. **D** *Oak Tree Guest House*, 30 Caledon St, T8745931, T082-8964797 (mob). A turn of the century family home which has been faithfully restored. Double rooms with en suite bathroom, TV and mini bar, central location, ideal for shops and restaurants, ask for Gail. Recommended.

D-E *Cosy Corner*, 12 Rens St, T8740710, www.cosy-corner.co.za B&B with old-fashioned rooms, TV, en suite, dinner available on request, garden views, no children under 10, owners are also tour guides so know all there is to know about the area. **E-F** and **B** *George Tourist Resort*, York St, T8745205, F8744255. Huge complex with self-catering chalets, rondavels and caravans. Shady sites with power and water, indoor pool and outdoor heated pool, gym, sauna, tennis courts, crazy golf, shop, laundry, room for 300 caravans! Double the price during peak season. **F** *George Backpackers*, 29 York ST, T8747807, F8746054. New hostel in a good location on the main road. The building has recently undergone a facelift so everything still looks in good shape. Dorms and doubles, bright and airy, some with mountain views, broad lawn for camping at the back, braai area, breakfasts on request. Only backpacker option in town.

Eating
• *on map*

Copper Pot, 12 Montagu St, Blanco, T8707378. Closed for lunch Sat and Sun. Excellent and elegant seafood restaurant serving very fresh grilled fish, as well as slightly different dishes – try the Mauritian curry. Award-winning wine list. Recommended. *Chilli Groove*, in shopping centre on corner of Cathedral and York streets, T3820931, Mexican restaurant and cocktail bar, usual range of Tex-Mex dishes, plus pizzas. *Crafty Chameleon*, 79 Market St, T8744027, quirky coffee shop serving soups, sandwiches and salads, plus a couple of more substantial dishes. *De Oude Werf*, 53 York St, T8735892. Comfortable dining area, good choice of typical South African dishes, daily venison specials, considerably better than the average steakhouse, lively atmosphere. *Fong Ling*, 69 Fichat St, T8840088. Taiwanese and Chinese dishes, some exotic seafood dishes. *Geronimo Spur*, 118 York St, T8734279. Steakhouse chain, generous portions, popular with families. *Herman's Pub*, 70 Courtney St, T8732052. Grill house serving good pub meals in an old-fashioned setting. *Kingfisher*, 1 Courtenay St, T8733127. Fresh seafood dishes, some meat dishes including good ostrich, also has a good selection of pasta and pizzas on offer. *Marshall's*, corner of Market and Meade streets, T8740918. Quality steakhouse serving good pub lunches, carvery on Sun, live music at weekends, outside seating on deck. *The Old Townhouse*, 20 Market St, T8743663. Good value, wide selection of meat and seafood, plus good salads. *Panarotti's*, 126 York St, T8747084. Pizza and pasta chain, very good value, friendly staff. *Red Rock*, Red River Centre, T8733842, pizza, pasta, steaks and seafood. *Reel and Rustic*, Davidson Rd, T8840707, popular seafood restaurant serving good fresh dishes. *St Moritz*, 16 Varing Rd, T8745993. Closes Sun. An emphasis on German-style meals, plus some seafood options, good quality. Recommended for anyone missing a more European-style meal. *Signalman's Arms*, Railway Station, T8730162. Good snacks, eat here before boarding the train. *Travel Bugs*, 111 York St, T8732009, lively café with an obsession with travel. Munch on delicious homemade cakes and sandwiches while poring over their selection of guide books and maps. Also has internet access and sells souvenirs. Recommended. *Wine Barrel*, 12 Montagu St, Blanco, bistro meals, part of the Copper Pot.

Arts and crafts *Der Lederhändler*, 3 Ring Rd, T8746935, shoes, belts, bags and other leather goods; *Touw Meubels*, 76 York St, T8735627, superior quality wooden furniture; *Woodcraft Furniture*, 34 CJ Langenhoven St, range of old-fashioned, well-finished furniture. *Strydom Gallery*, 79 Market St, an art shop with interesting exhibits as well as pieces for sale. **Shopping mall** *Marklaan*, between Market St and Meade St, shopping mall in converted store rooms arranged around open square. There is a coffee shop plus a couple of curio shops. A farmers' market is held Fri, 0700-1000 in the open square. *St George's Mall*, new slick mall with the usual clothes and food shops, Ster-Kinekor cinema and restaurants.

Shopping
George has a legacy of fine craftsmanship. Quality leather goods and wood furniture are a particular speciality in the town

Golf *George Golf Course*, CJ Langenhoven St, T8736116, par 72, 5,852 m, green fees about R60. *Fancourt Hotel and Country Club*, T8040000, F8040700, www.fancourt.com, par 71, 5,935 m, championship course designed by Gary Player, open to members and hotel guests only. **Hiking** There are over 20 recognized hiking trails around George and Wilderness. Details of hikes close to George are described below. For information on longer trails, call T8708323. **Watersports** The usual range of watersports are available along the coast. Check locally for demarcated areas for swimming and surfing. Children should be supervised in the sea as there are strong rip currents. One of the safest spots for swimming is in the Touw River mouth, Wilderness. There is good surfing in Victoria Bay. For scuba diving courses, charters and equipment hire, contact *George Scuba Diving Club*, T8746739, or T8708044.

Sports

Eco Bound, T083-7007907 (mob), prices don't include meals. *Eden Adventures*, T0448770179, www.edenadventures.co.za, excellent, good value adventure tours to Wilderness National Park. *Ingeloza Eco Tours*, T082-5746887 (mob). *Outeniqua Adventure Tours*, T082-7862144 (mob). *South Cape Travel*, 111 York St, T8746930, www.southcapetravel.co.za Very helpful local travel agent, can book flights, bus seats, local tours.

Tour operators

Local Car hire: *Avis*, T8769222; *Budget*, T8736259, airport T8769204.

Transport

Air George airport is 10 km from the town centre. There are flights to and from **Cape Town**, **Durban**, **East London**, **Johannesburg** and **Port Elizabeth**. For general information contact T8769310. *Avis*, *Budget* and *Imperial* all have a car hire counter in the terminal building. If you wish to leave your car at the airport there are a few lock-up garages available. *SAA & SA Express*, T8018434, fly the following routes in South Africa: **Cape Town** (1 hr), 3-5 flights a day, except Sat, 2 flights a day; **Durban** (2½ hrs), daily.

Rail The railway station is in the centre of town at the east end of Market St. Enquiries T8738202. The weekly service, called the *Southern Cross*, which runs between **Cape Town** and **Outdshoorn** stops here. **Cape Town** (13 hrs), Sun 1950, via **Hartenbos**, **Swellendam** and **Worcester**; **Port Elizabeth** (11 hrs), Fri 0658. Steam train: The *Outeniqua Choo-Tjoe* runs between George and **Knysna**, T044-8018289 or T044-3821361; see below.

Road 420 km to **Cape Town**, 320 km to **Port Elizabeth**, 61 km to **Knysna**, 55 km to **Mossel Bay**, 93 km to **Plettenberg Bay**, 151 km to **Tsitsikamma**, 60 km to **Oudtshoorn**. **Bus**: *Greyhound*, T021-5056363, coaches depart from St Mark's Sq. **Cape Town** (6 hrs), daily 0240; **Durban** (18 hrs), daily 0210; **East London** (9 hrs), daily 0315; **Knysna** (1 hr), daily 0210; **Port Elizabeth** (4 hrs): daily, 0210.
   Intercape, T021-3804400, coaches depart George station, on Station St, or from St Mark's Sq. **Bloemfontein** (9 hrs), daily 1810; **Cape Town** (6 hrs), daily 1115, 0030; **Durban** (18 hrs), daily 1400, 0130; **East London** (9 hrs), daily 1400, 0130; **Kimberley** (9 hrs), Mon, Thu, Fri, Sun 1515. **Knysna** (1 hr), daily 1400, 0130; **Oudtshoorn** (2 hrs), daily 1800; Mon, Thu, Fri, Sun 1515. **Port Elizabeth** (4 hrs), daily 1400, 0130; **Johannesburg** and **Pretoria** (17 hrs), 1800; Mon, Thu, Fri, Sun 1515.
   Translux, T021-4493333, coaches depart from St Mark's Sq. **Beaufort West** (4½ hrs), Fri 1600, 1700, Wed, 1700, Mon, Tue, Thu, Sun, 1800; **Bloemfontein** (10 hrs), Fri 1600, Mon, Tue, Thu 1800; **Cape Town** (7 hrs), daily 0030, 1210; **Durban** (11 hrs), daily 0105; **Johannesburg** and **Pretoria** (17 hrs), Tue, Wed, Fri, Sun 1715; **Kimberley** (9 hrs), Tue, Wed, Fri, Sun 1715; **Knysna** (1 hr), Sun

Western Cape

0850, Tue, Wed, Fri 1035, Mon, Thu, Sat 0735, daily, 1400; **Oudtshoorn** (2 hrs), daily shuttle 0115, Tue, Wed, Fri, Sun 1715; **Port Elizabeth** (4 hrs), daily 0105; **Swellendam** (3 hrs), daily 0030.

Baz Bus, T021-4392323, www.bazbus.com This is the best value budget bus service along the Garden Route. For towns towards Port Elizabeth, service collects pre-booked passengers at approximately 1400. Towards Cape Town, departs at about 1500. All seats need to be booked in advance. Daily service between Cape Town and Port Elizabeth in both directions. Another cheap option is the privately run *Garden Line Bus*. For information and timetables, T044-8760074.

Directory **Banks** All the principal banks, *First National*, *Nedbank*, *Standard*, and *ABSA Bank* are in York St. **Communications** *Travel Bugs*, 111 York St, T8732009, internet café and travel shop. **Post Office**: York St. **Useful services** Casualty: T8745122, 8746770. **Police**: Courtenay St, T8736262, T10111. Taxi: *Zeelies Taxis* T8746707.

Around George

Local hiking trails

The mountains which enclose the Garden Route make excellent hiking country. They are wild and remote and in places a real challenge

The **Cradock and George Peaks** trail starts from the old Witfontein forest station. Follow the Cradock Pass through some coniferous plantations and keep an eye out for the signpost for the peaks; it should be reached after about 1¼ hours. If you see yellow ox-wagon markers you are on the wrong path. The route to the peaks only splits at the 'Nek' where there is another signpost. If you are too tired to continue, the view at this point is still highly rewarding. The climb to George Peak (1,336 m) and back should take seven hours; the round trip is 17 km long. Cradock Peak (1,578 m) takes about nine hours, and is a 21 km round trip. Both hikes are tough going and should not be attempted alone or without sufficient drinking water, food and waterproof clothing.

Tierkop Trail also starts from the old Witfontein forest station, and is a 30 km route of average difficulty. There is a basic overnight hut, *Tierkop*, which can sleep 12. It ends at the Garden Route Dam, and goes via Pepsi Pools. **NB** We have received reports of attacks on tourists at the Garden Route Dam – check with George tourism before you leave. Permits are available from Cape Nature Conservation in George.

Herold's Bay & Victoria Bay
Colour map 7, grid B2

If you are based in George and wish to spend a quiet day by the sea, these small resorts are only a short drive away. Victoria Bay (2 km off the N2) is an excellent place to surf during the winter. It has a narrow cove with a broad sandy beach and a safe tidal pool for children. Herold's Bay (8 km from the N2) has a larger sandy beach. The village is on a wooded ridge looking down on the bay.

Price codes: see inside front cover

Sleeping **C** *Lands End*, The Point, T044-8890123. 4 double rooms with en suite bathroom, TV, 2 self-contained apartments with sun deck, self-catering, or breakfasts served on an open veranda overlooking the sea, beautiful location, fishing and surf equipment hired out, ask for Rod or Shanell. **C** *The Waves*, 6 Beach Rd, T/F044-8890166. 15 mins from George, a superior B&B right on the beach, 3 double rooms with en suite bathroom, separate family cottage available (B&B or self-catering). Recommended. **D** *Sea Breeze*, Victoria Bay, T044-8890098, F8890104. 94 rooms, modern development of flats and chalets, short walk from the beach.

Little Karoo & Montagu Pass

If you have been travelling along the coast from Cape Town, a short diversion into the Little Karoo is well worth the effort. Starting in George, the most direct route is the N9 via the **Outeniqua Pass**. Having reached the summit (799 m) it quickly becomes apparent why the narrow coastal belt is referred to as the Garden Route. The dry undulating terrain is a stark contrast to the lush coastal region, no more than 15 km away. From the top of the pass it is 35 km to **Oudtshoorn**, the capital of the Little Karoo (see page 265). Close by there are three ostrich farms and the **Cango Caves**.

Montagu Pass was the fourth pass over the Outeniqua range. It was opened in 1847 and took over four years to complete

Returning from Oudtshoorn, a scenic and interesting route through the mountains is via **Montagu Pass**. Travelling on the N12 from Oudtshoorn, look out for a left turn just before the road starts to climb up to Outeniqua Pass. This is the N9 (formerly the R62) and will be signposted to Uniondale and Willowmore. Look out for a right turn for Herold and Montagu Pass. Before the road starts to climb it goes through a fertile valley full of hops and fruit trees. The area is ideal for hop growing since it is sheltered from strong winds and rarely has hail. Harvest time is during February and March. This road is gravel so take care after rain. For much of the route there is a low stone wall along the side of the road, and several stretches are single track. Fortunately, very little local traffic uses this road. Near the summit the road passes under a narrow bridge – the railway line linking George with Oudtshoorn – an amazing engineering feat when you look out across the valley below. Halfway along the road are the ruins of a blacksmith's shop, and before the road links up with the main road into George you'll see the old toll house. **NB** This was closed at time of writing as the road was being repaired. Check with the tourist office in Oudthoorn or George if it is open again.

One of the most popular and enjoyable day trips is a ride on a steam train between George and Knysna. This picturesque branch line was opened in 1928. The 67-km journey gives you an extraordinary view of some spectacular coastal scenery and forests, passing through Wilderness National Park and along the Goukamma Valley. The journey ends crossing Knysna Lagoon via a long bridge. There are daily trains from Monday-Friday in each direction, stopping at Wilderness, Sedgefield and Goukamma. ■ *Depart Railway Museum, George, at 0930. Journey time to Knysna, 2½ hrs. Return journey to Knysna costs R60 per person adults, R45 children under 16. Snacks are available on the train. Further information, T044-8018289, in Knysna T044-3821361. You must book at least 24 hrs in advance.*

Outeniqua Choo-Tjoe
This is the train that appears in many of the South African tourist brochures, and includes the famous curved bridge across the mouth of the Kaaimans River

One of the most enjoyable drives in the region, the Seven Passes Road, or the Old Passes Road, is the name given to the original road between George and Knysna. It starts 3 km out of George, just before *Pine Lodge*. The route was surveyed and built by Thomas Bain in 1867, and like so many of his engineering projects is still in use today. Much of the road follows the foothills of the Outeniqua Mountains. When it was built the engineers not only had to cut their way through dense forest but negotiate the fast flowing rivers coming out of the mountains. The seven passes which give the road its name are: the Swart River, Kaaimans, Touw River, Hoogekraal, Karatara, Homtini and Phantom. At each pass the road winds down the gorges to a narrow bridge at the bottom. The stone bridges over the Silver and Kaaimans rivers have been declared national monuments.

Seven Passes Road

After crossing the Swart River, which flows out of the Garden Route dam, the road rises through the forest up on to a plateau. 5 km from the turning is the entrance to Saasveld, a college of forestry founded in 1905. The descent to the Kaaimans River was a major obstacle for Bain in 1867. Loaded wagons slid on their brake shoes to the bottom before being hauled up by 32 oxen on the other side, the ground so soft that the wheels had gouged out 3 m-deep channels. Shortly after the road crosses the Silver River, there is a junction with White Road for **Wilderness**. After crossing the fourth river, Touw, the road reaches the turn-offs to the Woodville, Bergplaas and Kleinplaat forest stations. Just before Woodville there is a turn-off north leading to a giant yellowwood tree which is thought to be more than 800 years old. It is 31 m high and has a girth of 9 m. A picnic site and a short trail into the forest have been laid out close by. At Bergplaas there is a right turning which leads down to the lakes, **Langvlei** and **Rondevlei**, before joining the N2 outside **Sedgefield**.

The next two passes are the **Hoogekraal** and **Karatara**. The village of **Karatara** was established in 1941 as a centre for woodcutters who could no longer practice their skills as attitudes towards the forests and trees changed. The **Homtini Pass** is a beautiful wooded valley which ends by the turning for the village of Rheenendal. After another 1 km there is a left turning signposted for Millwood, Goldfields and Bibby's Hoek. The rest of this route into Knysna is described in the West of Knysna section (see page 301).

Wilderness

Phone code: 044
(NB Always use
3-figure prefix)
Colour map 7, grid B2

This appealing little town is an ideal base for exploring the Garden Route. Except for the few hectic weeks at Christmas and New Year, it is generally very relaxed and has an excellent range of accommodation. The advantage of staying here is that you are also within a day's drive of all the interesting sights of the Little Karoo. The highlight, however, is **Wilderness National Park**, a quiet, well-managed park, with three levels of self-catering accommodation available and a campsite.

The town doesn't have much of a centre, but stretches instead up the lush foothills of the Outeniqua Mountains and along leafy streets by the lake and river. The supermarket, restaurants, post office and tourist office are by the petrol station, where the N2 crosses the Serpentine channel. The **Outeniqua Choo-Tjoe** steam train stops at the station on the beach side of the main road.

Wilderness Tourism Bureau, Leila's Lane, turn left by the post office, T/F8770045, www.wildernessinfo.co.za, is open Mon-Fri, 0830-1800, Sat, 0800-1300, Sun 1500-1700. It's a very helpful office, especially when it comes to finding suitable accommodation. The staff here are well-aware of the problems of finding good value accommodation during the peak season – if you think you may have problems finding somewhere, don't hesitate to contact them.

History The first European to settle in the district was a farmer, Van der Bergh, who built himself a simple farmhouse in the 1850s. It was in 1877 that the name was first used, when George Bennet purchased some land where the present-day *Wilderness Hotel* stands. He named it as he saw it, a 'wilderness' of dense bush and forest. At this time the only road access was from the Seven Passes Road between George and Knysna. Bennet cut a track from this road to his new farmhouse. In 1905 Montagu White bought the homestead from Bennet and converted it into a boarding house. It was not a great success: the area was undoubtedly beautiful, but the swimming was dangerous and access was still a problem.

When the property changed hands in 1921 the farmhouse-cum-boarding house had further conversions made to it and so the *Wilderness Hotel* came into being. In 1907 the railway line from Mossel Bay reached George and six years later, Oudtshoorn. It was not until 1928 that the great engineering feat of building the link between George and Knysna was completed. This is the route the **Outeniqua Choo-Tjoe** steam train still runs along, including the famous curved bridge across Kaaimans River. By 1928 a second hotel had been built by the river, which is now known as the *Fairy Knowe Hotel*. In 1985 the original *Wilderness Hotel* was destroyed in a fire – the new building is the smart four-star *Wilderness Hotel*.

Sleeping If you are just passing through we recommend you check the availability of chalets or log
Price codes: cabins in the Wilderness National Park. For longer stays speak to the local information office.
see inside front cover
A *Wilderness*, T8771110. Smartest hotel in the area, large with over 150 rooms, restaurant, swimming pool, great views all round. **B** *Bruni's Guest House*, 937 8th Av, Wilderness East, close to the *Holiday Inn*, T8770551. Thatched house with views of the ocean, strong links with Germany. **B** *Holiday Inn Garden Court*, 4 km east of Wilderness off the N2, 28 km from George airport, T8771104, F8771134. 149 a/c rooms, formula style rooms, Garden grill, McGinty's pub, swimming pool, tennis, crazy golf, volleyball, the only hotel in the area right on the beach. **B** *Villa Sentosa*, overlooks the Serpentine channel, T8770378, www.sentosa.co.za An elegant retreat with 7 luxurious rooms housed in a magnificent modern house, set in the hills behind the national park. All the rooms have large windows providing plenty of light and panoramic views. Spacious lounge with plush furnishings, the atrium at the entrance sets the scene, heated swimming pool surrounded by a sundeck with views towards the ocean, B&B, can also organize picnic hampers, airport transfer. Recommended. **B-C** *Clairewood Chalets*, 7 km from Wilderness, T8771150, airbpgrj@uafrica.com 4 chalets of varying sizes set on a 16-ha private estate, with swimming pool and tennis court. Peaceful position with views across the Outeniqua Mountains. **B-C** *Fairy Knowe*, Dumbleton

Rd, T8771100, F8770364. 42 rooms, some thatched rondavels, peaceful location on Touw River, close to Wilderness National Park, restaurant, bar, canoes, pedalos and tennis.

C *The Pink Lodge*, 45 die Duin, T8770263, F8771839, www.pinklodge.co.za B&B or self-catering in a great position right on the beach, spacious en suite rooms, rolling lawns, a very relaxing spot. Recommended. **C-D** *Dolphin Dunes*, Buxton Close, T/F8770204, dolphindunes@mweb.co.za Approaching from George, turn right off the N2, 2½ km after the Caltex petrol station. A fine upmarket guesthouse with 4 tasteful, double rooms, en suite bathrooms, fridge, TV, telephone, private access to the beach. One of the rooms has a self-catering option and wheelchair access. **C-D** *Moontide Guest Lodge*, Southside Rd, T8770361, F8770124, moontide@intekom.co.za 4 en suite thatched cottages set under milkwood trees in a beautiful garden overlooking the lagoon. Each cottage has been tastefully decorated with Kilim carpets and fine furniture. Easy access to the hiking trails in the national park and a short walk from the beach. A well-appointed and well-run guesthouse. Recommended. **D** *Albatross Guest House*, PO Box 485, T/F8771716 or T082-4583178 (mob). 2 double rooms with en suite bathroom, plus self-catering flat, nicely decorated, spotlessly clean, run by Shirley and Eloff who are very friendly, overlooks the beach, access is via the *Holiday Inn* turn off from the N2, after which there are signposts. Recommended.

F *Blue Lake*, Island Lake Rd, 5 km from Wilderness, T8821040, emilyone@cksmail.com Backpacker joint overlooking the wetland lakes, fairly new, very relaxed, home cooking, internet access, travel desk, popular but we've had mixed reports. **F** *Fairy Knowe Backpackers*, just off Waterside Rd, T8771285, fairybp@mweb.co.za A great set-up in 2 farm houses surrounded by gardens, clean attractive rooms, dorms and doubles, bar, great breakfasts, nightly camp fires and braais. Also has a travel desk. A very relaxing place which is ideal to rest up at for a few days. Recommended. *Baz Bus* stops here, or you can travel by the Outeniqua Choo-Tjoe steam train from George or Knysna. The station is a request stop so tell the conductor you wish to get off at Fairy Knowe station. **F** *The Wild Welcome*, 479 10th Av, T/F8771307, www.wildwelcome.com Hostel just 100 m from the beach, with dorms, double rooms and camping. TV, video, pool, free surfboards and mountain bikes.

Western Cape

Eating

Wilderness does not offer a great deal of choice but most hotels and hostels offer meals. The majority of domestic visitors will self-cater. *Kingfisher*, 1 George Rd, behind the Caltex garage, T8770288. Family restaurant serving seafood and meat dishes; the grilled musselcracker and stuffed ostrich are good. Friendly service but strange setting – the restaurant is part of the petrol station building. *Wilderness Grille*, George Rd, T8770808. Seafood, steaks and pizza, good breakfasts, outdoor terrace. *Wiesenhof Café*, opp Caltex garage, T8771403. Pub and café serving breakfast, snacks and simple meals, also a travel agent.

Transport

Road 450 km to Cape Town, 18 km to George, 43 km to Knysna, 75 km to, Plettenberg Bay. **Bus**: the *Baz Bus*, T021-4392323, www.bazbus.com, will collect and drop-off at budget accommodation in Wilderness. See Knysna transport, page , for full details.

Rail The *Outeniqua Choo-Tjoe* steam train stops here on its journey between Knysna and George. There is 1 train in each direction every day except for Sun. Towards **Knysna** (2 hrs), 1005; towards **George** (40 mins), 1619.

Wilderness National Park

This is one of the most relaxing places to stay along the Garden Route. Since the accommodation is provided by South African National Parks (SANPARKS), it is also excellent value, especially for four or more people. The main attraction is the water and the birdlife in the reed beds but there are some excellent hikes as well and a beautiful sandy beach.

Colour map 7, grid B2

Ins & outs

Getting there Just east of Wilderness off the N2, a gravel road drops down the edge of the hill to the main camp next to a river. You can also approach the camp from the gravel road which follows the railway a little further inland.

Park information Open 0800-1300, 1400-1700; during school holidays and Dec-Jan, 0700-2000. R8 for day visitors. There's a small shop (0800-1300, 1400-1700), which sells cool drinks, including beer and wines, plus a deep freeze with meats and eggs, firewood also available. The reception area has a clear map of the camp and useful information on the surrounding countryside. The shop is next door in the same building. There is a supermarket in the small commercial centre of Wilderness close to the post office, 4 km. This is also the closest restaurant. Driving towards Knysna the closest place to eat at is the *Holiday Inn Hotel* which has a choice of restaurants and bar.

Tour operator *Eden Adventures* is a good-value adventure tour operator that organizes daily trips to the national park. Activities on offer include kayaking, kloofing, mountain biking nearby, abseiling and walking tours. The guides are very knowledgeable about the environment and are happy to answer endless questions. Recommended. T877178, www.eden.co.za

The park The Wilderness National Park covers 2,612 ha and incorporates five rivers and four lakes as well as a 28-km stretch of the coastline. The series of freshwater lakes are situated between the Outeniqua foothills and sand dunes which back on to a beautiful, long sand beach. As this is such a stunning and unique ecosystem, additional land around the national park is also protected and managed by South African National Parks (SANPARKS) – this additional area is referred to as the National Lake Area. The four lakes are known as Island, Langvlei, Rondevlei and Swartvlei. There is a bird hide on Langvlei and Rondevlei. There is also a second parks office beside Rondevlei.

There are two ways in which to enjoy the beauty of the surrounds, on foot or in a canoe. The former takes you further, but is tiring in the middle of the day. The latter is perfect for exploring the area and ideal for seeing birds, but can be even more

Western Cape

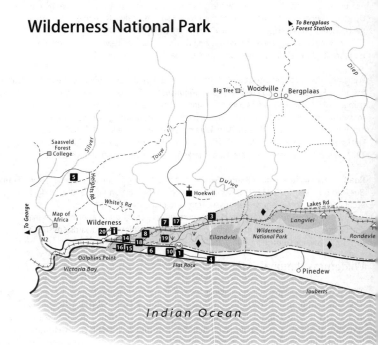

Wilderness National Park

■ Sleeping	6 Dolphin Dunes	11 Landfall
1 Albatross Guest House	7 Ebb & Flow Camp	12 Lake Pleasant
2 Beervlei Hiking Hut	8 Fairy Knowe & Fairy	13 Lakeside Lodge
3 Blue Lake Backpackers	Knowe Backpackers	14 Moontide Guest Lodge

tiring than walking. There are five trails in the park. The **Pied Kingfisher Trail** is a circular route which can be completed in four hours. It follows the river in one direction and the beach on your return. The other walks are also forest walks, except for the **Dune Molerat** trail which takes you through dune fynbos. Each of the accommodation units should have a folder which has full details of all the possible hikes and routes you can go on in the park; maps are also included.

The main camp has canoes and pedalos for hire – a small fee is payable at the reception. One of the more interesting short routes is to continue up the Touw River past the *Ebb and Flow Camp*. This quickly becomes a narrow stream and you have to leave your canoe. A path continues along the bank of the stream through some beautiful riverine forest.

Twice a day the **Outeniqua Choo-Tjoe** can be seen as it crosses the Touw River by *Ebb and Flow* campsite.

The accommodation is laid out in 2 camps which are divided by the railway and the Serpentine River channel. They are known as the *Wilderness Camp* and the *Ebb & Flow Camp*. All the park's accommodation must be vacated by 0900. Arriving visitors can have access from 1200. **Reservations**: T044-8771197, F8770633, www.george.co.za/parks, reservations@parks-sa.co.za Bookings can also be made in person at 2 offices in Cape Town, either at the V&A Waterfront Tourist Office, Clock Tower Centre, or in the Cape Town Tourism Centre on the corner of Castle and Burg streets.

Wilderness Camp has the following choice which will suit all budgets: **B-C** *Log Cabins*, 7 self-contained cabins on stilts, all have views across the river and the reed beds, 2 bedrooms, bathroom, kitchen, comfortable lounge area and a veranda, full of character. Good value for 4

Sleeping
■ *on map*
Price codes:
see inside front cover

Western Cape

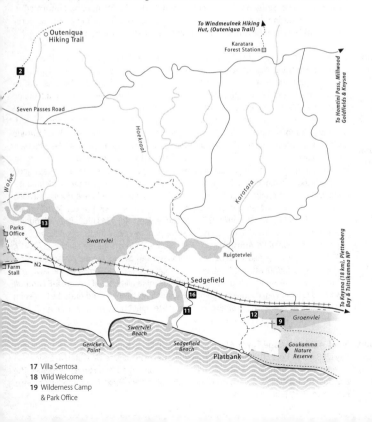

17 Villa Sentosa
18 Wild Welcome
19 Wilderness Camp
& Park Office

people especially with a seasonal discount. **B-C** *Cottage*, 2 bedrooms and sofa bed, bathroom, fully equipped kitchen, lounge, modern bungalows with no appeal when you compare them with the log cabins, better value for a group of 6. **D** *Chalavans*, small caravan with anteroom fixed on one side, this room has a kitchen and an extra bed, a cheap but soulless option. **F** *Campsite*, thick grass with patches of good shade on the banks of the river, beautiful setting and good facilities, an excellent campsite, full of character as long as it is not too full. *Ebb & Flow*, a short walk from the office, this is a smaller campsite beside the Touw River where it emerges from the hills. A beautiful and peaceful spot but its geography means that cold air collects in the narrow valley, and the sun only shines in the camp for a few hrs. There is a mix of simple self-catering units: **E** *Huts*, 1 room, 2 single beds, 2-plate electric stove, fridge, plus a shower, for 2 people, or a cheaper option with no en suite shower. **F** *Camping*, plenty of grass and shade, wash block, no communal kitchen and no electric points.

Sedgefield

Phone code: 044
(NB Always use
3-figure prefix)
Colour map 7, grid B2

Unless you turn off the N2, all that can be seen of Sedgefield is a collection of curio shops and snack bars. Between the main road and the beach is the **Swartvlei Lagoon**, South Africa's largest natural inland salt-water lake. The bulk of the lake lies on the inland side of the N2. Where the road crosses the river you will see a low level railway bridge, an ideal setting to take photographs of the Outeniqua steam trains. The lake is a popular spot for watersports and birdwatching, although the two pastimes don't always go well together. The village itself is of little interest, but the country around the lakes is spectacular and very peaceful. On the Knysna side of Sedgefield is another lake, **Groenvlei**, a freshwater lake lying within the **Goukamma Nature Reserve**. **Sedgefield Tourism Bureau**, T/F3432658, has good information on accommodation and can organize tours on the lake, including a popular ferry which runs between the different restaurants and lodges around the shore.

Sleeping

Price codes:
see inside front cover

As with all villages
along this stretch of
coast, prices are
considerably higher at
Christmas and rooms
need to be booked
well in advance

There is a choice of overnight stops and holiday cottages in the village and around the lakes.

B *Lake Pleasant*, east of Sedgefield on the edge of Groenvlei, T3431313, F3432040, www.lake-pleasant.co.za Comfortable hotel set right on the lake, with 17 rooms with en suite bathroom, and 8 luxury suites (worth the extra cost), all with lake views. Smart lounge furnished with antiques, restaurant with a menu to match the setting – great lunch stop if you're passing through. Swimming pool, tennis court, gym, health spa. Perfect for birdwatchers with some hides by the lake, rowing boats for hire. Recommended. **B-C** *Lakeside Lodge*, 6 km west of Sedgefield (look out for Pine Lake Marina sign), T3431844. Beautiful setting with lawns stretching down to the lake, 6 rooms with en suite bathroom, all lake-facing, honeymoon garden flat has self-catering facilities, dining room, no evening meals, good breakfasts, bar, swimming pool. A perfect base from which to explore the Garden Route, good value for long stays outside the peak season. Recommended. Next door is the *Club Mariner* which has a full range of watersport equipment plus a sauna, jacuzzi, gym, squash court, tennis and beauty therapist. **C** *Forest Lodge*, Main Rd, T3431269. B&B, TV lounge, attached restaurant closed Sun evening, popular pub, takeaway meals, good for an overnight stop. **C** *Sedgefield Arms*, Pelican Lane, off the N2 in the village centre, T3431417, F3431535, www.sedgefieldarms.co.za A comfortable mix of self-catering cottages suitable for 2-6 people, or B&B. Attached restaurant and pub, good spot for lunch on the lawn, bar, swimming pool, all set in leafy gardens, good value for families out of season. **E-F** *Landfall Resort*, T3431804. Well maintained campsite with plenty of shade and grass. Self-catering cottages also available. This is an excellent campsite right on the estuary, a short distance from the beach. A good, cheap option.

Transport

Road 473 km to **Cape Town**, 41 km to **George**, 20 km to **Knysna**, 52 km to **Plettenberg Bay**, 288 km to **Port Elizabeth**. **Bus**: *Translux*, T021-4493333, services stop at Sedgefield Garage, 15 mins to Knysna. See Knysna transport section, page 300, for timetable details. The *Baz Bus*, T021-4392332, www.bazbus.com, will stop in Sedgefield if requested in advance. See Knysna transport for details.

Western Cape

Considering the number of nature reserves and national parks along the Garden Route, this delightful reserve has had a relatively low profile. The reserve was established to protect 2,230 ha of the hinterland between Sedgefield and Buffalo Bay. This includes Groenvlei or Lake Pleasant, a large freshwater lake, and a 13 km sandy beach with some magnificent sand dunes covered in fynbos and patches of forest containing milkwood trees. The **Goukamma River** estuary is the main attraction in the eastern part of the reserve. Groenvlei was originally a river estuary, but it has been cut off from the sea by the large sand dunes. The lake is now fed by natural drainage and springs, and is surrounded by reed beds which are excellent for birdwatching. Rowing boats can be hired to paddle into the reed beds and take you closer to the nesting birds. More than 75 species have been identified. Look out for a few small mammals such as blue duiker, bushbuck and bontebok.

Goukamma Nature Reserve

Ins and outs There are 2 points of access, one at each end of the reserve. Just east of Sedgefield, look out for the turning for the *Lake Pleasant Hotel*, Platbank (on the beach), and the *Groenvlei Bushcamp*. Beyond the hotel the road divides; take the left turning by the dunes which takes you to the bushcamp and the Groenvlei Conservation Station. A 4-km hiking trail starts close by which runs along the lake shore. If you are feeling energetic, there is a 14-km trail starting from the same point which takes you across the reserve to the Goukamma River in the eastern sector, although this leaves you with the problem of return transportation. On any of the walks in the reserve, always carry plenty of drinking water and keep an eye out for snakes, especially amongst the sand dunes. The second point of access is much closer to Knysna. Look out for the Buffalo Bay signpost where the N2 crosses the Goukamma River, and the railway crosses the N2.

Gates open 0800-1700. There is a picnic spot by the river. This is where the hike across the reserve ends. There is a third hike which leads down to the beach and along the coast. Be very careful if you go into the sea as there are dangerous rip currents.

Sleeping B-C *Groenvlei Bushcamp*, reservations, Goukamma Nature & Marine Reserve, Box 331, Knysna 6570, T044-3830042, goukamma@mweb.co.za Beautiful camp hidden away in the milkwood forest with 6 thatched chalets each sleeping 4, communal bathrooms, living area and kitchen are linked by broadwalks, the furnishings are made from wood or reeds. It is a short walk to the lake where you can swim and watch the sun set. There is no electricity; light is provided by gas or paraffin lamps. You must bring all your own food and bedding. Camp is open all year round. This is one of the most relaxing camps you could hope to stay in. *Cape Nature Conservation* have done an excellent job of creating a beautiful camp in a perfect setting with particular attention paid to the environment. Strongly recommended.

Price codes: see inside front cover

Knysna

Knysna (the 'K' is silent) is the self-proclaimed heart of the Garden Route. It is no longer the sleepy lagoon-side village it once was – far from it – but is nevertheless a pleasant spot to spend a day or two. The town itself is fully geared up for tourists, which means a lot of choice in accommodation and restaurants, as well as over-crowding and high prices. It remains quite an arty place though, and many artists and craftspeople have gravitated to the region, plenty of whom display their products in craft shops and galleries. Nevertheless, development is booming, with a slick waterfront development, complete with souvenir shops and fast-food outlets, setting the pace. If you're trying to choose between Knysna and Plettenberg Bay as a base, Knysna offers more amenities and activities, while Plett is far more relaxed and has the better beach. Both get very busy during high season.

Phone code: 044 (NB Always use 3-figure prefix) Colour map 7, grid B2

Getting there *Baz Bus* runs from Knysna towards Cape Town and towards Durban. There's a daily service in either direction between Cape Town and Port Elizabeth, 5 times a week. The best way to arrive is by the *Outeniqua Choo-Tjoe* train, which sweeps across the still waters of the lagoon. The station is in Remembrance Av close to the lagoon.

Ins & outs

Western Cape

Getting around The centre of town is compact and easy to find your way about, although you'll need transport to see the sights. If you don't have your own transport, the best way to get to popular sites such as the beach at Brenton, or The Heads, is to contact *Rikki's*, T3826540.

Tourist offices *Knysna Tourism Bureau*, 40 Main St, T3825510, www.knysna-info.co.za Open daily, 0900-1700. Next door is *Knysna Tourism Accommodation Booking Service*, T3826960, booking@mweb.co.za, which can make reservations for accommodation, tours and public transport.

Sights Although there are a couple of sights and museums in the town, Knysna's highlights are its natural attractions. The main feature of the town is the **lagoon**, around which much of Knysna life revolves. **The Heads**, the rocky promontories that lead from the lagoon to the open sea, are quite stunning. The **Knysna National Lakes**, over 15,000 ha of protected area, are also wonderful to explore, comprising islands, seashore and beach. This fragile ecosystem is bound to suffer from the ever-expanding tourist industry; of particular concern is the rich variety of aquatic life in the lagoon. This has not been helped by the construction of large retirement residential suburbs such as Belvidere Estate and Leisure Island – the latter should never have been built upon.

The **Maritime Museum** is on Queen Street, housed in the Old Gaol, the first public building built by the Colonial Government in the 1870s. Most of the collection focuses on fishing methods used along the coast with a variety of nets and tackle on display. The highlight is in fact a fish, or to be more precise, a *Coelacanth*. This is a

Knysna

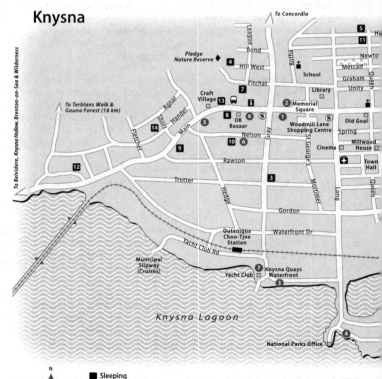

Sleeping
1 Ashmead Resort & Pirate Restaurant
2 Backpack
3 Caboose
4 Gallery Guest House
5 Falcon's View Manor
6 Highfield Backpackers
7 Knysna Manor House
8 Protea Knysna
9 Mike's Guest House
10 Overlander's Lodge
11 Peregrin
12 Rolling Waters
13 Wayside Inn
14 Yellowwood Lodge

prehistoric fish that was believed to be extinct, but a live specimen was famously caught by a fisherman in 1938. There is also an art gallery, tearoom and gift shop. ■ *Mon-Fri 0930-1630, Sat 0930-1300. Small entrance fee.*

Millwood House is a single storey wooden building similar to those that once made up the gold mining community of Millwood (see below). The house was originally built in sections and re-erected here. It is now a National Monument, and houses the local history museum, including a display depicting the goldrush days. ■ *Mon-Fri 0930-1630, Sat 0930-1230.* Next door is Parkes cottage, a similar wooden house, which was moved three times before arriving at its present site. Originally erected in Millwood village, it was moved into Knysna when the gold ran out. In 1905 it was moved to Rawson Street, and then finally in 1992 it was moved to its present site to house the extension to the local history museum.

The **Outeniqua Choo-Tjoe** steam train runs from Knysna to George, a journey of 2½ hours through some spectacular countryside. For background details see page 289. There is one train a day to George, at 1415, except Sunday. Trains stop at Goukamma, Sedgefield and Wilderness. You must book at least 24 hrs in advance. This can also be used as a cheap option for travelling between the two towns; an advantage it has over some of the bus services is that the station at each end of the line is relatively close to the town centre. ■ *Return journey to George costs R60, adults. Guests of the backpackers can get a discount on the train.*

There are two **St George's Churches** in Knysna, the old and the new. Both ran into financial difficulties during construction. To complete the old church the Bishop of the Cape Colony, Robert Gray, persuaded six local businessmen to come up with the necessary £150. The church was consecrated in October 1855. The interior has a timbered ceiling and a fine yellowwood floor. In the 1920s it was decided that a second church needed to be built to accommodate the local congregation. It was 11 years between the foundation stone being laid and the church being consecrated by Bishop Gwyer of George in April 1937. Construction had been delayed due to lack of funds when the walls were only 6 ft high. The community was very proud of the fact that all the materials used in the construction were local – the stone for the walls was quarried from the other side of the lagoon in the Brenton hills. Most of the interior fittings are made from stinkwood, and commemorate local worthies.

One of the more unusual attractions is a tour around the **Knysna Oyster beds** culminating in a tasting session. To get there, follow the road to Thesen's Island, and take a left just after the timber factory. ■ *Phone ahead to check if tours are running, T3826941, www.oysters.co.za*

Featherbed Nature Reserve is the unspoilt western side of **The Heads**. This is a private nature reserve with a restaurant and can only be reached by a ferry service which runs from the

To Plettenberg Bay (32 km) & Port Elizabeth (224 km)

High

6

Montague

Main

Church

Pitt

Clyde

Bokmakierie

Market

Green

Cove

Strand

Tide

2

George Rex Dr.

Union

To Mitchell's Brewery (250m)

1

Thesen's Island

To Woodburn Resort, Leisure Isle & the Heads

● **Eating**
1 Anchorage
2 Havana Bar
3 Health's Bells
4 Knysna Oyster Co
5 La Loerie
6 Longbarn Tavern
7 Oyster Catcher
8 Persello's

Western Cape

municipal jetty close to Knysna railway station. The reserve is home to South Africa's largest breeding herd of blue duiker (*Cephalophus monticola*), an endangered species. Also of interest is a cave once inhabited by the Khoi, which has been declared a National Heritage Site. Adrenaline junkies might also want to try abseiling The Heads. On arrival you are given a ride from the jetty to a high point with excellent views, where meals are served at a restaurant. The rest of your time is spent walking or watching the birdlife, before the ferry returns you to Knysna.
■ *T3810590, www.featherbed.co.za*

Sleeping
■ *on maps, pages 296 and 302*
Price codes: see inside front cover

It is difficult to find accommodation during the Christmas and New Year period unless you book 6 months in advance

As one of the most popular holiday centres along the Garden Route, there is plenty of choice of accommodation, both in type and location. The centre of Knysna is on the northern margin of the lagoon. To the east of town, George Rex Dr leads to Leisure Island and The Heads. Along and off this road are a number of guesthouses and B&Bs. To the west, the suburbs follow the shores of the lagoon and the Knysna River; a left turn immediately after crossing the White Bridge takes you to the fashionable village of Belvidere. A little further on is Brenton followed by the popular seaside resort of Brenton-on-Sea. The list below only includes places found near the town centre and in the vicinity of The Heads. Given the lack of local public transport only properties close to the centre are easily accessible for those without their own transport.

Town centre and The Heads A *Falcon's View Manor*, 2 Thesen Hill, T3826767, F3826430, www.falconsview.com Small, up-market hotel with 9 spacious double rooms (non-smoking), en suite bathrooms, TV, tastefully decorated and furnished to an exceptional level of comfort, relaxing on the veranda overlooking the lagoon is a perfect way to spend a day, swimming pool, neat gardens, a classic Victorian house. Recommended.

B *Leisure Isle Lodge*, 87 Bayswater Dr, Leisure Isle, T3840462, F3841027, www.leisureislelodge.co.za Spacious rooms, heated swimming pool, views across bay, gardens stretch to waterfront, a short drive from The Heads. **B** *Protea Knysna Quays*, Waterfront Dr, T3825005, F3825006, kynsna@mweb.co.za Usual large hotel, with comfortable a/c rooms, restaurant, cocktail bar, lounge, attractive swimming pool. Close to the Waterfront. **B** *Under Milkwood*, T3840745, F3840156, admin@undermilkwood.com 16 luxury self-catering log chalets at Knysna Heads set in a grove of milkwood trees, can sleep 6 people, excellent kitchen facilities. Not all have views of the lagoon. Plenty of light, relaxing sun deck, recommended if you plan on spending a week in the district. Out of the town, but still close to all the amenities. **B** *Wayside Inn*, 48 Main St, T/F3826011. Smart set-up in the centre of town with a colonial theme. 15 luxury rooms with iron beds and sisal carpets, fans, fine African art on show, private balconies, wicker furniture, TV, superior picnic hampers can be made to order. Several readers have commented on the lack of a lounge area. Friendly and helpful staff. **B** *Yellowwood Lodge*, 18 Handel St, T3825906, F3824230, www.yellowwoodlodge.co.za Lovely guesthouse in one of Knysna's older houses with 10 thoughtfully decorated rooms. Ask for an upstairs room – they have relaxing balconies. Delicious buffet breakfasts, immaculate garden with views across town and lagoon, strictly non-smoking household. Loses some of its appeal when full, look out for the flagpole. **B-D** *Ashmead Resort*, George Rex Dr, T3841166, F3841173. Log cabins and modern brick cottages set in mature gardens overlooking lagoon, bright lobby and lounge, stark restaurant, bar, miniature golf, swimming pool, popular domestic family holiday venue.

C *Heron Water Lodge*, 33 Cearn Dr, Leisure Isle, T3840624, play.knysna@pixie. co.za A friendly and comfortable B&B with 4 spacious double rooms with en suite bathrooms, 2 of the rooms overlook the lagoon. Sun deck, bar, swimming pool, boat hire, generous, filling breakfasts. Recommended. **C** *Knysna Manor House*, 19 Fitchat St, T3825440, F3824389. A solid stone house, a short walk from town centre, all rooms have en suite bathrooms, B&B or self-catering. **C** *Oyster Creek Lodge*, The Point, T3820808, www.oystercreeklodge.co.za Attractive log lodge set right on the lagoon and surrounded by trees. Comfortable well-appointed rooms, en suite, with views of the lagoon. Ask for Mandy. **C** *Rolling Waters*, 120 Old Cape Rd, T3825217, F3825871. Town house on the edge of the lagoon, all rooms have en suite bathroom and face the water. Enjoy breakfast from the first floor dining room. Private jetty has a small motor boat to hire plus a canoe. **C-D** *Gallery Guest House*, 10 Hill St West, T3822510, F3825212. 3 double rooms in an old house overlooking the lagoon. Breakfast is served on the peaceful balcony. The owner, an artist, has some works on display in the lounge.

Invisible elephants

No guide to Knysna would be complete without a mention of the Knysna elephants. They have come to represent the last stand of wildlife against man in the region. Just over 100 years ago the forests were full of wild animals. Today the elephants live deep in the forest and few people will see them. Little is known about their numbers or their characteristics. They belong to the same species as the savanna elephant but from living in the forest their lifestyle and habits have changed, and they are thought to now resemble the forest elephant found in the equatorial forests of Central Africa. In July 1994 some new elephants were introduced into the forest to try and guarantee the survival of elephants in the region. At the time there were thought to be only seven of the original magnificent animals remaining.

The **Terblans Nature Walk** through the Gouna Forest, 16 km north of Knysna, is a short walk through an area thought to be frequented by the Knysna elephants. Follow the bushpig markers. Happy hiking – you may just see more than the Knysna lourie.

See also page 303

Western Cape

D *Caboose*, corner of Gray and Trotter streets, T3825850, F3825224. Cramped rooms with en suite bathroom which are based upon a train compartment, swimming pool, B&B, sheltered parking, fun concept but not the best value. **D-E** *Mike's Guest House*, 67 Main St, T3821728, dolphin@mweb.co.za Townhouse with 5 rooms with en suite bathroom, TV lounge, kitchen, good value, a short walk from centre. Hard to miss as you drive in from the lagoon.

E-F *Highfield Backpackers*, 2 Graham St, T3826266, highfields@hotmail.com Quiet backpackers set in 2 townhouses, dorms and doubles, pub, kitchen, courtyard with pool, travel centre. **F** *The Backpack*, 17 Tide St, T3827766. Well-run lodge a short walk to town centre, dorms and doubles, kitchen, satellite TV, space for a couple of tents. **F** *Overlander's Lodge*, T3825920, overlanders@cyberperk.co.za Large dorms, clean bathrooms, TV room with good video collection, small swimming pool, well-stocked kitchen, pool table, good for camping, fun atmosphere but not to everyone's liking. Management are very helpful in organizing local and national trips. **F** *Peregrin*, 16 High St, T3823747, peregrin@cyberperk.co.za Great backpacker lodge in a large townhouse. Colourful dorms, double rooms, kitchen, bar, garden with small pool, TV room, very friendly and helpful staff, fun party place. Recommended, despite the limited bathroom space. **F** *Woodbourne Resort*, George Rex Dr, T3840316. Some self-catering chalets, medium size caravan park, well-grassed and shaded, camping allowed but expect to pay triple rates to camp during peak periods.

Knysna is well-known for its seafood, especially its excellent oysters which are cultivated in the lagoon. During the peak season, it is not uncommon to wait an hour or more before getting a table – be sure to book ahead at the better-known restaurants.

Eating
● on maps, pages
296 and 302

Anchorage, T3822230, Main St, in the Garden Route Centre. Seafood platters, prawns, oysters and steaks all washed down with excellent draught Mitchell's beer. *Crabs Creek*, T3860011, Belvidere Rd, close to White Bridge off the N2. Seafood tavern, excellent seafood and good value. Pleasant outdoor terrace overlooking the river. *Havana Bar*, Main Rd. Stylish Cuban-themed bar and restaurant, nice seating on a terrace overlooking Main Rd, selection of Cuban and Tex-Mex dishes, cocktails. *Health's Bells*, Knysna Quays, T3827931. Health food shop and vegetarian café. *Knysna Hollow*, Welbedacht Lane, T3825401. Up-market restaurant serving a mix of South African and French cuisine, good seafood. *Knysna Oyster Co.*, T3826941, www.oysters.co.za Has an attached seafood restaurant, perhaps the best place to try Knysna's famous oysters. *La Loerie*, 57 Main Rd, T3821616. Closed Sun. Cosy, family-run restaurant serving excellent seafood dishes and some meat choices. Good value considering the food. Recommended by readers as the best in town. *Longbarn Tavern*, Nelson St, T3823839. Lively pub and restaurant serving good value pub lunches, live music some nights. *Oyster Catcher*, Knysna Quays, T3829995. Another place to try oysters, at working quays. *Paquitas*, Knysna Heads, T3840408. Relaxed family restaurant, pizza, pasta, seafood and steaks, but the main reason for coming here is for the stunning views of The Heads.

152 Old Cape Rd, T3822251. Closed Sun, pasta and steaks, lively bar and restaurant with a special German menu, someone plays the piano to entertain you while you eat, overlooking small lake off the Salt River. *Persello's*, 41 Main St, T3822665. A small and simple Italian-owned restaurant which serves excellent pasta and takeaway pizza. *Pink Umbrella*, 14 Kingsway, just out of town on Leisure Isle, T3840135. Al fresco dining. A pleasant change from standard high cholesterol fare – only seafood or vegetarian dishes. This place is a must for vegetarians who have been travelling in South Africa for a few weeks and have been living on toasted cheese sandwiches. Recommended.

Entertainment **Cinema** *Knysna Movie House*, Pledge Sq, Main St, T3827812. Daily shows of new releases. **Shopping** Keeping in tune with Knysna's reputation as a cultural arts and crafts centre are a number of galleries and craft shops. Check at the tourist office for special exhibitions. *Birds of Africa*, Waenhout St, carved wooden birds. *Bitou Craft*, Woodmill Lane Centre, Main St, local arts and crafts. *Metalcraft Gallery*, 19 Clyde St, modern pieces. *Metamorphosis*, 12 Main Rd, interesting selection made from recycled cans and other materials. *Spring St Gallery*, 19 Spring St. There is also a good *African craft market* set up on the side of the road as you enter Knysna on the N2 from George, with an extensive range of carvings, baskets, drums and curios.

Sports **Golf** There is an 18-hole, par 73, course off George Rex Dr. T3822391. **Scuba diving** *The Heads Adventure Centre*, Bottom Car Park, Knysna Heads, T3840831, PADI courses, equipment rental, daily trips to reefs and to the Paquita wreck in the lagoon.

Tour operators *Eco Afrika*, 11 Horne Dr, T3840479, T082-9250716 (mob), township tours and nature-viewing trips. *Featherbed Ferries*, T3821693/7, boats depart from the municipal jetty for the Featherbed Nature Reserve, daily from 1000, and also do ½-hr tours around the Heads. *The Heads Adventure Centre*, Bottom Car Park, Knysna Heads, T3840831, scuba trips, abseiling, canoeing and kayaking. *John Benn Cruises*, T3821693, pleasure cruises on Knysna Lagoon, great way of seeing the area, but can get a bit rowdy when the live entertainment is in full swing and the bar is doing great trade. Boats leave from the municipal jetty, trips lasts about 2 hrs. *Forest Explorers*, T083-7025103 (mob), trails around the remaining tracts of indigenous forest in the area. *Knysna Forest Walks*, T3980102, walks and trails through the forest. *SAA City Centre*, Woodmill Lane, T3821161, well-organized travel agent and tour operator. *Top Tours*, T3826806, T082-4905806 (mob), a local all-purpose tour operator, can arrange day trips along the Garden Route, as far as Cango Caves in the Karoo. Also run an airport transfer service for George. *Brenton Blue Tours*, T082-6570448 (mob), specialize in running a shuttle service to George airport and meeting the Outeniqua Choo-Tjoe steam train. Can also arrange tours in a/c vehicles to all the popular sites.

Transport **Rail** *Outeniqua Choo-Tjoe* steam train running between Knysna and **George**. Station is on Remembrance Av close to the lagoon. One train a day, T044-3821361. You must book at least 24 hrs in advance.

Road 932 km to **Bloemfontein**, 500 km to **Cape Town**, 61 km to **George**, 1,350 km to **Johannesburg**, 100 km to **Mossel Bay**, 120 km to **Outdshoorn**, 32 km to **Plettenberg Bay**, 244 km to **Port Elizabeth**, 90 km to **Tsitsikamma National Park**. **Bus**: *Greyhound*, T021-5056363, coaches depart from Burns Toyota Garage. **Cape Town** (8 hrs), daily, 0145; **Port Elizabeth** (3½ hrs), daily, 0145.

Intercape, T021-3804400, coaches depart from Burns Toyota Garage. **Pretoria** and **Johannesburg** (14 hrs), daily 1645, via **Oudtshoorn** (2 hrs), **Beaufort West** (4 hrs), **Kimberley** (9 hrs), 1400, via Garden Route.

Translux, T021-4493333, coaches depart from Burns Toyota Garage. **Bloemfontein** (11 hrs), Mon, Tue, Thu 1700, Fri 1500; **Cape Town** (9 hrs), daily 1010, 2335; **Durban** (11 hrs), daily 0200; **George** (1 hr), daily 2335; Mon, Thu, Fri, Sun 1630, 1700, Fri 1500, Wed, Fri, Sun 1600; **Johannesburg** and **Pretoria** (16½ hrs), daily 1715, Mon, Tue, Wed, Fri, Sun 1630; **Mossel Bay** (1 hr), daily 1010, Mon, Thu, Sat 1630; **Oudtshoorn** (3 hrs), Tue, Wed, Thu, Fri, Sun 1630; **Port Elizabeth** (3 hrs), daily 1440.

Baz Bus, T021-4392323, www.bazbus.com Budget bus running from Knysna towards Cape Town or Durban. Knysna is used as an overnight base. Daily service in either direction between Cape Town and Port Elizabeth. 5 times a week between Port Elizabeth and Durban.

Internet *Imaginet Internet Café*, next to the Spar off Main Rd, open daily 9am-7pm. **Laundry** *Wash Tub*, 20 Gray St, reliable laundry service, ironing and dry cleaning, closed Sat afternoons and Sun. **Useful services** Ambulance: T10177. **Emergency pharmacy**: T3826314**Private Hospital – with a casualty**: T3841083. **Police**: T10111. **Sea Rescue**: T3840211.

Directory

West of Knysna

These villages on the western shores of the lagoon are in many ways really smart suburbs of the Knysna. Brenton has the great attraction of having the nearest sandy beach (Brenton-on-Sea), making it very popular during the school holidays. There is a fine hotel and a limited selection of seaside cottages. Belvidere is primarily a leafy residential suburb along the banks of the river as it enters the lagoon. A large proportion of the village is made up of the relatively new Belvidere Estate, a prestigious development on 67 ha, made up of large houses and gardens.

The small village church, **Belvidere Church**, is a popular attraction in the area and is a miniature replica of a Norman church. It was built in 1855 from local stone and timber, with picturesque stained-glass windows and stinkwood fittings. The **rose window** on the west side was installed in 1955. Further along the road past the church is the seaside resort of Brenton-on-Sea with its wonderful stretch of yellow sand and wild seas – the closest beach to Knysna. The beach is dominated by a hotel of the same name (see below).

Belvidere, Brenton & Brenton-on-Sea
Phone code: 044
(NB Always use 3-figure prefix)

Some of the glass within the window of Belvidere Church is from the bombed ruins of Coventry Cathedral in England

Sleeping **A** *Belvidere Manor*, Duthie Dr, Belvidere, T3871055, F3871059, manager@belvidere.co.za 21 smart cottages arranged around a swimming pool in shady gardens, with private verandas with views across the lagoon, sleeping 2-4 people. Some have a study; all are individually furnished and have log fires. The manor house, from 1834, houses the reception and an elegant dining room. Friendly and attentive staff. **B** *Brenton-on-Sea*, Agapanthus Av, T3810081, F3810026, www.brenton.on.sea@pixie.co.za Overlooking the striking beach at Brenton-on-Sea. Choice of rooms or 14 self-contained, open plan, thatched chalets, private verandas with sea views. JJ's restaurant, with a carvery in the evenings, is very popular. Good seafood lunches and a terrace overlooking the beach, although it can get very noisy with families during the holidays. **C** *Camelot*, 28 Lower Duthie Dr, Belvidere Estate, T/F3871393. 2 large upstairs suites with views across the lagoon, TV, fridge, breakfast is served outside during the summer, peaceful location, secure parking, good value. Recommended. **C-D** *Seaside Chalets*, T3810032. Set back from the beach in the quiet village, self-catering for up to 6 people, ideal for spending time near the beach.

Price codes: see inside front cover

Eating *Crabs Creek*, T3860011, 8 km from Knysna, 200 m off the N2 on the Belvidere road. A mock Tudor building beside Knysna River, secluded country pub in a garden of oak trees, sensible prices, good selection of wines, mostly seafood but of a very high standard, one of the better restaurants in the area and good value at the price. Recommended. *O'Pescador*, T3860036. Book during holiday season. Mozambique-style menu, including beer-baked prawns and chicken peri-peri, plus some spicy fish dishes. Another one which is clearly a cut above most places in the area, not cheap but the food quality is worth it. Highly recommended.

On the southern slopes of the Outeniqua Mountains, behind Knysna, are the remnants of the grand forests which first attracted white settlers to the region. No longer a single expanse, the patches go under a variety of names which can be confusing: Diepwalle Forest, Ysternek Reserve, Goudveld State Forest, and Millwood Creek (and Jubilee Creek) Nature Reserve. As a whole, these state forests are often referred to as the **Knysna Indigenous Forests**. Today the indigenous forests are noteworthy for the variety of birdlife and their magnificent 'big trees'. Trees of special interest

Knysna Forest & Millwood Goldfields

Western Cape

include the yellowwood, assegai, stinkwood, red alder, white alder and the Cape chestnut. A variety of short walks have been laid out in the forests. In some areas horse riding is allowed.

About 25 km from Knysna, in the **Goudveld State Forest**, are the remains of an old mining town, **Millwood**. This was the site of a minor goldrush in the 1880s, just before the gold was discovered at Pilgrim's Rest and Johannesburg. The first gold was discovered here in 1876 when a local farmer picked up a nugget in the Karatara River. This triggered the usual manic influx, and by 1887 Millwood had a court building, three banks, 32 stores, six hotels and three newspapers. By 1900 most people had left as the reefs became too difficult to mine. Today only one building survives, along with some mining machinery which has remained untouched for over 60 years. For a long time abandoned and forgotten, Millwood is gradually being developed into a tourist attraction, with its perfect combination of the mystical fascination with gold and the beauty of the lush surrounding forest.

■ *To reach the mine, take the Phantom Pass road out of Knysna. Just before the village of Rheenendal take a right turn, signposted for Millwood, Goldfields and Bibby's Hoek. Entrance is between 0600-1800.* To the right of the car park is the complex of reduction works machinery; the larger pieces are a steam engine and a boiler. Further up the slope is a shaft and a short Co-Co Pan rail track. In addition to the mine buildings, there are a few picnic spots and short paths leading into the forest – you only have to walk a few yards before being completely enveloped by trees.

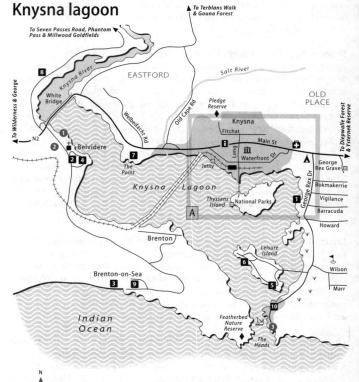

Knysna lagoon

Detailed map
A *Knysna*,
page 296

■ Sleeping		4 Camelot	5 Heron Water Lodge	8 Phantom Forest	● Eating
1 Ashmead Resort		6 Leisure Isle Lodge	9 Seaside Chalets	1 Crabs Creek
2 Belvidere Manor		7 Oyster Creek Lodge	10 Under Milkwood	2 O'Pescador
3 Brenton-on-Sea				3 Paquitas

Just before the village of **Rheenendal**, on the **Old Passes** or **Seven Passes Road**, are a couple of delightful cottages on the border of the state forest (see below). They are ideal for anyone wishing to spend time exploring and hiking in the forested hinterland around Knysna rather than sitting on a beach. Look out for the signpost for Millwood, Goldfields and Bibby's Hoek.

Sleeping AL *Phantom Forest*, T044-3860046. Signposted from the Phantom Pass road. Superb collection of luxurious tree houses set in the forest. This lodge is a fairly new addition to the Knysna area and offers ultra-stylish accommodation set high above the lagoon. Tree houses are eco-friendly and stylishly decorated, with double beds, private terraces overlooking the trees and luxurious bathrooms – the showers are open to the forest. Individual houses are connected by walkway to the excellent restaurant, bar, lookout points, and pool. Attentive, helpful staff, the perfect place to experience the forest. Highly recommended. **C** *Forest Edge*, T044-3884704. 2 holiday cottages, self-contained and fully equipped, sleeping 4 people. Linen and towels are provided and there is a fireplace, telephone, braai facilities and mountain bikes available for hire. You can walk straight into the forest from here. Collect the keys from 'Blue Hills' which is on the road to the right, just after Phantom Pass as you head inland.

Price codes:
see inside front cover

East of Knysna

Starting from the Diepwalle forest station is the 18 km Elephant Walk, an easy going, level hike which gives a clear insight into the forest environment. The trail is marked by elephant silhouettes and takes around seven hours to complete. The hike is made up of three loops, but it is possible to complete only one or two loops. The three paths are simply known as Routes I, II and III, and are 9, 8 and 6 km long, respectively. Apart from the (very slim) possibility of spying the rare Knysna elephant (see box page 299), of which there are 3 on record at present, the main attractions are the giant forest trees, particularly the Outeniqua yellowwood. There are eight such trees along the full trail – the largest, at 46 m, is known as the **King Edward VII Tree**, and stands just off the R339 by the Diepwalle picnic spot at the end of Route I and the start of Route II. The end of the **Outeniqua Trail** (see page 304) meets with Route III. Before setting out you must sign in at the forest station where maps are on offer. There is no charge but the hike is only open between 0700-1800. The R339 passes through the middle of the forest en route to the **Ysternek Nature Reserve**, see below.

Diepwalle Forest & Elephant Walk

Noetzie is a small village on the coast with an outlandish collection of holiday homes built to look like castles from Medieval Europe, complete with towers and battlements. On the curiosity scale they rate quite high, but unfortunately you can only see them from the outside, as they are all private homes. A further 5 km beyond the Noetzie turning is another turning to the right; a gravel road passes through a eucalyptus and pine plantation to a picnic spot which overlooks the Brackenhill Falls. This is where the Noetzie River plunges into a narrow gorge with flourishing plants growing in the spray on the steep sides.

Noetzie & Brackenhill Falls

About 25 km from Knysna, as the R339 makes its way north over the Outeniqua Mountains into the Karoo, this reserve passes through a band of montane forest which was once typical of the whole region. Today only a few patches remain and the 1,212 ha Ysternek Reserve exists to conserve an area rich in mountain fynbos and wet mountain forest, with some impressive tree ferns. The area is administered by the Diepwalle State Forest, but apart from a special picnic spot and a few paths, the region remains unspoilt. The picnic spot is known as the *Dal van Varings*, Valley of the Ferns, deep in the forest. From here you can walk to a high point, **Spitzkop** view, which overlooks the canopy of surrounding forests – on a clear day you can see as far as Humansdorp.

Ysternek Nature Reserve
Late spring and summer, from Oct-May, are the best months for walking in the forest

This small park is a refuge for orphaned elephants. Visitors are taken on tours around the forest area and are allowed to touch and play with the little elephants.

Knysna Elephant Park

Although the animals are 'free-range' they are very used to human contact, making it a wonderful experience for children. This is also the only chance you'll have of seeing elephants in the area – the indigenous ones are far too elusive. ■ *Daily, 0830-1630, T044-5327732, kep@pixie.co.za*

The Outeniqua Trail

Up until February 1993 this was one of the longest and most strenuous hikes in South Africa; a 140-km trail from Witfontein to Diepwalle Forest Station. But now the ground covered over the first three days is no longer part of the recognized trail. The shortened route is still 90 km long and takes a minimum of five days to complete. As with most long trails there are a couple of chances to finish the hike at an earlier stage. There are paths linking **Windmeulnek hut** with **Karatara Forest Station** and from **Farleigh hut** to the village of **Barrington** on the Seven Passes Road. The new route starts from **Beervlei** in the Bergplaas State Forest where an extra path has been cut to the first overnight hut, Windmeulnek; the route still ends at the **Diepwalle Forest Station**, however, there are plans to extend the hike by two further days and continue the path out of the hills towards the Harkerville Forest Trail, south of the N2, and east of Knysna, on the coast. The easiest approach to Beervlei is to take the Hoekwil road opposite the *Holiday Inn Garden Court* on the N2, 4 km east of Wilderness, after a steep climb this links with the Seven Passes Road. Alternatively the start point can be reached via the Seven Passes Road direct from George or Knysna.

Nature Reserves The principal incentive for completing the second half of the trail is that the path cuts through small sections of the **Lily Vlei Nature Reserve** and the **Millwood Creek Nature Reserve**. Both are usually closed to the public. The Knysna elephants are thought to spend most of their time in these remote and isolated areas. In Lily Vlei Reserve there is 50 ha of virgin forest full of interesting plants; Millwood Reserve has some fine specimens of yellowwoods and stinkwoods. With such a diverse range of plants the hiker also has a better chance of seeing some of the more rare forest birds.

Trail information Permits are available from the Department of Water Affairs and Forestry, Demar Centre, Main Road, Knysna, T044-5825466. A detailed map is available from the same office. Given the altitude and the forest there is a good chance of rain or a damp mist throughout most of the year, this is not a walk to embark upon without good waterproof clothing and the usual set of additional warm clothing. The best period for hiking is from June to January when the fynbos are likely to be in flower.

Sleeping There are 6 overnight camps: *Beervlei* (at the start), *Windmeulnek*, *Farleigh*, *Millwood*, *Rondebossie*, and *Diepwalle*. Each hut can sleep up to 30 people, bunks with mattresses, fireplaces and wood are provided.

Plettenberg Bay

Phone code: 044
(NB Always use 3-figure prefix)
Colour map 7, grid B2

Plettenberg Bay, or 'Plett', as it is commonly known, is one of the most appealing resorts on the Garden Route. Although it is modern and has little of historical interest, the compact centre is attractive and the main beach beautiful. Plett has become fashionable in recent years, and during the busy Christmas season the town transforms. Wealthy families descend from Johannesburg and the pace can get quite frenetic – expect busy beaches and long queues for restaurant tables. For the rest of the year the pace is rather calmer and the resort becomes just another sleepy seaside town. There are three beaches which are good for swimming, but the coastline is spoilt by the multi-storey hotel on a sand bar between two beaches.

Ins & outs
See transport section for more details

Getting there For such a popular seaside resort the transport to/from here is not very good. During the peak season many of the more wealthy visitors will fly in. For short trips to other towns along the Garden Route the *Baz Bus* represents the best value and most convenient schedule. If you are on a tight budget there are good hitching opportunities along this stretch of the coast, but it is not recommended that you hitch beyond Port Elizabeth.

Tourist offices **Publicity Association**, PO Box 894, 12 Kloof St, T5334065, F5334066, www.plettenbergbay.co.za A helpful office with quite a detailed website. Open, Mon-Fri, 0900-1700; Sat, 0900-1300. Slightly longer hrs during the peak summer season.

In 1630 a Portuguese vessel, the **San Gonzalez**, was wrecked in the bay. This was 20 years before Jan van Riebeeck's arrival at the Cape. The survivors stayed here for eight months, during which time they built two smaller boats out of the wreckage, and one of the boats managed to sail up the coast to Mozambique. The survivors were eventually returned home to Lisbon, but they left behind a sandstone plaque on which they had inscribed the name *Baia Formosa*. Today a replica can be seen in Plett in the same place that the first was left by the sailors. (The original is now on show in the South African Museum in Cape Town.) The Portuguese had a number of names for the bay, but none stuck for very long. Later the Dutch also gave the bay several different names, such as Content Bay and Pisang River Bay. But it was only in 1778 when Governor Joachim van Plettenberg opened a timber post on the shores of the bay, and named it after himself, that a name stuck.

> **History**

It remained an important timber port until the early 1800s when the Dutch decided to move operations to Knysna since it was a safer harbour. For a period the bay became famous as a whaling station but all that remains of this operation are a blubber cauldron and slipway. Most of the buildings were destroyed in a fire in 1914.

The tourist office gamely tries to promote some sights to visit but the attraction of this area is the sea and the outdoors. Aside from the three beaches, Robberg, Central and Lookout, there is excellent deep sea fishing, while the **Keurbooms River lagoon** is a safe area for bathing and other watersports. The dunes around the lagoon are now part of a nature reserve. The main streets in town are just a collection of modern shopping malls and restaurants, but there are a few old buildings still standing which represent a little of the town's earlier history: St Andrew's Chapel, the remains of the Old Timber Store (1787), the Old Rectory (1776), the Forest Hall (1864) and the Dutch Reformed Church (1834).

> **Sights**

Taking a sailing trip upstream on the **Keurbooms River Ferry** is a great way to spend a few hours. You are ferried 5 km along the river through a spectacular gorge overhung by indigenous trees and other flora. At the furthest point from the jetty there is an optional 30-minute walk, with a professional guide, through the forest. This is the ultimate eco-experience and a relaxing way of being introduced to the plants, sights and sounds of the forest. Make sure you are wearing sturdy footwear if you intend to join the walk. ■ *Keurbooms River Ferries, T044-5327876, www.ferry.co.za Daily trips, 1100 and sundown; times change seasonally, so phone ahead to check. Boat trip plus walk lasts for 2½ hours. Adults R60 per person. Lunches, picnics and drinks can be organized in advance. The ferry departs from the jetty under the bridge, across the Keurbooms River just east of Plettenberg Bay. Each ferry can carry up to 30 people. They are shaded and have a toilet on board. Highly recommended for nature lovers.*

Milkwood This is a 3 or 5 km trail in and around the town. Follow the yellow footprints. The trail starts from the car park off Marine Drive and takes you via Piesangs River lagoon, Central beach, and Lookout beach. At this point the shorter route turns back through the centre of town via some of the historical buildings, while the longer route continues via Keurbooms Lagoon and round the back of town.

> **Local hikes**
>
> *Nearby are 5 designated trails, a pleasant alternative to the beach*

Robberg Nature Reserve There are three possibilities ranging from 2 to 9 km on this loop along the peninsula which forms the western boundary of Plettenberg Bay. Permits are available at the entrance gate. Follow the 'seal' markers. Parts of the trail follow the cliffs and caution is advised. There are plenty of prominent view-points from where it is possible to see whales and dolphins in the bay. Recommended. Allow at least four hours for the full route.

Wittedrift A 10-km drive, this takes the N2 towards Nature's Valley. Turn left immediately after crossing the Bitou River (R340 signposted Avontur), and follow signs for Wittedrift (5 km). A variety of loops start from the village high school. There is a basic overnight hut by the river which can be booked at the Wittedrift butcher. The paths follow the Bitou River and its wetlands. To reach the other two trails involves about a 25-km drive.

Kranshoek Take the N2 towards Knysna. Take the Kranshoek turning in Harkerville; just after crossing the river there is parking and a picnic site on the left. The full length of the trail is 9 km, but a shorter (3 km) walk is also possible. The route is indicated by white footprints. Half of the trail is in the Kruisfontein State Forest, and the rest is along a rocky beach. It is possible to swim in the sea here.

Nature's Valley This network of paths lies 25 km from Plettenberg Bay. Maps are available at the *De Vasselot* campsite. One of the trails (a steep climb), goes past **Forest Hall**, a manor house built by William Newdigate in 1864. The house is open

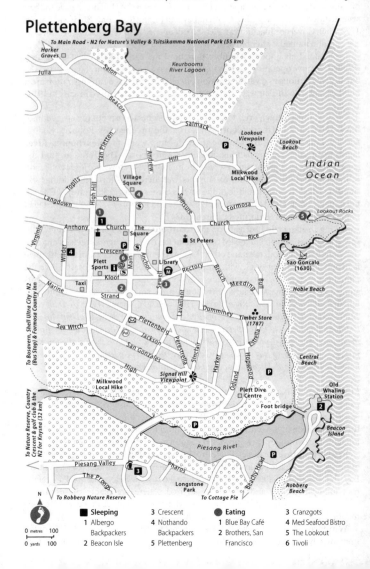

Plettenberg Bay

To Main Road - N2 for Nature's Valley & Tsitsikamma National Park (55 km)

Harker Graves
Julia
Salon
Beacon

Keurbooms River Lagoon

Salmack

Lookout Viewpoint
Lookout Beach

Indian Ocean

Van Pletten
Andrew
Hill
Milkwood Local Hike

Toplis
High Hill
Village Square
Gibbs
Swinsure
Formosa

Lookout Rocks

Langdown
Anthony
Church
The Square
Church
Rice
5

Sao Goncalo (1630)

Virginia
Wilder
Crescent
Plett Sports
Anchor
Library
Rectory
Breach
Meeding
Butt

Hobie Beach

Marine
Taxi
Kloof
Strand
Sewell
Lavalliant
Dumminey

Timber Store (1787)

Sea Witch
Plettenberg
Jackson
San Gonzales
High
Peresttrela
Sinchar
Estrela
Hopwood
Odland

Central Beach

Milkwood Local Hike
Signal Hill Viewpoint
Plett Dive Centre
Foot bridge

Old Whaling Station
2

Beacon Island

Piesang River

Piesang Valley
The Prongs
Pharos
Beachy Head

Robberg Beach

To Nature Reserve, Country Crescent & golf club & the N2 for Knysna (32 km)
To Bosaven, Shell Ultra City - N2 (Bus Stop) & Formosa Country Inn

Longstone Park
To Cottage Pie

N
To Robberg Nature Reserve

0 metres 100
0 yards 100

■ Sleeping	3 Crescent	● Eating	3 Cranzgots
1 Albergo Backpackers	4 Nothando Backpackers	1 Blue Bay Café	4 Med Seafood Bistro
2 Beacon Isle	5 Plettenberg	2 Brothers, San Francisco	5 The Lookout
			6 Tivoli

to the public and there is a tea garden. The Salt River mouth is a particularly beautiful spot. Birdwatchers may get the chance to see the **Narina Trogon** (*Apaloderma narina*) in the riverine forest.

During Christmas it is difficult to find a bed unless you have booked well in advance. Along with Knysna, there is an unbelievable transformation here during the mid-summer rush (see Holidays and Festivals section, page 49, for school holiday dates). For the rest of the year, hotels and B&Bs cry out for guests. In an effort to attract visitors during the winter months, several special package deals have been introduced. If you have the time and the patience it is worth checking these out.

Sleeping
■ *on map*
Price codes:
see inside front cover

AL-A *The Plettenberg*, 40 Church St, T5332030, F5332074. 40 a/c rooms, lounge and dining rooms furnished with antiques, swimming pool, sea views, smartest in area, everything you would expect in a small exclusive top class hotel. **A** *Hunter's Country House*, 10 km towards Knysna, T5327818, F5327878, www.hunterhotels.com 20 thatched suites with fireplace, antique furnishings and private patio, 3 dining rooms, 2 swimming pools, one of the top country hotels in the country which has won awards for food and service, a special place to treat yourself to. Recommended.

B *Beacon Isle*, Beacon Isle Crescent, T5331120, F5333880. Multi-storey building dominating the bay, right on the water between two beaches, 200 rooms, 3 restaurants – *Captain's Cabin* (à la carte) and *Quarterdeck* (burgers and pizza), swimming pool, tennis, also a timeshare resort. **B** *Blue Hills Guest House*, PO Box 1566, Plettenberg, 7 km from Plettenberg Bay towards Knysna, T/F5327741. 5 double rooms with en suite bathroom, lounge with a lovely log fire in cold weather, large covered patio with braai area, tennis, swimming pool, croquet lawn, delightful views across the foothills of the Tsitsikamma Mountains, B&B, run by David and Ros, evening meals by arrangement. Recommended. **B** *Formosa Bay Hotel*, just off N2 opposite Shell Ultra City, T5332060, F5333343. 34 chalets set in mature gardens, *Seven Cellars* restaurant, cocktail bar, swimming pool, tennis. **B** *Stone Cottage*, T5331331, T083-5902092 (mob). Beautifully restored 19th-century cottage, tastefully decorated rooms with wooden floors, full of antiques and old photographs, deck overlooking the main beach. **B-C** *Bosavern*, 38 Cutty Sark Av, T5331312, www.bosavern.co.za Ultra-modern and stylish guesthouse overlooking Plett Bay, comfortable rooms with private balconies, minimalist bathrooms, lounge with fireplace, pool. **B-C** *Cottage Pie*, 16 Tarbet Ness Av, T5330368, www.cottagepie.co.za Homely but up-market guesthouse offering well-appointed rooms, very comfortable and cosy. Pool, bougainvillea bedecked terrace. Slightly out of town, but close to Robberg Beach. Healthy or full English breakfasts served, evening meals on request. Friendly owners Frik and Nerine are happy to arrange excursions. Recommended. **B-C** *Strombolis Inn*, 8 km from Plettenberg Bay on the N2 between Knysna and Plettenberg Bay. T5327710, F5327823, strombolis@visit.co.za Accommodation is in private timber cottages, each with en suite bathrooms and tea/coffee facilities. There is a choice between standard cabin rooms and luxury lodges – all rates B&B. Meals are prepared by a team of professional chefs using fresh home-grown ingredients. Recommended. **B-C** *The Crescent*, Pharos Link, PO Box 191, T5334490, F5334491, crescenthotels@pixie.co.za Simple block with 26 double rooms with en suite bathroom, TV, restaurant, bar, lounge area, good value for the town.

E-F *Abalone Beach House*, Keurboomstrand, follow Keurboomstrand signs from N2, turn in to El Remo and continue to the top of the hill, T5359602, beachhouse@global.co.za Great new guesthouse and backpackers set in a modern house right by the beach. 3 doubles and one dorm, spotless, comfortable rooms, TV area, kitchen, balcony and terrace with hammocks. Delicious nightly braais, buffet breakfast. Deserted stretch of beach, free surf boards. Feels like staying in a family home. Recommended. **E-F** *Nothando Backpackers*, 3/5 Wilder St, T5330220, deios@global.co.za Dorms, double rooms, camping, B&B. Clean, cheap and friendly, plus offering plenty of activities with discounts. Beds have duvets, some rooms are en suite. Small kitchen, large TV lounge, Far Side Bar with braai and pool table. African meals available. Good at organizing activities. Highly recommended. **F** *Albergo Backpackers*, 8 Church St, T5334434, www.albergo.co.za Centrally located hostel with dorms, double rooms and a camping area. Garden with hammocks and nightly bonfires, TV/video lounge, 2 kitchens, travel centre.

Western Cape

Eating
● *on map*

All the hotels have their own restaurants and bars. Those listed here are all within walking distance of the town centre

Blue Bay Café, Lookout Centre, Main St, T5331390.Seafood, pasta and sandwiches, good coffee. *Brother's*, Melville Shopping Centre, corner of Main St and Marine Dr, T5335056. Restaurant with attractive terrace overlooking Marine Drive, light lunches and seafood. *Cranzgots*, corner of Strand and Main streets, T5331660. Simple Italian place serving good pizza, pasta and steaks, eat in or take away. There is also a cosy bar. *The Lookout*, T5331379. Popular seafood restaurant perched on the rocks overlooking Lookout beach, perfect location, excellent seafood, soups, salads and steak, also has a busy bar, lively, bustling atmosphere. Recommended. *Med Seafood Bistro*, Village Sq, T5333102. A la carte seafood, good light lunches, huge seafood platters, nice ambience. *San Francisco*, Melville Shopping Centre, corner of Main St and Marine Dr. Coffee shop and restaurant serving excellent breakfasts, sandwiches and salads, good coffee, shady seating on outdoor terrace overlooking the bustle of Marine Drive. *Tivoli's Coffee Shop*, Main St. Continental-style light meals and fresh cakes.

The following restaurants are a short drive from the town centre along the N2 highway. *Hunter's Country House*, 10 km towards Knysna, T5327818. Excellent food served in an old wine cellar, pricey but worth it, recommended for special occasions, booking essential. *The Islander*, 7 km towards Knysna, T5327776. Seafood buffet in tropical surrounds, some poultry and meat dishes, booking advised, closed Tue. *Stromboli's Inn*, 10 km towards Knysna. Good selection, excellent food and friendly, attentive service.

Shopping

There are a wide range of souvenir shops reflecting the town's popularity with domestic visitors. The only products which could be regarded as a speciality of the area are those made from wood and paintings. *African Market*, Main St, crafts and clothing. *The Art House*, 1 Melville's Corner, Main St, crafts, fabrics and pottery. *Lookout Gallery*, Main St. *Old Nick's*, on the N2 outside Plettenberg Bay going east. Group of galleries, craft workshops and studios, with shops and a restaurant. Look out for the ceramics and Zimbabwean sculpture at the *Porcupine*.

Sports

Canoeing and watersports The Keurbooms River is a safe and designated area for canoeing and waterskiing. It is possible to hire canoes from **Nature & Environmental Conservation**, 7 Zenon St, T5332125 and go on an overnight trail up the river as far as *Whiskey Creek hut*. There is a slipway by the bridge where the N2 crosses the river. Within the bay, sailing boats can be launched off Hobie Beach. There are several companies who charter boats and organize dolphin watching trips: *Dolphin Adventures*, T0833405; *Ocean Adventures*, T5335083; *Ocean Safaris*, T5334963.

Diving and snorkelling Conditions are best for diving during the winter months of Sep and Oct. The average water temperature is between 16°C and 18°C, while visibility ranges between 5 m and 10 m. There are not many tropical fish but due to an abundance of planktonic matter there is a colourful reef life. One of the more exciting dive sites is Groot Bank, about 12 km northeast of Hobie Beach. The reef is 35 m off-shore and is best reached by boat. The maximum depth is 25 m and there is a whole variety of rock formations to explore, including tunnels and caves. There is a good chance of seeing parrotfish, ragged-tooth sharks and steenbras. At the southern end of Plettenberg Bay is the wreck of the *MFV Athina*, a Greek trawler which sunk in Aug 1967. It should only be dived in the calmest of conditions as there is a strong surge and the danger of suction. For those who enjoy snorkelling, there is a popular spot in front of the *Beacon Isle Hotel* known as *Deep Blinders* – behind the reef is a sandy area where you might see stingrays. Inflatables leave from the hotel.

There are two dive companies in Plett: *Beyond the Beach*, T5331158, T082-7733344 (mob), run daily dives and rent equipment; *Diving International*, T5330381, T082-4906226 (mob).

Fishing There are several recognized good rock angling sites along the coast – Beacon Island, Robberg Beach, Lockout Rocks, and Nature's Valley. Elf, Galjoen and Steenbras are the most frequent catch. Deep sea fishing is also possible. *Plett Angling Club*, T5359740.

Golf *Plettenberg Bay Country Club*, T5332132. Lush 18-hole course in the middle of a private nature reserve, *Piesang Valley*. Tennis and bowls also available. A challenging 9-hole course has been laid out at Goose Valley.

Horse riding *Equitrailing*, Wittedrift Rd, T5330599, lessons as well as guided trails through the forest.

Western Cape

Plett Eco Adventure, 5 Kloof St, T5333732, info@plettbay.com *Why Not Travel*, Main St, **Tour operators**
T5332873, whynot@global.co.za, local tours.

Air The airport, 10 km from town, was recently upgraded. *SA Airlink*, T044-5339041, oper- **Transport**
ate flights between Plettenberg Bay and Cape Town or Johannesburg; **Cape Town** (75
mins): 1 flight daily, 2 on Sun; **Johannesburg** (2 hrs): 1 flight daily, 2 on Sat.

Road 525 km to **Cape Town**, 93 km to **George**, 32 km to **Knysna**, 171 km to **Mossel Bay**,
236 km to **Port Elizabeth**. **Bus**: *Baz Bus*, T021-4392323, www.bazbus.com, departs daily
towards **Port Elizabeth** and **Cape Town**. Continuing on from Port Elizabeth to **Durban**, the
service runs 5 times a week.

Banks *First National*, 22 Main St, T5332070; *Nedbank*, Nedbank Pl, Main Rd, T5011200; *Standard*, 17 **Directory**
Main St, T5332110. **Communications** There is an *Internet Café*, just next to the Melville Shopping
Centre, on Main Rd. *Post Office*, Plettenberg St, by police station.

East of Plettenberg Bay

If you are in a hurry, stay on the N2 – there is a good stretch of road, although you
have to pay a toll of R8.50. The more spectacular route is a deviation via the village of
Nature's Valley along the R102, which branches off the N2 just after the settlement
known as The Crags.

Sleeping A *Hog Hollow Country Lodge*, PO Box 503, 16 km east of Plettenberg Bay off the
N2 main road, Plettenberg Bay, T/F044-5348879, F5348879, hoghollow@global.co.za One
of the finest lodges along the Garden Route. It has 9 double rooms and 3 suites, all with ceiling fans and decorated with locally made wall hangings and wood carvings. Each room has
its own wooden deck overlooking the Matjies River gorge and Tsitsikamma mountains. The
suites have a mini bar, hand-made wooden beds and a spacious lounge with an open fireplace for log fires in the winter months. Good evening meals are served around a communal
table in a relaxed manner. Swimming pool with stunning views, library/lounge in the main
house. The lodge also organizes 3-hr boat trips around the bay to view whales and dolphins
– if you're lucky you may be able to swim with the dolphins. There are also a number of walking trails through the forest surrounding the lodge which are very popular with birdwatchers. Recommended.

This is a primate reserve where the attractions are free to move about the forest. Visi- **Monkeyland**
tors are advised to join a guided walk which takes in various water holes in the forest.
Guides have a keen eye for spotting animals. If you don't wish to join a tour, the day
centre has a good view point and the restaurant serves up a tasty lunch. Great for
kids. ■ *Daily, 0800-1800, free entrance, but you pay R60 for a guided tour.
T044-5348906, www.monkeyland.co.za To get there, turn off the N2 at the Forest
Hall turning. Monkeyland is a further 2 km down the road.*

This small village has one of the most beautiful settings along the Garden Route. **Nature's Valley**
Since the N2 toll road was opened in 1984, most traffic bypasses this sleepy commu- *Phone code: 044*
nity. The village is surrounded on three sides by the **De Vasselot** section of the *(NB Always use*
Tsitsikamma National Park (see below). The approach by road is particularly *3-figure prefix)*
spectacular. The R102 dropping 223 m to sea level via a narrow gorge, the *Colour map 7, grid B3*
Kalanderkloof, twists and turns through lush green coastal forest. At the bottom is a *The Baz Bus stops in*
lagoon formed by the sand dunes blocking the estuary of the **Groot River**. A right *Nature's Valley most*
turn leads into the village, made up of a collection of holiday cottages and a beach *days of the week*
shop. Note that there are no banks in Nature's Valley. There are several braai spots
on the sandy beach, but be warned that swimming in the sea is not safe. Canoes, rowing boats and yachts can all be sailed on the Groot River and lagoon, but fortunately
power boats are prohibited.

Western Cape

Sleeping **C-F** *Hiker's Haven*, 411 St Patrick St, T044-5316805. A large stone guesthouse with thatched roof, 3 double rooms with individual garden access, 12-bed dorm in the loft which connects to a TV lounge and bar area, self-contained kitchen. We've had some bad reports from budget travellers. **F** *Utopia*, 280 Forest Dr, T044-5316683, utopiabp@worlonline.co.za Alternative to *Hiker's Haven*, backpacker accommodation in an A-frame house in the forest, close to trails.

Groot River & Bloukrans Passes As the road starts to climb out of the Groot Valley it passes the *De Vasselot Rest Camp* on the right. This is the only camp at the western end of the Tsitsikamma National Park (see page 314 for booking details). Many visitors will end up here because this is one end of two of the Garden Route's most spectacular hiking trails, the **Tsitsikamma Trail** and the **Otter Trail**. Look out for a poem by JP Rudd, *Ode to a tree*, on a stone slab underneath the magnificent yellowwood directly across the road from the entrance to the De Vaselot Nature Reserve. From the top of the Groot River Pass the road continues for 6 km before crossing a second river valley, the Bloukrans Pass. Here it descends 183 m into the narrow gorge before crossing the river and climbing up again. 10 km further on the R102 rejoins the N2 highway. **Bloukrans River Bridge** has become a popular stopping point along the N2 since the opening of the world's largest bungee jump. The bridge is apparently the highest in Africa, and the drop into the gorge is quite spectacular. Expect to pay upwards of US$100.

Sleeping Close by is the **E-F** *Bloukrans Lodge*, T042-2811450, offering a good range of accommodation including 2 dorms sleeping 8, and 2 self-catering chalets with open-plan kitchens sleeping 4 or 6. Good value, very friendly.

Storms River
Phone code: 042
(NB Always use 3-figure prefix)
Colour map 7, grid B3

This small village has several smart lodges catering for visitors to the Tsitsikamma National Park and hikers wishing to head to the inland mountains. Next to the Storms River bridge is the **Total Village**, a popular stopover with petrol pumps, curio shops, a restaurant, small museum and the Tsitsikamma info office. If you are approaching from the Port Elizabeth side it is worth stopping briefly here to pick up some local tourist leaflets, especially if you have plans to hike in the region. There is a viewing platform to look down into the river gorge. Administratively, this is the first town in the Eastern Cape Province, but it is also regarded as the first and last town along the Garden Route, hence our including it here. For more **information** contact *Tsitsikamma Information* at the Total Village, T042-2803561, F2803563. This is a helpful office and can provide information and local bookings for a whole variety of adventure activities. The Baz Bus stops at Storms River when requested. There is a daily service along this part of the N2.

Price codes:
see inside front cover

Sleeping **B** *The Armagh*, T5411512, F5411510. Comfortable graded guesthouse with 6 double rooms with en suite facilities, guest lounge, craft shop. Attached restaurant has a good local reputation. Run by Johan and Marion who will tell you everything there is to know about the area. **B** *Tsitsikamma Lodge*, 8 km east of Storms River bridge, T042-2803802, www.tsitsikamma.com Luxurious selection of 22 timber log cabins, plus several honeymoon suites. Each log cabin has an en suite bathroom with spa bath, TV, telephone. Set in forested grounds and colourful gardens, cosy restaurant serving buffet lunches, swimming pool. The short 'strip-tease' trail into the forest brings you to some enticing cool pools. The whole complex is of a high standard and well run, the ideal base from which to start the two famous hikes, the Otter and Tsitsikamma trails – the management will transport you to the start and collect you at the end after 4/5 days for a small fee, a very useful service. **D** *Witels Guesthouse*, PO Box 47, Witelsbas, T/F042-2803770, T082-5781090 (mob). 6 double rooms with en suite bathroom, self-catering cottage, dinners on request, accepts credit cards, clean and friendly, run by Rika and Pietjas. Turn off the N2 opposite the *Tsitsikamma Lodge*. Recommended. **F** *Rainbow Lodge*, T042-2811530. Informal budget B&B with some backpacker accommodation, dorms, doubles, secluded gardens with pool and braai area.

The Otter Trail The trail is one of the great trails managed by the South African National Parks (SANPARKS) in South Africa, it was also the first of its kind to be laid out. The

41-km trail is unidirectional, it runs between Storms River Mouth rest camp in the Tsitsikamma National Park and the village of Nature's Valley at the western end of the national park. It takes five days and four nights to complete. It closely follows the coast and care should be taken close to the cliffs. None of the sectors are that long, but it is still fairly strenuous in parts since you have to cross 11 rivers and there are some steep ascents and descents at each river crossing. The longest stretch is between Oakhurst and André huts, which can take seven hours to complete, although it is only 14 km in length. Apart from the natural beauty and the birdlife the trail passes some fine waterfalls and Strandloper caves, look out for the fine large old hardwood trees which have escaped the dreaded axe.

Trail information Permits are available from South African National Parks (SANPARKS) offices in Cape Town, T021-222810 and in Pretoria, T012-3431991. This is a very popular hike, booking opens 13 months in advance; your best chance of a permit is a cancellation during school term time. The offices also provide excellent maps which are packed full of background information and advice to help make your experience an enjoyable one. Of the 11 river crossings, the Bloukrans River, presents the most problems. Check tide tables, you will at least have to wade, or even swim across. So waterproofing for your rucksack is vital. The route is marked with painted otter footprints. Only 12 people can start the trail each day, groups should consist of a minimum of 4. It costs R175 per person, this includes 4 nights in the hiking huts as well as the permit.

Sleeping There are 4 overnight camps, *Ngubu*, *Scott*, *Oakhurst* and *André*. At each site there are 2 log huts each sleeping 6 people in bunk beds, mattresses and firewood are provided. Take time to enjoy the trail, respect the environment and leave with positive and happy memories.

Price codes: see inside front cover

Tsitsikamma National Park

This is one of the most popular national parks in the country, second only to Kruger. It consists of beautiful stretches of lush, coastal forest and is known for its excellent birdlife. Not only is the forest protected, but the park boundaries reach out to sea for 5½ km in the eastern sector. No boats are allowed in this area, nor is spearfishing permitted and no shells (even dead ones) may be removed or disturbed.

Colour map 7, grid B3

Getting there The turn-off for Storms River camp is on a straight stretch of road, easy to miss if driving fast. A surfaced road leads down to the reception centre on the coast. The last part of this drive is a beautiful, steep descent through lush rainforest, a marked contrast to the coniferous plantations along the N2 toll road. If you are travelling along the R102, the turning is just beyond the sawmill at Boskor. If you are approaching from the Port Elizabeth side, the turning is 4 km after the small village of Storms River.

Ins & outs
590 km to Cape Town
180 km to Port Elizabeth
55 km to Plettenberg Bay
90 km to Knysna

The **De Vasselot** camp can only be reached from the R102; when approaching from Knysna take the Nature's Valley turning at Kurland (R102). If you miss this turning you cannot turn off the N2 toll road until it meets with the other end of the R102, at which point you are only 8 km from the turning for Storms River camp. When approaching from Port Elizabeth look out for signs for Nature's Valley, R102. De Vasselot camp is clearly signposted 3 km outside the village of Nature's Valley.

Information Information and enquiries: T042-2811607. **Storms River Mouth** gate open: 0530-2130; **De Vasselot** gate open: 0700-2100. Office hours: 0800-1300, 1400-1800, T042-5411607. All visitors pay a small entrance fee. Shop hours: daily, 0800-1800, stocks gift items as well as groceries, wines and beer. *Jabulani Restaurant* hours: 0730-1000, 1200-1500, 1800-1930, you must make reservations for evening meals by 1700. Swimming pool, card telephone, occasional films shows on the park ecology.

Climate The best time to visit is between Nov and Feb. Bear in mind that although this is midsummer, you can expect rain at any time. Annual rainfall is in excess of 1,200 mm; Jun and Jul are the driest months, while May and Oct are the wettest.

The park, flora & fauna The park stretches 80 km along the coast between Nature's Valley and Oubosstrand. For most of its length it is no more than 500 m wide on the landward side. At the western end, where the Otter Trail reaches the Groot River estuary, the park boundary extends 3 km inland. It was established on 4 December 1964 in response to an appeal for the creation of more marine parks and reserves, made during the First World Conference on National Parks in Seattle in 1962. The main administrative office is at Storms River camp, which is almost the midpoint of the park. Apart from the short walk to the Storms River suspension bridge, the land east of the office is closed to the public. In the immediate vicinity of the camp there are several other short hikes (see below) which provide ample opportunity to explore the forest and look out for birds. West from the camp is the famous **Otter Hiking Trail** (see page 310), which follows the coastline all the way to De Vasselot, the second park camp at the western extremity of the park. The rest of the parklands are inaccessible to the public. To the west of Nature's Valley is the 'De Vasselot' section.

A cross-section of the coastlands would reveal the Tsitsikamma Mountains, 900-1,600 m, whose slopes level off into a coastal plain or plateau at about 230 m, and then the forested cliffs which plunge 230 m into the ocean. The slope is only precipitous in a few places; elsewhere along the coast it is still very steep, but there is enough soil to support the magnificent rainforest which the park was in part created to protect. The rainforest is the last remnant of a forest which was once found right along this coast between the ocean and the mountains. The canopy ranges between 18 m and 30 m and is closed, which helps hikers since little sun reaches the footpath – note that you'll have to use fast film if you wish to take photos. The most common species of trees found here are milkwood, real yellowwood, stinkwood, Cape blackwood, forest elder, white pear and candlewood, plus the famous Outeniqua yellowwood, a forest giant. All are magnificent trees which combine with climbers such as wild grape, red saffron and milky rope to create an outstandingly beautiful forest.

In the forest itself 35 different bird species have been recorded, while in the park as a whole over 220 species have been identified. Spotting birds in a forest environment can be hard work – the most reliable means of identification is by song, not something you learn overnight. The most colourful bird in the forest is the Knysna lourie, *Tauraco corythaix*. Its call is a "korr korr korr", and in flight it has a flash of deep red in its wings, with a green body and distinct crest. In the vicinity of the Storms River campsite and the Groot River estuary you will see an entirely different selection of birds: over 40 species of sea bird have been recorded here. The most satisfying sighting is the rare African black oystercatcher, with its black plumage and red eyes, beak and legs.

With such steep slopes and dense forest you will only come across a few small mammals. The species that do occur include caracal, bushbuck, blue duiker, grysbok, bushpig and the Cape clawless otter. The blue duiker and the Cape clawless otter are the most rare and you should consider yourself very lucky if you glimpse either. The blue duiker is the smallest antelope in South Africa – the adult male stands less than 30 cm high and weighs about 4 kg, although the female is slightly bigger. They live in forest and thick bush along the coast, feeding on forest fruits and flowers which are dropped from the canopy by feeding monkeys, or birds such as the Knysna lourie or rameron pigeons. Each animal lives alone in a territory of about 6 ha in extent. The most likely time to see them is at dawn or dusk in an open clearing which they are known to frequent – ask one of the park rangers about recent sightings. The Cape clawless otter is also very rare and considered an endangered species. They feed on fish and sea crabs, emerging from their dens in the early evening.

Hiking in the park

Tsitsikamma is home to one of the best hiking trails in South Africa, the Otter Trail, see page 310 for details

The Tsitsikamma Trail This is a trail of average difficulty which runs through the foothills of the Tsitsikamma Mountains. The full trail is 65 km long, it starts from the Kalander hut in Nature's Valley and finishes at the suspension bridge over the Storms River. Shorter hikes are possible, there are paths connecting the trail with Bloukrans Forest Station, Lottering Forest Station and Boskor sawmill. All three points are close to the R102. The full hike takes four nights and five days to complete. Having a hut at the start of the trail, Kalander hut, is ideal in allowing one to start the first day very early and not have to worry about transport to the start and preparing all your equipment. The path passes through pine plantations (which are a bit dull), patches of moist indigenous forest and open fynbos country which looks its best in spring and early summer. Patches of the highveld are deliberately burnt to protect plantations from fires. You may swim in all streams except for the Kleinbos and Lottering rivers which supply drinking water to people downstream.

Trail essentials Since April 1993 the lands through which the Tsitsikamma hiking trail pass are managed by the South African Forestry Company Ltd (SAFCOL). Permits are issued by the Regional Forestry Manager, SAFCOL, Private Bag X537, Humansdorp, T042-351180. The trail is far less popular than the Otter Trail . Bookings are accepted from within six months of the time you wish to hike, you can appear in person at the office in the Downing and Attwood Building, Main St, Humansdorp. An excellent map of the route is produced by the Department of Water Affairs and Forestry. This includes details of the terrain, the availability of drinking water and background information on the flora and fauna of the Tsitsikamma Mountains. The trail is sign-posted by white footprints, blue footprints indicate short deviations to a swimming pool or source of drinking water, yellow footprints indicate connecting routes – for example there are paths between the Keurbos hut and Lottering Forest Station; and from Boskor sawmill to Heuningbos overnight hut. The longest day's stretch is 17 km, between Kalander and Blaauwkrantz huts. You can only walk in one direction, from west to east. Numbers are limited to 30 people per day, ideally there should be a minimum of 4 people in a hiking group.

Sleeping There are 5 overnight huts, *Kalander*, *Blaauwkrantz*, *Keurbos*, *Heuningbos* and *Sleepkloof*. Each of the huts can sleep 30 people in bunk beds, mattresses and firewood are provided. Drinking water is available at the huts, but use it sparingly. Fires can only be lit in the cooking shed. You are not allowed to camp along the trail, you must spend each night in a hut.

De Vasselot Camp Across the Groot River from the camp are six trails in the Grootkloof Forest. There are a number of large trees here and the birdlife is excellent, although there's the usual problem of catching sight of them in the first place. The best spots are in clearings and along streams. Note that there are a large number of streams in the forest which can be difficult to cross after heavy rains. South of the camp the river estuary broadens into a lagoon which is a popular spot for watersports. Fortunately no powerboats are allowed on the water, and exploring the limits by canoe is great fun.

Storms River Camp There are four different trails in the vicinity of the camp. The most popular, and strongly recommended, is a 1-km walk along a raised boardwalk from the restaurant block to the mouth of the Storms River. The last part of the walk involves a steep descent – there is a solid handrail, but the wooden steps can be slippery after rains, as can other parts of the walk. At the bottom is the suspension bridge which appears in many pictures promoting the Garden Route. The views from this point are excellent, especially at midday when there is a clear view of the narrow river gorge extending back inland. The path continues on the other side of the bridge, although it is no longer protected by planks and the damage is clearly evident. From here you can climb the hill for superb views; there are over 300 steps and the path is narrow and steep. Look out for identification labels on the trees as the path winds through the forest. This is a great opportunity to see the trees which a century ago were in great demand for household furniture and building projects – much of the reason for the extensive deforestation in the area. Allow at least an hour for the walk to the bridge and back.

The other trails close to the camp are the **Lourie Trail**, 1 km through the forested slopes behind the camp, the **Blue Duiker Trail**, 3.7 km further into the forest, and the **Waterfall Trail**, a 3-km walk along the first part of the **Otter Trail**, hikers without a permit have to turn back at the waterfall.

The latest addition to the park is the **Dolphin Trail**, a three-day guided trail. This is a far more upmarket hike – luggage is transported from one night stop to the next, accommodation is in luxurious lodges, all meals are included (with pre-packed picnics for lunch), and the entire hike is professionally guided. This trail is far more expensive, at R2,200 per person for three days. For more information, T042-2811607. For bookings, call T012-3431991.

Behind the restaurant is the rather unusual **Underwater trail**, which can be completed with scuba equipment or a mask and snorkel. You can see a good cross-section of the marine life found along the south coast, but conditions are not ideal so few people complete the trail. If you do want to give it a go, the best time of year is in the summer, although conditions are rough for most of the year and visibility is rarely more than 10 m. The water is fairly cold, so be sure to wear a wetsuit.

Sleeping This is a very popular national park, particularly with South Africans, so during the school holidays it is almost impossible to find accommodation here. Reservations must be made up to 12 months in advance. Fortunately there is plenty of accommodation along the Garden Route. If you're staying in Knysna, for example, the park can still be reached within a 1-hr drive. There are also several private lodges close to the main entrance (see above).

All of the park's accommodation must be vacated by 0900. Arriving visitors have access from 1200. There are 2 rest camps in the park: *Storms River Mouth*, the main camp with a full range of facilities, and *De Vasselot*, a very basic camp close to the settlement of Nature's Valley. Reservations, Pretoria, T012-3431991, F3430905 or at reservations@parks-sa.co.za Bookings can also be made in person at 2 offices in Cape Town: the V&A Waterfront Office, Clocktower Centre, or at Cape Town Tourism in the city centre, corner of Castle and Burg streets. Closer to the time of your intended stay contact: T042-2811607. Credit card bookings are accepted over the telephone. If the park is full there are several options just outside the park limits, see above. Seasonal discounts apply to all forms of accommodation between 1 May and end of Aug. Price quoted for all sheltered accommodation includes breakfast.

Storms River Mouth On a narrow strip of land between ocean and forested hills, this is one of the most beautiful settings of all the national parks. At the end of the surfaced road is the reception area which also has a shop and restaurant. The nearest petrol is available at Storms River bridge. Accommodation here is a mix of: **C** *Log Cabins*, with 2 bedrooms, can sleep a maximum of 6 people, fully equipped kitchen with fridge and stove, bedding provided, bathroom, lounge area; **D** *Oceanettes*, with 2 bedrooms, fully equipped kitchen, bathroom, lounge, a little less smart and comfortable, but ideal when you are likely to spend most of the day outdoors; **E** *Forest Cabins*, sleeps 2, no kitchen, breakfast is extra, very basic; and **F** *Camping*, terraced lawns in a beautiful location right on the shoreline, exposed when the wind blows. There are a few shady trees, and it is a real thrill to peer out of your tent at dawn and watch the waves crashing on the rocks right in front of you. There are twice as many sites for caravans, braai sites but no electric points, laundry, and central wash blocks.

De Vasselot This camping and caravan site is 40 km west of Storms River Mouth. The site is set in an indigenous forest on the banks of the Groot River, and has a wash block, hot water, laundry, no electricity, no shop or restaurant, all supplies can be bought in Nature's Valley village, 3 km away.

Tour operators A great way of seeing the forest from a new angle is with *Tsitsikamma Canopy Tours*, T042-2811836, www.treetoptour.com These canopy tours involve climbing up to a platform from where you are attached to a steel rope (plenty of safety equipment is used to prevent falls). From here you glide between different platforms attached to forest giants, giving extraordinary views from high above the ground. Recommended. An excellent local operator is *Stormsriver Adventures*, T042-2811836, www.stormriver.com Organize a number of tours in the Tsitsikamma region, including guided hikes, abseiling, tubing and scuba diving.

Eastern Cape

5

Eastern Cape

The Eastern Cape, although far less visited than many parts of South Africa, is a fascinating region of wild, empty beaches, forested mountains and the sun-baked plains of the Karoo. **Port Elizabeth** *is a major industrial centre, but with surprisingly good beaches, and acts as a gateway to the Garden Route, the lush coast stretching towards Cape Town, and* **Tsitsikamma National Park**. *A short drive from here is* **Jeffreys Bay**, *where the long beach and perfect waves attract surfers from around the world. Just west of Port Elizabeth lies the* **Baviaanskloofberge**, *a rugged wilderness area which offers challenging hiking in forested hills.*

To the north is a variety of game reserves and national parks, including **Addo Elephant Park** *with its extraordinary herds of elephant,* **Mountain Zebra Reserve**, *a haven for the endangered mountain zebra, and* **Shamwari Game Reserve**, *where you can catch a glimpse of the Big Five. Further inland lie the mystical landscapes of the* **Amatola Mountains** *and the sharply contrasting* **Karoo**, *with its surreal semi-desert conditions and 19th-century towns.*

The eastern region is known as the **Transkei**, *a traditional Xhosa area with a rugged, virtually deserted coastline, known as the* **Wild Coast**. *This is far less developed than much of the rest of South Africa's coast – instead of full-blown resorts, there are small seaside villages backed by protected stretches of verdant coastal forest and windswept dunes.*

Port Elizabeth

Phone code: 041
(NB Always use
3-figure prefix)
Colour map 7, grid B4

Port Elizabeth – usually referred to as 'PE' – is a major port and industrial centre, and the biggest coastal city between Cape Town and Durban. The centre of town, known as 'Central', is an attractive grid of Victorian houses and green spaces (burnt brown in summer) but the rest of the city – a modern sprawl of shopping malls, office blocks and apartments stretching between wealthy suburbs and industrial docks – is less aesthetically pleasing. The main tourist area is along the long beaches of Algoa Bay, and although the endless soft-sand beaches are enticing, the holiday flats and apartment blocks creeping on to the flat land behind them are less so. Nevertheless, Port Elizabeth is celebrated for its long hours of sunshine and the warm waters of the bay, making it a good place to try some watersports. It also has a large student population, lending to the city a lively edge with a particularly vibrant bar and clubbing scene.

The other great pull of the city is the fact that within an easy day's drive there are three parks open for game viewing: Addo Elephant Park (see page 340), Zuurberg National Park (page 342) and the Shamwari Game Reserve (page 350). Although Shamwari is a private reserve and has a development with some very smart camps, it is open to the public for day visits so long as you book in advance. Here is the only opportunity you'll have in South Africa of seeing the Big Five without having to worry about malaria. Combine this with the fact that you can fly back to Cape Town in less than an hour and it becomes obvious why Port Elizabeth is rapidly growing as a popular tourist destination.

Ins and outs

Getting there
For more detailed
information, see
Transport, page 331

Port Elizabeth Airport is 4 km from the city centre along Alister Miller Drive. Visitors staying in the tourist areas at Humewood Beach and Summerstrand can reach the airport without having to negotiate the city centre. Most of the major hotels provide a courtesy bus. There is no public transport from the airport into town, but taxis and hotel transport are available at the airport terminal. The mainline **railway station** is on the edge of the town centre on Station St, by the harbour and just off Strand St, which runs parallel to Govan Mbeki Av. *Greyhound* coaches arrive at the rear car park, 107 Govan Mbeki Av and in front of Edgars at the Greenacres Shopping Centre. *Intercape* coaches arrive at the corner of Flemming and North Union streets or at the Edgars entrance to Greenacres Shopping Centre. *Translux* coaches arrive by the Ernst and Young Building, and the railway station, Strand St.

Getting around

Local buses depart from Market Square Bus Station, beneath the Norwich Union Centre Building, Strand St. *Algoa Bus Company* operates a regular central city service between the beachfront, city centre, St George's Park, Rink St, Greenacres and The Bridge Shopping Complex – Route O.

Tourist offices

Port Elizabeth Publicity Association, Donkin Lighthouse Building, Belmont Terr, T5858884, F5852564, www.ibhayi.com, 24-hr information, T5860773. Open Mon-Fri, 0800-1630; Sat and Sun, 0930-1530. A useful and well-placed office with bookings and information on accommodation, nightlife, tours and travel throughout the Eastern Cape. There are also offices in Brookes Pavilion and the Boardwalk, both on Marine Dr. *Eastern Cape Tourist Board*, 25 Donkin St, T5857761, www.ectourism.org.za has excellent regional information.

History

The city was established in 1820 when the first British settlers landed in the bay. The town became a port and a trading centre catering for the early settlers who were gradually moving inland. During the first half of the 20th century, Port Elizabeth expanded and became an important trading and manufacturing city. The main exports were mineral ores, citrus fruits and wool. Ford General Motors opened its first assembly plants here in the 1920s. As an industrial city it is understandable that tourists don't want to spend a great deal of time here. However, with the massive

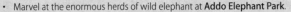

Things to do in Eastern Cape

- Marvel at the enormous herds of wild elephant at **Addo Elephant Park**.
- Learn to surf on the **world's best right-hander** in Jeffreys Bay.
- Hike through the indigenous forests of the mystical **Amatola Mountains**.
- Relax on a deserted beach on the **Wild Coast** in the Transkei.
- Visit the historical **desert towns** of the great Karoo.

growth in tourism along the Garden Route, the city has experienced similar growth and most of the visitors to the area start or finish their journey here.

Sights

The 5 km **Donkin Heritage Trail** has been created to show visitors the most impor-   **Central** tant monuments, buildings, gardens and churches around the city centre. An excellent guidebook is available from the information office and contains 47 places of historical interest. A few of the more interesting buildings are mentioned below – they are not in the order you might come across them on the trail. The trail starts in Market Square opposite the City Hall.

Market Square is probably PE's most attractive corner, with a couple of fine buildings and the beginning of bustling Govan Mbeki Avenue. **City Hall** was built between 1858 and 1862; the clock tower was added in 1883. While part of the hall is still used by the council, it is also now a lecture and concert hall for public performances. Look out for a replica of the Diaz Cross in Market Square. This was donated by the Portuguese Government to commemorate the arrival of Bartholomeu Diaz in Algoa Bay in 1488. The **Main Public Library** dominates the new corner of Market Square. This fine early Victorian building, with its terracotta façade shipped out from the UK, dates from 1837 and started life as a courthouse. It was not until 1902 that it was officially opened as the public library. Outside by the road is a fine marble statue of Queen Victoria, erected in 1903. Once inside, visitors have the opportunity to view some beautiful early books. Call the librarian in advance if there is a specific topic you wish to research. ■ *Open 0900-1700. T5858133.*

The **Monument to Prester John** stands in Fleming Square, behind City Hall. It is dedicated to the mythical king-priest, Prester John and the Portuguese explorers who discovered South Africa. It was unveiled in 1986 by the Portuguese Ambassador and is thought to be the only monument in the world depicting Prester John. The monument is in the form of a large Coptic cross.

South of City Hall, near the *Translux* bus station, at 27 Baakens Street, is the **Wezandla Gallery and Craft Centre**, hard to miss with its brightly painted exterior. This is an interesting collection of African art, some of which is for sale: wire and wood sculptures, woven baskets, pottery, crafts and curios. Many of the items are the works of local craftsmen. ■ *Mon-Fri 0900-1700; Sat 0900-1300. T5851185.*

The **Campanile** (Italian for 'bell tower') is a 53 m high tower close to the docks down by the railway station. It was built to commemorate the landing of the 1820 Settlers, and was once the highest structure in PE, but today there are a number of modern buildings that are taller. The views of the city and harbour remain impressive though, and if you're fit you can climb up 204 stairs to the observation room at the top. It contains the largest carillon of bells in the country as well as a chiming clock, and the tower is a useful reference point on the coast. ■ *Tue-Sat 0900-1230, 1330-1630; Sun 1400-1700.*

Castle Hill Museum is housed in one of the oldest buildings in the city, at 7 Castle Hill Road. It was built in 1827 for the Reverend Francis McCleland as the Rectory. The cottage has been restored to look like an early-Victorian home, complete with a slate roof, yellowwood floors and 19th-century furniture and household goods.

Eastern Cape

■ *Mon 1400-1700, Tue-Fri 1000-1300, 1400-1700; Sat 1000-1300, T5822515. Minimal entrance fee.*

Donkin Reserve is a public park in Central, high up on a hill with views of Govan Mbeki Avenue and the harbour. On the inland side of the park is the fine façade of the *Edward Hotel*; on the other side is a lighthouse and an unusual pyramid. The lighthouse dates from 1861 and is today home to the tourist office, a very helpful and friendly information centre. The rest of the lighthouse building can be opened on request. The odd-looking pyramid is actually a touching memorial erected by Sir Rufane Donkin in memory of his wife after whom the city was named – Elizabeth. Local folklore is rather more sinister and suggests that her heart was buried in the pyramid. Rufane Donkin, a British colonialist and the former Cape Governor, was sent to administer PE in the late 19th century, but his wife Elizabeth never actually saw the town.

South of Donkin Reserve, on Belmont Terrace, is **Fort Frederick**. This was the first stone building in the Eastern Cape, completed in 1799. From its high point it overlooks the mouth of the Baakens River. It was built to stop any French troops from landing in the river mouth and thereby helping the rebels at Graaff-Reinet. No shot has ever been fired from, or at, the fort. ■ *Open daily, sunrise to sunset, free entrance.*

Northwest of Donkin Reserve, on Raleigh Street, is the **Jewish Pioneers' Memorial Museum**, which houses a collection of memorabilia celebrating the history of the Jewish community in Port Elizabeth. The house was originally the Raleigh Street

Port Elizabeth Central

To N2 Highway

	Sleeping				Eating
	1 Calabash Lodge		4 Jikeleza Lodge		1 Aviemore
	2 Edward & Causerie		5 Millbrook House		2 Chatter's Bar & Grill
	Restaurant		6 Port Elizabeth		3 Keg & Fox
	3 Heritage Inn		Backpackers		4 Ranch

0 metres 200
0 yards 200

Synagogue which served the city's Jewish community between 1912 and 1954. In addition to some personal effects there are some very interesting old photographs on display. ■ *Sun only, 1000-1145. Free entrance. T5833671.*

On Park Drive, at the western fringes on the city centre is **King George VI Art Gallery**. Most of the collection is of 19th- and 20th-century British art, but there are also some good monthly contemporary exhibitions, accompanied by films and lectures. Other displays include a collection of Oriental miniatures as well as pottery and sculptures. ■ *Mon-Fri 0830-1700, Sat-Sun 1400-1700, 1st Sun of every month, 0900-1400, free entrance. T5861030.*

Equine lovers may wish to sneak a peek at the **Horse Memorial** standing on the corner of Russell and Cape roads. This fine sculpture was created after the Boer War. Between 1899 and 1902 thousands of horses died, more often through fatigue and starvation than from being slain in actual battle. There is an inscription on the memorial that reads, "The greatness of a nation consists not so much in the number of its people or the extent of its territory as in the extent and justice of its compassion." The statue shows a man kneeling in front of a horse with a bucket in his hands making as if to feed or quench the horse's thirst.

Southeast of the city centre, off Marine Drive in Humewood, is **Bayworld**, a museum complex. There are three attractions: the Main Museum, the Oceanarium and the Snake Park. Respective opening hours differ slightly as do their entrance charges. Like all museums they are popular with school groups, but there isn't much to keep anyone else (or children for that matter) distracted for long. ■ *T5861051.*

Outside Central

See also Algoa Bay & The Beaches page 332

Eastern Cape

5 Rome
6 Up the Khyber

The **Main Museum** is a mix of natural and cultural history. Look out for the southern right whale skeleton, and the fully rigged models of early sailing ships. There is also a collection of objects collected from wrecks in and around Algoa Bay. The rest of the collection focuses on fossils and early man. ■ *Daily 0900-1630. Small entrance fee.*

Oceanarium is PE's aquarium, with displays of over 40 species of fish, as well as a ragged tooth shark tank, rays, turtles and African penguins. The most interesting part of the complex is the dolphin research centre, with seal and dolphin presentations daily at 1100 and 1500. The centre has a successful breeding programme – one of the most popular attractions is baby dolphin Thunzi who recently turned one. ■ *Daily 0900-1300, 1400-1700. Entrance: adults, R20, children, R10. Certified scuba divers can dive in the shark tank on Wed at 1430. Book ahead on T5835316.*

The **Snake Park** houses a collection of exotic reptiles in realistically landscaped glass enclosures, including some rare and endangered species. Inside the **Tropical House** you follow a path through woodlands with paths, bridges, waterfalls and streams. Birds are free to fly around within the giant enclosure. ■ *Daily 0900-1700. Entrance: adults, R7, children, R4. Reptile demonstrations take place daily at 1000 and 1400 in season.*

A rather esoteric museum outside the centre is the **Port Elizabeth Air Force Museum**, a collection of aircraft memorabilia and three reconstructed aircraft. ■ *At the southern side of Port Elizabeth airport, on Forest Hill Dr, Southdene, T5051295.*

Settler's Park is not what you would expect to find in the middle of South Africa's fifth largest city. Running through the town is the Baakens River Gorge which is surrounded by a well kept 54 ha green park. The valley runs for 7 km and is full of interesting birds, plants and even some small buck. Unfortunately, despite the tranquil setting you must be wary since there are the occasional muggings, so don't come here alone. The park has three entrances: How Avenue, just off Park Drive; Chelmsford Avenue, just off Target Kloof; or Third Avenue, Walmer. Look out for the recommended walks by each entrance, such as the 8 km Guinea Fowl trail.

Essentials

Sleeping
■ *on maps, pages 320 and 324*
Price codes: see inside front cover

During the last couple of years Port Elizabeth has experienced a rapid expansion in tourist accommodation. Much of this has been in the seaside suburbs of Humewood and Summerstrand, and if you're looking for something close to the beach, it's perfect. The seafront area, however, is a modern and ugly stretch of high-rise blocks and shopping malls. The centre, around the Donkin Reserve, has more character and is far more appealing.

Central and Walmer The centre of PE, around the Donkin Reserve, has a number of quiet back streets lined with some finely restored Victorian houses. The leafy suburb of Walmer is on the far side of St George's Park and southwest of the centre and is very convenient for the airport, but not for anyone wishing to spend time on the beach.

A *Hacklewood Hill Country House*, 152 Prospect Rd, Walmer, T5811300, F5814155, www.pehotels.co.za This luxurious guesthouse is housed in a late-Victorian manor house, with 8 a/c tasteful double rooms, each with massive en suite bathrooms, some non-smoking rooms, TV with M-net. There are also beautiful mature gardens with swimming pool and tennis court, plus secure covered parking. There are some special touches which make this a fine choice: guests, for example, are encouraged to select their wine from the impressive cellar. Advanced booking essential during the peak season.

B *Country Club 39*, 39 Church Rd, Walmer, T5815099, F5814458, club39@icon.co.za A large, purpose-built complex, clean and well-equipped, with 11 a/c double rooms, all with en suite bath or shower, TV with M-net, lounge, laundry service, good size swimming pool with a tidy outhouse, floodlit tennis court, gardens, only 5 mins from the airport and close to the shops. **B** *The Edward*, Belmont Terr, Central, T5862056, F5864925, edward@cyberhost.co.za This building is a fine example of late 19th-century architecture, and is one of Port Elizabeth's famous landmarks, its elegant façade bordering the Donkin Reserve. The hotel was recently taken over by the Protea chain. There are 110 comfortable double rooms with en suite bathroom, telephone and TV, some with good city views. Furnishings are old-fashioned and dreary. The *Causerie* restaurant is rather fussy but nevertheless an excellent carvery. There is also a bar, lounge, laundry service and secure covered parking. What the hotel may lack in style, it makes up for in character. **B** *Oak Tree Cottage*, 112 Church Rd, Walmer, T/F5813611, duff@global.co.za A well-run B&B with 3 double rooms with en suite bathroom, 1 with private bathroom, TV lounge, swimming pool, shady gardens, laundry. Lunch and dinner on request, a touch more expensive than similar set-ups, secure parking, close to the beach, ask for Duff or Joy.

C *Two King George's*, 2 King George's Rd, Millpark, T3741825, F3731164. A mock Tudor family home with plenty of space for guests. 6 double rooms with en suite bathroom, mini bar and TV, 1 single room, non-smoking room available. There is also a study and a lounge, plus sizable gardens with a swimming pool. Extra meals available on request. Close to the cricket ground in St George's Park but located on a main road, secure electronic gates. A popular guesthouse, well-managed and friendly, ask for Dave or Danielle. **C-D** *Valley Guest House*, 10 Jutland Cres, St George's Park, T5862188, F5822579, T083-6263253 (mob). 4 double rooms, 2 with en suite bathroom, 1 with private bathroom. The 4th room is a honeymoon suite with a bath spa. Each is clean, light and airy, with TV. There is also a homely lounge with a shaded veranda and views of the mature gardens full of birds. Evening meals available on request, and guests can request use of a fully equipped kitchen. Secure parking, a short drive from the airport, friendly, close to the cricket ground, ask for Marilyn. Excellent value when compared with similar establishments. Recommended.

D *Calabash Lodge*, 8 Dollery St, Central, T5856162, F5850985, calabash@iafrica.co.za Clean and comfortable guesthouse in an ideal location for central sights. Double rooms and family rooms with en suite bathroom, free pickup from airport, station and bus terminal. Friendly, helpful, also run an excellent tour company. Recommended by several readers. Ask for Tandi or Paul. **D** *Millbrook House*, 2 Havelok Sq, Central, T5853080, F5823774, millbrook@eastcape.net Delightful B&B in a leafy square in the centre of town. Victorian house with iron-wrought balconies, peaceful setting, perfect for seeing the sights. Family-run with 5 charming double rooms, 4 are en suite, 1 has private bathroom, all have ceiling fans, TV with M-net, clean, bright and airy. Small garden with pool, lounge, free airport pickup. Liz and Miles are very friendly and welcoming, and are happy to help with questions about the Eastern Cape. Excellent value. Recommended.

E *Heritage Inn*, corner of Western and Alfred roads, T5825275, F5825280. Large, functional B&B in a good location in the centre of town. Range of double rooms with en suite bath or shower, TV, telephone, decent furnishings. A couple of comfortable dorm rooms with single beds (thankfully no bunks) and shared bathrooms. Clean and practical place, good buffet breakfasts, some outdoor tables on shady terrace overlooking the street.

F *Jikeleza Lodge*, 44 Cuyler St, T5863721, F5856686, winteam@hinet.co.za Double rooms, dorms, kitchen, pleasant backyard, internet access, free pick up across town, close to shops and some restaurants. Helpful set-up, keen to organize transport and tours. **F** *Port Elizabeth Backpackers*, 7 Prospect Hill, Central, T5860697. Attractive old building with bright and airy dorms, some double rooms, well-equipped kitchen, good location as one of the few central backpackers, small backyard, good travel centre.

Humewood and Summerstrand Most of the resort hotels and smart guesthouses are south of the city centre in the suburbs of Humewood and Summerstrand.

These suburbs are located between the town centre and Cape Recife. Although a rather unattractive development, it is safe to walk around at night

A *The Beach*, Marine Dr, Summerstrand, T5832161, F5836220, reservations@pehotels.co.za Luxurious, low-rise hotel right on the beach. 63 well-appointed rooms, good restaurant, bar, golf, large pool, laundry, secure parking, tidy gardens, good service, just across the road from Shark Rock pier, a short drive from the centre. Rather more low-key than other hotels in the area. **A-B** *Marine Protea*, Marine Dr, T5832101, F5832076, marine@pehotel.co.za Large, unattractive high-rise block just across from the beach. 66 a/c rooms and 7 suites, en suite bathrooms, TV with M-net, comfortable but unimaginatively furnished, some rooms have great views of Pollock Beach and Algoa Bay. The *De Kelder* restaurant has a good local reputation. Good service in comfortable and luxurious surrounds, secure covered parking, no swimming pool, free bus transfer to the airport.

B *Humewood*, 33 Marine Dr, T5858961, F5851740, humewood@intekom.co.za Attractive old-fashioned seaside building right on King's Beach. 65 rooms, most of which are sea-facing with a small private balconies. There's the pleasant *Sandpiper* à la carte restaurant, and the *Quarterdeck* pub is a popular drinking haunt for local students. The morning coffee shop has a pleasant ambience and some seats on a terrace overlooking the street. A bus provides transfers to the airport or the city centre. Lacks a proper garden for children to play in and enjoy. **B** *Holiday Inn Garden Court King's Beach*, La Roche Dr, King's Beach, T5823720, F5855754, margaretm@southernsun.com Huge white building which dominates the area, 283 a/c rooms with en suite bathrooms, TV, restaurant, swimming pool, courtesy bus for trips away from the beach. **B-C** *Kingfisher Guest House*, 73 Brighton Dr, Summerstrand, T5832150, F5832512, www.kingfisherpe.co.za Family-run B&B close to the beach, with 4 double rooms with en suite bathrooms, 1 double room with private bathroom, TV, lounge, disabled facilities, laundry, swimming pool, peaceful garden to relax in, secure parking, evening meals available

Eastern Cape

on request, ask for Ken. **B-C** *King's Tide*, 16 Tenth Av, Summerstrand, T5836023, kingstide@crowcollection.co.za Stylish B&B with 10 suites, good breakfasts, comfortable and friendly. Ask for Hester. **B** *Summerstrand Inn*, Marine Dr, Summerstrand, T5833131, F5832505, hotsummer@icon.co.za Large hotel with 237 spacious a/c rooms, TV, views of Humewood Golf Course, leafy gardens offer privacy around the pool area. *Palm Grill* restaurant, cosy residents' bar, 4 conference rooms, courtesy bus offered.

C *Brighton Lodge*, 21 Brighton St, Summerstrand, T5834576, F5324104. This is a very comfortable guesthouse where each of the 9 bedrooms has been decorated from a different period, all have en suite bathrooms, TV and a private entrance, convenient location for both the beaches and the airport, ask for Felicity. Recommended. **C** *Fifth Avenue Beach House*, 5th Av, Summerstrand, T5832441, F5832479. Guests have the choice of being in the main house or in a neat complex with a balcony overlooking the swimming pool. 10 double rooms with en suite bathroom, TV, phone in all rooms, no smoking in the house. Garden has a tropical feel with several mature palm trees. Ask for Anthea. A friendly and good-value set up. Recommended.

D *Driftsands Guest House* 2 Marshall Rd, Humewood, T5860459, F5856513. 4 double rooms with en suite bathroom plus a private suite with ocean views, guest lounge has TV with M-net, neat gardens, secure parking, bicycles available for a ride along the nearby beach, evening meals can be provided on request, good value. **D** *Margate Place*, 5 Margate St, Summerstrand, Humewood, T5835799, F5835264, mplace@mweb.co.za B&B set right on the beach. 7 double rooms with en suite bathroom and TV. Laundry, swimming pool in a private garden, self-catering also possible, ask for Cornell Lamprecht.

E *Formula 1*, Marine Dr, T5856380, corner of La Roche Drive and Marine Dr. This hotel is basic and bland, but is good value in an emergency. 88 basic rooms in an unattractive building a block from the beach. **E** *Port Elizabeth Caboose*, Brookes Hill Dr, Humewood, T5860088, F5860087, www.caboose.co.za A large budget set up with 130 rooms in a well-built timber log building with a train theme. Each bedroom is built like a 1st-class train compartment; the more expensive ones have the added luxury of a shower, basin and toilet. The interior consists of cosy wood panelling. There are a couple of vending machines in the hotel lounge from which you can buy snacks.

F *Ikhayalam Lodge*, 25 Windermere Rd, Humewood, T5825098, leterbarendse@ cybertrade.co.za Homely, clean set-up a block away from the beach and nightlife, with dorms and doubles, meals on request (excellent home-made potjie), lovely gardens, bar. **F** *King's Beach Backpackers*, 41 Windermere Rd, Humewood, T5858113, kingsb@ agnet.co.za An excellent hostel set 2 blocks back from the beach and close to restaurants,

Humewood & Summerstrand

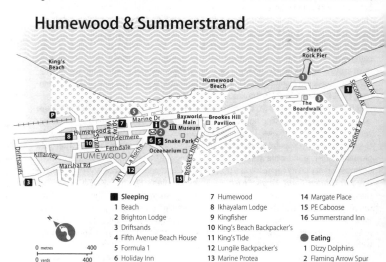

■ Sleeping	7 Humewood	14 Margate Place
1 Beach	8 Ikhayalam Lodge	15 PE Caboose
2 Brighton Lodge	9 Kingfisher	16 Summerstrand Inn
3 Driftsands	10 King's Beach Backpacker's	
4 Fifth Avenue Beach House	11 King's Tide	**● Eating**
5 Formula 1	12 Lungile Backpacker's	1 Dizzy Dolphins
6 Holiday Inn	13 Marine Protea	2 Flaming Arrow Spur

0 metres   400
0 yards   400

bars and clubs. Small and friendly with clean, comfortable dorms, slightly cramped double rooms set in individual buildings in the garden, and camping space on the lawn. Excellent kitchen facilities including free bread and jam, TV and video lounge, internet access, laid-back bar, travel centre. Also has reduced weekly rates, secure off-road parking, 24-hour check-in and free pickups. This is the best backpacker option in Port Elizabeth and one of the best along the whole coast. Recommended. **F** *Lungile Backpackers*, 12 La Roche Dr, Humewood, T5822042, T082-8256181 (mob). Lively lodge set in a fine modern house about 10 mins' walk from Humewood Beach and the beachfront nightlife. There are dorms in the main house and double rooms in separate wooden cabins at the back. Also has a garden with pool, TV and video lounge, bar, pool table, laundry, and a clean kitchen. Mandy, the very friendly manager, often lays on an evening braai in the garden when guests are up for it. Great value. Recommended.

Out of town Just to the south of the city centre, the coastal suburbs merge with the town. However, beyond Cape Recife there are a number of small seaside holiday villages all of which provide a pleasant alternative to staying in the city. **B-C** *Lovemore Retreat*, 434 Sardinia Bay Rd, Lovemore Park, T3661708, F3662304. Smart new complex in the forest at the edge of the nature reserve. 8 rooms, shaded terrace, heated indoor swimming pool, jacuzzi, sauna. The grounds are a joy to explore with a boardwalk to a small waterfall, views across the bay, all less than 15 mins from the airport. Recommended.

All of the accommodation listed below is no more than 30 mins' drive from the centre of town

  C *Erin's Glenn Country Cottage*, off Sardinia Bay Rd, Walmer, T3662316, F3661902. 2 B&B or self-catering cottages, with en suite double rooms, peaceful garden, away from the town and close to the beach.

  D-F *Beachview Caravan Park*, Seaview Main Rd, Beachview, T3781884, F3781885. 35 mins from city centre. 116 luxury caravan sites with power points and private ablution facilities, also some self-contained sea-facing cottages, with TV and bedding provided on request. Restaurant, shop on the premises, plus tennis courts, trampolines, miniature golf, children's playground, safe tidal pool, rock fishing and braai facilities. Recommended for a long stay. **D-F** *Maitland River Caravan Park*, Seaview Main Rd, Beachview, T3781884, F3781885. At the foot of the famous Maitland dune 'mountain', 35 mins from city centre. Log cabins as well as 20 sheltered caravan sites with braai facilities. Try your hand at sand-skiing or -boarding, a local favourite pastime. The Maitland Hiking Trail runs through the dunes, and the resort is opposite a hang glider and parasail launch pad. **D-F** *Seaview Guest Farm*, New Seaview Rd, T3781764, sgft@global.co.za Simple set-up with 6 self-catering chalets, open-plan with kitchen facilities, sleep 4, also large dorms sleeping up to 56 but aimed at school kids. **D-F** *Van Stadens Holiday Resort & Caravan Park*, Van Stadens River Mouth, Linton Grange, T/F7761059. 30 mins from Port Elizabeth, 25 mins to Jeffreys Bay. Self-contained cottages with TV, sheltered caravan sites, all with sea and river view, restaurant, shop, conference centre, trampolines, miniature golf, children's playground, located on the river mouth, close to the Van Stadens Wild Flower Reserve. Recommended. **D-F** *Willows Caravan Park*, Marine Dr, Schoenmakerskop, T3661717, F3661878. A large, self-contained complex with more than 170 caravan sites, sea-facing chalets and rondavels with TV. Café serves snacks on the site during the day, plenty of extras for children: tidal pool, trampolines, miniature golf, children's playground, rock fishing, tractor rides, 4-wheel mini motor bikes, tennis courts. Very popular in season.

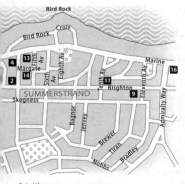

3 Lai Kung
4 The Mediterranean & Zorba's
5 Up the Khyber

All other restaurants are in the large entertainment centres, marked on the map

Eastern Cape

Eating
● *on maps, pages 320 and 324*

Port Elizabeth claims to have the highest per capita ratio of restaurants in South Africa, which for tourists means a wide choice without the inflated prices of Cape Town or Johannesburg

There are two purpose-built 'entertainment' centres, *Brooke's Hill Pavilion* and *The Board-walk*, where you will find a wide selection of restaurants and bars under one roof (see below for details). These are similar to modern shopping malls – there is ample parking and visitors can feel more secure than they would wandering the streets at night. Away from these centres, most of the restaurants are either in the old city centre or close to the seafront in the suburbs of Humewood and Summerstrand.

Aviemore, 12 Whitlock St, T5851125. Closed Mon and Sat lunch and all day Sun. Elegant establishment serving South African country fare, including fresh game and seafood dishes influenced by French, Italian and Thai cuisine. Recommended for a treat. *Blackbeard's Lookout*, Brookes Hill Pavilion, corner of Marine Dr and Brookes Hill Dr, Summerstrand, T5855567, F5851024. Closed Sun, reservations advised for evening meals and weekends. An à la carte seafood restaurant which has been run by the same family for 3 generations. Great ocean views and impressive fish tank displays, extensive range of seafood, steak, Italian, vegetarian and poultry dishes. Recommended. *Causerie*, *The Edward Hotel*, Belmont Terr, Central, T5862056. Good for a buffet and carvery (on Sun) served in an old fashioned atmosphere, good value and plenty to eat. *The Connaught*, *Marine Protea Hotel*, Marine Dr, Summerstrand, T5832101. A quality restaurant serving good seafood and meat dishes – everything you'd expect in a 4-star hotel. Excellent weekend carvery. *Dizzy Dolphins Café*, 1 Shark Rock Pier, T5834536. Trendy cocktail bar and restaurant serving a good range of seafood, steaks and salads. Popular with a young, lively crowd. *Flaming Arrow Spur*, below the *Holiday Inn*, Gardenhof Sq, T5861432. Surprisingly good steaks, Tex-Mex, varied salad bar and some seafood dishes, but excessively cheerful and family-oriented. *Lai Kung*, Boardwalk, Summerstrand, T5831123. Large Chinese restaurant serving a huge range of dishes. *The Mediterranean*, Dolphin's Leap, 9 Marine Dr, T5823981. Fashionable seafood restaurant on the second floor of a complex overlooking the beach. Good grilled fish, calamari, some meat dishes, balcony with outdoor tables, good service. Booking essential at weekends. *The Ranch*, corner of Russell Rd and Rose St, T5859684. Above-average steak house serving a range of large and tasty steaks. Not for vegetarians! *Rome*, 63 Campbell St, facing Russell Rd, Central, T5862731. Well-known for their pastas and pizzas which are cooked in a traditional Italian wood-burning oven. Good size portions served in a friendly manner, fun atmosphere, good value, check for the special daily pizzas, all round one of the better options in town. Recommended. *Royal Delhi*, 10 Burgess St, Central, T3738216. Closed Sun and Sat lunchtime. A very popular local curry house serving a full range of Indian dishes. Large groups can eat in their own separate dining room. *Sabatino's*, 35 Westbourne Rd, Central, T3731707. A medium-priced Italian option. The quality of the food is matched by the ambience and attentive service. Recommended. *Sandpiper*, *Humewood Hotel*, 33 Beach Rd, Humewood, T5858961. A popular hotel restaurant serving traditional home cooked table d'hôte meals. *Tapas al Sol*, Brookes Hill Pavilion, T5862159. Lively tapas bar, serving a limited range of tapas, plus steaks, pasta and salads. Turns into a boisterous bar and club late at night. *Up the Khyber*, Western Rd, Humewood. Cheap curries, burgers and steaks in a great setting right above the beach. Just a short walk from some of the backpacker hostels. *La Vigie*, 168 Cape Road, Mill Park, T3745464. Closed Sun and Sat lunch. A smart art deco restaurant in awell-respected guesthouse. French-style menu which makes good use of local fresh ingredients. Excellent wine list. Recommended. *Zorba's*, Dolphin's Leap, 9 Marine Dr, new Greek restaurant specialising in meze and seafood. Romantic interior, good food, but arrogant service.

Coffee shops & tea rooms

Café Dulce, Boardwalk, Summerstrand, T5831193. Great coffee shop selling tasty sandwiches, salads, milkshakes and ice creams. *Kafeehaus Maran*, Brookes Hill Pavilion, corner of Marine Dr and Brookes Hill Dr, Humewood, T5855328. Good coffee, cakes and snacks. *Lemon Tree*, 58 Pearson St, Central, T5864782. A converted Victorian greenhouse provides the ideal setting for afternoon teas. Worth tracking down. *Tiffany's*, Marine Dr, Humewood, T5823989. Tea garden serving snacks and cakes. *The Verandah*, *Beach Hotel*, Marine Dr, Humewood, T5832161. Attractive Mediterranean-style patio serving snacks and light meals.

Port Elizabeth has a good choice of late night bars and clubs, often offering meals in the early evening and live music or DJs later. Oddly, the biggest night out is Wed, although Fri and Sat come a close second.

Most of the nightlife is focused at 2 major entertainment centres, *The Boardwalk* on Marine Dr by Shark Rock Pier and *Brookes Hill Pavilion* on the corner of Beach Rd and Brooke's Hill Dr in Summerstrand. These areas are safe to walk about at night, which is much of their appeal. In Central, the busiest area is along Parliament St, but be wary of walking here at night – stick to taxis.

52, 52 Parliament St, T083-2485852 (mob). Hugely fashionable bar with attached restaurant. Ultra-stylish décor, expensive drinks and a well-heeled crowd. Its main appeal is its relaxed ambience and live DJs – check out the funk night on Sat. *After Party*, 324 Kempston Rd, T083-2992096 (mob). Hip-hop and R&B club, gets going earlier than most clubs, at about 2200. *The Blinking Owl*, 306 Cape Rd, Newton Park, T3653591. Lively pub serving good meals, either pub grub or à la carte. There's a very popular happy hour from 1900-2000. *Barney's Tavern*, The Boardwalk, T5834500. Atmospheric bar with live music every night as well as on Sat and Sun afternoons on 'The Deck'. *Chatters Bar & Grill*, Grace St, Central, T5850001. Closed Sun. During the day people tend to just pop in for a quick drink or for lunch, but come the evening it gets very busy. Look out for the 'happy hour' at the bar when you can save a few coins on your drinks. Does not suffer from the dress code syndrome. *Cool Runnings*, Brookes Hill Pavilion, T5840011. Trendy chain with a beach-bar theme. Pub food, great chips, live music on some nights, drum evenings, DJs, vibey place attracting a young crowd. *The Keg & Fox*, 31 Clyde St, T5854547. Open 1200 to midnight, smart dress code in the evening. English-style pub and bar with a mixed crowd – there's less emphasis on testosterone-fuelled drinking sessions than in other pubs. Good range of beers including imported labels. Unlike pubs in England, the restaurant side is as important as the bar, so make sure to book a table at weekends. *Kwaito House*, Parliament St. 3-storey Kwaito club, great chance to dance to Kwaito in the basement, or more commercial stuff upstairs. Pool tables, great atmosphere, but expect to attract quite a bit of attention if you're white. *O'Hagan's Pub & Grill*, 5-Ways Central, 60 Cape Rd. A chain of outlets similar to the Keg group, but with an obvious Irish theme. Good meals and a fine selection of beers, including a few draught beers and Guinness (don't expect too much if this is your preferred tipple back home). Lively atmosphere, where the crowd gets younger as the night progresses. *Quake*, 9 Eastbourne Rd, Central. Sports bar showing all the big games. Good range of beers. *Tapas al Sol*, Brookes Hill Pavilion, T5862159. Tapas bar and pub with extended happy hour on Thu, DJs on Fri and Sat. *Tarantino's*, The Boardwalk, T5831699. Popular student haunt, so expect a late night. Lively bar and club playing dance music and commercial house.

Cinemas The cinemas in PE tend to have a/c and are comfortable, with a wide range of screenings to choose from each day. All the latest releases from Europe and the US are shown, and sometimes films are released here before Europe. Check the local newspapers for screenings. There is no longer an arts cinema in Port Elizabeth. *Ster-Kinekor Complex*, The Bridge Mall, Cape Rd, T3634340, bridge@sterkinekor.com Largest cinema complex in Port Elizabeth, 10 screens. *Walmer Park Nu-Metro*, Walmer Park Shopping Complex, T3671102. 8 screens.

Feb *Shakespearian Festival*, a selection of plays are put on at the Mannville Open-Air Theatre in St George's Park. The theatre is named after the late Helen and Bruce Mann, who first instituted the festival. A most enjoyable way to pass a summer's evening. *Prickly Pear Festival*, at Cuyler Hofstede farm museum in Uitenhage. Crowds of over 25,000 turn up each year to enjoy traditional food such as pancakes, ginger beer, potjiekos, jam, spitbraais, fish braais, curry bunnies, and home-made pudding. Not to be missed if you are in the area – this is a golden opportunity to try real South African cooking. Look out for the local beer tent.

March *Splash Festival*, 4-day beach festival focusing on watersports, surfing competitions, live music and fireworks. Very popular annual event and fundraiser for the Community Chest. www.splashfestival.com

Apr *Arts and Crafts Fair*, held in Walmer Town Hall. An annual event designed to provide local artists with their first opportunity to display and sell their products. A good place to find some unique pieces at bargain prices.

Oct *Addo Rose Show*, a massive display with over 25,000 blooms on show, including new varieties. An enjoyable day out for anyone keen on gardens.

Nov *Evening Post Mini Marathon*, a 10 km fun run for residents to help raise money for charity.

Dec *Opening of the Summer Entertainment Programme*, very much for families. The Mayor gets the show rolling by turning on the Christmas Lights and there is a giant firework display on the beach. There follow pleny of activities for children to get involved in throughout the season. There is also an annual 4-day ski-boat race from Port Elizabeth to East London.

Shopping   **Flea markets** *Art in the Park*, first Sun of every month, St George's Park, located along Park Drive. An open-air exhibition of craft stalls and local art. *Humewood Beach front*, between the King's Beach parking area and McArthur's Baths.

Shopping malls Like all South African cities, Port Elizabeth has its share of American-style shopping malls. The main appeal of these malls is their practicality – they are safe to walk around and provide shelter from the sun. *The Bridge Shopping and Entertainment Centre*, giant up-market centre, built over a main road with great views from its elevated position. There are 8 cinemas in the Movie Complex, ATMs, restaurants, coffee shops and fast food outlets, plus a smart fashion mall for those with spare cash. Most units are open Mon-Fri, 0900-1730, and longer over the weekend. *Greenacres Shopping Centre*, Cape Rd, Greenacres, Port Elizabeth's favourite. Easily accessible with all well-known chain stores, similar mix to The Bridge. *Walmer Park Shopping Centre* on Main Rd, Walmer, popular amongst the local residents, once again everything is here. *Pier 14 Shopping Centre*, 444 Govan Mbeki Av, North End, a central location, decorated along a nautical theme, but more down-market than the others.

Sports   Port Elizabeth has excellent facilities catering for sports, especially waterports, golf, tennis, yachting and athletics, although these seem to be limited to wealthy areas – you won't come across them on a township tour. It is also a great city in which to watch sport, as it is home to both the Eastern Province Rugby Union and the Eastern Province Cricket Board. Each of these has an internationally recognized stadium: Telkom Park Stadium and St George's Park Cricket Oval.

Canoeing *Avoca River Camp*, T042-2340421. Offer canoeing, fishing and birdwatching, 2-man canoes are used and you travel with the river flow which is generally quite quick and easy-going on the arms.

Cricket Port Elizabeth is home to the Eastern Province Cricket Board. Matches are played at St George's Park Cricket Oval, also now known as the Crusaders Ground. The first test match played here was between South Africa and England on 12 Feb 1889, which was also the first test match to be played in Africa. St George's is a pleasant old stadium and an enjoyable venue to watch cricket. The two ends are known as the Duckpond End and the Park Drive End. There has been a cricket club here since 1843. The following international matches will be played at the Crusaders' Ground during the **2002-03 season**. West Indies v New Zealand, World Cup, 13 Feb 2003; England v Namibia, World Cup, 19 Feb, 2003; Australia v England, World Cup, 2 March 2003. *Crusaders Ground*, PO Box 12327, St Georges Park. Ticket enquiries: T5851646, F5864259, admin@epcricket.co.za

Diving See St Croix Islands and other scuba dive sites below, page 333.

Horse riding Note that some of these are a 30-min drive from the city centre. *Afrikara Safaris*, T6832985, afrikaras@bigfoot.com Hiking, horse riding trails, packages organized. *Heavenly Stables*, Sardinia Bay Rd, T041-3661038. Beach rides and trails. *Rothman Place*,

Lovemore Park, Sardinia Bay, T041-3675234, T82-6511825 (mob). 35 years established, beach and trails rides, lessons. *Springmount Trails*, T041-4680403. Operate from a campsite 79 km from the town. There are 2 major racecourses, *Arlington*, home of the St Andrew's Racing Club, and *Fairview*, headquarters of the Port Elizabeth Turf Club. There are races every Fri afternoon at one of the 2 courses.

Mountain biking The 2 trails outlined below can be attempted if you are staying in town for several days. For organized trips, contact T3687254. If you are in your own car then contact this club for details of routes laid out in the forests around Port Elizabeth, such as the Longmore Forest Mountain Bike Trail.

Baakens River Trail: a 23 km circuit right in the middle of Port Elizabeth. This is a unique valley; although surrounded by an urban environment, it has plenty of examples of indigenous vegetation. The trail starts from the car park at Dodds Farm, off 9th Av, Walmer, and ends at Abelia Crescent in Sunridge Park. No special skills or experience are necessary. This is an ideal trail for a weekend outing. Follow the marked concrete bollards with a bicycle painted on them.

The Swartkops Trail: 22 km circular route in the Swartkops Valley Nature Reserve, a 850 ha reserve on the northern outskirts of town. The reserve was created in 1993 to protect an area of threatened valley bushveld as well as local bird breeding colonies. This is a much more difficult trail with sections where some riders are likely to push their bikes up the escarpment. You will need to wear a helmet and have a full puncture repair kit – do not ride this trail alone. The route is marked by a blue arrow and bicycle motif on concrete bollards; the start is at the Corobrik brick factory next to the Bramlin-Markman Highway.

Rugby Port Elizabeth is home to the *Eastern Province Rugby Union* which was founded in 1888. Matches are played at Telkom Park (formally known as Boet Erasmus Rugby Stadium), which has a capacity of around 34,000. A unique feature at the stadium is a steam train placed on top of an open stand overlooking the field, which has been converted into a bar. For more information contact the local rugby union on T5835245, eprugby@asa.org.za

Sailing Algoa Bay is world renowned in sailing circles. There are predominantly 2 prevailing winds which either produce very rough and choppy conditions or calm and flat conditions. Because of the speed at which the weather has been known to change, you should always contact the weather office before going out, T2311668. The following clubs charter boats and can organize sailing cruises: *Algoa Bay Yacht Club*, T5854058, F5860095; *The Port Elizabeth Beach Yacht Club*, T5833449. **Algoa Bay Sailing Week**, is a national sailing regatta. Racing yachts from all over South Africa compete for 5 days around buoys in front of Shark Rock Pier. There's plenty going on in the nightclubs around this time.

Scuba diving There are a number of good dive sites around Port Elizabeth, and you shouldn't have any trouble finding a dive buddy or joining a group going out in a boat. The best time for diving within Algoa Bay is during the winter months of May until Sep. Average visibility is between 8-15 m in winter. One of the major appeals of the region is the variety of dive sites – there are colourful reefs, drop-offs, shipwrecks and corals. The tourist office has a useful leaflet, *Dive Port Elizabeth*, outlining the major dive sites. See Around Port Elizabeth below for details of some of the best sites. Diving outfits based in and around Port Elizabeth: *Diver's Alert Network (DAN)*, T0800-020111. *Ocean Divers International*, Boardwalk Centre, T5831790, www.odipe.co.za PADI courses and equipment. *Pro Dive*, Walmer Park, T3687880, T083-6598485 (mob), dive@prodive.co.za 5-star dive centre, courses, charters, equipment hire, 1-day 'resort' courses. There is a recompression chamber on the *SAS Donkin*, T082-3214789 (mob), as well as at the PE Hyperbaric Unit, T5831189 or T082-9275678 (mob).

Soccer Between Feb and Oct there are afternoon games every weekend. Remember that there is a fundamental sporting division in South Africa: rugby and cricket is for whites; soccer is for blacks. These ridiculous divisions mean that local whites often discourage white visitors who want to see a match – ignore them, but contact the tourist office about safety issues for visitors. The principal venues are the Gelvandale Stadium in Liebenberg Rd; the Westbourne Oval in Westbourne Rd; the Moore Dyke Playing Fields in Schauder and the Gelvandale Playing Fields, in Stanford Rd. For match details contact *The Eastern Province Football Union*, T4513716.

Surfing Good waves on this stretch of coast aren't restricted to Jeffreys Bay. The Pipe in Algoa Bay is one of the most popular spots, as is Millars Point further to the west. One drawback of the waves closer to town is the crowded beaches and the industrial backdrop. The best person to talk to about local conditions is Turtle Morris based at *Surf Centre*, T5856027.

Swimming The beaches around Port Elizabeth are very clean, but the sea temperature rarely gets above 21º C. Away from the large hotels there are a couple of excellent municipal swimming pools. *McArthur Baths*, King's Beach Promenade, T5863412, Sep-Apr: daily, 0700-1700. Tidal pool, children's water chute, splash pool, freshwater pool, permanent life guard, restaurant and snack bar. *St George's Park Baths*, St George's Park, T5857751, Sep-Apr: Mon-Fri, 0700-2100; Sat, 0900-1800; Sun, 1030-1800. Olympic size pool with diving facilities, children's pool, restaurant, snack bar.

Windsurfing Experienced windsurfers have the opportunity to go out at Noordhoek, where they are totally exposed to the ocean swell, but it is important to check the tides. There are excellent reef breaks and cross-shore conditions when the southwest wind blows. Off Hobie Beach the conditions are much calmer, particularly when there is a southwest wind. Be careful at all times to avoid the designated public bathing areas. The Swartkop River Mouth is a good area for beginners as the conditions are calm. For daily updates on wind speed and conditions, contact T4862317. Some of the larger hotels on the beach front in Summerstrand and Humewood have equipment to rent out to residents.

Tour operators Most of the companies offer a similar range of local tours; shop around, and apart from the price, check what sort of vehicle you'll travel in (in the summer it's not much fun being stuck in the back of a Land Rover without a/c), how many people will be in the group, and if the price includes entrance fees, guides and refreshments. In general, there are 3 types of tours on offer: historical town tours which may involve walking; township tours, which are growing in popularity; and wildlife tours, with visits to one or more of the local game reserves (Addo Elephant National Park and Shamwari Game Reserve are the most popular), plus birdwatching and horse riding trips. *Afrikara Safaris*, T6832985, afrikaras@bigfoot.com Hiking, horse riding trails, packages organized. *Birdwatching and Eco-Tours*, T4665698, gary@baytours.co.za Specialist wildlife and birdwatching tours. *Calabash Tours*, 8 Dollery St, Central, T5856162, calabash@iafrica.com Excellent day tours around the city, including visits to various townships. Tours include visits to local artists and self-help projects. Also run day tours to Addo Elephant Park, Shamwari Game Reserve and visits to the beaches. Minimum 2 people. Good value. Highly recommended. *Friendly City Tours*, T5851801, T083-2709739 (mob). Daily historical and sightseeing tours of Port Elizabeth's monuments, tours last up to 1½ hrs, plus visits to Addo from R150 per person, includes entrance. *Fundani Cultural Tours*, 69 Theko St, Kwa-Magxaki, T4542064, T082-9646563 (mob), cultours@iafrica.com Cultural tours of the townships, tours last from 2-3 hrs and cost from R250 per person. They generally involve visits to places of historical and cultural importance, viewings of local art and a stop at a shebeen for a drink and a meal. Travel is by minibus taxi. *Gaylards Safaris*, T4680055. Organize 4-day tours of the Eastern Cape for birdwatchers. *Molo Tours*, A75 Witbooi St, Walmer township, T5817085, molotours@mweb.co.za Specialize in tours around Walmer township. Mzolisi, the guide, is from this township, and consequently knows his stuff. This tour focuses on walking through the streets, allowing a higher level of participation with the people you see. *Springbok Atlas*, 1st Floor, Port Elizabeth Airport, Alister Miller Dr, T5812555, F5812550. Well-established company providing coach tours throughout South Africa.

The following are travel agents: *American Express Travel*, Moffat Retail Park, T3688000, F3688020. *Maritime Sure Travel*, 11 Uitenhage Rd, Maritime House, North End, T4845540,

F4872803, marisure@iafrica.com *Pentravel*, Walmer Park, T3686151, F3686162. *Rennies Travel*, Murray and Roberts, Ring Rd, Greenacres, T3630989, F3632097.

Local Bus: Services depart from Market Square Bus Station, beneath the Norwich Union Centre Building, Strand St. Timetables are available from the information kiosk at the entrance. *Algoa Bus Company* operates a regular central city service between the beach-front, city centre, St George's Park, Rink St, Greenacres and The Bridge Shopping Complex – Route O. For timetables and information, call T0801421444.

Transport

See also Ins and outs, page 318

Car hire: *Affordable*, T3681594. *Avis*, airport counter, T5017200, toll free, T086-1021111. *Budget*, airport counter, T5814242, F5815531. *Economic*, 104 Heugh Rd, Walmer, T5815826, F5815840. *Imperial*, T0861131000, airport counter, T5811268, F5813919. Offers extensive services within South Africa. *National*, T5811123. *Res Q*, T0118676552, www.resqrentacar.co.za *Tempest Car Hire*, 23 Heugh Rd, T5811256, F5811248, www.tempestcarhire.com *United Car Hire*, 90a Heugh Rd, T/F5814525.

Taxi: *Hurters Radio Cabs*, T5855500. Well-established local company, book a taxi in the evening to save waiting around. *UNICAB*, 15 Rink St, T5853030. Also provide airport transfer service.

Long distance Air: transport into town centre, *Supercab Shuttle*, T4575590. Will drop you off at most hotels and guesthouses. The *Leopard Express*, T4841057, runs a bus to Grahams-town via the airport on Fri, Sat and Sun. Several car hire groups have a counter in the termi-nal, see above for contact numbers. Local airlines have an office in town as well as at the airport, see Directory below for details.

Port Elizabeth Airport is 4 km from the city centre along Alister Miller Dr. Flight information: T5077319

SA Airlink, T5339041, 011-9781111, www.saairlink.co.za To **Bloemfontein** (80 mins): Mon-Fri, 1 flight a day. **East London** (45 mins): Mon-Fri, 3-4 flights daily; Sun, 1 flight a day.

South African Airways, T5071111, www.flysaa.co.za To **Bloemfontein** (80 mins): Mon-Fri, 1 flight a day. **Cape Town** (80 mins): Mon-Fri, 6 flights a day; Sat and Sun, 2 flights a day. **Durban** (70 mins): daily, 4 flights a day. **East London** (45 mins): Mon-Fri, 3 flights a day; Sun, 2 flights a day; no flight on Sat. **Johannesburg** (90 mins): Mon-Fri, 7 flights a day; Sat, 4 flights a day; Sun, 3 flights a day.

If you change aircraft in Johannesburg or Durban it is possible to fly to the following domestic destinations, all within a day: Kimberley, Margate, Nelspruit, Phalaborwa, Pietermaritzburg, Pietersburg, Richards Bay, Sun City and Umtata.

Rail The mainline station is in the town centre on Station St, just off Strand St which runs parallel to Govan Mbeki Av. *Spoornet* information office, The Bridge, Greenacres, T086-000888. For train schedules and fares. **NB** The service to Cape Town only starts in Oudtshoorn. So at present there is only 1 train a day from Port Elizabeth. There is, however, an interesting local steam service, the Apple Express. The *Algoa Express* service departs daily at 1430 for **Johannesburg** (18½ hrs), via **Cradock** (4½ hrs), and **Bloemfontein** (12 hrs).

Timetable enquiries: T5072662

Road 72 km to **Addo Elephant Park**; 643 km to **Bloemfontein**; 763 km to **Cape Town**; 295 km to **East London**; 124 km to **Grahamstown**; 246 km to **Graaff-Reinet**; 79 km to **Jeffreys Bay**; 1,050 km to **Johannesburg**; 150 km to **Port Alfred**; 74 km to **Shamwari Game Reserve**. **Bus**: *The Baz Bus*, T021-4392323, www.bazbus.co.za Provides the best budget bus travel service along the coast between Cape Town and Durban. Port Elizabeth tends to be the midway point where the bus will stay overnight. In other words, if you start the day in Cape Town and are heading towards Durban, Port Elizabeth is the furthest you can get in a single day. All of the backpacker hostels are well-informed about the service.

Computicket, Information kiosk, Greenacres Shopping Mall, T3744550. Sells coach tickets as well as tickets for concerts and major sports events nationwide.

Greyhound, the office is at 107 Govan Mbeki Av, T3634555, tickets and information or *Computicket Office*, Greenacres Centre, T3744550. Coaches arrive/depart from the rear car park, 107 Govan Mbeki Av, and in front of Edgars at the Greenacres Shopping Centre. **Cape Town** (11 hrs): daily, 2145. **Durban** (13 hrs): daily, 0655. **Grahamstown** (2 hrs): daily, 0655. **Johannesburg** and **Pretoria** (17 hrs): daily, 1630, 1700.

Eastern Cape

Intercape, the office is in the Flemming Building behind the Old Post Office, corner of Flemming and North Union streets, T5860055, or T021-3864400. Tickets and information, reservations must be made 72 hrs before departure. Coaches depart/arrive from the corner of Flemming and North Union Streets or at the Edgars entrance to Greenacres Shopping Centre. **Cape Town** (10 hrs): daily, 0615, 1930. **Durban** (10 hrs): daily, 1830, 0630. **Graaf Reniet** (4 hrs): daily, 1730. **East London** (5 hrs): daily, 1830, 0630. **George** (4 hrs): daily, 0615, 1930. **Johannesburg** and **Pretoria** (13½ hrs): daily, 1730. **Knysna** (3 hrs): daily, 0615, 1930. **Plettenberg Bay** (2½ hrs): daily, 0615, 1930.

Sunshine Express, T082-9562687 (mob). A 24-hr door-to-door mini bus service to **Jeffreys Bay**. Also available for group hire – for example, a group of surfers could hire the bus for a day to take them to a particular bay which can only normally be accessed by private transport.

Translux, the office is in the Ernst and Young Building, Ring Rd, Greenacres, T3921333, for information and reservations. Coaches start/finish their journey by the railway station in the centre of town. All routes also make an additional stop by the Ernst and Young Building in the outer suburbs. If arriving by bus check with your hotel which is the most convenient stop for their location. To **Cape Town** (10 hrs): daily, 0615, 2005, via **Plettenberg Bay**, **Knysna**, **Mossel Bay** and **Swellendam**. **Cradock** (4 hrs): Mon, Fri, 1730. **Graaff-Reinet** (4 hrs): Tue, Wed, Thu, Fri, Sun, 1845. **Johannesburg** and **Pretoria** (15 hrs): daily, 1745. **Durban** (13½ hrs): daily, 0640. **East London** (4 hrs): daily, 0640. **Grahamstown** (2 hrs): daily, 0700.

Directory   **Communications Main Post Office**: 259 Govan Mbeki Av, T5084000, open Mon-Fri, 0800-1630, Sat, 0830-1200. There are coin and card telephones by the post office with direct dialling to overseas countries. You can access the internet at all the backpacker lodges. Otherwise, there is an internet café known as *Fantasia Internet* at The Bridge Shopping Centre, T3634681. **Embassies and consulates Germany**: Govan Mbeki Av, T4872840, F5847908. **UK**: First Bowring House, Ring Rd, Greenacres, T3638841, open Mon-Fri, 0900-1230. **Medical Services Chemists**: *Mediscore Pharmacy and Medicine Depot*, 322 Cape Rd, Newton Park, T3652366. An emergency late night chemist. **British Airways Travel Clinic**, 19 Westbourne Rd, T3747471. **Hospitals**: *Provincial Hospital*, T3923911. *St George's Hospital*, T3926111.

Around Port Elizabeth

Algoa Bay &   A combination of natural conditions and man-made developments means that
The Beaches   Algoa Bay is one of the most popular stretches of coast in South Africa. The water is clean, warm and calm for most of the year, making it an ideal spot for watersports. Around the city there are smart hotels and shopping developments and the whole area is within an hour's flying time of other major cities. The beaches around the city are commonly referred to as the northern and the southern beaches; each beach has its own character and is frequented by different groups of people.

The **three northern beaches** include **New Brighton**, a good spot for swimming and fishing. There are changing rooms and life guards, and along the promenade you can buy drinks and a snack. To get here by car, take the N2 towards Grahamstown and look out for the Brighton Beach sign. **Bluewater Bay** can also be reached from the N2; look out for the signpost after crossing the Swartkops River. This is a long stretch of white sand with good swimming, but the life guards are only present during the summer months. **St George's Strand** is known for its sand dunes and some attractive picnic spots.

There are **six southern beaches** which come right up to the city centre. **King's** is the closest to the city, lying between the harbour and the Humewood suburb. Being so close to the city and several major hotels, it can get very busy. The swimming is safe and boogie-boarding is allowed; there are also life guards and all the necessary changing facilities. This is probably the best beach for families as there is a go-kart track, mini-golf, children's playground and plenty of kiosks and snack bars behind the beach. In contrast, **Humewood** is a quieter beach. The swimming is good and there is plenty of shade to relax under. At the other side of the main coastal road is

Happy Valley, an ornamental garden with ponds and green lawns. The next beach, **Hobie Beach**, is marked by Shark Rock Pier. In the evenings this is a busy area due to the presence of **The Boardwalk**, an entertainment centre (see Bars & clubs above). The swimming is safe and each year the local body surfing, beach volleyball and boardsailing championships are held here. **Pollock Beach** is the last beach before Cape Recife. This is one of the better surfing spots along the coast. There is a car park and a wash block for surfers and as it is further from the city, it's not nearly as busy here. On the other side of Cape Recife are two more sheltered beaches, each with a village overlooking them, **Schoenmakerskop** and **Sardinia**. Sardinia Bay has the most beautiful beach near Port Elizabeth. It is a Marine Reserve and has become a popular spot for snorkelling and scuba diving.

The Apple Express

This historic narrow gauge steam train, similar to the *Outeniqua Choo-Tjoe* in the Western Cape, carries tourists on day trips through some beautiful countryside. The booking office is in the Station Building, Humewood Road Station and the Spoornet information centre. The train service is operated by a voluntary, non-profit making society formed solely for the restoration and maintenance of the famous narrow gauge trains. The trains run on a track which is only 2 ft, or 610 mm, wide. The full extent of the railway suitable for the trains is 310 km – there is a line between Port Elizabeth and Avontuur in the Langkloof plus a branchline to Hankey and Patensie. At recognized points the train stops to allow passengers to stretch their legs and buy a cool drink from the *Apple Tavern* buffet coach in the middle of the train.

NB At time of writing, the Apple Express was out of service while work was being completed on the tracks. Contact the Port Elizabeth tourist office for details of whether it is running again. Before work began, there were only irregular services; trips ran roughly every second weekend of the month, usually to **Thornhill** and back. Other destinations could be organized for large groups with several months' advance notice.

St Croix Islands & other scuba dive sites
See also Diving section on page 51

The best scuba diving in the area is in the vicinity of the St Croix Islands, 20 km from Port Elizabeth harbour. The average dive is along a slope with a maximum depth of 30 m. There are a few caves, drop-offs and gullies. The islands and the surrounding waters are protected by nature conservation; fishing and spearfishing are forbidden and it is **forbidden to land on the islands**. A consequence of this has been a flourishing population of jackass penguins, gulls, terns and cormorants on land, while the surrounding waters are rich in marine life, providing a plentiful diet for the birds. Some of the largest fish in the area have been recorded here. A permit is required from Cape Nature and Environmental Conservation to visit the islands for diving purposes; this can be issued at the same time as you charter a boat for the trip.

Other popular local dives are located at, or are known as: **Thunderbolt Reef**, **Sardinia Bay**, **Devil's Reef**, **Roman Rock** and **Philip's Reef**. There are also some good wreck dives including: the **Pati**, on Thunderbolt Reef; the **Inchcape Rock** wreck – this steel hull from 1902 suffers from poor visibility; the **Western Knight** wreck (experienced wreck divers only); and the **Haerlem** wreck, a navy vessel sunk in 1987 for divers. The last is a very popular wreck, resting at a depth of 21 m and attracting visitors from all over South Africa.

Dive operators The following can organize daily trips to the best scuba sites: *Ocean Divers International*, Boardwalk Centre, T5831790, www.odipe.co.za, and *Pro Dive*, Walmer Park, T3687880, T083-6598485, dive@prodive.co.za

Eastern Cape

West of Port Elizabeth

Sardinia & Sylvic Bay Nature Reserve

Sardinia and Sylvic Bay Nature Reserve is only 20 km from Port Elizabeth and is a small protected area of beautiful coastal dunes stretching across wide beaches to the Indian Ocean. Its stunning setting makes it understandably popular with holidaymakers and anglers. Dolphins are often seen close to the beach along this coastline. No vehicles are allowed inside the reserve.

Van Stadens Wild Flower Reserve

The reserve has an information centre and a picnic site. For more information contact the Reserve Manager, T041-9555649

The N2 from Port Elizabeth to Humansdorp passes directly through the middle of the wild flower reserve. The turning into the reserve is 35 km from Port Elizabeth. Established to protect and propagate indigenous flora, the area is also worth visiting for its butterflies and birds. The best time to visit is between February and August when many of the plants are in bloom. Some of the flowering plants to look out for include the ground orchids and the proteas. The southern part of the reserve is an interesting area of forest with many ironwood and wild pomegranate trees, as well as a rare tree species, the Cape star-chestnut.

There are two short walks through the different ecosystems of the reserve: the **River Walk**, 3 km, passes the nursery and follows the course of the Van Stadens River; whilst the **Forest Walk**, 2 km, enters an area which has been replanted with proteas. From the highest point of the walk there are good views of riverine forest in the valleys leading into the gorge below.

Loerie Dam Nature Reserve

For more information on the trails, permits and accommodation, contact T042-2830437

On the N2 between Port Elizabeth and Humansdorp there is a turning to the reserve via the village of Loerie, 10 km north of the N2. The protected area is part of the Baviaanskloof range of mountains and is spectacular to explore on foot. There are a number of trails here, some of which pass through wild, forested and inaccessible ravines. The summer months are too hot for serious hiking, but the conditions during the winter tend to be cool and dry and therefore much more pleasant.

The **Gonaqua Trail**, 30 km, is a two-day circular trail passing through the Otterford State Forest. The walk involves some steep climbs in the mountainous area approaching the Baviaanskloof. The patches of indigenous forest are the most interesting areas to walk through. Look out for the exotic tree orchids and colourful woodland birds such as the Knysna lourie or the Narina trogon. The **Wild Goose Trail**, 7 km, is a shorter, one-day trail passing through areas of thick forest.

Sleeping A maximum of 18 people are allowed on the trail each day. **F** *Robinson Hut*, at Loerie Dam, has basic facilities and sleeps 18. There is also a *Trail Hut*, for overnight hikers on the Gonaqua Trail.

St Francis Bay

Phone code: 042 (NB Always use 3-figure prefix) Colour map 7, grid B4

This bay was named by the Portuguese explorer Manuel Perestrelo in 1575. It is famous for its waves and attracts surfers from all over the world. The bay is also popular with shell collectors who come in search of the rare Indo-Pacific shells which are washed ashore by currents. Between Port Elizabeth and Jeffreys Bay, the Maitland and Gamtoos River Mouth Nature Reserves are easily reached from the N2.

The village of St Francis Bay is 20 km from Humansdorp, just off the R330. Less than 40 years ago there was nothing here except for fine, white sand beaches and a mule track which ran from Humansdorp to the lighthouse at Cape St Francis. These days a very prosperous collection of whitewashed and thatched holiday homes line the beach just south of the Krom River Mouth. For **tourist information**, contact the *St Francis Bay Publicity Association*, T2940076, www.stfrancistourism.com

The village is bounded on one side by a series of canals linked to the Krom River. There is a marina development to complement the smart holiday homes, and a nearby dam, the Churchill, which supplies Port Elizabeth with much of its water. Just a few minutes away is Cape St Francis, another small village with some budget accommodation options.

Sleeping A *The Beach House*, 4 Frank St, T2941225, www.stfrancisbay.co.za Beautiful guesthouse set right on the beach. 4 luxurious and stylish rooms, 2 with ocean views, 2 overlooking the pool, excellent breakfasts, also evening meals by prior arrangement, attentive unfussy service. Ask for Caroline. Recommended. **A** *Sandals*, T2940551, donnelly@agnet.co.za Smart, comfortable guesthouse just a few mins from the beach. Attractive thatched house with 10 colourful rooms, B&B, pool, sundeck, garden, breakfast served on terrace overlooking the pool, conference facilities. Ask for Barbara or Doreen. **B-C** *St Francis Bay Hotel*, Diana Crescent, T2940800, www.stfrancisbayhotel.com Upmarket hotel with B&B, double rooms with en suite bathrooms, TV, some self-catering apartments, conference facilities. **B-C** *Thatchwood*, 63 Lyme Rd, T2940082, F2941998. Smart and comfortable guesthouse overlooking the local golf course. 4 double rooms with en suite bathroom, meals served on the lawn or from an open dining room, no TV ensures plenty of peace, guests have the delightful option of a sunset boat cruise in St Francis Bay, with champagne and fresh oysters. **C-F** *Cape St Francis Resort*, Da Gama Rd, Cape St Francis, T2980054, seals@iafrica.com Good value holiday resort with a range of accommodation, from superior thatched cottages to caravanning and camping plots, good amenities, self-catering facilities, restaurant. **D** *Duxbury*, 8 George Rd, T2940514, F2940833. A neat little family house right on the beach. 2 double rooms with bath, 1 double room with shower, non-smoking room, TV lounge. The garden is protected from the wind and is the ideal place to spend a day reading or catching up on letter writing. Good value, ask for Sheila. **F** *Seal Point Backpackers*, Da Gama Rd, Cape St Francis, T2980284, sealsbackpackers@ webonline.co.za Great-value backpacker lodge with well-kept self-catering apartments, each with TV, en suite bathrooms and open-plan kitchen, plus balconies with seaviews. Good restaurant and bar downstairs serving cheap meals, braai area, pool, popular with surfers. Organize booze cruises on the canal.

Price codes:
see inside front cover

Eastern Cape

Maitland Nature Reserve

Facing St Francis Bay, the reserve is a small strip of coastal forest near the estuary of the Maitland River. This was the site of a number of lead mines in the 19th century but as these were abandoned so was the whole area, thankfully giving the forest a chance to recover. The reserve is now renowned for its birdlife and is an excellent forest for seeing paradise flycatchers and Knysna louries. October, when many of the forest plants are either flowering or in fruit, is one of the best months to visit.

The 3-km **Sir Peregrine Maitland Trail** is a leisurely walk through forest along an old wagon trail; the 9-km **De Stades Trail** covers the length and breadth of the reserve, passing through small areas of dune forest and open grassland.

Sleeping F *Maitland Camping Site*, is just beyond the reserve next to the mouth of the Maitland River. The reserve is 35 km west of Port Elizabeth and can be reached via the N2 or via Seaview Main Road along the coast. **Reservations** for the trails and for the campsite should be made through the *Algoa Regional Services Council*, Nature Conservation Division, Port Elizabeth, T041-58597111.

Gamtoos River Mouth Nature Reserve

This reserve, 10 km south of the N2, consists of a large area of wetlands surrounding the lagoon formed by the Gamtoos River as it enters the sea on St Francis Bay. The area is rich in birdlife and is a good place to spot osprey. Just outside the reserve there is a caravan park and a camping site.

Jeffreys Bay

Jeffreys Bay, or 'J Bay' as it's known locally, is surf central. Home to the 'perfect wave', this is an internationally acclaimed surfing spot and a major playground for self-respecting surf rats. In the evenings, the local bars buzz with talk of supertubes and perfect breaks. Unsurprisingly, J Bay attracts more than its fair share of long-term resident travellers, but away from the beach, there's little going on in town. There are numerous surf shops selling a wide range of boards and wetsuits, as well as Billabong and Quicksilver factory outlets, but when surf's up don't be surprised to find many of the local businesses closed.

Phone code: 042
(NB Always use
3-figure prefix)
Colour map 7, grid B4

The origins of Jeffreys Bay date to 1894, when a trading post was established here by Joseph Avent Jeffrey, a whaler from the island of St Helena. The trading post received goods by sea and supplied settlers living inland in the Langkloof. Little of the original settlement remains and today Jeffreys Bay is a sprawl of unattractive bungalows and holiday homes. Out of season in summer, when most of the coast is at its liveliest, the resort is a quiet and desolate place and there's little of the surfing scene or nightlife you might expect. In winter, however, when the waves are at their best, the town comes back to life. July is also when the **Billabong Country Feeling Surf Competition** is held – the event draws surfers from across the globe and the town gets packed out. This is a major surfing event, and you'll get to see some of the best surfers in the world compete.

Ins & outs   **Getting there** The town is served by the *Baz Bus* (see Transport below for details).

Tourist office *Jeffreys Bay Tourism*, PO Box 460, Da Gama Rd, T2932588, F2932227, www.jeffreysbaytourism.com Open, Mon-Fri, 0830-1700; Sat, 0900-1200. Helpful and enthusiastic, but note that backpacker hostels tend to have more practical information when it comes to the surfing scene. For updated info on the surfing conditions, T082-2346323 (mob).

Sights   The waves here are definitely the main attraction, but as an alternative, the **Shell Museum** makes for an interesting visit. The collection is incredibly large and has many rare examples of Indo-Pacific and Southern Cape shells found on nearby beaches. The position of Jeffreys Bay along the coast happens to coincide with the meeting point of two opposing ocean currents, which explains why so many unusual shells have been found on the local beaches. Some shells have been carried all the way down the western coast of Africa. The collection was put together over a 30-year period and left to the town by Charlotte Kritzinger.

Aston Bay, Paradise Beach and the **Kabeljous River Estuary** are only a short drive away and make a pleasant change from the main beach in Jeffreys Bay.

Sleeping   As the best-known surfing spot in South African, Jeffreys Bay attracts large numbers of surf-
■ on map   ers from all over the world. Consequently, there is a good range of budget accommodation
Price codes: here. Each backpacker place has its own scene and you're bound to come across people who
see inside front cover   are staying there for the whole season.

B-C *Diaz 15 Holiday Apartments*, 15 Diaz Rd, T/F2931779. Selection of 2- or 3-bedroom luxury self-catering apartments, with fully equipped kitchens with microwave, large lounge with open balcony overlooking the beach, 2 bathrooms, TV with M-net, linen included, towels available on request, perfect for families looking for a high standard of comfort right on the beach, walking distance to the shops and restaurants. Very popular, so be sure to phone several months in advance. **B-C** *Savoy Protea*, 16 Da Gama Rd, T2931106, F2932445, www.proteas.co.za 37 small rooms, TV, pool in central courtyard, separate restaurant next door, poor value when compared to similar hotels elsewhere in South Africa. **B** *Stratos*, 11 Uys St, T2931116, F2933072. A modern brick house on the seafront set in a quiet residential district. 7 luxury double rooms with en suite shower/bath, TV, non-smoking room, solar heated swimming pool. Swiss owners, German spoken.

C *Eastview*, 24 Spekboom St, T/F2961484. Small B&B with 2 double rooms, views across beach, ask for Hanny. **C** *Mount Joy*, 31 Mimosa St, T/F2961932. Comfortable, modern B&B, balconies with views across bay. **C-D** *The Guesthouse*, 17 Flame Cres, Wavecrest, T2931878, F2932778, faber@global.co.za Variety of accommodation available: a self contained flat which can sleep up to 4 people, with a fully equipped kitchen and TV; a Honeymoon suite with an oval bath and champagne on arrival in your room; plus 3 other double rooms with bathrooms. Set in a secure walled garden, close to the beach and a shopping centre. Madelaine gives excellent advice, information and hospitality. Recommended.

D *Dirkies Dream*, 10 Flame Cres, T/F2933909. Has a range of self-catering apartments set right on the beach. Sleep 2,4 or 6, each with kitchen, bathroom and satellite TV, great sea views, lock-up garage. **D** *Lighthouse*, 45 Da Gama Rd, T/F2932142. Self-catering and

B&B with shared bathroom, run by Barbara from Liverpool, UK. Recommended. **D** *Supertubes*, 6 Pepper St, T2932957, supertubes@agnet.co.za Laid-back B&B set 30 m from the beach, double rooms with en suite bathroom, set across 3 houses. Meals are available on request. Ask for Maresa.

F *Aloe Afrika*, 10 Mimosa St, T/F2962974. Simple wooden chalet close to the beach. Run by surfers for surfers. **F** *Island Vibe*, 10 Dageraad St, T2931625, ivibe@lantic.co.za This hostel has an excellent location at the top end of Jeffreys Bay, perched high up with views across two beaches, steps down to the beach. Dorms and doubles, kitchen, bar, café serving set evening meals and good breakfasts. The place has a big surfer scene, so don't expect to get much sleep. Music from the bar pumps out through the night. Very popular and perfect for a couple of day's partying, although it could do with a clean. Also has a good travel centre and internet access. **F** *Jeffreys Bay Backpackers*, 12 Jeffrey St, T2931379, F2961763, backpac@netactive.co.za This was the first backpacker place to open in Jeffreys Bay. It is well-run and remains popular, but there are rather too many rules to follow. It does have a good location in the centre of town, and is very clean. Small dorms, 5 double rooms, camping in garden, 3 showers, off-street parking, reductions can be negotiated for long stays, well-stocked and clean kitchen, bedding provided when necessary, close to Main Beach, short walk to the shops, restaurants and bars in the town centre. *Baz Bus* stop. **F** *Jeffreys Bay Caravan Park*, Da Gama Rd, T2931111. A large municipal site with 169 sites plus all the facilities expected in a park set up for family holidays, plenty of shade, individual power points, and all located on the beach. **F** *Peggy's Place*, 8a Oribi St, near town centre, T2932160. Dorms, rondavels, kitchen, great when Peggy is around, large garden to relax in when not surfing.

Breakers, Ferreira St, T2931801. Fairly smart seafood restaurant right on the beach, slightly more expensive than other restaurants in town but good fresh dishes. Note that the kitchen closes at 1430, so late lunches aren't an option. *Café Havana*, Malhoek Centre, Da Gama Rd, T2931510. Beer garden, light lunches, popular local spot. *Le Grotto*, Jeffrey's St, T2932612. Popular corner restaurant serving fresh seafood, steaks and burgers, good catch of the day. *Red Creek Spur*, Da Gama Rd, next to *Savoy Protea Hotel*. Successful formula menu and décor, good steaks and Mexican fare, unimaginative salad bar, open Mon-Sat 1100-2300, Sun 1200-2200. *Sunflower Café*, 20 Da Gama Rd, T2932168. Café and restaurant serving great range of light meals, including plenty for vegetarians. Delicious milkshakes and homemade cakes, good

Eating
● *on map*

Eastern Cape

Jeffreys Bay

To Eastview & Port Elizabeth

To Humansdorp & Port Elizabeth

To Eastview & Port Elizabeth

Golf Course

Bowls

Indian Ocean

Impala

Mopane
Acorn
Olive
Myrtle
Gazelle
Sable
Petunia
Tulip
Azalea
Strelitzia
Heide
Verbena
Da Gama
Diaz
Uys
De Reyger
Jeffrey
Schelde
Francis
Oosterland
Goedehoop
Salamander
Drommedaris
Supermarket
Shell Museum
Woltemade
Prospect
St Croix
Pell
Da Gama
Diaz
Main Beach

N

0 metres 250
0 yards 250

■ **Sleeping**
1 Diaz 15 Holiday
  Apartments
2 Jeffreys Bay
  Backpackers
3 Jeffreys Bay
  Caravan Park

4 Lighthouse
5 Peggy's Place
6 Savoy Protea
7 Stratos

● **Eating**
1 Breakers
2 Café Havana
3 Le Grotto
4 Red Creek Spur
5 Sunflower Café

evening meals such as grilled calamari or pasta. Also has internet access. Recommended. *Die Walskipper*, Marina Martinique Harbour, out of town towards St Francis Bay, T082-8009478 (mob). Open daily from midday to midnight. As befits a popular surfing venue, this open-air restaurant attracts a fun crowd in season. During the winter months Phillip and Grace bring coal stoves to the beach. The menu consists of good local dishes with fresh ingredients and homemade breads. Recommended.

Transport **Road** 78 km to **Port Elizabeth**, 20 km to **Cape St Francis**, 20 km to **Humansdorp** (N2), 206 km to **Knysna**, 1,062 km to **Durban**. **Bus**: *Baz Bus*, T021-4392323, www.bazbus.com Backpackers budget service which calls in at hostels to collect/drop off. They should have room to carry your surfing equipment but let them know in advance. **NB** Services going towards Port Elizabeth start early in Cape Town, and Jeffreys Bay is the last drop off/pick up before the bus crew spend the night in Port Elizabeth. Services travelling towards **Cape Town** start from either **Cintsa/East London** or **Port Elizabeth**. Only the bus starting in **Port Elizabeth** will take you through to **Cape Town** in 1 day; the bus from **East London** only travels as far as **Knysna** in the day.

Greyhound, T041-3634555 and *Translux*, T041-3921333, only run services as close as **Humansdorp**, 20 km from Jeffreys Bay on the N2. From here, you have to hitch or take a local taxi. It may be possible to arrange for your accommodation to collect you for a small charge.

Sunshine Express, T2932221. A local door-to-door service running only to/from **Port Elizabeth**. Expect to pay R60 per person one way if there are other people on the bus. If you are alone, the cost will double. Booking ahead essential.

The Langkloof

Three mountain ranges lie to the north of the N2 and Jeffreys Bay: the Kougaberge, the Baviaanskloofberge and the Grootwinterhoekberge, known collectively as 'the Langkloof'. The valleys of the Langkloof are referred to as 'the Kouga', and this is from where modern man is thought to have first emerged. The region became the meeting point of San hunter-gatherers and Khoi pastoralists – known collectively as the Khoisan. Their rock art stands testament in overhangs and caves throughout the area. The Langkloof was first settled by European farmers in the 1750s.

One of the most fascinating routes to take through the Langkloof is to follow the gravel road along the Baviaanskloof River Valley between Patensie and Willowmore. The road meanders through a landscape dominated by the red sandstone hills on either side. The hills are rich in proteas, ericas, orchids and the 'drie-bessie-bos', an endemic plant which can only be seen in this area. As the road climbs further up the river valley, the scenery becomes more rugged with the mountains rising to over 1,600 m. The **Boskloof Hiking Trail** and other excellent trails are a good way to explore this wild mountain landscape.

Humansdorp to Willowmore

Humansdorp
Phone code: 042
(NB Always use 3-figure prefix)
Colour map 7, grid B3

Local tourist information is provided by the Humansdorp Publicity Association, T2951361

Like many small towns in South Africa, Humansdorp came into being after the local farming community in the 1840's put pressure on the government to provide a church and focal point for the region's residents. It was only when a local farmer, Matthys Human, offered 606 ha of his farm *Rheeboksfontein*, in 1849, for a settlement that the government allowed a town to be laid out. Half of the land was immediately sold to endow a church. Humansdorp soon developed into an important local agricultural centre. Sadly, in February 1869, a massive fire broke out which destroyed most of the coastal forest from Port Elizabeth through to George. The patches of woodland that survived still bear the scars. Not surprisingly, farming in the area suffered a severe setback.

For most visitors today, the town's only relevance is as a gateway to the Garden Route, or as the nearest place served by long distance coaches heading to Jeffreys Bay. Indeed, the town is a modern sprawl and has little to hold visitors for long, although the soon-to-be-opened **Kouga Cultural Centre** may have a positive impact. (The term 'Kouga' refers to the area between the Garden Route and the Sunshine Coast, and means 'Place of Dreaming'.) This multi-media centre is part of the 'African Renaissance' initiative, and will be devoted to cultural exhibitions and events, such as Khoisan art, traditional healing, and dance and music. ■ *For more information contact T2951111, kougaculture@intekom.co.za*

Sleeping **C-D** *Palm Court Hotel*, T2952458. Pleasant small town hotel, restaurant, bar. **D** *Loubser B&B*, 5 Asegaai St, T2951588. Small, friendly B&B. **D** *Pontac B&B*, 1 Nieshout Cres, T2951463, F2952632. 2 bedrooms, ask for Mrs Skein. **E-F** *Ben Marais Caravan Park*, T2952499, F2950567. A medium size caravan and campsite, with some self-catering bungalows, electric points, lights, hot water, laundry, recreation hall.

Festivals There is a **Fynbos Festival** held here every year in September.

Transport **Bus**: *Greyhound*, coaches depart from the *Touristo restaurant*. **Cape Town** (11 hrs): daily, 2315, via the **Garden Route**. **Durban** (15 hrs): daily, 0530. **Port Elizabeth** (1 hr): daily, 0530.

The Kouga and Baviaanskloof Mountain Ranges form part of the two State Forests. These are some of the wildest areas for hiking in the Eastern Cape, their red sandstone mountains having been eroded into a spectacular landscape. Hikes here are strenuous and involve some long climbs, but the rewards are well worth it. The mountains are a maze of cliffs and ravines inhabited by baboons and tortoises; the trails here pass through thick areas of woodland where you can see the unique Baviaanskloof cedar. Views from the top of the range look over the acacia woodland to the fruit farms in the valleys below. Eland and Cape mountain zebra have recently been reintroduced.

The Baviaanskloof Mountains start about 50 km north of Humansdorp. The road enters the Gamtoos River Valley, passing through the villages of **Patensie**, 29 km, and **Hankey**, 40 km. This is a quiet, agricultural area producing tobacco, vegetables and fruit. The road continues past the Paul Sauer Dam and continues on towards Willowmore, 200 km, passing between the two State Forests. This road meanders along the Baviaanskloof River through some spectacular countryside. (There is a **tourist office** in Tolbos which has information on the Gamtoer Tourist Route and hiking in the area. Access to the mountains themselves involves crossing private farmland; arrangements for this can be made through Cape Nature Conservation.) Summers here tend to be too hot for long hikes – the scenery is still worth seeing, so it makes sense simply to drive through the area. March to November is cooler and more suitable for hiking.

Baviaanskloof Wilderness Area & Cockscomb State Forests

Reservations for trails and sleeping should be made through *Cape Nature Conservation*, Baviaanskloof, T044-9451090. There are a number of different trails, most of which involve crossing private farmland before reaching the mountains. Details of how to get the necessary permissions are available here. **F** Geelhoutbos Huts, 5 6-bed huts for overnight hikers.

Humansdorp to Uniondale

Following the N2 westwards from Humansdorp, there is an exit on the R62 to Joubertina after 36 km. The R62 passes through the small villages of Assegaibos and Kammiebos before reaching Joubertina (80 km). This small agricultural village on the Wabooms River grows apricots, peaches and pears. The village is interesting in its own right, but hikers wanting to explore the Langkloof should press on to Le Ferox Paradis, see below.

Joubertina
Phone code: 042
(NB Always use 3-figure prefix)
Colour map 7, grid B3

Eastern Cape

Sleeping C *Kloof Hotel*, Main St, T2733310. Offers B&B accommodation on the outskirts of the village, swimming pool.

Le Ferox Paradis Private Nature Reserve This is a private nature reserve on a farm lying between the Kouga Mountains and the Baviaanskloof. A number of hiking trails have been set out within the reserve passing through a magnificent rocky and forested landscape. Apart from the numerous birds found here, you may see klipspringers, bushbuck and mountain reedbuck.

There are two relatively easy day walks: the 6 km **Gorge Walk**, and the 14 km **Aloe-Fynbos Trail**. Both start near the Braamrivier Farm and are well-signposted. The **Skrikkerivier Wilderness Trail** is an open area of bush in the reserve through which this unmarked trail passes. The hiking trails are open to the public all year round and a maximum of 20 people are allowed on each trail. March to November is the popular hiking time here, as the heat is less intense than in the summer.

Ins and outs Take the P1822 out of Joubertina heading north into the Kouga Mountains; after 30 km the road passes the Braamrivier Farm from where the reserve is signposted. Reservations for hiking and accommodation should be made through Le Ferox Paradis Nature Reserve, T042-2732079. **Sleeping** C *Farm House*, rooms and meals are available in the farmhouse. There is a field in which you can camp (**F**) with some basic facilities.

Port Elizabeth to Graaff-Reinet

Groendal Wilderness Area, Addo Elephant Park and Zuurberg National Park lie just to the north of Port Elizabeth and can easily be visited on a day excursion. The R335 from Port Elizabeth leads to Addo and Zuurberg, whilst the R368 leads to Uitenhage, 24 km, and on to Groendal.

The fastest route north into the Karoo is via the N2 from Port Elizabeth which connects with the N10 heading to Cradock and Middelburg. The R63 leaves the N10 at Cookhouse and heads west to Somerset East and Graaff-Reinet (see page 346 for more information).

Groendal Wilderness Area

The entrance to the wilderness area is 8 km west of Uitenhage

This large area of wilderness forms part of the Groot Winterhoek Range. The terrain here is extremely rugged and the area is best explored on foot. The ravines, forests and mountains are good places for spotting forest birds and hikers might also see some of the smaller buck such as bushbuck, duiker, grysbok and mountain reedbuck. The main physical features of Groendal are Srydomsberg Peak at 1,180 m, the Swartkops River and Groendal Dam.

There is a network of well-marked trails around Groendal, some of which are temporarily closed due to erosion caused by overuse by hikers. The 14 km **Blindekloof Trail** is a comfortable day's walk through a thickly forested ravine. The **Upper Blindekloof Trail**, 36 km, and the **Dam Trail**, 38 km, are both circular trails which penetrate further into the Groot Winterhoek Range. The forests and ravines here are still inhabited by leopards, and the wild nature of the terrain and steep climb means that you have to be fairly fit to enjoy these trails.

Permits for the hiking trails are available from the *Nature Conservator*, Groendal Wilderness Area, Cape Nature Conservation, Uitenhage, T041-9925418. A maximum of 12 people are allowed on each trail. There is no established campsite but there are caves to sleep in on the overnight hikes.

Greater Addo National Park

Colour map 7, grid B4

Addo, covering 12,000 ha, is a genuine highlight of the Eastern Cape and highly recommended. The park was established in 1931 to protect the last 11 surviving elephant in the area – at present there are over 320 inhabiting the unique Spekboom environment. The relative flatness of the bush and the large number of elephant

Addo's fruity elephants

For many years the elephants in the Addo Elephant Park were fed oranges and other citrus fruits in an attempt to stop them wandering into neighbouring farmland. The experiment was successful in that the elephants stayed within the reserve, however the feeding caused other problems as most of the herd lived within a small area around the feeding posts which caused overgrazing and aggressive behaviour as the elephants competed for the oranges. Feeding was stopped in 1978, but visitors are still prohibited from bringing citrus fruits into the reserve as the elephants have developed a taste for them.

present mean that they are easily seen. To add to this, there are a couple of water-holes which can be accessed by car, and visitors will often see several herds drinking at one time – this can mean watching over a hundred elephant, quite a magnificent experience. Although you'll see them at any time of year, one of the best times to visit is in January and February, when many of the females will have recently calved.

Other animals which one can see within the park are eland, grysbok, kudu, ostrich, jackal, Cape buffalo and red hartebeest. Black rhino are also present but are rarely seen. Over 185 species of birds have been recorded here. Look out for the flightless dung beetle, unique to the park and found wherever there's elephant dung. Addo has ambitious plans for the future – more land has been acquired and lions will be introduced from Kruger in the next few years. The plan is to extend the park all the way to the coast, allowing people to see the Big Seven (this includes the great white shark and the southern right whale) in one day, all in a malaria-free environment.

Getting there The park is 72 km from Port Elizabeth and can be reached by taking the **Ins & outs** R335. The park is also well-signposted off the Port Elizabeth to Grahamstown road.

Getting around The weather here is usually warm and dry and visits to the park are enjoyable all year round. There are 43 km of gravel roads which are open to the public from sunrise to sunset for game viewing. There are also two hides, one of which overlooks a floodlit water hole and can be booked for the night. The other hide tends to be busier as it is near the restaurant, but it is good for birdwatching as it overlooks a small dam. After heavy rains visitors in a saloon car may find some of the roads closed to them. Although it is convenient driving in your own car, it is a good idea to pay for a tour in a four-wheel drive, as the guides are very knowledgeable and know where the animals are best found. This can save considerable searching time. Night drives can also be booked. To book a four-wheel drive tour or night drive, call T042-2351123. Booking essential.

Park information Entrance gates open daily 0700-1900; office hours open daily 0700-2000; R30 entry fee; restaurant open daily 0800-2100, serves light snacks and meals; shop open daily 0800-1900, sells a selection of groceries, meat, bread and wines; petrol (no diesel) 0730-1700; laundry, telephone and postal services are also available. Swimming pool and tennis courts. Note that it is illegal to leave your vehicle anywhere other than at signposted climb-out points. The speed limit is 40 km/h. **Information and accommodation bookings**, T042-2330556, F2330196, addoelephantsres@parks-sa.co.za 4WD tours and night drives are offered on a first-come-first-served basis. Book your seat when you check in. Bookings can also be made in person at the two National Parks offices in Cape Town, either at the tourist office in the Clocktower Centre, V&A Waterfront, or at Cape Town Tourism, corner of Castle and Burg streets, a short walk from Green Market Square in the city centre.

The Spekboom Trail, 12 km, passes through a fenced-off area of the national park **Hiking** from which the elephants have been excluded. This is a circular trail which climbs

Eastern Cape

gradually uphill through the *spekboomveld*. From the top of the hill there are clear views over Addo's unique landscape. There is some small game within the enclosed area and the birdlife is spectacular.

Sleeping
Price codes:
see inside front cover

All units have to be vacated by 0900, and can be occupied from 1100 on the day of arrival

Each cottage has bedding, towels and soap, a/c and braai facilities. **B** *Guest cottages*, 6-bed cottages with 2 en suite a/c bedrooms, fully equipped kitchen and a living room. There are only 2 such cottages, known as Hapoor and Domkrag. **C** *Bungalow*, suitable for 4 people, bathroom plus a kitchen. **D** *2-bed huts*, simple units with a shower, fridge and toilet. There is a fully equipped communal kitchen. **F** *Camping*, a maximum of 6 people can occupy any 1 campsite. The grounds are well-grassed and there is plenty of shade. Communal kitchens have hot plates, power points and hot water.

A very luxurious alternative is the privately owned **L3** *Gorah Elephant Camp*, T042-2351123, www.gorah.com This camp has a private concession covering 4,500 ha but can also access the rest of the park. Accommodation is in huge, luxurious tents with a colonial theme, complete with four-poster beds, en suite bathrooms and terraces overlooking the park. Meals are served in a superbly renovated farmhouse, overlooking a waterhole frequented by elephant, buffalo and antelope. The price includes all meals, guided game drives and night drives. This is a highly recommended camp – the only drawback is that the service is rather over-attentive.

Zuurberg National Park
This is a beautiful part of the Winterhoek Mountains which is rich in birdlife and vegetation

Game is being reintroduced into Zuurberg and although there are chances of seeing some of the small buck, none of the more spectacular large mammals are here. The area is better known for its plantlife. This is the only place in the world where you can find the Zuurberg cushionbush and the Zuurberg cycad. Most of the park is covered with large areas of false fynbos consisting of low-lying bush. The valleys are filled with thick evergreen forest where there are many yellowwood and white stinkwood trees.

Ins and outs Zuurberg is 32 km from Addo Elephant Park. Access is via the R356. Trail permits and accommodation reservations can be made directly at, T042-2330581, F2331212.

Hiking and riding There is a 12-km walking trail which climbs up from the Forester's Office through a forestry plantation into an area of fynbos. The overall terrain consists of dry, rocky scrub inhabited by kudu, mountain reedbuck and grey rhebock. It is also possible to ride through the fynbos and Alexandria forests. For novice riders there is a popular 1-hour trail through easy terrain. If you are more experienced you can be taken out by a guide for a 5-hour trail on Basuto pony/Boerperd crossbreeds. All the necessary equipment is provided, but it is important to book in advance.

Price codes:
see inside front cover

Sleeping There is a simple **D-E** *Bush Camp* in the reserve, with 4 tents, each sleeping 8 people, plus an open kitchen, self-catering only, T042-2330581. For more luxury, you'll have to stay outside the park. **B-E** *Zuurberg Mountain Inn*, T042-2330583, F2330070, zuurberg@addo.co.za, is directly opposite the original entrance to the Zuurberg National Park. There are 20 double rooms; some are in the original main building while the rest are delightful individual spacious lodges under traditional thatch in the Zuurberg Village. Restaurant with magnificent views, swimming pool, tennis conference centre. Highly recommended as a base for exploring the Greater Addo National Park. Attached budget rooms for backpackers. Mountain bikes for hire.

Eastern Cape Karoo

The surreal Karoo landscape, clear air and desert sunsets are evocative of the very heart of South Africa. The archaic scenery, created from sedimentary rock around 250 million years ago, is rich in fossils and San paintings. This is an area of vast open spaces studded with scrub and cacti, craggy mountains looming in the distance. Despite its barren appearance, this is mainly a farming area, known for its sheep, cattle, angora goats and horses. The most beautiful place to experience the Karoo is in the Valley of Desolation next to the historical town of Graaff-Reinet.

Somerset East was named after Lord Charles Somerset, Governor of the Cape, and is a neat agricultural town typical of the Karoo. The town has a few historical buildings and faces the Bosberg Mountains. The Somerset **museum** recreates the atmosphere and lifestyle of a Victorian parsonage. It is set amongst beautiful rose gardens, the petals of which are used to make rose petal jam which is on sale in the museum shop. ■ *Small entry fee.* The **Walter Battiss Art Museum** is also here and has the world's largest collection of this South African artist's work. ■ *Mon-Fri, 0900-1700.*

Somerset East
Phone code: 042
(NB Always use 3-figure prefix)
Colour map 7, grid A4

The reserve has a fenced-off area where kudu, mountain reedbuck, and mountain zebra can be seen. Its major bonuses are the views of koppies stretching out into the distance beyond Besterhoek Valley, and the birds which are attracted to the dam. There is a two-day **hiking trail** which circles the reserve. Both days involve leisurely walking as the total distance of the trail is only 15 km. The first day of the trail is spent climbing up through the remains of indigenous woodland to the hiking hut near Kebe's cave. On the second day the trail reaches the highest point of the reserve at Blaukop, 1,622 m, from where there are views of Somerset East and the surrounding countryside. The trail then descends through fynbos back to the park entrance. **Permits and maps** of the trail are available from the tourist office in Somerset East, T2431448.

Bosberg Nature Reserve

Only 10 people are allowed on the trail at any one time

Sleeping There are several game farms and guesthouses in the area. **B-C** *Darlington Lake Lodge*, T/F2433673. 5 double rooms with en suite facilities furnished in a colonial style. Weather permitting, meals are served outdoors in a traditional *boma*. Wide range of activities on offer, skiing, parasailing, wave tubing, horse rides, fishing and white water rafting.

Price codes: see inside front cover

This small Karoo town is made up of an attractive grid of wide roads lined with Victorian bungalows. It was once a frontier town and has three Victorian churches. The **Dutch Reformed Church** on Stockenstroom St was opened in 1868 – visitors from London should have a closer look it is based upon St Martin in the Fields, on Trafalgar Square. Cradock is now better known for its connections with the author Olive Schreiner who wrote *The Story of an African Farm*. The **Olive Schreiner House**, 9 Cross St, T8815251, can be visited and illustrates aspects of her life. ■ *Mon-Fri, 0800-1245, 1400-1630, small entrance charge.* There is also a trail leading to her grave on Buffelskop Mountain, off the R390, 25 km south of the town. Cradock Spa, Marlow Rd, is a series of indoor and outdoor pools set around some natural sulphurous springs and is an ideal place to visit after hiking in the Winterberge.

For **tourist information**, contact the Cradock Tourist Office, Town Hall, Stockenstroom St, T8812383.

The **Fish River** is one of the top whitewater rivers in the world and the Sunseeker canoe marathon is held here. *Amanzi Adventures*, T2950305, T082-3362958 (mob), organizes whitewater rafting trips. There are also two short circular hiking trails beginning at Cradock Spa. The 10 km **Fish River Trail** follows the Fish River into town, crossing over the bridge and returning on the opposite bank. The **Eerstekrantz Trail**, 5 km, is a hike up the mountain opposite to the spa resort.

Cradock
Phone code: 048
(NB Always use 3-figure prefix)
Colour map 7, grid A4

Sleeping C *Die Tuishuise*, 36 Market St, T8811322, F8811164, tuishuise@eastcape.net Characterful guesthouse based in a series of historical buildings on Market St, each restored and decorated in a different style. All of the houses are fitted out with a fully equipped kitchen and lounges and are ideal for self-catering families or two couples travelling together. All rooms have en suite bathrooms and the staff are very friendly and helpful. Delicious, huge breakfasts are served in a Victorian dining room. A good evening meal can be had in the Victoria Manor hotel at the end of the street, also owned by *De Tuishuise*. Recommended, almost worth a detour alone. **C** *Victoria Manor Hotel*, Market St, T8811650,

Price codes: see inside front cover

Eastern Cape

tuishuise@eastcape.net Lovely old town inn set in a 3-storey white-washed Victorian build-ing. Full of character, with old-fashioned furnishings, a good restaurant, bar, tearoom and attached curio shop. **D** *Heritage House*, 45 Bree St, T8813210. Delightful old farmhouse with 3 comfortable and stylish double rooms, all en suite, and 2 airy cottages set on wide lawns. The owners are animal-lovers so don't be surprised to see a rescued springbok foal tottering around the garden, and don't be alarmed by the 3 m-long Burmese python (thankfully kept in a tank). Good breakfasts, friendly owners, the perfect spot to relax and soak up the Karoo atmosphere for a few days. Recommended. **D** *New Masonic Hotel*, Stockenstroom St, T8813115, F8814402. Characterless block with 24 rooms, restaurant, bar. Last resort if the guesthouses are full. **D** *Palm House*, 26 Market St, T8814229. Old fashioned Victorian bunga-low with 3 rooms, en suite, no smoking, old-style furnishings, high ceilings, lovely old dining room, TV lounge, good breakfasts, very friendly owners. Recommended.

Eating *1814 Restaurant*, Stockenstroom St, T8815390. Simple place serving large lunches and takeaways, one of the most popular local restaurants. *Fiddler's*, Voortrekker St, T8811497. Next to the Total garage, good meaty fare. Frequented by local farmers and the like. *Lemoenhoek*, Mortimer Rd, 6 km out of town along the R337, T8812514. Excellent meals in the most unlikely of places, well-worth the stop. Mix of quality karoo dishes with a continental touch. Fine wines also on offer.

Transport Rail: bookings, T086000888. The *Algoa Express*, runs daily to **Johannesburg** (13½ hrs): 1911, via **Bloemfontein** (7 hrs). To **Port Elizabeth** (4½ hrs): daily, 0445. **Road Bus**: *Translux*, coaches depart from Struwig Motors, Voortrekker St. The only bus that runs is to **East London** (5 hrs): daily, 1545. Otherwise there are daily buses from Pretoria to **Middelburg** daily except Tue and Sun, arriving at 0240, from where you can get a local mini-bus taxi the next day.

Mountain Zebra National Park
Colour map 7, grid A4

The plains and mountains of this Karoo landscape support a wide variety of mammals, including black wildebeest, kudu, eland, mountain zebra, red hartebeest, springbok and caracal. The Rooiplat Plateau is a good area for seeing the zebra. Over 200 species of bird have been recorded here, and less appealingly, this is also the home of the giant earthworm.

The national park was established in 1937, when the mountain zebra was facing extinction; there are now over 200 of them here, making it the largest herd of mountain zebra in the world. There are currently several studies being done to create a greatly enlarged reserve which will protect several different environments in the area.

Ins and outs The park is 25 km west of Cradock in the foothills of the Bankberg. The reserve is signposted from the Cradock to Middelburg road. It is 280 km from Port Elizabeth and about 800 km from Cape Town.

Park information Gates open Oct-Apr 0700-1900, May-Sep 0700-1800; office hours Oct-Apr 0700-1900, May-Sep 0700-1800, T048-8812427, F048-8813943, nellieg@parks-sa.co.za There is a fully licensed à la carte restaurant open daily 0700-1900, which also serves snacks; shop open daily 0700-1900, sells a good range of groceries, wines, curios, books and firewood; the park also has a swimming pool (resident guests only), post office, telephones and petrol. **Accommodation reservations**, by telephone only, Mon-Fri; Pretoria, T012-3431991, F3430905 or via email at reservations@parks-sa.co.za Bookings can also be made in person at 2 offices in Cape Town, either the tourist office at the Clocktower Centre, V&A Waterfront or in the Cape Town tourist office, corner of Castle and Burg streets in the city centre.

The weather in this part of the eastern Karoo is generally warm and dry all year round. However, there are extremes of weather and it does get cold at night during the winter months when it has been known to snow on high ground; daytime temperatures during the summer can also be very high. The average annual rainfall for the park is 390 mm.

Hiking & game viewing

Game viewing can be done by car during daylight hours on the 37 km of tracks which cross the reserve. Otherwise the park can be explored on foot. There are a number of circular day walks starting at the rest camp. The **Mountain Zebra Hiking Trail** is 31 km long and takes three days to walk. The hike passes through the Fonteinkloof and Grootkloof Gorges and climbs up to the top of the Banksberg, from where there are magnificent views of the Kompassberg in the distance. There are two overnight huts with showers which sleep a maximum of 12 people. Hikers must bring their own sleeping bags, food and cooking equipment.

Sleeping **B** *Doornhoek Guest House*, a restored Victorian farmhouse built in 1836, registered as a national monument. The house sleeps up to 6 people in 2 cast iron double beds and 2 single beds. All 3 bedrooms have an en suite bathroom. The house is decorated in a Victorian style, with pine floors, stained-glass windows, open fireplaces for the winter months, a fully equipped kitchen and to complete the feeling of isolated luxury the house is set in its own valley. **C** *Cottages*, these self-catering cottages are rather more functional. Each has 2 bedrooms, a bathroom, living room and a partially equipped kitchen. **F** The camping area is set amongst good shade trees. There is a communal wash block and kitchen facilities. A maximum of 6 people are allowed on each site. Some sites have power points for caravans.

Price codes: see inside front cover

This small agricultural town is a convenient base for hikers intending to tackle the Compassberg, which rises to 2,052 m. The Compassberg is the highest point in the Sneeuberg Mountain range and was named in 1778. **Grootfontein Agricultural College** has a small museum where historical and agricultural implements are on display. For **tourist information**, contact the Middleburg Publicity Assocation, T8422188.

Middelburg
Phone code: 049 (NB Always use 3-figure prefix) Colour map 7, grid A4

The **Compassberg Hiking Trail** is a 48 km, 3-day circular trail around the foothills on the northern side of Compassberg. The first night is spent in a cottage at the base camp, the second night is at a farmhouse and the final night is in a stone mountain hut. A maximum of 12 hikers are allowed on the trail at a time; T8422418 for bookings. The **Trans Karoo Hiking Trail** passes through an area of Karoo wilderness, rich in birdlife and San art, on a private farm. The trails start and end at Rietpoort and there is a choice of 2- or 3-day trails, the longest being 42 km. Accommodation is in self-catering huts and tents; a maximum of 12 hikers are allowed on the trail at a time. T8431506 for bookings.

Sleeping **B** *Country Inn*, corner of Meintjies and Loop streets, T8421126, F8421681. Lovely old building with 23 double rooms, shady verandas, restaurant, bar. **C** *Middelburg Lodge*, Meintjies St, T8421100, F8421681. 22 double rooms, restaurant and swimming pool. **C** *My Home Your Home*, T8422072, T082-4936576 (mob). Small B&B, large gardens.

Price codes: see inside front cover

Transport **Bus** *Translux*, coaches depart from Volkstad Motors. **Johannesburg** and **Pretoria** (10 hrs): Thu, Fri, Sat, Sun, 2310, via **Bloemfontein** (4 hrs). **Port Elizabeth**, Tue, Thu, Fri, Sat, Sun, 0245, via **Graaff-Reinet** (1½ hrs).

This small village has become famous through the work of Helen Martins and her Owl House. Helen was a local eccentric who lived a hermit-like existence, devoting her time to her art and the study of Eastern philosophies. Most of the surfaces on the inside of the house are decorated with finely ground glass of many colours. At the back of the house is an enclosed area known as the Camel Yard, filled with hundreds of sphinxes, camels and other figures made from cement and glass. Her house and its grounds, along with much of her art is now a **museum**. The village is only 50 km from Graaff-Reinet and can easily be visited in a day. ■ *Museum open daily 0900-1700, adults R7, children, R4. For further information contact the local Information Office, T8411623 in Muller St.*

Nieu Bethesda
Phone code: 049 (NB Always use 3-figure prefix) Colour map 7, grid A3

A day trip worth doing while you are here is going to view the ancient **San rock art**, discovered in nearby Ganora. Contact *Ganora Excursions*, T84113002, for more details.

Price codes:
see inside front cover
Sleeping D *House No 1*, 1 Cloete St, T8411700. Attractive old-style guesthouse, very comfortable rooms with antique furnishings, polished wooden floors, en suite, lounge, dining room. **F** *Owl House Backpackers*, Martin St, T8411642, owlhouse@global.co.za Pleasant budget alternative with creatively decorated dorms and double rooms, cottage, camping, kitchen, bar, home-cooked meals, run by a friendly couple. *Baz Bus* drop off.

Graaff-Reinet

Phone code: 049
(NB Always use
3-figure prefix)
Colour map 7, grid A3

Founded in 1786, Graaff-Reinet is the oldest town of the Eastern Cape, and lies between the Sneuberg Mountains and the Sundays River. The town was originally described as nothing more than a collection of mud huts, but years of prosperity from farming are reflected in the local architecture – over 200 of the town's historical buildings have been declared national monuments. Today it is surprisingly smart, with row upon row of perfectly restored houses, leafy streets and a quiet, bustling atmosphere. Nevertheless, Graaff-Reinet remains a small provincial town; don't expect much in the form of entertainment, and remember that this is deep Karoo country – some locals even claim that there are still lions in the area. **Tourist information** is available from *Graaff-Reinet Publicity Association*, corner of Church and Somerset streets, T8924248, www.graaffreinet.co.za Open, Mon-Fri, 0800-1700; Sat and Sun, 0900-1200. The office recently lost its funding, so it remains to be seen if it will stay open.

The town was originally established as an administrative centre to control the frontier districts for the government in the Cape. Mauritz Woeke was sent as governor or landrost in 1785. He chose the site of Graaff-Reinet because of its water supplies and fertile soils. The town grew to become an important trading centre on the new frontier and there was a boom in sheep farming during the 1850s, when English settlers first brought Merino sheep to the region.

Sights

The earliest surviving historical buildings, mostly square and originally thatched but now roofed with corrugated iron, are on **Cradock Street**. The buildings are typical of Karoo architecture and were designed to be cool during the blistering summer heat. They have thick white-washed walls and shuttered windows.

All of the town's
museums are open
Mon-Fri 0900-1230,
1400-1700, Sat and
Sun 0900-1200, unless
otherwise stated

A walk down **Parsonage Street** and **Church Street** passes many of Graaff-Reinet's most interesting historical buildings. **The Drostdy** is a fine example of classical Cape architecture designed by Louis Thibault. It was built in 1806 and was the site of the local council for 40 years. In 1855 it was bought by Captain Charles Lennox Stretch and converted into a hotel. The modern *Drostdy Hof Hotel* was restored in 1977.

Reinet House on Parsonage Street was completed in 1812 and became the parsonage for the Dutch Reformed Church. It was opened to the public as a historical museum in 1956, displaying what a period home looked like. It is still decorated with original yellowwood and stinkwood furniture, and boasts the world's largest vine. Several extensions have been added to provide additional space for the museum's collection – the final addition to the complex was a brandy still, built in 1990, now used to demonstrate the distillation of *withond*, a local brand of fire-water from the early settler days.

Opposite is the **Old Residency Museum**, which was originally a town house built early in the 19th century. It became the magistrate's residence in 1916. Today it houses the Jan Felix Lategan Memorial collection of sporting rifles as well as Middellandse Regiment memorabilia. Closed Sun. The **John Rupert Little Theatre**, also on Parsonage Street, was originally the church of the London Missionary Society. It became an art gallery during the 1970s and is now a theatre.

The **Old Library Museum** on Church Street was built in 1847 although new wings were added last century. The building is now a museum with displays of period costumes and a collection of fossils. The tourist information office is also here. The **Hester Rupert Art Museum** is next to the Old Library and makes a

Eastern Cape

pleasant change from the nostalgia of the other museums. The art gallery contains a collection of South African contemporary art.

The **Graaff-Reinet Pharmacy** on Caledon Street is a Victorian chemist's shop which still has many of its original fittings. There are a number Victorian chemists which have been converted into tourist attractions in South Africa, but this one is considered to be amongst the finest.

Graaff-Reinet

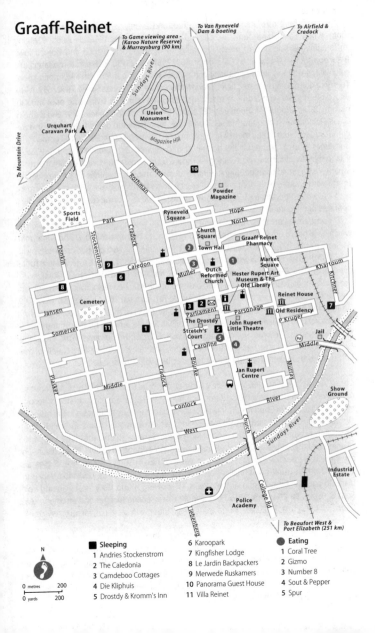

Eastern Cape

■ **Sleeping**
1 Andries Stockenstrom
2 The Caledonia
3 Camdeboo Cottages
4 Die Kliphuis
5 Drostdy & Kromm's Inn
6 Karoopark
7 Kingfisher Lodge
8 Le Jardin Backpackers
9 Merwede Ruskamers
10 Panorama Guest House
11 Villa Reinet

● **Eating**
1 Coral Tree
2 Gizmo
3 Number 8
4 Sout & Pepper
5 Spur

Sleeping

■ *on map, page 347*
Price codes:
see inside front cover

A *Drostdy*, 30 Church St, T8922161, F8924582, drostdy@intekom.co.za Beautifully restored historical building, designed by Louis Thibault in 1804. The rooms are at the back of the main house in an appealing complex of 19th-century cottages known as *Stretch's Courts*, originally the homes of emancipated slaves. There are 50 slightly fussy rooms, but all en suite and a/c. The *Camdebo Restaurant* has a good reputation (see below) and the attached *Kromm's Inn* services snack meals throughout the day. There is a lovely secluded garden where you can have pre-dinner drinks, as well as a pool and secure off-street parking.

B *Andries Stockenstroom Guest House*, 100 Cradock St, T/F8924575. This guesthouse was originally built in 1819 and has been restored and lavishly decorated. There are 4 double rooms with en suite bathrooms and a/c, and a superb dining room (residents only) serving an imaginative selection of meals including kudu, springbok, ostrich and guinea fowl. **B** *Karoopark Guest House*, 81 Caledon St, T8922557, F8925730. B&B accommodation in a colonial style manor, plus self-catering cottages set in a large garden with a swimming pool. There is a doll museum located here. **B** *Kingfisher Lodge*, 33 Cypress Grove, T8922657. A luxurious guesthouse with 5 double rooms, non-smoking room, TV, swimming pool and safe parking. **B** *Die Kliphuis*, 46 Bourke St, T8922345. Die Kliphuis was built in 1857 and is one of Graaff-Reinet's most beautiful historical buildings. Breakfasts and dinners are served in a traditionally decorated dining room with a roaring fire. The rooms overlook a Karoo garden with fruit trees and a pomegranate hedge. **C** *Villa Reinet*, 83 Somerset St, T/F8925525, villa_reinet@worldonline.co.za New guesthouse set in an old church hall – a national monument – with broad corridors, high ceilings and comfortable furnishings. There are 2 double rooms with en suite bathroom and large French doors leading on to a garden, 1 apartment with its own lounge, and 6 garden cottages. Breakfast is served in the cosy kitchen or under a pear tree in the garden.

D *Camdeboo Cottages*, 16 Parliament St, T8923180. A small group of historical buildings which have been converted into 8 self-catering cottages. Recommended. **D** *The Caledonia*, 61 Somerset St, T8923156. A self-catering cottage sleeping up to 5 people; breakfasts available. **D** *Panorama Guest House*, Magazine Hill, T8922233, F8922412. Large modern motel overlooking Graaff-Reinet, with a swimming pool, restaurant and conference facilities. The rooms are modern units with TV, a/c and bathroom; the attached restaurant serves a generous buffet most evening weekdays. **D** *Merwede Ruskamers*, 100 Caledon St, T8923749. Double and single rooms, swimming pool and safe parking, meals included. **F** *Le Jardin Backpackers*, 103 Caledon St, T8925890, F8925890. Simple set-up with dorms and double rooms, shared bathrooms, self-catering available. **F** *Urquhart Caravan Park*, T8922136. Large park with clean, modern facilities for campers and caravans. There are a couple of chalets, some with kitchen, and very simple but excellent value rondavels.

Eating

● *on map, page 347*

Coral Tree, 3 Church St, T8925947. Great location opposite the church. Very popular restaurant serving a good range of typical Karoo dishes – try the Karoo lamb or kudu steaks. Recommended. *Drostdy*, 28 Church St, T8922161. Excellent romantic restaurant set in the historical *Drostdy Hotel*. Beautiful setting with high ceilings, polished wooden floors and candle light. Great nightly buffets with a fine range of local Karoo dishes – shame about the silly period clothing that the waitresses have to wear. *Gizmo*, 40 Caledon St, T8923041. Italian restaurant serving excellent-value pizzas, salads and pasta dishes. Friendly, fast service. A pleasant change from the usual 'traditional' restaurants. *Number 8*, 8 Church St, T8924464. Very popular pub and grill house, good simple steaks, TV showing sports, busy local watering hole. *Sout & Peper*, 90 Church St, T8923403. Simple place serving lunches and afternoon teas. *Spur*, 22B Church St, T8923202. Good value steak house with salad bar, friendly service.

Sports

Sporting facilities around Graaff-Reinet including fishing, golf, hiking, horse riding and paragliding. There are a number of farms in the area offering eco-tourism experiences on foot or on horseback. *Camdeboo Safaris*, Sondagsrivierhoek, T8459002. **Paragliding** There are good thermals near Desolation Valley. Contact T8910929 for more information on equipment hire and the chance of a flight over the mountains and desert. Expect to pay in the region of US$80 for a 30 mins flight.

Ganora Excursions, based in Nieu-Bethesa, T049-8411302, ganora@xsinet.co.za Excellent **Tour operators** small operator based in nearby Nieu-Bethesa, with guides specializing in trips to view ancient San rock art, as well as walking trails and fossil walks. Recommended. *Irhafu Tours*, T082-8442890 (mob), irhafutours@yahoo.com Specializes in tours to the local township, the birthplace of Robert Sobukwe. *Karoo Connections*, T8923978, karooconnections@ intekom.co.za Well-organized local tour operator offering a wide range of trips, including township tours, trips to San rock art, Karoo farm visits, hot-air balloon trips over the desert and horse riding.

Road 251 km to **Port Elizabeth** 90 km to **Murraysburg**. **Bus**: *Intercape*, services **Transport** depart/arrive from the *Kuklu Motors* in Church St, T021-3804400. **Port Elizabeth** (3 hrs): daily in high season, 0445. **Plettenburg Bay** (7 hrs): daily, 0430 (via **George** and **Knysna**). **Johannesburg** and **Pretoria** (10½ hrs): daily, 2115 (via **Bloemfontein**).

Translux, T041-3921333, coaches depart from Kudu Motors in Church St. **Cape Town** (10 hrs): daily, 2235. **Johannesburg** and **Pretoria** (12 hrs): Tue, Wed, Thu, Fri, Sun, 2155; Wed and Fri, 2230 (via **Kimberley**); Tue, Wed, Thu, Fri and Sun, 2245; via **Bloemfontein** (5 hrs): Mon, Thu, Sat, 2310; **Knysna** (7 hrs): Mon, Thu, Sat 0430; **Port Elizabeth** (3½ hrs): Tue, Wed, Thu, Fri, Sun, 0415.

Around Graaff-Reinet

The Karoo Nature Reserve covers 16,500 hectares and virtually surrounds **Karoo Nature** Graaff-Reinet. The landscape is typical of the Karoo, with spectacular rock forma- **Reserve** tions, peculiar desert flora and interesting game and birdlife – if you're in the area, *Colour map 7, grid A3* do not miss the spectacular views of the Karoo from the Valley of Desolation. There are three main areas within the reserve: the Valley of Desolation to the west; a game *Entrance to the* drive area to the north; and the eastern hiking area. To reach the park, take the road *reserve is free.* in the direction of Murraysburg. You will pass a large dam, which has picnic sites *Open from 0600-2000* and is popular with tourists who come here to sail and windsurf. After 5 km you pass the entrance to the Valley of Desolation on your left, and after 8 km you reach the entrance to the game reserve, on the right.

The **Valley of Desolation** is the highlight of the reserve, offering stunning views of the Karoo in all directions to the horizon, with stark rock formations looming in the foreground. From the entrance to the Valley, drive up to the first viewpoint – the views are at their best from here. Looking out over the harsh landscape gives you a good idea of the overwhelming obstacles that the *Vortrekkers* managed to overcome. If you continue up the road, you come to a carpark and a short 1½ km hike, with stunning views of the mountains and the chance of seeing black eagles and dassies. Back down off the main road, there is a 19 km **game drive**, where you may see Cape buffalo, kudu, mountain zebra and springbok. The **Eerstefontein Day Walks** start at the Spandau Kop Gate. There is a choice of three walks of 4 km, 11 km or 14 km. The walks pass through a wilderness area where you can see black wildebeest, kudu and springbok. Permits are acquired at the gate. The **Driekoppe Trail** is an overnight trail which passes through the mountainous eastern area of the reserve. This area is rich in wildlife, and hikers can see klipspringers, kudu, mountain reedbuck and mountain zebra. The overnight hut sleeps 10 hikers. The trail should be booked in advance through the Karoo Nature Reserve on T8923453.

A short distance from Graaff-Reinet are the weathered remains of a giant crater cre- **Kalkkop** ated by a meteorite more than 200,000 years ago. Research has shown the original **Impact Crater** hole to have been several hundred metres deep. Over time the crater has been filled with limestone deposits, but the circular ridge, with a diameter of 640 m, is still visible. ■ *To get there, follow the N9 in the direction of Aberdeen for about 30 km; at Aberdeen, turn left on to the R338 until you reach a right-hand turn marked as Aberdeen Road. From here there is a dirt track that leads to the crater – it should be signposted.*

Port Elizabeth to East London

There are two routes to East London from Port Elizabeth. The quickest is on the N2 via Grahamstown. An alternative route is to take the R72 coastal road. Whichever you choose, it will mean missing out on some of the sights and spectacular scenery. There are two very compelling reasons for following the N2: a visit to the superb Shamwari Game Reserve, and to see the old colonial town of Grahamstown.

Shamwari Game Reserve

Colour map 7, grid B5 This is a privately owned reserve which in many aspects resembles the private reserves of Mpumalanga along the boundary of Kruger National Park. The park has been well-stocked with game from all over the region, including black rhino, elephant, buffalo, leopard, lion and antelope of all sizes. The reserve covers an area of 14,000 ha; there are four different lodges within the boundary. All are part of the same operation.

Ins & outs **Getting there** Driving out from Port Elizabeth, follow the signs for the N2, Grahamstown. After 65 km take a left turn, signposted Shamwari. This gravel road is the R342; after 7 km take a right turn. It is then a further 2 km to the entrance. Driving from Grahamstown, the R342 turning is about 58 km along the N2.

The reserve There are two very significant factors which have made this reserve such a success in a short time period. Firstly, unlike Kruger National Park, Pilansberg National Park or any of the private reserves which stock the Big Five, Shamwari is **malaria free**. Secondly, it is very close to the Cape where many visitors to South Africa now spend their whole holiday. It is possible to fly up to Port Elizabeth in less than an hour from Cape Town (four times a day). Distances are suddenly more practical – it is only 835 km from Cape Town to the reserve, whereas a trip to Kruger is over 2,000 km.

If you are just here for the day, "**Kaya Lendaba**", a traditional African **Healing Village** is well worth a visit. The village is helping to preserve methods and recipes, most of which would otherwise have been lost. ■ *Daily tour at 1100, booking essential, T042-8511196.*

Sleeping There are 5 luxury camps within the reserve – all are expensive. Each is completely
Price codes: self-contained and independent of the others. Rooms have to be vacated by 1100 and arriv-
see inside front cover ing guests will normally be allowed to occupy their rooms from 1400. Current rates per person are between R2,500 and R3,500, although between May and Sep some rates drop to R1,500. Nevertheless this is still one of the most expensive game reserves in South Africa. **Reservations**: PO Box 32017, Summerstrand, Port Elizabeth, T042-2031111, F2351224 **NB** Day visitors are welcome, but you must make advance reservations.

L4 *Bushman's River Lodge*, a small lodge at the centre of the reserve. The rooms are set in restored settlers' cottages. Maximum of 8 guests. Swimming pool and a personal ranger service. **L4** *Eagles Cragg Lodge*, the most central of the 4 camps. Maximum of 8 guests. This is a restored settler's cottage which has been divided into 4 rooms with twin beds and an en suite bathroom with shower. Private swimming pool, ranger who acts as a guide on game drives and as an armed guard on walking safaris. **L4** *Highfield*, near the eastern boundary of the reserve just north of *Eagles Cragg*. Maximum of 8 guests. Also a faithfully restored settler's cottage, converted into 4 luxury rooms, each with twin beds, en suite bathroom with a shower, private pool, ranger. **L3** *Long Lee Manor*, this is the manor house near the main entrance on the western side of the reserve. Largest of the 4 camps, although it never feels crowded. There is a curio shop with the usual collection of books, trinkets and T-shirts. The rooms here are in the Manor House, Palm Court or Sidbury Suites. All of the rooms have under-floor heating, ceiling fans, a/c, TV, telephone. There are 20 rooms, and a maximum of 38 guests can stay here. The accommodation consists of the following: *The Garden suite*, mix of double rooms and twins, all en suite; *Fowlds Room*, a really unusual treat with a 4 poster bed, en suite bath and shower;

outside there is a swimming pool and a floodlit tennis court for a cool evening game; down by the Bushman's River, at a point known as Hippo-pool, is a covered *lapa* where guests can watch the animals drink while they enjoy a meal. **L4** *Lobengula Lodge*, at the northern extremity of the reserve, this is the most luxurious of the 4 complexes. It has a thatched roof and has been decorated to the highest standard. Six rooms and a maximum of 12 guests can stay here. Five rooms have en suite bath and shower plus a/c and under-floor heating; the 6th room is the most expensive option in the whole of the reserve – *The Pretorius Suite*. Separate lounge with super a/c and fan, plus under-floor heating; the bedroom has a double bed and en suite shower and bath. The swimming pool has a sunken cocktail bar.

Grahamstown

Grahamstown is first and foremost a student town. At the top end of the High Street is one of the country's major centres of learning, **Rhodes University**. The presence of the University has a significant impact on this small town and during term time the town's pubs and bars are packed with students. It is a pleasant town to wander around and there are a number of interesting little shops along the High Street.

Despite the English feel to the town centre the other side of the valley is dominated by a poor, dusty and badly serviced township where the majority of the African residents live. The proximity of the two sides of town makes the contrast more apparent than in some of the bigger towns and cities where the townships are distant from the town centre.

*Phone code: 046
(NB Always use
3-figure prefix)
Colour map 7, grid B5*

Eastern Cape

Getting there The town has good transport links and is served by *Greyhound* and *Translux* buses (see page 356).

Ins & outs

Tourist offices *Eastern Cape Nature Conservation*, T6227216. The local Grahamstown offices are a good source of information on accommodation and hiking trails in the inland nature reserves. *Tourism Grahamstown*, 63 High St, T6223241, F6223266, www.grahamstown.co.za Open, Mon-Fri, 0830-1700; Sat, 0900-1100. A well-organized centre with accommodation booking facilities for the entire region. The staff here can also organize and book a variety of local tours. There is also a *Translux* desk at the office. A worthwhile local scheme is 'Step-On Guides' under which locally registered guides join you in your own vehicle and show you around the various sights.

Grahamstown was established around a fort which had been built here after the Fourth Frontier War. It was founded in 1812 and named after Colonel Graham. Within two years it was a busy border settlement. The **1820 Settlers** began to arrive after the end of the Fifth Frontier War, during which Grahamstown had been besieged by Xhosa warriors. Despite the continual threat of armed conflict and problems of security, the town had evolved into the second largest settlement in the whole of southern Africa by 1836.

History

One factor behind the town's rapid growth was that the majority of the 1820 settlers were ill-prepared to be farmers, let alone in an environment of which they had no knowledge. As soon as they realized farming was not going to bring them wealth and security they gave it up and returned to the town to take up the jobs they were trained to do. Grahamstown quickly established a thriving industry based around blacksmiths, carpenters, millers and gunsmiths. Having settled back in the town, the skilled settlers quickly built a series of elegant stone buildings which remain grand specimens of the era's architecture today. Of particular note are the buildings around Church Square, but elsewhere there are churches and fine private homes. The culmination of all this is a smart town centre with a distinctly English atmosphere.

When you look at a map or walk about the town centre you quickly come across a variety of different museums: the Observatory Museum, Natural Science Museum and the History Museum, along with Fort Selwyn and the Provost. These displays are all part

Sights

of one museum, the **Albany Museum**. The collection grew with the development of the town and presents a fairly complete picture of the town's history.

The **Observatory Museum**, on the right hand side of Bathurst Street as you look up towards the City Hall, is a unique building. Inside is a collection of Victorian furniture, household goods and silver, but the highlight is the entertaining Camera Obscura. This a rare specimen, claiming to be the only Victorian Camera Obscura in the southern hemisphere, and projects an image of Grahamstown on to a screen. Visitors are led up a tiny spiral staircase to a small room on the roof, where an enthusiastic guide pivots the camera to show a 360 degree view of the town, pointing out major sights as he does so. There is also an Observatory and a Meridian Room, from which astronomical time can be calculated. The clock is a miniature of one that was made in 1883 for the Royal Courts of Justice in London. An obscure piece of trivia is that the painting on the pendulum is 'Father Time', from the weather vein at Lords Cricket Ground, London; the artist is a well-known Frontier Artist, Frederick Timpson l'Ons. For anyone interested in the history of the diamond industry, the building is loosely connected with the drawn-out identification of the Eureka diamond back in 1869 (see page 692). From the outside the building has a magnificent presence. There are three floors of balconies, each with ornately carved arches and railings, enough to give a hint of how it would have looked in its heyday. ■ *Mon-Fri 0930-1300, 1400-1700, Sat 0900-1300, R8.*

The **Natural Science Museum** is on Somerset Street. It houses a couple of objects of interest, although most of the displays are aimed at children. Some of the more interesting exhibits include a large iron meteorite which came down in a shower in Namibia, a Foucault Pendulum and some dinosaur fossils. There are regular temporary exhibitions, and this is one of the main venues for the Scifest, a science and

Grahamstown

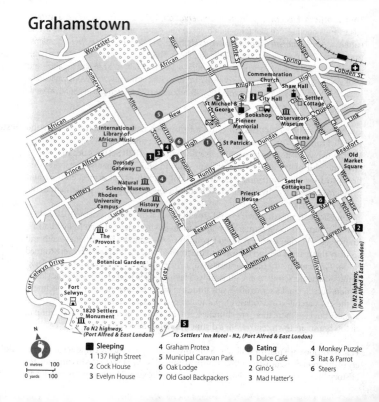

■ Sleeping		● Eating	
1 137 High Street	4 Graham Protea	1 Dulce Café	4 Monkey Puzzle
2 Cock House	5 Municipal Caravan Park	2 Gino's	5 Rat & Parrot
3 Evelyn House	6 Oak Lodge	3 Mad Hatter's	6 Steers
	7 Old Gaol Backpackers		

technology festival held in March. There is a café in a courtyard at the back. ■ *Tue-Fri 0930-1300, 1400-1700, Sat 0900-1300, R8. Entrance by donation.*

The **History Museum** is in a building opposite the Natural Science Museum on Somerset Street. It houses an interesting collection outlining the area's history, including beadwork displays from the Eastern Cape, traditional Xhosa dress, 1820 settler history and some art galleries, with regularly changing contemporary exhibitions. ■ *Tue-Fri 0930-1300, 1400-1700, Sat 0900-1300, R8. Small entrance fee.*

The **Provost**, off Somerset Street, at the western end of town in the botanical gardens, is a quadrangle building with a double-storeyed tower at its apex. It was built in 1837 by the Royal Engineers to act as a military prison; their actual instructions were to build a "fortified barrack establishment". A lot of thought went into the overall design of the complex as the architects of the time sought to come up with a design where, from the central tower, it would be possible to view as many prisoners as possible with minimal manpower. In January 1838 the first 20 convicts were brought here. They were mutineers, and after they had shot one of their officers, Ensign Crowe, they were executed on the parade grounds. The building was proclaimed a National Monument in 1937.

Fort Selwyn is on Fort Selwyn Drive, at the western end of town close to the Settlers Monument. During the sixth Frontier War in 1834 parliament decided that it would be necessary to protect the barracks. The Royal Engineers who built the fort were commanded by Major Charles Jasper Selwyn. Between 1841 and 1868 the fort was used as an Artillery Barracks and a semaphore link – a mast was erected in the northeast corner – but then the army gave up using the building in 1870. During the Anglo-Boer War the fort served in the defence of Grahamstown, but by the 1920s it had once more been left to run down and become overgrown. It was not until the 1970s that the building finally got the restoration work it deserved and this was due to it being proclaimed a National Monument. Although it stands on the property of the Department of Nature and Environmental Conservation, it was given to the Albany Museum to use as exhibition space to further promote the history of Grahamstown. ■ *Open by prior appointment only. T6222312.*

The **1820 Settlers Monument** is, oddly, a large modern office block with rather a totalitarian feel to it. There is a series of rooms which include a conference hall, theatre and a restaurant. It overlooks the city and completely dominates its surrounds on Gunfire Hill. It was opened in July 1974, but in 1994 disaster struck and fire gutted the whole complex. The memorial is surrounded by the **Wild Flower Garden** which has displays of indigenous plants. The Botanical Garden has a recreation of a nostalgic old English garden, but more interestingly there is a huge collection of aloes, cycads, proteas and tree ferns. ■ *Daily 0800-1630, T62227115.*

An interesting new collection is the **International Library of African Music (ILAM)**, on Prince Alfred St. ILAM is a publishing and research centre for traditional African music, and houses a fascinating collection of musical instruments – there are over 200 traditional African instruments from across the continent. ■ *Mon-Fri 0830-1245, 1400-1700, T6038557.*

The **Cathedral of St Michael and St George** occupies its rightful position in the centre of town on Church Square. The style of this building is what is described as Early English Gothic, a 13th-century style, which the Victorians chose to revive in the late 19th century. Like similar buildings in Europe, the cathedral took generations to complete. Work started in 1824 and the first useable form was opened in 1830 as a single room church. In 1952 the Lady Chapel was completed and so the cathedral had taken 128 years to build. Look out for the memorial tablets which together provide a vivid history of Grahamstown as the frontier of the empire.

The **Priest's House**, on Beaufort Street, was built as a residence for the bishop and the clergy of the Catholic church. It is one of the finer buildings in Grahamstown and like the Observatory Museum has a connection with the identification of the Eureka diamond (see above). Because of this connection, the De Beers Group rescued the house in 1981, helped to partially restore the building and then oversaw the establishment of the **National English Literary Museum**. These days the research carried out behind the scenes is proving to be an important component in the understanding of the role of English as a national language of South Africa. There is a comprehensive collection of scholarly books, articles and press-clippings as well as a good bookshop. The house is also of interest. The façade is typical of the Cape during the 1800s – flat, with a colonnaded neo-Georgian portico.

The **Shaw Hall** is behind the Observatory Museum, but still in the High Street. It was inaugurated in December 1832 as a Methodist Church, and had three galleries and room for over 800 members. Once the Commemoration Church had been completed in 1850, the first building was turned over for use as a meeting hall. The Reverend William Shaw was a local missionary worker. The most important role the building played was on 25 April, 1864, when the Governor of the Cape Colony, Sir Philip Wodehouse, convened a session of parliament in the hall. This was part of a programme of tacit support for a movement that was trying to break away from the western part of the province and set up an independent government. Although nothing ever came of the idea, it was a clear indication of how serious the government took the threats of secession, since this was the only time that the Cape parliament ever sat outside of Cape Town.

Township tours The large township in Grahamstown is known as **Rhini** and lies to the east of the town across the river. Not surprisingly, most local whites will never have visited this part of their town and will know very little of it. Tourists, however, are offered a choice of township tours, with visits to a 'traditional' Xhosa family for a meal, as well as visiting craft centres and shebeens. Although these tours can seem rather tasteless and voyeuristic, some of them do bring income to the townships and provide a far broader view of the town. It's a good idea to choose a walking tour, rather than one in a mini-bus – this allows a greater degree of interaction with people, removing, to a degree, the sense of voyeurism. Mbuleli Mpokela organizes half-day tours, T6370630, T082-9795906 (mob).

Excursions The **Thomas Baines Nature Reserve** offers canoeing, fishing, sailing and windsurfing at Settlers Dam. There are 15 km of dirt tracks which pass through fynbos and bushveld inhabited by bontebok, black wildebeest, buffalo, eland, impala and white rhino – due to the elusive presence of the latter, walking is only allowed by the Oldenbergia Trail overnight hut. The reserve is 15 km from town next to the Great Fish River Reserve Complex. ■ *Contact the Eastern Cape Nature Conservation office for more information, T6227216, F6227270.*

Ecca Nature Reserve, is a small reserve, also 15 km from Grahamstown on the road to Fort Beaufort with two short nature trails.

Sleeping
■ *on map, page 352*
Price codes:
see inside front cover

B *Evelyn House*, High St, T6222366, F6222424, evelynhouse@albany.com A very fine guesthouse in a local landmark building dating from the 1800s. 4 double rooms, 2 luxury suites, a/c, laundry service, M-net TV, swimming pool, sauna, gym, secure off-street parking. Well-appointed accommodation, good value. Recommended. **B-C** *The Cock House*, 10 Market St, T/F6361287, cockhouse@imaginet.co.za Beautifully restored 1820s national monument with 7 double rooms with en suite bathrooms. Luxurious guesthouse with a good à la carte restaurant attached with a comfortable lounge and library. Peter and Belinda have clearly made a good impression – Nelson Mandela has stayed here twice. The first floor veranda is a particularly fine feature. Recommended.

C *137 High Street*, 137 High St, T6223242, 137highstr@xsinet.co.za Stylish hotel in a good location close to restaurants and sights. 7 luxurious rooms, en suite bath or shower, good service, attractive historical building, restaurant downstairs serving excellent breakfasts and snacks, as well as more substantial meals. **C** *Amberleigh*, 37 Southey St, T6224724, T082-7733983 (mob). Small B&B in a quiet suburb close to the university. 1 double room with en suite and 1 twin, choice of B&B or self-catering. **C** *Aucklands Country House*, T6222401, F6225682, www.aucklands.co.za A fine country house 8 km from the town centre off the N2 towards Port Elizabeth. 6 spacious rooms with en suite bathrooms, set in beautiful grounds with a swimming pool, tennis court, croquet lawn – horse riding and hikes nearby. Excellent meals, friendly owners. An extremely well-run guesthouse. Strongly recommended. **C** *Carlisle*, 1 Parker St, T6223980, louisa.clayton@ru.ac.za B&B in a fine old stone town house dating from the 1840s. 2 double rooms, non smoking, separate entrances. Swimming pool, off-street parking. Set in a peaceful mature garden. Recommended. **C** *Graham Protea*, 123 High St, T6222324, F6222424, grahotel@intekom.co.za Rather unattractive building but in a good location on the High St. 27 rooms with en suite bathrooms, TV, lounge. *Oasis* restaurant has a good local reputation, cocktail bar, laundry service, secure parking, comfortable town hotel within a short walk of the shops and sights, cheaper than most Proteas.

D *Atherfold's*, 16 Jacobus Uys Way, T6223393. Self-catering and B&B, a short drive from shops and university. 2 double rooms in the house with private bathrooms, 1 garden cottage with lounge, TV and kitchenette. Packed lunches available on request. **D** *Oak Lodge Guest-house*, 95 Bathurst St, T6229123, F6229124, oaklodge@albanyhotels.co.za Large historical building with a range of accommodation aimed at budgeting groups. 21 rooms, some sleeping 8, TV lounge, gardens, swimming pool, braai area, bar, secure parking. Tours arranged. A short walk from the town centre. **D** *The Hermitage*, 14 Henry St, T6361503. Beautifully restored house, a fine example of a villa built in the 1820s by an early British settler. 2 double rooms with en suite bathrooms and sitting room with TV, private entrance to each elegant suite. The neat gardens are a perfect complement to the house, breakfasts served on a veranda. Good value, strongly recommended, ask for Bea or Dick.

F *Municipal Caravan Park*, Grey St, T6036072. On the outskirts of town on the N2 heading towards Port Elizabeth. 48 sites for tents or caravans, communal ablution block and laundry room. The chalets and rondavels sleep up to 5 people in each. They are good value and should be reserved in advance. **F** *Old Gaol Backpackers*, Somerset St, T6361001, gsapelt@yebo.co.za An unusual and excellent place to stay. This is the only backpackers in Grahamstown, and is housed in an old Victorian gaol. Double rooms are in individual cells, complete with thick stone walls, domed ceilings, tiny barred windows and original graffiti. The dorms are housed in the communal cells. There is also a lounge with kitchen, TV room and nightly braais. The building is listed, so no work can be done on the original structure. While this gives the place a run-down (and rather too authentic) feel, the cells are spotless and the beds comfortable. Highly recommended as an atmospheric and unique backpackers.

Eating
● *on map, page 352*

The Cock House, 10 Market St, T6361287. Closed Sun lunch. Excellent restaurant which is part of a smart town guesthouse. Plenty of attention is given to presentation and quality of the country cuisine. If you don't fancy eating then enjoy a beer in the cosy bar with a light snack. *Calabash*, 123 High St, T6222324. Popular traditional South African restaurant specializing in Xhosa hotpots. Also have seafood, steaks and venison. *Dulce Café*, 112 High St. Café and ice cream parlour, excellent sandwiches made to order, ice cream sundaes, milkshakes and salads. *Ginos*, 8 New St, part of the *Victoria Hotel*. Good selection of pizza and pasta dishes, very popular, open daily. *Mad Hatter's*, 118 High St. Great café serving cooked breakfasts, sandwiches, good cheap burgers, delicious home-made cakes. *Monkey Puzzle*, Botanical Gardens, T6225318. Small restaurant serving average steaks, seafood and pasta. Cheap meals, shady beer garden overlooking the botanical gardens is very popular with boozy students, the place to head for a big night out. *Rat & Parrot*, 59 New St. A popular bar, choice of beers, meals also served, good value for lunch. *Steers*, High St. Cheap hamburgers and toasties, busy outlet found in most towns.

Many of the quality restaurants in town are in the main hotels. There are also plenty of cheap cafes and takeaways catering to the large student population

Festivals

In early **July**, Grahamstown hosts the famous 11-day *Standard Bank National Festival of Arts*, T6227115. This is undoubtedly one of the top cultural events in the country. Over 50,000 visitors are attracted to the town to watch a range of shows, which include theatre, dance, fine art, films, music, opera and an increasing variety of traditional crafts and art. Like many festivals, there are official events plus a huge range of fringe shows. The centre of the festival is the 1820 Settlers Monument. During this period accommodation gets booked very quickly, so book several months ahead, or phone the tourist office to check if any private homes are letting out rooms. During the festival the whole atmosphere of the town changes,

Check with the local tourist office for the exact dates and programme details

Eastern Cape

so if you are in the country at this time it is well worth a visit. In late **March** the town also hosts a large *Scifest*, T6223402, 4 days of lectures, exhibitions, work shops and sci-fi films.

Transport **Road Bus**: *Greyhound*, T041-3634555. Buses depart from the corner of Bathurst and High streets by the conference centre. **Cape Town** (12 hrs): daily, 1915, via **Plettenberg Bay**, **George** and **Swellendam**. **Durban** (12 hrs): daily, 0910, via **East London**, **Umtata**, **Kokstad** and **Port Shepstone**. **Port Elizabeth** (2 hrs): daily, 2105.

Leopard Express, T046-6224589. A quick daily return service to **Port Elizabeth**.

Translux, T041-5071333. Coaches depart from outside the *Conference Centre*, Bathurst St. The town tourist office acts as a local booking agent. **Cape Town**: daily, 1740, via **Graaff-Reinet**. **Durban** (12 hrs): daily, 0825, via **East London**, **Umtata**, **Kokstad** and **Port Shepstone**. **Port Elizabeth** (2 hrs): daily, 0825.

Coast Road to Port Alfred

Alexandria
Phone code: 046
(NB Always use
3-figure prefix)
Colour map 7, grid B5

The coastal route follows the R72. Around 100 km from Port Elizabeth is the small town of Alexandria, a farming centre for pineapple and chicory growers. The dune forests between Alexandria and the coast are a unique environment and interesting to explore on a hike. The **grave of Nonquase** is on a nearby farm. In 1856 Nonquase had a vision in which her ancestors claimed that a mass slaughter of cattle and the destruction of crops would liberate the Xhosa from the ever encroaching European settlers. This sacrifice had disastrous consequences and many thousands of people died of starvation. Nonquase herself was forced to spend the rest of her life in hiding.

Alexandria
State Forest
Nature Reserve

On the coast to the south of Alexandria between the Bushman's River and the Sundays River is an area of dunes and coastal forest. There is no large game here but this is the habitat of the hairy-footed gerbil which is unique to this area. The forests are good for birdwatching and along the coast it is possible to see dolphins and the Damara tern. There are many easy trails passing along the beach and into the forest. The longest trail, for which permits are necessary, is the **Alexandria Trail**. It is 36 km long and is a well-marked two-day circular trail. The first day takes you from the base camp at Langebos through forest down to the coastal dunefield which extends for 120 km up the coast. One night is spent in the hut at Woody Cape. In the morning the trail then heads back across farmland in the Langevlakte Valley and back to Langebos.

Permits for the trail are available from the Alexandria Conservation Office, T046-6530601. Maximum 12 people, a popular trail over weekends. Take precautions against ticks. **F** *Hiking Huts*, there are 2 huts, both sleeping 12 people on bunks and mattresses; the hut at base camp has toilets and cold showers, whilst at the overnight hiking hut at Woody Cape you'll be using rain water to wash with.

Island
Conservation
Area

This area lies next to the Alexandria Forest. The woodland here is similar to the tropical forests in KwaZulu Natal but has adapted to the drier conditions of the Eastern Cape. There are more than 40 different species of tree which can be seen from several trails which cross the forest.

The **Bosbock Walk**, 16 km, is a good day's walk through indigenous dune forest. The walk begins and ends at the Forester's House and there are several short cuts back to the entrance if you decide you've had enough. Contact the Alexandria Conservation Office, T046-6530601, for details of permits.

Kenton-on-Sea
Phone code: 046
(NB Always use
3-figure prefix)
Colour map 7, grid B5

The R72 continues from Alexandria for 30 km to Kenton-on-Sea, between the estuaries of the Bushman's and the Kariega Rivers. This is a pleasant seaside town with a beautiful beach, huge sand dunes and a lagoon. The pace of life is slow here, despite the resort being very popular with domestic travellers. The town caters mainly for family holidays and the emphasis is on organized entertainment, not nightlife. Activities are low-key and include walking on the beach, tennis, squash, bowls, golf, angling and a popular canoe trail up the Bushman's River. The local birdwatchers club is a mine of information on local sites. **Tourist information** is available at *Kenton-on-Sea Tourism*, T6482418, mcnulty@xsinet.co.za The Intercape Coach stops here.

There is a monument 6 km from the centre of town which is a replica of a stone cross erected there by Bartolomeu Dias. There is a short walking trail which leads here. **Joan Muirhead Nature Reserve** was created in 1960 to protect the land between the Bushman's and the Kariega Rivers. At 20 ha it is relatively small but this stretch of high dunes covered in thick forest is a very pleasant area to explore on foot.

Emlanjeni Reserve is a private nature reserve set beside the Bushman's River. It offers luxury accommodation to guests but it is open to the public for day visits. The reserve is well-stocked with game and is rich in birdlife. *T046-6481203 for reservations*

Sleeping Most of the accommodation around Kenton-on-Sea consists of self-catering cottages and holiday homes. Prices rise sharply during the South African holiday season. **D** *Burke's Nest*, 38 Van der Stel St, T6481894, jlburke@border.co.za Cottage and self-contained flat set in gardens, secure parking, B&B or self-catering. **D** *Woodside*, 27 Bathurst Rd, T6481802, tgen15@mweb.co.za Homely and old-fashioned B&B, 2 mins from beach, en suite rooms, TV, breakfast served on a sunny terrace, braai area. *Price codes: see inside front cover*

Eating The *Homewoods*, T6481363, Eastbourne Rd, Kenton. A split-level restaurant and bar right by the Kariega river. Check out their fresh seafood. *Sandbar*, Bushman's River Mouth, T6482192. A floating restaurant open daily.

Tour operators *Kelly's Tours*, T6482545, organizes tours throughout the region including scuba diving, game viewing, historical tours and accommodation.

Port Alfred

Port Alfred consists almost entirely of holiday homes and bungalows nestling into dunes. It is one of the largest holiday resorts on this stretch of coastline, and overlooks large expanses of water in all directions: the Kowie River, the lagoon and the smart Royal Alfred Marina, where many local people keep their power boats. The town's history is closely linked to the 1820 Settlers and there is a small **Methodist church** 1 km out of town whose cemetery makes for an interesting visit. Many of the names on the gravestones are those of original settlers. *Phone code: 046 (NB Always use 3-figure prefix) Colour map 7, grid B5*

The weather on this coast is mild all year round and Port Alfred has a wide range of facilities to offer tourists. Walks through the **dune forests** are always pleasant but for the more intrepid, there is a **scuba diving school** which organizes trips to nearby reefs, as well as facilities for **canoeing** and **game fishing**. The **Fish River Casino** and **St Francis Spa** are both nearby and are popular excursions from town. The regional **tourist office** is the Port Alfred division of *Ndlambe Tourism*, Van der Riet St, T6241235, patourism@intekom.co.za Open Mon-Fri, 0830-1600; Sat, 0830-1200.

The **Oribi Hiking Trail** is a network of guided trails on Kasouga Farm, 3 km from Port Alfred. The farm has two B&B cottages known as Oribi Haven. All the trails are relatively easy walks across rolling dunes overlooking the sea. The longest possible walk here is around 20 km, but the guides are flexible and quite happy to go on shorter walks to specific areas. The wildlife which inhabits the area is mostly small mammals like the bushpig, duiker and jackal. The range of birdlife is a mixture of coastal and grassland species. ■ *Reservations for accommodation and information on walks from Oribi Haven, T6482043, www.oribihaven.cjb.net*

Eastern Cape

Eastern Cape

Sleeping

■ on map
Price codes:
see inside front cover

There is no longer a backpacker hostel in Port Alfred, but there are 3 camp sites

B *Halyards*, Royal Alfred Marina, off Albany Rd, T6242410, F6242466, ramch@intekom.co.za Smartest hotel in Port Alfred, provides luxury accommodation for the wealthy set during peak holiday periods. During quiet periods, however, you should find some bargain room rates on offer. Spacious a/c rooms with all mod-cons, good views of the marina. 2 restaurants, bar, swimming pool, pleasant grounds. **B** *Victoria* , PO Box 2, T6241133, F6241134. Comfortable family-run hotel just off the coastal road. Old-fashioned rooms, mainly aimed at business people, restaurant, conference facilities. Should be possible to negotiate discounts during the quiet season.

C *Albany Guest Farm*, T6751179. 4 km off the R72 between Port Alfred and East London. Although this farm is 23 km outside Port Alfred, it is a lovely spot and well worth a stay. There are 3 luxurious cottages, with rustic décor, bathrooms, self-catering or B&B, tennis courts, good views. Recommended. **C** *Ferndale Guest Lodge*, 13 Ferndale Rd, T/F6244894. Attractive colonial-style Cape building with 4 comfortable en suite rooms, TV, private entrances, secure parking, full breakfasts included. **C** *Ferrymans*, Beach Rd, T/F6241122. An old hotel situated right on the beach next to the river. Double rooms with en suite bathrooms. Good value restaurant and a lively bar, both of which tend to be popular with local residents over the weekend. *Settlers Sands*, T6241110, info@remaxkowie.co.za Self-catering chalets. **C-D** *Coral Guest Cottages*, PO Box 2427, T6242849. Settler-style cottage with 2 en suite double rooms, with fridge and TV, sunny veranda, off-street parking. Ask for Cynthia.

D *First Stop*, 15 van Riebeek St, T6344917. Spotless en suite rooms with TV, secure parking, 24-hr breakfasts. **D** *Kowie Beach Cabanas*, right on West Beach, T6245222, F6244455. Self-catering beach cabins, two double bedrooms, well-equipped kitchen. Popular during local school holidays, book well in advance.

E-F *Medolino Caravan Park*, 23 Stewart Rd, T/F6241651, dvicyor@global.co.za This is a medium sized park with 68 sites, managed by Club Caraville. Well-grassed and plenty of shade, electric points, electric lights and a well-equipped laundry and heated pool. Tents are allowed and you can hire a caravan.

F *Riverside Caravan Park*, Mentone Rd, T6242230. A pleasant site on the banks of the Kowie River, tents not allowed, TV lounge, laundry, pool, electric points, grassy, self-catering. **D** Chalets also available for hire, 29 caravan sites. **F** *Willow's Caravan Park*, right next to the bridge in the centre of town, T6245201. Camping and caravan sites with electric points, central wash blocks, lush grounds. Gets very busy over the Christmas period. Not too far to walk to the beach for families.

Eating

● on map

Barnacles, Royal Alfred Marina, T6245330. Popular pub overlooking the water, specializes in steaks and has nightly entertainment, including live music and karaoke. *Buck & Hunter*, Main St, T6245960. Relaxed restaurant serving good seafood, steaks and pub

Port Alfred

N

0 metres 100
0 yards 100

■ **Sleeping**
1 Coral Guest Cottages
2 Ferndale
3 Ferrymans
4 Halyards
5 Kowie Beach Cabanas
6 Victoria Protea
7 Willow's Caravan Park

● **Eating**
1 Barnacle's
2 Buch & Hunter
3 Butlers
4 Guido's on the Beach

lunches. *Butlers*, 25 Van der Riet St, T6241398. Restaurant-cum-pub with a lively atmosphere. Pub snack menu served on the open deck overlooking the river, or eat inside in a slightly more formal setting with a more pricey menu. The fresh fish is excellent. *Guido's on the Beach*, West Beach, T6245264. Open daily till late. The restaurant serves great pizzas and pasta dishes along with seafood and steaks. There is a busy bar upstairs with great views across the waves. *The Halyard*, Halyards Hotel, Royal Alfred Marina, T6242410. One of the smartest options, good seafood and traditional meat dishes, good service and views across the marina.

Canoeing *Kowie Canoe Trail*, information, T6242230. A very popular 22 km trail in the **Sports** Kowie Nature Reserve. See below for full details. Recommended – great for a few days break from the road.

Eco-tours There are several local nature guides who will take you bird watching or game viewing, usually on foot. *Anne Williams*, T6751976. *Paul Martin*, T4665698, apmartin@global.co.za

Horse riding The roads that access the most beautiful and remote beaches and river valleys are poor, which means that horses are often the best mode of transport. If you have never ridden before, this is a good place to learn. *Rufanes River Horseback*, T6241469, T082-6971297 (mob). Trails through rolling hills, milkwoods, dunes and along beaches. Experienced guides, can pace to any level. Ask for Dave or Allison. *Three Sisters Farm*, 15 km along the R72 towards East London, T6751269. Beach trails, forest dune trails, family outings, as well as 2-3 day safaris with game viewing on horseback.

Scuba diving *Keryn's Dive School*, T6244432. A variety of courses available, plus daily dives for certified scuba divers. The nearby reef has some fine corals and there are some popular wreck dives. The water is not too warm and nor is the visibility that good.

Bus The only bus that runs from Port Alfred is the *Minilux*, T043-7413107, Tue and Thu, 0845 **Transport** from *Halyards Hotel*, to **Port Elizabeth** and **East London**. The *Baz Bus* no longer stops here.

Banks *Standard Bank* and *First National*, both in Govan Mbeki Av. **Medical Services** Chemists: **Directory** *Port Alfred Pharmacy*, Govan Mbeki Av. **Emergencies** Medical, police or fire: 10111.

This reserve lies along the banks of the Kowie River, about 5 km from Port Alfred on **Kowie Nature** the Bathurst road. It passes through a thickly forested canyon and offers walking **Reserve** trails and a well-run canoe trail, which has turned this into one of the most popular nature reserves in the region.

The **Kowie Canoe Trail** is about 24 km in total and takes two days to complete. The first day is spent paddling 22 km up the Kowie River from Port Alfred to the forests of the Kowie Nature Reserve where you then spend the night in the reserve hut. On the second day you can attempt the 8 km walking trail, following yellow 'footprints'. One of the more popular parts of the hike is a steep climb up the escarpment from where you are rewarded with a perfect view of the horseshoe bend in the river below. Look out for the small mammals found here, such as duiker and bushbuck; both are very shy and well-camouflaged. There are plenty of shorter walks across the gentle hills and through the forests along with a number of picnic sites, braai facilities and toilets. Please remove all your litter, and collect any bottles and cans left by less considerate visitors.

The trail is easily completed in half a day, which can be followed by canoeing back to Port Alfred. Canoes can be rented in town. If you have any queries ask in advance when you collect the canoes. It should take no more than 4 hours to reach the hut, but if you are not a regular in a canoe give yourself plenty of breaks – your arms will be stiff by the end of the day. Make a note of when the tide will be coming in and going out and try to plan your trip to coincide with the flow each time. This will make the journey far more fun and less tiring.

Permits for the Kowie Canoe Trail and overnight hut are available from the local Cape Nature Conservation office in Port Alfred, T046-6242230. Like many reserves in South Africa, the

Eastern Cape

number of people allowed on the trail at any one time is limited. In this case the limit is 12. As noted above, this trail is very popular and consequently it can get fully booked up to 6 months in advance, especially over weekends. However, it is always worth checking to see if there have been any last minute cancellations or no shows. Rates are R80 per person, including the hire of a 2-person canoe. **F** *Horseshoe Reserve Hut*, is a simple hut sleeping up to 12 people. Remember to bring all your camping supplies; the only cooking facilities are a braai area.

King Williamstown

Phone code: 043
(NB Always use 3-figure prefix)
Colour map 7, grid B6

The London Missionary Society established a mission station here in 1826 and over the years the town has grown into an important commercial centre. There are some old Victorian buildings here, but little else to keep you for long. Most travellers visit King Williamstown on their way to East London or Stutterheim and Hogsback. For **tourist information**, contact the *King Williamstown Municipality*, T6423450.

King Williamstown Nature Reserve is a small reserve lying just north of town. It is an area of dense bush with several well-marked nature trails. **Pirie Forest** is 12 km further on, on the road to Stutterheim. This is an area of thick yellowwood and white stinkwood forest and is the start of the **Amatola Hiking Trail** (see page 361).

Sleeping **B** *Crown Hotel*, T6423025, has a restaurant as does **B** *Grosvenor Lodge*, T6047200.

Transport **Bus** *Greyhound*, T041-3634555. Coaches depart from the Engen One Stop (Wimpy), Cathcart St. **Cape Town** (16 hrs): daily, 1745. **Durban** (10 hrs): daily, 1040, 1125. **East London**, daily, 0600. **Johannesburg** and **Pretoria** (12 hrs): daily 1800, 2000. **Port Elizabeth** (3 hrs): daily, 0545.

Translux, T041-3921333. Coaches depart from the BP service station on Alexander Rd. **Cape Town** (16 hrs): daily, 1620, 1700. **Durban** (5 hrs): daily, 0945. **East London** (45 mins): daily, 1755.

Amatola Mountains and the Cape Midlands

Colour map 7, grid A5

The mountainous region lying between Stutterheim and Fort Beaufort is a beautiful area of rolling hills, lush indigenous forests and waterfalls. The strange and magical landscape was an inspiration for Tolkien whilst creating Middle Earth for his 'Lord of the Rings'. Sadly, some areas have now been replaced with pine plantations. Nevertheless, there remains an abundance of unharmed forest, criss-crossed with trails and perfect for hiking.

Ins & outs **Getting there** From King Williamstown to Queenstown there are two routes. The first follows the R63 west to Fort Beaufort and then heads north along the R67 to Queenstown. The second route heads north via Stutterheim and Cathcart via the N6. The Amatola Mountains can be reached from both sides. Queenstown is one of the easiest points of entry as it is connected by coach services running inland from Port Elizabeth and East London to Bloemfontein and Johannesburg. For further information, see page 364.

The **best time to visit** the area is during the spring or autumn, as in winter it can get very cold and it is not unusual to have snow in May. Most of the rain tends to fall during the summer months.

Hogsback

Phone code: 045
(NB Always use 3-figure prefix)
Colour map 7, grid A5
Altitude: 1,200 m

The quiet village of Hogsback lies in the centre of the Amatola mountains, surrounded by rolling hills covered in forest reserves. The village itself has no real centre, but is made up of a string of cottages, hotels, tea gardens and craft shops dotted along several kilometres of gravel road. Tucked away down the side lanes are some beautiful gardens, more reminiscent of rural England than inland Africa. The beautiful surroundings and slow pace of life makes this a delightful spot to rest up for a few days and explore the forests.

Hiking in the Amatola Mountains

Amatola Hiking Trails Permits for hiking in the Amatola Mountains are available from Contour, PO Box 186 Bisho, 5600, T0401-952115. They will provide maps and brochures for the trails. The Amatola Hiking Trail begins 23 km from King Williamstown and ends 3 km from Hogsback. The trails are strenuous and do involve steep climbs up to grasslands on the plateau. The forested areas are some of the most beautiful sections of the trail. The high forest canopy is shady and cool during hot weather. The many pools and waterfalls are also attractive and are a good place to spot rare amphibians. The trail passes through the **Auckland Nature Reserve** where bird watchers should look out for the red-billed hornbill, African orioles and Knysna parrots.

The best time of year to walk the trail is during the summer months. The trail is only open to a maximum of 16 people at any one time. Hikers need to be totally self-sufficient, the overnight huts are only fitted with mattresses.

Stutterheim and Kologha Hiking Trails Permits are available from Kubusi State Forest, Stutterheim, T0436-31546. The trail is 35 km long and takes two days. The hike starts at Isidenge Forest Station and descends through yellowwood forest past many waterfalls to an overnight hut close to the Gubu Dam. The hut has cooking facilities and an ablution block. The hike ends the next day at Kologha Forest Station. The Eagles Ridge Hotel is a few kilometres from the end of the trail.

Eastern Cape

There are several theories as to how the area got its name. One is that a peak in the Hogsback range resembles the back of a hog when viewed from a particular angle. The other is that the founder was a Captain Hogg who had been based at **Fort Mitchell**. The Xhosa name for the peaks is *Belekazana* (to carry on the back), as another view from a different angle resembles a woman carrying a child on her back. There are three peaks which can be seen from the village, Hog One (1,836 m), Hog Two (1,824 m) and Hog Three (1,937 m). The highest peak in the region lies to the north of Hogsback and is known as Elandsberg (2,019 m).

There is a helpful **tourist office** on Main Road next to the Purple Chameleon pub, open Mon-Fri 1030-1230, 1500-1700, and Sat 1030-1230. For enquiries out of office hours, call T9621234.

One highlight in the surrounding forests are the spectacular **waterfalls**. The most popular falls are known as **Madonna and Child**, **Kettle Spout** and the **39 Steps Falls**. The Madonna and Child falls are a 30-minute walk from a car park on Wolfridge Road, 5 km from the village centre. The easiest falls to visit are the 39 Steps, which are 10 minutes' walk from the end of Oak Avenue. Look out for a green pig with a red triangle. If you're staying at *Away with the Fairies* (see Sleeping below), there's a good one hour walk to the **Swallowtail Falls**, where you'll pass an impressive 'big tree' and see plenty of vervet monkeys and birdlife.

A short distance from the centre of the village is the church of **St Patrick on the Hill**. The original chapel dates from 1935. Just beyond the church is a track off to the right, Gaika Road, which leads up to the view point **Gaika Kop** (1,963 m). The path is not very easy to follow – get a local map from one of the hotels before you set off.

Some of the finest views are from **Tor Doone** (1,565 m), weather permitting. The easiest path follows the fire break at the end of Oak Avenue. Look out for markers with a yellow pig and a single green stripe; the contour path is marked with a green pig and yellow dot. Allow a minimum of two hours to get to the top.

NB If you are here during the winter months, remember that the weather gets very cold at night. Even in summer, the nights are cold and a warm clear morning can quickly develop into low cloud and thunderstorms which may take a day or two to clear. If in doubt, check with local people who should be able better to interpret the vagaries of the weather.

Local hikes
If you wish to go further afield ask at the tourist office for details of the longer hiking trails in the area. See box above for more information on hiking in the area

Sleeping
■ *on map*
Price codes
see inside front cover

In addition to the options listed below there are more than 20 different self-catering establishments. If you plan on hiking in the region, these may be more convenient than staying in a lodge or hotel where meal times are fixed. Contact the local tourist office for further details. Be sure to book ahead during local school holidays.

C *Arminel Mountain Lodge*, T9621005. 24 log cabins with en suite facilities, excellent restaurant serving meals based on local fresh produce. Room rates include evening meal. Extensive gardens, swimming pool, tennis. The management is very friendly and keen to further promote this beautiful area which few overseas travellers visit. Recommended. **C** *Hogsback Inn*, Wolf Ridge Rd, T9621006, F9621015. Old-fashioned rural retreat with 31 comfortable (if chintzy) rooms. There is a good restaurant and a cosy, traditional pub, as well as a swimming pool and tennis court. Log fires greatly add to the ambience. Very friendly and a good place to meet local folk. **C** *King's Lodge*, Main Rd, T9621024, F9621058. 25 rooms with en suite bathroom, popular restaurant, bar, fine wood-panelled lounge and reception area. Large garden with a swimming pool and tennis court. Self-catering rooms also available. **D** *Hyde Park Chalets*, Main Rd, T9621069. Self-catering set-up with comfortable chalets, double rooms, en suite bathrooms and kitchens, nice green surrounds. **F** *Away with the Fairies*, T9621031. One of the best hostels in the country, a friendly, relaxed and well-run place. Well-kept, brightly painted dorms, double rooms, one new caravan (sleeps 2), well-equipped kitchen, clean bathrooms and cosy lounge with fireplace. The surrounding gardens are beautiful with plenty of camping space and a gate that leads to forest trails. There's a lively bar, great breakfasts and evening meals, daily guided walks and sundowner trips, 3 weekly shuttles to Sugarshack in East London. The manager, Dan, makes sure that everyone feels very welcome and that there's always plenty to do. Highly recommended. **F** *The Edge*, off Woodside Rd, T9621159. Well-kept caravan and camping site with plenty of leafy plots, cooking facilities, some self-catering chalets. Make sure your tent is waterproof and that you have a good sleeping bag. It often rains in the summer and nights can be cold due to the altitude.

Hogsback

Sleeping
1 Arminel Mountain Lodge
2 Away with the Fairies
3 Hogsback Inn
4 Hyde Park Chalets
5 King's Lodge

Eating
1 High-on-the-Hog
2 Purple Chameleon

Eastern Cape

Eating
• *on map*

The main hotels include dinner in their room rate, so there is not much of a choice for eating out at night. If you are staying at a guesthouse, check if evening meals are available.

High-on-the-Hog, Main Rd. The only local restaurant, with good nightly specials. Great soups (don't miss the creamed butternut), steaks and pasta dishes. Fairly new, so prices are still low. ***Purple Chameleon***, Main Rd. Simple pub serving hearty lunch and dinner, focus on steaks and burgers, popular local drinking hole.

Shopping

There is one supermarket, a bottle store and a petrol station in town (**NB** that there aren't any banks). Otherwise, there are several craft shops which sell gifts as well as delicious locally made jams. Look out for ***Stasways Pottery***, Plaatjieskraal Rd; ***Storm Haven*** and ***Arminel Crafts*** on Main Rd. When you first arrive in the village you are likely to be greeted by local Xhosas selling their crafts. Look out for the clay animals: kudu, horses and hogs are the most common. These items are not found elsewhere in South Africa.

Directory

Communications Internet: You can access the internet at the cyber café in *Amatola Guesthouse* on Main Rd. **Post Office**: Main Rd. Open Mon-Fri, 0900-1300; 1400-1600. There are public **telephones** next door which take phone cards. **Useful addresses** The **police station** is next to *King's Lodge*. **Forest fires**, T9621055.

Eastern Cape

Fort Beaufort
Phone code: 046
(NB Always use 3-figure prefix)
Colour map 7, grid B5

Fort Beaufort came into being as a garrison fort in 1823 during the Fifth Frontier War. The fort was built as part of a chain of forts designed to protect the eastern borders of the colony. Today the town is an important farming centre for the large citrus farms located along the Kat river. Cattle ranching and sheep farming are also important to the local economy. The town **museum** in Durban Street has some interesting displays recording the events of the various Frontier wars. **Tourist information** is available from the *Publicity Association*, Historical Museum, Durban Street, T6451555.

Sleeping C ***Savoy Hotel***, Durban St, T6451146. 8 en suite rooms, restaurant, bar, swimming pool. A straightforward town hotel. There are several B&Bs in town, ask at tourist office.

Fort Fordyce Nature Reserve

This small mountain reserve, 14 km north of Fort Beaufort on the R67, is named after Lieutenant Colonel Fordyce, a British soldier killed here during the bloody Frontier Wars. It is stocked with Burchell's zebra, wildebeest, mountain reedbuck, red hartebeest, kudu and bushbuck, plus a few smaller mammals such as blue duiker, klipspringer and wild cat. The vegetation is a mix of open grassland and patches of indigenous hardwood forests in the steep ravines. There is a good network of clearly marked trails, plus some magnificent views of the Hogsback Mountains.

Sleeping There is a simple overnight hut with a fridge and hot water. Check with the Publicity Association in Fort Beaufort, T046-6451555, to ensure that the hut is still open. Many remote hiking huts have not been maintained in recent years as funds are directed to more pressing needs in the new South Africa.

Cathcart
Phone code: 045
(NB Always use 3-figure prefix)
Colour map 7, grid A5

On the slopes of the Windvogelberg, Cathcart is named after Sir George Cathcart who was the governor of the Cape between 1852-54. The first settlers purchased land in the area in 1858 at the end of the Eighth Frontier War between the colonial powers and the Xhosa. Initially the town developed as a centre for cattle and merino sheep farms; these days it also acts as a popular base from which to explore the Amatola Mountains. Visitors to the area will find a corner of South Africa that few travellers have seen. A new tourist office was being built at time of writing; in the meantime visitors can contact the local library for **tourist information**, T8431022.

Sleeping C ***Royal Hotel***, Caernarvon St, T8431145. With a restaurant.

Transport Train *The Amatola Express*, runs daily to **Johannesburg** (17 hrs): at 1522, via **Queenstown** and **Bloemfontein**. To **East London** (3 hrs): daily at 0517.

Bus *Greyhound*, T041-3634555. Coaches depart from the Eastern Cape Agricultural Co-op. **Bloemfontein** (5 hrs): daily, 1900. **East London** (2 hrs): daily, 0430. *Translux*, T041-3921333. Coaches depart from the Eastern Cape Agricultural Co-op. **Cape Town** (13 hrs): daily, 1805. **East London** (2 hrs): daily, 0520, 0650. **Johannesburg** and **Pretoria** (11 hrs): daily, 1850.

Queenstown
Phone code: 045
(NB Always use 3-figure prefix)
Colour map 7, grid A5

Queenstown is the largest town in the Cape midlands and was named after Queen Victoria. Like many settlements in the area, it only started to thrive once the Frontier Wars had ended. However, the central square in the town was designed with defence in mind. Known today as the Hexagon, the square has six main streets radiating off it like spokes on a wheel. The idea was that defenders would have a clear line of fire to the outskirts of town from the fortified central square. There are two small museums in town, the **Frontier Museum** and the **Queenstown Collectors'**. Most of the collection is devoted to the achievements of the early settlers and the Frontier Wars. For anyone interested in South African place names, the library is well worth a visit. It contains a collection compiled by the Reverend Charles Pettman, a local Methodist minister.

Ask at the tourist office for directions and access to some local **rock art** which is reported to be some of the finest in South Africa. For **tourist information** on Queenstown, Cathcart and Tarkastad contact the *Queenstown Publicity Association*, 8 Owen St, T8932265.

Sleeping C *Hotel Hexagon*, 4 Hexagon Rd, T4513015. Comfortable hotel with 49 rooms, en suite, TV, restaurant, bar and café. C *Jeantel Hotel*, Shepstone St, T4513016. 24 rooms, en suite, TV lounge, a Chinese restaurant and bar.

Transport Rail: *The Amatola Express*, runs a daily service to **Johannesburg** (16 hrs): departs at 1655, via **Bloemfontein** (8 hrs). To **East London** (5 hrs): departs daily at 0400, via **Cathcart**.

Road Bus: *Greyhound*, T041-3634555. Coaches depart from Shell Ultra City on Cathcart St. Towards **Johannesburg** and **Pretoria**, daily, 1945, 2215, via **Bloemfontein** (5 hrs). To **Port Elizabeth** (5 hrs): daily at 0415, via **Grahamstown** (3 hrs).

There is also a *Translux* coach service, T041-3921333, also departing from Shell Ultra City. To **Port Elizabeth** (4 hrs): daily, 0315; **Johannesburg** and **Pretoria**, (10 hrs), via **Bloemfontein**, daily, 2315.

Tsolwana Game Park

This unusual park covers an area of typical semi-arid Karoo grasslands. Several exotic species have been introduced here and it is possible to see Corsican mouflon, Himalayan tahr and Indian black buck. Some of the more traditional game park animals are also interesting to spot including Cape mountain zebra, giraffe, springbok, steenbok and, if you're lucky, white rhino. It is possible to organize a hike in the reserve, but you have to be accompanied by a game ranger. Contact: The Director, Tsolwana Game Reserve, Queenstown, T0408-22104.

Tsolwana is 55 km south of Queenstown on the road to Whittlesea. 20 km after leaving Queenstown there is a signpost to the park down the Upper Swart Kei Road. The last few kilometres of the journey are on a dirt road.

Price codes: see inside front cover

Sleeping There are 3 lodges here all of which are self-catering. T0401-952115. Meals can be prepared but this must be arranged in advance. Close to the main entrance and park offices is **A-B** *Indwe Lodge*, which can sleep a maximum of 8 people. This is a converted farmstead dating from the 19th century. **A-B** *Otterford Lodge*, can accommodate up to 10 people and has a tennis court. It is located along the banks of the Swart Kei river. **A** *Lilyfontein Lodge*, can sleep 16 people and has a swimming pool. This is a fine old farmhouse with a characteristically large veranda. Each lodge is fully serviced. Advance reservations are advised. Further into the park there are 2 simple self-catering camps equipped with only a wood stove and a cold shower. **E** *Pumlani Trail Camp* and *Fundani Trail Camp*. Reservations as above.

Witteberge

The Witteberge Mountains are rather grandly known as the 'Switzerland of South Africa', forming part of the southernmost limits of the Drakensberg. It is the heart of South Africa's skiing industry but is probably more interesting for its Khoisan paintings. The road heading into the Witteberge passes through the small towns of Elliot, Lady Grey and Rhodes.

This small mountain town is handily placed for visiting the 32-m long gallery of Khoisan paintings on Denorbin Farm, on the road to Barkly East. Thompson Dam is a popular local picnic spot, and just out of town is the start of the 39-km long **Ecowa Hiking Trail**. Like many such trails the number of hikers are restricted. Contact the local tourist office for full details. For **tourist information**, contact the *Elliot Publicity Association*, T9311011.

Elliot
Phone code: 045
(NB Always use 3-figure prefix)
Colour map 7, grid A6

Sleeping C *Mountain Shadows*, 25 km north of Elliot on the R58, T9312233, T9311139.

This is one of South Africa's few ski resorts as there are snowfalls on the mountains here most winters. This area is popular with visitors all year round, attracting skiers in winter and fly fishermen in the summer. This is also a good area to see Khoisan paintings, and there are some good hiking trails.

There is a well-known **steam railway (Zigzag Railway)** which descends from Barkly East to Lady Grey and then on to Aliwal North, a total distance of 160 km. The route is so steep that the line has eight switchbacks. The Town Clerk's Office will arrange excursions for steam train enthusiasts. Trains usually leave from Aliwal North very early in the morning and arrive in Barkly East around 1300. For **tourist information** contact the *Barkly East Tourism Association*, T8392265.

Barkly East
Phone code: 045
(NB Always use 3-figure prefix)
Colour map 4, grid B4
Altitude: 1,183 m

Sleeping C *Old Mill Inn*, White St, T9710277, has B&B.

Rhodes is a peaceful little mountain ski resort, with good access to nearby Tiffindell, the most popular ski area in South Africa. There is a ski lift, snow-making machines and ski hire. The peak of Ben MacDhui overlooks the town and stands at 3,000 m high; there is a hiking trail here during the summer with superb views. Contact T9710446 for trail information. The resort is also popular during the summer with fly fishermen, mountain bikers and riders. For **tourist information** contact T7879090, tiffindell@global.co.za (winter), T9749004 (summer).

Rhodes
Phone code: 045
(NB Always use 3-figure prefix)
Colour map 4, grid C5

Sleeping C *Rhodes Hotel*, T9749305. Charming old-style hotel, B&B rates, tennis court, local tours and horse riding organized.

Lady Grey lies in a forested valley surrounded by the high peaks of the Witteberge. For **tourist information** contact the municipality, T6030019. The **Karringmelkspruit Vulture Reserve** is 12 km south of Lady Grey on the road to Barkly East. Over 500 Cape vultures breed on the cliffs of this reserve.

Lady Grey
Phone code: 051
(NB Always use 3-figure prefix)
Colour map 4, grid B4

Sleeping C-D *Mountain View Country Inn*, T6030421, F6030114. A pleasant rural retreat with a lovely view over the town towards the mountains. Family and double rooms with en suite bathroom. Nicely decorated, excellent homemade food, especially the scones and marmalade.

Aliwal North lies on the south bank of the Orange River. The hot springs have been turned into a health spa with pools, saunas and a gym. **Buffelspruit Nature Reserve** lies to the east of town, where a limited number of game animals can be seen. For **tourist information** contact local municipality, T6332441.

Aliwal North
Phone code: 051
(NB Always use 3-figure prefix)
Colour map 4, grid C4

Sleeping B *Aliwal Health Springs*, T6332951. Restaurant, swimming pool, tennis courts. **B** *Spa Hotel*, T6342189, F6342008. Closest hotel to the springs, has a restaurant. **C** *Balmoral Hotel*, T6332453. B&B.

Transport Bus: *Greyhound*, T041-3634555, coaches depart from *Balmoral Hotel*. **Pretoria** and **Johannesburg**, daily, 0015, via **Bloemfontein**. **Port Elizabeth** (7 hrs): daily at 0145. *Translux*, T041-3921333. Depart from *Balmoral Hotel*. **East London** (5 hrs): daily, 0255, via **Queenstown**, **Johannesburg** and **Pretoria** (8 hrs): daily at 2155, via **Bloemfontein** (2½ hrs).

East London

Phone code: 043
(NB Always use
3-figure prefix)
Colour map 7, grid B6

East London is South Africa's only river port and a major industrial centre, with an economy based on motor assembly plants, textile and electronics industries. Nevertheless, the city centre has a certain energetic appeal to it, as well as a handful of attractive historical buildings. There are also surprisingly beautiful beaches which get very busy with domestic tourists over Christmas. Nahoon Beach is best known for its excellent surfing, and the city has attracted a real surfing community in recent years. Despite this, most travellers only pass through on their way to other coastal resorts or to the Amatola Mountains.

Ins and outs

Getting there **Ben Schoeman Airport** is 11 km from city centre. There is transport to and from the centre
For all transport with an airport shuttle service which runs to the centre of town, T082-5693599 (mob). The
details, see page 370 larger car hire groups have a counter at the airport. The **railway** terminus is on Station St;
information, T7002118 or T7402020. There are **bus** services to most South African cities from
Greyhound, *Intercape*, *Minilux* and *Translux*. The *Baz Bus* also stops here.

Tourist offices The main tourist office covers the region from East London to King Williamstown, and is
known as *Buffalo City Tourism*, Old Library Building, 35 Argyle St, T7226015, F7435091,
www.buffalocitytoursim.co.za Open, Mon-Fri, 0830-1630; Sat, 0900-1200. *Wild Coast Holiday Reservations*, T7436181, F7436188, meross@iafrica.com Efficient setup which can
organize accommodation throughout the Transkei region; worth contacting if you are looking to spend a few quiet days on this beautiful wild coast. Free service. For information on the
Amatola region, the mountainous region centred around Hogsback, stretching from Cathcart to Fort Beaufort, contact *Eastern Cape Tourism*, T7439511, www.ectourism.co.za

Sights

The town centre is a modern, bustling place, but there are several historical monuments: the Colonial Division Memorial is in front of the City Hall; the German Settler Memorial is on the Esplanade; and there are War Memorials on Oxford Street.

The **Ann Bryant Art Gallery** is on St Marks Road, in an interesting Edwardian
building dating from 1905. The collection was originally mostly of British artists but
now has many fine contemporary South African works. An arts and crafts fair is held
here on the first and second Sunday of each month. ■ *Mon-Fri 0900-1700, Sat
0930-1200. Entry free. T7224044.*

The **East London Museum**, on Oxford Street, has a surprisingly interesting
range of natural history exhibits. The highlights of the museum include the world's
only dodo egg, and the coelacanth which was trawled up off the Chalumna River in
1938. The coelacanth, known as the Fossil Fish, was thought to have been extinct for
80 million years until it was rediscovered earlier this century. The museum also has
some good displays on Xhosa culture and customs, as well as a section devoted to
Nguni beadwork. ■ *Mon-Fri 0930-1700, Sat 1400-1700, Sun and public holidays
1100-1600. Small entry fee. T7430686.*

Gately House was built in 1876 by John Gately, one of East London's first mayors. The house was donated to the city in 1966 and is now a town house museum decorated with original Victorian furnishings. It is at 1 Park Gates Road. ■ *Tue-Thu 1000-1300, 1400-1700, Sat and Sun 1500-1700. Small entry fee. T7222141.*

Latimer's Landing is a waterfront development on the Buffalo River whose restaurants, shops and flea markets were a major tourist attraction when the scheme first opened. It is currently out of favour with local businesses, who have chosen to open elsewhere in town. Latimer's Landing was named after Doctor Argery Courteney Latimer, who was the curator of the East London Museum in 1938 when the coelacanth was first rediscovered.

West Bank Village is the oldest surviving area of East London with some interesting **West Bank** old buildings on Bank Street and near the entrance to the harbour. **Hood Point** **Village** **Lighthouse** was built in 1895 and is a typical Victorian lighthouse with a steel upper gallery and keyhole windows. ■ *Mon, Wed, Fri 1400-1600, Sat 0900-1100. Small entry fee. T7003056.* **Fort Glamorgan** is a vaulted brick building on Bank Street, closed to the general public but devotees of Victorian military architecture can get permission to visit the fort through Major Du Toit on T7311610. The fort was built in 1847 during the Seventh Frontier War to defend the supplies that were being sent to the inland garrisons from the Buffalo River Mouth. A monument to honour **Steven Bantu Biko** was unveiled by Nelson Mandela on 12 September 1997 in Oxford

Eastern Cape

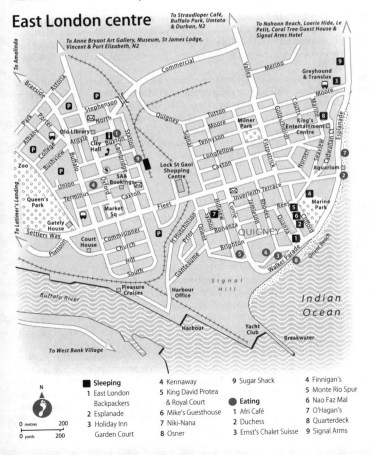

East London centre

To Straudloper Café, Buffalo Park, Umtata & Durban, N2

To Nahoon Beach, Loerie Hide, Le Petit, Coral Tree Guest House & Signal Arms Hotel

To Anne Bryant Art Gallery, Museum, St James Lodge, Vincent & Port Elizabeth, N2

To Amalinda
To Latimer's Landing
To West Bank Village

Indian Ocean

Buffalo River

N

| 0 metres | 200 |
| 0 yards | 200 |

■ **Sleeping**
1 East London Backpackers
2 Esplanade
3 Holiday Inn Garden Court
4 Kennaway
5 King David Protea & Royal Court
6 Mike's Guesthouse
7 Niki-Nana
8 Osner
9 Sugar Shack

● **Eating**
1 Afri Café
2 Duchess
3 Ernst's Chalet Suisse
4 Finnigan's
5 Monte Rio Spur
6 Nao Faz Mal
7 O'Hagan's
8 Quarterdeck
9 Signal Arms

Coelacanth – back from the dead

The discovery of a living Coelacanth off the coast of East London in 1938 provided scientists with a link to prehistoric times. At first it was thought that they shared a common connection with lungfish and land vertebrates but on closer examination it became obvious that the fish had hardly changed since the Devonian period, 350 million years ago. It had been assumed that it had become extinct after some 290 million years. The fact that a living specimen was trawled from the deep destroyed this theory but the fish became known as a living fossil. Named **Latimeria chalumnae**, this lobe-finned fish grows to about 1.5 m and can weigh about 68 kg. It is bright blue in colour and produces large quantities of oil and slime. Its four fins resemble legs and these have some rotating movement which allows them to crawl along the seabed. They also have very powerful jaws.

More fish have been found near the Comoros Islands which lie to the north of the Mozambique Channel between Madagascar and mainland Africa. After all the excitement, it turned out that the Comores had been eating coelacanth for years. So much for coming back from the dead!

Street outside the City Hall. At the time this marked the 20th anniversary of his death while in police custody.

Bridlesdrift Nature Reserve Bridlesdrift Nature Reserve is a small reserve on the banks of Bridlesdrift Dam which attracts many species of waterbirds. There are some interesting walks and a bird hide here. Bridlesdrift Dam is also popular with people from East London who come here at weekends to fish and sail. ■ *The reserve is 25 km west of East London on the R346.*

Umtiza Nature Reserve Named after the unique Umtiza trees which grow here, this reserve is a small area of protected indigenous forest along the banks of the Buffalo River. There are three circular trails in the reserve, the longest of which is 6 km. All the trails are well-signposted and are relaxing walks through woodland and mature cycads. Samango monkeys, duiker and bushbuck live in the forest as well as numerous woodland bird species. ■ *For more information, T043-7369909. The reserve is 15 km west of East London on the R346*

Essentials

Sleeping
■ *on map, page 367*
Price codes:
see inside front cover

B-C *Esplanade*, 6 Clifford St, Beachfront, T7222518, esphotel.iafrica.com 74 rooms, recently refurbished, family holiday style hotel. **B** *Holiday Inn Garden Court*, corner of John Bailie Rd and Moore St, T7227260, F7437360, hicgeastlondon@southernsun.com Modern block set back from the beach, 173 standard a/c rooms, with balcony, some have great views of the beach, non-smoking room, restaurant, bar, swimming pool, curio shop, secure parking, on the seafront. **B** *King David Protea*, 27 Inverleith Terr, T7223174, F7436939, kingdavidhotel@ iafrica.com Comfortable city centre option aimed at business travellers, with 80 rooms, some of which are more luxurious and thus more expensive, TV, lounge. *Kasbah* restaurant serves à la carte French dishes, also *El Bistro* coffee shop, 3 bars, secure covered parking. **B** *Kennaway Hotel*, Esplanade, T7225531, F7433433. A large modern block overlooking the Indian Ocean and Orient Beach, with 71 rooms, non-smoking room available, restaurants, bar, lounge, a bit dull but fine ocean views.

C *Mike's Guesthouse*, 22 Clifford St, T7433647, F7430308, mikes@his.co.za Welcoming guesthouse by the Esplanade, cosy rooms with en suite bathrooms, TV, lounge, kitchen, braai area, free pickup from airport. **C** *Osner*, Beachfront, T/F7433433, osaccom@iafrica.com A soulless modern development by the beachfront, with 111 en suite rooms, restaurant, bar, swimming pool, gym, sauna, sensibly priced. **C-D** *St James Lodge*, Southernwood, T7431766. Newly established upmarket B&B, centrally situated in a quiet area of town, en suite rooms with TV, secure parking.

D *The Coral Tree Guest House*, 5 Gleneagles Rd, Bunkers Hill, T/F7352664. 3 double rooms with en suite facilities and fan cooled, TV, lounge, non-smoking room, swimming pool, B&B only, ask for Felix or Petro. **D** *Loerie Hide*, 2b Sheerness Rd, Bonnie Doon, T/F7353206. Cottage for 2 tucked away in a beautiful garden, fridge, TV, the grounds border the Nahoon riverine forest, swimming pool, close to the beaches, a short drive from the city centre.

Budget accommodation   Most of the backpackers staying in East London are here for the surf. Others tend to move on to Cintsa, 38 km up the coast. **F** *East London Backpackers*, 11 Quanza St, Quigney, T7222748, www.elbackpackers.co.za Small, spotless set-up, with spacious dorms, double rooms, TV room, courtyard with plunge pool, braai area, kitchen, bar, internet facilities, secure parking, local tours arranged. Well-maintained and friendly and in a good location by Orient Beach. **F** *Niki-Nana*, 4 Hillview Rd, T7228509, www.nikinana.co.za New, comfortable lodge close to the beach, pubs and restaurants. Dorms and double rooms, kitchen, TV and video room, pool table, saltwater pool, braai area, internet access, arrange day trips, free airport pickup. Hard to miss with the lime green and zebra-striped exterior! **F** *Sugar Shack*, Esplanade Rd, Eastern Beach, T7228240, sugarsk@iafrica.com The best choice in East London, great backpackers in a lively location by the beach. Always popular and parties most nights. Dorms, double rooms, and camping possible, 4 showers, well-stocked kitchen, free town pick up, free surf and boogie boards, free surfing lessons, good value daily adrenaline-fuelled activities organized. Ideal location with a number of local pubs and clubs in walking distance. Recommended. Run a daily shuttle to *Away with the Fairies* in Hogsback.

Eating
● *on map, page 367*

Afri Café, 59 Cambridge St, T083-5480317 (mob). Genuine Xhosa takeaway food, including Ulusu with pap and grilled meat with Xhosa bread. *Buccaneers*, Eastern Beach, Esplanade, T7271349. Popular pub and grill house, serving steaks, seafood and salads, gets very lively at night (see below). *Ernst's Chalet Suisse*, Orient Beach, T7221840. Closed Sat lunch and Sun evening. Probably the best food in town, friendly and efficient service. Local fish and traditional Swiss dishes available. *The Duchess*, Aquarium Complex, Esplanade. Coffee shop and ice cream parlour. *Finnegan's*, 40 Terminus St, T7225585. Good value for steaks, burgers and seafood dishes. *Monte Rio Spur*, Esplanade. Steakhouse chain which serves family meals and large portions, the ribs and salads are often good value. *Nao Faz Mal*, Windsor Cabanas, T7432225. Authentic Mozambican and Portuguese dishes, relaxed place, good seafood and peri-peri chicken, popular place so book ahead. *O'Hagan's*, Esplanade, T7438713. Steaks and salads with an Irish theme, occasional good imported beers, upstairs bar, part of a successful chain, mix of young office types and backpackers. *Le Petit*, 54 Beach Rd, Nahoon, T7353685. Closed Sat lunch and Sun. Classic French dishes, pub lunches and game including buffalo, ostrich and crocodile. *Quarterdeck*, Orient Pavilion, Esplanade, T7435312. A busy seafood dining room and bar with live music 3 times a week, Wed, Fri and Sat. Good value, well worth a visit if you are on a tight budget but still want to eat well. *Santa Monica*, Esplanade, is a noisy bar with large video screens, there is a busy snack bar serving fried chicken dishes, very popular with surfers. *Signal Arms*, Railway Station, Station St, T7436882. Steakhouse and busy pub with an above average choice of imported beers. Nothing fancy, but the majority of residents keep coming back. Always a good sign. *Strandloper Café*, 95 Old Transkei Rd, T7354570. Cheap and cheerful fish 'n' chips. *Sunset*, Blue Lagoon Timeshare, Beacon Bay, T7474821. Good seafood dishes.

Entertainment

Cinemas *Vincent Park*, multi-screen cinema showing the latest blockbuster releases and a selection of art house films.

Nightclubs *Buccaneer's*, Eastern Beach, Esplanade, T7271349. Very popular venue on the beach close to O'Hagen's and next to the Sugar Shack backpackers. Live music, food, bar, popular with surfers and backpackers. *Jaggers Nightclub*, in the *King David Hotel*. *O'Hagan's*, Esplanade, T7438713. Irish-themed pub, good imported beers and Guinness, bar upstairs gets very busy especially at weekends, mix of young office types and backpackers. *Numbers*, King's Entertainment Centre, Esplanade, T7439274. Tacky but popular club, different themed nights.

Eastern Cape

Shopping *Lock Street Gaol* is an unusual shopping centre in that the original building was built in 1880. The cells were transformed into shops in 1979. Check out the African Curios shop for a good selection of items to take home. *Vincent Park Centre* is a modern shopping mall which holds an arts and crafts market every Sunday from 0900-1300.

Sports **Cricket** The East London cricket ground, Buffalo Park, is South Africa's newest international venue. It is a short distance from the beach and is the smallest of the current test match grounds in the country, with a capacity of 15,000. The first international cricket match played here was during the Indian tour of 1992/93. *Buffalo Park*, PO Box 803, Buffalo Drive. Ticket enquiries: T7437757, F7433393, bordercb@iafrica.com The following international matches will be played at Buffalo Park during the 2002-03 season: England v Holland, World Cup, 16 Feb 2003; South Africa v Canada, 27 Feb, 2003.

Hiking *Strandloper Trail*, managed by the *Standloper Ecotourism Board*, T043-8411046, strandloper@net4u.co.za Guides can be hired for this popular 5-day hike along the coast.

Horse riding *Glendale Trekking Centre*, Schafli Rd, T7385141. *Welcome Stables*, Igoda Beach, T7374055.

Scuba diving The best time of year for diving is during the winter between May-Aug. The dives around Nahoon Bay and Three Sisters are 8-15 m deep, over pinnacles, ledges and caves. The reefs are colourful and have soft corals, sponges and reef fish. Nahoon Reef is good for snorkelling but popular with surfers. For information on dive courses and trips, contact Alan Grimmer, T7482958.

Surfing The best-known surf break is Nahoon Reef, with a reputation as having the most consistent break in the country. Easterns, in front of the Sugar Shack backpackers, is the most consistent beach break in the area, with regular tubes. There are good breaks all the way up the Wild Coast – for more info, contact David Malherbe, wackypt@iafrica.com or ask at backpacker lodges.

Tour operators *African Magic*, T7343168, www.africanmagic.co.za Four-wheel drive tours, also cultural and historical tours around the whole country. *Amatola Tours*, 20 Currie St, Quigney, T7430472, info@amatour.co.za Local and city tours. *Let's Travel*, Kenneway Building, Esplanade, T7432983. *Xhosa Land Tourism*, T7432904, xhosalandtoursim@telkomsa.net

Transport
For information and timetables on local bus services: T7221251

Local Car hire: *Avis*, T7362250. *Budget*, 9 Breezyvale Rd, T7362364. *Hertz*, Shop 8, Greenfields Centre, 79 Jan Smuts Av, Greenfields, T7025701, T0861600136. *Imperial*, Settlers Way, Greenfields, T7362230. *Wild Coast Rentals*, T7225094. Four-wheel drive for all the local rough roads and beaches. A number of these companies also have offices at the airport.

Taxi: *Border Taxi*, Gladstone St, T7223946. *Herman's Taxis*, Union St, T7227901.

Information: T7060306
Passenger services: T7060211

Long distance Air: *SA Airlink*, reservations, T011-9781111, www.saairlink.co.za Fly to **Bloemfontein**, Mon-Fri daily, via **Port Elizabeth**. **Port Elizabeth** (50 mins): Mon-Fri, 3 flights daily; Sun, 1 flight a day.

South African Airways, Caxton House, 6th floor, Terminus St, T7060211, www.flysaa.co.za Below is a summary of their direct domestic flights. **Cape Town** (2 hrs): Mon-Fri, 5 flights a day; Sat and Sun, 2 flights a day. **Durban** (1 hr): Mon-Fri, 4 flights a day; Sat, 2 flights a day; Sun, 1 flight. **Johannesburg** (80 mins): 5 flights a day. **Port Elizabeth** (50 mins): Mon-Fri, 3 times a day; Sun, 1 flight a day; no flights on Sat.

If you change aircraft in Johannesburg or Durban it is possible to fly to the following domestic destinations, all within a day: Kimberley, Margate, Nelspruit, Phalaborwa, Pietermaritzburg, Pietersburg, Sun City and Ulundi.

Rail The *Amatola Express* service departs daily at 1200 for **Johannesburg** (20 hrs), via **Queenstown** (4½ hrs) and **Bloemfontein** (13 hrs).

Road From East London it is 584 km to **Bloemfontein**, 1,099 km to **Cape Town**, 674 km to Durban, 395 km to **Graaff-Reinet**, 1,002 km to **Johannesburg**, 310 km to **Port Elizabeth**, 207 km to **Queenstown**, 235 km to **Umtata**. **Bus**: *Baz Bus*: T021-4392323, www.bazbus.com A hop-on, hop-off service for backpackers. The bus will collect and drop off at any of the local backpacker hostels. A good, reliable service with friendly drivers who know a bit of the local background in addition to the route.

Greyhound, T043-7439284. Coaches depart from Windmill Park on Moore St. **Bloemfontein** (7 hrs): daily, 1700. **Durban** (9 hrs): daily, 1300, via **Umtata**, **Kokstad** and **Port Shepstone**. **Cape Town** (14 hrs): daily, 1655, via **Port Elizabeth**, **Knysna**, **George** and **Swellendam**. **Johannesburg** and **Pretoria** (14½ hrs): daily, 1700. **Port Elizabeth** (4½ hrs): daily, 1655.

Intercape, BP Garage, Fleet St, T7269580. Coaches depart from Windmill Park in Moore St going to **Port Elizabeth** (4 hrs): daily, 1515, via **Fish River Sun**, **Port Alfred**, **Kenton-on-Sea** and **Alexandria**. The service arrives in Port Elizabeth in time to connect with the service to either Cape Town or Johannesburg/Pretoria.

Minilux, T7413107. Coaches depart from the tourist office, 35 Argyle St and from Major Square in Beacon Bay going to **King Williamstown**, **Grahamstown**, **Port Alfred** and **Port Elizabeth**.

Translux, T7001999. All services depart from Station St and Windmill Roadhouse on Moore St. **Cape Town** (15 hrs): daily, 1505, 1540, via **Queenstown**, **Graaff-Reinet**, **Beaufort West** and **Worcester**. **Durban** (9 hrs): daily, 1040, via **Umtata**, **Kokstad** and **Port Shepstone**. **Johannesburg** and **Pretoria** (13½ hrs): daily, 1645, via **Queenstown**, **Aliwal North** and **Bloemfontein**. **Port Elizabeth** (4 hrs): daily, 1540, via **Grahamstown**.

Banks *Rennies Travel*, Caxton House, Terminus St, T7260698. Agents for Thomas Cook, will change **Directory** TCs, also act as the local agent for South African Airways. Branches of *Standard Bank*, *First National* and *ABSA* have ATMs and exchange facilities along Oxford St. **Communications** Internet: *Beacon Cyberhouse*, corner of Sherwood and Batting Rds, Beacon Bay, T3786423. **Medical Services** Chemists: late night services from *Berea Pharmacies*, Pearce St, T7353336. Open Mon-Sat until 2200, Sun and public holidays until 2100. *Devro-Kem Pharmacy*, 9 Anlyn Spar Centre, T7401120. Open daily until 2100. *Fleetway Pharmacy*, 102 Fleet St, Quigney, T7432155. Open daily until 2100. **Hospital**: *East London Private Hospital*, 32 Albany St, T7223128.

The Wild Coast

The former Transkei homeland is an area of rolling grasslands wedged between the Great Kei River in the south and the Umtamvuma River in the north. The beautiful Wild Coast stretches for 180 km from East London to Port St Johns. Its inland borders are the Drakensberg and the Stormberg Mountains, and dotted between are small villages, brightly painted kraals and endless communal pastureland. It remains a traditional area – most people speak only Xhosa, there is widespread poverty, and tourists are few. The Great Kei River was originally the border between South Africa and the independent homeland of Transkei, and as the N2 crosses the Kei River 65 km north of East London, the difference in the standard of living between the two areas is striking. Years of overpopulation and under-investment have taken their toll in the former Transkei. The landscape is deforested and seriously eroded and the roads are in terrible condition. There are few tourist amenities here, certainly when compared to the Garden Route, and you will get a more realistic picture of the poverty that still blights South Africa.

Ins and outs

The N2 is Transkei's main road and is fairly well-surfaced, although stretches are peppered with small potholes. The two other roads in the region which can be travelled with a standard road vehicle are the roads leading east off the N2 to Port St Johns and to Coffee Bay. There is an extensive network of unsurfaced roads connecting numerous villages and farms, but these have serious potholes and should only be attempted in a four-wheel drive vehicle.

Between East London and Port St Johns are a selection of isolated seaside villages, with a few hotels and plenty of backpacker accommodation. An excellent way of seeing the most

Getting around
Do not drive through the Transkei after nightfall. The roads are bad, cattle roam free and there have been some reports of attacks on tourists

Eastern Cape

inaccessible areas of the Wild Coast is by doing a four- or six-day hiking or horse riding tour with *Amadiba Adventures*. This is a community-based tour company offering excellent trips up the coast and inland. Local guides are very knowledgeable about the area, and much of the tour involves contact and overnight stays with local families. All proceeds go back into local community-based projects. For more information, contact T031-2055180, cropeddy@iafrica.com

East London to the Kei Mouth

The coast immediately to the north of East London has been named 'The Romantic Coast' by the local tourist board, and its relative wildness makes the statement ring true. Although the coast is being developed for tourism there are still some considerable stretches of the coastline which are protected nature reserves. There are thick dune forests and windswept open beaches stretching to wild waves. The coastal resorts nearest to East London can get crowded during the South African school holidays, but for the rest of the year it is quite surprising how isolated and quiet this coast really is. The best time of year to see the region's birdlife is from September to November; the wild flowers are best from August to September.

Ins & outs   **Getting around**   The resorts of Gonubie, Cintsa, Haga-Haga, Morgan's Bay and Kei Mouth are all within an hour's drive of East London. Public transport to these resorts is virtually non-existent, but as the hoteliers on the coast regularly visit East London to collect supplies, you can often get a lift to the coast by telephoning ahead to arrange transport. The *East Coast Shuttle*, T043-7405718, runs a service to Kei Mouth via some of the other coastal resorts, but requires a minimum of 6 passengers. Expect to pay in the region of R60 per person.

Gonubie   This tourist resort overlooks the Gonubie River and the lagoon. It is only 20 km *Postal code: 5256*   northeast of East London and has become a popular suburb with commuters. Its *Phone code: 043*   main attraction for tourists is that it offers a wide range of sporting facilities includ- *(NB Always use*   ing some of the best scuba diving along this coast. For **tourist information** contact *3-figure prefix)*   *Gonubie Publicity Association*, T7404000. *Colour map 7, grid B6*

Kwelera Nature Reserve lies 10 km to the north of Gonubie and is an area of sand dunes and dune forest facing the sea. The highest dune here rises just over 250 m above sea level. The forests are inhabited by vervet monkeys, bushbuck and numerous forest birds. There is a small picnic site which is popular with local visitors who come here to fish and surf.

Gxulu Nature Reserve and **Cape Henderson Nature Reserve** are similar areas to Kwelera, but they are further up the coast. These reserves are only accessible on foot. Gxulu can be reached from the car parks at the mouths of the Gxulu and the Igoda Rivers, but Cape Henderson is best visited whilst walking the Strandloper Trail (see page 374).

Sleeping B *Blue Water Lodge*, 9 Arthur St, T7402019, hotel with B&B. **C** *Gonubie Hotel*, 141 Main Rd, T7404010. Hotel overlooking the beach. **E** *Gonubie Resort and Caravan Park*, T7059748. Caravan and camping site with shared washrooms, some chalets.

Inkwenkwezi   This private game reserve has a combination of forest dunes and bushveld, and is **Game Reserve**   home to an impressive range of imported game, including rhino, wildebeest, giraffe, warthog, Eastern Cape kudu and an abundance of birdlife. Visitors are required to leave their cars at the entrance, and are then transported by four-wheel drive around the reserve. A range of trips can be organized, including night drives. There are also walking trails available, and some accommodation in a tented camp. There is a good restaurant, the *Emthombeni*, and a bar overlooking the river valley. ■ *Inkwenkwezi is 33 km from East London. Take the N2 towards Umtata and turn off at the Brakfontain exit. Turn left into the East Coast Resort Rd. A sign for the reserve is 20 km on the left side. Reservations essential, T043-7343234.*

The Strandloper Trail

*The trail stretches 60 km along the Ciskei coast between Gonubie and Kei Mouth and is an ideal long walk along the beach for anyone looking for a peaceful but energetic few days. (Most visitors cover the full distance within five days.) The trail passes through **Kwelera** and **Cape Henderson Nature Reserves**, so there is always a chance of viewing some wildlife.*

*The trail is managed by the **Standloper Ecotourism Board**, T043-8411888. Hikers have to pay R40 per person per day, if you choose to take a guide (recommended, both because of their excellent local knowledge but also from a point of view of safety), the charge is R50. Aside from the usual list of essential hiking and camping equipment make sure you also have a copy of the local tide tables. In several places the trail crosses river mouths which are quite treacherous in places and should only be crossed at low*

tide or at the beginning of an incoming tide.

*There are four huts along the trail, Beacon Valley, Cape Henderson Log Cabin, Double Mouth and Pumphouse. The trail fee includes the cost of using these huts and their basic facilities. The trail also passes close to several resorts, accommodation can be booked via the excellent **Wild Coast Holiday Reservations** office in East London, T043-7436181, F7436188, meross@iafrica.com A popular stop amongst backpackers is **F Buccaneer's Retreat** at Cintsa, PO Box 14, Cintsa 5275, T/F043-1383012, beach cottages and a backpackers' dormitory on a beautiful stretch of unspoilt coastline, kitchen facilities, canoes, lifts to and from East London, lagoon, an excellent hostel which is used a lot by the Baz Bus, which sometimes remains overnight here. Strongly recommended.*

Eastern Cape

The combined villages of Cintsa East and Cintsa West nestle on lush hills rolling down to a lagoon and a wide stretch of deserted beach. Although popular during the Christmas holidays, the resort is blessedly isolated for the rest of the year and offers relaxing outdoor activities such as canoeing and horse riding. There are a couple of backpacker hostels which lay on more adventurous pursuits including kloofing and surfing, but the main appeal here is lazily exploring the shell-strewn beach, forests and tranquil lagoon.

Cintsa
Phone code: 043
(NB Always use 3-figure prefix)
Colour map 7, grid B6

Sleeping C-D *SMKV Cottages*, T7385000, www.smkv.co.za Range of fully equipped thatched cottages of varying sizes, pool, braai area, overlooking lagoon, connected to the excellent *Michaela's Restaurant*. **D-F** *Buccaneer's Backpackers*, T7343012, cintsabp@ iafrica.com Superb backpacker lodge set in forests overlooking the lagoon and beach. A 2 km dirt track leads to the secluded site, with a choice of dorms, doubles, fully equipped self-catering cottages and camping on platforms beneath trees. There is a lively bar, pool, kitchen, volleyball court, free canoes and surfboards, excellent home-cooked evening meals and free daily activities. Very relaxing spot in a beautiful setting and well-run, if slightly over-priced. Recommended. **F** *Moonshine Bay*, T7343590. Large backpackers with well-decorated dorms, doubles, and camping. Bar, terrace, meals served.

Price codes: see inside front cover

Further along the coast lies this tiny seaside resort, 72 km from East London. Its name is said to be derived from the sound the waves make as they ceaselessly wash the shoreline. Like all the nearby resorts, this is a peaceful spot to spend a few days and lose track of time.

Haga-Haga
Phone code: 043
(NB Always use 3-figure prefix)
Colour map 7, grid A6

Sleeping C *Bosbokstrand Private Nature Reserve*, T8411640. **C** *Haga-Haga Resort*, Mariner's Way, T/F8411670, haga@intekom.co.za A large family-run complex situated on a rocky headland. 30 self-catering cabanas plus a cottage for backpackers. Restaurant, bar, TV lounge, swimming pool, tennis, safe tidal pools. Run by Sandy and Neil. **C** *Club Wild Coast*, T/F8411781. Choice of self-catering villa or B&B. Peaceful location on a private beach. Swimming pool.

Eastern Cape

Wild Coast Hiking Trail

The Wild Coast Hiking Trail is 280 km long and it takes 14 days to walk its entire length. The trail follows the coastline down isolated beaches and along the many clifftops. As the trail passes through several nature reserves, the opportunities for seeing wildlife are exceptional.

The prospect of walking for 280 km is quite a challenge but it is possible to walk shorter sections. The section from **Silaka Nature Reserve** to **Coffee Bay** is very popular. Not only is it a beautiful stretch of coastline but both ends of the trail are accessible by public transport.

There are more than 60 estuaries of varying size on the Transkei coast. It is important to be aware of the tides and of sharks when crossing an estuary. Remember that sharks tend to feed at dawn and dusk, and whilst crossing estuaries, try to cross at low tide or on an incoming tide. If the conditions are not right walk upstream and find a shallow area to ford the river. It is a

good idea to bring an inflatable mattress to float your pack on whilst crossing rivers.

The trail has been divided into five sections running from north to south and overnight huts have been located 12 km apart. Each hut has 12 bunks, pit latrines, a cooking area, water and firewood. Supervisors at the huts will inspect permits. The maximum number of people allowed in each group is 12. A series of three maps, available when booking, cover the entire trail. It is not unknown for hikers to be mugged whilst walking on this trail so it is a good idea to do the walk with a fairly large group of people.

Applications for bookings should be made in writing at least 21 days in advance to: The Director, Environmental Conservation, Private Bag X5002, Umtata. Bookings by phone or in person are also possible at short notice, T047-53112711, or Room 3-117, Botha Sigcau Building, Owen St, Umtata.

Morgan's Bay
Phone code: 043
(NB Alwaus sue 3-figure prefix)
Colour map 7, grid A6

This is a perfect resort for a peaceful beach break and a taste of the Transkei. The village itself is tiny and somewhat isolated and has little more than a hotel, the local store, a bottle shop and a petrol pump. The surrounding countryside is a conservation area and is ideal for hiking along the cliffs or strolling along the beach where deep currents wash up unusual shells.

There is a useful **tourist information** office by the Shell Ultra garage just after the bridge where the N2 crosses the Great Kei River. The office can provide general information on the Wild Coast and East London. **The Pont** is a car ferry which crosses over the Kei River. It is open from 0630-1730 and charges R25 per car. The dirt track on the other side leads to the resort of Kei Mouth, 8 km (see below).

Price codes:
see inside front cover

Sleeping **C** *Morgan's Bay Hotel*, Beach Rd, T8411062, www.morganbay.co.za This is a family-run hotel which markets itself as an affordable family holiday hotel. There are 30 good-value rooms; prices vary with the tourist season but the service maintains its high standard throughout the year and off-season is excellent value. The hotel has a pool and views across the bay and gardens which extend down to the beach. Inside there is a comfortable lounge, a quiet reading room, a dining room with an extensive breakfast buffet and an à la carte menu in the evenings. Travellers with children have the option of a separate dining room and child minders, and backpackers are offered special deals with collection from East London on the weekly run to collect supplies. There is also a caravan park and camping facilities. **C-F** *Mitford Resort*, 14 Beach Rd, follow the road past the *Morgan's Bay Hotel*, T/F8411510, www.morgans-bay.com Excellent choice of rooms to suit all budgets and group sizes. Some comfortable en suite rooms, self-catering chalets, and a backpacker lodge is also attached. Restaurant, home-cooked meals on request, pub and internet access.

This quiet seaside resort has a couple of supermarkets, some curio shops, a butcher, two bottle stores and a petrol station. There are no banking facilities. Nearby are some municipal tennis courts and a golf course.

Kei Mouth
Phone code: 043
(NB Always use 3-figure prefix)
Colour map 7, grid A6

The **Kei River** is navigable upstream for a short distance by boat or canoe, although sandbanks make it difficult at times. A popular river trip is to Picnic Rock, about 8 km upstream. The journey passes a private game reserve on the Ciskei side where it is possible to spot game. The cliffs around Cob Hole on the Transkei side of the river are quite dramatic and the patches of forest further on are rich in birdlife. There is a spot on the eastern bank of the river with a small creek and a landing stage. The path from here climbs up a riverbed through forest and at the end of the trail is a deep pool with two waterfalls where you can swim – this is **Picnic Rock**.

Sleeping C *Kei Mouth Hotel*, PO Box 8, Kei Mouth, 5260, T8411017. A neat complex right on the beach with 30 double and family rooms, a restaurant, 2 bars, TV lounge and swimming pool. The pool and gardens are protected from the sea breeze by mature tropical trees. Nearby you can go fishing, horse riding, canoeing and play golf. **D** *Suncoast Cabanas*, PO Box 19, Kei Mouth, 5260, T/F8411102. 9 self-catering cabanas neatly arranged around a central garden with a swimming pool and braai sites. Each unit has 2 double rooms, TV, well-equipped kitchen and a wall safe. There is also a bar and a laundry on the site. Shops and the beach are a short walk away. **D** *Suncoast Cabanas*, Main Rd, T8411102. Good-value self-catering cottages. **F** *Kei Mouth Caravan Park*, T8411004. Camping and space for caravans, usual facilities.

Price codes:
see inside front cover

North from Kei Mouth

There are two possible routes leading on from Kei Mouth. After crossing the pont, the R366 heads uphill for 9 km where it joins the R48/1 from Kentani. The road then divides heading inland to Kentani or seawards to **Qolora Mouth**. The road back to **Butterworth** and the N2 passes through a deforested area dotted with small farms; this road is in terrible condition and although it is just over 50 km to the N2, it is only just negotiable in a standard road vehicle – the top speed possible is around 30 kmph. The other route to Qolora Mouth (16 km) is best attempted in a four-wheel drive vehicle.

This is the first town that the N2 passes on its way through Transkei. It is a hectic and unappealing stretch of supermarkets and discount stores, and has little to keep you there for long. Founded as a Wesleyan mission station in 1827, it is the oldest town in the Transkei, although little of its history is evident today. At the end of the Frontier Wars in 1877, traders began to settle here and the town has grown to become a small industrial centre. One attraction worth stopping for are two nearby waterfalls just outside of town. The falls are spectacular after the rains when the water drops over 100 m over the **Bawa Falls** and 80 m over the **Gcuwa Falls**. If you are driving north towards Durban and arrive here shortly before dark you should stop for the night at the reasonable **C/D** *Wayside Budget Hotel*, T047-4914615. All rooms a/c with TV and en suite facilities. Restaurant, bar, secure underground carpark. Most of the other restaurants in town are fast-food takeaways.

Butterworth
Colour map 7, grid A6

From Butterworth, the **N2** continues north to **Umtata**, 135 km. There is a turning just north of Butterworth which goes to **Qoboqobo**, 34 km, and **Kentani**. This road is only surfaced for the first 10 km, after which the surface is rocky and full of pot-holes, but in good weather it can just be negotiated without a four-wheel drive. The road divides at Kentani; the road heading south goes to **Qolora Mouth**.

Qolora Mouth has a private airstrip and is accessible by light aircraft. The alternative is to travel the 16 km by four-wheel drive on the dirt road from the ferry over the Kei River. The hike up the Gxara River heads 4 km inland to the pool where Nonquase, a young Xhosa girl, saw visions and communed with her ancestral spirits. She heard voices telling her that the dead would rise and destroy the European invaders if the

Qolora Mouth
Phone code: 047
(NB Always use 3-figure prefix)
Colour map 4, grid C5

Eastern Cape

Xhosa destroyed all their cattle and crops. This disastrous prophesy lead to the deaths of thousands of people through starvation, and Nongqawuse had to spend the rest of her life in hiding. She is buried on a farm near Alexandria.

Price codes: see inside front cover

Sleeping C ***Seagulls Beach Hotel***, PO Box 61, Kei Mouth,T4980044, T082-5569238 (mob), www.seagulls.co.za Beachfront hotel with 40 double rooms with en suite bathroom, TV, private patio, some with sea views. The rooms are in small single storey units dotted around the grounds. Restaurant, bar, swimming pool, direct access to a sandy beach. The central reception block houses a TV lounge, snooker table and the *Anchor Inn* bar. Guests can enjoy canoeing, wind surfing and fishing in the nearby lagoon. Further afield it is possible to go horse riding and play golf. **C** ***Trennery's***, T4980004, F4980011. Thatched chalets set in large shady gardens full of mature trees, seafood restaurant, swimming pool, canoeing, boating, golf, tennis, fishing, bowls, snooker table and a small shop. One of the finest settings along this stretch of coast. Recommended.

Nxaxo Mouth

The road heading north from Kentani goes to Nxaxo Mouth, which lies at the confluence of the Nxaxo and Nqusi Rivers. The area has a lagoon and is dotted with swamps and islands. The estuary is rich in birdlife and there are hiking trails through a small strip of coastal forest to a colony of crowned cranes. Listen for the distinctive calls of groups of trumpeter hornbills which inhabit the forest.

Eastern Cape

Price codes: see inside front cover

Sleeping C ***Wavecrest***, PO Box 81, Butterworth, T047-4980022, www.wavecrest.co.za An excellent hotel in a beautiful setting on the edge of a lagoon, with 35 thatched bungalows, bar, seafood restaurant, watersports, deep sea fishing, private airstrip. Good value, recommended.

Mazeppa Bay

Phone code: 047 (NB Always use 3-figure prefix)
Colour map 7, grid C5

This small holiday resort is named after the *Mazeppa*, a coastal trading ship that used the bay as a point to unload trading goods. There is a suspension footbridge to the island from where you can see Clan Lindsay Rocks, the site where the *Clan Lindsay* was wrecked in 1898. **First Beach** is good for swimming, and the waves on this stretch of coast attract local surfers. Just back from the beach are the shell middens left by strandlopers. August is a busy month when many people come here for the shark fishing. The nearby **Manubi Forest** has 7 km of trails passing through patches of yellowwood and sneezewood trees.

Price codes: see inside front cover

Sleeping C ***Mazeppa Bay Hotel***, T4980033, F4980034, mazeppabayhotel@sainet.co.za Accommodation is a mix of double rooms, family rooms and rondavels, all with sea views and private surrounds. The central building has a restaurant, the *'Red Blanket'* bar which serves snacks, a TV lounge, snooker table and terrace. The whole complex sits on a green ridge covered with tropical vegetation, overlooking a broad sandy beach. Also prides itself on having its own island, accessible by an ancient swing bridge. Anglers have a choice of rock, lagoon or river fishing. Free collection from East London airport. Recommended. The **F** ***Forestry Department Camping Park*** has camping facilities and ablution blocks.

Qora Mouth

Phone code: 047 (NB Always use 3-figure prefix)
Colour map 4, grid C5

The N2 highway continues north from Butterworth until it reaches Idutywa. There is a turning at Idutywa to Willowvale, 32 km, from where there is a track which passes the village of Nyokana and leads to Qora Mouth. This road should only be attempted in a four-wheel drive. Qora Mouth is a small collection of houses, hardly large enough to be called a village, and is known for its kob fishing. The river mouth here marks the ecological boundary between the sundu palms whose habitat lies to the south of the river, and the lala palms which only grow to the north.

Price codes: see inside front cover

Sleeping C ***Kob Inn***, PO Box 18137, Quigney 5211, T4990011, www.kobinn.hypermarkt.net Access is via a poor gravel road, 66 km from Idutywa on the N2. Isolated, comfortable hotel set on rocks above the sea. Rooms are a mix of 10 thatched cottages with 1 or 2 bedrooms and en suite bathroom. There is a restaurant which specializes in seafood, and a bar. The swimming pool is perched on rocks overlooking the ocean, and the extensive gardens are surrounded by coastal forest. There are a couple of shady beaches nearby plus the Qora River which is ideal for canoeing. Deep sea fishing trips can be organized from the hotel.

This reserve covers an area of riverine forest, grassland and beach. It provides a habitat for the Cape clawless otter and a wide range of water birds. There is a hiking trail to the Mbanyana Falls.

Cwebe Nature Reserve

Sleeping C *The Haven*, PO Box 566, Umtata 5100, T047-5760006, F5760008 or T082-6909284 (mob). Set in the middle of Cwebe Nature Reserve, a beautiful isolated spot just a short walk from the beach. Rooms are thatched cottages randomly spread out around the central dining block and swimming pool, tennis court. Rates include meals. Close by is a lagoon formed by the Mbanya River just before it flows into the sea.

At the mouth of the Nenga River, Coffee Bay is easily accessible (there is a tarred road here) and is well-known for its good surf, making it a major stop on many backpacker routes. Nevertheless, development has been low key and it remains a quiet and laid-back place. The name of Coffee Bay comes from the coffee trees which grew here briefly in the 1860s after a ship ran aground with a cargo of coffee beans.

Coffee Bay
Phone code: 047
(NB Always use 3-figure prefix)
Colour map 4, grid C6

The **Hole In The Wall** is a famous natural feature and well worth a visit. An enormous tunnel has been eroded by the sea through a cliff which lies just off shore. A small holiday resort has sprung up by the beach here.

It is possible to hike from Coffee Bay to Port St Johns. This is part of the **Wild Coast Hiking Trail** (see page 374) and permits have to be obtained in advance. The hike should take four to five days; check for the latest information at the backpacker hostels in Coffee Bay or Port St Johns. Unfortunately they do not seem prepared to work together, believing that if a backpacker stays at one place they will not visit the other, but instead continue their travels up or down the coast.

Sleeping C *Anchorage Hotel*, PO Box 982, Umtata 5700, T/F5340061. Bungalows, seafood restaurant, bar, horse riding and hiking. There is a coastal road from Coffee Bay to the hotel, but some sections are extremely rough and the ford over the Umtata is impassable when the river is in flood. An alternative route is to drive from Umtata towards Ngqeleni, taking the dirt road to the coast. **C** *Hole In The Wall*, PO Box 13135, Vincent 5217, T/F043-7260582. Small hotel set by the beach overlooking the Hole in the Wall. 23 thatched cottages, 23 en suite double rooms, restaurant, bar, TV lounge, braai area and shop. **C** *Ocean View Hotel*, PO Box 566, Umtata 5100. T/F5752005, oceanview@coffeebay.co.za Comfortable set up perched on a headland above the main beach, double rooms with terraces, swimming pool, bar, restaurant. Golf and horse riding nearby. Deep sea fishing charters. Trips can be arranged to a traditional Xhosa village.

Price codes:
see inside front cover

F *The Coffee Shack*, T5752048, coffeeshack@wildcoast.co.za Daily shuttle to Shell Ultra City in Umtata. Popular party place set right on the beach. Mix of dorms and double rooms, good kitchen facilities, pub which gets very noisy at night, great seafood suppers and big breakfasts, plenty of activities on offer. Great spot for a couple of wild days by the beach. Recommended. **F** *Hole in the Wall Backpackers*, T083-3178786 (mob), F5750010. Great setting by the beach, with dorms, doubles, camping, a pool, volley ball, nightly seafood braais and a bar. Pick-up from Shell Ultra City by prior arrangment. **F** *Bomvu Backpackers*, T5752073, www.bomvubackpackers.com Another party lodge set in tropical gardens with decks and hammocks. There are dorms and double rooms, a restaurant and a bar. An alternative place, with yoga lessons, drum sessions, monthly full-moon parties and Xhosa song and dance performances. Strong emphasis on surfing – claims to have the only surf shop on the wild coast.

Transport Hostels will collect backpackers from the Shell Ultra City on the N2 outside Umtata. Hotel may also pick up guests by prior arrangement. The only public transport to Coffee Bay are minibus taxis, which leave from Circus Triangle in Umtata (see below).

Umtata

Phone code: 047
(NB Always use 3-figure prefix)
Colour map 4, grid C5

Umtata is a sprawling, modern town with a small grid of historical buildings at its core. Founded in 1871, it was the capital of Transkei from 1976 to 1994 and has grown to be a busy administrative centre. The N2 passes through the city centre where some of the oldest buildings are located. Most of the hotels are also in the central district, as is the tourist information office, the *Wild Coast Reservations* office and the *Nature Conservation* office. The Nelson Mandela Museum, opened in 2000, is the latest addition to the city's (limited) sights, and is definitely worth a stop.

Ins & outs   **Tourist offices** *Department of Nature Conservation*, corner of York Rd and Victoria St, Private Bag X5002, T5311191. Information and booking for the Wild Coast Hiking Trail and Nature Reserves. Open, Mon-Fri, 0800-1630. *Wild Coast Tourism*, 64 Owen St, T5315290, F5315291, ectbwc@icon.co.za Very helpful office supplying regional and city information. *Wild Coast Reservations*, 3 Beaufort St, T5325344, F5323766. Open, Mon-Fri, 0800-1800. Excellent central reservations office which can provide advice on accommodation throughout the region. Useful when trying to find out about some of the more remote hotels.

Sights   Housed in the Bunga building, the site of the Transkei Parliament, is the **Nelson Mandela Museum**. This is the third component of a museum honouring Nelson Mandela. The first component is at Mvezo, where Mandela was born and includes his old homestead. The second is the Youth and Heritage Centre, in Qunu where he grew up. Plans are still underway for this section, but will include a resource centre and library. The third component is here in Umtata and is a moving and insightful look at Mandela's life and his struggle against Apartheid. The displays focus on his autobiography, *Long Walk to Freedom*, with extracts complemented by photography, personal items, letters and video footage, including a short excerpt from an interview he gave in 1961. Although the displays are rather confusing from a chronological point of view, they give a good overview of Mandela's life. Other displays include international awards and honorary degrees that he received, portraits and sculptures of him, and diplomatic gifts he received during his term of office. The staff are very enthusiastic about the museum and are happy to answer questions. ■ *Mon-Fri 0900-1600, Sat 0900-1230, free entrance, T5325110, mandelamuseum@intekom.co.za*

The **Transkei Museum** is a block north, on Victoria Street, and features local displays including traditional dress, local crafts and some stuffed animals.

Nduli Nature Reserve   Only 3 km north of Umtata next to a holiday resort, the reserve has been used as a distribution centre for game being transported around the former Transkei to other reserves. There is usually a good selection of animals which can be seen from the 20 km road used for game drives. ■ *Daily 0700-1700. Small entry fee.*

Luchaba Nature Reserve   Luchaba Nature Reserve is a few kilometres north of town and lies next to Umtata Dam. The reserve is small but this area of marshes and grassland is a fascinating place to see this region's birdlife. Stanley bustard are common here, as are crowned cranes, both of which breed here. The reserve has also been stocked with blesbok, red hartebeest and Burchell's zebra. ■ *Daily 0800-1630. Small entry fee.*

Sleeping
Price codes:
see inside front cover

It is far preferable to stay in nearby Coffee Bay or Port St Johns and visit Umtata on a day trip. There is no backpacker accommodation here

B *Holiday Inn Garden Court*, National Rd, T5370181, F5370191, luckies@southersun.com 113 a/c room, TV, swimming pool, restaurant, bar, 1 km from Nduli Game Reserve. **B** *Savoy Hotel*, corner Stanford Terrace and Sutherland St, T5310791, jhotels@sainet.co.za Double rooms with TV, Spur restaurant, bar, recently renovated. **B** *Hotel Umtata Protea*, 36 Sutherland St, T5310721, F5310083, umtpro@wildcoast.co.za Double rooms with a/c, TV, restaurant, bar. **B-D** *Herington House*, 46 Vukutu St, T5325692, herrington@wildcoast.com Comfortable hotel with double rooms, en suite bathrooms, B&B, ask for Lorraine. **C** *White House*, 5 Mhlobo St, Southridge Park, T/F5370580. B&B in a modern residence located south of the town just after the Shell Ultra City.

Eating Most of the restaurants in town are either connected to the hotels or specialize in fast food. *Nando's*, York St. Very good variety of peri-peri chicken. *Spur*, Queenstown Rd. Quality steak house connected to the *Savoy* Hotel. *Steers*, Sutherland St. Burgers, toasties and fries.

Tour operators *Swift Travel*, City Centre Bldg, York Rd, T5311641, F5311646. Can organize local accommodation bookings, car hire, onward transport reservations. *Travel World 2000*, Leeds St, T5312011.

Transport **Local Car hire**: *Avis*, KD Matanzima Airport, T5360066, F5360067.

Long distance Air: KD Matanzima Airport, 17 km from the city centre. *SA Airlink*, T5360024, 011-9781111, www.saairlink.co.za Operate direct flights to **Durban** and **Johannesburg**. Expect to pay a nominal departure tax. Johannesburg (90 mins): 2-3 flights per day.

Bus: *The Baz Bus*, T021-4392323, www.bazbus.com Passengers who are going to hostels in Coffee Bay and Port St Johns should get off at the Shell Ultra City, just to the south of Umtata centre. Hostels should pick you up from here (by prior arrangement) and may charge a fee. Minibus taxis also run to both resorts, and leave from Circus Triangle in town. It is **not** advisable to try and hitch this route. Avoid driving here after dark, as there have been violent incidents.

Greyhound, T043-7439284. Coaches depart from Shell Ultra City on the N2 highway. **Cape Town** (18½ hrs): daily, 1655, via **Port Elizabeth** (7 hrs) and **East London** (3 hrs). **Durban** (6 hrs): daily, 1500, via **Port Shepstone** (4½ hrs). **Pretoria** (12 hrs): Mon-Sat, 1815.

Intercape, T041-5860055. Coaches depart from Shell Ultra City on the N2 highway. **Cape Town** (18½ hrs): daily, 1230, 2300, via **Port Elizabeth** (7 hrs) and **East London** (3 hrs). **Durban** (6 hrs): daily, 0215, 1415, via **Port Shepstone** (4½ hrs).

Translux, T043-7001999. Coaches depart from Shell Ultra City on the N2. **Durban** (6 hrs): daily, 1400, via **Kokstad** (2½ hrs) and **Port Shepstone** (4½ hrs). **Port Elizabeth** (7 hrs): daily, 1235, via **East London** (3 hrs) and **Grahamstown** (5½ hrs).

Directory **Medical Services** Hospitals: *St Mary's Private*, 30 Durham St, T5325902. 24-hr service.

Eastern Cape

Umtata

```
0 metres   200
0 yards    200
```

■ Sleeping   ● Eating
1 Savoy Hotel & Spur   1 Nandos
2 Umtata Protea   2 Steers

Port St Johns

Phone code: 047
(NB alwauys use
3-figure prefix)
Colour map 4, grid C6

This small, peaceful town on the banks of the Mzimvubu River has a laid-back atmosphere which may have something to do with the fact this is a major cannabis-growing area. Its bohemian feel has attracted many artists and, more recently, backpackers, who tend to hang around for a while. Consequently, there's a good selection of budget accommodation here, much of which is self-catering. There aren't many restaurants in town but the local produce such as papaya, avocado pears, pecans, macadamia nuts and the fresh fish sold on the beach calls for cooking facilities.

Portuguese ships stopped here to pick up water on their journeys up the coast and the town itself is named after the *Sao Joao* which was wrecked here in 1552. A trading post was built in 1846 and in 1878 the British established a military outpost here and built Fort Harrison.

There are two beaches – **Second Beach** is the most attractive; a beautiful stretch of soft sand, backed by smooth, forested hills. As a pleasant contrast to most beaches visited by tourists, the majority of sunbathers and swimmers here are black. There are two nature reserves within easy reach of town: Silaka (see below) and Mount Thesiger, which has a small herd of wildebeest belonging to an unusual sub-species which has no mane. The warm, sulphurous springs at Isinuka are just outside of town.

The **tourist office** is on Town Entrance Square, just to the right as you enter the town, T5641187, toursimpsj@wildcoast.co.za

Sleeping

Price codes:
see inside front cover

B-C *Umngazi River Bungalows*, T/F5641115. About 25 km west of the town, off the R61 back towards Umtata. Thatched luxury bungalows facing the estuary, restaurant, bar, shop, swimming pool, wide range of watersports including sunset cruises up the river, conference centre, fly-in packages. Full board rates. **C** *Bulolo Holiday Resort*, Second Beach, T5641245, F5641314. Self-catering chalets in lush gardens right on the beach. Small shop, windsurfing, boating and fishing. **C** *The Jetty*, PO Box 64, 5 km from the town centre on the banks of the Umzimuabu river, T5641072. A small, peaceful guesthouse with 4 double rooms and a family room. B&B or self-catering possible. The house is set in a fruit orchard and is the perfect location for a few relaxing days. Recommended. **D** *Gwyneth's Barn*, First Beach, T/F5641506, T082-9204278 (mob). Short walk from the beach. Self-catering units for 4 to 8 people. Well-equipped with all mod cons, including satellite TV for sports junkies. The units are set in wild gardens with private terraces and a braai area. Great ambiance. **D** *The Lodge*, Second Beach, T5641171. B&B, 3 double rooms, good sea views and some facilities for backpackers. The location and view are something to write home about – over a long lazy day or two. Also has a reputation for quality food. **D** *Outspan Inn*, Main Rd, T/F5641057. A local favourite with 9 double rooms, at the mouth of the Umzimvubu river. The restaurant has a good reputation and is worth visiting. Reception also act as an unofficial local information centre.

E-F *Ikaya*, Second Beach, PO Box 32, T5641266. A fine, small guesthouse-cum-backpackers. One of the last places at the end of the dirt road on Second Beach. The building is surrounded by tropical indigenous bush, and the gardens extend down to the beach. A mix of double rooms and small dorms, with self-catering facilities. Next door is a hand-dyed clothing workshop – Jakotz Clothing. Worth a visit if you're planning on spending some time in PSJ. Secure parking. **F** *The Island*, 341 Berea Rd, T5641958. Friendly and well-run backpacker lodge with a good range of rooms, including dorms and some comfortable en suite doubles. There's a restaurant and chill-out room, plus a TV/video room, bar, camping and shuttles to Second Beach. **F** *Jungle Monkey*, Berea Rd, T5641517. Recently refurbished hostel with dorms, doubles, bar, TV room. **F** *Amapondo Backpackers*, Second Beach, T082-6307905 (mob), F5641083. A last resort in terms of backpacker lodges here. There's a chilled ambience and the staff are very friendly, but the place is dirty and rundown. Dorms, doubles, kitchen, bar, nightly meals. **F** *The Kraal*, Mpande, T043-6832384. Signposted from road to Port St Johns. The Kraal is a 20 km drive along a bad dirt road, but is well worth the trip. Shuttles to Umtata by prior arrangement. Set on an isolated hill above a beach and lagoon, the lodge is made up of 3 traditional Xhosa rondavels with dirt floors, no electricity and 'eco-loos'. Dorms only, camping space. Communal kitchen where you can buy all your supplies, superb meals

Eastern Cape

served, hot showers, wonderful views over the sea. A genuine retreat and perfect for experiencing village life in the Transkei. Recommended.

Bus *Transtate* run a daily bus service to **Durban** via **Lusikisiki**. Backpackers using the *Baz Bus* may be able to arrange a pickup from Umtata to their hostels; otherwise there are local minibus taxis, costing about R25. (See Transport, Umtata.) **Transport**

This reserve is on a gravel road 4 km south from Port St Johns. Although the reserve is small, the tropical atmosphere of the trails weaving through the tangle of thick forest is unmissable. Blesbuck, blue wildebeest and Burchell's zebra have been reintroduced. There is a beautiful stretch of rugged coastline and just off the beach is Bird Island, a breeding colony for sea birds. **Silaka Nature Reserve**
Colour map 4, grid C6

Sleeping 14 self-catering bungalows, 2 bedrooms, kitchen, bathroom. For reservations, T047-5311191 or T047-5641177. You will have to book in advance to stay here.

Some 30 km south of Port St Johns, on a good dirt road, this reserve covers 772 ha of evergreen forest, lagoon, saltmarsh and rocky seashore. A network of paths has been laid out from which you can see wildlife, including blesbuck, blue wildebeest, Burchell's zebra, Cape clawless otter and monitor lizards. The birdlife here is particularly rich and the African jacana, black duck, Cape batis, dabchick, green pigeon, long crested eagle, olive bushshrike and yellowthroated longclaw have all been seen here. **Hluleka Nature Reserve**
Colour map 4, grid C6

The reserve is open to visitors daily from 0600-1800. 12 self-catering chalets on stilts, each sleeping 6 people. There is a small shop here with postal facilities. For reservations contact *Department of Nature Conservation*, in Umtata, T047-5311191.

Eastern Cape

North to Port Edward and Durban

The reserve covers an area of 8,000 ha between the Msikaba and Mtentu Rivers. The grasslands here are known for their gladioli, ground orchids and watsonias. There are good chances of seeing blesbuck, blue wildebeest, eland, gemsbok and red hartebeest feeding. **Mkambati Nature Reserve**
Colour map 5, grid C1

Ins and outs The reserve lies on the coast between Port St Johns and Port Edward. The road from Port St Johns passes through the villages of Lusikisiki, Flagstaff and Holy Cross. There are plans to surface the road to Mkambati, but until that happens it is best to do the journey in a four-wheel drive vehicle.

Entry and sleeping For reservations contact the *Department of Nature Conservation*, in Umtata, T047-5311191. The reserve is open from sunrise to sunset, small entry fee. There is a small shop here selling a limited range of tinned foods and firewood. **E** 5-bedded self-catering log cabins, overlooking the Msikaba River, swimming pool. North of the reserve, near Port Edward, is **B** *Wild Coast Sun*, PO Box 23, Port Edward 4295, T039-3059111, www.suninternational.co.za Modern, brash, luxury hotel with casino, cabaret, cinema, championship golf course, beach and watersports.

The forested ravines along the Msikaba River are lined with thick riverine forest and the unique Pondo coconut or Mkambati palm. This is the only place in the world where it grows. Cape vultures nest on the cliffs above the Msikaba River gorge. Gurney's sugarbird, the greater double collared sunbird, the red-shouldered widow and many other woodland birds can be seen here. Canoe trips, horse riding and hiking are the best way to see this area of forested ravines and coastal grasslands. There are some spectacular waterfalls. **Wildlife**

KwaZulu Natal

6

KwaZulu Natal

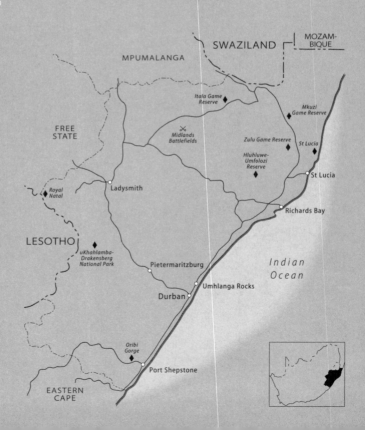

KwaZulu Natal, both one of South Africa's most popular holiday destinations and its greenest provinces, extends from the Drakensberg Mountains in the northwest to the humid sub-tropical coast in the southeast. The mountains in the **uKhahlamba-Drakensberg National Park** *rise steeply to over 3,000 m and although the park doesn't have the large numbers of game of other game reserves in KwaZulu Natal, it does have an extensive network of relatively undiscovered trails. Zululand is another fascinating area, where traditional Zulu lifestyles are still evident and have endured the onset of the 20th century and the game reserves are amongst South Africa's finest.* **Hluhluwe and Umfolozi Game Reserve** *is the most well-known and has become famous for its rhino conservation programme, which has brought the rhino back from the brink of extinction. Maputaland lying to the north of Zululand is also an extraordinary area of undisturbed African wilderness, with remote game parks and pristine coastlines not generally on the tourist trail. However, the variety of wildlife experiences on offer here is on a par with Kruger, but without the crowds. The landscape of the central region, dotted with small industrial towns and flat farmland, may be uninspiring but it is an area that has lived through the Zulu Wars, the Zulu-Boer War, the Anglo-Zulu War and lastly the Boer War. There are numerous battlefield sites but* **Isandlwana**, **Rorke's Drift** *and* **Blood River** *are amongst the most evocative. And as if all that weren't enough, KwaZulu Natal's* **beaches** *have attracted South African tourists for many years. The areas around Durban and the south coast are heavily developed while the coastline extending from the north of Durban to Maputaland is much less intensely developed. Long empty expanses of beach are backed by thick tropical dune forests – an excellent place for interesting wildlife encounters.*

Ins and outs

Getting around Travel within KwaZulu Natal is not complicated, the main areas of interest are connected by either the N2 or the N3. The N2 runs along most of the coast from Port Shepstone in the south, through to Durban, Zululand and Maputaland in the north. The N3 heads inland from Durban towards Pietermaritzburg, skirting the Battlefield Route to the East, and the uKhahlamba-Drakensberg National Park in the west, eventually reaching Gauteng. The roads in Maputaland are gradually being surfaced but there are still vast tracts of wilderness which are best explored in a four-wheel drive. The most accessible reserve is Sodwana Bay where the colourful tropical reefs have become South Africa's most popular diving destination. The battlefield sites in the centre of the province are isolated and best experienced on a guided historical tour.

Tourist information *Tourism KwaZulu-Natal*, at *Tourist Junction*, in Durban (see below for address), T031-3047144, F3056693, kzn@iafrica.com, www.zulu.org.za is the regional tourist office, open Mon-Fri 0800-1630. They have an innovative fax-on-demand service for tourist information in four languages, check out the website for more details.

There is a good range of **accommodation** throughout the province, and *KZN Wildlife* accommodation in the game reserves is particularly good value.

Durban

Phone code: 031
(NB Always use 3-figure prefix)
Colour map 5, grid B2

The overwhelming impression of Durban is of a busy modern city suffering from too much traffic and too many people. Very few of Durban's original buildings remain, and the centre is dominated by mirror-clad high-rise buildings whilst the surrounding hills are covered by a dense suburban sprawl. In spite of this, Durban's history is fascinating and although it is difficult to appreciate visually, the town has been the site of some epic historical events. A good way to discover what went on and where is by taking one of Durban Africa's historical tours.

Ins and outs

Getting there
For more detailed information, see Transport, page 402

Durban International Airport is well-connected to international air routes and is a practical alternative point of arrival in South Africa to Johannesburg. It is 16 km from the city centre, and transport into Durban takes about 30 mins. Behind Durban **railway station** on NMR Av (M12) is the **Motor Coach Terminal** for major long distance coaches; *Translux, Intercape*, and *Greyhound*, plus the *Margate Mini Coach*.

Getting around
By day, the centre is safe to walk around, but there is a serious danger of being mugged here after dark

Modern Durban has developed into South Africa's largest sea port and is also one of its main tourist centres. The approach to Durban passes through coastal tourist resorts, industrial areas, townships and eventually reaches the city's business centre. The extensive beachfront and all the most important landmarks are within easy walking distance in the city centre. In addition to local **bus** services, there are **taxi** ranks next to the City Hall and on the beachfront.

Tourist offices *Tourist Junction*, Station Building, 160 Pine St, T3044934, F3043868, funinsun@iafrica.com, www.durbanexperience.co.za, www.bookabedahead.co.za Open Mon-Fri 0800-1700, Sat 0900-1400. The Junction offers a comprehensive service for tourists, facilities here include hotel and tour bookings, coach and rail bookings, foreign exchange, a curio shop, a café. *Durban Africa* is the city tourist information office which is very helpful and has a full range of leaflets. They also run their own city tours. The websites are highly developed and informative, and have online booking for accommodation. Advance bookings for accommodation in wildlife parks and nature reserves throughout South Africa can also be made with the *KZN Wildlife & South Africa National Parks* (SANPARKS), office Mon-Fri, between 0800-1600, when they are online, or with their respective head offices in Pietermaritzburg and Pretoria. There are another two smaller tourist offices; one on the Golden Mile seafront

Things to do in KwaZulu Natal

- Explore the little-visited region of **Maputaland**, a remote and magical place of shimmering lakes, forests, bush, and pristine tropical beaches, it's one of the most unspoilt wilderness areas left in South Africa.
- Follow the route of the Basotho traders and cross into the mountain kingdom of Lesotho over the **Sani Pass**, on a 4x4 tour or hike. Celebrate the ascent with a glass of mulled wine in the bar at the lodge at the top – Africa's highest pub.
- Dive to the coral gardens, overhangs, and caves teeming with colourful tropical fish in the reefs off **Sodwana Bay** and **Aliwal Shoal**.
- Catch the turtle season in the **Greater St Lucia Wetlands National Park** from December to February. See these ancient creatures crawl on to the beach at night, under the watchful eyes of KZN Wildlife rangers.
- Visit the largest shopping mall in the Southern Hemisphere, the **Gateway Shopping Mall** outside Durban. With floor space equivalent of 17 rugby pitches and the world's first manmade surf park, and a skate park designed by the world skate boarding champion amongst its myriad attractions, it's Ab Fab darling.
- Sleep in the excellent KZN Wildlife accommodation in the **uKhahlamba-Drakensberg National Park**, declared a World Heritage Site in recognition of its environmental value to mankind.

opposite the *Beach Hotel*, T3322595, open Mon-Fri 0800-1630, weekends 0900-1630; the other is in Durban Airport in the domestic arrivals hall, T4501000, open daily, 0830-1600.

History

The area around the bay was once covered with mangrove forests and inhabited by pelicans, flamingos and hippos. The earliest inhabitants of what is now Durban were members of the Lala tribe who fished in the estuary and hunted and grew crops in the fertile tropical forests along the coast (as well pioneering new characters for BBC children's TV...).

The first Europeans to land here were Portuguese explorers en route to the east. On the 25 December 1497, Vasco da Gama sighted land and called it Natal, though this was probably off the coast of present day Transkei. The Portuguese cartographer Manuel Perestrello mapped the coast of Natal in 1576, but it was nearly 200 years after the earliest European sighting that the first trading ships arrived. In 1684 the *Francis* began a new era when she sailed to Natal to buy ivory.

The first Europeans to live here were the survivors of two shipwrecks. In 1686 the Dutch Eastindiaman, the *Stavenisse* ran aground at Umzinto. The survivors walked north until they reached the Bay of Natal where they met up with the survivors of the *Good Hope* which had been driven ashore in a storm in 1685. The two groups lived there for a year in a hut built on the Bluff, the first European building in Durban.

After the relative success of the first trading expedition, the Dutch East India Company planned to open a trading post here (after buying land off Chief Inyangesi for 1,000 guilders worth of beads, copper rings and iron). But after a few technical hitches involving the estuary's sandbars, trade in this area was never really developed and in 1730 the Dutch established an alternative trading station at Delagoa Bay.

The first British traders arrived in 1823 on the Salisbury, spurred on by news of Shaka, the powerful chief of the Zulus, and his Empire. Lieutenant Francis and George Farewell arrived in the Bay of Natal and were blown over the sandbars in a storm. They returned again in May 1824, with Henry Francis Fynn and a group of other adventurers, and set up their first camp in what is now known as Farewell Square. Henry Fynn was the first European trader to make contact with Shaka, though the imminent arrival of European traders had been reported to Shaka about a year previously by a Xhosa translator, John Msimbithi, who had left Farewell's first aborted party after an argument with one of the traders. Fynn and the other adventurers claimed (falsely) to be envoys of King George and were well-received by Shaka. Fynn became a favourite of the Zulu royal household after he had helped Shaka recover from a stab wound sustained during a battle. In thanks Shaka granted Fynn a huge tract of land, over 9,000 sq km.

Fynn and his young colleague Nathaniel Issacs ran this area as their own personal fiefdom, taking many Zulu wives and fathering dozens of children. Fynn declared himself King of Natal and wielded power in the same brutal manner as his infamous neighbour, Shaka. Even though Fynn and his companions broke many Zulu laws, including the prohibition on all but the King from trading in ivory, they were treated with great respect by Shaka (though the chiefs they bought the ivory from were invariably executed by Shaka).

Both Fynn and Issacs were keen for the British to annex the area as they believed they would make a killing from selling off their land. They decided, therefore, to emphasize the bloodthirsty and brutal nature of Shaka's reign in their memoirs. This also had the added benefit of excusing their own greed and brutality, reports of which had reached the British authorities in the Cape. But the British administration did not play ball and so the settlement of Port Natal continued to remain small.

Ten years later when the missionary Allen Gardiner arrived, there were still only 35 settlers. Thirteen of them attended his first service where they decided to name the settlement after Sir Benjamin D'Urban, governor of the Cape Colony. But this obvious attempt to get the Cape Colony to officially recognize Durban met with no response.

It was not until the establishment of the Voortrekker republic of Natalia in 1838 that British saw their interests as being under threat. The capital of Natalia was in Pietermaritzburg, but settlements had also been established at Weenen and Durban, giving the Voortrekkers access to the sea. The possibility of a viable independent Voortrekker republic wasn't acceptable to the Cape Colony and an expeditionary force was sent from the Cape in 1842. Although they were besieged by the Voortrekkers on their arrival, by June of that year the parliament in Pietermaritzburg had accepted British rule. The Cape Colony annexed Natal in 1844 and appointed a governor. The security given by becoming part of the Cape Colony encouraged many new settlers in search of land to come to Durban.

The continued presence of an Indian population in Durban gives the city a distinctive multicultural atmosphere

The development of the sugarcane industry in the 1860s encouraged the growth of Durban as a port and gave the city one of its most unique characteristics. Initially the sugarcane industry suffered from a lack of cheap labour because most Zulu were content to continue living by farming and other traditional economic activities. So the planters imported a large number of indentured labourers from India (living under conditions not dissimilar to slavery). After working off their 5-year indenture contracts some returned home but a number remained in Natal. Many continued farming, and eventually came to dominate the local fruit and vegetable market. Others established small businesses and gradually built up important trade connections with India. These ex-indentured labourers were joined by a number of more affluent traders, mainly from Gujarat, who arrived direct from India to set up a business.

Sights

City Centre

The 3 main areas of interest to tourists are the city centre around Farewell Square, the Indian district around Queen Street and Grey Street, and the Golden Mile on the beachfront

The small area surrounding City Hall between Commercial Road and Smith Street in central Durban is one of the city's more interesting spots. The colonial buildings and gardens offer a striking contrast between Durban's past and the present. High rise office blocks tower over the remains of Durban's older buildings where pastel coloured art deco shops are dwarfed by mirrored skyscrapers. The city centre's eclectic mixture of architectural styles is the responsibility of Lord Holford, the town planner who developed the city centre during the 1970s. Lord Holford was originally from South Africa but became one of England's most notorious town planners when he created many of the soulless city centres built in England during the 1960s. He

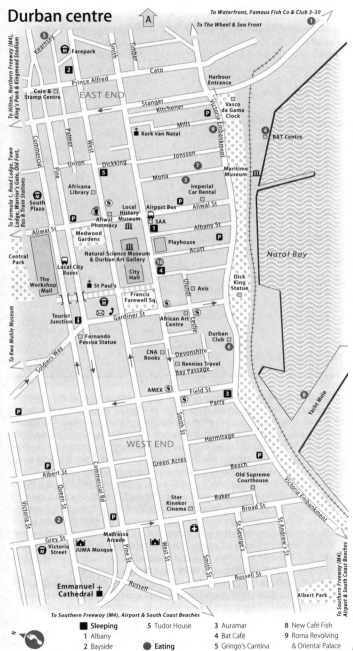

Durban centre

KwaZulu Natal

Sleeping
1 Albany
2 Bayside
3 Riviera
4 Royal

5 Tudor House

Eating
1 100 on Point
2 Aangan

3 Auramar
4 Bat Café
5 Gringo's Cantina
6 La Dolce Vita
7 Maitre Pers

8 New Café Fish
9 Roma Revolving
   & Oriental Palace
10 Royal Grill & Ulundi

Related map
A Durban beach
front, page 393

★ 24 hours in the city

Head down the **Golden Mile** at dawn, except for the few early rising surf fanatics and muscular life guards limbering up, you will have the wide promenade, sandy beaches and crashing waves to yourself, before the crowds, holiday resort tackiness, and humidity set in. Breakfast at one of the small cafés where the surfers congregate to swap wave stories.

Explore the **Indian shopping district** off Grey Street, an exotic, cross-cultural, shopping experience, where the tangy aroma of eastern spices mingles with the colourful fabrics, trinkets, and jewellery in the courtyard bazaars. Make sure you remove your shoes in the **Juma Masjid Mosque** on Grey Street, the largest in the Southern Hemisphere. Relish the cool tranquility here before heading back on to Durban's hectic streets. Enjoy an African shopping experience at **Victoria Market**, where curios and souvenirs can be haggled over, and a famous Durban bunny chow sampled at one the traditional food stalls.

Catch the bird show at **Umgeni River Bird Park**, the only one of its kind in the world. Some of South Africa's largest and rarest birds, including the Blue Crane (South Africa's national bird) are on display in this innovative free-flight show.

Sink a couple of cold Castle lagers and watch the sun go down on the deck of the **Bat Café** in the small craft harbour. If you're lucky you may catch some township jazz here before heading to one of Durban's top Indian restaurants to sample a fine Durban curry. The best are the **Jewel of India**; with cushions and low tables where you can kick off your shoes and relax, the **Oriental Palace**; 31 floors up with great city views, and **Ulundi**; where days of colonial Natal are echoed with turbaned waiters and rattan furniture.

Florida Road in Morningside and **Musgrave Road** in Musgrave, are Durban's current hip and happening café-lined streets. Take your pick of trendy late night bars, open-air restaurants, pubs, live music venues, all conveniently located for a pub crawl next door to each other on these two suburban streets.

returned to South Africa to help redesign city centres as part of the Apartheid programme of forcing different races to live in separate suburbs. He thus helped destroy the bustling Indian atmosphere of the city centre when thousands of Indians were moved out. The original plans for the new centre also involved the demolition of the City Hall and the old railway station. However, vociferous protests by conservationists managed to prevent this from happening and these two fabulous buildings now take pride of place amongst Durban's historical monuments.

Francis Farewell Square is the hub of this area and is named after the first British settler, who built his home here out of wattle and daub in 1824. The town has since grown around this spot. Today the square with its bustling street market is part of the busy city centre. At night however, the empty square rather incongruously resembles a Victorian cemetery as this is where most of Durban's commemorative statues have been placed. There is a Cenotaph to those who died in both World Wars, a memorial to the dead of the Boer War, and statues of Queen Victoria, in commemoration of her Diamond Jubilee, and Natal's first two prime ministers.

The **City Hall**, on Smith Street, faces directly onto the Francis Farewell Square. This is one of Durban's most impressive buildings and reflects the town's municipal might at the turn of the century. The building was completed in 1910 and in its day this neo-baroque building was one of the British Empire's finest city halls in the southern hemisphere. The main entrance is on Farewell Square and the hall inside is decorated with an interesting collection of portraits of all of Durban's mayors. What is particularly appealing about this building are the palms lining the street outside which soften the edges and give it a more luxuriant and colonial ambience. You will also find the Natural Science Museum and Durban Art Gallery here.

The **Natural Science Museum** has a grand colonial entrance adorned with palm trees. The largest collection inside is the gallery full of stuffed African mammals. Some of these are so old they are on the verge of becoming antiques in their own right. More interestingly the museum also houses an extremely rare Dodo skeleton and South Africa's only Egyptian mummy. The KwaZuzulwazi Science Centre has an excellent series of displays dedicated to the Zulu culture. ■ *Mon-Sat 0830-1600, Sun 1100-1600. Free entry. Gift shop and the Waterhole Coffee Shop plus internet facilities. T3112256.*

The **Durban Art Gallery** has a collection of work by local artists dating from the beginning of this century. There are also regularly changing exhibitions of contemporary art and handicrafts. ■ *Mon-Sat 0830-1700, Sun 1100-1700. Free entry. City Hall, on the upper floor. T3112265.*

The Playhouse is directly opposite the Smith Street entrance to the City Hall. It was built in 1935 and was originally used as a bioscope, which seated 1,900 people. The lounge bar became popular with visiting sailors during the 1970s and was notorious for its heavy drinking sessions and the occasional fight. The cinema was eventually forced to close after a fire and has now been restored and converted into an arts complex with five theatres. ■ *T3043631.*

St Paul's Church was originally built in 1853, however it was rebuilt in 1906 after a fire. The church is purely British in architectural style and inside there are commemorative plaques to Durban's early settlers. The chapel of St Nicholas on the left side of the aisle was part of the Mission to Seamen between 1899 and 1989. And very incidentally, Reverend Wade, who was rector of the church between 1952 and 1961, was the father of tennis one-hit-wonder Virginia Wade, who won the ladies singles title at Wimbledon in 1977.

The **Post Office**, built in 1885, was originally Durban's first town hall. There is a plaque on the southern corner of the building, which commemorates Winston Churchill's speech after his escape during the Boer War.

Tourist Junction used to be the site of the old railway station. The building was completed in 1899, is modelled on a traditional British Victorian Railway Station and is one of the few left standing in South Africa. The architects designed the station in England at the same time as they drew up the plans for another station in Canada. They were dispatched to South Africa and Canada but had unwittingly mixed up the plans for each station. Consequently the station in Durban had a sloping roof to cope with the heavy snowfall of Canada, and the one in Canada, a flat high roof to circulate the air in the heat of Durban. The Canadian roof soon collapsed under heavy snow!

During the Apartheid years this station design suffered from what was perceived to be a major fault. This was the fact that there was no way in which people of different races could effectively be stopped from mixing before getting onto the train. The regime's response to this was to design the Apartheid railway station. In these stations black and white people had separate entrances, separate ticket offices and separate access routes to their separate carriages. While visiting a modern South African railway station it is interesting to see the remains of Apartheid architecture in the surprising number of apparently superfluous access routes.

The **Fernando Pessoa Statue**, is directly opposite the Tourist Junction on the other side of Gardiner Street. The bronze statue commemorates Fernando Pessoa who lived in Durban during the early years of his life between 1896 and 1906. On his return to Portugal he lived in poverty whilst teaching English in Lisbon. He went on to become Portugal's most celebrated and complex modern poet.

The Workshop, also on Commercial Road, lies directly behind the Old Railway Station and is an enormous shopping mall which has been built inside the railway station's old train sheds. With the transition of major shops to the Pavilion and Gateway malls in the suburbs, the Workshop has suffered a decline in recent years and is starting to look somewhat shabby, the shops here are not at all interesting.

Around 500 m north of The Workshop, on Ordnance Road, near Warrior's Gate, is the **Kwa Muhle Museum**, housed in the Old Pass Office. It's a fascinating and

The interior of the station has been entirely remodelled and now offers a comprehensive range of facilities

KwaZulu Natal

moving exhibition of what it was like to be an African under the old regime. A collection of waxworks of figures in hostels along with a series of photographs of incidents and riots of the past 25 years. Another display features the Indian merchants of Grey Street, here you can learn more about the first trade union, the Grey Street mosque, a replica of Victoria Street beer hall, the Bantu Social Centre, and *bunny chow* (see page 400). ■ *Mon-Sat. T3112223, T3006250.* **Warriors' Gate**, on Old Fort Road, has an excellent collection of battlefield relics from the early Zulu Wars and the Boer War. ■ *Tue, Fri and Sun 1100-1500, Sat 1000-1200. T3073337.* The **Moth Museum of Military History** is also located here, a large collection of military memorabilia mostly from the First and Second World Wars. ■ *Tue-Sun 0830-1630. Small entry fee. T3073337.*

Indian District

This is a good 20-min walk west from the centre down Commercial Rd or Pine St or take a taxi to Victoria St

The area around Victoria Street, Queen Street and Grey Street is one of the oldest areas of Durban still standing. The pastel coloured shopping arcades were built in the 1920s and 30s by Indian traders. Originally they were designed so families could have their homes over their shops. In 1973, however, legislation was introduced which prohibited Indians from living in the area (though not from carrying out their business). Family labour living above the shops was seen as integral to their success and the legislation was deliberately introduced in an effort to reduce their competition with white-owned businesses. With the new legislation much of the residential population was forced to move out to Chatsworth or Phoenix, the wealthier traders moved to Westville. Thankfully the new residential rules did not succeed in destroying the Indian-owned businesses and many have continued to prosper. Many of the shops are still here catering for Durban's Indian population selling spices, saris and other goods from India but it is now very much a commercial rather than residential area.

Durban Cultural and Documentation Centre is well worth a visit if you are interested in the history of the Indian Community in South Africa. There are displays on the indentured Indian community, Ghandi in South Africa, culinary art, and traditional clothing. ■ *Daily except Sat. On the corner of Epsom Rd and Derby St. T3097559.*

Victoria Street Market is on the corner of Queen Street and Victoria Street. The original market was destroyed in 1973 by fire and has been replaced by a modern market. Unfortunately the new building is rather dingy and made from concrete. There are over 170 stalls inside selling African curios, leather goods, fabrics, copper, and spices. The main attraction of the stalls here are the spices and dried beans imported from India. Upstairs are a variety of food stalls serving up delicious snacks such as bunny chow, samoosas, and Durban curries. This is well worth a wander around but it gets extremely busy so beware of pickpockets and don't take anything valuable with you. ■ *Mon-Fri 0600-1800. Free entry. T3064021.*

The entrance to the **Madressa Arcade** is on Grey Street. The arcade was built in 1927 and houses shops selling suitcases, radiocassettes and Indian fabrics. There are two unusual shops here, one of which sells the latest African hits on record, the other specializes in dried monkey heads and other paraphernalia of African magic.

The **Jumma Muslim Mosque**, on Queen Street and Grey Street, was also built in 1927 and is the largest mosque in the southern hemisphere. ■ *Open to all, guided tours available with the Islamic Propagation Centre. T3060026.*

Victoria Embankment

The Victoria Embankment was originally built in 1897 and was a grand and desirable residential area facing a beautiful stretch of beach. Unfortunately very little of this remains today and at first glance the Embankment seems like any other busy road lined by skyscrapers.

Starting at the eastern end of the Embankment is the ornate **Da Gama Clock**. Very much a product of its time and a good example of Late Victorian design, this large cast iron clock was erected to commemorate the 400th anniversary of Vasco da Gama's discovery of the sea route to India in 1487.

A short walk further on at the junction of Gardiner Street and the Victoria Embankment is the **Dick King Statue** which commemorates Dick King's epic

Durban beach front

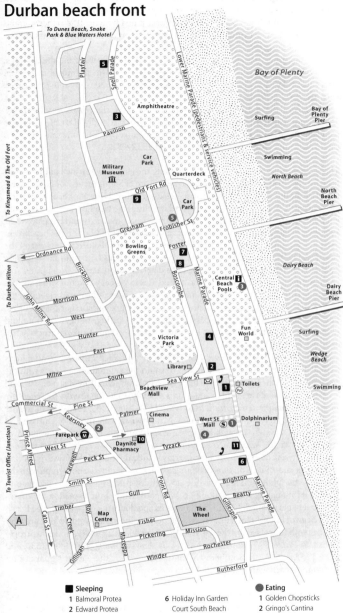

To Dunes Beach, Snake
Park & Blue Waters Hotel

Playfair

Snell Parade

5

Lower Marine Parade (pedestrians & service vehicles)

Bay of Plenty

Amphitheatre

Surfing

Bay of
Plenty
Pier

3

Pavilion

Swimming

Car
Park

North Beach

North
Beach
Pier

Military
Museum

Quarterdeck

Old Fort Rd

9

Car
Park

5

Frobisher St

Gresham

Foster

Bowling
Greens

7

Dairy Beach

Ordnance Rd

8

Boscombe

Marine Parade

Central
Beach
Pools

Dairy
Beach
Pier

North

Brickhill

John Mine Rd

Morrison

West

Hunter

East

Fun
World

Surfing

Milne

South

Victoria
Park

Wedge
Beach

Library

Swimming

Sea View St

4

2

Beachview
Mall

1

Toilets

Commercial St

Pine St

Pol

Kearsney

Palmer

Cinema

West St
Mall

Dolphinarium

Farepark

2

M

4

West St

Daynite
Pharmacy

10

Tyzack

11

Peck St

6

Smith St

Brighton

Beatty

Timber

Roy

Gull

Point Rd

Map
Centre

The
Wheel

Gillespie

Marine Parade

Cato St

Gilligan

Creek

Mazenppa

Fisher

Mission

Pickering

Rochester

Winder

Rutherford

To Kingsmead & The Old Fort

To Durban Hilton

To Tourist Office (Junction)

Prince Alfred

Farewell

KwaZulu Natal

Related map
A Durban centre,
page 389

N

0 metres   100
0 yards   100

A

■ **Sleeping**
1 Balmoral Protea
2 Edward Protea
3 Holiday Inn Crowne Plaza,
  Jewel Of India & Darumo
4 Holiday Inn Garden Court
  Beach & Saagries
5 Holiday Inn Garden
  Court North Beach
6 Holiday Inn Garden
  Court South Beach
7 Palace
8 Parade & Orient Restaurant
9 Pavillion
10 Seaboard Protea
11 Tropicana

● **Eating**
1 Golden Chopsticks
2 Gringo's Cantina
3 Joe Kool's
4 Maharajah
5 Scalini

10-day ride to Grahamstown in 1842 whilst Durban was under siege. The **Durban Club** is on the opposite side of the embankment and was built in 1904. This is one of the few original buildings left on the Victoria Embankment. It is rather a grand building and does give one an inkling of what the Victoria Embankment must once have been like.

The **Maritime Museum** has a minesweeper, the *SAS Durban*, and the two tugs, the *Ulundi* and the *JR More*. Entrance is on the docks opposite the junction of Aliwal Street and the Victoria Embankment. ■ *Mon-Sat 0830-1530, Sun 1100-1530. Small entry fee. T3112230.*

Just beyond the Maritime Museum is the **BAT Centre**, right on the harbour front. This is a popular arts centre with a bar plus the 'cheap & friendly' *Bat Café*. There are some unique arts and crafts in the *Bat Shop*. The centre overlooks the water and one can usually enjoy some jazz most evenings. ■ *T3329951.*

The Beachfront

The beachfront area is not safe to wander about in after dark

The most popular seafront area extends along the length of Marine Parade. Traditionally known as the **Golden Mile**, it's a favourite of South African holidaymakers with a pronounced seaside resort feel to it. High-rise hotels line the beachfront overlooking gardens and a promenade beyond which are the beaches. Behind the hotels is a built up urban area which in recent years has become seedy and is a place to be avoided at night. Because of this, there is a huge police presence on the beachfront itself. Gangs of policemen equipped with firearms and bulletproof vests patrol the beach and there's a police station on the promenade. This is an unusual sight for a holiday resort, but hopefully is enough of a deterrent to ensure the area is safe.

To see the beachfront at its best it is a good idea to visit at weekends when crowds of people come to enjoy the attractions. The **flea market** at the northern end of the Lower Marine Parade is a hive of activity with stalls selling Indian snacks and curios. The beaches are divided into areas designated for surfing, boogy boarding and swimming. All the beaches are protected with shark nets and lifeguards are on patrol daily between 0800-1700.

The Promenade along Lower Marine Parade and Snell Parade has numerous tourist attractions. Running from north to south the entertainment starts with the flea market and the **Snake Park**. The park has a large collection of snakes from all over the world which are kept in aquariums. ■ *0900-1630. Small entry fee. There are daily snake handling demonstrations at 1000, 1130, 1300, 1400, 1500. The snakes are fed at weekends after the demonstrations.* **Minitown**, a scale model of Durban and **Waterworld**, a waterpark with a number of slides and pools are a short walk down the seafront. ■ *T3376336. All their profits go to charity.*

There are several stands where the extravagantly dressed **Rickshaw** drivers wait for tourists, the options on offer are either a quick and painless photograph with the driver, or the photograph and a ride up and down Marine Parade, negotiate to around R15. Slightly further along on Wedge Beach is **Fun World**, a children's amusement park with a chairlift, roundabouts and dodgems. Also on Wedge Beach is the **Seaworld and Dolphinarium**. The performing seals and dolphins are very popular with tourists as are the aquaria stocked with turtles, sharks and other tropical fish. ■ *Daily 0900-1800. Entry R40. Daily shows at 1000, 1130, 1400, 1530, and 1700. T3373536.* At the southern end of the Promenade there is an **Aquapark** on Addington Beach with a slide over 100 m long.

Berea

This residential district, to the west of the City Centre, is one of Durban's oldest and most prosperous. On Sydenham Road, in Upper Berea, are the **Botanic Gardens**. The gardens were founded in 1849, they cover almost 15 ha and are a classic example of a Victorian botanical garden. There are some impressive avenues of palms crossing the park and good displays of orchids and cycads. The tea garden, open 0930-1615, is a pleasant place to relax. The KwaZulu Natal Philharmonic Orchestra perfroms by the lake on Sundays during the summer, bring along a picnic and enjoy the music in fine tropical grounds. ■ *Daily 0730-1745, orchid house 0930-1700. Free*

KwaZulu Natal

entry. A set tour leaves from the information centre on the last Sun of every month at 0930. T2011303. Two other smaller parks are **Mitchell Park**, at the end of Musgrave Road, which are public gardens with an open air café, aviaries and a few animals; and the **Japanese Gardens**, on Prospect Hall Road in Durban North.

The **Killie Campbell Collection** is a museum and African library in a Cape Dutch house built in 1914 which still has most of its original decorations. There are some fine examples of Cape furniture and early South African oil paintings, displays of African sculpture, weapons, musical instruments and a rare collection of paintings by Barbara Tyrrell. Most of the paintings are of Africans dressed in their traditional costumes during the 19th century. The paintings form part of a unique record of what people actually wore before contact with European settlers. ■ *220 Marriott Rd, T2073711. The main house is open to the public by appointment only, Tue and Thu 0800-1300. Free entry. The library and its outstanding reading room are open for researchers, Mon-Fri 0900-1600. For tours of the library, T2073432. The friendly staff will let most people in who express a broad genuine interest in the collection.*

The **Hare Krishna Temple of Understanding** is an ashram opened in 1969, but the futuristic marble temple set in extensive ornamental gardens was only opened to the public in 1975. There is an excellent vegetarian restaurant here serving everything from light snacks to large curries. ■ *Open daily. Free entry. South of the centre on Ambassador Rd, and can be reached from the N2. T4033328.*

Chatsworth

In contrast to the rampant building boom of the 1980s, during which many of Durban's historical buildings were demolished, the Metropolitan Open Space System was being developed at the same time by local conservationists as a green lung for the Durban area. The idea behind MOSS is to protect wilderness areas within Durban and the suburbs. The scheme has so far designated more than 20 reserves varying in size from the tiny Crestholme Nature Reserve of 6 ha to the 1,700 ha of the Shongweni Resources Reserve. Most of the reserves have walking trails and all are easily accessible from the town centre.

Nature reserves
Entrance staff at the reserves should have maps and guides to hand out for all the various walking trails

KwaZulu Natal

Burman Bush Nature Reserve, in Morningside, is a relatively small reserve, only 50 ha, but is an important patch of dense coastal bush that has grown and flourished virtually untouched since the 1850s, and has a large population of vervet monkeys. There are three trails in the reserve, all clearly marked by coloured arrows. To get there from the centre of town follow Umgeni Rd, after 2 km you will reach a junction with Argyle Road, take a left here and then the third right into Windermere Road. Burman Nature Reserve is 3 km at the end of this road. Next to the car park is a Visitors' Centre (Mon-Fri, 0730-1600), public toilets, plus some picnic and braai sites.

Also off Umgeni Rd, on the opposite side to Burman Bush Nature Reserve is the **Umgeni River Bird Park**. This is well worth a visit with over 3,000 exotic and indigenous birds from flamingos to finches, and magpies to macaws. The free flight show is very unusual. Many large birds such as owls, raptures, vultures, and a rare blue crane, make an entrance on to the stage and then fly over the heads of the audience to perches at the top of the open-air auditorium. Sit at the top for great photography of the birds in flight. This successful show is thought to be one of its kind and can also be seen at the Monticasino's bird park in Johannesburg. ■ *Daily, 0900-1700. Entrance fee R30. Free flight show, Tue-Sun 1100 and 1400, tea garden. 490 Riverside Rd, T5794600.*

Kenneth Stainbank Nature Reserve is a fascinating place to visit because although it is a fairly large area of woodland and grassland next to a dam, the 253 ha reserve is completely surrounded by Durban and is an ideal place to examine man's effect on the environment. Expect to see impala, zebra, duiker and bushbuck along with a colourful variety of birds. There are 13 km of walks including one designed for the physically challenged. Night game drives can be organized, the highlights of the drive are the rare sightings of nocturnal mammals such as the bushbaby and genet, birdwatchers have an opportunity to see species like the nightjar and wood owl. ■ *Daily 0600-1800. Small entrance charge. At 96 Coedmore Av, Yellowwood Park, T4692807. Night drives available if booked in advance.*

Krantzkloof Nature Reserve is one of the larger reserves only 26 km from Durban. It is a well-defined and thickly-forested gorge, cut by the Emolweni River. Trails descend into the forested gorge where there are three waterfalls, the highest of which is 90 m. There is no large game here, but there is some interesting birdlife. ■ *Daily 0600-1800. At 152 Kloof Falls Road, T7647412.*

Silverglen Nature Reserve is another city park tended for by the Municipality, the largest area of public land within the city limits, comprising dense bush and open coastal grasslands. This used to be a popular place to visit with several walking trails. However we hear that this is not a safe place to visit any longer, and is notorious as a dumping ground for the bodies of victims of gang warfare. Avoid.

Shongweni Resources Reserve, is the largest nature reserve close to Durban and although it is not stocked with the more spectacular large African mammals it is a good place to see birds. Rhino and buffalo may be introduced here soon. The reserve is 30 km from Durban along the N3. After taking the Shongweni-Assagay exit off the N3, follow the signs to Shongweni and the dam. There are 15 km of hiking trails past weathered rock formations in the gorges and through grasslands around the dam. It is possible to go horse riding and canoeing here but both activities need to be booked in advance. ■ *Daily 0600-1800. At Shongweni Dam, T7691283.*

Excursions Durban's good motorway connections open up a range of day trips within driving distance from the city centre, although good public transport connections are limited to the South Coast, Pietermaritzburg and Umhlanga.

To the north inland on the N3 are the **Valley of a 1000 Hills**, **Pietermaritzburg**, the **Natal Midlands** and the **Battlefields**. To the south on the N2 are the surfing beaches and tourist resorts heading to **Port Shepstone** and **Margate**. To the north along the N2 lie **Umhlanga** and the coastal resorts of the north coast, whilst just inland from the N2 is the historical Zulu town of **Eshowe**.

The area was supposedly named the Valley of 1,000 Hills by the writer Mark Twain on a visit to South Africa at the end of the 19th century

The **Valley of a 1000 Hills** is an easy 35 km drive from Durban. Follow the N3 north out of the city but leave at the Westville/Pavilion Mall exit and join the old Pietermaritzburg road, R103, through the suburbs of Kloof and Hillcrest. Here you will pick up signs for the Valley of a 1000 Hills Meander. The Comrades Marathon runs along this road in June, a gruelling 90 km between Pietermaritzburg and Durban. Many tour operators run inexpensive half-day tours to this region. Between Durban and Pietermaritzburg the landscape quickly climbs some 700 m over a series of rolling hills characteristic of the suburbs around the two cities. From Botha's Rest, there are many viewpoints on the R103 from which to see the valley unfold, the fertile hills are dotted with settlements and farms and the encroaching townships closer to Durban. The valley has historically been a Zulu stronghold, and in the early 19th century was a refuge for dispossessed Zulus who had lost their farmland through battle further north.

If you want to stay in the area contact Kwababa, the KwaZulu Natal B&B Association, T5613795, F5612088

The R103 runs along the lip of the valley and tourism has literally gone into overdrive along this road with a variety of craft shops, restaurants, B&Bs, guest houses, and several Zulu cultural villages. The more popular of these is **PheZulu Safari Park**, at Botha's Hill. There are commanding views of the valley from here, a reptile farm, a small game park with zebra and antelope, curio shops (one specifically for children), the *Crocokraal* restaurant which specializes in croc steaks, and the *Mbizo* restaurant that serves traditional *potjies* (stews). The main attraction is the Zulu show. Visitors are taken into traditional beehive shaped huts where the various beliefs, rituals and artefacts are explained, before watching an impressive dancing display. However, there's nothing like a camera-toting coach party whose only focus is on the bare-breasted dancers to put you off this sort of thing and there are other more authentic Zulu 'experiences' in KwaZulu Natal. ■ *Daily, show times 1000, 1130, 1400, 1530. T7771000.*

Essentials

As a popular holiday destination there are plenty of agencies dealing with B&B and **Sleeping** self-catering accommodation close to the centre. The quality of the self-catering holiday apartments varies enormously, so always check with an agency, who should have pictures, and expect to be able to negotiate a low season and long term special rate. Make sure you check the security, remember it's not the same as a hotel where there are guards and cameras and staff all day long around the building. Try to avoid the apartment blocks around Gillespie St, which runs parallel with south beach, this area becomes quite unsavoury at night. Accommodation Reservation Service at the *Tourist Junction*, 160 Pine St, T3044934, F3043868, funinsun@iafrica.com, www.bookabedahead.co.za

City centre and Beachfront AL-A *Durban Hilton*, 12 Walnut St, next to the ICC, ■ *on maps,* T3368100. All the trappings you'd expect from a modern 5-star 'name' city hotel. A recent *pages 389 and 393* addition, but aims to be the best. **A-B** *Protea Hotel Edward*, 149 Marine Park, T3373681, *Price codes:* F3321692. 60 double a/c rooms, 30 a/c single rooms, 11 suites, non-smoking room available, *see inside front cover* restaurants, bar, pool, secure covered parking, one of the most luxurious of the beachfront hotels, reopened after a major rebuilding programme in 1996, a 5-star hotel, but let down by the immediate surrounds and the continued problems of petty crime. **A** *Royal*, 267 Smith St, T3336000, F3076884. A/c, TV, restaurant, swimming pool, the hotel originally built on this site in 1842 was made of wattle and daub, over the years the hotel has expanded and modernized, with luxurious 5-star service in central Durban. Has an excellent Indian restaurant.

B *Holiday Inn Garden Court – North Beach*, 83/91 Snell Parade, T3327361, F3374058. 270 a/c rooms, TV, restaurant, swimming pool, sauna, secure parking, a large modern hotel with good seaviews on the upper floors. **B** *Holiday Inn Garden Court – Beach Hotel*, 167 Marine Parade, T3373341, F3329885. A massive complex with 344 a/c double rooms with ensuite facilities, restaurant, swimming pool, a modern, smart and centrally located hotel. Recommended. **B-C** *Tropicana*, 85 Marine Parade, T3374222, F3682322. 80 a/c rooms, M-Net TV, *Seven Palms* restaurant, serves buffet meals or an excellent carvery, for seafood in smarter surrounds try the *La Concha* restaurant, *Clippers Café Bar* serves light meals on the terrace, swimming pool, secure covered parking, *Zululand Tours* based here – recommended for organizing all your transport and sightseeing in the region. Major renovations in 1997. **B-C** *Holiday Inn Garden Court - South Beach*, 73 Marine Parade, T3372231, F3379381. 414 rooms, a/c, TV, restaurant, swimming pool, is very popular with South African family holidaymakers, gets very busy.

C *City Lodge*, corner of Brickhill Rd and Old Fort Rd, T3321447, F3321483. Standard quality chain lodge with usual facilities, not much to do to keep you hanging around the hotel, mainly used by conference delegates at the nearby ICC. The cheaper, no-frills, **D** *Road Lodge*, is round the corner, TT3048202, F3048265. **C** *Palace Hotel*, 211 Marine Parade, North Beach, T0860-333666, F3328307. A/c, TV, restaurant, swimming pool, is a good value self-catering hotel with holiday apartments sleeping up to 6 people. **C** *Seaboard Protea*, Nedbank Circle, 577 Point Rd, T3373601, F3372600. 255 a/c rooms with TV, mix between ensuite doubles and self-catering flats for up to 4 people, restaurant, lounge, swimming pool, secure parking. **C** *Tenbury*, corner of Erskine Terr and South Beach Av, T/F3351900. Self-catering flats, a/c, TV. **C** *Bayside*, 116 West St, T3320460. Recently refurbished central hotel, old house with wooden floors and wide balconies looking out over the traffic, en suite rooms, a/c, TV, secure under cover parking. **C-D** *Tudor House*, 197 West St, T3377328, F3377060. 28 rooms, a/c, TV, restaurant, does look rather run down from the outside, but is actually quite pluckily decorated on the inside. **D** *Albany*, corner of Smith St and Albany Grove, T3044381, F3071411. 72 simple a/c, en suite single and double rooms, TV, restaurant, pub, good central location opposite City Hall and Playhouse. **D** *Riviera*, 127 Victoria Embankment, T3013681, F3013684. A bland hotel despite its excellent location, harbour views, TV, phone, some family rooms, under cover parking, sports bar with pool table, tacky *Bimbo's* 24-hr fast food restaurant, better to eat elsewhere.

E *Pavilion*, Marine Parade, T3377366, F3682322. TV, restaurant. **E** *Formule 1*, next to the railway station and long distance coach station, T3011551, F3011552. Budget rooms for up

KwaZulu Natal

to 3 pax, ideal for late arrivals but nothing to keep you there other than sleeping, book to guarantee a room since there are few budget options of this kind.

Backpackers
Baz Bus collect and drop off from all backpacker hostels if booked in advance

F *Anstey's*, 477 Marine Dr, Bluff, T/f4671192. The Bluff is the section of Durban that sticks out to sea on the opposite side of the entrance to the port. Anstey's is a new hostel so we would welcome reports. Dorms, self-catering apartmants sleeping 4, bar with pool table, meals. Arrange their own city tours of Durban, beach horse rides, surfboards. The lodge is opposite the *cave rock*, thought to be the most hollow wave in South Africa – surf dudes should head here. **F** *Brown Sugar*, 6 Kinnord Pl, 607 Essenwood Rd, Essenwood, T2098528. A massive colonial mansion with some of the best views in Durban. Rooms all over the place. In a good safe part of town, but very mixed reports, it's a case of either loving it here or not being able to get out fast enough. You'll know your likes better than us, check it out if tempted by the house. It could be worth it. **F** *Hippo Hide*, 2 Jesmond Rd, Berea, T2074366, F2074366, michelle@hippohide.co.za A small tidy lodge set in a pretty indigenous garden, double rooms, some en suite, dorms, relaxed atmosphere, rock pool with outside bar and pleasant deck, close to shopping centres and restaurants on Musgrove Rd. Michelle, the on site owner, is fastidious about keeping the place clean, and helpful in pointing you in the right direction in and around Durbs. **F** *Nomads*, 70 Essenwood Rd, Berea, T/F2029709, nomadsbp@netralink.com Dorms, double rooms, self-catering facilities, *Bambooza* bar, swimming pool, pool table. Good friendly backpackers' place in a safe area within easy walking distance for shops and places to munch. Run by Paul and Leigh who know their travel stuff and are always happy to help out. *Baz Bus* stop. **F** *Tekweni Backpackers*, 169 Ninth Av, Morningside, T3031433, F3034369, tekweni@global.co.za Dorms and double rooms, small swimming pool and bar out front, 'smokers' area outback along with the tents, full laundry facilities, internet access. Often in a party mood, quieter doubles available next door. The excellent *Tekweni Ecotours*, T3031199, are based here. They offer a full range of tours for ornithologists, surfers and big game watchers in their own well-kept combis. Their Durban tour is worth going on to help get a feel for the place. A popular hostel in an ideal location, one of the best in Durban at present. 30 mins' walk from beach, or a 10 mins' bus ride. **F** *Traveller's International Lodge*, 743 Currie Rd, Morningside, T/F3031064, travelers-lodge@saol.com Dorms, double rooms, excellent kitchen with all you need to conjure up a fresh meal – but often cook an evening meal for guests. Small outdoor bar and pool table, email access. Free pick up from bus/train station. An often recommended hostel with close ties with the *Baz Bus*, very clean, has no swimming pool or night manager, but we still feel one of the best current options in Durban. Colleen takes a genuine interest in her visitors and a short chat with her will help set you up for an enjoyable stay in Durban. Very helpful when setting up day tours and longer safari deals into Zululand. High standards.

Durban suburbs

The attraction of staying in the suburbs is that they are at a higher altitude and therefore cooler and less humid. Accommodation offered here tends to be in hotels aimed more towards the business traveller, or luxury B&Bs, by no means all unreasonably priced, but you will need a car. They are too numerous to list in full, contact the **Tourist Junction**, www.bookabedahead.co.za or **Kwababa**, the KwaZulu Natal B&B Association, T5613795, F5612088, sugarfld@iafrica.com

Westville **B** *Westville*, 124 Jan Hofmeyr Rd, T2666326, F2668559. Recently refurbished to high standards, 42 a/c rooms, TV, the *Cape Southeaster* restaurant is fast becoming well-renowned for its excellent Cape and French cuisine, swimming pool, squash courts, big sports bar. An upmarket businessmen's hotel but suitable for the tourist who doesn't like the beach scene. **D** *Wellington Views*, 19 Wellington Rd, T/F2629094. Small B&B in a cozy home, pool, office facilities, ask for Chene.

North Berea and Morningside **B-C** *Elephant House*, 745 Ridge Rd, Berea, T289580. 2 double a/c rooms with ensuite bathrooms, TV, non-smoking room, lounge, laundry service, mature tropical gardens, B&B, other meals on request, this house is a National Monument, the tale goes that it is the oldest house in Durban and it got its name after it was once attacked by elephants (for charging too much for trunk calls?). **B-C** *Quarters*, 101 Florida Rd, T3035246, F3035269. 25 a/c double rooms, ensuite facilities, TV, guest lounge. 4 historic homes have been converted into a fine hotel with plenty of character. Residents can relax in the brasserie which is open for light meals throughout the day, sit in a shaded courtyard or a simple modern bar. Most rooms have a small veranda overlooking gardens with palm trees and colour. Central location, close to restaurants, recommended.

C *Brown's*, 132 Marriott Rd, Berea, T2087630, F2087630. Ask for Penny, 2 suites with ensuite bathrooms, B&B, TV, comfortable and homely furnishings, lounge, laundry, pool, peaceful garden to sit out in, short walk to the beach. **C-D** *Rosetta House*, 126 Rosetta Rd, T/F3036180. 4 double roooms, TV, secure parking, a fine old town house. **C-D** *Triple Five*, 555 Essenwood Rd, T/F2096787. 3 a/c en suite double rooms, TV lounge, garden jacuzzi, dining area, self-catering kitchen, secure off street parking.

Durban North C-D *Mentone*, 7 Humber Crescent, Durban North, T5643108, F5633986. 2 small apartments with a/c, TV, swimming pool, secure parking. Easy access to shops and restaurants. **C** *Sunrise on Broadway*, 55 Broadway, Durban North, T5639871, F5638230. B&B, pool, use of internet facilities.

Glenwood C *Bali on the Ridge*, 268 South Ridge Rd, Glenwood, T2619574, F2619476. Close to the University of Natal, spectacular views of the city and harbour, elegantly furnished with many ethnic pieces, comfortable stylish a/c rooms, TV, bar fridge, pool. Recommended. **B** *Ridgeview Lodge*, 17 Loudoun Rd, Glenwood, T2029777, F2015587. 7 double rooms each with a/c and en suite bathrooms. An elegant house with excellent guest facilities. Secluded lush gardens with swimming pool. Close to restaurants and shops. Airport transfer can be arranged. Recommended.

City centre *Famous Fish Co*, King's Battery, Point Waterfront, T3681060. A highly popular outfit with several outlets throughout the town. Worth finding, secure parking while you eat. Quality fresh seafood served with an engaging smile. Watch the ships negotiate the narrow entrance to Durban's port from here. *Gringo's Cantina*, 28 Kearnsey Rd, T3320519. Tacos, tequila and beer, very trendy. *La Dolce Vita*, Durban Club, Victoria Embankment, T3018161. Italian style menu with plenty of seafood and good wines. A long term quality favourite in Durban. *Maharajah*, Palm Beach Hotel, 106 Gillespie St, T3373451. A good selection of authentic Indian curries and tandoori dishes. Recommended. *Mykonos*, 156 Essenwood Rd, T2025636. Lively atmosphere with Greek dancing and plate breaking. Eat as much as you can buffet with an extensive selection of dishes. *New Café Fish*, yacht mole, Victoria Embankment, T3055062. Set out into the water with yachts moored within arms reach, upstairs bar great for a sundowner and view of the working harbour, seafood a speciality, some salads and steaks. *Oriental Palace*, John Ross House, Victoria Embankment, 31st floor, below the revolving restaurant, T3683751. Quality curryies served with a magnificent harbour view. Vast vegetarian menu and the tandoor items are worth investigating. Book to avoid disappointment during busy periods. *Roma Revolving*, John Ross House, Victoria Embankment, T3376707. Closed Sun. Revolving restaurant on the 32nd floor, seafood and pasta, heavily laden dessert trolley, unparalleled views of Durban at night. *Royal Grill*, 267 Smith St, T3336000. Excellent steaks, part of the Royal Hotel. *Ulundi*, Royal Hotel, 267 Smith St, T3336000. The top end of the scale, days of colonial Natal are echoed here, turbaned waiters, rattan furniture, ceiling fans, grills and traditional Durban curries.

Eating
● *on maps, pages 389 and 393*

Beachfront *Darumo*, *Holiday Inn Crowne Plaza*, 63 Snell Parade, T3371321. Beautifully prepared Japanese seafood dishes, you can watch your meal being prepared at the *hibachi* and *teppanyaki* tables. *Golden Chopsticks*, Marine Parade, T3328858. A popular beachfront restaurant with seaviews, reasonably priced meals. *Jewel of India*, 63 Snell Parade, *Holiday Inn Crown Plaza*, T3621300. Worth visiting on a night in Durban. Excellent and tasty dishes served with tandoor breads. There is a side room with cushions and low tables where you can kick off your shoes and relax with a drink. Recommended. *Saagries*, Marine Parade, *Holiday Inn*, T3227922. Good range of Durban and Indian curries, reservations necessary. Recommended.

KwaZulu Natal

Bunny Chow

One of the more popular and delicious takeaway meals in Durban is Bunny Chow. A half loaf of bread with the middle scooped out and filled with curry. The scooped out bit is then used as a spoon, which soaks up the sauce. The dish was originally created by innovative chefs for black caddies, commonly known as bunnies, who were not allowed to use the crockery or cutlery at certain exclusive golf clubs in the old apartheid days.

Durban suburbs Durban's most popular night time hives of activity are currently in Florida Rd in Morningside and Musgrave Rd in Berea. On both these roads, all the popular bars and restaurants are next to each other making for a convenient night out with plenty of choice. *A Timbuktu*, 200 Florida Rd, Morningside, T3121435. Seafood and sangria are the specialities in this startlingly pink restaurant. *Aldo's*, 62 Kensington Drive, Durban North, T5630454, closed Sun. A popular well-established Italian restaurant owned by Aurie from the Turin area. Wide range of pasta and veal dishes. Outdoor terrace. *Christina's*, 134 Florida Rd, Morningside, T3032111. Open for dinner Tue-Fri only, breakfast, teas and lunch Tue-Sat. This is a training restaurant, but is still very popular and manages to maintain a good standard of French cuisine. Menus are as varied as the students curriculems and presentation is a strong point. Good value Sat buffet lunch. Outdoor shaded patio is pleasant in the summer. *Coimbra*, Queensmead Mall, Umbilo, T2055447. Closed Sun. A good range of authentic regional Portuguese dishes one of the best of its kind in Durban, good wines, busy pub with live music at the weekends. *Gulzar*, 71 Stamford Hill Road, Greyville, T3096379. A good venue to sample traditional Natal Indian curries such as mutton with beans, the prawn curry is excellent, if they are not to your taste there are plenty of North Indian dishes to choose from. A long narrow room with Eastern charm. *Langoustine by the Sea*, 101 Waterkant Rd, Durban North, T5637324. Large bright restaurant on the coastal road facing the sea, seafood is their speciality but there's something for everyone here, the extensive menu including steaks, pizzas, pasta, curries and Thai dishes too. There is a small theatre attached, frequent local plays, worth checking if there's anything on that interests you.

Bars, cafés & bistros *Bat Café*, in the BAT Centre, small craft harbour, Victoria Embankment, T3682029. Relaxed venue with a deck overlooking the harbour, often with live music. African menu from samp and beans to boerewors rolls. *Bean Bag Bohemia*, 18 Windermere Rd, Greyville, T3096030. Coffee shop on the ground floor, restaurant upstairs in an old converted Durban town house, quirky décor, fun place in the evenings when the bar attracts a well to do crowd, plenty of snacks with strong Mediterranean bias. Recommended. *Bistro 136*, 136 Florida Rd, Morningside, T3033440. Classic bistro atmosphere and menu with plenty of filling dishes to choose from. *Legends Café*, Musgrave Centre, Musgrave Rd, T2010733. Enjoyable mix of oriental and European dishes, popular venue for some time, the inside is decorated with posters of movie stars, bar and kitchen open late. *Joe Kools*, North Beach, T3329697. Right on the beach opposite one of the more popular surf sites, lots of outside terraces lit with strobe lights at night, popular bar and restaurant with the surfing fraternity. *Zacks*, Musgrave Centre, Musgrave Rd, T2014768. Open all day from breakfast, bar closes late, light meals from bruschetta to steak, pastas and burgers.

Nightclubs Club 3-30, 330 Point Rd, T3377172. Open Fri and Sat 2200. One of South Africa's top clubs with regular 3-30 events happening in London. A mass of different dance floors. *Dusk til Dawn*, corner of Umbilo Rd and Clarke Rd. Beanbag and incense ambience, music from the 70's through to electronica 90's. *Night Fever*, 121 Argyle Rd, Greyville, T3098422. Tue, Fri, Sat, 2000 until late, commercial dance music, attracts lots of rugby fans. Tue is commonly referred to as 'Pig's Night' – pay one entrance fee and drink as much as you can between 2000-2330. *100 on Point*, 100 Point Rd. Fri and Sat from 2100, R&B, retro, house, live bands, over 25s.

Wildlife of East and Southern Africa

"Well, make up your mind", said the Ethiopian, "because I'd hate to go hunting without you, but I must if you insist on looking like a sunflower against a tarred fence."

"I'll take spots, then," said the Leopard; "but don't make 'em too vulgar-big. I wouldn't look like Giraffe – not for ever so."

"I'll make 'em with the tips of my fingers," said the Ethiopian. "There's plenty of black left on my skin still. Stand over!"

Then the Ethiopian put his five fingers close together (there was plenty of black left on his new skin still) and pressed them all over the Leopard, and wherever the five fingers touched they left five little black marks, all close together. You can see them on any leopard's skin you like, Best Beloved. Sometimes the fingers slipped and the marks got a little blurred; but if you look closely at any Leopard now you will see that there are always five spots—off five fat black finger-tips.

"Now you are a beauty!" said the Ethiopian. "You can lie out on the bare ground and look like a heap of pebbles. You can lie on the naked rocks and look like a piece of pudding-stone. You can lie out on a leafy branch and look like sunshine sifting through the leaves; and you can lie right across the centre of a path and look like nothing in particular. Think of that and purr!"

How the Leopard got his spots
Just So Stories, Rudyard Kipling

Wildlife of East and Southern Africa
Text: adapted from original version by Margaret Carswell with additional material from Sebastian Ballard. Photographs: BBC Natural History Unit Picture Library, Bruce Coleman Collection, gettyone Stone Images, Gus Malcolm.

3

Contents

The big nine

It is fortunate that many of the large and spectacular animals of Africa are also, on the whole, fairly common. They are often known as the "Big Five". This term was originally coined by hunters who wanted to take home trophies of their safari. Thus it was, that, in hunting parlance, the Big Five were Elephant, Black Rhino, Buffalo, Lion and Leopard. Nowadays the Hippopotamus is usually considered one of the Big Five for those who shoot with their cameras, whereas the Buffalo is far less of a 'trophy'. Also equally photogenic and worthy of being included are the Zebra, Giraffe and Cheetah. But whether they are the Big Five or the Big Nine, these are the animals that most people come to Africa to see and with the possible exception of the Leopard and the Black Rhino, you have an excellent chance of seeing them all.

■ **Common/Masai Giraffe** *Giraffa camelopardis* (top). Yellowish-buff with patchwork of brownish marks and jagged edges, usually two horns, sometimes three. Found throughout Africa in several differing subspecies. ■ **Reticulated Giraffe** *Giraffa reticulata* (right). Reddish brown coat and a network of distinct, pale, narrow lines. Found from the Tana River, Kenya, north and east into Somalia and Ethiopia. Giraffes found in East Africa have darker coloured legs and their spots are dark and of an irregular shape with a jagged outline. In southern Africa the patches tend to be much larger and have well defined outlines, although giraffes found in the desert margins of Namibia are very pale in colour and less tall – probably due to a poor diet lacking in minerals. ■ **Buffalo** *Syncerus caffer* (above). Were considered by hunters to be the most dangerous of the big game and the most difficult to track and, therefore, the biggest 'trophy'. Generally found on open plains but also at home in dense forest, they occur in most African national parks, but like the elephant, they need a large area to roam in, so they are not usually found in the smaller parks.

■ **Cheetah** *Acinonyx jubatus* (left). Often seen in family groups walking across plains or resting in the shade. The black 'tear' mark is usually obvious through binoculars. Can reach speeds of 90km per hour over short distances. Found in open, semi-arid savannah, never in forested country. Endangered in some parts of Africa but in Namibia there is believed to be the largest free-roaming population left in Africa. More commonly seen than the leopard, they are not as widespread as the lion. ■ **Lion** *Panthera leo* (below). Nearly always seen in a group and found in parks all over East and Southern Africa. ■ **Leopard** *Panthera pardus* (bottom). Found in varied habitats ranging from forest to open savannah. They are generally nocturnal, hunting at night or before the sun comes up to avoid the heat. You may see them resting during the day in the lower branches of trees.

Wildlife of East and Southern Africa

■ **Black Rhinoceros** *Syncerus caffer* (right). Long, hooked upper lip distinguishes it from White Rhino. Prefers dry bush and thorn scrub habitat and in the past they were found in mountain uplands such as the slopes of Mount Kenya. Males usually solitary. Females seen in small groups with their calves (very rarely more than four), sometimes with two generations. Mother always walks in front of offspring, unlike the White Rhino, where the mother walks behind, guiding calf with her horn. The distribution of this animal has been massively reduced by poaching and work continues to save both the Black and the White Rhino from extinction. You might be lucky and see the Black Rhino in: Etosha NP, Namibia; Ngorongoro crater, Tanzania; Masai Mara, Kenya; Kruger, Shamwari and Pilansberg NPs and private reserves like Mala Mala and Londolozi, South Africa.

■ **White Rhinoceros** *Diceros simus* (right). Square muzzle and bulkier than the Black Rhino, they are grazers rather than browsers, hence the different lip. Found in open grassland, they are more sociable and can be seen in groups of five or more. More common in Southern Africa due to a successful breeding programme in Hluhluwe/Umfolozi NP, South Africa. The park now stocks other parks in the region. ■ **Elephant** *Loxodonta africana* (above). Commonly seen, even on short safaris, throughout East and Southern Africa, though they have suffered from the activities of war and from ivory poachers. It is no longer possible to see herds of 500 or more animals but in Southern Africa there are problems of over population and culling programmes have been introduced.

Wildlife of East and Southern Africa

■ **Hippopotamus** *Hippopotamus amphibius* (top). Prefer shallow water, graze at night and have a strong sense of territory, which they protect aggressively. Live in large family groups known as "schools". ■ **Mountain zebra** *Equus zebra zebra* (above). Smallest of the three zebras shown here, with a short mane and broad stripes, it is only found in the western cape region of South Africa on hills and stony mountains. ■ **Common Zebra (Burchell's)** *Equus burchelli* (left). Generally, broad stripes (some with lighter shadow stripes next to the dark ones), which cross the top of the hind leg in unbroken lines. The true species is probably extinct but there are many varying subspecies found in different locations across Africa, including: **Grants** (found in East Africa) **Selous** (Malawi, Zimbabwe and Mozambique) and **Chapman's** (Etosha NP, Namibia, east across Southern Africa to Kruger NP). ■ **Grevy's Zebra** *Equus grevyi,* (bottom left) larger than the Burchell's Zebra, with narrower stripes that meet in star above hind leg, generally found north of the equator. Lives in small herds.

Wildlife of East and Southern Africa

Larger antelopes

On safari the first animals that will be seen are almost certainly antelope, on the plains. Although there are many different species, it is not difficult to distinguish between them. For identification purposes they can be divided into the larger ones which stand about 120 cm or more at the shoulder, and the smaller ones about 90 cm or less.

■ **Common** *Kobus ellipsiprymnus* and **Defassa** *Kobus defassa* **Waterbuck** 122-137cm (right). Very similar with shaggy coats and white marking on buttocks. On the Common variety, this is a clear half ring on rump and round tails; on Defassa, the ring is a filled in solid white area. Both species occur in small herds in grassy areas, often near water. Common found in East and Southern Africa, Defassa only in East.

■ **Nyala** *Tragelaphus angasi* 110cm (above). Slender frame, shaggy, dark brown coat with mauve tinge (males). Horns (male only) single open curve. As the picture shows, the female is a very different chestnut colour. Like dense bush and found close to water. Gather in herds of up to 30 but smaller groups more likely. Found across Zimbabwe and Malawi.

■ **Eland** *Taurotragus oryx* 175-183cm (right). Noticeable dewlap and shortish spiral horns (both sexes). Greyish to fawn, sometimes with rufous tinge and narrow white stripes down side of body. Occurs in groups of up to 30 in both East and Southern Africa in grassy habitats.

■ **Sable antelope** *Hippotragus niger* 140-145cm (left) and **Roan antelope** *Hippotragus equinus* 127-137cm (bottom left). Both similar shape, with ringed horns curving backwards (both sexes), longer in the Sable. Female Sables are reddish brown and can be mistaken for the Roan. Males are very dark with a white underbelly. The Roan has distinct tufts of hair at the tips of its long ears. Found in East and southern Africa (although the Sable is not found naturally in East Africa, there is a small herd in the Shimba Hills game reserve). Sable prefers wooded areas and the Roan is generally only seen near water. Both species live in herds. ■ **Gemsbok** *Oryx gazella* 122cm (below). Unmistakable, with black line down spine and black stripe between coloured body and white underparts. Horns (both sexes) straight, long and look v-shaped (seen face-on). Only found in Southern Africa, in arid, semi-desert country. Beisa Oryx occurs in East Africa.

■ **Greater Kudu** *Tragelaphus strepsiceros* 140-153cm (above). Colour varies from greyish to fawn with several white stripes on sides of the body. Horns long and spreading, with two or three twists (male only). Distinctive thick fringe of hair running from the chin down the neck. Found in fairly thick bush, sometimes in quite dry areas. Usually live in family groups of up to six, but occasionally larger herds of up to about 30. ■ **The Lesser Kudu** *Tragelaphus imberis* 99-102cm is considerably smaller, looks similar but lacks the throat fringe of the bigger animal. Has two conspicuous white patches on underside of neck. Not seen south of Tanzania.

Wildlife of East and Southern Africa

■ Brindled or Blue Wildebeest or Gnu *Connochaetes tauri- nus* (right)132cm. Often seen grazing with Zebra. Found only in Southern Africa. ■ **The White bearded Wildebeest** *Connochaetes taurinus albojubatus* is generally found between central Tanzania and central Kenya and is distinguished by its white 'beard'.

■ Hartebeest, 3 sub-species, (right) and **Topi** (above). In the Hartebeest the horns arise from boney protuberance on the top of head and curve outwards and backwards. **Coke's Hartebeest** *Alcephalus buselaphus* 122cm, also called the **Kongoni** in Kenya, is a drab pale brown with a paler rump. **Lichtenstein's Hartebeest** *Alcephalus lichtensteinii* 127-132cm, is also fawn in general colouration, with a rufous wash over the back, dark marks on the front of the legs and often a dark patch near shoulder. The **Red Hartebeest** *Alcephalus caama* is another subspecies that occurs throughout Southern Africa, although not in Kruger NP. **Topi** *Damaliscus korrigum* 122-127cm. Very rich dark rufous, with dark patches on the tops of the legs and more ordinary looking, lyre-shaped horns.

Smaller antelopes

■ **Impala** *Aepyceros melampus* 92-107cm (left). Bright rufous in colour with a white abdomen. From behind, white rump with black lines on each side is characteristic. Long lyre-shaped horns (male only). Above the heels of the hind legs is a tuft of thick black bristles (unique to Impala), easy to see as the animal runs. Black mark on the side of abdomen, just in front of the back leg. Found in herds of 15 to 20 in both East and Southern Africa.

Wildlife of East and Southern Africa

■ **Thomson's Gazelle** *Gazella thomsonii*, 64-69cm (left) and **Grant's Gazelle** *Gazella granti* 81-99cm (above). Superficially similar Grant's, the larger of the two, has slightly longer horns (carried by both sexes in both species). Colour of both varies from bright to sandy rufous. Thomson's Gazelle can usually be distinguished by the broad black band along the side between the upperparts and abdomen, but some forms of Grant's also have this dark lateral stripe. Look for the white area on the buttocks which extends above the tail on to the rump in Grant's, but does not extend above the tail in Thomson's. Thomson's occur commonly on plains of Kenya and Tanzania in large herds. Grant's Gazelle occur on rather dry grass plains, in various forms, from Ethiopia and Somalia to Tanzania.

Wildlife of East and Southern Africa

■ **Vaal Rhebuck** *Pelea capreolus* 75cm (right). Sometimes confused with the Mountain Reedbuck where the two species coexist. The Rhebuck has a long, slender neck and a woolly coat and narrow, pointed ears. Brownish grey in colour, its underparts and the tip of its short bushy tail are slightly paler. The horns (male only) are quite distinctive: they are vertical, straight and almost parallel to each other. It lives in family groups of up to 30. They are usually found in mountainous or hilly regions where there are patches of open grasslands. ■ **Springbuck** *Antidorcas marsupialis* or Springbok, 76-84cm (below). The upper part of the body is fawn, and is separated from the white underparts by a dark brown lateral stripe. A distinguishing feature is a reddish brown stripe which runs between the base of the horns and the mouth, passing through the eye. The only gazelle found south of the Zambezi River. You no longer see giant herds, but you will see Springbuck along the roadside as you drive between Cape Town and Bloemfontein in South Africa.

■ **Steenbok** *Raphicerus campestris* 58cm (right). An even, rufous brown colour with clean white underside and white ring around eye. Small dark patch at the tip of the nose and long broad ears. The horns (male only) are slightly longer than the ears: they are sharp, have a smooth surface and curve slightly forward. Generally seen alone, prefers open plains, often found in more arid regions. A slight creature which usually runs off very quickly on being spotted. Common resident throughout Southern Africa, Tanzania and parts of Southern Kenya. ■ **Sharpe's Grysbok** *Raphicerus sharpei* 52cm (bottom). Similar in appearance to the Steenbok, but with a white speckled rufous coat. Nose dark brown, white belly. Horns (male only) are very short and sharp, rising vertically from the forehead. Prefers stony and hilly country, often seen amongst kopjies, could be confused with the klipspringer. Lives alone except during the breeding season. Often seen under low bushes, which they browse upon, looking for new shoots and any small fruits. Limited distribution in East Africa, but common along the mountainous areas of the rift valley. In South Africa you are likely to see the **Cape Grysbok**.

Wildlife of East and Southern Africa

■ **Oribi** *Ourebia ourebi* 61cm (left). Slender and delicate looking with a longish neck, sandy to brownish fawn coat. Oval-shaped ears, short, straight horns with a few rings at their base (male only). Like the Reedbuck it has a patch of bare skin just below each ear. Live in small groups or as a pair. Never far from water. Found in East and Southern Africa. ■ **Kirk's Dikdik**, *Rhynchotragus kirkii* 36-41cm (below). So small it cannot be mistaken, it is greyish brown, often washed with rufous. Legs are thin and stick-like. Slightly elongated snout and a conspicuous tuft of hair on the top of the head. Straight, small horns (male only). Found in bush country, singly or in pairs, East Africa only.

■ **Bohor Reedbuck** *Redunca redunca* 71-76cm (above). Horns (males only) sharply hooked forwards at the tip, distinguishing them from the Oribi (top). Reddish fawn with white underparts and short bushy tail. Live in pairs or small family groups, in East and Southern Africa. Often seen with Oribi, in bushed grassland and always near water. ■ **Suni** *Nesotragus moschatus* 37cm (left). Dark chestnut to grey fawn in colour with slight speckles along the back. Head and neck slightly paler with a white throat. Distinct bushy tail with a white tip. Longish horns (male only), thick, ribbed and sloping back. One of the smallest antelope, they live alone and prefer dense bush cover and reed beds in East and Southern Africa.

Wildlife of East and Southern Africa

■ **Gerenuk** *Litocranius walleri* 90-105cm (right). Disinct long neck, often stands on hind legs to browse from thorn bushes. Likes arid, semi-desert conditions. Only found in Kenya and possibly Uganda.

■ **Bushbuck** *Tragelaphus scriptus* 76-92cm (below). Shaggy coat with variable pattern of white spots and stripes on the side and back and 2 white, crescent-shaped marks on front of neck. Short horns (male only) slightly spiral. High rump gives characteristic crouch. White underside of tail is noticeable when running. Occurs in thick bush, especially near water. Either seen in pairs or singly in East and Southern Africa.

■ **Klipspringer** *Oreotragus oreotragus* 56cm (bottom right). Brownish-yellow with grey speckles. White chin and underparts, short tail. Distinctive, blunt hoof tips. Short horns (male only). Likes dry, stony hills and mountains. Found only in Southern Africa.

■ **Common (Grimm's) Duiker** *Sylvicapra grimmia* 58cm (above). Grey fawn colour with darker rump and pale colour on the underside. Dark muzzle. Prominent ears divided by straight, upright, narrow pointed horns. This particular species is the only duiker found in open grasslands. The duiker is more commonly associated with a forested environment. Common throughout Southern and East Africa, but difficult to see – it is shy and will quickly disappear into the bush.

Other mammals

Although the antelopes are undoubtedly the most numerous animals to be seen on the plains, there are many other fascinating mammals worth keeing an eye out for. The following are some of the more common mammals that you may see in East and Southern Africa.

■ **Warthog** *Phacochoerus aethiopicus* (left). Almost hairless and grey with a very large head, tusks and wart-like growths on face. Frequently occurs in family parties and when startled will run at speed with their tails held straight up in the air. Often seen near water caking themselves in the thick mud which helps to keep them both cool and free of ticks and flies. Found in both East and southern Africa.

Wildlife of East and Southern Africa

■ **African Wild Dog** or **Hunting Dog** *Lycaon pictus* (above). Easy to identify since they have all the features of a large mongrel dog: a large head and slender body. Their coat is a mixed pattern of dark shapes and white and yellow patches, no two dogs are quite alike. Very rarely seen, they are seriously threatened with extinction. Found on the open plains around dead animals, but not a scavenger. They are in fact very effective hunters, frequently working in packs. ■ **Dassie** (left, above Rock hyrax, left below Tree hyrax) *Dendrohyrax arboreus*. There are three main groups of this small, guinea-pig-like rodent: the rock hyrax, the yellow spotted hyrax and the tree hyrax. Tree hyraxes are nocturnal and feed in trees at night. They have longer fur than the rock hyrax. The rock hyrax, also nocturnal, lives in colonies amongst boulders and on rocky hillsides, protecting themselves from predators like eagle, caracal and leopard by darting into the rock crevices if alarmed. Found only in Southern Africa.

Wildlife of East and Southern Africa

■ Bat-eared fox *Otocyon megalotis* (right). Distinctive large ears (used for listening for prey underneath the surface of the ground) and very short snout are unmistakeable. Greyish-brown coat with black markings on legs, ears and face. They are mainly nocturnal, but can be seen lying in the sun near their burrows during the day. Found in East and southern Africa.

■ Civet *Viverra civetta* (right). Yellowish-grey coarse coat with black and white markings and black rings around eyes. Nocturnal animal rarely seen and quite shy. Found in woody areas or thick bush. ■ **Black-backed Jackal** *Canis mesomelas* 45cm (bottom). Foxy reddish fawn in colour with a noticeable black area on its back. This black part is sprinkled with a silvery white which can make the back look silver in some lights. Often seen near a lion kill, they are timid creatures which can be seen by day or night.

■ **Serval** *Felis serval* 50cm (left). Narrow frame and long legs, with a small head and disproportionately large ears. Similar colouring to a cheetah, but the spots are more spread out. Generally nocturnal, they are sometimes seen in bushy areas, near rivers or marshes. Found in both East and Southern Africa. ■ **Spotted Hyena** *Crocuta crocuta* 69-91cm (below). ■ **Brown Hyena** *Hyaena brunnea* (opposite page, centre). High shoulders and low back give characteristic appearance. Spotted variety is larger, brownish with dark spots, a large head and rounded ears. The brown hyena, slightly smaller, has pointed ears and a shaggy coat, more noctural. Found in both East and Southern Africa.

Wildlife of East and Southern Africa

■ **Caracal** *Felis caracal* (left). Also known as the African lynx, it is twice the weight of a domestic cat, with reddish sandy colour fur and paler underparts. Distinctive black stripe from eye to nose and tufts on ears. Generally nocturnal and with similar habits to the leopard. They are not commonly seen, but are found in hilly country, sometimes in trees, in both East and Southern Africa.

Apes

Baboons

■ **Chacma** *Papio ursinus* (top). Adult male slender and can weigh 40kg. General colour is a brownish grey, with lighter undersides. Usually seen in trees, but rocks can provide sufficient protection from predators. Occur in large family troops, have a reputation for being aggressive where they have become used to man's presence. Found in East and Southern Africa. ■ **Hamadryas** *Papio hamadryas* (right). Very different from the other two species, the male being mainly ashy grey with a massive cape-like mane. The face and buttocks are bright pink, and the tail does not appear broken. Females lack the mane and are brownish in colour. ■ **Olive Baboon** *Papio anubis* (top, opposite page). A large, heavily built animal, olive brown or greyish in colour. Adult males have a well-developed mane. In the eastern part of Kenya and Tanzania, including the coast, the Olive Baboon is replaced by the Yellow Baboon *Papio cynocephalus*, smaller and lighter, with longer legs and almost no mane in adult males. The tail in both species looks as if it is broken and hangs down in a loop.

Wildlife of East and Southern Africa

■ **Vervet** or **Green Monkey** *Cercopithicus mitis* (above). Appearance varies, most commonly has a black face framed with white across the forehead and cheeks. General colour is greyish tinged with a varying amount of yellow. Feet, hands and tip of tail are black. They live in savannah and woodlands but have proved to be highly adaptable. You might think the Vervet Monkey cute: it is not, it is vermin and in many places treated as such. They can do widespread damage to orchards and other crops. On no account encourage these creatures, they can make off with your whole picnic, including the beers, in a matter of seconds. Found in East and Southern Africa. ■ **Chimpanzee** *Pan troglodytes* (left) and the **Gorilla** *Gorilla gorilla* (centre, page 16) are not animals you will see casually in passing, you have to go and look for them. They occur only in the forests in the west of the region in Uganda, Rwanda and Zaire. In addition there are some Chimpanzee in western Tanzania.

Reptiles

■ **Blue-headed Agama** *Agama atricollis* (opposite page, top) and **Orange-headed Agama** *Agama agama* (right) up to 20cms long. Only the males have the brightly coloured head and tail. They run along walls and rocks and are frequently seen doing 'press-ups'. You will notice them around your lodge or camp site. They make lovely photos, but are not easy to approach. The Blue-headed is the most common and more widespread of the two.

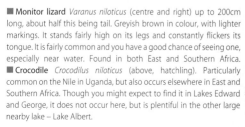

■ **Monitor lizard** *Varanus niloticus* (centre and right) up to 200cm long, about half this being tail. Greyish brown in colour, with lighter markings. It stands fairly high on its legs and constantly flickers its tongue. It is fairly common and you have a good chance of seeing one, especially near water. Found in both East and Southern Africa.
■ **Crocodile** *Crocodilus niloticus* (above, hatchling). Particularly common on the Nile in Uganda, but also occurs elsewhere in East and Southern Africa. Though you might expect to find it in Lakes Edward and George, it does not occur here, but is plentiful in the other large nearby lake – Lake Albert.

■ **Green Chameleon** *Chamaeleo gracilis* (below). Well-known and colourful reptiles, there are several species of Chameleon, but this is the most common and is fairly widespread. ■ **Tree Frogs** *Hylidae*, (bottom). There are many different sorts of tree frog. They are all small amphibians which are not often seen, but occasionally one can be found half way up a door post or window frame which it has mistaken for a tree. They are usually bright green or yellow, often with pretty markings.

Wildlife of East and Southern Africa

Water and waterside birds

Wildlife of East and Southern Africa

Africa is one of the richest bird areas in the world and you could spot over 100 species in a single day. The birds shown here are the common ones and with a little careful observation can all be identified, even though they may appear totally strange and exotic. To make identification easier, they have been grouped by habitat. Unless otherwise stated, they occur both in East and Southern Africa.

■ **Greater Flamingo** (96) *Phoenicopterus ruber* 142cms (right). The larger and paler bird of the two species found in Africa has a pink bill with a black tip. ■ **Lesser Flamingo** (97) *Phoenicopterus minor* 101cms, deeper pink all over and has a deep carmine bill with a black tip. Both occur in large numbers in the soda lakes of western Kenya.

■ **Hammerkop** (81) *Scopus umbretta* 58cms (top left). Dull brown in colour with a stout, moderately long bill. Distinctive large crest which projects straight backwards and is said to look like a hammer. A solitary bird usually seen on the ground near water – even roadside puddles. Builds an enormous nest in trees, large and strong enough to support the weight of a man. ■ **Pied Kingfisher** (428) *Ceryle rudis* 25cms (above). The only black and white kingfisher. Common all round the large lakes and also turns up at quite small bodies of water. Hovers over the water before plunging in to capture its prey. ■ **Blacksmith Plover** (258) *Vanellus armatus* 30 cms (right). Strongly contrasting black, white and grey plumage. White crown, red eye, black legs. Common resident found around the margins of lakes, both freshwater and alkaline, also close to rivers and cultivated lands. Distinct, high-pitched call which it utters when it that feels its nest or young are threatened.

■ **NB** The number in brackets after the birds' names refers to the species' 'Roberts' number, which is used for identification purposes in Southern Africa. This code is not used in East Africa, but it can still help in cases where the same species has a different local name.

Wildlife of East and Southern Africa

■ **Fish Eagle** (148) *Haliaeetus vocifer* 76cms (left). This magnificent bird has a very distinctive colour pattern. It often perches on the tops of trees, where its dazzling white head and chest are easily seen. In flight this white and the white tail contrast with the black wings. It has a wild yelping call which is usually uttered in flight. Watch the bird throwing back its head as it calls. ■ **Goliath Heron** (64) *Ardea goliath* 144cms (below). Usually seen singly on mud banks and shores, both inland and on the coast. Its very large size is enough to distinguish it, but the smaller **Purple Heron** (65) *Ardea purpurea* 80cms, which frequents similar habitat and is also widespread, may be mistaken for it at a distance. If in doubt, the colour on the top of the head (rufous in the Goliath and black in the Purple) will clinch it.

■ **African Jacana** (240) *Actophilornis africana* 25cms (left). This is a mainly chestnut bird, almost invariably seen walking on floating leaves. Its toes are greatly elongated to allow it to do this. Its legs dangle down distinctively when in flight. Found in quiet backwaters with lily pads and other floating vegetation.

■ **Paradise Flycatcher** *Terpsiphone viridis* male 33cm, female 20cm (right). Easily identified by its very long tail and bright chestnut plumage. The head is black and bears a crest. The tail of the female is much shorter, but otherwise the sexes are similar. It is seen in wooded areas, including gardens and is usually in pairs. In certain parts, notably eastern Kenya, its plumage is often white, but it still has the black head. Sometimes birds are seen with partly white and partly chestnut plumage. ■ **Egyptian goose** (102) *Alopochen aegyptiaca* (below) 65cm. Brown to grey-brown plumage. Distinct chestnut patch around the eye and on the centre of the breast; wings appear white in flight. Red/pink legs and feet. This is a common resident found throughout the region except in arid areas. Occurs in small flocks and pairs. Most likely to be seen around the margins of inland waters, lakes, rivers, marshes, pans and cultivated fields.

■ **Crowned Crane** (209) *Balearica pavonina* 100cms (right). It cannot really be mistaken for anything else when seen on the ground. In flight the legs trail behind and the neck is extended, but the head droops down from the vertical. Overhead flocks fly in loose V-shaped formation. Not a water bird, but quite common near Lake Victoria, it also occurs in much of the rest of East Africa as well.

Birds of the open plains

■ **Ground Hornbill** (463) *Bucorvus cafer* 107cm (left). Looks very like a turkey from a distance, but close up it is very distinctive and cannot really be mistaken for anything else. They are very often seen in pairs and the male has bare red skin around the eye and on the throat. In the female this skin is red and blue. Found in open grassland.

■ **Bateleur** (146) *Terathopius ecaudatus* 61cm (above). A magnificent and strange looking eagle. It is rarely seen perched, but is quite commonly seen soaring very high overhead. Its tail is so short that it sometimes appears tailless. This, its buoyant flight and the black and white pattern of its underparts make it easy to identify. ■ **Secretary Bird** (118) *Sagittarius serpentarius* 101cm (left). So called because the long plumes of its crest are supposed to resemble the old time secretaries who carried their quill pens tucked behind their ears. Often seen in pairs hunting for snakes, its main source of food.

■**Ostrich** (1) *Struthio camelus* 2m (right). Male birds are predominantly black, while the females are usually a dusty dark brown. Found both in national parks and on open farm land. The original wild variety has been interbred with subspecies in order to improve feather quality. In South Africa the region known as the Little Karoo was once the centre of a boom during which millions of birds were kept in captivity. The Ostrich is sometimes seen singly, but also in family groups.

■ **Kori Bustard** (230) *Otis kori* 80cm (top left). Like the Secretary Bird, it quarters the plains looking for snakes. Quite a different shape, however, and can be distinguished by the thick looking grey neck, caused by the loose feathers on its neck. Particularly common in Serengeti National Park and in the Mara. ■ **Red-billed Oxpecker** (772) *Buphagus erythrorhynchus* 18cm (above). Members of the starling family, they associate with game animals and cattle, spending their time clinging to the animals while they hunt for ticks. ■ **Cattle Egret, Forktailed** (71) *Bubulcus ibis* 51cm (right). Follows herds and feeds on the grasshoppers and other insects disturbed by the passing of the animals. Occasionally too, the Cattle Egret will perch on the back of a large animal, but this is quite different from the behaviour of Oxpeckers. Cattle Egrets are long legged and long billed white birds which are most often seen in small flocks. In the breeding season they develop long buff feathers on the head, chest and back.

Woodland birds

■ **Superb Starling** *Spreo superbus* 18cm (left) and **Golden-breasted Starling** *Cosmopsarus regius* 32cms (below). Both are common, but the Superb Starling is the more widespread and is seen near habitation as well as in thorn bush country. Tsavo East is probably the best place to see the Golden-breasted Starling. Look out for the long tail of the Golden-breasted Starling, and the white under tail and white breast band of the Superb Starling. Both are usually seen hopping about on the ground.

■ **Little bee-eater** (444) *Merops pusillus* 16cm (above). Bright green with a yellow throat, conspicuous black eye stripe and black tip to a square tail, lacks the elongated tail feathers found in many other species of bee-eater. Solitary by day, but at night often seen bunched in a row. Favours open woodlands, streams and areas where there are scattered bushes which can act as perches. Look out for Carmine bee-eater colonies in sandbanks along rivers. This beautiful bird is an intra-African migrant. ■ **Drongo** (541) *Dicrurus adsimilis* 24cm (left). An all black bird. It is easily identified by its forked tail, which is 'fish-tailed' at the end. Often seen sitting on bare branches, it is usually solitary.

Wildlife of East and Southern Africa

■ **Red Bishop** (824) *Euplectes orix* 13cm (right). Brown wings and tail and noticeable scarlet feathers on its rump. Seen in long grass and cultivated areas, and often, but not invariably, near water. Almost equally brilliant is the **Blackwinged Bishop** *Euplectes hordeaceus* 14cm. Distinguished by black wings and tail and obvious red rump. ■ **Red-cheeked Cordon-bleu** *Uraeginthus benegalus* 13cm (below). Brown back and bright red cheek patches. They are seen in pairs or family parties and the females and young are somewhat duller in colour than the males. They are quite tame and you often see them round the game lodges, particularly in Kenya and parts of Uganda and Tanzania but not in Southern Africa.

■ **Red-billed Hornbill** (458) *Tockus erythrorhynchus* 45cm (above). Blackish-brown back, with a white stripe down between the wings. The wings themselves are spotted with white. The underparts are white and the bill is long, curved and mainly red. Use the tops of thorn trees as observation perches. ■ **White-crowned Shrike** (756) *Eurocephalus rueppelli* 23cm (right). Black wings, tail and eye stripe, brown back. Throat and breast white, with a distinct white crown. Always seen in small parties, making short direct flights from one vantage point to the next. Walks confidently on the ground amongst debris in the dry bush country they tend to favour. Look out for them in 'feeding parties' in acacia woodlands. Similar in appearance to the White-headed Buffalo Weaver *Dinemellia dinemelli* 23cm, though not related.

■ **Helmeted Guinea Fowl** (203) *Numida meleagris* 55cm (left). Slaty grey with white speckles throughout, bare around the head which is blue and red with a distinct horny 'casque' – the helmet. A common resident in most countries, found close to cultivated lands and open grasslands. Highly gregarious, during the day the flocks tend to forage on the ground for food; rarely do they take to flying and even then it is usually only for a short distance. At night the birds roost communally, making a tremendous din when they come together at dusk. Look out for them near water, they tend to approach the source in single file.

■ **Red-billed Francolin** (194) *Francolinus adspersu* 35cm (below). Medium sized brown bird, finely barred all over. Legs and feet red to orange, yellow eye with bare skin around it. This particular species is found throughout central and northern Namibia, Botswana and western Zimbabwe. Other similar species with only minor variations are found throughout East and Southern Africa. An annoying bird which makes itself known at dawn around campsites with a harsh cry that speeds up and then suddenly stops.

■ **D'Arnaud's Barbet** *Trachyphonus darnaudii* 15cm (above). Quite common in the dry bush country. A very spotted bird, dark with pale spots above, and pale with dark spots below. It has rather a long dark tail which is also heavily spotted. Its call and behaviour is very distinctive. A pair will sit facing each other with their tails raised over their backs and wagging from side to side and bob at each other in a duet. All the while they utter a four note call over and over again. "Do-do dee-dok". They look just like a pair of clockwork toys.

■ **Lilac-breasted Roller** (447) *Coracias caudata* 41cm (left). The brilliant blue on its wings, head and underparts is very eye-catching. Its throat and breast are a deep lilac and its tail has two elongated streamers. It is quite common in open bush country and easy to see as it perches on telegraph poles or wires, or on bare branches.

Urban birds

The first birds you will see on arrival in any big city will almost certainly be the large numbers soaring overhead. Early in the morning there are few, but as the temperature rises, more and more can be seen circling high above the buildings. The following (with the possible exception of the Quelea) are often seen in either in towns or near human habitation, although you may see them elsewhere, such as arable farmland, as well.

■ **Black-headed Weaver** *Ploceus cucullatus* 18cm (right). Male has a mainly black head and throat, but the back of the head is chestnut. The underparts are bright yellow and the back and wings mottled black and greenish yellow. When the bird is perched, and seen from behind, the markings on the back form a V-shape. Often builds its colonies in bamboo clumps.

■ **Marabou Stork** (89) *Leptoptilos crumeniferus* 152cm (above, with fish eagle devouring a flamingo). Overhead, its large size, long and noticeable bill and trailing legs make it easy to identify. Although this bird is a stork it behaves like a vulture, in that it lives by scavenging.
■ **Hooded Vulture** (212) *Neophron monachus* 66cm (right). Medium size vulture, dark brown, pink head. This is one of the smallest of the vultures and is unable to compete with other vultures at a carcass. Often solitary, feeding on small scraps of carrion as well as insects and offal.

■ **Red-billed quelea** (821) *Quelea quelea* 13cm (left and below). Similar colour and markings to a common sparrow, black face and a distinct thick red bill. Widespread throughout tropical Africa, a quiet bird when alone or in pairs. Best known for their destructive abilities around harvest time. They gather into flocks of several hundreds of thousands and can wipe out a seed crop in a single day. When they reach plague proportions they are treated as such and destroyed.

Wildlife of East and Southern Africa

■ **Scarlet-chested Sunbird** *Nectarinia senegalensis* 15cm (above). Male is a dark velvety brown colour with scarlet chest. Top of the head and the throat are iridescent green. The tail is short. One member of a large family of birds which are confusingly similar (particularly the females), rather like the weavers. Often perches on overhead wires and in parks and gardens, especially among flowers, allowing you to get a good look at it.
■ **African Pied Wagtail** (711) *Motacilla aguimp* 20cm (left). Black and white with a white band over the eye, black legs. Common where resident throughout the region. Associated with human habitation, sports fields, city parks and drains, also seen on sand bars along river beds. A very tame bird which you may be able to approach in some hotel gardens.

Cinemas *Nu Metro*, have multi-screen cinemas at the *BP Centre*, corner of West St and **Entertainment**
Aliwal St, T3379320, and the *Pavilion*, mall in Westville, T2650001. *Ster-Kinekor*, cinemas
can be found in many of the suburban shopping malls, check press for details.

Theatres *The Playhouse*, 231 Smith St, T3699444 for information on what's on. Has 5
auditoriums showing regular performances. An eclectic range of shows ranging from Shake-
speare to contemporary political satire and modern dance. It has recently been suffering
from financial hardship and it would be a shame to see *The Playhouse* close, as there are too
few quality theatres in South Africa.

African Art Centre, Tourist Junction Station Building, 160 Pine St, T3047915. This is one of **Shopping**
the best places in Durban to buy Zulu beadwork, baskets and ceramics, the shop is a
non-profit making outlet for rural craftspeople. *Antiques and Bygones*, 437 Windermere Rd,
Morningside, T3038880. Sell a range of silver jewellery and European antiques. *Haribhai's
Spice Emporium*, 31 Pine St, T3326662. Open daily, has a large selection of imported spices
and other Indian foods. *Matombo Art Gallery*, also at the Tourist Junction, T3049968. Good
quality but expensive Zimbabwe stone sculputures. *The Wheel*, 55 Gillespie St. Once a mall
worth visiting a few years ago, it now suffers from being located in an area that has become
rapidly unsafe. There are no decent shops anymore and the area should be avoided.

With the demise of the area between the beachfront and the city centre, around Point Rd
and Gillespie Rd, most of the shops have moved to the shopping malls in the suburbs, which
are becoming a regular aspect of day-to-day life in South Africa. The *Pavillion*, T2650558, in
Westville has 320 shops and restaurants, and a cinema, or head north out of town to *Gateway*, T5662332, in Umhlanga Rocks. This is supposedly the largest shopping mall in the
Southern Hemisphere and a full day could easily be spent here. A huge variety of shops and
restaurants, 18 screen cinema, Imax theatre, impressive climbing wall, surf waves, championship skateboard park, and all sorts of other treats. Something for everyone...a place that
has to be seen to believed.

Cricket Durban's first test match was played in January 1910 at a ground then known as **Sports**
Lords. This ground no longer exists, it was replaced by the current ground, Kingsmead, in
January 1923. Kingsmead is home to the KwaZulu Natal provincial cricket team, it is a modern stadium with large grandstands, only a small area of grass banks remains. All of Durban's
big matches are played at this popular venue. The weather for matches is generally good but
being close to the sea there is always a chance of rain or poor visibility. *Kingsmead*, PO Box
47266, Greyville, 4023. Ticket enquiries: T3329703, F3325288, dolphins@natalcricklet.co.za

Diving Operators dive from Durban or can arrange trips to other sites such as Sodwana
Bay or the Aliwal Shoal. *Dive Nautique*, T082-5532834 (mob); *Dive Factory*, T3012241.

Surfing There are several designated surfing and boogie boarding beaches along the
seafront, and plenty of surf shops on the South Beach promenade have boards for hire. *Surf
Zone*, Ocean Sports Centre, North Beach, T3685818, board rental. *Tekweni Ecotours*,
T3031199, arrange day trips to classic wave sites up and down the coast.

Golf *Windsor Park Municipal Golf Course*, T3122245, is next to the Umgeni River just
north of Durban. 18 holes, phone for teeing off times for visitors, equipment can be hired
here by the day or by the week.

Horse racing Race meetings are held on Tue, Wed or Thu, and Sat from 1200-1700 at
one of KwaZulu Natal's 3 racecourses operated by the *Golden Circle Turf Club*. Night racing at
Greyville on Wed, Thu, and ocassionally Sat, 1715-2115. *Greyville*, T3141500; *Clairwood
Park*, T4691020; and *Scottsville*, T033-3453405. Smart casual dress is fine for all but the most
exclusive racetrack restaurants.

Scenic flights *Court Helicopters*, T5639513. Helicopter tours of Durban. *La mercy
Microlight Flights*, T083-5974222 (mob). Short flights over Umhlanga Lagoon, ideal for
whale spotting, lessons also available. *Blue Sky Paragliding*, T7651318. Flights Wed-Sun in
the Valley of the 1000 Hills, weather permitting.

City tours *Durban Charter Boat Association*, Fuelling Jetty, Yacht Mole, T3011115. Offer a **Tour operators**
wide range of boats, for small speed boat diving trips and deep sea shark fishing to luxury

booze cruises. *Durban Ferry Services*, T3011953. Sundowner cruises and harbour tours. *Durban Watersports Centre*, Vetch's Beach, T3377238. A wide range of watersports, sailing, surfing, dolphin and whale watching, sea kayaking, hourly or daily rates, instruction available, restaurant on site. *Durban Africa*, contact the Tourist Junction, T3044934. Tours throughout the day Mon-Fri, a choice of Oriental Walkabout or Historical Walkabout. *Coloured Experience*, T082-6731923 (mob). Historical city and coloured township tours. *Exec-u-tours*, T5726483. Budget city tours, day trips to Shakaland, St Lucia, battlefields. Unusual 'Creepy Crawly' tour to the Natal Sharks Board in Umhlanga, Umgeni Bird Park, and Snake Park. *Jikeleza Tours*, T7021189. Township tour starting at the Kwa-Muhle Museum to understand the nature of Apartheid, before visiting the Umlazi or Nanda township. Also evening trips with local guides for drinks at the township *shebeens*. *Islamic Propagation Centre*, T3060026. Offer guided tours of the mosque on Queen St. *Sugar Terminals*, 51 Maydon Rd, Maydon Wharf, T3658153. 4 daily tours, Mon-Fri at 0830, 1000, 1130, and 1400, an unusual and industrial visit to Durban's massive sugar terminals.

KwaZulu Natal Province tours *Far and Wild Safaris*, 477 Essenwood Rd, T2083684, F2074700. Luxury safaris to Hluhluwe and Umfolozi, fly-in day trips also possible. *Tekweni Ecotours*, 169 Ninth Av, Morningside, T3031199, F3034369. Durban's alternative tour operator catering for surfers, birdwatchers and vegetarians. As well as regular tours to Hluhluwe, Umfolozi and St Lucia game parks, they also offer a week-long surfers' trip through Transkei down to Jeffreys Bay, and tailor-made bird trips. There are also a number of cultural day and overnight trips to Zululand. Consistently good reports, recommended. *Strelitzia Tours*, T2669480, F2669404. A comprehensive range of tours in the province from 1-3 days with regular departures. Day trips to townships, Valley of the 1000 hills, Durban city.

Transport   **Local Bus**: *Margate Mini Coach*, T039-3121406, after hours T082-4559736 (mob). Operates a service along the south coast to Margate, very convenient if you are staying here. *Mynah*, information office on corner of Aliwal St and Pine St, T3095942. This is a frequent local bus service with routes around the city centre, the beachfront and Berea, average fare R2. *Umhlanga Express*, T5612860. Minibus taxi service to Umhlanga Rocks (20 mins), good rates for a group, surcharge for surfboards and luggage.

See also under   **Car hire**: *Avis*, *Royal Durban Hotel*, Toll Free reservations; International, T08610-34444; *'Air' below*   Domestic, T08610-21111. *Berea Car and Bakkie Hire*, 331 Berea Rd, T2023333, F2018914, bereacar@saol.com *Budget*, 108 Ordnance Rd, T0860-016622. *Hertz*, 13 The Avenue East, Toll Free, T0861-600136. *Europcar*, *Holiday Inn Garden Court*, North Beach, domestic reservations, Toll Free, T0800-011344. *Imperial*, 34 Aliwal St, domestic reservations, Toll Free, T0800-011344. *Rent-a-drive*, T3324987, F3322201. Cars, mini-buses, bakkies. *Tempest*, 47 Victoria Embankment, T3685231, F3686466. *Maharani*, 30 Playfair Rd, North Beach, T3686563. *Woodford*, 41 Woodford Grove, Stamford Hill, T3127311, F3128532, woodford@icon.co.za Good range of hire options and broad range of vehicles.

Taxi: *Aussies*, 33 Cato St, T3097888. *Eagle*, 34 Brickhill Rd, T3378333. *Mozzie Cabs*, T3036137. *Falcon*, T3096771, T0800-323334, toll free.

Durban International   **Long distance Air**: at present there are only a limited number of international flights which *Airport: T4516667,*   fly direct into **Durban International Airport**. But if your planned visit to South Africa only *for flight information*   entails spending time within the Durban and KwaZulu Natal region, if possible it makes *14 km south of the*   sense to fly direct into Durban. This airport is far less hectic than Johannesburg or Cape Town *city centre*   and on arrival you can quickly find yourself settled in the city with the minimum of hassle. If you are budget conscious, you will find that many backpacker hostels offer free airport collection/transfer service. Alternatively there are plenty of private companies providing airport transfer services. *Airport Bus Service*, T4651660, operate an hourly service between 0530 and 2000. Their coaches depart from the corner of All St and Smith St, next to the AS office. *Magic Bus*, T5611095/6, F5614423. A pre-booked transfer is much cheaper than just showing up. *Cheetah Coaches*, T033-3422673, and the *Margate Mini Coach*, T039-3121406, after hours T082-4559736 (mob), will also call in at the airport for advance bookings. If you have been unable to arrange a collection at the airport ask your hotel to organize a collection, before you start your travels.

Comair/British Airways, T4507000, central reservations, T011-9210111, fly between Durban and **Johannesburg** up to 10 times per day, first departure approx 0630, arriving in Johannesburg within an hour. There are 4 flights per weekday between Durban and **Cape Town**, 1 on Sat, 2 on Sun, the flight takes just over 2 hrs. *South African Airways*, information, T4503388. Plenty of daily flights to Cape Town and Johannesburg along with flights to other principal South African cities.

Kulula.com, booking online at www.kulula.com (no phone but a desk at the airport), is South Africa's new no-frills, budget airline, currently offering the cheapest flights between Johannesburg and Durban. The airline runs on the same principle as the European budget airlines, no tickets, reservations through the website, no on-board refreshments etc. Fares from R300 one-way to Johannesburg. The number of daily flights is ever-increasing as its popularity grows.

Kulula's fares are little more than the cost of equivalent long distance bus fares

Car hire at the airport: *Avis*, T4081777, Toll free, T08610-2444; *Budget*, T3049023, Toll free, T0860-016622; *Hertz*, T4694247; *Imperial*, T4690066, Toll free, T0800-131000. **NB** Each company has a counter in either the domestic or international terminal. There is a tourist information office in the domestic arrivals hall, T4501000, open daily 0830-1600.

Virginia Airport, for helicopters and light aircraft, is 10 km north of Durban, T5644144 for flight information. Private charter flights operate from here to the larger game reserves in KwaZulu Natal. *East Coast Airways*, T5649344, operate from here. *Imperial*, T5641758, have a few hire cars at this airport.

Rail: Trains for Durban arrive at the **New Durban Station**, NMR Ave. Reservations T0860-008888, Enquires (Spoornet), T3613388. The *Trans Oranje* service departs Wed at 1730 for **Cape Town** (36 hrs), via **Bloemfontein** and **Kimberley**. The *Trans Natal* service departs daily at 1830 for **Johannesburg** (13 hrs), via **Pietermaritzburg** (2 hrs) and **Ladysmith**, (6 hrs).

Road: *Greyhound*, T3097830, bus services depart from the Motor Coach Terminal by New Durban Station. **Cape Town** (24 hrs): daily, 0700 (via **Umtata**, **East London**, **Port Elizabeth**, **Knysna** and **Swellendam**). **Cape Town** (22¾ hrs): daily 1130 (via **Harrismith**, **Bloemfontein**, and **Beaufort West**. **Pretoria** and **Johannesburg** (8½ hrs): daily, 0800, 1000, 1030, 1400, 1600, 2230, 2300 (the 1000 coach is a slower stopping service). **Richards Bay** (3 hrs): daily, 0900; this service continues to **Johannesburg** (12 ½ hrs) (via **Piet Retief** and **Ermelo**). *Intercape*, T3092144. To **Cape Town** (24 hrs): daily, 1600 via **Bloemfontein**, daily 0530 and 1600 via **Port Elizabeth**. To **Johannesburg** and **Pretoria** (11 hrs): daily, 0630, 1200, and 2030. *Margate Mini Coach*, T039-3121406, after hours T082-4559736 (mob), departs Durban Station Translux Terminal, advance booking essential, service to **Margate** (2 hrs), departs up to 3 times per day, fewer services at the weekend, via **Durban Airport**, **Scottburgh**, **Hibberdene** and **Port Shepstone**. Expect to pay approx R85 return, R65 single, Durban to Margate. *Luxliner*, T3059090, toll free 0800003537. To **Johannesburg International Airport** (7 hrs): daily, 0830, and to **Margate** (2½ hrs): daily, 1730. *Sodwana Shuttle*, T2669878, a local minivan running between **Durban** and **Sodwana Bay** via **Richards Bay** (north coast). Minimum of 6 people. *Translux*, T3088111, F3617963. **Cape Town** (20 hrs): daily, 1100 (via **Bethlehem** and **Bloemfontein**), daily, 0630 (via **Port Elizabeth**). **Johannesburg** and **Pretoria** (9 hrs): daily, 0745, 0830, 0930, 2230; Fri, Sun, 0850: Mon, Fri, Sun, 1400. *Baz Bus*, the most efficient and comprehensive budget bus service for backpackers from overseas; National hotline, T021-4392323. Further information can be obtained via their website or contacting the principal office in Cape Town, www.bazbus.com There are 3 different services running out of Durban each week. Check at the back of this book for exact timings or look up the latest timetable on their website. There is a service to **Port Elizabeth** which runs 5 times per week in both directions. This bus has a video to help pass the time. The second service runs 3 times per week to **Johannesburg** and **Pretoria**, via the **Northern Drakensberg**. Finally the third bus runs 3 times per week to **Pretoria** and **Johannesburg** via **Zululand** and **Swaziland** in both directions.

If the only bus journey you plan on making is to travel directly between Durban and Cape Town, with no stops, the Greyhound ticket is half the price of the Baz Bus

KwaZulu Natal

Directory **Airline offices** *Air Zimbabwe*, Musgrave Centre, Musgrave Rd, T2016061-5, F2017809. *Comair/BA*, T4507000, F4081808. *East Coast Airways*, Virginia Airport, T849344. Private air charters. *Lufthansa*, 66 Kensington Dr, Durban North, T5646684, F5646687. *Singapore Airlines*. 305 Musgrove Rd, T2024303, F2024333. **South African Airways**, airport, T4503388, reservations T2501111. *Swazi Express*, T4081115-6. *Virgin*, T2016061, airport.

Banks *ABSA*, T0800-111155. *First National*, T0800-111722. *Nedbank*, T0800-110929. *Standard Bank*, T0800-020600. *American Express*, Pavilion Mall, T2651455; 151 Musgrave Rd, T2028733. Open Mon-Fri 0800-1700, Sat 0830-1200. *Rennies*, 333 Smith St, T3055722. Foreign exchange and *Thomas Cook* representative. Also has offices at: *Bhoda Centre*, 72 Prince Edward St, T3055038. *Shop 7*, Sanlam Centre, Musgrove Rd, T2027833. *Shop 155*, The Pavillion, Westville, T2650751. *Mastercard*, T0800-990418. *Diners Club*, T0800-112017.

Consulates *Belgium*, 2 Sunrise Close, Morningside, T3032840, F3120434. *Germany*, (Honorary Consul), 2 Devonshire Pl, T3055677, F3055679. *Italy*, 14th floor, Embassy House, 199 Smith St, T3684388, F3684504. *Mozambique*, 320 West St, T3040200, F3040774. *Netherlands*, ABSA Bldg, corner of Field St and West St, T3041770, F3045716. *Sweden and Norway*, 702 Musgrave Centre, 115 Musgrave Rd, Berea, T2026911, F2012283. *United Kingdom*, 19th Floor, The Marine, 22 Gardiner St, T3032840, F3074661. *USA*, Durban Bay House, 333 Smith St, T3044737, F3018206.

Medical services **Chemists**: *Aliwal Pharmacy*, corner of Aliwal St and West St, T3375770. *Daynite Pharmacy*, corner of West St and Point Rd, T3683666. Open daily 0800-2230. **Medical emergencies**: T0800-333911. *The Medicine Chest*, 155 Berea Rd, T3056151. Open daily 0800-2400. *South Beach Medical Centre*, Rutherford St, Point, T3323101. A multi disciplinary centre, open 24 hrs. Practical central location. **Hospitals**: *Addington Hospital*, (Principal State Hospital), Erskine Terrace, South Beach, T3322111. *City Hospital Ltd*, 83 Lorne St, T3143000, F3272000. 24-hr emergency service. *Entabeni Private Hospital*, 148 South Ridge Rd, T2041300. (Be prepared to pay, or prove ability to do so, from the outset). *The Travel Doctor*, 45 Ordnance Rd, International Convention Centre, T3601122, F3601121. Vaccination centre and a good place to pick up anti-malarials.

Useful services/numbers **City Police**: T3064422. **Mountain Club of South Africa**: T082-9905877 (mob). **KZN Wildlife**: T033-8451000, F8451001. **Police Tourism Unit**: T3682207/3325923. **Sea Rescue**: T3372200. *The Visa Shop*, 10th Floor, ABSA Building, 78 Field St, T3041419, F3041481. **Weather**: T082162.

KwaZulu Natal south coast

The landscape south of Durban includes a fertile subtropical region stretching from the southern tip of the Drakensberg Mountain Range to the Indian Ocean. The Umzimkulu, the Umkomaas and the Elands rivers wind their way from the Drakensberg escarpment through the rolling hills of KwaZulu Natal to the sea. This was one of the first areas to be settled by the British during the last century and continuous agricultural development has left its mark on the landscape. Some of South Africa's largest pine and eucalyptus plantations extend for mile after mile around Harding, whilst nearer to the coast sugarcane and banana plantations dominate the scenery. A strip of subtropical forest runs down the coast bordering onto the beach. Excellent roads also make the Strelitzia and Hibiscus coastlines one of South Africa's most popular holiday destinations and this part of the coastline, which runs for 160 km all the way from Durban to Port Edward, has been heavily developed for tourism, getting very busy at weekends and during school holidays.

The main attractions inland are the nature reserves at Oribi Gorge and Umtamvuna, whilst along the coast dolphin watching and scuba diving on the Aliwal Shoal and on the reefs south of Port Shepstone thrill an ever growing number of enthusiasts. A wide range of sporting facilities are available at all the resorts and visitors also come for the numerous golf courses, tennis courts and long, safe beaches.

Strelitzia Coast

The Strelitzia Coast is one of the more built up areas south of Durban. Driving down the N2 the road passes Durban's international airport and goes through an extensive industrial belt. The lagoons beyond Amanzimtoti have been spared the relentless pace of development and these havens of tropical vegetation are sanctuaries for the coast's prolific birdlife.

Amanzimtoti, or 'toti', only 22 km south of Durban, is effectively a suburb. This Zulu name translates as "sweet waters", which is how Shaka announced the waters from the river to be on tasting. A wide range of holiday accommodation is available here amongst the high-rise flats and holiday homes facing the beach. **Inyoni Rocks** and **Pipeline Beach** are the two main beaches for swimmers and sunbathers. Sporting facilities in Amanzimtoti include tennis, golf, bowls and angling. Canoes and pedalos are available for hire on the lagoon. **Funland,** just back from the beach, is an amusement arcade on five floors with video games, fruit machines and the usual collection of fast food outlets. Behind the beach is a busy main road and on the outskirts of town there is a large chemical factory and an explosives factory. For **Tourist Information,** contact the *Amanzimtoti Publicity Association*, 95 Beach Rd, T9037498, F9037493. They can fax you a complete list of accommodation.

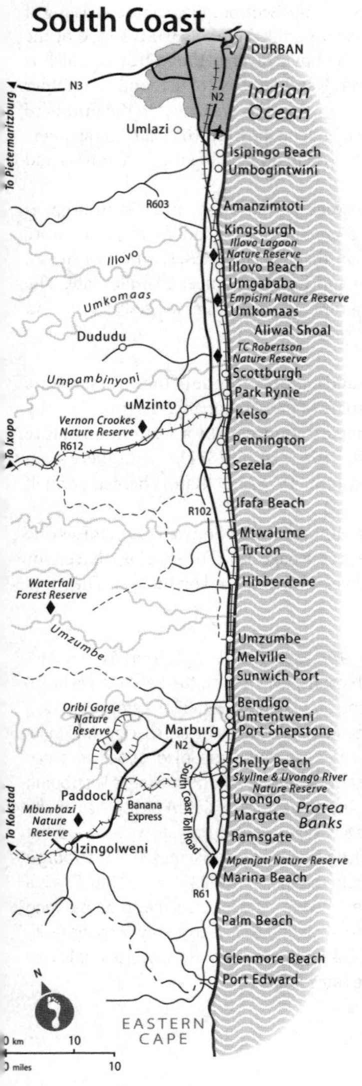

South Coast

Amanzimtoti
Phone code: 031
(NB Always use
3-figure prefix)
Colour map 5, grid B2

Sleeping B-C *Happy Days*, 65 Beach Rd, T9033246, F9033482. Beach front holiday flats with a restaurant and bar in the complex. **B-C** *Stella Maris*, 73 Beach Rd, T9035477, F9035479. Self-catering flats with TV, swimming pool for guests. **B-C** *Cabanas Mio*, 123 Beach Rd, T/F9036583. Holiday flats in a big block, all with superb views, including a beach facing balcony, TV, restaurant on site, swimming pool. **C** *Ezulweni Holiday Flats*, 71 Beach Rd, T9033493. 8 self contained flats sleeping up to 7 people. **C** *The View Guesthouse*, 9 Hillside Rd, T9031556, F9038820. Luxury guesthouse in smart suburb, sea views, nice pool area, jacuzzi, four poster beds, B&B, evening meals on request.

Eating *Clearwaters Spur*, 97 Beach Rd, T9038813. A busy western-style saloon bar selling enormous steaks and large amounts of beer. *Keg & Hedgehog*, 417 Kingsway, T9037390. A lively pub atmosphere selling a good range of beers and pub meals. *Oasis Tropical*, 73 Beach Rd, T9034834. Popular seafood restaurant. *Valentino's*, Beach Road, T9037015. Beachside bar, good value breakfasts and snack lunches.

Between Amanzimtoti and Umgababa are a series of coastal resorts known collectively as Kingsburgh. The 8-km stretch of beaches is known for good ski-boating conditions, surfing and its variety of different bathing sites. Visitors can swim in a lagoon, in tidal pools, or at

Price codes:
see inside front cover

Most accommodation
is in self-catering
apartments.
Thousands of local folk
spend their annual
beach holiday here,
swimming, soaking up
the sun and partying

KwaZulu Natal

Kingsburgh
Phone code: 031
(NB Always use
3-figure prefix)
Colour map 5, grid B1

one of the protected beaches: **Warner**, **Illovo** and **Winkelspruit** (see below). Travelling down the coast from Amanzimtoti the first beach you reach is **Doonside**, across the Little Manzimtoti River is Warner Beach.

Price codes:
see inside front cover

Sleeping C *Bela Vista Hotel*, 175 Kingsway, T9161800. 32 rooms, some with en suite bathroom, restaurant, bar, popular evening venue. **F** *Angle Rock Backpackers*, 5 Ellcock Rd, T9167007, F9167006, anglerock@iafrica.com Dorms, double rooms, excellent kitchen, laundry facilities, full size snooker table, swimming pool in a private garden full of palm trees and a great tropical feel, they promise if the pool is green you stay for free, owners can organize trips to help you get the best out of the region, building is situated on the beach, very good reports, served by the *Baz Bus*, recommended as the place to stay south of Durban, call in advance for pick ups from Durban stations and airport.

Kingsburgh to Scottburgh

There are a string of resorts between Kingsburgh and Scottburgh, mainly consisting of retirement homes, holiday flats and time-share units. **Winkelspruit**, is one of the more developed parts of the area. Across the Lovu River is **Illovo** beach, which is backed by a lagoon at the mouth of the river. **Karridene**, is at the mouth of another river, the Msimbazi. **Umkomaas** is the last resort in this area, next to the **Empisini Nature Reserve**, where a small dam has been built on the river which attracts an interesting variety of birdlife. The reserve can be reached by taking the Umkomaas and Widenham exit off the N2.

On the Old South Coast Road between Umkomaas and Scottburgh is **Crocworld**. The central idea behind this theme park is crocodiles, there are more than 10,000 here, some of which end up in the *Crocodilian Restaurant* as steaks, whilst others are exported to Hong Kong and Europe to meet a similar fate. The most exciting part of a visit here is feeding time, the crocodiles are fed at 1100 and 1500 daily. ■ *Daily 0830-1630. Small entry fee.*

Scottburgh
Phone code: 039
(NB Always use 3-figure prefix)
Colour map 5, grid B1

Scottburgh is only 35 km south of Durban and has become one of the busiest resorts on the Strelitzia coast. The beach by the estuary of the Mpambanyoni is protected by shark nets and is very popular. The beaches are connected by a seafront miniature railway. The **tourist office** is on Scott St, T9761364, F9783114. And there's an **internet café**, *East Coast Access*, at 177 Scott St, T9782539. Rates charged per half hour, open 0900-1730.

The Aliwal Shoal lies just north of Scottburgh, and after Sodwana Bay, this is one of South Africa's most popular diving areas (see page 53). The shoal is a haven for marine life and offers a good selection of dives on wrecks and on the reef. The caves here attract ragged tooth sharks each winter.

Price codes:
see inside front cover

Sleeping B *Cutty Sark Protea*, Beach Front, T9761230, F9762197. 55 rooms, TV, 2 restaurants, bar, swimming pool, tennis and squash courts, gym, set on the beach in well-kept tropical gardens. C *Blue Marlin Resort*, 180 Scott St, T9783361, F9760971. Large resort on a hill overlooking the beach, pool, gardens, 2 bars, inclusive of buffet meals, spacious and functional rooms, have weekly specials for senior citizens so, as you can imagine, activities lean towards bingo, bowls and bridge. **D-F** *Charles Hoffe Caravan Park*, overlooks Scottburgh beach, 2 km from the nearest restaurant and supermarket, T9760651. A pleasant small site with some self-catering chalets and rooms in a small block, not all sites are well-shaded, but clean ablution block and laundry service, booking essential in peak times. **D-F** *Scottburgh Caravan Park*, on the seafront, a short walk from the shops, T9760291, F9762148. This is a typical giant caravan park, over 300 stands, designed to cater for the family groups during school holidays, the park has several swimming pools and is close to plenty of sports facilities. In the peak season you would have to book, but for a visitor from overseas it is very unlikely you would wish to stay here when the camp is full.

The Hibiscus Coast

Extending from Scottburgh to Port Edward, there is less industrial development along this stretch of coast but the overall impression driving down the coast is of a long line of caravan parks and holiday homes set in a lush subtropical strip of forest.

The typical African landscape of grassland and thornveld supports many animals and this is one of the best reserves to see blue wildebeest, eland, impala, nyala, oribi, reedbuck and zebra near to the south coast. The wide range of habitats here supports over 300 species of bird. The reserve is also known for having several species of cisticola. These little brown birds are notoriously difficult to differentiate and are best identified by their calls. There is also a breeding colony of the considerably easier to spot and more beautiful crowned crane. **Vernon Crookes Nature Reserve**

Ins and outs To reach the nature reserve from the N2 take the R612 heading inland towards Ixopo. There is a signpost to the reserve 8 km after passing Umzinto. The road passes through eucalyptus and sugarcane plantations.

The reserve is open from sunrise to sunset; entry fee R10; enquiries T039-9742222; reservations for the camp should be made through KWN Wildlife, T033-8451000, F033-8451001.

Sights The land which makes up the reserve was established in 1973 after being used for cattle and mule ranching for many years. The reserve is now beginning to recover after years of intensive land use and now consists of coastal forest, swampland and grassland. The best time of year to see the reserve's wild flowers is during the spring in September and October. There are some magnificent displays of orchids, lobelias and watsonias. Another rare plant for KwaZulu Natal which can be seen here is the honey-scented protea which is at the southern limit of its range. There are seven walks of varying lengths here, the longest of which is 6 km. A network of dirt roads crosses the park and there are picnic sites, a dam, and view points to stop at. Guided walks and night drives are available throughout the year.

Sleeping D-E *Nyengelezi Camp*, is a self-catering camp with 5 huts with 2 beds in each, and a unique 10-bed tree house, which must be booked as one facility, there is a communal kitchen equipped with cutlery and crockery, cooking utensils, fridge and freezer, and an ablution block. You only need to bring food. *Price codes: see inside front cover*

This is a pleasant, small village with a great restaurant and a backpackers' place to chill out at by the beach. Driving from Durban turn off the N2 at Hibberdene and follow the R102. Turn right at the sign for Umzumbe Fairview Mission and then look out for the sign after a further kilometre. **F** *The Mantis & Moon*, Station Rd, T/F039-6846256, T083-5350884 (mob). Dorms, double rooms, camping, pool table, candle-lit bar, great music, free use of surf boards, courtyard with a wild garden, outside hot tub, rooftop deck for a sundowner and a spot of dolphin watching, all on a quiet sandy beach. Recommended. On the *Baz Bus* route. **Umzumbe Village**

Port Shepstone

Located at the mouth of the Umzimkulu River, Port Shepstone is the largest town on the south coast. It is more of an industrial centre than a tourist resort. The first European visitors to this point of the coast were the sailors of the *Nossa Senhora de Belem* who were shipwrecked here in 1635. They spent about a year here building boats for their journey back to Angola. Port Shepstone itself was founded in 1867 and the port was built by Norwegian settlers in 1886. The port hasn't been developed to any great extent as the river keeps on silting up and in the long term railways have proved to be a cheaper form of transport. *Phone code: 039 (NB Always use 3-figure prefix) Colour map 5, grid C1*

KwaZulu Natal

Banana Express The *Banana Express* is a vintage steam train which runs between Port Shepstone and Paddock, 550 m. The narrow gauge railway was opened in 1907, it is now one of the few remaining steam journeys a visitor can make in South Africa. Trains run as far as Paddock station, 39 km from the coast (the station is listed as a national monument).

The route from Port Shepstone follows the coast for about 6 km before the track starts to wind its way up into the green hills covered with banana and sugarcane plantations. Visitors can choose between two excursions. If your time is limited there is a 2-hour round trip to the historic village of Izotsha. A full day outing takes you up to Paddock station where a braai lunch is served at the station; after you can explore the countryside before returning to the coast – the total excursion lasts 5½ hours. Both trips stop at the **Zakhele Craft Training Centre**. The shorter tour departs at 1100 on Thu, R40, the trip to Paddock departs at 1000 on Sat, R100, there are more departures during holiday periods. An interesting alternative is to take the train as far as Plains station where you are met by a Conservancy Ranger. The ranger will act as your guide as you explore the spectacular **Oribi Gorge Nature Reserve**. After a braai at the boma you rejoin the train for the journey back down to the coast. Whichever journey you choose you will be rewarded with views of the coast and farmlands you would never see from the road. ■ *For further information and bookings contact, T039-6824821, after hours T6950520.*

Sleeping
■ *on map*
Price codes:
see inside front cover

B *Kapenta Bay*, 11-12 Princess Elizabeth Dr, T6825528, F6824590. 50 rooms, all suites, bland modern block overlooking the beach, large swimming pool, secure parking, typical resort setup. **C-F** *Pepper Pots*, 60 Commercial Rd, T6950852, F6950750. Self-catering chalets, backpackers dorm, caravan and camping sites, bar, restaurant, TV lounge, walking distance to the beach, smaller and not quite as sprawling as the usual beachside resorts. **F** *The Spot*, T6951318, F6950439. Local backpackers served by the *Baz Bus*. Dorm, 2 double rooms and camping. Surf boards for hire, 20 m from the beach in a quiet suburb.

Transport
128 km from Durban

Road *Baz Bus*, T021-4392323, info@bazbus. com Runs 5 times a week between Durban and Cape Town. **Towards Cape Town**: bus collects every morning except Wed and Sat – overnights at **Port Elizabeth**, and completes the journey to **Cape Town** the following day, scheduled to arrive in Cape Town by 2200. **Towards Durban**: bus collects every evening except Wed and Sat, scheduled to arrive in Durban by 2115. Passengers for hostels in **Port Edward** and **Margate** will be collected and dropped off at the *Spur Silver Lake Restaurant*. For the latest, precise information, on their routes and schedules check the web page: www.bazbus.com

Greyhound, central reservations, T011-2498900. Coaches depart from Engen service station, Pick n' Pay Centre. To **Umtata** (5 hrs), **East London** (7 hrs), **Grahamstown** (9 hrs), **Port Elizabeth** (11 hrs). To **Cape Town** (25 hrs): daily, 0835. To **Durban** (1½ hrs): daily, 1940.

Luxliner, T011-9144321, toll free T0800-003537, operates a service between Margate and Johannesburg International Airport via Port Shepstone and Durban. To

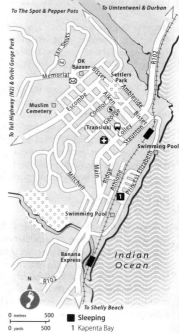

Port Shepstone

To The Spot & Pepper Pots
To Umtentweni & Durban

To Toll Highway (N2) & Oribi Gorge Park

Jan Smuts
Bisset
OK Bazaar
Memorial
Settlers Park
Ambleside
Escombe
Aiken
Comter
George
(Translux)
Colley
Staunton
Muslim Cemetery
Mitchell
Main
Ridge
Athlone
Princess Elizabeth
Swimming Pool
Swimming Pool
Banana Express

Indian Ocean

R102

N

To Shelly Beach

0 metres   500
0 yards   500

■ **Sleeping**
1 Kapenta Bay

Margate (30 min): daily, 1945, **Durban International Airport** (1½ hrs), **Durban** (2½ hrs), and **Johannesburg International Airport** (9 hrs): daily, 0800.

Margate Mini Coach, reservations T039-3121406, after hours T082-4559736 (mob). Coaches depart from the *Silver Lake Spur Restaurant*, and will pick up or drop off at set bus stops on the main route between **Durban** and **Margate**. Also operates and connects to the *Flutterbus*, which continues on from **Margate** to the *Wild Coast Casino* in the **Eastern Cape**.

Translux, central reservations, T012-3154300. Coaches depart from *Silver Lake Spur Restaurant*. To **East London** (8 hrs), **Grahamstown** (10 hrs), **Port Elizabeth** (12 hrs), **Cape Town** (24 hrs): daily, 1600. To **Durban** (1½ hrs): daily, 0800.

Port Shepstone to Margate

The towns and villages on this southernmost stretch of coast are the last of the chain of resorts that feel like seaside holiday camps before the R620 enters the Wild Coast. The hiking in Umtamvuna Nature Reserve, diving on Protea Banks, the reefs off Shelly Beach, whale and dolphin watching, and golfing are the highlights of this region.

The **Wild Coast** lies to the south of Port Edward, on the other side of the former border over the river Umtamvuna. This used to be part of the former homeland of Transkei, though since the abolishment of the homelands is now part of the Eastern Cape Province. The contrast between the former homeland and Natal could hardly be more marked, and crossing the old border is like crossing into another, albeit much poorer, country. Road conditions deteriorate immediately and this is not a good route for access to the Wild Coast unless you are driving a four-wheel drive vehicle. The alternative route to the Wild Coast is along the N2 via Kokstad and Umtata to Port St Johns on a tarred road. There have been recent cases of armed robbery and violent assault on tourists travelling through the Wild Coast and it is essential to plan your journey to make sure you set off in time to arrive well before nightfall. It is extremely dangerous to travel at night.

For a detailed description of the Wild Coast, see page 371

Shelly Beach is a 5 km south of Port Shepstone on the R620. It is quite a large suburb with one of the region's biggest shopping malls and has wide variety of shops, restaurants and a cinema. The beach here is popular as a launch site for various fishing and diving charters.

Shelly Beach
Phone code: 039
(NB Always use 3-figure prefix)

Sleeping C *Shelly Lodge*, Siege Lane, T3157280/1, F3155117. Comfortable rooms, TV, phone, the family room has a balcony with sea views, bar, restaurant, pool. **C** *Ayton Manor*, 2½ km inland, after driving under the N2, take the first right, T/F6850777. A B&B guest lodge set in a fine country house on a sugar estate, finalist in a local accommodation award, elegantly decorated, private balconies and separate entrances, TV, fridge, microwave, bar, pool, children will like the working farmyard. **E** *Greyfare*, 38 Frere Rd, T/F3157446, ask for Arlene. 6 modern spacious flats for 1-4 people, private balconies or secluded patios, fully equipped, TV, lovely small pool and garden, breakfast available on request, walking distance to beach, shops and cinema, ridiculously cheap rates, recommended for excellent value for money. **F** *Shelly Caraven Park*, T/F6850764, 35 sites with power points around a small dam, 1 self-catering family chalet, TV lounge, pool.

Price codes: see inside front cover

Uvongo, 12 km south of Port Shepstone, is built on cliffs looking out to sea and is one of the more pleasant resorts on the south coast. The beach, protected by shark nets, is safe for swimming and surfing. The waterfall at the nearby **Uvongo River Nature Reserve** is a pleasant place for a picnic. The 23 m high waterfall tumbling over cliffs into the beachside lagoon is the reserve's main feature. ■ *Open from sunrise to sunset.*

Uvongo
Phone code: 039
(NB Always use 3-figure prefix)
Colour map 5, grid C1

Sleeping and eating C *Casa Uvongo Holiday Flats*, T3150553. Souless but functional holiday flats. **C** *Costablanca*, T3151203. A B&B guest lodge with a restaurant and swimming pool. *Gavin's Seafood Grill*, corner of Foster St and Colin St, T3176192. Bring your own wines to

Price codes: see inside front cover

KwaZulu Natal

accompany the freshly grilled seafood. *Stephward Estate*, 17 Peter St, T3155926. Nursery and tea gardens renowned for their rather decadent Champagne breakfasts and French gateaux.

Margate

This town began to be developed as a small tourist resort in 1919. What must have originally been a secluded palm fringed beach has more recently been turned into another highly developed family beach resort popular with holidaymakers from Gauteng, which is beginning to rival Durban for numbers of visitors. A range of cultural and sporting entertainment aimed at a mass tourist market is available, as well as a wide selection of restaurants, bars, night clubs, and seaside shops. From the junction with the South Coast Toll Road, the link road immediately enters the tourist zone passing the mini golf and holiday homes on the way into town. In the centre high-rise flats crowd down towards the beach front, which gets particularly crowded during school holidays, when one can hire pedalo boats and canoes or watch basket weaving demonstrations.

Hibiscus Coast Publicity Association, Panorama Parade, Margate Beachfront, T3122322, F3121886, open Mon-Fri 0800-1630, Sat 0900-1200, is a helpful **tourist office** with good information on accommodation and entertainment, well worth a visit if you are planning on spending some time in the area. Regional office with information on most towns in the area.

The **Riverbend Crocodile Farm and Art Gallery**, 8 km south of Margate, breeds around 200 Nile crocodiles which are kept in pits before being turned into the belts, wallets, and handbags which are for sale in the curio shop. This tourist complex also has a tea garden, a farm stall and an art gallery. ■ *Daily 0830-1700. Feeding time Sun 1500. T3166204.*

Sleeping
Price codes:
see inside front cover

As Margate comprises
almost entirely blocks
of holiday flats, a
useful organization
is Fun Holidays,
T3122553, F3172732,
a central reservations
agency for
self-catering
accomodation

B *Kennilworth-on-Sea*, Marine Dr, T3120342. Guest lodge and dive resort with good seaviews near the beach, swimming pool. Recommended. **B** *Margate*, 71 Marine Dr, T3121410, F73318. 69 a/c rooms, TV, restaurant, swimming pool, tennis, comfortable family hotel set in mature gardens overlooking the beach. **B** *San Lameer*, Lower South Coast Main Rd, T3120011, F3120157. 40 a/c rooms, 15 villas, restaurant, bar, 2 swimming pools, private 18-hole golf course, a luxury complex overlooking the San Lameer Lagoon. **B-C** *The Beach Hotel*, Marine Dr, T/F3121483. 35 a/c rooms, TV, restaurant, swimming pool. **C** *De Villiers Holiday Cottages*, Marine Dr, T3120311. **C-D** *Oppiestrand Flats*, 18 Lagoon Rd, T3120622. TV, restaurant. **F** *Margate Backpackers*, 14 Collis St, T/F3122176. Dorms, doubles plus camping in the garden. Bar and pool table. Easy going setup, on the *Margate Mini Coach* run from Durban, or free pick-ups from Port Shepstone. A colourful old-style town house with the ideal veranda to chill on. Short walk from the beach, can arrange surfing and diving.

Eating

Eat & Meet, Granada Building, Marine Dr, T3122213. Seafood restaurant, vast menu and vast quantities of food. *La Capannina*, Marine Dr, T3171078. Pizza and seafood, open Tue-Sun lunch and dinner, closed Sat lunchtime. *Larry's*, corner of O'Connor Dr and Panorama, Beachfront, T3121929. Busy pizza terrace overlooking the beach. *7 Seas*, William O'Connor Dr, T3174349. Beachfront restaurant and bar with live music.

Entertainment

Cinema *Casino*, Marine Dr, T3120741. 3 screens.

Shopping

Southern Explorer, is a route around town visiting the studios of local artists. *OK Mall*, has wide range of shops and services including banks, chemists and a supermarket.

Sports
Being the main tourist
centre on the south
coast Margate is a
good place from which
to organize activities

Diving *African Dive Adventures*, T082-4567885 (mob), F3157799, afridive@ africa.com Offers a wide range of NAUI diving courses, dives take place at the Protea Banks where schools of hammerhead and Zambezi sharks are regularly seen. **Fishing** Fishing is allowed off the pier and off Margate Rocks, there are plenty of tackle shops in town. **Golf** *Margate Country Club*, T3176146, open Tue-Sat 0800-1700, Sun 1400-1700. 18-hole course, visitors welcome. **Microlights** *Microlight Flips*, from Margate Airport, T082-7747784 (mob). Ask for Derek. Hire and lessons. **Surfing** Designated surfing and boogie-boarding areas are on Main Beach and at Lucien Point. Boards can be hired from a number of shops in town. **Swimming** Main Beach is shark-protected and therefore the safest and most popular area for swimming.

Local Bus *Margate Mini Coach*, for reservations contact T3121406, after hours T082-4559736 (mob). To **Durban** (2 hrs), via **Port Shepstone**, **Hibberdene**, **Scottburg** and **Durban Airport**. *Flutter Bus*, runs a regular service to the **Wild Coast** on Sun. **Car hire** Offices all located at the airport, *Avis*, T3120094. *Budget*, T3173202. *Imperial*, T3121346.

Transport

Long distance **Air**: **Margate Municipal Airport**, is 2 km from the town centre. Information, T3120560. The *Margate Mini Coach* service calls in at the airport to meet incoming and departing flights. The only scheduled service using the airport is operated by *SA Airlink*, central reservations, T011-9781111. **Johannesburg** (1½ hrs): daily 1340, Sun 1750.

Ramsgate is only 2 km from Margate and now practically a suburb, but the beach here is a little quieter. It has a tidal pool and shark nets and is popular for surfing.

Ramsgate
Phone code: 039
(NB Always use
3-figure prefix)
Colour map 5, grid C1

Sleeping and eating C *Surf Edge Holiday Flats*, 218 Marine Dr, T3120631. A variety of fully equipped self-catering flats sleeping 4-6 people, nothing special but good value for a family or group of friends, undercover parking, private path to the beach. **D** *Wailana Beach Lodge*, 436 Ashmead Rd, T/F3144606. 1 km to both Ramsgate and Margate centres, easy walking distance to all amenities, nice gardens with hammocks and pool, B&B, en suite rooms, TV, fan, sun deck, evening meals on request, much more friendly than the standard blocks of holiday flats in the area. *The Bistro*, T3144128, Marine Dr. A good selection of seafood. *The Lobster Pot*, Marine Dr, T3149809. Good value 4-course Sun lunch, wide selection of seafood and curries. *La Capannina*, Marine Dr, T3171078. Authentic Italian restaurant, the chef actually comes from Italy, know locally for the *Tripa alla Florentine* (tripe stew) and roast lamb.

Southbroom is a popular resort with subtropical trees coming down to the beach. There is safe swimming in a tidal pool and waterskiing and just down the coast is a beautiful 5 km stretch of sand at Marina Beach. **Mpenjati Nature Reserve** is 18 km from Margate just south of Southbroom and is popular with windsurfers, canoeists, and fishermen. The reserve covers a small area of coastal forest and wetlands along the edge of the lagoon and is good for spotting wetland and woodland birds. There are some leisurely walking trails along the Mpenjati River and around the lagoon.

Southbroom
Phone code: 039
(NB Always use
3-figure prefix)

Sleeping A-B *Protea San Lameer*, Lower Main Rd, between Southbroom and Port Edward, T3130011, F3130157. 40 luxury rooms, 13 2-4-room Italian style villas, 1 8-room lodge, set next to a palm-fringed lagoon and 18-hole golf course, stunning pool with surrounding wooden deck, theme evenings in restaurant decorated to resemble, somewhat strangely, an Arabian tent, all the facilities expected of a quality member of the Protea group. **B-C** *Nature's Cottage*, Churchill Rd, T/F3168533. Charming log house encircled by large verandas with cane furniture, set in a patch of indigenous forest. The house has 3 bedrooms, 2 of which open up on to the deck, separate dining room, 2 Victorian bathrooms overlooking the wall of trees, lounge with TV, fully fitted kitchen with deep freezer and separate scullery. On request, breakfast can be delivered to the house at a time of your choice. For a family or group this is a great place to be based away from it all, and still be close enough to explore the beaches, local nature reserves, and resort towns.

Price codes:
see inside front cover

This small tourist resort has a large palm-fringed beach backing onto tropical forest. It is a convenient place to stay when visiting **Umthamvuna Nature Reserve**. The **African Mzamba Village**, south of town on the R61 just after crossing the Umtamvuna River to the Wild Coast, is a small theme park laid out as a Xhosa village and sells

Port Edward
Phone code: 039
(NB Always use
3-figure prefix)
Colour map 5, grid C1

KwaZulu Natal

handicrafts. If you are interested in coffee, daily tours are held at the **Beaver Creek Coffee Estate** on the opposite side of the N2, T3132347, showing the process of picking, fermenting, drying and roasting the beans. Several blends are available for tasting.

The Port Edward Holiday Letting Agency, T3132026, F3132032, is a useful booking agent for self-catering beach cottages and flats

Sleeping It is worth noting that Port Edward is only 5-min drive to the Wild Coast Casino resort and offers much more affordable accommodation. **B-C** *Estuary Country Hotel*, 1 km before Port Edward on the N2, clearly signposted, T3132675, F3132689. A combination of hotel rooms in a restored Cape Dutch manor house, most with balcony overlooking the estuary, some self-catering units. Bar, pool, the *Fish Eagle Restaurant* is open to non-residents, ownership by an Austrian family, interesting and varied South African and European menu. **C-D** *Umtamvuna River Lodge*, T3132313, F3132326, small B&B. **D-F** *TO Strand*, T3192729, 93 self-catering chalets, camping and caravan sites, shop restaurant, own pool, standard resort close to the beach. **F** *Vuna Valley Backpackers*, 9 Old Pont Rd, T3132532, F3132141, T083-99269999 (mob). A small setup that can only accommodate 12 people in a dorm and 1 double room, camping, email, laundry, shared ablutions, very peaceful, bordering Uthamvuna Nature Reserve and close to the beach, can organize Wild Coast excursions from here. Run by Brett and Bernice.

Transport *The Flutterbus*, T039-3121406. Operates a daily service from **Margate** to the *Wild Coast casino.*

Umthamvuna Nature Reserve

This is the southernmost and one of the less visited reserves in KwaZulu Natal and the day hikes down into the sandstone gorge are well worth the effort it takes to get there. The sheer walls of lichen-covered rock, dropping down into thick rainforest at the bottom of the gorge, are the centre of this dramatic landscape. There is no big game here but the reserve is known best for its displays of wild flowers in the spring and its colony of Cape vultures. The reserve was established in 1971 along the border between Transkei and KwaZulu Natal and covers a 19 km stretch of the Umthamvuna River. It is usually fairly easy to spot bushbuck, blue and common duiker and the ubiquitous chacma baboons. The shy Cape clawless otters do inhabit the reserve but the most visitors ever see of them are the white calcareous droppings found along river banks.

Ins & outs **Getting there** Umthamvuna is 8 km north of Port Edward on the road to Izingolweni. There are 2 entrances to the reserve; the first turning, off the Izingolweni road leads to the southern gate; the second turning 5 km further on leads to the northern gate.

Information Opening times, Apr-Aug 0700-1700, Sep-Mar 0600-1800. Small entry fee. Enquiries, T039-3132383. A simple map, bird check list and some ecology information leaflets are available at the entrance. There is no accommodation in the reserve, the nearest hotels are in Port Edward.

West from Port Shepstone The road heading inland from Port Shepstone passes through banana and sugar plantations. The region is a densely populated farming area crowded with Zulu huts and smallholdings. There are two routes to Oribi Gorge (21 km). The fastest route is to follow the N2; just past Oribi Flats East there is a signpost to the park on the right hand side of the road. The alternative route is slightly longer and involves turning off the N2 onto a minor road 7 km outside of Port Shepstone. This road leads to Oribi Flats (21 km), and to the *Oribi Gorge Hotel*. The road passes through some rugged scenery along the Umzimkulweni River Valley.

Soobramanya Temple The temple is a tiny green building with a corrugated iron roof 1 km before the Portland Cement Factory. This is an enchanting place to break your journey, apart from the beautiful views over subtropical woodland a stop here offers a rare insight into Natal's history. The temple was built around the turn of the century by Indian

KwaZulu Natal (side margin)

labourers working on the nearby sugar plantations and is a good example of early Natal temple architecture. The site has all the traditional elements of a South Indian shrine. There is a Kodi pole, a lingam stone and a fig tree in the courtyard in front of the main building, whilst inside the shrine are the bronze statues representing the deities of the Hindu pantheon.

Although the Indian community has now moved to Port Shepstone the temple is still lovingly cared for and is the site of some colourful ceremonies. The faithful congregate here every Easter and haul a temple chariot from the Umzimkulweni River at the bottom of the valley up to the hilltop shrine. The temple tends to be closed during the week so the best time to visit is at weekends when weddings are held.

Oribi Gorge Nature Reserve

Established in 1950 to protect this area of thick woodland and towering cliffs where the *Colour map 5, grid C1* Umzimkulu and Umzimkulweni rivers meet, the Oribi Gorge is 24 km long and 5 km wide. The views from the top of the sandstone cliffs, some of which are up to 280 m high, look out over the forest which clings to the sides of the ravines below. The atmosphere in the gorge is of a secluded rugged wilderness. The cliffs provide nesting sites for many birds of prey and the forest, home to the African python, is so thick that although leopard are thought to live here they are never seen. One of their prey, the Samango monkey, can sometimes be seen in small groups. Favouring dense, evergreen jungle, the Samango has a dark brown face and longish hair in marked contrast to the more familiar vervet monkey. **Birdlife** here is prolific and this is a good place to see some interesting forest species. Knysna louries, narina trogons, trumpeter hornbills, grass owls, bat hawk, seven eagle and five kingfisher species can all be seen here. Ironically, oribi are not common in the reserve and are very rarely seen.

Samango Falls, Hoopoe Falls and Lehr's Falls are the most spectacular **waterfalls** in the gorge and are best seen after heavy rain when vast quantities of water come crashing down into the ravines below. There are several clearly marked hikes from 1-9 km.

Getting there Oribi Gorge Nature Reserve is 21 km west of Port Shepstone via the N2.The **Ins & outs** road leading to the nature reserve passes through an extensive agricultural area of sugarcane fields, eucalyptus plantations and cattle pastures which have almost entirely replaced the indigenous woodland in the last 100 years. The contrast between the outlying farmland and the untouched African bush in the gorge is striking.

Getting around A series of tracks lead to viewpoints over the gorge. There are stunning views from Oribi Heads, Horseshoe Rock, Camel Rock and the Overhanging Rock from where you can see the forests and cliffs of the gorge with the Portland Cement factory in the distance. **Warning** Don't leave valuables in your car when you walk to the edge of the gorge as there have been cases of petty theft from visitors' cars. There is a tarred road which winds down 4 km from the hutted camp to a picnic spot next to the bridge crossing the Umzimkulweni River. There are some impressive views of the gorge, giving a clear idea of just how deep it really is.

Information Access to the gorge costs R10. The reserve is open 24 hrs, however the camp office is only open from 0800-1230 and 1400-1630. The camp shop sells wildlife books, souvenirs, charcoal, firewood and a limited range of food. The Umzimkulweni River is not safe to swim in as it is infected with bilharzia. There is a pleasant swimming pool to cool off in the camp. Fresh meat, vegetables and cheese are available from a farm shop just by the entrance to the reserve. The nearest petrol station is 4 km away in Paddock.

Apart from the numerous hiking trails, Oribi Gorge is also the ideal location for a **Activities** number of adventure sports. *Orib-x-treme*, T6870253, based at the *Oribi Gorge Hotel* (see below) offers **white water rafting** trips and **black water tubing** (large inner tubes), on the Umzimkulu River, and **abseiling** from Lehr's Waterfall. The waterfall has a 170 m drop and is quite spectacular in its own right. If you can get a group together, *Orib-x-treme* organizes sun-downers and a braai at the top of the falls, from which there is a 110 m abseil, the last 66 m being a free abseil during which you can feel the spray of the falls on your back. This is advertised as the highest abseil in the world – debatable, but even so it's a sheer cliff face next to a very powerful waterfall – dare you!

Sleeping
Price codes:
see inside front cover

C *Oribi Gorge Hotel*, T/F039-6870253. 8 double rooms, small family hotel, restaurant, snooker, swimming pool. The hotel, built in the 1870s, is a colonial building circled by a veranda and feels like an African country house. The restaurant serves burgers, steaks, pies and pub food. There is a pleasant beer garden where you can eat outside under the trees. The gorge can also be seen from the viewpoints on farmland adjoining the hotel which is only 17 km from the hutted camp. A number of activities can be arranged from here (see above). Follow the scenic route through the gorge and on leaving the reserve head towards Port Shepstone. The hotel is on the northern side of the gorge and is clearly signposted. An alternative route from the N2 is to take the turning on the road signposted to Oribi Flats, continuing along this road the turning to the hotel is then signposted down a dirt road next to a coffee estate. After 1 km the road opens out into mature tropical gardens. **C-D** The *Hutted Camp* has 6 2-bed huts, a 7-bed hut, and 10-bed rustic cottage over looking the gorge. Each is equipped with fridge, kettle, crockery and cutlery but no cooking facilities. The camp cooks will collect your food to prepare meals between 0630-1330 for breakfast and lunch, and 1630-1830 for supper. It is a good idea to buy your own food and drink before you arrive as there is not always much choice locally. Reservations for the hutted camp should be made through KWN Wildlife, T033-8451000, F033-8451001.

Camping F There is a small campsite with an ablution block opposite the office. Reservations for camping should be made through the camp manager, T039-6791644.

The Sugar Coast and Dolphin Coast

The area between Umhlanga and Tugela Mouth is promoted as either the Dolphin Coast or the Sugar Coast. Like the coastline to the south of Durban it is possible to miss many of the sights and small coastal settlements if you remain on the N2 highway. If you have time, travel on the original main road and pass through the beach resorts until you find one that feels just right for you. After Umhlanga Rocks most of the resorts are far smaller than those found on the south coast. While there are plenty of new hotels and resorts the overall feel is more relaxed and far less developed than the south coast. The beaches are all excellent but remember that there are sharks along the coast and people do get attacked. Always ask whether your beach is protected by shark nets, as some have been removed in recent times. If the sea is not your thing, the local tourist offices can point you in the direction of the numerous tropical nature reserves. Seldom overrun with visitors these well-run protected areas provide some fine birdwatching opportunities and there is always the chance of spotting some of the more shy small mammals in the woodlands. Finally there are some stunning golf courses to play.

Ins & outs
Following the N2 north from Durban, the road passes through vast sugarcane and eucalyptus plantations. The inland towns of Verulam, Tongaat and Stanger have large resident Indian populations and are processing centres for the area's industries. The old coast road runs northwards parallel to the sea passing through the beach resorts of Umhlanga Rocks, Ballito and Salt Rock.

Umhlanga Rocks

Phone code: 031
(NB Always use 3-figure prefix)
Colour map 5, grid B2

This trendy holiday resort is only a short drive north of Durban, of which it is now virtually a suburb. Following the same line of thinking as Gauteng, many Durban businesses have moved to office parks in the hills at the top of the resort and locally Umhlanga Rocks has been dubbed Sandton-by-the-Sea. The Gateway shopping mall,

Durban's premier shopping emporium and supposedly the largest shopping mall in the Southern Hemisphere, is also here (see page 401).

The main attractions of Umhlanga Rocks are that it is neither as dangerous nor as sleazy as the beachfront in Durban and during the off season it is considerably less crowded. Lagoon Drive and Marine Drive run parallel to the coast and many of the best hotels are here. Umhlanga Lagoon lies just to the north of town where there are beautiful expanses of wetland, forest and undisturbed open beach.

Sugar Coast & Dolphin Coast

The towns name means "Place of Reeds" in Zulu, this is with reference to the reeds that are washed down the river to the north of the town and then end up on the pristine beaches. The area was once covered with a dune forest, which was home to wild animals and no one else. Sadly this is no more, and only small pockets of the original vegetation have been preserved in the nature reserves as mentioned above. The land originally was part of a large sugar estate, *Natal Estates Ltd*, owned by Sir Marshall Campbell. The estate was managed from Mount Edgecombe in the interior, a track was built from here to the coast and local farmers began to lease small plots on the beach and build holiday cottages. The first cottage was built in 1869 and was known as the Oyster Box, today the *Oyster Box Hotel* occupies the site. In the 1920's an Irishman, Marcus McCausland, built the first hotel, the *Victoria*, these days it is known as the *Umhlanga Rocks Hotel*. This marked the start of the town's development and it has remained a popular and smart resort within easy reach of Durban. The **Sugar Coast Tourism Association**, can help with booking accommodation and provide advice on how best to visit the nature reserves. They also have a selection of maps and brochures. It's on Chartwell Drive, T5614257, F5616943, info@sugarcoast.co.za Open Mon-Fri 0800-1630, Sat 0900-1200.

Crocodile Creek is between Umhlanga and Ballito; turn off the Old Main Rd (R102) close to Maidstone Golf Course. As well as displaying crocodiles the park also has snakes and some tortoises. Between Dec-Mar, it is possible to see baby crocs hatching. The curio shop sells plenty of goods made from the skins, check the quality of the handiwork before being tempted, it may also be worth getting an idea on prices elsewhere beforehand, its easy to think

Sights

you're always getting a good deal here. Not surprisingly the coffee shop has crocodile on the menu. For anyone interested in a bite, they taste a bit like chicken (what else!) ■ *Open daily, except Sat out of season, 0930-1700. Small entry fee. Guided tours at 1030, 1130, 1230, 1430 and 1530. The crocodiles are fed daily at 1100 and 1500. T032-9443845.*

The **Sharks Board** on Herrwood Drive, studies the lifecycles of the sharks which live in the sea off the coast of KwaZulu Natal and investigates how best to protect bathers with various forms of netting. Umhlanga Rocks became the first beach to erect shark nets in 1962 following a series of attacks along the whole coast in December 1957. Today the Sharks Board is responsible for looking after more than 400 nets, which protect nearly 50 beaches. Tours at the Sharks Board, the only organization of its kind in the world, begin with a 25-minute video on the biology of sharks and their role as top predators in the marine food chain. This is followed by a shark dissection, if you feel you can handle it, to see what can only be described as the internal machinery. The Display Hall has a variety of replicas of sharks, fish and rays, including that of an 892 kg shark. If this shark experience whets your appetite further, it is possible to arrange to go out on the Sharks Board ski boat with the staff as they go about their daily servicing of the shark nets off Durban's Golden Mile. ■ *Video and dissection Tue, Wed, Thu at 0900 and 1400, Sun 1400. The Display Hall and curio shop are open Mon-Fri 0800-1600. T5660400.*

A very popular local landmark is the **Umhlanga Lighthouse**. The distinct red and white circular concrete tower stands 21 m above the beach and acts as a fixed point to help ships, waiting to dock in Durban harbour, confirm their exact position in the outer anchorage. The tower has stood here since November 1954. The lighthouse occupies the centre point on the beach standing right in front of the Oyster Box Hotel. The lighthouse has never had a keeper, it is operated by the owner of the Oyster Box Hotel from controls in the hotel office.

Hawaan Nature Reserve is 4 km north of Umhlanga Rocks at the end of Newlands Drive. During the 1920's William Alfred Campbell, son of Sir Marshall who had founded the sugar estates, used to stage an annual hunt in this unique forest environment. It was not until 1980 that 60 ha were protected as part of the nature reserve. Within the reserve there are 4 km of leisurely guided walks through an unusual area of mature coastal forest. Walks can be organized with the *Umhlanga Wildlife Society*.

Umhlanga Rocks

Sleeping
1 Beverly Hills Sun Inter-Continental
2 Breakers Resort
3 Cabana Beach
4 Cathy's Place
5 Holiday Apartments
6 Jessica's
7 Licorna Beach
8 Oyster Box
9 Umhlanga Rocks
10 Umhlanga Sands

Eating
1 Angelo's
2 Curry Place
3 Cottonfields
4 George & Dragon
5 Razzmatazz

Contact the tourist office for further information, T5614257. **Umhlanga Nature Reserve** is only 1 km from Umhlanga at the end of Lagoon Drive. The entrance to this small private reserve is on the far side of Umhlanga Lagoon. Entry to the reserve is free. There are trails here passing through dune forest, which circle the lagoon. The area is rich in birdlife and you can also see bushbuck, duiker and vervet monkeys. ■ *Daily 0600-1800. T5614257 for more information 0700-1200, 1300-1630.*

A *Beverly Hills Sun Inter-Continental*, Lighthouse Rd, T5612211, F5613711. 95 rooms, a/c, TV, restaurants and *Cabin Cocktail* bar, swimming pool, fitness centre, close to tennis and squash courts a smart hotel overlooking the beach, afternoon tea served daily.

    B *Breakers Resort*, Lagoon Dr, T5612271, F5613711. 80 rooms, a/c, TV, restaurants, swimming pool, tennis, the hotel itself isn't particularly attractive, but it is quiet and overlooks Hawaan Forest and Umhlanga Lagoon. **B** *Cabana Beach Resorts*, Lagoon Dr, T5612371, F5613522. 217 rooms, a/c, TV, restaurants, swimming pool, large holiday complex with Spanish-style self-catering villas. **B** *Oyster Box*, Lighthouse Rd, T5612233, F5614072. 80 rooms, a/c, TV, restaurant, swimming pool, tennis, original building dates from the 1940s and was always popular with British travellers visiting the colonies, the hotel retains its colonial atmosphere but has been in need of refurbishment in recent years. Spectacular setting behind dunes, beach and lighthouse. **B** *Umhlanga Sands*, Lagoon Dr, T5612323, F5612333. A/c, TV, restaurant, pool. **C** *Umhlanga Rocks*, Lagoon Dr, T5611321, F5611328. TV, restaurant, swimming pool.

    B&B and self-catering There is a large selection of holiday apartments, most of which are rented out by the week. During the off season it may be possible to organize shorter lets in the middle of the week. A couple of local agents who specialize in self-catering units are listed below along with a small selection of local B&Bs. *Umhlanga Accommodation*, Sanlam Centre, corner of Chartwell Dr and Lighthouse Rd, T5612012, F5613957, is an agency for letting holiday flats and chalets. *Umhlanga & Coastal Letting*, Granada Centre, T5615838, F5615835. Contact well in advance if you are planning on renting a family size apartment during any local school holidays. Short and long term lets as well as time share.

    D *Cathy's Place*, 18 Stanley Grace Cres, T5613286. B&B or self-catering cottages, TV, swimming pool. All just a short walk from the beach and shops. **D** *Honeypot Cottage*, 11 Hilken Dr, T5613795, sugarfld@iafrica.com Smart B&B rooms with TV, bar fridge and email access. Satour accredited. **D** *Jessica's*, 35 Portland Dr, T5613369. B&B rooms in the house, self-catering cottages in the garden. Email facilities. Close to shops and restaurants. **D** *Licorna Beach*, 82 Lagoon Dr, T5612986. Self-catering unit with TV, a/c and use of a swimming pool. **D** *Paulette's Place*, 38 Hilken Dr, T5612716, paulettes@icon.co.za Double rooms with en suite facilities, private lounge and entrance, all with sea views. Swimming pool set in a typical tropical coastal garden, secure parking. B&B or self-catering.

Al Firenze, 21 Ray Paul Dr, T5725559. Pasta and seafood with a lively terrace. Takeaways available. *Angelo's*, Granada Centre, Chartwell Dr, T5613245. Italian cooking, BYO. *The Cabin*, *Beverly Hills*, Lighthouse Rd, T5612211. Pricey dinner and dance in an extravagant blue and gold stateroom, every evening except Sun. *Miami Spur*, *Umhlanga Sands Hotel*, T5611370. Large steaks for breakfast, lunch and dinner. Pub and bar food, popular local chain, mixed results, sometimes the beer and salad are excellent, other times not so good. *Cottonfields*, 2 Lagoon Dr, T5612744. Freshly cooked Natal seafood and meat dishes. *George & Dragon*, 16 Chartwell Dr, T5615850. Good pub lunches and selection of draught beers. *The Curry Place*, Chartwell Centre, T5615796. Indian takeaway. *Lord Prawn*, Umhlanga Plaza, T5611133. Has been recommended for its seafood dishes. *Ming Bow*, Chartwell Centre, Chartwell Dr, T5613789. Chinese, good value set menus. *Pescador*, *Cabana Beach Hotel*, Lagoon Dr, T5612371. A good Portugese-style restaurant with some excellent fish dishes on the menu. *Razzmatazz*, *Cabana Beach*, 10 Lagoon Dr, T5612371. Closed Sun, unusual game and seafood dishes, try the daily specials.

Sleeping
■ *on map*
Price codes:
see inside front cover

Eating
● *on map*

KwaZulu Natal

Shopping The enormous *Gateway*, shopping mall is on the fringes of Umhlanga but is technically part of Durban. *Granada Centre*, Chartwell Dr, is a large modern shopping mall. *La Lucia Mall*, Armstrong, is very popular with an immense selection of shops.

Sports **Diving** There are two interesting wreck dives at the *T-Barge* and the *Fontao*. Both sites are at around 20 m deep where visibility is good. The boats were sunk to create artificial reefs and provide habitats for tropical fish. *Dive Nautique* PO Box 1264, Umhlanga Rocks 4320, T082-5532834 (mob). Local dive charters, can also organize dolphin viewing boat trips, their shop is at the *Surf Life-saving Club* on the beachfront. **Golf** *Mt Edgecombe Country Club*, T5395330 for details on temporary membership. **Quad-biking** *Guided Quad Trails*, T082-4775837 (mob). Off road trails for beginners and advanced riders.

Tour operators *Natal Sightseeing Tours*, Granada Centre, Chartwell Dr, T5615322, F5613479. Variety of day tours, 2-day Zululand game reserve tours. *Travel Eve*, Sanlam Centre, T5611050, F5611052. General travel agent. *Uthola*, T082-9212374 (mob), uthola@iafrica.com Upmarket 1-3 day adventures with experienced guides to the game parks to the north, the battlefields, Midlands Meander, expect to pay around R800 per day.

Transport **Road Bus**: *Umhlanga Express*, T5612860. To **Durban** (20 mins), picks up passengers at the major hotels on Lagoon Dr and Marine Dr, and the kiosk on Chartwell Dr, opposite *Sugar Coast Tourism*. This is a mini-bus taxi so is only good value for a largish group. *Greyhound*, central reservations, T011-2498900. Operates a daily service between **Durban** and **Pretoria**. Coach stops by the Swiss Chalet, opposite the *Cabana Beach Hotel* at 0920 for **Pretoria** (13 hrs), (via **Richards Bay**, **Vryheid**, **Piet Retief** and **Evander**).**Car hire**: *Forest Drive*, 40 Forest Dr, La Lucia, T5628433. Low cost daily rental rates but very small amount of free mileage, you could be stung here if you drive big distances. *Imperial*, T5614501. *Master Rent*, T5611296. **Taxi**: *Umhlanga Rocks*, T5611846.

Directory **Banks** Branches of all the major banks can be found in the shopping malls. *Rennies Foreign Exchange*, La Lucia Mall, T5628510. Agents for *Thomas Cook*. **Communications** Post Office: Tanager St, next to Civic Offices, open Mon-Fri 0830-1630, Sat 0800-1200. **Useful numbers** Ambulence/Fire: T5611297. **Medical Emergencies**: T10177, T3013737. **Pharmacy**: all-hours, T5613491. **Sea Rescue Service**: T3372200. **Weather Info**: T082162.

Heading north to Zululand

Ballito
Phone code: 032
(NB Always use 3-figure prefix)
Colour map 5, grid B2

In the 1950s Ballito was just one of many small quiet coastal resorts to the north of Durban. Over the past few years there has been rapid change and development along this stretch of coast. Large resorts are still being built and places like Ballito, Salt Rock and Shakas Rock are now outdoing Umhlanga Rocks. At present these developments cater for the domestic market. However, there is no reason why you can't enjoy a seaside holiday here like many other families. For **tourist information**, contact the *Dolphin Coast Publicity Association*, T/F9461997, info@thedolphincoast.co.za, near the Ballito exit off the N2, next to the BP service station. Open Mon-Fri 0830-1630, Sat in season 0900-1200. It's well worth calling in here if you plan on spending some time in the area. They can fax a list of accommodation in the area.

For a **microlight trip** along the Dolphin Coast contact *Dolphin Coast Microlight School*, the runway is 2 km north of the N2, T082-6595550 (mob). Daily flights, 5 min (R75), 15 min (R200), 30 min (R300).

Price codes:
see inside front cover

Sleeping and eating *Coastal Holiday Letting*, T9462155. Holiday flat agency for all budgets.
B *Boathouse*, 33 Compensation Beach Rd, T9460300, F9460184. Luxury guest house right on the beach, 19 beautifully decorated rooms, TV, phone, a/c, the bar is a great place to have a sundowner and spot dolphins. Recommended. **B-C** *Shortens Country House*, Compensation Rd T9471140, F9471144. Country club with 18-hole golf course, tennis, squash, pool, 5 min from beach, award winning restaurant, pretty tea garden, comfortable a/c rooms. **D** *Dolphin*

Caravan Park, T9462187. Caravans and camping overlooking the sea. *Galley on the Rocks*, Compensation Beach Rd, T9460597. Excellent seafood, overlooking beach.

Salt Rock is named after a rock near the hotel where the Zulus used to collect salt. The nearby Shaka's Rock is a cliff overlooking the sea from which Shaka is rumoured to have thrown his enemies. There is good snorkelling at Tiffany's Reef and Sheffield Reef.

Salt Rock
*Phone code: 032
(NB Always use
3-figure prefix)
Colour map 5, grid A6*

Sleeping C *Salt Rock*, Basil Hluett Dr, T5255025, F5255071. A friendly hotel with a beautiful location, restaurant, bar and swimming pool. Popular local haunt for rugby fanatics on Sat nights, expect a rowdy time during the playing season. **D** *Beach House*, 3 Osborne Dr, T/F5258309. Double rooms with ensuite facilities, TV, internet access, garden, swimming pool, sundeck overlooks the beach, secure parking. Ask for Sue or Kevin. Recommended.

From **Umhlanga Rocks** take the road towards the N2 via Mount Edgecombe. The R102 heads inland from this intersection and passes through the towns of Verulam, Tongaat and Stanger. These large inland towns are at the centre of the sugar processing industry. The descendants of the indentured labourers who were brought here from India in the 1860s give the region a distinct Indian atmosphere and although the towns now are predominantly industrial centres, the Hindu temples and Indian markets are interesting to see. Accommodation is available here, but the beach resorts on the coast are more pleasant places to stay.

**Tongaat,
Verulam
& Stanger**
*Phone code: 032
(NB Always use
3-figure prefix)*

In Tongaat, the **Juggernath Puri Temple** is 23 m high and can be seen from miles away. There are no windows in the tower, but inside, as the eye adjusts to the darkness, the Vishnu statue gradually becomes visible. **Shri Gopalal Temple** is just outside of Verulam on the road to the *Packo* food factory. The temple was opened by Gandhi in 1912, and catered for wealthier and more educated Gujurati immigrants. **Subramanyar Alayam Temple** is set in a beautiful tropical garden just north of town as you reach the railway bridge. A good time to experience the atmosphere of the temple is at weekends when many weddings are held.

*It is customary to
remove your shoes
before entering the
temple buildings*

   Stanger is a busy commercial centre surrounded by extensive sugar plantations. The original settlement here was founded by Shaka as a capital and was known as KwaDukuza. At its height there were up to 2,000 beehive huts surrounding Shaka's royal kraal. Shaka was murdered here by his half-brothers Dingaan and Umhlangana on 22 September 1828. A monument was erected in Shaka's memory in 1932. For further information on Shaka, see page 734. It is rather incongruously set in the town's central Victorian garden. Albert Luthuli, who won the Nobel Peace Prize in 1960, was restricted to living here for his political activities with the ANC. He died here in 1967. The *Greyhound* service stops at Stanger Shell garage. Pretoria, via Richards Bay, daily at 1000, Durban at 1925.

Just over 20 km north of Stanger on the N2, a signposted dirt track leads through sugar plantations up to the entrance of this reserve where there is a parking area and a picnic site. Near to the reserve are the remains of Fort Pearson and the Ultimatum Tree. Fort Pearson was used as a base from which British troops invaded Zululand in 1879. The Ultimatum Tree was where Shepstone read out the ultimatum to Cetshwayo's izindunas giving them 20 days to disband their armies, pay fines in cattle, and to conform to the coronation vows which Shepstone had imposed on Cetshwayo, but to which Cetshwayo had never agreed. These demands and others were totally unreasonable to the Zulus and non compliance with the ultimatum was used by the Colonial authorities as an excuse for war. ■ *Entry, R15 per person. T032-4861574. There are 7 km of walking trails through the orchids and butterflies of which there are over 110 species, and a small cultural museum at the picnic site portraying traditional dress and culture of the Zulu people. There's also a crocodile dam, feeding Sat at 1400 during summer. F 50 sites for tents or caravans and an ablution block. It is worth being fully prepared for camping as there are no other facilities available.*

**Harold
Johnson
Nature
Reserve**

KwaZulu Natal

Zululand

For many visitors, Zululand, homeland of Shaka and one of the most most evocative regions of South Africa will be forever associated with the classic movie starring Michael Caine as the redoubtable British officer fighting in vain against hugely superior numbers of Zulu warriors. Today, this region extending from the northern bank of the Tugela River up to Mkuze and Maputaland, is rather more peaceful and well worth a visit with its coastline of long, unspoilt tropical beaches and large expanses of grassy, rolling hills away from the coast. Gone are the vast herds of migrating elephant, wildebeest and springbok, victim in part to the many battles fought over this wealthy province and despite being one of the more traditional areas of South Africa, it has thriving industrial cities and vast areas of sugarcane and eucalyptus plantations. However, game reserves at St Lucia and Hluhluwe-Umfolozi are still natural magnets for tourists and around 6% of KwaZulu Natal is managed by KZN Wildlife as conservation areas which they refer to as "islands in a sea of development".

Ins and outs

Getting there The route into the Zulu heartland follows the N2 north from Stanger to the village of Gingindlovu. From here the R68 goes inland to Eshowe (26 km) while the N2 continues north to Mtunzini (18 km), Empangeni (50 km), Richards Bay (62 km), St Lucia (130 km), and Hluhluwe-Umfolozi (150 km).

Getting around Facilities for tourists are well-developed, there are numerous game ranches offering luxury accommodation and game watching, and scuba diving and deep sea fishing are available in the coastal resorts. The N2 highway connects it to Durban in the south and Mpumalanga in the north. Travel between the reserves within the area is swift giving visitors the opportunity to visit several reserves in a few days.

Gingindlovu
Phone code: 035
(NB Always use 3-figure prefix)
Colour map 5, grid B2

Gingindlovu, which means "the swallower of the elephant", was originally a military kraal established by Cetshwayo after the Battle of Ndondakusuka where he defeated his half-brother Mbulazi and gained control of the Zulu Kingdom. Today Gingindlovu is a small modern commercial centre surrounded by farmland.

Price codes: see inside front cover

Sleeping F *Inyezane Backpackers*, T/F3371326, inyezane@ethniczulu.com A hostel that helps to open up this fascinating region for the budget traveller. There is a variety of accommodation available to suit your budget: 3 dorms with bunk beds located in rondavels, for couples seeking some privacy or anyone fed up with the general noise of others sleeping, there are 3 double rooms and 2 small single rooms, kitchen and dining area. The whole site is on an expansive sugar farm, a short walk from the huts is a large dam, swimming here is not possible because of bilharzia. There are a number of treats here, mud baths, open-air herbal steam bath, and an art studio where you can paint your own T-shirt or sarong, or make paper from animal dung. This is an alternative but well-run backpackers hostel which will provide the ideal introduction to Zululand and the local customs and history. On the *Baz Bus* route.

Amatikulu Nature Reserve Unlike the other small reserves in this area, Amatikulu does have some big game as giraffe, zebra and waterbuck have been reintroduced and it is the one of the few places to see animals grazing close to the sea. The reserve covers approximately 2,000 ha of forested dunes overlooking the sea and, until it is fully developed, is a beautiful place to combine game watching with a beach holiday. The reserve has only recently been opened to the public. So far only the tented camp has been built, but there are plans for a golf course, hotels and holiday homes. There are game drives and walking trails but the most interesting way to see the reserve is by canoeing up the Amatikulu River.

The reserve is signposted from the N2, from where a dirt road leads towards the sea and the entrance 6 km from Gingindhlovu on the coast.

Sleeping Reservations to stay here should be made through *KZN Wildlife*, T033-946696, F033-421948. **E** *Zangozolo Tented Camp*, has 4 2-bed tents on raised wooden platforms overlooking the sea, a shared ablution block is connected by a wooden walkway, there is no shop here so bring all your own food and supplies, fridge and freezers are supplied and meals are prepared for you by the camp cooks.

Price codes: see inside front cover

Central Zululand

This region of Zululand is famous for its rich cultural heritage. The museums and battlefield sites are the main attractions and the best way to gain an insight into the region's fascinating history.

NB Although there are a number of Zulu battle sites and graves around the villages of Melmoth, Ulundi, and Babanango to the north of Eshowe on the R66, this stretch of road is notorious for having one of the highest rates of car-jacking incidents in KwaZulu Natal.

Zululand game reserves

KwaZulu Natal

Eshowe

Phone code: 035
(NB Always use
3-figure prefix)
Colour map 5, grid B2

Eshowe is an historical inland town named after the sound of a breeze passing through bushes. Situated on a hill, the town has pleasant views over Dhlinza forest and is an administrative centre for the surrounding sugarcane growing region. The historical origins of Eshowe are based around a kraal called Eziqwaqweni which was established here by Cetshwayo. In 1860 the Norwegian missionary Reverend Oftebro was allowed to open a mission station here which was occupied by the British in 1879 while they planned an attack on Ulundi. The Zulus briefly gained the upper hand here when they laid siege to the garrison for 10 weeks. Eshowe was relieved by Lord Chelmsford in April 1879, but not before the Zulus had managed to burn the mission station down. **Tourist information** from *Eshowe Publicity Association*, Osbourne Rd, T4741141, F4744733.

Sights

Dhlinza is a must
for birdwatchers,
65 species have been
recorded in the forest
including the
endangered spotted
thrush and
Delegorgue's Pigeon

Dhlinza Forest Nature Reserve is next to the municipal caravan park. It is a 250 ha area of dense hardwood forest, ferns and creepers where Shaka supposedly hid his wives and children during attacks. There are two short walking trails here through orchids, wild plum and milkwood trees, and knarled vines that are clearly labelled, which in turn attract a number of birds and butterflies. A new addition and the first of its kind in South Africa, is a 125 m wheelchair-accessible timber boardwalk, which takes you through the tree line to the 20 m viewing platform that overlooks the canopy of the forest. This is quite ingenious and a joy to walk up, giving you a real monkey's eye view of the world. ■ *Daily, Sep-Apr 0600-1800, May-Aug 0800-1700. Small entry fee which includes guide. Visitor centre, kiosk, picnic site.*

See also Sleeping
below for the
Skakaland Protea

Shakaland, 14 km north of Eshowe on the R66, is a very popular Zulu theme park with daily cultural shows which include Zulu dancing and tours of a traditional village where tribal customs such as spearmaking, the beer ceremony, and Sangoma rituals are explained. A full lunch in the *Shisa Nyama Restaurant* is included in the price, a good place to try some traditional African food. ■ *Daily, 3-hr tours at 1100, 1230. Entry fee R150. T4600912.*

On Fort Nongqai Road is the **Zululand Historical Museum**. Fort Nongqai was built in 1883 and served as a residence for the Natal Native Police who acted as bodyguards for Sir Melmoth Osborn, the Resident for British Zululand. It is a square fort with high towers on each corner. The museum has displays on John Dunn and his 49 wives and on the Bambata rebellion. John Dunn was the first European settler in what is now KwaZulu Natal. He became an honorary chief and was granted land by the Zulus, ruled at the time by Cetshwayo. His 49 wives gave him 117 children. ■ *0900-1600. Small entry donation.*

Vukani Collection Museum, is near the post office and tourist office, T4745274. While there are antique items on display, this is actually an exhibition of the Vukani Association, a body of over 1000 Zulu craftspeople run and owned by the crafters themselves to manage the pricing and quality of their products. Some award-winning artists exhibit here and crafts include carvings, pottery, basketry, and the famous Zulu beadwork. ■ *Mon-Fri 0900-1300. Small donation.*

Sleeping

Price codes:
see inside front cover

B-C *Shakaland Protea*, T4600912, F4600824. If you are staying the night the Shaka experience follows through in the adjacent *Protea* hotel, where Zulu dancers escort you to your beehive-shaped hut. The evenings are spent sampling the local brew *tshwala* around the campfire while being entertained with dancing and story telling. The en suite huts are huge with all the mod cons expected of a *Protea* hotel. **C** *Amble Inn*, 116 Main St, Eshowe, T4741300. 11 rooms, restaurant offers hearty English meals like roast beef and Yorkshire pudding or steak and kidney pie for lunch and dinner. **D** *Kwabhekithunga/Stewarts Farm*, 36 km from Eshowe on the R34 towards Empangeni, T4600644. 12 Zulu kraals, swimming pool. Like the *Protea* at Shakaland, this overnight stay is accompanied by dancing and traditional food. **C-D** *Royal*, 9 Osborn Rd, Eshowe, T4741117, F4741119. 24 rooms, a/c, TV, restaurant. Town hotel that is starting to look a bit frayed around the edges. **D** *Chennells*

Guesthouse, 36 Pearson Av, Eshowe, T4742894. A fine old farmhouse with double en suite rooms, swimming pool, peaceful setting. **D** *The Chase*, 1 ½ km south of town on the John Ross Highway, T4745491. Holiday farm B&B accommodation. **E** *Eshowe Caravan Park*, next to the entrance of the Dhlinza Forest Nature Reserve, T4744664. 24 sites. **F** *Zululand Backpackers*, 38 Main St, T4744919, F4742691, eshowe@zululand.co.za Part of the *George Hotel*. Dorms, kitchen, showers, double rooms, camping possible, M-Net TV, pool table, swimming pool, close to shops and banks, best to come here on the *Baz Bus* since we heard reports of people being charged for Durban pickups. Has an excellent reputation for organizing local tours, such as visits to traditional Zulu weddings, mountain bikes available for hire, ask about Walter Cele who used to work here and has apparently got a smallholding now where he is willing to take in a few backpackers, this is an excellent way to check out local rural life.

KZN Kaleidoscope, T/F4742348, ask for Henry Bird. Out-of-the-way tours to Zulu graves and battle sites, or a day tour of all the sites mentioned above including lunch and wine for around R300. *Zululand Eco-adventures*, T4744919, ask for Graham Chennells. A registered guide involved in community projects for many years. Unusual cultural tours of the surrounding countryside moving from village to village, no shows are visited, see contemporary traditional life as it is. Interesting projects include the Eshowe Skills Centre, a papermaking project, and the Rotary Classroom Project (the building of 2,000 classrooms in the region). Graham is a Rotary Club member and the ex-mayor of Eshowe who has intimate knowledge of the Zulu people. Highly recommended for more of an insight into Zulu traditions than the usual all-singing all-dancing tourist traps.

Tour operators

From Eshowe the R66 heads north through the **Nkwalini Valley** to **Melmoth** (52 km). About 30 km out of Eshowe look out for a left turn, D256, where there is a signpost with a wagon wheel and a large 'S'. This road will take you to one of the more interesting lodges in Zululand where you can experience an authentic and relaxing introduction to the Zulu culture.

Simunye Zulu Lodge

Follow the gravel road for 12 km until you reach an old trading post. This is the assembly point for guests before they are taken down into the valley to the **B** *Protea Simunye Zulu Lodge*, T035-4503111, F4502534, PO Box 248, Melmoth 3835. You must be at the trading post by 1530, from where you travel for 1 hour on horseback, donkey or ox wagon. (If you don't wish to enter into the spirit or are a bit frail you can request a four-wheel drive transfer.) The lodge is simple and traditional, rooms are stone huts, there are open air rock baths and light comes from candles and oil lamps. In the evening music, singing and dancing is performed by the local people. The lodge is not cheap but rates include all meals, guides and demonstrations.

Coastal Zululand

The N2 highway continues up the coast towards Richards Bay, St Lucia, Hluhluwe-Umfolozi and Maputaland. This is the most popular area of Zululand for visiting tourists. The coastal region has a subtropical climate; it is hot and humid from December to March and warm and dry from April to November.

Mtunzini means "the shady place", and is a pleasant resort at the mouth of the Umlalazi River facing the lagoon. The town is set in an area of coastal forest and mangrove swamps. John Dunn, who had become a Zulu chief in his own right and was one of Cetshwayo's advisors, lived here with his 49 wives and 117 children. There is a pleasant Country Club here, T3401779, open to day visitors. Facilities include tennis, squash, and a pretty 9-hole golf course edged with palm trees, clubs can be rented. There is a good view of the ocean and Umlalazi Game Reserve from the club house bar and restaurant.

Mtunzini
Phone code: 035
(NB Always use 3-figure prefix)
Colour map 5, grid B2

The best source of **tourist information** is at *Zini Arts & Crafts*, off the main street on Station Rd, T/F3401630. Open Mon-Fri 0800-1700 and weekends in holiday season. An after-hours phone number is displayed on the door. Helpful for accommodation recommendations and activities within a day's drive from Mtunzizi.

Raffia Palm Monument marks the southernmost point for this giant palm. The Raffia is monocarpic and only produces seeds once in its 25-year life cycle. It is thought that the seeds were brought here from Maputo and were planted in 1910 by a District Magistrate. There is a wooden boardwalk which meanders through the palm forest. The rare palmnut vulture breeds here.

Price codes:
see inside front cover

Sleeping B *Trade Winds*, T3402533, F3401629. 26 rooms, a/c, TV, restaurant, swimming pool. The principal hotel in town. **C** *Highfield Country Home*, 7 km from town off the N2, however you must get to it from Mtunzini on the old Durban road, T3401731. 4 double rooms with exquisite bathrooms, TV, meals on request, pool, set in a beautiful farmhouse in 4 ha of parklands, sea views, ask for Willie or Sarco. International visitors return here year after year. Recommended. **C** *Mtunzini Chalets*, T3401953, F3401955. 22 beach chalets, log cabins, set in dune forest, meals available, chalets sleep 6 people, swimming pool. This is the only accommodation on the beach. **E** *Forest Inn*, on the N2, T3401828. 42 rooms, a/c, TV, restaurant, swimming pool, may sound OK on paper but very poor reports. **E-F** *Casa Benri Caravan Park*, 1 Cyclid St, T3401997. At the end of the village in a beautiful tropical setting, plenty of grass and shade, safe, quiet location, 15 mins' walk to a peaceful white sandy beach. Unfortunately the shared ablutions blocks are very poorly maintained. **E-F** *Xa Xa Caravan Park*, at the top of town, T3401843. Further from the beach but much better looked after.

Umlalazi Nature Reserve

Umlalazi is a small but popular nature reserve with South African tourists and when full can accommodate at least 300 people who come here for fishing, windsurfing and the beaches. There are no shark nets but swimming is permitted. The natural ambience of the reserve is best felt when it is less crowded and it is easier to appreciate the long tropical beaches and walks along the banks of the lagoon and mangrove swamps. This reserve is particularly interesting to birdwatchers in search of the rare palmnut vulture and the woolly necked stork, both of which breed here. ■ *Gate hours, 0500-2200. The reserve is 132 km north of Durban, 2 km to the east of Mtunzini and is signposted from the N2.*

Price codes:
see inside front cover

Sleeping C 13 5-bed self-catering chalets, reservations through *KWN Wildlife*, T033-8451000, F033-8451001. **F** Camping, 38 sites, ablution block, electric points. Reservations, T035-3401836.

Empangeni

Phone code: 035
(NB Always use 3-figure prefix)
Colour map 5, grid B2

Empangeni is named after the Zulu word of 'pangaed' meaning grabbed – due to many people being taken by crocs on the banks of the Mpangeni River, on which the town is situated. Shaka grew up in this area before the Norwegian Missionary Society mission station opened in 1851. The town has developed into a busy industrial centre and has been pulping wood since the first eucalyptus plantations were established in 1905. The University of Zululand is on the left of the motorway. **NB** The area is undergoing a series of name changes. Officially Empangeni and Richards Bay, 18 km away, have now joined together as one municipal area, referred to jointly as the city of **Umhlathuze**. It will be some time before this change is reflected on maps or sign posts so for the time being we will refer to these towns by their old names, but they are practically joined and share many of the same facilities.

Game reserves
There is little accommodation in the town itself, but on the R34 heading inland there are private game ranches

Thula Thula Game Lodge is west of Empangeni and north of the small village of Heatonville. Take the R34 for 8 km before turning onto the road to Heatonville, which is a further 10 km. Thula Thula is signposted down a gravel road from Heatonville. The reserve is a large private game ranch in the Enselini Valley that was originally used for the cultivation of cotton and cattle pastures. It was converted in 1964 and now offers game drives, and bush walks through flat acacia covered thornveld. Some of the larger mammals you can expect to see are white rhino, elephant, giraffe, kudu, nyala and other antelopes.

Sleeping AL *Elephant Safari Lodge*, T7928322/3, F7928324. Exclusive safari lodge with 7 luxury thatched chalets beautifully decorated in an ethnic style. Rates are all-inclusive of meals and game drives, pool, outside dining in rustic boma. The lodge will arrange private picnic lunches in the bush accompanied by an armed ranger.

Price codes:
see inside front cover

Nyala Game Ranch is on the R34 from Empangeni to Nkwalini; 22 km along this road there is a turning right onto the D130. The reserve is signposted from here. Established in 1962, this was the first game private reserve in Natal. Many of the techniques used in running a game farm were first developed here. The reserve offers horse riding, mountain biking, clay pigeon shooting, hiking, game drives (day and night) and hunting.

Sleeping C-D There are 3 self-catering camps here. *Mbondwe* and *Hlati* are both rondavels with fully equipped kitchens, TV lounge, and a swimming pool. *Umvumvu*, is a rustic bush camp with no electricity, paraffin is used for cooking and lighting, T7928185, F7928185 for reservations.

Price codes:
see inside front cover

Enselini Nature Reserve is a small reserve on the banks of the Enselini River. Follow the N2 north from Empangeni and you get to the reserve after 13 km. The **Nkonikini Trail**, 7 km, passes along raised platforms over the swamp and through grasslands where game has been reintroduced. Here you can see giraffe, nyala, waterbuck, wildebeest, and zebra. This is an interesting reserve to visit and a good chance to break the monotony of driving through the vast plantations that line the N2. At the reception centre there is a picnic site. Maps and information leaflets are available.

From Empangeni the R34 heads east, crossing the N2, and reaches **Richards Bay** (18 km) through a flat landscape of sugarcane and eucalyptus plantations. On the horizon you can see rows of pylons and the high chimneys of industrial complexes. If the wind is blowing inland the fumes can be particularly strong and at some point on the R34 you will pass through them. The N2 continues north to St Lucia (80 km), and Hluhluwe-Umfolozi (106 km).

Greyhound, central reservations, T011-2498900. Coaches depart from the museum in Turnbull St, towards **Durban** (3 hrs): daily, 1735. **Johannesburg** and **Pretoria** (9 hrs): daily, 1215.

Transport

Richards Bay

Richards Bay is a modern town built principally to house people working in the port and the nearby industrial plants. First impressions of the town are of an extensive, centreless suburban sprawl built with car drivers in mind. However, the attraction of Richards Bay as a tourist centre is that many of Zululand's major nature reserves such as Hluhluwe-Umfolozi, Mkuze and St Lucia can be visited from here on day trips. **NB** Officially Empangeni and Richards Bay have now joined together as one municipal area, referred jointly as the city of Umhlathuze. It will be some time before this change is reflected on maps or sign posts so for the time being we will refer to these towns by their old name.

The original Richards Bay was a small holiday resort just north of the lagoon on the mouth of the Mhlatuze River. Development on the wide lagoon and natural harbour began in the 1960s as an alternative to Durban, which was becoming too busy and slow. Richards Bay has grown into an important industrial centre exporting mineral ores and coal. Massive tankers arrive here to discharge oil for Gauteng through the oil pipeline.

Phone code: 035
(NB Always use
3-figure prefix)
Colour map 5, grid B2

KwaZulu Natal

What used to be a wild river estuary inhabited by hippos, crocodiles and migrant birds has now become a highly developed modern port which plans to be one of the largest in South Africa. Approaching the town on the R34, one is immediately struck by the massive industrial processing complexes on either side of the road. The R34 continues to head east; after 2 km there is a turning on the right onto Main Road where the shopping malls, banks, the post office and hospital are all located on the junctions of Bullion Boulevard and Krugerrand. Following the R34 for a further 4 km brings you to Meerensee, a green suburban area where you will find most of the hotels.

Meerensee is a pleasant place to stay and is next to small areas of dune forest and long tropical beaches which stretch north for 60 km towards Mapelane. The furthest beaches are only accessible in a four-wheel drive vehicle but Alkantstrand, Five Mile and Newark beaches are all on the edge of town and have picnic spots. The Small Craft Harbour and the Tuzi-Gazi Waterfront has been developed for tourism. Here you will find a selection of restaurants, curio shops and the helpful **tourist information** office, T7880039, F7880040, rbtour@uthungulu.co.za Open Mon-Fri 0800-1600, Sat 1000-1400. It's a very friendly and helpful office, tucked away from the hotels and shops, with a few restaurants nearby. Come here for information on the whole region, as the municipal offices in the smaller towns are of little use.

Sights   Some unusual and free tours are available here organized by *Richards Bay Minerals* who had intended to strip mine titanium bearing sand dunes in the northern sector of the Greater St Lucia Wetland Park. As these plans were environmentally sensitive, they were understandably the source of some controversy and have been

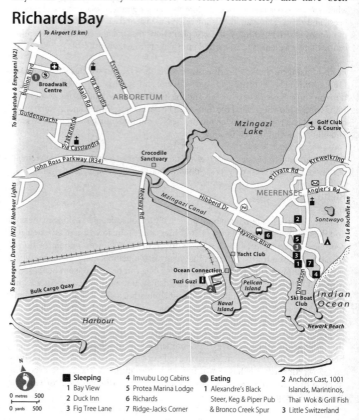

Richards Bay

successfully opposed by environmentalists. There are three tours on offer during which you can see dune mining and smelting in action as well as visiting mined areas in the process of rehabilitation. While you may be somewhat blinded by science, the tours offer an interesting insight to the huge industrial plants that surround the town. Tours must be booked at least a day in advance. ■ *Richards Bay Minerals*, *T9013444, F9013442. A choice of 3 industrial tours lasting from 2-3 hrs.*

Bay Crocodile Sanctuary is on the Mzingazi Canal opposite the entrance to the Small Craft Harbour. The sanctuary consists of a 500 m long raised walkway through swamp forest which is rich in birdlife. From this safe vantage point you can see crocodiles in their natural habitat. Other facilities include the *Croc Roc* restaurant, curio shop and plant nursery. ■ *T7532555.*

B *Protea Marina Lodge*, corner of Davidson Lane and Launder Lane, T7531350, F7531361. 68 rooms, a/c, TV, restaurant and bar, an expensive modern businessman's hotel, but it does serve good breakfasts. **B** *The Ridge – Jacks Corner*, Davidson St, T7534312, F7534321. 14 luxury rooms in an upmarket guest house, well-positioned pool with views of the ocean and harbour. **C** *Richards Hotel*, T7531301, F7532334. Modern hotel, 100 rooms, swimming pool, restaurants, a rather bleak setting on a road junction, special offers at weekends. **C** *Bay View Lodge*, 24 Davidson Lane, T/F7533065. 12 rooms, a/c, restaurant and bar, swimming pool, a small apartment block. **C** *Fig Tree Lane*, 20 Davidson Lane, T082-9505666 (mob), F7532174. Pleasant, tin-roofed self-catering family cottages under the shade of a grove of fig trees, TV, a/c, fully equipped kitchens, or B&B. **C-D** *Imvubu Log Cabins*, Hibbert Dr, T7534122, F7534120. 34 self-catering cabins, 1-2 bedrooms, set in lovely woodlands next to a lake (watch out for crocs), just a few steps from the beach, you wouldn't know you were so close to town. Recommended. **D** *Duck Inn*, 3 Dageraad, T/F7534147. 5 rooms, B&B, garden, secure parking. **D** *La Rochelle Inn*, 10 Angler's Rd, T7531903, F7533173. 4 double a/c room, M-Net TV, 2 swimming pools, garden, secure parking. **D-F** *Harbour Lights Resort*, on a sugar estate 8 km from the N2 turn off to Richards Bay, T7966239, F7966753. 7 rather frilly self-catering apartments with separate lounges and TV. Good value backpackers accommodation in dorms or beehive huts sleeping 6 people, shared ablutions, bar, pool, email facility, meals on request, local tours. Caravan and camping sites also available. Free pick ups from Empangeni and Richards Bay bus stops.

Sleeping
■ *on map*
Price codes:
see inside front cover

The town caters mainly for business travellers and hotels are overpriced. New B&Bs are springing up and offer a cheaper alternative

Anchors Cast, Small Craft Harbour, T7880219. Seafront bar and restaurant. *Blue Dolphin*, Alkant Strand, T7535553. Family restaurant, right on the beach, not a bad place to have a beer in the heat of the day, but other than that resembling little more than a beach front kiosk. *Bronco Creek Spur*, Boardwalk Centre, T7895647. Steakhouse chain, also do takeaway, open late. *Keg & Piper*, United Buildings, Bullion Blvd, T7891063. Pub food and cold beers, big screen sports. *Little Switzerland*, Blue Sereh Centre, Davidson Av, T7532208. Continental dishes. *Marintinos*, Tuzi Gazi Waterfront, T7880312. Portuguese fish and chicken, nice setting. *1001 Islands*, Small Craft Harbour, T7880020. Crayfish, langoustines and prawns. *Thai Wok Food House*, Quay Walk, Tuzi Gazi Waterfront, T7880525. Local version of Thai food, some tasty seafood dishes. Open daily. *The Grill Fish*, Tuzi Gazi Waterfront, T7880110. Quality seafood restaurant right in the harbour, excellent grills.

Eating
● *on map*

Cinemas *Numetro*, Boardwalk Shopping Mall, Krugerrand.

Entertainment

There are a number of shopping malls in the centre of town, the largest of which is the **Boardwalk** where facilities include banks, chemists, supermarkets, restaurants, a wide range of shops and a cinema.

Shopping

East Coast Safaris, T082-4591637 (mob), contact Peter Van Wyk. Registered guide for all the local attractions. Game park tours start from R300 per day. *Esseness Safaris*, T/F7924114, contact Steve Gibson. Tours to the game parks in the north, deep-sea fishing, horseriding. *Rennies Travel*, Boardwalk Centre, T7890589. *Thomas Cook* agent, foreign exchange.

Tour operators

KwaZulu Natal

Transport **Air** A small airport, at the northern edge of town, 5 km from the centre, serves business more than the average tourist. *SA Express*, T7860301, fly 4 flights a day to Johannesburg. From Johannesburg it is possible to fly direct to all other domestic destinations.

Road **Bus**: the *Baz Bus*, T021-4392323, info@bazbus.com, www.bazbus.com Runs up the coast along the N2. *Greyhound*, central reservations, T011-2498900. The coaches depart from Steers, by the Total Service Station in Anglers Rod St. **Durban** (3 hrs): daily, 1800; **Pretoria** and **Johannesburg** (10 hrs): daily, 1120. *Sodwana Shuttle*, T031-2669878. Can stop here on request, a private minivan shuttle service running between **Sodwana Bay** and **Durban**. The service runs on request from Durban for a minimum of 6 people. **Car hire**: all offices at the airport; *Avis*, T7896549, *Budget*, T7860986, *Imperial*, T7860309, *Hertz*, T7861201. **Taxi** *Pronto*, T7895460. *Falcon*, T7899050.

Directory **Banks** *Ned Bank* and *Standard Bank* are both on Bullion Blvd. **Medical Services** Pharmacy: after hours T7892301. **Hospitals**: *The Bay Hospital*, Krugerrand Central Business District, T7891234.

Richards Bay to St Lucia

Mapelane National Park
Colour map 5, grid A3

This park was established in 1897, but was later handed over to the Department of Forestry. After the campaign waged by the Wildlife Society of Southern Africa the threat of strip-mining the titanium-rich dunes was averted. This small coastal reserve is popular with fishermen who can launch their speedboats here. There is a safe beach for swimming and licences are available to collect mussels, oysters and crayfish. Swimming or wading in the Umfolozi River is prohibited as there are too many crocodiles.

Ins and outs Look out for the small village of Kwambonambi, 30 km north of Empangeni on the N2. There is a turning heading east from Kwambonambe to the Kwambonambi Lighthouse, from here it is a further 50 km to Mapelane along a narrow dirt track which is in very bad condition. Four-wheel drive vehicles are recommended but vehicles with high road clearance can also get through in dry weather. Gates open Oct-Mar 0600-1900, Apr-Sep 0600-1800, office hours 0800-1230, 1400-1630, entry fee R20.

The **Mapelane Trail** is 2 km long and climbs up a large dune from where there are views over the reserve. The forests and the swamp are wild and impenetrable but the dirt roads passing through the reserve are also good for walking. The road approaching the camp enters a natural tunnel created by the thick tropical forest. New trails are planned for the area, but the existing trails through dune forest, swamp forest and through the Umfolozi Swamp to the crocodile hide are a fascinating way to explore the area.

Price codes:
see inside front cover

Sleeping **C** 10 5-bed log cabins, self-catering, with kitchen, bathroom, dining room and lounge. The cabins are set on a large forested dune with views over a large beach and the sea. Reservations through *KZN Wildlife*, T033-8451000, F033-8451001. **Camping** **F** 45 sites, ablution blocks. Food and petrol are not for sale at the camp, it is therefore essential to plan on being self-sufficient and bring all your supplies with you. Campsite reservations T/F035-5901407.

St Lucia

Phone code: 035
(NB Always use 3-figure prefix)
Colour map 5, grid A3

The holiday resort of St Lucia lies to the south of Lake St Lucia and is surrounded by the Greater St Lucia Wetland National Park. St Lucia is the largest seaside holiday destination on this part of the coast and is particularly popular during the South African school holidays. Many tourists arrive with large high powered speedboats and jetskis and, until recently when beach driving was thankfully banned, to burn up and down the beach in their four-wheel drive vehicles. The resort is always noisy and overcrowded at Christmas and the thousands of people enjoying a boisterous beach holiday do make it hard to believe that this is actually part of a nature reserve. The

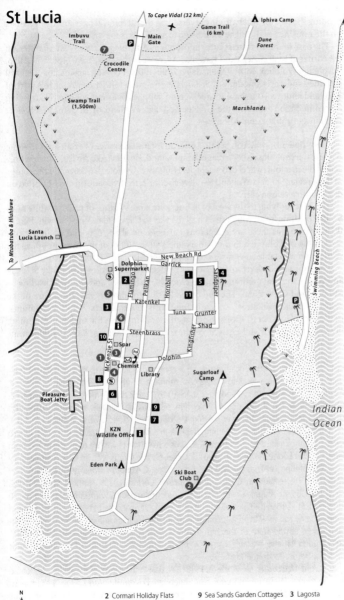

St Lucia

To Cape Vidal (32 km)

Game Trail (6 km)

Iphiva Camp

Imbuvu Trail

Main Gate

Dune Forest

Crocodile Centre

Swamp Trail (1,500m)

Marshlands

Santa Lucia Launch

To Mtubatuba & Hluhluwe

New Beach Rd

Garrick

Dolphin Supermarket

Flamingo

Pelikan

Hornbill

Sandpiper

Katenkel

Tuna

Grunter

Shad

Steenbrass

Kingfisher

Spar

McKenzie St

Chemist

Dolphin

Library

Sugarloaf Camp

Pleasure Boat Jetty

KZN Wildlife Office

Swimming Beach

Indian Ocean

Eden Park

Ski Boat Club

KwaZulu Natal

N

Not to scale

Sleeping
1 Aspidura Holiday Flats
2 Cormari Holiday Flats
3 Jo-a-Lize Lodge
4 Lalapanzi Guest Lodge
5 Maputaland Guest House
6 Namib Safari Lodge
7 Ndiza Lodge
8 St Lucia Bibs Backpackers
9 Sea Sands Garden Cottages
10 Tight Lines Rest Camp
11 Wetlands Guest House

Eating
1 Alfredo's
2 Boat House Fish & Grill
3 Lagosta
4 Paradiso
5 Quarterdeck & Key West Bar
6 St Lucia Pizza
7 Zulu & I

best time to appreciate St Lucia and its surrounding wetlands is off-season. **NB** At the time of writing, soon after the ban on beach driving in February 2002, regular 4x4 owning holidaymakers threatened not to go to St Lucia any longer. This caused a public and well-televised series of demonstrations by the tourist industry in St Lucia, wanting the ban on beach driving reversed, as they feel it will have an adverse affect on their businesses. It will be interesting to see if this is the case.

The best source of **tourist information** is at *Advantage Cruises and Charters*, on the corner of McKenzie St and Katonkel Av, close to the *Spar*, T5901180, F5901053, advantage@zululink.co.za Open daily 7000-1900. Booking agents for all local activities and accommodation. St Lucia is the main tourist centre in this part of Zululand and is a good base to stock up on supplies before staying in self-catering accommodation either in the Greater St Lucia Wetland or in game reserves at Hluhluwe-Umfolozi and Mkuzi.

Sights   The tour operators based in St Lucia offer an interesting range of excursions to some of the less frequently visited areas of Maputaland, such as Lake Sibaya, which is only accessible in a four-wheel drive vehicle. Hluhluwe-Umfolozi, Mkuzi and the camps of the Greater St Lucia Wetland are all well-connected by road and can be visited on day trips in a saloon car.

The beaches lying to the west of St Lucia are large swathes of pristine white sand backed by dune forest which stretch all the way to Cape Vidal. Visitors swim here at their own risk as there are dangerous currents, no shark nets and no lifeguards. Swimming is prohibited in the estuary and within 100 m of the river mouth as the strong unpredictable currents, sharks and crocodiles make it too dangerous.

The approach to the resort crosses the bridge over the outflow from Lake St Lucia and passes the main entrance to the crocodile sanctuary and the road leading to Mfabeni and Cape Vidal. The end of the R618 leads directly into the centre of the resort on McKenzie Street, which is lined with supermarkets, banks, restaurants, bottle shops, handicraft shops and boat charter companies for anglers. Continuing down past the end of McKenzie Street the road leads to the large *KZN Wildlife* camp-sites at Sugarloaf and Eden Park.

Sleeping   In such a popular South African resort the accommodation is cheap by international stan-
■ *on map , page 429*   dards, however there is almost always a shortage of beds so book well in advance.
Price codes: **C** *Lalapanzi Guest Lodge*, 7 Sandpiper St, T5901167. Large double rooms with en suite facil-
see inside front cover   ities and fridge full of cool drinks, TV lounge, self-catering facilities, swimming pool, lush tropical garden, secure off street parking. **C** *Maputaland Guest House*, Kabeljou Av No 1, T/F5901041. TV, restaurant, swimming pool set in a large tropical garden in a quiet suburb away from the main drag. Recommended. Wide selection of wildlife tours organized from here. **C** *Ndiza Lodge*, Hornbill St, T5901113. B&B, double rooms with en suite bathroom, TV plus self-catering cabanas, a good size for families. **C** *Aspidura Holiday Flats*, Garrick St, T5901077. TV, restaurant. **C** *Sea Sands Garden Cottages*, 135 Hornbill St, T5901082, F011-7896565. 7 cottages, a/c, TV, restaurant, swimming pool. **C** *Wetlands Guest House*, 20 Kingfisher St, T/F5901098. Family run B&B set in quiet suburbs between the beach and shops. 3 large rooms with en suite bathroom, the high ceilings and wood floors help main-tain a cool temperature in the hot summer months. Guest lounge with bar and TV. Self-catering flat also available. Large swimming pool with child protection fence. Ask for Derick or Hettie. Recommended.

C-D *Jo-a-Lize Lodge*, McKenzie St, T5901224. B&B in the centre of the village. 20 double ensuite rooms, TV, swimming pool, recommended. **D** *Namib Safari Lodge*, McKenzie St, T5901133, F5901256. 20 2-room self-catering chalets, a bit close to one another but spacious inside, min 2 people, max 7, lounge and braai area, TV, pool. **D** *Tight Lines Rest Camp*, McKenzie St, T5901087. Double rooms with TV, backpacker rooms with shared bathroom, restaurant. **F** *St Lucia Bibs*, McKenzie St, T5901056, F5901360. Small dorms, double rooms, twins and camping. Great kitchen and self-catering area, *Spar* shop next door for supplies, evening meals on request. Braai area, rock swimming pool, relaxing gardens with hammock and bar area, email/internet access. Run well-organized and guided day trips to Hluhluwe and other local sights. Free transfer to beach. Chris does an excellent job, with the overall emphasis on making sure all guests have a good time and feel relaxed. On the *Baz Bus* route.

Camping There are 2 *KZN Wildlife* campsites on the edge of town, reservations T5901340, F5901343. **F** *Sugarloaf Camp*, 92 sites, swimming pool, ablution blocks. **F** *Eden Park*, 20 sites, ablution block. There is a shop selling a wide range of guides and curios and a restaurant serving light meals.

Alfredos, McKenzie St. Good Italian food, occasional live music, tables inside and out, all adds to the easy going fun atmosphere. *Key West*, McKenzie St. Late night cocktail bar with music. *Lagosta*, next to *Spar*, McKenzie St, T5902197. Takeaway seafood snacks, great value, fish pies, paella, fish & chips. *Paradiso*, McKenzie St, T5901190. Good value breakfasts, set back from the street on an open courtyard, unusual Austrian dishes. *Quarterdeck*, McKenzie St, T5901116. Fancy burgers, best feature is watching the world go by from the balcony, friendly service. *St Lucia Pizza*, 13 McKenzie St, T5901048. Unlicensed pizza restaurant, good size deep pan or thin crust. *Zulu & I*, at the crocodile centre just out of town, T5901144. Nice setting if you don't mind the snakes in the glass cases. Open all day, tasty seafood dishes, crocodile pasta and daily croc specials.

Eating & bars
● *on map, page 429*

Advantage Charters, T5901259. Explore Lake St Lucia on a 2-hr boat ride or try whale watching in season, estuary trips depart from the jetty behind Bibs Backpackers. Whale watching trips run Jun-Nov when humpback, mink, and occasional southern right whales travel along the coast heading for the warmer breeding waters of Mozambique. Expect to pay around R300, which is refundable if no whales are spotted. *Maputaland Tours*, T5901075. Organize day trips to the game reserves and snorkelling and fishing trips to Cape Vidal, Sodwana Bay, Lake Sibaya. All equipment is provided. Overnight tours to Kosi Bay.

Tour operators

Road Passengers using the *Baz Bus* can be dropped off at *Bib's Backpackers* on Mckenzie St. **Car hire** Most car hire offices in Richards Bay will drop off and collect in St Lucia.

Transport

Banks The *First National Bank*, T5901008, and *Standard Bank*, T5901044, on McKenzie St.

Directory

Greater St Lucia Wetland Park

The Greater St Lucia Wetland Park was declared a World Heritage Site in 1999, the first place to be awarded this status in South Africa. The protected area is the largest estuarine lake system in Africa. The variety of flora and fauna here, including 105 species listed in the Red Data Book, compares favourably with the Okavango Delta or Kruger National Park. St Lucia has therefore become one of South Africa's most popular tourist resorts.

Colour map 5, grid A3

The birdlife is outstanding and a staggering 420 species have been recorded here

Ins and outs

The park falls into 3 main areas in the southern region accessible from St Lucia. These are: **St Lucia Public Resort and Estuary National Park**, which is a good area to see crocodiles, hippo, impala, waterbuck, wildebeest and zebra. The second area is the coastline up to **Cape Vidal**, 32 km from St Lucia with interesting trails and the prospect of good swimming at the beautiful Cape beach. The third area is the **western shore** of the lake, which is much quieter than the other two but affords the opportunity to explore the lake by boat. The Greater St Lucia Wetland Park extends north and encompasses all the coastal parks from Sodwana Bay to Kosi Bay Nature Reserve on the border of Mozambique. These are dealt with in the Northern Maputaland section, see page 442.

KwaZulu Natal

Sleeping
See also each park area's Sleeping section

Reservations for all self-catering accommodation and wilderness trails within the park can be made up to 12 months in advance through *KZN Wildlife Reservations*, T033-8451000, F8451001. For postal reservations, write to The Reservations Officer, *KZN Wildlife*, PO Box 13069, Cascades, Pietermaritzburg 3202. Bookings can also be made directly through the website, www.kznwildlife.com Reservations for campsites must be made through each individual camp. There are only limited supplies available in the camp shops so it is essential to bring your own food, the nearest supermarket is in St Lucia; if you are staying at Charters Creek, Fanie's Island or one the camps around False Bay, the nearest shops are in Hluhluwe.

Best time to visit

Each season in the wetlands has its own attraction. From Nov-Feb there tends to be more rain making the vegetation greener. Jun-Aug is the best time for birdwatching as this is the breeding season. The best months for walking are Mar-Nov when it is less hot and humid. The school holidays are always a popular time for South African tourists to visit and accommodation at these times should be booked in advance.

Warning Visitors to the park should be aware of some of the dangers presented by the wildlife. When hiking around the lake, watch out for hippos and poisonous snakes. When swimming stay away from the estuary, which is inhabited by crocodiles and Zambezi sharks. St Lucia is a malarial area and prophylactics should be taken.

History

The land now occupied by the park has had human inhabitants since the Early Iron Age. Archaeological excavations have uncovered the remains of settlements and middens. Large areas of forest were cleared to provide charcoal for iron smelting and it is possible that the grass-covered dunes seen today were originally cleared at that time. St Lucia was named by the Portuguese explorer Manuel Perestrello in 1575 although European influence in the area was minimal until the 1850s. Up to that time the area was inhabited by a relatively large population of Thongas and Zulus who herded cattle and cultivated the land.

Professional hunters began visiting the lake in the 1850s in search of ivory, hides and horns which were at one point the Colony of Natal's main source of income. So successful were these hunters that within 50 years the last elephant in this region had been shot. Amongst the big game hunters here were William Baldwin, Robert Briggs Struthers, 'Elephant' White and John Dunn who recorded having shot 23 seacows in one morning and a total of 203 seacows in the following 3 months. Hunting parties would kill hundreds of elephants, crocodiles and hippos on each expedition.

During the 1880s the British government annexed St Lucia in a move which would foil the Boers from the New Republic in their search for access to the sea. It was after this that land was distributed to settlers and that missions were founded at Mount Tabor, Cape Vidal and Ozabeni.

St Lucia lake, along with Hluhluwe and Umfolozi was one of the first game reserves to be established in Africa in 1895. Further moves to protect wildlife also took place in 1944 with the addition of False Bay Park to the protected area, and in 1975 South Africa signed the international RAMSAR Convention to protect wetlands. It was then that the Greater St Lucia Wetland region was declared. More recently land was recovered by the park when in 1987 the Eastern Shores State Forest was returned to the Natal Parks Board. Conservation measures have continued in the 1990s, and many conservation initiatives were introduced when St Lucia won World Heritage status in 1999. One of the most important of these has been the recent national ban on beach driving in Feb 2002, enraging many South African 4x4 owners.

In spite of these measures to protect St Lucia, the survival of the lake system has been under constant threat since the turn of the century. One of the most intractable problems has been the effects of agriculture on the lake's water supply. Land reclamation, drainage canals, the diversion of the Umfolozi River and the damming of the Hluhluwe River for irrigation have all contributed to the silting up of the lake. In

The Turtle Season

The Turtle Season along the coast of the Greater St Lucia Wetland Park usually runs from Novemebr too March, when giant leatherback and loggerhead turtles come on to the beach to nest, some weighing up to 900 kg. The turtles nest up to 10 times in a season and the hatchlings arrive by February. During the season the turtles are protected by KZN Wildlife who monitor them carefully and protect them from predators such as honey badgers and jackals. Their nesting site continues north into Mozambique. For more information on the turtles see page 447. Since the ban on beach driving, KZN Wildlife has granted a single concession to a St Lucia eco-tour operator to run trips to see the turtles at night when they come on to the beach to lay their eggs. **Shaka Barker Tours**, *McKenzie St, T5901162, F5901070, shakabarker@stlucia.co.za A minimum of 4 and a maximum of 10 people are required and advance booking is essential. The tour departs at 1830 and returns at 0300 the following morning, expect to pay R500, which includes supper and night drives in search of genets, leopard, bush babies, chameleons, and hippos grazing at night. The drive heads north past Cape Vidal towards Leven Point, which is normally restricted to visitors. Once at the breeding site it is possible to get close to the turtles and it's not uncommon to see crocodile and snakes on the beach. This is a very special wildlife experience conducted in an eco-friendly way and highly recommended.*

KwaZulu Natal

the 1960s salinity levels increased to such an extent during a series of droughts that the water in the lake system was twice as salty as sea water. Plants, fish and crocodiles started to die in ever increasing numbers. So far regular dredging of the estuary has protected the wetland system but without effective water management by farmers upstream the lakes could still dry up.

Another problem is the vast pine plantations in the region that were first planted in 1954. The thirsty pines consume a lot of water and as a result, over the last 20 years the level of Lake St Lucia has dropped by 2 m to the present average depth of only one metre. When St Lucia won it's status as a World Heritage Site in 1999, a five-year plan was put in process to remove all the pine trees and revert the land back to indigenous flora. While five years may have been a little ambitious, the pine trees that are being chopped down are not being replaced and vast tracks of land can be seen with evidence of new growth of indigenous plants and trees. This in turns stimulates the wildlife populations, and St Lucia is expected to look a lot more natural in a decade or so.

Wildlife

The area now known as the Greater St Lucia Wetland Park consists of a number of formerly separate nature reserves and state forests. These are still referred to locally under a bewildering array of old and new names, but the greater area is considered to be South Africa's third largest park. The entire 328,000 ha reserve starts south of the St Lucia Estuary and stretches north to the border of Mozambique, encompassing 280 km of coastline. Fringing this coastline are vegetated sand dunes exceeding 180 m in height and estimated to be over 30,000 years old. These are the second highest vegetated dunes in the world, after Fraiser Island in Australia.

On the land
There are chances of seeing buffalo, kudu, waterbuck, one of the few black rhinos and leopards

The Mkuze, Mzinene, Hluhluwe and Nyalazi rivers flow into the northern end of the lake system. The lakes are shallow and interspersed with islands and reedbeds and reach a maximum of 3 m in depth although large areas are only up to 1 m deep. A narrow channel connects the lakes to the estuary and the sea. The lake's shores are bounded by papyrus, reeds, mangrove and forest swamps. The other inland areas in the park are grasslands with zones of thornveld, coastal and dune forest.

Ecotourism in the Greater St Lucia Wetland Park

The expectations of what ecotourism can realistically achieve in helping to conserve the Lake St Lucia ecosystem will seriously be put to the test over the next few years. The two main threats to the environment here are the local farmers who want to move back onto their lands within the park and Richards Bay Minerals whose plans to mine the dunes for titanium have recently been foiled.

Five thousand local farmers were forcibly removed from their land to make way for the Eastern Shores State Forest and a missile testing range. As 73% of people in Zululand are living in poverty the local farmers are keen to return to farm the fertile soils within the park. But agriculture and cattle grazing could silt up the wetland and destroy the park. The plans to develop ecotourism will be expected to benefit these farmers but the lack of skills and educational qualifications means that few local people will find work in tourism. The proposed forms of employment so far are the sale of

handicrafts and the establishment of performances of singing and dancing troupes. Whether the income from these activities will satisfy the aspirations of local farmers remains to be seen.

Richards Bay Minerals were granted a government licence in the 1970s to strip mine 17 km of forested dunes in the Eastern Shores area. In 1993 an environmental survey recommended that mining should not go ahead and that the area should apply for protection as a World Heritage Status site. In April 1996 the cabinet, under pressure from both international and South African environmental activists, decided not to allow Richards Bay Minerals to strip mine in St Lucia. The planned R6bn investment in titanium mining will not now take place.

This, however, has not solved the problems of local farmers who, having lost both their land and the chance of massive investment in the area, now have only tourim rely on tourism to make a living.

In the water Lake St Lucia is a nursery and feeding ground for fish and crustaceans. As salinity changes in the water from fresh to salt water so do the corresponding ecosystems. Fresh water attracts tilapia, catfish and ducks whilst saltier water attracts pelicans and herons. Zambezi and black tipped sharks come into the estuary to breed. Although game is being reintroduced to the area the animals which are most often seen are the large populations of common reedbuck, hippopotamus and Nile crocodile. There are an estimated 2000 crocs in the entire lake system, and it is thought that is the only place in the world where sharks and crocodiles share the same water.

In the air The birdlife is the main attraction here. As well as the species often found in the dune forests and grasslands of the reserve many unusual migrant birds can also be seen. Southern African waterbirds migrate depending on regional droughts between Bangweulu and Kafue in Zambia, the Okavango Delta in Botswana, the Zambezi Delta in Mozambique and the wetlands of Maputaland and St Lucia. The St Lucia waters are high in nutrients and support large populations of pinkbacked and white pelicans, greater and lesser flamingos, ducks, spoonbills and ibises.

The pelicans arrive every autumn to feed on migrating mullet in the Narrows, north of St Lucia Village. Around 6,000 pelicans nest at the northern end of the lake where visitors can see their courtship displays.

St Lucia Public Resort and Estuary National Parks

For Sleeping in this area see page 430 These areas directly surround St Lucia village. There is a 12-km network of self-guided trails, which start in the area near the Crocodile Centre. As the trails extend from the Indian Ocean to the estuary they cross several different habitats such as dune forest, grasslands, mangroves and swamps. The trail leading from the Crocodile Centre to the estuary takes you to some good hippo-viewing riverside

KwaZulu Natal

spots. The grasslands to the north of the village are a source of ncema grass, traditionally used by Zulus to make sleeping and sitting mats. The cutting season starts on 1 May when thousands of people come for the annual harvest.

The Crocodile Centre, is next to the entrance gate to Cape Vidal where a small display highlights the important role crocodiles play in the ecosystem of the park. The Nile, long snouted and dwarf crocodiles which are kept here in pens are all endangered in the wild, and are part of an international breeding programme to protect them. The curio shop here is one of the best in St Lucia with a good selection of books and leaflets on the area. The *Zulu & I* restaurant is also here. ■ *Mon-Fri 0800-1630, Sat 0830-1700, Sun 0900-1600. Small entry fee. T5901386. The crocodiles are fed once a week on Sat at 1500, which follows a snake demonstration at 1400.*

Launch Tours

The *Santa Lucia* is an 80-seater catamaran with a bar which departs from the jetty next to the bridge. The tours last for 90 minutes and travel up the estuary past thick banks of vegetation as far as the Narrows. There are good chances of seeing hippos and waterfowl. Migrating mullet are often seen leaping out of the water during the autumn when they move from the lake into the sea. The 80-seater boat which belongs to the South African National Parks (SANPARKS) is the only boat allowed into the remote area of the estuary. ■ *Daily tours at 0830, 1030, 1400. R80 per person. Book in advance during holiday season.*

Cape Vidal

Ins & outs

Gates to Cape Vidal area open Oct-Mar 0500-1900, Apr-Sep 0600-1800; office hours 0800-1230, 1400-1630, T035-5909012; entry fee R20, vehicle R35. The small shop at Cape Vidal sells a good range of wildlife identification books, T-shirts and souvenirs, however there are only a couple of narrow shelves stocked with food. Petrol and firewood are also on sale in the camp (see page 436). If you are staying overnight stock up in St Lucia village, otherwise Cape Vidal makes an easy day trip from town. Only 100 vehicles per day are allowed past the gate and the speed limit is 40 kph. This is in an effort to try and protect the region, and at long last beach driving has been banned

The park

Cape Vidal is 32 km from St Lucia Village along a road heading north from the park gates and the crocodile centre next to St Lucia. The road passes through an area of pine forest, known as Mfabeni, which is gradually being harvested and allowed to return to its natural state (see Wildlife above). It is not unusual to see kudu amongst the pine trees and cheetah have been reintroduced to this area to control reedbuck.

There are three interesting places to stop off at on the way to Cape Vidal. **Mission Rocks** and the old Second World War Royal Airforce observation post on **Mount Tabor** are 16 km from St Lucia and are signposted off the dirt road. **Mfazana Pan** is a short distance further on. There is a small layby on the left of the Cape Vidal road and a signpost marking a trail down to the pans where there are two hides. It is possible to see hippos, crocodiles, reedbuck, an area of rare forest fig woodland and amazing birdlife around the pan. Snorkelling and scuba diving are allowed at Mission Rocks but there are no facilities here so it is essential to bring your own equipment. The rock pools here are full of life and are best seen at low tide.

Cape Vidal is an area of vegetated dunes along what must be one of the most spectacular beaches in KwaZulu Natal. The sand is pure white and the warm Indian Ocean inviting. There are two interesting short trails near the camp and the rocks just off the beach are teeming with tropical fish and the shallow water is safe to snorkel in. Thanks to the daily limit of cars into the reserve, the beach is never crowded even at the busiest of times. The camp has facilities for launching powerboats and is popular for game fishing, but as Cape Vidal marks the beginning of a marine reserve that stretches north to the Mozambique border, anglers require permits and many fish are on a tag and release system.

Mziki Trail The Mziki Trail links Cape Vidal with the St Lucia Estuary. It is about 40 km long and takes three days to cover, although it is split into three sections for day hikes. The walks pass through a wide range of habitats from wetlands, forests, and coastlines, where you can expect to see large flocks of birds, reedbuck and hippos. (Ticks and mosquitoes can be a problem.) Recently there have been efforts to relocate elephants to this region from the western shores of False Bay. However, they tend to wander back to their original home on the other side of the lake. If there are elephants, you will only be able to hike these trails accompanied by a guide who leaves Mission Rocks daily at 0830. Check with the office first.

South Coast Loop This 10 km hike passes through dune forest and pine plantations reaching the sea at Rangers Rocks. From here the trail returns along the coastline to Mission Rocks. The trail then heads back to Mount Tabor through dune forest. Kudu are often seen on this trail.

Mfazana Pan Loop This 10-km hike also starts at Mount Tabor, it crosses the road to Cape Vidal and heads for the hides at Mfazana Pan, from there it heads north through grassland to the shore of Lake St Lucia.

North Coast Loop At 18 km this is the longest day hike which heads north along Mount Tabor Ridge to Bokkie Valley and then returns back along the coast past Bat's Cave and on to Mount Tabor.

■ *Reservations for the day trails should be made through the Officer in Charge, T5909002, F5909090. Maps and a detailed booklet are available from the parks office in St Lucia. The 3-day hike costs R1,380 per person, including all meals. A maximum of 6 people is allowed in each group and advance booking is essential through KZN Wildlife, T033-8451000, F033-8451001.* **NB** *It is important to be aware that the trail is also used by hippos who can be extremely dangerous to humans. If you do come across one on the path move away quietly, hide or if possible climb up a tree – not a bush or a sapling, but a tree! Access to the trails is limited to a daily maximum of eight people per trail, minimum group size is four.*

Sleeping *Cape Vidal Camp*, reservations, *KZN Wildlife*, T033-8451000, F033-8451001. **B** *Log Cabins*,
Price codes: 18 5-bed log cabins, and 12 8-bed log cabins, all are self-catering with fully equipped kitch-
see inside front cover ens, dining rooms, terraces and bathrooms, the cabins are set under pine trees on the dunes 200 m from the beach. **D** *Camping*, reservations, T5909016. 50 sites set amongst the pines. Shared ablution block, power points and an area for cleaning fish. It gets very overcrowded with fishermen here during the high season. Minimum charge of R212 per day, this is very expensive by local standards and there are better options closer to St Lucia town. **Lake Bhangazi A** *Bush Camp*, sleeps 8 people, a game guard and cook look after you during your stay, walks into the wilderness area accompanied by the game guard can also be organized, the bush camp is on the opposite side of Lake Bhangazi and has spectacular views over the lake, reedbeds and forest, at 10 km from the main camp it is relatively peaceful and an ideal place from which to explore on foot.

Western Shores

The camps on the Western Shores are smaller and less often visited than the coastal areas of the park. Access to these camps is via the N2 north of St Lucia.

Charter's Creek Charter's Creek has a boat launching area and is popular with fishermen who come
You can hire boats to here in search of kob which can grow up to 20 kg in weight. There are two circular
explore the lake y walks here which are good for seeing wildlife. There are chances of seeing bushbuck,
without a motor. bushpigs, red and grey duikers, nyala, warthogs, hippos and crocodiles. The area is
A 20-seater launch also rich in birdlife: cisticolas and warblers can be seen in the wetland areas next to
cruises the lake daily the lake. Swimming in the lake is prohibited because of the danger of crocodiles.
for trips lasting 1 hr ■ *Entrance gates open Oct-Mar 0500-1900, Apr-Sep 0600-1800; office hours 0800-1230, 1400-1630. Entry fee R20, vehicle R35. There is a small shop, a swimming pool, a laundry room and petrol is available for sale. 20 km north of Mtubatuba on the*

N2 there is a clearly signposted turning to Charter's Creek, from here it is another 18 km of which the last six km are on a dirt road.

Sleeping Reservations, *KZN Wildlife*, T033-8451000, F033-8451001. **C** 1 7-bed chalet, **D** 4-bed huts, **D** 4 3-bed huts and **E** 2 2-bed hut, all on a low hill with views out over the lake. Although a small shop sells tinned food it is probably more interesting to bring your own supplies as there are braais next to the lake and cooks who prepare meals for you. Each hut has a refrigerator and food can be stored in the camp freezer.

There are two easy walking trails from the camp that follow the edge of the lake. Remember to look out for hippos and crocs

Fanies Island is quieter than Charter's Creek and has amazing views over the large areas of reedbeds and channels in the lake. Although the camp does have conference facilities and is popular with fishermen the overall atmosphere of the camp is peaceful. There is 5 km walking trail along the shores of the lake, small rowing boats can be hired, or cruise the lake for an hour on the 20-seater launch. With sufficient numbers boat tours depart daily at 0830. ■ *Entrance gates open Oct-Mar 0500-2000, Apr-Sep 0600-2000; office hours 0800-1230, 1400-1630, enquiries and reservations for camping, T035-5509035, F5509051. Entry fee R20, vehicle R35. The shop sells a small selection of tinned foods, drinks and petrol. To get there follow the signs to Charter's Creek from the N2, before reaching Charter's Creek there is a signposted turning which heads north for 13 km.*

Fanies Island

Red duikers are often seen wandering through the camp and flamingos can be seen on the lake

Sleeping Reservations, *KZN Wildlife*, T033-8451000, F033-8451001, **E** 12 2-bed rondavels and **B** 1 7-bed cottage, all with fridges, meals are all self-catering and prepared by cooks in one of the kitchen blocks. **Camping** **F** 20 pitches, 2 ablution blocks. Reservations, T5509035.

Price codes: see inside front cover

False Bay is the northernmost camp on the lake. The accommodation here is more basic than at the other camps but this is offset by the splendid landscape in which visitors are allowed to walk freely. The surrounding sand forests are similar to Mkhuze Game Reserve and are inhabited by the rare suni antelope and nyala. The banks and marshlands along the Hluhluwe River are rich in birdlife. ■ *Gates open Oct-Mar 0500-2000, Apr-Sep 0600-2000, office hours 0800-1230, 1400-1630. Entry fee R20, vehicle R35. From the N2 take the turning to Hluhluwe village, the road from here continues a further 15 km to the park and is well-signposted.*

False Bay

A good place to see flamingos and pink-backed pelicans, breeding from Dec-Apr

This is one of the few camps that can be booked direct and not through *KZN Wildlife*, T5620425. **Sleeping** **E** *Dugandlovu Rustic Camp*, 4 4-bed huts, cold showers, paraffin lamps, gas cookers, freezer, braais, firewood, bring your own bedding, fully equipped kitchen. There is a small shop selling cold drinks and tinned food, petrol is available. **Camping** **F** 40 sites next to the lake, ablution blocks only.

A viewing platform near the camp looks over the lake. Launch tours e are only available to camp residents

Hluhluwe-Umfolozi Game Reserve

This is one of Africa's oldest game reserves and the only park in KwaZulu Natal where you can see the Big Five. It has been managed as one unit since Hluhluwe and Umfolozi were connected by the Corridor. Hluhluwe is named after the umHluhluwe or thorny rope, a climber which is found in the forests of this area. The aerial roots hanging from the Sycamore figs where the Black Umfolozi and the White Umfolozi rivers meet give the area its name. Umfolozi is named after 'uMfula walosi' or the river of fibres. The park has a variety of landscapes; thick forests, dry bushveld, and open savannah, that is home to a number of species of game including healthy populations of rhino and the rare nyala. What is unusual about the park is the hilly terrain, which provides a great vantage point for game viewing.

Colour map 5, grid A2

KwaZulu Natal

Ins and outs

Getting there Hluhluwe-Umfolozi is 280 km north of Durban just off the N2. There is a turning at Mtubatuba leading west on the R618 (50 km) to the Umfolozi entrance and a turning opposite the exit to Hluhluwe village which leads (14 km) to the northern Memorial Gate entrance. This is an easy park to visit on a day trip if you are staying anywhere in the Maputaland or St Lucia regions.

Information **In Umfolozi** Park gates open Oct-Mar 0500-1900, Apr-Sep 0600-1800; office hours 0800-1230, 1400-1630 daily. Entry fee R30, vehicle R35. There are souvenir shops selling gifts and books on natural history at Masinda and Mpila Camps. All the accommodation is self-catering. There are no shops or restaurants in the reserve so it is necessary to bring all your own supplies with you, the nearest shop is in Mtubatuba. Night drives, R90, and game walks, R60 can be booked through the camp office. Petrol is sold at Mpila Camp.

In Hluhluwe Same opening hours as above. The camp reception office at Hilltop is open daily 0700-1930, there is also a curio shop here and a small supermarket. Guided walks, R60, and night drives, R90, can be booked at reception. Petrol and oil are on sale here. There is a smart restaurant serving buffet meals and light snacks, open until 2100. The tables on the shady outdoor terrace are in a superb setting overlooking the reserve, the game burgers are highly recommended. The new 40-seater launch on the Hluhluwe River departs from the Maphumulo Picnic Site, R60 pp, 0900 and 1500, book at Hilltop reception or just turn up. Guided launch tours last 1½ hrs.

Best time to visit The climate is hot in summer and mild in winter. The best times to see the park are between Mar and Nov. The park's vegetation is lush, during the summer months the weather is hot and humid. The park is then more beautiful to look at but the thick vegetation does make it more difficult to see the game. During the winter months the climate is cool and dry and you

KwaZulu Natal

Hluhluwe-Umfolozi Game Reserve

Sleeping		
	3 Masinda Camp & Lodge	7 Munyaweni
1 Gqoyeni	4 Mndindini	8 Nselweni
2 Hilltop Camp &	5 Mpila Camp & Reception	9 Sontuli
Mtwazi Lodge	6 Muntulu	

might even need a sweater in the evenings. Game congregates at the waterholes and rivers. The landscape is very dry with less vegetation making it easier to see game.

History

The confluence of the Black and White Umfolozi rivers is where the Zulu King Shaka dug his hunting pits. Once a year game was driven into the area and would fall into the pits, where it was speared by young warriors eager to prove their courage. Consequently, Hluhluwe and Umfolozi were established as protected areas as long ago as 1895. Since then the parks have suffered a number of set backs such as temporary de-proclamation and the massive slaughter of thousands of game animals in a campaign to eliminate tetse fly. Aerial spraying of the chemical DDT did eventually eliminated the tetse fly but at great cost to the environment.

In 1947 the newly formed Natal Parks, Game and Fish Preservation Board took control of the parks, and reintroduced locally extinct species such as lion, elephant, and giraffe. The biggest conservation success story is the white rhino, which has been brought back from the brink of extinction. It is estimated that the entire world population of southern white rhinos in 1895 was only 50, all of them living in this area. The early protection of the rhino from hunting allowed numbers to grow to such an extent that since the 1960s, surplus rhino have been transferred to other areas as part of the internationally famous 'Operation Rhino'. Today, it is estimated that Hluhluwe-Umfolozi is home to 50% of the world's population of white rhino.

Wildlife

This is one of the best reserves in KwaZulu Natal for seeing wildlife

The varied landscapes of Hluhluwe and Umfolozi provide a wide range of habitats which support large numbers of big game. The Big Five are present, and there are large populations of three rarely seen animals; the white rhino (1680), the black rhino (376), and the nyala (9540). Despite the thriving hippo populations in nearby St Lucia, there are less than 20 hippo in this park because the rivers move too fast.

Hluhluwe is the northern sector of the reserve and has a hilly and wooded landscape and elephant are often seen in the area around the Hluhluwe Dam where the thick forests are inhabited by the rare samango monkey. There are some areas of savanna in this sector where white rhino and giraffe can be seen feeding. Umfolozi, in the south is characterized by thornveld and semi-desert, and the grasslands here support large populations of impala, kudu, waterbuck, giraffe, blue wildebeest and zebra. The predators here are rarely seen but cheetah, lion, leopard and wild dog are all present. Over 300 species of birds including the rare bateleur eagle have been recorded in Hluhluwe-Umfolozi and bird lists are available from the camp offices.

An extensive network of dirt roads crosses the reserve which can easily be negotiated in a saloon car. There are hides at Mphafa waterhole and Thiyeni waterhole but much of the best game viewing can be done from a car. Good areas for viewing game are the Sontuli Loop, the corridor connecting Umfolozi to Hluhluwe and the areas around the Hluhluwe River.

Hiking in the reserve

Day Walks

One of the most exciting ways to see wildlife here is on foot. Guided walks can be booked at the camp offices. There are choices of two self-guided walks and two daily guided walks with a game guard from Hilltop and Mpila camps lasting 2-3 hours. Children are not permitted.

Wilderness Trails

The wilderness area was established in the southern section of the park in 1959. The area is now totally undisturbed by man and the trails enter an area that used to be part of traditional royal Zulu hunting grounds. There are no roads here and access is only allowed on foot.

KwaZulu Natal

These trails are extremely popular and should be booked well in advance

There are three wilderness trails all of which cross the wilderness area and you must be accompanied by game guards. Food, drinks, water bottles, cutlery and cooking equipment, bedding, towels, daypacks, backpacks and donkey bags are all provided by *KZN Wildlife*. (Vegetarians are not catered for so it is necessary to bring your own food and separate cooking equipment.) Although seeing game on foot is not always as spectacular as viewing from a car, it tends to be a more intense experience and there is little that can compare with the excitement of tracking rhino through the wilderness.

Cost per person, R1725

Traditional Trail This trail takes place between March and November and lasts for three days and four nights. On the first and last nights you stay at *Mdindini Camp* and both the other nights at a trail camp in the wilderness area. The first day's walk is spent going to the trail camp. Hikers' luggage is carried by donkeys which leaves you free to walk comfortably. The terrain is quite hilly and involves crossing rivers and climbing hills. The day walks from the trail camp cover up to 15 km a day so you need to be quite fit and have a comfortable pair of walking boots.

Cost per person, R975

Weekend Trail The Weekend Trail is run throughout the year. The trails begin on Fridays and depart from *Mpila Camp*. You will spend two days game walking with day packs, covering up to 15 km per day. The walks during the summer months are shorter because of the heat. From December to March the weather is really too hot for walking so the emphasis is on game viewing, birdwatching from hides and on swimming in rock pools.

Cost per person, R1830

Primitive Trails follows a similar route as the Traditional Trail except you carry all your own equipment. Inexplicably, and rather outrageously, it is more expensive!

■ *There is a maximum of 8 people on the Wilderness Trails. Reservations for all accommodation and wilderness trails within the park can be made up to 6 months in advance through KZN Wildlife Reservations, T033-8451000, F8451001; KZN Wildlife, PO Box 13069, Cascades, Pietermaritzburg 3202. Bookings can also be made directly through the website, www.kznwildlife.com*

Essentials

Sleeping
Price codes: see inside front cover

In Umfolozi The bush lodges and bush camps are only available to one group at a time and are therefore quieter and more private than the larger tourist camps; although booking a bush camp is quite expensive, when the cost is divided between a group (up to 8 people) the camps do offer exceptionally good value for money. Each bush camp is self-catering and comes with a cook, a caretaker and a game ranger who will take you on guided bush walks.

A *Masinda*, 9-bed lodge, 2 bathrooms, kitchen with cook, lounge, dining room. **A** *Gqoyeni*, 8-bed bush lodge, 4 thatched cottages on stilts connected by raised wooden walkways to the living and cooking areas, the camp has its own viewing platform overlooking the river where there are good chances of seeing crocodiles and lions, and elephants in the summer. **B** *Mpila*, 2 7-bed cottages, fully equipped and self-catering. **B** 6 5-bed chalets, fully equipped and self-catering. **C-D** 12 4-bed rest huts with a communal ablution block. **D-E** 7 2-bed and 2 4-bed safari camps, pre-erected tents, shared ablution block, the cheapest option. Mpila Camp is set on a hilltop and has views of the surrounding countryside, meals are prepared by camp cooks in a central kitchen. **A** *Nselweni*, 8-bed bush lodge, overlooks the Black Umfolozi, 4 thatched huts on stilts with a central lounge area, kitchen and ablution block. **A** *Sontuli*, 8-bed bush camp, also overlooks the Black Umfolozi, 4 A-frame huts, a central lounging area, kitchen and an ablution block. **C** *Mdindini*, 8-bed tented bush camp, open Dec-Feb for use during the Traditional guided hike, see above.

All accommodation here is self-catering; bring your own supplies as the supermarket at Hilltop Camp only has limited basic supplies

In Hluhluwe **AL** *Muntulu Bush Camp*, 8-bed bush lodge, overlooking the Hluhluwe River, verandas, central viewing lounge, cook, caretaker and game guard, probably the most luxurious camp. **AL** *Munyawaneni*, 8-bed bush lodge, the lodge is built on the banks of the Hluhluwe River and is a good area for seeing elephant. **A** *Mtwazi Lodge*, 1 9-bed lodge, with a lounge, dining room, 3 bedrooms, garden, cook and a game guard who will take you on walks into the bush. **A-D** *Hilltop Camp*, four types of accommodation available covering a wide price range and varied facilities: **A** 22 4-bed chalets, **C** 7 2-bed chalets, **C** 20 2-bed units (not self-catering), **D** 20 2-bed rest huts. This is a large camp with excellent views stretching out over the bush with over 200 guests staying here when it is full. Although this doesn't have the exclusivity of the smaller bush camps, the central lounge, restaurant, bar and veranda make for a relaxing end to the day.

Hluhluwe

Hluhluwe is a small village in an area surrounded by large luxury game farms. It is within easy reach of many of the local game parks and only 15 km to St Lucia's False Bay, a good base to explore the region. An international game auction is held here annually by *KZN Wildlife*. *Ilala Weavers*, T5620630, is a quality handicraft shop selling traditional basketwork and beadwork decorated with geometric patterns based at the **Thembalethu Craft Village**. This adjoining Craft Village, however, is very disappointing with its mock up of huts where a Zulu family stands to attention for the benefit of tourists. One of the many tribal or cultural 'experiences' found in KZN that really isn't genuine. The *Savannah Restaurant*, T5620836, is also found here, but despite its good local reputation, we had a very poor meal here.

The **Dumazulu Traditional Village**, a short drive from Hluhluwe, has been established to preserve traditional Zulu crafts. There are displays of Zulu dancing, spear making and basket weaving.

Phone code: 035
(NB Always use 3-figure prefix)
Colour map 5, grid A3

Ins & outs

Getting there Passengers using the *Baz Bus* are dropped off and picked up outside of the tourist office. *Baz Bus*, T021-4392323, info@bazbus.com, www.bazbus.com **Tourist office** *Hluhluwe Tourism Association*, next to the Engen garage, T5620966, F5620351. Open Mon-Fri 0800-1700, Sat 0900-1300, Sun 1000-1200. Can book accommodation.

Sleeping
Price codes: see inside front cover

A *Bushlands Game Lodge*, T5620144, F5620205. 20 luxurious wooden cabins set in lush gardens overlooking the swimming pool. The lodge is signposted from the N2. Fly-in package deals from Johannesburg and Durban are available, they last up to 4 days and include visits to the game reserves, scuba diving and game fishing tours.

B *Gazebo Safari Lodge*, a short drive from Hluhluwe village, off the road to False Bay, T5621066, F5620358. 7 double en suite rooms, TV, a/c, verandas with stunning views of the bush. Restaurant, bar, lounge, swimming pool, game drives to nearby reserves. A modern brick building which lacks the character that similar safari lodges have. **B** *Hluhluwe Inn*, 104 Bush Rd, T/F5620251. 64 a/c rooms, TV, tennis, swimming pool and volleyball, smart modern hotel decorated with African motifs, 2 restaurants serving an à la carte menu or a buffet, occasional performances of Zulu dancing in the evenings around the pool. **B** *Hluhluwe River Lodge*, approx 15 km from Hluhluwe village off the road to False Bay Park, T5620246, F5620248. 8 double A-frame thatched chalets with great views. Central lodge houses a dining area, bar, lounge, curio shop and library. Swimming pool. A high quality private lodge offering the perfect introduction to this diverse region. Recommended. **B** *Protea Zulu Nyala Game Lodge*, 15 km on the Mzinene Rd, T/F5620169. Recently taken over by the Protea group, the lodge is in its own game reserve on top of a mountain top overlooking the hills. 35 rooms with thatched roofs and terraces facing the bush. Restaurant, tennis, snooker, and a beautiful large swimming pool. Waterholes have been built to attract game, which can be seen from hides. Game can be viewed by open Land Rover, horseback, on foot, or river cruises on the Mzinene River. The **B** *Protea Zulu Nyala Heritage Hotel*, is 5 km closer to Hluhlwe on the same road and on the fringes of the same game reserve, T5620177, F5620582. A beautifully restored colonial building, 53 twin a/c twin rooms, restaurant, 2 bars, curio shop, pool, tennis, clay-pigeon shooting. Also 10 luxury 'Hemmingway' style tents in the extensive gardens. Both these Protea establishments come highly recommended.

C-D *Sand Forest Lodge*, 10 km from Hluhluwe village, T5622509, F5622550. A quality game farm within an ancient sand forest. 4 self-catering cottages, en suite double room, kitchenette, veranda overlooks a neat lawn with acacia trees; variety of simpler self-catering log cabins on stilts in the forest with separate kitchen. Central bar, swimming pool and thatched lapa. Game walks and drives plus visits to Zulu villages. Good value and peaceful setup.

KwaZulu Natal

E *Ezulweni Lodge*, T5622100. Caravan park and camping site, huts available.
E *Kwamanzi Waterpan Haven*, 10 km from Hluhluwe village, just before False Bay, via the D540. Log cabins or en suite chalets, communal kitchen for self-catering, meals available. Run by a friendly Swiss lady, worth checking out for an insight into what can be seen and enjoyed in the area. This place is popular with overland trucks, good value. **F** *Isinkwe Backpackers* Look out for the 'Bushlands' turnoff on the N2, 40 km north of the St Lucia/Mtubatuba turning, the lodge is a further 2 km down this road, T5622258, F5622273, isinkwe@saol.com Free pickup from the *Baz Bus* in Hluhluwe village. A neat hostel with dorms, double rooms, rustic rooms and camping. Swimming pool and a new bar area for star gazing. Check out the beehive as a different place to spend the night. Great home made meals served up most nights. Laundry. Provide well-organized day trips to all the local sights.

Tour operators *Dinizulu Safaris*, T5620025, F5620209. An established family outfit with excellent knowledge of Zululand and its parks. Recommended. *Wild Cat Adventures*, T/F5620838. Tours to private and national game reserves with qualified guides.

Maputaland

Named after the Maputa River which flows through southern Mozambique Maputaland covers an area of 9,000 sq km stretching north from Lake St Lucia to the Mozambique border, and east from the Indian Ocean to the Lebombo Mountains. One of South Africa's least developed regions, Maputaland has still preserved a traditional African atmosphere. The land is unsuitable for intensive modern agriculture and the small farmsteads which dot the landscape are connected by a rough network of roads. The whole region is part of the 1.3 million ha St Lucia-Maputaland Biosphere that encompasses the Maputaland Marine Reserve, and the Greater St Lucia Wetlands Park National Park, which includes all the regional game reserves up to and including Hluhluwe-Umfolozi to the south.

The climate varies from being tropical in the north to subtropical in the south and this has created a fascinatingly diverse range of ecosystems, from the forested Lebombo Mountains at 700 m to the low lying expanses of the coastal plain. Maputaland's features include Lake Sibaya, South Africa's largest freshwater lake, mangrove swamps, coral reefs, dune forest, riverine forest and savannah. And seeing Maputaland's last wild elephants from a Land Rover in Tembe or diving on the reefs at Sodwana Bay are among South Africa's ultimate wilderness experiences.

Ins and outs

Getting there Maputaland is well-connected by road on the N2 highway. By car it is only a 3-hr drive from Durban or 6 hrs from Johannesburg. From Hluhluwe, leave the N2 at the Ngwenya-Sodwana exit, the Lower Mkuzi Road runs along the southern boundary of Mkhuze Game Reserve. The road passes a number of luxury private game lodges. The tarred road continues on to Mbazwana and Sodwana Bay (90 km) (see page 446).

Mkuze

Phone code: 035
(NB Always use 3-figure prefix)
Colour map 5, grid A2

This small modern town next to the N2 has a supermarket, bank and petrol station. The **Maputaland Tourism office** office is just off the N2 on the right side of the road as you drive into town. T5731439, F5731448, maputaland@uthungulu.co.za Open Monday-Friday 0900-1730, Saturday 0930-1330. The office has general information on nearby parks and accommodation. The *Ghost Mountain Inn* (see below) provides information on Sundays and after hours.

B *Shukuza Game Ranch*, T082-5662441 (mob), F5731014. The entrance to the ranch is next to the airstrip and the tourist information office. There are 4 thatched huts with 2 beds each. Safari tours, game drives and overnight excursions can be organized from here. **C** *Ghost Mountain Inn*, T5731025, F5731359. The inn is near the N2 next to the northern entrance to Mkuze. 38 rooms, a/c, TV, restaurant and swimming pool. The inn offers some very good value 2 and 3 day packages from around R1000, which includes all meals, accommodation and tours to local game farms as well as to Mkuzi, Hluhluwe, St Lucia, Lake Sibaya and Tembe. Hikes up to Tshaneni are also possible, as are sunset booze cruises on the nearby dam. This inn is hugely popular as a base for birdwatchers. Advance booking is essential. The inn also owns **C** *Moyeni Lodge*, a remote self-catering lodge sleeping up to 8 people, very private, set up in the mountains with impressive views. And **F** *Tribe Africa*, a new backpackers' place on the *Baz Bus* route, TT5731474. 4 doubles, 4 dorms, shared bathroom, kitchen, lounge with TV, cosy converted house on the next plot to the inn, if you ask nicely can use their pool. Finally, *Tribe Africa Tours*, are also based here, T5731474. Very professional local operator, canoe trips, game drives, specialist birding safaris, snorkelling trips to a lagoon near Kosi Bay, cultural tours. All in all a fantastic place to stay catering to all budgets and you will never be short of something to do.

From Mkuze there is a dirt road heading south parallel to the N2 which leads to the turning to **Mkhuze Game Reserve** (20 km). There is an alternative northern route on dirt roads from Mkuze to **Sodwana Bay** (120 km), passing through Ubombo, Tshongwe and **Mbazwana**. The drive to Mkuzi passes through sisal plantations before entering a beautiful rustic area. The road winds through gently rounded hills

Sleeping
Price codes:
see inside front cover

Mkhuze to Mkhuze Game Reserve

KwaZulu Natal

Maputaland game reserves

Sleeping
1 Baya Camp
2 Kosi Forest Lodge
3 Ndumo Wilderness Camp
4 Rocktail Bay Lodge
5 Sodwana Bay Lodge
6 Tembe Elephant Lodge
7 White Elephant Lodge
8 Zulu Nyala Lodge

dotted with aloes and acacias. Donkeys and cows graze on the meadows at the side of the road and wander about freely. The road is in good condition but after rain it is crossed by numerous streams.

Mkhuze Game Reserve

Colour map 5, grid A3   The reserve was established 1912 and covers an area of 36,000 ha. This flat and dry landscape consists of open grasslands, dense forests, coastal dunes and pans. The area to the north is tropical whereas the southern part of the reserve is more temperate. The protected area conserves a representative cross-section of the Maputaland ecosystem. Mkhuze is not visited as often as Hluhluwe and Umfolozi as there are not so many rhinos, but it is less crowded and there are some good opportunities to go on guided bush walks and see some of Maputaland's more unusual animals.

Ins & outs   **Getting there**   The exit to the reserve is clearly signposted from the N2. It is 335 km from Durban and 145 km from Richards Bay.

Information   Park gates open 0500-1900, Oct-Mar, 0600-1800, Apr-Sep. Office hours 0800-1230, 1400-1630, except Sun, 0800-1230, 1400-1600. Entry fee R30 per person, vehicles R35. Enquiries T035-5739004. Some frozen food is for sale in the curio shop and there is a selection of books on natural history and postcards. There are well-produced and informative leaflets available here on birds, trees, walks and drives. Petrol is for sale at the entrance gate. Reservations for camping sites should be made here.

Wildlife

This is one of the best places to see the shy antelope nyala – nearly 8,000 live here

Mkhuze is an excellent place to see some of Maputaland's big game. Elephant, giraffe, blue wildebeest, eland, kudu, black and white rhino, cheetah, leopard and hyena are all present in the reserve. As part of the Mozambique coastal plain Mkhuze attracts many tropical birds often seen further north. Over 450 species have been recorded here, representing seven percent of the world's total number of species. Look out for Neergard's sunbird, the yellowspotted nicator and the African broadbill.

Many aquatic birds visit the pans here during the summer when you can see woolly-necked storks, herons, flamingos, pink-backed and white pelicans, ibises, spoonbills and jacanas from the hides overlooking the pans. A good way to see Mkhuze's birds is to organize a birding walk with a park ranger from the camp office, or go on a specialized birding tour, arranged from the Ghost Mountain Inn.

Vegetation   An interesting variety of different vegetation communities grow on the soils of the reserve. The valleys of the Lebombo Mountains are forested but large areas of the reserve are covered in bushy thorn thickets and open grassland. In the swampy ground bordering Nsumo Pan the vegetation is made up of reedbeds, fig trees and fever trees. The smooth yellow bark of the fever tree was once thought to be a source of malaria by early travellers. The connection is valid as it thrives in the same swampy areas as the mosquito. The tree's leaves and seed pods attract giraffes.

Fig Forest Trail   The Fig Forest Trail is next to Nsumo Pan. This rare forest is one of the last surviving areas of fig tree forest in South Africa and thrives on the flood plains of the Mkuze River. It is not necessary to be accompanied by a guide on this 3 km walk which begins by passing through a patch of umbrella thorn trees and ilala palms. The path then crosses over a swing bridge and enters the fig tree forest. The atmosphere of the forest is magical, some of the trees are up to 25 m high and 12 m around the base and attract a number of interesting birds.

Game viewing   An 84 km network of roads crosses the reserve, passing through areas of thick bush which are not ideal for game viewing, the grasslands, however, are more open and animals are easier to see. The best game viewing areas are the **Loop Road**, the **Nsumo Pan**, and the **airstrip**.

Formation flying: DDT on the fly

The old airstrip in Mkhuze was used as a base from 1944 by the South African Air Force. They experimented with spraying techniques by flying planes in formation over the bush spraying DDT. The plan was to eliminate the tsetse fly which spreads sleeping sickness or nagana, which is lethal to cattle.

Wild animals are immune to sleeping sickness but they are thought to spread the disease. Before DDT controlled the tsetse fly,

38,000 game animals were shot in an attempt to wipe out the threat to cattle on neighbouring farms. The long term effects of the DDT on Mkhuze's wildlife are not known, but the powerful lobby which existed in the 1930s demanding the abolition of game reserves because of the tsetse fly threat were prevented from opening up the land to farming. Thereby saving the reserve.

There are four game viewing hides next to the Kubube, Kumasinga, Kwamalibala and Kumahlala pans. The game viewing here is excellent and you can watch the game coming down to drink. There are car parks nearby where you can leave your car and walk to the hides. The Kwamalibala Hide is regarded as one of the best viewing sites, but then you can never be sure where the animals are going to be.

The prices for the following are for the whole lodge or cottage, when split amongst a group they offer quite good value. Reservations through *KZN Wildlife*, T033-8451000, F8451001, PO Box 13069, Cascades, Pietermaritzburg 3202. Bookings can also be made through the website, www.kznwildlife.com   Camping is booked directly, T035-5730003.

Sleeping
Price codes:
see inside front cover

A *Nhlonhlela*, the luxury 8-bed bush lodge looks out over the fever trees and Nhlonhlela Pan. There is a central lounge and kitchen where a cook will prepare your meals and a game guard for guided bush walks. *Mantuma*: **A** 2 7-bed cottages, 5 5-bed bungalows, **C** 4 3-bed chalets, **E** 6 3-bed rest huts. This is the largest camp, the buildings are set amongst natural gardens and are not fenced off from the reserve so game does sometimes wander through. There is a pool here. Meals are prepared for you by camp cooks, they will accept food for cooking up till 1800, the kitchens close at 1930. *Umkumbi*: **A** There are 4 safari tents each containing 2 beds, an en suite shower and a toilet. There is a cook here to prepare your meals and a game guard to take you on guided bush walks. The bush camp is open to the public only from Oct-Mar as it is in the Controlled Hunting Area. *Tented Camp*: **D** 10 tents each sleeping 2 people.

Camping F There are 10 pitches for campers next to the Emshopi entrance gate. The site has an ablution block but no kitchen area so bring your own cooking equipment.

Northern Maputaland

A further 10 km along the N2 from Mkhuze is the exit for Jozini. (The N2 continues north towards Lavumisa (40 km) on the frontier with Swaziland.) After leaving the N2 the road passes through Jozini. This is the last place of any size that visitors will stop at before continuing on to the reserves in northern Maputaland, it is a good idea to fill up on petrol and buy any last minute supplies whilst you are here.

NB This is an endemic malaria area

The road east from Jozini crosses the Lebombo Mountains and the Maputaland coastal plain. The northern route to Sodwana Bay (120 km) and Lake Sibaya passes through Tshongwe and **Mbazwana**. This small village has grown along with tourism in Sodwana Bay. There is a colourful market here selling fruit and handicrafts. It is 15 km from here to Sodwana Bay along a sealed road.

Jozini to Lake Sibaya & Sodwana Bay

The dirt road to Sodwana can be tackled without a four-wheel drive vehicle but the stretch between Mbazwana and Lake Sibaya can be difficult after rain.

Sodwana Bay

Colour map 5, grid A3   Sodwana's major attraction for visitors are the diving opportunities it offers on the world's southernmost tropical reefs. Diving has recently become so popular here that over 100,000 dives a year are made on these reefs. Sodwana is popular with visitors all year round. Divers prefer April to September, whereas fishermen tend to congregate here in November and December. December and January are the best times to see the turtles laying their eggs. Sodwana does get very busy and crowded especially during the school holidays when the accommodation is fully booked months in advance.

Ins & outs   **Getting there**   Sodwana Bay is 350 km from Durban and is well-signposted from the N2, approaching from the south on the N2 take the Ngwenya/Sodwana Bay exit. The road is tarred and goes through Mbazwana to Sodwana Bay (80 km). From the N2 in the north take the turning to Jozini and Mbazana. Follow the dirt road to Sodwana Bay (120 km).

Information   Entrance gates open 24 hrs; entry fee R20. The supermarket stocks bread, tinned food and beach gear. Petrol and oil are for sale. Freezer drawers are available for hire and should be booked in advance.

KZN Wildlife turtle viewing trips are held nightly between Dec and Jan, they cost R70 per person and should be booked at reception the day before. The turtle tours look for loggerhead and leatherback turtles laying their eggs on nearby beaches.

Diving   The coral reefs at Sodwana lie just offshore and teem with colourful tropical fish.
For more detailed dive facts and recommendations, see the Diving section in the Essentials chapter, page 51   Amongst some of the more unusual sightings made off this coast are the loggerhead, leatherback and hawksbill turtles, honeycomb moray eels, dolphins, whale sharks, stingrays, humpback whales and black marlins. **Two Mile Reef** is very popular with divers, it is 1½ km long and nearly 1 km wide, depths range from 9-34 m. There are numerous dive sites to explore here and anemones, triggerfish, sponges and fan-shaped gorgoniums can be seen in this area of overhangs and caves. The dives at **Five Mile Reef** and **Seven Mile Reef** are at around 22 m, and both are renowned for their corals. Access to Five Mile Reef is limited, but it is worth trying to get on a dive to see this protected area with its delicate miniature Staghorn Coral Gardens. Only divers with good buoyancy control will be allowed to dive here. **Nine Mile Reef** is only open for a limited number of dives. well-known for its soft corals. There are some large caves which can shelter Pyjama Sharks. Depths range from 5-24 m.

The closest snorkelling site to Sodwana is on **Quarter Mile Reef**, 500 m off Jesser Point. Further south down the coast are **Algae Reef** (5 km) and **Adams Reef** (10 km). These are shallow rocky reefs with good visibility inhabited by tiny tropical fish.

Sleeping   B *Sodwana Bay Lodge*, T035-5710095, F5710144. Accommodation is in 20 twin-bedded
Price codes: see inside front cover   thatched huts on stilts overlooking woodland, restaurant serving seafood (what else) bar, game fishing trips available. The lodge offers a number of all-inclusive diving package deals, the PADI courses are very popular and can be booked in advance from Durban, the courses include transport to and from Durban (toll free T0861-000333). A large operation which can provide all your needs while staying here.

Reservations for hutted accommodation through *KZN Wildlife*, T033-8451000, F8451001, PO Box 13069, Cascades, Pietermaritzburg 3202. Bookings can also be made through the website, www.kznwildlife.com Camping is booked directly, T035-5710051-4. **B** 10 8-bed and 10 5-bed self-catering fully equipped log cabins. **F** The main campsite here has an amazing 413 sites. This is a noisy and overcrowded campsite and the staff are not the most friendly you will come across. **F** *Gwalagwala* is a smaller campsite with 33 sites, luxury sites are available here with their own water and electricity supplies. **F** *Sodwana State Forest*, open camping. Reservations are essential during school holidays and can be made up to 12 months in advance. Minimum charge for camping, R140/night, expensive by local standards.

Maputaland Turtles

*Five species of turtle can be found off the Maputaland coast but the **loggerhead** and the **leatherback** turtles are the only ones to breed here. The turtles arrive between October and February migrating vast distances from as far afield as Madagascar, Kenya and the Cape. There are two theories as to how the turtles return to the beaches where they were born after spending at least 15 years at sea. One proposes that the turtles are guided by the earth's magnetic fields, whilst the other holds that they use their sense of smell to find the right beach.*

After mating offshore the female turtles, who can weigh up to 900 kg, struggle through the surf and up the beach to lay their eggs. Egg laying takes place at night and after digging a hole in the beach the female will lay around 100 eggs. She then covers the nest with sand and returns to the sea.

Incubation takes around 60 days, the tiny turtles then hatch together and dig their way to the surface. Few hatchlings live to become adults and the threat of being eaten by predators begins immediately with ghost crabs and jackals waiting to catch them before they can reach the sea. About one turtle in 500 will survive.

The Maputaland Marine Reserve has played a vital role in rescuing the loggerhead and the leatherback from extinction. The beaches along this coast are an important breeding area and years of protection have finally resulted in increasing numbers of turtles returning each year to breed.

*In season, KZN Wildlife organizes tours to see the turtles from Sodwana Bay. In St Lucia, KZN Wildlife has granted a single concession to, **Shaka Barker Tours**, T035-5901162, who run nightime trips which include supper and gamedrives.*

Tours A good way to see Sodwana is to go on a dive and accommodation package which can be booked from Durban or Johannesburg. *Coral Divers*, T035-5710209, F035-5710042, come consistently recommended. Budget dive packages including transfers from Durban and accommodation. PADI courses start from R1250.

Transport This is a relatively remote part of the coast and until recently it was only accessible to people with their own transport and preferably a four-wheel drive vehicle. The *Baz Bus*, T021-4392323, info@bazbus.com, www.bazbus.com, drops passengers off in **Hluhluwe** on its way north to **Swaziland** 3 days a week. *Coral Divers*, (see above) meet the bus here and transfer passengers to **Sodwana Bay**. You must call in advance for a pick-up.

Lake Sibaya
Colour map 2, grid C6

Lake Sibaya is the largest freshwater lake in South Africa and was previously connected to the sea. The lake is now surrounded by swampy reed beds and patches of forest which provide varied habitats for the many species of birds which can be found here. A long strip of thickly forested dunes run between the Indian Ocean and the lake.

The tropical birdlife is Lake Sibaya's main attraction, there are two hides overlooking pans a short walk from the camp. Kingfishers, cormorants and fish eagles are often seen, as are the lake's hippos and crocodiles. The lake is very quiet as no public boating is allowed. Camp boats are available for hire and are an excellent way to see the reedbeds and woods around the shores of the lake.

Sleeping Reservations through *KZN Wildlife*, T033-8451000, F033-8451001. **D** *Baya Camp*, looks out over the lake and is shaded by umdoni trees. It is self-catering and has 3 4-bed huts and 4 2-bed huts. The camp is solar powered so the battery powered electric lights sometimes run out after a long cloudy spell. There is a fully equipped communal kitchen, plus a lounge area and 2 shared ablution blocks. The small swimming pool at the camp is there to prevent people from being tempted to swim in the lake where you can find crocodiles, hippos and bilharzia. Meals prepared by camp cooks at the following times or braai for yourself,

Reservations are essential given the small size and beautiful setting

KwaZulu Natal

breakfast 0700-0830, lunch 1200-1300, dinner 1700-1830. You need to bring all your food with you. No provisions at the camp, firewood is available, nearest shop and petrol at Mbazwana 16 km.

From **Mbazwana** a track heads north to Mseleni and the forest station at **Manzengwenya**. This route can only be negotiated with a four-wheel drive vehicle and passes through the **Sileza Forest Nature Reserve**, an untouched wilderness area of extensive grassland and pans. This area is not yet open to the public but there are plans to build bush camps here in the near future. From **Manzengwenya** the dirt track heading south towards **Lake Sibaya** leads to **Mabibi** (10 km).

Mabibi Coastal Camp The camp is set in one of the most isolated stretches of the Kosi Bay Coastal Forest Reserve and is the ideal place for an idyllic tropical beach holiday. The path connecting the camp to the beach passes through thick tropical forest rich in birdlife and lying just offshore is a fascinating area of rarely visited coral reefs and rock pools. It's only possible to visit here if you have hired a four-wheel drive and are fully self sufficient camping in a warm humid environment. Entry, R20 per person, R15 vehicle.

This is an endemic malaria area

Sleeping E There are 10 campsites, each with shade netting, braai area, surrounded by tropical forest. There is an ablution block and an area for braais 10 mins' walk from the beach. Reservations, T035-5920142. Report to the office on arrival, which closes at 1600. The nearest petrol and supplies are 60 km away at Mbazwana.

Lala Neck, Rocktail Bay & Black Rock From **Manzengwenya** there is a dirt track running north parallel to the coast which leads to three secluded beach resorts. **Lala Neck** (8 km), **Rocktail Bay** (12 km) and **Black Rock** (20 km). These are renowned for being amongst the ultimate game fishing sites in South Africa. **Lala Neck** and **Black Rock** have clear waters that offer spectacular opportunities for snorkelling and diving, with good chances of seeing turtles and sharks as well as hundreds of colourful tropical fish. There are no facilities here as yet but there is a day entry fee of R20 per person, R15 per vehicle, though there isn't always anyone here to pay.

Price codes: see inside front cover

Sleeping AL *Rocktail Bay Lodge*, 12 km north of Manzengwenya along a dirt track running parallel with the beach. A luxury bush camp set amongst dunes and coastal forest a few hundred metres from the beach and the Indian Ocean. A wide range of activities are available including birdwatching, snorkelling, swimming, fishing and four-wheel drive trips to nearby beaches and Lake Sibaya. The highlight of a stay here is a night-time search for egg laying turtles on the beach just below the lodge. Reservations should be made through *Wilderness Safaris*, PO Box 5219, Rivonia 2128, T011-8071800, F011-8072110, enquiry@wilderness.co.za

Ndumo Game Reserve

Ndumo is a low lying and humid tropical floodplain renowned for its magnificent birdlife and large numbers of crocodiles and hippos. Ndumo is one of the wildest and most beautiful reserves in South Africa and its verdant wetlands have been compared with the Okavango Delta.

This area had been heavily hunted since the 1850s with the government of the day offering rewards for the elimination of 'vermin'. Early hunters left records of having seen large herds of game here, however, within 50 years many of them had been shot. One of the species which has recovered well is the nyala which was hunted here by Courtney Selous. He visited this region at the turn of the century to capture nyala for London Zoo.

Ins & outs **Getting there** The reserve is 14 km beyond the village of Ndumo on a rough dirt road and lies along the border of Mozambique.

Getting around The roads are in good condition and visitors can drive around the reserve in their own cars or travel by Land Rover with a guide. There are five game viewing hides to stop at and a leaflet is available for a self-guided car trail. A good way to see Ndumo is on one of the tours organized by the reserve. It is possible to go on five different guided walks with a game ranger. The walks cater for all tastes and specialize in birdwatching, game viewing and tree spotting. Visits to the Pongola Fig Forest and Shokwe Pan are recommended. Walks should be booked the day before at the camp office.

Information Park gates are open Apr-Sep, 0600-1800, Oct-Mar, 0500-1900; office hours 0800-1300, 1400-1600. Entry fee R30 per person, R35 per vehicle. Reservations for the park camp (see below) should be made through *KZN Wildlife*, T033-8451000, F033-8451001.

Wildlife

The reserve was initially established in 1924 to protect the hippos which lived here. As human activity has decreased the animal population of the park has increased dramatically. Some species have been reintroduced, but the varied flora of the reserve which includes numerous pans and reedbeds interspersed with patches of riverine forest and mixed woodland provides habitats for many different species.

The pans at Banzi and Nyamithi are fascinating areas to experience the atmosphere of an African tropical swamp. There are many waterbirds to look out for on the pans including some rare tropical species at the southern limit of their habitats. Thousands of birds congregate here in the evenings and it is possible to see flocks of flamingos, geese, pelicans and storks.

Buffalo are occasionally seen in the swampy areas of the reserve, but nyala, hippo and crocodiles are present in large numbers. The vegetation in the rest of the reserve is really quite thick and does make game viewing difficult. Black rhino and suni antelope thrive in these thickets but they are very rarely seen.

Sleeping
Price codes: see inside front cover

D The park camp has 7 huts with 2 beds each, the huts are fully equipped with a refrigerator, bedding and cutlery, plus a **B** 6-bed lodge with all equipment. Meals are prepared for you by camp cooks, it is essential to bring your own food as there is none for sale here. There is a small store 2 km from the park which sells basic supplies and petrol.

AL *Ndumo Wilderness Camp* is a privately run luxury safari camp on the edge of Banzi Pan. The small exlusive camp is in a part of the wilderness area of the reserve which is not open to the general public although it is possible to go on guided walks through magnificent fig tree forests full of colourful and noisy birdlife. There are 8 tented rooms with en suite bathrooms. The camp is raised up on wooden walkways shaded by large fig and fever trees. The bar and dining area overlook a flood plain. Reservations should be made through *Wilderness Safaris*, PO Box 5219, Rivonia 2128, T011-8071800, F011-8072110, enquiry@wilderness.co.za

Tembe Elephant Park

The reserve was established in 1983 to protect this area's elephants. They used to migrate over the border into Mozambique but suffered greatly at the hands of poachers. When created there were only an estimated 130 elephants left. This herd is reckoned to be the only indigenous elephants in KwaZulu Natal. Rangers estimated the rhino population to be down to only 65 animals. The protected area, 30,000 ha, at Tembe is a vast impenetrable wilderness of sand forest, thick bush, and the Muzi Swamp. This is a very special place to visit, but you will need to plan well advance given the strict access controls.

Colour map 2, grid C6

Ins & outs

Tembe lies on the border with Mozambique between Ndumo Game Reserve and Kosi Bay. It is 72 km from Jozini and although the road is tarred as far as the entrance to the park the roads inside are so rough that only four-wheel drive vehicles are allowed in. Day entry fee, R30 per person, R35 vehicle. Gate hours: Apr-Sep, 0600-1800, Oct-Mar, 0500-1900.

KwaZulu Natal

Wildlife In addition to overnight visitors staying in the luxury lodge (the only accommodation within the park) only a further five groups of day visitors in a four-wheel drive vehicle are allowed into the park each day. Each group is accompanied by a park ranger and there are good chances of seeing Tembe's abundant game and birdlife. Some of the more common species to be seen include, giraffe, elephant, waterbuck, black rhino, white rhino, kudu, eland, wildebeest, zebra, nyala, serval, hippo, red duiker, reedbuck, warthog, jackal, hyaena and buffalo. If you are lucky you may see the small, shy, suni antelope and a leopard. There are two hides in the reserve, one at Ponweni by Muzi swamp, this overlooks an elephant crossing point, the second overlooks Mahlasela Pan. There is also a self guided walk within the Ngobazane enclosure area.

Sleeping
Price codes:
see inside front cover

AL *Tembe Elephant Lodge*, is the official concessionaire of *KZN Wildlife*, T031-2029090, F031-2028026. The bush camp consists of luxurious tents with 2 beds each on raised wooden platforms tucked away in secluded areas. There are hot showers with glass walls that look out over the bush, small pool with thatched roof and relaxing veranda. Rates include meals and game drives, which are also available to day visitors by prior arrangement. Transfers from Durban can be arranged.

Kosi Bay Nature Reserve

Colour map 2, grid C6 Kosi Bay is one of South Africa's favourite wilderness destinations. The protected area is over 25 km long and consists of four lakes separated from the sea by a long strip of forest covered dunes. Lakes Amanzimnyama, Nhlange, Mpungwini and Sifungwe, are part of a fascinating tropical wetland environment. Lake Amanzimnyama is a freshwater lake whose water has been darkened due to decomposing plants. The shores of the lakes are bordered with reedbeds, ferns, swamp figs and umdoni trees. Five species of mangrove thrive in the estuary where local fishermen have built traditional fishing traps.

Ins & outs There is a rough dirt road leading to the park though a four-wheel drive vehicle is not necessary. However, access to Kosi Mouth itself is through deep sand when a four-wheel drive is needed. Entry R20, vehicle R15. The nearest petrol station and supermarket are at Kwangwanase. There are several walks through the reserve with a guide which can be booked through the camp office. A good way to explore the lakes is to hire a canoe, although it is best to steer well clear of the hippos. The Kosi Bay Hiking Trail (see below) is very popular and can be fully booked up to 6 months in advance, a maximum of 10 people are allowed on each trail. Reservations through *KZN Wildlife*, T033-8451000, F8451001.

The tropical climate here can be debilitatingly hot and humid. The best time to visit is in Aug and Sep, which are coolest months and tend not to be so humid.

Wildlife The lakes are inhabited by hippos and crocodiles, which can be seen basking in the sun around Lake Amanzimnyama. There are no large mammals here but you are likely to see samango and vervet monkeys. The tropical climate is a boon to reptiles and two species of monitor lizard, the Rock and the Nile, are often seen. Many of the snakes which live here are poisonous. The gaboon adder, boomslang, green mamba and forest cobras are all found here.

Many aquatic birds are attracted to the lakes and over 200 species have been spotted here. Rarities include the palmnut vulture and Pel's fishing owl.

The research station at Bhanga Nek has been tagging turtles and protecting nesting sites since 1963. Leatherback and loggerhead turtles arrive on these beaches after lengthy journeys from as far away as Madagascar and the Cape.

Kosi Bay Hiking Trail The four-day trail is 34 km long and is probably the best way to see the Kosi Bay Nature Reserve. Hikers are accompanied by a guide who leads the group through the entire ecosystem. The distances covered every day are quite short so this gives ample time to relax and enjoy the atmosphere of the lakes.

The first day begins with a 6-km walk from Nhlange Camp through coastal forest to the lake mouth. The crossing to Makawulani Camp is a wade through 1 km of waist-deep water. From here there is an excursion to the coral reef at Kosi Mouth for a spot of snorkelling. The second day's walk is along a 10-km beach to Bhanga Nek where during the summer months it is possible to see turtles landing in the evenings to lay their eggs. On the third day there is a short 6-km walk which passes through a raphia palm forest inhabited by palmnut vultures.

The last night is spent in the rondavels at Sihadla Camp. On the fourth and final day after crossing the Sihadla River on a raphia palm raft the trail heads back to the base camp through 11 km of magnificent swamp forest.

You must bring all your own dried food, cooking utensils, crockery and sleeping bags, only tents are provided. It is a good idea to bring a snorkelling kit with you too. As an optional extra it is possible to spend one more night at the base camp after walking the trail.

AL *Kosi Forest Lodge*, Reservations T011-4633376, F011-4635308. This has recently been upgraded to a luxury all-inclusive safari camp, and although we haven't visited since refurbishment, the usual high standards of these types of exclusive camps are expected. Excursions to Banga Nek, Kosi Mouth and Black Rock for birdwatching, snorkelling, hiking and boating can be arranged. **B-C** There are 3 thatched lodges here with either 6, 5 or 2 beds. All 3 lodges are fully equipped and self-catering. **Camping F** There are 15 pitches and an ablution block set amongst the trees near the lake. For camping, book direct, T035-5920236, F035-5929512.

Sleeping
Price codes:
see inside front cover

Returning to the N2 via Jozini the highway heads north towards **Pongola** and **Swaziland**. The R69 heads west off the N2 at Candova. The gravel road goes as far as **Magudu**. From there the R69 is tarred leading to the **Itala Game Reserve**. This section of the R69 is a fascinating drive through rural Zululand. The road passes through lowlying grasslands and cattle ranching country. In November and December, after the rains, the countryside is green and lush and rich in birdlife.

Pongola Nature Reserve

When driving north along the N2, the Pongola dam can be seen lying to the east with the Lebombo Mountains in the background. The entrance to the small Pongola Nature Reserve is clearly signposted off the N2. This large area of bush surrounding the dam has recently been declared a biosphere reserve and there are plans to introduce large game into the area. It's hugely popular with fishermen in search of barbel, carp, and the elusive tigerfish that reside in the dam. The landscape is rolling grasslands interspersed with acacias and patches of thick bush. There is a beautiful stretch of lush riverine woodland along the Pongola River and the dam itself attracts thousands of aquatic birds during the winter months, probably the best time to visit as the tracks within the reserve become impassable after rain in the summer months. ■ *Entry fee, R20, vehicle, R35.*

Phone code: 034
(NB Always use 3-figure prefix)
Colour map 2, grid C5

AL *White Elephant Lodge*, T/F4351117. A luxurious all inclusive game lodge, 8 en suite elegant safari tents, the highlight being the open air baths, game drives, guided mountain biking, boat cruises, tiger fishing. **F** *Camping*, T4351012. 20 basic campsites, ablution block, cold water only. Both these places are next to the dam within the reserve.

Sleeping
Price codes:
see inside front cover

The village of Pongola is 35 km north of the Pongola Nature Reserve along the N2. This is a small industrial region where most of the people are employed by the neighbouring cane and cotton plantations and sugar mill. Interestingly, this was the site of the first game reserve in Africa, proclaimed by Paul Kruger in 1894, which comprised 17400 ha of farmland between Swaziland, the Lebombo Mountains, and the Pongola River. The Anglo-Boer War doomed the existence of the reserve but the Pongola Nature Reserve was reinstated in 1964.

Pongola

KwaZulu Natal

Sleeping **B-C** *Pongola Country Lodge*, 14 Mielie St, T4131352, F4131353. Hardly a country lodge as it's next to an industrial area in the village but pleasant inside. 47 rooms, some on the small side, en suite, TV, a/c, phone, pool, extensive gardens, restaurant, bar. Game drives on local private game farms can be arranged. **C-F** *Pongola Caravan Park*, 219 Hans Meyer St, PO Box 539, T 4131789, F4132505. 9 luxury self-catering chalets, TV, a/c, shady and grassed caravan and camping sites, all sites have electric points, spotless ablution block, mini-golf course, small kiosk with basic camping supplies, ideal base for exploring the region as well as Swaziland. Recommended.

Crossing into Swaziland
This is one of the busiest crossings into Swaziland

The N2 continues to **Golela** and the frontier with Swaziland. From here it is possible to head north into Swaziland through Lavumisa (see page 825). The alternative is to head west into **Mpumalanga** along the N2 towards **Piet Retief**.

The border post is open daily from 0700-2200. You will need a valid passport. A road tax is also levied here. If you are driving a hired car ensure you get a letter from your car hire firm confirming that you can take the car out of South Africa. Lavumisa is not a very interesting place and most people pass straight through. Fuel and snacks are available here and there is a basic hotel. Continuing on into Swaziland is relatively easy as many local buses ply the route between Lavumisa and Manzini.

Itala Game Reserve

Phone code: 034
(NB Always use 3-figure prefix)
Colour map 5, grid A2

The reserve was established in 1972 after the Natal Parks Board began buying farms on the land lying between the top of the escarpment at Louwsburg and the Pongola River Valley. After years of overgrazing the land had seriously deteriorated and very little wildlife remained. In the last 25 years Itala has been transformed into one of KwaZulu Natal's most spectacular reserves.

Ins & outs **Getting there** From Durban travel north on the N2 as far as Pongola. From here take the R66 and then the R69 for 73 km and the park entrance is near the village of Louwsburg. From Gauteng the easiest route is via the N2 to Pongola, though the park can also be approached via Vryheid from the Battlefield region. (The park is 74 km east of Pongola, 400 km north of Durban and 500 km from Johannesburg.)

Getting around There is a network of dirt roads looping around the reserve which offer good game viewing by car. Large herds of grazers are often seen on the grasslands near the airstrip, look out for white rhino and tsessebe and particularly cheetah, which favour grass airstrips because of their openness. For visitors wanting to see the park on foot, guided day hikes can be booked at reception.

Information Gates open Oct-Mar 0500-1900, Apr-Sep 0600-1800. Entry fee R20 per person, vehicles R35. Reception office at Ntshondwe Camp, open daily 0700-1930, T034-9075105. There is a swimming pool and restaurant at Ntshondwe Camp serving meals and takeaways, the camp shop sells a limited range of tinned and dried food, wildlife books and charcoal and petrol is on sale next to the main gates. Completely self-catering, bring all your supplies with you. The nearest shop is in Louwsburg (5 km). Guided game drives and game walks can be booked through camp reception.

Climate The climate is warm all year round but it can get cold in the evenings from May-Aug when there are occasional frosts. Most of the rain falls in the summer months of Nov, Dec and Jan.

Wildlife & vegetation The reserve's landscapes are mostly large areas of low lying grasslands at 400 m rising up through steep sided forested valleys to granite cliffs at 1,450 m. The streams rising in these mountains flow down into the Pongola River. The steeply rising terrain has created several different ecosystems from deep narrow valleys, boulder outcrops, to cliff faces, with an interesting diversity of wildlife. Twenty new species have been reintroduced into the reserve including a herd of young elephants and the only herd of tsessebe in Natal. Animals commonly seen are dassies, eland, giraffe, kudu, steenbok, tsessebe, white rhino, blue wildebeest and zebra. The following animals are present here but are rarely seen: cheetah, elephant, klipspringer, leopard, nyala and black rhino. There is no lion.

Some 320 species of bird have been recorded, including black eagle, bathawk, bald ibis, martial eagle, and brown-necked parrot. Some interesting plants to look out for in season are the flowering aloes trees, unmistakable in June and July when they come into bloom. Their large orange flowers are an important source of nectar at this time of year and they attract birds and insects.

Sleeping
■ on map
Price codes:
see inside front cover

Reservations for Ntshondwe Camp and bush camps through: *KWN Wildlife*, T033-8451000, F033-8451001, PO Box 13069, Cascades, Pietermaritzburg 3202. Bookings can also be made through the website, www.kznwildlife.com Reservations for camping should be made through The Officer in Charge, Itala Game Reserve, PO Box 42, Louwsberg 3150, T034-9075239, F9075303.

Ntshondwe Camp C *Luxury Lodge*, sleeps 6 people in 3 luxurious double bedrooms, the lodge is self-catering and has its own cook. **D** *Chalets*, 41 2, 4 or 6-bed chalets, they are all self-catering, with fully equipped kitchens, a lounge and dining room, bathroom and bedrooms, guests cook for themselves. **D** *Rondavels*, 28 2-bed units with no cooking facilities, includes breakfast, Ntshondwe Camp has been built recently on the Ngoje Plateau and the chalets and luxury lodge both have amazing views looking out over the reserve, there is a swimming pool here, surrounded by boulders.

Bush Camps The camps are all self-catering, are supplied with bedding and have a fully equipped kitchen, the lodges are thatched and built from natural materials. The camps are set by themselves in the bush and guests can game watch from the comfort of their verandas in front of the huts or go on a game walk accompanied by a guard, the walks should be booked the day before. **B** *Mhlangeni*, sleeps 10 people in 2 lodges, and is set in a rocky area overlooking the Ncence River, Mhlangeni is set well away from the busiest areas of the park

The rivers at Thalu and Mbiso camps are not infected with bilharzia and are safe for swimming

KwaZulu Natal

Itala Game Reserve

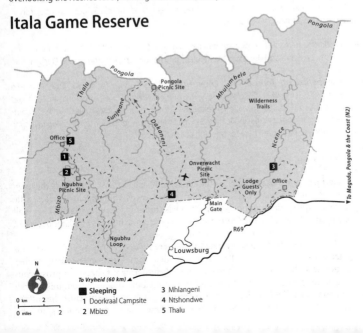

N

0 km   2
0 miles   2

■ **Sleeping**
1 Doorkraal Campsite
2 Mbizo
3 Mhlangeni
4 Ntshondwe
5 Thalu

To Vryheid (60 km) ▲

and is renowned for its game viewing. **F** There are 3 small camping sites here for the completely self-sufficient. **C** *Mbizo Bush Camp*, sleeps 8 people in 2 lodges, it overlooks the rapids on the Mbizo River.

Camping There is a small campsite, which is 17 km from Ntshondwe, with a basic kitchen and an ablution block with cold showers. The campsite sleeps a maximum of 20 people and is near the Camp Office, situated in the west of the reserve on the banks of the Thalu River. The river is not infected with bilharzia and there are some pleasant pools for swimming below the campsite.

Pietermaritzburg

Phone code: 033
(NB Always use
3-figure prefix)
Colour map 5, grid B1
Altitude: 647 m

This attractive Victorian city centre dates from the late 19th century when it was the capital of the Colony of Natal and the red brick buildings are strikingly similar to many English provincial city centres. Pietermaritzburg is the joint capital of KwaZulu Natal with Ulundi and was named after the Voortrekker leaders Gert Maritz and Piet Reteif who settled here in 1838 after the Battle of Blood River. Today it is an important trading centre for the local farming industry and is home to the University of Natal and many other technical colleges. During term time the city has a studenty feel about it with a number of youthful distractions such as cinemas, bowling alleys and nightclubs.

Ins and outs

Getting there Pietermaritzburg is only 80 km from Durban on the N3 and can easily be visited in a day. International flights leave from Durban International Airport on the outskirts of Durban. The airport is only 45 mins' drive from Pietermaritzburg. **Oribi Airport** is 6 km from the centre of town, there are daily domestic flights to Johannesburg and Durban operated by *SA Airlink*. The **railway station** is on the corner of Church St and Pine St. This is a rough part of town, arrange in advance to be collected if arriving by train. **Long distance buses** stop here on the route between Durban and Johannesburg. Pietermaritzburg lies on the *Baz Bus* route, Durban-Johannesburg via the Northern Drakensberg, and *Sani Pass Carriers* run regular shuttles to the Southern Drakensberg.

Climate The climate here is subtropical with heavy rainfall in Dec, Jan and Feb. The rest of the year tends to be warm and dry and makes a pleasant change from the humidity in Durban.

Tourist offices *Pietermaritzburg Tourism*, 177 Commercial Rd, T3451348, F3943535. Open Mon-Fri 0800-1700, Sat 0800-1300, closed Sun. The original building was completed in 1884 and used to be the local police station. The tourist office is conveniently situated and has a comprehensive range of maps and leaflets as well as an accommodation service. *Capital Coach Bookings* also has a desk here for booking coach tickets.

History

Pietermaritzburg was founded as the capital of Natalia in 1838. Originally the town was laid out in the same way as other Cape Dutch towns, with thatched houses, wide streets, large gardens and irrigation channels running down the streets. The small rural capital was a trading centre for farmers and game hunters and later became a stopover for wagon trains heading for the interior.

The republic of Natalia only lasted a few years and the British arrived in 1843 and established a garrison here. The safety provided by the garrison encouraged other settlers to arrive from Britain and Germany. Pietermaritzburg became a prosperous Victorian town and many of the most interesting buildings date from this period. The administrative buildings of the Colony of Natal are in the city centre. Just off the city centre in Pietermaritz Street there are some fine Victorian houses built by wealthy merchants. The houses are basically unaltered and retain interesting architectural details such as the verandas decorated with cast iron lace work and the hardwood windows with brass fittings.

Sights

The city centre is the site of Pietermaritzburg's most impressive Victorian buildings, civic gardens and war memorials. The old buildings are not all open to the public but it is possible to walk around most of the sites in a morning and experience the traditional British atmosphere of the town.

The City Hall, on the corner of Commercial Road and Church Street, was built on the site of the Volksraadsaal in 1900. It has attracted questionable fame by being recognized by *Ripley's Believe it or Not* US TV series as the largest all brick building in the southern hemisphere and is decorated with stained glass windows, portraits and busts of famous people.

City Hall

Opposite the City Hall, this building was completed in 1879 and was first used as a post office until in 1906 when it became the site of the Supreme Court. Renovation

Tatham Art Gallery

KwaZulu Natal

Central Pietermaritzburg

To Rehoboth Chalets & Natal Midlands, Drakensberg. N3

To Durban, N3, (80 km)

To Redlands Lodge & Hotel, Gateside, Cascade Centre & the offices of KZN Wildlife

To Scottsville, Hotels, Quiny's, Nedbank Centre, Caravan Park & Alexandra Park

To Tockwith Cottage

Berg
Church
Loop
Boshoff
Municipal Offices
Pietermaritzburg
Symonds
St Andrews
Drummond
Supreme Court
Otto
Prince Edward
Ndlovu Square
City Hall
Longmarket
Methodist
Voortrekker Museum
Dutch Reformed
Churchill Square
Archbell
Terry
Henrietta
Local Buses
Taxis
Translux & Greyhound
AA
Burger
Commercial
Settlers House
Foresters'
Colonial Building
Gallwey
Princess
Archives
Presbyterian
Standard
Bank
Levy
Tatham Gallery
Gandhi Statue
Old Legislative Assembly & Council
Change
Greys Inn
Fraser
Watson
Old Stock Exchange
Old Stock Exchange
Theatre
Timber
Harwin's Arcade
Perks
Witness La
Natal Museum
Murray
Pol
Tenpin Bowling Alley
Club
Cheetah Coach
Killarney
Buchanan
Carbinet
Printing Office
Drury
Lambert
Cathedral
St Peter's
Chapel

To Botanical Gardens
To Railway Station
To Macrorie Museum & Jailbreak Café

N

0 metres 200
0 yards 200

Sleeping
1 City Royal
2 Crown
3 Imperial Protea & Garden Room

4 Ngena Backpackers

Eating & Drinking
1 Café du Midi
2 Crowded House

3 Da Vinci's
4 Els Amics
5 Golden Dragon
6 Locker Room

work started during the late 1980s and in 1990 it was inaugurated as the new home for the Tatham Art Gallery.

The original collections are of French and British Victorian art and although the landscapes are fairly pleasant there is nothing particularly striking about them. But the gallery does have some interesting and unusual works, including a Stanley Spencer landscape called *Near Nareta, Bosnia*, and paintings by Degas, Renoir, Braque and Picasso. There is a large highly ornate ormolu late Victorian clock at the top of the stairs on the first floor which is worth seeing. During chiming a screen is raised to reveal a clockwork blacksmith and some bellringers moving in time to the chimes. The South African Gallery is the most interesting and has an innovative collection of contemporary art on show. These eclectic works are a refreshing change from the worthy but somewhat staid collections of Victoriana. There is a trendy tea room on the first floor overlooking the gardens serving, er, tea and cakes. ■ *Tue-Sun 1000-1800. Small entry fee. At 60 Commercial Rd, T3421804.*

Voortrekker Museum The museum is on Church St, on the site of the original Church of the Vow and has a collection of period farm machinery, furniture and Voortrekker relics. There is an interesting display which ponders on the subject of Kruger's gold. Apparently Kruger's war chest disappeared en route to Lorenço Marques (Mapato – modern day capital of Mozambique) and there has been some speculation as to its final destination and the possibilities of recovering it. Another unusual item to look out for in this museum is a pair of enormous Voortrekker trousers. The former Longmarket Street Girls' School building has been incoporated into the site, and now houses more culturally significant exhibitions on Zulu heritage, traditional sculpture, and the life of Prince Imperial of France, Louis Napoleon, who stayed in Pietermaritzburg before being killed by a Zulu ambush near Ulundi during the Anglo-Boer war. His death in South Africa ended the Bonaparte dynasty. ■ *Mon-Fri 0900-1600, Sat 0900-1100, closed Sun. Free entry. T3946834.*

Welverdient House, the thatched house opposite the Voortrekker Museum, was moved from Edendale, a farm outside the city, in 1981. It used to be the house of Andries Pretorius, the victor at the battle of Blood River, and gives a good idea of the spartan conditions the early Voortrekkers lived in.

Supreme Court Gardens The Supreme Court Gardens are opposite the City Hall and are the site of several war memorials. **The Memorial Arch** is flanked by two field guns captured from the Germans by South African forces in Southwest Africa in 1915. The **Zulu War Memorial** has a cannon next to it which was cast in Scotland in 1812 and used to be fired to let the citizens of Pietermaritzburg know that the mail had arrived.

The old **Colonial Building**, is 100 m further on. Built in 1899, it is decorated with Natal's coat of arms, featuring a wildebeest and Pietermaritzburg's coat of arms, featuring an elephant. The statue of **Gandhi**, commemorating the centenary of his arrival in South Africa (1893) is directly in front of the Colonial Building. The **Presbyterian Church** built in 1852 is opposite the Colonial Building and was the first British church in Pietermaritzburg.

Continuing up Church Street past City Hall is **Edgar's Store** which has been restored and is decorated with a cast iron lace veranda. From Church Street enter the Lanes on Timber Street where you can see **Harwin's Arcade**. The arcade was built in 1904, and has a skylight running through it illuminating the second-hand bookshops.

The Lanes are a network of alleyways between Longmarket Street and Church Street. They were originally the site of Pietermaritzburg's legal and financial centre. The lanes themselves used to be private rights of way to the small offices behind the Supreme Court. Today they are lined with small shops and cafés and administrative buildings dating from the turn of the century.

Timber Street leads into Longmarket Street, turn left here and return to Commercial Road. This route passes the impressive **General Post Office**, opened in 1903 and the offices of the **Natal Witness**, South Africa's oldest newspaper established in

Mahatma Gandhi

Gandhi was asked by a journalist when he was on a visit to Europe what he thought of Western civilization. He paused and then replied: "It would be very nice, wouldn't it". The answer illustrated just one facet of his extraordinarily complex character. A westernized, English educated lawyer, who practised in South Africa from 1893 to 1914, he preached the general acceptance of some of the doctrines he had grown to respect in his childhood, which stemmed from deep Indian traditions – notably ahimsa, or non-violence. From 1921 he gave up his Western style of dress and adopted the hand spun dhoti worn by poor Indian villagers, giving rise to Churchill's jibe that he was a 'naked fakir' (holy man). Yet if he was a thorn in the British side, he was also fiercely critical of many aspects of traditional Hindu society. He preached against the iniquities of the caste system which still dominated life for the overwhelming majority of Hindus. Through the 1920s much of his work was based on writing for the weekly newspaper Young India, which became The Harijan in 1932. The change in name symbolized his commitment to improving the status of the outcastes, Harijan (person of God) being coined to replace the term outcaste. Often despised by the British in India he succeeded in gaining the reluctant respect and

ultimately outright admiration of many.

Gandhi arrived in South Africa in 1893 to practice law but soon became involved in South African politics after being a victim of racial prejudice himself when he was forcibly removed from a whites only train carriage in Pietermaritzburg. He founded the Natal Indian Congress in 1894 to fight for the freedom of the indentured Indian labourers that were working in the sugar plantations, docks and railways. He moved to a farm just outside of Durban with his family and followers in 1903, to produce a resistance magazine called Indian Opinion, and his fame as an opponent to the rising racial prejudice saw him negotiating with General Jan Smuts in person. Thousands of indentured workers went on strike when the government passed a law to ban Indians entering the Transvaal in 1907, which led to the Indian Relief Bill in 1914 that finally emancipated the Indians. With the fight over, Gandhi returned to England in July 1914 and never saw South Africa again.

His death at the hands of an extreme Hindu chauvinist in January 1948 was a final testimony to the ambiguity of his achievements: successful in contributing so much to achieving India's Independence, yet failing to resolve some of the bitter communal legacies which he gave his life to overcome.

1846. The **Old Legislative Assembly** and the **Old Legislative Council** are on the left hand side. On the right is Witness Lane which leads to the Natal Museum.

The Natal museum, at 237 Loop Street, has a more diverse collection of objects than **Natal Museum** many other South African museums. The natural history gallery has many animals, which date from the foundation of the museum. The last wild elephant shot in Natal in 1911 is on display here as are two fine specimens of the black and white rhino. The first treasure chest of the Colony of Natal can be found here, it is an old iron chest which used to travel around the colony by wagon and was used to collect the Native Hut Tax. The colony's finances were at times so desperate that the chest held less than a pound.

Upstairs there are two other interesting galleries, the anthropology gallery and the marine life gallery. The anthropology displays include a fascinating section on the Ashanti people of the Gold Coast donated by Major Matthew Nathan, Governor of Natal. There is a wooden stool decorated with strips of gold, which the Major obtained while stationed there. The stool is a sacred object, which was demanded by the British as a token of surrender. The collection of brass weights is particularly beautiful, they were used for weighing gold and were moulded from natural objects such as snails, ground nuts and grasshoppers. The marine gallery has an unusual

KwaZulu Natal

collection of fishes, teeth and displays on cetaceans. ■ *Mon-Fri 0900-1630, Sat 1000-1600, Sun 1100-1500. Small entry fee. T3451404.*

At the other end of Longmarket Street is **St Peters Church**. The church has now become a museum and has displays of European stained glass. The church was built in 1857 after Colenso split with the Church of England. Bishop Colenso is buried in front of the altar. From here, turn left into Chapel Street, then left into Loop Street. At number 11 is the **Macrorie House Museum**, where Bishop Macrorie lived from 1870 to 1892. The house is decorated with period furniture, and houses a collection of Victorian costumes. ■ *Mon 1100-1600, Tue-Thu 0900-1300, closed Sun. Small entry fee. T3942161.*

Butterflies for Africa, is on Willowton Rd, you will need to ask the tourist office for directions. It's a large enclosed butterfly house with a variety of local and exotic butterflies, a butterfly garden and nursery, craft and coffee shop, art gallery. This is primarily a place where local people buy plants for their gardens that attract butter-flies but its rather a pleasant spot and worth a stop. ■ *Tue-Fri 0900-1630, Sat 0900-1530, Sun 1030-1600, closed Mon. Small entry fee. T3871356.*

Sights outside the city centre

Alexandra Park lies to the south of the city centre and can be reached by following Commercial Road past the Voortrekker Cemetery. Alexandra Park was founded in 1863 and has large public gardens with a beautiful old cricket pavilion built in 1898. Two other interesting antique features here are the Victorian bandstand and a cast iron water trough for watering horses. An open-air art show is held here every May.

World's View lies to the west of town and you can get to it by following the Old Howick Road (R103), past the Country Club golf course and into World's View Road. There is a commemorative plaque at World's View next to the Voortrekker Road which is a national monument and follows the route taken by the early Voortrekkers. The short trails follow the path of an old railway line and pass through pine and wattle plantations where it is possible to see interesting birdlife and small buck. There are magnificent views of Pietermaritzburg from the top of the hill.

KwaZulu Natal Botanical Gardens are at 2 Swartkops Road, Mayors Walk. The park was founded in 1870 and following a fine Victorian tradition has a collection of plants from all over the world. The most interesting feature in the gardens is the new **Zulu Muthi Garden**. This was created with the help of local traditional healers and includes a traditional beehive-style healers hut. This is a 'living display' to inform visi-tors about traditional plant-use and associated conservation issues. It is not just for visitors, it is planned for local traditional healers to attend courses in the sustainable use of traditional medicine plants. This is an ideal place for a leisurely stroll along the garden's network of paths or an afternoon tea outside the Gardens Tea Rooms next to the ornamental lake. ■ *Open daily from sunrise to sunset. Small entry fee. T3443585.*

Queen Elizabeth Park Nature Reserve, off the Howick road on the outskirts of Pietermaritzburg, is small but it does have a network of short walking trails from which you can see blesbock, impala, white rhino and zebra. The flora here is particu-larly interesting; the park has been a wildflower reserve since 1960 and has stunning displays of colour in the spring.

The headquarters of *KZN Wildlife* is located within the park. *KZN Wildlife* is a parastatal nature conservation body comprising the former Natal Parks Board and the KwaZulu Department of Nature Conservation. The service manages 79 formerly protected areas within the province and administers 29 'hutted' camps and 35 camping grounds. See page 461 for reservations and booking details for all accom-modation and hiking permits for parks and reserves throughout the province. This includes many of the Drakensberg resorts, as well as excellent wildlife reserves such as Itala and Hluhluwe/Umfolozi.

The Ferncliffe Trail is 12 km from the city centre, drive to Town Bush Valley and turn into Warwick Road. There is a network of short trails which takes less than 2 hours to cover. The trails pass through moist indigenous forest to a waterfall where there are many different ferns and lichens. ■ *Information, T3421322.*

Trainspotters will be interested in the **Natal Railway Museum** at Hilton Station, which is part of the Umgeni Steam Railways and run by volunteers. The museum has a fine display of railway memorabilia and a number of coaches and locomotives dating from the 1930s. Some of the highlights of the museum include a sleeper coach from 1903, a bullion coach from 1937 and a 36 ton steam crane. The trains are taken out on runs to Howick and Cedara on the last Sunday of each month. ■ *Daily 0800-1600. Small entry fee. T3431857 for information and ticket reservations.*

Essentials

A-B *Redlands Lodge and Hotel*,1 George Mcfarlane Lane (off the Old Hilton Rd), T3943333. A small luxury hotel which is regarded as the best in town. Set in the grounds of an old farm. Beautiful gardens. Relaxing atmosphere in the winter months when there are log fires and sweet smelling flower arrangements throughout the reception and lounge. Restaurant also has a good reputation. Recommended. **B** *Imperial Protea*, 224 Loop St, T3426551, F3429796. 61 rooms, TV, a/c, secure parking, restaurant and bar, the restaurant is recommended for its game dishes, oldest hotel in town and recently refurbished to high Protea standards. The Imperial Crown Prince of France, Louis Napoleon stayed here during the Anglo-Boer War.

C *Ascot Inn*, 210 Woodhouse Rd, Scottsville, T3462346, F3462940. Self-catering cottages set in a large garden with 2 swimming pools. Restaurant and bar also available on site. **C** *City Royal*, 301 Burger St, T3947072, F3947080. Spacious double rooms, a/c with en suite facilities, TV. Choice between 2 restaurants, bar, plus an open air terrace for drinks. Secure parking. Positive reports from some readers. **C** *Crown Hotel*, 186 Commercial Rd, T3941601, F3941690. 14 rooms, TV, a/c, secure parking. **C** *Gables*, 216 Woodhouse Rd, Scottsville, T3460792, F3461264. Comfortable B&B or self-catering units, TV, converted stables of a former racehorse stud, small restaurant and bar with one set meal each night. **C** *Gateside*, 11 Quarry Rd, Hilton, T3431536. Self-catering or B&B suites decorated in a colonial-style. Overlooks a trout dam, swimming pool. Ask for Richard or Debbie. **C** *Rehoboth Chalets*, 276 Murray Rd, Hayfields, T3962312, F3964008. 25 self-catering chalets of various sizes, TV, linen provided, breakfast available on request. Colourful gardens with swimming pool, tennis and braai facilities. A well-run complex which caters for both the local businessman and tourists alike. **C** *Sweetholme*, 9 Taylor Rd, Scottsville, T460897. Self-catering garden cottage, garden and swimming pool.

D *African Dreamz*, 30 Taunton Rd, Wembley, T3945141, F3455937. A very comfortable self contained B&B or self-catering, TV, private entrance, secure parking, access to swimming pool and a tennis court all set in a large garden just 2 km from the city centre. Ask for Isolde or Gianni. Recommended. **D** *Fairfields*, 24 Fairfield Av, Scottsville, T/F3865554. Double rooms with separate bathroom, private entrance, swimming pool, laundry service. Good value. 3 km south of city centre. **D** *Prince's Gate*, 227 Prince Alfred St, Scottsville, T3450159. 12 self-catering units, open plan kitchen/lounge, TV, a/c, small garden, good value, central location. **D** *Tockwith Cottage*, 208 Chapel St, T3425802. A small cottage with a veranda, sleeps 4, TV, swimming pool and garden, plus 2 double B&B rooms in the main house. Ask for Megan.

F *Ngena Backpackers*, 293 Burger St, T/F3456237, T082-3747920 (mob). Dorm, double rooms, all with a/c, kitchen, games room and a great lounge. A small upmarket backpackers right in the centre of town, which should do well given that there is no competition. The long distance bus stops are a few minutes walk away, *Sani Pass Carriers* and *Baz Bus* stop here, ideal if you don't have a car. All tours can be arranged.

Els Amics, 380 Longmarket St, T3456524. Serves Catalan and Mediterranean food, the fish dishes here are particularly good. *Café du Midi*, near Commercial Rd and Boom St, T3945444. Quiet Parisian style with excellent haut cuisine meals. Small bar inside, pleasant open courtyard. Upmarket, but well worth it. Booking essential most evenings and at weekends. *Da Vinci's*, 117 Commercial Rd, T3455172. Italian menu, good value. Well-managed with a pleasant atmosphere and attentive service. Up-market cigar bar with live dance music daily from 10 pm, jazz on Sun. One of the few places open on a Sun in town. *Garden Room*, at the Protea Imperial Hotel, Loop St, T3426551. All you can eat buffet breakfasts and dinners, good value for the very hungry. *GardensTea Rooms*, T3442207. Light snacks overlooking the

Sleeping
■ on map, page 455
Price codes:
see inside front cover

There are lots more B&Bs; check the tourist office for details

KwaZulu Natal

Eating
● on map, page 455

There is a wide choice which will suit all budgets. At the weekend it is necessary to book for more expensive restaurants. Many places close on Sunday ornamental lake in the Botanical Gardens, carvery on Sun lunchtime, open 1000-1600. *Golden Dragon*, 121 Commmercial Rd, T3457745. Only serves Chinese dishes. Regarded by backpackers as one of the best value places in Africa. Worth checking out. *Head Hogs*, Victoria Centre, T3450935. Innovative combination of a hairdressers and coffee shop, breakfasts, light lunches and cut and blow dry. *Jailbreak Café*, corner of Burger St and Pine St, T3943342. Located in the old prison, café and tea garden, cakes, lunches, small craft shop, open 0800-1600. *Spar*, N3 truck stop at the Pietermaritzburg exit. We have been informed by students at the university here that the cheapest and best burger in town can be found at the 24-hr *Spar* at this service station. The *Kwagga Burger* is apparantly enormous, delicious, and is served with practically a packet of bacon on top! *Quincy's*, in the new shopping mall in Victoria Rd, T3454339. Expensive restaurant but beautifully prepared food. Coffee shop in the day.

Entertainment   **Bars and clubs** *Crowded House*, Commercial Rd. The dance club in town. Though like most clubs it may well have closed down by the time the next edition of this book comes out. Very popular with the students from the university. Alternative live music. Thu night is 'Pig night' – you pay your entrance, get given a glass for the night and then drink as much as you like until midnight. *Locker Room*, Commercial Rd. The town sports bar which also has a dance floor. Good place to come and play some pool. Frequent African bands. **Cinemas** *Numetro* (8 screens), Cascades Centre near the new *Grey's Hospital*. *SterKinekor*, Nedbank Centre, 50 Durban Rd, near the University. **Ten pin bowling** *Club Lanes*, Club Lane, T3428220.

Tour operators   *African Link*, 241 Commercial Rd, T3453175, F3453172. All round tour operator and travel
The tourist office agent, bus tickets, Hilton steam train tickets, township tours. *Countryside Tours*, T/F3868753.
has a full listing of Organize a number of day tours around the Natal Midlands area. Pietermaritzburg Tour, visits
registered guides for the city centre, botanical gardens and parks, 3 hrs; Valley of a Thousand Hills Tour, see a croco-
tours of the city, dile park and Zulu dancing, 3 hrs; Midlands Meander, visits to Howick Falls, and a drive around
Drakensberg, and the Midlands with views of the Drakensberg, 8 hrs; Durban Tour, visits to the beachfront,
Battlefields Umhlanga Rocks, and Valley of a Thousand Hills, 8 hrs, longer 4- and 6-day tours to Sani Pass, Natal Battlefields, St Lucia and Hluhluwe, Kruger, Namaqualand and the Garden Route can also be arranged. *Eco-Tours*, 3 The Hide, 525 Chase Valley Rd, T/F3471344. Interesting tours to some of the less-visited nature reserves near Pietermaritzburg, including Weenen Game Reserve, 9 hrs; Umgeni Valley Game Reserve, 5 hrs. *PMB Heritage*, T3443260. One of the leading operators visiting the Battlefields Route. Recommended.

Transport   **Local Car hire**: *Avis*, *Imperial Hotel*, T3866101. *Budget*, *Imperial Hotel*, T3428433, Toll free 0800-16622. *Hertz*, toll free T0861-600136. **Taxi**: *Junior*, 31 Gresham Cres, T3945454. *Wilken*, 6 Broughton Pl, T3971700.

Long distance Air: **Durban International Airport** is a 45-min drive from Pietermaritzburg. There is a small town airport, 6 km from the centre, on the Oribi Rd. *SA Airlink*, T011-9781111, to **Johannesburg**, Mon-Fri, 7 flights, Sat, 2 flights, Sun, 3 flights; to **Durban**, Mon-Fri, 2 flights.

Rail: The railway station is on the corner of Church St and Pine St, T8972350. This is a rough part of town, arrange in advance to be collected if arriving by train. The *Trans Natal* runs between Durban and Johannesburg. **Johannesburg** (11 hrs): daily, 2051, via **Ladysmith** (3½ hrs), **Durban** (2½ hrs): daily, 0551.

Reservations and   **Road Bus**: *Baz Bus*, T021-4392323, info@bazbus.com, www.bazbus.com A very success-
tickets for all buses ful budget bus for backpackers. Ngena Lodge in Pietermaritzburg lies on the *Baz Bus* route,
through Capital Coach Durban-Johannesburg via the **Northern Drakensberg**. This service runs 3 times per week.
Bookings, in the tourist To **Johannesburg**, Tue, Fri, and Sun, 1000; to **Durban**, Wed, Fri, and Sun, 1615. *Cheetah*
office, T3423026 *Coaches*, reservations from Main City Building, 206 Longmarket St, T3424444. Departs from Ulundi car park, Loop St. **Durban** and **airport** (1¼ hrs): Mon-Fri 0745, 1300, Fri, 1500, 1730, Sat, 0800, 1315, Sun, 1500. *Greyhound*, central reservations T011-2498900. Coaches depart

from McDonald's on the corner of Burger St and Commercial St. **Durban** (1-hr): daily, 0430, 0500, 1450, 1730, 1825, 2020, 2200. **Butterworth** (7½ hrs): Daily, 2335; **Johannesburg** and **Pretoria** (7½ hrs): daily, 0000, 0915, 1110, 1200, 1510, 1700, 2330. *Luxliner*, central reservations, toll free T0800-003537. Coaches depart from the Premier Caltex service station on Commercial Rd. **Durban** (1-hr) daily, 1545; **Johannesburg International Airport** (7½ hrs) daily, 0955. *Sani Pass Carriers*, T/F033-7011017 for bookings. Daily service to **Underberg**, expect to pay approx R90 each way. Worth it if you wish to get close to the Drakensberg Mountains without your own transport. The bus picks up and drops off at *Ngena Backpackers* and the *Imperial Hotel* mid-morning, daily except Sun. *Translux*, central reservations T021-3154300, coaches depart from the Premier Caltex service station on Commercial Rd. **Cape Town** (17 hrs) daily, 1200. **Durban** (1-hr) daily, 0435, 1415, 1615, 2000. **Johannesburg** and **Pretoria** (8 hrs) daily, 0850, 0940, 1045, 1505, 2335.

Banks *Rennies Foreign Exchange*, Park Lane Centre, Commercial Rd, T3943968. *Standard Bank*, 211 Church St, T3452421. **Internet facilities** *Hive Media Café*, Nedbank Centre, 50 Durban Rd, Scottsville, T3428988, open Mon-Fri 0900-1800, Sat 1000-2100, Sun 1000-1600. **Medical Services Hospitals:** *Greys*, T8973000. *Medicity*, T3426773. **Nature Reserve offices** *KNZ Wildlife*, PO Box 13053, Cascades 3202. T033-8451000, F8451001, bookings@kznwildlife.com www.wildlife.com This is the central reservations office for all the accommodation within the various nature reserves and conservation areas throughout the KwaZulu Natal. Do not confuse this office with the South African National Parks, SANPARKS (see pages 128 and 534), who are responsible for parks such as Kruger, Tsitsikamma and Addo Elephant Park. All the parks offices are open between 0800-1900 (Oct-Mar) and 0800-1800 (Apr-Sep). Advance booking opens 6 months in advance. Some of the popular camps are booked up well in advance during the local school holidays, making it difficult for overseas visitors to get reservations on their arrival in South Africa. However, if you are sure of your exact dates of travel then there is no reason not to contact this office from overseas and make a reservation. Credit card bookings will be accepted. Their website is rapidly developing and many bookings can be made online. Although it is always advisable to book in advance you can turn up on the day looking for accommodation, but you may not be allowed to occupy a room before the end of the day in case this central office passes on a last minute reservation to the individual parks. Overall, the accommodation represents very good value for money and is in a good state of repair.

Directory

Natal Midlands

The Midlands covers the region between Greytown and Richmond, Pietermaritzburg and Estcourt. The many rivers flowing off the Drakensberg escarpment have created a well-watered fertile landscape which originally supported a large healthy population of Zulu cattle herders and farmers in the lowlands. San migrated between here and the Drakensberg following the herds of eland according to the changes of the seasons. Later the fertile territory attracted first the Voortrekkers and then British immigrants in the 1850s, all of whom fought for control of the land.

Predominantly a rural, agricultural area, there are farms here cultivating wattle for tanning and paper pulp, horse breeding studs, and cattle and sheep ranches. The N3 bisects the Midlands and the majority of traffic passes through on its way between Gauteng and Durban. However, by taking the alternative R103, the Midlands towns and countryside can be explored at leisure by following the Midlands Meander route, a tourist initiative highlighting the multitude of craft outlets, country restaurants, and rural retreats.

Ins and outs

Midlands Meander There is an excellent map and leaflet available in the region's tourist information offices promoting a series of routes for visiting the Midlands by car. The meander is reminiscent of a drive through English countryside on a Sunday afternoon, and is one of South Africa's local tourism success stories. Over 410 places are marked on the map and include a selection of bed and breakfasts, craft shops and restaurants. The antique shops,

Getting around

KwaZulu Natal

potteries and weavers are good places to buy some unusual but decidedly European-style gifts. **Tourist information** from the *Midlands Meander Association*, T/F033-3308195, info@midlandsmeander.co.za, www.midlandsmeander.co.za

Howick

Phone code: 033
(NB Always use
3-figure prefix)
Colour map 5, grid B1

Howick has grown up around what was originally a fording point across the Umgeni River on the wagon route to the interior. The first building here was completed in 1850 when an inn was built and a ferry established. The town today is small and quiet, being something of a backwater. The original settlement was named by the colonial secretary Earl Grey after his English home of Howick.

Sights

The 95-m high **Howick Falls** are popular with South African tourists who stop off here for a break whilst travelling on the N3. In 1951 they were proclaimed a national monument. To the Zulu people the waterfall is known as *kwaNogqaza*, 'the place of the tall one'. There is a path to the bottom of the falls, but beware of slippery rocks. A 105 m abseil is the newest activity at the falls, contact *Over the Top*, T082-7363651 (mob). There is an open air café and a tourist information office above the falls. The nearby caravan park and picnic site is rather run down – previous visitors having left their litter here. The **tourist information** office, T3305305, F3308154, is open daily 0930-1600, and staffed by a group of friendly volunteers all over the age of 70!

The Howick Museum is just next to the falls in a new building and has a display of Victorian furniture and farm machinery. There is also an interesting collection of military badges. Next door is an excellent craft and curio shop, *Craft Southern Africa*, T3305859. This is well worth a look if you are still searching for presents to take home. ■ *Tue-Fri 0930-1530, Sat 1000-1300, Sun 1000-1500. Small entry fee.*

Sleeping & eating
Price codes:
see inside front cover

B *Old Halliwell Country Inn*, Curry's Post Rd, T3302602, F3303430. A traditional English-style country hotel and restaurant. **B-C** *Penny Lane Guest House*, 11 km from Howick on the R103 towards Lidgetton, T2344332, F2344617. 10 tastefully decorated rooms with plenty of space, fan-cooled, satellite TV and heaters for the winter months. The guest lounge has a log fire and a bar, here the décor has more of an African feel. During the summer months guests can enjoy a swimming pool and a tennis court. Delicious home cuisine which makes good use of local fresh produce. Recommended. **B-C** *Shafton Grange*, 12 km from Howick towards Rietvlei, T/F3302386. A fine old farmhouse built in 1852, 5 rooms with en suite facilities, lounge. The attraction here is horseriding or polo on the 52 ha farm, there are 21 stables and people from Johannesburg bring their horses here on holiday. This is also home to the South African Lipizzaner stud, which breeds the white stallions used by the Lipizzaner School in Gauteng, affiliated to the Spanish Riding School in Vienna, Austria. These are magnificent horses and any equestrian lover is welcome to visit the stables even if not staying here. **D** *Garden Cottage*, 33a Fraser St, T3306454. Quiet B&B, 2 double rooms with kettle and toaster. **D** *Howick Falls Hotel*, Main St, T3302809, F3305997. 19 simple rooms in one of Howick's oldest buildings, don't expect too much but its cheap, quite a good Greek restaurant on site. **E-F** *Braeside*, Shafton Rd, T3305328. House set in an enormous wild garden overlooking the Umgeni Valley. A variety of family suites, single rooms and dorms, self-catering or B&B, owned by a European couple Pia and Kech, Spanish, French, Italian and German speaking. Budget accommodation for families and backpackers.

Midmar Nature Reserve
The Midmar Mile swimming contest is held here every Feb. In 2002 it attracted over 10,000 entrants. It's now the world's largest inland swimming race

From Howick the R617 crosses the N3 and passes Midmar Public Resort Nature Reserve (7 km), and follows on to Bulwer (90 km), and Underberg (120 km). There is a small game park on the banks of the dam where it is possible to see blesbok, oribi, springbok, red hartebeest, reedbuck, black wildebeest and zebra. The dam is a popular holiday resort with numerous sporting facilities on offer including power boating, jet skis, windsurfing, and yachting. Sunset cruises can be organized with advance notice. There is a small shop open at weekends and peak periods where bikes, windsurfs and canoes can be hired. Day visitors are permitted.

KwaZulu Natal

Sleeping D *Chalets & Rustic Cabins*, 47 self-catering units on the shoreline, including a 6-bed chalet equipped for the handicapped, contact *KZN Wildlife*, T033-8451000, F033-8451001, for reservations. **F Camping** There are 3 separate campsites, *Orient Park*, *Munro Bay*, and *Dukududku*, all with ablution blocks, T033-3302067 for reservations.

Transport Road: The fastest route north from Howick to **Mooi River** (37 km), **Estcourt** (60 km), and the **Free State** is on the N3. An alternative scenic route is to take the R103 through **Nottingham Road** (29 km) to **Mooi River** (48 km).

The Nottingham Regiment was stationed near here during the 19th century and gave their name to this small farming settlement. This is a quiet rural area known for its trout fishing and holiday farms.

Nottingham Road
Phone code: 033
(NB Always use 3-figure prefix)
Colour map 5, grid B1

Sleeping and eating B *Rawdons*, Old Main Rd (R103), T2666044, F2666048. 25 double rooms, en suite bathroom, TV, restaurant, swimming pool, bowls, tennis, trout fishing, rich furnishings, a luxurious, thatched English-style country hotel. **B-C** *Thatchings*, Curry Post Rd T2666275, F2666276, thatchings@futurenet.co.za Award-winning rural guesthouse set in a huge garden. 7 en suite rooms with TV and a lot of extra attention from the hosts, Carole and Richard. Evening meals available on request. During wet and cold weather guests can enjoy the use of a snooker table, when its fine there is a golf course nearby as well as trout fishing on the farm. Recommended. **C** *Nottingham Road Hotel*, Nottingham Rd, T2666151, F2666167. 12 rooms, an old fashioned hotel with gardens and pub food, new owners are making major improvements, big TV sports screen and log fires in the pub, rooms to be upgraded shortly. *Nottingham Road Brewery Co*, Old Main Rd, T2666044 ext 150. Rustic brewery with some enticingly named brews; *Tiddly Toad Lager*, *Pie-eyed Possum Pilsner*, *Pickled Pig Porter*, hand-brewed beers using spring water. Tastings and shop open 0800-1700 daily.

Transport Road: The R27 heads west towards the Drakensberg reserves at **Kamberg** (48 km), and **Loteni** (70 km). This road is a rough dirt track which can become impassable after rain, check on road conditions before starting out.

The Mooi River flows through this small farming community from the Drakensberg Mountains to the Tugela River. This is a well-known stud farming area which is smaller than the Cape, but has a higher proportion of winners.

Mooi River
Phone code: 033
(NB Always use 3-figure prefix)
Colour map 5, grid B1

Sleeping and eating B *The Bend Country House & Nature Reserve*, T2666441, F2666372. A variety of lodge rooms and cottages, country meals, indoor swimming pool, horse riding and hiking, 5 km of the Mooi River runs through this reserve, trout fishing on 6 dams. **C** *Sierra Ranch*, Greytown Rd, T2631073. Restaurant, swimming pool, the resort is 16 km outside of Mooi River and offers a wide range of sporting activities including river tubing, the accommodation is in chalets, rondavels or the bunkhouse. **F** *Riverbank Caravan Park*, T2632144. Camping on the banks of the river. *Station Master's Arms*, T2631238. Closed Mon, pub meals and railway memorabilia.

Transport Road: The central Drakensberg resorts are well-signposted from Mooi River. The road to **Kamberg** (42 km), goes via Rosetta. The road to **Hillside** and **Giant's Castle** (64 km), is tarred as far as Ncibidwana Store, after which it becomes a well-surfaced dirt road. From Mooi River the N3 heads north to **Estcourt** (23 km), **Spioenkop** (55 km), and the **Free State**.

Estcourt

Estcourt is a thriving industrial town and is the site of South Africa's largest sausage factory. The first buildings in Estcourt were an inn and a trading store built next to a ford on the wagon route into the interior. The first fort was built here in 1849 to protect local cattle farmers from raids by San. A small village gradually grew up around

Phone code: 036
(NB Always use 3-figure prefix)
Colour map 5, grid B1

KwaZulu Natal

the fort, which was named in 1863 after the British MP, Thomas Estcourt, who had promoted settlement in this area. This is a quiet modern town not usually visited by tourists. People travelling to self-catering accommodation in the Drakensberg can stop here to buy food at the supermarkets before heading off into the mountains.

Bushmens River Tourism, Old Civic Building, Harding St, T/F3526253, open Mon-Fri 0900-1600, is an excellent **tourist office**, stacked full of brochures from all over the country. Well worth a stop if you are passing through town, it also has internet facilities and a craft shop. *Greyhound* and *Translux* buses stop outside.

Fort Durnford has interesting displays on military history and a good section on fossils. In the grounds you can look around a reconstructed Amangwane Zulu kraal. The fort itself was built in 1874 in order to protect local residents from feared Zulu attacks. This is an impressively solid building which overlooks the modern town. ■ *Daily, 0900-1200, 1300-1600. T3523000.*

Price codes:
see inside front cover

Sleeping **C** *Blue Haze Country Lodge*, 6 km from Estcourt, T3525772. 7 rooms, swimming pool, meals on request. **C** *Willow Grange*, Old Main Rd, T3524622. Rondavels, swimming pool, tennis, restaurant and bar, 12 km from the centre of town. **D** *Oak Cottage*, 95 Albert St, T3521129. 2 garden flatletts sleeping 4 people, breakfast on request, German spoken. **D** *Peach Palace*, 38 Lorne St, T3524706. 3 rooms, B&B accommodation in a Victorian town house. **D** *Rockyside Farm*, on the Colenso Rd, T/F3525332. 2 double en suite rooms, B&B. **F** *Wagendrift Public Resort Nature Reserve*, T3525520. Wagendrift Dam is 5 km from the city centre on the road to Ntabamhlopem, there are 2 campsites with a total of 37 sites, ablution blocks, the reserve is a popular holiday resort and has facilities for power boats and fishing, canoes are available for hire. It is a small area of acacia and grassland inhabited by blesbok, bushbuck, kudu, reedbuck, impala and zebra. There are some short walking trails and a feeding site for vultures. The remains of trenches dug during the Boer War can still be seen.

Transport **Bus**: *Greyhound*, central reservations T011-2498900. **Durban**, daily, 1700; **Johannesburg** and **Pretoria**, daily, 1230. *Translux*, central reservations T012-3154300. **Johannesburg** and **Pretoria**, daily, 1100. **NB** *Translux* do not operate a service to Durban from Estcourt.

uKhahlamba-Drakensberg Park

Originally the Nguni
people called the
mountains
uKhalamba or the
'Barrier of Spears', an
apt description of the
escarpment which
rises sharply from the
rolling hills of Natal

The Drakensberg Mountains, which form the backbone of the uKhahlamba-Drakensberg Park, are considered one of the premier tourist attractions of South Africa. In November 2001, UNESCO awarded this formidable mountain range of diverse flora and fauna, San rock paintings and staggeringly beautiful mountain scenery the status of a World Heritage Site. KZN Wildlife, the conservation body that despite going through a series of name changes over the years, has looked after this heritage for decades and succeeded in striking a balance between protecting the fragile resources and giving visitors an opportunity to appreciate the full spectrum of natural beauty. There are numerous points from which to explore the Berg, ranging from fully equipped holiday resorts to campsites, mountain huts and isolated caves which are suitable overnight shelters.

Ins and outs

Getting there
& around
Colour map 5, grid A4

The mountain range runs along the border between Natal and Lesotho. The greater uKhahlamba-Drakensberg Park, now all one administrative area, extends from the Royal Natal National Park in the north to Sehlabathebe National Park, part of Lesotho, in the south. The protected area is 180 km long and up to 20 km wide. **Road Car**: budget travellers who are keen to explore the mountains would be advised to hire a car, there just isn't a widespread public transport network. The **most popular resorts** of the Drakensberg are easily reached from Johannesburg, Pretoria or Durban within 2-3 hrs by car on the N3. The various resorts are well-signposted from the motorway along a network of minor roads heading west into the mountains. The resorts in the **far south** of the Drakensberg are best approached via Underberg on the R617 from Pietermaritzburg or the R626 from Kokstad. The **Central Drakensberg** resorts are well-signposted from Escourt (see above). The road to Hillside and Giant's Castle (70 km), is tarred as far as the White Mountain Lodge, the last section is on a well-maintained dirt road. To reach Monk's Cowl and Cathedral Peak rejoin the N3 and take Central Berg turn-off, follow the minor road past Loskop (38 km), to the junction with the R600. Monk's Cowl (20 km), and Cathedral Peak (42 km) are clearly signposted from here. The **Northern Drakensberg** resorts can be reached by taking the N3 as far as the Northern Berg turn-off (17 km). From here the R74 goes through Winterton (39 km), and Bergville (58 km), and on to the Royal Natal National Park (114 km). There is an alternative route from Winterton to Monk's Cowl and Cathedral Peak. The **Battlefields Route** lies to the northeast of Estcourt. Follow the R103 north as far as Frere (17 km), and then join the R74 leading to Colenso (35 km), and Ladysmith (56 km).

Bus: the *Baz Bus*, T021-4392323, info@bazbus.com, www.bazbus.com, runs through the Drakensberg 3 times a week. From **Johannesburg**, Wed, Fri, Sun; from **Durban**, Tue, Fri, Sun. It stops at *Ampitheatre Backpackers*, in the northern berg and Winterton in the central berg, where a shuttle can be arranged to *Inkosana Lodge*, near Monk's Cowl. In the southern berg, *Sani Pass Carriers*, T/F7011017, toll free T0800-167809, run to/from **Underberg/Sani Pass**, and **Pietermaritzburg**, R90 one-way, daily except Sun. The minibuses leave from *Sani Pass Hotel*, *Sani Lodge*, and the *Himeville Arms* in Underburg, between 0830-1030 each morning and drop off and pick up from *Ngena Backpackers* and *Protea Imperial Hotel* in Pietermaritzburg. They arrive back in Underberg/Sani Pass early the same afternoon. Connections for onward inter-city coach or *Baz Bus* travel can be made on the same day in Pietermaritzburg.

KwaZulu Natal

Entry fees There is an entry fee that includes a community levy and an emergency rescue levy, that is payable each time you enter a protected area administered by *KZN Wildlife*. This fee is included in the cost of accommodation within the parks so therefore only day visitors will pay an entry fee at the gate. Current rates for day visitors vary from R8-10 depending on the park and in some, there is a R35 fee for a car. If you are planning to visit a number of parks on day trips, it may be a good idea to obtain a **Golden Rhino Passport** from the *KZN Wildlife* office in Pietermariztburg, which permits a car and 4 people unlimited free entry for one single fee per annum. The Golden Rhino Passport is half price from 1 Aug.

Climate The weather in the Drakensberg can be divided into two main seasons: summer and winter. Although the weather tends to be pleasant all year round, the altitude and the mountain climate shouldn't be underestimated. Climatic conditions can change rapidly and snow, fog, rain and thunderstorms can develop within minutes, enveloping hikers on exposed hillsides.

Winter May, Jun, Jul and Aug are the driest months of the year and also the coolest. There will always be some rain during the winter months which, when it's cold enough, will occasionally fall as snow. Daytime temperatures can be as high as 15°C whilst at night temperatures will often fall below 0°C.

Summer Nov, Dec, Jan and Feb are the wettest months in the Drakensberg. The mornings tend to be warm and bright, but as the heat builds up clouds begin to collect in the afternoon. The violence of the thunderstorms when they break is quite spectacular. The lightning flashes, torrential rain and ear-splitting thunderclaps are unforgettable. Daytime temperatures average around 20°C and the nights are generally mild with temperatures not falling much below 10°C.

History

San The earliest human inhabitants of the Drakensberg were the San who lived here as hunter gatherers. The only visible traces of their existence which can still be seen today are the rock shelters that they lived in at certain times of year. It is thought that groups of San would gather at these sites to exchange goods, arrange marriages and carry out shamanic ceremonies.

For the rest of the year they dispersed into smaller family groups moving slowly in search of food. The women gathered edible plants and looked after children whilst men hunted. Part of the reason for the success of their lifestyle was its relative simplicity. The few goods that they needed could be made from locally available materials. Clothing was made from hides, poisons for hunting from crushed insects and plants, and other tools from bone, flint and wood.

Anthropological studies of modern hunter gatherers in Australia and the Amazon estimate that they only spend about 20 hours a week collecting enough food to survive. Considering the relative abundance of food at that time it seems likely that the Drakensberg San had a similar working week, dedicating much of the rest of their time to rock painting, singing and dancing.

The San came under increasing pressure towards the end of the last century as new settlers established themselves on their land. Opportunities for hunting decreased as European immigrants shot such large numbers of game and gradually the San were forced to adapt. They abandoned their stone tools and hunting poisons in favour of horses and guns and became cattle rustlers. Their raids on farms in Natal were so successful that the raiders were often hunted down and shot.

Attitudes of Europeans towards the San during the last century couldn't be more different to the rather romantic view in which they are held today. They were regarded as being less than human and were often shot on sight whilst their children were used as slaves. The last records of San being seen in the Drakensberg date from 1878 just before the Natal government began auctioning plots of land at the base of the mountains themselves. Although the San's way of life ended completely it is possible that they were not all killed, some of them may have survived as refugees in Lesotho or as slaves on farms in Natal.

Colonial The first Europeans to see the Drakensberg were a group of Portuguese sailors whose ship the Santo Alberto was wrecked on the Transkei coast in 1593. They had decided to head inland on their way back to Lourenço Marques and reported having seen snow-covered mountains in the distance.

Almost 250 years later the first hunters, missionaries and farmers began to arrive. The Voortrekkers arrived from the Orange Free State in the north moving down into Natal through what was later to be called Oliviershoek Pass whilst the settlers from the Eastern Cape moved up from the south. As the land gradually fell under their control the Drakensberg's natural resources were subject to the settler's rapacious exploitation. The timber and sheep farming industries were particularly successful in the short term, but their effects on the delicate ecosystem of the Drakensberg were eventually to lead to the creation of the national park.

Modern The first area of the park to receive protection was the Giant's Castle Game Reserve in 1903. Over the years more land was acquired and given a protected status as the ecological importance of the Drakensberg became more apparent.

One of the main reasons for creating a national park here is that the Drakensberg escarpment is the source of many of the rivers which flow through Natal. The Tugela, the Mkhomazi and the Mzimkhulu are three of the most important sources of water in Natal. During the 1950s damage caused by deforestation and overgrazing was proved to be affecting the water supply. The indigenous vegetation of the Drakensberg was shown to play an essential role in holding water from torrential seasonal rain and preventing flash floods. The root systems in the soil release the water gradually throughout the year providing Natal with a regular water supply.

The park today protects a unique area of Afro-montane and Afro-alpine vegetation and access to this delicate ecosystem is restricted in order to prevent further damage. Unlike other national parks the best way to view nature here is either on foot or on horseback. Trails have been laid out for hikers to prevent soil erosion and

Cave paintings

The sandstone caves of the Drakensberg are one of the best places in the world to see rock art. Most of the paintings that survive are on the walls of rock shelters. There are traces of paintings on exposed rocks but they have been heavily weathered and very few of them are distinguishable. The paintings tend to be quite recent and are probably only 200 to 300 years old, but they do form part of a long standing tradition and some of the earliest cave paintings in Southern Africa date from 28,000 years ago.

The pigments used by the San were made from natural ochre mixed with blood, fat or milk. Artists would carry their pigments in antelope horns hanging from their belts. The San here were particularly prolific and there are hundreds of caves throughout these mountains which are covered with layer upon layer of paintings. Some of the most beautiful of South Africa's cave paintings can be found in the Drakensberg.

There have been numerous attempts at interpreting the meaning of these paintings. One of the more outlandish theories held by European archaeologists at the beginning of this century was that they had been drawn with the help of migrating Carthaginians.

Other more recent theories hold that the paintings are either little more than well-executed graffitos illustrating scenes from daily life or that they were used in sympathetic magic.

The most recent research has drawn from ethnographic records from the end of the last century and interviews with the remaining San people in this century. The eland features largely in San mythology and is one of the most frequently painted subjects. It seems unlikely that the eland were painted as part of a hunting ritual using sympathetic magic as the eland is not often found in food debris from archaeological excavations. It is thought that the eland in some way represents god.

The most prevalent current theory holds that the paintings of human figures dancing which show people with nose bleeds hallucinating geometric patterns, are people taking part in shamanic rituals who are in a state of trance.

There are also other paintings which seem to deal with more mundane matters. The scenes of San collecting wild honey, hunting pigs or being chased by a leopard reveal aspects of a way of life which has now disappeared.

accommodation within the park is limited to certain areas. In 2001 UNESCO awarded the park with the status of a World Heritage Site in recognition of its universal environmental value to mankind.

Landscape

The Drakensberg have been created as part of a geological process which began around 140 million years ago when Africa was still part of Gondwanaland. Massive eruptions of lava spread from an area near where Lesotho is today reaching as far as the Natal coastline. The lava flows solidified over sandstone and have gradually been eroded back over millions of years. Today the bands of rock revealed by the erosion show layers of different coloured sandstones capped by basalt. The Drakensberg are divided into two areas known as the High Berg and the Little Berg.

The **High Berg**, covering the area which rises steeply up to the plateau, is the more interesting of the two with its spectacular scenery of high peaks and cliffs. The top of the escarpment averages around 3,000 m in altitude and forms the western boundary of the park along the watershed between Natal and Lesotho.

The **Little Berg** lies at lower altitude and consists of the spurs of sandstone which stretch out towards the plains of Natal. The landscape here is of rolling hills and grassland divided by forested ravines. The Little Berg is the most popular area for hiking and many of the *KZN Wildlife* resorts are located here.

KwaZulu Natal

Wildlife and vegetation

The different wildlife habitats in the Drakensberg vary according to altitude which can range from the subtropical at around 1,000 m to the Afro-alpine at over 3,000 m. All the Drakensberg resorts have a relatively representative cross-section of the Drakensberg ecosystem. The wealth of plantlife in the Drakensberg is quite staggering; over 1,500 plant species have been identified here amongst which 350 of them are endemic. By far the best time of year to see the *veldt* is during the spring, when the grass is green and lush and many of the orchids, irises and lilies will be in flower. Plants on the high plateau are hardy, small alpine plants consisting mostly of grasses, shrubs and succulents.

The **wildlife** is not as easy to spot as in some of South Africa's other wildlife reserves as the land simply cannot support such large numbers of animals. Viewing wildlife here is more the province of the enthusiastic naturalist rather than the casual observer. The large mammals likely to be seen are the eland, baboon, and some of the small antelope such as klipspringer and duiker. Red hartebeest, blesbok, bushbuck and oribi are present but are seen less often as they only inhabit certain areas. Leopard, lynx, serval, aardvark, aardwolf and porcupine, are thought to be present but are almost never seen, even by park staff or regular hikers.

Birdlife in the Drakensberg is particularly rich as it is possible to visit several different ecosystems within a relatively small area. Over 300 species have been recorded here, most of which live below 2,000 m. The best time to see the birds is during the summer whilst they are courting and nesting. This is their most active time of year and their most colourful as the birds will have their breeding plumage.

The rarest birds live at higher altitudes on the summit plateau where it is possible to see species such as the Orange-breasted rockjumper, the Drakensberg siskin, the Bald Ibis, the Cape vulture and the Lammergeyer. Conditions are so harsh in this environment that only 54 species have been recorded here. The environment in the Little Berg is less extreme and many species of bird common to other parts of KwaZulu Natal can be seen here. There are few hides in the park, and Lammergeyer Hide at Giant's Castle, tends to be booked up months in advance. However, the gardens around the *KZN Wildlife* camps are often planted with indigenous trees, which attract many birds to your doorstep.

Activities in the Drakensberg

The Drakensberg have been a popular destination for South African tourists since the 1930s. Hiking, horse riding and mountaineering are the traditional Drakensberg sports but new activities like mountain biking and hang gliding are increasingly becoming available. Many of the larger resort hotels also offer a wide range of sporting facilities such as tennis, squash, bowls, golf and swimming.

Climbing   The Drakensberg is a relatively undiscovered mountain range by the standards of international climbing. This was due mainly to the sports boycott imposed on South Africa during the Apartheid regime. Many international climbers chose not to climb here in protest against the Mountain Club of South Africa's membership policy. With the advent of a more enlightened outlook in South Africa, mountaineers are beginning to rediscover the challenges of climbing in the Drakensberg. For more information on climbing contact Steve Cook, at the KwaZulu Natal division of the ***Mountain Club of South Africa***, T031-7010155.

Fishing   Trout were introduced into the rivers of the Drakensberg around the turn of the century and over the years fly-fishing for trout has become a popular pastime. Fishing licences are available from *KZN Wildlfe*, T033-8451000, F8451001.

Golf   Keen golfers will no doubt be pleased to know that the Northern and Central Berg have four golf courses either attached to private resorts or nearby. In good mountain weather the

Snakes

There are only three poisonous snakes in the Drakensberg all of which will do their best to avoid people. The Puff Adder and the Rinkhals or Spitting Cobra are the most likely to be disturbed whilst basking as they are more common at lower altitudes. The Berg Adder lives higher up and is therefore less frequently encountered. The venom of all three snakes is potentially lethal although deaths in fact are very rare. The best course of action is to keep an eye out for where you are stepping and to avoid contact with them at all costs, they are protected species after all.

In the unfortunate event of a bite take the victim to a hospital as soon as possible (see Health, page 69).

---

backdrop for each of these courses takes some beating. Green fees are very reasonable, call in advance to check on availability of equipment hire. *Cathedral Peak Hotel*, T036-4881888, 9 holes. *Monk's Cowl Country Club*, T036-4681918, 9 holes. *Ampitheatre Golf Club*, T036-4386308, 9 holes. *Champagne Sports Resort*, T036-4681088, 18 holes.

There is a hang gliding and paragliding school at Bulwer, T039-8320224.

Hang gliding

The Drakensberg hiking trails offer hikers numerous opportunities to explore this unique mountain environment. Trails vary between short well-marked leisurely strolls to challenging hikes at high altitude lasting several days. The majority of visitors to the Drakensberg prefer to complete a number of day hikes and stay overnight in *KZN Wildlife* camps.

Hiking

Experienced hikers have compared some of the longer hikes to hiking in the Himalayas, where several days are spent in isolated wilderness areas at altitudes of up to 3,000 m. Some of the longer hiking trails can last up to 10 days crossing through isolated and challenging mountain passes such as the Mnweni and Ifidi, which are amongst the wildest and most beautiful trails along the Northern Berg. Planning ahead is essential for longer hikes as overnight caves and mountain huts have to be booked in advance. It is recommended that all overnight hikers read *KZN Wildlife*'s brochure, *Its Tough at the Top – Hiking Safely in the Drakensberg*.

Weather conditions The climate of the Drakensberg is one of extremes, weather conditions can change in minutes and snow, rain or fog can quickly descend on a clear and sunny day. The best weather for hiking is during the winter months as the weather tends to be cool and dry, but there is the danger of snow. The summer months are less popular as violent thunderstorms gather most afternoons. The advantage of summer hikes is that the landscape is greener and wildlife will be more abundant.

The most common problems to watch out for are the effects of intense sunlight at high altitudes. Sunstroke and dehydration are best avoided by wearing a sun hat, using a high protection factor suncream and by carrying enough water.

Guided hikes are a realistic option considering the advantages they offer, the most obvious one being that you are unlikely to get lost. A good guide will know how to deal safely with the problems caused by extremes of weather or the dangers of being mugged. Other more mundane logistical problems like food, equipment hire, and most importantly, a lift back to where you parked your car will also be taken care of for you. Contact any of the tourist offices in the Drakensberg region who will be able to arrange a guided hike.

Equipment Apart from the common sense items of equipment mentioned in the Hiking section of Essentials, see page 58, such as a comfortable pair of boots and a sunhat there are some items which will be particularly useful in the Drakensberg.

Camping stoves are essential as fires are not allowed in the park. Although fuel for most camping stoves is available in South Africa, it is unlikely to be available in the small stores in the resorts. Petrol is available for multi-fuel stoves from some of the larger resorts. Camping gas and other fuels should be bought in advance from a camping shop in a large urban

KwaZulu Natal

centre such as Durban or Pietermaritzburg. Meths stoves: it is better to buy meths from a pharmacy than a supermarket, it is much better quality.

Resort shops and the local stores up in the mountains have a limited selection of tinned **food** and unless you bring your own food you might end up living off processed bread, baked beans and pilchards in tomato sauce. The best idea is to bring most lightweight dry food from Pietermaritzburg or Durban as even towns like Estcourt or Mooi River can have a surprisingly limited selection. If you are an experienced hiker and have all the necessary equipment it is worth considering bringing your own favourite dry meals with you from home.

It is not always necessary to carry a **tent** as you can sleep in caves or mountain huts. Remember these always need to be booked in advance. It is easier to find caves to sleep in during the week as they tend to get full at weekends. Unfortunately caves are not always marked accurately on maps and they can be difficult to find. If you can't find your cave before nightfall a bivibag or a back-up tent will protect you from the cold and damp. On overnight hikes a **trowel** or a **spade** are necessary for digging toilets to prevent litter and pollution. Dig a hole well away from streams and make sure everything is properly buried.

Clothing The most exciting Drakensberg hikes are the ones up to the summit plateau. The clothing you carry with you should protect you from the weather you are likely to encounter over 3,000 m. An anorak made from waterproof breathable fabrics like Goretex will be useful all year round, whilst in winter layers of thermal underwear, fleece, a woolly hat and gloves should prepare you for possible sub-zero temperatures. Even on short day hikes in the Little Berg a waterproof jacket and a sweater can be invaluable if it rains.

Permits are necessary on all but the shortest walks and are available from camp offices for a small fee. Maximum group size is 12 people and the minimum size is three. It is a good idea to go in a group as some hikers have had all their equipment stolen on reaching the plateau. Mountain registers are located at all the trail heads and should be filled in even for short day walks. A map, a compass and a good knowledge of map reading are essential.

Maps There is a series of three 1:50,000 maps published by the old Forestry Department which cover the Drakensberg area. These are sometimes referred to as the 'Slingsby' maps, but while they may still be available in some shops they are now out of print. *KZN Wildlife* are gradually replacing these with a new series of six comprehensive 1:50,000 maps, which usefully also cover the Lesotho side of the mountains. Contact *KZN Wildlife* in advance.

Horse riding The full length of the Berg is negotiable on horseback, by way of trails and bridleways. Riding is available in the *KZN Wildlife* parks of **Rugged Glen** and **Spioenkop**, which can be arranged at the parks office. The current rates for horse rides organized by *KZN Wildlife* are R35 per hour

Many of the large resort hotels on the boundaries of the national park offer riding as an activity, and several include overnight adventure rides for groups of five or more into the parks. Contact the local tourist office or ask the people where you are staying to point you in the direction of the nearest operator, of which there are many.

Mountain biking Mountain biking is a relatively new sport in South Africa and so far only three areas of the Drakensberg have designated trails where mountain bikes are permitted. These are Cathedral Peak, Champagne Valley and Underberg. The facilities for mountain bikers in Cathedral Peak and Champagne Valley are fairly limited and consist basically of a network of jeep tracks on which cyclists are allowed to ride.

The route to Sani Pass and back is one of South Africa's epic mountain bike rides. The 20 km climb up to the Lesotho border is a truly challenging ascent along a trail cut out of the rock. The altitude at the highest point of the trail is around 2,800 m from where there are spectacular views over the sheer cliffs and gorges of the Mkhomazana Valley. There are also a number of more sedate rides around Underberg itself. Unfortunately, we have as yet to find anyone who rents out bikes in any of these areas so they are restricted to people who bring their bikes on holiday.

Sleeping

Accommodation within the national park is run by *KZN Wildlife* They offer a wide range of facilities from luxury lodges and chalets through to campsites, mountain huts and caves. All of the *KZN Wildlife* camps are basically self-catering and although there are some camp shops, which do sell food, the choice is limited. It is far better to come prepared and to buy your food beforehand in the nearest large town.

The land bordering the national park is increasingly being developed for tourism and a number of self-contained holiday resorts and timeshares have sprung up. These tend to offer numerous sporting and entertainment facilities but they are sometimes rather distant from the Drakensberg Mountains themselves. The other option for accommodation outside the park is to stay in one of the B&B guesthouses which are becoming more popular and are more economical.

The problem with accommodation outside the park is that you can find yourself staying up to 20 km away from the park entrance. Apart from the inconvenience of travelling to the park on day visits, the main disadvantage of this is that the scenery is completely different. Instead of staying within striking distance of the peaks and cliffs of the high Drakensberg you could find yourself staring disconsolately at the gently rolling hills and farmland of the Natal Midlands.

Reservations for *KZN Wildlife* accommodation can be made through the central booking office in Pietermaritzburg, PO Box 13053, Cascades 3202, T033-8451000, F033-8451001, bookings@kznwildlife.com Payment can be made over the phone by credit card, or alternatively book online through the website which is also an excellent source of further information, www.kznwildlife.com Camping reservations must be made directly with the officer in charge of the campsite.

KwaZulu Natal

The Northern Berg

The scenery of the Northern Berg is exceptional in its grandeur and is featured on many postcards. The Royal Natal National Park is the most popular of all the resorts in the Drakensberg and though there are some good hikes outside the park, they don't really compare with the sheer majesty of those within the park boudaries.

Phone code: 036
(NB Always use
3-figure prefix)
Colour map 4, grid A6

Royal Natal National Park

The highlight of any visit to the park must be the first views of the massive rock walls which form the Amphitheatre. The Eastern Buttress (3,009 m) is the southernmost peak of the 4 km of cliff face which arcs northwards towards the Sentinel (3,165 m) forming an impressive barrier. On the plateau behind the Amphitheatre is Mont-aux-Sources (3,299 m) named by French missionaries in 1836. This mountain is the source of five rivers; the Elands which flows into the Vaal; the Khudeda and the Singu leading into the Orange River in the Free State; and the Tugela and the Bilanjil which lead into Natal.

The most impressive of these is the Tugela which plunges over the edge of the Amphitheatre wall dropping around 800 m through a series of five falls. The gorge created by the waters of the Tugela is a steep-sided tangle of boulders and trees which at a point near the Devil's Tooth Gully has bored straight through the sandstone to form what appears to be a tunnel around 40 m long.

The national park was established in 1916 when farms around the Amphitheatre were bought by the government to protect the land. Tourism started around this time and the park has been perennially popular since then. Queen Elizabeth II visited the park in 1947, 5 years before she became Queen, since then both the national park and the (now closed) hotel are prefixed by the word 'Royal' in memory of this visit.

Getting there The National Park can be reached on tarred roads from Harrismith (60 km), or Bergville (40 km). The route is well-signposted from the N3. **Ins & outs**

Information Office and visitors' centre open daily 0800-1630. Park entry fee R15 per person, T036-4386303. The number of day visitors is controlled to prevent overcrowding in the park, however this only tends to be a problem at weekends and on holidays. The visitors' centre and gift shop sells a good selection of books, T-shirts, a very limited range of tinned goods, curios, alcoholic and soft drinks, maps, and quite often fresh trout. Petrol is also available here.

Hiking There are over 130 km of walking trails around Royal Natal National Park many of which are easy half-day strolls. Even the hikes that don't climb up to the top of the escarpment wind through beautiful countryside of grassland dotted with patches of yellowwood forest and proteas set against the stunning backdrop of the Amphitheatre. The KZN Visitors' Centre sells hiking maps and a leaflet describing the many possible walks around the park. Permits are also available here. Soil erosion has increasingly become a problem as more and more hikers visit the park. In an attempt to control soil erosion some paths may occasionally be closed to hikers.

Mont-aux-Sources The 20 km hike up to Mont-aux-Sources at 3,299 m can be completed in a strenuous day's walk. The path starts at Mahai Campsite and heads steadily uphill following the course of the Mahai River. The path climbs steeply around the eastern flank of the Sentinel (3,165 m). Just after the Sentinel Caves is the notorious chain ladder, built in 1930, which takes you up a 30 m cliff face. Once on top Mont-aux-Sources is only 3 km away and involves no more serious climbing.

On a clear day the views from the top of the escarpment are splendid as they stretch out over KwaZulu Natal. The hike up to Mont-aux-Sources is restricted to 100 people per day because it is so popular. Unfortunately, the consequences of so many visitors has meant that a considerable amount of litter has collected along the trail.

Royal Natal National Park

Lesotho

In the Drakensberg area the border between South Africa and Lesotho follows the watershed along the top edge of the escarpment. As there are no boundary markers it is quite possible that you will inadvertently enter Lesotho once you reach the summit plateau. It is therefore essential to carry your passport with you at all times in case you meet one of the mounted border patrols on the Lesotho side.

Tugela Gorge The walk up the gorge is a 14 km round trip which begins at the car park below Tendele Camp. The path heads up the gorge and follows the Tugela River passing through strands of sourveld and yellowwood forest. Higher up along the valley there are rock pools which are ideal for swimming in. After around 6 km at the entrance to the gorge there is a chain ladder, from here you can either wade through the gorge or climb up the ladder and walk along the top. There are magnificent views here of the Devil's Tooth, the Eastern Buttress and Tugela Falls. Beware of heavy rain on this walk as flash flooding through the gorge is extremely dangerous.

Cannibal Cave The 8-km trail heads north from the road leading to Mahai Campsite. The route follows the Goldie River for 1 km before crossing over and following the ridge north again until it passes close to Sunday Falls. The path then rises over Surprise Ridge and on to the Cannibal Cave (see box).

The walks from the **Rugged Glen** Campsite are mostly over rolling hills and although there are some amazing views of the amphitheatre they don't really compare with the hikes leaving from the Thendele and Mahai camps. Horseriding is available from Rugged Glen into the mountains lasting between 2-3 hours and leave from the stables daily at 0900, 1000, 1400. The cost is R35 per hour. The rides are very popular during the holiday period and it is best to book in advance at the stables, T4386422.

NB The *Royal Natal National Park Hotel*, is currently closed, supposedly for refurbishment, though no work has started as yet and it is unclear when and if it will reopen. Hopefully the hotel will reopen in the future as it in a stunning location with magnificent views of the amphitheatre, this is where Michael Caine and the film crew stayed during the filming of *Zulu* in the early 1960s.

A-C *Thendele Hutted Camp*, camp office open daily 0800-1230,1400-1600, T036-4386411. The cottages and bungalows have cooks whilst the chalets are self-catering with fully equipped kitchens, a coal fire, with a private terrace and braai overlooking the amphitheatre. The views from this camp make it one of the most popular in the Drakensberg and it is 90% full throughout the year, reservations should be made in advance through the central office in Pietermaritzburg, T033-8451000. There is a curio shop here selling books, T-shirts, jackets, boots and other souvenirs.

Camping **F** *Mahai*, T036-4386303. The campsite has pleasant lawns and is bordered by large pine trees and a stream, there is a spacious camping area with 40 sites with power points, 2 wash blocks and an area for open camping, good views of the Drakensberg and footpaths leading straight up into the hills make this camp very popular, it is crowded and noisy at weekends. After a busy weekend the camp can appear to be very untidy and in need of a good clear up, especially during the school holidays. **F** *Rugged Glen*, is a small campsite to the north of the park, with 10 sites shaded by pine trees and a central ablution block. There are no other facilities here. Reservations for camping at both sites should be booked through the Officer-in-Charge, Royal Natal National Park, Pvt Bag X1669, Bergville 3350, T4386310, F4386231.

Sleeping in the park
*Price codes:
see inside front cover*

KwaZulu Natal

Cannibal Cave

This large cave overlooking a quiet valley is accessible on foot either from Mahai Campsite or Rugged Glen. The remains of some San paintings can still be seen.

During the Zulu wars refugees from the Zulu wars escaped into the mountains and lived in these caves. These years were so turbulent that people were unable to plant crops and as game became scarcer the refugees were forced to eat passing travellers or even their own children. Rumour has it that the bodies were hung up from the cave roof to keep them fresh, to save them for later.

The cannibals lived here for around 20 years, eventually becoming such a threat that they were hunted and killed by the Zulus.

Outside the park

Ins & outs From Royal Natal National Park the R74 heads east to Bergville, 41 km, and Winterton, 62 km. The R615 heads north off the R74 14 km from the park gates. After 11 km it reaches the top of Oliviershoek Pass from where it is a further 37 km to Harrismith.

Oliviershoek Pass The pass was named after Adriaan Olivier who was one of the first Voortrekkers to descend from the Orange Free State in the 1830s. He claimed a farm for himself at the foot of the pass. As the R615 ascends to the top of the pass it begins to climb up through pine forests. Although the mountains here aren't as spectacular as Mont-aux-Sources, they do have their own quiet charm and it is worth stopping off at one of the few restaurants and hotels on this road. The pass isn't as crowded as the national park and at 1,730 m it is higher than the other resorts and does have a wilder feel to it. Once over the pass the road circles round Sterkfontein Dam and then descends to Harrismith.

Sleeping outside the park
Phone code: 036
(NB Always use 3-figure prefix)

■ *on map*
Price codes:
see inside front cover

A *Little Switzerland*, look out for the signposted turning off the R74 next to the petrol station, just below Oliviershoek Pass, T/F4386220. 66 thatched cottages and self-catering chalets. A large luxury self-contained resort offering a choice of sporting facilities including riding, fishing, water skiing, canoeing, tennis and swimming. Recent additions include indoor heated pool and gym. More suited to local family holidays than the overseas visitor just passing through. **A-B** *Alpine Heath*, below Oliviershoek Pass, follow signs along the Northern Berg Rd, T4386484, F4386485. 100 luxurious 3-bedroomed self-catering chalets with lounge, 2 bathrooms, and private patio, TV. A fully self-contained resort offering a range of activities, 2 pools, gym, sauna, restaurant. **A-B** *The Cavern*, 10 km, follow the signs heading off the R74 towards the Royal Natal National Park, T4386270, F4386334. The resort is a large complex set amongst gardens and woodland offering accommodation in 55 luxury thatched cottages, a wide range of activities are on offer including horse riding, bowls, swimming and a weekend disco. Rates include all meals and guided hikes. A superb location, with well-kept mature gardens and an overall friendly and welcoming atmosphere. Like many resorts in the Drakensberg it's probably more suited to family groups where you are looking for everything on one site. Nevertheless, a couple of nights spent here will not disappoint.

C-D *Drakensville Resort*, from Oliviershoek Pass, the turning is on the left towards Jagersrust, T4386287, F4386524. A large holiday camp with 70 self-catering chalets, each with 3 beds, sporting facilities include water skiing, fishing, riding, tennis, squash and mini golf. Camping also possible. **D** *Caterpillar & Catfish*, at the top of Oliviershoek Pass, great views, T/F4386130. A pine panelled mountain lodge in a restored trading post, tucked under some large pine trees, new owners have refurbished this place to the highest standards, decorated with African antiques, stripped pine, and handmade furniture. 8 comfortable en suite bedrooms and a massage room, ideal for weary hikers, huge buffet breakfasts, guided hikes to some fascinating rock art, fishing in a well-stocked trout dam. Beautifully decorated piano bar and 24-seater restaurant offering 30 different trout dishes and specializing in Cajun cooking. People from Gauteng come here for Sunday lunch, gaining a fast-growing good reputation, stay here while the excellent rooms are still cheap. Recommended.

F *Ampitheatre Backpackers*, 17 km, at the top of Oliviershoek Pass, T4386106. Excellent new backpackers and the highest hostel in the country with fantastic views. A converted sandstone house, log fires, dorms, doubles and camping, hearty home-cooked meals, packed lunches to take with you on over 30 hikes in the area. Call for collection from Bergville or Harrismith. Linda and Isle run a shuttle on weekdays from here to *Malealea Lodge* in Lesotho, if you are short of time this is the perfect way to spend a couple of days in the mountain kingdom. On the *Baz Bus* route. Recommended.

This quiet country town is in the centre of a maize and dairy farming area. Most visitors to Bergville will either be passing through en route to the resorts in the Northern Drakensberg or be heading northeast towards Ladysmith and the Battlefields. The main reason for stopping here is to visit the helpful **tourist office**, and supermarket and petrol station to get last minute supplies before entering the Drakensberg. The *Drakensberg Tourism Association* is on Thatham Road, T4481557, F4481088, info@drakensberg.org.za Open Mon-Fri 0900-1700, Sat 0900-1200. An excellent regional office which now produces some very useful maps and brochures to help visitors make the most of the region, can book accommodation.

Bergville
Phone code: 036
*(NB Always use
3-figure prefix)*
Colour map 5, grid A4

Northern & central Drakensberg

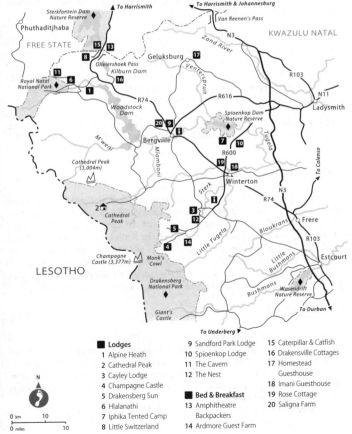

KwaZulu Natal

Sleeping **A-B** *Sandford Park Lodge*, on the R616 to Ladysmith, T4481001, F4481047. 25 en suite rooms, some are separate rondavels the rest are in an old converted coach house. Meals and drinks are served in *Pete's Pub*. Neat gardens around the house, large swimming pool, horse riding, hiking and canoeing. Run by Vanessa. Rates are for dinner, B&B. One of the finest lodges in the region, full of character, the oldest part of the coach house dates from 1850. **D** *Homestead Guest House*, off the R616 towards Ladysmith, T4481328. 12 double rooms with en suite facilities, TV, swimming pool, excellent value, an ideal location from which to explore either the Battlefields or the mountains. Ask for Bernice or Phil. **D** *Saligna Farm Lodge*, off the R616 heading towards Woodstock Dam, T4481302. Self-catering or B&B, evening meals also available on request. Double en suite rooms, great views. **D** *Drakensberg Inn*, Tatham Rd, Bergville, T/F4482946. 17 double rooms, TV, restaurant. Fine for an overnight stop, but there are plenty of rural places with character, for longer stays, to choose from. **F** *Bergville Caravan Park*, T/F4481273, on the R74 just south of town. There are 10 bungalows, 2 rondavels and a campsite next to the Tugela River, in the low season and during the week the resort offers considerable discounts on accommodation.

Eating All the large mountain resorts have restaurants and bars on site. Much of the other accommodation is self-catering, as a result there is a lack of choice for eating out in the region between the N3 and the mountains. *Bingelela*, a short drive out of town towards Woodstock Dam, T4481336. A la carte restaurant with good value meals to restore oneself after a day's hiking. There are two coffee shops within the village offering similar light meals and drinks. Both are also part of a craft shop. Closed evenings. *Candles & Antiques*, T4481339 and *Koffiepot*, T4482946.

Shopping Within the village there are several supermarkets and fresh food outlets from which to stock up before heading off into the Drakensberg. Most of the parks accommodation is self-catering and the shops at any campsite will only stock a few basics. Away from the village look out for farms selling their own produce as well as a few interesting craft centres. *Tevreden Cheese Making Farm*, take the R74 out of the village towards the Northern Berg, take a left turn after approx 7 km, T4481840. The name says it all, hikers may find a few tasty supplies.

Directory **Banks** *First National Bank*, South St, T4481037. **Medical Services** *Bergville Pharmacy*, T4481053. **Useful services** Car Breakdown Service: *BP Garage*, T4481786. **Police:** T4481095, T10177.

Central Drakensberg

The Giant's Castle Nature Reserve is the most spectacular of the Central Berg resorts. It has three camps: Giant's Castle, Hillside and Injasuti. The views of this section of the Drakensberg are of a range of mountains and basalt cliff faces rising up to 3,000 m and stretching out to the north and south for over 30 km. Further north, the road to Monk's Cowl with its string of top class resorts, curio villages, golf courses, and small villages is one of the most heavily developed areas of the Drakensberg. While you may see more tourists in this region, the scenery is no less spectacular and access is easier than other areas of the park. This is also home to the internationally famous Drakensberg Boys' Choir.

Cathedral Peak

Phone code: 036
(NB Always use
3-figure prefix)
Colour map 4, grid B6

Cathedral Peak is the main point of access to some of the wildest areas of the central Drakensberg and is popular with mountaineers and hikers. The park is surrounded by peaks with views of the Cathedral Spur and Cathedral Peak (3,004 m), the Inner and Outer Horns (3,005 m), and the Bell (2,930 m). An alternative to hiking round the peaks is to take the road suitable for cars heading up Mike's Pass from where there are views of the Little Berg.

The sheltered valleys of what is now Cathedral Peak are thought to have been one of the last refuges of the San in the Drakensberg. There are a large number of San cave painting sites in this area although not all are marked on maps. Leopards Cave and Poachers Cave in the Ndedema Gorge have especially good galleries of paintings and are well worth the effort of visiting.

An earlier name for Cathedral Peak was Zikhali's Horn, named after Zikhali who escaped to Swaziland after his father Matiwane was killed by Dingaan. During the years that he and his tribe spent there they assimilated many aspects of Swazi culture. Swazi influences can still be seen today in the way that traditional huts are built.

Ins & outs

Cathedral Peak is well-signposted from Bergville and Winterton. The road is not tarred all the way but is usually passable even after rain. It goes through communal farmlands before reaching the resort.

The reception office at Mike's Pass is open from 0700-1900 daily. The curio shop and information office are open from 0800-1630 daily, T4881880. Entry fee R15 per person, vehicles to Mike's Pass R35. The shop sells a limited range of basic groceries, otherwise the nearest supermarket is at Winterton. Maps are available in the information office and show a number of walks departing from the *Cathedral Peak Hotel*. Petrol can be bought at the hotel. *KZN Wildlife* reservations (Pietermaritzburg), T033-8451000, F033-8451001.

Hiking

The Cathedral Peak area is growing in popularity with hikers. There is a good network of paths heading up the Mlambonja Valley to the escarpment from where there are trails heading south to Monk's Cowl and Injasuti or heading north to Royal Natal National Park. The campsite at Mike's Pass or the *Cathedral Peak Hotel* are good bases from which to set out exploring the area on a series of day walks. For keen hikers there are designated caves and mountain huts on the longer trails. The 10 km hike to the top of **Cathedral Peak** (3,004 m) is one of the most exciting and strenuous hikes in this part of the Drakensberg, and the views from the top of the Drakensberg stretching out to the north and south are unforgettable.

Horse riding

Horses can be hired for short rides from the *Cathedral Peak Hotel*, T4881888.

Mountain biking

There are some 70 km of dirt roads in the Cathedral Peak area which can be used by mountain bikers. The routes are by no means extreme but they do pass through some spectacular scenery. The views from the top of Mike's Pass are as exhilarating as the 5 km ride back down. As yet there is nowhere to hire bikes so the trails are restricted to those who bring their own.

Cave paintings

There are several caves within easy walking distance of the hotel with paintings showing fascinating scenes from the San's world. Mushroom Hill has two particularly interesting scenes, one is of two mythical human figures with animal heads and hooves holding what are thought to be early musical instruments, the other is a more lighthearted scene of some San scrambling away from an irate leopard. Xeni Shelter, 2 km beyond Mushroom Rock and also easily reached from the hotel, shows a group of people and a few antelope. Ladder Shelter shows San ladders with a small picture of a man climbing up the rock face.

Junction Shelter has a number of interesting scenes of men crossing on a rope bridge, a baboon hunt and some human figures dancing. Eland Cave is a large cave with many splendid paintings, but more mysteriously, a San hunting kit was found here in the 1920s, which had apparently been left behind on a shelf of rock. To protect the rock art in the parks, the sites can only be visited with a guide, which can be arranged at the hotel.

Sleeping
■ *on map, page 475*
Price codes:
see inside front cover

A-B *Cathedral Peak Hotel*, is at the end of the road past the entry gates, T4881888, F4881889, info@cathedralpeak.co.za 90 luxurious double rooms, several restaurants and bars, swimming pool, 9-hole golf course, horse riding, sqaush, 10 m climbing tower, and tennis. This hotel is an all round resort, popular for weddings, and has traditionally been used as a base by hikers and climbers because of its stunning location close to the high peaks of the Drakensberg.

KwaZulu Natal

Camping The 12 sites are opposite the information office, this is a secluded campsite up in the mountains with a quiet, tranquil feel to it. The facilities here are simple, there is only an ablution block for campers. The campsite is popular so it is advisable to book up to a month in advance. Camp gates are open daily from 0600-1800, and until 2100 on Fri. **F** There are at least 15 caves near here in which hikers can camp. They should be booked well in advance. Officer in charge, Cathedral Peak, Private Bag X1, Winterton 3340, T4881880, F4881677.

Winterton
Phone code: 036
(NB Always use
3-figure prefix)
Colour map 5, grid A4

This small regional centre was originally known as Springfield, but in 1910 it was renamed in honour of the secretary for agriculture in Natal at the time, HD Winter. In 1905 the future prosperity of the village had been assured when the Natal government built a weir across the Little Tugela River to divert water for agriculture. Today the village remains an important centre for dairy farms as well as being the last centre for supplies for tourists visiting either the Cathedral Peak or Monk's Cowl areas of the Drakensberg National Park. It is worth a quick stop to look around its pleasant tree-lined streets, small museum, and gather some local information. The petrol station and the supermarket are on the junction of the R74 with the road leading into the centre of village.

Tourist information is currently available at *Cannan Cellars*, a wine and coffee shop opposite the Winterton *Spar*, T4881988, open Mon-Fri 0830-1630, Sat 0900-1200. At the time of writing the building of a new tourist office and craft outlet was being discussed, the proposed location is on the junction of Springfield St and the road to Monk's Cowl. For the time being, the Bergville office can help with a broader range of enquiries.

The small **museum** has displays illustrating the natural history of the Drakensberg. ■ *It is supposed to be open Mon-Fri 0900-1500, 2 Sats per month, 0900-1200, but often isn't. Small entry fee.*

Many of the accommodation alternatives will pick up from buses at the Midway service station on the N3, phone ahead to arrange a lift

Sleeping and eating C *Ardmore Guest Farm*, T/F4681314. Run by Paul and his family. Superb views with lovely gardens. B&B, 7 double en suite rooms, has an excellent local reputation for home cooked meals. Self-catering available or full board. Also home to a well-known ceramic art studio with some very special designs. Always worth a visit with tea garden on site, recommended by several readers.

D *Bridge Lodge*, 18 Springfield Rd, T/F4881554. 7 rooms, restaurant serves snacks and pub food. **D** *Glade Farm Lodge*, close to Spioenkop Dam, T4881424. 6 double rooms with en suite facilities, B&B or self-catering. **D** *Imani Guest House*, turn off Springfield, drive past the library and out of the village on the Colenso road, look out for signs on the left, T4881265. B&B, ensuite rooms, evening meals available on request. **D** *Lilac Lodge Cottages*, Springfield Rd, T4881025. B&B or self-catering, TV, swimming pool. A fine old house set in a large garden within the village. **D** *Purple House*, 10 Springfield Rd, T4881025. B&B with attached coffee and crafts shop. **D** *Swallow's Nest*, 1 Bergview Dr, T/F4881009. Two double rooms, with fans and heaters, shared bathroom, separate toilet. Plus a garden cottage which can sleep 4, with a fridge and microwave. TV lounge for communal use, breakfasts served in the homely dining room. All set in a landscaped garden. A short walk from restaurant at the Bridge Lodge for evening meals. Ask for Molly. Good value, recommended. *Cannan Cellars*, opposite the *Spar*, T4881988. Local tourist information outlet, fine wine shop, small tea room with 5 tables. *Cheesery*, 6 Springfield Rd, T4881296. Farm shop specializing in various cheeses, free tastings. *Purple House*, 10 Springfield St, T4881025. Light lunches, afternoon teas and cool drinks or hot coffee in the winter months.

Shopping There are several craft shops along the R600 to Champagne Valley and Monk's Cowl. *Ingkar Art Gallery & MG Traders*, just after the junction with the D160, towards Monk's Cowl. A couple of curio shops promoting local ethnic arts and crafts, worth checking out for some more unusual pieces. Plenty of mountain images. *KwaZulu Weavers*, 12 km from Winterton towards Monk's Cowl, T4881658. Colourful handmade crafts at sensible prices, check the quality on some of the larger pieces. *Rainbow Room*, off the R600 just after the *Nest Hotel*, heading towards Monk's Cowl, T4681801. An unusual selection of hand made crafts, unfortunately the larger pieces are a bit too big to take home for overseas visitors. Run by Inger. *Thokiza*, 13 km from Winterton, a one-stop tourist centre, *Drakensberg Tourism* has an office here, T4881207. Useful if you still haven't decided on accommodation in Champagne Valley, 9 shops selling arts and crafts, fishing equipment, fine wines, and a coffee shop. Recommended.

Road Bus: the *Baz Bus*, T021-4392323, info@bazbus.com, www.bazbus.com Calls in 3 times a week in both directions between **Johannesburg** and **Durban**, drops off and picks up outside of the *First National* Bank. A shuttle can be arranged from here to *Inkosana Lodge*, near Monk's Cowl. **Car**: two roads from Winterton lead towards the Drakensberg resorts; heading north the R74 goes via Bergville, 22 km, to the **Royal Natal National Park**, 62 km. Two km south of Winterton on the R600 there is a signposted turning to **Cathedral Peak**, 43 km. The R600 continues on to **Monk's Cowl** (Champagne Valley), 35 km. To reach **Injasuti**, take the turning to Loskop off the R600, before reaching Loskop there is a dirt road on the right. Follow the signposts to Injasuti from here. Heading southeast, the R74 crosses the N3 to **Estcourt**, 43 km.

Transport

Most of the Drakensberg National Park is more or less inaccessible to travellers who have not hired a car

This 6,000 ha game park is a popular tourist resort for boating and fishing. Almost all the game here has been reintroduced and there is a good chance of seeing white rhino and buffalo. With this in mind visitors must be careful when walking in the open around their campsite. Other animals one can expect to see include giraffe, kudu, mountain reedbuck, waterbuck, blesbok, impala, zebra, eland, duiker and steenbok. The area is particularly rich in birdlife and more than 270 species have been recorded here. Anglers can fish the reservoir from the dam or from the shore.

Spioenkop Dam Nature Reserve

Phone code 036 (NB Always use 3-figure prefix) Colour map 5, grid A4

KwaZulu Natal

Information The reserve is 14 km north of Winterton on the R600. Office and booking accommodation, T4881578, F4881065. PO Box 140, Winterton. Gates open Oct-Mar 0600-1900, Apr-Sep 0600-1800. Entry R15 per person. All the accommodation here is self-catering so visitors need to bring their food and drink. The closest shops are in Winterton, 14 km.

Sights In 1906 Liverpool Football Club named the new stands after Spioenkop in memory of those who died during the Boer War. The stands overlooking the home end at Anfield are still called the Kop to this day. The famous battlefield (see box next page) overlooks the dam and is clearly visible from the reserve. There are several self-guided trails through the reserve including one to Spioenkop battlefield. **Riding** Horses can be hired daily at 0800 and 1400 for rides through the park to see game. R35 per hour.

Sleeping D *Iphika Tented Camp*, can sleep up to 4 in 2 large 2-bed tents, the camp also has a lounge area with fireplace and kitchen, it is set in the reserve and it is possible to go on game walks from here, Spioenkop battlefield is only a short walk from here, but up a steep slope. **E** *Chalets*, the hutted camp closed down some years ago and most of the chalets were dismantled. However, 5 still remain and can be hired out but they're very old. Each have 3 twin bedrooms, kitchen, bathroom, and are fully-equipped. Accommodation is cheap but quite frankly they should also have been knocked down and there is better accommodation in the area notably at Spioenkop Lodge, see below. **F** *Camping*, 30 sites next to the dam with power points, slip ways for launching of boats, popular with anglers.

The accommodation in the park is sometimes listed in tourist brochures as 'Spioenkop Chalets & Caravan Park'

Nearby Private Accommodation B-C *Spioenkop Lodge*, located on the R600 between Winterton and Ladysmith, T/F 4881404. 15 double rooms, fully inclusive, set on a farm close to Spioenkop. This delightful country lodge makes for an excellent base from which to explore the surroundings. Canoe rides on the nearby Tugela river, sundowner cruises on Spioenkop Dam, horseriding and battlefield tours all available. Run by Raymond and Lynette. Recommended.

Spion Kop

The battle of Spion Kop, 24 January 1890, was yet another embarrassing defeat for the British at the hands of the Boers and had a marked impact upon British public opinion.

After the disaster of Colenso, (see page 503) Redvers Buller had been replaced as Commander-in-Chief of British forces in South Africa by Field Marshall Lord Roberts (whose son had been killed at Colenso). However, he remained in control of British forces in northern Natal and was determined to relieve the besieged Ladysmith. Buller had ample supplies and equipment and some 30,000 British troops facing just 8,000 Boers, under the command of General Botha. Buller's plan was simple. One division under General Warren would cross the Tugela at Trichardt's Drift and outflank the Boer positions in the Rangeworthy Hills. In the meantime a brigade under General Lyttelton would ford the Tugela at Potgieter's Drift and head due north to meet up with Warren near Dewdrop and totally surround the western section of the Boer forces blocking the British advance on Ladysmith.

At first the advance went according to plan. The Tugela was effectively bridged and a cavalry force made good progress on a wide outflanking arc to the west. Warren's main force, however, found the route too difficult for their wagons and halted at the foot of the Rangeworthy Hills. Warren decided that the best course of action was a direct assault on the hills to dislodge the Boer positions so his column could advance without coming under fire from the heights. Surveying the terrain he decided to occupy the highest peak on the ridge – Spion Kop.

The initial advance under cover of darkness was highly successful and the small troop of about 70 Boers guarding the peak were easily dislodged. Furthermore heavy mist at dawn allowed the British time to construct defensive positions. At this point, however, things started to go badly wrong. Despite the extra time afforded by the mist, the British were unable to construct deep trenches due to the hard surface of the peak and when the mist lifted at about 0700 their true position became apparent. Despite

taking the highest peak the shallow British defences meant they were exposed to Boer rifle and field gun fire from all sides and especially from the Twin Peaks to the east. The British soon suffered extremely heavy losses, especially amongst the Lancashire Fusiliers. Despite these losses the British troops managed to hang on to the peak throughout the day, rallied by Lieutenant-Colonel Thorneycroft who became the defacto commander of the force whilst his superiors dithered.

Hearing of the problems at Spion Kop the brigade under General Lyttelton's command, who had successfully crossed the Tugela at Potgieter's Drift, decided to storm the Twin Peaks instead of pushing north towards Dewdrop as originally planned. The assault was a success and by sunset the British held most of the heights. General Buller, however, made the incomprehensible decision of ordering Lyttelton to withdraw becasue his assault was not according to the original plan. Under the safety of night Thorneycroft was also ordered to bring the shattered remnants of his troops down from Spion Kop and all British forces was ordered to retreat back across the Tugela.

Some 1,750 British troops were either killed, wounded or captured at Spion Kop compared to about 300 Boers. What made the defeat for the British so stinging, however, was the fact that the battle was theirs for the taking. Unbeknownst to them, the Boer forces, discouraged by the British troops' victory at Twin Peaks, had actually been slipping away from Spion Kop at the same time as the British were withdrawing. It was only the efforts of General Botha that persuaded many of the Boers to stay and, at the break of dawn, they were very surprised to see two of their number waving from the peak abandoned by the British. Had Buller and the other commanders had the ability to adapt their initial plan and strengthen the British positions on Spion Kop and Twin Peaks instead of withdrawing surely it would have been a famous victory instead of an ignominious defeat.

Monk's Cowl

The road to Monk's Cowl passes through one of the most developed areas of the Drakensberg. Looking down from Monk's Cowl the view of KwaZulu Natal is dotted with hotels, golf courses and timeshare developments and the area is locally dubbed 'Champagne Valley'. However, Champagne Castle, Monk's Cowl and Cathkin Peak are still impressive features in this landscape and several interesting long distance hikes begin from here.

Phone code: 036
(NB Always use
3-figure prefix)
Colour map 4, grid B6

Information Park gates open Oct-Mar 0500-1900, Apr-Sep 0600-1800. Camp office open daily 0830-1230, 1400-1630, T036-4681103. Entry fee R15 per person. The nearest supermarket is opposite the *Champagne Sports Resort* (9 km).

The short hikes around Monk's Cowl do get busy as so many tourists just come to visit for the day. A map is available from the office and the paths are clear and well-signposted. Places to visit include **Nandi's Falls** (5 km), **Sterkspruit Falls** (2 km), and **The Sphinx** (3 km). The paths cross areas of proteas and some woodland.

The hike up to **Champagne Castle** (3,377 m) is a 20 km, two-day hike which involves a steady slog uphill but no climbing skills. From the camp the trail rises up and follows the Mhlawazini Valley circling around Cathkin Peak and Monk's Cowl. There is a campsite just below Gray's Pass. A path winds steeply up the pass for 2 km to the top of the escarpment.

From here it is possible to walk to the top of Champagne Castle or to visit the cliffs at Vulture's Retreat where a colony of Cape vultures breed. The return journey follows the same path back.

Hiking

KwaZulu Natal

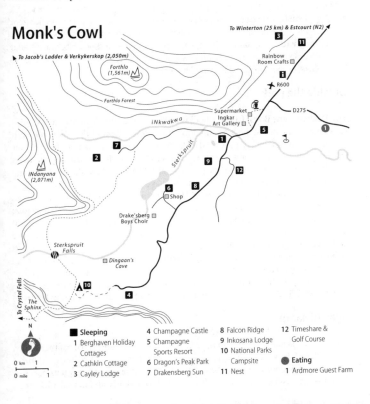

Monk's Cowl

To Winterton (25 km) & Estcourt (N2)
3 **11**

Rainbow
Room Crafts ▣

i

↑ R600

To Jacob's Ladder & Verkykerskop (2,050m) ▶

Forthlo
(1,561m) ⛺

Forthlo Forest

Supermarket ▣
Ingkar
Art Gallery ▣   — D275 —

iNkwakwa

5   **1**

1

iNdanyana
(2,071m)   **9**

7   **12**

2

6 ▣ Shop   **8**

Drake'sberg ▣
Boys Choir

Sterkspruit
Falls 〰

▣ Dingaan's
Cave

10 ▲   **4**

To Crystal Falls

The
Sphinx

◀◀

N
↓

0 km   1
0 mile   1

■ **Sleeping**		
1 Berghaven Holiday Cottages	4 Champagne Castle	8 Falcon Ridge	12 Timeshare & Golf Course
2 Cathkin Cottage	5 Champagne Sports Resort	9 Inkosana Lodge	
3 Cayley Lodge	6 Dragon's Peak Park	10 National Parks Campsite	● **Eating**
	7 Drakensberg Sun	11 Nest	1 Ardmore Guest Farm

Sleeping

■ *on map, page 481*
Price codes:
see inside front cover

All the accommodation listed below is outside the park and signposted off the R600. The distances shown are the distance from each hotel to the entrance of Monk's Cowl. **B** *Cayley Lodge*, 22 km, T4681222, F4681020. 24 double rooms, swimming pool. The lodge is set amongst extensive lawns with views over Champagne Castle and Cathkin Peak, plenty of activities are available here including horse riding, birdwatching and trout fishing. **B** *Champagne Castle* 2 km, T4681063, F4681306. 47 rooms, restaurant, horse riding, tennis, swimming pool, a traditional Drakensberg resort in a spectacular mountain setting. **B** *Drakensberg Sun*, 12 km, T4681000, F4681224. 148 rooms, 30 chalets, canoeing, horse riding, tennis, swimming pool, the hotel is surrounded by mountains and overlooks a small reservoir. **B-C** *The Nest*, 13 km, T4681068, F4681390. 55 rooms in thatched chalets with private veranda, restaurant, bar, guest lounges, swimming pool, bowls, horse riding. Rates include all meals as well as afternoon tea, a complete resort where guests base themselves for several days and explore the mountains at leisure.

C *Champagne Sports Resort*, 9 km, T4681088, F4681072. 60 rooms, restaurant, golf course, tennis, horse riding, swimming pool, a smart modern resort with all the latest facilities. **C** *Berghaven Holiday Cottages*, 8 km, T4681212, F4681102. Self-catering holiday cottages with 2, 4 or 6 beds. **D** *Dragon's Peak Park*, 4 km, T4681031, F4681104. 30 chalets, 34 campsites, a busy holiday camp offering a wide range of organized entertainment, there is a small supermarket here and a petrol pump. **D** *Cathkin Cottage*, 13 km, follow directions for the *Drakensberg Sun*, after the hotel turn right into Yellowood Dr, T4681513. 2 double rooms with en suite facilities and private entrance. B&B with a fridge, TV and secure parking. Run by Val and Ian. Ideal location to take advantage of the many facilities provided by the big hotels. **E** *Inkosana Lodge*, 7 km, easy access via a good surfaced road, T/F4681202. 4 small dormitories, double rooms, some en suite, camping, large dining area, vegetarian food available, tours, email access, laundry, horse riding, evening meals, large modern bungalow. The backpackers has fine views towards the mountains and is set in a large garden planted with indigenous plants, guided hikes lasting up to several days can be organized from here. Free collection from the *Baz Bus* in Winterton. Short walk to local shops and restaurants. Edmund is the owner.

Camping within the park F There are 15 pitches and an ablution block next to the camp office. Reservations for this campsite should be made through the Officer in Charge, Monk's Cowl, Private Bag X2, Winterton 3340, T4681103

Outside the park

The **Drakensberg Boys' Choir** school is on the right of the R600 towards Monk's Cowl and is one of the most beautiful locations for a school in the whole of South Africa. The school is highly accredited in its own right, but is most famous for the choir that has performed all over the world over the last 25 years. In the past, boys between 9-15 have performed in front of the pope and 25,000 people at the Vatican City, sung with the Vienna Boys' Choir in Austria, and have been proclaimed top choir three times at the World Festival of Choirs. ■ *During term-time they perform on Wed, 1530, in the school's impressive auditorium. Bookings are essential, T4681012.* **Falcon Ridge** is a rehabilitation centre for rescued birds of prey, mostly injured through flying into power lines. The daily show is interesting and there is the opportunity to don a glove and have your photo taken with a large raptor. ■ *Daily bird shows 1130. Turn off just before* Champagne Castle Hotel. *T082-7746398* (mob). There is an airfield opposite the *Champagne Sports Resort* from where you can take short **helicopter flights** over the mountains. Contact, *Chopper Flying Services*, T4881300, or *NAC Scenic Helicopter Flights*, T082-5723949 (mob), a 20-minute scenic flight should cost approx R400 pp.

Injasuti camp

Phone code: 036
(NB Always use
3-figure prefix)
See Giant's Castle map

Injasuti is an isolated camp high up in the Central Drakensberg, part of the Giant's Castle Nature Reserve. The valley is covered with large areas of yellowwood forest and grassland. Looming over the camp are the awe inspiring mountain peaks of Champagne Castle (3,248 m), Monk's Cowl (3,234 m) and Cathkin Peak (3,149 m).

Some of the highest peaks in South Africa are nearby, all of which soar up to well over 3,000 m. Mafadi (3,446 m), Injasuti Dome (3,410 m), The Injasuti Triplets, Eastern Triplet (3,134 m), Western Triplet (3,187 m), Injasuti Buttress (3,202 m) are all magnets to South Africa's climbers. The game in Injasuti Valley used to be abundant and the Zulu word 'Injasuti' actually means 'well-fed dog' as hunting parties here were often so successful. San also thrived here and left many cave paintings as a testament to their passing.

Ins & outs The reserve is signposted from Winterton and Loskop, the last 30 km of the journey are on a dirt road. Park gates open Oct-Mar 0500-1900, Apr-Sep 0600-1800. Camp office open daily 0800-1230, 1400-1630, T036-4317848. Entry fee R15 per person. There is no shop here so visitors need to bring all supplies with them. Reservations for campsites and caves should be made through the Officer in Charge, Injasuti, Private Bag X7010, Estcourt 3310, T/F4317848, for huts and chalets contact *KZN Wildlife* reservations office in Pietermaritzburg, T033-8451000, F033-8451001.

Hiking There is a selection of trails for day hikes beginning at the campsite and following the Injasuti Stream to the southwest. Poacher's Stream is a tributary of the Injasuti and this path leads off Boundary Pool (3 km) where it is possible to swim. Following the Injasuti further up the valley are Battle Cave (5 km), Junction Cave (8 km) and Lower Injasuti Cave (8 km).
Giant's Castle is a three-day hike from Injasuti following the contour path south. The trail can be exhausting but it does pass through spectacular mountain scenery including Popple Peak. Reservations for sleeping at Lower Injasuti Cave and Bannerman Hut have to be made beforehand.

Battle Cave There is a daily guided walk, 7 km, departing at 0830 to Battle Cave and other San sites which should be booked the day before, these are limited to a minimum of 4 and a maximum of 20 people, R35 per person. Battle Cave is named after one of the paintings in this shelter which shows two groups of San attacking each other. Figures are shown running into the fight with arrows flying between them. There are hundreds of other paintings on the cave walls of animals that used to live here. A family of lions, numerous eland and rhebok, an elephant and an antbear are depicted.

Sleeping D *Chalets*, 17 6-bed chalets, fully equipped for self-catering, linen provided. **E** *Cabins*, which are a basic 8-bed dormitory. Electricity between 1730 and 2200 only. **Camping F** There are 20 sites and shared ablution blocks.
Price codes: see inside front cover
Caves F *Lower Injasuti Cave*, *Upper Injasuti Cave* and *Grindstone Cave*, can all be used by hikers for overnight stops but should be reserved in advance. No fires allowed, very basic facilities. Come well-equipped.

Hillside Camp

Part of the Giant's Castle Nature Reserve, Hillside Camp is much lower than Injasuti but there are formidable views and a number of interesting hikes.
Phone code: 036 (NB Always use 3-figure prefix)

Ins & outs Hillside is 32 km from Giant's Castle main camp and 47 km from Estcourt. Both Hillside and Giant's Castle can be reached either from Estcourt or from Mooi River. From Estcourt take the road to Wagendrift and Ntabamhlope, after 35 km you will reach the White Mountain Resort (see next page) from where both camps are well-signposted. Park gates open daily 0800-1800. Entry fee R15 per person. Reservations for camping should be made through the Officer-in-Charge, Hillside, PO Box 288, Estcourt 3310, T3538255, between 0900-1200 only. Advance booking for Hillside Camp is recommended as it is popular all year round. The camp doesn't have many facilities; in fact as there is no electricity, petrol is not for sale and the shop sells only a limited selection of tinned goods, it is essential to bring all supplies from Estcourt.

Hiking There are several day walks from Hillside Camp which vary between a short stroll in the immediate vicinity to serious all-day hikes up into the Berg. The **Forest Walk**, 5 km, passes through grassland and forested areas just around the camp. The path crosses over the Mtshezana River where there is a popular spot for swimming.

The hike up to **Tree Fern Cave**, 12 km, follows the Mtshezana River up to eMasthanini Ridge from where the path begins to climb steeply. On the ascent to Tree Fern Cave there are amazing views of cliffs and gorges; from the cave itself the views stretch out down the Injasuti Valley over forests and tree ferns. The return to the camp is back along the same path used to go up.

Tom's Cave, 17 km, is a circular walk which can also be completed in one day. This path rises up to the Ntondolo Flats, crosses the Shayake River heading west past a kraal before reaching Tom's Cave. The return is along the eMasthanini Ridge and back down to the camp. A leaflet is available here with details of the walks and information about the area.

Sleeping **E** There is a rustic hut with 8 beds and a fully equipped kitchen. Towels, sheets and blankets
Price codes: are not supplied. The hut must be booked through *KZN Wildlife*, T033-8451000,
see inside front cover F033-8451001. **Camping F** There are 25 sites for tents or caravans and an ablution block with hot and cold water. Apart from braai areas there are no other cooking facilities.

On the road to Giant's Castle and Hillside from Estcourt is **B-E** *White Mountain Resort*, T/F3533437. A friendly family holiday camp with a variety of full-board rooms, self-catering chalets, dorms, camping and caravan sites. The resort is self-contained and offers a wide range of organized activities. It is a long way from the higher parts of the Drakensberg and if you want to see the mountains it's better to find accommodation somewhere else. There is a small supermarket here and petrol is also available.

Giant's Castle

Phone code: 036 This reserve was established in 1903 when there were only 200 eland left in the whole of
(NB Always use KwaZulu Natal. Over the years the reserve has successfully helped the eland popula-
3-figure prefix) tion in the Drakensberg to recover and at present there are around 600 in the reserve.
Colour map 4, grid B6
The Drakensberg escarpment towers over the campsite here. A wall of basalt cliffs rise up to over 3,000 m and the peaks of Giant's Castle (3,314 m), Champagne Castle (3,248 m) and Cathkin Peak (3,149 m) can be seen on the skyline. The grasslands below the cliffs roll out in a series of massive hills, which give rise to the Bushman's River and the Little Tugela River.

On the drive to the camp from the park gates, the road passes through a cutting which exposes layers of brown, red, yellow and purple rock. These are the Molteno Beds, layers of sandstone deposited 200 million years ago where plant and dinosaur fossils have been found.

Ins & outs The road to Giant's Castle is signposted from Mooi River (64 km) and Estcourt (65 km) on the N3. The road from Estcourt is tarred for most of the way whilst the mostly dirt road from Mooi River should be avoided in wet weather. From Mooi River take the road to Ncibidwana Store, 46 km, and then follow the signs. Park gates open Oct-Mar 0500-1900, Apr-Sep 0600-1800. Camp office open daily 0800-1230, 1400-1630. Entry fee R20 per person. Information T3533718. Accommodation here is self-catering, but cooks are provided to prepare simple meals for you in a central kitchen. The camp shop sells a wide range of books and curios but only a limited selection of dried and frozen food. Petrol is for sale by the main gate. There is a farm shop next to the park gates selling fresh and smoked trout otherwise the nearest supermarket is in Estcourt.

Wildlife Rolling hills of sourveld grasslands dominate the landscape of the reserve. Eland, blesbok, mountain reedbuck and oribi are some of the mammals you are likely to see. The area around the camp has a network of short paths through riverine forest and wetlands which supports many species of birds. The malachite kingfisher,

Gurney's sugarbird and the various sunbirds are often spotted here and grey duiker can sometimes be seen walking around the camp.

There are numerous inter-connected hikes crossing the reserve, the shorter walks explore the forests and river valleys within a few kilometres of the camp, whilst the longer ones take up to three days and can reach areas as far afield as Injasuti and the escarpment.

The more challenging walks to **Langalibalele Pass**, 12 km, **Bannerman Pass**, 20 km, and **Giant's Castle** involve a long uphill struggle to reach the top of the escarpment. The hike up to Giant's Castle at 3,314 m takes three days and means using Giant's Hut as a base camp for two nights. The second day's hike from the hut up to Giant's Castle Pass, 12 km, rises up through scree slopes and loose rubble. From the top of the pass it is a further 1 km to the peak. Giant's Hut is 10 km from the main camp and there are several well-marked paths which lead to it.

World's View The 7 km hike up to World's View (1,842 m), follows a path north along a ridge overlooking the Bushman's River. The climb up to the top is not too strenuous and the views from there looking over Wildebeest Plateau to Giant's Castle and Cathkin Peak are well worth the effort. The best time to see the peaks of the mountains is early in the morning as clouds tend to descend in the afternoon.

Lammergeyer Hide The hide is only open over weekends between May and September. This is a popular attraction and advance booking is necessary. A

Hiking
A comprehensive leaflet detailing the hiking choices is available from the camp office

KwaZulu Natal

Giant's Castle

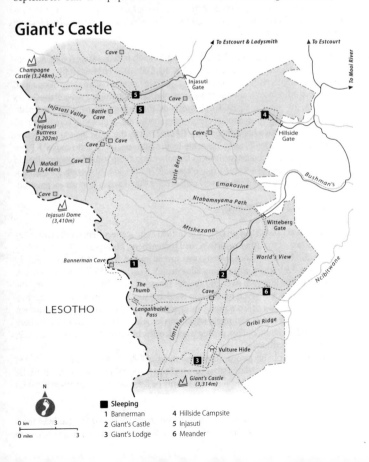

To Estcourt & Ladysmith   To Estcourt

To Mooi River

Cave

Champagne Castle (3,248m)

Injasuti Gate

5

Cave

Injasuti Valley

Battle Cave

5

Injasuti Buttress (3,202m)

Cave ☐ Cave

Cave

4

Hillside Gate

Mafadi (3,446m)

Cave

Little Berg

Emakosine

Bushman's

Cave

Injasuti Dome (3,410m)

Ntabamnyama Path

Mtshezana

Witteberg Gate

Bannerman Cave

1

World's View

2

Ncibitwone

The Thumb

Cave

6

LESOTHO

Langalibalele Pass

Umtshezi

Oribi Ridge

Vulture Hide

3

Giant's Castle (3,314m)

N

0 km   3
0 miles   3

■ **Sleeping**
1 Bannerman
2 Giant's Castle
3 Giant's Lodge
4 Hillside Campsite
5 Injasuti
6 Meander

☛ ## Lammergeyers

Lammergeyers are one of the world's rarest vultures, living mainly in isolated high mountain areas in the Pyrenees, the Atlas Mountains of Morocco and the Middle East. However, there are around 200 pairs of Lammergeyers in the Drakensburg and Lesotho, and a visit to the hide at Giant's Castle is one of the best ways to see them.

They live on a diet of dried bones, waiting for a carcass to be cleaned by other vultures before they will start to feed. The Lammergeyer flies off with bones from the carcass and drops them onto rocks below. The bones crack open enabling the bird to feed on the marrow inside.

The Lammergeyer is an endangered species still under threat as local farmers leave poisoned carcasses out in the wild to kill jackals, these carcasses naturally attract vultures who in their turn are poisoned.

maximum of 6 people are driven up to the hide in a parks vehicle in the early morning. You are then left to make your own way back to the camp on foot. In addition to the magnificent lammergeyer you can expect to see the lanner falcon, jackal buzzard, Cape vulture and the black eagle. ■ *Advanced bookings, T3533718. R100 per person, for a minimum of 4 people.*

The **Main Cave** is half an hour's walk from the camp and has a large wall covered in paintings and a simple display on the archaeology of the cave and the San who lived there. ■ *The cave must be visited with a guide, which can be arranged at the camp office, R15 per person.*

Sleeping
■ *on map, page 485*
Price codes:
see inside front cover

Giant's Castle is popular all year and accommodation tends to be full at weekends. Advance bookings through *KZN Wildlife* is recommended, T033-8451000, F033-8451001.

A *Giant's Lodge* is further up the valley and secluded from the hutted camp, sleeping up to 7 people, this luxurious lodge has its own cook and has uninterrupted views of the Giant's Castle peaks. The hutted camp has **B** *Cottages* and **C** *Bungalows* with between 2 to 6 beds, bathroom, fridge and an area to eat and prepare snacks, the camp can accommodate 68 people, one of these is a honeymoon suite. **F** *Rustic Hut* by the picnic area surrounded by trees offers basic facilities for up to 10 people, foam mattresses, fridge and a cooker. **F** There are 4 mountain huts at about 4 to 5 hrs walk from the camp, *Giant's Hut*, *Centenary Hut* and *Bannerman Hut*, sleep 8 people each, and *Meander Hut* sleeps 4. All the huts are at an altitude of around 2,000 m and can get very cold at night. Bunks and mattresses are provided.

Kamberg Nature Reserve

The reserve was established on farmland in 1951. The scenery here is not as spectacular as at some of the other resorts in the Drakensberg, however the Clarens Sandstone around Kamberg does have its own special appeal. The reserve is at relatively low altitude, the highest point being Gladstone's Nose at 2,265 m, and is therefore known for its birdlife with over 200 species recorded here. The wetlands along the Mooi River provide a haven for the rare wattled crane which breeds here. Stanley's bustard which grows up to a metre in height can also be spotted in the adjacent grasslands. Some of the mammals which can be seen on walks through Kamberg include eland, blesbok, duiker, red hartebeest, oribi, black wildebeest, grey rhebuck, and mountain reedbuck.

Kamberg is probably known mostly for its trout fishing; there is a hatchery open to the public and several dams stocked with brown and rainbow trout which can be fished all year round. The Mooi River can only be fished during the season between September and April.

Ins & outs **Getting there** Kamberg is 48 km from Nottingham Road travelling via Rosetta. The route is well-signposted all the way and only the last 19 km of the journey are along dirt roads. It is also

Langibalele Pass

During the 1870s many Africans went to work in Kimberley including members of the Hlubi. Langibalele's Hlubi clan had bought guns with the money earned from working the diamond fields and the government of Natal was not happy with the idea of black people owning guns. In 1874 they issued an ultimatum demanding that Langibalele hand them over, so Langibalele and his clan fled into Lesotho to escape the situation.

Hundreds of colonial troops from the 75th regiment and 8,000 native recruits were sent after Langibalele. They caught up with a group of Hlubi tribesmen on the pass where a brief skirmish took place. The colonial troops fled leaving three dead and one wounded officer, a Colonel Durnford.

In revenge for this fracas the colonial troops hunted down the stragglers and shot around 200 elderly men and women. The younger Hlubi who were caught were sent into forced labour on the farms in Natal. A neighbouring tribe, the Putini, did not escape the vengeance. They were accused of sympathizing with the Hlubi so their kraals were burnt down, their cattle were confiscated and they too were sent into forced labour in Natal.

Langibalele was eventually betrayed and handed over to the Colonial authorities. After trial he was sent to Robben Island for life.

possible to reach the reserve from Mooi River (42 km) by taking the turning off the N3 to Rosetta. To reach Highmoor follow the signs to Kamberg from Nottingham Road. After 30 km there is a T-junction where one road heads south to Kamberg the other heading north to Giant's Castle. Take the road north and after 500 m there is a signposted turning to Highmoor.

Reserve gates open Oct-Mar 0500-1900, Apr-Sep 0600-1800. Camp office open daily 0800-1230, 1400-1630. All visitors must report to the office on arrival. Entry fee R15 per person. Food and petrol are not for sale at the camp. The nearest shops and petrol station are 42 km away in Rosetta.

Hiking The trails around Kamberg are quite leisurely and involve no steep climbs. The **Mooi River Trail**, 4 km, has been designed with wheelchair access in mind, and is a relaxing stroll past willows and eucalyptus trees along the banks of the Mooi River. There are some longer trails such as the hike up to **Emeweni Falls**, other two-day hikes are planned, ask at the camp office for the latest details. Always make sure you have warm clothing, conditions can change very quickly in this area and try and hike in groups of 3 or more people.

Cave paintings Check at the office for details about guided walks to the San paintings. There are several rock art sites, but the two main sites worth visiting for the variety and quality of the paintings are Game Pass Shelter and The Kranses.

Game Pass Shelter is approximately a 7 km walk from Kamberg. The sheer number of paintings here is impressive. Among the many scenes on the rock wall is one of a human with hooves instead of feet holding the tail of a dying eland. This is thought to have shamanic meaning and to be connected to a trance-like state. Just outside the shelter there are some fossilized dinosaur footprints.

The walk to the Kranses group of caves is a 12 km round trip. Apart from these there are also several other interesting caves to visit. The Kranses has a long sheltered rock wall covered in paintings of eland. Among these are some smaller scenes showing a group of people, some of whom are carrying shields. It is known that the San didn't use shields so they must be paintings of cattle herders, possibly the Amazizi, who moved up into the Drakensberg and lived peacefully with the San.

Sleeping
Price codes:
see inside front cover

Reservations should be made through *KZN Wildlife*, T033-8451000, F033-8451001. **C** *Stillerust Rustic Cottage* has 10 beds; but the minimum charge is for 6 people. The cottage is 8 km from the main camp and is self-catering and fully equipped with a gas stove, a fridge and gas lighting. Bring your own bedding. **C** 1 chalet with 6 beds; **C** 1 chalet with 5 beds; **C** 1 rustic cottage with 10 dorm beds (must be booked as a whole unit), **F** 5 Rest Huts with 2 beds, communal lounge area. The accommodation in the main camp does not include kitchens as all cooking is done for you by camp staff, it is however essential to bring all your own food with you. The huts and the cottage do have fridges; freezers are available for storing food in the camp kitchen. **Camping F** It is possible to camp on overnight hikes.

Backpackers with their own means of transport might be tempted to explore this region from the relatively new lodge, **F** *Drakensberg International Backpackers Lodge* T033-2637241, F2632737. The actual address is 'Grace Valley Farm' on the Highmoor Rd, there are signposts but call for directions if you don't have a good road map. 18 dorm beds, 2 double rooms, camping, TV lounge, kitchen, bar, email facility, laundry service, horse riding, evening meals provided. Lovely farm surrounded by mountains. Owned by Lionel who will run local tours on request, pick up from Mooi River Wimpy, also offers shuttle service to Durban for groups.

Highmoor   This reserve is known mostly for its trout fishing. The area surrounding the campsite consists of rolling hills and grassland and has views of the escarpment. **F** Open campsites and caves only. T033-2637240. Entry fee R15 per person. Plan on being totally self-sufficient.

Southern Drakensberg

Underberg is the main access point to Southern Drakensberg resorts. Maps do show a network of roads linking Mkhomazi Wilderness Area to Howick and Mooi River, however these roads become impassable if it rains and even in the best conditions they are only suitable for four-wheel drive vehicles. The quickest way to the resorts is to stay on surfaced roads. Most people will inevitably pass through Underburg or neighbouring Himeville, which are sleepy farming villages but have a good variety of pubs, restaurants, and shops, and are convenient stop-offs for provisions en route to the KZN Wildlife camps or backpackers at the bottom of the Sani Pass.

Bulwer   Bulwer is a small village in the foothills of the Drakensberg set amongst pine planta-
Colour map 4, grid B6   tions. There is little of interest for tourists here but it is one of the few centres for paragliding in the Drakensberg. Contact *Wildsky Adventures*, T039-8320224, wildsky@pixie.co.za, for course information. They also offer a number of other activities including mountain bike hire, abseiling, and fishing, and have simple accommodation in log cabins available to those who are undertaking paragliding courses. From here the R617 begins to climb into the mountains and there are some spectacular views of the mountains in the distance.

Reichenau   The old Catholic mission station was originally run by Trappist monks. Today there
Mission   is a convent and a thriving farm school here. The best time to visit the mission is at the weekend as it tends to be quiet during the week. The highlight here for visitors is the Zulu Mass held every Sunday. The church has no organ so all the hymns are purely choral and the singing is amazing. Most of the people here are Zulu speakers, only the nuns and priests speak English. This is generally a quiet place but it is possible to hike or ride up to the old mill or to see the waterfall and go swimming in the river. Guides are available for the local rock art sites and fishing is permitted in the trout dam. The turning to the mission is signposted 20 km from Bulwer towards Underburg. The simple **guest cottage F**, sleeps up to 20 people. There is a large kitchen with cold water, a gas cooker, a fridge and cutlery, a lounge and dining area. You need to bring your own food or either western-style or Zulu traditional food can be prepared with advance notice. T039-7011631.

Underberg

This small market town was founded in 1886 when a trading store was opened here. It is still very much the main service centre for this part of the Drakensberg and visitors will find this an ideal base from which to plan trips into the mountains. The junction with the road to Himeville is where the banks, supermarkets and the tourist information office can all be found.

Phone code: 033
(NB Always use
3-figure prefix)
Colour map 4, grid B6

Despite its relative isolation *Sani Pass Carriers*, offer transport to/from Underberg which helps make this beautiful area of the Drakensberg accessible for budget travellers. An extra incentive for visiting the area is to cross into Lesotho via the Sani Pass border post

Ins & outs

Tourist information *Sani Saunter*, at the White Cottage shopping centre, T/F7021902, info@sanisaunter.com Produce a leaflet packed with information on activities and accommodation in the Southern Drakensberg.

For B&B accomodation around Underburg, contact *Underburg Hideaways*, T3431564, pc@futurenet.co.za, who act as agents for a number of establishments. **C** *Rougham Farm Cottage*, Bushman's Nek Valley, T7011631. A large stone built self-catering cottage on a farm, B&B available on request, working farm, with organic dairy and vegetables for sale. **C** *Splashy Fen*, T7011932. Trout farm and guest cottage, site of the renowned music festival (see below). **C** *Eagle Rock Mountain Retreat*, T7011757. 4 self-catering guest cottages sleeping 2-12 people, magnificently positioned on a mountain plateau, overlooking the Mzimkulu River, private with log fires. **D** *Torridon*, on the road to Bushman's Nek, T7011637. B&B sleeping 8 people overlooking the Mzimkulu River, trout-fishing and swimming in the river. Recommended. **D** *Underberg Hotel*, Main Rd, T7011412. 18 rooms, restaurant and pub serving snacks, outdated and gloomy small town hotel.

Sleeping
■ *on map*
Price codes:
see inside front cover

Most accommodation
around Underberg
consists of B&Bs or
self-catering chalets on
local farms bordering
the Drakensberg

KwaZulu Natal

Bunters, Main St, T7012603. Affordable family à la carte menu in relaxed pub. *Mike's Restaurant*, 46 Main St, T7011565. Closed Sun evening, serves breakfast, lunch and dinner, seafood specials on Mon and Tue night. *Underberg Pub*, Main Rd. Part of the *Underberg Hotel*, serves pub grub and bar meals just like a pub in England, this is where the local farmers come to drink, there's sport on the satellite TV, rock music and plenty of beer, for a good meal try the freshly grilled trout. *White Cottage Coffee Shoppe*, White Cottage Shopping Centre, T7011589. A rustic tea room serving light snacks.

Eating
● *on map*

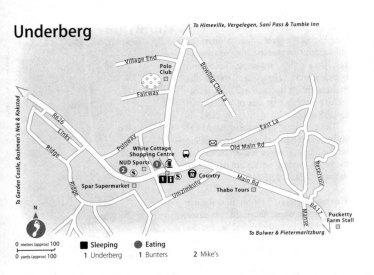

Underberg

To Himeville, Vergelegen, Sani Pass & Tumble Inn

Village End
Polo Club
Bowling Club La
Fairway
R626
Links
Ridge
East La
Potsway
White Cottage Shopping Centre
Old Main Rd
NUD Sports
Spar Supermarket
Country
Main Rd
Umzimkulu
Thabo Tours
Ridge
Reservoir
Manse
R617
Pucketty Farm Stall
To Garden Castle, Bushman's Nek & Kokstad
To Bulwer & Pietermaritzburg
N
0 metres (approx) 100
0 yards (approx) 100

■ **Sleeping**   ● **Eating**
1 Underberg   1 Bunters   2 Mike's

Festivals *Splashy Fen festival* is a small folk music festival held each **May** on Splashy Fen Farm. Over the years it has become more popular and it now attracts a broad selection of modern musicians as well as South Africa's teepee people.

Shopping The *Underberg Country Market* and the *Pucketty Farm* shop are well worth a visit if you are staying in self-catering accommodation. The Underberg Country Market is opposite the Shell service station and sells a wide range of fresh vegetables, fruit and home-made jams. The Pucketty Farm shop is 500 m out of town on the road to Bulwer and sells organic food, farm bread, eggs, yoghurts and cheeses.

Camping equipment *NUD Sports & Saddlery* on Main St and *NCD Trading* on the road to Himeville both sell hiking boots and camping equipment. In the *White Cottage Shopping Centre*, a mini shopping mall with a rather twee white picket fence, are a number of craft shops and a coffee shop.

Tour operators *Major Adventures*, T7011625, *Sani Pass Tours*, TT7011064, and *Thaba Tours*, T7012333, all offer daily 4x4 day trips up to the top of Sani Pass (see Tours under Sani Pass below). **Horse riding** Day trips on horseback are available from the hotels at Sani Pass, Drakensberg Gardens, Bushman's Nek and Coleford Nature Reserve. *Khotso Horse Trails*, is 10 km from Underburg on the road to Drakensberg Gardens, T/F7011502, contact Steve and Eva. Mountain rides for beginners and advanced riders, specialist adventure rides and cattle round-ups. **E** Accommodation is available in dorms in a log cabin with shared kitchen and bathroom or in self-catering thatched chalets.

Transport **Bus** *Sani Pass Carriers*, bookings T/F7011017, toll free T0800-167809. Run between **Underberg**, **Himeville**, **Sani Pass**, and **Pietermaritzburg**, R90 one-way, daily except Sun. The buses are minibuses not large coaches, they they pick up from *Sani Lodge*, *Sani Pass Hotel*, the *Himeville Arms* and *Underburg Hotel*, between 0830-1030 each morning, and drop off and pick up from the *Ngena Backpackers* and the *Protea Imperial Hotel* in Pietermaritzburg. They arrive back in Underberg early the same afternoon. Connections for onward inter-city coach or *Bas Bus* travel can be made on the same day in Pietermaritzburg.

Directory **Medical Services** Pharmacy: T7011034. **Hospitals:** *Riverview Hospital*, T7011911. Private hospital with 24-hr emergency service.

Himeville

Phone code: 033
(NB Always use
3-figure prefix)
Colour map 4, grid B6
Altitude: 1,600 m

Founded in 1893, Himeville is a small prosperous village reminiscent of England. Arbuckle Street runs through the village centre where there is a supermarket, post office, museum, hotel and petrol station. *Himeville Arms* is the main hotel; its distinctive Tudor architecture wouldn't be out of place in an English village.

There is a small **museum** in the old fort and prison. It is an early sandstone building with exhibits on settler history and one of the better displays on San. ■ *0830-1230, daily except Mon. T7021184.*

Himeville Nature Reserve This small reserve is set on the outskirts of Himeville where there are two dams surrounded by grassland. The 105-ha protected area is a home for water birds and the occasional blesbok and black

Himeville

To Ripon Country Cottage & Sani Pass

Clayton

Tennis Club

George

To Strathmore Cottages & Cobham

Thomas

Arbuckle

Sutton

Dartnell

To Himeville Nature Reserve

Dartnell

New

To Underberg

N

0 metres (approx) 400
0 yards (approx) 400

■ **Sleeping**
1 Himeville Arms
2 Robin's Nest

● **Eating**
1 Rose & Quail

wildebeest; look out for three different species of crane which have been bred here in captivity. The dams are popular with trout fishermen and it is possible to hire rowing boats, but you must provide your own rods. ■ *Day visitors, R10.*

C-D *Ripon Country Cottage*, contact the *Rose & Quail*, T7021154. Self-catering or B&B accommodation on a rose farm north of Himeville, sleeps up to 10 people. **C-E** *The Himeville Arms*, Arbuckle St, T/F7021305. Restaurant, swimming pool, recently underwent refurbishment having changed ownership. Rooms rather gloomy in summer, but cosy in winter thanks to well-stocked log fires. Cheaper backpacker beds in shared rooms. Good lunchtime bar menu. Local birdwatchers meet here at 1730 on the first Mon of every month. **E** *Tumble In*, Arbuckle St, T7011556. 4 en suite budget double rooms, separate entrance, secure parking.

Sleeping
■ *on map*
Price codes:
see inside front cover

   Camping F There are 10 pitches and an ablution block overlooking the dam in Himeville Nature Reserve, hot showers and baths. No electricity, gas lights only. Supplies can be bought in the village a short walk from the campsite. Reservations should be made through The Officer-in-Charge, Himeville Nature Reserve, PO Box 115, Himeville, 3256, T7021036, F7020007. Office hours, 0700-1300; 1400-1700, daily.

Rose & Quail, Arbuckle St, T7021154. Open Mon-Fri 0900-1630, Sat 0830-1230, serves light lunches and snacks, there is also a small shop here selling farm produce and home baked cakes. *The Trout House*, at the *Himeville Arms* on Arbuckle St, T7021305. An à la carte country restaurant. Recommended. The pub in the hotel is the main focal point in town, pub lunches and evening bar meals.

Eating
● *on map*

Road Bus: *Sani Pass Carriers*, T/F7011017, toll free T0800-167809. Picks up and drops off at the *Himeville Arms* (see under Underburg for details).

Transport

KwaZulu Natal

Cobham

Cobham is a fascinating wilderness area and is an ideal base for many exciting hikes. The land rising up towards the escarpment has been gouged with steep sided gorges filled with thick yellowwood forest. The view above the cliffs of the escarpment is of the Giant's Cup lying between Hodgson's Peaks and of the Drakensberg stretching out to the north and south. The Mzimkulu River rises here and flows to Port Shepstone. This area is relatively undisturbed by human activity and the clean waters of these high Drakensberg streams are a sanctuary for otters. The Cape clawless otter and the spotted-necked otter both inhabit this area. People very rarely see them, as they are very shy animals but they tend to be active at dusk and dawn. White droppings on riverbanks are a sign of their presence, the distinctive colour comes from the calcium of the crab shells which make up a large proportion of their diet.

Getting there On the road between Underberg and Himeville there is a signposted turning down the D7 on a dirt road to Cobham (14 km). Park gates open Oct-Mar 0500-1900, Apr-Sep 0600-1800. Office hrs 0800-1630 daily, T033-7020831. Entry fee R15 per person. There is a curio shop here, otherwise plan on being totally self sufficient. The nearest shops and supermarkets are in Underberg. Nights here do get cold all year round so it is a good idea to bring some warm clothing. Hiking permits for the Sani Pass area including the Giant's Cup Hiking Trail are available from this office. Caves should also be reserved here. For your own safety, a mountain rescue register must be filled in.

Ins & outs

Siphongweni Shelter The trail is a hearty 12 km round trip. The path follows the Pholela River into the valley between Siphongweni (2,258 m) and Emerald Dome (1,971 m). After 6 km there is a path heading south which rises steeply up towards Siphongweni Rock and the shelter. The paintings here have been declared a national monument and are well-known for the pictures of men on horseback. Other paintings of interest include scenes of men in canoes spear fishing and what appears to be a dancing baboon.

Hiking

Lake District A network of paths head up from Cobham into what is known as the Lake District. This is a unique part of the environment in the Drakensberg which is dotted with tarns. These upland lakes are surrounded by lush grassland and attract many waterbirds including the rare wattled crane. It is a 15 km walk up to the lakes and once there it is worth spending a couple of days exploring the area. There are several caves to sleep in which can be reserved in advance. These can accommodate a maximum of 12 people – fires are not allowed in the caves, or anywhere else within the wilderness area.

Hodgson's Peaks The 20 km walk up the Pholela River Valley to Masubasuba Pass at 3,050 m, is the most challenging hike from Cobham. It is possible to complete the hike in two days by sleeping at the top of the Pass and returning the next day. However, the hike is quite strenuous enough and is best tackled in three days. Gorge Cave and Spectacle Cave make an ideal base camp from which to tackle the final ascent up the steep sides of the rock amphitheatre on a day trip.

Sleeping
Price codes:
see inside front cover

Camping **F** The campsite here is very basic with an open area for setting up tents and you need to be totally self-sufficient. There are 8 toilets but no showers. **F** *Trail Huts*, there are 5 30-bed trail huts on the Giant's Cup Hiking Trail. Reservations for campsites and caves should be made through the Cobham Office, PO Box 168, Himeville 3256, T033-7020831. Cost, R48 per person per night.

Sani Pass

Phone code: 033
(NB Always use 3-figure prefix)
Colour map 4, grid B6

The road from Himeville to Sani Pass (15 km), rises steadily through rolling hills covered in grassland and patches of pine plantation until it passes the Sani Top Chalet and the 3,000 m peaks on the escarpment come into view. This is the only road leading into Lesotho on its eastern border with South Africa. Sani Pass was originally used by traders transporting goods by mule into Basutoland. A trading post was opened in the 1920s at Good Hope Farm at the bottom of the pass, which was the closest store to Mokhotlong in Lesotho. Then the Sani Pass was little more than a bridalpath, but it was upgraded to a road in 1955 after the first 4x4 Landrover managed to complete the ascent. Maize and trade goods, including a fair number of guns, were taken up, whilst wool and hides were taken down. Trade still continues on this route, although these days most traders supplying shops in Lesotho now have their own 4x4s and prefer to drive to the larger warehouses in Pietermaritzburg to stock up on goods. The Good Hope trading post closed in 1990 but the remains of the buildings can still be seen at the bottom of the pass. The Pass is a popular attraction with tourists and organized trips are available up to the top. The road is one of the most dramatic in Africa, and the top of the pass is so high that it has a distinct Alpine climate. The flora and fauna have adapted to this harsh environment and some of the Drakensberg's rarest species can be found here. Hodgson's Peaks, at 3,256 m and 3,229 m, the Twelve Apostles, and Sani Pass at 2,874 m present a formidable range of peaks and are at their most beautiful after snow.

Climate May, Jun and Jul are the best months to explore the many hiking trails in the park. The mild and sunny weather at this time of year is ideal for walking, rain is unusual but there are occasional snowfalls. Night-time temperatures at the top of the pass can descend to -16°C, although temperatures lower down the pass seldom go below -5°C. During the summer months of Nov, Dec and Jan, the park is greener and more beautiful due to the thunderstorms every afternoon.

Hiking
Survey maps can be borrowed from Sani Lodge for a deposit of R50

The most rewarding hike in this area must be the day hike up to the top of Sani Pass at 2,874 m. There is a car park at the South African border post from where it is a further 14-km hike to the top. The trail is quite straightforward and just involves following the road. The views from the top are spectacular.

KwaZulu Natal

There are a number of shorter walks, which visit **Gxalingwena**, **Kaula** and **Ikanti Shelter**. These are cave-like dwellings that are home to a number of San rock paintings. New regulations stipulate that for the protection of the paintings, they must only be visited with a registered guide. These can be arranged from the Sani Pass Hotel or Sani Lodge.

Tours

A number of operators organize day tours from Underberg, and the *Sani Pass Hotel* and Sani Lodge, over the border to Lesotho. Travellers are taken up the road to the top of Sani Pass by Land Rover. The road is terrifyingly steep and winding but the views are outstanding. The tours are a good way to discover local history and wildlife and include a visit to a Basotho village to see sheep shearing, maize cultivation, or beer making. A picnic lunch in the Black Mountains or lunch at the *Sani Top Chalet* is included, and most definitely a glass of warming mulled wine at the pub at the *Sani Top Chalet* – at 2874 m it is the highest pub in Africa!

In spite of its isolation you should expect full border formalities at Sani Pass. The crossing is normally quick and easy but you will need your passport. The route up to the pass was originally made by using dynamite to blow a road out of the rock. The road is so rough that saloon cars are not allowed past the border post. Access to the pass is restricted to four-wheel drive vehicles, motorbikes, mountain bikes and people on foot. The South African border post is open daily 0800-1600, the Lesotho border post is open daily 0700-1700. If you are hiking, the walk between the two borderposts takes about 3 hours.

KwaZulu Natal

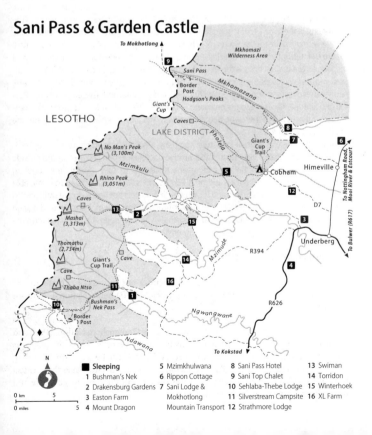

Sani Pass & Garden Castle

Sleeping		
1 Bushman's Nek	5 Mzimkhulwana	8 Sani Pass Hotel	13 Swiman
2 Drakensburg Gardens	6 Rippon Cottage	9 Sani Top Chalet	14 Torridon
3 Easton Farm	7 Sani Lodge &	10 Sehlaba-Thebe Lodge	15 Winterhoek
4 Mount Dragon	Mokhotlong	11 Silverstream Campsite	16 XL Farm
	Mountain Transport	12 Strathmore Lodge	

Interestingly, there are no customs and immigration officials at this border and all formalities are conducted by the police. This could be due in some part to the high incidence of *dagga* (marijuana) smuggling. We have heard reports of some overnight hikers on the *KZN Wildlife* trails coming across Lesotho smugglers with great bags of *dagga* hiding in the mountains awaiting nightfall so they can cross into South Africa undetected.

Sleeping

■ *on map, page 493*
Price codes:
see inside front cover

B *Sani Pass Hotel*, Sani Pass Rd, 22 km from Underberg, T7021320, F7020220. This is a large resort hotel offering accommodation either in the hotel building or in luxury cottages in the gardens, sporting facilities include squash, tennis, bowls, riding and swimming. Large restaurant with a reasonably priced set menu, unfortunately the meals are based on rather uninspiring English cuisine, tinned peaches and ice cream for dessert and the like. Despite its beautiful location, accommodation is overpriced. The **D-F** *Sani Top Chalet*, is at 2,874 m at the top of the pass next to the Lesotho border post, T033-7021158, T082-7151131 (mob). A combination of double rooms in the main building or backpacker bunks in rondavels out back. The hotel has a licensed pub (the highest in Africa) and dining room warmed with roaring wood fires, overlooking the dramatic road below. When it does snow it is possible to hire skis from the hotel. Don't expect too much as the skis are rather dated models and have seen a lot of use. **F** *Sani Lodge*, 19 km from Underberg on the Sani Pass road, call for collection from Underberg, T7020330, F7021401. If you are coming from Pietermaritzburg, travel with *Sani Pass Carriers* see page for details, who drop off here. This is one of the best backpackers away from the big towns in South Africa, always have good memories. It is the ideal place to base yourself at and explore the Drakensberg. There are 4 small dorms, 5 large double rooms with pine ceilings and good insulation, 2 private rondavels, a 22-bed dorm for large groups, and plenty of space to pitch a tent or two, outside hot shower with tremendous views of the mountains. In the large kitchen there is all you need to prepare your own meals, comfortable lounge with open fire for the winter months when it can get very cold, and a veranda with a superb uninterrupted view of the Drakensberg escarpment. Aside from the location, one of the lodge's great attractions is the good, healthy food. Breakfast, lunch, and evening meals available at very reasonable rates, plus packed lunches, there is help yourself chocolate cake, perfect after a day's walking, the *Giant's Cup Tea Garden* is attached. The lodge is run by Russell and Simone who are experts on hiking in Lesotho. Recommended. Some people complain about access, but then who needs a highway and a daily bus service leading into the middle of a beautiful wilderness?

Also based here is a small local tour company, *Drakensberg Adventures*, T7021401, suchet@futurenet.co.za Here Russell and Simone pool their expert knowledge and provide visitors with all the information and means necessary to fully explore the southern Drakensberg mountains. Russell is author of *A Backpackers Guide to Lesotho* and a formidable guide for the Sani Pass excursion and local hikes. Simone lets her hands do the walking and offers Aromatherepy massages. On offer are 4x4 tours, hikes to San rock art, horse riding and of special interest, visits to local Zulu families where you can spend the night and have the opportunity to learn in a relaxed and friendly environment.

Mkhomazi Wilderness Area

Garden Castle and Bushman's Nek (see below) are the access points to the Mzimkhulu Wilderness Area which borders Sehlabethebe National Park in Lesotho.

Vergelegen Vergelegen is one of the more remote reserves in the Drakensberg National Park and as such receives few visitors. Thaba Ntlenyana on the Lesotho side of the border is the highest mountain in Southern Africa at 3,482 m and can be seen from the top of the escarpment in the reserve. The rugged mountain terrain here makes this an ideal base from which to explore the mountains on some of the most inaccessible and demanding hiking trails in the Drakensberg.

Ins and outs Entry fee R15. There is a camp office at Vergelegen where hikers can register, otherwise facilities such as petrol or basic food supplies are not available here and visitors should plan on being completely self-sufficient. Permits are needed for hikes which leave from Vergelegen. Overnight hiking permits cost R20 per person.

Hiking The Pyramid is a short 3 km walk from the camp to a free standing peak at 1,782 m. This is an ideal place to get for good views of the reserve before tackling some of the more challenging hikes to **Lynx Cave**, 14 km, **Mkhomazi Pass**, 18 km, and **Nhlangeni Pass**, 22 km.

Nkangala The 23 km hike is a fascinating if strenuous way to explore the Mkhomazi Wilderness Area. Some hikers prefer to do the trail in two days. The trail follows the Mlahlangubo omhoane River Valley through indigenous forest passing streams and waterfalls up to the rock arch on Nkangala Ridge. The network of paths in this valley make it possible to choose a different route back down.

Sleeping D 2 self-catering chalets with 5 beds each. Reservations through *KZN Wildlife*, T033-8451000, F033-8451001. **Camping F** It is now possible to camp overnight within the reserve on long distance hikes.

Price codes: see inside front cover

The landscape at Loteni is mainly rolling grassland rising up towards the High Berg and Redi Peak at 3,298 m. The grassland is interspersed with patches of protea woodland, tree ferns and the rare Berg bamboo. The demand for timber in the first half of this century resulted in most of the indigenous woodland being cut down leaving large areas of grassland. The land was then used for grazing and as farmland until the 1950s when it was bought by the KwaZulu Natal Parks Board. The original farmhouse (at the camp) was built in 1905 and is now the **Settlers' Homestead**

Loteni

KwaZulu Natal

Mkhomazi Wilderness Area

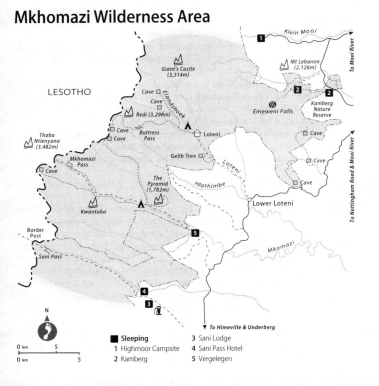

■ **Sleeping**
1 Highmoor Campsite
2 Kamberg
3 Sani Lodge
4 Sani Pass Hotel
5 Vergelegen

Museum where the lifestyle of the early settlers has been recreated. Wagons, farm tools and period furniture are on display here.

Ins and outs The reserve can be reached either from Himeville or from Nottingham Road; both access routes are along rough dirt tracks which can become impassable during heavy rains. The most popular route is the signposted dirt track from Himeville which heads north for 45 km towards Loteni Store and the reserve. The Nottingham Road track heads southeast for 60 km to Loteni Store from where there is a signposted turning for the last 10 km to the reserve.

Park gates open Oct-Mar, 0500-1900, Apr-Sep, 0600-1800. Entry fee R15 per person, T033-7020540. Permits for overnight hiking cost R20 per person. There is a camp shop here which sells hiking maps and permits, otherwise the nearest shop is at the Loteni Store 14 km from the entrance to the camp. Petrol is not available here.

Best time to visit Streams cutting down through the rock have formed narrow wooded gorges which have been stocked with brown trout. The trout season lasts from Sep-Apr and during these months accommodation at weekends can be fully booked. Spring is also a popular time for visitors who come to see the magnificent wild flowers.

Hiking There are three leisurely day hikes around Loteni. The path from the campsite heading up the Loteni River Valley passes the eMpophomeni Falls and reaches a fork in the river after 5 km. The path splits here; the right hand path follows the Loteni River into a narrow gorge to **Ash Cave**, which is a further 3 km; the path to Yellowwood Cave follows the left hand trail up the Ka-Mashilenga tributary for another 2 km. Both routes pass through areas of indigenous forest.

There are two longer overnight hikes to **Redi Peak**, 13 km, and to **Hlathimbe Cave**, 17 km. Although the distance in kilometres on these trails seems relatively short, both these trails involve strenuous climbs and it is best to plan on spending at least one night camping. As the trails climb up into the mountains they are less clearly marked and difficult to follow without a map.

The path to Redi Peak ascends Buttress Pass where it heads north. The path itself stops just short of the summit of Redi Peak which at an altitude of 3,298 m offers magnificent views over Natal.

The trail to **Hlathimbe Cave** is a continuation of the ascent to Redi Peak, although there is an alternative less strenuous route up which was originally used by San driving back cattle from their raids on farms lower down the Loteni Valley. From Hlathimbe Cave you can see The Fingers and Hlathimbe Pass.

During hot weather it is worth remembering that it is safe to **swim** in the Loteni River when it is not in flood. There are some natural pools a short walk from the camp although the water flowing straight off the mountains can be icy.

Sleeping
■ *on map, page 495*
Price codes:
see inside front cover

C 2 self-catering cottages with 6 beds, and **E** 12 self-catering bungalows, with either 2 or 3 beds. All the accommodation is fully equipped; there are two freezers in the camp kitchen which can be used by guests, electricity from 1700-2200 only. **C** *Simes Rustic Cottage*, sleeps 10, although the minimum charge is for 6 people. The cottage originally belonged to a farmer called Symes who lived there for 43 years. The small dam nearby has been stocked with brown trout and is exclusively for the use of visitors staying at the cottage. The cottage is now self-catering and has a gas supply but visitors are expected to bring their own bedding. **Reservations** through *KZN Wildlife*, T033-8451000, F033-8451001. **Camping F** The 10 sites are a secluded 2 km from the hutted camp. The only facilities there are an ablution block with hot and cold water. Reservations for campsites should be made through the Officer in Charge, Loteni, PO Box 14, Himeville 3256, T/F033-7020540.

Transport Returning to Underberg the R626 continues south, 5 km out of Underberg there is a turning on the right to Garden Castle, which is then a further 30 km away. Bushman's Nek is 45 km from Underberg and is also signposted off the R626.

The Giant's Cup Hiking Trail

The trail covers 60 km in five days averaging around 13 km per day. The trail runs from Sani Pass to Bushmen's Nek and follows the contours round the edge of the escarpment. Nights are spent sleeping in well-equipped huts with wood burning stoves and hot showers. The trail costs R48 per person per day plus a daily park entry fee of R15. The trail never climbs above 2,000 m and must be one of the most leisurely ways to explore the Drakensberg. It crosses some of the most beautiful areas of the Southern Drakensberg

where apart from the mountain scenery it is also possible to see Lammergeyers, blue cranes, eland, and other wildlife. On completing the trail it is possible to arrange a pick up by Russell at Sani Lodge if you are staying at the lodge before and after the trail. Reservations for the trail should be made through KZN Wildlife, PO Box 13053, Cascades 3202, T033-8451000, F033-8451001, bookings@kznwildlife.com, in Pietermaritzburg where maps and information are available.

Garden Castle is the southernmost reserve in the Drakensberg Park, a wild area with few visitors where you are likely to see eland, grey rhebok and reedbuck. The landscape consists mostly of grassland with patches of proteas and tree ferns with some bush along river valleys. There are many tarns in this part of the Drakensberg where waterbirds and wildlife can be seen. There are magnificent views up into the mountains on a clear day with the mountain peaks of **Walker** at 3,322 m, **Wilson** at 3,342 m and the **Rhino** at 3,051 m towering over the reserve.

Garden Castle
*Phone code: 033
(NB Always use 3-figure prefix)
See map page 493*

KwaZulu Natal

Ins and outs From Underburg the park is clearly signposted. There are two entrances, one at Drakensberg Garden (34 km), and at Bushmen's Nek (45 km). The police border post with Lesotho at Bushmen's Nek is open daily from 0800-1600, though this is only really open to local people and tourists rarely use this route.

Park gates open, Oct-Mar, 0500-1900, Apr-Sep, 0600-1800. Entry fee R15 per person. In addition to the standard park entry fee, hikers must pay an overnight hiking fee of R20 plus R48 per person per night if they choose to stay in one of the three overnight huts along the trail. Each of these huts can accommodate up to 30 people. During the winter months hikers are strongly advised to stay in these huts. There can be heavy snowfalls and very cold nights. Overnight hikers must complete the Mountain Rescue Register before starting their hike and make sure they sign in on return. There are plenty of caves to spend the night in, but no fires are allowed anywhere within the reserve. Bookings for the caves can be made through The Officer in Charge, Garden Castle, PO Box 378, Underberg 3257, T033-7011823, F7011822. The office has a small shop which sells basic supplies, permits and hiking maps, otherwise the nearest shops are in Underberg. Petrol is not available here.

Hiking The highest peak in this area which can be hiked up in a day is the strenuous 11 km trail leading up to **Mashai Pass** (peak 3,313 m) and **Rhino Peak** at 3,051 m. **Engagement Cave** and **Sleeping Beauty Cave** are only 4 km from the Parks Board office, and are easily visited in a morning. From here it is also possible to join the Giant's Cup Hiking Trail (see below).

The **Giant's Cup Hiking Trail** starts at Sani Pass and ends at Bushman's Nek (see box on page 497). Hikers will find themselves at the Swiman Hut at Bushmen's Nek on the last night of the five-day hike. There are many options for day hikes around Bushman's Nek to various caves including **Thomathu Cave**, 10 km, and Lammergeyer Cave, 11 km.

Sleeping In the park: Huts F There are 3 rustic huts on the Giant's Cup Hiking Trail and 12 **Caves F** in the park available to hikers, all of which should be booked in advance through the parks office, T033-7011823.

Price codes: see inside front cover

Outside the park: B-D *Penwarn Country Lodge*, PO Box 253, Underberg, T033-7011777, F033-7011342. A luxury converted barn close to Bushman's Nek, 25 km from Underberg. 5 en suite bedrooms, 3 simple self-catering log cabins plus a basic cave dwelling for the adventurous and budget minded. This is a comfortable mountain farm offering a wide range of activities: canoeing, fly fishing, mountain biking, hiking and hunting by special arrangement. Excellent food and a warm homely atmosphere during the winter months. Recommended.

Battlefield Route

This area of vast open landscape in northern KwaZulu Natal is made up of large plains and savannah grasslands interspersed with acacias. Small granite koppies dot the landscape and there are large plateaux stretching to the horizon. It is the stage on which three major wars have been fought. The battlefield sites of the clashes between Boers, Britons and Zulus can all be visited, although some are little more than a small commemorative plaque and may be a mite disappointing if you've travelled a long way to reach them. This is also a hard-working area, with numerous large farms raising cattle and sheep, industrial towns in the north, coalfields around Dundee and a giant steelworks in Newcastle.

The battlefield sites themselves are not always as spectacular as might be expected. There is often little left to see except war graves and monuments to the dead and probably the best way to appreciate the history behind the battles is to go on an organized tour (it is possible to do a tour of the major battlefield sites in a day). Two of the best museums dealing with these events are the Siege Museum at Ladysmith and the Talana Museum in Dundee. Of the wars fought between the Voortrekkers and the Zulus, the most interesting battlefield site is Blood River, east of Dundee. Two of the most interesting historical sites of the Anglo-Zulu War are Isandlwana and Rorke's Drift. The best Boer War sites to visit are Talana, the Siege of Ladysmith, and Spioenkop.

Ladysmith

Altitude: 1,015 m
Phone code: 036
(NB Always use 3-figure prefix)
Colour map 4, grid A6

Ladysmith is a quiet rural town surrounded by cattle and sheep ranches. The town is well-connected by road and rail to Durban and Johannesburg, and although there is some industrial development, the town centre has a modern shopping complex, Victorian buildings and the Siege Museum is a good place from which to start a visit to the Battlefields Route. In recent years, the town centre has undergone a transformation, and has much more of a vibrant African feel to it. For the black population, Ladysmith is much more famous for the Ladysmith Black Mambazo band, which is phenomenally popular in South Africa, rather than the somewhat stuffy battlefield sites.

Ins & outs **Getting there** Ladysmith is on the N11 and is well-connected to the highway network. The N11 heads north to Newcastle (100 km), Volksrust (153 km), and into Mpumalanga. 26 km south of Ladysmith the N11 connects with the N3, which in turn leads north into the Free State and south to Durban. The N11 also connects at this junction with the R616 leading to the Northern Drakensberg.

Tourist office *Ladysmith Information Bureau*, at the museum, Murchison St, T/F6372992. Open Mon-Fri 0900-1600, Sat 0900-1300. There is a good selection of maps and leaflets on the Battlefields. The bureau is also very helpful with booking accommodation and advising on Battlefield Tours. Guided tours can also be booked from Durban, Pietermaritzburg and Dundee.

The Voortrekkers first arrived in 1847 and established a small republican settlement on the banks of the Klip River. However, it was only a matter of months before the area fell under the British sphere of influence. Ladysmith originally consisted of a trading post and a small village known as Windsor, named after George Windsor the trader who was first based here. The name was later changed, in 1850, to honour the wife of Sir Harry Smith, governor of the Cape.

British settlers began to arrive during the 1850s to farm in the area. One of Ladysmith's first industries was a lard factory set up by two Scotsmen who culled the region's vast herds of zebra and melted down their fat. Ladysmith grew in importance as a trading centre because it was on the trail connecting the diamond and gold mines of the interior, Kimberley and Barberton, with Port Natal on the coast.

Ladysmith is most famous for being besieged by General Piet Joubert for 120 days during the Boer War (see box next page). The British garrison of 12,500 men was cut off for the duration. Food and water were in such short supply that by the end of the siege the daily bread ration for each person was only 230g.

Ladysmith's historical monuments are on the main square by the Town Hall on Murchison Street. **The Town Hall** on the corner of Murchison Street and Queen Street is a classic Victorian municipal building which was completed in 1893. During the siege it was converted into a hospital until the clock tower was hit by a 6 in shell. The patients were then moved to the Dutch Reformed Church. The Town Hall was then repaired in 1901 after the end of the siege. There is a small museum here with a gallery of photographs illustrating Ladysmith's history up to the present day.

Sights
A walk around the town centre to see these sights will take less than 2 hrs

Siege Museum is next to the Town Hall, on Murchison Street. This is a fascinating museum which reconstructs scenes from the Siege of Ladysmith and the Boer War. There are displays of weapons, uniforms and household goods that were in use during the siege. ■ *Mon-Fri 0900-1600, Sat 0900-1300. Small entry fee. T6372992.*

There are four field guns on Murchison Street just outside the museum. **Castor** and **Pollux** are the two guns sent from Cape Town at the outbreak of the Boer War for the defence of the town. **Long Tom** is a replica of the Creussot Fortress Guns

KwaZulu Natal

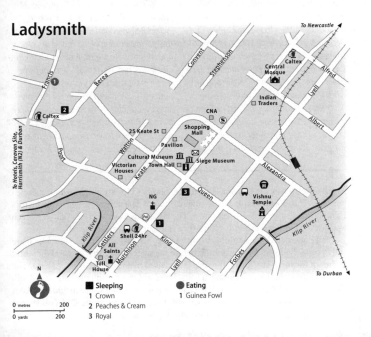

Ladysmith

Sleeping
1 Crown
2 Peaches & Cream
3 Royal

Eating
1 Guinea Fowl

To Newcastle

To Durban

0 metres 200
0 yards 200

The siege of Ladysmith

The siege of the British in Ladysmith by Boer forces lasted from early in the Anglo-Boer War, October 1899, until February 1900 – 118 days in total. The British forces in northern Natal, under General White, had been forced to withdraw into Ladysmith after a series of defeats at the hands of Boers from both the Free State and Transvaal. The Boer forces had taken up positions in approximately a 6 mile radius around the town, but made few attempts to defeat decisively the 10,000 remaining British troops. The Boers, under the command of Piet Joubert (ably assisted by his tactically minded wife) did make one major assault on the British defences at Bester's Ridge on 6 January 1900. The British were, however, able to repulse the attack, though it placed a further strain on their already stretched resources.

The Boer forces decided to concentrate on starving-out the British or shelling them into submission whilst they held off any British attempts to relieve the town from the south by establishing secure defensive positions in the hills overlooking the Tugela River. For the besieged British troops the defence of Ladysmith required patience and organization rather than heroics. In December 1899 General White had been ordered to try to break-out and join up with the British forces under Buller attempting an advance through Colenso – but details of when the advance was to take place were never relayed to him and the first he knew of the attack actually happening was when he heard the artillery fire. After the losses sustained in the defence of Bester's Ridge in

January 1900, White was unable to offer any support to General Buller's forces in their attempts to relieve Ladysmith and all his troops could do was sit tight and survive the bombardment as best they possibly could.

Conditions for the town's inhabitants, whether military or civilian were harsh. Food and other provisions were in short supply and what was available became exceptionally expensive. Tins of condensed milk, for example, could fetch up to a pound and bottles of whisky seven pounds. One source of comfort for the civilians and wounded was that the Boer commanders allowed them to set up a camp and hospital at Intombi some four miles southeast of the town so that they were spared the heavy artillery bombardment of the town centre. News of Buller's numerous blunders at Colenso, Spion Kop and other battles along the Tugela did nothing for morale, however, and many inhabitants felt it was only a matter of time until they had to give in to the Boers.

In February 1900 Buller's substantial army at last had some success in assaults on the Boer positions along the Tugela. On 27 February the British succeeded in taking Pieter's Railway and Terrace Hills overlooking the railway crossing of the Tugela at Colenso and the Boer forces surrounding Ladysmith rapidly lost morale. As news of the decisive defeat of General Conje's forces in the northern Cape filtered through to the Boer lines their resolve snapped and they fell back towards Elandslaagte, many in fact returning home, leaving the path clear for Buller's troops to at last relieve Ladysmith.

which were used by the Transvaal Republic to bombard Ladysmith from the surrounding hills. The Boers destroyed the original gun at Haenertsburg when Kitchener's Fighting Scouts threatened to capture it. The last gun is a German *Feldkanonne* which was captured in German South West Africa and sent back as a war trophy.

Walking south down Murchison Street there are two historical hotels which are still in use. The *Royal Hotel* was built before the siege during the gold and diamond rushes of the interior. During the siege it was used by the press corps as a base. The *Crown Hotel* is the site of Ladysmith's first hotel which was built of wattle and daub. The earliest battlefield tours, on horseback, could be booked here in 1904. Further down Murchison Street, on the corner with Princess Street, is the **Old Toll House** where wagon drivers paid a toll before entering town.

Walking north up Murchison Street to the junction with Albert Street visitors can see what is left of the old Indian district. Before the introduction of the Group Areas Act this used to be a thriving trading area. **Surat's House**, **Seedat's** and **Asmal's Stores** were all magnificent buildings in the 1920s when they were built. These buildings fell into disrepair when the Indian traders were forcibly relocated to the 'Oriental Plaza'. Just next door are two other buildings from the same period, the **NGR Institute** is a magnificent structure built in 1903 to house railway workers, and the **Central Mosque**, completed in 1922 with its beautiful fountain and courtyard surrounded by palm trees.

A refreshingly non-historical site is the new **Cultural Museum**, 25 Keate St behind the town hall. Housed in a restored Victorian house, there is a collection of cultural and natural history exhibits, a township shack, and a tribute to the Drakensberg Boys' Choir. There is also a hall totally dedicated to the **Ladysmith Black Mambazo** – the world-renowned group that became South Africa's most successful band. The music-filled hall contains the footprints of the members of the band eternalized in concrete and life-size cut outs of the band on a mock-up stage. ■ *Mon-Fri 0900-1600, Sat 0900-1300. Small entry fee. T6372231.*

Sleeping
■ *on map, page 499*
Price codes:
see inside front cover

Town centre C *Bullers Rest Lodge*, 61 Cove Cres, T6310310, F6373549. B&B in a family atmosphere fine views of the mountains, chalets with double & single rooms, ensuite facilities. The *Boer War Pub* has a fine collection battlefield artifacts. Located near the site of the Naval Gun Shield, also a short walk from the golf course. Run by Andy & Sheila, ask to hear the story about the cellar. Recommended. C *Ladysmith Motel*, Durban Rd, T/F6376908. TV, functional chalets sleeping 4 people in a motel next to the airfield. Restaurant and bar. C *Crown Hotel*, 90 Murchison St, T6372266, F6376458. Mix of modern double & single rooms with en suite facilities, a/c, TV, comfortable grill restaurant and bar serving buffet dinners. C *Royal Hotel*, 140 Murchison St, T/F6372176. 71 rooms decorated in colonial style, TV, a/c, 4 restaurants – one of which is regarded as the best in town, 3 bars, swimming pool and garden. Busy town centre hotel with an interesting history.

D *Peaches & Cream*, 4 Berea Rd, T6310954. B&B accommodation. D *Bonnie Highlands*, Cresswell Rd, T6378390. 5 double rooms in a fine old town house. Evening meals on request. The peaceful gardens make for the perfect base to return to at the end of a day exploring the Battlefields. D *Hydeswood Farm*, Hyde Rd, T/F6355012. Farmhouse B&B, satellite TV, swimming pool, overlooks the battlesite at Nicholson's Neck. Evening meals available on request. Abundant birdlife in the gardens. Ask for Jeannette or Peter.

Out of town C *Woodlands Lodge*, 23 km from Ladysmith, follow the Ezakheni road out of town, after 17 km turn left onto the D46 gravel road and follow signs, T/F6319026. Accommodation consists of 6 double rooms, with en suite bathrooms, rooms are light and spacious. If you wish to self-cater there is a spotless fitted kitchen with all necessary equipment. At the end of the day you can choose between 2 lounges to enjoy a sun downer. Upstairs the lounge opens onto a large veranda overlooking the garden; the downstairs lounge has a large open fire place for the winter nights, a popular feature at any time. This is a working farm with plenty of cattle and limited wildlife, if you want to, you can work from horseback and assist the owners with some of the daily tasks. On a more sedate level, guests can play a game of tennis or try their hand at bass fishing in one of three dams on the farm, these dams are also excellent spots for a bit of twitching. D *Naunton Guest House*, 4 km from town centre off the Newcastle Rd (N11), T/F6313307. Double rooms with en suite facilities, TV, cosy pub, eve meals available on request. A pleasant alternative to suburban B&B's. D *Rietkuil Country Cottages*, 12 km out of town off the Newcastle Rd (N11), T/F6319021. 3 6-bed chalets with TV, fridge and coffee machine. All with private patio, braai facilities and set in fine gardens with mountain views. Evening meals on request.

Eating
● *on map, page 499*

Guinea Fowl, Shop 13, Marco Centre, Francis Rd, T6378163. Steakhouse, known for their excellent ribs. Good value and friendly. The *Royal Hotel*, 140 Murchison St, T/F6372176 has four restaurants to choose from: *Mario's Famiglia Restorante*, serves pasta and pizzas; *Royal Carvery*, serves a selection of steaks and has a large buffet; *Swainsons*, an elegant á la

KwaZulu Natal

carte dining room which reputedly servers the best meals, giant Sun lunch buffet, good choice for the rest of the week; and *Tipsy Trooper*, casual atmosphere, good pub lunches. *Santa Catalina Spur*, Oval Shopping Centre, T6311260. Family restaurant serving big portions of steak, ribs, and chicken.

Tour operators *Liz Spiret*, T6377702. *John Snyman*, T6310660. Tours of the battlefields: Isandlwana, Rorke's Drift, Blood River and Spioenkop Battle.

Transport **Rail** Enquiries, T2712020. The *Trans Natal* departs to **Johannesburg** and **Pretoria** (7 hrs), daily at 0020; and **Durban** (6 hrs), daily 0217; the *Trans Oranje* departs to **Cape Town** (28 hrs), on Thu 2320; to **Durban** (6 hrs), Mon 0122.

Road **Bus**: *Greyhound*, central reservations T011-2498900, coaches depart from Ted's Service Station (next to *Wimpy*), to **Durban** (3 hrs), daily at 1615; to **Johannesburg** and **Pretoria** (7 hrs), daily at 1350. *Translux*, T012-3154300, coaches depart from Ted's Service Station. **Johannesburg**, and **Pretoria**: daily, 1145. **NB** *Translux* do not operate a southbound service.

Directory **Medical services** Hospitals: *La Verna Private Hospital*, T6310065.

South of Ladysmith

The region lying to the south of Ladysmith is where many of the Boer War Battlefields are located. The sites are often marked by monuments to the dead and the graves of those who fell. The Siege Museum in Ladysmith will help to arrange tours or provide a detailed map if you have your own car.

Colenso
Phone code: 036
(NB Always use 3-figure prefix)
Colour map 4, grid A6

The town was named after John William Colenso, the Anglican Bishop of Natal from 1853 to 1883. The first advance by British troops trying to break the siege at Ladysmith was foiled here by General Louis Botha in a battle fought along the Tugela River. It was to be a further two months before Ladysmith was relieved. The small **RE Stevenson Museum** is next to the Borough Offices. It concentrates on the Battle of Colenso, with exhibits of weapons, medals and photographs. There are also two vintage steam engines and a steam tractor. ■ *Tue-Fri 0900-1600, Sat-Sun 0900-1200, closed Mon.*

It's an easy excursion from Ladysmith, but there are a couple of accommodation options in Colenso

Sleeping **D** *Aloes Game Farm*, 12 km from N3 Colenso turnoff, T4222834, F4222592. Rustic self-catering cottage, sleeps up to 5 people. Birdwatching, game drives, fishing. Ask for George or Lynda. Close to Weenen Game Reserve. **D** *Battlefields Hotel*, 75 Sir George St, T4222242. B&B, restaurant, secure parking, in a historic building used as a commandeering post during the Anglo-Boer War.

Weenen Game Reserve

The 6,500 ha reserve is 20 km south of Colenso on the R74 to Weenen. It is the core area of the much larger Thukela Biosphere Reserve. The reserve has been hailed as a conservation success in as much as it has succeeded in converting heavily eroded farmland into an area where the flora and fauna indigenous to the Natal Midlands have been re-established. This is one of the many reserves created during the Apartheid era where local farmers were forcibly relocated to homelands and, as the farmers have received little benefit from the conversion of their farms into a nature reserve, there is still some controversy surrounding it.

Ins & outs **Getting there** Travelling up from Durban on the N3 take the Estcourt junction and then follow the R74 to the reserve, 25 km. Alternatively, approaching from Ladysmith follow the R74 to Colenso and then on to Weenen.

Colenso

In December 1899 the British Commander-in-Chief Redvers Buller, newly arrived in Natal, was keen to lift the siege of Ladysmith. After the initial Boer advances the war in Natal had reached stalemate, with the Boers unable to break out south towards Durban and the British unable to cross the Tugela and move north towards Ladysmith and Newcastle. At first Buller had told London that a frontal assault on the Boer positions overlooking the rail crossing of the Tugela at Colenso was impossible but by 15 December, he had changed his mind.

At Colenso Buller had 18,000 British troops at his command compared with only 6,000 Boer commandos under Louis Botha. British reconnaissance, however, had not realized the full extent of the heavily fortified Boer positions.

Out of range of Boer rifles, the Naval Guns, called up to support the Royal Artillery, pounded Boer positions above the Tugela to the west of Colenso before the first advance of the battle by the Irish Fifth Brigade, under Fitzroy Hart. The British had been informed by African guides that there was an easy ford of the river at the cusp of a sharp meander to the west of Colenso but when Hart and his troops arrived at the river they discovered it strewn with barbed wire and, under intense Boer rifle fire, they were forced to retreat, suffering heavy casualties.

The second British advance, under General Henry Hildyard, was to attempt to take the railway crossing directly to the north of Colenso. It got off to a disastrous start, however, and never looked likely to achieve its objective. The Royal Artillery had been sighted too close to Boer lines and when they opened fire in advance of the main assault the gunners were decimated by Boer rifle fire. With their ammunition exhausted the surviving gunners were forced to abandon the guns and take cover in a dried watercourse. A six gun Naval brigade on the British right flank, far enough to the rear to avoid the Boer rifles, was able to keep firing but without full artillery cover Hildyard's troops were fatally exposed. Some British troops managed to make it as far as the wagon bridge just to the west of Colenso but, suffering heavy losses, were ordered to retire.

The British attack had been a disaster and Redvers Buller was renamed in the angry British press, 'Reverse' Buller.

KwaZulu Natal

The vegetation here is mostly grasslands interspersed with acacia woodland. Many of **Wildlife** the larger game animals have been reintroduced while some of the smaller species have recolonized the area themselves. One of the great attractions is the opportunity to view both black and white rhino, which are endangered species and can no longer be seen in some of the better known large national parks of Africa. Elephant have recently been introduced and other more common species include the following; kudu, giraffe, roan antelope, zebra, eland, buffalo, common reedbuck, klipspringer, red hartebeest, grey duiker, bushbuck, steenbok, hyena, mountain reedbuck, black-backed jackal, wildebeest and ostrich can all be seen. Leopard are present but are rarely caught sight of. This is a good reserve for birdwatchers, more than 250 species have been recorded here including korhaans, blue crane and the scimitarbilled woodhoopoe.

Viewing There are three short walking trails, three picnic sites, a 47 km network of game viewing dirt roads, 4x4 trails, and the Isipho Hide which can be rented at night for game viewing over a water hole. There is also a feeding point for vultures. But one of the great treats here is the opportunity to go on an early morning guided walk when you can view buffalo and black rhino, some of the grandest beasts in the bush. These walks last up to 3 hours and if possible are best booked before you arrive at the reserve.

Camping F 12 pitches for tents and caravans are near the entrance gate. There is an ablu- **Sleeping** tion block plus one A-frame hut, sleeping 5 people, which has an entertaining feature – an *Price codes:* exclusive picnic site overlooking a waterhole. The small shop here only sells a limited range *see inside front cover* of food so visitors should bring supplies with them. Reservations should be made through

The Officer-in-Charge, PO Box 122, Weenen 3325, T036-3547013. Further supplies are available in the village of Weenen 8 km from the reserve.

North of Ladysmith

The battlefield route passes through a sparsely populated region divided into cattle ranches. This is the area of Isandlwana, Rorke's Drift and Blood River. The R602 leaves the N11 26 km north of Ladysmith and shortly passes the village of Elandslaagte where there is a signpost leading to the site of the Battle of Elandslaagte. On the 21 October 1899 British forces abandoned the village and the railway station. They had kept it open to enable the Dundee garrison to retreat back to Ladysmith. (The site is open daily.) The R602 continues to Dundee through a vast treeless plain with plateaux rising up in the distance. The small mining and farming town of Glencoe, just before Dundee is named after the village in the Highlands of Scotland, where some of the first miners came from.

Dundee

Phone code: 034
(NB Always use 3-figure prefix)
Colour map 5, grid A1
Altitude: 1,247 m

This modern town has built up around the coal mining deposits which were first exploited here on a large scale in the 1880s. The town centre has unfortunately fallen victim to South Africa's town planners and has little to distinguish it from other towns in the Midlands. Dundee is a convenient base from which to explore the well-known battlefield sites at Isandlwana, Rorke's Drift and Blood River.

Ins & outs *Tourism Dundee* is the tourist office at Civic Gardens, Victoria St, T2122121 ext 262, F2182837, tourism@dundeekzn.co.za Open Mon-Fri 0900-1645, Sat 0900-1200. A helpful office with information on accommodation and excellent advice on how best to view the battlefields depending upon your time, budget and level of interest. Ask about personal tour guides. This is an excellent initiative, which greatly enhances the visitors understanding and appreciation of the area.

Sights **MOTH Museum**, on the corner of Beaconsfield Street and Wilson Street, is one of the best private collections of military memorabilia in South Africa and includes pieces from the Anglo-Zulu War. ■ *Open Fri evenings or arrange an appointment through the tourist office. The museum is usually visited on organized tours.*

The Battle of Talana Hill took place on the 20 October 1899 and was the first major battle of the Boer War. British forces had been sent to Dundee to protect the coal field from the advancing Boers. General Lucas Meyer, moving down from the Transvaal, took the hill and began bombarding the British. The counter attack succeeded in forcing the Boers off the hill but only at great cost to the British who lost 255 soldiers including their commanding officer General Penn Symons. **Talana Hill Museum**, 1 km north of town on the R33, has been built on the site of the battle, there is a self-guided trail up which visits the remains of two British forts and the Boer gun emplacements. The path passes a cairn where General Penn Symons was wounded.

The main building is a modern museum with good displays on the Zulu Wars and the Anglo-Boer War. The industrial section includes the **Consol Glass Museum** which has an extensive display of glass products illustrating the changes in taste from highly decorative Victorian vases, passing through the abstract bowls of the 1950s to the crisp designer products of today. The **Chamber of Mines Coal Museum** has re-created scenes of early mining in Dundee with many of the original tools on display.

Many of the outlying buildings are original. The **Peter Smith Cottage** has been restored and decorated with period furniture, the workshop and stables outside have a collection of original blacksmith's tools and several wagons. **Talana House** has historical displays on the lifestyles of the Zulus and the early settlers in Dundee. Both these buildings were used as dressing stations during the Battle of Talana Hill.

■ *Mon-Fri 0800-1630, Sat 1000-1630, Sun 1200-1630. Free entry. T2122654. The Miner's Rest restaurant and curio shop is in the gardens behind the new building. A typical miner's cottage of the 1920s, serving teas and light lunches.*

The battlefield sites around Dundee can easily be visited on day trips. However, the sites themselves are often little more than a War Memorial in a windswept field. The best way to appreciate the sites and the epic events that took place in this region is to take a guided tour with a qualified historian. Battlefield Tours can be organized from the tourist offices in both Ladysmith and Dundee, and at the Talana Museum in Dundee (above). Expect to pay around R150 per person for a half-day tour. The major sites are clearly signposted and can be reached from Dundee or Ulundi. The sites are quite isolated and access to them is along dirt roads. Allow enough time to return in daylight as the bad roads and wandering cattle are dangerous at night. **Battlefield excursions**

Blood River is 48 km from Dundee. Take the R33 northeast as far as Dejagersdrif, there is a turning here on the right leading to Blood River. The last section of the journey is on a dirt road. This is one of the more interesting sites as there is something more to see than a simple grave or monument. A replica laager has been built on the site to commemorate the battle. The laager is quite unusual in that the 64 wagons are made of bronze and are equipped with replica bronze spades, lamps and buckets. The scale of the replica is just larger than life-size. There is a café here serving drinks and snacks which has a selection of historical leaflets on sale. ■ *Daily 0800-1700. Small entry fee. T6321695.*

Isandlwana is 80 km from Dundee. Take the R68 west of here passing through Vant's Drift and Nqutu, the dirt road leading to Isandlwana is clearly signposted south of Nqutu. The 24th Regiment were defeated here by 25,000 Zulu warriors on the 22 January 1879. Cairns mark the places where British soldiers were buried (see box on page 508). ■ *Daily 0800-1600. Small entry fee. T2710634.*

Rorke's Drift is 42 km from Dundee and is clearly signposted off the R68 between Dundee and Nqutu. Rorke's Drift was the site of a Swedish Mission next to a ford over the Buffalo River. The missionaries built two small stone buildings, a house and a storeroom which was also used as a church. They were commandeered by the British at the start of the war and converted into a hospital and a supply depot. Only 110 men were stationed there when two survivors of Isandlwana arrived warning about an imminent attack. Four thousand Zulus arrived 1½ hours later

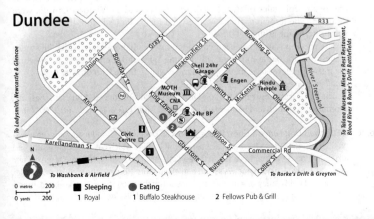

Dundee

0 metres 200
0 yards 200

■ **Sleeping**
1 Royal

● **Eating**
1 Buffalo Steakhouse   2 Fellows Pub & Grill

KwaZulu Natal

Blood River

1838 had been a difficult year for the Voortrekkers in Natal. In February their leader Piet Retief was beaten to death at the Zulu king Dingane's kraal and shortly afterwards about 500 members of a Voortrekker party at Bloukrans River were killed in a Zulu ambush. The majority of the dead were in fact 'coloured' servants but subsequent generations of Boers honoured the defeat by naming the site Weenen – meaning 'weeping'. Voortrekker attempts at reprisals against the Zulus similarly failed and in a battle near the Buffalo River Piet Uys, another Voortrekker leader, was killed. It was only with the arrival of Andries Pretorius and a party of 60 experienced commandos later in the year that Voortrekker fortunes began to take a turn for the better.

On the 9 December Pretorius set out with 468 men and three cannons to confront Dingane's army. Before setting out he reportedly stood on a gun carriage and made the famous vow that if God gave them victory "we would note the date of victory to make it known even to our latest posterity in order that it might be celebrated to the honour of God". Many historians doubt if the vow was ever really made; certainly it was not commemorated until many years after the event. Nevertheless the vow has taken on an important place in Afrikaner traditions.

On the 15 December Pretorius' scouts reported a heavy Zulu presence nearby and he ordered the column to move their wagons into the tried and tested Voortrekker defensive laager. This involved lashing all the wagons together into a ring and protecting all cattle, horses and stores in the centre. This allowed trekkers to hide in and under the wagons and fire out at any approaching attackers. Pretorius had formed his laager on the banks of the Ncome River with a deep gully to the rear and an open plain to the front. He placed the three cannons at points along the perimeter of the laager to give them a clear line of fire across the open ground. Early in the morning of the 16 December the Zulu army, estimated at about 10,000, began its attack.

Wave upon wave of Zulu soldiers charged the laager but their short spears, so effective in hand to hand combat, were useless against the trekkers' rifles and the grapeshot from the cannons. Finally the Zulu attack faltered and Pretorius sent out a party of mounted commandos to pursue the shattered Zulus. The trekkers were merciless and shot every Zulu in sight, including more than 400 hiding in a small ravine. No prisoners were taken and something like 3,000 people were killed. No trekkers had been killed and only three were injured – including Pretorius who was stabbed in the hand. So many Zulu soldiers were shot whilst trying to flee back across the Ncome River the waters ran red – hence the name Blood River.

and launched the assault on the mission station. The defence of Rorke's Drift is one of the epic tales of British military history and 11 Victoria Crosses were awarded. The ferocious attack was resisted for 12 hours before the Zulu impis withdrew, losing around 400 men.

The mission station has been converted into a small museum which illustrates scenes from the battle complete with flashing lights and sound effects. Just beyond the museum there is a cemetery and a memorial to those who died. ■ *0800-1700. Small entrance fee. Coffee shop. T6421687.*

The **ELC Craft Centre**, at Rorke's Drift, sells locally produced Zulu crafts: baskets, ceramics, dyed cloth and hand-made carpets. ■ *Mon-Fri 0800-1630, Sat 1000-1500.*

Sleeping

■ *on map, page 505*
Price codes:
see inside front cover
Some of the places
listed here are out
of town

A *Fugitive's Drift Lodge & Guest House,* approx 50 km south of Dundee towards Greytown on the R33, T6421843. Offers a choice between the lodge which has 11 double rooms and luxury farmhouse accommodation in 2-bed cottages all on a private game reserve. Fully inclusive, birdwatching, game walks and battlefield tours. Home to the well-known battlefield guide, David Rattray, who has set the standard for the region for everyone else to try and follow. A must for anyone with a keen interest in the local history.

B-C *Penny Farthing Country House*, Greytown Rd, T/F6421925. The farmhouse is 31 km south of Dundee on the R33, there is a choice of rooms in either the old fort, the colonial sandstone farmhouse or the garden cottage, this luxury B&B caters for up to 14 guests and offers battlefield tours and hiking, swimming pool, reservations are essential. **C** *Lennox Cottage*, a few kilometres out of town off the R68 towards Nqutu, T/F2182201. A comfortable guesthouse with 9 double rooms with en suite bathrooms and lots of space. Plenty to keep yourself occupied in the gardens, a swimming pool, tennis court, plus a snooker room. This has been recommended to us as an ideal base for exploring the battlefields. **C** *Royal Inn*, 61 Victoria St, T2122147, F2182146. 13 a/c double rooms, 5 singles and 3 good sized family rooms. A la carte restaurant, bar, a small modern hotel. **C** *House on the Park*, 24 Melville St, T/F2181893, T082-4572563 (mob), jeremy@trustnet.co.za B&B consisting of garden chalets some with en suite bathrooms. 1 double and 4 twin rooms all set in a neat garden with swimming pool. Children welcome. An added benefit from staying here is that your host is a registered local tour guide with expert knowledge of the Battlefields, ask for Jeremy. Secure parking.

D *Corner Cottage*, 130 McKenzie St, T2122814, F2122166. 3 double rooms and 2 twin rooms, some rooms shared bathroom, all separate from main house. A central B&B with secure parking. **D** *Kamnandi Guest House*, 91 Victoria St, T2121419. 3 double rooms with en suite bathrooms, old Victorian house. Swimming pool, secure parking. German spoken, ask for Marilyn. **D-E** *Bergview Lodge*, corner of Chard St and Browning St, T2122566, F2181203. 10 double rooms, all with en suite bathrooms, separate entrance. Lounge with a bar, satellite TV, evening meals on request, secure parking. **D-E** *The Stables*, 96 McKenzie St, T2182514. Self-catering unit with 1 double room and 1 twin room, lounge, TV, all separate from the principal house. B&B also available. **F** *Dundee Caravan Park*, Union St, T2182486. A medium size site which like many parks in the country, will be very busy during holiday periods, expect plenty of children. 40 sites each with a power point, plus 10 other sites. Limited facilities, but only a short walk from local shops and restaurants.

Buffalo Steakhouse, 5 King Edward St, T2124644. It may be a small town, but the meat and portions are great. Like so many outlets in the country, you have to like your meats. *Fellows*, Victoria St. Pub with restaurant attached serving up a good grill.

Eating
● *on map, page 505*

Travel House, 70 Gladstone St, T2122117, F2122427. Long distance coach tickets, hotels and car hire. **Local Tour Guides** *Elizabeth Durham*, T034-2122387. French speaking local expert and guide. *KZN Battlefield Promotions*, T2122654. *Paul Garner*, T2121931. Enjoyable tales of the San paintings found throughout the area. *Edelgaard Haschke*, T2181844 (German and English). *Jeremy Krone*, T082-4572563 (mob). Battlefield tours with the added benefit that you can continue the discussions at the *House on the Park* B&B which is owned by Jeremy. *Pat Rundgren*, T2124560.

Tour operators

Newcastle

This is a major industrial town based on coal and steel industries. It was established in 1864 by a Dr Sutherland from Newcastle in England who was trapped on the swollen banks of the Ncandu River during his honeymoon. To pass the time he planned a township for the site, named streets after the then government, and filed his plan on return to Peietermaritzburg. There is little in this modern town to attract tourists but the nearby mountain ranges with peaks such as Koningsberg and Kanskop rising to over 2,000 m, have become a popular destination for hikers. Newcastle is well-connected by road and rail and local taxis will take hikers out to the farms which organize the private hiking trails. Inexplicably, Newcastle has one of the largest Chinese communities in South Africa. **Tourism Newcastle** is on Town Hall, Scott Street, T3153318, F3129815. Open Mon-Fri 0900-1600, Sat 0930-1030. A useful range of brochures and information on hiking and birdwatching.

*Phone code: 034
(NB Always use
3-figure prefix)
Colour map 5, grid A1*

Fort Amiel was built in 1876 and used for military operations until 1902. It was built by a detatchment of the Staffordshire Volunteers (80th regiment) and named after

Sights

KwaZulu Natal

Isandlwana

On the 11 January 1879 three columns of British troops entered Zululand in an attempt to destroy the strongest and most self-reliant independent African states in southern Africa. When the Zulu leaders learned of the British invasion they gathered together their regiments and on the 17 January the Zulu king Cetshwayo addressed 2,000 warriors, telling them to engage the British and throw them out of Zululand. The march to confront the British began almost at once.

On the 22 January the Zulu army had settled down in a deep valley some six kilometres south of Isandlwana to wait until the state of the moon was more auspicious to make an attack on the British. The British had set up camp at the foot of the Isandlwana pinnacle of rock, guarded by 822 British and colonial troops and 431 African Levies of the Natal Native Contingent. The British, confident of their superiority, had not bothered to construct any defensive positions to protect the camp. When a small British cavalry unit, scouring the land to the south of their camp, spotted some cattle being herded by Zulu scouts they gave chase. Within moments they reached the lip of a valley and pulled up in terror when they saw the entire Zulu army seated in complete silence.

The Zulu force could now no longer wait out the day and, as one, jumped to their feet and immediately began an advance on the British camp, using their tried and tested two pronged attack. At first the British managed to check the headlong charge of the right-handed Zulu horn, with shrapnel and rifle fire extracting heavy Zulu casualties. But then the Zulu left overran fierce resistance of the small advanced line of the British right, made up mainly of African Levies, and was able to outflank the main body of the British troops. The British attempted a second stand but then fell back into the main camp as the Zulus surged forward on both fronts. As the Zulu force entered the camp the British fixed bayonets and engaged in hand to hand combat. The Zulu technique of throwing their assegais from a short distance was especially effective at these close quarters and the British were rapidly defeated. The last small pockets of resistance were on the western slopes but as ammunition ran out they soon gave way. By early afternoon it was all over, with only a handful of the 1,200 British forces lucky enough to escape.

their commander Major Charles Frederick Amiel. After the original plans for the fort were found in a London museum in 1985 the fort was completely rebuilt. The museum houses displays on the Boer War and has an interesting section on Rider Haggard. There is a Boer War cemetery just outside the museum. ■ *Mon-Fri 1000-1600, Sat 0900-1300. Memel Rd.*

Hiking in the Newcastle area
Popular with hikers from Gauteng, trails tend to be fully booked at the weekends, the best time to walk is during the week

The hiking trails in the mountains around Newcastle are mostly organized trails on private farmland. The farms are widely spread out in the region and often isolated.

Bushmanskrantz Trail Comfortable day hikes for beginners along Paradise Valley, passing through woodland and visiting San paintings. ■ *Contact T3154300.*

Geelhout Trail A 12 km trail in Normandien Pass going through yellowwood forest and along mountain streams. Overnight huts are also available. ■ *Contact T034-3186560.*

Ncandu Trail A tough two-day hike through the Normandien Mountains starting from Mullers Pass. Overnight accommodation is in an old cattle post with kitchen facilities and a shower. ■ *Contact T034-3511753.*

Moorfield Trail Hikes through a deep gorge with waterfalls, passing indigenous forests, San paintings and fossils. Overnight accommodation in chalets and a campsite. Closed on Sunday. ■ *Contact T058-940702.*

Eikenhof Trail Two-day hike through Mullers Pass and along the Ncandu River, accommodation is in a thatched self-catering chalet. Game and birdlife. ■ *Contact T034-3571346.*

Holkrans Hiking Trail The trails pass through a rocky area of indigenous forest and tree ferns inhabited by duiker and mountain reedbuck. There are many San paintings in the area. The birdlife here includes the rare rameron pigeon, eagles, woodpeckers and secretary birds. There is a choice of two overnight huts, both of which have hot showers, a fridge, and a braai, firewood is in short supply so it is best to bring a camping stove. The accommodation is self-catering, so bring food and sleeping bags. The best time of year to hike here is during the winter when the days are warm, it can get too hot for comfortable walking in the summer and it tends to rain. A maximum of 30 hikers are allowed on the trail at one time. There is a small grocery shop on the farm to buy any last minute supplies. ■ *Costs approx R150 per person. Contact Mr DCP Van Niekerk, PO Box 2734, Newcastle, T/F034-3511600. The farm is near Normandien 25 km to the southwest of Newcastle, the best time to book is during the week as it tends to be fully booked at weekends. There is also a shorter mountain bike trail here but you need your own bike.*

B *Newcastle Inn*, corner of Victoria St and Hunter St, T3128151, F3124142. 167 double rooms with en suite facilities, cocktail bar, restaurant, swimming pool. Used to be a *Holiday Inn*, time will tell if standards will be maintained. **B** *Majuba Lodge*, 27 Victoria St, T3155011, F3155023. Luxury chalets, swimming pool, 'Shape Up' gym and a driving range for golfers (T082-4847547 (mob)), friendly set-up. **C** *Cannon Lodge*, Allen St, T3152307. 22 double rooms with en suite facilities, phone, fan, TV, room service. Much lower rates at the weekends. Next to the *Keg & Cannon* pub and restaurant. **C-D** *Hilldrop House*, 15 Hilldrop Rd, 3 km out of town, T/F3152098. 20 en suite double rooms, TV, pub, log fires, large pool, evening meals on request. Beautiful house which used to be the home of Sir Rider Haggard, whose novel 'Jess' (1887) was based on his experiences at Hilldrop, now a National Monument set in 3 ha of indigenous forest and gardens. Request the forest rooms, which have private balconies and separate entrances. Recommended. This is not to be confused with **D** *Hilldrop B&B*, further up the road, T3124263. 2 double en suite rooms in a plain house. **Guest farms & camping** Many of the farms offering hiking trails have camping facilities and overnight huts, see Hiking above.

Sleeping
Price codes:
see inside front cover

Chinshu, Beares Arcade, Scott St, T3124013. Chinese food. *Keg & Cannon*, Allen St. Bar and restaurant, huge interesting menu and hearty portions. Nice outside terrace. Busy at the weekend and late nights. *Pint & Pigout*, corner of Allen St and Harding St, T3152468. Located in a turn-of-the-century manor house, Adams fireplaces, oregon pine floors. Pub food, good steaks and beers. Satellite TV, friendly service.

Eating

Park Tours, T3126006. The only travel agent in town, *Greyhound*, tickets and information.

Tour operators

Air A charter airline, *New Heights*, operates a fairly regular service between **Johannesburg** and a local airfield near Newcastle approximately 3 times a week. Call the *Park Tours* office (above) to see if there are spare seats and for information on fares.

Transport

Rail The *Trans Natal*, enquiries, T2712020, departs to **Durban** (8 hrs), daily at 2355; to **Johannesburg** (5 hrs), daily at 0234.

Road The N11 continues north from Newcastle towards Volksrust, 53 km and Mpumalanga, and south back to Ladysmith, 100 km. **Taxi/car hire:** *Avis*, T3121274. *Imperial*, T3122806. *William's*, 100 Victoria Rd, T3150556. Shuttle service to trains and airport, car hire and taxi service to surrounding sites of interest. **Bus:** *Greyhound*, central reservfations, T011-2498900, coaches depart from the Shell Service Station, Allen St, to **Durban** (5 hrs) daily at 1505, via **Ladysmith** and **Pietermaritzburg**; to **Johannesburg** and **Pretoria** (5 hrs), daily at 1510. *Translux*, central reservations, T012-3154300, also depart from the Shell Service Station, to **Johannesburg**, and **Pretoria**, daily at 1320. NB *Translux* does not stop at Newcastle on the route south to Durban.

KwaZulu Natal

Majuba Battlefield   Majuba Battlefield is 43 km from Newcastle on the N11 to Volksrust. The site is sign-posted from the highway. A 2 km dirt road leads to the battlefield where there is a caravan park, a youth hostel and a small museum. Majuba is the site where the British were defeated by the Boers in 1881. There is a short (45 minutes) trail heading up Majuba Mountain from where there are spectacular views of Volksrust, Newcastle and the surrounding countryside.

The N11 continues north from here into Volksrust and Mpumalanga Province.

Gauteng

7

512

Gauteng

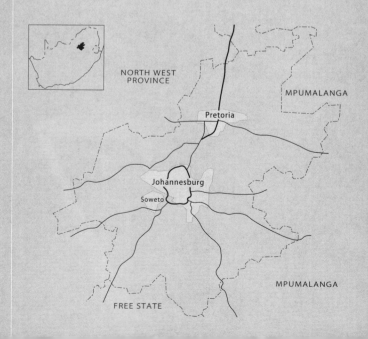

The province of Gauteng – Sotho for 'place of gold' – is one of the wealthiest areas of land in the world, yet it is dominated by large areas of impoverished townships such as the notorious Soweto. (During Apartheid these areas didn't feature on maps at all, despite being home to millions of people.) The province, is also the smallest in the country, and home for 45% of South Africa's white population. Today, the two principal cities of Gauteng remain Johannesburg and Pretoria and both city centres have gone through a change of identity in recent years. With the reinstated freedom of movement for all South African citizens and the demise of Apartheid, black South Africans are at last permitted to live where they choose. Many hundreds of thousands have moved from the townships and into what were once white-only areas. As a result the city centres now have a distinctive and cultural African feel . Despite the well-publicised chronically high crime rates, these city centres represent urban African living at its most intense. But, undeniably, the crime has had an adverse effect on the business community – many offices and shops have moved out of the city centres into suburban business parks and shopping malls – implying that many of the racial social and economic boundaries have not yet been completely addressed in the brave new South Africa. But do not be deterred from going to Johannesburg and Pretoria: these are places not to be avoided but understood, and a visit to a township and an upmarket shopping mall in the suburbs contribute equally to this understanding.

Arrival by air

Johannesburg International Airport is 25 km from the city centre and 35 km from the northern suburbs. All the terminals are next to each other in one long building.

Facilities for passengers at International Arrivals and International Departures include food courts, shops, and a variety of banks. Rennie's/Thomas Cook and American Express branches are open 0530-2130 and there are a number of ATM machines to withdraw Rand on your credit card. In International Arrivals, there is a cell phone and South African SIM card hire counter and a post office. (Remember that because many flights leave nightly to Europe, the airport post office has the facility to put post on the next flight for a small extra fee above the cost of postage. This is as close to overnight delivery you can get save sending with a courier service.)

The duty-free shops in International Departures are extensive and the terminal is beginning to resemble a typical South African shopping mall.

Transport to and from the airport The new Parkade Centre is opposite the main terminal building across from the pick-up/drop-off zone. This is where the multi-storey car park and all the car hire offices and shuttle bus companies are located. Most international flights from Europe arrive early in the morning and depart in the evening, which along with the domestic commuter traffic sees the airport at its busiest at these times of the day. It is advisable to pre-book an airport transfer at these times. Expect to pay between R75-120 for a one way transfer depending on the time of day/night. Regular taxis can be found outside the main terminal building but tend to be more expensive than the shuttle services and drivers often do not know the way without direction. **Airport Link Taxis**, T011-8039474. **Shuttle services**: Magic Bus, T011-6081662, drops off at the major hotels.

Pretoria Airport Shuttle, T011-3220904, drops off at Sammy Mark's Square in Pretoria but for an extra fee will take you to your final destination within reason. **Lux Express**, T082-4474324 (mob), drops off at the following hotels in Sandton: Protea Wanderers, City Lodge and Town Lodge. All the hotels located within the environs of the airport offer a free pick up shuttle service, and a drop off service for a nominal fee. Opposite the main terminal building are a series of hotel bus stops where the hotel shuttles come and go, but in quieter times of the day you may need to phone the hotel to tell them you are waiting. The following backpackers hostels offer free pick ups from the airport if you phone ahead. In Johannesburg: **Airport Backpackers**, **Backpackers Ritz**, **Rockey's of Fourways** and **In-Africa**. In Pretoria: **Pretoria Backpackers**.

Car hire at the airport Avis, T011-3945433. **Budget**, T011-3942905. Europcar, T011-3948832. **Hertz**, T011-3902066. **Imperial**, T011-3944020.

Sleeping There are several airport hotels within a few kilometres that all provide free pick-ups. The closest ones are, the **A** Intercontinental, T011-9615400, F9615401. A new five star hotel directly opposite the terminal building. You can push your trolley from the airport into your room, flight arrival and departure information throughout the hotel, gym and beauty salon available for passengers on long waits between flights. **B** Holiday Inn Crown Plaza, T011-9751121, F9755846. 365 rooms, restaurant, pool. **B** City Lodge, T011-3921750, F3922644. Modern, well-run hotel for the business traveller, restaurant, pool, 4 km from airport. **B** Holiday Inn Garden Court, T/F011-3921062. **C** Town Lodge, T011-9745202. F9745490. **D** Road Lodge, T011-3922268, F3924820.

Ins and outs

Climate The lands on which Johannesburg and Pretoria are located are known as the highveld, with an average altitude of over 1,500 m. The weather here can be quite extreme, in the summer it can get very hot. At this time the rains coincide with the summer months, which gives rise to the occasional spectacular electric storm that can flood a town or village in a matter of minutes. In the middle of winter, during June and July, you can expect frosts and this is not the time of the year to stay in Gauteng. Johannesburg also suffers from some unpleasant haze before the arrival of the first rains when the winds blow loose sand from all the mine workings into the atmosphere. On certain days you might think you are in a fog but this brown haze is just fine soil particles. Despite this, Johannesburg is surprisingly a city full of trees, there are over six million on pavements, parks and private residences (the city resembles a rainforest on pictures taken from satellites, making it one of the greenest urban areas in the world).

In the past five years the pattern of tourist arrivals into South Africa has changed. Increasingly people fly direct into Cape Town, and when there is no direct flight from their home country they fly into Johannesburg International airport and then transfer on to a Cape Town flight. This means that the choice of accommodation in Johannesburg and Pretoria is now way behind that in the Cape, and while the standards are OK, most is in chain style hotels.

Where to stay

In Johannesburg there are now no hotels in the old commercial centre. All the new developments have taken place north of the city centre in the northern suburbs such as Sandton and Rosebank. In Pretoria there has been a gradual relocation of hotels, restaurants and nightlife to the new developments in Hatfield and Brooklyn. All of this makes it a little confusing for the first time visitor who expects to be staying in the town centre but then finds themselves staying in a district they had never heard of.

Neither city is worth spending too much time in if you are on a relatively short holiday, but there is a variety of interesting sights, and like the other big cities of Cape Town and Durban, excellent shopping and eating opportunities, which with the tumbling value of the Rand are well worthwhile making time for.

Johannesburg

Johannesburg is the largest financial, commercial and industrial centre in South Africa and is now also the capital of Gauteng, one of the nine new provinces of the country. The city is just over 100 years old and since the gold rush, has grown into one of the wealthiest cities of the world. Settlers from all over the world have been arriving in Johannesburg since the first weeks of the gold rush, including people of Eastern European, British and African descent. At one time, this mixture of cultures produced a vibrant cosmopolitan atmosphere, but Apartheid changed all that, creating deep divisions in society that remain evident today. For despite Apartheid's demise, Johannesburg is still on the whole segregated, albeit no longer by legal requisite. The city centre and neighbouring suburbs such as Hillbrow, are largely home to the urban black population, a condensed area of overcrowded high rise flats where poverty and crime is rife. Soweto is a large sprawling township of rudimentary government housing and informal settlements, home to the majority of Johannesburg's black commuters, where African culture and street life is at its most intense and vibrant. Most white residents live in the attractive and affluent northern suburbs. Because of the high crime rate, people here lead a paranoid lifestyle behind high walls and razor wire fences in palatial neighbourhoods and modern shopping malls. You are unlikely to find yourself arriving in the city centre, and instead will probably be whisked off to Johannesburg's smart residential suburbs, but it is well worth seeing the city's other areas, to understand fully how the its diversity has evolved.

*Phone code: 011
(NB Always use
3-figure prefix)
Colour map 2, grid B3
Altitude: 1,763 m*

Gauteng

Ins and outs

Johannesburg International Airport, formerly known as Jan Smuts, is in Kempton Park, 25 km from the city centre on the R24. Enquiries: T9216262. International and domestic flights both leave from one large complex, within which are several terminals. The airport is located between Johannesburg and Pretoria and both cities can be reached by car in 30 minutes. The **railway station** and the main **bus terminal** are at the Park City Transit Centre.

Getting there
For more detailed information see Transport, page 531 and Arrival by air box, previous page

24 hours in the city

Start the day with a sumptuous breakfast at **Fourno's Bakery**, they open at 0700 but the chefs have been busy baking pies, breads, and pastries from midnight. A great place to watch Jo'burg's high-fliers conduct power breakfasts over trendy coffees. Don't miss a mind-expanding morning tour of **Soweto**, South Africa's oldest and most famous township. Drop in at Mandela's former home which is now a museum, drink a cool Castle lager in a Shebeen, and visit the memorials dedicated to the struggle against Apartheid.

Lunch at **Rosebank Mall** before hitting the shops. Jo'burger's love their shopping malls and Rosebank has an excellent African Craft Market and a lively rooftop flea market on a Sunday.

Take an afternoon drive out to the **Lion Park** where you can get close to a number of lions and play with some cubs. Continue on to the **Lesedi Cultural Village**. After the 2-hour tour of four authentic African villages recreated from the Xhosa, Zulu, Pedi, and Sotho tribes, enjoy traditional dancing from over 60 performers around a large fire and a dinner of game meat such as impala or crocodile.

Crack open a good bottle of South African wine at the stylish **Blues Room** in Sandton, one of the best jazz and blues venues in Gauteng before heading to **Melville**, Jo'burg's hip and happening nightlife district. Two streets of bars, restaurants, and late night lounges where all the trendy people go to be seen.

If you're feeling peckish in the wee small hours of the morning, try the nachos at **Catz Pyjamas**, Jo'burg's original 24-hour bistro and cocktail bar.

Getting around Municipal buses ply certain routes during rush hour only, but you have little chance of getting a seat on these as they are often booked by regular passengers. Mini bus or commuter taxis follow the same routes as the municipal buses but these services are not safe due to the ongoing 'taxi wars' and high accident rate. On the whole it is safer to stick to radio taxis. Unfortunately, Johannesburg is a city where you really do need a car to get around.

Orientation **City centre** The once-prosperous central business district is today a grim area of mostly abandoned office blocks and flyovers where very few of Johannesburg's original buildings are left standing. Violent crime is a serious problem here and businesses have mostly moved out to the safer northern suburbs. However, a visit to the city centre is well worthwhile for an insight on how Johannesburg has developed over the decades, but due to safety concerns, it is only recommended that you go on an organized tour. Two buildings which give some idea of what Johannesburg was actually like are the Post Office, built in 1897, and the City Hall, built in 1915, opposite each other on Rissik Street.

Suburbs Johannesburg's affluent suburbs are clustered around the main freeway to Pretoria, the M1, and on the surface could be on the edge of any modern city. The hills to the north of the city centre are home to large residential areas with rows of mansions, well-tended gardens and shopping malls. What is unusual are the lengths that residents have to go to protect their property. The fences topped with razor wire, the guard dogs and armed response warnings emphasize the insecurity under which these people live. In the extreme, some residents have clubbed together to pay to cordon off their whole block or street with boom gates guarded by a private security company.

These suburbs are safer than the city centre and accommodation for tourists, from B&Bs to the major 5-star hotels has followed the businesses to the suburbs. Particularly **Rosebank**, a few kilometres north of the city, and **Sandton**, almost a city in its own right further north off the M1 to Pretoria. Many of the sights, shopping malls and entertainment complexes are also in the suburbs so there is little reason to venture into the city centre for facilities. To the east of Rosebank are the trendy suburbs of **Melville**, **Parkhurst**, and **Parktown**, where most of Johannesburg's more popular restaurants and nightlife are located along with more of the obligatory shopping malls.

In contrast, the largest of the suburbs is **Soweto**, the infamous township southwest of the city, simply named because of it's location, South West Township. Soweto is linked to the city by a number of freeways that carry hundreds of thousands of commuters to the city centre and shops and businesses in the northern suburbs each day. Adjoining Soweto to the south, are smaller townships where other communities were relocated during Apartheid; the coloureds were forced to move to **Eldorado Park**, and the Indians to **Lenasia**.

Gauteng Tourism Authority, Rosebank Mall, T3272000, F3277000, tourism@gauteng.net **Tourist offices**
South Africa Tourism, T9701669, F3941508. In the international arrivals hall of Johannesburg airport.

Modern Johannesburg

The city centre of Johannesburg is surrounded by some 600 suburbs covering approximately 500 sq km. The population of greater Johannesburg is roughly 2.9 million excluding Soweto. As it is almost impossible to estimate the population of Soweto due to the constant arrival of people from the rural areas and illegal immigrants looking for work, the population of greater Johannesburg including Soweto is put at somewhere between 7 and 10 million.

During the height of Apartheid the African population of Johannesburg were all evicted to the new townships, such as Soweto, built on the outskirts of the city. The most infamous forced removal was the bulldozing of an area to the west of Johannesburg called Sophiatown. This was an area of slum housing near to the city centre and was home to a diverse population of Africans, Coloureds and 'poor Whites'. During the 1940s and 1950s there was a huge outburst of a new African urban culture in Sophiatown based mainly on the influence of American jazz musicians. This cultural explosion attracted Bohemian Whites and a huge number of African writers, journalists and politicians. To the Apartheid planners the area stood for everything they opposed, the government had to get rid of it because it proved that people could live together, and in the mid-1950s the entire population was removed and the bulldozers were sent in, in the same manner as Cape Town's District Six was razed to the ground in 1966. A new White suburb was built on the ruins of Sophiatown - and in a gesture that was crass even by the standards of Apartheid they named the new suburb Triomf – Afrikaans for 'triumph'.

Since the mid-1980s this forced movement of Africans from the city centre to the townships has been reversed. The breakdown of influx controls led to the rapid growth of the African population of Johannesburg city centre, especially in Hillbrow, which has one of Africa's highest population densities. Since the end of Apartheid this trend has continued and has been bolstered by the arrival of new immigrants from outside South Africa's borders. Today downtown Johannesburg feels very much like an authentic African city, to rival say, Nairobi or Dar es Salaam, though sadly not without its own new set of problems.

The modern city centre is dominated by high-rise office blocks surrounded by the prosperous suburbs to the north and the townships like Soweto to the south. In spite of Johannesburg's overall wealth, the office buildings in the city centre are now virtually derelict. Because of the rising crime rate over the last two decades, shops and businesses have gradually closed and been relocated to the new shopping malls and office parks in the suburbs. Even the Carlton Hotel, (the second tallest building in Africa after the Sheraton Hotel in Cairo, the Holiday Inn, and the Stock Exchange have closed or moved out, and many of the skyscrapers stand empty. There can't be any other capital city in the world that has literally had its guts ripped out.

This is not a city which tourists can casually discover wandering around on foot, or exploring by public transport. Most of the backpackers hostels and hotels offer half day tours explaining how the city grew from farmland, to gold mines, to a

Gauteng

City of gold

The high plateau on which Johannesburg was built was originally an arid place inhabited by a few Boer farmers grazing cattle and cultivating maize and wheat. This harsh and isolated landscape was transformed after the discovery of gold in 1886. During the 1880s, prospectors began arriving in the Eastern Transvaal attracted by reports of gold in Barberton and the mountains of the Eastern Drakensberg. George Harrison arrived from the Cape and travelled north to look at an abandoned gold mine on a farm in the Witwatersrand. He was employed to build a farmhouse at Langlaagte but in his free time he continued his search for gold. He discovered Main Reef in March of 1886 and travelled to Pretoria to register his claim. Within weeks hordes of prospectors and fortune hunters began to arrive and officials of the Pretoria government were quickly sent to inspect the diggings and to lay out plans for a town.

Johannesburg expanded at a phenomenal rate and within three years

had become the largest town in the Eastern Transvaal. Confidence in Johannesburg's future was so great that traders in other regions of South Africa dismantled their wood and corrugated iron buildings and transported the component parts to reassemble them in the new boom town. The Star *newspaper relocated to Johannesburg from Grahamstown and transported its printing press across the veld by ox wagon. The gold rush attracted people from all over the world and Johannesburg became a cosmopolitan town where vast fortunes could be made overnight. Gambling dens, brothels and riotous canteens lined the streets and hundreds of ox drawn wagons arrived daily to deliver food, drink and building supplies.*

The mines expanded as new technologies opened up the deeper deposits of gold and Johannesburg was gradually transformed from being a gold rush boom town to being a large modern industrial city.

financial hub of Southern Africa. The tours take in the city sights such as the Market Theatre complex, Museum Africa, and the viewing platform on the top floor of the Carlton Centre, which has a 360 degree view of all of Johannesburg. They also go to Nelson Mandela's present house in the ultra-rich Houghton region through to the decaying inner city suburbs of Hillbrow or Yeoville.

Sights

In the city centre **Museum Africa**, at 121 Bree Street, T8335624, is an excellent new museum focusing on the black experience of living in Johannesburg. There are displays on the struggle for democracy and on life in the goldmines and the townships, with excellent mock-ups of both a mining shaft and an informal settlement to give you the feel of these environments. There is also a new gallery dedicated to San rock art, and a display on the life of Mahatma Ghandi. The photography gallery on the fourth floor has an interesting collection of early photographs of Soweto. This is well worth the visit and most Johannesburg city tours allow at least a couple of hours here. ■ *Tue-Sun 0900-1700, small entry fee.*

The **KwaZulu Muti Museum of Man and Science** is on the corner of Diagonal (14) and President streets. The muti shop has been here since 1897 and sells products used in traditional herbal medicine and magic and is a slightly unnerving place, especially for the superstitious. Muti is a form of witchcraft practised exclusively by witch doctors, which is not only used to treat physical ailments with unconventional medicine, but also for far more soul-searching or sinister endeavours. Whilst largely not understood by the outside world, their mystical powers are highly revered amongst much of the African community. The ingredients on sale include the usual mixture of leaves, seeds and bark but some of the more specialized requirements are also here. Monkey skulls, dried crocodiles and ostrich feet hang from the ceiling before being used as part of a cure. Again city tours stop at this shop, which interestingly still has a 'non-white' sign above it. (During Apartheid, every public facility from shops, businesses, to entrances to train stations, and park benches, were separated and labeled for use by 'whites' or 'non-whites'.) ■ *Mon-Fri 0730-1700, Sat 0730-1300. T8364470.*

The **Market Theatre Complex** next to Museum Africa, was once a hive of activity but is now just a poor shadow of its former self. Apart from the theatre, people used to come to visit the street cafés, restaurants and shops selling antiquarian books, vintage records and the galleries selling contemporary art. The well-known Saturday flea market, which is held in front of the Complex, is now very poor, selling only shabby clothes, kitchen stuff and no curios in sight. There is talk of reviving the area and The Central Improvement Project has been set up to investigate ways of improving many of the city centre areas and make them more attractive and safe.

South African Breweries' (SAB) **World of Beer** will appeal to anyone who enjoys the golden nectar. SAB now dominate the African beer industry and control many local breweries throughout southern and eastern Africa. *Castle Lager* is probably now the most popular beer between Cape Town and Cairo. The 90-minute tour covers the brewing process, a greenhouse that nurtures ingredients, and a variety of

Johannesburg centre

Gauteng

● **Eating & drinking**
1 Guildhall

0 metres 200
0 metres 200

mock-up bars from a township *Shebeen* to a *honky-tonk pub* from Johannesburg's mining camps. ■ *Open Tue-Sat 1000-1800. R10 including 2 complimentary beers. 15 President St, T8364900.*

Outside the city centre Twenty years ago few people would have believed that the **Apartheid Museum** would ever have existed. Fortunately today South Africa has the opportunity to exhibit a regime that is well and truly in the past. The museum opened in December 2001 and we were one of the first to visit, when the museum was not entirely finished and the organization of the exhibits not finalized. We would be interested to hear from anyone who has visited more recently. Nelson Mandela officially opened the museum in April 2002. There are several 'spaces' which you are briefly introduced to by a guide before wandering around each one by yourself, and the entire route through the museum from the birth of Apartheid to the present day is described as 'the journey'. When paying your entry fee you are issued with a white or non-white ticket that takes you through two different entry points to symbolize segregation. The building itself has an innovative design to reflect the cold subject of Apartheid – harsh concrete, raw brick, lots of steel bars and barbed wire.

A 15-minute introduction video takes you briefly through Voortreker history to the Afrikaner government of 1948 who implemented Apartheid. The 'spaces' are dedicated to the rise of nationalism in 1948, pass laws, segregation, the first response from townships such as Sharpeville and Langa, the forced removals and the implementation of the Group Areas Act. The rise of Black Consciousness and other liberation movements, the student uprisings in Soweto in 1976, and political prisoners and executions, (here there is a replica solitary confinement cell and 131 nooses hanging from the ceiling that represent the 131 political executions that occurred during Apartheid). The reforms during the 1980s and 1990s are well-documented including President FW DeKlerk's un-banning of political parties, Mandela's release, the 1994 election, sanction lifting, and the new constitution.

The last 'space' is called the *Deposition Studio*. Here you are invited to stand before a video and leave your own deposition relating to your own experience during Apartheid, or overall feelings of the museum, which is later played to other museum visitors. One of the more interesting 'spaces' is the *House of Bondage*, named after a book of photographs published in 1967 by Ernest Cole and banned in South Africa at the time. A white photographer, he managed to class himself as a Coloured in order to go into the townships and take the pictures. The black and white photographs are stark, harsh, tragic and beautiful and the images are outstandingly memorable.

What is immediately striking about this museum are the several hundred TV screens showing footage of the various events during the Apartheid regime. Most of the displays of the museum are actually on televised screen, which is highly unusual for a museum but then this is a subject that is so recent, most of it was captured on camera. It is a very visual experience and a must for any visitor to South Africa to fully understand what is a very recent past. Highly recommended. ■ *The museum is next to Gold Reef City. Open Tue-Sat 1000-1700, closed Sun. Entry R20. T4961600.*

The **Johannesburg Zoo** has over 400 different species of birds and animals set in an area of parkland and gardens. The ponds attract free ranging aquatic birds, which come here to breed. All the enclosures have recently been upgraded and the night tours to see the nocturnal animals are fun, ending with marshmallows and hot chocolate around a bonfire. There is a small restaurant here selling light meals and refreshments. ■ *Daily 0830-1730. Small entrance fee. Jan Smuts Av, Parktown, T6462000.*

Near to the Johannesburg Zoo is the **South African National Museum of Military History**. This building has exhibits on the role South African forces played in the Second World War including artillery pieces, aircraft and tanks. There is a more up-to-date section illustrating the war in Angola with displays of modern armaments including captured Soviet tanks and French Mirage fighter planes. ■ *T6465513. Daily except Mon, 0900-1630. Small entry fee. 20 Erlswold Way, Saxonwold.*

Gold Reef City is built on the site of one of Johannesburg's mining areas. The most interesting part of the experience is the visit to the original miners' cottages and the tour of the gold mine. Assuming you are happy going underground, the tour to the fifth level, about 220 m deep, is very interesting. This tour takes you down number 14 shaft, one of the richest deposits in its day. Unfortunately Gold Reef City is basically a theme park with amusement arcades and fun fair and only offers a sanitized version of mining history. Entrance to 23 rides are included in the tour price. A visit to Gold Reef City is often included as part of an organized tour of Johannesburg.
■ *Closed Mon. Mine tours, 0900 and 1330. Entry fee R115. Northern Parkway, Ormonde, T2486800.*

Probably the most popular excursion from Johannesburg is to the (in)famous township of Soweto, lying 13 km from Johannesburg city centre and the largest urban living space in South Africa. In the last census conducted in 1996, the population was put at between 3.9 and 4.2 million, but in reality this figure is much higher. Short for South West Township, people first moved here in 1904 from Sophiatown where there was an outbreak of plague. The township increased in size dramatically in the 1950s and 1960s when blacks were forced to relocate from the city centre into designated areas. Since then the population has steadily grown as people from the rural areas have come to the city in search of work. It is also a place where illegal immigrants from Nigeria, Mozambique, Zimbabwe and other parts of Africa can live in relative anonymity. Consequently, it is almost impossible to estimate how many people live here.

Soweto
They used to say that when Soweto sneezes, the whole country catches cold

Today Soweto covers an area of 135 square km and in an area this size, and with one of the highest concentrations of people in Africa, there is only 1 fire station, 1 hospital, and 350 schools. Despite this, the Baragwanath Hospital is the largest hospital in the world with over 5,000 beds and 15-20,000 employees. It is estimated that half of Soweto's residents were born here and it also attracts unfortunate fame for it's large proportion of AIDS patients and victims of street violence.

There are large areas in Soweto of tidy, neat rows of houses, where residents are aspiring professionals with middle class attitudes and modest ambitions of decent housing, medical care and education for their children. In fact, Soweto has the highest concentration of millionaires in the country and ironically, one of the most successful BMW dealerships. But there are also the sprawling mixtures of poverty-

Gauteng

Soweto

stricken dwellings where people's aspirations are less hopeful, and unemployment is as high as 90%. Squatter camps, hostels, and areas of rudimentary two-roomed government-built houses make up the majority of township dwellings. Many still don't have basic amenities such as running water, electricity and sanitation. For every 7,000 people who live in these areas, there are approximately 90 toilets and five taps, and each shack sleeps 8-10 people. The present government is trying to provide more, but it cannot happen overnight. Each month up to 20,000 people flood into Soweto fleeing rural poverty and desperate for jobs. This influx places enormous pressure on already stretched public resources.

There are many important historical sites to see including Nelson and Winnie's former home before Mandela was incarcerated, a tiny three-roomed house that was rebuilt after being bombed several times by the South African Defence Forces. Today it houses a small museum and it is not difficult to imagine the Mandela family hiding beneath the kitchen table as the white policemen that watched them from across the street shot regular bullets through the window. On the same road is Archbishop Desmond Tutu's former home, the only street in the world where two Nobel Peace Prize winners have lived.

See page 530 for a list of tour operators who run tours to Soweto

What were once Apartheid areas for the displacement of undesirables, the townships now represent real homes; Soweto is almost 100 years old, virtually the same age as Johannesburg itself. It is still not safe to visit alone but tour companies have been running successful tours for over 5 years. The tours are fascinating and the informative guides are township residents. There are a number of operators, which can be arranged by all hotels and hostels. Expect to pay in the region of R200-300 for a half-day tour.

Excursions from Johannesburg

Lesedi Cultural Village is an easy day trip from Johannesburg or Pretoria. Four authentic African villages have been recreated from the Xhosa, Zulu, Pedi, and Sotho tribes and there are two 2½-hour tours each day. These include an audio-visual presentation on all aspects of tribal life, music, singing and traditional dancing from over 60 performers around a large fire in an ampitheatre. The morning tour includes lunch and the afternoon tour includes a dinner of game meat such as impala or crocodile. ■ *Lesedi is on the R512, 12 km north of Lanseria Airport, T012-2051394. Tours run at 1130 and again at 1630 and include meals. The **C-D** Protea Hotel Lesedi, part of the cultural village provides en suite accommodation in traditional bomas or rondavaals decorated with Ndebele crafts.*

The lions are accustomed to vehicles and don't think twice about strolling right up to a car – keep windows at least half closed

The **Lion Park**, en route to Lesedi (above), is worth a stop for the excellent photo opportunities. You are unlikely to get closer to lion than here. There are over 50 in the park including many cubs and a rare male white lion. Although they are bred in captivity, they are well-cared for and have ample room in the drive-through enclosures. Walks and close encounters with cubs are on offer. ■ *Open Mon-Fri 0830-1700, Sat-Sun 0830-1800, entry car + 4 people R90, cub enclosure R10, walk on the wild side R50, restaurant and curio shop. 30 mins drive from Johannesburg on the Old Pretoria-Krugersdorp road, T4601814.*

Sterkfontein Caves are an important anthropological site in a dolomite hill discovered in the late 19th century when blasting for a lime quarry. The caves form part of the Cradle of Humankind World Heritage Site, which covers much of western Gauteng where many important anthropological finds have been unearthed. But it was not until 1936 that the most important find was made, the first adult skull of the ape-man Australopithecus africanus transvaalensis, 'Mrs Ples' for short, estimated to be over 3.3 million years old, was found by Dr Robert Broom. The caves consist of six chambers all connected by passages, in one of the chambers is a large lake with crystal clear water, 40 m below the surface. In 1958 the caves were donated to the University of the Witwatersrand. In addition to viewing the lake and learning about the various fossil remains there are the usual impressive stalactite formations. ■ *Daily tours of the caves Tue-Sun from 0900-1600, café. The caves are off the N14 from Randburg towards Hartbeetspoort Dam, T9566342.*

The **Witwaterserand Botanical Gardens** are 30 minutes drive from the city centre on the banks of the Emmarentia Dam in Roodepoort, T9581750. It's a pleasant place to visit for a quiet stroll away from the bustle of the city. The gardens are planted with oaks, cherry trees and a mixture of exotic and indigenous plants. The nursery with over 2,500 species of succulent plants is a fascinating area and the nearby ponds attract wild birds. It is possible to see yellowbilled ducks, Egyptian geese and crested grebes. ■ *Open daily 0800-1700. Small entry fee.*

Essentials

The increase of violent crime in central Johannesburg has meant that visitors are choosing to stay in hotels in the northern suburbs. There are no accommodation choices left in the city centre anymore, and those that still exist in the central suburbs of Yeoville, Hillbrow, or Berea are not recommended for tourists.

Sleeping
■ on maps, pages
523 and 524
Price codes:
see inside front cover

Northern suburbs AL+ *Saxon*, 36 Saxon Rd, Sandhurst, T2926000, F2926001. Voted the World's Leading Boutique Hotel twice since it opened in 2000. 26 suites including one named after Nelson Mandela, who spent 7 months in this hotel editing his book, *The Long Walk to Freedom*. Set in 6 acres of beautifully tended grounds, gigantic heated swimming pools, state of the art gym, 2 wine cellars, and every other luxury imaginable with a price tag to match. Stunning. Expensive by South African standards, but not when compared to the same quality in Europe, so definitely worth a mention. **AL** *The Michelangelo*, 135 West St, Sandton Sq, T2827000, F2827171. 242 superior rooms, includes a variety of giant suites, residents' lounge, restaurants, bar, heated swimming pool, fitness centre, shops, one of the latest luxury additions to Sandton and which has contributed to the area becoming one of the smartest new centres of Johannesburg. Plenty of restaurants, shops and offices in the immediate surrounds. A newish hotel which aims to be recognized as one of the top luxury hotels

Gauteng

Sandton

■ Sleeping	5 Park Plaza Santon	● Eating
1 Balalaika Protea	6 Road Lodge & Town Lodge	1 Blues Room
2 City Lodge	7 Santon Hilton	2 Butcher Shop & Grill
3 Holiday Inn Garden Court	8 Santon Sun/Towers	3 O'Galito & Graasroots
4 Michaelangelo	& Daruma Restaurant	

0 metres 500
0 yards 500

in the world with prices, facilities and service to match. **AL** *Sandton Hilton*, Rivonia Rd, Sandton, T3221888, F7846291. 329 luxury rooms, includes the latest Hilton feature – a separate executive floor with its own lounge-cum-club room where business folk can breakfast and have snacks throughout the day. 2 restaurants, bar, health club, swimming pool, tennis court, extensive conference facilities, all set in a beautiful landscaped garden, close to smart shopping malls in Sandton. **A** *Balalaika Protea*, Maude St, T3225000, F3225021. 325 a/c rooms, some with jacuzzi, 2 restaurants, 2 swimming pools, garden courtyard, next to the Village Walk shopping mall. **A** *Sandton Sun/Sandton Towers* *Inter-Continental*, corner of 5th and Alice streets, T7805000, F7805002. 565 rooms, 4 restaurants, 2 swimming pools, a modern high-rise building next to a shopping mall, excellent views from the top floor, hotel split in two, the luxury wing is known as 'The Towers'.

Rosebank to Hyde Park

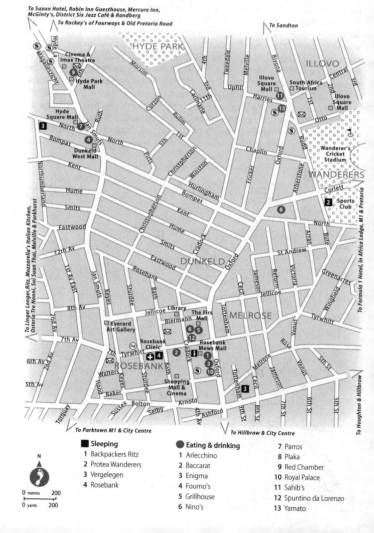

Sleeping
1 Backpackers Ritz
2 Protea Wanderers
3 Vergelegen
4 Rosebank

Eating & drinking
1 Arlecchino
2 Baccarat
3 Enigma
4 Fourno's
5 Grillhouse
6 Nino's
7 Parros
8 Plaka
9 Red Chamber
10 Royal Palace
11 Sahib's
12 Spuntino da Lorenzo
13 Yamato

0 metres 200
0 yards 200

Gauteng

B *Holiday Inn Garden Court*, corner of Katherine St and Rivonia Rd, T8845660, F7832004. 157 rooms, restaurant, swimming pool, impersonal modern hotel, close to the Sandton City shopping mall. **B** *Park Plaza Sandton*, 84 Katherine St, Sandton, T7847707, F7844364. 138 rooms spread over 3 sprawling wings. Large, airy a/c rooms, 2 pools, gym, though service unexceptional. Has the advantage of motel-style parking outside the ground floor rooms. Free airport pickup and drop off. **B** *Protea Wanderers*, corner of Corlett Dr and Rudd Rd, Illovo, T7705500, F7705555. Directly opposite Wanderers cricket stadium. Quality hi-tec modern hotel, but lacking in character save for the fresh apple placed in each room! Rooms have individual office station with leather chair, phone in bathroom, electronic safe, trendy African and sporting motifs, nice pool area except for the traffic noise from the busy road below. **B** *Rosebank*, corner of Tyrwhitt and Bath avenues, Rosebank, T4472700, F4473276. Mid-range independent hotel with 318 a/c rooms, renowned Chinese restaurant, swimming pool, gym, sauna, within walking distance of the main shopping malls. **B** *Sunnyside Park*, Prince of Wales Terr, Parktown, T6437226, F6420019. 96 rooms, restaurant, swimming pool, converted mansion with new annexes, pleasant old fashioned atmosphere let down by an indifferent service. **B** *Vergelegen*, 6 Tottenham Av, Melrose Estate, T4473434, F8805366. Superb luxurious guesthouse set in beautiful and intimate gardens, 100 m from Rosebank Mall. Each of the 9 rooms have French windows leading out to a private terrace, under floor heating, individually decorated with antiques and tapestries in a 1930's colonial theme. Several comfortable lounges and conservatories, floodlit tennis court, cosy bar. A lovely family atmosphere and very much a home from home, makes a pleasant change from the chain hotels. Breakfast included, dinner on request. Recommended.

C *City Lodge*, Katherine St, Sandton, T4445300, F4445315. 106 single rooms, 53 double rooms, all a/c with TV, lounge area, non-smoking rooms available, gardens, pool, restaurant, bar, good value for location, close to business district and shops. **C** *Robin Inn Guesthouse*, 62 Valley Rd, Robin Hills, T/F7932583. 4 rooms, en suite facilities in an annexe, cool beers kept in the kitchenette, swimming pool, all meals available, this is an excellent guesthouse that stands out from many of the other options in the region. Jonita and Brams provide fresh flowers every day in your room as well as leaving biscuits and home-made cake for you to enjoy at the end of a day sightseeing. Strongly recommended. **C** *Mecure Inn*, Corner of Republic and Randburg Waterfront roads, T3263300, F7894175. 104 rooms with lots of extras including fridge, modem point, and an innovative internet station with keyboard attached to the TV. Narrow rooms and minuscule bathrooms but comfortable and excellent value for money. Breakfasts only, arrangement with 4 restaurants in the adjacent Randburg Waterfront mall to bill your hotel account. **C** *Town Lodge*, corner Grayston Dr and Webber Rd, Sandton, T7848850, F7848888. **D** *Road Lodge*, corner of 10th Av and Rivonia Rd, Rivonia, T8035220, F8032778. Both unimaginative but good value hotels (of the same chain) for town centre. **E** *Formula 1*, 1 Marie St, Bramley Park, T8875555, F8875632. Economical soulless accommodation units. Same rate for up to 3 people in a room.

Budget accommodation All the backpackers hostels have travel desks offering budget tours to local destinations such as Soweto, Johannesburg city centre, and Kruger, as well as being agents for *Baz Bus* and tours throughout the rest of Africa. They offer free pick-ups from the airport and the train and coach station, help on car hire deals and vary from looking like a student squat to good value, quiet rooms in a town house.

Backpackers hostels can arrange all travel arrangements

In a city as large as Johannesburg there are many options and new places appear every year, while others suddenly go out of business. Avoid touts at the airport. Not only is it illegal to tout, but you could be in danger of being ripped off by an expensive airport transfer and not know in advance where the backpackers is located. It's better to arrange a free pick up from a reputable hostel. Here we list some backpackers hostels which we know have been in business for several years and to the best of our knowledge can still be recommended. They are all served by the *Baz Bus*.

F *Backpackers Ritz*, 1A North Rd, Dunkeld West, T3257125, F3252521, ritz@iafrica.com One of Johannesburg's most well-established hostels. Large house in a secure neighbourhood with garden and swimming pool. Dorms, double rooms, travel desk, Soweto and city tours, internet access, individual safes plus long term baggage storage, helpful place to start

Gauteng

your visit to South Africa from. Meals available. Close to shops and entertainment at Hyde Park and Rosebank, all in a safe suburb away from the city centre, 30 mins from airport, free pickup, call before leaving home. YHA discount. Used by overland trucks. Comprehensive website, www.backpackinafrica.com For all budget travel in Southern Africa right the way up to Nairobi. Highly recommended. **E-F** *In Africa Lodge*, 20 Swartkops Cres, Buurendal, Edenvale 1609, T6095874, F6097818. A small backpackers in a homely house near the airport, run by pleasant people who genuinely take good care of their guests. Free transport to/from the airport. Dorm, smart double rooms, garden with pool. **F** *Airport Backpackers*, 3 Mohawk St, Rhodesfield, Kempton Park, T/F3940485. Only 2 km from the airport, close to the end of the runway, consequently planes flying low overhead. Dorms, double rooms and camping. Internet facilities, swimming pool, free pickup and drop off, free basic breakfast. One of the cheapest backpackers in Jo'burg but not particularly well-maintained. Not much to do locally, no shops or restaurants close by. **F** *Eastgate Backpackers*, 41 Hans Pirow Rd, Bruma, T6162741, F6151092. Close to the airport, free pickups. Dorms, double rooms, garden, relaxed atmosphere, very close to the Eastgate shopping mall, Burma flea market, and restaurants. **F** *Rockey's of Fourways*, 22 Campbell Rd, Craigavon, Sandton, T4654219, F4672597. Formely Rocky Street Backpackers of Yeoville. This well-established backpackers has relocated to the safer northern suburbs and is in walking distance of the Fourways Mall and Montecasino complex. Doubles and 30 dorm beds in large comfortable house. Camping available in 3 acres of gardens, large pool, bar with open fire, meals available, free airport pick up.

Eating
● *on maps, pages 523 and 524*

You will find many of the restaurants and bars within the confines of a shopping mall. To experience the ambience of street side eating and drinking, one of the best places to go to at night is **Melville**, in the northern suburbs off the M1. At the centre of this suburb, are a couple of streets with countless bars and restaurants to explore. At present they are safe and everything is within walking distance of each other. A few years ago Rocky St in Yeoville was the best place to go, but this is no longer the case and the area has witnessed a severe decline, you are advised to avoid it.

General *Baccarat*, 53 Admiral Court, Rosebank, T8801835. Quality French restaurant, romantic dimly lit corners, tasty treats such as Roquefort and mushroom pate, venison, oxtail in red wine, duck in orange sauce. *Browns of Rivonia*, 21 Wessels St, Rivonia, T8037605. Meals served in the courtyard of an old farmhouse, expensive but extensive menu includes roast lamb, salmon timbale, mustard sirloin and crêpes. Free tour of the wine cellar, which has over 40,000 bottles. *Butcher Shop & Grill*, Sandton Sq, Sandton City, T7848676. The sawdust on the floor fools nobody, this won an award as South Africa's Best Steakhouse in 2001, they get through 5 tonnes of quality steak each week. Tourists can buy cooler bags of vacuum-packed meat to take home on the plane, there's also a duty-free branch at the airport. If you like melt-in-the-mouth fillets and prime aged sirloins, head here. Recommended. *Linger Longer*, 58 Wierda Rd, Wierda Valley, T8840465. Closed all day Sun and lunch on Sat, one of Johannesburg's top restaurants serving an imaginative mix of delicate meals. *McGinty's Irish Pub*, Randburg Waterfront, Randburg, T7894572. Part of yet another chain, but authentically decorated as a traditional Irish pub. Guiness and Kilkenny on tap. Inexpensive huge portions of wholesome pub fare, pork knuckles, lamb shanks, liver and onions, steak and kidney pie and sausages and mash. *The Grillhouse*, The Firs, Oxford Rd, Rosebank, T8803945. South Africa is famous for its quality steaks and this restaurant is hugely popular for its melt in the mouth fillets and succulent sauces. Exposed brick and chunky, wooden furniture, excellent service and a lively atmosphere. Opposite and under the same ownership is *Katzy's* late night piano bar and cigar lounge, which has live music most nights and is fast making its way onto Jo'burg's nightlife circuit. Vast selection of Cognacs and malt whiskies. You would never know you're in a shopping mall.

African *Carnivore*, 69 Drift Boulevard, Muldersdrift, 30 mins' drive (approx 30 kms) from Johannesburg centre on the N14, T9572099. Zebra skin chairs, hot cast iron plates and slabs of meat carved off Masaai spears, make this a popular place with tourists who come for the ultimate African eating experience. The menu includes rare treats of marinated game meat such as crocodile, impala, kudu, ostrich, warthog and zebra. *Gramadoelas*, Market Theatre Complex, T8386960, closed Sun and Mon lunch. Good selection of South African dishes including sosaties, bobotie and melk tert, for starters there are mopani worms served in peri-peri sauce, other dishes from Morocco, Zanzibar and Ethiopia, the decor is an appealing Cape Dutch style, many famous visitors including Queen Elizabeth II in 1999, reservations recommended.

Mediterranean *Arlecchino*, Oxford Rd, Rosebank, T8802615. Tasty pizzas served with Italian wines in an open-air courtyard. *Spuntino da Lorenzo*, corner of Tyrwhitt and Cradock avenues, Rosebank, T7888750/2. Affordable wood fired pizzas, gluton free and whole wheat pasta, 70 pasta sauces, and a huge vegetarian menu. Small intimate Italian restaurant so booking advisable. *Ritz*, 17 3rd St, Parktown North, T8802470. Charming setting in a large conservatory, interesting Italian dishes without the usual reliance on pasta, reservations recommended, closed Sun. *Mozzarella's Italian Kitchen*, 6c 7th St, Melville, T4826910. In the heart of vibey Melville, big pasta portions, relaxed atmosphere. *Osteria Tre Nonni*, 9 Grafton Av, Craighall, T3270096. Closed Mon, Sun, expensive but sophisticated north Italian cuisine, home-made pasta, fresh seafood and rich creamy sauces, reservations recommended. *O'Galito*, Village Walk mall, Sandown, T7834930. Seafood specialist, excellent prawn and crab curries, Portuguese dishes incorporating African game meat, crocodile and ostrich. *Parros*, Hutton Court, 291 Jan Smuts Av, Hyde Park, T8804410. Traditional Greek dishes, late night bar, plate throwing at R1 per plate, the pieces are swept up and reused to make more disposable plates, good for a rowdy group but not an intimate time. *Plaka*, 3 Corlett Dr, Illovo, T7888777. Popular Greek taverna, that spills out on to the pavement, meze, succulent lamb dishes, retsina, end a smashing time with plate throwing.

Indian *Sahib's*, 2 branches at; 83 4th St, Melville, T4826670, and Illovo Sq, Rivonia Rd, T4474043. Unpretentious cheap curry houses, wide range of bunny chows, roti wraps, tandoori grills, and biryanis, Sunday buffet lunches for under R40 are unbeatable value.

Oriental *Daruma*, Sandton Sun/Towers Hotel, T7805157. Formal Japanese restaurant that serves some of the best sushi in Johannesburg, if not the African continent, according to some. Extensive menu with price tag to match. *The Royal Palace*, corner of Oxford Rd and Baker St, Rosebank, T4473381. Chinese, good value buffet lunches. *Red Chamber Mandarin Restaurant*, Hyde Park Mall, Jan Smuts, T3256048. Good value, wide choice of regional dishes, including Mandarin where wheat rather than rice is the staple. *Soi*, corner 7th and 3rd avenues, Melville, T7265775. Smart, trendy setting, Thai, Vietnamese, delicate dishes. *Suan Thai*, 11 Main Rd, Melville, T4822182. Another Melville quality restaurant, authentic Thai cooked by a Danish chef! Very hot curries, mango and coconut ice cream for dessert, live jazz some Sun evenings. *Yamato*, 196 Oxford Rd, Illovo, T8809781. Traditional Japanese restaurant, recommended for large groups, closed Sat lunchtime.

Vegetarian There are few specific vegetarian restaurants in Jo'burg, but almost every menu, particularly in Italian and Indian restaurants, has an excellent variety of vegetarian dishes. Usually denoted with a 'V'. *Graasroots*, Village Walk mall, Sandown, T8847220.

Gauteng

Breakfasts, snacks and lunch only. Healthy eating from this shopping mall stall, no meat, dairy or egg. Pastas, salads, bagels, cakes. Pumpkin and leek, or wild mushroom and port soups are recommended.

Bars & cafés *Bassline*, 7 7th St, Melville, T4826915. Popular South African jazz venue, nightly except Mon until 0200. *Blues Room*, Village Walk Mall, Sandown, T7845527. One of the best jazz and blues venues in Gauteng despite the steep cover charge. A stylish basement bar and restaurant, catering for the more mature music lover who is looking for a decent meal, a bit of a boogie, and intact eardrums at the end of it. Recommended. *District Six Jazz Café*, Randburg Waterfront, Republic Rd, T7899809. Cape Malay meals and live jazz on Wed, Fri and Sat nights. *Guildhall*, Meischkes Building, Market St, T8365560. An old fashioned bar with original wood panelling and Victorian décor. This is an historic miners pub in the centre of downtown Jo'burg, only visit with someone who is familiar with the area. *Fourno's Bakery*, Dunkeld West Centre, Jan Smuts Av, T3270009, open Mon-Fri, 0700-1800, Sat-Sun, 0700-1400. A firm favourite for cheap eats with other branches at the airport, Fourways, and Southgate malls. The bakers arrive at midnight to prepare the delicious range of pastries, cakes, croissants, quiches, and pies. Big breakfasts, trendy coffees, a great place at the weekends for a spot of people watching. *Kippies*, Market Theatre Complex, Bree St, T8343743. Light meals and township jazz. *Nino's*, 22 Cradock Av, Rosebank, T4474758, open 0700-1800 daily. Large, open, street side eating area, reasonably priced coffee and panini sandwich bar, opposite the Rosebank Sunday fleamarket, good place to start the day with a fat 3-egg omelette.

Nightclubs *Catz Pyjamas*, corner of 3rd and Main streets, Melville, T7268596. Jo'burg's original 24-hr bistro and cocktail bar, funky atmosphere, famous nachos and potent sangria, fun place in the wee early hours of the morning. *Enigma*, 187 Oxford Rd, Rosebank, T6823457. Current popular club with the well-heeled northern suburbs elite, open Tue and Wed – garage, acid-jazz, Fri and Sat – hip hop, soul, R&B, funk, R50 cover charge. *Monsoon Lagoon*, at *Ceaser's Casino* next to the airport, T9281290. Huge special events venue, TV show and fashion parties, upmarket mainstream club, over 23s, layers of dance floors, bars, and lounges, lavish and totally over the top. *Punter & Trouserleg*, corner of 5th and Main streets, Melville, T7261030. Open Mon, Wed-Sat, 1700 'til late. A small club/bar in trendy Melville, commercial music, aggressive bouncers, lots of students looking for drinks specials such as bottomless wine, cheap beer and shooters, expect things to get messy.

Entertainment

Entertainments listings are published in the local papers, the Mail and the Guardian and the bi-monthly magazine, SA City Life

Computicket, T3408000, F3408900. A central booking agency for tickets to the cinema, theatre, concerts, sports events, and city tours. They have kiosks in most of the large shopping malls. A safe way to see evening and late night shows is to travel by taxi directly to the door of the venue, on your return phone a radio taxi and walk directly from the entrance to the venue into the waiting taxi. Don't loiter around in the street waiting for a taxi in case you draw attention to yourself.

Cinemas All the latest Hollywood and European releases can be seen at the many multi-screen cinemas in the shopping malls. Check the local newspapers for complete listings. *Nu Metro*, T3254029 for information and bookings. *Ster-KineKor*, T3408200 for information and bookings. *IMAX Theatre*, Hyde Park Mall, Hyde Park, T3256182. Giant screen 5-storeys high with surround sound system, showing films on wildlife, mountains, deserts and seas. 4 shows daily during the week, 5 at the weekends.

Theatres *Civic Theatre*, Loveday St, Braamfontein, T4033408. Modern theatre building with four auditoriums, frequent performances of South African plays. *Market Theatre*, Bree St, T8321614. 3 auditoriums, famous for its controversial political plays during the 1980s.

Shopping **African art** *African Craft Market of Rosebank*, Cradock Av, Rosebank, T8802906. Open 0900-1700, closed Mon. The former street traders have now been housed in one ethnic inspired building in the centre of the popular Rosebank Mall. Curios from all over Africa, and as everyone is now under one roof, credit cards are accepted and shipping arranged. Street performers, musicians, and on Thu evenings, African food and cabaret. Recommended. *Art Africa*,

62 Tyrone Av, Parkview, T/F4862052. Ethnic arts, African antiques, strong emphasis on recycled art products, open Mon-Fri 0900-1800, Sat 0900-1500. *Everard Art Gallery*, 6 Jellicoe Av, Rosebank, T7884805. Open Mon-Sat 0900-1800. A private gallery selling contemporary South African art and wildlife paintings. *Kim Sacks Gallery*, 153 Jan Smuts Av, Parkwood, T4475804. Open Mon-Fri, 0900-1700, Sat-Sun 1000-1500. A selection of quality ethnic art from all over Africa and contemporary South African prints, sculptures, beadwork, and ceramics.

Camping equipment *Cape Union Mart*, Hyde Park Mall, Jan Smuts Av, T3255038, and 10 other branches throughout Johannesburg's various shopping malls. Outdoor equipment, clothing and books. Everything from mosquito nets to thermal gloves. *Drifters Adventure Centre*, Sandton City Mall, Sandton, T7839200. Specialist clothes and equipment for hikers or people going on safaris.

Camera equipment *Kameraz*, Rosebank Mews, Oxford Rd, Rosebank, T8802885. Open Mon-Fri 0800-1700, Sat 0800-1400. One of the largest dealers in new and second hand camera equipment in Gauteng. New and used accessories and lenses, and specialists in insurance claims. On the first Sun of every even month they hold a fleamarket of second hand equipment, and on the first Sun of every odd month, an exhibition and sale of work from local photographers.

Gold Krugerrands, South Africa's notorious gold coins can now be bought as an investment or simply as a souvenir. They can be ordered at most banks or can be bought over the counter at the *Scoin Shop*, 5th Floor, Twin Towers, Sandton City Mall, T7848551, F7848662.

Shopping malls Enormous modern shopping malls have taken Johannesburg by storm and visiting one is almost inevitable as they not only have shops but cafés, restaurants, banks, chemists, post offices and cinemas. As the city centre has deteriorated, shops and entertainment facilities have moved into these pre-constructed shopping emporiums, some of the biggest and two of most impressive are *Eastgate Mall*, near the airport and *Hyde Park Mall*, Jan Smuts Av, Hyde Park, T3254340. This is luxury shopping, where the ladies of Johannesburg who lunch, lunch, and is also home to the city's only IMAX theatre. *Rosebank Mall*, corner of Cradock and Baker streets, Rosebank, T7885530. The large open air plaza lined with cafés is ideal for sitting in the sun and watching people go by, it has much more of a village feel than the average indoor shopping mall, there is a busy and excellent fleamarket on the roof every Sun selling crafts and snacks, open 1000-1700. Daily curio markets are held at the *African Craft Market* on Cradock Av. *The Zone*, open 0900-0100 daily includes a games arcade, fluorescent ten-pin bowling, a bar and pool hall. *Sandton City Mall*, corner of Sandton Dr and Rivonia Rd (also attached to Sandton Sq by a walkway), T7837413, has international exclusive stores and trendy restaurants around an attractive square. *Randburg Waterfront*, corner of Republic Rd and Hans Strijdom Dr, T7895052. 55 restaurants, 360 shops, a musical fountain with 1,000 nozzles shooting spouts of water 30 m up into the air, fun fair, boat rides, the mall is almost a tourist attraction in its own right. One of the first supermalls to open in Johannesburg but now looking somewhat tacky.

Cricket *Wanderers' Stadium*, PO Box 55309, 21 North St, Illovo, Johannesburg 2116. Ticket **Sports** enquiries: T7881008, F8806229. This is one of South Africa's premier cricket grounds and regular international matches are played here in season.

Golf There are at least 14 golf courses around Johannesburg and several of South Africa's top courses are open to visitors during the week. *Glendower Club*, Marais Rd, Bedford View, T4531013. Beautiful location in a bird sanctuary, 20 mins from the city centre. *Houghton Golf Club*, 2nd Av, Lower Houghton, T7287337. Many major tournaments are held here including the South African Open. *Royal Johannesburg Golf Club*, Fairway Av, Linksfield North, T6403021. 2 courses east and west, South African Open held on the east Course, 30 mins from the city centre. *Wanderers Golf Club*, Rudd Rd, Illovo, T4473311. One of the oldest courses in South Africa, quite challenging, hosts the South African PGA Championship, near the city centre.

Rugby *Ellis Park*, Staib St, Doornfontein, T4028644, F4028144. This is the home of the Gauteng Strikers and the Cats, and matches are played here regularly during the season. The stadium seats 60,000 spectators and is a rowdy day out for the Boers who bring their braais and beers with them for a day's party.

Gauteng

Tour operators   **Local tours** *A'Zambezi Tours*, T4626620. Tours of Johannesburg and the surrounding area. *Airtrack Adventures*, T9572322. Game viewing in hot air balloons over the Crocodile River and Cradle of Humankind region. *Chamber of Mines*, T4987100. Visits by request only, to operating gold mines outside of Johannesburg, in a different league to the sanitized theme park at Gold Reef City, visitors here get taken 1 km underground into the industrial heart of a working mine to see the miners in action. *Expeditionary Force*, T012-6672833. Historical tours of Johannesburg and Pretoria, known for their insight and depth. Recommended. *Gold Reef Guides*, T4961400. Tours of Soweto and Gold Reef City. *Karabo Tours*, T/F8805099, T083-5290065 (mob), karabotours@iafrica.com Affordable in-depth Soweto tours (R200, 4 hrs) with a guide who was an active 12-year-old in the 1976 school children uprisings; historic Pretoria tours (R260, 4 hrs); Gold Reef City (R200, 4 hrs); Lion Park (R200, 4 hrs); comprehensive Johannesburg city tours (R200, 4 hrs); Lesedi Cultural Village (R350, 5 hrs), picks up at all hotels and hostels in the northern suburbs, discount for booking multiple tours. Recommended, to show you the important and fun sights if you only have a day or two in Johannesburg. *Jimmy's Face to Face Tours*, 130 Main St, Budget House, T3316109. One of the original Soweto tour operators. *Lords Travel & Tours*, T7915494, F7935011. City tours, Soweto, Pilanesberg and Sun City, Lesedi and packages to Kruger.

Southern Africa tours *The Bundu Bus*, T6750767. Budget 4-day tours to Kruger and the Panorama region, R2,100-2,800 per person, choose from camping or chalet accommodation. *Drifters*, PO Box 48434, Roosevelt Park 2129, T8881160, F8881020. Well-organized overland tours between Johannesburg and Cape Town, visiting the Garden Route, Swaziland, Zululand, the Drakensberg and Kruger, 18 days, E1,345 per person; they also run long distance tours to Namibia, Victoria Falls and Nairobi. *Sunway Safaris*, T/F8037400. Small group budget overland and camping tours in minibuses, 17 days Johannesburg to Cape Town via Kruger, Swaziland, Drakensberg, Garden Route, from US$995 per person. 4-day/3-night Kruger tours from US$265. *Ventures for Africa*, PO Box 3005, Cresta 2118, T4768842, F4761437. Professionally organized hiking tours. *Wagon Trails*, T011-9078063, F9070913, wagon.trails@pixie.co.za Some of the best value camping tours to Kruger for anyone who wants an enjoyable as well as informative trip; 4 days, 3 nights, with night drives and bush braais – R1,380, including pickup/drop off from Johannesburg and Pretoria, strongly recommended, the editors were most impressed with this conscientious company. Regular departures to Kruger and further afield adventure tours to Zimbabwe and Mozambique.

There is a special tour during the 2003 Cricket World Cup in South Africa, which will follow the matches around the country

Shongololo Safari Train Hotel The *Shongololo Express* is a hotel train, which only travels at night leaving you free to explore and enjoy each new stop during the daytime. At each stop you can join a day or half-day side trip, all included in the overall price. The train carries its own comfortable vehicles and guides, who unload the combi minibuses whenever necessary.

The train has 7 accommodation carriages, the maximum number of guests it can carry is 108. There is a dining car and an air conditioned lounge/bar carriage. The sleeping compartments are compact but functional and bathrooms are located on each corridor. The *Shongololo* is not as luxurious or formal as, say, the *Blue Train* – expect the train equivalent of a hotel 3 star rating– and consequently more affordable.

There are three tours: one in Namibia; one that departs from Johannesburg and finishes in Victoria Falls in ZimbabweTh; and a third tour, the Shongololo Good Hope, which is a comprehensive 16-day tour of South Africa between Pretoria and Cape Town. It runs in both directions and also links up with the Victoria Falls leg. The following is a summary of the southbound route; Pretoria – Hazyview region (two days are spent off the train and include a full day in Kruger) – Swaziland – Northern Zululand (leave the train to visit Hluhlwe/Umfolozi Game Reserve) – Southern Zululand (battlefield sites/St Lucia National Park) – Durban – Drakensburg (the train stops at Ladysmith to visit the Royal Natal Park) – Bloemfontein – Port Elizabeth – Oudtshoorn (Cango Caves and ostrich farm) – Garden Route (the train stops at Mossel Bay which is a convenient base from which to explore the region) – Stellenbosh (wine estates) – Cape Peninsular – Cape Town.

There are fixed departure dates throughout the year and all prices are inclusive of meals and excursions. Current rates for the Shongololo Good Hope are; €1,990 per person sharing,

€2,190 single in a coupe. Contact any major travel agent that deals with South Africa or directly at PO Box 1558, Parklands, T011-4862824, F011-4862909, shongo@mweb.co.za

Local Bus: *Magic Bus*, T6081662. Runs a shuttle service between the major hotels in Sandton and the airport. *Municipal Bus Service*, T8382125, for information on local bus services within Johannesburg.

Transport
See also Ins and outs, page 515

    Car hire: *Avis*, toll-free T0800-021111 for the nearest branch. *Britz Africa*, T3961860. Contact for camper vans and motorhomes – good all-inclusive deals. *Budget*, T3923929 or toll-free T0800-016622 for nearest branch. *Leisuremobiles*, T7921884. Camper vans and fully equipped safari 4-wheel drive. *Imperial*, T8834352 or toll-free T0861-131000. *Maui Camper Hire*, T3961445, F3661757. For 4-wheel drive and fully-equipped camper vans, rates from R700 per day. *Tempest*, T3961080. *U-Drive*, T4023309. Motorbike hire only.

    Taxi: there is a taxi rank at the Park City Transit Centre otherwise you will have to phone for a taxi, always agree on a price before travelling. *Maxi*, T6481212. *Midway*, T3122111. *Rose's*, T4030000. One reader recently recommended *Mohammed Taxis*, T8558876, as a cheap option for getting to Durban. Check with your hostel to make sure this is a reliable company and service.

Long distance Air: all **domestic departures** leave from Terminal 5 of Johannesburg International Airport. *Comair*, *Intensive Air*, *Kuhula.com*, *Nationwide*, *SAA*, *SA Airlink* and *SA Express*, cover the country between them. *SAA*, T9781111, in conjunction with *SA Airlink*, T9781111, and *SA Express*, T9785569, is the largest local carrier and has regular daily flights connecting Johannesburg with other major towns within South Africa.

For details of arrival by air see box on page 514

    Kulula.com, www.kulula.com (no phone but a desk at the airport) is South Africa's new no-frills, budget airline, which currently has flights between Johannesburg and Durban and Cape Town. The airline runs on the same principle as the European budget airlines, no tickets, reservations through the website, no on board refreshments etc, and currently has the cheapest fares, from R300 one-way to Durban, R450 one-way to Cape Town. The number of daily flights is ever-increasing as its popularity grows. Note, these fares are little more than the cost of long distance bus fares between the cities.

    At the time of writing, *Intensive Air*, T9275111, F8807404, were also offering competitive fares between Johannesburg and Cape Town. Daily flights, expect to pay R850-R1,250 for a return ticket.

    BA Comair, reservations, T9210222. Operate in conjunction with *British Airways*. **Cape Town**: Mon-Fri, 13 flights a day, Sat, 6 flights, Sun 11 flights; **Durban**: Mon-Fri, 9 flights a day, Sat, 4 flights, Sun, 5 flights; **Harare**: daily at 1230; **Port Elizabeth**: Mon-Fri, 4 flights a day, Sat-Sun 2 flights; **Victoria Falls**: daily at 1215; **Windhoek**: daily except Tue at 1200; and **Ndola**: 4 times a week, and **Lusaka**: daily, both in Zambia.

Rail The railway station is in the Park City Transit Centre. Sales & Ticket Offices: Pretoria, T012-3348470; Johannesburg, T7732944; Nelspruit, T013-7529257; Bloemfontein; T051-4082941; Kimberley, T053-8382631; Port Elizabeth, T041-5072400; Cape Town, T021-4493871. Even though rail travel is relatively slow the train service is popular and seats should be reserved well in advance.

    The *Algoa* service departs daily at 1430 to **Port Elizabeth** (19 hrs), via **Bloemfontein** (6½ hrs), **Cradock** (14 hrs), and **Addo** (18 hrs).

    The *Amatola* service departs daily at 1245 to **East London** (20 hrs), via **Bloemfontein** (6½ hrs), **Queenstown** (15 hrs), **Cathcart** (17½ hrs), and **Stutterheim** (19 hrs). The *Bosvelder* service departs daily at 1900 to **Messina** (14½ hrs), via **Pretoria** (1¼ hrs), Pietersburg/Polokwane (7½ hrs), and **Louis Trichardt** (12 hrs).

    The *Komati* service departs daily at 1810 to **Maputo** (Mozambique), via **Nelspruit** (10¼ hrs), and **Komatipoort** (13 hrs). At the time of writing there was a daily shuttle service running between the border and Maputo in both directions.

    The *Trans Karoo* service departs daily at 1230 to **Cape Town** (28 hrs), via **Kimberley** (10½ hrs), **Beaufort West** (18 hrs) and **Worcester** (24½ hrs).

Gauteng

The *Trans Natal* service departs daily at 1830 to **Durban** (13½ hrs), via **Ladysmith** (7½ hrs) and **Pietermaritzburg** (11 hrs).

Local trains: run between Johannesburg and **Pretoria** every 30 mins, *Metro services*, T7735878. However, violent robbery on these trains is so frequent we would advise against using this service. Rather take the bus. A new high speed rail link between Johannesburg and Pretoria via the airport has recently been given the go ahead, though planning and construction is likely to take several years.

Luxury trains: the main operators of epic luxury train journeys are *Blue Train*, T012-3348459, F3348464, www.bluetrain.co.za and *RovosRail*, T012-3158242, F3230843, www.rovos.co.za For full details see the Pretoria rail transport section.

There are currently no phones inside the bus station, leave all valuables with someone you trust when you go out to phone

Road Bus: *Translux*, *Intercape*, *Greyhound*, and all the smaller bus companies depart and arrive from the Park City Transit Centre, which is also where the railway station is, in central Jo'burg. The surrounding area is notoriously bad for muggings. We have heard of too many tales of incidents for this not to be taken seriously. Be extra careful in the terminal and don't go outside unless you are meeting a pre-arranged taxi or lift. If you have to wait at all, insist on sitting in one of the bus company waiting areas which are normally guarded. If you are waiting for a pick up from, say, one of the backpacker hostels, they will usually suggest you sit in a restaurant such as *Steers*. The price of a cup of coffee is well worth it for a safe environment. We have heard of muggings in the terminal toilets so ensure a friend is looking after your belongings somewhere safe if you need to use the toilets. Many of the buses depart and arrive late at night or early in the morning, ensure you are dropped off or picked up immediately after the relevant times. Many of the public phone booths are located outside the terminal, arrange a pick up before your arrival.

All the bus companies listed below have frequent departures between Johannesburg and Pretoria throughout the day (1 hr). You cannot pre-book this short journey, but it is never a problem to get a stand-by ticket, expect to pay around R40.

Greyhound, T2498900 reservations and enquiries. To **Bulawayo** (12 hrs), Mon, Wed, 0800, Fri, 2200. To **Cape Town** (17 hrs), daily at 1730 via **Bloemfontein** (5½ hrs). **Durban** (7 hrs), departs daily at 0830, 1000, 1100, 1400, 1600, 2200, 2300, the 1000 service stops at **Newcastle** (4½ hrs) and **Ladysmith** (6 hrs). **Durban** via **Vryheid** and **Richards Bay**, daily, 0815. **Harare** (Zimbabwe) (16 hrs), Mon, Wed, Fri, 2230 via **Pietersburg** (4 hrs) and **Masvingo** (Zimbabwe) (12½ hrs). To **Nelspruit** (5 hrs), daily, 1545. **Port Elizabeth** (15 hrs), daily 1745 via **Bloemfontein** (5½ hrs), and **Grahamstown** (11½ hrs).

Intercape, T012-6544114 information and enquiries. To **Durban** (7 hrs), departs daily at 0800, 1330, 2200. **Cape Town** (15 hrs), daily at 1400, 1730 via **Bloemfontein** (4½ hrs). To **Port Elizabeth** (14 hrs), daily 1730. To **Plettenberg Bay** (13 hrs), daily, 1730. To **Upington** (9 hrs), daily at 0715 via **Kuruman** (6 hrs). The Upington service connects with coaches to **Windhoek** (Namibia).

Translux, T012-3154300 reservations and enquiries. To **Blantyre** (Malawi) (31 hrs), Wed, Thu, Sat, Sun, 1000, via **Harare**. **Bloemfontein** (6 hrs), daily 0855. **Bulawayo** (Zimbabwe) (14½ hrs), daily, 2100. **Cape Town** (18 hrs), daily, 1245 via **Kimberley** and 1845 via **Bloemfontein**. **Durban** (8 hrs), daily at 0800, 0930, 2230, Thu, Fri, Sun, 1400. **Maputo** (Mozambique) (7½ hrs), daily, 0900, via **Nelspruit** (4 hrs). **Plettenberg Bay** (16½ hrs), Tue, Wed, Fri, Sun, 1745 via **Kimberley**, Mon, Thu, Sat, 1745 via **Bloemfontein**. **East London** (12 hrs), daily at 1815. **Harare** (Zimbabwe) (13½ hrs), Tue, Thu, Fri, Sun, 2200. **Lusaka** (Zambia) (27 hrs), Tue and Fri, 0900 via Harare. **Port Elizabeth** (14 hrs), daily 0830.

Luxliner, T9144321, toll free T0800-003537, runs a daily service from the Parkade Centre at Johannesburg International Airport, to **Margate**, via **Durban**, departs 1030.

Budget buses: *Baz Bus*, T021-4392323, F4392343, info@bazbus.com The best option for the backpacker to get about most of South Africa on the cheap. Reservation hours Mon-Fri, 0800-2100, Sat-Sun, 0800-2000 or book through any backpackers hostel. This is a hop-on, hop-off service which runs from door to door of the popular backpacker hostels. Passengers just need to confirm where they wish to be collected from before they continue their route, there are no restrictions on the period of validity nor on how many times you can hop-on, hop-off. See page for full details of the service. From Johannesburg the bus runs to **Durban**, via the **Drakensberg** on Wed, Fri and Sun, and **Swaziland**, via **Nelspruit** on Mon, Wed, and Sat. For more up-to-date information on the *Baz Bus* check out their website, this can also help with other links concerning travel on the cheap in South Africa: www.bazbus.com

Airline offices *Air France*, T7701600. *Air Malawi*, T6220466. *Air Namibia*, T3902876. *Air Tanzania*, T6161870. *Air Zimbabwe*, T6157017. *Alitalia*, T8819600. *American Airlines*, T3255777. *Air Botswana*, T4476078. *British Airways*, international flights, T0860-011747 (toll free SA only), domestic flights T9210222. *Cathay Pacific*, T7977700. *Delta Airlines*, T4824582. *El Al*, T8803232. *Egypt Air*, T8804126. *Emirates*, T3031900. *Ethiopian Airlines*, T2898114. *Ghana Airways*, T6224005. *Kenya Airways*, T8819667. *KLM*, T0860-247747 (toll free SA only), T8819696 (international). *Lineas Aereas de Mozambique*, T6224889. *Lufthansa*, T6459111. *Malaysia Airways*, T8809614. *Qantas*, T4418550. *SAA*, T9781111. *Sabena*, T7787000. *Swissair*, T7787000. *Singapore Airlines*, T8808560. *Virgin Atlantic*, T3403500. *Air Route Adventures*, T7948967, F7947296. Offer flights and package deals with the following historic aircraft, Douglas DC-3 Dakota and DC-4 Skymaster.

Directory

   Banks *American Express*, Sandton City Mall, T8849195; 33 Bath Av, Rosebank, T8808382; Eastgate Mall, Bedfordview, T6223914; Hyde Park Mall, T3254424. *Rennies Travel*, Sandton City Mall, T8844035; Rosebank Firs Mall, T7880502; and Eastgate Mall, Bedfordview, T6162077. Agents for *Thomas Cook*, no commission on Thomas Cook TCs. There are *Rennies Travel*, and *American Express*, bureaux de change at Johannesburg International Airport, open daily 0500-2100. All the major banks have foreign exchange facilities, most shopping malls will have a bank where you can cash TCs and change money or withdraw money from your credit card at an ATM. *First National*, T0800-111722; *Nedbank*, T0800-110180; *Standard Bank*, T0800-123000.

   Communications Post Office: *Postnet*, T0800-110226, toll-free for customer services. **Internet**: there is an extraordinary lack of internet cafés in Johannesburg, but you will be able to get access at most hotels and backpacker places.

   Embassies and consulates Consulates: *Belgium*, T4476434. *Botswana*, T4033748. *France*, T3313478. *Mozambique*, T3272938. *Norway*, T4424613. *Swaziland*, T4032050. *Switzerland*, T4427500. *UK*, T3270015.

   Medical services Hospitals: north eastern areas, T4884911; southern areas, T4350022; Sandton and environs, T7092000. *Rosebank Vaccination Station*: 63 7th Av, Parktown North, T7882016. Open Mon-Fri, 0730-1800, Sat 0830-1300. Useful stop to update vaccinations and pick up anti-malarials before heading to the Kruger region. **Emergencies**: Air Mercy Ambulance, T4841616; Ambulance T999, Randburg T7891111, Sandton T8832800.

   Useful services *Bed and Breakfast Association*, T012-4802001. Booking agency for B&B accommodation in Johannesburg and Pretoria. *South African National Parks (SANPARKS)*, 643 Leyds St, Muckleneuk, Pretoria, T012-3431991, F021-3430905, open Mon-Fri 0800-1545. It is a good idea to visit the office in person to book accommodation in the National Parks in advance (see Pretoria, page 534). **Fire Brigade**: T10111, T6242800. **Immigration**: 77 Harrison St, T8363228. Extensions for a holiday visa cost R390 and take 10 working days, an onward ticket and proof of funds are required, this office is in a notorious part of town, expect lengthy queues. **Police**: T10111. **VAT Refund**: T4847530. **Weather**: T082162.

Gauteng

Pretoria

The name Pretoria was given to the new settlement by Marthinus Wessel Pretorius, in memory of his father, Andries Pretorius, who had led the Voortrekkers in the bloody massacre of the Zulus at Blood River. Today it is the administrative capital of South Africa and the third largest city in the country. Despite being almost joined to Johannesburg 56 kms to the south by a band of green belt towns, the atmospheres of the two cities couldn't be more different. While Johannesburg was built on gold and industry, Pretoria's existence was founded on the Vortrekker period of South Africa's turbulent past and retains the rather stern, bureaucratic atmosphere from the years as capital of the state machine. While it is safer than Johannesburg, downtown Pretoria, like most major cities in South Africa, has gone through a transformation in recent years. With the demise of Apartheid, black South Africans are again permitted to live and work freely within the city centre, and it has a much more of an African feel about it. Despite

*Phone code: 012
(NB Always use
3-figure prefix)
Colour map 2, grid B3
Altitude: 1,363 m*

this, the city centre was designed with corporate and governmental bodies in mind, and there is little to see, most of the historical sights are dotted around the surrounding hills.

Ins and outs

Getting there
For more detailed information see Transport, page 545

The centre of Pretoria is about 45 km from Johannesburg International Airport. The easiest way to travel to and from the airport is to take the Pretoria Airport Shuttle. There is a Metro commuter train service between Pretoria and Johannesburg but we **strongly advise against** using this due to problems of theft and security. Take the bus instead. *Intercape*, *Greyhound* and *Translux* have several departures between the 2 cities per day, and although these cannot be booked it is never usually a problem getting a stand-by seat.

Getting around
There is little of interest in the city centre, which is nothing more than a collection of high rise office blocks, and the majority of Pretoria's interesting sights are dotted around on the surrounding hills

While there is a good local bus service which everyone uses to get into work, it does not take you to the various monuments in the city's suburbs. The easiest way to appreciate the city sights is to spend a day driving around before you return a hired car. Alternatively take an inexpensive half-day city tour with a guide, you will get much more out of sites such as the Vortrekker Monument with someone who is knowledgeable about its history. During the day taking a municipal bus that runs between the centre and suburbs is a safe and cheap way of getting about town. **Church Street** is Pretoria's main through road running from east to west and at 26 km long is considered to be one of the world's longest streets. From the city centre it leads east to **Arcadia** where many of the embassies and the Union Buildings are located. To the south of here is **Sunnyside**, which until recently was home to most hotels and nightlife. However, the area has suffered a severe decline in recent years, comparable to Yeoville or Hillbrow in Johannesburg, where crime is endemic and gangs dealing in drugs control the streets. There is little reason to venture into this area anymore, so it is best to avoid it. Most restaurants, hotels, nightclubs, and backpackers have closed or relocated to the safer suburbs of **Hatfield** and **Brooklyn** a few kilometres further east where the colleges, universities and sports stadiums are also located. Both are attractive suburbs dotted with parks and gardens, and streets lined with Pretoria's distinctive jacaranda trees.

Climate
Pretoria has a pleasant climate with warm to hot summers and mild sunny winters. The sun shines throughout the year except during the rains. In winter the daily temperature averages 19°C, the days are still and the skies are clear blue and cloud-free. In the evening it can get a bit cool, local residents will tell you it's cold as they walk about in thick warm clothes. The average annual rainfall is 741 mm, usually falling during the months from Nov to Mar. The best time to visit is during the spring in order to see the jacarandas in full bloom, however, most months are pleasant except for Dec to Feb when heavy rain can cause a few problems.

Tourist offices
The *Pretoria Tourist Rendezvous Centre*, is in The Old Netherlands Bank Building, Church Square. Located here is the municipal *Pretoria Tourism Information Bureau*, T3374430, F3262243, open Mon-Fri, 0800-1600, and *Travel the Planet*, T3374415, F3262325, open Mon-Fri, 0800-1800, Sat-Sun, 0900-1200. A new privately run reservation and information service for tours in and around Pretoria. The municipal office used to be a very poorly run and had little to offer the visitor to Pretoria. However it seems to have improved with the arrival of Travel the Planet, who also provide an information service for both offices at the weekend. Between the two offices you should get the information you are looking for.

South African National Parks (SANPARKS), 643 Leyds St, Muckleneuk, (postal address: Box 787, Pretoria 0001). **Reservations**: T3431991, F3430905 or via email at reservations@parks-sa.co.za Open for telephone bookings: Mon-Fri, 0800-1730; Sat, 0800-1500; Sun, 0900-1400. Bookings can also be made at the offices in Cape Town, T021-4222810, F021-4246211, or Durban T031-3044934, F031-3043868.

The Pretoria office is the main office in the country which handles all bookings for accommodation and special long distance hikes such as the Otter Trail in Tsitsikamma National Park. The following parks have overnight accommodation which can be booked in advance: Addo Elephant, Augrabies Falls, Bontebok, Golden Gate Highlands, Kgalagadi Transfrontier

Park, Karoo, Kruger, Mountain Zebra, Tsitsikamma, West Coast and Wilderness National Park. There is a curio shop selling Parks Board items in this office.

History

From the outset Pretoria has been closely involved with political upheaval in South Africa, culminating with the inauguration of President Nelson Mandela at the Union Buildings on 10 May 1994. These buildings were only built in 1913, but the suburbs started to take shape as soon as the city had been named. As with all South African cities the first building of any substance to emerge was the church. In August 1854 work had started on a church right by today's Church Square. The first streets were laid out by Andries du Toit, a self-taught surveyor, while the first suburb was known as Arcadia, which was developed by Stephanus Meintjes who in turn was commemorated by naming the hillock nearby, *Meintjeskop*.

During the 1860s, as the city was steadily growing, Marthinus Pretorius, who had been made president of the republic, tried to unite the Orange Free State with the Transvaal. He failed, resigned as president and was replaced by the Rev Thomas Francois Burgers in 1870. Under Burgers the city developed in certain areas, schools and parks were built, but the political problems remained unresolved. The British eventually annexed the Transvaal in April 1877, and their first action was to establish a garrison which in turn attracted a large number of immigrants who brought money with them. New buildings were built and the fortunes of the city began to look more promising. However, during the Transvaal War of Independence the British withdrew and the city was taken over by the dominant Paul Kruger who was to cause countless problems once the gold had been discovered.

At the end of the Anglo-Boer War Pretoria was named as the capital of the British colony, and under such conditions it continued to prosper so that when the Union of South Africa was created in 1910, Pretoria was made the administrative capital of the new state. Shortly afterwards, the Union Buildings were built to house the new government. The growth of the town was now closely related to the expanding civil service and its status as an important city assured. The city has remained a centre for government and today most overseas diplomats are based in Pretoria. The city is also headquarters to the defence forces and home to the University of South Africa (UNISA). Today it has over 125,000 students throughout the world and is regarded as one of the largest correspondence universities in the world.

Like Johannesburg, Pretoria has large township areas to the north west and north east of the city. The greater Pretoria area covers some 632 square miles and the population is estimated at 1.3 million. The metropolitan council has recently reorganized itself to unite the previously segregated areas under one council administration. The greater area is now called Tshwane, which means 'we are the same'. Technically this is the new name for Pretoria but like other regional name changes in South Africa, it will be some time before this is widely recognized.

Sights

Overall the sights of Pretoria are not that many and most visitors tend only to spend a couple of days here before pushing on into the countryside and enjoying their holiday. If you have to spend some time here there's the Voortrekker monument and a couple of museums worth visiting. The other major attraction is Sun City, a couple of hours' drive away, though most people go on an excellent value day tour. Other sights such as the Lion Park, Witwatersrand Botanical Gardens, and Lesedi Cultural Village are dealt with in the Johannesburg section (see page 522) but are just as easily accessible from Pretoria.

Every spring the appearance of the city is transformed by 60,000 flowering jacaranda trees, the parks and gardens are covered in a mauve blanket

The oldest buildings in Pretoria can be found in **Church Square**, which was once a Vortrekker marketplace. A statue of Paul Kruger stands in the middle of the

In the centre

pigeon-filled square surrounded by late 19th-century banks and government offices. The most interesting of these is the **Palace of Justice**, where Mandela was tried during the Treason Trials.

Transvaal Museum, on Paul Kruger Street, is a typical city centre natural history museum. This is a leading centre of zoological research, particularly in terms of taxonomy and systematics. If you can convince them that you have any relevant academic credentials, you may get to see some of the more interesting pieces of the collection. The Bird Hall houses the Austin Roberts Collection, where you can see some of the birds, for example forest birds, which you may only hear in the field. The world-renowned hominid fossil, Mrs Ples, *Australopithecus africanus*, is kept here, but you must get special permission if you wish to view it. ■ *T3227632. Mon-Sat 0900-1700, Sun 1100-1700. There is a coffee shop in the entrance lobby.*

The **Treaty of Vereeniging** ending the Anglo-Boer War (1899-1902) was signed in **Melrose House**, on 275 Jacob Maré Street, on 31 May 1902, between the British High Command and Boer Republican Forces. The house was originally built in 1886 for George Heys, who made his fortune from trade and a stagecoach service to the Transvaal. It is regarded as one of the finest examples of Victorian domestic architecture in South Africa; marble columns, stained-glass windows and mosaic floors all help create a feeling of serene style and wealth. The house was restored after being bombed by ri ght-wingers in 1990. Today the grounds are used for the occasional classical concert. Inside the house there is a fine collection of objects made by Boer prisoners of war who were sent to St Helena. ■ *Tue-Sun, 1000-1700. Closed Mon. There is a small café in the converted stables.*

President Kruger House, on Church Street West, is where President Kruger lived between 1884-1901. The museum collection displays many of the family possessions and objects relating to the Anglo-Boer War. During the war the European governments sent him presents as they voiced their support for the Boers, but Kruger needed arms and soldiers, not decorative items. Also on show is a State coach and his private railway carriage. ■ *T3321266. Tue-Sat 0830-1600, Sun 1100-1600. Small entrance fee.*

Pretoria Zoo is on the corner of Paul Kruger and Boom streets, the entrance is on Boom Street. Look out for all the curio sellers crowded by the gate. ■ *Daily, summer 0800-1730, winter 0800-1700. T3283265. Entrance is R30 per person, which includes admission to the aquarium. Rides on the cable car are R15 extra.*

Difficult to miss if you are walking about in the centre of town, is **Strijdom Square**, an open square that used to be dominated by a massive bust of JG Strijdom covered by a curved concrete roof like a piece of canvas. However, this has turned out to be not such a spectacular architectural feat after all as it recently collapsed! At present a pile of rubble is all that remains, only time will tell if it will be rebuilt. Strijdom was Prime Minister between 1954 and 1958 when the government started to place heavy restrictions upon the ANC and banned the Communist Party. Eight people were shot dead here by right-wing activists in the early 1990s. Today, however, it is a popular meeting place at lunchtime, on one corner stands the tall ABSA Bank building and the excellent State Theatre takes up the rest of the block. Local buses and taxis all stop in front of the square.

Burgers Park is the most central of the city parks, between Van der Walt and Andries streets. This is a fine Victorian park, which was first laid out as a botanical garden in the early 1870s. Today the park is a popular place for people to relax in the shade at lunchtime and at the weekend. More than 100 years later it is now graced with some fine mature trees; India rubber trees, Phoenix palms and jacarandas. Amongst the old trees is a fish pond, rose garden, tea garden and a '**florarium**'. The florarium was opened in the 1970s to house a collection of exotic plants in contrasting environments. The eastern part of the building houses subtropical plants, including palms, anthuriums, philodendrons, bromeliads and orchids. In the southern section ferns, camellias, orchids, fuchsias, begonias and primulas grow in a cool, moist climate; an arid room exists to display plants from the Karoo and Kalahari regions of South Africa. Elsewhere in the garden is a statue of remembrance for the officers and men of the South African Scottish Regiment who were killed during the First World War. The park is named after President TJ Burgers, whose statue stands in one corner. ■ *Winter 0600-1800, summer 0600-2200.*

African Window is a very interesting and creatively designed museum, at 149 Visagie Street, between Bosman and Schubart. The cave paintings and rock art

Greater Pretoria

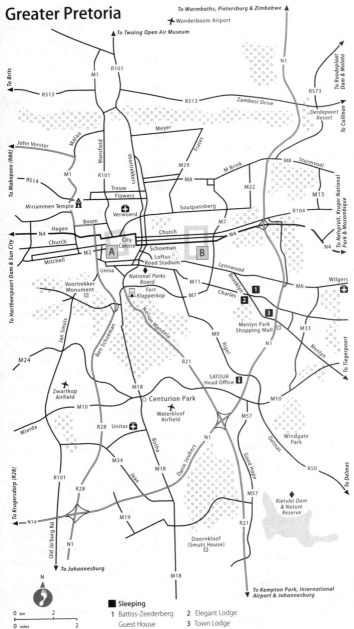

Gauteng

Detailed maps
A Central Pretoria,
page 539
B Hatfield & Hillcrest,
page 542

Sleeping
1 Battiss-Zeederberg Guest House
2 Elegant Lodge
3 Town Lodge

displays are particularly interesting. They are clear and provide good explanations of the hows and whys of such an art form. Another exhibit worth checking out is the history and development of the Hananwa people from the Blue Mountain before the arrival of the first Europeans in Africa. There are also some exciting temporary exhibitions. ■ *Daily 0900-1700. Free entry. T3246082. The main entrance hall contains a curio shop and restaurant.*

Sunnyside **Pretoria Art Museum** in Arcadia Park houses a fine collection of South African art
& Arcadia and 17th-century paintings. The collection includes works by Pierneef, Frans Oerder and Anton van Wouw, plus the Michaelis Collection. Space for exhibitions. ■ *Tue-Sat 1000-1700, Wed 1000-2000, Sun 1400-1800, closed Mon. Guided tours are available, contact T3441807. Teas and light meals available.*

The magnificent complex of the **Union Buildings** sits on top of Meintjeskop overlooking the centre of the city. The gardens were packed with people when Nelson Mandela addressed the nation after his inauguration as first black president on 10 May 1994. The building, designed by Herbert Baker who had already designed St George's Cathedral and Rhodes Memorial in Cape Town, was completed in 1913. Baker went on to help Edwin Lutyens in the planning of New Delhi, India. The Union Buildings in Pretoria influenced his designs for the new Government Secretariat and the Imperial Legislative Assembly. Baker had first used the local red sandstone in 1909 for Pretoria Railway station to test its suitability for such grand buildings. The gardens below the buildings are pleasant to walk about, but the best reason for coming here is for the city view. Look out for the statues of South Africa's famous generals: Botha, on horseback, Hertzog and Smuts. Also found on the hill is the Pretoria War Memorial, Delville Wood Memorial and the Garden of Remembrance. ■ *In Arcadia, less than 1 km east of the city centre, catch a bus along Church St and get off by the gardens directly below the buildings. There are a number of curio sellers in the carpark.*

Around the **Miriammen Temple** is a pleasant reminder of the importance of the Indian popula-
suburbs tion in South Africa. The temple is one of the oldest buildings in Pretoria, it was built in 1905. The imposing *gopuram* (tower) is made from layers of stone, figures of gods, demons and goddesses, it stands 12.5 m high. The temple is devoted to Miriammen, the Hindu goddess of infectious diseases such as smallpox. You are free to enter most areas but remember to remove your shoes. ■ *Follow the N4, Proes St, from the city centre for 2 km, turn right into Seventh Street. Open daily all day.*

The sheer size and design of the **Voortrekker Monument** will ensure that this building is never completely forgotten, but the ceremony held here on 16 December has now become a very low key affair. (Few people turn up at the monument on the day and the national holiday is now referred to as Day of Reconciliation, with different reasons for celebration.) The monument was completed in 1949 after 11 years of work. The building itself is a huge stone square built from granite quarried in the Northern Province, measuring 40 m by 40 m at its base and standing 40 m high. Inside is the cavernous Hall of Heroes guarded by a carved head of a buffalo above the entrance, thought by most to be the most dangerous animal in Africa. It was created to commemorate the Great Trek of the 1830s, when the Afrikaners headed inland with just their ox wagons and little idea of what lay ahead of them. However the date of 16 December is particularly significant, and until the election of the new government this was a very important public holiday for the Boer, the Day of the Covenant. At exactly midday a ray of sunlight falls onto a large slab of stone in the centre of the basement (rather like a tomb), spotlighting the carved words: "Ons Vir Jou, Suid Afrika" (We are for you, South Africa). The date celebrates the bloody massacre of the Zulus at Blood River a short distance from Dundee in KwaZulu Natal (see page 456). Inside the hall is a 92 m long frieze with 27 panels depicting episodes from the Great Trek. A narrow staircase, and a new elevator, lead up into the roof where on a clear day the views of Pretoria and the highveld are quite special, although this view is definitely not for anyone who suffers from vertigo. Outside, the surrounding wall recreates the circular laager of 64 ox-wagons that can be seen at the site of the battlefield. There are three busts of Great Trek leaders, Piet Retief, Andries Pretorius and Hendrik Potgieter.

Central Pretoria

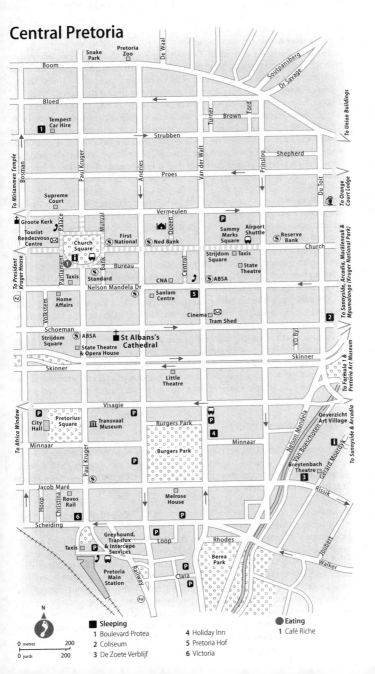

■ Sleeping
1 Boulevard Protea
2 Coliseum
3 De Zoete Verblijf
4 Holiday Inn
5 Pretoria Hof
6 Victoria

● Eating
1 Café Riche

Above the car park is an open air café, a shop, bureau de change, internet facilities, and a small museum devoted to the lives of the trekkers. The museum contains Johannes Uys's Bible, some interesting photographs, a superb multi-panelled tapestry, a reconstruction of an early homestead and a smaller version of the reliefs in the monument. ■ *The monument is south of the city, just off the R28. Mon-Sat 0800-1700, Sun 1100-1700. Small entrance charge. There are usually a few taxis close to the entrance to take you back to the city.*

The best reason for coming to **Klapperkop Fort** is to enjoy the excellent view from the high vantage point. You can walk about the battlements but the rest of the fort is closed to the public. A separate building houses a museum on South Africa's military history. There is an old steam locomotive in the car park, plus a couple of tanks in the grounds. The fort was built to guard the southern entrance to the town, but no resistance was put up when the British entered the town in May 1900. ■ *Daily, 1000-1530, free entrance. The fort is just on the southern outskirts of town, off the R28 on J Rissik Dr. A small road winds up the side of a wooded hill, and there are several parking spots popular with young couples. Near the top take a right fork, if you drive past a reservoir you will have overshot, it is not clearly signposted. A couple of guards require you to sign in at the gate, no charge.*

Parks & gardens

Pretoria is well-known for its parks and gardens and the city takes a lot of pride in its magnificent open space

Gauteng

Jan Celliers Park, also known as Protea Park, is west of Queen Wilhelmina Road in Groenkloof and is the furthest of all of them from the city centre. The park is on a natural slope and is made up of rock gardens, mixed borders, groups of trees and a water garden; two ponds are linked by a series of 14 small waterfalls. Aside from being a relaxing place to pass your time, the park is worth visiting if you are keen on wild flowers and wish to see a number of South Africa's indigenous flora close up.

Springbok Park, in contrast, has a much more informal layout. Located between Schoeman and Pretorius streets in Hatfield to the east of the city centre towards the N1, this park was declared a national monument in 1979. It was first planted in 1905 when WH Lanham was planning the suburb of Hatfield. A stream flows through the grounds and there are some fine trees from different regions of the country.

Venning Park is a neatly planned garden known for its immaculate rose beds. Like Springbok Park it is found between Schoeman and Pretorius streets, but slightly closer to the centre of town. Regular pruning demonstrations are held for the rose enthusiast. An avenue of palm trees ends beside a pleasant tea garden and restaurant; the park is close to the diplomatic enclave and many families come here over the weekend.

Essentials

Sleeping

■ *on maps, pages 539 and 542*

Price codes: see inside front cover

There is not such a great choice of quality hotels in Pretoria. The more relaxing places to stay are guesthouses and a few are starting to open their doors in the suburbs of Hatfield, Brooklyn, and Lynnwood. Although they are not necessarily a cheap option, they offer a change from standard business traveller hotels.

A ***Victoria***, corner of Paul Kruger and Scheiding roads, T3236054. 10 a/c suites, fireside pub, elegant restaurant restored to its 1920s splendour, palm trees and fountains add to the dining experience, this small luxury hotel is now part of the Rovos Rail group and the majority of guests will have just finished a luxury steam journey or be about to start one. This is the most exclusive hotel in town, but due to its position and size it lacks many of the facilities a much larger 5-star hotel would have. However, the fittings and the service are of the highest standard; a perfect complement to the luxury trains. **A-B** ***Holiday Inn***, Beatrix and Church streets, T/F3411571. 242 a/c rooms, non-smoking rooms, restaurant, bar, secure parking, smart large city hotel (don't be put off by the tinted exterior, but ostensibly for business travellers), short walk from shops and restaurants, small garden in the middle around the swimming pool. **A-B** ***Kloof House***, 366 Aries St, Waterkloof, a suburb off the N1 to the southeast of the city. T4604600, F4604585. 7 luxury rooms in a select guesthouse close to the diplomatic enclave, city views, B&B, dinner by arrangement, high rates probably aimed for the international diplomatic market.

B *La Maison*, 235 Hilda St, Hatfield, T4304341, F3421531. This is regarded as one of the best guesthouses in Gauteng and consists of 6 large en suite bedrooms. The house is a grand white Victorian mansion, close to many diplomatic missions, the restaurant is also highly regarded and has won awards for outstanding cuisine, lush gardens, swimming pool. Recommended if you can afford it. **B** *Protea Hatfield Lodge*, 1080 Prospect St, Hatfield, T3626105, F3627251. 64 en suite rooms, standard Protea quality, TV, a/c, pool, bar, great location in the throng of shops, restaurants of Hatfield. **B** *Protea Manor*, corner of Burnett and Festival streets, Hatfield, T3627077, F3625646. Almost across the road from Hatfield Lodge (above) in an equally good location, everything you could possibly need is close by. 42, a/c en suite rooms with mini-bars and writing desks, luxurious English club-style décor, no restaurant or bar, but rates include full English breakfast. **B-C** *Boulevard Protea*, 186 Strubben St, T3264806, F3261366. 100 a/c rooms, restaurant, ladies' bar, swimming pool, recently refurbished, not such a safe area at night, use taxis. **B-C** *Mutsago Guesthouse*, 327 Festival St, Hatfield, T4307193. Smart house with garden and swimming pool. 14 double rooms with en suite bathroom, TV and minibar. Close to Hatfield Square, very convenient. Recommended.

C *Arcadia*, 515 Proes St, T3269311, F3261067. 139 a/c rooms, quality city centre hotel, clean, well-managed, restaurant, bar, lounge, part of the Arcadia shopping complex, a fun area to stay to in, plenty of restaurants nearby, short walk to the Union Buildings. **C** *Battiss-Zeederberg Guest House*, 3 Fook Island, 92 20th Street, Menlo Park, T/F4607318. 5 double rooms, each opens onto a calm courtyard, B&B but self-catering possible. This has to be one of the more unusual places anyone will stay at in South Africa. It's the original home of the artist Walter Battiss, whose work remains on the walls and the floors as a reminder of his love for San paintings, painted blue, yellow, emerald green and turquoise. Much of the artist's character is still evident. No children, secure parking. Need your own car to get into town, but a short drive from the N1 and Menlyn Park shopping mall (see Greater Pretoria map). **C** *Best Western*, 230 Hamilton St, T/F3413473. 132 a/c rooms, TV, restaurant, open air terrace and coffee shop, a standard town centre hotel for the business traveller, efficient and functional, central location. **C** *Elegant Lodge*, 83 Atterbury Rd, Menlo Park, T3466460, F3466459. Attractive business hotel with easy access to the N1. Tastefully decorated, en suite, TV, internet line, small pleasant restaurant, room service no extra charge, escape the traffic on the main road in the pretty courtyards. **C** *Orange Court Lodge*, 540 Vermeulen St, T3266346, F3262492. 18 self-catering apartments, serviced daily, can sleep up to 5 people, quiet but close to all the shops and sights, secure off street parking, good value if you don't mind self-catering setup, breakfasts available to order. **C** *Tiptol Guest House*, 345 Clark St, Waterkloof, T/F3461934. Comfortable and spacious bedrooms with en suite bathrooms, short walk from the Brooklyn Plaza shopping complex, secure off street parking, good local advice, need your own transport, southeast of city centre, ideal if you are departing from the airport. **C** *Town Lodge*, Atterbury Rd, Menlo Park, T3482711, F3482820. Functional but uninspiring modern chain hotel just off the N1 and close to Menlyn Park Mall. **C-D** *Pretoria Hof*, corner of Nelson Mandela Dr and Van de Walt St, T3227570, F3229461. Good value double room for city centre, restaurant, bar, price includes English breakfast. **D** *That's It*, 5 Brecher St, Sunnyside, T3443404. 4 neat but bare non-smoking bedrooms, TV lounge, standard B&B, swimming pool, thatched garden seating area, useful location for dealings with foreign embassies but be wary in Sunnyside at night, easy bus route into the town centre, more suited to a longer stay. **D** *Formula 1*, 81 Nelson Mandela Dr T3238331. Could be anywhere in the world, soulless but good value for 3 people sharing a shoebox, clean, plenty of hot water, just sleep here while organizing your trip. **D** *Hotel 224*, corner of Schoeman and Leyds streets, T4405281, F443063. A mix of 224 single and double rooms in a tower block, all a bit small, some have TV, restaurant, bar, secure parking, short walk from the Union Buildings, cheap but rather seedy city centre hotel.

Backpacker hostels The majority of backpackers stay in Johannesburg, where admittedly there is a far greater choice of accommodation and more travellers to exchange tips and tales with. However, there are good backpacker's facilities to be found in Pretoria, which are conveniently located within walking distance or a short taxi ride from the nightlife in Hatfield and the major sporting venues, and are on the *Baz Bus* route.

F *Hatfield Backpackers*, 1226 Park St, Hatfield, T3625501, F3621785. Dorms, double rooms, excellent kitchen, bar, gardens for camping, internet facilities. Special deals for overseas students looking for a homely base for several months while they study in Pretoria. 2 min walk from buzzy Hatfield Square and Plaza. **F** *Pretoria Backpackers*, 425 Farenden Rd, Clydesdale, T3439754, F3432524. The oldest backpackers in town, which has recently relocated from Sunnyside to brighter premises next to the Loftus Rd rugby stadium. 2 houses around the corner from each other, 2 dorms, several doubles in garden huts or in the main house, nicely decorated with a guest house feel, beauty salon offering lots of treats after a few weeks' hard travelling, lovely tropical gardens with fish ponds and gazebos, pool, travel desk. Organize their own local tours of Pretoria, Sun City/Pilansberg, Lesedi Cultural Village, which are good value when there are enough takers. Staff will accompany guests to football and rugby matches at Loftus Stadium. **F** *Word of Mouth*, 430 Reitz St, Sunnyside, T3437499, F3439351, info@wordofmouthbackpackers.com 2 small dorms, several double rooms plus double huts in the garden, small camping area hidden from road. Satellite TV and video lounge, laundry, individual safes plus a long-term baggage storage facility, bar with pool table plus internet café. Free airport pick-up if staying 2 nights or more. Useful website provides information both on South Africa and travel all the way up to Nairobi: www.travelinafrica.co.za The downside is, Sunnyside is no longer such a salubrious area, other backpackers hostels have moved elsewhere.

Hatfield & Hillcrest

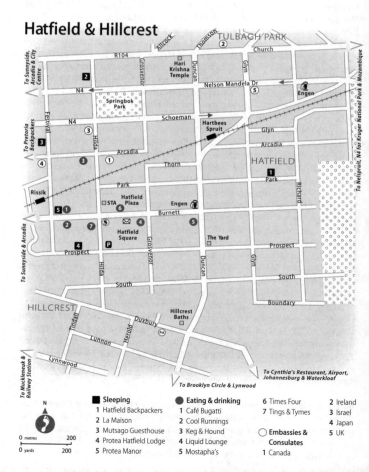

Sleeping
1 Hatfield Backpackers
2 La Maison
3 Mutsago Guesthouse
4 Protea Hatfield Lodge
5 Protea Manor

Eating & drinking
1 Café Bugatti
2 Cool Runnings
3 Keg & Hound
4 Liquid Lounge
5 Mostapha's
6 Times Four
7 Tings & Tymes

Embassies & Consulates
1 Canada
2 Ireland
3 Israel
4 Japan
5 UK

The city centre has a few places to eat in at night, and nightlife in general takes place away from the city centre. During the day there are plenty of sandwich bars and fast food outlets serving the office workers brigade. The best places to go to at night are **Hatfield** and **Brooklyn**. At the centre of these two suburbs are large modern developments with countless bars and restaurants. At present they are safe and everything is within walking distance of each other. A few years ago Esselen Street in Sunnyside was the best place to go, but this is no longer the case and the area has witnessed a severe decline, our advice is to avoid the area. Closer to the town centre there are a couple of smart restaurants in the **Oeverzicht Art Village**.

Eating

● on maps, pages 539 and 542

In a city as spread out as Pretoria, the restaurants tend to be found in or near the large shopping malls (see Shopping below)

Cynthia's, Maroelana Centre, near Pretoria Country Club, in Maroelana, in the southern suburbs off the N1, T4603229. Closed Sat lunch, Sun evening. Heavy furnishings, more suited to a colder climate, you can dine in the wine cellar here, excellent food, sometimes served in an unknown combination, the fish dishes are particularly good, try the Maputo prawns if on offer, also pub lunches and take-outs. Recommended. *Farm Inn*, Lynnwood Rd East, Lynnwood Manor, T8090266. Inviting country inn with famous buffet and carvery for Sunday lunch, worth the drive out, but avoid if there's a wedding on. *Gerard Moerdyk*, 752 Park St, Arcadia, T3444856. Closed Sat lunch and Sun. A bizarre combination, the menu consists entirely of South African dishes, ostrich, snoek, crocodile mousse, springbok pie, mealie bread, but the décor is silk curtains, pink walls, antiques, crystal and silver, all a bit delicate and elegant when compared to the menu, but this is a popular and worthwhile place to eat at. Recommended. *La Madeleine*, 122 Priory Rd, Lynnwood, T3613667. Closed Mon, Sun and Sat lunch. Not cheap, but then this has been regarded as one of the top restaurants in South Africa for over 20 years, recently relocated from Sunnyside. Fine cuisine, oysters, langoustine, foie gras, award-winning wine list. Somewhere to come and celebrate your holiday before returning to the routine of work back home; the meals are classical French and will depend upon what the markets have to offer, this is a perfect example of what can be done with all the lovely fresh produce that grows in South Africa, reservations essential. The new premises has 4 double rooms for overnight accommodation. *Mostapha's*, 478 Duncan St, Hatfield, T3423855. Moroccan dishes, lots of lamb, saffron, and couscous, shabby interior but it adds to the atmosphere. *Natassa & Melina's*, Brooklyn Sq, Brooklyn, T3465317. Greek taverna upstairs in the modern mall. Outside dining area plus cramped area inside which is a bit bright. Generous portions, tasty food, but suffers from indifferent service at times, they seemed to have their favourite clientele. *Oriental Palace*, 410 Schoeman St, Arcadia, T3222195. Very authentic Indian restaurant, chefs imported from Pakistan and north India to prepare genuine dishes, this is not food found at the local Indian take-away, be prepared to experiment, tandoori breads, Indian ice-cream, everything Halaal, no alcohol allowed. *Pachas*, Club Two Shopping Centre, Hazelwood, in the southern suburbs off the N1, T4605063. Closed Sat lunch and Sun, fun venue for the young with a bit of money, prime steaks, unusual salads, strong French influence on the sauce front, always a surprise. *Vilamoura*, 273 Middel St, Brooklyn, T3461650. Closed all day Sun, and Sat lunch. Smart-casual Portuguese restaurant with over the top décor. Big portions of Mozambique/Portuguese dishes and seafood platters for Africa. *Villa Paolo*, Waterkloof Mall, T4601202. Closed Tue and Sat lunch, all day Sun. A quality Italian bistro with plenty of charm, caters well for the vegetarian, wood burning pizza oven, regarded as one of the best of its kind, attracts people from Jo'burg. Recommended. *Wangthai*, 281 Middel St, Brooklyn, T3466230. Authentic and elegant Thai restaurant, huge menu, lots of choice for vegetarians, not cheap but excellent food, sister restaurant in the prestigious Sandton Sq in Jo'burg.

Café Bugatti, Burnett St, Hatfield. This appears to be one of the most popular venues in Hatfield to be seen at on a Sunday morning. Al fresco tables plus a bar and restaurant inside. Good friendly service that puts this place ahead of many other similar establishments. Very much the young wealthy set's choice: great if you want to watch Pretoria watching at itself. *Café Riche*, Church Sq (southwest corner), T3283173. Restored historical building reminiscent of European café society, abundant breakfasts and teas, late night dinners, thought to be the oldest café in Pretoria. *Gala Deli*, Brooklyn Mall, T4602641. Family-run deli still packed

Cafés & coffee shops

Gauteng

with Italian folk which is always a good sign, lots of traditional Italian goodies, breakfast and lunch daily, dinner Fri-Sat. *Times Four*, Burnett St, Hatfield. Good value breakfasts, plus the usual selection of hamburgers and drinks.

Pubs & bars Again, by far the best areas to head for in the evening and at weekends are **Hatfield** and **Brooklyn**, both to the east of the town centre. Ask the taxi to take you to Hatfield Square, from here there are dozens of places to explore, all within a short walk of each other.

Cool Runnings, Burnett St. A chain of bar-cum-restaurants that attract the trendy young crowd, live reggae music Sun evenings. Currently one of the 'in' places, always busy at the weekend. Cocktails and imported beers, definitely one of the better late night venues. *Devine Lounge*, Menlyn Park Mall, T3681361. Award-winning wine list, fab cocktails, a plethora of sofas, great jazz on Sun, don't expect to stay too late as it's still in a shopping mall. *Hillside Tavern*, 320 Hillside Rd, Lynnwood, T3481402, closed Sat lunch. Pub and steak restaurant, substantial bar with wide choice of beers and ciders. *Keg & Hound*, 1077 Arcadia St, Hatfield. Good choice of imported beers, plus a snack menu. Popular pub atmosphere amongst the local university students, late nights at the weekend. *Liquid Lounge*, 141 Burnett St, Hatfield. Stylish late-night cocktail bar, music has a chilled vibe, somewhere you can actually talk. *Tings & Thymes*, just off Burnett St in Hatfield Plaza, Hatfield, T3625537. Small bar with mix of live music, can get very crowded, best to arrive mid-evening to guarantee a table, great cocktails, middle eastern and vegetarian meals, fun place. Recommended.

Nightclubs *Boston Tea Party*, Menlyn Park, T3653625. Large conference venue during the day and live music, comedy, and DJ venue at night. Phone first to find out what's on, impressive bar, this place holds 1,000 people. *Upstairs at Morgan's*, Burnett Rd, Hatfield, T3626610. Thu-Sat from 1930. Commercial dance music from the 1960s-90s. Expect the likes of foam parties and pig nights (all you can drink) regularly.

Entertainment *Computicket*, Hatfield Plaza, Burnett St, Hatfield, T3623542; Sammy Marks Sq, Church St, T3289333. Advance booking for all events, pop concerts, major sports finals, theatre etc, a nationwide company.

Cinemas *NuMetro*, Menlyn Park, T3681300, 15 screens; and Hatfield Plaza, T3625899. *IMAX*, Menlyn Park, T3681186. Giant screen with wrap-around sound, showing wildlife and landscape films. Also at Menlyn Park is the *Drive-in*, on the rooftop of the shopping mall, nightly at 1800. 4 original Chevvy convertibles can be hired by special arrangement if you don't have your own car. *Ster Kinekor*, Tramshed, Van der Walt and Schoman, T3204300. *Sterland*, Beatrix St, Arcadia, T3417568. 12 screens to choose from, all a/c and comfortable.

Shopping The easiest way to shop is to go to one of the large covered shopping complexes. They are very popular and include everything a visitor might need. You will find banks and ATMs, supermarkets, shops, travel agents, restaurants, cinemas and chemists. Some of the popular centres are: *Brooklyn Mall*, 338 Bronkhorst St, New Muckleneuk, T3461063 and *Hatfield Plaza*, Park St, Hatfield. A lively flea market is held here at the weekend. *The Tramshed*, corner of Van der Walt and Schoeman streets, though avoid this area after dark, and the *Sanlam Centre*, Andries St in the town centre. Pretoria's premier new mall is *Menlyn Park*, Atterbury Rd, Menlo Park, T3488766. 300 shops and restaurants, 15-screen cinema, IMAX theatre, bowling alley, and a unique drive-in cinema.

Oeverzicht Art Village, between Gerard Moerdyk St, Kotze St and Van Boeschoten Lane, T4402320. This is a delightful small pocket of old Pretoria. All the houses date from between 1895 and 1920 and have been perfectly restored. Since it is such a small area it is very easy to miss, and strangely, it does not seem to be promoted. It is a mix of galleries, antique shops and restaurants. At the south end of Gerard Moerdyk St is the Breytenbach Theatre.

Sports *Cricket* *Centurion Park*, PO Box 7706, Hennopsmeer 0046. Ticket enquiries: T6631005, F6633329, info@ncu.co.za The ground where international matches for Pretoria are now played at, is 23 km from the centre of town, off the R21 to Johannesburg. This makes access without your own transport a little difficult but special shuttle buses may be provided for important matches at weekends. Before your arrival in Pretoria ask the manager of the back-packers you have chosen to stay at (or your hotel!) if they have any information about transport to/from the ground. The ground is home to Northern Transvaal provincial cricket team, it is a modern circular stadium dominated by a huge single grandstand. The rest of the boundary is just grass banks which are great fun for picnics and braais and groups having a fun day out, but make sure you have some form of protection from the sun, there is no shade.

Rugby Pretoria is the home town for the Northern Transvaal Rugby Union, T3444011. All their matches are played at *Loftus Versveld Rugby Stadium*, Kirkness Street, Sunnyside.

Tour & tour operators

Apart from city tours, the most popular day trips from Pretoria are to **Sun City, Pilansberg National Park** and the **Gold Mines**. Expect to pay in the region of R250 per person for a half-day tour of the **city**, which takes in the major sights such as the Voortrekker Monument and Union Buildings.

At the weekend many Pretoria residents head out for the **Magaliesberg Hills** and **Hartbeespoort Dam**, less than an hour by car. The rugged terrain is popular amongst hikers, and the mountains are perfect for hang gliders and ballooning. The dam is surrounded with holiday homes, caravan parks and holiday resorts. If you don't have a car, some tour operators can arrange trips to this region, a pleasant contrast to the popular Sun City.

American Express Travel, 4 Brooklyn Mall, Bronkhorst St, New Muckleneuk, T3463580. *City Tours*, T3471000. Sightseeing tours of Pretoria. *Expeditionary Force*, T/F6672833. Specialize in historical city tours, an excellent learned approach to the city. *Holidays for Africa*, T3485339. City tours or longer trips to Kruger. *CM Louw City Tours*, Andreas St, T083-2513874 (mob). Conducted tours in a 14-seat a/c kombi van, city centre and historical or longer trips to Sun City and Kruger, reasonable rates for 4 or more people. *Rennies Travel*, 15 Sanlam Centre, T3202240. National chain, all purpose travel agent plus Thomas Cook bureau de change, useful for reconfirming flights. *Sakabula*, 54 Charles St, Brooklyn, T4605251. For half day city tours. *Tokologo*, T3300464. Local trips plus longer outings to Mpumalanga and KwaZulu Natal. *Travel the Planet*, Church Sq, T3374415, F3262325. Located in the historic Old Netherlands Bank building, a new reservation and booking service attached to a coffee shop. All tours in and around Pretoria, frequent special offers, useful stop for general travel arrangements and long opening hours, Mon-Fri, 0800-1800, Sat-Sun, 0900-1200. *Ulysses*, T3444377, F3444399. City tours, day trips to Sun City and Pilanesberg, and Lesedi Cultural Village. *Visions of Africa*, T9975420, F9974618. Reasonably priced 2-3 day Kruger tours, 3-day Cape Town packages including tours and flights from R3,300 per person.

Transport
See also Ins and outs page 534

Local Bus: *Municipal* buses run between the city centre and the suburbs. Timetables are available in chemists and from the service information office in Church Sq, T3080839. *Translux, Greyhound*, and *Intercape* buses run between Pretoria and Johannesburg (1 hr). Although they are long distance coaches, there are several departures throughout the day. They cannot be pre booked but seats are always available, expect to pay around R40-60 standby. You can then connect with other buses or trains at Johannesburg's Park City terminus.

Car hire: assuming they have a car available most companies can organize a car hire within 30 mins. You require a driver's licence with a photograph and a credit card; the latter makes the deposit requirements much easier. Companies with offices at the airport should deliver to your hotel in Pretoria. Look out for long weekend deals, it is possible to get a Fri-Mon deal which, for example, would enable you to spend 2 days game viewing in Kruger; with 4 people this works out cheaper than an organized tour. *Avis*, T3251490; *Budget*, T3414650; *Imperial*, T3427867; *Tempest*, T4302724.

Taxi: there are always taxis in front of the railway station, on Prinsloo opposite the tourist office, and on Church St by Strijdom Square. You cannot wave down a taxi, restaurants and clubs will always order one by telephone. Most are reliable and should use their meters with a minimum of fuss. One of the best companies at present is **A-Class**, T3228147. There are several other companies also at work, but far less reliable.

☞ Luxury meals on wheels: Blue Trains and Rovos Rail

*South Africa has several rival rail companies offering luxury train travel. These trains are the ultimate in comfort (that can fit into a carriage) but special attention is also given to the quality of food and service. For many years the **Blue Train** has been known outside of South Africa for its excellent food. But recently a new company has entered the market, **Rovos Rail**. Based in Pretoria their trains are made up of restored and converted old rolling stock. Their interiors are magnificent – it is difficult to believe you are on a train – and their presence has undoubtedly influenced the current refurbishment of the Blue Train. The national rail company, Spoornet, has a subsidiary company running luxury steam outings, the **Union Limited Steam Safari Train**, T021-4054390, which is the cheapest of the three luxury services. Cape Town to Pretoria costs US$2,200.*

***Blue Train**, central reservations: PO Box 2671, Joubert Park 2044, T012-334 8459, F012-334 8464. Regional office: Jo'burg, T011-7744469; Pretoria, T012-3152436; Cape Town, T021-4052672; Durban, T031-3617550. There are five types of accommodation, only the cheapest option has communal shower*

*and toilet facilities. The train can carry 92 passengers, the dining car has room for 46 guests, there is also a lounge car with 34 seats. The Blue Train departs three times a week at 0850 to **Cape Town** (15 hrs), via **Kimberley** (8 hrs), **Worcester** (12 hrs) and **Wellington** (14 hrs). Cape Town to Pretoria costs US$2,200.*

*Two new services have been introduced, to **Nelspruit** and **Victoria Falls** (Zimbabwe). At present there are only one or two trains per month. The journey to the Victoria Falls takes two days, this includes stops for game viewing and sights. The single fare is about US$1,000 per person.*

***Rovos Rail**, reservations Victoria Hotel, PO Box 2837, Pretoria 0001, T012-323 6052, F3230843. Each train consists of up to 19 restored coaches, the maximum number of passengers it can carry is 70. The dining car is characterized by seven pairs of carved wooden, roof-supporting pillars and arches, it can comfortably seat 44 diners. The observation and bar coach dates back to 1936 and there is room for 30 guests. If you don't wish to leave your suite there is full room service. The journey price includes all meals and drinks, all tours and guide fees,*

Airport arrival/ departure enquiries: T011-9216262

Long distance Air: follow the R21 out of Pretoria to **Johannesburg International Airport**. The easiest way to travel to/from the airport is to take the *Airport Shuttle*, T3220904. An efficient daily service which runs between 0715-2015. The shuttle runs between **Sammy Marks Square** and Terminal 3, domestic arrivals. When going to the airport call the shuttle a good hour or more in advance, they will collect from most major Pretoria hotels. Full one way fare, R95.

For details of luxury train services, see box

Angry commuters set fire to the railway station in 2001, the station was still in a state of repair at the time of going to press

Rail: not all of the long distance trains depart from Pretoria, if you are going to Durban, East London, Bloemfontein, or Port Elizabeth you will have to start your journey from Johannesburg. There are plenty of Metro commuter trains throughout the day between Pretoria and Johannesburg but **avoid this service at all times**, this is not a safe way to travel. It is better to take the bus.

There is a booking office to the right in the main railway station building. **Sales and ticket offices**: Pretoria, T012-3348470; Johannesburg, T011-7732944. **NB** Trains do get fully booked, especially at the start and end of school and university terms. Pretoria is particularly busy because of the large university here, UNISA. Try and book long distance trips, such as Cape Town, as far in advance as possible. The main train services are known as 'Name Trains'.

The *Bosvelder* departs daily at 2036 to **Messina** (13 hrs), via **Pietersburg** (6 hrs) and **Louis Trichardt** (10 hrs).

The *Komati* departs daily at 1940 to **Maputo** (Mozambique) (15 hrs), via **Nelspruit** (8 hrs).

The *Trans Karoo* departs daily at 1010 to **Cape Town** (28 hrs), via **Kimberley** (9½ hrs), **Beaufort West** (18 hrs), and **Worcester** (25 hrs). All trains have dining cars.

and any entrance charges, all you need money for is tipping the staff at the end of your journey. Rovos Rail also own the **Victoria Hotel**, opposite Pretoria railway station. It is the ideal place to stay overnight at the end of a journey. Even if you don't stay, it is a smart place to treat yourself to a meal.

Pretoria to **Cape Town** is the most frequent service. The journey will last two days, it includes two stops for guided tours, one in Kimberley to look around the Kimberley Mine Museum and the famous Big Hole, the second at the perfectly preserved Victorian Karoo town, Matjiesfontein, where passengers have breakfast at the Lord Milner Hotel just like they would have done 80 years ago. The service leaves Pretoria on Saturday afternoon and arrives in Cape Town on Monday, 1800, platform 24. For the reverse journey the train departs from Cape Town on Friday morning and arrives in Pretoria at midday on Sunday.

Pretoria to **Victoria Falls** (Zimbabwe) via Bulawayo where there is a short outing to the Matobo Hills. For the round trip the train leaves Pretoria on Monday morning, arrives at Victoria Falls on Wednesday morning, leaving early Wednesday evening, stops again in Bulawayo on Thursday morning, arrives back in Pretoria Friday, 1600.

Cape Town to **Knysna**, via George, with an excursion to Oudtshoorn and the ostrich farms. This is a particularly beautiful 600 km journey since the railway line has to negotiate all the mountains surrounding Cape Town. At George you transfer to special lounge cars which are attached to the Outeniqua Choo-Tjoe, for the leg to Knysna. This is one of the most charming stretches of railway in South Africa. The round trip lasts for two nights, three days.

Pretoria to **Komatipoort** with a transfer by minibus to Skukuza in Kruger National Park; there is an optional leg to continue to the Mozambique capital, Maputo, a further 90 kilometres from Komatipoort. After two days' game viewing in Kruger National Park you return via the same route.

There is also an epic 12-day safari from **Cape Town** to **Dar-es-Salaam** in Tanzania, taking you via Kimberley, Bulawayo, Victoria Falls, Lusaka (in Zambia) and on to Dar. There is only room for 68 passengers.

Road 500 km to Zimbabwe border (**Beitbridge**), 474 km to **Bloemfontein**, 1492 km to **Cape Town**, 688 km to **Durban**, 1060 km to **East London**, 1078 km to **Harare** (Zimbabwe), 58 km to **Johannesburg**, 530 km to **Kimberley**, 1406 km to **Knysna**, 1133 km to **Port Elizabeth**.

Bus: the bus stand is to the left of the railway station (as you face it) in the 1928 Building. *Translux, Greyhound* and *Intercape* all have an office here, open during normal office hours. Each company has a waiting room, there are toilets and a drinks machine; only *Translux* stay open in the evening until their last bus and passenger has left. Do not expect such a conscientious service from *Greyhound* who also acts as agents for *Blue Arrow*, a Zimbabwe company which runs buses to Bulawayo, Victoria Falls, Masvingo and Harare. If you are planning on using these services it would be sensible to pick up as many timetables as possible from these offices.

Greyhound, central reservations, T011-2498900. To **Bulawayo** (10½ hrs), Mon, Wed, 0845, Fri, 2245. **Cape Town** (18 hrs), daily, 1630, via **Bloemfontein** (6½ hrs), daily, 1200, 1500, via **Kimberley** (7 hrs). **Durban** (8 hrs), daily at 0645, 0845, 0930, 1230, 1400, 2130, the 1000 service stops at **Newcastle** (5½ hrs) and **Ladysmith** (7 hrs). To **Durban** via **Vryheid** and **Richards Bay**, daily, 0645. **Harare** (Zimbabwe) (15 hrs), Mon, Wed, Fri, 2315, via **Pietersburg** (3 hrs) and **Masvingo** (Zimbabwe) (11½ hrs). **Nelspruit** (5 hrs), Mon-Sat, 1645. **Port Elizabeth** (16 hrs), daily, 1630, via **Bloemfontein** (6½ hrs) and **Grahamstown** (12½ hrs).

Intercape, reservations, T6544114. To **Durban** (8 hrs), departs daily, 0630, 1200, 2100. **Cape Town** (16 hrs), daily, 1230, 1600, via **Bloemfontein** (4½ hrs). **Port Elizabeth** (15 hrs), daily, 1600. **Plettenberg Bay** (14 hrs), daily, 1600. **Upington** (10 hrs), daily, 0600, via **Kuruman** (7 hrs). The Upington service connects with coaches to **Windhoek** in Namibia. *Translux*, T3154300. To **Blantyre** (Malawi) (30 hrs), Wed, Thu, Sat, Sun, 0800, via **Harare**. **Bloemfontein** (7 hrs), daily, 0815. **Bulawayo** (Zimbabwe) (13½ hrs), daily, 2200. **Cape Town** (19 hrs), daily, 1130, via **Kimberley**, and 1635, via **Bloemfontein**. **Durban** (9 hrs), daily at 0630, 0815, 2035, 2115, Thu, Fri, Sun, 1245. **Maputo** (Mozambique) (8½ hrs), daily, 0650, via **Nelspruit** (5 hrs). **Plettenberg Bay** (17½ hrs), Tue, Wed, Fri, Sun, 1615, via **Kimberley**, Mon, Thu, Sat, 1615, via **Bloemfontein**. **East London** (13 hrs), daily at 1645. **Harare** (Zimbabwe) (15½ hrs), Tue, Thu, Fri, Sun, 2300. **Lusaka** (Zambia) (26 hrs), Tue and Fri, 0945, via **Harare**. **Port Elizabeth** (15 hrs), daily 1615.

For further details about routes and conditions of transport see page 42

Budget buses: at present the *Baz Bus* is the only budget transport for backpackers which will pick up and drop off at hostels in Pretoria. This is an ideal service for the budget traveller, once you have purchased your ticket you only have to telephone a day in advance to organize collection from your hostal. At the end of each leg of your journey the bus will drop you off at your next choice of overnight accommodation. Reservations, T021-4392323, F4392343, info@bazbus.com, www.bazbus.com

Directory

Banks Main Branches: those listed here are in the city centre. All banks have outlets in the many shopping malls dotted about the suburbs. *ABSA* bank tend to charge the highest commission rates for TCs. *First National*, Church Sq, T3091000; *Ned Bank*, Church St, T3386000; *Standard*, Church St, T3398900; *ABSA*, Van der Walt St, T3377300; *American Express*, Brooklyn Shopping Centre, T3462599; *Rennies Travel*, Sanlam Centre, corner of Andries and Pretorius streets, T3202240.

Communications Internet: *Odyssey internet-cafe*, branches at, Burnett St, Hatfield, T3622467, and Menlyn Mall, T3681259, late opening hours.

If you have problems in contacting a diplomatic mission enquire at the Department of Foreign Affairs (Protocol division), T3251000

Embassies and consulates *Australia*, 292 Orient St, Arcadia, T3423740, F3428442; *Austria*, 105 Nicolson St, Brooklyn, T4602483, F4601151; *Belgium*, 625 Leyds St, Muckleneuk, T4403201, F4403216; *Botswana*, 24 Asmos St, T3424761, F3421845; *Canada*, 1103 Arcadia St, Hatfield, T4223000, F4223052; *Denmark*, 8th floor Sanlam Centre, corner Nelson Mandela Dr and Andries St, T3220595, F3220596; *Finland*, 628 Leyds St, Muckleneuk, T3430275, F3133095; *France*, 807 George Av, Arcadia, T4297000, F4297029; *Germany*, 180 Blackwood St, Arcadia, T4278900, F3439401; *Ireland*, Tulbagh Park, 1234 Church St, Colbyn, T3425062, F3424752; *Israel*, Dashing Centre, 339 Hilda St, Hatfield, T3422693, F3421442; *Italy*, 769 George Av, Arcadia, T4305541, F4305547; *Japan*, Sanlam Bldg, 353 Festival St, Hatfield, T3422100, F4303922; *Lesotho*, 1 T Edison St, Menlo Park, T4607648, F4607649; *Malawi*, 770 Government Av, T3420146, F3420147; *Mozambique*, 199 Beckett St, Arcadia, T4010300, F3436714; *Namibia*, 702 Church St, T3445992, F3445998; *Netherlands*, 825 Arcadia St, Arcadia, T3443910, F3439950; *Norway*, 1166 Park St, Hatfield, T3426100, F3426099; *Portugal*, 599 Leyds St, Sunnyside, T3412340, F4403071; *Russian Federation*, Butano Bldg, 316 Brooks St, Menlo Park, T3621337, F3620116; *Spain*, 169 Pine St, Arcadia, T3443875, F3434891; *Swaziland*, 170 Pine St, Arcadia, T3441917, F3430455; *Sweden*, 1166 Park St, Hatfield, T4266400, F4266464; *Switzerland*, 818 George Av, Arcadia, T4306707, F4306771; *UK*, 255 Hill St, Arcadia, T4831200, F4831302; *USA*, 877 Nelson Mandela Drive, Arcadia, T3421048, F3422299; *Zambia*, 570 Ziervogel St, Arcadia, T3261847, F3262140; *Zimbabwe*, 798 Merton St, Arcadia, T3425125, F3425126.

Medical Services Ambulance: T10177, T3106400, T4277111. Hospitals: *Starcare Muelmed Hospital*, T4402362; *Wilgers Hospital*, T8070019. Medical clinics: *College Medical Centre*, corner of Mears and Rissik streets, Sunnyside, T4402622.

Useful addresses Police: T10111. Visa extensions: *Dept of Home Affairs*, Struben St, T3268081, F3232416. Always ask for 3 months when coming into South Africa, an extension will cost R390 and will take 10 working days. You will need to produce an onward ticket and proof of funds. **Weather**: T082162.

North West Province

North West Province

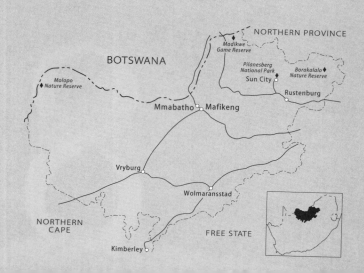

Driving through the North West Province could, for some visitors, be a tiring and perhaps boring experience. Much of the region is flat Kalahari grasslands with few features and for most of the year there is little green to be seen. But dotted about the landscape are small farming areas that in the early days of the white man were important centres. Much of this region was in the Western Transvaal, one of the areas the Voortrekkers came to settle in at the end of the Great Trek, and towns such as **Mafikeng** and **Rustenburg** have a fascinating history. The remote bushveld region is home to 16 nature reserves and game parks, all relatively remote, diverse and most certainly less visited by the overseas visitor and all over an altitude of 1,000-2,000 m, ensuring no threat of malaria.

These are poorly promoted outside of the province, and yet all lie in unique environments. Aside from the well-publicized **Pilanesberg National Park** there are also **Borakalalo National Park**, **Botsalano Game Reserve** and **Madikwe Game Reserve**. In Madikwe you can see the Big Five and enjoy accommodation of the highest standard, along with easy transfers from Johannesburg and Pretoria.

In addition to the wildlife, there are the **Magaliesberg Mountains**, less than one hour's drive from Pretoria, and full of wild hiking trails and comfortable holiday resorts. Further west you will come across private game farms, which provide an insight into life in the bushveld on the edge of the **Kalahari**.

Finally, the province has one of the most well-known 'features' of South Africa – **Sun City**, an amazingly extravagant gambling resort built to entertain the wealthy South African in the days when they were unable to travel overseas. This is a place where the phrase, 'you have to see it to believe it' rings remarkably true.

North West Province

Ins and outs

Tourist Information

North West Parks and Tourism Board, is 5 km north of Mmabatho and clearly signposted at Military Village, Khupe Complex, Mmabatho, T3861225-9, F3861158, nwptb@iafrica.com, www.tourismnorthwest.co.za, open Mon-Fri, 0800-1640. This office is responsible for promoting tourism throughout the province. Contact them in advance for information, they have a range of useful brochures, particularly on the little known parks. Their website is like many such sites, in so much as its coverage of the province is patchy. Some places have been very well-covered, while other important tourist centres don't get a look in.

The Central Region

Mafikeng and Mmabatho

*Phone code: 018
(NB Always use
3-figure prefix)
Colour map 1, grid B6
Altitude 1,278 m*

Mmabatho is a modern town only created in 1977. Before the free elections were held in South Africa and the new political boundaries came into effect, Mafikeng was in the old Western Transvaal and Mmabatho was the capital of the homeland known as Bophuthatswana, and as such had severall government buildings built there. When the North West Province was created, it was decided to keep Mmabatho on as the regional capital. However, there has been a gradual shift of power back to the principal town in the region, Rustenburg. As a new and rather garish concrete town, Mmabatho lacks the atmosphere of Rustenburg, and although the majority of government offices are still here there remains an air of artificiality and incompleteness. Dusty open ground between isolated buildings waits for the city to grow around it, and the poverty of the former homeland of Bophuthatswana remains evident. The whole town is dominated by a sports stadium of Olympic proportions, which is in itself quite an impressive architectural specimen. But the likeliest reason for visiting here is to explore the historical town of Mafikeng, another hot and dusty commercial centre on the highveld, but one with an interesting early history, and plenty of buildings which help tell its story.

There are several different sources of **tourist information** in the two towns, each has a slightly different collection of practical information on offer, contact in advance for specific information. **Mafikeng Museum**, (see also Sights below) on the corner of Martin and Robinson streets, Mafikeng, T3816102, is a useful centre for finding out what to do in the town, however for regional information you are better off calling in at the **North West Parks and Tourism** office in Mmabatho (see above). **Mafikeng Tourist Information and Development Centre**, is just off Mandela Drive by the entrance to Cooke's Lake, T3813155-7, open Mon-Fri 0830-1800, Sat 0830-1200. The office is presently closed for refurbishment after being destroyed by fire but should be up and running again by the time of publication.

History

Mafikeng was founded as a British administrative centre in 1885, when Sir Charles Warren was sent to the region with a military force to occupy and bring peace to this frontier territory. Only 20 km away was the Goshen Republic, an independent state created by a group of European mercenaries who had been given farms by the local Rolong tribe. The name of the new settlement came from the Tswana *maFikeng*, 'place of boulders'. The surrounding territory became known as British Bechuanaland, with Mafikeng as the centre for the local farmers, traders and hunters. At the time this was still very much frontier territory, occupied by a rough crowd and policed by the tough Bechuanaland Border Police.

On 14 October 1899, a Boer force under the command of General JP Snyman besieged the town, and so started the period of events that was to put the town on the map for all time. The **Siege of Mafeking** lasted 217 days until 17 May 1900 when the town was relieved by a combined force of Rhodesian troops from the north and Imperial troops from the south. At the time the siege captured the imagination of the

Things to do in the North West Province

- Visit **Madikwe** a beautiful park that in a few years' time will surely be regarded as one of the major game reserves in the country.
- Try you luck at the outrageously over the top **Sun City** with its casinos, hotels and restaurants, not to mention the man-made rainforest, the bridge that trembles in a mock earthquake, two golf courses and a water park that can generate surfing waves, all located in a dry bushveld valley, of course.
- On a good day, see the Big Five, amongst others, in **Pilanesberg National Park**, an extinct volcano similar in geography to the Ngorongoro Crater in Tanzania.
- Cheat, and sleep at the **Sundown Ranch** between Rustenburg and Sun City, rather than actually in Sun City. Visit the lion park, where you are guaranteed a close view.
- Meander through the **Magaliesberg Mountains**, where the people from Gauteng come to play at the weekends in rustic camps hidden amongst mountain streams.

British public in England – the Anglo-Boer War was the first war to be reported in such detail back to England, with pictures, cartoons and newspaper articles. It was during the siege that the British commander, Colonel RSS Baden-Powell, made his name and conceived the idea for the Boy Scout movement.

Although the siege lasted for a long period it was never that violent and the Boer forces could have easily overrun the town in the early days when they completely outnumbered the British force. There was never any fighting on a Sunday and most contact between the two sides was in the form of patrol raids to test each other's lines. Baden-Powell proved himself to be very competent in organizing the defences, but in later years was criticized for his treatment of the black troops. At the start of the siege he constructed a series of trenches and forts around the town; in the centre of town bomb-proof shelters were constructed for the civilian population. Baden-Powell based himself in *Dixon's Hotel*: to keep in touch with the lines an elaborate system of telephones, flag signals, heliographs and pigeons was used. One of his well-documented ideas was to place life-size dummies in observation posts around the town. Throughout the siege the Boers thought that they were holding down a large British force, in fact the opposite was true, at the peak over 6,000 burghers were involved with the siege of Mafeking. The Boer commander, General Cronje believed that he was pinning down a British force planned for the invasion of the Western Transvaal. In fact Mafeking was an insignificant centre but it became an important focal point and when the siege had been lifted, the Boer resolve seemed to weaken and the towns of Ladysmith and Kimberley were relieved soon after.

After the war, Mafikeng returned to life as a sleepy border town. Up until 1965 it was the centre for the British administration of the Bechuanaland Protectorate. This was a fairly unique set-up where the government for one state, Bechuanaland, was in fact located in a foreign country, South Africa. In 1965 the government moved to Gaborone and on 30 September 1966 Botswana became an independent republic, led by Sir Seretse Khama. Today the town is the centre for the local cattle industry and a minor tourist centre. Although the relics from the Boer War are most interesting, the town suffers from being off the well-beaten tourist trail.

Sights The **Mafikeng Museum**, corner of Martin and Robinson streets, Mafikeng, T3816102. Has an excellent series of displays relating to the Siege of Mafeking, but there are also some informative exhibits, which trace the history of the region along with the culture of the indigenous peoples. **Mafikeng Cemetery** contains the graves of British servicemen, the Town Guard and South African troops. The most prominent grave is that of Andrew Beauchamp-Proctor, South Africa's most highly decorated First World War airman. **Kanon Kopje**, is the site of a fort on the southern

North West Province

Siege Sidelines

During the long days of the seven month siege of Mafikeng from 13 October 1899 to 17 May 1900, the English schoolboys in this colonial town became a mite undisciplined – especially when their school closed because of the daily bombardment of the town by artillery shells. The commander of the British forces in Mafikeng, Colonel Baden-Powell, whose small force was having difficulty defending the town, had an idea. He organized boys, aged between 9 and 15 years, into a disciplined Siege Cadet Corps and put them to non-combat use. Their tasks included carrying supplies and messages between the front line and command posts, delivering post within the town, assisting the aged, and acting as observers for the regular soldiers. They were given uniforms and bicycles, and sport and military drills all played a part in fostering self-discipline and responsibility. Despite the dangers there was only one casualty during the siege among the cadets, that of nine-year-old Frankie Brown, who was killed by an exploding shell; his grave can be seen in Mafikeng cemetery. Baden-Powell went on to found the Boy Scout movement at Brownsea in southern England in 1907. He said of the boys of Mafikeng, "These lads proved by their achievements that, if trusted, boys can be relied upon to act as men when needed."

The impact of the war between Briton and Boer on the majority of the southern African population is also often forgotten. Neither side made much use of African soldiers directly, though a great many were employed (or forced to work) as porters, transport handlers and messengers. Nevertheless it was inevitable that they were caught up in the war and a great many were killed, either directly or as a result of disease and starvation, and many more had their livelihoods destroyed.

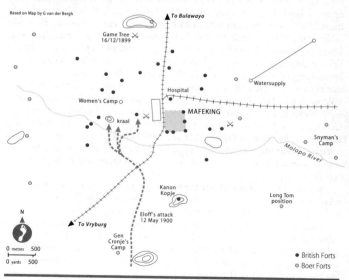

banks of the Molopo River built during a conflict between the Goshen Republic and the Barolong Boo Tshidi. The fort has been restored along with some cannons and guns and there are panoramic views of Mafikeng and its surrounds.

The **Imperial Reserve**, an area just outside the town contains the administrative buildings from three different local governments; the Bechuanaland Protectorate, the Tswana Territorial Authority and most recently the Republic of Bophuthatswana. The **1902 Engineering Works** is a site of disused and derelict factories and machinery, which for some unfathomable reason the South African Tourist Board has declared a tourist site and awarded it with a sign. Finally **The Mafikeng Game Reserve**, lies at the edge of town but the entrance is 10 km out on the Zeerust road at Manyane Game Lodge (see Sleeping below). The reserve contains large populations of plains game, white rhino, buffalo, and giraffe and the principle circuit takes only 2 hours to drive around. ■ *Open 0700-1800. T3817874.*

Essentials

Apart from the obligatory Spur, found in most of South Africa's small towns, there are few restaurants but unusually, most of the guest houses have their own excellent à la carte restaurants, which are open to non-residents and where the local people go out to eat.

Sleeping & eating
■ *on map*
Price codes:
see inside front cover

B *Mmabatho Tusk*, Nelson Mandela Dr, Mmabatho, T3891111, F3861661. Newly renovated, several restaurants, swimming pool, casino and health centre with spa and sauna facilities. Once an important gambling centre when gaming was illegal in South Africa but legal in the homelands, now looking somewhat out of place.
  C *Ferns Guest House*, 12 Cook St, Mafikeng, T/F3815971. 20 double rooms, a/c, en suite bathroom or shower, TV, guest lounge, bar, laundry service, swimming pool, secure parking, a modern quality guesthouse, good value. The smart restaurant is probably one of the better places to eat at in town. **C** *Buffalo Park Lodge*, corner of Botha and Molopo roads, T3812159, F3811359. Modern guest house with 20 simply decorated rooms, TV, en suite, very popular bar and restaurant, home cooked meals and a good Sunday lunch. Can get noisy when there are a few local farmers in the bar at the weekends. **C-D** *Bush Fern Lodge*, 3 km out of

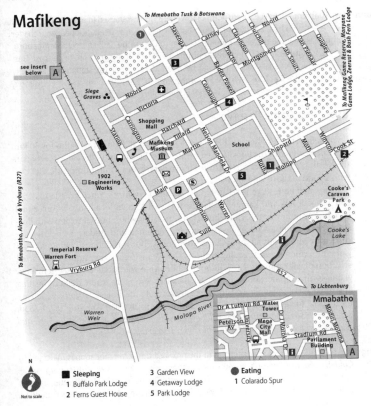

Mafikeng

North West Province

N
Not to scale

■ **Sleeping**
1 Buffalo Park Lodge
2 Ferns Guest House
3 Garden View
4 Getaway Lodge
5 Park Lodge

● **Eating**
1 Colarado Spur

Mafikeng on the Zeerust road, T3815971, F3816764. 12 a/c rooms, TV, decorated in an African theme, lively pub, evening meals on request, same ownership as Ferns in town.

D *Garden View*, corner of North and Havenga streets, Mafikeng, T3813110. Mix of double rooms, single rooms and self-catering units. Swimming pool, tennis and sauna. Good guest house which is more like a small hotel, breakfasts extra. Attached restaurant and bar. Rooms with shared bathroom represent great value. **D** *Getaway Lodge*, 39 Tillard St, Mafikeng, T3811150. 33 rooms, 28 with en suite bathroom, TV, fridge, good reasonably priced restaurant, relaxing gardens. A comfortable and centrally located guest house. **D-F** *Manyane Game Lodge*, 10 km from town on the Zeerust road, T3816020, F3816075. A selection of chalets, some self-catering, and camping at the entrance of the Mafikeng Game Reserve. Small shop with basic provisions, crocodile farm. In the gardens at the entrance gate is an interesting collection of carvings in the roots of upturned baobab trees. **F** *Cooke's Lake Caravan Park*, next to the lake just south of town, Mafikeng. A dusty caravan site for camping, little grass but sufficient shade, 24-hour reception, electric points, braais, laundry, all other facilities close by in the town.

Shopping *Mega City*, is a modern shopping centre close to the parliament buildings in Mmabatho. Outside the centre are a selection of Batswana curio sellers with some fine marula, mopane and ebony carvings.

Tour operators *Dumagole Tours and Safaris*, T3849197. Helpful local operator that can arrange tours in the region. *Heartland Northwest Safari Trail*, T3862222. This organization is run by Makikeng's Institute of Hotel and Tourism Management, which offers two guided self drive tours over 4 days specializing in bird watching and history.

Transport **Air** Mafikeng Airport is 17 km north of town, T3851141. *SAA* used to operate a scheduled

Public transport is almost non-existent and there are no scheduled flights, buses or trains, you will need a car to explore this region

service between here and Johannesburg but this has recently been dropped, only charter companies now use the airport. **Road** 217 km to **Gaborone**; 287 km to **Johannesburg**; 320 km to **Kimberley**; 200 km to **Rustenburg**; 156 km to **Vryburg**; 70 km to **Zeerust**. **Bus:** there are regular local services running between Mafikeng railway station and Megacity shopping centre. **Car hire** *Avis*, T3851114. *Imperial*, T/F3851000, both at Mafikeng airport, but since there are now no scheduled flights these offices are in danger of closing.

Botsalano Game Reserve

If you follow the R52 Ramatlabama border road north from Mmabatho for 30 km you will see signs for the Botsalano Game Reserve. Like many of the game reserves in the North West Province this is a little known park in beautiful countryside, stocked with a good range of wild animals.

The 5,800 ha reserve is set in typical Kalahari country – open grasslands with patches of acacia and karee woodlands. It is well-known locally for its successful breeding program for the white rhino. In the past this whole border region with Botswana was teeming with game and hunters, but man and rinderpest nearly succeeded in wiping out all the indigenous animals. But through restocking, natural game movements and breeding projects the area is once again home to a varied selection of wild animals. In addition to white rhino you can hope to see gemsbok, eland, springbok, steenbok, giraffe, jackal, hartebeest, zebra, kudu, duiker, warthog and impala. Hiking is allowed and there are several waterholes and dams which are ideal spots for game viewing in this environment. ■ *Open Apr-Aug 0600-1830; Sep-Mar 0530-1900. Hunting is still permitted in the reserve and between April and August it may well be closed for this purpose. T3862433.*

Sleeping Like some of the other national parks in the province the accommodation is managed by

Price codes: see inside front cover

Golden Leopard Resorts, central reservations, PO Box 6651, Rustenburg 0300, T014-5556135/6, F5557555/8, goldres@iafrica.com There is one simple self-catering camp at the entrance gate of the park. **D-E** *Mogobe Camp*, 4 tents with 2 beds in each, bedding supplied, there is a fully equipped kitchen; at the weekend all 4 tents have to be taken by the same booking. The camp is in a typical shady thicket overlooking Mogobe Dam.

Zeerust

Zeerust is a small centre for the local sheep and cattle industry. There is little of interest in the town but you may find yourself here en route to Botswana and it is a useful overnight stop between Gauteng and Gaberone. If you are hitching around the region this is the best point to look for lifts into Botswana as many trucks stop over here. The commercial centre is along Church St, where you will find banks to change money, supermarkets, and snack bars at the 24-hour petrol stations.

Phone code: 018
(NB Always use
3-figure prefix)
Colour map 1, grid B6
Altitude: 1187 m

C-E *Abjaterskop*, Rustenburg Rd, T/F6422008. 19 a/c rooms, with en suite bathroom, TV, restaurant, bar, lounge, swimming pool, gardens, secure parking, rates include meals, the most comfortable and friendly local option within the town. Camping and caravan site and much cheaper accommodation in simple, but rather grim, rondavels round the back. **D** *Marico Bosveld*, 5 President St, T/F6423545. Pretty B&B with 9 en suite rooms, TV, ladies bar, secure motel style parking, evening meals on request.

Sleeping
& eating
Price codes:
see inside front cover

Madikwe Game Reserve

Madikwe is the fourth largest game reserve in South Africa. More than 75,000 ha in extent, it has the second largest elephant population and it lies within a malaria-free zone. At present the park is not open to the passing day visitor, but for anyone visiting with one of the concessionaires they will undoubtedly have one of the most enjoyable and exclusive game viewing experiences possible at present in South Africa. Future plans to open a section of the park to day visitors is being considered once internal roads have been improved sufficiently for all vehicle use. This is a beautiful and up-and-coming park and something that it is hoped will be a great boost to tourism in the North West Province in general.

Colour map 1, grid A6

Getting there Although the reserve lies entirely within South Africa it is only 35 km from the Botswana capital, Gaborone. The northern limits of the park are marked by the international border, while the southern limits coincide with the Dwarsberg Mountains. Most of the park lies between the main road to Botswana and the Marico River to the east. If you are driving from the Gauteng district, take the N4 west through Magalies, Koster, Swartruggens, and Zeerust where you will turn right onto the R49 following signs to Gaborone. 100 km from Zeerust, just before the border crossing, turn right on to a sand road for 12 km to the Tau Gate. There are other gates at Derdepoort and Abjaterskop. Visitors should establish entry points before departure. An air charter service operates from Pretoria.

Ins & outs

Entry requirements Day visitors are presently not allowed into the reserve. In order to visit the park you must book through one of the lodges/camps listed in Sleeping below. Gate times by arrangement for pre-booked visitors only.

Best time to visit Most of the rain falls during the summer between Nov and Mar. Up to 600 mm is expected in the south, but as you move across the plains northwards, the annual rainfall is on average about 100 mm less. During the summer it can get very hot in the day – this is not the sort of weather for walking in. However, during the winter while it may be dry, it can be very cold at night. If you visit the park before the rains arrive, there is always the chance of finding the animals close to the water points, however the vegetation in the park is brown and dull, and the birdlife is not nearly so prolific.

One of the great features of the reserve is its diverse geology which has resulted in a broad mix of habitats suitable for a wide range of animals to live in. In the northern part of the reserve the land is a level savannah plain. Running across the middle of

Wildlife

the park, and in effect dividing it in two is the Tweedepoort escarpment. Above the escarpment is an undulating plateau covered with dense vegetation, a marked contrast to the grasslands below the escarpment. At the southern edge of the park is a more extensive range of rocky mountains, the Dwarsberg range. These are similar in appearance to the Magaliesberg but have been severely eroded over the years, the highest point being only 1,228 m. The final distinct environment is provided by the perennial Marico River along the eastern boundary, where an aquatic and well-vegetated environment exists.

When the lands started to be prepared for inclusion into a game reserve only a few of the indigenous species had survived the years of hunting and farming as well as the rinderpest outbreak. Back in 1836 the hunter William Cornwallis came across the first known sable in the Marico Valley and wrote of large herds of elephant and prides of lion frightening the local farmers. In 1991 **Operation Phoenix** was launched – one of the largest game translocation programmes in the world. By 1996 more than 10,000 animals from 28 species had been successfully released into the reserve. It now remains to be seen whether the right ecological environment has been created in order that this animal population can naturally increase to the envisaged numbers.

Before the start of the programme the following animals were recorded as still being present within the reserve: steenbok, duiker, kudu, brown and spotted hyena, leopard, and a few cheetah. Operation Phoenix was an ambitious programme that benefited from the lessons learnt from other game translocation projects. During the drought in the early 1990s entire breeding herds of elephant were moved from the Gona-re-Zhou game reserve in Zimbabwe to Madikwe. These animals are now thriving. Other species to have been brought in from other parts of South Africa include zebra, lion, buffalo, white rhino, spotted hyena and the rare wild dog. Visitors to the park are able to view these animals either during game drives or on morning walks with a guide and experienced tracker. A special feature of the reserve is the introduction of community projects, which will allow local communities to benefit from, and contribute to, a number of aspects of ecological management within the reserve.

Madikwe Game Reserve

Based on a map by Des Webster

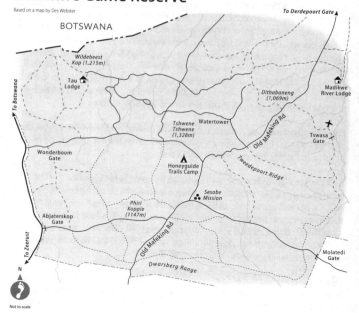

Madikwe is a low-density tourism facility and the lodges are built as far away as possible from each other. Staying here, you have a great sense of having the whole game reserve to yourself.

AL *Madikwe River Lodge*, T014-7780891/2, F7780893. A lot of care and thought has gone into the décor of the 16 luxury split level chalets, each has an en suite bathroom, a lounge area with bar fridge and a private balcony overlooking the Marico River. The central lodge has a fine thatched roof and is partly hidden by the riverine forest, here there is a lounge area with a small wildlife reference library, an open bar and the restaurant. There's a small swimming pool is above the river. The lodge is connected by a wooden bridge with a small island in the river where meals are served in a reed boma. An excellent lodge with plenty of atmosphere and a helpful and friendly staff, strongly recommended. **A** *Mosetlha Bushcamp*, T011-8026222. The price is based upon a weekend for 2 in the park including all meals and activities, but not alcoholic drinks and transport to the reserve and it is currently the least expensive of the 3 options. The camp is in the middle of the park close to the Tswene Tswene Hills, game drives or guided walks are available each day, the guides are exceptionally good and are expert at bringing the bush to life even when you are not viewing the more dramatic animals. At the end of a weekend you should be relaxed and able to appreciate the bush in a new light. Recommended as one of the less fancy lodges but nonetheless friendly and well-run. **A** *Tau Game Lodge*, T018- 3659027. 30 luxury chalets with en suite bathrooms, private wooden view/sun deck, swimming pool. The lodge is located close to an Inselberg complex known as the *Majwaneng Hills*, the chalets are arranged in an arc looking out onto a large seasonal waterhole, this is an area of acacia woodland with plenty of animals to be seen on the open grass plains close by; game drives, guided walks and all meals are included in the rates.

If you wish to view the park from a different angle there is always the option of going up in a hot air balloon at dawn. *Bill Harrop's Balloon Safaris*, T011-7053201, F011-7053203. Operates from here whenever there is sufficient demand. At the end of the flight you are treated to a champagne breakfast on the ground before being driven back to your camp. *Honeyguide Trails*, PO Box 78690, Sandton 2146, T083-6539869 (mob), F011-8023643, ask for Chris Lucas. Organize tours, usually bringing guests out from Johannesburg or Pretoria. It is possible to drive to the entrance where their vehicles will then take you to the camp. Booking is essential during school holidays. This is a good value package and is run in a friendly and easygoing manner. Recommended.

Sleeping
Price codes:
see inside front cover

Tours

North West Province

The Western Region

West to Setlagole

After leaving Mafikeng the R49 leads across a large expanse of featureless savannah broken only by the occasional stands of acacia trees. For most of the year this is a hot and dusty region just waiting for the rains. Most of the country is given over to farming cattle, maize and surprisingly, groundnuts. About 71 km from Mafikeng, around Setlagole, there are several private **game farms** which attract visitors for game viewing as well as hunting. These lodges provide some excellent game viewing opportunities that few visitors are aware of. There is a choice between simple self-catering bush camps or luxury lodges where everything is included in the price. On a couple of the farms it is possible to go boating and fishing on the dams, but in most cases people come here to view game or hunt. Where the emphasis is on game viewing you can walk in the bush and go out on night drives when the countryside reveals another world of wildlife.

Be careful when driving through this rather featureless landscape not to fall asleep at the wheel, and always lookout for wild animals suddenly running out in front of the car

Game farms A-B *Makgoro Game Ranch*, T053982 ask for 6811. An exclusive thatched lodge overlooking a dam, sleeps 8. **B** *Nonen Ranch*, T053982 ask for 8131. 2 thatched chalets, self-catering only, room for up to 8 people, hunting and hiking opportunities.

Sleeping
Price codes:
see inside front cover

Stella A further 110 km from Mafikeng is Stella, the largest settlement between Mafikeng and Vryburg. This is a typical quiet farming centre where nothing seems to be going on when you just drive through. However, every October the town wakes up for the national **Cattle and Beef Festival** which attracts farmers from all over the country.

Vryburg

Phone code: 053
(NB Always use
3-figure prefix)
Colour map 1, grid C5

No matter which direction you approach from, the size of Vryburg often takes visitors by surprise. After miles of flat dry savannah, you suddenly stumble upon this busy commercial centre, seemingly in the middle of nowhere. This is an important cattle centre where an auction is held every Friday, the cattle are trucked in from the surrounding countryside, many destined for the local canning factory. **Tourist information** is available at the Municipality, Market St, upstairs in the municipal building, T9272200, F9273482. It has information on the town only but is very helpful. Ask for Clemintine.

History The early history of Vryburg is interesting in so far as it provides a vivid picture of life along the frontier of the British Empire just over 100 years ago. Before the arrival of any proper form of authority in the region there was a protracted war between the Tlapin people of Chief Mankwarane and the Koranna Khoikhoi led by David Massouw. In an effort to win the conflict, Massouw offered a collection of European mercenaries farms as their share of the loot and eventually 416 farms were given away. Shortly afterwards in August 1883 the ex-mercenaries proclaimed their block of farms to be a new independent republic, which would be known as Stellaland. The capital of this new republic was Vryburg, the 'town of freedom'. Despite being short-lived the Stellaland Republic is interesting inasmuch as a postal service was organized, with their own postage stamps (rare collectors' items), and a flag was designed. This flag was sent to Queen Victoria after an expeditionary force under Sir Charles Warren had occupied the area in 1885 and the republic had been merged into British Bechuanaland. It was later returned to Vryburg and is on display in the town's museum.

Vryburg

To Stella & Mafikeng
To Leon Taljaardt Nature Reserve,
Swartfontein Resort & Botswana
To Cattle Auctions
To Station
To Wolmaransstad & Potchefstroom
To Kuruman & Upington
To Airport, Kimberley & Agriculture Showgrounds

Molopo · E Frylinck · Fincham · Noord · Sports Ground · Boshoff · Du Plessis · Noord · French · East · Livingstone · De Kock · Ulmer · Nelson · Mackenzie · Royden · Warren · Moffat · Stella · Market · Delarey · Vry · Kerk · Market · Pol · Voortrekker · Vry · Sports Ground

N   Not to scale

■ **Sleeping**
1 Grobler
2 International
3 Kilphuisie Guest House
4 Lockerbie Lodge
5 Ngulube Lodge
6 Schoon Guest House
7 St Quintin Lodge

● **Eating**
1 Durado Spur
2 Saddles
3 Steers

Leon Taljaardt Nature Reserve is the municipal game reserve 5 km from the town centre, to the left, off the Botswana road. It's a pleasant small reserve which was created in 1968 and named in honour of the local mayor. It has gradually been stocked with a mix of species, not all of which ever occurred naturally in this area. The countryside is quite flat with a few rock outcrops and a dense vegetation cover which makes game viewing difficult after the rains when the bush is in leaf. Walking is not allowed, with luck you can expect to see buffalo, white rhino, black and blue wildebeest, eland, gemsbok, impala, red hartebeest, Burchell's and mountain zebra and waterbuck. Accommodation is provided by *Swartfontein Holiday Resort*, see details below. ■ *Gate hours Apr-Aug 0700-1500, Sep-Mar 0700-1800. Small entrance fee.*

Sights

B-C *The International*, 43 Market St, T/F9272235. 37 a/c rooms with en suite bathrooms, TV MNet, Gallery restaurant, popular local pub, swimming pool, conference facilities. Very average and rooms need upgrading, also own *St Quintin Lodge* and *Lockerbie Lodge* (see below) which are better options for the same rate. The central reservations number for all three is the same. **B-C** *Lockerbie Lodge*, Vry St behind the International, T/F9272235. 12 double rooms with en suite bathroom, comfortable TV lounge with an open fire for winter, self-catering kitchen, pool, the lodge is an annex to the *International Hotel*, guests have a short walk if they wish to dine in the restaurant. This hotel, now a listed historical building, was established in 1890 and was used by Cecil Rhodes. **B-C** *St Quintin Lodge*, Vry St next door to the Lockerbie, T/F9272235. 15 doubles with same ownership and facilities as above. More geared for conference delegates. **C-D** *Ngulube Lodge*, 81 Vry St, T9270700, F9270808. 15 double rooms of exceptionally high standard, quite a surprise in this remote town. Very modern and spacious, individually designed in a building that is a converted dental practice. TV, a/c, ladies bar, lapa and braai area, attractive breakfast room, family run and very friendly. Recommended. **D** *Schoon Guest House*, 14 Ulmer St, T082-4102067 (mob). 1 double room with en suite bathroom, 2 double rooms with shared bathroom, cosy TV lounge, bar fridge, swimming pool, braai area, secure parking. A quiet base for exploring the area, with a very helpful service providing picnic/braai hampers, this is a well-run and friendly guesthouse. Recommended. **E-F** *Swartfontein Holiday Resort*, 5 km from town off the R378, T9274261. 14 self-catering chalets with 2 or 4 beds, kitchen, dining area, camping is possible, swimming pool, peaceful site with some large shady trees, acts as the accommodation for the adjacent Leon Taljaardt Nature Reserve (see above).

Sleeping
■ *on map*
Price codes:
see inside front cover

Durado Spur, T9274724. As part of the Spur chain you are assured of quality steaks and ribs, generous portions, salad bar, open for meals all through the day. *Gallery and Bullring Bar*, T/F9272235. Principal town à la carte restaurant and pub in the *International Hotel*, choice will depend in part on how busy the hotel is. *Saddles*, Market St. Similar set up and menu as the Spur, a/c, good for a cold beer in the heat of the day. *Steers*, Market St. Fast food takeaways, steaks and burgers, long distance coaches depart from outside.

Eating
● *on map*

Road 250 km to **Botswana** (Bray); 420 km to **Johannesburg**; 212 km to **Kimberley**; 156 km to **Mafikeng**; 400 km to **Upington**. **Bus**: *Intercape*, T012-6544114, buses arrive and depart from outside *Steers Restaurant*, Market St . To **Pretoria** (5 hrs): Mon, Tue, Thu, Sat, 1015, via Potchefstroom; **Upington** (4½ hrs): Tue, Thu, Fri, Sun, 1500, via Kuruman.

Transport

Molopo Nature Reserve

This is a remote reserve on the Botswana border, which was proclaimed in 1988, and falls under the responsibility of the North West Province Parks and Tourism Board, PO Box 4488, Mmabatho 2735, T018-3861225-9, F018-3861158. If you have already travelled extensively in South Africa by the time you reach this corner of the North West Province you are bound to have a strong sense of the diversity and contrast of land and the way of life for people in the country. Driving around on the fringes of the Kalahari, this hot and dusty region with few signs of habitation, feels like a million miles away from the Cape or the coast in KwaZulu Natal. This will

Colour map 1, grid B5

North West Province

almost certainly be one of the most remote and wild corners of South Africa that you'll get to see. Although the region is not well-known for its wildlife there are huge herds of antelope roaming the area. One border of the 24,000 ha park is made up by the Molopo River, which also happens to be the international border with Botswana. The river rarely flows, maybe once every 45 years, but there is plenty of water in the ground. It is the presence of the water just below the surface that helps keep the vegetation alive, which in turn accounts for the concentration of wild animals. As you drive up to the reserve the road passes through lands that were part of the former Bophuthatswana Homelands, and here evidence of what impact overgrazing and poor range management can have on the land is painfully clear.

The park is in an area of dry thornveld, and by protecting the land there is sufficient grazing and browsing to support a mix of wildlife including gemsbok, red hartebeest, kudu, springbok and eland – if you are very lucky you may also see cheetah, leopard and brown hyena. Given the remoteness and the fact that few tourists ever get to this part of the country, very little has been spent on developing the park or facilities for the visitor.

To make ensure that you are allowed to visit the park contact the Officer-in-Charge at the Park Office, T082-5747427

Reserve information If you wish to stay here you have to be completely self sufficient, and the network of roads are only suitable for 4x4 vehicles. The *Motopi Camp* accommodates 8 people on a self-catering basis, and *Phiri Camp* has 9 campsites spread over a wide area. Walking is allowed anywhere in the park with prior permission. But for your own safety you must let the park wardens know exactly what your intended route will be and also carry sufficient water. Do not walk during the summer when it is too hot, and remember that in the winter months it can freeze at night. Gate times 0600-1800. This is a non-malarial region. 250 km north of Vryburg, 7 km west of the village of Vostershoop.

Tour operators *Molapo Safaris*, T018-2976290.

The Eastern Region

Pretoria to Botswana The first part of the N4, which heads westwards from Pretoria, is a toll road and therefore avoided by most local traffic. If you do not wish to pay the toll, which is only a few Rand, then follow the signs for the alternative route via the R27. Just before the toll road reaches Hartbeespoort Dam it ends and traffic rejoins the R27. After passing through Hartbeestpoort, this road rejoins the N4 towards Rustenburg. The N4 is currently being upgraded to a freeway through to Botswana, however at the time of writing not all the sections had been completed (hence the first toll out of Pretoria). This road is all part of the planned Trans-Kalahari highway, the Botswana section has recently been completed, which will eventually link Pretoria with Walvis Bay in Namibia.

Hartbeespoort Dam

Phone code: 021 (NB Always use 3-figure prefix) Altitude: 1,200 m Colour map 2, grid C2

The proximity of Johannesburg and Pretoria (35 km), has made this dam in the Magaliesberg Mountains a popular water sports resort and weekend retreat. Around the shoreline are smart marinas and large private homes overlooking the lake. For **tourist information**, contact The Hartbeespoort Dam Information Shop, on the Damdoryn Crossroad next to the curio market, T2531741. Open Tue-Sun 1000–1700. (There is an old information sign in town that leads you to the library, ignore this as they will only redirect you to the Information Shop.)

The dam was built in 1923 in a narrow gorge where the Crocodile River cuts through the Magaliesberg Mountains, which are estimated to be 100 times older than Everest. In the early 1970s the dam wall was raised, thus increasing the lake to its present size. There are two major canals, which conduct water away from the dam into a series of smaller canals which irrigate the farmlands around Brits. The old main road from Pretoria runs through the village of **Schoemansville** on the north shore of the lake before crossing the dam wall and continuing to **Rustenburg** and **Sun City**.

The Hartbeespoort Dam Snake and Animal Park in Schoemansville, remains a popular attraction for visiting families from Gauteng. There are various reptiles as well as lions, cheetahs, chimps, hyena, panthers and Bengal tigers, most in inadequate cages and in an area of Africa that is an inappropriate location for many of the species on display. At the weekend and on public holidays there are rather antiquated performances by chimps and seals. This is little more than a cooped up zoo and there are far more pleasurable places in South Africa to view animals in their natural environments. ■ *The entrance is on the main road, Scott St, opposite the Squires Restaurant and Lake Motel , T2531162. The park is open daily, 0800-1700.*

The **Hartbeespoort Dam Cableway** was erected at one of the highest points of the Magaliesberg Mountains 1,600 m above sea level. The total length of the cableway is 2.3 km and the ride takes about 6 minutes. This is also a popular spot for hang gliding and paragliding and there are great views of the dam from the picnic site at the top. ■ *Open Mon-Fri 0900-1530, Sat-Sun 0900-1700. The entrance is on the R513 just outside of town towards Pretoria, T2531706.*

Sleeping & eating
Price codes:
see inside front cover

C *Waterside Country House*, 70 Waterfront Road, T/F 2530123. Hardly a country house but more of a rather jumbled collection of self-catering rooms in the owner's back garden. Fridge and microwave, TV, meals on request. Not particularly good value but close to the dam. **C-F** *Ring Wagon Inn*, T/F2591506. 6 chalets attached to furnished ox-wagons, en suite bathroom, homely restaurant, swimming pool, cheaper beds available in a backpackers dorm built out of an old double decker bus, situated high up in the hills with nice views and hiking trails. **D** *Squires Grill and Lake Motel*, 1 Scott St, opposite the Snake and Animal park, T2531001. A simple affordable motel attached to the Squires Grill restaurant. 8 basic en suite rooms with TV. The restaurant has a large range of steaks and burgers. **D** *Berg & Dam*, 90 Scott St, T/F2530522. A very clean, modern, spacious B&B. Huge rooms with fully fitted kitchenettes and large showers, pretty gardens, secure parking, meals on request. Recommended.

Brits
Colour map 2, grid B2

Brits is a medium sized industrial centre which is surrounded by highly productive farmlands irrigated from the Hartbeespoort Dam. However, most people are only likely to see Brits if they are heading north for the little known Borakalalo Nature Reserve, one of several excellent reserves tucked away in the North West Province (see below). There is a **cheetah research station** here, though, which is famous for being the first such place where cheetah were successfully born in captivity. ■ *Tours can be arranged by appointment only, no casual visitors, T5041921.*

Borakalalo Nature Reserve

Colour map 2, grid B2

This is a pleasant nature reserve almost due north from Pretoria which is primarily known for the excellent fishing in the Klipvoor Dam. The reserve surrounds the dam, however the lands on the northern shore have been restocked with a variety of wild animals so that visitors now have a choice of hiking, game viewing and fishing at Borakalalo, also known as 'the place where people relax'.

Getting there From Brits take the R512 and then the right turning signposted Lethlabile. After Lethlabile follow the signs for Jericho, at Jericho take a right at the T-junction and then the first left signposted Legonyane. The reserve is signposted along this road. The entrance is about 50 km from Brits.

Ins & outs
Fill up with petrol before arrival if you plan to do several game viewing drives, there is no petrol here and the closest petrol station is 30 km from the entrance gate

Best time to visit The reserve receives most of its rain during the summer months, Oct through to Apr; the summer temperatures range from a very hot 37°C to an average of 20°C in the evening. During winter it can get much colder than most visitors from overseas would expect, if you are camping you will need jumpers and sleeping bags at night.

North West Province

Reserve information Gate hours: Apr-Aug 0600-1900; Sep-Mar, 0500-2000. Entrance charges: adults, R20; children, R12. There is a small refreshment shop at the park gate, however it is best to come with most provisions if you are self-catering. The day visitors' area has a picnic site with braai areas and washing up facilities plus clean toilets. Fishing licences for the day are issued at the gate on arrival, do not fish in the rivers.

Sights At 13,000 ha this was, for a time, the second largest national park in the former Bophuthatswana. Although it is closer to Pretoria than Pilanesberg National Park, it receives far fewer visitors, making it a favourite for some residents. Since the reserve was proclaimed in 1984, there has been a complete restocking programme replacing the animals that once roamed the plains; white rhino, buffalo, giraffe, zebra, eland, elephant, hippo, buffalo, nyala, leopard, crocodile, jackal, tsessebe, gemsbok and roan antelope are some of the animals you may see here today. There are over 350 species of bird in the park, enough to keep the keen ornithologist busy and happy. Several sturdy hides have been built where you can enjoy viewing the wildlife without being stuck inside a car.

By dividing the reserve into several areas, the management have ensured that each recreational activity does not interrupt another while at the same time making sure visitors' safety and the park environment are also protected. The Moretele River flows through the park which encompasses the 800 ha **Klipvoor Dam**. The dam has become a popular fishing venue after a record-breaking kurper was caught here. Boating and swimming are not allowed, there are crocodile and hippo in the park and the dam carries bilharzia. To the east of the dam is a wilderness area where there are no roads or man-made paths, the wildlife is free to roam undisturbed in this part of the park. To the southwest of the dam is the **game viewing** area, 50 km of gravel roads have been cut through the open savannah woodland, there is also another small dam where animals may be seen drinking – **Sefudi Dam**.

Hiking Trails One of the most pleasurable experiences in the park is to follow one of the self-guided walks through the riverine forest along the banks of the Moretele River, these vary from between 1-4 km in distance. Guides are available for the longer walks, which are usually made in the early morning and last up to 3 hours. One of the most enjoyable walks is a climb to the top of Pitjane Koppie where one is rewarded with views across the whole park. Maps of all the trails are provided at the entrance gate.

Sleeping There are 3 camps in the reserve, catering for every budget, all of which are operated by
Price codes: **Golden Leopard Resorts**, central reservations, PO Box 6651, Rustenburg 0300,
see inside front cover T014-5556135/6, F014-5557555, goldres@iafrica.com On arrival at the park confirm your reservation at reception.

A *Phudufudu Safari Camp*, 5 luxury tents. Set in a secluded corner with plenty of large shade trees, central dining area and lounge, plunge pool, the smartest and most luxurious of the 3 camps in the park, everything the visitor needs is here, and if not then you only have to ask your personal hostess/ranger. **D** *Moretele Camp*, has 2 camps of semi-permanent tents with basic furnishings. Self-catering facilities, fridges, and shared ablution blocks. You need to bring everything you need with you. **F** *Pitjane Camp*, a basic rustic camp right beside the dam, this is primarily used by anglers, camping sites have a braai area and a water tap, the central washblock is made from reeds but there is ample hot water and clean washing and toilet facilities, the camp has no electricity or fridges.

Rustenburg

Phone code: 014
(NB Always use
3-figure prefix)
Colour map 2, grid B1
Altitude: 1,160 m

Rustenburg, 'castle of rest', is one of the oldest towns in the region and was an important centre under the Transvaal Republic. Today it is a busy administrative centre for the many mining companies in the region. Due to it's proximity to Johannesburg and Pretoria, the Magaliesberg Mountains and the Rustenburg Nature Reserve have become popular weekend retreats for country-starved

Gautengers. While there is little to keep anyone in the town itself for long, there are the usual facilities and it is a useful stop en route to Magaliesberg's country hotels and guest houses, the gambling and entertainment resort at Sun City, and the park camps of Pilanesberg National Park.

Getting around Rustenburg is not on any of the commercial bus routes nor is it served by scheduled passenger train services. To visit and explore this region one needs to have a hired car. Being so close to Pretoria and Johannesburg there is plenty of choice and it should be possible to negotiate a good deal. To get the most out of the region one should allow for at least 3 nights in the area, this would enable a visitor to explore Pilansberg National Park, Sun City, the Magaliesberg Mountains and some of the historical sites such as Paul Kruger's farm.

Ins & outs
105 km to Pretoria; 112 km to Johannesburg; 48 km to Sun City via R27 and R565; 200 km to Mafikeng; 130 km to Zeerust

Tourist offices *Rustenburg Tourism Information and Development Centre*, corner of Van Staden and Kloof streets, T5970904, F5970907, on the outskirts of town, clearly visible when approaching from the Pretoria side on the N4. Open 0730-1800 Mon-Fri, 0800-1200 Sat, closed Sun. An excellent office that is well worth a stop when visiting the area, staffed by friendly and an enthusiastic team including tourism students on work experience schemes. The local accommodation is clearly presented with plenty of detailed photographs, the office also has some useful maps. This is a satellite office for the *North West Parks and Tourism Board* so they can also provide information on the whole region.

History

The first white settlers in the region were a group of burghers who had followed the Voortrekker leader Andries Pretorius from the Cape. Among the first Voortrekkers to start farming on the northern slopes of the fertile Magaliesberg were AH Potgieter and Casper Kruger, the father of the future President of the Transvaal, Paul Kruger. In 1851 the settlers were granted permission by the *Volksraad* in Potchefstroom to build a church on the farms Kafferskraal and Witpensfontein and so the new village of Rustenburg was born. This was only the second Dutch Reformed parish to be created north of the Vaal River.

During the short existence of the Boer Republic the town was for a while the capital before government was moved to Pretoria, and it was also an important education centre. On 16 March 1852 it was the scene of the reconciliation between Andries Pretorius and Hendrik Potgieter, two of the leaders of the splintered Great Trek vortrekkers. This was an important occasion as far as peace within the Republic was concerned because Pretorius had gone to the Orange Free State and Potgieter to the Eastern Transvaal and Mozambique. Reconciling their differences helped unify the two states (Orange Free and Transvaal) as a strong force against the British.

Sights

This is the third oldest town in the region and as such has some sights of historical interest. As you drive around the region visiting a few of the local museums and perhaps a couple of the battlefields from the Anglo-Boer War you gain a greater insight into the early history of the Voortrekkers and the conditions under which they lived and survived. Despite many aspects of their behaviour and government it is difficult not to admire what they achieved in unfamiliar and hostile terrain with little knowledge of what lay ahead of them. A little over 100 years ago, every river and mountain represented an obstacle to be overcome, plus the region was teeming with wild animals that would attack domestic cattle and oxen.

Hervormde Church Square is the square where the reconciliation between Andries Pretorius and Hendrik Potgieter took place. The meeting actually took place where the church now stands.

Kwaggapan Look-out Tower stands in a park to your left as you drive into town from the Pretoria direction. This is a stone cylindrical tower, which offers panoramic views of the town. The entrance is from Heystek Street but although the tourist office insists it is open from 0800-1600, the gate is often mysteriously locked.

The Statue of Paul Kruger and **The Rustenburg Museum** have recently moved from the centre of Rustenburg to the Kedar Country Hotel and **The Paul Kruger**

North West Province

Country House Museum 18 km northwest towards Sun City on the R565. (See Excursions below.)

Statue of a Voortrekker Girl is in Plein Street opposite the Hervormde Church, the girl is holding a candle and represents the introduction of Christianity to the area.

Excursions **Paul Kruger Country House Museum** is at Boekenhoutfontein, the farm where Paul Kruger lived as an obscure farmer before he became the president of the Transvaal Republic from 1883 until the end of the Anglo-Boer War. Four buildings have been preserved and restored as museums to the life of Paul Kruger and the earliest farmers in the Transvaal. The oldest building is a cottage built in 1841 by the first owner of Boekenhoutfontein, this is a single storeyed building with a thatched roof and stone patio out front. When Paul Kruger moved here in 1863, he built a new thatched homestead for his family, known as the 'Pioneer House'. To its right stands the main homestead, a double storey stone building built in 1872 in typical Eastern Cape style. The house contains many of Kruger's possessions along with an assortment of period furniture from other homes. The fourth house dates from 1892, this was built for Kruger's son Pieter.

Of the original 500-ha farm, 32 ha have been kept as part of the museum; the gardens have been partially restored and visitors are free to stroll around looking at the birds and plants, picnic areas have been laid out. The old **Rustenburg Museum** has moved here and has a small but interesting collection of local historical items. The Statue of Paul Kruger used to stand in front of the information office in Rustenburg but this has also been moved to Boekenhoutfontein. Sculpted in bronze by a French artist, Jean Archand, the statue was first discovered in Paris in 1919 by General Louis Botha and General Jan Smuts. They wanted to donate it to the Union Government with the intention that it would occupy a central position in Church Square in Pretoria but the statue was too small for the large open space and was donated to Rustenburg. ■ *Open Tue-Fri 1000-1600, Sat-Sun 1000-1400 T014-5733218, minimal entrance charge. The Pioneer House contains the 1872 Restaurant, but opening times are sporadic and depend on how many guests are staying at the Kedar Lodge next door. 18 km northwest of Rustenburg, off the R565, en route to Sun City, look out for a left turning just after Phokeng.*

Sleeping
■ *on map, page 569*
Price codes:
see inside front cover

As you drive around the centre of Rustenburg you will not come across a *Town Lodge, Protea Hotel* or *Holiday Inn* – the usual range of business/tourist hotels that you would expect to find in a South African town.

Most of the local hotels are located beyond the built up area towards the spectacular Magaliesberg Mountains

Although Sun City and Pilansberg National Park remain the principal draw for tourists to the region, many people find the price of their rooms too high. Consequently visitors are always looking for alternatives nearby. The *Sundown Ranch Hotel*, is the closest hotel to Sun City, a comfortable complex which is less than 10 mins drive from the gates (see below). After this, the best value place to stay at is one of the fine country resort hotels in the Magaliesberg range, close to Rustenburg. The *Rustenburg Residential Accommodation Association* is a useful organization: a group of B&Bs have clubbed together to man a central cell phone number for enquiries and reservations T082-4856816 (mob).

B *Orion Safari Lodge*, 7 km from centre on Donkerhoek road, T/F5971361. 131 a/c rooms, restaurant in a converted railway carriage, bar, swimming pool, floodlit tennis courts, squash, gym, the principal town hotel on a ridge behind the city centre close to Rustenburg Kloof. Offer game drives into Rustenburg Nature Reserve and horse riding. Good rates for single occupancy. **C-D** *Ananda Country Lodge*, T5973875. A combination of 68 hotel rooms, thatched chalets and a well-shaded campsite, all set in the lee of the Magaliesberg, restaurant, bar, 3 swimming pools, tennis courts, bowls, squash, golf nearby. A short distance from town so often overrun with conference delegates. **B-C** *Kedar Lodge*, 20 km from Rustenburg towards Sun City on the R565, T/F5733218. 27 double rooms with en suite bathroom, open log fires, individual plunge pools, rustic stone shower rooms. A peaceful group of cottages next to the historic farm of President Kruger, zebra and ostrich within the grounds. The 1872

North West Province

Restaurant is in Kruger's house, designed for conferences during the week. Fishing trips can be organized from here. **C** *Sundown Ranch*, 33 km from Rustenburg centre, on the R565, T5731000, F5731055. This is only 10 km from Sun City and Pilanesberg National Park and a much cheaper option than the accommodation choices within the resort. 101 double rooms, 2 restaurants – *Stage Coach Grill* and *Pilanesberg* restaurant, swimming pool in a pleasant palm courtyard, outdoor bar, tennis courts, squash, bowls, horse trails and a lion park where for a small fee you are guaranteed a close view and even play with some lion cubs. Rates include dinner and breakfast, tremendous value. A perfect base for exploring the area. Recommended. Next door is **D** *Sundown Ranch Chalets*, T5733131, F5733104. 91 simple self-catering chalets accommodating 2-6 people, large pool area. Most of these are time-share units so they are only, inexplicably, available for hire on Friday and Saturday nights!

C-F *Rustenburg Kloof*, 7 km from centre on Donkerhoek road, T5941037-9. 88 chalets with either 1 or 2 bedrooms, there are 7 different price bands which vary according to the facilities, the most expensive chalets are fully equipped with a/c, bathrooms, TV, microwave oven – bedding is provided in all the chalets, discounts of up to 30% possible out of season. There is also an enormous caravan and camping park with plenty of grass and shade. The facilities include tennis courts, 3 swimming pools, mini golf, a games room, small supermarket, a kiosk for light meals, including breakfast, a bar, and a shop. Overall good value, but a very popular holiday camp during local school holidays. The entrance to Rustenburg Nature Reserve is close by, the best budget place to stay in town if you have a car. **D** *Bergsig Lodge*, 7 Peperboom Av, T/F5933343. 4 double rooms with en suite facilities, ceiling fans, TV lounge, MNet, separate entrance, braai area, swimming pool, well-kept garden with shady corners, ideal for local sights and town centre, winners of a national accommodation award, secure parking. Top of the range B&B, recommended. **D** *Joan's B&B*, 61 Wildevy Av, Protea Park, T5932086. Straightforward B&B in a private home in a peaceful residential district, call in advance to guarantee a room, full English breakfast served the next day.

Bistro & Brouwerij, 5 km from the town centre on the R30, turn of the Pretoria road by the Ultra City, T5992592. Pub lunches and Indonesian cuisine, a real treat is to try the Dutch beer brewed on the site. Recommended. *Dros*, Von Vielligh St, opposite Rustenburg Square mall, TT5925439. Lively bar and restaurant with a huge menu of pizzas, steaks, seafood, and massive breakfasts. Very little choice for vegetarians though. Good venue for a few cold beers in the evening. *San Francisco*, 16 Pretorius St, T5923652. An excellent coffee shop open every day, in addition to a superb selection of coffees you can also enjoy cakes and snack lunches. **Eating**

Rustenburg Travel, Steen St, T5920251, F5971280. Useful local booking agent. *Wise Guy's Travel*, 140 Kruger St, T5929256, F5925674. Useful agent for local car hire and tours, will also organize domestic and international flights. **Tour operators**

Internet *Vodacom Store*, in the Waterfall Shopping Mall, at the far end of the mall next to *Pick 'n Pay*. Only one terminal, so you might have to queue. **Useful addresses** Ambulance: T5943334. Hospital: T22112. Police: T10111. **Directory**

Rustenburg Nature Reserve

This is a very popular mountain reserve at the summit and along the northern slopes of the Magaliesberg range, 400 m above Rustenburg. The reserve is regarded as an important recreational area as well as a valuable educational environment for visitors from Johannesburg and Pretoria, just over 100 km away. Because it it so close to the large cities, the number of visitors is tightly controlled and anyone wishing to camp or enjoy the longer hiking trails needs to book up to six months in advance. *Colour map 2, grid B1*

Getting there From the centre of Rustenburg follow Wolmarans St (from the junction with Van Staden by the Municipal Offices), through the residential suburbs to the very end where it then curves to the left and becomes Boekenhout Rd. Follow this road out of town until you come to a T-junction, the right is signposted for the *Ananda Hotel*, take a left turn. Shortly after **Ins & outs**

North West Province

passing Rustenburg Kloof, just before the entrance gates to the *Orion Safari Lodge*, is a right turn to the main gates of the reserve. The reserve is not clearly signposted in the centre of town.

Reserve information Gate hours: Sep-Mar 0530-1900, Apr-Aug 0600-1830. Small entrance charge. Hiking charges: R90 per person. Confirmed bookings for the huts must be paid for in full at least a month before the booked date. The overnight hike is very popular at weekends and during school holidays, it will nearly always be necessary to book at these times. However, overseas visitors are unlikely to have any problem getting on the trail in the middle of the week at the last moment. Bookings through the Reservations Officer, Rustenburg Nature Reserve, PO Box 20382, Protea Park 0305, T5332050.

Climate Hikers suffer from seasonal extremes, in winter it gets very cold at night, during summer it is so hot that it is important you carry sufficient drinking water.

Wildlife & vegetation The land was originally part of Rietvallei farm, which once belonged to President Paul Kruger. The reserve was proclaimed in 1967 after the council had been given the land by one of Kruger's descendants. In 1981 the nature reserve was extended to include an adjoining farm to the east and today the total area protected is 4,257 ha. From the top of the reserve you can see the flat bushveld to the south, while the ridge of the mountains disappears east towards the Hartbeespoort Dam and Pretoria. Between the mountain ridges is a hidden valley basin which acts as a natural catchment area, the streams flowing out of here are cool and refreshing all year round.

The valley floor is a mix between a reed swamp and stands of trees such as acacia, boekenhout, and syringa. Higher up, on the plateau and along the ridges the vegetation cover is more sparse and consists mainly of open grasslands, along the short day trail you can see the rare and endemic *Aloe peglerae*. In the narrow gullies or kloofs that have been cut out by water flowing off the summit you will find tree ferns. Amongst all this a few species of antelope had managed to survive man's encroachment before the reserve was proclaimed; these were grey duiker, klipspringer and mountain reedbuck. Subsequently the following animals have been reintroduced: impala, oribi, bushbuck, sable, waterbuck, steenbuck, kudu, zebra and red hartebeest. While you may well see these animals while walking it is unlikely that you will also see jackal, leopard, hyena and caracal, which are also known to live in the mountains. Most of these creatures are nocturnal and will be frightened off well before an unsuspecting hiker comes along. Finally there are the raptors which live high up along the rocky cliff faces, an ideal environment for such birds. Scops owl, martial eagles and black eagles can be viewed along with an important breeding colony of the endangered Cape vulture.

Hiking There are currently three marked hiking trails in the reserve. Two of the trails are open for day visitors, the third trail requires spending a couple of nights in the reserve. The first of the day trails is known as the **Peglarae Interpretive trail**. This is about 5 km long, but involves walking over some steep and rocky land in places. The path starts 200 m from the visitors' centre, and is marked with yellow Peglarae aloe stickers. Hikers should buy a copy of the trail booklet which will explain the various unique and interesting features at numbered points along the trail. If your time is short this is a most interesting walk that should appeal to most people.

The second day trail is known as the **Vlei Ramble**. This is the shortest of the designated walks, and merely involves a 2 km walk along a path to a viewing hut which overlooks the sheltered valley where you have a good chance of seeing quite a few of the antelope drinking and grazing; follow the yellow arrows from the offices.

The longest hike, known simply as the **Rustenburg Overnight Trail**, is 44.8 km long, and two days and two nights are spent in the reserve. On the first day you arrive in the afternoon and spend the first night in Kudu Hut, which is at the start of the trail. The next morning you start the hike and end up at the Red Hartebeest Hut at the summit of the ridge, a distance of 19.5 km. On the second day the path follows a circular route back to Kudu Hut, a distance of 25.3 km. Numbers are limited to protect the environment. Only 10 people are allowed on the trail at any time.

F *Hiking Huts*, there are 4 huts sleeping 4 people, between the 2 bedrooms is a communal seating and dining area with a table and chairs. Meals have to be cooked by wood fire over a braai, cooking pots, buckets to collect water and two lamps are provided. There is also a veld toilet close by. Water by Kudu Hut comes from a tap, there is a mountain stream close to Hartebeest Hut. During the winter months a sleeping bag will be necessary for your comfort.

Sleeping
Price codes:
see inside front cover

Rustenburg, the Magaliesberg & Sun City

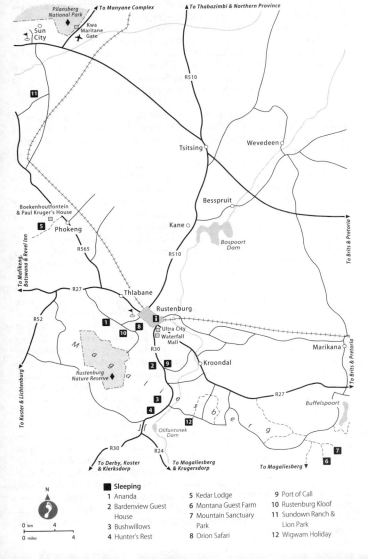

North West Province

Sleeping
1 Ananda
2 Bardenview Guest House
3 Bushwillows
4 Hunter's Rest
5 Kedar Lodge
6 Montana Guest Farm
7 Mountain Sanctuary Park
8 Orion Safari
9 Port of Call
10 Rustenburg Kloof
11 Sundown Ranch & Lion Park
12 Wigwam Holiday

Magaliesberg Mountains

Colour map 2, grid C1   The Magaliesberg are a range of flat topped quartzite mountains which roughly extend from Pretoria to just beyond Rustenburg. In 1977 the area was declared a Natural Heritage Site and along with the Hartbeespoort Dam this is an important recreational area for the residents of Pretoria and Johannesburg. The whole region receives more visitors than any other part of the country, but almost all are local residents.

Ins & outs   **Getting around**   Approaching Rustenburg from Pretoria the main road splits into a one-way system by the showgrounds. If you drive straight through town on Van Staden St take a right at the junction with Malan St. This road becomes the R510 and goes north across the plains to Pilansberg. After 51 km take a left turn, follow this road for a further 5 km past some factories and take a right turn by the petrol station. The entrance to **Pilansberg National Park** and **Manyane Camp** is just on the left. If you are heading for **Sun City** follow Van Staden St straight out of town, past the golf course to your left, and then take the R565 signposted Phokeng and Sun City, shortly before Sun City you will pass a left turn for Pilansberg National Park. The entrance to Sun City is just after a large shopping mall by the staff housing complex. To explore the **Magaliesberg** take the R30 shortly before entering the town from Pretoria. This road leads up into the mountains to **Olifantsnek**, a gap in the Magaliesberg created by the Hex River, there are plenty of hotels and resorts along this road.

History   When the first white hunters came to the region they named the hills the 'Cashan Mountains', a corruption of Khashane, the name of the local chief. They were renamed by the Voortrekkers who named the range after another local leader, Mohale, but whose name they spelt as Magalie.

The region witnessed a number of bloody battles during the 19th century. The first major conflicts were between Mzilikazi, leader of the Ndebele, and the local peoples when he arrived here from modern day KwaZulu Natal. At a later date the mountains were the scene of several important battles during the Anglo-Boer War. One of these was the **Battle of Nooitgedacht**, 13 December 1900, in which the British forces suffered their heaviest defeat since their arrival in July 1900. Three hundred men were killed and a similar number taken prisoner, and the Boers managed to seize 70 full wagons, 200 tents, plenty of ammunition, 300 mules, some cattle and over 400 horses. The gorge where the battle took place is just off the R560 close to Hekpoort.

Wildlife & vegetation   The range is about 160 km long, the highest point is 1,852 m but they are no more than 400 m above the surrounding countryside. The difference in elevation is sufficient to ensure that they receive a relatively high rainfall, and because of this they are regarded as an important watershed. The rainfall also means that they are well vegetated with some remaining stands of forest. However, most of the wild animals that once lived in the hills have long since been hunted out. Today the ledges on the south facing cliff faces are important nesting sites for the endangered Cape vulture. In contrast, the north facing slopes are no more than a gentle climb cut by plenty of mountain streams and well-vegetated kloofs. The range forms the natural divide between the cool highveld to the south and the warm bushveld to the north.

Hiking   Hiking remains the most popular pastime in the region and maps and permits are available from most resorts. This is also an excellent area for gliding, horse riding, or even hot air ballooning. *African Air Adventure*, T012-2071376, and *Bill Harrope's Original Balloon Safaris*, T011-7053201. Both offer flights over the Magalies Valley by micro light or balloon respectively. Most of the holiday resorts are equipped with a complete range of sports facilities, including golf courses, tennis courts and gyms. Pick up a map for the 'Magalies Meander' at the tourist office in Rustenburg, which lists craft shops, accommodation, sports, and restaurants within the region, or visit www.magaliesburg.co.za

Most of the hotels and lodges listed below are located at the western end of the mountains, within a short drive of Rustenburg. Bookings and further information can be provided by the Rustenburg tourist office, T041-5970904.

Sleeping & eating
■ *on map, page 569*
Price codes:
see inside front cover

B *De Hoek*, turn off the R563 by Poort Caf, and follow the signs for Bekker Schools, T041-5371198, F5374530. A double-storey stone house set with 7 double rooms in a large garden which borders the Magalies River, the dining room is one of the central features with a fine mahogany table, well-known for the excellent cuisine. Recommended. **B** *Hunter's Rest*, 14 km from Rustenburg centre, on the R30, T041-5372140, F5372661. Quoted room rates are for full board, 94 spacious rooms with private patio, rooms are arranged up the side of the hill in a mix of extensions and it is a bit of a hike from the furthest room to the restaurant. Bar serves good range of imported beers and has an English pub feel and design, large swimming pool surrounded by sun chairs and a well-kept garden, curio shop, tennis, sauna, squash, fitness centre, bowls, horse riding, mini golf, 9-hole golf course with some water hazards. This is a large complex which is a popular conference venue, the full range of sporting activities are ideal for a relaxing couple of days when you may not wish to travel or go sightseeing. Fun for children as well with a creche, games room and pet farm. Recommended. **B** *Mount Grace*, approaching Magaliesberg village on the R24 from Johannesburg take a right turn 2 km past the information office, T041-5771350, F5771202. 65 double rooms with en suite bathrooms, rooms are in a variety of thatched cottages set in a beautiful garden with lakes and waterfalls, swimming pool, tennis, once a month a classical music concert is held here. Excellent food, Johannesburg airport transfers available, children under 10 not permitted. Recommended. **C** *Wigwam Holiday Hotel*, 14 km from Rustenburg centre, T041-5372147/8, F5372164. Mix of large a/c rooms or one of 7 rather hideous looking 'wigwam' style units which stand out on the mountain side and sleep up to 5 people. Restaurant, bar, neat colourful gardens, this is a large holiday resort with a complete range of recreational facilities: 2 swimming pools, 4 tennis courts, 9-hole golf course, bowling green, squash court, sauna, games room, mini golf and a choice of hikes in the Magaliesberg behind the complex, better suited for a long stay than a single night. **C-D** *Montana Guest Farm*, PO Box 107 Kroondal, T041-5340113. 8 self-catering chalets surrounded by the natural woodlands of the Magaliesberg, swimming pool, pub and games room, no restaurant, bring all your own food, a small and friendly retreat with some excellent local hikes. **C-F** *Mountain Sanctuary Park*, PO Box 187, Kroondal, T041-5340114, F5340568. This is a private farm in the mountains 35 km from Rustenburg, which was converted into a nature reserve for visitors over 30 years ago. The owners have created a simple rest camp and have instigated a careful restocking programme. The number of visitors is controlled and there are strict regulations designed to preserve and maintain this mountain wilderness, so early booking is advised even for day visits (there is a small charge for day visitors). The accommodation consists of self-catering chalets which are fully equipped and furnished, visitors must provide bedding, towels, soap and food, there are a number of different sizes; there are also on-site caravans for 2 or 4 people, each one has its own cooking area but the washing facilities are in a communal block; finally there are a limited number of shady campsites with electric points and braais. A stunning pool has been cleverly built from natural stone on the lip of the valley offering fantastic views. This sanctuary is an excellent place to come and stay at to explore the mountains, and guests have access to over 1,000 hectares of hiking country. It is possible to appreciate most aspects of the Magaliesberg within the boundaries of the sanctuary. There are several mountain streams which have pools suitable for swimming in and it is possible to walk up to the face of the cliffs. A peaceful and beautiful spot if you are self-sufficient, recommended. **E** *Bushwillows*, 12 km from Rustenburg centre, off the R24, T/F041-5372333. A modern family home with 2 double rooms with en suite bathroom and own entrance, upstairs 4-bed family suite, TV guest lounge, swimming pool in the mature gardens, B&B only, friendly people, at the end of a long woody lane, ask for Bill. **E-F** *Port of Call*, T041-5372128. Small rest camp next to the *Port of Call* German and Austrian restaurant on the R30, 12 km from Rustenburg. Simple self-catering rondavels or camping, pool, pretty gardens, pub and restaurant next door. **F** *Revel In*, this backpackers and campsite is probably the most remote backpackers in South Africa, 38 km west of Rustenburg off the N4 towards Swartruggens, turn right at Bokfontien and travel up a dirt road for 6.5 km, T082-7971702 (mob). Set on a beautiful farm, hiking trails to natural springs, bar with a reggae feel, stone and thatch rustic bungalows, some with sunken baths made from rock, open fires, a bunk house with 16 dorm beds, home made furniture, pool, self-catering kitchen. Owner used to manage nightclubs in Johannesburg and Cape Town, now promoting this place as an outdoor music festival venue to compete with Rustlers Valley in the Free State. Several festivals throughout the year that draw revellers from the big cities, including an annual reggae concert and New Year's Eve festival. Phone ahead for details. Probably the cheapest accommodation within one hour's drive of Sun City. If you are staying here when there isn't a festival on, you are likely to have the place to yourself.

Sun City

Phone code: 014
(NB Always use
3-figure prefix)
Colour map 2, grid B1

This is one of the most luxurious resorts in South Africa. Tucked away in North West Province, on the fringe of the Kalahari, no expense has been spared in creating a fantasy world with superb recreational facilities and a collection of hotels most people will only imagine in their dreams. The result is a garish, neon-lit, extravaganza of kitsch in the middle of the bush, with every conceivable tacky tourist attraction available to idle away the hours. While Sun City may not appeal to everyone and certainly wouldn't win any Eco-Tourism awards (the power and water consumption must equal a small country) it is worth a brief visit to experience the sheer indulgence and incredibility of its location. A giant theme park, the whole complex is unashamedly over the top, and after Soweto and the Kruger National Park, Sun City (somewhat ironically) and Pilanesberg National Park are South Africa's third most visited tourist attraction.

The complex has five hotels, numerous restaurants and fast food outlets, two golf courses, a water park which can generate surfing waves, a man-made rainforest, casinos and plenty of entertainment halls. The first part of the complex was opened in December 1979, when the central features were the *Sun City Hotel* and a golf course designed by Gary Player. A lot of the emphasis was placed upon the gambling element, as the hotel was in the homeland of Bophuthatswana where gambling was legal, unlike the rest of South Africa at the time. Wealthy people had to travel to what were then, the designated black homelands, to gamble, and like all of the other casino resorts that were built in the homelands at the time, the contrasts between the this luxury and impoverished townships and rural areas, were, and still are, evident. A sharp physical reminder of the inequality of the old South Africa.

In the same year **Pilanesberg National Park** opened, but it only had a few resident animals at this early stage. Even the developers were surprised by the success, a year later the second phase was complete – the 284-room *Sun City Cabanas* for families. In 1980 the famous **Sun City Million Dollar Golf Challenge** was founded, and over the years this has attracted most of the world's top golfers. In December 1984 the third hotel was opened – *Cascades*. Around this hotel a lot of work was done with the gardens, 12 waterfalls and cataracts were built; but this was a drop in the ocean compared with what was to follow in the 1990s: The Lost City and the Valley of the Waves (see Sights and sports below).

However, things are not as rosy for Sun City as they once were. The resort has experienced a drop in visitors since the elections were held in South Africa. There are two possible explanations for this. Firstly the gambling laws have changed and gaming is now legal throughout South Africa, casinos have recently opened much closer to the major cities, and you no longer have to visit Sun City or other similar resorts in the former homelands in order to gamble. And secondly most South Africans who wanted to see Sun City have done so, and the novelty has worn off. The resort is now desperately trying to attract overseas visitors and by closing all but one of its casinos is successfully changing it's image from a gambling centre to more or an international leisure, entertainment, and conference destination. This is undeniably a bizarre place and has to be seen to be believed – whether you would want to spend a whole holiday here is another matter.

The image of Sun City that people are most likely to have seen is the **Palace of the Lost City**, a magnificent hotel. Work began in 1990, the 338-room hotel was completed in December 1992. This fantasy building is decorated with animal sculptures, mosaics, frescoes and hand-painted ceilings. There is even a bridge that trembles and spouts steam during a mock earthquake that occurs every half an hour. But it is the **Valley of the Waves** that creates the most interest. In the middle of the arid bush countryside the developers built a sandy beach complete with palm trees and a wave machine. Not only does the pool have the gentle motion of waves on the beach but it is possible to surf on artificially created 2 m waves. Day visitors have to pay extra to enter the Valley of the Waves, which is accessed from the Entertainments Centre.

Slightly less dramatic but still a tremendous feat is the **man-made forest** in front of the *Palace Hotel*. The forest is 25 ha in area, it has 1.6 million plants, trees and shrubs, the rainforest component has three layers with creepers and orchids growing in the canopy. While you cannot help but marvel at the forest, it seems and sounds slightly lacking when compared to a natural forest. (Even the rocks around the pools in the forest are not real, but have been moulded out of cement!)

You would have to be seriously indolent to find yourself with nothing to do at Sun City, just about every activity has been planned for guests. On the **sports** side there are the following options: two 18-hole golf courses, you can play the course the world's great players tackle every year; bowls; horseriding; mini golf; squash (three courts); tennis; mountain biking; jogging (two trails have been laid out around the golf courses); 10-pin bowling and swimming. At **Waterworld** a full range of water sports are on offer: jet skis; parasailing; canoes; mini-boats; sailing; pedalos; water-skiing; windsurfing and catamarans.

Other ways of entertaining yourself include cinema, gambling, theatre, concerts, slot machines, shopping, and a crocodile farm with over 7,000 crocs and the 3 biggest captive Nile crocodiles in the world. If you still can't occupy yourself after all that then there is a choice of restaurants and bars to suit everyone's taste and palate. Sun City is so vast that a 'sky-train' runs through the whole complex and shuttle buses run to and from the car park. There is even a daily Sun City tour, which departs from the Welcome Centre at 1400. It's not a bad idea to jump on this when you arrive to simply get your bearings. There is a small daily entrance fee, R50 per person, part of which is redeemable in tokens to spend inside. The Welcome Centre is in the middle of the complex and is a good place to start and pick up a map, T5571544.

North West Province

Sleeping
& eating
■ *on map, page 569*
Price codes:
see inside front cover

*See also page 566 for
more Sleeping options
outide Sun City*

None of the rooms are cheap (although you may find some good deals through tour operators, given the dropping numbers of visitors), but all are of a very high standard, the décor has had a lot of thought put into it and the service is some of the best you will receive in South Africa. Booking details are provided below. All the hotels listed below must be booked through central reservations and not contacted directly. Special off-season packages are sometimes available and children under the age of 18 sharing with two adults stay free.

Reservations The whole complex is part of the *Sun International Group* who have hotels in South Africa, Malawi, Namibia, Mauritius and Zimbabwe. Central reservations: 3 Sandown Valley Crescent, Sandown, Gauteng, PO Box 784487, Sandton 2146, T011-7807800, F011-7807449 www.suninternational.co.za Sun City: PO Box 2, Sun City 0316, T5571000, F5571902.

AL *Palace of the Lost City*, T5573133. 338 a/c rooms, in a variety of formats ranging from twin rooms to luxury suites to family rooms. *Villa del Palazzo*, classic northern Italian cuisine, an excellent restaurant overlooking the pools; *Crystal Court*, Californian-style cuisine, live piano music, surrounded by the jungle, smart dress code; elsewhere in the hotel there are 3 bars and a poolside snack bar and bar; there is a selection of shops and a heated swimming pool. **AL** *The Cascades*, T5571000. 242 a/c rooms, TV, refrigerator, minibar, the bathrooms have jet baths, 24-hr room service, all the rooms face the gardens and the pools. *The Peninsula*, smart, international menu, live show during evening meal. *The Grotto*, pizza and pasta for lunch snacks only. *Fig Tree Coffee Shop*, open till late; there are 2 bars, *Vistas* and *Grotto*.

AL *Sun City*, T5571000. This is the original hotel which was refurbished in 1995. 341 a/c rooms overlooking the swimming pool and lush lawns; plenty of choice on the restaurant front: *The Harlequin*, à la carte, in the casino, casual dress; *The Calabash*, carvery and salad bar; *Sun Terrace*, fast foods during the day, formal restaurant at night; there are 2 cocktail bars. **AL** *Sun City Cabanas*, T5571000. 144 standard cabanas for 2 people; 236 family cabanas which can accommodate 4 people, all are fully a/c, TV, en suite bathrooms, the cottages are set in neat gardens close to a lake and Waterworld. This is the cheapest option available throughout the whole complex, but there is nothing cheap or inferior about the facilities; *Morula* restaurant for steaks and grills; *Palm Terrace*, an informal carvery; Pool Bar, Boathouse Bar, both casual dress.

Transport   **Air** 10 km from Sun City, close to Kwa Maritane Gate is **Sun City Airport**, built to serve the luxury resort. Information, T5521261. Buses connect with Sun City. *SA Airlink*, central reservations T011-9781111; to **Johannesburg** (40 mins), daily except Tue and Sat, 1330. The flights from Johannesburg arrive 35 min before. **Car hire** Offices at the airport. *Avis*, T5521507. *Imperial*, T5521244.

Pilanesberg National Park

Phone code: 014
(NB Always use
3-figure prefix))
Colour map 2, grid B1

This is the fourth largest national park in South Africa, close to Johannesburg and Pretoria. All the major animals can be seen here on a good day, and it's all artificial. The park was created in 1979 to complement the new luxury development being built at Sun City. The two have been closely linked ever since.

Ins & outs   **Getting there** Follow directions for Sun City, if coming from Johannesburg it is quicker to take the N1 north until it joins the N4 and then head west for Rustenburg. From Rustenburg the R510 heads north towards Sun City Airport and the park. Pretoria is about 140 km from the park. It can be visited as a long day trip from Pretoria, but most visitors stay at least one night in the region and combine a trip to Pilanesberg with Sun City.

Park information Gate hours: Nov-Feb 0530-1900; Mar-Apr 0600-1830; May-Aug 0630-1800; Sep-Oct 0600-1830. Entrance charges: adults, R20; children, R15; car R15. At the Manyane Complex there is a restaurant, swimming pool, shop and mini golf. All enquiries dealt with by the park office, T 5555356. Guided tours are available if you are visiting Sun City on a day trip and do not have your own transport. *Game Trackers*, in the Welcome Centre in Sun City, T5571544, organize game drives in open-top vehicles leaving early morning, afternoon and at night (warm clothes required), the drive can last up to 3 hrs, if it's not too busy you don't need to book and can just turn up at the Welcome Centre. Balloon safaris and hiking trails can also be arranged from here. By taking a guided tour you are almost certain to see most of the animals since the rangers are in constant radio contact and monitor the movements of the Big Five, and you are likely to be travelling in a vehicle with high seats and good viewing. This is a **malaria free** zone.

History   The park was created in somewhat controversial circumstances. Until the 1970s the
& sights   Pilanesberg area was occupied by a large number of farmers. The story goes that the Bophuthatswana government decided to create a game reserve to attract foreign visitors and the money they would bring, and the reserve was completed in December 1979, one week after the first visitors had arrived at Sun City. Local publications record that the farmers happily agreed to move to new farms, but this was evidently not the case. Many of the Tswana people had to be removed from the lands by force, and were made to live in abject poverty outside the park boundaries.

The stocking of the reserve was known as 'Operation Genesis', a complex and ambitious project. The animals came from all over southern Africa in what was a bit like an exotic shopping spree; elephant and buffalo from Addo National Park, 17 black rhino from the Natal Parks Board, eland from Namibia, white rhino from Natal, Burchell's zebra and waterbuck from the Transvaal and red hartebeest from the Northern Cape and Namibia. As a transition zone between the Kalahari sandveld and the bushveld, it was also the natural habitat for a number of rare species already in existence, including brown hyena, Cape hunting dog, and sable antelope. As you drive around the 55,000 ha reserve you now have a good chance of seeing all the large animals including rhino, elephant, lion, cheetah, buffalo and the occasional leopard. A lucky visitor might see the same range of wild animals here as they would on a visit to Kruger, however, the scenery and the size of the herds is much more impressive in Kruger. Nevertheless it has been a remarkable programme, and since 1979 more than 6,000 animals have been successfully introduced to the park.

The park encompasses the caldera of an extinct volcano, which is similar in geography to the Ngorongoro Conservation Area in Tanzania. The crater is surrounded by three concentric rings of hills, in the centre is a lake, Mankwe Dam, where you can see crocodile and hippo. The hills have plenty of rocky wooded valleys, which gradually give way to open savannah grasslands. This variety of habitat is ideal for wild animals, and a rewarding birdwatching environment where over 340 species have been recorded, some extremely rare. A number of walk-in viewing hides have been constructed at strategic locations. Excellent tar and gravel roads traverse the park and maps and game check lists are available at each of the four gates; Manyane, Bakgatla, Bakubung, and Kwa Maritane, the last being the closest to Sun City.

Sleeping

Two of the camps in Pilansberg are run by *Golden Leopard Resorts*, central reservations, PO Box 6651, Rustenburg 0300 T5556135/6, F5557555/8, goldres@iafrica.com These camps are a mix of campsites, self-catering chalets, and permanent tents with a central restaurant and bar block. Children under 12 stay for free. NB Two of the Golden Leopard Resorts camps have recently closed because of guests driving too late in the evening and disturbing the animals. Consequently the number of accommodation options within the park has reduced dramatically so advance booking is advised particularly during school holidays. The 3

■ *on map*
Price codes:
see inside front cover

There are several camps within the park, but advance booking is essential

North West Province

Pilanesberg National Park

N

0 km   5

0 miles   5

■ Sleeping
1 Bakgatla Complex
2 Bakubung Lodge
3 Kwa Maritane
4 Manyane Complex
5 Metswedi Camp
6 Tshukudu Lodge

exclusive lodges are part of the **Stocks Hotels Group**, PO Box 3410, Rivonia 2128, T011-8064145, F8064105 or T014-6521861, F6521621.

Golden Leopard Camps C-E *Manyane Complex*, T011-4655423, F4651228. 60 2, 4 or 6-bed self-catering thatched chalets with kitchen, lounge, bathroom, braai, there are a couple of swimming pools amongst the chalets for residents' use only, behind the chalets is a caravan and campsite, electric points, clean washblocks and shade trees; central restaurant block open for all meals, bar, central swimming pool, children's playground. The camp is some open savanna grasslands with a few trees dotted about, when full there are too many people here, but outside of the school holidays this is a good value place to stay. There is a day visitors' complex with a shop, picnic area, swimming pool, a couple of walk-in aviaries, a 4x4 track, walking trails, and mini-golf. The camp is a few hundred metres from the Manyane Gate. **B-E** *Bakgatla Complex*, T011-4655423, F4651228. 60 self-catering chalets similar to those at Manyane. Each chalet can sleep a maximum of 5 people, all are a/c and are fitted with a kitchen, en suite bathroom, lounge area plus a private patio and braai area. At the centre of the complex is a large swimming pool, picnic site and kiosk. There are also a limited number of caravan and campsites available, which will suit people on a tighter budget who are self-sufficient. A maximum of 6 people per site, advance booking for sites with electric points essential. The campsites have a central kiosk plus a small bar, there are also freezing facilities for fresh food. This camp is at the north west of the park close to the Bakgatla Gate.

Stocks Resorts AL *Tshukudu Game Lodge*, T5521861, F5521621. The location of this luxury lodge is something very special, if you are going to spend money to stay in the area then this should be your first choice. This is a small lodge, room for 12, in the middle of Pilanesberg National Park on the slope of a steep rock outcrop. The accommodation consists of 6 stone thatched chalets half way up the hill, they have been beautifully furnished in a sympathetic manner that several other lodges could learn from, slate floors, wicker furniture and a fireplace, the beds are on an elevated platform, sunken double bath with a view to enjoy while washing, lounge area with bar fridge, books and magazines – the chalets are linked to the main lodge on top of the outcrop by a winding stone staircase, this climb may be too steep for some guests, from the top you have clear views across the park and a floodlit waterhole, restaurant, bar, swimming pool. **A** *Bakubung Lodge*, T5521861, F5521621. On the edge of the park, 10 km from Sun City, this is a large complex, 76 rooms, 50 chalets all with en suite bathroom, restaurant, bar, curio shop, tennis court, swimming pool, game drives and hikes are extra but well worth it, price includes all meals, there are superb views of the surrounding bush and a waterhole with resident hippos, a free shuttle runs to Sun City every couple of hours. **A** *Kwa Maritane*, T5521820, F5521147. Quoted rates are for dinner, B&B. A smart bush lodge with 155 a/c rooms, each with a TV, high thatched ceilings, and a private veranda to watch the sun go down and listen to the sounds of the bush. Meals can be taken in the restaurant or from an outdoor braai. At any time guests can enjoy good close up game viewing at a nearby waterhole, a unique underground hide is reached via a 180 m tunnel from the lodge. Activities for guests include game drives and guided walks, within the camp complex are 2 swimming pools, floodlit tennis courts, table tennis, a sauna and a gymnasium. There is a regular free shuttle to the Sun City complex where guests can take further advantage of the wide range of facilities on offer, including golf and the 'Valley of the Waves'.

North West Province

Mpumalanga

Mpumalanga

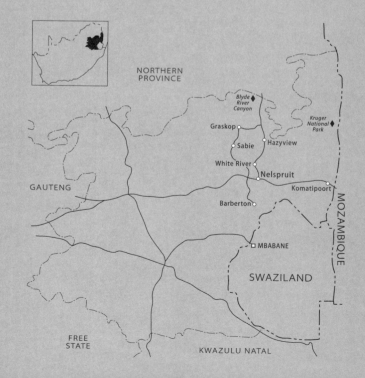

*Mpumalanga, 'place of the rising sun', is one of South Africa's most popular tourist destinations. The **Kruger National Park** is in a class of its own in terms of the opportunities it gives visitors to savour some truly spectacular game viewing moments. It is, of course, possible to do Kruger and see the Big Five in an afternoon but a longer stay in the park gives you a much greater understanding of the wilderness and the chance to see a variety of animals in the park's different habitats.*

*For those who tire of seeing so much wildlife in Kruger, the forests and waterfalls of the **Eastern Drakensberg** make a pleasant change from the heat of the Lowveld. Here you will find small, pleasant towns such as Graskop and Sabie, clustered around the top of the spectacular **Blyde River Canyon**, the third largest in the world. Further into the mountains is the ancient gold mining town of **Pilgrim's Rest** where you can visit buildings that have remained unchanged for almost a hundred years. Further information about the early gold rush can be found in the historical town of **Barberton** set in the hills close to Swaziland. The province also has many **waterfalls** and **isolated valleys** to explore, and is fast becoming South Africa's premier adventure destination with a vast range of outdoor activities such as quad biking, hiking, white water rafting, and horse riding on offer.*

Ins and outs

Getting around
See also Nelspruit Ins and outs section below

The two main areas of interest for tourists in Mpumalanga are the Kruger National Park and the Eastern Drakensberg or 'Panorama Region', where you will find the Blyde River Canyon. The public transport network doesn't link the towns and sights effectively so the best way to visit the more isolated beauty spots is to hire a car, and it's possible to do a leisurely circuit in two or three days. However, unlike the Northern (Limpopo) and the North West Provinces, where car hire is almost the only option, there are alternatives here for the budget traveller. The *Baz Bus* picks up and drops off at backpacker hostels in Nelspruit. From here it is possible to arrange pick-ups by other hostels and there are many tour operators to choose from who run inexpensive 2-3 day tours combining Kruger and the Panorama region.

Orientation

The **Lowveld** is the strip of land which extends eastwards from the foot of the Drakensberg escarpment to the border with Mozambique. It begins below the foothills of Swaziland and stretches as far north as the **Blyde River Canyon** and the border with the Northern (Limpopo) Province. Most of the region is a low lying humid plain, crossed by many small rivers and broken up with ridges of hills, none of which rise above 600 m.

Kruger National Park is a classic lowveld region with its savannah landscape, umbrella thorns and herds of slowly moving game. The lands immediately to the west of Kruger are known for their superb game viewing. This is the area where one will find the greatest concentration of luxury private game reserves; lodges such as **Mala Mala** and **Londolozi** are world famous. Nowhere in the world can visitors enjoy game viewing in such luxury.

Along the rivers which flow eastwards off the escarpment into Kruger are several irrigation schemes. Although the actual land under cultivation is not that extensive this is an important area for the growing of tropical fruit. The **plantations**, a major source of employment, produce bananas, avocados, mangoes, lychees and citrus fruits. When any of the produce is being harvested there are plenty of small stalls along the roadside selling some delicious fresh produce, perfect for anyone about to enter Kruger on a self-catering trip.

NB Visitors to this region must take a **malaria** prophylactic. Look at a map and imagine a straight line running from Nelspruit in the south directly north to the border with Zimbabwe in the Northern Province. Anywhere to the right or east of this line is an endemic malarial area. Kruger National Park is regarded as medium risk, especially during and just after the rainy season when there is a lot of free standing water. Advice is available from the very useful malaria information line based in Nelspruit, T7527889.

Tourist Information

Mpumalanga Tourism Authority, PO Box 679, Nelspruit 1200, T7527001, F7595441, mtanlpsa@cis.co.za, www.mpumalanga.com This is the regional office, located next door to the Mpumalanga Parks Board, 5 km west of Nelspruit on the N4, turn off at the Shell Halls Gateway service station. Open Mon-Fri 0800-1630. If you phone at the weekend there is a recorded message with a phone number of the person who is on duty and who can be contacted immediately. Impressive service! Contact this office before you leave home for general advice and information.

To Nelspruit and Barberton

The journey down the N4 between Gauteng and Eastern Mpumalanga crosses a vast area of cattle ranching country interspersed with the industrial towns like Witbank and Middleberg. This stark landscape seems to stretch out endlessly and most travellers drive straight through. Look out for the large coal-fired power stations to the south. The first magnificent views over the Lowveld are at **Machadodorp**, where the road starts to drop into the Elands River Valley passing through the towns of **Waterval Boven** and **Waterval Onder**. This is a beautiful stretch of road with high cliffs on either side and the railway carved into the sides of the valley in places. Dotted along the valley are plenty of country hotels and motels which catch the holiday traffic en route to Kruger Park and Mozambique.

Things to do in Mpumalanga

- Explore the **Panorama Region**, a leisurely day trip along the top of the Blyde River Canyon escarpment and take a photo at the view point at the Three Rondavels, where a lip of rock juts out over the third largest canyon in the world.
- Break the monotony of driving around endlessly in search of the Big 5 in **Kruger National Park** and go on an organized night drive.
- Pan for gold at **Pilgrim's Rest**, or catch the National Gold Panning Championships at the end of November each year, when the village hosts a festival lasting 4-5 days.
- Browse in the secondhand bookshop in **Sabie**. One of the best in all of South Africa, this place is stuffed full of interesting books and collectors items. A number of books that were banned during Apartheid have resurfaced in this shop.
- Take a tour with Zozi, an enterprising and entertaining guide who runs tours of the **Matsulu township** on the edge of Kruger. An extraordinary insight into African rural life and how the local people manage to live alongside the animals of Kruger.
- Eat sumptuous pancakes in **Graskop**. *Harrie's* was the first pancake house but many more have followed suit.

Nelspruit

Nelspruit developed around the railway when the line between Pretoria and Lourenço Marques (now Maputo) was completed in 1891. A railway station was built here on farmland bought from Gert, Andries and Louis Nel; three brothers who used to bring their cattle here every year for the winter grazing. Briefly the capital of the Transvaal Republic after Paul Kruger abandoned Pretoria in 1900 during the Boer War, Nelspruit is now the industrial centre of the Lowveld and a processing point for the fruit, tobacco and beef farms of the surrounding region. The town has a lush tropical atmosphere with broad streets lined with acacias, flamboyants, bougainvillea and jacaranda trees. Although there is not much to keep you for long here, most people travelling to Kruger, the Eastern Drakensberg, Mozambique and Swaziland will have to pass through and it's a good place to get things done. Despite still not being that densely populated, Nelspruit has grown rapidly over recent years and the suburbs are very spread out. New business parks and Mpumalanga's largest shopping mall and casino have been built on the road to White River, 20 kms away, with access to everyone in the corresponding region. As a consequence, Nelspruit recently extended its municipality by joining with neighbouring White River and Hazyview to form the Mbombela Municipal Region – meaning 'a lot of people put together in a small space'! This is now the provincial capital of Mpumalanga Province.

Phone code: 013
(NB Always use 3-figure prefix)
Colour map 2, grid B5
Altitude: 716 m

Mpumalanga

Getting there Nelspruit is linked by road, rail and air with the rest of South Africa and there are good facilities here for tourists to plan trips to Swaziland, the Panorama region as well as safaris in to Kruger National Park and the more expensive private game reserves. **Nelspruit Airport** is on Kaapsche Rd, T7413192, 12 km from the town centre. Although this is only a provincial airport it has a steady flow of traffic due to the proximity of Kruger National Park, in addition to the national airlines there are plenty of small private charter companies flying visitors into the private game reserves. The new **Kruger Mpumalanga International Airport (KMIA)** is presently under construction and is expected to be operational by September 2002 (see box page 586). There is a daily train service between **Pretoria/Johannesburg** and **Komatipoort** (border post with Mozambique). The *Baz Bus* runs from **Johannesburg**, **Pretoria**, and **Swaziland**.

Ins & outs
See also Transport, page 585

Getting around Nelspruit has excellent road links to Mpumalanga's major tourist attractions. The nearest entrance gates to Kruger are less than 80 km away on the N4 (east), and the R538 through White River (north), and a day trip to see the southern sector of the park is quite feasible. The gold rush town of Barberton is 43 km to the south on the R40, and a visit here could be combined with a day trip over the border to Swaziland. The mountain resorts of Sabie and Graskop are equally accessible and make a pleasant change from the heat of the Lowveld. It's worth bearing in mind that all these places have an excellent range of accommodation and that many people prefer not to stay in the centre of town. The shopping centres in town are convenient for stocking up on food and equipment before setting off to stay in self-catering accommodation in Kruger.

Tourist information *Lowveld Tourism Association*, Civic Centre, 1 Nel St, T7551988, F7551350, after hours T082-7354888 (mob), open Mon-Fri 0800-1630. Situated in the municipal building, this is the main office for the town and the immediate region, it is also a useful place to visit for information on Kruger Park safaris, car rental and accommodation throughout Mpumalanga. *Mpumalanga Tourism Authority*, PO Box 679, Nelspruit 1200, T7527001, F7595441, mtanlpsa@cis.co.za, www.mpumalanga.com, is the provincial office, 5 km from town (see previous page).

Sights just outside of town

The Lowveld National Botanical Gardens are relatively small but have a very important and unique collection of plants. There are a number of trails you can follow which take you through different collections of plants. If you turn left after entering the gardens you will see a boadwalk which takes you through a newly established 3-ha **Tropical Rain Forest**. At the far end of the path is an open area of marshland which is all good birdwatching country. There is a booklet available which provides a concise introduction to rain forests and why they are so important.

At the other end of the gardens is the **Cycad collection**, the largest of its kind in Africa, and the **Riverside Trail** – a 1-km walk along the banks of the Crocodile River. Take the guide which goes with the trail because this helps identify the plants and shrubs along the way which are typical of what the whole countryside around Nelspruit once looked like before the impact of man. **NB** The path follows the river gorge and it is steep and uneven in parts. ■ *T7525531, open daily 0800-1700. Small entrance charge. A little further into the gardens is the Cascades Cafe, T7524201, open daily 0800-1700, Sun lunch is a popular time. There are also braai and picnic facilities. To get there, follow the R40 to White River, cross the railway, take a right turn at the crossroads by the traffic lights, 2 km out of town. This road quickly becomes a gravel track which passes over a narrow bridge on the Crocodile River before reaching the gardens.*

Croc River Reptile Park is a relatively new addition to the local sights, and like so many other crocodile parks in southern Africa, claims to be the largest of its type in the whole continent! A lot of effort and expense has gone into creating an exciting (especially for children) attraction. The reptiles are on show in a variety of houses, each with a different environment, rather like the greenhouses in a botanical garden. The turtle pond, crocodile pool and fishpond, are all linked by a cascading waterway. Inside the tropical house is a 9 m high waterfall and an aquarium with some dwarf crocodiles from Central America. The reptile gallery houses 88 indigenous and exotic species. Visitors can view two snake pits from the safety of an elevated walkway. There is also a desert house with a realistic desert landscape. ■ *Open daily 0900-1700. Entrance fee, adults, R30, children, R15. Daily handling demonstrations at 1100 and 1500. T7336096. The park is north of town, off the R40 towards White River.*

The entrance to **Sudwala Caves** is on a forested hillside in the Houtbosloop Valley. Only the first 2.5 km of the cave system has been explored and it is thought that the passages could lead much further into the mountains.

A tour explores the first 600 m of the cave system where many of the stalactites and stalagmites are lit by coloured spotlights. The rock formations have been given Biblical names such as Lot's wife, the Devil's pulpit and the weeping Madonna. One of the most interesting formations is the Gong, which resonates through the cave chambers when struck. ■ *T013-7334152, open daily, 0830-1630. A 90-min tour costs R30 per person. Keen cavers can organize a special visit to the Crystal Chamber. The tour takes place on Sat and lasts for 5 hrs, but this tour must be booked in advance.*

The caves are 36 km north west of Nelspruit and can be reached by following the N4 westwards. After 30 km turn on to the R539 (Sabie) and follow the signs for the caves.

The Sudwala Dinosaur Park has a rather uninspiring collection of life-size concrete dinosaurs. The special effects of 'Jurassic Park' have led people to expect rather more from their dinosaurs these days and the collection no longer has the appeal it might once have had. In keeping with the theme there are some live crocodiles on show. ■ *T013-7335268, open daily, 0800-1730, small entry fee. The collection is next to the Sudwala Caves, see entry above for directions. Gift shop and Pierre's Restaurant, open daily 0800-1800, for cold drinks, snacks and lunches. Stunning views over Sudwala Valley.*

Sleeping
■ *on map*
Price codes:
see inside front cover

B-C *Lakeview Country Lodge*, 4 km south of town, 5 mins from the airport, T/F7415058. Very smart, self-contained cottages, with TV, on the banks of the Nelsloop river. Evening meals available on request in a lovely open air restaurant surrounded by sub-tropical gardens. **B-C** *Shandon Lodge*, 1 Saturn St, quite a distance from the town centre, follow Ferreira St out of town towards Uitkyk, T/F7449934. 5 double rooms with en suite shower, 1 suite, TV, non-smoking room, lounge, laundry service, swimming pool in a mature garden, a fine old house full of character with shade veranda running around the house. Recommended.

C *Bundu Park*, off the R40 White River road, T/F7581221-3, central reservations, T011-2073600. 30 a/c rondavels, TV, lounge, restaurant, bar, swimming pool, sauna, tennis, set in large gardens, play centre and farmyard for kids. Recently taken over by the good value Aventura resort chain, so more improvements expected. **C** *Klipspringer Lodge*, Uitkyk Rd, T7440195, F7449002. 14 rooms, restaurant decorated with hunting trophies, open-air bar, swimming pool, a beautiful bush setting 14 km south of Nelspruit. **C** *La Roca Guest House*, 56 van Wyk St, T7526628, F7526205. 3 double rooms with en suite bathroom, 2 single rooms, each has a private balcony with views across the Lowveld, TV, bar fridge, ceiling fans, lounge, swimming pool, will collect from town centre and airport, one of the best new guesthouses in the area. Recommended. **C** *Jörn's Guest House*, 62 Hunter St, T7523855, F7522426. Large

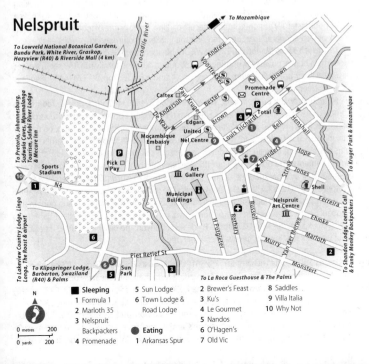

Nelspruit

Mpumalanga

guesthouse run by a German couple, comfortable rooms, lounge, bar, swimming pool, no young children. **C** *Mercure Inn*, corner of Graniet St and N4, T7414222, F4414290. Part of a successful quality French chain. 104 fully equipped, self-catering, luxury, single storey units, TV, a/c, airport transfers, large conference facilities. Impressively spacious, beautifully furnished lounge and bar, open to one side to the attractive pool area, harps on a bit about having the largest pool in Nelspruit. Probably phone first to check that no conferences are scheduled as it can get overrun with delegates. Otherwise excellent quality for a mid range hotel, with the benefit of having self-catering facilities. **C** *The Loerie's Call*, 2 du Preez St, T7524844, F7532115. 4 spacious double rooms with en suite bathroom, minibar, all in separate building, private terrace with views across the Crocodile River valley, non-smoking room, TV, laundry service, B&B, swimming pool, gardens. **C** *Palms Guest House*, 25 van Wijk St, T7554374. 3 double rooms, 3 single rooms all with en suite bathroom, TV, Mnet, lounge areas, B&B, all meals available on request, swimming pool, sauna, gardens, secure parking, comfortable and relaxing. **C** *The Roost*, 21c Koraalboom St, T7411419, F7411421. 9 smart double rooms with en suite bathroom, TV, MNet, overhead fans, swimming pool, spacious old house which is popular with the regular business traveller, secure parking, plenty of atmosphere. Recommended. **C-D** *Town Lodge & Road Lodge*, corner of Gen Dan Pienaar and Koorsboom streets (turn right at main traffic lights when approaching from Pretoria), T7411444, F7412258. 106 a/c rooms, cramped en suite bathroom, TV, non-smoking room available, bar, small swimming pool with terrace seating area, a clean modern businessman's hotel, breakfast extra, but plenty of good choice, very popular during holiday periods when advance booking advised, part of a successful mid-range chain. **C-D** *Linga Longa*, Karee Cres, T7511942, F7581173. 4 double, en suite, non-smoking, luxury rooms, TV, bar, B&B, lovely verandas, pool, tasteful house in the suburbs.

D-F *Safubi River Lodge*, 45 Graniet St, PO Box 4310, T7413253. 7 self-catering chalets, fully equipped kitchen, bathroom, lounge, TV, secure parking, braai in the garden. Also a 40-site camping and caravan park on the banks of the Gladdespruit. Large peaceful and secure, swimming pool plus communal kitchens for self-catering. **D** *Promenade*, Louis Trichardt St, T7533000, F7525533. 71 a/c rooms with en suite bathrooms, TV, non-smoking room available, a smart hotel in a Spanish-style hacienda, restaurant, bar, terrace overlooks a small pool, tastefully designed interior, secure parking, in the centre of town, but suffers from a lack of recreational space. Cheap rates for the quality, recommended.

E *Marloth 35*, 35 Marloth St, T7524529. Double rooms with en suite bathroom set away from main house, private, swimming pool, secluded gardens, family run B&B set in a quiet residential suburb. **E** *Formula 1*, corner of N4 and Kaapsehoop St, T7414490. Soulless modern sleeping units.

F *Funky Monkey Backpackers*, 102 Van Wijk St, T7440534. Dorms, double rooms and camping. Plenty of room in the house. Swimming pool and pool table. Lorna knows plenty about the local area and can help organize trips to Kruger or Blyde River Canyon, on the *Baz Bus* route. **F** *Sun Lodge*, 7 de Villiers St, T/F7412253, T082-4535930 (mob). Garden chalet plus double room in main house, dorms, pool set in colourful lush gardens, close to shops and restaurants. This used to be a guesthouse but with the addition of a dorm room is reinventing itself as a backpackers, on the *Baz Bus* route. **F** *Nelspruit Backpackers*, 9 Andries Pretorius St, T7412237, F7552311. Dorms, 2 double rooms, kitchen, laundry, bar, pool table, swimming pool. Good location next to a nature reserve, close to restaurants and pubs in the Sunpark Centre. Free pick up service from town, on the *Baz Bus* route. Excellent base from which to explore the area. Day trips to Blyde River Canyon and other local treats, see under Tour operators (below) for details. Recommended.

Eating & bars
● *on map*

Arkansas Spur, Louis Trichardt St, T7523619. Steakhouse. *Brewer's Feast*, off Piet Retief St, next to the *Formula 1 Lodge*, T7414674. Roadside restaurant and takeaway open all day. Bargain breakfasts. *Café Mozart*, 56 Promenade Centre, Louis Trichardt St, T7522637. Closed Sun, French cuisine, fondue is a speciality. Popular locally. *Ku's*, Sunpark, T7413989. Economically priced Chinese dishes, takeaway service. *Le Gourmet*, 24 Branders St, T7551941. The local French style cuisine. *Livingstone's*, at the *Emnotweni Casino* next to the *Riverside Mall*, T7570021. If you can stand the noise of the 200-odd slot machines the food is good quality, bar and snack menu 24 hours. *Mediterranean*, Riverside Mall, T7570170. Good value seafood restaurant, part of a chain found throughout the country. *O'Hagen's*, Sunpark, corner of General Dan Pienaar and Piet Retief streets, T7413584. Good Irish theme pub chain, wide selection of imported beers, open-air terrace and music, wholesome pub meals. *Saddles*, Bell St, T7526688. A very popular steakhouse, excellent value for money. *The Old Vic*, 38 Nel St, T7522264. A pub in a converted church in the centre of town, open from 0800 for breakfasts until late, bar menu, DJs at the weekends. *Villa Italia*, corner of Paul Kruger and Louis Trichardt streets, T7525780. Standard Italian. *Why Not*, Bester St, T7522549. Pasta and pizza just on the edge of town, cheap and cheerful. Good value. Recommended if your budget is tight.

The *Promenade Shopping Centre* between Louis Trichardt and Henshall streets, was the **Shopping** premier shopping mall in town but now many of the shops and restaurants seem to have closed and probably moved to the new *Riverside Mall*, 5 km out of town on the White River road, T7570080. This mall contains the usual mix of shops, restaurants, banks, department stores and a few other services. It proudly boasts to be the largest shopping centre in Mpumalanga. Also here is the *Nu Metro* 8-screen cinema, T7570300. Next door is the new *Emnotweni Casino*. After a long period of gambling being illegal in South Africa new ventures such as this are being built across the country. Most visitors will probably not be that impressed by such complexes with all their mirrors and glitter, but for many South Africans they serve as a reminder that they are now living in a new country.

Green Rhino, T7511952, F7501638, greenrhino@mweb.co.za, national adventure operator. **Tour operators** Tours from 1-7 days throughout the region. *Harvey World Travel*, Riverside Mall, T/F7570883. Reliable national chain of general travel agents, flight sales. If you don't have a car *Vula Tours*, T7412826, *Safarilandia*, T082-3389055 (mob), *Old Vic*, T7440993 (ask for Dave), *Pachedu*, T/F7411350, and *Dabula Mangi Safaris*, T083-4490330 (mob), all run affordable day trips to Kruger, the Panorama region, and Sudwala Caves. Expect to pay around R450 per person per day. For the budget traveller try booking a tour through *Nelspruit Backpackers*, 9 Andries Pretorius St, T7412237. Will pick up from anywhere in Nelspruit if you are staying elsewhere. 2-day/1-night Kruger tour, R890 pp, 3-day/2-night, Kruger/Panorama tour, R1250. A comprehensive tour of the region is recommended. *Spectra Ventures*, T7441582, F7449764. 2-hr canoe trips with wine on the picturesque Lake Longmere near White River, half-day hiking trips to Blyde River Canyon. Min 8 people.

Local Car hire: all offices are at the airport terminal building, 12 km out of town. *Avis*, **Transport** T7411087, F7414308; *Budget*, T7413871, F7411213; *Europcar Inter Rent*, T7412350; *Imperial*, T7413210, F7412834; *Tempest*, T7553483, F7413062. **Taxi**: *City Bug*, T7553792.

Long distance Air: *SA Airlink*, T7413536. Central reservations, airport, T011-9781111, town office, *Dana Agency*, corner Louis Trichardt and Paul Kruger streets, T7533571, F7526060. 8 flights a day to **Johannesburg** and 1 to **Durban**. *Nelair Charters*, T7412012, F7412013.

Rail: the *Komati Express* is a daily service running between **Pretoria/Johannesburg** and **Komatipoort** (border post with Mozambique). Departs Nelspruit at 0415 daily. Daily service departs Nelspruit at 2039 for Pretoria.

Road: from Nelspruit it is 43 km to **Barberton**; 92 km to **Graskop** (via Sabie, R37); 58 km to **Hazyview**, 355 km to **Johannesburg**; 107 km to **Komatipoort**; 173 km to **Mbabane** (Swaziland), 200 km to **Maputo** (Mozambique); 55 km to **Numbi Gate** (Kruger Park); 322 km to **Pretoria**. *Baz Bus*, T021-4392323, F021-4392343 has services towards **Johannesburg** and **Pretoria** (8 hrs) Tue, Thu, Sat, picks up between 1130-1200; **Swaziland** (3 hrs) Mon, Wed, Sat, picks up 1415. **NB** The *Baz Bus* stops at *Nelspruit Backpackers, Sun Lodge,* and *Funky Monkey Backpackers*. *Kruger Park Backpackers* in Hazyview offer a free pick up from the bus by prior arrangement. *Greyhound*, T7532100, the office is in the foyer of the *Promenade Hotel* on Louis Trichardt St, coaches depart from outside the hotel. **Pretoria** and **Johannesburg** (5 hrs) Mon-Sat 0730, Sun 1615. *Lowveld Link*, T7501174, combis for **Pretoria** and **Johannesburg** depart Mon-Sat at 0730, Sun 1100. *Panthera Azul*, T011-3377430. Bus service between **Johannesburg** and **Maputo**. Service stops outside the Promenade Centre. *Translux*, central

Mpumalanga

Mpumalanga

Kruger Mpumalanga International Airport (KMAI)

Kruger Mpumalanga International Airport (KMAI) is the new R270 million airport for the region which is presently under construction 25 km from Nelspruit towards Kruger, 10 km from the Maputo corridor (N4) and a short drive to Kruger's Numbi and Malelane gates. It's due to be operational by September 2002, when domestic traffic will be moved from the present airport at Nelspruit and Skukuza Airport within the Kruger National Park. Both these airports will be closed to commercial traffic when this happens. Although the airport company hasn't negotiated any deals at the time of printing, they are hoping to increase domestic routes including a direct flight to and from Cape Town, and international routes between here and Victoria Falls and Nairobi by December 2002.

The runway and airport will have the capacity to accept flights from Europe without connecting through Johannesburg. This is also expected to take some pressure off Johannesburg International Airport. The development is interesting in that 10% ownership of the airport has gone directly to the local community and R5 per passenger passing through will contribute to improving local infrastructure and medical and educational facilities in the poorer regions such as the townships. KMAI will be able to accept night flights and flight tests have confirmed that there is no noise impact on Kruger. People in the local tourism industry are bordering on the ecstatic about the new airport and the possible impact it will have on tourism in the region and it will be interesting to see what new options may open up. There are no contact numbers or flight details for the airport as yet but to follow progress visit www.kmiairport.co.za

reservations, T012-3154300, coaches depart from the *Promenade Hotel*. **Pretoria** and **Johannesburg** (5 hrs): daily, 1115. **Maputo** (4 hrs): daily, 1315.

Directory **Banks** *American Express*, Riverside Mall, T7570400. Open Mon-Fri 0900-1800, Sat 0900-1700, Sun 1000-1400. **Communications** *Alpha Internet Café*, Riverside Mall, Open Mon-Thu 0900-2200, Fri-Sat 0900-2300, Sun 1000-2100. **Medical Services** Hospitals: *Rob Ferreira Hospital*, T7413031. *Medi-clinic*, T7447150. **Consulate** Mozambique Consulate, CVA building, Bester St, T7532089. Open Mon-Fri, 0830-1500. Visas take 3 days but can be issued on the same day or within 24 hrs for an extra fee, you will need to bring 2 passport-size photos and then fill in the application form at the embassy. Expect to pay in the region of US$15 but double this for same day issue. Alternatively visas are now issued at all Mozambique borders, costing R170 or US$25. **Useful services** Ambulance: T10177, T7533331. **Chemist**: after hours, T7525721. **Mpumalanga Parks Board**: T7595301. **Police**: T10111, T7591000. **Snake Bite Rescue**: T082-3377863 (mob), F7525741.

Nelspruit to Komatipoort and Mozambique

The N4 heads east from Nelspruit to Komatipoort (104 km), past the villages of Kaapmuiden, Malelane and Hectorspruit. The road follows the Crocodile River Valley through an area of fruit plantations at the bottom edge of Kruger National Park. This valley is one of the hottest areas of South Africa with year-round temperatures averaging between 25-30°C.

Malelane
Phone code: 013
(NB Always use 3-figure prefix)
Colour map 2, grid B5

A dusty town with a sprawling shopping centre, Malalane is the hub of a sugarcane and fruit growing area. The R570 continues north through the village to the entrance to Kruger Park at Malelane Gate. The Matsamo/Jeppes Reef border crossing into Swaziland (open 0700-1800), is 38 km south of Malelane on the R570. **Tourist information** is available at the *Kruger Park South Tourism Association*, in *Daph's Leather Shop*, Spar Mall, T7901031. It's a helpful private office with a collection of brochures and will book local accommodation.

Sleeping and eating **B** *Buhala Country House*, 6 km east off the N4, T7904372, F7904306. 8 double rooms, 1 suite, a luxury bush hotel, lounge, restaurant, bar, swimming pool, fishing on the banks of the Crocodile River, now actually inside Kruger Park since fences have been removed, finalist of a national award as best country house for the last 5 years. **B** *Serenity Mountain and Forest Lodge*, T7527365, F7527361. While most of the lodges in this region are concentrated on the fringes of Kruger and the Crocodile River, this lodge is in an unusual location in a patch of rain forest high up in the hills in the opposite direction, off the R570 toward the Jeppe's Reef border with Swaziland. 2 camps of luxury thatched chalets, en suite, TV, private verandas overlooking the butterfly-filled forest, unusual sunken bar. Beautiful spot, recommended. **B** *Malelane Sun Inter Continental Resort*, T7903304, F7903303. 40 double rooms, 60 triple rooms, all a/c with en suite bathroom, TV, restaurant, bar, large gardens with swimming pool, a huge complex next to Malelane Gate which copes with the overflow from the Kruger Park camps, peaceful setting on the Crocodile River. **B-C** *Thanda-Nani Game Lodge*, the turn off is 6 km east of Malalane, clearly signposted on the left of the N4, T7904543, F7904428. 6 a/c double rooms with en suite bathroom, lounge and dining area set under an open thatched area, swimming pool, a bush garden, this is a pleasant small private farm with a good range of wildlife which is an enjoyable variation to the full-on Kruger experience. **C** *Selati Guest Cottage*, 103 Selati Crescent, in a suburb north of town, T/F7900978. 6 a/c double rooms in a private house, non-smoking, TV, swimming pool, comfortable option before entering Kruger Park. **E** *Bezuidenhout Guest House*, in a quiet suburb north of town, T/F7900728. 6 very smart rooms, thatched house in pleasant gardens. Ask for Matilda.

For eating, try **Barney's Pub and Grill**, Impala St, T7901294. Town pub with regular pool competitions. **Crocafellas**, T7903415. Most unusual restaurant and pub just before the entrance to Kruger's Malalane Gate. A thatched boma built on stilts in a small lake full of crocodiles, look straight down at them from your table! Open 0700 until late, 500 gm T-bones a speciality, cheap Sunday buffet lunch.

Tour operators *Zozi's*, T7788849, T082-6681577 (mob). An enterprising and entertaining local guide who runs tours of the Matsulu township on the edge of Kruger. The site of the village was originally inside the park's boundary, but in 1968 the fences were removed and people were relocated from neighbouring farms to form the Matsulu community. Today, it's not uncommon to have an elephant stride through the village. Zozi shows you around in his taxi, and visits include a *shebben* (pub), a hairdressers where the art of African plaiting is demonstrated, a witch doctor who will 'throw the bones', and a school that has only 25 teachers for over 1,100 pupils. This excellent tour not only gives insight into African rural life, but also demonstrates how the local people manage to live alongside the animals of Kruger. Great fun and highly recommended.

Komatipoort

This is the last town in South Africa before the main road enters Mozambique at Lebombo. The town has always been close to the border between the two countries, and it has grown over the years as trade and the transport of goods between the coast and the interior has increased. In the early days it was just a campsite by the river crossing. But as soon as the railway arrived in 1890 it quickly developed into a permanent settlement. Coming up from Lourenço Marques (Maputo) this was the only place where the railway could pass through the Lebombo Mountains. From here to Pretoria the railway was built by a Dutch company who made their base at Komatipoort.

The Nkhomati Accord was signed here in March 1984 between Samora Machel, President of Mozambique, and PW Botha, Prime Minister of South Africa. The accord was intended to promote peace and co-operation between the two countries but met with limited success as Mozambique, along with the rest of Africa, was still a staunch opponent to the Apartheid regime and supported sanctions. Not far from here on the Komati flats is the **Marehall Memorial** which is a national monument marking the site where President Samora Machel tragically died in a plane crash. Not far from here on the Komati flats is the Marehall Memorial, a national

*Altitude: 137 m
Phone code: 013
(NB Always use
3-figure prefix)
Colour map 2, grid B5*

*Komatipoort is where
Mahatma Gandhi was
imprisoned in 1907
before managing to
escape to the coast*

Mpumalanga

monument marking the site where the president of Mozambique, Samora Machel tragically died in a plane crash in 1986. Joaquim Chissano succeeded him and his widow Graca Machel went on to marry Nelson Mandela a few years later.

These days the town is an important marshalling yard for the railways and a popular centre for supplies for visitors to Kruger National Park (**Crocodile Gate** is only 9 km away). Lying at the foot of the Lebombo Mountains at the confluence of the Komati and Crocodile rivers and little over 60 km from the Indian Ocean, the climate here is tropical and humid, with high summer temperatures as well as summer rainfall. Fortunately, however, the town's streets are shaded by poinciana and jacaranda trees, essential in the middle of summer.

Tourist information is available from *Info@Komatipoort*, 78 Rissik St, T7907218, F7907557, in *Duve*, a small but excellent African art shop and tea garden. A helpful office that can book local accommodation. Open Mon-Sat 0730-1800, Sun 0800-1700. There are also a number of supermarkets in the centre of town along Rissik St making it the ideal stop for anyone planning a self-catering trip into Kruger.

Sleeping
Price codes:
see inside front cover

C-D *The Border Country Inn*, 1 km from the border next to the *Komati Oasis* service station, T7907328, F7907100. Don't be put off by the neglected exterior or the derelict petrol station next door, the rooms inside are very pleasant with TV, a/c, pool, terrace restaurant, large gardens. **C-D** *Tree's Too*, 11 Furley St, T/F7908262. 6 large a/c en suite rooms under thatch, lounge, pleasant pool area, good evening meals on request, set in lush tropical gardens and palm trees. Recommended. **D** *Komati Guest House*, T082-6415923 (mob). Double rooms with en suite bathroom, swimming pool, evening meals available. **C-D** *Elephant Walk Retreat*, 8 km from town 50 m from Kruger's Crocodile Gate, T/F7907543. Basic self-catering chalets. Good option if you haven't been able to get bookings within the park. **E-F** *Komati Holiday Resort*, T7908040, F7907233. Self-catering chalets, caravan and campsite with plenty of shade from the fever trees, power points, swimming pool, the bar here can get busy with local trade, which is great, but be aware that this may threaten security.

Eating

For a small town this is quite a happening place for bars and restaurants and is well-known for its seafood, which arrives daily from Mozambique. *The Border Country Inn*, T7907328, hotel restaurant 1 km from the border, pleasant outdoor setting (watch the mosquitoes at night), indifferent service, but excellent prawns and calamari. *Hippo's Hide*, Rissik St, T7908155. Trendy bar and restaurant, fat sofas, reasonably priced menu, open all day for snacks and coffees, closes when the last person leaves. *Tambarina*, Rissik St, T7907057. A fun restaurant with a strong Portuguese feel. If you can't make it to the coast, the meals here are the next best thing. Guests from Crocodile Bridge camp in Kruger Park often dine here. Well worth a visit.

Transport

Rail The *Komati Express* is a daily service running between **Pretoria/Johannesburg** and **Komatipoort**. A daily shuttle service continues to the border that links with the train to **Maputo**, which departs from the Mozambique side. Customs and immigration will take at least 1 hr. However, *Spoornet*, South Africa's passenger rail network, has recently won the concession for the entire line between Johannesburg and Maputo. It is hoped that there will soon be a direct service between these two cities. **Johannesburg** (12 hrs): daily, 1807. **Road** 543 km to **Johannesburg**, 96 km to **Maputo**, 100 km to **Nelspruit**. The buses between **Pretoria/Johannesburg** and **Maputo** stop at the border post.

Directory

Banks *First National*, Rissik St, T7907343. Open for foreign exchange. *FX Bureau de Change*, at the *Komati Oasis* service station just before the border, T7907457. Open Mon-Sat 0700-1700, Sun 0700-1300. Poorer exchange rates compared to the bank, but after hours opening times. **Useful services Doctor**: T7907306. **Police**: T7907321 or 10111.

Crossing into Mozambique

The South African border post is at **Lebombo**, 3 km out of town. There is a viewpoint on a hill by the border from where one can look into Mozambique. **Border hours**: 0600-1900, 24 hours over the Easter and Christmas holiday periods. All visitors require visas for Mozambique, these are now issued at the border, US$25 or

R170. The new toll road between Nelspruit and Maputo has recently been completed on both sides, allowing time for the border crossing, the journey between the two cities takes around two and half hours. Komatipoort is 96 km from Maputo.

Barberton

This quiet colonial town is a pleasant place to spend a few days. It has an interesting gold mining past, there are several museums in the town centre and the Swaziland border is only 43 km away. Unlike the gold mining town of Pilgrim's Rest near Sabie, which is completely devoted to tourism, the old corrugated iron roofed mining buildings and cottages in Barberton are very much part of the working commercial town. Lone Tree Hill, on the outskirts of Barberton, is one of the most popular hang gliding centres in South Africa. It is set in the De Kaap Valley where some of the oldest sedimentary rock formations in the world have been found (4,200 million years). The Makhonjwa Mountains around Barberton are covered in grasslands and woods and are an extension of the southern Drakensberg.

Phone code: 013
(NB Always use
3-figure prefix)
Colour map 2, grid C5
Altitude: 877 m

The road into Barberton passes the shacks and vegetable plots of the local farmers before entering the quiet wealthy garden suburbs on the edge of town. The old abandoned mining centre, suitably named Eureka City, is tucked up in the hills at the back of the town. The main sights are all within walking distance and the hiking trails start from the edge of town.

Tourist information is available from *Barberton Information Bureau*, PO Box 33, Crown St, Market Square, T7122121, F7125120. Open Mon-Fri 0800-1300, 1400-1630, Sat 0830-1200. This is a friendly and helpful office with good information on tours and accommodation in the area, check here for up-to-date information on excursions to Swaziland.

The De Kaap Valley was originally known as the Valley of Death due to the many prospectors who had died here of malaria. Barberton is most famous for being the site of South Africa's first large-scale gold rush. Pioneer Reef was discovered in 1883 by 'French Bob', but it was after Graham, Henry, and Fred Barber found a reef which sparkled in the sun in 1884 that the gold rush really began. By 1886 over 4,000 claims were being worked in the valley and Barberton became a wild frontier town of corrugated iron shacks, gambling dens and whisky bars.

History
Cockney Liz, a
notorious prostitute
and resident of
Barberton, would
dance on a snooker
table every night
whilst being
auctioned off to
the highest bidder

Barberton quickly became a wealthy town. South Africa's first stock exchange opened here in 1887 and many of Barberton's most attractive colonial buildings were built during the gold rush. Unfortunately, the gold rush only lasted a few years, the stock market crashed after too many speculators were sold shares in bogus companies and investors lost fortunes in the Transvaal and Britain. By the outbreak of the Boer War, Barberton had been virtually abandoned by the miners who had moved on to the new gold rush at Witwatersrand. However, in recent years the industry has been revived and four gold mines operate within the area; Sheba Reef, Fairview, New Consort, and Agnes, providing employment for much of the local community.

The historical sites within the town have been clearly mapped out by Barberton's tourism initiative, *The Heritage Walk*. Pick up a map at the tourist office. The walk starts from **Barberton Museum** and ends at the **Steam Locomotive**. The sights have been listed below in order of the walk. Only **Belhaven House Museum** and **Stopforth House Museum** have an entry fee, R10 pp, but you only need pay at one to cover entrance to the other.

Sights
The historical buildings
are all within walking
distance of Market
Square

Barberton Museum, 36 Pilgrim St, is the town's local history museum with displays on geology, mining, and cultural history of the area. A well-meaning but odd mixture of exhibits alongside modern artwork. ■ *Open daily, 0900-1600*. **The Blockhouse**, on the corner of Lee Road and Judge Street, is a small fort built in 1901 during the Boer War as part of the defence of Barberton. It is made from wood and corrugated iron and is one of the earliest examples of its kind. **Belhaven Museum**, Lee Road, is a

Mpumalanga

large Edwardian mansion built in 1904 set in mature gardens, the interior is decorated with period furniture and gives an interesting insight into the comfortable lifestyles of Barberton's middle class. ■ *Tours Mon-Fri, 1000, 1100, 1200, 1400 1500.* **Fernlea House**, Lee Road, was built in the 1890s from wood and iron, the materials were part of a kit sent from England. The house is in a beautiful setting at the bottom of a wooded valley on the edge of Barberton. It is decorated with period furniture and has displays on Barberton's famous botanists. ■ *Open Mon-Fri 0830-1300, 1330-1600.*

Rimer's Creek was a popular recreational spot for the townsfolk, particularly on Wednesdays when it was frequented by the barmaids of the town

The walk passes **Rimer's Creek**, the site where, on 24 June 1884, David Wilson the mining commissioner, broke a bottle of gin over a rock to christen the new town of Barberton. **Stopforth House**, 18 Bowness Street, belonged to James Stopforth, a baker and a general dealer, and was built in 1886. The Stopforth family lived here until 1983. ■ *Tours Mon-Fri, 1000, 1100, 1200, 1400, 1500.* The **De Kaap Stock Exchange** on Pilgrim Street was built in 1887. All that remains of the original structure is the façade, which has been declared a national monument. **The Globe Tavern**, on Pilgrim Street, is an interesting building completed in 1887 and restored in 1979. Now home to *Ragamuffin's* coffee and gift shop.

The Lewis and Marks Building, on Pilgrim Street and completed in 1887, was Barberton's first two-storey building and housed the *Bank of Africa*. It's now *Bernstein's* Restaurant and Pub. **Market Square**, is a quiet place shaded by trees with whitewashed colonial buildings on all four sides. The open air *Victoria Tea Gardens* is a pleasant place to sit and watch the world go by. In front of the town hall is a statue of **Jock of the Bushveld**, the faithful dog of Percy Fitzpatrick during his days as a transport rider. The **Magistrate's Court**, General Street, was completed in 1911 to house all the government departments. However, the government employees were highly critical of the building because the architects forgot to include lavatories in the plans. The **steam locomotive** on General Street, by the entrance to the caravan park, used to run between Barberton and Kaapmuiden. The engine was identified from an old photograph and found in Port Elizabeth and brought to Barberton by it's own steam.

The **Aerial Cableway** crosses town and is clearly visible climbing the mountains that border Swaziland. It was built in 1938 to transport asbestos 20 km over mountainous terrain from the Havelock mine in Swaziland to the railhead in Barberton. It is still in use today and now takes coal, transported to Barberton from Witbank, back to Swaziland on the return journey to fuel the mine.

Walking trails There are two short local walking trails starting from the centre of town; the **Rose Creek Walk** and the **Fortuna Mine Walk** (2 km). The Fortuna Mine Walk starts on Crown Street and passes through a 500-m tunnel, which is part of an old mine. There is no lighting inside the tunnel so bring a torch.

Sleeping
■ *on map*
Price codes:
see inside front cover

B *Sweet Home Guest Farm*, T7123978. The guest farm is 10 km from Barberton on the road to Badplaas, a self-catering cottage on a farm below the Makhonjwa Mountains, sleeps up to 10, horse riding and hiking, reservations recommended. **C** *Digger's Retreat*, 14 km out of town on the R38 to Kaapmuiden, T7199681. 6 double rooms and 4-bed rondavels, restaurant, swimming pool, hiking and birdwatching. **C** *Digger's Rest Guest Cottage*, Sheba Rd, T7122995. 4 double rooms, sleeps 8, self-catering. The whole cottage must be taken, so suitable for large groups only. **C** *Fountain Baths Holiday Cottages*, 48 Pilgrim St, T7122707. Self-catering, swimming pool, gardens. Recommended. **C** *Gracefarm Cottages*, T7125068. 10 km from Barberton on the Badplaas road. B&B or self-catering, gardens, swimming pool. Relaxing rural location with some good birdwatching. **C-D** *Kloofhuis*, 1 Kloof St, T7124268. Central location just behind Bellhaven House, a short walk from the tourist office. 1 double room with en suite bathroom, 2 twin rooms with shared bathroom. Cosy B&B in a perfect setting overlooking the town. Relaxing on the veranda at the end of the day in this fine Victorian home will probably tempt you to stay an extra day. Ask for Steve or Magda. **D** *Phoenix Hotel*, 20 Pilgrim St, T/F7124211. A/c, bar lunches and à la carte restaurant, 3 pool tables, *Jocks Tavern* is a lively bar. The building dates from the time of the gold rush and it is said that Paul Kruger was entertained here after meetings with the miners. The hotel was so popular in its day that on occasions guests had to sleep on or under the billiards table. Today it's looking a bit dated but in true historic style. To get a TV, pay R12 extra. **D** *Olivia's Guest Villa*, 33 Norman Nader St, T7123365. B&B in a quiet suburb. 2 double a/c rooms, lounge, secure parking. French and German spoken. **D** *William George House*, 1 Bok St, T/F7125886. 8 double en suite rooms, TV, minibar, pool, B&B but choice of early breakfast or takeaway brunch, evening meals on request, pretty colonial house with 50 m of covered veranda. **D-F** *Caravan Park*, Fitzpatrick Park, T7123323. Chalets, caravans and camping set in the neatly maintained public gardens with a swimming pool, tea garden and laundrette. Recommended.

Eating
● *on map*

Bernstein's, 22 Pilgrim St, T7124896. Housed in the historical Lewis and Marks building, open lunch until late, affordable mixed menu, good fish and steaks. *Cheers*, 30 President St, T7123226. Open 1100-1400, 1700-2300, light snacks and à la carte menu, part of the Barberton Club Building, gloomy 50s-style décor, roof garden, pool table. *Gold Mine*, Eureka Centre, Nourse St, T7124373. Open daily 1200-1500, 1800-late, good steaks. *John Henry's Pub and Ragamuffin's*, President St, in the historic Globe Tavern, T7126735. A la carte menu at the weekends, light meals the rest of the week. Good place to have a cold beer and imagine what went on in this tavern during it's hey-day. *Victoria Tea Garden*, Market Square, T7124985. Charming open-air café serving toasted sandwiches, juice and light snacks.

Tour operators

Eureka City Ghost Town Tours, General St, T7125055. With sufficient numbers of people, this tour departs from Barberton daily at 0900 and returns at 1630. Transport is in a 4x4

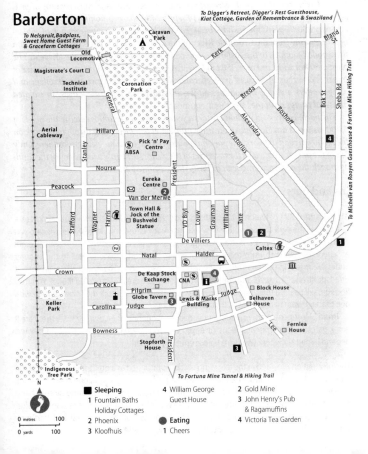

Barberton

To Nelspruit, Badplass,
Sweet Home Guest Farm
& Gracefarm Cottages

To Digger's Retreat, Digger's Rest Guesthouse,
Kiat Cottage, Garden of Remembrance & Swaziland

To Michelle van Rooyen Guesthouse & Fortuna Mine Hiking Trail

Caravan Park

Old Locomotive

Magistrate's Court

Technical Institute

Coronation Park

Aerial Cableway

Hillary

Pick 'n' Pay Centre

ABSA

Nourse

Eureka Centre

Van der Merwe

Peacock

Stanley

General

President

Kerk

Breda

Alexandra

Boshoff

Pretorius

Bok St

Sheba Rd

Brand St

Town Hall & Jock of the Bushveld Statue

Stafford

Wagner

Harris

VD Blyt

Louw

Grauman

Williams

Tate

De Villiers

Natal

Halder

Caltex

Crown

De Kock

De Kaap Stock Exchange

CNA

Block House

Keller Park

Pilgrim

Globe Tavern

Lewis & Marks Building

Judge

Belhaven House

Carolina

Judge

Lee

Fernlea House

Bowness

Stopforth House

President

Indigenous Tree Park

N

To Fortuna Mine Tunnel & Hiking Trail

Mpumalanga

0 metres   100
0 yards   100

■ **Sleeping**
1 Fountain Baths Holiday Cottages
2 Phoenix
3 Kloofhuis

4 William George Guest House

● **Eating**
1 Cheers

2 Gold Mine
3 John Henry's Pub & Ragamuffins
4 Victoria Tea Garden

open sided vehicle and includes drinks and informative guide. Visit Eureka City, the abandoned mining town, and walk a short way underground into the gold mine itself. The drive goes through some spectacular mountain scenery and is recommended for an all round historical picture of the region. *Inhlava Tour Guide Services*, Pilgrim St, T7127462. Local guides for the town's Heritage Walk around the historical buildings, and township tours. The municipality has funded training for disadvantaged local people to become South African Tourism registered guides for the area, a community project that is well worthwhile supporting. *Pyramid Flight School*, contact Brian Young, T/F7411580, T082-3378206 (mob). Microlight courses and flights over the lowveld.

Transport **Road** 78 km **Kruger** (Malelane Gate), 45 km to **Nelspruit**, 42 km **Swaziland**. There is no public transport to Barberton. The only options are to hitchhike or take a taxi from Nelspruit.

Directory **Useful services** **Ambulance**: T7125002. **Medic-clinic**: T7124279. **Police**: T7122233 or 10111.

Kruger National Park

Colour map 2, grid B5

The park is in an endemic malaria area. You are advised to take anti-malarial medication and use insect repellent. Malaria information T013-7527889

The Kruger experience is unique in the way it conjures up a romantic view of African history; of a landscape inhabited from the earliest times by San, iron age villages, slave traders, ivory poachers and gold prospectors, of vast herds of game migrating across the lowveld with the seasons. The reality of modern Kruger as a conservation area is equally fascinating: 500 bird species, 114 reptile, 49 fish, 33 amphibian, 146 mammal and over 23,000 plant species have been recorded here in an enormous region of wilderness extending from the Crocodile River in the south to the Limpopo in the north, from the wooded foothills of the eastern escarpment to the humid plains of the lowveld. The park is 60 km wide and over 350 km long, conserving 21,497 sq km, an area the size of Israel. The needs of tourists are well-catered for, the game viewing is excellent and Kruger offers a choice of holidays either in luxury private game lodges, in isolated bushveld camps or in the larger well-equipped public camps.

The park receives 1.5 million visitors a year and the park camps cater to the needs of 5,000 visitors a day. In spite of the huge number of people passing through the park on the 2,600 km road network, the park has managed to keep its magical atmosphere. Only 5% of the park is affected by the activities of the visitors and only a few areas in the south approach the overcrowding seen in East Africa's game parks.

Ins and outs

Getting there **Air** *SA Airlink* flies between Johannesburg and Nelspruit and Phalaborwa, both airports are just outside the park and are within easy reach of many of the entry gates. In either case you will need to arrange for a car hire at the airport since there is no local public transport. Details of scheduled flights to/from the 2 airports, and car hire, are listed in detail in this chapter under Nelspruit (page 585) and in Phalaborwa (page 664). There are other airports at Hoedspruit, and Skukuza Camp within the park but there are no scheduled flights. You may find yourself passing through these airports if you have booked an all-inclusive package with one of the private game reserves that includes flights.

Road Most people arrive in Kruger by road on a tour or in their own vehicle. There are 8 entry gates and unlimited options of approach. Which area you end up staying in will depend in part on where you were before entering the park.

Getting around The information provided in the following section is intended as a guide for the whole of the national park. Given its huge size many visitors to Kruger tend to stay in one area of the park on each visit. Unless you are staying for more than a couple of nights it is impossible to combine effective game viewing with visiting all areas of the park. It is for this reason that after this introduction the park has been divided into 3 areas: Southern, Central and Northern, with a description of each of the different camps within these areas.

Kruger National Park: gate opening times

National Park gates		Camp gates	
January-February	0530-1830	January	0500-1830
March	0530-1800	February	0530-1830
April	0600-1730	March	0530-1800
May-August	0630-1730	April	0600-1730
September	0600-1800	May-August	0630-1730
October	0530-1800	September	0600-1800
November-December	0530-1830	October	0530-1800
		November-December	0430-1830

Best time to visit

Kruger's climate changes through the year with each season bringing its own advantages. The park looks its best after the **summer** rains when the new shoots and lush vegetation provide a surplus of food for the grazers. Migratory birds are attracted to the area and display their more colourful breeding plumage. The birdwatching in summer offers good opportunities to see courtship rituals and nesting. The animals get healthier on their new diet and the herds of grazers give birth to their young. Visitors can see playful foals and calves of zebra and elephant. The disadvantages of summer are that the thick foliage and tall grasses do make it harder to spot animals and daytime temperatures can rise to a sweltering 40°C, afternoon rains are also common.

The **winter** months are good for game viewing because the dry weather forces animals to congregate around waterholes, and you will also see more animals because there is less foliage (the dry leafless panorama of apparently dead woodland stretching as far as the eye can see is an awesome sight). However, the animals tend not to be in the best condition. The winter months of Jun, Jul and Aug are more comfortable with daytime temperatures of around 30°C, nights can be surprisingly cold at this time of year as temperatures descend to 0°C. This is a good time of year to visit the northern areas of the park which can be unbearably hot in the summer.

Kruger is at its most crowded during the South African school holidays. Accommodation within the park will be completely full and the heavy traffic on the roads can mar the 'wilderness' experience.

Entry requirements

Most of the camps are at least an hour's drive from the nearest entrance gate, you should always make sure you arrive in time to get to the camp. At the park gate your booking will be checked before you are allowed into the park, especially during the busy periods when all the accommodation, including campsites, gets booked up. You could be fined if you arrive at the camp gate after it has closed. There is a speed limit of 50 kph on the surfaced roads. **Park entrance** is: R30 per adult, R24 per car. **NB** This price has not gone up since 1997, a full review of entry fees is expected in Nov 2002.

Services & opening hours

Reception hours: Apr-Jun 0800-1800; Mar, Sep and Oct 0800-1830; Nov-Feb 0800-1900. **Shop hours** are the same as reception. The shops have a steady trade with the camp staff, on payday you will see all the staff in their green jumpers collecting baskets full of chicken and beer. The closer you are to Skukuza the fresher the produce will be, that is not to say that the dairy products in Shingwedzi will be bad, but they are more likely to run out. Other useful items on sale include: firewood and braai lighters, frozen meats, tinned vegetables, jams, beer, wines, spirits, cool drinks, books and a few curio items. If you don't have a cool box in your car and you are self-catering it is still possible to buy all you need for a meal from the shop each day.

Restaurant hours: Breakfast 0700-0900; Lunch 1200-1400; Dinner 1800-2100. Once the cafeteria has closed the only evening meal available will be buffet for R60. Some of the camps also have a bar. At small camps, or when there are very few guests, you will be asked to order your evening meal in advance, this allows for taking food out of the deep freeze and helps to limit waste, while still providing you with a choice of meals in the depth of the bush.

Mpumalanga

Bush fires

A series of bush fires were started by lightning in Oct 1996 burning an estimated 15% of Kruger. Radio stations in Johannesburg reported that entire herds of impala had been barbecued, but the reality was that light winds gave the majority of animals ample time to escape the flames. The burnt areas of dense grass and shrubland will make room for new shoots to germinate and are part of the natural life-cycle of the park.

After several days the menu may seem a bit limited but efforts are being made to improve the food in some camps as they are gradually given more autonomy.

Petrol is available at all the camps during office hours, the mark-up is not that unreasonable. As is the case throughout South Africa, petrol cannot be paid for by credit card. Make sure you have sufficient cash while staying in the park.

See also Sleeping section page 597 Some of the camps have a **swimming pool** for residents, this is most welcome during the summer months, it is also an added attraction if you choose to base yourself at a camp for several days and just want to rest up in the middle of the day. In the camping area there are **laundry blocks** and excellent clean **showers** with plenty of hot water. The **communal kitchens** have power points, instant boiling water machines, electric rings and a washing sink. It is your responsibility to clean up after yourself. Always secure rubbish to minimize the baboon threat. Once the animals start to steal from a camp the only way to solve the problem is to shoot them, please take note of the signs which say **Do Not Feed The Baboons**.

Park history

The first area of what was to become Kruger National Park was officially protected in 1898 by President Kruger when he established the Sabie River Game Reserve. This consisted of what is now the southern sector of Kruger, the lands extending between the Crocodile and the Sabi rivers. This is still one of the best game viewing areas, with zones of mountain bushveld, bushwillow woodlands, thorn thickets and marula savanna.

The land covered by the Sabie River Game Reserve had always been under-populated as tsetse fly, malaria and bilharzia made it difficult for people or cattle to survive for any length of time. The early inhabitants were San and the Baphalaborwa tribes who had little effect on the region's wildlife.

The Voortrekkers of the Transvaal Republic wanted to secure a trading route to the sea which was not controlled by the British. Hendrik Potgieter travelled from the Orange Free State to the coast of Mozambique in 1836 and set up a trade route with goods being carried by porters. European explorers first crossed the Transvaal Lowveld in the 1850s opening the area up for slave traders and ivory hunters who established staging posts here.

Trade with settlers on the highveld increased to such an extent that porters could not cope with the larger volumes of goods. 'The Old Wagon Road' was a trail forged through the bush by the Voortrekkers which forded rivers and bypassed the toughest mountain ranges. The transport riders were amongst the most romantic figures of the Lowveld and were known for their reckless skills for driving wagonloads of goods hauled by teams of oxen to the most isolated outposts. The railway linking Pretoria and the coast was completed in 1895 and ended an era for the transport riders as goods began to be transported by train.

The game reserve was established in 1898 to protect wildlife from the threat of 'biltong hunters' who were visiting the lowveld in ever increasing numbers during the dry season. Hunters had already slaughtered vast herds of animals throughout South Africa and this was an early attempt to preserve an undisturbed wilderness. A police sergeant at Komatipoort was given the daunting task of protecting the entire area from poachers.

Mpumalanga

Major James Stevenson-Hamilton

James Stevenson-Hamilton, Kruger's first game warden, was appointed at the end of the Boer War. He established his headquarters at the end of the railway on the branch line from Komatipoort to the Sabi River. The headquarters were then called Sabi Bridge and have grown to become Skukuza camp.

He began his work with two other rangers and spent years patrolling the reserve on horseback and on foot. His main duties were to encourage a healthy game population and to rid the park of poachers. However, his deep love of the African bush inspired him to campaign to increase the size of the park and to ensure the continued protection of the wildlife within its borders. He retired in 1946 after spending 44 years working in Kruger.

James Stevenson-Hamilton's philosophy on nature was that man's attempts to manage the park only interfered with natural processes. He believed that all the creatures within the park deserved to live regardless of temporary effects and that the balance of nature would always be preserved. His interest was to protect the park from any of man's activities and to compare the results with what mankind achieved outside of the park.

The game reserve was reproclaimed by the British in 1903 increasing the size of the park with both the Shingwedzi Game Reserve, the area between the Letaba and the Luvuvhu rivers, and the 5,000 sq km of unworked ranches between the Sabi and the Letaba rivers. The new area under protection covered roughly the same area as Kruger does today.

Even at this stage the park's boundaries were not totally secure and demand for land threatened the survival of the game reserve. Hunters wanted access to the park, soldiers returning from the First World War expected land for sheep farming, prospectors looking for gold, coal and copper wanted mining rights and South Africa's vets were campaigning for a mass slaughter of wildlife to prevent the possible spread of tsetse fly and other diseases.

The seeds of creating a self-financing national park which was open to visitors were unwittingly sown by South African Railways when they opened a new tour running from Pretoria to Lorenço Marques which stopped at places in the reserve where game rangers would take tourists into the bush. The first tourists arrived in 1923 and the visits became such a popular feature of the holiday that park visits were used as publicity by the railways. Public support for a national park empowered the conservationist lobby and public access was finally allowed in 1926. The Bill on National Parks was passed after borders for the new national park had been negotiated and an administrative board organizing construction of roads and access to visitors was established. The public would pay towards the development of the park through the fees charged to visitors.

The first cars arrived in 1927 and were able to travel by road through Sabi Bridge between the Olifants and Crocodile rivers. Visitors were expected to fend for themselves and made their own thorn bush camps to stay in. The animals reacted well to visitors in cars as long as they stayed inside them, but night driving was stopped almost immediately as too many animals were being killed. The first camp was built for tourists at Pretoriuskop after the chaos of the early years when tourists had been known to spend the night in trees hiding from predators.

By 1946 38,000 tourists a year were visiting Kruger and in 1947 Princess Elizabeth and Princess Margaret visited the park on their Royal Tour of South Africa where they stayed in the first luxury lodges. The publicity surrounding the tour ensured that a visit to Kruger became a fixture on every tourist's trip to South Africa. By 1955 over 100,000 people were visiting Kruger each year.

Kruger has grown to accommodate the huge numbers of visitors, more roads have been tarred and more picnic sites and public camps have been built. The land

Mpumalanga

area available to the park's wildlife increased in 1994 when the game fences between the private reserves on Kruger's western border were taken down allowing the animals to roam freely in an extra 2,000 sq km of bush.

Wildlife

Wildlife management   Although to the visitor the park appears to be an untamed wilderness where the wildlife exists without any interference from humans, all aspects of the ecosystem are carefully monitored and in so far as it is possible, controlled. Wildlife has been managed here from the beginning with the culling of lions to encourage the growth of the populations of grazing animals. Windpumps have been built at waterholes in dry areas so that game congregates in large enough numbers to attract the public. Animals which had disappeared from Kruger have gradually been reintroduced. Four white rhino were reintroduced in 1961 from Rhodesia, a couple of years later a further 96 were brought in from the Natal Parks board. The programme has been so successful that there are now over 2,000 in the park. Black rhino were reintroduced in 1971, 40 years after they had last been seen here. Other animals which have been re-established include tsessebe and roan.

Game viewing

Kruger is one of the few places in South Africa where it is possible to see all the Big Five: lion, elephant, buffalo, black rhino and leopard

The highest concentrations and variety of game are around Lower Sabie, Satara and Skukuza. Although it is certainly a thrill to see the more impressive animals the sheer number of different species here makes the park very special.

The best times for game viewing are after dawn and just before dusk as animals tend to lie up during the heat of the day. It is easy to spend several days at Kruger viewing the game in different areas and stopping at rest camps, picnic sites and view points to break up the journey.

The roads are only open to the public during daylight hours and are subject to speed limits which are monitored by radar. There is a network of tarred and dirt roads linking the camps. Game viewing takes time, so it is best not to travel over 20 kph or the chances are you'll have passed the animals before you've had a chance to see them. The temptation is to head for the most isolated dirt tracks and to neglect the tarred roads as being 'more developed'. This is a mistake because cars are quieter on tarred roads and the animals living near them are more used to traffic. Also, the run-off from tarred roads makes the vegetation greener and attracts more animals. Spending hours on end in a car driving around Kruger does get exhausting and visiting one of the get out points and passing a few hours' game viewing at a waterhole makes a pleasant alternative. Kruger shops sell almost every identification guide available on the wildlife in the park. Their own publications, the map, the travel guide and the comprehensive 'Find it' guide are an excellent introduction to the geology, history, vegetation and wildlife of Kruger.

Planning a safari   Kruger offers visitors the opportunity to travel uninterruptedly through the African bush for several days. The ultimate journey through Kruger is to drive the entire length of the park staying at the bushveld camps. The costs of self-catering accommodation, food and car hire shared between four people often works out cheaper than an organized tour.

Game drives   People visiting Kruger for the first time can find the bush a daunting place. Many of the animals are hard to identify and you can get the feeling that you're missing things. A guided tour with a game ranger does help to get a deeper understanding of the wilderness and most camps offer guided day drives and night drives. These are very popular and should be booked in advance at camp reception as soon as you arrive to check in. A half day drive costs R115 per person, and a whole day costs R150 per person. Night drives cost R100 per person, with a minimum of four people and they usually depart around 1700. Make sure you have warm clothing; a thick jumper would not be excessive during the months May-August. The drives finish in time for guests to have an evening meal at the camp restaurant. Some camps now offer a late drive after dinner, departing at 2030 and lasting for up to 3 hours, at R100 per person.

There are limited opportunities to walk through Kruger because there are only seven trails but seeing the park on foot is the most exciting way to experience the wilderness and places on the hiking trails are booked up months in advance. A maximum of eight people go on each trail and they are accompanied by an armed ranger. Hikers spend all nights at the same bush camp and go out on day walks. The trails are only up to 15 km long which gives hikers ample time for game viewing. Food, water bottles, sleeping bags, rucksacks and cutlery are all provided.

Wilderness trails

The wilderness trails are run twice a week on Sunday and Wednesday and last for two days and three nights and cost R1,075 per person each day. For reservations contact the *South African National Parks* (SANPARKS) offices, bookings can be made up to a year ahead and places fill up quickly. The best time of year for hiking is from March to July when the weather is dry and daytime temperatures are cooler.

The Bushman Trail is a good area for seeing white rhino and wild dogs but the walks also visit nearby San paintings. The camp is in an area of mountain bushveld, southwest of Kruger in an isolated valley surrounded by koppies. Hikers stay in thatched bush huts. Hikers check in at Berg-en-Dal which is an hour's drive by Land Rover from the camp.

The Napi Trail passes through a variety of habitats following the banks of the Biyamiti River through thick riverine bush and crossing through mixed woodlands. This is a good area for seeing both the black and white rhinos, duiker, jackal, kudu and giraffe. Hikers check in at Pretoriuskop.

NB Several trail huts get damaged during the floods

The Metsi-Metsi Trail camp is in an area of mountain bushveld near the N'waswitsontso River. The trail also visits areas of marula savannah where many plains animals are seen. Hikers check in at Skukuza.

The Nyalaland Trail passes through a vast expanse of mopane scrub, dotted with baobabs, aloes and koppies. The wildlife here is unique to this sector of the park and nyala are often seen. The birdlife here is spectacular. The hutted camp is shaded by kuduberry trees next to the Madzaringwe Stream. Hikers check in at Punda Maria.

The Olifants Trail crosses through a region of classic African plains, it is excellent for seeing large herds of buffalo, wildebeest and zebra. The hutted camp overlooks the Olifants River and is 1½ hours by Land Rover to Letaba. Hikers check in at Letaba.

The Sweni Trail is southeast of Satara overlooking the Sweni River and crosses through knobthorn and marula savannah where large herds of buffalo, wildebeest and zebra can be seen. The interesting species to spot are cheetah, lion, kudu, sable and steenbok. Hikers check in at Satara.

The Wolhuter Trail passes through lowveld savannah where it is possible to see some of the rare species such as lions, cheetah, black and white rhino, roan, sable and wild dog. The trail is named after the park ranger Harry Wolhuter, who killed a lion with his knife in 1903. The bush camp has wooden huts and is near the Mlambane River. Hikers check in at Berg-en-Dal.

Sleeping

Within the confines of Kruger National Park all the accommodation is currently owned by South African National Parks (SANPARKS), Pretoria (with one exception Jock Safari Lodge, see

See also individual area Sleeping sections

Mpumalanga

Cashing in on Kruger

In a recent move by SANPARKS to investigate the possibility of earning more revenue from Kruger National Park, the former Jock-of-the-Bushveld Camp has been given over to a private concessionaire, and is now Jock Safari Lodge. All-inclusive rates are comparable to those of the private game reserves, where pampering and exclusivity comes hand in hand with game watching with a price tag to match. This is a worrying move by SANPARKS. Whilst there will always be a market for top class lodges, if other concessions are granted to private operators within the park, many of the present camps maybe be offered out to new management and be in danger of

becoming out of reach financially to anyone other than the top-of-the-range-tourist, and more importantly, to local visitors including many families and school groups.

The other significant issue is that as a private concession this is the only place in Kruger where off road game viewing is permitted. This is a controversial issue. While vehicles must stick to the roads in every other region of the park so as not to invade or damage the animals environment, why is it OK to break these barriers in an area where a tourist has more money to spend? It remains to be seen how SANPARKS will proceed with this initiative.

box). Although there is a choice in the type of accommodation available all the room rates are very reasonable when one considers where you are and what you are getting. **NB** The accommodation rates haven't changed since 1997, a full review of accommodation rates is expected in Nov 2002. If you are looking for luxury then the South African National Parks (SANPARKS) camps are not the place to come to. Outside the boundaries of Kruger are the well-publicized luxury camps where on average you can expect to pay over R2,500 per person/night, sharing. This does include 3 meals and all your game drives with guides.

Reservations Reservations can be made in person or by telephone Mon-Fri at SANPARKS head office in Pretoria, T012-3431991, F012-3430905 or via email at, reservations@parks-sa.co.za Alternatively go to the satellite office at the Tourist Junction in Durban, T031-3044934, F3043868, funinsun@iafrica.com, www.durbanexperience.co.za, www.bookabedahead.co.za. See pages 386 and 534 under these chapters for further details. The direct line for each camp is included under the description of the camp. This number can be used for making a booking only 48 hrs or under prior to your arrival. All other bookings have to be made through the central office in Pretoria. Once you are in the park it is always worth calling a day ahead or even early morning to see if there have been any cancellations. Outside of the school holidays it should always be possible to stay in the camp of your choice. **NB** *Punda Maria* is considerably smaller than other camps and it is therefore more likely to be full.

Jock Safari Lodge **L2** *Jock Safari Lodge* This camp is the only one in the park under private ownership and must be booked independently. T011-7844144, F011-7844172, bluemtnres@icon.co.za The camp is in an area of mixed woodland between Malelane and Skukuza. The cottages have recently been refurbished to the highest standard to compete with the lodges in the private game reserves. The 12 luxury rooms are decorated with prints of the original illustrations from the novel, *Jock of the Bushveld*. Each has its own private viewing deck overlooking the Mitomeni and Biyamiti rivers. Rates include game drives, bush walks, and all meals.

Main Public Camps There are 12 main public camps where the majority of overnight visitors stay in the park. Most of the accommodation is in the form of chalets or cottages which can sleep between 2 and 12. The differences between them is not always that clear, although the cottages tend to have more space. If you are self-catering then you will have the choice between a separate fully equipped kitchen, a kitchenette or the use of a communal kitchen. The units with just a kitchenette do not have any cutlery or crockery. All accommodation comes with a refrigerator, bedding and towels. If in doubt always check when booking over the telephone exactly what you will be getting. More precise details of the choices are listed under the separate

Mpumalanga

entry for each of the camps. Some of the older camps have a tired feel to them but nevertheless the grounds are clean and well-kept and when compared to game viewing in other major parks in Africa they represent excellent value. As noted above most camps have a shop which stocks enough for a couple of days self-catering, and if you don't wish to cook there is always a restaurant at most of the camps. During the school holidays the atmosphere is more like a holiday camp and you can easily forget you are in the middle of a game reserve full of wild animals. The facilities from one camp to the next vary slightly but in most cases they include a shop, petrol, a restaurant or cafeteria, laundrettes, toilets, braai areas with seating, public telephones and an office with information on the other camps. The main public camps are: *Berg-en-Dal*, *Crocodile Bridge*, *Lower Sabie*, *Pretoriuskop*, *Skukuza*, *Letaba*, *Mopani*, *Olifants*, *Orpen*, *Satara*, *Shingwedzi* and *Punda Maria*.

Private Camps

The private camps are smaller and more remote, and do not have facilities such as shops, restaurants, or petrol stations. Many do not have electricity and rely on solar power

The 5 private camps offer secluded luxury accommodation. These camps are ideal for a large group of friends since the whole camp has to be taken with each booking. Each camp has a different choice of accommodation but they all sleep a minimum of 12 people, while some have room for as many as 19 – which could be 4 families with children. Jackalbessie is designed for conference groups. Reservations for these camps should be made well in advance as they offer exceptionally good value if the maximum number of people stay in the camp. The camps are located away from the main public camps, but are close enough for visits to the shops for supplies, they are powered by solar panels which also provide hot water. Although they are privately owned all bookings are dealt with by the South African National Parks (SANPARKS) as for any other accommodation within the park. The 5 camps are: *Jackalbessie* (sleeps 32), *Malelane* (sleeps 19), *Boulders* (sleeps 12), *N'Wanetsi* (sleeps 16) and *Roodewal* (sleeps 19).

Bushveld Camps

There are 5 bushveld camps, these are smaller and offer more of a wilderness experience than the main camps, but they also have far fewer facilities. Staying in these camps is one of the best ways to experience Kruger but it does involve a degree of advanced planning. The chalets are all self-catering with fully equipped kitchens, bedding and towels are provided, each chalet can sleep up to 4 people. The 5 camps are: *Biyamiti*, *Shimuwini*, *Talamati*, *Bateleur* and *Sirheni*.

Campsites

Although most of the main public camps have a separate area for caravans, camping and camper vans, there are 2 separate campsites for those people who don't want to share their game viewing experience with a large estate of buildings and all the trappings of the main camps. The only facilities here are what you would expect at any municipal campsite in South Africa, a washblock and communal kitchen facilities, however, each camp has a totally different character. The 2 sites are known as *Maroela* and *Balule*.

Kruger tours

Organized tours of Kruger are widely available throughout South Africa and can be booked in Cape Town, Durban, Johannesburg and Nelspruit. The variety of tours on offer can be baffling so it is a good idea to

Mpumalanga

shop around to get the type of tour you want. Prices vary according to the quality of accommodation, the length of the tour and whether you travel by minibus, open air Land Rover or air conditioned coach.

Tour operators These tours depart and finish in either Johannesburg or Durban, there are many other operators offering 1-2 day tours from the Panorama towns, see these sections for details. *Bundu Bus*, T011-6750767, F6750769. Backpacker tours, regular departures from Johannesburg, 4-8 day overland tours including Kruger. *Indabushe*, T011-4782483, F4762571. 3-5 day all inclusive tours from Johannesburg. *Strelitzia Tours*, 23 Serpentine Dr, Westville 3630, T031-861904, F031-2669404. 5-day tour visiting Hluhluwe, Swaziland, Kruger, and Eastern Transvaal, R3,500 per person, ex-Durban. *Viva*, T011-4768842, F4768835. 3-5 day budget and camping tours, upgrades available to a private lodge. *Wagon Trails*, T011-9078063, F9070913, info@wagon-trails.com Some of the best value camping tours for anyone who wants an enjoyable as well as informative trip; 4 days, 3 nights, with night drives and bush braais – R1380, including pickup/drop off from Johannesburg and Pretoria, strongly recommended, the editors were most impressed with this conscientious company. Regular departures to Kruger, and further afield adventure tours to Zimbabwe and Mozambique. *Wildlife Safaris*, T011-7914238, F7922080. 3-day Kruger tours from R2600, 4-day Kruger/Panorama tours from R3350. Also Sun City transfers.

Southern Kruger

The greatest concentrations of game can be found in southern Kruger and many visitors only ever see this section of the park. The landscape here is more varied than the rest of the park and supports a wider range of animals. The black and white rhinos, wild dogs and lions as well as large numbers of giraffe, impala, wildebeest and zebra attract the greatest number of tourists and most of Kruger's large camps are here.

Ins & outs The entrance gates at **Crocodile Bridge** and **Malelane** are on the southern boundary of the park and are clearly signposted from the N4 running between Nelspruit and Komatipoort. The entrance gates at **Numbi** and **Paul Kruger** are on the southwestern boundary. Numbi Gate is signposted off the R538 between Nelspruit and Hazyview. Paul Kruger Gate is on the R536 from Hazyview.

Berg-En-Dal Near the entrance at Malelane Gate, this large, modern camp has a rather austere
113 km to Lower Sabie institutional feel to it. It is set in a hilly landscape, wooded with acacias, marulas
213 km to Orpen and jackalberry overlooking the Matjulu Dam. There is some interesting game in
92 km to Pretoriuskop this area including giraffe, kudu, white rhino, zebra and wild dog. **Facilities**
165 km to Satara include swimming pool, in-camp trail, environmental centre showing wildlife
72 km to Skukuza films, petrol station, camp shop, restaurant, telephones and laundrette; open to day visitors. The camp accommodates 300 guests when full and offers day and night game drives. The cottages at this camp are slightly larger than the other camps and are more comfortable for three or four people. **Bookings** (48 hours before arrival) T013-7356016.

Price codes: **Sleeping AL** *J le Roux*, 8-bed guest cottage. **AL** *Rhino*, 6-bed guest cottage. **B** *Cottages*, 6
see inside front cover beds, 1 bathroom. **B** *Rondavels*, 3 beds, bathroom, kitchen. **Camping**: **F** camping and caravan park, 70 sites, ablution blocks, kitchen units.

Biyamiti This bushveld camp is in the far south of Kruger on the banks of the Mbiyamiti
26 km to River. It is set in an area of crocodile thorn thicket inhabited by impala, kudu,
Crocodile Gate bushbuck, black and white rhino, lion and leopard. The camp accommodates 70
45 km to Malelane people in 15 cottages. Day walks and night drives with a trained guide can be booked on arrival at the camp.

Sleeping A *Cottage*, 5 beds, 2 bedrooms, self-catering. **B** *Cottage*, 4 beds, self-catering.

Mpumalanga

The camp is next to the park's southern gate. It is a small camp set in acacia woodland. The road from here to Lower Sabie is a good area for seeing large herds of buffalo, kudu, impala, wildebeest and zebra. Lion and cheetah can sometimes be spotted following the large herds. There is a hippo pool on the dirt road to Malelane where elephant and other animals come to drink.

Facilities include petrol station, camp shop, telephones, laundrette; open to day visitors. Night drives are run from here, they need to be booked at the rest camp. These drives are also open to people staying outside the game reserve. Day walks are available from Crocodile Bridge. These hikes will be governed by existing hiking regulations for the park. Guests staying at Crocodile Bridge can now visit a restaurant located just outside of the park. The procedure is usually as follows, guests are picked up from their accommodation approximately 1 hour after the gates have closed and taken to the restaurant in a parks vehicle (take warm clothing). Although the drive back is short, it can often turn into a free mini night drive. Guests have been known to see hippo, leopard, gennet, civet, impala, elephant and more just along the 1 km stretch of road back to the camp. You are not allowed to travel to the restaurant in your own vehicle. **Bookings** (48 hours before arrival) T013-7356012.

Sleeping B *Chalets*, 3 beds, self-catering. **Camping**: F camping and caravan park, ablution block, kitchen units.

Crocodile Bridge

34 km to Lower Sabie
175 km to Orpen
125 km to Pretoriuskop
127 km to Satara
77 km to Skukuza

Kruger Park southern sector

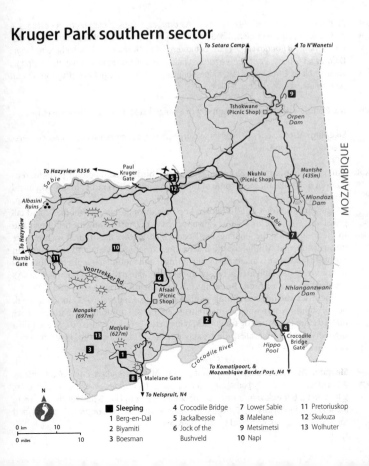

Sleeping

1 Berg-en-Dal
2 Biyamiti
3 Boesman
4 Crocodile Bridge
5 Jackalbessie
6 Jock of the Bushveld
7 Lower Sabie
8 Malelane
9 Metsimetsi
10 Napi
11 Pretoriuskop
12 Skukuza
13 Wolhuter

Mpumalanga

Jackalbessie Jackalbessie is a smart private camp with electricity and cottages with air condition-ing. This is the largest of such camps and is let out for small conference groups. It is on the Sabie River 8 km from Skukuza. This is one of the best game viewing areas in Kruger with impressive numbers of animals passing through the thorn thickets to the river. There are chances of seeing black and white rhino, lions, leopards and wild dog. There are no facilities such as shops, post office and petrol here but the larger public camp, Skukuza, is only a short drive away. **A** *Cottages*, four beds, self-cater-ing. The camp accommodates 32 guests.

Lower Sabie The region around Lower Sabie is part of a classic African savannah landscape, with
113 km to Berg-en-Dal grasslands, umbrella thorn and round leaf teak stretching off into the distance. This
141 km to Orpen is one of the best regions of Kruger for seeing game. Giraffe, kudu, wildebeest, zebra,
53 km to waterbuck and elephant are common around Lower Sabie. It is also regarded as a
Paul Kruger Gate good area to see rhino. It is possible to join a three-hour night drive plus a bush braai
213 km to Phalaborwa in a boma a few kilometres from the camp. Bookings should be made on your arrival
90 km to Pretoriuskop at the office. Game is attracted here by water at the Mlondosi and Nhlanganzwani
342 km to Dams and the Sabi River. The camp overlooks the Sabi River and is a good base for
Punda Maria game drives. The accommodation here is impersonal but the camp itself is fairly
93 km to Satara peaceful. In February 1998 a fire burnt down the shop, reception area and cafeteria.
43 km to Skukuza A smarter complex has since been built, which has improved facilities. **Bookings** (48 hours before arrival): T013-7356056.

Price codes: **Sleeping AL** *Keartland*, 7-bed cottage. **A** *Cottages*, 5 beds, 2 bathrooms. **A** *Cottages*, 4
see inside front cover beds, 2 bathrooms. **B** *Chalets*, 3 beds, bathroom, fridge, hot-plate. **B** *Chalets*, 2 beds, bath-room, fridge. **B** *Rondavels*, 2 beds, bathroom, fridge. **B** *Huts*, 2 beds, bathroom, fridge. **D** *Cottages*, 2 beds, a/c, fridge, veranda, ablution block. **E** *Cottages*, 2, 3, 5 beds, a/c, fridge, ablution block. **E** *Hut*, 1-bed, a/c, fridge, ablution block. **Camping**: **F** camping and caravan park, ablution blocks, kitchen facilities.

Malelane Malelane is a luxury private camp set in a rugged area of mountain bushveld.

Sleeping AL *Malelane*, 19 beds in 5 luxury cottages, communal kitchen, solar powered, check in at Berg-en-Dal.

Pretoriuskop This is the oldest camp in Kruger and is also the third largest. There are plans for ren-
92 km to Berg-en-Dal ovation but at the moment some of the accommodation is rather institutional and
125 km to run down.
Crocodile Bridge The game drives around Pretoriuskop pass through marula woodland and tall
90 km to Lower Sabie grassland. There are good game viewing areas to the north along the Sabi River and
184 km to Orpen to the south along the Voortrekker Road which follows the original wagon route
140 km to Satara through the veld. Rhino are often seen close to Numbi Gate and the mountain
49 km to Skukuza bushveld landscape is inhabited by klipspringer and mountain reedbuck. More ani-mals congregate in this area in the summer rather than in the winter but this is always a rewarding area for game. **Bookings** (48 hours before arrival) T013-7355128.

Facilities include swimming pool made out of natural rock, in-camp trail, petrol station, camp shop, restaurant, telephones, laundrette. Night drives are offered from Pretoriuskop for guest staying in the camp. It is also possible to join a night drive at Numbi Gate if you are staying outside the park in the Hazyview Area; bookings T013-7355133.

Price codes: **Sleeping AL** *Bryant Boma*, 9-bed guest cottage. **AL** *Pierre Joubert*, 8-bed guest cottage.
see inside front cover **A** *Cottages*, 6 beds, 2 bathrooms, self-catering. **B** *Cottages*, 4 beds, 1 bathroom, self-catering. **B** *Rondavels*, 2 beds, bathroom, fridge, hot-plate. **B** *Rondavels*, 2, 4 beds, bathroom, fridge. **E** *Huts*, 2, 3, 5, 6 beds, a/c, fridge, ablution block. **Camping**: **F** camping and caravan park with ablution blocks and kitchen units.

Mpumalanga

Immigration control? Maneaters of Kruger

In South Africa, national parks seem to be used strategically. Much of South Africa's border with Mozambique is taken up by the Kruger Park. The proposed Maputaland National Park would add to this extensive cordon sanitaire along this sensitive border. Soldiers along the Mozambique border, inside the park, claim that they often find the remains of refugees eaten by lions. In 1989 the head warden of the park reported that between 6,000 and 10,000 refugees cross the park every year, spending about 24 hours

walking across. Park officials have complained that Kruger Park lions are becoming man eaters, and that a park warden was killed in 1989 by a lion displaying uncharacteristic behaviour which may have indicated previous exposure to human flesh.

In August 1997 four lions were darted when it was noted they were acting strangely towards Parks Personnel, on closer examination it was found that the stomachs of each lion contained human remains. They had to be shot.

Kruger's largest camp is the administrative centre of the park. The camp has grown to such an extent that it's possible to forget that you're surrounded by a national park. In spite of all the development Skukuza is still at the centre of Kruger's prime game viewing area and is a good base for game drives. The road heading northeast towards Satara has high concentrations of game.

The camp has become a base for arriving in Kruger and is connected by air to Johannesburg for charter companies. **Facilities** here cater to almost every need and include a supermarket, petrol station, car wash, airport, restaurant, bank, post office, telephones, doctor, laundrette. There is also an open air cinema, a good information centre and library, a golf course and a small nursery selling indigenous plants including baobabs. (Yes – you are still in a game park). **Bookings** (48 hours before arrival) T013-7356159. *Kruger Emergency Road Services* are based here, T7355606. The service is not equipped to do any major repairs, but if you break down within the park they will tow you to the nearest garage outside of the park. There's also a **golf course**: bookings and reservations T013-7355611. R60 for 18 holes, R40 for 9 holes.

Skukuza
72 km to Berg-en-Dal
77 km to Crocodile Bridge
43 km to Lower Sabie
137 km to Orpen
213 km to Phalaborwa
49 km to Pretoriuskop
342 km to Punda Maria
93 km to Satara

Sleeping **AL** *Moni*, 8-bed guest cottage. **AL** *Nyathi*, 8-bed guest cottage. **AL** *Volksas*, 8-bed guest cottage. **AL** *Waterkrant*, 8-bed guest cottage. **A** *Cottages*, 6 beds, 2 bathrooms, self-catering. **A** *Cottages*, 4 beds, 2 bathrooms, self-catering. **B** *Cottages*, 4 beds, 1 bathroom, self-catering. **B** *Chalets*, 2 beds, self-catering. **B** *Chalets*, 3 beds, bathroom, fridge, hot-plate. **B** *Rondavels*, 3 beds, bathroom, fridge. **B** *Huts*, 3 beds, bathroom, fridge. **E** *Furnished tents*, 2, 4 beds, ablution block, kitchen units. **Camping**: **F** camping and caravan park, ablution block, kitchen units.

Price codes: see inside front cover

Central Kruger

The central area of Kruger is quieter than the south. There are large areas of flat mopane woodland inhabited by herds of buffalo, elephant, wildebeest and zebra. The camp at Olifants is in a spectacular location.

Orpen Gate and **Phalaborwa Gate** are on the western boundary. Orpen Gate is on the R531 from Acornhoek and Phalaborwa is on the R71 route from Pietersburg and Tzaneen.

Ins & outs

Balule is near the Olifants River and is one of Kruger's wildest camps. It is little more than a patch of cleared bush surrounded by an electrified chain link fence. Visitors camping next to the fence can see animals wandering by only yards away. There are very few facilities here for cooking but this is an ideal site for a braai in the bush. The

Balule

smell of barbecued meat attracts hyenas who patrol the fence all night in search of scraps. Balule is 11 km from Olifants where visitors must check in.

Sleeping E *Huts*, 3 beds, no electricity, ablution block, kitchen units. **Camping**: **F** basic campsite with ablution block and braai sites, firewood is on sale here.

Boulders
54 km to Letaba
31 km to Mopani
54 km to
Phalaborwa Gate

This unfenced private camp is in an area of acacia, knobthorn and mopane woodland. The camp blends in beautifully with its environment and is set amongst massive granite boulders. The thatched buildings are raised on stilts and have a veranda from which to observe the wildlife wandering through the camp.

Sleeping AL *Boulders*, 12 beds in 4 bungalows, communal kitchen, solar power, check in at Mopani.

Kruger Park central sector

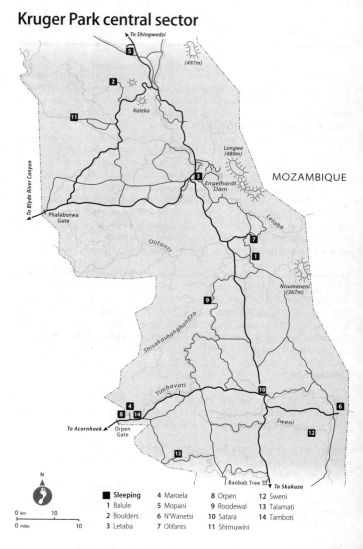

Sleeping		4 Maroela	8 Orpen	12 Sweni
1 Balule	5 Mopani	6 N'Wanetsi	9 Roodewal	13 Talamati
2 Boulders	6 N'Wanetsi	10 Satara	14 Tamboti
3 Letaba	7 Olifants	11 Shimuwini	

The Magnificent Seven

The herds of elephant which roam around Kruger migrating from east to west are one of the park's biggest attractions. The population was estimated at 7,500 in 1992, and has grown substantially from the 986 elephants found during the aerial census of 1959. Elephants have voracious appetites and will eat bark, fruit, leaves and roots. The damage caused by feeding elephants is easy to spot and they have played an important role in the creation of the African landscape. However, too many elephants in a restricted area can cause serious damage to trees and shrubs.

The air conditioned Prospectors Museum at Letaba has an amazing display on elephants. There is a small theatre showing wildlife videos and a large hall dedicated to the lifecycle of the elephant.

The most impressive section of the museum must be the 'Magnificent Seven'. These were Kruger's finest elephants who became famous for their exceptionally large tusks. The skulls and tusks are accompanied by a photo of the elephant and a map showing each animal's range.

Letaba

234 km to Berg-en-Dal
117 km to Orpen
51 km to Phalaborwa
176 km to Punda Maria
69 km to Satara
162 km to Skukuza

Letaba is one of the larger public camps in Central Kruger and is a pleasant place to visit whilst travelling through this area. This is a large neatly laid out camp on the banks of the Letaba River. The restaurant is in a magnificent setting for watching the game come down to drink. Some interesting species can be seen here, most notably the large herds of elephant, but the list also includes cheetah, lion, ostrich, roan, sable, steenbok and tsessebe. There is good game viewing to the east of Letaba along the river and at Engelhardt Dam. The two hills rising in the distance to the east of the dam are Longwe, 480 m, and Mhala, 465 m. They are flanked by some beautiful round-leaf teak woodland and baobabs. Middelvlei windmill is 20 km north of Letaba on the H1-6 and provides the only source of water for miles around. **Bookings** (48 hours before arrival) T013-7356636. **Facilities** include mini supermarket, good restaurant, laundrette, petrol station, Kruger Emergency Road Services, there is a short nature trail around the camp. Night drives are offered from the camp.

Sleeping AL *Fish Eagle*, 8-bed guest cottage. AL *Melville*, 9-bed guest cottage. A *Cottages*, 6 beds, 2 bathrooms, self-catering. B *Chalets*, 2, 3 beds, bathroom, fridge, hot-plate. B *Chalets*, 2 beds, bathroom, fridge. B *Rondavels*, 2, 3 beds, bathroom, fridge. D *Huts*, 4 beds, a/c, fridge, veranda. E *Furnished tents*, 4 beds. **Camping**: F there is a large shadeless camping and caravan park with ablution blocks and kitchen units.

Price codes:
see inside front cover

Maroela

This large camping site is 4 km from Orpen Gate. There are no facilities here. There is a shop less than 3 km away at Orpen Camp which is one of the few main camps which does not have a camping area or restaurant. All the accommodation at Orpen is self-catering. F camping and caravan site, ablution blocks, kitchen units.

Tamboti

Not far from Maroela is another tented camp offering accommodation in furnished safari tents for two to four people. This is the ideal spot for people looking for a complete bush experience without having to bring all the equipment. There is no restaurant or shop here. Check in is at Orphen Gate, the site is on the banks of the Timbavati River.

Mopani

281 km to Berg-en-Dal
47 km to Letaba
86 km to Olifants
74 km to Phalaborwa Gate
258 km to Punda Maria
209 km to Skukuza

This is one of Kruger's largest new public camps set on a rocky hill overlooking the Pioneer Dam. It is only a few kilometres south of the Tropic of Capricorn set on a seemingly endless plain of mopane shrub. This area is inhabited by elephant, buffalo, giraffe, roan, tsessebe, sable, wildebeest, zebra, lions and hyenas who are attracted here by the year-round waters of the dam. The chalets at Mopani have been made from natural materials and are more pleasant than some of the older camps. **Facilities** include swimming pool, nature trail, petrol station, shop, restaurant, cafeteria, laundrette. **Bookings** (48 hours before arrival) T013-7356536.

Mpumalanga

Sleeping AL *Xanatseni*, 8-bed guest cottage. **B** *Chalets*, 2, 3 beds, self-catering.

N'wanetsi This luxury private camp is close to the Mozambique border and the Lebombo Mountains. The camp is set in a rugged area of mountain bushveld overlooking the N'wanetsi River.

Sleeping AL *N'wanetsi*, 16 beds in 6 huts, communal kitchen, ablution block. Check in at Satara.

Olifants This peaceful camp is in a spectacular setting high on a hill overlooking the fever

219 km to Berg-en-Dal
147 km to Lower Sabie
102 km to Orpen
158 km to Paul Kruger Gate
83 km to Phalaborwa Gate
212 km to Punda Maria
147 km to Skukuza

trees and wild figs lining the banks of the Olifants River. The game drives in the immediate area pass through flat mopane woodland in the north and a hilly area of rocks and woodland in the south where klipspringer are often seen.

Olifants is one of Kruger's most attractive camps blending into the surrounding woodland, the thatched chalets are shaded by large old sycamores and sausage trees. The thatched veranda perched on the edge of the camp looks down into the river valley and is a superb place for game viewing. **Facilities** restaurant, shop, information centre, wildlife films, petrol, laundrette, open to day visitors. **Bookings** (48 hours before arrival) T013-7356606.

Sleeping AL *Ellis-Nshawu*, 8-bed guest cottage. **AL** *Doherty*, 8-bed guest cottage. **B** *Cottages*, 4 beds, self-catering. **B** *Chalets*, 2 beds, self-catering. **B** *Chalets*, 2 beds, bathroom, fridge, hot-plate. **B** *Rondavels*, 2, 3 beds, bathroom, fridge.

Orpen Orpen is a small camp just past the entrance gate on the western central plains set amongst acacias, marulas and aloes. The road passing along the Timbavati River offers the chance of seeing giraffe, kudu, sable, white rhino, wildebeest and zebra. The area around the camp is known as a good place to see leopard, lion and cheetah.

The camp itself is not particularly attractive and time in Kruger can be better spent in the other camps. **NB** All the accommodation at Orpen is self-catering, there is no restaurant at the camp, basic supplies can be bought from the camp shop during office hours. **Facilities** include petrol station, camp shop, and it's open to day visitors. **Bookings** (48 hours before arrival) T013-7356355.

Sleeping A *Cottages*, 6 beds, self-catering. **D** *Huts*, 3 beds, ablution block, communal cooking area.

Roodewal Roodewal is a private camp on the Timbavati River, 29 km from Olifants and 42 km from Satara. The camp has a platform built around a nyala tree which overlooks a waterhole. **AL** *Roodewal*, 19 beds in one cottage and five A-frame huts, communal kitchen and dining room, check in at Satara.

Satara Satara, Kruger's second largest camp, is rather incongruous in that it looks like a

Berg-en-Dal 15 km;
Crocodile Bridge
127 km; Letaba 69 km;
Lower Sabie 93 km;
Orpen 48 km; Paul
Kruger Gate 104 km;
Pretoriuskop 140 km;
Punda Maria 245 km;
Skukuza 93 km

motorway service station in the middle of the bush. The institutional atmosphere of the accommodation is softened by the trees and lawns. Satara is set in the flat grasslands of the eastern region which attract large herds of wildebeest, buffalo, kudu, impala, zebra and elephant. There is good game viewing on the road to Orpen. **Bookings** (48 hours before arrival) T013-7356306. **Facilities** include petrol station, car wash, Kruger Emergency Road Service, camp shop, cafeteria, restaurant and laundrette. Open to day visitors. Night drives, starting at 2030, R70 per person.

Sleeping AL *Rudy Frankel*, 8-bed guest cottage. **AL** *Stanley*, 9-bed guest cottage. **AL** *Wells*, 6-bed guest cottage. **A** *Cottages*, 5, 6 beds, self-catering. **B** *Chalets*, 2 beds, bathroom, fridge, hot-plate. **B** *Chalets*, 3 beds, bathroom, fridge. **B** *Rondavels*, 3 beds, bathroom, fridge. **Camping**: **F** camping and caravan park, ablution blocks, kitchen units.

Mpumalanga

The name Shimuwini means 'the place of the baobab'. The quantity of game in this region of bushwillow and mopane woodland is not as great as in the south of Kruger. However, this is still an interesting wilderness area with a good variety of game. There are good possibilities of seeing sable and eland as well as the more common animals such as giraffe, kudu, wildebeest and zebra. The private access road leading to Shimuwini follows the Letaba River where elephant can sometimes be seen bathing. The riverine forest around the camp is good for birdwatching.

Shimuwini bushveld camp overlooks the Shimuwini Dam. Visitors to the camp have private access to the dam which is surrounded by giant sycamore trees. There is a hide here from which to see crocodiles, hippo, waterbuck and waterbirds. The camp consists of a row of thatched cottages shaded by appleleaf trees and acacias. The bushveld camp was badly destroyed by flood waters and was one of the last to reopen in the park – in late 2000.

Shimuwini
66 km to Letaba
118 km to Olifants
52 km to Phalaborwa

Sleeping A *Cottage*, 5, 6 beds, self-catering. **B** *Cottage*, 4 beds, self-catering. The camp can accommodate up to 70 visitors and offers day and night game drives.

The camp is set on the banks of the Nwaswitsonto River which is normally dry. The grassland and acacia woodland along the western boundary attract kudu, giraffe, sable and white rhino. Klipspringer can be seen on the rocky outcrops. There are two hides in the camp for game viewing and birdwatching. The camp accommodates 80 visitors, and offers day and night game drives.

Talamati
30 km to Orpen Gate

Sleeping A *Cottage*, 6 beds, self-catering. **B** *Cottage*, 4 beds, self-catering.

Northern Kruger

The northern sector of Kruger was originally called the Shingwedzi Game Reserve, which covered the region between the Letaba and the Luvuvhu rivers. The reserve was added to the park in 1903 but the park wasn't opened to the public until 1933 when a road was built from the bridge over the Letaba River to Punda Maria. The first rangers' camp on the banks of the Tsende River was totally isolated and run by Major AA Fraser who lived with a pack of dogs and survived on whisky and tobacco.

This is a dry and remote region rarely visited by tourists. Because there is no year-round water supply, there isn't the same density of animals as in the south. But the area does support animals unique to this part of Kruger including Sharpe's grysbok, tsessebe, sable, nyala and leopard. The landscape is covered with mopane woodland, jackalberry, sausage tree, leadwood and baobab.

The Luvuvhu River offers some of the best wildlife viewing. The river banks are lined with ironwood, ebony and sycamore fig. Huge pythons thrive in the thick forests and some of the largest crocodiles in Kruger can be seen in the Luvuvhu River.

The bridge over the Luvuvhu is an excellent spot for birdwatchers after heavy rains. Many birds are attracted to the fruit trees, some of the unusual species which can be seen here are the Cape parrot, Basra reed warbler, tropical boubou and yellowbellied sunbird. Two interesting raptors here are Ayre's eagle and Dickinson's kestrel. The picnic site at Mooiplaas between Letaba and Shingwedzi overlooks a waterhole on the Tsende River where game can often be seen.

Punda Maria Gate and **Pafuri Gate** are in the far north of the park. Punda Maria Gate is on the R524 and can be reached from Louis Trichardt. Pafuri Gate is in the far north and can be reached from Venda. **NB** The far north of Kruger Park was the most severely damaged by the floods in February 2000. Two large rivers flow through the area, each was seen to carry more water than ever before. At one stage the Luvuvhu river was 2.8 km wide and the Limpopo 15 km at the confluence. All the roads and bridges in the area had to be completely rebuilt, all of which have been completed.

Ins & outs

Mpumalanga

Bateleur
37 km to Shingwedzi
Bateleur is an isolated bushveld camp surrounded by a vast area of mopane and acacia woodland with the Phonda Hills (400 m) lying to the north. Visitors to the camp have exclusive access to the two nearby dams, Rooibosrand and Silverfish both of which are good areas for game watching especially for sable and nyala. There is a viewing platform nearby overlooking a waterhole which is best seen after the rains. The camp is solar powered and accommodates up to 34 visitors, offering day and night game drives.

Sleeping A *Cottages*, 6 beds, self-catering. **B** *Cottages*, 4 beds, self-catering.

Shingwedzi
This is the most northerly large camp, most of the chalets are brick units arranged in a large circle looking in on an open area which has no grass, just a shady area of short mopane trees. The restaurant has a pleasant outside terrace where one can sit during

Kruger Park northern sector

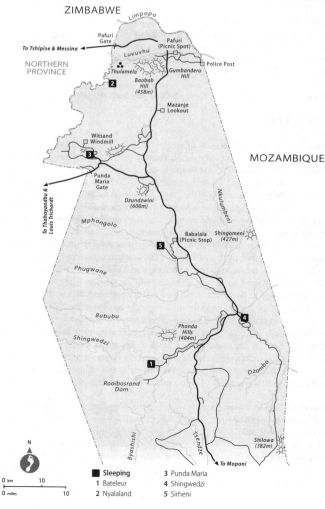

Hermits

In the early years of the park the region was a massive wilderness which attracted hermits. During the 1940s a hermit lived naked by the Olifants River for five years. He made his home in enlarged aardvark holes and lived off fruit and game. The park authorities left him in peace, partly because there were not enough people to catch him – he could run and hide too well through the bush – and partly because he wasn't causing any trouble.

However, he was eventually caught after he began stealing equipment from the

rangers. A group of them tracked him to his shelter and surprised him late one night while he was sleeping next to his fire. The hermit luckily escaped and the rangers recovered the knives, pots and pans that he had stolen.

Finally, an anti-poaching patrol caught the him after surprising him on the banks of the Olifants River. He stumbled whilst trying to escape and the rangers grabbed him and tied him up. Unfortunately he was prosecuted for poaching and committed to a lunatic asylum.

---

the day and look out over the Shingwedzi River. There is plenty of space in the campsite, but there is limited shade and virtually no grass; the site is well away from the cottages and chalets. The best game viewing in this area is around Kanniedood Dam and the riverine forest along the banks of the Shingwedzi. Many animals from the surrounding areas come here for water. There is a bird hide south of the camp on the S134 overlooking the river. **Facilities** include a restaurant, cafeteria, shop, petrol, information centre, swimming pool and laundrette. Night drives can be booked at reception.

Sleeping A *Cottage*, 4 beds, self-catering. **B** *Chalets*, 2 beds, bathroom, fridge. **C** *Chalets*, 2 beds, self-catering. **C** *Rondavels*, 2 beds, bathroom, fridge. **E** *Huts*, 3 beds, fridge, veranda, ablution blocks, kitchen facilities. **Camping**: **F** camping and caravan park, ablution block.

Price codes: see inside front cover

This peaceful rest camp hidden by dense woodland is the northernmost large public camp in Kruger. It is situated in a unique area of sandveld dotted with baobabs, white seringa and pod mahogany. There are spectacular views of the surrounding landscapes from the top of Dzundzwini (600 m). There is good game viewing near the camp on the Mahonie Loop and up by the Witsand windmill. Look out for nyala and kudu. The game drive north to Pafuri passes through mopane shrubveld inhabited by roan, sable and tsessebe. The bridge over the Luvuvhu River is a top place for birdwatchers where many species of bird are attracted to the fruit trees along the banks of the river. This is the only area in the park where you can see and enjoy Mopani Forest.

Punda Maria was named after the zebra that Captain JJ Coetzer saw when he first arrived here, he mistakenly believed punda maria to be the Swahili word for zebra, it is in fact *punda milia*, but the first name has stuck. **Facilities** include restaurant, shop and petrol. The short Paradise Flycatcher nature trail wanders around the camp. **Bookings** (48 hours before arrival) T013-7356873.

Thulamela has turned out to be an important Late Iron Age archaeological site in the northern corner of Kruger Park close to the Levuvhu River. It is an important site that has forced people to reconsider their understanding and interpretation of the local regional history.

Sidney Miller was responsible for the excavation project which was sponsored by the Gold Fields Foundation. Aside from clearing all the vegetation and collecting items such as spearheads, pots, beads, bracelets and harpoons, the team embarked upon an ambitious project of rebuilding some of the stone walls which had originally been built over 400 years ago. The whole site lies on the top of a sub-plateau which is reached after a steep 25 minutes' climb. It is estimated that more than 1,500 people lived here. The stone enclosure was a royal palace which during its heyday in the Khami period was an important commercial centre of a powerful agro-pastoral

Punda Maria
By far the most pleasant of camps in Kruger, but you will never see as much game in this area as you will in the south of the park

The camp is 8 km from the Punda Maria Gate Berg-en-Dal 415 km; Letaba 176 km; Mopani 130 km; Phalaborwa Gate 201 km; Shingwedzi 71 km; Skukuza 342 km

Mpumalanga

Crooks' Corner and the Ivory Trail

In the 1900s this area of Transvaal was a favourite haunt for poachers and hunters who lived at the confluence of the Limpopo and the Luvuvhu rivers on the borders of Rhodesia, Mozambique and the Transvaal. Their base here was known as Crooks' Corner and was on the 'Ivory Trail'. The camp itself was little more than a few

corrugated iron shacks where traders, poachers and bandits would congregate. Its location near the three borders meant that whenever the authorities came to apprehend anyone they could cross a border and escape to another jurisdiction. Punda Maria was originally built for the park rangers to obstruct the 'Ivory Trail'.

kingdom. Evidence collected at Thulamela points towards a thriving metal-working community producing spearheads and hoe blades in iron as well as more delicate items from copper and gold. During the 16th century it is likely that Thulamela traded with people from Zimbabwe and possibly traders who travelled up the eastern coast as far as Egypt. There are two daily guided walking tours with a ranger to Thulamela which depart from the Pafuri picnic spot. **Bookings** at Sirheni, Shingwedzi, Punda Maria, and Pafuri Gate.

Gumbandevu Hill used to be a traditional centre for rain makers where offerings of livestock and snuff were given in return for rain. The sounds of a goat being sacrificed at the base of the hill helped to summon the spirits which made rain. The hill is still thought to be haunted and is always greener than the surrounding area.

This is a small camp and is often booked at weekends

Sleeping The food in the restaurant is better than other camps. **B** *Cottages*, 4 beds, self-catering. **B** *Chalets*, 2 beds, self-catering. **B** *Rondavels*, 2 beds, bathroom, fridge, ablution block, communal kitchen. **Camping: F** camping and caravan park, ablution block.

Sirheni
28 km to Shingwezi
48 km to Punda Maria

This is a bushveld camp overlooking Sirheni Dam. It is surrounded by mopane and acacia woodlands. This is a good game viewing and birdwatching area inhabited by eland and sable. Giraffe, kudu, elephant and lion are also here but not in the same concentrations as they are in southern Kruger. The road approaching the camp from the south on the S66 passes through the alluvial plains and riverine forest of the Mphongolo River, inhabited by leopard, nyala and waterbuck. It is signposted off the H1-7. **Bookings** (48 hours before arrival) T013-7356806. The camp accommodates up to 80 visitors and offers day and night bush drives.

Sleeping A *Cottages*, 6 beds, self-catering. **B** *Cottages*, 4 beds, self-catering.

Approaching Kruger National Park from Zimbabwe

Unless you are starting your journey from a hotel in **Beitbridge**, the route into Kruger National Park from Zimbabwe is a long one. Just outside the **Pafuri Gate** in the northern part of the park is **D-F** *Waller's Camp*. This camp does very well during the holidays, when visitors coming from Zimbabwe who do not have a reservation for **Punda Maria** or **Shingwedzi**, but wish to visit Thulamela, end up staying a couple of days.

Nelspruit to Blyde River Canyon

Colour map 2, grid B5

The route north of Nelspruit gradually climbs up into the Eastern Drakensberg, generally referred to as the Panorama region. This is an area of pretty towns filled with country restaurants and craft shops, all within easy reach of the spectacular Blyde River Canyon, the third largest canyon in the world. The mountains are a pleasant change from the heat on the plains of the Lowveld.

Adventure activities

There is more to Mpumalanga than game viewing and tea shops. The Panorama region is a land of cliffs, waterfalls, forests, mountains, and valleys. In true South African outdoor lifestyle tradition, these environments are perfect for hiking, mountain biking, quad biking, horse riding, ballooning, micro-lighting, white water rafting, abseiling – even gorge swinging or *kloofing* (a combination of rock hopping, waterfall diving, and bum sliding). Many of these activities are listed in the relevant areas, though there are a number that can be tried at several locations throughout the Panorama region.

Tour operators

There are so many tour operators in this region, it is impossible to list them all. The best way to book an activity in the Panorama region is to go through *Big 5 Country*, a division of the *Lowveld Tourism Association*, Nelspruit, T013-7378191, F7378384, goldenm@mweb.co.za, www.big5country.com This is a central reservations organization that represents most of the activity operators in the area.

White Water Rafting

The tamest rafting routes for the whole family or feint hearted are on the lower **Blyde River**, 3 km of mild rapids, or the **Sabie River**, 3-hr trips through well-wooded banks, finishing with a

Blyde River Canyon & Drakensberg

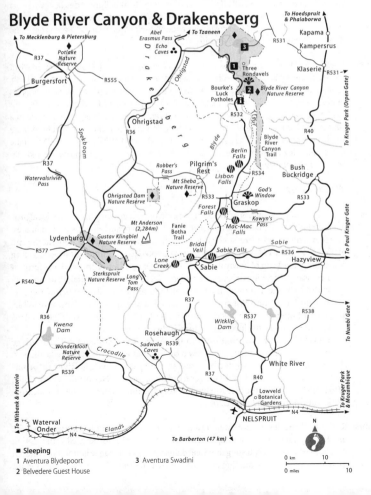

■ Sleeping
1 Aventura Blydepoort
2 Belvedere Guest House
3 Aventura Swadini

Mpumalanga

35 m abseil if desired. A day on the **Olifants River** takes you over Grade 2-3 rapids and the odd Grade 4 rapid that can be avoided if you walk around. Arguably the best river action in South Africa is at the **northern section of the Blyde River**, 8 km of intense rapids with the occasional Grade 5, which can also be walked around. A 5-km ferry trip on the Blydepoort Dam is usually included on this day trip. For the adrenaline junkie, day or multi-day trips on Blyde River and Olifants River offer a combination of exciting rapids and gentle paddles through some spectacular scenery, over-night in either riverside bush camps, local accommodation or a combination of both. There is a choice of rafting trips between 1-3 days.

Expect to pay around R150 for the shorter tips, or R300-400 per day

Operators There are several operators, and when choosing you are advised to check that they are members of the *South African River Association* (SARA). All the tourism offices in the Panorama region can supply further information and make reservations. *Big 5 Country*, central reservations (as above). *Hardy Ventures*, T7511693, F7511693, T083-6318633 (mob), ask for Stephen Hardy, a choice of 3 rivers for all ages and experience. *Otter's Den White Water Rafting*, T015-7955250, T082-5722223 (mob). Olifants and Blyde River rafting.

Scenic flights The Blyde River Canyon region and the Sabie Valley look even more impressive from the air. **Helicopter** trips from 15 min to 1 hr fly right into the canyon and dip down to the various waterfalls in the region, R500-1500 pp. Early morning (1-hr) **balloon rides** float wherever the wind maybe going over the Sabie Valley, R1300 pp, and **micro light** flights from Hazyview take in Graskop, God's Window, and the Sabie River, R350 pp. Reservations and detailed information from *Big 5 Country*, (as above).

Quad biking Quad biking (4-wheel motorbikes) is an up and coming sport in the Sabie valley, excellent fun and totally exhilarating. One or 2 hour guided trails run through scenic indigenous bush, plantation areas, along the Sabie River and other streams. For those who have never ridden a motorbike before, opt for an automatic bike. Riders must be over 16 with a car licence, but passengers can be younger. Goggles and helmets are provided, and quite often drinks or a light snack. There are several operators in the region but when choosing ensure they are adequately insured. Expect to pay around R300 for 1 hr and R400 for a 2-hr ride. Any of the tourist offices in the Panorama region can be contacted for reservations and further information, or *Big 5 Country*, (as above).

White River

Phone code: 013
(NB Always use 3-figure prefix)
Colour map 2, grid B5
Altitude: 800 m

This small country town is at the centre of a citrus fruit growing area, fresh local produce includes macadamia nuts, pecans, cashews, avocados, litchis and mangoes. The first settlers here were Boer cattle ranchers who arrived in the 1880s, at the end of the Anglo-Boer War a new settlement was created to accommodate a new farming community made up of newly demobilized soldiers. Although the land was fertile it was necessary to provide irrigation in order to realize its full potential. With an average size of 40 ha the holdings were too small to support a family, just before the outbreak of the First World War a syndicate started to buy up as much land as possible. The scale of operations changed overnight, by 1915 there were over 60,000 citrus trees planted, and so the local agricultural industry was born.

Lowveld Tourist Information is in the White River Museum at Casterbridge Farm, 2 km from town on the Hazyview road. It's only a small desk littered with brochures and leaflets, but worth a browse if you are passing. **White River Information**, Kruger Park St, 1 km from the centre of town towards Nelspruit, PO Box 2387, T/F7500845, is a private office run by a friendly and informative couple. Local information and accommodation bookings.

Sights **Rottcher Wineries**, is more than just a winery. Why not tour the nuttery, visit the macadamia nut farm, or tour the Nutcracker Valley Nut Factory as well as the visiting the Orange Winery. Try tasting the sweet golden Avalencia orange liquor. For children there is a riding school offering pony and horse rides each day. ■ *In the heart of the*

Nutcracker Valley a short distance from White River. T7513884, F7513472. Open Mon-Fri 0800-1700; Sat 0800-1500; Sun in season 0900-1300. Tours 1000 and 1400. Garden restaurant open through the day. Expect plenty of nut dishes.

There is a selection of luxury of high standard B&Bs and guest farms within a 20 km radius of White River, check with *White River Information*, for details and bookings.

Sleeping
■ *on map*
Price codes:
see inside front cover

A *Hulala Lakeside Lodge*, 22 km from White River on the R40 towards Hazyview, T/F7641893. Situated on a peninsula in a lake that gives the feeling of being on an island, this lodge has recently been renovated to the highest standard. 12 luxury suites, private lounge, fireplace, TV, secluded patios overlooking the garden or lake, fine dining in the restaurant, pool, 2 bars. The most popular activity is boating but powerboats are banned, maintaining some peace and tranquillity. However, there is a choice of canoes, rowing boats, specially adapted boats for anglers, or the nightly sundowner cruise. A romantic setting, recommended for couples. **B** *Balcony Guest House*, 51 Frank Townsend St, T7512015, F7512481. 2 double a/c rooms with en suite bathroom, TV, non-smoking, 2 suites, all set in a fine old double-storey house with an elegant upstairs balcony, a lot of thought has gone into the décor, which is a mix of modern fittings with antique furnishings, each room has its own unique character, mature gardens, swimming pool, all very ornate, even the breakfast room would not be out of place in a museum. Very smart and recommended. **B** *Greenway Woods*, T7511094, F7513512. An all suite hotel set in the beautiful countryside, swimming pool, on a championship golf course, each suite has 2 bathrooms, there is an open fireplace in the lounge, a popular conference venue, relatively new, needs to age a bit before developing the full character of the location. **B** *Igwala Gwala Country Lodge*, 5 km to the south of town off the R40, PO Box 103, T7501723, F7501999. 5 garden suites, each with own entrance and private terrace, glorious large swimming pool, beautiful mature gardens, has a reputation for providing all you can possibly eat breakfasts if you so wish. Highly recommended. **B** *Kirby*

Mpumalanga

White River

To Hazyview, Bag-dad Café, Kruger Park - Numbi Gate (R40) & Canterbury Farm

To Kirby Country Lodge, Plaston & Karula Hotel

To Bird Sanctuary & Danie Joubert Dam

To Balcony Guest House

To Sabie & Nelspruit & Tourist Information

Klepersol   Rudolf

Mopanie

Kiaat

Imbula   Protea   Theo Kleynhans   Tom Lawrence   Kasting   Petani   Cemetery

Tamboot   Ruimsig

Baobab   Maroela   Norwin   OK Bazaar   Sanlam Centre   Ferreira Park   J Theron

Caltex

Engen   Standard   Kruger Park

Tom Lawrence   Willem Swanepoel   Peter Graham   Kraal Kraft   United

Total   CNA   First National

Alec van Belgen   Hennie van Til   Thabo   ABSA   Impala Building   Local Minibuses

Town Hall   Tour d'Afrique

Caltex   Library   Swimming Pool

Kruger Park   Cornwell   Danie Joubert   Engen

N

0 metres   200
0 yards   200

■ **Sleeping**
1 Gleighnelly Country Lodge
2 Legogote Lodge

3 Linga Lodge

● **Eating**
1 Meating Place

2 Savannah Moon
3 Steers
4 Tambuti

Country Lodge, leave town by Kruger Park Rd, follow the signs for Plaston, PO Box 3411, T7512645, F7501836. 9 double rooms with en suite bathroom or shower, lounge, restaurant, bar, swimming pool, beautiful mature gardens with plenty of colour, rates quoted are fully inclusive. **B-C** *Winkler*, 5 km from White River, off the road to Numbi Gate, T7515068, F7515044. A weird-looking circular central building, with 2 'arms' of rooms. 82 double rooms with en suite bathroom, 5 suites, TV, a/c, non-smoking room available, a large but extremely comfortable complex, restaurant, bar, swimming pool, tennis, bowling green. Some rooms have private service hatch for room service delivery – very decadent!

C *Gleighnelly Country Lodge*, Tom Lawrence St, T7511100, F7511200. Hardly a country lodge, as it is in the middle of town, but not an unpleasant setting overlooking the park. Newly built businessman's hotel of usual quality, TV, a/c, spacious rooms, pool, close to town restaurants and pubs. **C-D** *Legogote Lodge*, 10 Kiepersol St, T7501254, F7501207. Restaurant, bar, swimming pool, a large modern hotel with 2-bed bungalows or 4-bed family bungalows. **C-D** *Karula*, Old Plaston Rd, PO Box 279, 1 km from town centre, T7512277, F7500413. 42 double rooms with en suite bathroom, TV, restaurant, bar, swimming pool, tennis, billiard room, a slightly dated, old fashioned hotel but nevertheless it is popular and has an excellent local reputation. A perfect base from which to explore the region. Rates include set 5-course dinner so brush up on use of silverware. **E-F** *Flamboyant Rondavels*, 6 km towards Nelspruit, T7581133. Basic huts behind a supermarket and service station, private shower, fridge, pool, pay extra for a kitchen. Simple overnight budget accommodation if you have a car. **F** *Lalela Backpackers*, 6 km from White River, off R40 towards Nelspruit, T7512812, T082-7763669 (mob). A new backpackers on a farm at the top of a picturesque valley with great views from the pool and terrace. 1 dorm in the main house, outside kitchen and braai area, ablution blocks, camping, 6 unique tepees in the garden sleeping 2-4 people, these can get unbearably hot in the summer but cosy in the winter when coal fires are supplied inside. We have had good recommendations so far. Are presently renovating another house into B&B accommodation. Free pick-ups from White River and Nelspruit.

Eating
● *on map*

Unlike other South African small towns that are overrun with the usual chicken or burger chains, White River has a variety of good quality individual restaurants and the local people seem to enjoy the restaurant scene. Even if you are not staying here, it is worth making sure you pass through at lunchtime. *Bag-dad Café*, out of town on the R40 at the Safari Junction shopping centre, T7511777. Open for breakfast, lunch and dinner, bookings essential for dinner, delicious homemade pies and breads, takeaway service and specially prepared picnic hampers. *Greenway Woods*, T7511094. Luxury hotel restaurant in a lovely setting, with a price tag to match. If you want to splash out, this is the place to go but check first to ensure the hotel is not overrun with conference delegates. *Meating Place*, corner of Tom Lawrence and Peter Graham streets, T7501076. New restaurant and lively pub popular with the local people. *Savannah Moon*, corner of Tom Lawrence and William Lynne streets, T7511727. Smart restaurant and casual pizza counter, plus a ladies bar, good for pub lunches. *Tambuti*, 11 Kruger Park St, T7512895. Game meat, steaks, prawns, special offers on pub lunches during the week. *10 Green Bottles Bistro*, at Casterbridge Farm, 2 km out of town towards Hazyview, T7501097. Mixed menu in pleasant, atmospheric converted farm building. Pretty outside terrace that gets very busy during the day with passing traffic.

Shopping

Casterbridge Farm, 2 km from White River on the R40 to Hazyview. A small shopping centre in some converted farm buildings. Railway sleeper teak furniture, leather goods, art galleries, ceramics, *10 Green Bottles* restaurant (see above), bookshop, and the small Barnyard Theatre – worth checking out local productions if you are staying in the area. The White River Museum is situated here, a collection of fine vintage cars loaned by a local collector; interesting if you like cars, but don't be misled by the museum's name, there is nothing on display here from the area. Across the road is a similar tourist centre (see below). *Safari Junction*, opposite Casterbridge Farm, 2 km from White River on the R40 to Hazyview, Mon-Sun 0830-1800. A small shopping centre selling African handicrafts, furniture, safari clothes and books. The nursery sells a fascinating selection of bonsais grown from indigenous trees, small indigenous African butterfly sanctuary that is worth a look, free of charge.

The delicatessen sells home-made jams, cheeses, chocolates, and fresh trout. The *Bag-dad Café* is also here (see above).

Balloons Over Africa, T/F7525265. Contact Kevin for info on 1-hr flights. *Katambora Safaris*, T/F7513339. Backpacker priced day and night safaris into Kruger. *Mfafa Safaris*, T7501782/3, F7501909. Kruger tours. **Tour operators**

Road White River is 20 km from **Nelspruit** on the R40. The entrance to Kruger Park at **Numbi Gate** (35 km), is signposted off the R538 heading north towards **Hazyview** (40 km). **Sabie** (45 km) and **Graskop** (70 km) are northwest on the R537. **Bus:** *Lowveld Link*, T7501174. Combi service to **Johannesburg** (5 hrs), and **Pretoria** (4 hrs), via **Nelspruit** (30 mins), departs Mon-Sat at 0700, Sun at 1100. **Car hire:** *Avis*, T7411087; *Imperial*, T7413210; *Budget*, T7413871. Will deliver a car to you in White River. All companies have offices at Nelspruit Airport. **Transport**

Useful services **Ambulance:** T7532285. **Medical Centre:** T7500063. **Police:** T7500888. **Directory**

Hazyview

Hazyview lies on the banks of the Sabie River in the hot lowveld country on the southwestern border of Kruger. It is a large area of banana plantations. While the facilities for tourists here have been growing since the first visitors to Kruger in the 1920s and the 1930s, the village was only promulgated as late as 1959 when the first post office was established. There is a wide range of accommodation from timeshares and caravan parks to luxury private game reserves, should the facilities in the park be fully booked.

Phone code: 013
(NB Always use 3-figure prefix)
Colour map 2, grid B5

Panorama Tourist Information, at the Simynye Centre, T7377414, F7377410, info@saftour.co.za, is another helpful regional office, part of the same association that has offices in Sabie and Graskop. Contact in advance for all accommodation and activity bookings, agents for *Avis*, knowledgeable about many of the private camps in Kruger.

It is possible to take a 'cultural tour' of a village where a **Shangana** family lives, descendants of Chief Shoshangana, an important turn of the century tribal leader of the region. Not a gawking tourist experience quite often seen in other 'cultural villages' around the country, this family is keen to prolong their rich traditions and tribal dignity for as long as possible, and if it is tourism that helps them do this, then it is well worthwhile supporting. Tours follow a path through the bush to the village, where a guide explains the family's way of life before moving on to a kraal for a lesson in traditional medicine. On the midday tour a traditional lunch is included, and in the evening, a festival dinner is served inside the huts where the history of the Shanganas is presented by singers and dancers. Try and go to the evening festival, the display is visually spectacular and moving, and the food is quite delicious, a recommended African experience for adults and children alike. ■ *Daytime tours by arrangement between, 0900-1700; midday tours, phone and book for lunch; Evening festival, 1800 in summer, 1715 in winter, bookings essential. T7377000, 5 km from Hazyview on the R535 to Graskop.* **Sights**

A *Sabi River Sun*, PO Box 13, T7377311, F7377314, on the R536 to Sabie. 60 rooms, 74 self-catering chalets, a luxurious riverside setting in 85 acres of private bushveld, restaurants, bars and a full range of sporting facilities. **B** *Hazyview Protea*, on the R40 to White River, PO Box 105, T7377332, F7377335. 48 rooms, 28 self-catering chalets, bars, restaurants, swimming pool, full range of sporting facilities. Pleasant country hotel. **B** *Hippo Hollow Country Estate*, off the R40 en route to Paul Kruger Gate, T7376624, F7377673. Selection of self-catering thatched cottages, or hotel rooms, overlooking the Sabie River, restaurant, guests bar, curio shop. Watch the hippos on the lawn at night. **C** *Rissington Inn*, T7377700, F7377112. Comfortable double rooms with en suite facilities. Neat gardens, views of the **Sleeping**
Price codes:
see inside front cover

Mpumalanga

river, swimming pool. Recommended. **C** *Safari Lodge*, on the R40 to White River, PO Box 79, T7377113, F7377258. 2 beds, 4-bed family rooms and rondavels in quest farm-style accommodation, restaurant, bar, indoor swimming pool.

C *Chestnut Country Lodge*, 11 km out of Hazyview off the R40 to White River and Nelspruit, T7378195, F7378196, info@chesnutlodge.co.za A comfortable rural retreat with 8 double rooms with en suite facilities, simple clean rooms, TV, each with a private patio, 1 family suite for 4 people. Evening meals available on request. In front of the swimming pool is a raised wooden platform, the ideal spot for a sundowner or just to watch the birds from. Homely lounge with reference library bar. All only 15 mins' drive from Numbi Gate, making this a perfect base for visitors to Kruger Park who wish a little more comfort and privacy than the national park camps can offer. Often have off-season special deals. Recommended. **C** *Eagle's Nest*, signposted off the R536 to Sabie, T7378434. Self-catering flats, swimming pool, good bushveld views and hikes. **C-D** *Under African Skies*, T/F7376793. Charming garden self-catering flat in quiet residential neighbourhood, good views over the Sabie valley, suitable for a family staying for a few days to explore the region. **F** *Big 5 Backpackers*, just south of Hazyview on the R40, T083-7262140 (mob) or T011-6223663 (office hours). Dorms with thatched roof, double rooms, camping, swimming pool, laundry, tours can be organized to most of the local popular tourist spots, collection from the bus station. **F** *Kruger Park Backpackers*, on the junction of the R40 and the road leading to Numbi Gate, 200 m past the Caltex garage, T7377224. The accommodation is in Zulu huts (with running water and electricity), Kruger and Drakensberg tours are organized from here. This is one of the few hostels in the vicinity of Kruger Park that will collect *Baz Bus* passengers from Nelspruit. There is no charge for this if you subsequently join one of their tours. Most restaurants are in the hotels. *Stuck in the Mud*, 3 km on the R536 to Sabie, T083-7490737 (mob). Farm pub, hearty meals, good salads, open Wed-Sun 1200-late. Famous for their bagel burgers.

Tour operators *Ukuzwana Horse Trails*, Farmhouse Lodge, 10 km from Hazyview on the White River road, T083-3559894 (mob). Daily 1-2-hr rides on a game farm.

Transport **Road** Hazyview is 36 km north of **White River** on the R40. The entrance to Kruger at **Numbi Gate** (16 km) is signposted south of town off the R538; the entrance at **Paul Kruger Gate** (43 km) is on the R536. **Sabie** is 34 km west of Hazyview on the R536. **Graskop** is 24 km west of Hazyview on the R535. The R40 continues north into the Northern (Limpopo) Province to **Acornhoek** (56 km), **Orpen Gate** (100 km), and the private game reserves on Kruger's eastern boundary. The R536 climbs up from the lowveld around Hazyview onto the edge of the Drakensberg escarpment at Sabie.

Directory **Communications** Internet: *Simunye Centre*, T7377811. **Useful services** Ambulance: T10177. **Doctor**: T7377321.0 **Police**: T7377328.

Sabie

Phone code: 013
(NB Always use
3-figure prefix)
Colour map 2, grid B5
Altitude: 1,020 m

Once a gold mining town, Sabie has little left to show of this glistering age, and is now an equally prosaic timber-processing centre. Nevertheless, it is one of the more attractive towns in the region, its main road lined with pleasant craft and coffee shops and its setting a pretty valley ringed by mountains and a landscape dominated by pine and eucalyptus plantations.

Ulusaba means 'River of Fear'. Its crocodiles and strong currents had given it a reputation as a notoriously dangerous place when the propectors turned up

Prospectors first found gold in this region during the 1870s, but it wasn't until 1895 that gold was found at Sabie. The land here belonged to a big game hunter named Glynn who discovered the gold whilst on a picnic at Lower Sabie Falls. Glynn and his friends began shooting at a row of empty bottles on an outcrop of rock – the bullets chipped away at the rock revealing flecks of sparkling gold. This led to an influx of fortune hunters who came and camped on the banks of the Sabi River. In the process of mining gold, many indigenous forests were chopped down to meet the demand for mine props and firewood. Fortunately, the farsighted mine manager, Joseph Brook Shires realized that manmade forests were necessary and planted the first commercial trees in 1876. Planting continued into the next century and created forestry jobs during the 1930s depression.

Today, Sabie lies in one of the largest manmade forests in the world. Driving around this region one is immediately struck by just how many square miles of forest have been cultivated. The endless rows of neatly planted trees are impressive but the remaining patches of indigenous forest give a good indication of just how beautiful these mountains were less than 100 years ago.

Panorama Tourist Information, in the Sabie Market Mall in the centre of town, Main St, T7641125, F7641134, info@saftour.co.za, www.saftour.co.za, is open Mon-Fri 0900-1700, Sat-Sun 0900-1300. One of a trio of excellent, friendly, and very helpful tourism offices covering the Panorama region – the other two are in Graskop and Hazyview. Can book all accommodation and activities and suggest itineraries. A stop at any one of these superb offices is a must before embarking on a tour of the region. *The Old Trading Post*, 494 Main St is a curio shop with some good value African crafts as well as maps, books and gifts. Next door is *African Travel and Central Reservations*, PO Box 494, T/F7642641, a very helpful source of information on the region with an up-to-date database on local accommodation. **The Forestry Museum**, Ford

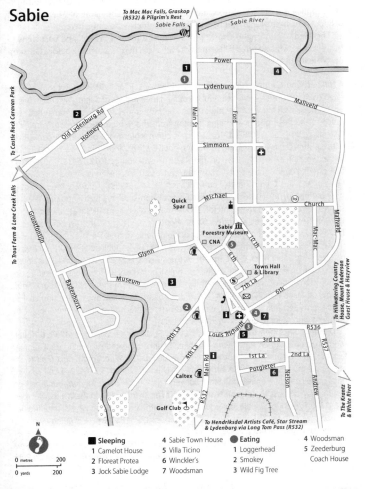

Mpumalanga

■ Sleeping	● Eating
1 Camelot House	4 Sabie Town House	4 Woodsman	1 Loggerhead	4 Woodsman
2 Floreat Protea	5 Villa Ticino	2 Smokey	5 Zeederburg
3 Jock Sabie Lodge	6 Winckler's	3 Wild Fig Tree	Coach House
	7 Woodsman		

Street, T7641058, open Mon-Fri 0900-1600, has displays on the development of South Africa's plantations and the timber industry. Refurbished during 1997, the new buildings are also home to a satellite office of SAFCOL (Forestry Department), T7641058, for information on hiking and mountain bike trails in the region.

Excursions

The tourist office has leaflets on day hikes in the area which visit local waterfalls

Mountain biking is becoming increasingly popular in the forests around Sabie and is being promoted by the tourist board. 13 km, 22 km, and 45 km guided and self-guided trails have been marked out by the forestry department (SAFCOL) T7641058, which include challenging ascents and high speed downhill runs over loose shale, tree felling remnants and eroded gullies. The national MTB championships have been held here in previous years. For more information contact Panorama Tourist Information or Denzil Lawrie, at *The Bike Doc*, corner Louis Trichardt and Main streets, T082-8785527 (mob), F7641034. He has bikes for hire, experienced guides, and special tours to ride on game farms on request.

Mac Mac Falls and **Mac Mac Pools** are 11 km from Sabie on the road to Graskop. The twin falls are 56 m high. Over a thousand miners rushed to the farm in 1873 after gold was discovered above the falls. Originally there was a single fall, but in their eagerness to get to gold, some miners tried to divert the fall's flow. An over enthusiastic application of dynamite created the second fall. The name of Mac Mac Falls originates from the large numbers of Scottish miners who came here.

The road continuing to Graskop passes over a natural bridge, and past signs to Bonnet Falls, Maria Shires Falls, and Forest Falls. There is a turning before Graskop onto the R533 to Pilgrim's Rest.

Sleeping

■ *on map, page 617*
Price codes:
see inside front cover

A *Hillwatering Country House*, Marula St, T7641421, F7641550. A sumptuously decorated country house set in a beautiful garden on the outskirts of Sabie, each room has its own terrace with views of the mountains, the restaurant is highly recommended with much of the fresh produce coming straight from the garden. **B-C** *Floreat Protea*, Old Lydenburg Rd, T7642160, F7642162. A large modern motel on the banks of the Sabie River, with a buffet/carvery restaurant, swimming pool. **C** *Misty Mountain Chalets*, 24 km from Sabie, west of Long Tom Pass on the R532 to Lydenburg, T013-7643377, F7641482. Self-catering or B&B chalets, plus a cosy pub and restaurant, the endangered blue swallow nests on the site. **C** *Villa Ticino*, Louis Trichardt St, T/F7642598. 4 double rooms with en suite bathroom, B&B, TV lounge, swimming pool, non-smoking, pleasant gardens with a superb view across the valley and forests, German spoken, centrally located, next door to *Wild Fig Tree* restaurant. **C** *Azalea Guest House*, Cycad St, off the Lyndenburg road, T/F7643147. Upmarket guest house, 8 spacious double rooms, TV, 1 self-catering townhouse with 2 bedrooms and bathrooms perfect for a family, pool, quiet suburb, nice views of forests and Sabie River. **C-D** *Camelot House*, 75 Nelson St, T7641744. Spacious double rooms with en suite bathroom, generous English breakfasts, TV lounge, swimming pool, games room, braai facilities, very friendly, a short walk from the shops. **C-D** *Jock Sabie Lodge*, off Main St, T742178, F7643215. 6 acres of attractive lawns, self-catering chalets, large rooms, restaurant, used to have poor reports but recently taken over by new management who seem to be making improvements.

D *Mount Anderson Guest House*, 74 Cycad St, Mt Anderson, T/F7641758. 6 double rooms each with an en suite bathroom, fans, TV, indoor heated swimming pool, tanning facilities, an 'upmarket' guesthouse. Recommended. **D** *The Woodsman*, next door to the restaurant and book shop of the same name, 94 Main St, T7642015, F7642016. Self-catering units or B&B, modern uninspiring block but very comfortable inside, underground parking, central location close to restaurants and shops. **D** *The Krantz*, 2 km on the White River road, T7641330, F7643135. Double rooms with en suite bathroom in the house, self-catering garden cottage with terrace, award winning garden, excellent B&B where evening meals can also be arranged, secure parking, ask for May or Peter. **D** *Sabie Town House*, Power St, T7642292, F7641988. A comfortable B&B with secure parking, swimming pool, braai area, peaceful house in the suburbs, overlooking the Sabie valley. **E-F** *Castle Rock Caravan Park*, T7641242. Municipal caravan park, ablution blocks, cooking facilities.

Hendriksdal Artists Café, 15 km from Sabie on the road to Hendriksdal, T7642309. Open for lunch Tue-Sun, dinner Tue-Sat, superb rural Italian cuisine, specializes in meals from Tuscany. Expensive by local rates, reservations recommended. *Loggerhead*, corner of Main Rd and Old Lydenburg Rd, T7643341. Closed Mon and Sun evenings, busy, established steakhouse with a friendly atmosphere when the log fire is burning. Fresh de-boned trout a speciality. *Smokey*, 9th Lane, T7643445. Breakfasts, burgers, ribs, steaks, pizzas and pancakes. *The Wild Fig Tree*, Main St, T7642239. Quality restaurant serving light lunches and more ambitious meals in the evening, choice of cool interior or shaded veranda, plenty of choice, including fresh trout, game meats such as guinea fowl, crocodile, warthog, and some delicious home-made sweets, good choice for vegetarians. If you are spending the night in Sabie this is the place to have your evening meal, restaurant open until 2100, recommended. Curio shop next door full of overpriced but good quality items. *The Woodsman*, 94 Main St, T7642204. Open daily, smart restaurant and bar on the outskirts of town, emphasis on Greek food, but local trout and steaks also available, sit outside on the terrace for a few beers in the evening.

Eating
● *on map, page 617*

The second hand bookshop next door to the *Woodsman* restaurant is one of the best in all of South Africa. The small shop is stuffed full of interesting books and there are many collectors' items. The African section is particularly superb with many turn-of-the-century volumes on the great explorers, controversial titles from the 1950s and '60s on the rise of Apartheid, and atlases from the days when most African countries were still colonized. A number of books that were banned in South Africa during the Apartheid years have resurfaced in this shop. Well worth a browse.

Shopping

Useful services Doctor: T7642134. **Hospital:** T7641222. **Police:** T7641211.

Directory

Lydenburg

This quiet agricultural town is typical of the central region of Mpumalanga. The descent from **Long Tom's Pass** west to Lydenburg opens up vistas of rolling grasslands, cattle ranches and wheat growing country stretching out into the distance. Approaching from the south, the town is often described as the gateway to the Lowveld. On the other side of Long Tom Pass you are over the escarpment formed by the Drakensberg, which marks the boundary between the highveld and the lowveld. (Beware of fog at the top of Long Tom's Pass and in the winter months it is quite possible for the pass to be blocked by snow.) **Tourist information** is available at the reception desk of *The Lydenburg Museum*, during museum opening hours, 1 km from town on the R37 to Sabie, T2352121. Don't expect too much, as this is not an official tourist office or booking agent, but they will help with local information if they can.

*Phone code: 013
(NB Always use
3-figure prefix)
Colour map 2, grid B4
Altitude: 1,469 m*

Mpumalanga

Lydenburg Museum is a fascinating museum with well-presented displays on the history of the Lydenburg region from the Stone Age to the present day. It is famous for being the first home to the **Lydenburg Heads** (see box next page), and is unusual amongst South Africa's provincial museums in that it has displays illustrating South African history before the arrival of the Voortrekkers. This is undoubtedly one of the best displays we have seen away from the big city museums. ■ *Open Mon-Fri 0800-1300, 1400-1600, Sat-Sun 0800-1700, small entry fee. 1 km from town on the R37, T2352121.*
   Next to the museum entrance is the **Gustav Klingbiel Nature Reserve**. Here you have the opportunity to view some small antelope and a vulture's restaurant within the 2,200 ha reserve, while walking on one of several short hiking trails that start from the museum. If you are interested, ask at the museum for directions to some iron age sites and the remains of some early trenches from the Boer War.

Sights
*The museum distils its
own 'mampoer' – a
local brew similar to
brandy or schnapps –
ask for a free taste if
you dare*

C *Forget Me Not*, 101 Voortrekker St, T2354016. 3 double rooms with en suite bathroom, non-smoking, all meals available at this B&B if ordered in advance, lounge, laundry service,

**Sleeping
& eating**

The Lydenburg Heads

The Lydenburg Heads are a collection of seven clay heads which date back to AD 590. They are unique pieces in the history of South African art and some of the earliest sculptures of the human form. The clay heads have only ever been found in this region and it is thought that they may have been used in initiation ceremonies.

The heads were first discovered in 1957 by Ludwig von Bezig on a farm near Lydenburg. Ludwig was 10 years old when he found the pieces of pottery but it wasn't until five years later that he became interested in archaeology. He returned to the farm several times between 1962 and 1966 where he found the pieces of the broken heads. When they were reconstructed he had seven heads of different sizes, one of which had the snout of an animal.

The heads on display in the Lydenburg Museum are replicas of the originals which can be seen in the South African Museum in Cape Town.

---

secure parking. **D** *An-Mari*, 7 Sterkspruit St, T2351454. 3 double rooms with en suite bathroom, non-smoking, TV lounge, evening meals available on request. **D** *Stassenhaus Guesthouse*, 66 Vortrekker St, T2351865, T082-4668616 (mob). 2 double rooms in smart bungalow in the centre of town. **E-F** *Laske Nakke Resort*, 2 km on the Dullstroom road, T2352886, F2351690. Self-catering chalets or budget en suite rooms, caravan park, 2 pools, bar, simple restaurant. Don't be put off by the sad looking concrete blocks, the rooms are OK inside. Each has an ancient black and white TV that only picks up SABC1 – South Africa didn't get TV until 1973 and there are still some sets around from this time that were only designed to receive the first channel. **Eating** *Jocks Country Stalls*, on the right of the R36 as it heads out of town towards Dullstroom. A small shopping centre with a few restaurants and takeaways including a pancake house and a fish restaurant specializing in local trout

Transport While the town may not receive too many overnight visitors it lies on an important route which takes traffic from the highveld down to the lowveld country. Lydenburg is 66 km from the N4. With Pretoria and Johannesburg on one side and Kruger Park on the other side, much traffic passes through here en route to **Sabie** and **Hazyview** on the R37, and **Hoedspruit**, **Tzaneen**, and **Phalaborwa** in the Northern Province on the R36.

Pilgrim's Rest

Phone code: 013
(NB Always use 3-figure prefix)
Colour map 2, grid B4

Since the gold mines closed (see below) Pilgrim's Rest has been totally reconstructed as a living museum to preserve a fascinating part of South Africa's cultural heritage. The small miners' cottages with corrugated iron roofs and wooden walls line the main street and the atmosphere of a small mountain town with its magistrate's court, local newspaper, schoolhouse and church is not difficult to imagine. However, the main street today is lined with gift shops, restaurants and hotels giving Pilgrim's Rest the atmosphere of a theme park instead. Coach loads of tourists come to spend the day here so the best time to see Pilgrim's Rest is early in the morning or in the late afternoon after the day-trippers have gone. Although most of the buildings are strung out along one long street, the settlement has a very clear division between the smart and prosperous Uppertown and the more plain Downtown. Many visitors never actually visit the lower part of town, which is just as interesting in its own way.

Pilgrim's Rest Tourist Information Centre, is on Main St, Upper Town, T7681211, F7681113, accommodation reservations, T7671377. It's open daily 0900-1245, 1315-1630. There is a small display here on the town's history and gold panning techniques, and there are another three small village museums within walking distance. Bookings for village tours can be made from here, but always in advance of your arrival.

The history of Pilgrim's Rest is a fascinating tale of gold fever in southern Africa during the late 19th century as prospectors opened up new areas in search of a fortune. In fact the town was so named by one of the first prospectors, William Trafford, because he believed that his wandering days in search of gold had finally ended. The first gold was found by a lonely prospector, Alec 'Wheelbarrow' Patterson, in a fertile valley then known as Lone Peach Tree Creek, during September 1873. After Trafford announced that he had also found gold, the newspapers quickly spread the word and by the end of the year more than 1,500 prospectors had pitched their tents along the creek. They came from Grahamstown, Kimberley, the coastal towns and a few from overseas.

Pilgrim's Rest

Some of the best finds were made in 1875, however, the region continued to produce gold until 1972 when the last mine was closed. In 1881 a financier, David Benjamin, formed the *Transvaal Gold Exploration and Land Company* which effectively ran the gold fields until they were closed. Although there were poor years there were also some bountiful periods; in the 1890's a particularly rich reef – the Theta Reef – was discovered. Over a period of 50 years the reef yielded more than 5 million ounces of gold. Mining ceased in 1972 when most of the reefs were depleted and in 1986 Pilgrim's Rest was declared a National Monument and restoration of the old mining buildings began.

Pilgrim's Rest is a small village and most of the sights are within walking distance. Alternatively, you can take a ride on the **Zeederberg Omnibus** that runs the kilometre between Uptown and Downtown, a restored horse drawn coach now pulled by a tractor. Historical displays and exhibits are found at the Information Centre, and three other **Village Museums** housed in old miner's cottages. ■ *Open, Mon-Sun 0900-1245; Sat 1345-1600; entry R5.*

The **Diggings Site Museum** is at the top of uptown where the coaches park. A visit here is well worthwhile to gain insight into the lives of the diggers and prospectors during the gold rush at the end of the 19th century before the first gold mining company took control of the town. Life was far from easy for these fortune seekers, who slept on grass mattresses in makeshift tents, often sick with malaria and exposure, and in a place where lawlessness and violence was rife. Gold panning is demonstrated and visitors can have a go themselves. The National Gold Panning Championships are held in Pilgrim's Rest at the end of November each year, when the village hosts a festival lasting 4-5 days. The World Gold Panning Championships are due to take place here in 2005. ■ *Guided tour with gold panning demonstration, Mon-Sun, 1000, 1100, 1200, 1400, and 1500, R5. Tickets available at the Information Centre.*

The Alanglade Period House Museum is north of the village on the Mpumalanga escarpment. Built in 1915, the house is typically early 20th century and was the official mine manager's residence for Pilgrim's Rest up until 1972. Today it is furnished with objects from the period between 1900-1930, including Edwardian, art nouveau, and art deco pieces. ■ *Guided tours only, Mon-Sat, 1030 and 1400, R20. Tickets available at the Information Centre.*

Robber's Pass The pass is 9 km from Pilgrim's Rest on the R533, the pass rises 650 m in altitude in only 9 km. Gold bullion and mail from Pilgrim's Rest was taken to the commercial banks in Lydenburg by coach twice a week via the pass north of town. The first major robbery took place here when two masked gunmen on horseback held up the stage-coach and disappeared with £10,000 worth of gold bullion.

The second robbery in 1912 was not so successful. The armed robber was Tommy Dennison, a local barber, who carried out the crime and returned to Pilgrim's Rest to celebrate. He was soon arrested and spent five years in jail in Pretoria. On his release he came back and went into business at The Highwayman's Garage.

Sleeping
■ *on map, page 621*
Price codes:
see inside front cover

B *Crystal Springs Mountain Lodge*, T7685000, F7685024. A holiday resort high up in the hills off the R533 north of Pilgrim's Rest, luxurious self-catering chalets set in 5,000 ha of mountain bushveld, popular *Pointer's Rest* restaurant, bush *boma* braais, a full range of sporting activities including hiking, tennis, squash, birdwatching, health spa, gym, game drives. An all round resort in a convenient location to explore the region, rates drop considerably in the off-season months. Recommended. **B** *Inn on Robber's Pass*, 17 km above Pilgrim's Rest on the R533 heading towards Lydenburg, PO Box 1071, Lydenburg, T7681491, F7681386. 4 self-catering cottages plus 6 double rooms with en suite bathrooms in the converted stables, restaurant with fireplace which is put to good use during the winter, snack meals served in the pub, trout dams for fishing, excellent quiet rural retreat. **B** *The Royal*, Main St, Uppertown, T7681100, F7681188. 50 rooms, *Peach Tree* and *Digger's Den* restaurants, the original *Royal Hotel* is over 100 years old and dates from the time of the gold rush, the new hotel's corrugated iron roof and wooden structure have been renovated and the rooms are decorated with reproduction antique furniture recalling the spirit of the gold rush, other rooms are in small houses spread around the village. Restaurant is nothing special, but they serve excellent breakfasts. **B** *Mount Sheba*, 19 km from Pilgrim's Rest off the R533, T7681241, F7681248. Set in the Mount Sheba Nature Reserve. 25 double rooms with en suite bathrooms, lounge, *Potted Owl* pub, *Chandelier* restaurant, a luxury retreat high up in the hills, the morning air is always fresh and cool, one of the best places to stay at in the area. Rates include dinner and breakfast. Expect to pay significantly less during the low season. **B-C** *Beretta's*, T7681066, F768122. A collection of 3 original private homes which have been renovated and converted into luxury cottages. Guests are served tea and coffee in their cottage, meals are served at one of the restaurants in the village. *Belvedere Cottage*, sleeps 4-6, lounge, fireplace, veranda, Victorian style bathroom; *Russel House*, sleeps 6-8, wooden floors throughout, lounge and private veranda; *Beretta's Lodge*, 6 double rooms with en suite bathroom, guests share the lounge and veranda.

D *District Six Miners' Cottages*, T7681211. The cottages are on the hill above Pilgrim's Rest, 7 self-catering cottages with 4 or 6 beds, the cottages were built in 1920 and are decorated in the original style with brass bedsteads and period furniture, the views over the valley whilst having breakfast on the veranda make getting up easy for a change. The best value budget accommodation in the area, book in advance to avoid disappointment. Recommended. **F** *Caravan Park*, at the bottom of town at the endf of the main street on the shady banks of Blyde River, T7681427. Camping and caravan sites only, some pre-erected tents available, pool. A pretty spot but rather ominous charges such as higher rates for 'foreign backpackers', and loud music is charged at R150 an hour!

There is plenty of choice as to where to enjoy your meal, but the menus are all similar. As a popular tourist sight, the standards and quality of food and service are better than normal, but it all costs that little bit more.

Eating
● on map, page 621

Chaitow's Café, Main St, Uppertown, F7681389. Open daily 0900-1700. A trendy café and craft shop with an artistic ambience, ideal for snacks and light lunches, licensed. *The Inn on Robber's Pass*, 17 km from Pilgrim's Rest on the R533, T7681491. Meals made from fresh farm produce are served in the dining room or on the open veranda overlooking the mountains. A rare opportunity for vegetarians to enjoy good imaginative dishes. Recommended. Also has overnight rooms, see above. *Jubilee Potters & Coffee Shop*, Main St, Downtown, T7681151. Open 0900-1900, early closing Tue. Burgers and salads along with coffee and cakes. *Pilgrim's Pantry*, Main St, Downtown, T7681129. Local baker also acts as a coffee shop and handicraft shop. Their pancakes make for a pleasant light lunch, homemade jams, mustards, and pickles. *Scott's Café*, Main St, Uppertown, 0900-1700, T7681061. Choice of salads and hot dishes, quality country cooking making good use of local fruit and vegetables, also an Art Gallery. *The Vine*, Main St, Downtown, T7681080. Olde world pub-cum-restaurant with small *Ladies Bar*, very popular and typical of the town, hearty steaks and other typical local fare.

Graskop

This small mountain resort is just south of the Blyde River Canyon and even though there is a large selection of holiday accommodation here, the town is surprisingly quiet and makes a peaceful base from which to explore the region. Miners arrived here during the 1880s and established a camp but modern Graskop is surrounded by forestry plantations and is an important centre of the timber industry. Today Graskop attracts fame as home of the pancake – the infamous Harrie's restaurant started it all, and the stuffed sweet and savoury pancakes are renowned in South Africa. The local residents seem to have capitalised on this reputation, and there is now a line of pancake houses along the main street.

*Phone code: 013
(NB Always use
3-figure prefix)
Colour map 2, grid B5
Altitude: 1,430 m*

Panorama Tourist Association, is on Louis Trichardt St, T7671377, F7671975, info@graskop.com Open daily 0800-1700. One of the three privately run tourism organizations that cover the whole Panorama region (the other two are in Hazyview and Sabie). The offices collaborate exceptionally well and provide comprehensive information, reservations, and advise on the whole region. Internet access is also available here.

Graskop is 1,000 m higher than the lowveld plain at the bottom of the escarpment and temperatures here are normally up to 8°C cooler, night-time temperatures in winter often go below 0°C and even in summer a sweater can be useful. This is also one of the wettest regions in South Africa but most of the rain falls during the torrential thunderstorms in the summer months. This is the best time of year to see the waterfalls as the sheer force of the water crashing into the pools below is spectacular.

Climate

The road to Hazyview goes over Kowyn's Pass a few kilometres from Graskop. Before descending towards the Lowveld it passes Graskop Gorge and waterfall and there are views looking up to God's Window (see page 626). This is a fruit growing area of mangoes and litchis, which are sold at stalls on the side of the road in season.

Sights nearby

Jock of the Bushveld Trail is an 8 km circular trail starting from within *Graskop Holiday Resort*, along the trail you will pass a magnificent 500-year-old bearded yellowwood tree as well as several eroded sandstone formations mentioned in the story of 'Jock of the Bushveld', the walk can be completed in three hours.

The newest activity in the region and a sister company of the Gorge Swing over Victoria Falls in Zambia, the **Big Swing** and the **Zipliner**, are just out of town on the lip of the Graskop Gorge. The Big Swing is similar to a bungy jump, however, you step off the top of the cliff which creates more of an outward swing on the descent. After jumping the free fall is 60 m, equivalent to an 18-storey building, and lasts 2.5 seconds. Once the bungy cord has reached its optimum length, you are lowered

Mpumalanga

down into the rain forest at the bottom of the gorge, before a 10 minute walk back to the top via a wooden staircase and walkway. If your nerves have sufficiently recovered after the jump it is worth spending some time in what is a beautiful patch of indigenous forest, with a waterfall that you can swim beneath.

The Zipliner is referred to locally as the *foefie*, loosely translated from Afrikaans as 'something that's not real', and is equally terrifying as the Big Swing. This is a wire slide that runs 130 m across to the other side of the gorge, which you slide across in a harness underneath. ■ *Open 0900-1700, weather permitting, closed Mon, T082-4584457, or just turn up at the site. R230 for the Big Swing with complimentary Zipliner, R40 for the Zipliner only.*

Berlin Falls and **Lisbon Falls** are further north on the R532 heading straight out of Graskop. Berlin Falls are 45 m high, and the water cascades into a circular pool surrounded by forest. At 92 m, Lisbon Falls are the highest in the area, and the river is separated into three streams as it plunges into the pool below.

Sleeping
■ *on map*
Price codes:
see inside front cover

B *Lisbon Hideaway*, Lisbon Falls, on the R532 north of Graskop, T7671851. The chalets are next to the falls and there is a self-catering miners' cottage which was built in 1883 and is fully equipped. The other self-catering wooden chalets are on the banks of a stream. A comfortable base from which to explore this region. **C** *The Graskop Hotel*, Hoof St, T/F7671244. An excellent hotel in the centre of town, with a range of rooms at different prices, decorated with an attractive and unique mixture of modern and African furniture (from the shop next door), the main restaurant here is superb and it's worth making a detour simply to eat here, bar with large fireplace, pool in extensive gardens. **C** *Zur Alten Mine*, R532, just out of Graskop, T7671925, F7671181. B&B, luxury log chalets with fireplace and veranda, self-catering possible, German spoken, excellent location.

Graskop

To Lisbon Hideaway, Lisbon Falls, Berlin Falls, God's Window & Blyde River Canyon (48 km)

To Sabie (R532) & Pilgrim's Rest (R533)

Paul Kruger

First National

Tennis Court

Municipal Offices

Louis Trichardt Av

Doctors

Pilgrim's Rest Rd

Hoof

Kerk / Church

Oorwinning

President

Trienitz

Hugenot

Ray's Supermarket & Butchery

Pharmacy

Spar

Richardson

Monument

Pol

Total

Bloodriver

To Hazyview, (R533) (37 Km), Panorama Holiday Camp, Kowyn's Pass, Big Swing & Zipliner

N

Not to scale

■ **Sleeping**
1 Graskop
2 Graskop Holiday Resort
3 Log Cabin Village
4 Railway Coach & Summit Lodge

● **Eating**
1 Harrie's
2 Leonardo's Trattoria
3 Loco Inn
4 Notty Pine
5 Silver Spoon

D *Berlyn Peacock Tavern*, Berlin Waterfalls, T7671085. 4 double rooms with en suite bathroom, non-smoking room, dining room, bar, comfortable lounge, swimming pool, nearby hikes and horse riding, a fine old house in the country where the emphasis is on peace and privacy, no young children, open for afternoon teas. **D** *Log Cabin Village*, Louis Trichardt St, T7671974, F7671975. 8 wooden self-catering cabins with 2 bedrooms, furnished in comfort, TV, well-equipped kitchen, small private garden with swimming pool, situated on the main road right in the middle of town. Recommended for families. If you plan on staying here during the local holidays book in advance. **D** *Summit Lodge*, Mark St, T7671058, F7671895. 12 thatched rondavels, en suite, B&B, TV, 2 self-catering units, pool, à la carte restaurant, big friendly bar that hosts town pool competitions, family run and very hospitable. Helpful for local information and booking agent for several activities, run their own eco-friendly quad bike tours, members of SA Botanical Society and Wildlife Society of SA. Cheaper backpackers accommodation available in the **F** *Railway Coach*, same address as *Summit Lodge* above. A former Rhodesian Railways sleeper carriage, sleeps 1-4 people per compartment, unique and surprisingly comfortable despite the lack of space. An all round fun place to stay, can give excellent pointers to what to do in the region, excellent value for money. **D-E** *Graskop Holiday Resort*, T/F7671126. 52 self-contained chalets next to the R532, the views on the other side make up for their bland structure, room for 100 campsites plus 40 caravans, heated swimming pool, very popular during the holiday season since much of the other accommodation in the area has started to price itself beyond the domestic market, recommended if you just want somewhere to sleep and a the day out exploring. **E** *Panorama Restcamp*, on the road to Kowyn's Pass, T7671091. The holiday resort overlooks the Blyde River Canyon and has a selection of basic chalets and an amazing swimming pool perched on the edge of the escarpment.

Loco Inn, in an old railway building at the station, T7671961. Steaks, grills, probably the most lively pub in town. *Harrie's*, Louis Trichardt St, T7671273. Wide selection of pancakes, has somehow established a worldwide reputation, consequently pancake houses have erupted in Graskop and there is now a much wider choice. *Leonardo's Trattoria*, Louis Trichardt St, T7671078. Mon-Sat 0900-2100, Sun 1000-1500. Family-run Italian restaurant, pizza and wide selection of pasta dishes, tasty and good quality authentic meals. *The Silver Spoon Pancake Cabin*, corner Louis Trichardt and Kerk streets, T7611039. More of those pancakes, black forest gâteau and filter coffees. *Notty Pine*, 3 Pilgrim St, T7671030. Lunch and dinner, sophisticated dishes in a smart atmosphere, try the delicious freshly grilled trout, simple but effective décor, in winter months there is a lovely central fireplace, one of the best restaurants in the area, always worth having a meal here.

Eating
● *on map*

Useful services Chemist: T7671055, open all hours. **Doctor**: T7671124, after hours. **Emergency services**: T7671211. **First National Bank**: Kerk St, T7671280, the only bank in town, ATM outside will accept foreign credit cards for cash withdrawals, foreign exchange inside.

Directory

Blyde River Canyon

The Blyde River Canyon is the third largest in the world after the Grand Canyon in the USA and Fish River Canyon in Namibia. It is the product of the Blyde River, which tumbles down from the Drakensberg escarpment to the Lowveld over a series of waterfalls and cascades that spill into the Blydespoort Dam at the bottom. Blyde means 'river of joy', and the river was so named after Hendrik Potgieter and his party returned safely from Delagoa Bay (Mozambique) in 1844. While under the mistaken impression that the party had been killed, Vortrekkers who had stayed behind named the river where they were camping, Treur River ('river of mourning'). When Pogieter returned, they had to renamed it!

The winding canyon is 26 km in length and is joined by the similarly spectacular 11 km Ohrigstad Canyon near Swadini. The 27,000 ha Blyde River Canyon Nature Reserve extends from God's Window down to the far side of the Blyde River dam. The canyon itself starts just below Bourke's Luck Potholes, in places it is 750 m deep,

Colour map 2, grid B5

There are no roads crossing the reserve or linking the top and bottom of the canyon, but there are some short walking trails and plenty of view points along the R532

Mpumalanga

and for most of the time inaccessible. The R532 continues north from Graskop, where there are a series of signposts every few kilometres on the right leading to viewpoints, which overlook the Canyon and Lowveld beyond. The scenery here is truly spectacular and the viewpoints provide great opportunities to look across the valley at the sheer granite rock faces and ravines covered with thick forest.

The most famous of these is **God's Window**, a viewpoint right on the edge of the escarpment overlooking an almost sheer 300 m drop into the tangle of forest below. The views through the heat haze encompass the Lowveld, stretching as far as Kruger. There is a network of paths leading to the various viewing platforms. At the top of the hill there is a tiny patch of rainforest which survives in the micro-climate on the very tip of the ridge. At 1,730 m, **Wonder View** is the highest viewpoint accessible from the road, and **Pinnacle Rock** is a 30 m high quartzite 'needle' that rises dramatically out of the fern-clad ravine. From here it is possible to see the tops of the eight water-falls which take the Blyde River down 450 m in a series of falls and cascades to the bottom. The viewpoint at the **Three Rondavels** is by far the most dramatic. The canyon literally opens up before you with the Blydespoort Dam shimmering intensely blue at the bottom. This is a view not to be missed. The Three Rondavels are three circular rocky peaks on one of the mountains capped with grass and vege-tation, and looking distinctly like traditional African rondavel huts with thatched roofs. At **Bourke's Luck Potholes** (see box) there is a visitors' centre and kiosk ■ *Open 0700-1700, small entry fee.*

Sleeping
Price codes:
see inside front cover

As the main viewpoints are within an easy drive from Graskop, Sabie, and Pilgrim's Rest, there is little need for accommodation at the top of the canyon. If you are continuing to the bottom of the canyon and Blydespoort Dam, there is a wide range of accommodation around Hoedspruit in the Northern Province, see page 664.

B-C *Belvedere Guest House*, at the start of the canyon next to the old power station. Sleeps 9 in comfort, bring a good torch with you so you can identify some of the nocturnal creatures that come out in the evenings. From the outside veranda there are superb views and this is a very special place. One of the best kept secrets of the area and strongly recommended. NB Access to the house is very steep. Bookings must be made well in advance and it is managed by the Mpumalanga Parks Board, T7595432. The whole house has to be taken by one reser-vation, alternatively book through the Panorama Tourist Information office in Graskop. **C-D** *Aventura Blydepoort*, T7680155. Self-catering chalets, restaurant, shop selling a few provisions, bar, swimming pool, golf course, view points, this is a very popular family holiday resort, during the peak season you are unlikely to get a room without calling in advance, petrol is available at the gate.

North into Northern (Limpopo) Province

The R532 continues north from the top of the canyon until it joins the R36 and the road descends through the Strijdom Tunnel and north to Hoedspruit and Phalaborwa. **Echo Caves** are on the R36 continuing south to **Ohrigstad**. The caves extend 1.3 km into the mountain and are known for the echoes produced when the stalactites are tapped. Many human bones have been found inside, proving that at one time they were inhabited. A tour takes 45 minutes but the caves are in a poor state of repair and are often flooded. ■ *Open daily 0800-1700, R20 pp, T013-2380015.*

There are many places on the Northern Province side of the Strijdom Tunnel down in the Olifants Valley where one could easily spend a few days exploring, including the lower section of the Blyde River Canyon Nature Reserve around the dam. Once you have passed through the tunnel the road quickly climbs down and you will immedi-ately notice the rise in temperature. After a few days exploring the Hoedspruit area you can either continue into Kruger Park via Phalaborwa or Orpen Gates, or take the R36 to Tzaneen where another unexpected gem of a region awaits you. At present all of this area has barely been touched by tourism, and yet this is probably what many visitors to South Africa are looking for. Make the most of it before the crowds come. See the Northern (Limpopo) Province chapter, page 637 for further details.

Bourke's Luck Potholes

The potholes are an unusual rock formation resembling a Swiss cheese which have been created by the swirling action of whirlpools where the Treur and the Blyde rivers meet. The smooth cylindrical holes are 15 million years old and are carved out of quartzite. The deepest part of the ravine created by the holes is 30 m deep although individual holes don't get much deeper than 6 m.

'Bourke's Luck' comes from Tom Bourke, a prospector who worked a claim here in the vain belief that he would find gold. Gold was eventually found further downstream.

The holes are in a rocky area below the Visitors' Centre dotted with bushes and inhabited by dassies. There is a network of paths and footbridges from which to peer down into the ravine.

Private Game Reserves

Superb game viewing has led to the establishment of a number of private nature reserves and associated private game lodges. The reserves along the western border of Kruger offer some of the most exclusive game viewing opportunities in the world. Here you have the chance to see the Big Five in their natural environment and at the end of the day enjoy five-star luxury and cuisine. Each lodge has its own special setting and the guides help to ensure that your safari is a memorable one.

Ins and outs

Getting there
Access to the lodges is straightforward and guests are either collected from Phalaborwa or Skukuza airport from flights included in the package, or charter a light aircraft to the lodges' private airstrip. Alternatively it is possible to drive from Johannesburg by car which will take around 6 hrs. A few lodges have a special deal for day visitors, contact the local tourism offices in Hazyview or Hoedspruit for details.

Reserves
The principal private reserves are **Klaserie**, **Timbavati**, **Thornybush**, **Mala Mala**, **Sabi Sabi** and **Sabi Sand**, which together form the largest private game area in the world. The first three are in Northern Province, but are included here together with the Mpumalanga reserves. Within these reserves are several smaller reserves which have now been incorporated into a single wilderness area, some still retain their name which can be a bit confusing, for example Idube Game Reserve and Londolozi Game Reserve are now both part of the much larger Sabi Sand Game Reserve. In recent years the fences between all these reserves have been removed, including, most significantly, the western Kruger Park fence. This development has helped, in part, to restore natural east-west migration routes. While the ownership and management of the lodges are quite distinct from each other, the whole region is managed by a joint committee and staff of rangers. You may find yourself staying at a lodge within Sabi Sand Game Reserve, but during the day while game viewing you could quite easily end up in Mala Mala Game Reserve. Despite their exclusive status the work within these reserves is vital to the overall conservation of the area. Although Kruger is one of the largest national parks in Africa, an even greater area needs to be set aside in the long run to help preserve all types of wildlife in the region.

Lodges
Game viewing is the main activity in all the lodges and the daily programme has few variations. The day normally starts early with a game walk or a game drive through the bush until the heat becomes too intense, when the guests are taken back to their lodges to relax by the pool and to have lunch. At dusk there is another game drive followed by dinner under the stars. In between outings you can appreciate the full extent of the luxury of your surroundings: all the camps have platforms overlooking a waterhole or a river; there are comfortable lounge areas where one can enjoy a library of books and magazines about wildlife; and then there is always a welcoming swimming pool.

Mpumalanga

Where lodges do vary is in the quality of the service, the food and the wine list. Game viewing can also vary from lodge to lodge depending on how many vehicles patrol an area at any one time and on how much effort the rangers put into showing visitors the wildlife. Unfortunately some lodges emphasize spotting the Big Five to such an extent that you don't always get to spend enough time on other animals and birds in the wilderness.

Luxury bush camps & safari lodges

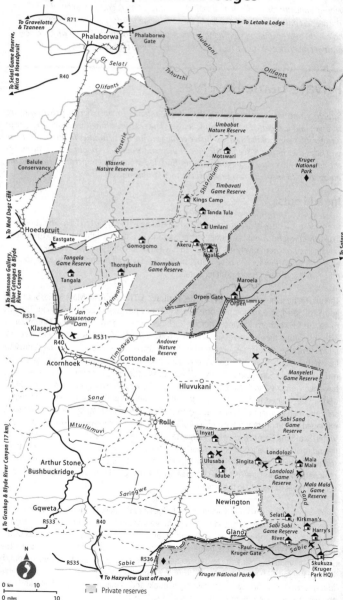

Mpumalanga

Most guests spend between two and three days at a lodge to get the most out of the game viewing. Special deals are available and it is worth looking out for fly-drive packages and discounts out of peak season. The daily cost of staying at a lodge can vary between R1,500 and R6,000 for 2 people sharing, prices include all meals, game walks and game drives. Reservations should be made well in advance because despite the high prices the most popular lodges are booked well in advance. (One of the great pleasures of game viewing within any of these reserves is that they are exclusive and the number of visitors limited.) During your walks or drives you are unlikely to see much evidence of other tourists. For anyone who has seen Kruger during the school holidays, or the crowds of vehicles in a game reserve in Kenya, this will always be a great bonus, and undoubtedly contributes to the game viewing experience.

There are too many lodges to list in full, and change of ownership appears to be frequent. If you intend to spend this much money on a private game lodge experience, it may be an idea to study some of the websites whilst choosing. Some of the images are very impressive.

Timbavati Game Reserve

Timbavati is a unique place in that it is possible to see a white lion, and there are also large herds of elephant, giraffe, blue wildebeest, zebra and impala. Open savannah, riverine forest, acacia, marula and mopane woodlands support a tremendous variety of wildlife including 240 species of bird.

Ins & outs

You can get to the lodges in the northern part of the reserve via the turning 7 km south of Hoedspruit off the R40. The nearest airport is Eastgate, although many of the lodges have a private airstrip. Camps in the southern areas are accessed by the turning 9 km north of Klaserie at Kapama, off the R40.

Sights

Timbavati is an area with a wealth of different habitats which shares a long boundary with Kruger extending from Orpen to the region just south of the Olifants River. The reserve was created in the 1950s from a group of privately owned farms where hunting was banned and game such as cheetah, sable and white rhino was reintroduced to re-establish game populations which were originally present in this area. There are several luxury lodges and camps dotted about the reserve, in comparison with other private lodges in the region these lodges tend to be in the middle price range.

Sleeping
For price guide, see inside front cover

L3 *Ngala*, Ngala Game Reserve is unusual insofar as it is in partnership with Kruger National Park as well as the Conservation Corporation. It is one of the most luxurious of the private game lodges. The lodge is on the Timbavati Flood Plain, a region known for its herds of elephant and prides of lion. Visitors in this part of the reserve experience two contrasting ecosystems; the open savannah grasslands, and the magnificent mopane woodlands, and the range of habitat means that the birdlife in this area is particularly interesting and varied. In September 1992 the management was taken over by the Conservation Corporation and it underwent a major refurbishment – it is now a member of the Small Luxury Hotels of the World. The accommodation is set in an area of mopane woodland and the shaded veranda overlooks a waterhole where many animals come to drink, there are 20 a/c cottages with en suite bathrooms, decorated with antique furnishings, the luxury *Safari Suite* has a lounge, dining area, along with its own swimming pool, and a private Land Rover. The lodge maintains an air of intimate formality with a maximum of 42 guests, meals are served under the trees in a paved dining area where fine wines, silver cutlery and crystal glassware add the finishing touches to restrained luxury in the African bush, there is a hide for guests who want to sleep out in the wilderness. **Reservations:** Private Bag X27, Benmore 2010, T011-8094444, F8094511, www.ccafrica.com

L2 *Motswari*, one of the smaller luxury camps, is located in the northern region of Timbavati and has exclusive access to a large area. The rangers here don't concentrate exclusively on the Big Five and there are choices of game viewing from a jeep, on foot or at hides overlooking waterholes, the camps send out only four game viewing jeeps at a time so you will have a vast area of wilderness to yourself. Game walking through the bush with an

Mpumalanga

armed ranger and a tracker following the *spoor* is one of the most exciting ways to see elephants and other game and is particularly good for birdwatching. The camp was completely renovated a few years ago and now consists of 11 thatched bungalows with en suite bathrooms and 4 executive suites. Throughout the camp are fine examples of African prints and carvings, there is a covered lounge area with a useful collection of field guides, a bar and a swimming pool. **Reservations**: PO Box 67865, Bryanston 2021, T011-4631990, F4631992, reservations@motswari.co.za, www.motswari.co.za

L1-L2 *Tanda Tula*, set in an area of thick acacia woodland, is not ideal country for seeing the Big Five but you will see some of the more unusual animals. This is one of the oldest lodges and with only 16 guests offers a more personal service. The accommodation consists of thatched bungalows and luxury East African safari tents furnished with wicker tables and chairs and electric fans. The bar on the veranda overlooks the swimming pool and a waterhole. In the evenings, weather permitting, guests meet for a barbecued dinner in the dried-up river bed in front of the camp. **Reservations**: PO Box 32, Constantia 7848, Western Cape, T021-7946500, F7947605, zinta@uitsig.co.za

L1 *King's Camp*, is an exclusive camp which enjoys easy access with Johannesburg via Eastgate Airport. 9 luxury en-suite thatched suites, with air-conditioning and mini-bar, lounge-dining room, bar, swimming pool, gym, game-viewing platform and deck overlooking a very active waterhole. A quiet day by the swimming pool is still bound to be a rewarding experience, and after the night drive enjoy your evening meal in the *boma*. **Reservations**: PO Box 427, Nelspruit, 1200, T013-7554408, F7533377, kings@kingscamp.com

L1 *Umlani Bush Camp*, offers a less sophisticated bush experience. The camp accommodates 10 guests in 6 thatched huts lit by paraffin lamps with an open-air bathroom, this is a lowveld area where kudu, nyala, giraffe, elephant, lion and white rhino can be seen. Game drives are run during the day and in the evenings but the emphasis is on the game walks where it is possible to gain a deeper experience of the wilderness. There is a tree house overlooking a waterhole which is good for birdwatching. **Reservations**: T012-3464028, F3464023, umlani@mweb.co.za, www.umlani.com

AL *Akeru*, is a private camp only 2 km inside Timbavati on the Eastgate road. Overlooking a waterhole, the camp has 4 twin, and 3 family thatched suites, pool, elevated loft area to watch the animals at the waterhole, lounge area and bar. Elmon, the general manager is thought to be one of the finest guides in Africa. Ask him about starring in a film with Brook Shields! Lower tariffs are available if you bring your own food, a chef is provided. Reservations: PO Box 69, Kiepersol 1241, T/F013-7511374, akeru@soft.co.za, www.akeru.co.za

A *Gomo Gomo Game Lodge*, is another pleasant bush camp with not too many frills and one of the more inexpensive options around, ask about specials. Here the emphasis is very much on enjoying the bush and the wildlife, rather than the luxury and the food and drink. A friendly camp where guests enjoy traditional South African fare under the open sky. There are 5 thatched rondavels with en suite bathrooms; the gardens are an interesting collection of aloes and other indigenous plants. Game drives and bush walks are all included in the price. Recommended. **Reservations**: T013-7523954, F7523002, gomo@netactive.co.za, www.gomogomo.co.za

Thornybush Nature Reserve

Thornybush started life as a private farm sharing a border with Timbavati, it has now been converted into a private game reserve of 11,500 ha. There are five game lodges here which also offer excursions to Kruger, Klaserie Dam and Mariepskop.

Ins & outs The main entrance is 9 km north of Klaserie off the R40, look out for the signs for Kapama and the Hoedspruit Cheetah project. The nearest airport is Eastgate at Hoedspruit.

Sleeping
Price codes:
see inside front cover

The first 3 lodges listed below are all part of the same company. **Reservations**: T011-8837918, F8838201, sales@thornybush.co.za, www.thornybush.co.za

L2 *Serondela Lodge*, is a delightful small lodge with just 4 a/c suites connected by wooden walkways which meet up at the Eagle's Nest. The lounge is at the centre of the camp where elephant, rhino and antelope can be seen visiting the waterhole and there is a secluded hide for birdwatching and game viewing. **L1** *n'Khaya Lodge*, is similar to Serondela, but slightly less expensive. The camp has 4 a/c suites which can be converted into singles if need be, each of the thatched chalets have been built well apart to ensure maximum privacy, the central lounge area has a large fireplace sunken into the floor and a high roof, dinners are eaten in a reed *boma* under the stars. **L1** *Thornybush Game Lodge*, is the largest lodge in the reserve but you can still enjoy a relaxing and private time in the bush here. The lodge has 16 a/c rooms with en suite bathrooms, the bar and the *boma* are a popular feature beside the Monwana River. Discuss with the camp rangers how you would most like to enjoy your game viewing; night drives, bush walks and morning drives are all possible, and in the heat of the day there is a refreshing swimming pool.

AL *Tangala*, is a small private lodge with just 5 a/c chalets with en suite bathrooms and a lounge area, each has a private veranda which overlooks a pool, the central eating area has an open terrace with a bar to one side, all tastefully decorated in colonial style. Game drives are available during the day and at night, when you have finished viewing game, there is an inviting swimming pool. **Reservations**: T015-7930321, F7930286, reservations@tangala.co.za

A *Kwa Mbili Game Lodge*, is a pleasant small lodge that offers comparatively cheap accommodation for the region, given that the game viewing and the service and food is as good as other lodges in the area this represents excellent value and is recommended to anyone who wishes to enjoy a more exclusive game viewing experience than one can have in Kruger. Game drives in open vehicles or bush walks are on offer, all in the company of experienced game rangers and trackers. The lodge has 6 thatched chalets and safari tents, all with en suite bathrooms, each has been carefully decorated with plenty of thought and taste, meals are enjoyed around a camp fire or on the open veranda where there is also a bar and a lounge area, there is also a swimming pool. **Reservations**: PO Box 1188, Hoedspruit 138, T/F015-7932773.

Mala Mala Game Reserve

Mala Mala was established as a safari lodge over 30 years, and this was one of the first private reserves to identify and cater for the top end of the luxury market. It is the most expensive private lodge bordering Kruger and has one of the best reputations for combining luxury service and game viewing; rates for the main camp start at US$600 per person sharing. This is truly a place to treat yourself, but remember the animals are not looking at your wallet when they choose to wander into view.

Guests have exclusive access to over 50 km of riverfront on the Sand as well as lands within Sabi Sand Game Reserve. The game and vegetation along the river is superb, this is some of the best game viewing in Africa and the fact that this is a perennial river is a great asset. Seeing the 'Big Five' is a central part of the Mala Mala experience and guests get a 'Big Five' certificate to authenticate their sightings.

Ins & outs The camps in the south of the reserve are approached from the R536, the Hazyview to Skukuza road. For the lodges to the north turn off the R40 about 15 km north of Hazyview. It is at least a further 50 km to the accommodation. The closest airport is at Skukuza.

Sleeping
Price codes:
see inside front cover

There are 3 camps to choose from, each with its own character. **Reservations**: Pvt Bag X284, Hillcrest 3650, Durban, T031-7652900, F7653365, reservations@malamala.com

L4 *Main Camp*, represents the best money can buy in the bush, perhaps what is most surprising is that there are so many rooms, there are smaller camps which are slightly less expensive but provide better value for money. Game drives are conducted in open Land Rovers with guides and a tracker, a regular feature is to enjoy your 'sundowner' from a picturesque spot in the reserve. The accommodation consists of 25 ochre coloured thatched rondavels, each with a 'his' and 'hers' bathroom, in the summer you have a quiet a/c, for winter there is heating, each unit has a safe, minibar and PABX telephone/intercom, the lounge area is decorated with elephant tusks, hunting rifles, spears and African memorabilia. The whole camp is set in a shady wood beside the river; meals are of international standard and a treat

Mpumalanga

in themselves, there is a swimming pool if you start to feel a bit too pampered. **L2** *Kirkman's Camp*, was the original farmhouse dating from the 1920s when the area was a cattle ranch belonging to Harry Kirkman. Kirkman was one of Kruger's first game rangers and the main house is decorated with early photos, hunting rifles and old maps of the Transvaal. The colonial atmosphere of Kirkman's Camp is rather more appealing than the impersonal modern luxury of Main Camp. The camp consists of 10 semi-detached a/c cottages, plus 4 twin rooms in the main house, all of the rooms have been furnished in the original 1920s-style, but with the modern air of luxury. **L1** *Harry's Huts*, in the southern corner of the reserve, away from the *Main Camp*, are the most intimate as well as cheapest of the 3 camps. The huts are functional and rather dated but they are in a beautiful setting overlooking the Sabie River, and the advantage of staying here is the access you have to the exclusive game viewing for which Mala Mala is so famous (the camp is very close to Kruger Park headquarters – Skukuza). There are 7 huts plus a central lodge which has been decorated in an Ndebele-style, open-air meals are a regular occurrence.

Sabi Sabi Game Reserve

Sabi Sabi Private Game Reserve is a relatively small area of land in the extreme south of the block of contiguous reserves which stretch all the way from the Olifants River to the Sabi River. Across the Sabi is Kruger National Park, and nothing could be more different from the camp at Skukuza in Kruger and the collection of private lodges and camps in Sabi Sabi.

Ins & outs Follow the R536 from Hazyview to Skukuza, turn off at Glano. The nearest airport is at Skukuza.

Sights In recent years the private game reserves and Kruger have removed most of their fences to allow the wildlife to migrate over a greater distance. This in turn has meant that guests on a game drive could quite easily follow the animals into a neighbouring reserve. Today it is the camps more than ever which define the overall character of each reserve, and it is here that Sabi Sabi has an excellent reputation by virtue of being the only private reserve on the perennial Sabie River. You are likely to see the Big Five and a selection of other game but we have heard it is possible to end up in a convoy of vehicles crowding around each sighting.

Sleeping
Price codes: see inside front cover

The 3 lodges which are part of Sabi Sabi Private Game Reserve have won multiple awards as Best Game Lodge in Southern Africa. **Reservations**: PO Box 52665, Saxonwold 2132, 85 Central St, Houghton Estate, Johannesburg, T011-4833939, F4833799, res@sabisabi.com, www.sabisabi.com

L4 *Bush Lodge*, is set amongst some trees along the banks of the Msuthlu River, overlooking a waterhole. There are 22 a/c chalets and 5 luxury suites, plus a swimming pool, around lawns and well-tended gardens. The main building is decorated with African art and animal trophies. **L4** *River Lodge*, set on the banks of the Sabie River are 21 thatched chalets and 2 suites, including the *Mandleve Treehouse Suite*. The whole camp is set in a beautiful cool patch of riverine forest made up of ebony, leadwood and jackalberry trees. Despite the number of guests this is a most relaxing setting. *Mandleve Treehouse Suite* has 2 bedrooms, 2 bathrooms, a lounge, dining room, outdoor sundeck, up in the trees you have total privacy. When you can tear yourself away from the beautiful setting and comfort there is a Land Rover with ranger and tracker for your own exclusive use. **L4** *Selati Lodge*, is the most expensive and exclusive of the 3 camps. There are only 7 stone and thatch chalets, and in order to maintain a feeling of bygone luxury, light is provided by oil lamp and the hot water for the bathroom comes from a gas geyser. One advantage of staying here is the excellent service you receive from the rangers – a most pleasant way to learn about the magic of the bush. **AL** *Nkombe Tented Camp*, a unique experience where visitors are lectured on a range of environmental bush management techniques by a team of experienced rangers. Held in an isolated camp for 8 people, strongly recommended if you wish to learn more about the surrounds.

Sabi Sand Game Reserve

Sabi Sand has the highest density of lodges and game viewing vehicles and is slightly more crowded than Timbavati or Thornybush. However, the Sand River has water all year round which does attract large numbers of game.

Ins & outs
Turn off the R40 about 15 km north of Hazyview, this is the same road for Mala Mala Game Reserve. It is at least a further 50 km to the accommodation. The closest airport is at Skukuza.

Sights
The reserve was established in 1934 by the owners of farms in this area but the first lodge wasn't opened to the public until 1962. The idea to develop this region for tourism took shape in 1965 and the plan for this area was not just to create a private extension of Kruger; the network of roads and game lodges enable the rangers to take guests to the wildest parts of the reserve. The quality of the game viewing here is superior to that of Kruger and the rangers are extremely knowledgeable about the wildlife and don't just concentrate on the Big Five. The game viewing experience here is intended to give visitors a deeper understanding of the wilderness.

Sleeping
Price codes:
see inside front cover
As noted above there are quite a few lodges within the reserve. Several of the concerns who operate private lodges have more than one camp, providing you with a choice in style as well as price. The camps have been grouped under the collective name.

Londolozi Along with Mala Mala, Londolozi is one of the best known and most exclusive luxury game lodges in the region. The highlight of a game drive here is the opportunity to see leopards. Leopards are some of the most elusive creatures but in Londolozi they have gradually become used to game viewing vehicles. There is naturally an emphasis on finding the Big Five, but the rangers here are willing to spend time searching for other animals. Londolozi operates 3 camps along the banks of the Sand River. As a separate small reserve it was the first game reserve to be accepted as a member of the *Relais et Châteaux*, now also a member of the Small Luxury Hotels of the World and managed by the Conservation Corporation. **Reservations:** Private Bag X27, Benmore 2010, T011-8094444, F8094511, www.ccafrica.com

L4 *Tree Camp*, is one of the best game lodges in Africa. The camp consists of 6 thatched chalets each with en suite facilities and private view platforms high in the trees above the Sand River. The furniture is made from old railway sleepers of beautifully polished hardwoods giving the camp a luxurious but ethnic feel. It is set amongst the rocks in a patch of riverine forest and has a platform on stilts over the river. **L4** *Bush Camp*, equally luxurious, but at ground level, has 8 spacious en suite thatched chalets along the river bank. There is a veranda on the river bank for comfortable game watching and the food and the wines are of the best quality. **L3** *Bateleur Camp*, slightly less expensive, is still a magnificent luxury camp. There are 8 chalets and 2 luxury suites, a swimming pool, lounge and dining area, all beautifully decorated and managed in a calm and unobtrusive manner. **L4** *Singita*, one of the newest resorts, has elevated game viewing and comfort in the bush to new heights. The country visited on game drives is the same as at Londolozi, so this is also one of the best places to stay at for spotting leopard. The rangers will also find the rest of the Big Five without neglecting the other animals in the reserve. The 16 guests are accommodated in 8 a/c guest cottages with enormous rooms decorated with hardwood furniture made from old railway sleepers. The lodge has a library and reading room, a bar, a well-stocked wine cellar, and an unusual pool cantilevered off a river bank. Dinners are formal and served in a magnificent setting on a raised platform shaded by trees overlooking a waterhole and grasslands. This won an award in 2001 as the World's Leading Game Lodge. Need we say more. **Reservations:** T011-2340990, F2340535, singita@singita.co.za, www.singita.com

Ulusaba There are 2 camps at Ulusaba, the *Safari Lodge* and the more expensive *Rock Lodge*. Both offer game drives and bush walks. The game viewing here tends to concentrate on the Big Five and the rangers in this area communicate with each other by radio so visitors don't have to spend hours patrolling the bush in search of animals and some good sightings

Mpumalanga

The railway lions

The entrance gate to Sabi Sand at Newington used to be the site of a layby on the Selati railway line. (The graves of the construction workers who died of malaria or were killed by wild animals can still be seen here.) This is an area which is known for its lions. When the railway was still running the problem was so serious for passengers waiting for trains that they were provided with ladders by the railway company so that they could climb to safety in the trees.

are more likely. This has recently been taken over by *Virgin*. **Reservations**: T013-7355460, F7355171, safaris@ulusaba.com, www.ulusaba.com

L3 *The Rock Lodge*, has an extraordinary setting on a kopje 200 m above the reserve. As you can imagine, the views of the plains below are quite spectacular. Pathways lead down the rock face to a veranda from where you can see the animals coming to drink at the Ulusaba dam. The lodge has 10 spacious a/c rooms with en suite bathrooms and colourful furnishings; there is a rock pool surrounded by a sundeck, and meals are enjoyed from one of the best vantage points. **L1** *Ulusaba Safari Lodge*, although much cheaper, still has a limited number of rooms and a friendly intimate atmosphere. There are 10 thatched chalets built on elevated wooden platforms shaded by wild fig trees, each has an en suite shower, and there is a rock pool by the river where guests can swim.

L2 *Idube*, is in a good area for spotting the Big Five, but there are several other lodges patrolling the same area for game so it is possible to bump into a group of other vehicles around the same animal. The lodge consists of 9 chalets, each with an en suite bathroom plus an outdoor shower, in a camp set in indigenous acacia gardens overlooking a waterhole, the thatched lounge has an ethnic feel and is decorated with hardwood beams and African art. The décor in the chalets is in a rather dingy 1970s-style, although the panoramic sliding windows do have good views out onto the bush. The camp is not too large and has a relaxed casual atmosphere where visitors and rangers eat together at the end of the day and exchange bush stories. **Reservations**: PO Box 2617, Northcliff 2115, T011-8883713, F8882181. **L2** *Inyati* is a lodge where game viewing is organized so that guests are likely to see the Big Five within 2 days. Even so, the variety of wildlife here and the experience of the rangers ensures that there is a lot more to game drives than just spotting the most spectacular beasts. The floating pontoon has a silent motor and takes guests on cruises along the Sand River, which offers an ideal opportunity for getting much closer than usual to the animals on the river bank. Being within a few metres of an elephant is an unforgettable experience. The setting of the lodge on the banks of the Sand River is perfect for game viewing over the lawns from the thatched veranda, and there is a wooden platform shaded by trees which overlooks the river where hippo can be seen and animals come down to drink. The lodge accommodates 20 guests in 10 luxury thatched huts decorated with African sculptures and fabrics. The facilities include the *Warthog Wallow Ladies Bar*, a swimming pool and a gym. The service is exceptional with good food and wine and the occasional touch of luxury when chilled champagne is served on safari. **Reservations**: PO Box 38838, Booysen 2016, T011-8805907, F7882406, Inyati@iafrica.com, www.inyati.co.za

There are several small private lodges in Sabi Sand which offer the same game viewing experience as any of the more expensive lodges. While they may not compare in terms of overall luxury, these camps are all very comfortable, serve excellent meals and in many ways are more friendly and relaxing since they are usually family concerns. They are often booked up as this represents the upper limit for most of the domestic tourist market but they are good value and will always provide a memorable experience.

AL *Chitwa Chitwa Game Lodge* is an excellent small lodge in the northern areas of Sabi Sand Game Reserve. The lodge is made up of 8 luxury rondavels with en suite bathrooms, meals are usually taken in an open *boma*; from the swimming pool you can watch a large dam which is a great draw for birdlife and wild animals, guests can enjoy game drives in open Land Rovers as well as bush walks with experienced guides, the camp has conference facilities and its own private airstrip. **Reservations**: T011-8831354, F7831858. Lodge direct line, T013-7355357, chitwaz@iafrica.com, www.chitwachitwa.com **AL-A** *Djuma Lodge*, this is a small private game reserve which has been swallowed into Sabi Sand Game Reserve, the camp is owned by Jurie and Philippa, who manage to run a friendly and relaxing bush retreat. **AL** *Djuma Bush Lodge*, 5 thatched chalets, central dining area and a swimming pool, 2 viewing decks, rates include all meals and game drives, good value. **AL** *Vuyatela*, 8 luxury suites with private plunge pool and viewing deck. **A** *Galago Camp*, self-catering camp suitable for a large family of group of friends. A field guide, tracker, and open vehicle are provided for exclusive use by the group. **Reservations**: T013-7355118, F7355070, djuma@djuma.co.za, wwwdjuma.com

10

Northern (Limpopo) Province

Northern (Limpopo) Province

Few first time visitors to South Africa see much of the Northern (Limpopo) Province. Until recently it had been poorly promoted and thus little was known of its hidden delights. However, it has more than its fair share of biological wealth. Aside from having a major chunk of the Kruger National Park within its boundaries, the province has 54 nature reserves and many private game farms, sustaining intricate African eco-systems. Much of the countryside is dry **bushveld**, but in contrast, the mountains around **Louis Trichardt** and **Tzaneen** are green and fertile and some of the most important agricultural districts in South Africa. Within the **Magoebaskloof** range, are spectacular waterfalls and patches of indigenous forest. This is a popular hiking area as well as a fun region to explore in a car. Further to the south is a region promoted as the '**Valley of the Olifants**', this is an area rich in wildlife, rivers, culture and history. A few days spent in the area around **Hoedspruit**, **Phalaborwa** and the **Drakensberg Escarpment** will introduce you to a beautiful area of South Africa that few visitors have enjoyed as yet.

Things to do in the Northern (Limpopo) Province

- Go twitching at the **Nylsvley Nature Reserve**, the largest and best-conserved floodplain in South Africa. It's not unheard of to see 200 species in one day.
- Have the wildest round of golf in **Phalaborwa** on the edge of Kruger. But watch out for hippos on the 17th hole.
- Explore the **Magoebaskloof Mountains** in autumn when all the wild flowers and cherry blossoms are out.
- Try *The Trading Post* restaurant near Hoedspruit, where each table has an in-built *braai*, to cook your own warthog on. Join the rangers from the local game farms and parks at the bar and listen to them swap snake stories.

Ins and outs

Getting around The N1, sometimes referred to as the Great North Road, is the only direct route which links South Africa with Zimbabwe and, in effect, the rest of Africa. Between Pretoria and the Zimbabwe border the road passes through 4 or 5 regional centres, which are linked by bus and train. However, these towns have few local attractions, and you really need a car to explore the countryside either side of the N1 to appreciate fully the appeal of the Northern (Limpopo) Province.

On leaving Pretoria the N1, passes through the Springbok Flats, a featureless plain between **Warmbaths** and **Potgietersrus**. Before the road reaches the provincial capital, **Pietersburg**, it runs parallel to the Waterberg plateau, an area which in recent years has seen the development of many private game reserves for hunting and game viewing. The route to the east of Pietersburg on the R71 will take you through the green and fertile **Magoebaskloof Mountains**, before continuing on to either the **Phalaborwa** and central Kruger, or the lowveld region of the Northern (Limpopo) Province where many private game reserves are situated. Continuing north of **Pietersburg** on the N1, the country is flat, typical bushveld country where the principal activity is cattle ranching, but as you approach **Louis Trichardt** the impressive Soutpansberg Mountains dominate the horizon and straddle the N1.

From Louis Trichardt most visitors will be faced with the choice of two routes, to turn off the N1 and head east through Venda to the northern camps in **Kruger**, or to continue over the mountains to **Messina** and **Zimbabwe**. The Great North Road cuts through Wyllie's Port and the two Hendrik Verwoerd tunnels in order to cross the Soutpansberg. On the northern side of the mountains the land quickly changes, much of the country is in rain shadow from the Soutpansberg and the temperatures are significantly warmer. As you approach Messina look out for groups of the distinctive baobab tree, a popular sight in these parts. From Messina it is only 12 km to the border at Beitbridge.

Tourist information Northern Province Tourism Board, Pietersburg International Airport, PO Box 1309, Pietersburg 0700, T015-2880099, F2880094, www.tourismboard.org.za Mon-Fri 0800-1630. This is the principal tourism office of the region. The regional officer is a very enthusiastic lady called Clara who has been on a one-woman mission over the last several years to promote the Northern (Limpopo) Province as a premier tourism destination. There is nothing she can't help you with and is available after hours and weekends at the restaurant that she owns upstairs from the office.

The African Ivory Route PO Box 2814, Pietersburg 0700, T2953025, F2912654. This is a new tourism innovative sponsored by the Northern Province Tourist Board. It's an adventure driving and camping route that covers most of the Northern (Limpopo) Province from the far north of Kruger National Park to the remote game farms towards the Botswana border. Certain sections of the route are open to all, while others are only accessible with a guide or tour operator. *The African Ivory Route* manages their own semi-permanent tents, liases with privately owned camps, and oversees central reservations from this office.

What's in a name?

The Northern Province has recently been renamed **Limpopo** *and many of the towns in the region were about to be, or had already been, re-named at the time of going to press. However, it will be a while, if not years, before this is reflected on maps and signposts in the area, so for this edition we have stuck to the old town names and will refer to what was the 'Northern Province' as 'Northern (Limpopo) Province'. Nevertheless, the name changes below are*

now 'official' and so worth knowing.
Pietersburg*: Polokwane ('place of safety')*
Messina*: Musina ('copper')*
Nylstroom*: Modimolle ('place of spirits')*
Potgietersrus*: Mokopane (named after the 1850s chief of the Tlou tribe)*
Warmbaths*: Bela-Bela ('boiling place')*
The following ones are about change 'soon':
Ellisras*: Lepalale*
Hoedspruit*: Marulaneng*
Louis Trichardt*: Makhado*

Background

South Africa is well-known as a mineral rich nation, but many people only think of the gold mines in the Witwatersrand and the diamond mines around Kimberley. However, the Northern (Limpopo) Province is one of the most mineral-rich regions in South Africa. As has already been noted in the North West Province chapter, the Bushveld complex contains the world's largest reserves of platinum, chrome and vanadium. There are also significant deposits of copper, titanium, nickel and iron ore. Dotted about the province are huge mines which would shock the average environmentalist from overseas. The town of Thabazimbi has suffered more than most, with the mining slowly destroying the surrounding hills. Residents here will tell you how the climate has changed as the hills have slowly been eaten away to extract the iron ore deposits. Despite the inherent beauty of the region one cannot help but be shocked as you approach Thabazimbi from the south. Another giant mine is to be found on the outskirts of Phalaborwa, where open cast mining has created a hole over 2 km long.

Mining

Most people would not associate the province with agriculture but the region is an important contributor to South African exports. Oranges and grapefruit form the largest citrus crops – 39% of total exports of South African oranges come from this region. The Letaba district, centred around Tzaneen, produces 36% of South Africa's tea, 75% of the mangoes and more than 60% of the avocados. Where the land lacks the water you will find cattle ranches and game farms which attract tourists as hunters as well as viewers.

Agriculture

Up the Great North Road

Warmbaths (Warmbad)

This resort town only exists because of the natural hot springs 'discovered' in the 1860s by Jan Grobler and Carl van Heerden whilst hunting in the region. (The local Tswana people called the springs *Biela bela*, "he who boils his own".) More than a staggering 2,000,000 people visit Warmbaths each year, making it one of the most popular domestic destinations in South Africa. The 50°C springs are rich in sodium chloride, calcium carbonate and are also slightly radioactive. The principal springs now lie engulfed within the massive Aventura Resort (see below) where visitors can enrol in a whole variety of different treatments at the spa. It is less than 1 hour's drive from Pretoria and the mild climate during the winter months ensures an average of 286 sunny days a year. If you are not planning on 'taking to the waters' there are plenty of other activities within the resorts. Nearby is the **Mokopa Reptile Park** and

Phone code: 014
(NB Always use 3-figure prefix)
Colour map 2, grid B2

Northern (Limpopo) Province

the **Thaba Kwena Crocodile Farm**, the largest commercial crocodile farm in South Africa. At the weekends, a free shuttle bus runs from town to the **Carousel Casino and Entertainment World**, 56 km from Warmbaths on the N1. There are also plenty of excellent **private game farms** worth visiting in the Waterberg region, many of which accept day visitors for game drives and meals. **Warmbaths Tourism Association**, a useful municipal office that can book local accommodation, is on the corner of Old Pretoria and Voortrekker streets in the Waterfront development. PO Box 205, T7363694, F7362890. Mon-Fri 0800-1700; Sat-Sun 0900-1200.

Sleeping
Price codes:
see inside front cover

A *Bonwa Phala*, 27 km out of town on the Thabazimbi-Rooiberg Rd, T7364101, F7364767. A luxury game ranch set in 3,000 ha of bushveld, 10 thatched chalets plus a self-catering tented camp, swimming pool. Price is for full board and all game drives, a typical example of a comfortable bush experience for tourists, for the visitor with a keen interest in wildlife. **A** *Mabula Game Lodge*, 35 km from Warmbaths off the Thabazimbi-Rooiberg Rd, T7340004, F7340001. A mix of timeshare, self-catering and full board double rooms, with restaurant, swimming pool, squash, tennis, gym, sauna, bush walks, game drives, horseback trails, luxury game farm with excellent facilities, recommended for a longer break. Day visitors are permitted for game drives and lunch. **B-D** *Château Annique*, Swanepoel street extension, 2 km from town, T/F7362847. 6 smart suites furnished with antiques set in a country house built by 2 Italian prisoners-of-war, all aspects are of the highest standard, swimming pool, immaculate landscaped gardens, private library, overall a smart exclusive bush retreat. Recommended. **C** *Elephant Springs*, 31 Sutter Rd, T7362101, F7363586. 40 a/c rooms with en suite bathroom, TV, lounge, 20 self-catering cabanas each with 3 bedrooms all set around a private swimming pool, all a short walk from the hot mineral springs across the road at Aventura. Also restaurant, bar, swimming pool, venue for large conference groups, pleasant old-fashioned wood décor helps create a relaxed atmosphere, the best value hotel in the town centre. **B-E** *Aventura Resort Warmbaths*, dominating the centre of town, T7362200, F7364712, central reservations T011-2073600. This resort contains the principal springs of Warmbaths and is so vast guests are required to wear plastic identity bracelets at all times! The caravan park alone extends for a couple kilometres to the edge of the town. Chalets and log cabins, 94 in total, surround 3 manmade dams, and there's a standard Protea 45-room hotel at the entrance gate. A selection of restaurants and bars, mineral pools, spa and hydro with a full range of beauty treatments, horseriding, squash, tennis, cable water ski circuit, water slides, go-karts, quad bikes, fishing. Advance booking is essential. Great, if a totally self-contained holiday park is for you. Day visitors permitted until 1700. **C-E** *Klein Kariba*, 1 km from town on the Pietersburg road, T7369800, F7363457. This is another huge resort in the attractive foothills of the Waterberg Mountains. Mix of over 250 self-catering chalets, log cabins, and hotel-style rooms with en suite bathrooms, restaurant, 3 heated swimming pools, mineral bath, squash court, horseriding, campsite has 80 sites equipped with electric points, shop and laundry. This place can get extremely busy during school holidays but recommended for families. **D** *Palmeira Guest House*, Knoppiesdoring Av, T7362558. Simple, self-catering units surrounded by pretty gardens in a quieter suburb.

Eating

Borveld, in the Bushveld Mall opposite *Shoprite*. Sports café with big TV screens, good value pizza and pasta. *Greenfields*, at the Waterfront development. Good for coffee, cakes and budget breakfasts. Closed evenings. *Lion and Elephant Country Inn*, 31 Sutter Rd, part of the *Elephant Springs* hotel, guests can choose between snacks at the bar or a larger restaurant menu. Lively atmosphere with a terrace from which to watch the world go by. *O'Hagans*, set in the Waterfront development close to the tourist office. A successful chain with mock Irish pub interiors, a good range of beers and a few hearty hot meals to choose from. *Spur Steak Ranch*, in the Aventura Spa. A reliable steak house chain found in most small towns, once you've eaten in one there will be no surprises.

Tour operators

Waterberg Escapes, T083-5097249 (mob), F011-4626937, waterberg@ode.co.za If you are staying in Warmbaths but want to explore the surrounding Waterberg Mountains, this operator can arrange a variety of tours, hikes, and abseiling.

Northern (Limpopo) Province

Rail The *Bosvelder* train service which runs daily between **Johannesburg** and **Messina** **Transport**
stops here. **Pretoria** (2 hrs): daily, 0228; **Messina** (11 hrs): daily, 2233, via **Pietersburg** and
Louis Trichardt. Road It is 27 km to **Nylstroom**; 205 km to **Pietersburg**; 56 km to **Pretoria**; 130 km to **Thabazimbi**.

Nylstroom

This is a small shaded town full of jacaranda and poinciana trees, which also happens to be the largest commercial centre in the Waterberg area. Groundnuts grown under irrigation and cattle are the principal sources of income. More recently a crop of table grapes has been developed in the district and each year there is a grape festival in January. The *NTK* is the largest agricultural co-operative society in the Northern (Limpopo) Province, here you can see groundnuts being sorted as well as peanut butter being made.

Phone code: 014
(NB Always use
3-figure prefix)
Colour map 2, grid B2

Nylstroom Visitors Bureau is in the library on the corner of General Beyers, Plein and Field streets, T7430957, F7430853. Mon-Fri 0900-1700, Sat 0900-1200. They are not particularly used to seeing visitors.

For a quiet rural centre Nylstroom has a surprising number of distinguished previous residents including South Africa's fifth prime minister (1954-58), JG Strijdom, who lived here while he was a member of parliament for the Waterberg constituency and during his time as an attorney. His house, **Strijdom House**, on Church Street, is now a museum devoted devoted principally to the former prime minister. ■ *Tue-Sat 0900-1300, 1400-1700, Sun 1400-1700.* The **Hervormde Kerk**, Calvyn St, is a national monument, built in 1889.

Sights

The Nylsvley Nature Reserve, 20 km out of town towards Naboomspruit, is the leading attraction of the area. A 1,600-ha floodplain along the Nyl River which is the largest and best-conserved floodplain in South Africa. The Nyl River (see box next page) rises in the hills near Nylstroom and eventually spills into the Limpopo. For much of its journey the river seems to lose its sense of direction and meanders back and forward forming the marshy floodplain, an important wetland eco-system, which reaches 6 km in width. The floodplain extends for nearly 70 km between Middlefontein and Moordrift and attracts numbers of up to 80,000 birds during the rains to breed. Consequently, this is a hugely popular bird watching destination with 365 recorded species and it's not unheard of to see 200 of these on a single day. Even if bird watching isn't your thing, this is a beautiful environment and mammals present include eland, tsessbe, kudu, waterbuck, reedbuck, zebra, and giraffe. It is possible to camp over night (see Sleeping below).

A birding festival and
bird census are held
here each year

B-C *Shangri-La Country Lodge*, Eerstebewood Rd, midway between Warmbaths and Nylstroom on a bushveld farm, T7175381, F7173188. Each of the 34 rooms in thatched cottages, with en suite bathroom, are spacious and tastefully decorated. The central block has all been restored and furnished with some fine antiques (there's an antique shop on the premises). Restaurant and bar, swimming pool, all set in lush gardens with views of the Waterberg. Recommended, however, a different atmosphere prevails when the place is taken over by conference groups. **D** *Komma Weer Guest House*, 17 Rupert St, T/F7175539. 4 simple en suite guest rooms in a modern house in a quiet suburb. **Camping F** *Eurosun Caravan Park*, Voortrekker Av, T7171328. A large unimaginative caravan park with120 caravan and campsites, electric points, laundry facilities, pool. There's also a simple campsite (**F**), T7431074, in the Nylsvley Nature Reserve for overnight visitors.

Sleeping
Price codes:
See inside front cover

Group Africa Super Tours, PO Box 2250, T7430957, F7430853. Inexpensive guided birding tours into Nylsvley Nature Reserve, pick-ups from most hotels in the area, 3-hr duration including brunch or supper. You will get much more out of the reserve if you go on a tour with a knowledgeable guide rather than by driving around yourself, recommended.

Tour operators

Northern (Limpopo) Province

The source of the Nile, I presume

The tale behind the foundation and naming of Nylstroom must rate as one of the most bizarre in South Africa. In the early 1860s a group of Voortrekkers from the vicinity of Great Marico in Western Transvaal resolved to continue their journey northwards until they reached the Holy Land, which was conceived as a means of finally escaping British authority. Their route followed the southeastern edge of the Waterberg plateau until they arrived at a river in flood flowing northwards. Consulting the maps in their family Bibles they concluded that the river

must be part of the Nile headwaters, and so the river was named Nyl. (After spotting a nearby hill resembling a pyramid, that settled it.) In February 1866 the village Nylstroom, 'stream of the Nile', was laid out on a farm on the southern bank of the river.

In fact the river was the headwaters of the Magalakwin, which flows north into the Limpopo. The 'pyramid' was an isolated hill known locally as Modimollo; coincidentally it was revered as a burial ground of local chiefs – today it appears on maps as Kranskop, 1,365 m.

Transport **Rail** The *Bosvelder* service which runs daily between **Johannesburg** and **Messina** stops here. **Pretoria** (3 hrs): daily, 0117; **Messina** (10 hrs): daily, 2307, via **Pietersburg** and **Louis Trichardt. Road** 178 km to **Pietersburg**; 95 km to **Potgietersrus**; 83 km to **Pretoria**; 27 km to **Warmbaths. Bus**: *Greyhound*, T012-3231154, coaches depart from by the *Wimpy* at the Engen Garage. **Bulawayo** (Zimbabwe) (10 hrs): Mon, Thu and Sun at 1020, Fri at 0020.

Potgietersrus

Phone code: 015
(NB Always use 3-figure prefix)
Colour map 2, grid B3

This is a busy centre for the surrounding agricultural area. Peanuts, cotton, wheat and oranges are major crops and the Zebediela Citrus Estate 55 km to the southeast is the largest citrus farms in the Southern Hemisphere. It is a modern town with few attractions, although the town does have an interesting past. However, if you do find yourself in the area with some time then the museum in the centre of the town, a cut above the average provincial collection, is well worth a visit. **Mogalakwena Bushveld Tourism** is next to the museum on Voortrekker Rd, PO Box 34, T4918458, F4918460. Closes at 1600.

Sights **Arend Dieperink Museum** has displays of furniture, clothes, guns and photographs of the early settlers in Transvaal, all on show in the Old Klip School (1917), a national monument. The *Australopithecus Africans* skull found in the Makapansgat Caves is part of an excellent palaeontological display. In the front courtyard there is an interesting collection of early farmyard machinery, ranging from small ploughs to large cumbersome tractors. ■ *Mon-Fri 0800-1630. Small entry fee. Voortrekker Rd, T4912244.*

Excursions **Ana Trees** 15 km from Potgietersrus on the R518 to Marken. A clump of apiesdoring trees *acacia albida* under which David Livingstone camped on one of his journeys. The biggest tree has a circumference of 6 m, they are considered a botanical rarity in this area.

The **caves of the Makapansgat Valley** are a unique archaeological site: nowhere else in the world is there such an extensive and complete record of hominid occupation. They provide a record of occupation from australopithecine times through the Stone and Iron Ages right up to the present day. In 1854 the local chief, Makapan, hid in the caves with his people to escape from the Voortrekker commandos. During the siege, which lasted from 25 October to 21 November, the Boer leader Piet Potgieter was killed by the warriors of Makapan and his body was retrieved by Paul Kruger, but over 1,500 of the warriors and their families died from starvation. After these events the local town changed its name from Vredenburg to Pieter Potgietersrus, and in 1935 it became Potgietersrus.

In 1925 the first archaeological finds were made by Prof Raymond Dart, following his discoveries a local teacher from Pietersburg, Mr Eitzman, sent Prof Dart a collection of rocks he had found near some lime kilns close to the caves. After close examination Dart realized they had stumbled across an important site and in 1936 the caves were declared a National Monument. In total there are seven caves plus a couple of other sites all of which have yielded thousands of bones and artefacts – the Cave of Hearths, Hyaena Cave, Rainbow Cave, Historic Cave, Buffalo Cave, Ficus Cave and Peppercorn's Cave.

■ *Makapansgat Caves, 19 km north of Potgietersrus in the Makapansgat Valley, can only be visited on a tour. Tours depart from the Arend Dieperink Museum every second Sat of the month at 0730, T4918458, maximum number 20, the tour lasts 4 hrs and visitors have to be reasonably fit as a climb of 300 m is involved, no children under 12.*

Percy Fyfe Nature Reserve is an important reserve about 35 km northeast of Potgietersrus. Percy Fyfe was a local farmer, who in 1933 bought a few head of blesbok from the Orange Free State to try and introduce the species to the region. After he donated the farm to the state in 1954 it has been used as a sanctuary to breed threatened antelope. Roan, sable and tsessebe have all been successfully bred here and then reintroduced to parts of the Waterberg range. There is also a simple campsite for overnight visitors.

Potgietersrus Game Breeding Centre is the game breeding centre for the National Zoo in Pretoria and rare species present include cheetah, roan antelope, black rhino, and pygmy hippos from West Africa. The main aim of the centre is to expand the National Zoo's breeding programmes of endangered species and supplement the zoo's populations. It is a member of the World Zoo Organisation, which focuses on the breeding of exotic, indigenous, and endangered wildlife. There is a network of roads throughout the 1,500 ha area of bushveld though dense vegetation makes game viewing difficult. At the entrance is a pleasant picnic area and small aviary, and an on site guesthouse is being considered. ■ *Mon-Fri 0800-1600, Sat and Sun 0800-1800. Small entry fee. 1 km north of town on the N1 to Pietersburg, T4914314.*

Potgietersrus

■ Sleeping — 1 Lonely Oak, 2 Oasis Lodge, 3 Orinoco, 4 Protea Park

● Eating — 1 Ginello's, 2 KFC, 3 Nando's, 4 Mambo's, 5 Oaks, 6 Spur

Not to scale

Sleeping

■ on map, page 645
Price codes:
see inside front cover

B-C *Protea Park*, 1 Beitel St, T4913101, F4916842. 96 a/c double rooms with en suite bathroom, non-smoking room, TV MNet, lounge, restaurant, bar, laundry service, swimming pool set in garden in the middle of the complex with a few decorative palms, regular quality hotel. **C** *Orinoco*, 66 Ruiter St, T/F4915891. Local 2-star hotel, a/c double rooms, TV MNet, restaurant, bar, swimming pool, special rates for children. **C-D** *Lonely Oak*, Hooge St, T4914560-2, F4914563. B&B, self-catering flatlets, in a dull block. **D** *Oasis Lodge*, 1 Voortrekker St, T/F4914124. Double rooms with en suite bathroom, ceiling fans, TV, restaurant, laundry service, shady garden with plenty of colour and palm trees. **E** *Jaagbaan*, on the N1, 10 km out of town towards Naboomspruit, T/F4917833. 5 double rooms with en suite bathroom, TV lounge, breakfast on request, a pleasant garden but rather overrun with small dogs. **Camping** **F** *Potgietersrus Caravan Park*, Voortrekker St. Shady sites with washblock and power points. **F** The Percy Fyfe Nature Reserve has a camp site for overnight stays.

Eating & drinking

Almost a full set of the standard chain outlets found in almost every town where there is insufficient local trade to sustain a private enterprise with character. Nevertheless your plate will always be full, either with steak or chicken. *Ginello's*, in the *Shoprite* mall, does good coffee and pancakes during the day, next door to an internet café. *KFC*, Vortrekker St. *Mambo's Theme Bar*, Protea Park Hotel, T4913101. Astonishingly large nightclub for a small town, attached to one side of the hotel, pub meals, club nights, sports viewing on giant screens. *The Oaks Pub, Grill and Breakfast Den*, Van Riebeeck Road, T4914355. Big menu, probably the best option in town, lively bar at night.

Festivals

If you happen to be here in Oct look out for the well-known *Biltong Festival* when a whole range of game biltong can be sampled.

Tour operators

Thabaphaswa Hiking & Mountain Bike Trails, PO Box 3078, T4914882. Tours throughout the Waterberg Mountains.

Transport

Rail The *Bosvelder* service which runs daily between **Johannesburg** and **Messina** stops here. **Pretoria** (3 hrs): daily 0158; **Messina** (9 hrs): daily, 0105, via **Pietersburg** and **Louis Trichardt**. **Road** 59 km to **Pietersburg**; 95 km to **Nylstroom**; 175 km to **Louis Trichardt**; 209 km to **Pretoria**. **Bus**: *Greyhound*, T012-3231154. Coaches to **Bulawayo** (Zimbabwe) (9 hrs): Mon, Tue, Wed Thu and Sun at 1120. **Johannesburg**: Mon, Thu, Sun at 1120, Fri at 0120. *Translux*, T012-3348000. Coaches to **Harare** (Zimbabwe) (13 hrs): Tue, Thu, Fri, Sun, 0140. **Johannesburg** and **Pretoria** (3 hrs): Mon, Wed, Fri at 1020; Sun at 0220. Buses leave from the *Wimpy* in Vortrekker Street.

Pietersburg

Phone code: 015
(NB Always use
3-figure prefix)
Colour map 2, grid B3
Altitude: 1,312 m

The regional capital of Northern (Limpopo) Province is a large modern town, founded in 1884 by Voortrekker Commandant-General Pieter Joubert, and the main agricultural and industrial centre for the thinly populated province. The town is located in a shallow hollow surrounded by level grass plains. There are a couple of rocky outcrops but the immediate countryside is rather uninspiring. However, it is a convenient base from which to explore a fascinating region which has yet to be really discovered and appreciated by the majority of tourists. The town enjoys a very pleasant climate where the summer temperatures are moderated by the altitude, in winter the average temperature is 20°C, the rainfall varies between 400-600 mm and falls during the summer months.

The **Pietersburg Marketing Company**, Civic Centre, Landdros Mare St, T2902010, F2902009, is responsible for tourism in and around Pietersburg and in the reception area of the office there is a good range of local promotional material. **Northern Province Tourism Board**, at the airport (see page 640), is responsible for promoting tourism in the whole province. Contact this office in advance to organize tours.

Northern (Limpopo) Province

As the regional capital the town has grown rapidly in recent years and is by far the **Sights** largest centre between Pretoria and Harare in Zimbabwe. If you have spent a few days in the surrounding countryside it can come as quite a shock as you drive into the busy centre with its wide tree-lined roads, traffic jams and tall buildings. It is quite tempting to immediately return to the peace of the bushveld, but there are a number of interesting museums and sights within the town which are well worth visiting. City walking maps are available at the tourist office.

The first stop for most visitors is likely to be the '**Irish House**', on the corner of Thabo Mbeki and Market streets, T2902180, which is home to the **Pietersburg Cultural Museum**. The history of the building is as interesting as the collection it houses. The building is a prefabricated steel structure from Germany which was imported by Aug Julius Möschke after his shop had been destroyed by a fire in 1906. It is a classic example of late Victorian architecture with wrought-iron decorations topped by a fine clock tower and weather vane. During the First World War Möschke was interned and on his return to Pietersburg he found his business to be bankrupt and was forced to sell the shop to James Albert Jones in 1920. It was Jones who named the building the Irish House, and over the years it grew into a very successful local fashion shop which imported the latest quality materials from Europe. The museum itself traces the history of the region from the Stone Age to modern times, it is a well-presented display in a spacious and airy building. ■ *Mon-Fri 0800-1600, Sat 0900-1200, Sun 1500-1700. Free.*

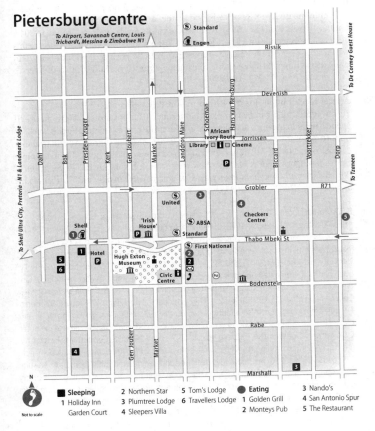

Pietersburg centre

To Airport, Savannah Centre, Louis Trichardt, Messina & Zimbabwe N1

To De Cormey Guest House

Standard
Engen
Rissik
Devenish
Schoeman
Hans van Rensburg
African Ivory Route
Jorrissen
Library
Cinema
President Kruger
Dahl
Bok
Kerk
Gen Joubert
Market
Landdros Mare
Biccard
Voortrekker
Dorp

To Shell Ultra City, Pretoria - N1 & Landmark Lodge

To Tzaneen

Grobler
R71
United
ABSA
Checkers Centre
Shell
'Irish House'
Standard
Thabo Mbeki St
First National
Hotel
Hugh Exton Museum
Civic Centre
Bodenstein
Gen Joubert
Market
Rabe
Marshall

Northern (Limpopo) Province

N
Not to scale

■ Sleeping		**5** Tom's Lodge	● Eating	**3** Nando's
1 Holiday Inn	**2** Northern Star	**6** Travellers Lodge	**1** Golden Grill	**4** San Antonio Spur
Garden Court	**3** Plumtree Lodge		**2** Monteys Pub	**5** The Restaurant
	4 Sleepers Villa			

On the other side of Vorster St from the Irish House, in the gardens which form the civic square, you will find another fascinating museum, the **Hugh Exton Photographic Museum**. Housed in the town's first Dutch Reformed Church, dating from 1890, this is a superb collection of prints and negatives which trace the first 50 years of Pietersburg – few towns have such a unique record of their past. Hugh Exton was a local photographer who had a studio in Pietersburg, the collection contains over 23,000 glass negatives. ■ *Mon-Fri 0900-1600, closed Sat, Sun 1500-1700. Free. T2902180.*

Another museum well worth a visit is the **Bakone Malapa Northern Sotho Open-air Museum**. This is quite unique for South Africa since it celebrates the life and traditions of the Bakone tribe and most museums one comes across seem to focus only upon the exploits of the white man in South Africa. Housed in a couple of lapas are displays illustrating various rituals and traditional artefacts, there is an excellent curio shop, kiosk and braai area. ■ *Daily 0830-1230, 1330-1530, closed Mon afternoon. Minimal entrance charge. T2952432. 9 km from the town centre on the Chuniespoort road (R37).*

In the **Pietersburg Art Museum** there is a fine collection of pictures and sculptures. Anyone interested in South African art should make time for it. ■ *Mon-Fri 0900-1600, Sat 0900-1200, closed Sun. Free. T2902177.*

Pietersburg Bird Sanctuary is an award winning sanctuary set around a couple of lakes in the acacia bush. There are numerous hides all around the lakes, more than 280 bird species have been recorded here. A must for any bird enthusiast. ■ *Daily, 0700-1800. R521. T2902331. It is 4 km north of town along Market St. Entry only on foot.*

Pietersburg Game Reserve is one of the largest municipal game reserves in South Africa, just on the edge of town where you can walk or drive around 3,200 ha and see 21 species of game. There are several hides and view points along the streams which flow through the reserve. Game drives can be arranged, phone ahead, and night drives run on Friday evenings during the summer. ■ *Daily 0700-1800. Next to the Caravan park, T2902331, F2902333.*

Local hikes A local hike of interest is the **Rhino** trail in Pietersburg Game Reserve. This is a 20-km trail, which can be completed in a single day, but most walkers choose to spend a night in the bush in order to enjoy the atmosphere at night, and the excellent opportunities for game viewing at dawn. There is also the shorter **Acacia** trail that can be completed in 5-7 hours. Overnight accommodation is available in a simple campsite (**F**), bring your own tent, there is also a basic hikers hut. ■ *There is a limit of 20 people per hike and a minimal fee per person, payable in advance. Further details available on T2902331, F2902333.*

Sleeping
■ *on map, page 647*
Price codes:
see inside front cover

B *The Ranch Hotel*, 25 km south of town on the N1, though there is no access off the N1, take the exit for the R101, T2905000, F2905050. A large holiday complex in the bush with 90 bungalows set in gardens with 1, 2 or 3 beds, and TV. Also a restaurant, bar, horse riding, golf, jacuzzi, swimming pools, tennis and squash. **C** *The Landmark lodge*, next to the N1 Shell Ultra City just south of town, T2557255, F2257256. Chain hotel, 80 a/c functional rooms, TV, pool, bar, buffet breakfast, internet provided through the TV and separate keyboard. Standard businessman's unimaginative hotel but conveniently located. **B-C** *Holiday Inn Garden Court*, Thabo Mbeki St, T2912030, F2913150. A functional hotel with 178 double a/c rooms, TV, non-smoking rooms. Also a lounge, bar, *Garden Grill* restaurant, swimming pool, cars parked in a fenced lot across the road. Limited facilities if you want to spend time at the hotel. **C** *De Cormey Guest House*, 48 Devenish St, T2971656, F2974236. Comfortable B&B with 8 rooms, TV, phone, evening meals available on request. **C** *Plumtree Lodge*, 138 Marshall St, T2956153/4, F2956150. Ten beautifully designed and decorated double rooms, a/c, en suite bathroom, TV, mini bar, phone, lounge in the rooms, laundry service, swimming pool, pretty gardens, relaxing and helpful. Exceptionally high quality. Recommended. **C** *Sleepers Villa*, 20a Bok St, T/F2915285. A rather bizarre looking house with a private walled garden and 5 rooms with bathrooms (but only separated with a screen), TV, lounge, meals available on request. Close to city centre, but over priced for the quality. **D** *Traveller's Rest*, 43 Bok St,

Zion City

One of the most significant modern day landmarks of the region, 30 km from Pietersburg on the R71 towards Haenertsburg, is the Zion City at Moria. Although there is nothing much for the visitor to see here, this is the seat of the Zion Christian Church, an entirely black denomination, which has the largest following of any denomination in Southern Africa. During Easter weekend each year, up to 2,000,000 followers congregate here from all over South Africa and Zimbabwe for mass worship, when they traditionally wear white robes. The sight of such staggering numbers in the Pietersburg region at this time is quite extraordinary.

T2915511, F2915585. 17 self-catering rooms, en suite, optional B&B, TV, bar, good value family rooms. **E** *Northern Star*, 46 Landdros Mare St, T/F2958980. Budget hotel in the centre of town, 23 en suite rooms, TV, parking extra, cheaper rates at the weekends. **E** *Tom's Lodge*, 45 Bok St, next door to *Traveller's Rest*, T2913797-8. Ten double rooms, fridge, TV, motel style parking, no meals, simple budget room close to the *Holiday Inn*, one of the better deals for the price. **E-F** *Pietersburg Game Reserve Caravan Park*, 5 km out of town along Dorp St, T2952011. 60 campsites for caravans and tents, 12 luxury rondavels, self-catering, clean ablution block, electric points, laundry.

Golden Grill, at the Shell Station on Thabo Mbeki St. Cheap roadside café and bar, burgers, South African *pap & vlies*, fish and chips. Convenient if you are staying at *Tom's Lodge* or the *Traveller's Rest* across the street. *Montey's*, 46 Landdros mare St, opposite the civic centre, T2958980. Lively local pub, pool room, bar meals. *Nando's*, 59 Schoeman St, Portuguese chicken dishes, fast foods. *San Antonio Spur*, Checkers Centre, Hans van Rensburg St, part of the steakhouse chain, reliable quality meals, salad bar, good value, open all day for meals. *The Restaurant*, 50 Dorp St, just out of the centre, T2911918. Fine dining with an international menu, Chinese, curries, South African steaks, set in a fine old building, clearly some thought has gone in to the décor. Recommended. *Villa Italia*, Savannah Centre, T2960857. An excellent selection of pasta dishes, one of the better options in town.

Eating & drinking
While there are still plenty of good places to visit in the city centre, there has been a gradual movement of nightlife and restaurants towards the Savannah Mall on Grobler St, a good walk from the centre

Concord, Checkers Centre, T2912177, F2958359. Flights and local accommodation agents. *Kudu Travels*, 53c Schoeman St, T2956483. *SA Tours & Bookings*, 89a Schoeman St, PO Box 357, T2970816, F2973937. Comprehensive brochure with a full range of half day, full day, and multi-day tours in the region. Recommended.

Tour operators

Air Pietersburg International Airport is only 3 km north of the city centre off the N1. A former air force base, which now has a 4 flights a day to **Johannesburg** (50 mins), during the week, 1 on Sat, and 3 on Sun. *SA Airlink*, reservations, T2880166, F2880165, central reservations T011-9781111.

Transport

    Rail Reservations, T2996203. The *Bosvelder* service departs daily at 2322 to **Johannesburg**, and at 0300 to **Messina**.

    Road 550 km to **Bulawayo** (Zimbabwe); 1,721 km to **Cape Town**; 116 km to **Louis Trichardt**; 204 km to **Messina**; 207 km to **Phalaborwa**; 275 km to **Pretoria**; 95 km to **Tzaneen**. **Bus**: **Greyhound**, T012-3231154. Coaches depart from Shell Ultra City on the outskirts of town. **Bulawayo** (Zimbabwe) (8 hrs): Mon, Thu and Sun at 1220, Fri at 0230. **Harare** (Zimbabwe) (11½ hrs) via **Masvingo**: Mon, Fri and Sun at 0300, Sat at 1800. **Johannesburg** (4½ hrs)L daily at 0130, Mon-Sat at 1005. *Translux*, T012-3348000. Coaches depart from ASMO building on Thabo Mbeki St. **Bulawayo** (10 hrs): daily, 0115. **Harare** (13 hrs): Tue, Thu, Fri, Sun at 0245. **Lusaka** (21 hrs): Tue, Fri, 1345. **Pretoria** and **Johannesburg** (4 hrs): Mon, Wed, Fri at 0930; Mon, Thu at 1030; daily at 0205. **Car hire**: all located at Pietersburg International Airport. *Avis*, T2880171; *Budget*, T2880169; *Imperial*, T2880097; *Sani 4x4 Rental*, T2880268.

Northern (Limpopo) Province

Directory **Communications** Internet: *Vodashop* in the Savannah Centre, T2963907. Only 1 terminal so expect to queue. Mon-Sat. *Business Basics*, Shop 17a, Middestad Centre, Market St, T2970246. **Useful services** Ambulance: T2930001. **Med Rescue**: T0800133789. **Pharmacy**: (opening hours 0800-2000): T2955737. **Police**: T10177. **Medical Service**: T2914171.

Routes north and east of Pietersburg

The **N1** continues north to **Louis Trichardt**, this section of the road has been upgraded to a dual carriageway, but is still a two lane road from Louis Trichardt to the Zimbabwe border. About 61 km from Pietersburg the N1 crosses the **Tropic of Capricorn**. There is a plaque to mark the spot, which unfortunately someone has decided should be covered with graffiti. If you are not heading for Zimbabwe or the northern camps in the Kruger National Park, an interesting alternative route out of Pietersburg is to take the **R71** to **Tzaneen** (95 km) and **Phalaborwa** (see page 655). This takes you into a beautiful area of South Africa that few people have seen as yet. Once in Tzaneen it is possible to take the **R40** south through the game farm region of the **Lowveld** to either **Blyde River Canyon** in Mpumalanga (see page 625) or central Kruger's **Orpen Gate** (see page 606).

The **N1** continues to the north winding through wooded valleys, after 21 km the highway passes through the **Verwoerd Tunnels**. The **R524** heads east from town through **Thohoyandou**, the former capital of the Venda homeland, to **Punda Maria Camp** (140 km), one of the most northerly camps in **Kruger National Park** (see page 592).

Louis Trichardt and around

Phone code: 015
(NB Always use 3-figure prefix)
Colour map 2, grid A4
Altitude: 984 m

The town was named after the Voortrekker leader, Louis Trichardt, who set up his camp near here in May 1836. He had travelled up to the Soutpansberg with another group of Voortrekkers under Hans Van Rensburg. After arguments between the two groups, Hans Van Rensburg led his people east in search of a route to Lourenço Marques. They disappeared into the wilderness and were never heard from again. Louis Trichardt remained in the area for a year before following Hans Van Rensburg east. This was one of the classic journeys of the Voortrekkers taking seven months to reach Lourenço Marques. It took them 2½ months to get down the Drakensberg escarpment and by the end of their trek 27 out of the original 53 Boers had died. Louis Trichardt and his wife survived the journey, but both died or malaria soon after.

The modern town is the centre of an agricultural area where tea, coffee, timber and subtropical fruits are the main crops. To the north and west is the Soutpansberg range of mountains which offer plenty of wilderness hikes, there are some pleasant country hotels and a number of farms in the area which have developed small camps for visitors in search of some peace and quiet.

The excellent Soutpansberg **tourist office** is just off the N1 on the right side as it heads north out of town. Mon-Fri 0800-1700, Sat 0800-1300. PO Box 980, Louis Trichardt, T/F5160040.

The Swiss Connection

During the early history of South Africa there were many different groups of Europeans exploring the dark continent for various reasons and in 1870 a group of Swiss missionaries visited, establishing a mission at Valdezia in 1875. In 1878 a farm was bought at Elim in order to start a hospital. **Elim Hospital** became one of the most important hospitals in southern Africa, over the years attracting many missionaries from Switzerland who stayed in the region and formed the basis of the Swiss community, which still exists today in the Louis Trichardt area.

By 1900 the hospital was serving an area of up to 300 km radius, including many farms and villages in southern Rhodesia (Zimbabwe). During the early years of the 20th century the presence of Elim Hospital ensured that an efficient postal service came to the region, and in 1920 the hospital had electricity before the town of Louis Trichardt. The final period of the hospital's fame and success followed the efforts and works of Dr Jean Rosset and Dr Odette Rosset-Berdez and this isolated bush hospital became world renowned for its eye treatment and surgery. Elim hospital is 25 km southeast of Louis Trichardt on the Gyani Road. It is presently being rebuilt and there are plans to re-establish a museum on the premises.

The Ben Lavin Nature Reserve is a protected area of indigenous woodland with 18 km of walking trails and hides. The reserve is a good place for birdwatching and has giraffes, wildebeest and other game indigenous to the area. There are also some interesting archaeological sites, which have been dated to around AD 1250. For the more energetic there are both hiking and mountain bike trails in the reserve. You will be provided with a booklet that helps interpret the environment you are likely to pass through. There are some new overnight huts along the hiking trail (see Sleeping below), which are fully furnished. When exploring the park on foot always remember to look out for wild animals. ■ *Daily 0600-1900. To get there, follow the N1 8 km south of the town and look out for the Fort Edward Rd, the reserve is 5 km along this road.*

Ben Lavin Nature Reserve
The tourist office tells us that there are rumours in town that the land may be sold off to build a new township

Soutpansberg is an impressive mountain range, whose name means 'salt-pan mountains', after a salt-pan and brine spring at the western end of the range. The sandstone range stretches for about 130 km east-west, the highest point is 1,753 m, known as Lejume. These hills have played an important role in the early history of the region, because of their altitude they receive an above average rainfall. Located along the high plateau are many Venda villages where many traditions have been preserved. Many of the valleys and lakes are considered to be sacred sights, the most well-known of these are the **Phiphidi Falls** and **Guvhukuvhu Pool, Lwamomdo Hill, Lake Fundudzi** and the sacred forest in the **Thathe Vondo Forest**. Many of these sights are difficult to find and you should enlist the services of a registered guide if you wish to visit them. This will also help ensure that you approach and treat the sights sensitively. Pick up the Soutpansberg Mountain Meander map at the tourist office, a self-drive guide to day trips in the area.

Soutpansberg mountains

Louis Trichardt

To Hangklip Forest

To Inn on Louis Trichardt, Mountain View, Clouds End, Messina & Zimbabwe

To Thohoyandou, Punda Maria (Kruger National Park) & Plaas Guest House (20 km)

To Tzaneen (R71), Pietersburg, Pretoria (N1), Ben Lavin Nature Reserve & Adam's Apple

N
Not to scale

■ **Sleeping**
1 Bergwater Inn
2 Carousel Lodge
3 Lutombo Guest House

● **Eating**
1 KFC
2 Shenandoah

Northern (Limpopo) Province

Hangklip Forest Reserve

The Hangklip Forest Reserve is 3 km west of town and is signposted off the N1. This is an area of indigenous forest around the base of the Hangklip, 1,719 m, a wall of rock rising over the forest. The top of the cliffs are some of the highest points of the Soutpansberg. There are several day hikes here through spectacular mountain scenery. The **Soutpansberg Hike** is a 21-km walk which you should allow two days to complete. Although this is a circular route all hikers must walk in the same direction, there is an **F** *Overnight Hut* which has room for 30, the maximum number of walkers allowed at any one time on the trail. ■ *For further details contact: The Forestry Office in Pretoria which takes bookings and issues permits for a number of hikes in the province, T012-4813615. The trail is graded as of average difficulty.*

Sleeping

■ *on map, page 651*
Price codes:
see inside front cover

B *Bergwater Inn*, 5 Rissik St, T/F5160262. 12 double a/c rooms with en suite bathroom, 11 single rooms, DSTV, restaurant favoured by the local people which is always a good sign, 2 bars, lounge, swimming pool, a whitewashed double-storey building overlooking a pond on the edge of town. **D** *Adam's Apple*, on the N1 highway 15 km south of Louis Trichardt, T/F5164817. 16 rooms with en suite bathroom, TV, restaurant, bar, lounge, pool room, swimming pool, breakfast included, an isolated roadside hotel set in well-kept gardens with views across the Soutpansberg Mountains. **C-E** *Clouds End*, follow the N1 north out of town, the hotel turning is to the left as the road starts to climb after the last residential area has been passed, T5177021, F5177187. 37 double rooms, a/c, en suite, TV, all in a variety of blocks dotted about the hillside, caravan park, restaurant serves excellent 5-course dinners with a few unusual dishes, bar and spacious lounge with large open fireplace, essential in the winter months, swimming pool, floodlit tennis court, extensive grounds, even a cricket pitch. A popular hotel though terribly old fashioned; think plastic bucket seats and other kitsch 1973 décor. Rates are for dinner, bed and breakfast, excellent service, probably the best value in town. Recommended. **C** *Dzhiawolala Cottages – Medike Mountain Reserve*, PO Box 513, T5160481, F5161138. 2 unique pioneer cottages in the Soutpansberg 37 km from Louis Trichardt towards Vivo on the R522, close to an impressive gorge cut by the Sand River, this is a Natural Heritage Site, excellent local hikes, rock paintings, mountain bike trails, a beautiful wilderness. Recommended. **C** *Mountain View*, N1, 9 km north of town, T/F5177031. 31 double a/c rooms, 6 triple rooms, TV, restaurant, bar, swimming pool, lounge, gardens, a great setting in the Soutpansberg but in need of refurbishment, due to be taken over by new owners. **C** *Inn on Louis Trichardt*, 11 km north of Louis Trichardt, T5177088, F5177020. Recently taken over by a successful Zimbabwe chain. 18 thatched rondavels dotted around beautifully tended gardens at the base of the Soutpansberg Mountains, enormous beds, en suite bathrooms, TV, phone, swimming pool, rates include dinner and breakfast. Terrace restaurant and bar, tea rooms and curio shop on the premises. The owners bought all the furnishings from one floor of the Carlton Hotel in Johannesburg when it closed down which has bought 5 star quality to the Inn. Recommended. **C** *Shiluvari Lakeside Lodge*, PO Box 560, T5563406, F5563413. A peaceful country lodge located in the Albasini Conservancy, 23 km from Louis Trichardt. Ideal for birdwatching, fishing and hiking, double rooms and chalets, full board rates available, restaurant, swimming pool. For the keen bird enthusiast the lodge offers boat trips during the day and at sunset on the dam, maximum 6 people. Recommended. **D** *Carousel Lodge*, 10 Industrial Rd, T/F5164482. 6 double rooms, all self-catering, TV, garden, operators for Kruger day trips, central position, but not particularly secure parking and as the address suggests, a big industrial area around the corner. **D** *Lutombo Guest House*, 141 Anderson St, T5160850, F5161846. 2 rooms with en suite bathroom, non-smoking, TV lounge, all meals available on request, gardens, swimming pool, good value B&B. **Camping D-F** *Ben Lavin Nature Reserve*, T/F5164534. Four self-catering chalets, 30 campsites, caravan park, electric points and lighting, plenty of shade. **E-F** *Makhado Caravan Park*, T5160212. Busy site during school holidays, in the middle of town next to the Indigenous Tree Park, 120 sites with electric points, hot water, plenty of shade, don't camp too near the streams as mosquitoes are a problem, improved greatly since private owners took it over from the municipality.

Apart from a few fast food outlets, the town is poorly served by restaurants. Try the hotel restaurants, which are open to non-residents. *Bergwater Hotel*, varied and changeable menu, has a good reputation with the local people. If you enjoy large meals try the restaurant at the *Clouds End Hotel*, a bit old fashioned, but good value meals, open 1900-2100. *Shenandoah Spur*, 102 Krogh St, T4470. Steakhouse chain, salad bar, burgers, ribs. This branch is well-overdue for refurbishment.

Country Mountain Trips, PO Box 3677, Louis Trichardt, T082-7688801 (mob). Hiking, 4x4 day trips, Soutpansberg tours. *Face Afrika Tours*, Lommies Emporium Building, 104 Burger St, PO Box 245, T/F5162076; T082-9693270 (mob), facaf@mweb.co.za For anyone planning a complete tour of the region with expert local knowledge. Strongly recommended. Chris Olivier, who is part of the team, is an expert on tourism throughout the province and a board member of The Northern Province Tourism Board. *Louis Trichardt Agencies*, in the Chequers Centre, T5165042. Local agent for all bus tickets. *Kuvona Cultural Tours*, T082-4659303 (mob). Tours to the tribal villages in the Soutpansberg. *Saddles Horse Trails*, PO Box 362, Louis Trichardt, T/F5164482. Horse trails in the Soutpansberg Mountains from 1-3 days, suitable for novices, overnight at bush camps, swim bare back with the horses. Recommended. Also do mountain bike and hiking trails.

Road 140 km to **Kruger Park** (Punda Maria Gate); 94 km to **Messina**; 116 km to **Pietersburg**. **Bus**: *Translux*, T012-3348000. Coaches to **Bulawayo** (8½ hrs): daily at 0245. **Harare** (10½ hrs): Tue, Thu, Fri, Sun at 0415. **Lusaka-Zambia** (20 hrs): Tue, Fri, 1515. This service arrives in Harare at 0200, not convenient unless you have friends who can meet the coach. **Pretoria** and **Johannesburg** (6 hrs): daily, 0020; Mon, Wed, Fri at 0725. *Greyhound*, T012-3231154. Coaches depart from Safari Motors, Caltex garage in Baobab St close to the tourist office. **Bulawayo** (Zimbabwe) (6½ hrs): Mon, Thu and Sun at 1340; Fri at 0350. **Harare** (10½ hrs): Mon, Fri and Sun at 0420, Sat at 1920. **Pretoria** (5½ hrs): daily at 2330; Mon-Sat at 0815. **Train** Railway Station, Vorster St, T5164202. The *Bosvelder* service stops here; towards **Messina** (3 hrs): daily, 0630; towards **Johannesburg** (11 hrs): daily, 1927.

Banks *First National*, 98 Krogh St, T5161540. *Standard*, 93 Krogh St, T5160291. *ABSA*, 295 Krogh St, T5160161. **Useful services** Chemist: T5164994. Hospital: T5160148. Police: T10111.

Venda

You are only likely to pass through this former homeland region if you are heading to the northern camps of Kruger from Louis Trichardt on the R524 or from Pietersburg/Tzaneen on the R81. The area looks more like rural Tanzania or Kenya than any other part of South Africa. Unlike Bophuthatswana in the North West Province, which the Apartheid government proclaimed a black homeland simply because they had no use for the inadequate land, Venda is fertile and green and produces tea, bananas, and mangoes. Despite this, and efforts made by the current government, the infrastructure is still poor, the roads are badly maintained, women and children fetch and carry water and firewood, the hillsides are overcrowded with huts, and most people rely on subsistence farming to make a living.

The VhaVenda culture is steeped in the spirit world and there are many important sacred, and private, sites in the region. The Venda people are regarded as some of the finest artists in South Africa, and are particularly renowned for their drum making. There is an **open-air drum workshop** off the R525 (approximately 50 km en route to Kruger's Pafuri Gate) in the far north that is worth visiting. **Thohyandou** is the former capital of the independent homeland and is the commercial and administrative centre for the district. It's name means 'head of the elephant' in tshiVenda. The town has a very infectious African feel about it, business, schooling, and life in general is conducted outdoors, the people are astoundingly friendly, and all the local produce from the region is sold along the colourful roadsides. The drive though Venda gives an interesting insight into the former political mind of South

Africa, which enforced poverty on black people in these particular homelands. If you would like to explore this region in detail, contact *Soutpansberg Tourist Office*, Louis Trichardt, T/F5160040, who can organize a tour with a local guide.

Sleeping
Price codes:
see inside front cover

There are few accommodation options here, apart from the **B-C** *Venda Sun Hotel and Casino*, PO Box 766, Sibasa 0970, T9624600, F9624541. A throwback to the days when gaming was legal in the independent homelands but illegal in South Africa, and wealthy people had to travel to these places to gamble. The resort has the usual quality facilities but is beginning to look out of place, frequented only by a few die-hard Afrikaner farmers who come for the Karioke and braai at Sunday lunchtime.

Messina

Phone code: 015
(NB Always use
3-figure prefix)
Colour map 2, grid A4

Messina was originally a mining camp set up around the copper mines which opened in 1905. The area was explored by prospectors after they had heard reports of abandoned mine workings. In fact archaeological evidence indicates that mines had been worked here for several centuries before they were abandoned at the beginning of the 19th century. The principal copper mines were closed eight years ago, but fortunately for the local labour force a new diamond mining operation was started up a few years ago. Nevertheless Messina is little more than a small *dorp* (the Afrikaner word for town or village) and, if you are coming from the south, this is a place most visitors will pass through without ever realizing they were here. But if you are arriving from Zimbabwe, particularly at night when the main street is lit up like a mini-Las Vegas, it appears to have all the trappings of the first world. For anyone who enjoys exploring the more remote and seldom-visited parts of South Africa the town is a good base from which to explore the local private game farms and the former homeland – Venda – to the east. There is also a good road across to the northern camps of Kruger via Tshipise, a route many Zimbabwean holidaymakers use. The Limpopo Valley Nature Reserve is in the process of being established and developed on the banks of the Limpopo River, though it is not open to the public yet. The reserve forms part of the Transfrontier Conservation area, which covers South Africa, Zimbabwe and Botswana. Also in the tube, so to speak, is a new tour to the local tomato paste factory! *Tigerbrand Food Processing*, T5340730, are the biggest producers of tomato paste in South Africa and are developing tours of their processing plant. Messina has the atmosphere of a frontier town with the main street lined with shops, banks, and fast food outlets. This is the last chance to buy South African products before crossing the border at Beitbridge into Zimbabwe, 12 km away. Both Messina and Beitbridge can get excessively hot during the summer months.

The **tourist office**, *Limpopo Valley Tourism*, on the corner of Whyte and Limpopo streets, T5343500, is useful for local accommodation bookings but it's a tiny office in comparison with the larger towns.

Sleeping
Price codes:
see inside front cover

B *Limpopo Safaris*, T/F5342403. 4 luxury double suites, a/c, lounge, swimming pool, a comfortable private game reserve which provides an excellent introduction to game viewing in the dry bushveld. Rates fully inclusive with game drives. **C-F** *Aventura Resort Tshipise*, 37 km from Messina, 105 km from Kruger's Pafuri Gate on the R508 or R525 from the N1, T5390634, F5390724. This is one of the chain of Aventura self-contained resorts. Conveniently situated en route to Kruger, adjacent to the Honnet Nature Reserve. Tennis, swimming pools, horseriding, hiking, mini golf, hot springs, laundry, shops and restaurants on site. Self-catering rondavels, TV, braai area, camping and caravan park with shared ablutions. It can get very hot here and summer temperatures are regularly over 40° C. **D** *Impala Lily Motel*, on the N1 as you approach town, T/F5340127. Good value a/c rondavels, en suite, TV, the most popular bar and restaurant in Messina. **E** *Limpopo River Lodge*, National Rd, T/F5340204. 12 double rooms, 7 single rooms, a/c, TV, budget simple rooms for traffic crossing the border with Zimbabwe. Buses stop here. **F** *Baobab Caravan Park*, on the left as you approach town from Louis Trichardt,

T5343504. Camp and caravan sites, electric points, laundry, well-grassed and shaded, busy over Christmas period, can get very crowded, booking advised. A greatly improved site since the management passed from the municipality into private hands.

Eating

Buffalo Ridge Spur, on Main St. Offers the predictable Spur fare of ribs, steaks, and fried chicken. If you are crossing into Zimbabwe, you might think you've finally seen your last Spur, but you'd be wrong, there's another one in Beitbridge! The best restaurant in town by far even if you're not staying there, is at the *Impala Lily Motel*, which has a huge menu with surprising variety from oysters to pork schnitzel. Lively bar which is the focal meeting place in town.

Tour operators

Far North, shares an office with *Limpopo Valley Tourism*, T5343500, F5343503. Camper van and 4x4 hire, a variety of tours in the region. *Manica Travel*, T5342220, on the main road at the north end of town. Agents for the *Translux* bus service and *Avis* car hire.

Transport

Rail The *Bosvelder* service departs daily at 1630 to **Johannesburg** via **Louis Trichardt**, **Pietersburg** and **Potgietersrus**. The train from Johannesburg is due to arrive at 0946. **Road** 12 km to **Beitbridge** (Zimbabwe border); 530 km to **Johannesburg**; 94 km to **Louis Trichardt**; 102 km to **Pontdrif** (Botswana border). **Bus**: *Translux*, T012-3348000. Coaches depart from the *Limpopo River Lodge*. **Bulawayo** (7 hrs): daily at 0415. **Harare** (9 hrs): Tue, Thu, Fri, Sun at 0540. **Lusaka-Zambia** (18 hrs): Tue, Fri, 1640. This service arrives in Harare at 0200, not convenient unless you have friends who can meet the coach. **Pretoria** and **Johannesburg** (7 hrs): Mon, Wed, Fri at 0615; Mon, Thu, 0715; daily 2305. *Greyhound*, T012-3231154. Services depart from the *Limpopo River Lodge*. **Bulawayo** (Zimbabwe) (5½ hrs): Mon, Thu and Sun at 1450; Fri at 0500. **Harare** (Zimbabwe) (9½ hrs): Mon, Fri and Sun at 0530; Sat at 2030. **Pretoria** (7 hrs): daily at 2200; Mon-Sat at 0715.

Getting to the border For the budget conscious traveller who has made it as far as Messina expect to pay no more than R10 for a ride to the border post. Once you have negotiated the South African side, you will either have to walk or hitch across the bridge over the Limpopo River. Allow yourself plenty of time to cross the border and find a lift towards Bulawayo, Masvingo, or Harare. Mini bus taxis to these destinations can be found waiting on the other side of Zimbabwe immigration.

When arriving from Zimbabwe there is a minibus taxi car park just outside the South African border post gates, from here you can get a lift to Messina where there is a daily stopping train to Johannesburg departing at 1630. Alternatively you can pick up one of the mainline bus services on either side of the border that operate between Harare and Johannesburg. The total unbroken bus journey between these 2 destinations is around 18 hrs.

Directory

Banks *First National*, Main Rd. *Standard*, corner of Main Rd and Emery St. *Bureau de change*, Main Rd next to the PO, T5343412. Open 7 days a week, 0700-1700. **Communications** Internet facilities: *The Computer Shop*, Main Rd, opposite *Shoprite*, T5341206. Open Mon-Fri 0830-1700. A useful first stop when arriving from Zimbabwe where internet access is not always as quick or reliable. **Useful services** Medical Centre: T5340557. **Police**: T10111. **Ambulance**: T10177.

Crossing into Zimbabwe

There is a duty-free shop selling a limited range of cigarettes and spirits plus a range of larger electrical items, and a VAT Refund office. This is particularly useful for tourists who can claim back the VAT on any unused items they are taking home with them. Formalities on the Zimbabwe side can be very slow, especially customs. During local school holidays it can take as long as 5 hours to clear all formalities and it gets very hot here during the summer. Avoid this border at opening time early in the morning, as this is when the buses arrive from both Johannesburg and Harare and there are lengthy queues. There is a new bridge across the Limpopo River, which has helped reduce traffic delays but there is a rather hefty toll, US$6.90. The original bridge is only used by pedestrians and the railway.

Beitbridge border
Open daily 0530-2230. 24 hrs over the Dec-Jan and Easter holiday periods

Ins and outs **Formalities** At present most hired cars from South Africa are not allowed into Zimbabwe. Third party insurance is required by law for all vehicles entering Zimbabwe. Short term policies can be bought at the border posts or offices of the AA, who are the sole representatives of Zimbabwean third party insurance in South Africa. Visitors from overseas countries must have an English translation of their licence plus a photograph.

Bona fide tourists in private vehicles must have a Vehicle Registration Certificate, they will normally be granted a temporary import permit free of charge provided the vehicle is licensed in its home country and has the appropriate number plates. If the vehicle has been borrowed, than a letter of authorization from the owner is required that has been certified by the police.

NB If you are travelling in a private vehicle be wary of petty thieves, especially on the Zimbabwe side, lock everything up and make sure anything on the outside is well-tied down. Do not under any circumstances accept help from touts in the car park who offer to sell relevant forms or 'look after' your car, all forms are available free of charge inside the border control building, and official uniformed security guards patrol the car park. There should be no problems for tourists but be prepared for some frustrating questions and delays from the officers in Zimbabwe customs, and under Zimbabwe's present political climate, do not state your occupation as that of journalist or any other media-related job.

East of the Great North Road

Colour map 2, grid A4 *As you drive north from Pretoria towards Zimbabwe much of the surrounding country-side seems to be flat and dull. Though this is not entirely true, you'll need to venture off the main road to discover the more interesting sights of the province. This is especially true of the country around the agricultural centre of Tzaneen. When you turn off the N1 at Pietersburg onto the R71 for Tzaneen there is a radical change in scenery.*

Ins and outs

Getting there Around Tzaneen is a range of hills known as the **Magoebaskloof**. Many of the slopes are **& around** covered with blue gum forest plantations, but in between there are lush valleys, dams and lakes full of fish and peaceful solitary country hotels. When you reach the small village of **Haenertsburg** you are faced with the choice of two possible routes to **Tzaneen**. The **R71** continues past **Ebenezer Dam** and winds through the beautiful forested **Magoebaskloof Valley** before reaching the verdant **Sapekoe Tea Estates (Middelkop)**; the other option is to follow the **R528** along **George's Valley**, 12 km from Tzaneen you will pass *Tenby Gardens*, open for light snacks and a wide range of curios and crafts. Whichever route you take, you are likely to be exploring the other later if you elect to stop over and spend a few days exploring this little-known region. Haenertsburg is the principle centre at the western end of the mountains, and Tzaneen is on the eastern side, they are linked by both valleys.

There are 2 possible routes east and south of Tzaneen, the R71 to **Gravelotte** and **Phalaborwa** (111 km) to enter Kruger at **Phalaborwa Gate**, or the R36 south towards **Hoedspruit** (120 km), the **Drakensberg escarpment** and Kruger's **Orpen Gate**. Both routes pass through the region known as the **Valley of the Olifants**, an area rich in private game farms and well worth visiting. If not entering Kruger, the route passes into the southern region of **Blyde River Canyon** in the Mpumalanga Province, see page 625.

The Magoebaskloof

Phone code: 015 One of the best times of the year to explore this mountainous area is in the autumn *(NB Always use* when all the wild flowers and cherry blossoms are out. Many of the country hotels *3-figure prefix)* will be fully booked, but this is a perfect time to pack a small picnic and spend the day *Colour map 2, grid B4* walking in the forests by mountain streams. Each valley is full of flowering plants and trees, and during December and January you can expect to see bright pink and mauve 'pride of India' trees, and over 200 species of orchid have been identified. The lower slopes are cultivated with tea and banana plantations, and gum tree forests, and the image is of one of a rolling green patchwork quilt. The villages and country cottages also retain this garden theme, even the police station in Haenertsburg is set in beautiful grounds with it's own flock of sheep and geese. Although it can't be visited, the tallest man-planted tree in the world is in Woodbush Forest Reserve, a blue gum eucalyptus and is estimated to be 100 m high. There are many nurseries with attached tea gardens dotted around the two principle valleys.

Before the region was peacefully settled it witnessed a brief bloody feud between the Transvaal government and the Tlou tribe of the chief Makgoba. In 1894 the followers of Makgoba retreated into the forests refusing to pay government taxes. The European soldiers were unable to dislodge the force and in the end it took a group of Swazi warriors, working for the government, to defeat Makgoba. In the final battle Makgoba had his head cut off.

There is **tourist information** at *Byadladi/Magoebaskloof Tourist Association*, Rissett St, Haenertsburg, T2764972, F2764797, mta@magoebaskloof.com Open Mon-Fri 0800-1700, Sat-Sun 0830-1200. A helpful office, which helps make visits to these slightly more remote areas such a pleasure. Can book accommodation.

Ins and outs The Magoebaskloof Hiking Trail is divided into two sections, known as the **Grootbosch** and the **Dokolewa**, both take three days to complete, are considered to be tough walks and should only be attempted by seasoned hikers. Permits must be obtained from the Department of Forestry (SAFCOL) in Pretoria, T012-4813615, as each trail has restrictions on the minimum and a maximum number of hikers. Both trails are circular which saves hikers from having to arrange for transport at the end of a walk back to their own

Magoebaskloof Hiking Trail

Magoebaskloof

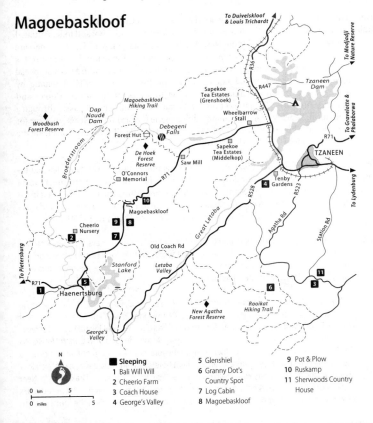

Northern (Limpopo) Province

■ Sleeping		
1 Bali Will Will	5 Glenshiel	9 Pot & Plow
2 Cheerio Farm	6 Granny Dot's	10 Ruskamp
3 Coach House	Country Spot	11 Sherwoods Country
4 George's Valley	7 Log Cabin	House
	8 Magoebaskloof	

vehicle. The **F** *Grootbosch-Dokolewa Hut* serves as a starting base for both sections, it is well-equipped with hot and cold water, a gas stove, cooking utensils, bunks and toilets.

Getting there From Tzaneen, the R71 passes the Sapekoe Tea Estates and a large dam on the right, shortly after is a sawmill, look out for a right turning just here to the **De Hoek Forest Station**. Follow a gravel road up into the forest, shortly before the station on the right is a parking spot for **Debegeni Waterfalls**. The falls are a series of cascades, which drop 80 m into a deep cool pool, a popular swimming and picnic spot. Care needs to be taken when swimming and scrambling amongst the rocks, some surfaces are very slippery. Lives have been lost here.

The **Grootbosch** section of the Magoebaskloof Hiking Trail is a difficult 50-km hike, the two overnight sites are simple *lapas*, with no immediate water supply. During the day it is important to look out for signs indicating where drinking water can be collected. Parts of the trail are very steep and much of the path is under the tree canopy, for this reason the hike is not recommended during the winter months. The best months to attempt this trail are September to November and March to April.

The **Dokolewa** section of the Magoebaskloof Hiking Trail is a slightly easier 36-km hike. The two overnight sites are simple huts with wood fires, bunks, mattresses and a fresh water supply. Parts of the trail are very steep, but it is a clearly marked path. The route alternates between plantation forest and patches of indigenous forest with plenty of view-points across the lowveld. If you are not so sure of your level of fitness then this is the easier of the two hikes to attempt.

Rooikat Hiking Trail This is the ideal trail for visitors who wish to spend a leisurely day walking in the cool mountains. The complete trail is an 11 km loop with a picnic spot and toilets situated midway. The trail starts by the New Agatha Forest station, permits and a map are available from here. There are plenty of opportunities for swimming, the forest is one of the last remaining patches of indigenous forest in the area and trees of special interest have been identified. Look out for some fine examples of Natal mahogany and matumi. If you are quiet you may get to see some bushbuck, duiker and samango monkeys. The last section of the trail is a bit dull since it passes through a plantation. Be wary of snakes when walking in the forest. You can leave your car for the day at the Forestry Office, T3074310. The **Letsodi Trail** starts and finishes at the Magoebaskloof Hotel, 1-2-hour strolls.

Pekoe View tea processing plant This tea processing plant is at the top of the magnificently green and lush tea plantation with a spectacular view down the valley over the tea bushes. Interesting tours of the plant depart Tuesday-Saturday at 1100, before tasting the tea in the tea garden along with their famous chocolate cake or excellent lunch menu, a peaceful and tranquil spot. ■ *Pekoe View is at Sapekoe's Middlekop Tea Estate, R71, T3053036.*

Sleeping
■ *on map, page 657*
Price codes:
see inside front cover

There are a range of accommodation options throughout the two valleys, if you are not staying in the more expensive hotels they are still worth visiting for lunch or afternoon tea. Remember when choosing accommodation, air-conditioning is not a priority in this area, rather fires and heating in the winter months.

A-B *Glenshiel*, 2 km from Haenertsburg on the R71, T2764335, F2764338. 15 luxury suites in a country lodge, each suite has open fireplaces, TV, the lodge is well-known for its excellent cuisine. Tennis, swimming pool, trout fishing, delightful gardens, walking trails, good service. Worth trying to bargain on the price out of season. Recommended. **A-B** *Coach House*, PO Box 544, Tzaneen, T/F3079342. Hidden away in the forests 15 km south of Tzaneen close to the Agatha Forest Reserve, 45 rooms, an excellent hotel with high standards, it has won four awards as the 'Best Country Hotel', all rooms have clear views across the Drakensberg. Neat and colourful gardens, swimming pool, much of the fresh produce served in the restaurant is grown within the grounds, it is possible to walk and join marked trails in the forest straight from the grounds, quiet location. The site is on the old Zeederberg Coach Run, the original coach house is close by, described in its day as 'a rough and ready wayside inn'.

B *Magoebaskloof*, off the R71, approximately 26 km from Tzaneen, T2764776, F2764780. 60 double rooms all with en suite bathroom, disabled access, ensure that your room has a view, at dawn the sun frequently rises above a carpet of mist which hangs over the forested valley, in fine weather you can dine on the lawns outside, *Red Post Box* pub also serves meals, swimming pool, activities include fishing, boating, tennis and golf close by. **B** *Sherwood's Country House*, PO Box 2033, 15 km from Tzaneen near Agatha, T015-3075512, F3074216. 5 double rooms and 2 suites with a small lounge and private veranda, each room has been carefully furnished in this fine Victorian country house, plenty of books in the lounge where one can relax in front of a warm fire during winter, excellent meals which benefit from all the home grown produce, extensive gardens which border the Agatha forests where there are numerous hiking opportunities. Recommended. **B-C-D** *Granny Dot's Country Spot*, 16 km from Tzaneen, off the Agatha road, T3075149, F3075927. Family-run B&B on a working farm. Each en suite room has a spectacular view of the Wolkberg mountains, a log fire warms the lounge during the winter months. Eve meals on request. An ideal base for anyone planning on walking the Rooikat Hiking Trail. Recommended.

C *Magoebaskloof Ruskamp*, 25 km from Tzaneen on the R71, T/F3054142/7. A cluster of rondavels perched high up on the R71 where it climbs over a winding pass. Self-catering or smaller B&B units, TV, heater, pool, sub-tropical gardens, excellent restaurant with a fantastic terrace overlooking the valley, but availability on the menu a bit hit and miss depending on how many people are staying. Finalist in a national award for varied accommodation.

D *Bali Wil Will*, 3 km out of the village Haenertsburg, T2762212. B&B or self-catering cottage available for up to six people. Meals available on request. Pleasant location off the main road on a farm. **D** *Cheerio Farm*, at the Cheerio Nursery, T2761802. Self-catering chalets or B&B rondavels. Swimming pool and tennis court. Perfect setting with fine views across the valley. **D** *Log Cabin*, off the R71, 8 km from Haenertsburg, T2762104. Variable rates depending upon numbers, room for up to 5 people. Breakfast extra. A suitable base for anyone contemplating the Magoebaskloof hiking trail. **D** *Pot & Plow*, off the R71, 10 km from Haenertsburg village, T2762104. 1 self-catering cottage and 1 double B&B facility. Next to a popular restaurant of the same name.

E-F *George's Valley Holiday Farm*, 12 km from Haenertsburg, R528, T/F2762002. New kid on the block and strongly supported by the tourism office. Stunning location next to the picturesque Letaba River and dam in George's Valley. 20 camping stands, basic loos and outside showers, no electricity but paraffin lamps available, 3 simple cottages, lower rates for longer stays, lots of outdoor activities.

Atholl Arms, in front of the tourist office in Haenertsburg, T2764712. Open breakfast til' late, **Eating** closed Mon. Hearty country fare, Sunday set lunch, cosy atmosphere. Join the local crowd for games evening on Thu. *Iron Crown Tavern*, Risset St, Haenertsburg. Pub serving bar snacks. *Picasso's*, a prominent wood cabin just off the main road through Haenertsburg. Comfortable restaurant and curio shop with a good choice of light meals, their pancakes are very popular. Open daily 0800-1700, but closed in evenings except for Fri-Sat, until 2100. Internet access. Always worth a brief stop. *Pot & Plow*, popular roadside restaurant and bar. Closed evenings. Check out the home made pies with some tasty salads.

Green Rhino, 38 Essenhout St Tzaneen, and an office at *The Wheelbarrow Farmstall*, **Tour operators** Magoebaskloof Road (R71), T3075979, F3072123, greenrhino@mweb.co.za Adventure operator for the region. Micro-lighting, quad-biking, tubing on the Lebata River, fishing, *kloofing* (a sport that has taken Cape Town by storm, a combination of hiking, rock climbing and sliding down waterfalls). To get to the *Wheelbarrow* from Tzaneen, drive across the Tzaneen Dam, turn left on to the R71 for 1 km, and will also pick up from most hotels in the surrounds. Recommended.

Northern (Limpopo) Province

Tzaneen

Phone code: 015
(NB Always use
3-figure prefix)
Colour map 2, grid B4

Tzaneen lies at the centre of a prosperous agricultural region on the eastern side of the Magoebaskloof Mountains. Consequently much of the countryside appears to be considerably greener than many parts of South Africa and the palm trees and banana plantations contribute to a tropical feel. *Tzaneen Tourism Centre* is at 23 Danie Joubert St, T3071294, F3071271.

History   This a relatively young town which only took a permanent form when the Selati Railway arrived in 1912, is now the second largest town in the Northern (Limpopo) Province after Pietersburg. Prior to this the first Europeans to arrive in the region and start farming were Conrad Plange and Heinrich Altenroxel from Germany. In September 1903 the Transvaal government bought their farms with the intention of using them as an experimental farm where new settlers were taught farming techniques before being given land to go and set up on their own.

After a public meeting on 11 June 1918 at the *Morgan Hotel* it was agreed that the area around the railway station was the best for a new township. In January 1919 plans were drawn up for 58 lots with streets which were to be not less than 60 ft wide. There are several versions of how the town was named. Louis Changuion when writing up the history of the town in 1994 concluded that the name was a very old Bantu name used to refer to the peoples and the area they lived in – Tsaneng. After the establishment of the government research farm the spelling appeared as 'Tzaneen Government Estate' in Agricultural Journals. The change in spelling is explained by how the German settlers wrote the sound when they heard the Bantu language being spoken; the sound 'ts' became 'tz' when written.

Sights   Do not be deceived by its size or the building, the **Tzaneen Museum** on Agatha Street, T3072425, is one of the best museums in South Africa, and as such it deserves far greater recognition and resources. The displays are in fact a private collection belonging to Jurgen Witt who has put together a unique collection of ethnological artefacts. Crammed into three small rooms is an amazing collection of pottery, pole carvings, drums, books, beadwork and other domestic items. Ask to be shown around by Jurgen and allow several hours for the tour. There is so much to learn about the area. ■ *Mon-Fri 0900-1700, Sat 0900-1300. Give generously to help towards the upkeep of the building.*

Hans Merensky Nature Reserve   Hans Merensky Nature Reserve is on the southern banks of the Great Letaba River, 68 km east of Tzaneen, on the R529 towards Giyani, T015-3868632. Founded in 1954 to protect various species of lowveld antelope, in particular roan and sable. The natural vegetation is described as mopane lowveld and there is a good chance of viewing giraffe, bushbuck, zebra, impala, duiker, impala, tsessebe, hippo, leopard, and blue wildebeest.

Sleeping
Price codes:
see inside front cover

If you are not staying in the Magoesbaskloof or in the surrounding country retreats, there are a few accommodation options in Tzaneen or on the road coming in from Phalaborwa. **C** *Tzaneen Country Lodge*, 17 km from Tzaneen on the R71 from Phalaborwa, T3043290-2, F3043290. 25 a/c functional rooms, DSTV, bar, restaurant, room service, can arrange local activities, fishing, bush walks etc. Large pretty gardens, outside restaurant that serves the passing traffic with pub lunches and good pancakes. **C-D** *La Borie Guest House*, 23b Circle Rd, T3075282, F3071352. 4 double rooms with en suite bathroom, TV, lounge, swimming pool, lunch and dinner available on request, lush gardens surround this family B&B, close to the commercial centre. **C-F** *Aventura Eiland*, Hans Merensky Nature Reserve, T3868763, 3868692. Central reservations, T011-2073600. 10 luxury rondavels with TV, a/c, 91 2-4 sleeper self-catering rondavels, 462 stand caravan and camping park, 150 with electric points, restaurant, bar, swimming pool, sauna, mineral pools, horse riding, water park, usual Aventura resort with inclusive facilities. **D** *Steffi's Sun Lodge*, 5 km before town from

Phalaborwa on the R71, T/F3071475. 6 rooms each with separate entrance, a/c, with en suite bathroom, TV, lounge, laundry service, large gardens, spacious rooms, relax on the shady veranda with a book and watch the traffic go by on the main road below. Run by a friendly German couple. **C-D** *Tamboti Lodge*, 18 Tambotie St, T/F3074526. 4 double rooms with en suite bathroom, 2 double rooms with private bathroom, non-smoking room, TV, lounge, swimming pool, a modern house in a quiet smart residential suburb, the garden has a real tropical feel with palm trees and orchids, a comfortable option for this type of accommodation, a short drive to the facilities in town.

   D *The Stoep*, 4 km from Tzaneen on the Deerpark road, turn off at the *Bananas for Africa* farm stall on the R71 from Phalaborwa, T3075101, T083-2559943 (mob). 5 double rooms with separate entrance, en suite bathroom, non-smoking room, TV, lounge, evening meals available on request, swimming pool with pleasant deck overlooking the valley, peaceful family-run farm setting. Ask for Johan or Hannie. **C-F** *Fairview Lodge & Caravan Park*, Old Gravelotte Rd, T3072679. A pleasant shady complex on a series of terraces above the Letaba River, the campsite has access to a restaurant, the chalets are divided into three categories, the cheapest are dark, dank units which should be avoided, however the new luxury chalets are good value as a self-catering unit, recommended to stay here if you are looking for an inexpensive base from which to explore the area, just out of town on the Phalaborwa road.

If you are staying at one of the country hotels there is no point in going into Tzaneen for a meal. During the day there are plenty of roadside tea gardens in the area which also serve snack lunches making good use of local fresh produce. There is nothing too special in the centre of town. *Addisons*, Arbor Park Business Centre, corner of Soetdoring and Geelhoout

Eating
● *on map*

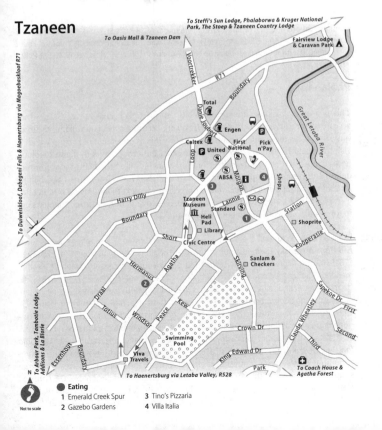

Tzaneen

Northern (Limpopo) Province

N
Not to scale

● **Eating**
1 Emerald Creek Spur
2 Gazebo Gardens
3 Tino's Pizzaria
4 Villa Italia

Hidden enemy

One interesting person who left his mark on Tzaneen was Dr Siegfried Annecke, a medical pioneer in the 1930s at the forefront in the battle against malaria. The annual number of patients at the time exceeded 4,000 and largely through his efforts, malaria was virtually eradicated in the region by 1966. However, it gradually returned and by 1972, 2,000 cases were reported between the Lowveld in the south,

and the east of Tzaneen.

The Malaria Institute in the centre of Tzaneen carries the name of Siegfried Annecke, and today is involved in research to combat and treat malaria and bilharzia. According to the map supplied by the institute, Tzaneen today is malaria free, but it is still endemic in parts of the Lowveld region of the Northern (Limpopo) Province and Kruger National Park.

streets, T3076261. Closed Sun, open from breakfast onwards, à la carte menu. *Emerald Creek Spur*, 16 Morgan St, T3071168. Standard quality steakhouse, no surprises. *Gazebo Gardens*, 30 Agatha St, T3071462. Coffee shop in a beautiful old garden, pleasant venue for evening cocktails. Recommended. *Tino's Pizzaria*, Agatha St, T3071893. Good Italian serving takeaway pizza.

Transport **Road** 95 km to **Pietersburg**; 112 km to **Phalaborwa**. There is no public transport linking Tzaneen with any other major centre so you really need a car or will have to join a day tour in order to visit the surrounding countryside.

Directory **Communications** Internet facilities: *Procom Internet Café*, 18 Peace St, T3074836. A short distance from the commercial centre, follow the one way street towards the swimming pool. Open Mon-Fri and Sat morning. **Useful services** Ambulance: T10177. **Chemist**: T3073790. **Hospital**: T3073790. **Police**: T10111.

Phalaborwa

Phone code: 015
(NB Always use 3-figure prefix)
Colour map 2, grid B5
Altitude: 450 m

This is a quiet Afrikaner town only 2 km from Kruger's Phalaborwa Gate, which accesses central and northern Kruger. If you are here in August you will find the town busy and full as the annual carnival takes place. It is a convenient base from which to visit Kruger and the luxury private game reserves, the airport has daily flights to Johannesburg and there are good facilities for tourists including a broad range of accommodation and restaurants, plus several car hire outlets. The well-informed and helpful *BaPhalaborwa Tourism Association*, is on Wildevy St next to the *Impala Inn*, PO Box 647, T/F7816770. Open Mon-Fri 0900-1800. Closed Sun. But, as the red triangle signs in town will warn you: watch out for those hippos.

Sleeping
■ *on map*
Price codes:
see inside front cover

Being so close to Kruger, there is a wide range of accommodation options in this town. **A-B** *Hans Merensky Club*, just out of town, at the Kruger end, off Koper Rd, T7813931, F7815309. 18 luxury a/c chalets set around a golf course, excellent restaurant. Recommended. **B** *Sefapane Lodge*, corner of Copper and Essenhout streets, T7817041, F7817042. Up market thatched self-catering chalets in a large indigenous garden, braai boma, restaurant, swimming pool with a sunken bar, have a meet and greet desk at the airport, fly in packages available, run day trips to Kruger and other regional tours. If you don't have a car this is a good mid-range option. **B** *Tulani Safari Lodge*, on the road to Mica, T7816541, F7696065. 20 chalets, a/c, restaurant, bar, swimming pool, tennis, hiking trails, bush drives. **C** *Impala Inn*, 52 Essenhout St, T7813681-4, F7815234. 60 double a/c rooms, restaurant, bar, swimming pool, central shady courtyard, walking distance to the shops and banks, 2 km from Kruger Park gate. Part of the Protea chain but very individual and personable. **C-F** *Lantana Hotel*, corner of Kiaat and Hall streets, T7815191, F7815193. 24 self-catering holiday flats, a/c, DSTV, restaurant, garden bar, swimming pool and caravan park. **C** *Selati River Lodge*,

Rooibos St, T7892021, F7810865. A/c rooms, swimming pool, restaurant, large gardens. **C** *Ingwe Park*, 3 km out on the Tzaneen road, T/F7813776. Restored old miner's camp, self-contained bungalows, TV, kitchen, swimming pool, hiking, bush trails on horseback, a fun bush lodge. Recommended. **C** *Steyn's Cottage*, 67 Bosvlier St, T7810836, F7815622. 12 a/c double rooms with en suite bathroom, TV, elegant lounge furnished with some fine antiques, rooms overlook a neat garden and swimming pool, excellent service, restaurant next door, one of the best mid-range options. Recommended.

D *Daan & Zena*, 15 Birkenhead St, T082-9208808 (mob). 14 double rooms, TV, swimming pool, garden cottage, comfortable B&B or self-catering, secure parking. Rates vary considerably between group or single occupancy. **D** *Raintree Cottage*, 1 Essenhout St, T7810995. B&B with attached tea garden, close to park gates, evening meals on request. **D** *Allins Travel Lodge*, corner of Palm and Essenhout streets, T7813805/6, F7813808. 16 holiday flats, 8 rather dire park homes, restaurant, bar, gardens with braai facilities. Indifferent service, the whole complex is surrounded by ominous looking razor wire fencing. **D-F** *Sholanaga Resort*, next to the Olifants river on the road to the mine, T7815069. Caravan and campsites, economic chalets, shady and well-grassed, electric points, laundry, swimming pool. **F** *Elephant Walk*, 30 Anna Scheepers Av, T/F7815860. A welcome backpackers place close to Kruger Park which also offers good value game viewing trips into Kruger Park. Choice of 13 bed dorm, double room, self-catering cottages, a flat or camping in the shady garden. Fully equipped kitchen, laundry, meals on request.

Eating
● *on map*

Buffalo Grill & Pub, Hendrick van Eck & Lekkerbreek Rd, T7810829. A lively and popular steak house serving large portions along with some chicken and fish dishes, the bar is also worth a visit at weekends for an outsiders insight into small town bush life. Steaks and cool beers. *La Gondola*, Phalaborwa Mall. Good value pasta and pizza. *La Werna*, 67 Bosvlier St, T7810836. Smart dining next to Steyn's Cottage, enjoyable selection of starters and main courses, meat and poultry dishes. Beautifully decorated intimate dining room, booking advised. Recommended. *The Guinea Fowl & Flying Olifant*, restaurant and pub in the *Impala Inn*, Essenhout St. A la carte menu and pub lunches. *The Roof Garden*, corner of Kiaat and Hall streets, T7815191. Part of the *Lantana Hotel*, closed Sun evening, open for light meals from 1100, also serves breakfast to non-residents, plenty of choice, steaks are your best bet. *Tiffany's*, Rooibos St, T7815562. A la carte restaurant, smart casual dress code, one of the best places for a meal, but still excellent value.

Sports

Golf *The Hans Merensky Country Club*, T7813931, clubhouse and pro shop, T7810449, is based around an 18-hole PGA championship golf course and is a must for golfers who can

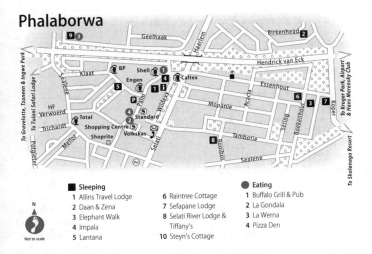

Phalaborwa

Not to scale

■ Sleeping
1 Allins Travel Lodge
2 Daan & Zena
3 Elephant Walk
4 Impala
5 Lantana
6 Raintree Cottage
7 Sefapane Lodge
8 Selati River Lodge & Tiffany's
10 Steyn's Cottage

● Eating
1 Buffalo Grill & Pub
2 La Gondala
3 La Werna
4 Pizza Den

Northern (Limpopo) Province

enjoy the unique experience of negotiating wildlife on the greens whilst they are playing. Watch out for the hippos on the 17th hole. Expect to pay about US$20 for a round with a caddie. Your caddie's local knowledge is particularly welcome here when you encounter wild game during your round, the odd antelope may be ok, but a few elephant are enough to put most people off their game! Call in advance to make sure there are no local matches and remember the best times to play are early morning or late afternoon.

Tour operators *Jumbo River Safaris*, T7816168. Organize a fun 3-hr boat trip on the Olifants River for the ever popular sundowner. Always a good chance of seeing game and some colourful water birds, assuming the group doesn't get too rowdy. *South Africa National Parks Board*, in Phalaborwa Mall, T7813828, F7813757. This is a useful satellite office of the Parks Board based in Pretoria. All rest camp reservations between 13 months and 48 hrs in advance must be made through the head office or here. Reservations less than 48 hrs must be made directly with the camp. See the Kruger National Park section on (page 592) for more details. This office, however, can assist with late bookings under 48 hrs by phoning the camps on your behalf. *Sure Turn Key Travel*, PO Box 647, T/F7816770. General travel agent with offices at the airport and Phalaborwa Mall.

Transport **Air** Phalaborwa Airport, 2 km from town centre and entrance to Kruger Park, T7815823, is currently reinventing itself as Kruger Park Gateway Airport and, recently refurbished, has got to be the most fabulously designed airport building in South Africa. The baggage reclaim is under a thatched roof, the seats in the waiting area are rocks, and the drinking fountain sprouts out from a tree stump. *SA Airlink*, T7815823, central reservations, T011-9781111. Operate the flights between **Phalaborwa** and **Johannesburg**, they are a partner of *South African Airways*. To **Johannesburg** (1 hr): Mon-Fri 0800, 1200, 1610; Sat 1200; Sun 1610. There are at 3 flights a day from Johannesburg, the flights arrive 30 mins before the flights listed above return to Johannesburg. Expect to pay around R1,000. **Road** 70 km to **Hoedspruit**; 200 km to **Nelspruit**; 219 km to **Pietersburg**; 480 km to **Pretoria**; 112 km to **Tzaneen**. **Car hire**: *Avis*, T7813169; *Budget*, T7815404; *Imperial*, T7810376, are all at the airport.

Directory **Banks** *Standard*, Palm St. *ABSA*, Wilger St. ATM's and foreign exchange available. **Communications** Internet facilities: *Net-o-Mania*, T7817812, in the Phalaborwa Mall on Palm St. Not open evenings or on Sun. **Useful services** Chemist: 24-hr, T7813805. **Hospital**: T7853511. **Police**: T7812400.

Hoedspruit

Phone code: 015
(NB Always use
3-figure prefix)
Colour map 2, grid B5

Hoedspruit is Afrikaans for *hat creek*, and the place acquired its name when, after a long trek over the mountains into the heat of the lowveld, one of the Vortrekkers removed his hat and threw it into the cool waters of the Sandspruit River and decided to stay. Where at first stood only an outpost shop and bank agency, today Hoedspruit is a busy little town, surrounded by game-rich country, and ever-present views of the Drakensberg escarpment. At the very south of the Northern (Limpopo) Province in the lowveld region, Hoedspruit is close to both the private game reserves around Kruger, and the Panorama region of Mpumalanga.

There is little of interest to keep you in town itself, but the main attractions and accommodation options are along the R531 towards Blyde River Canyon. *Central Lowveld Tourism Association*, is in the shopping centre just to the south of town on the R40, T7932481. A useful collection of brochures.

Bombyx Mori If you are heading towards Blyde River Canyon, this is well worth a visit, and is the
Silk Farm only silk farm in South Africa. During the tour skilled Shangaan women show visitors the intricate methods of commercial silk farming. Most of the labour is drawn from the local community, including the women who are responsible for the fine finished products sold in the farm shop. The cultivated silk is produced from the cocoons of the Bombyx Mori Silk Worm. This produces a silk, which is a soft creamy

Northern (Limpopo) Province

colour. The excellent farm shop sells a wide range of produce; silk scarves, blankets, silk filled duvets, and cushions, and there is a kiosk and tea garden. ■ *Mon-Sat 0900-1600, Sun in summer only 1100-1400. 5 daily tours 0900, 1030, 1200, 1330, 1500. Adults R20. T7955813. The farm is 23 km south of Hoedspruit on the R531.*

Hoedspruit Endangered Species Foundation

This is a unique project that conducts essential research on endangered species, in particular cheetah. There are daily standard tours lasting 2 hours, which begin with an informative video about the plight of some endangered species, before viewing cheetah, African wild dog, ground hornbills, and the 'vulture restaurant', where many wild vultures come to feed. The extended tour, which runs twice daily for 3 hours, also includes a visit to a breeding and rehabilitation camp for rhino and the rare Barbary lion. Booking is advised for both tours as many local school groups visit this centre. ■ *Mon-Sun 0800-1600, 2-hr tours depart on the hour at hourly intervals 0800-1500, 3-hr tours depart 0800 and 1400, small entrance fee, curio shop and tea garden on site. T7931633, F7931646, info@cheetahresearch.co.za The Endangered Species Foundation is 23 km south of Hoedspruit on the R531.*

Sleeping
Price codes:
see inside front cover

The accommodation listed below is at the bottom of Blyde River Canyon close to Hoedspruit. For information about accommodation at the top of the canyon, refer to the Mpumalanga chapter. All are situated within an hours drive of Kruger's Orpen Gate, so with an early start it is possible to get to Kruger in time for an early morning game drive.

B *Blyde River Canyon Lodge*, 28 km from Hoedspruit, turn off the R531 on to the road that leads to the bottom of the Blyde River Canyon Nature Reserve and Aventura Swadini, T/F7955305. A very intimate and individual lodge, 6 double thatched rooms with verandas, bar, pool, excellent cuisine. The whole building is constructed from natural materials, beautiful grounds, which the owners have gone to great lengths to keep totally indigenous, zebras, warthogs, and a herd of blue wildebeest wander across the lawns and through the car park! When we visited here we were actually shown around by a very enthusiastic guest who couldn't rate the place highly enough. Recommended. **C** *Blue Cottages*, PO Box 223, Hoedspruit, 37 km from Hoedspruit on the R527 towards Blyde River Canyon, T/7955075. 5 bungalows, 2 suites, set in a beautiful bush garden with orchards all around, swimming pool, each unit has been decorated with some unique pieces of artwork and African antiques from the owners private collection, self-catering possible or you can eat at the *Mad Dogz Café* on the main road. John Williams, the owner, has been instrumental in promoting the lowveld

Northern (Limpopo) Province

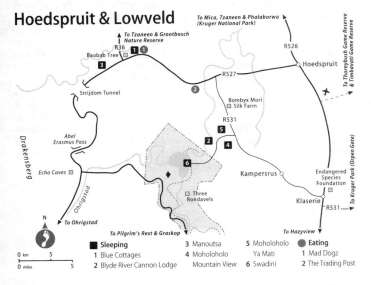

Hoedspruit & Lowveld

To Mica, Tzaneen & Phalaborwa
(Kruger National Park)

To Tzaneen & Grootbosch
Nature Reserve

R36

Baobab Tree ■ **1** ❶

3

R526

R527

Hoedspruit

To Thornybush Game Reserve
& Timbavati Game Reserve

Strijdom Tunnel

❷

Bombyx Mori
□ Silk Farm

R531

5

Abel
Erasmus
Pass

2

4

Drakensberg

Echo Caves □

6

Kampersrus

Endangered
Species
Foundation
□

To Kruger Park (Open Gate)

Ohrigstad

□ Three
Rondavels

Klaserie

R531 ▶

N

To Ohrigstad

To Pilgrim's Rest & Graskop ▼

To Hazyview ▼

| 0 km | 5 |
| 0 miles | 5 |

■ **Sleeping**
1 Blue Cottages
2 Blyde River Cannon Lodge

3 Manoutsa
4 Mololoholo
Mountain View

5 Mololoholo
Ya Mati
6 Swadini

● **Eating**
1 Mad Dogz
2 The Trading Post

and central Kruger region as a world recognized biosphere. Recommended. **C** *Moholoholo Ya Mati*, on the next property to the Blyde River Canyon Lodge, PO Box 1476, T7955236, F7955333. 3 chalets sleeping up to 6 people in each, TV, fridge, meals on request, 2 swimming pools, caravan park, chapel on site, popular for weddings. Lovely riverside setting, tea gardens, even if not staying it's worth a stop for tea. On the other side of the road is, **C-D** *Moholoholo Mountain View Camp*, PO Box 1380, T/F7955684. A 4,000 ha private reserve with wild lion, rhino and hippo. Free morning game walks with a ranger, night drives R40 pp. 9 self-catering chalets, meals on request, dining boma overlooks a waterhole, a good value, educational bush experience. **C-F** *Aventura Resort Swadini*, at the very base of Blyde River Canyon off the R531, adjacent to the Blyde River Nature Reserve and dam, T7955141, F7955178, central reservations T011-2073600. Part of the Aventura chain. South African Tourism award-winning resort in a stunning location. 78 chalets, 180 camping/caravan stands, shops, restaurants, swimming pools, tennis, mini golf, lots of hikes and a pleasant drive to viewpoints in the reserve, boat rides on the dam. As the crow flies, there is another Aventura resort, *Blydepoort* only a couple of kilometres away at the top of the canyon (see the Blyde River Canyon section in the Mpumalanga chapter), but they are actually over 100 km apart by road. **D-F** *Manoutsa Park*, a little further on from the *Blue Cottages* on the R531, T7955125, F7955012. Camping and simple self-catering thatched rondavels. **E** *The Trading Post*, see Eating below.

Eating   There are a couple of top class restaurants in this area. *Mad Dogz Café*, on the R527, east of the junction of the R527 and R36, T7955425, by the entrance for the *Blue Cottages* on the main road. The food here is some of the best in the region, an indication of how highly it is regarded is that at the weekend residents from Tzaneen will drive here for Sun lunch. There are very few eateries in South Africa which serve meals as good as this place: even if you are just passing through make time to stop off. *The Trading Post*, 26 km from Hoedspruit via Klaserie on the R531, T7955219. An attractive and unusual restaurant and pub owned by a friendly ex-game ranger and his French wife. A happy combination of the traditional South African way of cooking and the French social way of eating. If you have been in South Africa a while, you will be familiar with *braais* – here is the place to try it for yourself. Each table has an in-built gas *braai*, and you cook your meat to your liking. A selection of game meats such as warthog and crocodile, other ready prepared meat dishes, salads, and pizzas. There are occasional DIY fondue nights. This place is the focal meeting place for the rangers of the neighbouring game farms – go just to listen to them swap snake stories. **E** There are 2 simple chalets around the back for those who have had one too many for the road. The *braai* theme continues at breakfast, don't expect it early, when you can cook your own eggs.

Shopping   Next door to the *Mad Dogz Café* (see above) is the **Monsoon Gallery**. Like the café this is of the highest standard and is well-known, here you cannot help but find a fine piece of African art that you will want to take home, and all the packing and shipping can be arranged from here. There is also a shop here selling products from the *Bombyx Mori Silk Farm* (see above).

Transport   **Air**   Eastgate Airport is 7 km from Hoedspruit on the road to the Timbavati Game Reserve. *SA Express*, T7933681, central reservations T011-3942430. Operate daily flights between **Hoedspruit** and **Johannesburg**. To **Johannesburg**: Sun-Fri 1315; Sat 1415. From **Johannesburg**: Sun-Fri 1135; Sat 1235. The flights arrive about 25 mins before the flights listed above return to Johannesburg. **Road** 68 km to **Orpen Gate (Kruger)**; 74 km to **Phalaborwa**; 120 km to **Tzaneen**; 183 km to **Graskop (Mpumalanga)**.

Free State

11

Free State

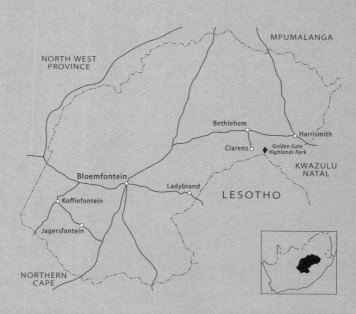

Between the Vaal River to the north and the Orange River in the south lies an undulating plateau and sparsely populated prairie land known as Free State. In the latter half of the 19th century the region was an independent Boer Republic governed by the Voortrekkers who had left the British Cape Colony in the 1830s. During this brief period of independence, Bloemfontein developed into a fine modern capital with many grand sandstone buildings. But the discovery of diamonds at Jagersfontein and Kimberley along with gold in the second independent Boer Republic of the time led to the outbreak of the Anglo-Boer War on 11 October 1899, a fact that has left its mark on the province, making it one of the most interesting areas of South Africa to visit from a historical point of view.

While there is not much to see in the arid farmlands to the west of Bloemfontein, the **Maluti Mountains** in the Eastern Free State hold many surprises. The scenery is spectacular as it rises to meet the lands of Lesotho, scattered with dams, mountain rivers and nature reserves, and connected by pretty rural villages with a wide range of accommodation choices and activities. At the centre of this area lies the spectacular **Golden Gate Highlands National Park**, where even during the summer months the hills are covered with snow.

The southern part of the Free State is known as the **Trans Gariep**, where many of the families who were part of the Great Trek first chose to settle after leaving the British controlled Cape Colony in the late 1830s. Here there are several battlefields from the Anglo-Boer War plus some small towns and museums which perfectly capture the atmosphere of the times.

Bloemfontein

Phone code: 051
(NB Always use
3-figure prefix)
Colour map 4, grid B3
Altitude: 1,392 m

The provincial capital of the Free State is the sixth biggest city in South Africa. It is also the judicial capital of South Africa, the Court of Appeal sits here. The city is located on the highveld plains surrounded by a group of flat-topped hillocks. It has warm, wet summers and dry, cold winters. The surrounding countryside is very fertile and an important farming region, maize being the principal crop. The city centre is an interesting mix of modern tower blocks built during the 1960s and 1970s with the State's mineral wealth, and a core of fine sandstone buildings dating from the late 19th century when Bloemfontein was the capital of the small independent Orange Free State Republic. Its central location, in South Africa, makes it an important transport centre, but few people actually spend time here. Like much of the Free State it has yet to figure on the tourist map, though fans of Lord of the Rings should note that JRR Tolkien was born here in 1892, moving to England when he was four years old. Despite having an interesting history, modern Bloemfontein has few visitor attractions, though it is a pleasant enough place to spend a couple of days in. As a small city it retains a friendly air and new shopping and eating developments are bringing people together. Because of the colleges and large training hospitals, there is a large youthful element and a number of trendy bars and nightclubs are opening up.

Ins and outs

This is an important centre for transport links, check timings carefully if you plan on changing bus or train. The general flow of traffic is between the Cape and Johannesburg. But from here you can head off west towards the Orange River Valley and Namibia; make the short journey eastwards to Lesotho; cut across the top of Lesotho into KwaZulu Natal; or journey around southern Lesotho into the Eastern Cape and the Great Karoo.

Getting there **Air** The airport is 10 km east of the city centre, off the N8, the Thaba Nchu road. The only transport available for transfers is taxis. Airport information, T4332901.

Rail Three different long distance trains stop in Bloemfontein each week, it is thus possible to travel to all the major towns in South Africa by train. While the train is very comfortable remember it is much slower than the bus, for example the journey from Cape Town takes 20 hrs by train, but only 11 hrs by bus.

Road Buses starting their journey from here tend to leave at a convenient hour, but buses stopping here to pick up and drop off passengers can pass through in the middle of the night or very early in the morning. The *Greyhound*, *Intercape* and *Translux* buses depart from and stop at the Tourist Centre on Park Rd (see below).

Tourist offices *Tourist Centre*, 60 Park Rd, PO Box 639, T4058490/8489, F4473859, blminfo@iafrica.com Open, Mon-Fri, 0800-1615, Sat, 0800-1200, helpful and knowledgeable staff who are keen to promote Bloemfontein as a tourist destination. *Trans Gariep Tourism*, directly next door to the above office, T4471362, F4471363, transgariep@intekom.co.za Open Mon-Fri, 0730-1600, closed weekends. This is the regional office and has a good selection of information on the Eastern Free State and Trans Gariep regions, strong supporters of cultural and community-based tourism projects.

History

There are several theories about the name Bloemfontein, but the accepted version is that the wife of Johannes Nicolaas Brits, one of the first settlers in the area who started to farm here in 1840, planted some flowers around the fountain which was used by everyone travelling across the central plains. In 1846 the Governor of the Cape Colony, Sir Peregrine Maitland, made a treaty with the Griqua chief, Adam Kok, by which the land between the Riet and Modder rivers be opened to European settlement. Major Henry Warden, the British resident in Griqua territory, was

Things to do in Free State

- Join Naval Hill Backpackers in Bloemfontein for a night of the **township jazz** in clubs which draw musicians from all over the world.
- Sleep in an old vortrekker ox wagon at the **Hoekfontein Ox Wagon Camp** near Ficksburg, and imagine what it was like on the Great Trek.
- Visit the caves, cliffs and green grasslands of **Golden Gate National Park**, all set against a backdrop of golden rocks.
- Go shopping in the craft shops and galleries of the small village of **Clarens** in the Eastern Highlands.
- Live it up on New Year's Eve at **Rustler's Valley**, one of South Africa's premier festivals and one of the most exciting alternative places to visit throughout the year.

instructed to move to the location to co-ordinate the new settlers. He chose Bloemfontein farm and the spot that had been developed by Brits. Brits received £37.10 in compensation, followed by £50 a few years later and a farm in Harrismith, which he also named Bloemfontein.

In 1848 Sir Harry Smith visited the new settlement and proclaimed the territory between the Orange and Vaal rivers as British, calling it the Orange River Sovereignty with Bloemfontein as its capital. Queen's Fort was built and the town started slowly to take shape. By 1853, Church Square and Market Square (now Hoffman Square) had been laid out. However, the surrounding countryside was still full of wild animals, which meant that travellers and farmers were in danger of attacks from lions, leopards and wild dogs. The British Government had decided the territory was hardly fit for habitation and not worth the trouble of maintaining. In 1854 the Bloemfontein Convention was signed, giving independence to the land between the Orange and Vaal rivers, and the British soldiers marched out of the town.

Josias Hoffman was the first President of the Republic of the Orange Free State and a *volksraad* (people's council) was elected to sit in the simple *raadsaal* (council chamber). This first council chamber can still be seen in St George's Street. President Johannes Brand followed him in 1863, under whom the town enjoyed 25 years of stable and prosperous independence when some fine government buildings were built. In 1890 the railway link with the Cape was finally completed and the town prospered further, though in 1904 there was a disastrous flood that cut the city in half and destroyed many buildings.

The discovery of diamonds at Jagersfontein and Kimberley along with gold, quickly led to the British wanting to re-establish control over these two regions. The Anglo-Boer War broke out and President Steyn of the Orange Free State sided with the South African Republic. When the British forces approached the town in March 1900 the Boer forces retreated to save the citizens and historic buildings. After the war was over, Bloemfontein became the capital of the Orange River Colony. In 1910, with the creation of the Union of South Africa, Bloemfontein aspired to be the country's capital; as it was it became the judicial capital, and remains so today.

Sights

Most buildings of note are within easy walking distance of each other along President Brand Street. Many of these grand sandstone buildings date from the second half of the 19th century when Bloemfontein was the capital of the small (in terms of population) Orange Free State Republic. (It is not possible to go inside all of them because some are still in use today.) On the corner of President Brand Street and Charles Street is the **Appeal Court**. Although Bloemfontein was designated as the seat of the Appeal Court with the advent of the Union in 1910, this building was only

The Tourist Centre produces a useful map showing 'The Rose Walk through Bloemfontein', which covers the major historical sites and takes about 1½ hrs

Free State

completed in 1929. It was built in a free-Roman style with corrugated Italian tiles on the roof and window ledges. Above the main entrance the helmet of Faith and the torches of Truth are portrayed.

Standing opposite is the neo-classical, Doric columned **Fourth Raadsaal** (Council Chamber) with its domed tower. This was the last home of the *Volksraad* (council) in the days of the independent republic and is now the seat of the Provincial Council. The impressive building was completed in 1893, and was designed by L Canning. Inside, the original coat of arms of the Free State carved out of wood hangs behind the seat of the Chairman, and the busts of six presidents are arranged around the chamber walls.

Nearby, on the corner of President Brand Street and Maitland, is the **Old Government Building**, now the **National Afrikaans Literature Museum**, an important collection of Afrikaans literature, and original manuscripts by leading poets and novelists. The original single storey building had a high clock tower and was built by Richard Wocke in 1875 to house a government office. A second storey was added and then in 1906 an extension designed by Herbert Baker was built at the back. Baker created the present form after a serious fire in 1908. ■ *Mon-Fri, 0800-1215, 1300-1600, Sat, 0900-1200.*

A short distance away, on the corner of President Brand Street and Fontein Street, opposite the fire station, is the **Supreme Court**. This seat of the Provincial Law Court was built in 1909 at a cost of £60,000. This is a stately and vast court building where many famous cases have been tried in recent years. ■ *Visits by appointment only, T4482128.*

Across the river, on the corner of President Brand Street and St George's Street, is the **Old Presidency**. This was home to the last three state presidents before the British invasion. It has now been converted into a concert hall and a museum depicting the lives of the presidents. It occupies the site where Brits erected his original farm buildings and where Major Warden built his first residence in 1846. ■ *Tue-Fri, 1000-1200, 1300-1600, Sat and Sun, 1300-1700. Free entrance, the original stables at the back have been converted into a coffee shop.*

Just around the corner, on St George's Street, is the **First Raadsaal (Council Chamber)**. This is a typical pioneers' building with a thatched roof, beaten dung floor and long white mud walls. It was opened in 1849 as the Government Schoolhouse, but was also used as a church and council chamber. After the creation of the Orange Free State Republic the inauguration ceremonies for the first two presidents, Josias Hoffman and Jacobus Boshof, were held here. The *volksraad*, or people's council, met here until 1856, hence the name First Raadsaal. In 1877 the building was given to the town to be used as a museum. ■ *Mon-Fri, 1015-1500, Sat-Sun, 1400-1700. Small entrance fee.*

Also on President Brand Street is **Jubileum Building**. It was built in the late 1920s by boys from a local orphanage to provide a venue for reading and refreshments for young Afrikaners. A variety of entertainments were staged here, including concerts and art exhibitions, as well as political rallies.

Back on Church Street, the **Twin-towered Church**, which was fully restored in 1985, is on the site of the first small church built in 1849. Inaugurated in 1880, the church played a major role as the venue for the inauguration ceremonies for the last three state presidents, JH Brand, FW Reitz and MT Steyn. In 1935 the western tower collapsed and the other tower was removed, only for residents then to complain that the absence of spires spoilt the church's appearance; so in 1942 the two spires were re-erected.

In **Hertzog Square**, outside the City Hall, is a memorial and statue of General Hertzog. He became Prime Minister of South Africa in 1929 and again in 1934. A founder member of the Afrikaans-supporting, right wing National Party in 1914, he introduced much of the legislation against non-whites.

The **National Women's Memorial** is an obelisk, 36.5 m high, built of sandstone from Kroonstad and resting at the foot of two kopjes on the outskirts of Bloemfontein on Monument Rd. On each side of the column is a bronze bas-relief depicting scenes from the suffering of women and children during the Anglo-Boer War. The monument was unveiled on 16 December 1923 to commemorate the 26,370 women and children who died in Concentration Camps as a result of the Anglo-Boer War.

Naval Hill was once outside the city, but is now almost completely engulfed by the expanding suburbs. The panoramic views of the city are worth the drive. At the top of this hill are the **Franklin Game Reserve**, the **Observatory Theatre** and a **White Horse**. The White Horse was laid out by soldiers during the Anglo-Boer War as a landmark for returning horsemen. There are eland, hartebeest and springbok in the reserve, and it is not uncommon to get very close to giraffe in the car park of the Observatory Theatre where they seek out shade.

South of the centre, on Church Street, is the **Queen's Fort**, or **Military Museum**. Following his victory over the Boers at the battle of Boomplaats, Sir Harry Smith decided to build a new fort on a more strategically situated hill, named after Queen Victoria. For the first 30 years of the Free State Republic it was left to fall into a state of disrepair. In 1879, Captain FW Albrecht was appointed to oversee the complete rebuilding of the fort and mounted four iron nine-pounder guns. During the Second Anglo-Boer War it was occupied by British troops and at the end of the war it was given to the South African Constabulary. After housing a military headquarters the building is now a museum. ■ *Mon-Fri, 0800-1600, Sun 1400-1600. Free entrance.*

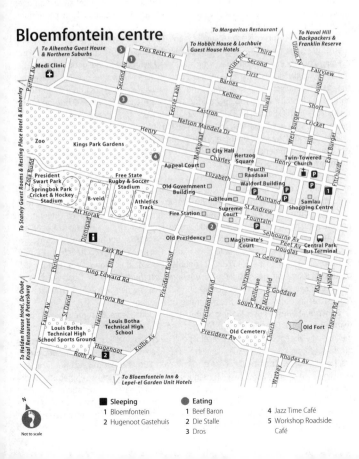

Bloemfontein centre

Sleeping ■
1 Bloemfontein
2 Hugenoot Gastehuis

Eating ●
1 Beef Baron
2 Die Stalle
3 Dros
4 Jazz Time Café
5 Workshop Roadside Café

Free State

Excursions

Whilst Bloemfontein has important 'white' historical sites, the nearby townships also have significance relating to the birth of the ANC and the legacy of the struggle. To see how life is lived in these places is interesting in its own right, and tours visit cultural and art centres, *Shebeens* (pubs), dance demonstrations, traditional restaurants, jazz clubs, and the various historical sites. There are three major townships outside of Bloemfontein. **Mangaung**, where the ANC was founded in 1912. **Botshabelo**, meaning 'place of refugees'. Estimated to be the second largest in the country after Soweto, established when Sotho and Xhosa people were forcibly removed from the Orange Free State towns. **Thaba 'Nchu**, was originally settled by Vortrekkers and later by Chief Moroka, the founder of the Barolong tribe and an important member of the early ANC. There is a rich Tswana culture here, particularly in the villages, which are still governed by chiefs and traditional courts.

Essentials

B *Bloemfontein*, Sanlam Plaza, East Burger St, T/F4038000. 113 a/c rooms, TV, restaurant, bar, shops, secure parking, swimming pool, owned by the Protea group, the principal hotel in the city centre, lacking in charm. **B** *Holiday Inn Garden Court*, corner of Zastron St and Melville Dr, T4441253, F4440671. 147 a/c rooms, non-smoking room, set around an open courtyard, restaurant, bar, swimming pool, disabled facilities, secure parking, comfortable hotel on the western outskirts of town.

C *City Lodge*, corner of Nelson Mandela St and Parfitt Av, T4442974, F4442192. 50 double rooms, 102 single rooms, a/c, good value town hotel, small rooms, choice of non-smoking, evening bar, pay extra for breakfast which is served in lobby lounge, good choice, eat as much as you like, no restaurant – a member of staff will advise on the evening choices, but they tend to send you to the nearest steak house – small swimming pool. Rooms tend to suffer from traffic noise when you open windows. Recommended for value. **C** *Haldon House*, Kwaggafontein, PO Box 10257, Drusana, T5233607, F5233742. 8 double rooms with en suite bathrooms, most have a separate entrance. This is a fine house set in a mature garden with a swimming pool and a large shade veranda. Evening meals can be arranged. Short drive from city centre. Recommended. **C** *Hobbit House*, 19 President Steyn Av, T4470663. 5 double rooms with en suite facilities, superior renovated guesthouse dating from 1925 and obviously named after Tolkien's creation, full of period furnishings. Evening meals available on request, after a day of exploring the city by foot the neat garden and swimming pool are a welcome sight. Recommended. **C** *Stately Guest Rooms*, 19 Jacobs St, T5224770, F5221610. 7 double rooms with en suite bathrooms, swimming pool, B&B or self-catering, TV, non-smoking room, disabled access. Rates are per room, which can sleep up to 4 people.

D *Alhentha Guest House*, 6 Rayton Ridge Rd, T/F5314367. 2 double rooms, a/c, a modern town house in a quiet suburb close to the Botanical Gardens. **D** *Bloemfontein Inn*, 17 Edison St, Hospital Park, T5226284, F5226223. 29 double rooms, 4 single rooms, TV, restaurant, simple budget rooms, off-street parking. **D** *Hugenoot Gastehuis*, T4300167. Good value guesthouse. **D-E** *The Resting Place*, 50 Scholtz St, T5225008. 1-5 person rooms, TV, breakfast on request, secure central guesthouse, swimming pool, sauna.

E *Lochbuie Guest House*, 28a Reid St, T4479528. 3 rooms, shared bathroom, use of fridge, swimming pool. **E** *Lepel-le Garden Unit*, 14 Usmar St, T4058489, F4473859. (The name means 'to lie like spoons'!) A cosy, peaceful poolside cottage, self-catering for 4 people, in a quiet suburb, private entrance, TV, contact Louise. Recommended. **F** *Naval Hill Backpackers*, Delville Rd, north of the city centre, follow West Burger street towards Naval Hill and Franklin Reserve, T4307266, F4474413. Regular users of backpackers will appreciate the different building, here the set up has been created in an old water pump station dating from 1901. Dorms in ingenious corrugated iron shacks within the old building, camping in the large grounds, one double private room with bush shower, large lounge and unusual underground eating area, pizza oven, excellent colourful set up. Will take people out at night to one of the township jazz clubs, which draws musicians from all over the world. Also runs a shuttle service to Lesotho – see transport section for details.

Eating & bars
● on map, page 673

Beef Baron, 22 Second Av, Westdene, T4474290. Well-established steakhouse, friendly service, good wine list. *De Oude Kraal*, something a bit special, but 40 km out of town, off the N1 to Cape Town, T5640636. Despite its location booking essential, famous for its typical South African food, such as 'boerekos'. *Dros*, 149 Zastron St, Westdene, T4487840. Good value restaurant and cellar bar, part of a successful group started a couple of years ago, fun atmosphere at the weekend.

Jazz Time Café, Waterfront, T4305727. Huge cocktail bar, outside terrace, excellent music, jazz, blues, big band, hubbly-bubbly pipes, extensive menu, try the *Zivas*, a Yemeni dough with a savoury filling, folded and toasted, open until midnight, a great place for an evening out. *Margaritas*, Baysvillage, 59 Milner Rd, Bayswater, T4363729. A good choice between fresh seafood and steaks, if you're not hungry then try a snack at the smart bar. *Workshop Roadside Café*, 109 President Reitz St, Westdene, T4472761. Trendy café with a giant TV screen, packed solid when there's a rugby match on, good value for the budget-minded.

Nightclubs
There are several universities and colleges in the city, consequently there is a large club scene

As in any major city, clubs go in and out of favour quickly and often change names or move location. For the latest information on what's in or what isn't, ask the waiters at the *Jazz Time Café* (above), also a good place to begin a night out. *Gringo's*, Bloomgate Centre, commercial music, large late night bar. *Reds*, Waterfront opposite Checkers, massively popular, rave, garage, open every night until 8 am. *Thump*, Second Av, huge dance floor, open until 6 am. *West End*, next door to Reds, dimly lit late night pool club and bar.

Shopping

Loch Logan Waterfront on First Av is an attractive outdoor shopping mall next to a lake and dam in Kings Park. Some of Bloemfontein's trendiest restaurants and bars are scattered along the boardwalk on the water's edge, there is a 6-screen *NuMetro* cinema. **Mimosa Mall** is on the corner of Nelson Mandela and Parfitt streets, a standard South African mall with the usual facilities, banks, food court, 4-screen *Ster-Kinekor* cinema, 2 internet cafés, *American Express* office.

Sport

Cricket International cricket matches are played at the Goodyear Park stadium which is part of the complex of excellent sports facilities to the west of the city centre close to the Tourist Centre. The cricket ground is a fun, small stadium, which has yet to be spoilt by towering modern stands. Here fans can still lounge around on grass banks as the game unfolds in front of them, a cool beer in hand. *Goodyear Park*, ticket enquiries: T4306365, F4472208. **Football and rugby** Next door to the cricket ground in Kings Park is the Free State Stadium, a neat modern stadium where international football and rugby matches are played. *Free State Stadium*, ticket enquiries: T4071701, F4473581.

Tour operators

Townships A full day tour visits all 3 townships, while a half-day tour visits 1 or 2, which can be combined with a half-day city tour. Contact the *Trans Gariep Tourism* office (above), or *Jumanji Tours*, T4511427; *Mipa Tours*, T4488786; *Poloko Tours*, T4300500; *Vuka Tours*, T082-9725927 (mob).

Battlefields For tour guides for the battlefields from the Boer War and the Zulu wars, try *Astra Tours*, PO Box 2818, T051-4302184, F4302097, johan@internext.co.za A recommended knowledgeable guide who also organize historical, tailor-made trips throughout Free State.

Transport

Local Car hire: *Avis*, T0800-21111, airport T4332331, *Gysie Pienaar Motors*, Nelson Mandela St, T4476185. *Budget*, airport T4331178. *Imperial*, T0800-131000, airport T4333511; *Safari Motors*, Zastron St, T4474202. *National/Alamo*, airport T4333577. **Taxis**: *Silver Leaf Taxis*, T4302005, for airport transfers.

Long distance Air *SA Airlink*, airport reservations office and flight information, T4333225, central reservations T011-9781111. Fly direct to the following towns: **Cape Town**: 5 times per day; **Durban**: 12 times per week; **East London**: 5 times per week; **Port Elizabeth**: 5

Free State

times per week; **Johannesburg**: 5 times per day. For other destinations within South Africa it is best to fly to Johannesburg and change.

Rail Part of the original station building from 1890 still remains. When buying a ticket pause to admire the teak pillars and staircase and the fine pine ceiling. Information T4084804. The *Algoa*, a 3 times a week service between **Port Elizabeth** and **Johannesburg**. **Johannesburg** (6½ hrs): Tue, Thu, Sat, 0233; **Port Elizabeth** (12 hrs): Tue, Thu, Sun, 2120. The *Amatola*, daily except Sat service between **Johannesburg** and **East London**. Towards **East London** (12½ hrs): daily, 1948; towards **Johannesburg** (7 hrs): daily, 0133. The *Diamond Express*, daily except Sat, service between **Bloemfontein** and **Johannesburg** (13 hrs), via Kimberley. Departs at 1700, arrives in **Kimberley** at 1950. The service from **Johannesburg** arrives in **Bloemfontein** at 0910. The *Trans Oranje*, once a week between **Cape Town** and **Durban**. Towards **Cape Town** (20 hrs): Thu, 0945; **Durban** (16 hrs): Tue, 1510.

Road 1,000 km to **Cape Town**; 415 km to **Johannesburg**; 186 km to **Kimberley**; 157 km to **Maseru**. **Bus**: *Intercape*, *Greyhound* and *Translux* offices are in the Tourist Centre on Park Rd where the buses stop. *Intercape*, T4471575. **Cape Town** (13 hrs): daily, 2330. **Johannesburg** (6 hrs): daily, 0630. **Plettenburg Bay** (11 ½ hrs): daily, 2330. **Port Elizabeth** (8 hrs): daily, 2330.

Greyhound, T4471558. **Cape Town** (12 hrs): daily, 2345. **East London** (7 hrs): daily, 0000. **Durban** (9½ hrs): daily, 2345. **Port Elizabeth** (9 hrs): daily, 2315. **Pretoria** (6½ hrs): daily, 0600, 0215.

Translux, T4083242. **Cape Town** (12½ hrs): daily, 2355. **Durban** (8 hrs): daily, 2230. **East London** (7 hrs): daily, 2355. **Johannesburg** and **Pretoria** (6½ hrs): daily, 0130, 1600. **Knysna** (11 hrs): Mon, Thu, Sat, 2305. **Port Elizabeth** (8½ hrs): Mon, Wed, Thu, Fri, Sat, 2245; Tue, Sun, 2240.

Lesotho transfers *Naval Hill Backpackers* offer a shuttle service to *Malealea Lodge* in **Lesotho**, (2 hrs) Mon and Fri, minimum 4 people. This returns on the same days, so it is quite feasible to stay at Malealea for 3 nights and return to Bloemfontein on the next shuttle. If you are short of time and are travelling between Cape Town and Johannesburg this is a good way to visit the mountain kingdom.

Big Sky Coaches, T5233620. Local commuter service to the **Lesotho Border**, (150 km) departing at 0600 daily from the Central Park bus station on East Burger St. R20 per person, pay on bus. Also to **Upington**, in the Northern Cape Province, every Fri, 1400, from the Tourist Centre, this service returns from Upington on Sun.

Directory **Banks** All the main branches are within the Mimosa Mall, corner of Nelson Mandela and Parfitt streets. **Medical services** Ambulance, Chemist, and **Medi clinic** all on T4046225/6.

Routes from Bloemfontein

There are several contrasting routes you can take when you leave Bloemfontein. **North** takes you across the veld to Johannesburg, most of the countryside is flat and scattered with ugly mine dumps. There is little to stop for between here and Gauteng. The N1 **south** passes by the early settler towns of the **Trans Gariep** region before entering the Great Karoo, there is a long way to go before you reach the first fertile valleys of the Cape. A short trip to the **west** along the N8 takes you to the mining town of Kimberley; further west the road skirts the fringes of the **Kalahari** en route to **Namibia**.

Finally the N8 to the **east** goes to the higher lands of Lesotho and what are known as the Eastern Highlands. Scenically this is the most spectacular countryside in the Free State. This is the main road to Maseru (140 km), the capital of Lesotho. Thaba Nchu is a huge township that used not to be signposted from the main road during Apartheid, despite the fact that all minibuses between Bloemfontein and Lesotho stop here. The lands around here were once part of the quasi-independent homeland known as Bophuthatswana, but it is all Free State today.

The Mighty Orange River

When you look at a map of South Africa it is immediately apparent that a large proportion of the country is sparsely populated, with only a few settlements of any size in the large province of the Northern Cape. Through this region flows one of the country's great rivers, the Orange River. It rises in the Drakensberg Mountains in northern Lesotho before flowing 2,250 km across the Great Karoo, entering the Atlantic Ocean at Alexander Bay. For most of its route it flows through arid country where the annual rainfall is less than 100 mm. From a very early date settlers dreamed of using the water for irrigation purposes and, after seeing it in full flood, for generating power. The first 32 km long canal was built in 1883 at Upington. In 1928 Dr AD Lewis, a government irrigation engineer, put forward a revolutionary plan to divert water from the Orange River into the Great Fish River and Sundays River via tunnels. The plan was too audacious and expensive for its time, but in 1944 serious field research began. The first dam was completed in 1971, the 88 m-high Hendrik Verwoerd Dam, now called the Gariep Dam; 130 km downstream a second dam was added, the Le Roux Dam. A canal running off the second dam provides water for 175,000 ha of agricultural land. A tunnel, 83 km long, takes water from the Gariep Dam south to the Great Fish River. The whole effect has been to take water out of one watershed and transfer it into another, where it flows in the opposite direction, but this time into areas of dense population, mining and intensive agriculture. A great engineering feat, and one that is in the process of being repeated on a much grander scale with the Lesotho Highlands Water Project.

Eastern Highlands

The countryside neighbouring the Lesotho border, dominated by sandstone outcrops and eroded river valleys, is the most dramatic and interesting in the Free State. The hills once provided shelter for the early San hunters who lived in the region and there are some fine examples of cave paintings as a record of this past. (You will need guidance from the local tourist offices to find and see the art.) The best way to appreciate the countryside is on horseback: the highlands are perfect hiking country and ideal for pony trekking and there is some great accommodation out of town on farms and in secluded valleys. Runing parallel to the Lesotho border, the R26 passes through all the towns of note in this region.

The region looks its best in the spring when the cherry orchards are in blossom. During winter there can be heavy snowfalls in the mountains

Ladybrand

A pleasant country town surrounded by a sandstone ridge full of San paintings and hidden caves, Ladybrand is the closest South African town to the Lesotho capital, Maseru (15 km). Along with Ficksburg and Wepener, the town was founded in 1867 after the war between the Boers and the Basothos to help guarantee peace in the Conquered Territory. It was named after Lady Catharina Brand, the mother of President Brand of the Orange Free State Republic. Sandstone from this area was used to build the Union Building in Pretoria.

Phone code: 051 (NB Always use 3-figure prefix) Colour map 4, grid B4

Maluti Route Tourism Office, Kerk St, T9245131, F9242636, malotiinfo@xsinet.co.za Open Mon-Fri, 0800-1700. The Maluti Route covers the Free State's Eastern Highlands, the Eastern Cape, and Lesotho so this enthusiastic tourist office is well worth a stop if you are planning to travel in any of these regions, they can provide an excellent booklet and map.

Tourist offices

There are two major **San rock painting** sites nearby that can be visited with a guide from the tourist office. One of 12 national monuments in the country, it is thought that they are the most concentrated San paintings in South Africa and range from between 5,000 and 250 years old. At **Modderpoort**, 15 km to the north, there is a

Sights

Free State

unique cave church dating from 1869. It was built by the Anglican Society of St Augustine, a small group of monks.

Sleeping
Price codes:
see inside front cover

C *Country Lodge*, 24 Joubert St, T9243209, F9242611. Double rooms with en suite bathrooms, a/c, TV. The rooms lead off from the restaurant and bar, so consequently it can get very noisy. **C** *Cranberry Cottage*, 37 Beaton St, T9242290, F9241168. 9 double rooms with en suite bathrooms, 4 elegant suites, TV. A smart award winning B&B in a restored Victorian country house. Additional rooms in the original ticket office and waiting rooms of Ladybrand Railway Station. All decorated with railway memorabilia and antiques. Recommended. **C-D** *Arbutuis Lodge*, 19 Prinsloo St, T083-3644988 (mob), F9242258. 2 doubles, 2 singles, housed in an historic sandstone house, B&B, garden full of flowers, neat veranda. **D** *Ladybrand Guest House*, 30 Nuwe St, T9241155, F9240305. Double rooms with en suite bathroom, modern B&B run by Paul and Sanet. **D** *My Housy*, 17a Prinsloo St. T9241010, F9242777. 5 double rooms with en suite bathroom, TV, heaters for winter and private entrance. A well-run B&B, ask for Jake or Sann. **D-E** *Traveller's Inn*, 23a Kolbe St, T/F9240191-3. A bit on the small side but economical rooms, en suite, TV, fans, restaurant with huge menu but many things must be ordered in advance. **D-F** *Leliehoek Resort*, T9240260, F9240305, 2 km from centre of Ladybrand, has self-catering units, caravan and tent sites – grassed and reasonably shady, full ablution facilities, swimming pool, a beautiful quiet place near some caves which contain some San paintings.

Ficksburg

Phone code: 051
(NB Always use 3-figure prefix)
Colour map 4, grid B5
Altitude: 1,629 m

Named after Cmdt-Gen Johan Fick, a hero of the Basotho wars, the town was founded in 1867 to occupy what was known as the Conquered Territory after the Basotho war. Its role was to prevent cattle rustlers coming over from Lesotho and to strengthen general control over the area. Interestingly, cattle rustling still occasionally occurs in this region. These days the small town has important trade links with Lesotho, but otherwise there is little of interest and it is only worth visiting for the **tourist office** (26 McCabe St, next to the Caltex garage, T082-5029292 (mob), open daily 0830-1300, 1400-1630) and basic supplies. A small **museum** commemorates the (not terribly interesting) life of General Fick, and a **Cherry Festival** is held here during the third week of November each year. ■ *Weekdays 1000-1200, 1400-1600.*

Sleeping & eating
A limited choice in town; many visitors choose to stay at one of the country lodges north of Ficksburg in the foothills of the Witteberge Mountains. The most popular area is Rustler's Valley (see below)

In town **C** *Bella Rosa*, 21 Bloem St, T/F9332623. 11 elegant suites make up this quality B&B set in a Victorian town house. Start the day with a delicious breakfast overlooking the mature gardens. A quiet and comfortable home, no young children. **C** *Hoekfontein Oxwagon Camp*, 10 km to the south of Ficksburg is a turning on to a gravel road, follow signs for 15 km, T9333915. Accommodation in original ox wagons arranged in a semi circle around a central eating and lounge *boma*. Double beds in the wagons themselves under white starched canvas roofs, also permanent tents, shared ablution block, meals available, horse riding, ox wagon drives, and abseiling in the neighbouring cliffs. Totally unique sleeping arrangement. Recommended. **D** *Highlands*, Voortrekker St, T9332214, F9332750. 37 rooms, TV, the *Rendezvous* restaurant on the 1st floor has a glassed-in veranda, but it's a very dank and dreary town hotel. **F** *Thom Park*, corner of McCabe and Bloem streets, T9332122. Plenty of grass and shade in this town centre caravan and camping site, some electric points, laundry, telephone, shops and restaurants a short walk away, but not much privacy due to its unshielded proximity to the main road. *The Bottling Co*, Piet Retief St, T9332404. Closed Mon evenings, pub and restaurant with good choice of beers.

North of Ficksburg About 15 km north of Ficksburg in the Witteberge Mountains are 3 contrasting rural retreats. Take the turning at Generaalsnek on to the S385, a gravel road winds its way into the hills, (all 3 have their own signposts at each junction).

B-C *Franshoek Mountain Lodge*, bookings usually dealt with by *Jacana Country Homes*, T012-3463550, F3462499. Prices include full board. A luxury rural lodge, bedrooms have 4-poster beds, thatched restaurant with cosy log fires. Plenty of emphasis on outdoor

Free State

pursuits, including polo, rock climbing, trout fishing, swimming pool, limited numbers, intimate atmosphere. Recommended. **B-C** *Nebo Holiday Farm*, at the junction of the S384 and S385, off the R26, T9333947, F9333281. 2-bed and 4-bed luxury chalets, TV, underfloor heating, plus self-catering cottages, quiet location on a sheep and cherry farm, quality restaurant and wine list, vegetarians will enjoy their meals here, swimming pool, ideal for hiking, fishing and bird viewing, everything you need to relax in comfort in the countryside. **C-F** *Rustler's Valley Mountain Lodge*, T/F051-9333939, www.rustlers.co.za Mix of rooms and dorms to suit all budgets and group sizes. In the warm months camping is possible, bar, restaurant serving some of the best vegetarian food in South Africa.

Rustler's Valley Festival For those in the know Rustler's Valley is one of South Africa's premier festival sites. Each year the New Year festival invites a range of different live bands and DJs to perform their latest material. This is a great opportunity to see some good live South African music and DJs in a safe setting. It's not Glastonbury or Roskilde, but it's an event well worth seeing if you are in South Africa at the time. For the budding musician Rustler's Valley is one of the most exciting alternative places to visit throughout the year and their website (see above) continually promotes a wide range of cultural activities and seminars for the faithful.

Fouriesburg

Phone code: 058
(NB Always use
3-figure prefix)
Colour map 5, grid A5

This is a small, untidy town 9 km from the Caledon River border post with Lesotho. Founded in 1892, Fouriesburg was named after Christoffel Fourie, the local farmer who originally owned the land. For a few months during the **Anglo-Boer War**, the town was the last seat of the Orange Free State's republican government and a stronghold of the Boer forces. As a consequence it was almost destroyed by the British army.

Sleeping and eating **C** *Fouriesburg Inn*, 7 Reitz St, T2230207, F2230257. 14 rooms, the only hotel in town, a comfortable, quiet overnight stop, small rooms opening on to sheltered veranda overlooking the church, a pleasant touch is being able to go into the original sandstone wine cellar and choose your wine before dinner. Restaurant offers a selection of mixed grills and salads, small dining room with plain pine tables. **C** *Carolina Lodge*, 3 km along the road to the Lesotho border, T2230552, F2230166. 17 rooms, fully licensed, an old style farm lodge, a holiday farm in the foothills of the Maluti Mountains, fresh farm cooking and plenty of outdoor activities, swimming pool, tennis, horseriding, hiking and mini golf. **C-D** *La Gratitude*, 6 Commisaris St, T2230017, F2230229. 5 rooms, 2 of which have en suite bathrooms, self-catering also available, tea garden, easy going B&B in the town centre.

Fouriesburg to Clarens

About 2 km south of Fouriesburg is the **Meiringskloof Nature Park**. Within the park there are short walks amongst the cliffs where there is a large open cave, '*holkrans*', once used as a hide-out during the Anglo-Boer War. For visitors with a head for heights there is a chain ladder which goes up a steep cliff face to a dam supplying water to Fouriesburg.

Travelling north from Fouriesburg there is a choice of two routes; 45 km direct to Bethlehem on the R26, or a much more interesting route, the R711 to Clarens, this also gives one the opportunity of visiting the Golden Gate National Park (page 681).

Surrender Hill is 7 km from Clarens on the R711. The name reminds the Boers of their most devastating defeat during the Anglo-Boer War, when on 29 July 1900, 4,314 Free State soldiers under the command of General Prinsloo were cornered in the mountains and surrendered to the British. Most of those captured were sent to India as prisoners of war. By the cliff is a memorial to the British soldiers who died here.

Clarens

Phone code: 058
(NB Always use
3-figure prefix)
Colour map 4, grid A5

This village was named after the Swiss resort on the shore of Lake Geneva where President Paul Kruger died in 1904. The settlement was only laid out in 1912 and has no historical past to explore but the relaxed feel of the place makes it the ideal spot to use as a base to explore the highlands. Tourism has taken over in this tiny, pretty village and a number of galleries, craft shops, and tea-rooms surround a grassed square

Free State

with a few sandstone buildings and large trees. It is the closest village to the Golden Gate National Park when approaching from the west, and the natural beauty of the area has attracted a number of artists to the region.

There are five quite well-preserved **cave paintings** on a farm called *Sonaapplaats* 20 mins' walk from town. In order to visit these paintings call in at the Clarens Tourist Centre who will phone ahead to let the farm owners know you are coming.

Tourist offices *Clarens Information*, Market St, T2561542, F2561643, clarens@dorea.co.za Open daily, 0900-1300, 1400-1700. Helpful, local booking agents for accommodation and activities. Clarens is a small community and the staff in this office know all the local artists and craftspeople, worth a stop if you are considering buying quality pieces.

Excursions Since the opening of the Katse Dam in Lesotho, part of the mammoth Lesotho Highlands Water Project (see the Lesotho chapter), to increase the feed of many South Africa's rivers, **Clarens Ash River** has experienced a surge of extra water from the new Trans Caledon Transfer Tunnel. The water exits the tunnel at 54 cu m per second and a series of rapids have developed on the river. It hasn't taken long for a **whitewater rafting** company to stake their claim. *Ash River Adventures*, T2561358, offer half-day, or early morning breakfast whitewater rafting runs for around R250.

A great way to see the local farmlands and enjoy views of Clarens from the hills above town, is on a **quad-bike tour**. *Sethuthuthu Tours*, (the name means motorbike in Sesotho) T2561569, runs quad-bike tours from one hour (R150) to a full day (R650) on trails connecting local farms. These trails are not for the thrill seeker as the pace is quite slow, but it is very pleasant to drive through the countryside and sandstone hills and on the longer tours there are some great views over the Free State and Maluti Mountains.

If you are heading for Golden Gate National Park from Clarens, the **Basotho Cultural Village**, T7210300, 10 km before the park gate on the right, is a worthwhile stop. Guided tours take you around a scattering of *bomas* and huts where traditional craft-making is demonstrated, local beer can be sampled, and a lively band provides entertainment.

Sleeping
In the village and along the R712 to Golden Gate National Park, there are over 60 places to stay. Here are just a few examples. Contact the Clarens Information and they will fax or email a complete list

In Clarens B *Country Lodge*, T/F2561354. 17 rooms, 8 chalets each with 2 bedrooms, restaurant, bar, swimming pool, gardens. B *Maluti Mountain Lodge*, Steil St, T2561422, F2561306. 10 rooms, 4 rondavels, M-Net TV, set in neat gardens, restaurant, fun pub atmosphere, swimming pool, popular as a weekend retreat. D *Clarens Inn*, Van Reenen St, T2561119. Self-catering cottage plus a dorm. Good value, central location. D *Patcham Place*, 262 Church St, T2561077. 3 double rooms with en suite facilities, TV, each has a private balcony and a separate entrance. The electric blankets and heaters serve as a reminder as to how cold it can actually get in this area during the winter months. Geoff and Delyse can also help you organize most local activities and get the most out of the stunning countryside. E-F *The Thistle Stop*, 58 Le Roux St, T/F2581003. A neat town house B&B with budget bunkhouse for backpackers.

Outside Clarens C-F *Bokpoort*, signposted 5 km out of Clarens on road to Golden Gate, a 3 km dirt road winds up into the hills on to a ridge where the farms and stables are laid out, T/F2561181, T083-6285055 (mob). There are 4 chalets and a 6-bed hikers' hut and camping, the shower block has plenty of hot water when the wood fires are burning, simple dining room and bar. Well-known for their excellent Western-style horse riding safaris in the Maluti Mountains, when you are treated to some superb countryside and real South African breakfasts. Recommended. D *Sediba Lodge*, 10 km south of Clarens just off the R711, T/F2561559. A delightful trout fishing lodge tucked away in a valley next to a small dam. In the evenings you can enjoy a sunset while admiring the sandstone mountains. Self-catering or meals provided with advance notice. Recommended.

Eating *Street Café*, Clarens. Snack meals and afternoon teas, open-air veranda, pub open late. *Sunnyside Guest Farm*, 12 km east of Clarens on the way to Golden Gate, 2 km off the R712,

PO Box 24, T2561099. Each Sun they organize an excellent braai and roast dinner along a shaded river bank. Costs R55 per person, bring your own drinks, make a reservation in advance as this is hugely popular locally.

Clarens Cottage, local handicrafts and jewellery, wildlife paintings, various exhibitions by local artists. *Clarens Meander Shops*, next to the Caltex garage as you approach town, has an interesting information office on the Lesotho Highlands Water Project, several craft shops and galleries, a farm stall selling home made treats, ATMs, and the fittingly named *Tourist Trap* café selling good coffees and pancakes. *Johan Smith Art Gallery*, colourful oil paintings of South African rural life by celebrated artist Johan Smith, also fine glass and ceramics. *Old Post House Gallery*, a smart gallery displaying paintings by local artist Alda van Biljon.

Shopping
For a small village Clarens has more than its fair share of craft shops and galleries. These are all within walking distance of President Square

Golf There is a 9-hole club on the outskirts of Clarens in the lee of the Rooiberg Hills, superb views from some holes. Guest members welcome, T2561255. **Horse riding** *Ashgar Connemara Stud*, T2561176. Trails of up to 6 hrs on offer. *Bokpoort* T/F2561181 (see under Sleeping above), offer the most exciting horse trails in the region. Their standard route lasts for 2 days, spending a night at a deserted homestead in the Maluti Mountains, the larger the group the better the value. This is a must if you like horse riding – like Lesotho just a few kilometres away, the countryside around here was made for horses.

Sports

Golden Gate National Park

A small (11,600-ha) national park on the edge of the Drakensberg and Maluti Mountains, the Golden Gate National Park is set in an area of massive sandstone rock formations. The eroded valleys have produced some spectacular shapes; caves, cliffs and green grasslands against a backdrop of golden rocks. This is a particularly special place at sunset when the colours of the rocks are at their most intense. The Caledon River rises in these mountains. It is a popular park given its proximity to Johannesburg (3 hours by car). The principal attractions are the hiking opportunities, the climbing and the spectacular rock formations. As you drive up to the first camp there are huge cliffs on either side of the road. The Rhebok Hiking Trail is also in the park, see below. The grasslands which dominate the sandstone slopes are known for their large variety of wild flowers in the summer months.

Colour map 4, grid A5

Getting there The common approach is the main road from Clarens, (15 km), which is surfaced all the way through the park. As you enter the park and approach the offices the road passes through a narrow valley with giant cliffs which give the name 'Golden Gate'. The sun shining on the oxides in the sandstone produces a brilliant golden hue to the cliff face.

Ins & outs
300 km from Bloemfontein, 15 km from Clarens, 54 km from Bethlehem

Information A public road runs through the middle of the park so there is no entrance fee. All enquiries can be dealt with at the respective camp receptions. If you have any questions concerning the park and its surrounds it is best to contact the Park Warden at Brandwag Restcamp, T058-2550012. Fuel is available at Glen Reenen, open 0700-1730. Glen Reenen Shop: open daily, winter 0730-1700, summer 0700-1730, stocks limited groceries, beer and wine, firewood and a few fresh items, maps and curios.

Climate The typical climate is cool rainy summers and cold winters with a high chance of snow. There is heavy snowfall on the high peaks while the valleys and surrounds remain untouched. Do not hike without suitable protective clothing in the winter. The park receives over 800 mm of rain annually so it is lush and green nearly all year.

You are unlikely to see many wild animals from the car, but once you get up into the wooded valleys and the quiet hills you may well see black wildebeest, Burchell's zebra, mountain reedbuck, blesbok, eland and grey rhebok. The larger raptors favour the high rocky cliff faces; look out for bearded vultures, jackal buzzards and black eagles.

Wildlife

Free State

Harrismith

Phone code: 058
(NB Always use 3-figure prefix)
Colour map 4, grid A6

Most visitors pass this town on the N3 en route to Durban. The town is dominated by a long flat mountain, the **Platberg**, 2,377 m. Each year on 10th October, a race is run up the mountain and along the top for 5 km before returning to the town. The origin of the race is very much part of local history. At the end of the Anglo-Boer War a Major John Belcher from the British Army referred to the mountain as 'that little hill of yours'. He was immediately bet that he could not run to the top in less than an hour. He duly won the bet, and the race, along with a trophy, was born.

The town was named after the British Governor Sir Harry Smith and nearby Ladysmith is named after his Spanish wife. The growth of the settlement was influenced by the discovery of diamonds at Barkly West and Kimberley in the 1860s, and gold on the Witwatersrand in 1886. Before the railway was built from the coast, at least 50 wagons a day used to stop over in the town.

Today it is still a popular stop for travellers between Gauteng and Durban, either overnight or for a break in one of the many service stations off the N3. Indeed in the one where all buses stop for a break, there is a public address announcer that broadcasts information on tourist sites on this major inter-city artery – throughout the toilets, restaurants and garage! More Disney than rural Africa but goes to show how seriously South Africa takes its, particularly local, tourism industry.

Tourist offices   The best source of info is at **Maluti Reservations**, at the Engen garage just out of town off the N3, T6222579, F6222591. Open daily, 0800-1700. This is a general travel agent, flights, bus tickets, agent for **Tempest**, car hire. Informative about the local area. *Translux, Greyhound, Intercape* and *Luxliner* stop at the Engen garage next door.

Excursions   **Mount Everest Game Reserve**, 21 km northeast of Harrismith on the R722 to Verkykerskop, is a private 1,000 ha reserve with the usual collection of antelope, which roam freely amongst the guest rondavels. C *Lodge & Chalets*, T6230235, F6230238. Accommodation consists of 10 luxury log cabins and some self-catering chalets, all with plenty of privacy. Facilities include a shop, restaurant, bar, and a swimming pool complex. There is a range of activities for the energetic visitor; horseriding, hiking, trout fishing, abseiling, rock climbing, and game drives.

Day trips can easily be made from here to the Northern Drakensberg   **Sterkfontein Dam Nature Reserve**, set in the foothills of the Drakensberg, covers an area of more than 7,000 ha and is one of the largest in South Africa. The entrance is off the R74 between Harrismith and Bergville. Accommodation is in **D-E** *Chalets* for 2-6 people as well as camping, T6223520. The local popularity of the reserve is illustrated by the fact that there are 360 camp sites. Most visitors come here for watersports and fishing. Hiking is possible and there are good opportunities for viewing raptors, and an interesting vultures' 'restaurant' that attracts Cape and Bearded vultures.

Sleeping & eating
Price codes: see inside front cover

C *Holiday Inn*, McKechnie St, T6221011. C *Sir Harry Motel*, McKechnie St, T6222151. 48 rooms, restaurant with copper pots, comfortable. **C-D** *Grand National*, corner of Warden and Boshoff streets, T6221060. 11 double rooms with en suite bathrooms, 19 single rooms, TV, restaurant, bar, secure parking, simple family-run country hotel, ideal for stopovers, excellent value. **C-D** *Rooikraal Inn*, T6231527, F6231661. 5 double rooms with en suite bathroom, comfortable B&B in a traditional rural sandstone house, evening meals on request. **F** *President Brand Caravan Park*, 2 km from town centre, T6221061. Perfect location on the banks of the Wilge River, good bird watching along the river bank, large site, well-grassed, half with shade, electric points, laundry, busy when holiday traffic is heading to or from Durban.

For eating, get away from the usual chains and service station road food, and try the ***Princess & Frog***, 17 Vowe St, T622476. Unusual for the area, a cosy double-storey Victorian house, fine French cuisine, limit of 12 people so advance booking essential.

The Trans Gariep

The Trans Gariep is the name given to the region to the southwest of Bloemfontein. This is rolling cattle and sheep ranch country, and a quiet seldom-visited corner of the Free State. It is in this region that the earliest Voortrekkers first settled. At the start of the 19th century this was classic wild animal country, with the plains full of game as far as you could see. In 1848 mail from Bloemfontein to Colesberg could not be despatched after 1600 because of the danger posed by wild animals. In 1860 a hunt organized for Prince Alfred, the second son of Queen Victoria, slaughtered nearly 5,000 wild animals on a single day. The wildlife never had a chance when competing with the farmers for this land. For information on accommodation in this area contact *Trans Gariep Tourism* in Bloemfontein, T051-4471362, F051-4471363.

The route outlined below takes you from Bloemfontein to Colesberg via some interesting rural towns as opposed to the direct route down the N1. It can easily be done in a full day

Koffiefontein

Phone code 053
(NB Always use 3-figure prefix)
Colour map 4, grid B2

This small sheep farming centre is on the Riet River. The name originates from the days when the settlement was on the transport route to Kimberley. Whenever transport riders passed through they stopped to make coffee by the town fountain. Today there is an ornamental fountain in the form of a pouring coffee pot to commemorate the transporters. In June 1870 a transport rider picked up a diamond by the fountain and the town enjoyed the rush and boom that always goes with diamonds. By 1882 there were four mining companies operating here. The legacy of the boom is a few fine old buildings, including the *Central Hotel* in Groot Trek Street. The open part of the diamond mine can be viewed from a lookout tower. During the Second World War the town was home for more than 2,000 Italians who were held in a prisoner-of-war camp. Little remains of the camp except for a wall which has been served with two wall paintings of Mussolini and the Italian king. The **Blue Diamond Tavern** is a well-preserved historical building still in use today. The **tourist office** is in the library, in the municipality building, T2050007, F2050128.

Jacobsdal

Phone code 053
(NB Always use 3-figure prefix)
Colour map 4, grid B2

This is famous for the **Landzicht Wine Cellar** (the first wine grapes to be grown outside the Cape Province in 1969). Cellar tours and tastings are possible here on request, T5910164, F5910145, and town has an annual wine festival in February. The Dutch Reformed Church, consecrated in 1879, enlarged in 1930 and now a national monument, was used as a hospital during the Anglo-Boer War. Look out for the bullet holes in the front door, vivid evidence of the many skirmishes which took place between the two sides in the area.

For visitors with a keen interest in the Anglo-Boer War there are two well-known battle sites just outside of Jacobsdal; Magersfontein and Paardeberg. Look out for an unusual British block house en route to Paardeberg. The **Battle of Paardeberg** occurred between 18-27 February 1900, when the Boers finally surrendered. More than 4,000 prisoners of war were taken, but perhaps more significantly the losses on the first day proved to be the highest for the British for any day during the whole war. More than 300 British troops were killed and over 900 wounded. This was an early indication of how bloody and brutal trench warfare could be.

Fauresmith

Colour map 4, grid B3

The drive across the plains to Fauresmith is through maize country; apart from a few poplar trees nothing else seems to be growing. Founded in 1842, Fauresmith is the second oldest town in the Free State. It is on the tourist map because of an unusual engineering feature: the railway line which was built right up the main street. An old steam engine still stands in the middle of the main street. Nearby the original small **Victorian town hall** is worth a quick look.

Jagersfontein

Phone code: 051
(NB Always use 3-figure prefix)
Colour map 4, grid B3

This is another old diamond centre. The first diamond was found by Mr JJ de Klerk in 1870 and the usual rush of miners were quickly on the scene. The village has retained much of the character from the boom years. All that remains today is a steep, deep hole (a volcanic pipe), which can be viewed from a platform. This is supposed to be the world's biggest vertical man-made hole. The mines are now closed,

Free State

but in their day they yielded some of the finest quality stones in the world. In 1893 the **Excelsior Stone** was found here; it weighed 971 carats and was the largest known stone until the Cullinan Diamond was found near Pretoria in 1905. Al Capone, the American gangster, had a large Jagersfontein diamond. In the early days of the settlement prisoners were tied to the trunk of a eucalyptus tree until the jail was built. Other places to visit include the small **Open Mine Museum** which has a few displays and early photographs from when the mine was operational. ■ *Daily, 0730-1600.*

Philippolis

Phone code: 051
(NB Always use 3-figure prefix)
Colour map 4, grid B3

The road between Jagersfontein and Philippolis is gravel in parts. It is much easier to approach from the south or the N1, 40 km to the east. Philippolis has many old buildings, which have been declared national monuments; they are all found along the one main street. The settlement is the oldest in the Free State and was founded in 1823 as a station of the London Missionary Society.

These days the town is still little more than one main street. Of particular interest is the **Dutch Reformed Church**, which has a grand pulpit made from wild olive wood, the library and some **Karoo-style houses**. The history of the region is portrayed in a typical Griqua cottage at the tiny **Transgariep Museum**, including an informative display on the life of Adam Kok and the Griqua tribe that once had a settlement here. ■ *Mon-Fri, 1000-1200.* The **ashes of Sir Laurens van der Post** are kept in the memorial gardens named in his memory. **Tourist Information**, 25 Kok St, T7730209, F7730157.

Price codes: see inside front cover

Sleeping **C** *Philippolis Lodge*, Voortrekker St, T7730422. This is a good value small town hotel with a restaurant, bar and secure parking. **E-F** *Old Jail*, T011-9731778, T082-5504421 (mob). This has to be one of the most unusual accommodation options in the country and although we didn't sleep here, we would be interested to hear from anyone who has. Accommodation is in individual cells in the oldest jail in the Free State, built in 1872. The cells are 2 m by 3 m with 60-cm thick outer walls, only 2 single 'prison' beds and 1 floor mat are supplied, cool in summer, hot in winter. The cells are virtually sound proof (though there is good cell phone reception), with heavy steel and wood prison doors (you do get to keep the key). If anyone has a hankering to experience what a 19th-century prisoner must have felt like, then this is the place to do it. Outside ablution block, braai areas, and kitchen with fridge and stove is available to the 'prisoners'. **D** *Die Waenhuis Guesthouse*, 26 Kok St, T7730157. This is an impeccably restored 19th-century Karoo farmhouse which is now listed as a national monument. It has 3 double rooms with en suite facilities. Recommended. **D-F** *Transgariep Getaway*, T/F7730088, 22 km out of town. Simple overnight self-catering guest farm for people travelling between Cape Town and Johannesburg, 3 en suite double rooms, shared kitchen, pool, cheaper basic backpackers' accommodation with shared ablutions.

Colesberg

The drive into Colesberg in the Western Cape is quite spectacular as it involves crossing the Orange River at Bothadrift, by the Serfontein Bridge. When you see the river in full flood you cannot help but admire the Voortrekkers who managed to cross this landscape, with no roads, in heavy ox wagons. Upstream from the Serfontein Bridge the Orange River flows out of the mighty **Gariep Dam**. The dam is the largest in South Africa and has become a popular destination for local holidaymakers. Formerly known as the Hendrik Verwoerd Dam; it may be a while before the name disappears from signposts and some maps.

Gariep Dam

Phone code: 051
(NB Always use 3-figure prefix)
Colour map 4, grid B3

At the western end of the lake is a small town, also called Gariep Dam. Since the completion of the dam wall in 1971, the town has evolved from a works camp. This is a sleepy little Afrikaner town, half of which is on top of a hill. It is worth going up to the top half for the commanding views of the lake and surrounding farmlands. At the eastern end of the lake is the Gariep Dam Nature Reserve. Each year in December the town hosts an **International Gliding Championship**. The competition has quickly gained a reputation for being the place to come and try to break world records. It is possible to arrange **kayaking trips** on the Orange River or **sunset cruises** on the dam. Contact *Big Sky River Adventures*, T7545055.

The local **tourist office** is in the library though is not especially informative, T7540071, F7540103. Open Mon-Fri, 0815-1300, 1345-1700.

The dam lies just off the N1 on the Northern Cape/Free State border, turn off at Donkerpoort, 40 km from Springfontein. The lake is over 100 km long and, in parts, 15 km wide, and the total shoreline is 435 km, most of which is protected by the **Gariep Dam Nature Reserve**. Primarily a watersports complex, it has excellent sailing and fishing. There is a fish hatchery nearby which supplies yellow fish, barbel and carp for the dam. The reserve exists in a unique environment. Before the dam was built, this was just a typical, arid Karoo landscape with the Orange River running through. With the construction of the dam and the flooding that followed, the landscape is quite bizarre. Hills rise out of the water. The lake has plenty of sheltered coves, and just away from the water the landscape reverts back to the typical desert environment. The reserve has been stocked with a variety of animals, including the endangered Cape mountain zebra. The best time to visit is either spring or autumn when the temperatures are not at their extremes.

Sleeping The main accommodation next to the dam is the large **C-D** *Aventura Gariep Resort*, T7540045, F7540135. Central reservations, T012-3462288. This is a smart caravan park and some stands have their own kitchen and bathroom, plus 56 chalets. There is plenty of grass and shade and all the facilities you'd expect at a family holiday resort, including a restaurant, bar, swimming pool, golf course and tennis. *Aventura* is for families and in the past had a strong Afrikaner bias. It is good value for an overnight stop out of season, but this is probably not the place to spend your holiday if you are visiting from overseas. **C** *Gariep Dam*, 2 Aasvoel Av, T7540060, F7540268. 23 double rooms with en suite bathrooms. A good value motel with restaurant, bar and parking. **D** *Bets*, 14 Rooibekkie St, T7540224. Guest house run by Bets Roothman. **D** *Green Doors Rooms*, 1 Fiskaal St, T7590190. B&B, caravan site, and restaurant, half way between the dam and village. If you want to get away from the canteen-style food at *Aventura*, eat here. **D** *Kate's Cottage*, 12 Swael St, T7540036. B&B in town, peaceful local base.

Price codes:
see inside front cover

Bethulie is a typical pleasant rural Free State town with an interesting history closely related to the development of South Africa. The original settlement, called Heidelburg, consisted of a mission station founded in 1829 by the London Missionary Society. It was taken over by the French Missionary Society in 1833 and renamed Bethulia – 'chosen by god'. A few of the original mission buildings still exist and are reckoned to be some of the oldest European-built houses in the Free State. The local museum is housed in **Pellissier House**.

Just outside of the town is a spectacular concrete **viaduct** across the Orange River. The 1,150 m road-rail bridge is the longest of its kind in South Africa, the railway is the main line to the port of East London.

Bethulie
Phone code: 051
(NB Always use 3-figure prefix)
Colour map 4, grid B3

Sleeping **C-D** *Royal*, Voortrekker St, T7630154. Principal town hotel with restaurant, bar. In dire need of refurbishment. **D** *Gariep*, 13 Oranje St, T7630180. Family-run guesthouse. **D** *Oppi-Koppi*, T7630388. Award winning B&B. **D** *T&T's Guest House*, 19 Joubert St, T7630643. Double rooms with en suite bathroom. Ideal location on the northern bank of Gariep Dam.

Price codes:
see inside front cover

The reserve lies between the **Orange** and the **Caledon rivers**. Most of the terrain is flat but there are prominent *kopjies*, which are covered with wild olive trees and bush guarri. Along the river banks are some beautiful large trees – Cape and weeping willows, white stinkwood and star apple. The reserve is one of the last places where you can still see large herds of plains game such as springbok, blue wildebeest, red hartebeest and blesbok. In addition you have a good chance of viewing white rhino, eland, gemsbok, kudu, zebra, impala, reedbuck and steenbok. Amongst the rock outcrops are some fine San paintings, but you will need a guide to find them.

Tussen Die Riviere Nature Reserve
Colour map 4, grid B3

This reserve is not that well-known but the game viewing and the hiking opportunities are excellent

Sleeping A *Letsatsi Game Lodge*, T4478865, F4478867. Relatively new and one of the best private game lodges in the province at this time. 35 luxury thatched chalets nestled in a *koppjie* with amazing views of the reserve and the mountains bordering Lesotho, 15 luxury tents in an exclusive bush camp connected by wooden walkways. Tastefully designed with elegant interiors, the main buildings have ingenious rooftop viewing platforms. Activities include mountain biking, helicopter flights, game drives, and horseriding. This is on a par with many of the luxury game lodges in northern KwaZulu Natal and around Kruger.

Northern Cape

12

Northern Cape

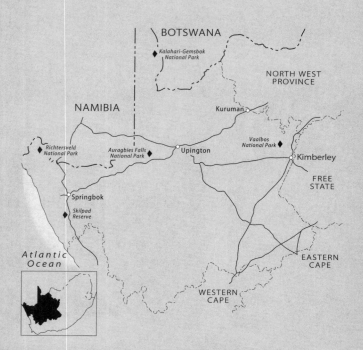

The Northern Cape is South Africa's largest state and one of its most beautiful, but compared to other areas of the country it remains tourist-free. Much of this has to do with the sheer harshness of the area – this is where the rock-strewn semi-desert of Namaqualand merges with the rolling red dunes of the Kalahari, where cruel heat pounds the parched wilderness for much of the year. But it is this sun-bleached emptiness and inaccessibility that gives the area its stark beauty, endless shimmering plains and hazy saltpans providing it with a real sense of isolation.

The state can be divided into three distinct regions: Namaqualand in the west; the Kalahari lying north of the Orange River; and the Karoo to the south. Despite the pervasive arid conditions, it is an area of excellent game viewing, with the magnificent **Kgalagadi Transfrontier Park** offering one of the finest national park experiences in Africa. In spring **Namaqualand** becomes the main attraction, when the valleys are transformed into carpets of vibrant colour as desert flowers explode from the earth with the first rains. The **Orange River** runs through much of the state, thundering over the surreal **Augrabies Falls**, the fifth largest in the world, and offering superb whitewater rafting. Lastly, this is diamond country, with the key town of **Kimberley** having a rich history and a number of sights, not least the colossal diamond mines. While the summer can be oppressively hot, the winter has pleasant daytime temperatures but frost at night, and the best times to visit are the more moderate seasons of spring or autumn.

Northern Cape

Kimberley

Phone code: 053
(NB Always use
3-figure prefix)
Colour map 4, grid A2

Kimberley, the capital of the Northern Cape, has a fascinating history and it is en route to some of the most beautiful and unspoilt wild country in South Africa – yet it is rarely visited by tourists. It is known first and foremost for its diamonds, and the flat land surrounding the town is pockmarked with mines. No longer the fortune-seeker's frontier town that it once was, Kimberley is today a bustling commercial centre with a surprising number of fascinating sights. The climate is one of hot summers, with occasional raging thunderstorms which account for most of the annual rainfall. The winters are warm but with cold nights and frosts in the morning.

Ins and outs

Getting there
For full details see transport on page 702

Air The airport is 10 km south of the town centre. There are daily flights to Cape Town and Johannesburg. **Rail** Three main line trains stop in Kimberley each week: The *Diamond Express*, *Trans Karoo* and *Trans Oranje*. **Road** *Greyhound* buses to Cape Town, Pretoria and Johannesburg start/finish their journey outside the Tourist Information Centre in Bultfontein St. All services also stop at the Shell Ultra City on the Transvaal Rd (N12) in the northern suburbs. *Intercape* and *Translux* coaches depart from the Shell Ultra City, Transvaal Rd.

Tourist offices & tour guides

Diamond Fields Tourist Information Centre, corner of Bultfontein and Lyndhurst streets, PO Box 1976, T8327298, F8327211. Open, Mon-Fri 0800-1700, Sat 0800-1200. The office has a list of local *Satour Registered Guides* for tours of the town, the surrounding region and the Kimberley Mine Museum. These include: Fiona Barbour, T8421018; Jean Bothomley, T8324712; Yvonne Dreyer T8421321; Steve Lunderstedt, T8314006; Dirk Potgieter, T8430017; Scotty Ross, T8324083; and Janet Welsh, T8328343.

For regional information, visit the *Northern Cape Tourism Office*, corner of Hemming and du Toitspan roads, just next to the Keg and Falcon Pub, T8322657, www.northerncape.org.za

History

The tremendous
wealth of the diamond
mines in Kimberley
was the basis on which
the modern economy
of South Africa was
founded

The early history of Kimberley is also the tale of the discovery of diamonds: a definitive turning point in the history of the country. The first significant find was in 1866 on a farm called *De Kalk* owned by Daniel Jacobs, near modern-day Hopetown. Jacobs' children gave a stone to their neighbour, Schalk van Niekerk. He in turn gave it to a trader, John O'Reilly, and asked him to find out the value of the stone. The stone ended up in Grahamstown in the hands of Dr Guyborn Atherstone, who found it to be a diamond of 21.25 carats, worth R1,000 and later named *Eureka*. In 1869 Schalk van Niekerk bartered for a larger stone from a Griqua shepherd – news soon spread of this stone and public interest began to grow. It came to be known as *The Star of Africa*, and in 1974 was sold in Geneva for over half a million US dollars.

In 1869 the search for diamonds was divided between two areas: the wet diggings, along the Vaal River; and the dry diggings on two farms some 40 km to the south. The Vaal River diggings attracted prospectors as the heat and drought of summer made conditions very tough on the farms at Bultfontein and Dorstfontein. In December 1870, the future of the region was finally determined when the children of Adriaan van Wyk found diamonds near their farm, Dorstfontein. The area was immediately engulfed with diggers and their equipment, including a party from Colesberg led by Fletwood Rawstone, known as the Red Caps. One night a servant appeared at his master's tent with a handful of diamonds. He had found them on the slopes of a hill on the nearby farm of Vooruitzicht, owned by the brothers Diederick and Nicolaas Johannes de Beer. The hill was named Colesberg Kopje, and within just a few months 50,000 diggers had turned the hill into a hole. Living conditions were very tough, and supplies expensive. In 1873 the name 'New Rush' was changed to Kimberley, in honour of the Earl of Kimberley, British Secretary-of-State for the Colonies. A twin town grew up around the Bultfontein and Du Toit's pan mines,

Things to do in the Northern Cape

- Follow the flower trail in **Namaqualand** and watch the sombre desert burst into a vibrant carpet of colour with the first spring rains.
- Hire a 4x4 and explore the jagged mountains and open spaces of the sun-baked **Richtersveld Mountain Desert Reserve**.
- Travel through the sandy expanse of the **Kgalagadi Transfrontier Park** – South Africa's most remote national park – and look out for the magnificent gemsbok or Kalahari lion snoozing amidst the red sand dunes.
- Watch colonies of **weaverbirds** build their house-sized nests on the lines of telegraph poles stretching endlessly across the Northern Cape.
- Scramble around the slippery moulded rock of the **Augrabies Falls**, and hike through their surreal cactus-studded, moonscape surroundings.
- Raft down the mighty **Orange River**, plunging down heart-pumping rapids and meandering through lush vineyards and green-fringed canyons.
- Don a hardhat and drop down an 800m shaft into one of Kimberley's working **diamond mines**.

called Beaconsfield, named after Benjamin Disraeli, the Earl of Beaconsfield. In 1912 the two towns amalgamated to become a city.

As the mines delved deeper, it became clear that individual claims would have to merge – there was simply no way of keeping them separate – at one point there were 1,600 separate claims in the Kimberley mine (now known as the Big Hole). In addition to the problems of mining logistics, the price of diamonds started falling because of over-production. It was at this point that Cecil John Rhodes and his partner Charles Dunell Rudd entered the scene. Together they began buying up claims in the De Beers mine, and in 1880 they founded the De Beers Mining Company. As Rhodes and Rudd expanded their operation, they came up against a man with similar ideas, Barney Barnato which led to an infamous power struggle only resolved when Rhodes paid Barnato a colossal pay off for his Kimberley Central mining Company (see box page 694). While the Big Hole stopped producing diamonds in 1914, three mines remain productive today: Dutoitspan, Bultfontein and Wesselton.

Sights

Most of Kimberley's attractions are in some way connected to the diamond industry. While there are some elegant Victorian buildings in town, there is far less evidence of the diamond wealth here than one might expect. Indeed, Kimberley was little more than a rough frontier settlement for much of its history; most of the diamond wealth making its way back to the civilized and comfortable climate of the Cape. Nevertheless, it is thought that in the 1890s more millionaires met together under the roof of the **Kimberley Club** than anywhere else in the world. The club still stands in du Toitspan Road close to the Africana Library. ■ *Private visits can be arranged, T8324224.*

While the suburb of **Belgravia** (see below) has a fine collection of Victorian houses, the rest of the city centre is made up of dull modern shops and office blocks. There are some early pictures of the centre at the **Kimberley Mine Museum** with the display on the siege of Kimberley. Today, the town's skyline is dominated by the **Telkom tower** and the De Beers headquaters, an ugly tinted glass building. More interesting is the equally unattractive **Harry Oppenheimer House** near the Civic Centre. This is the main diamond sorting centre in South Africa, and was designed to allow for optimum natural light to judge the stones by.

Close by is the pale yellow and white Corinthian style **City Hall**. A good way of getting from the City Hall to the Kimberley Mine Museum is by **tram**, there's a restored model dating from the early 1900s. It runs daily between 0900 and 1600, making the

A subtle reminder of the past is the irregular street pattern, which more or less runs true to the mud tracks which once criss- crossed a land filled with tented camps and diamond diggings

Northern Cape

Cecil John Rhodes

Cecil Rhodes was perhaps the ultimate British imperialist and played a central role in the history of southern Africa in the years after the discovery of diamonds at Kimberley.

He was born in the English town of Bishops Stortford in 1853 and was sent to Natal at the age of 17 to work on his brother's farm and to recuperate from bouts of tuberculosis. He was not, however, suited to a farming life and soon set off for the new diamond sites at Kimberley. From humble beginnings he began to prosper, slowly buying up shares in diamond buying concerns and through other schemes related to the diggings. With the money he earned from these businesses he went back to England, in 1872, to study for a degree at Oxford. Bad health forced him back to South Africa for a couple of years and he then alternated spells at Oxford with spells in South Africa and in 1881 he eventually managed to pass his degree. The contacts he made whilst at Oxford put him in an advantageous position in Kimberley and he was able to utilize British capital in his programme of gaining control of all the diamond mining activities. In 1880 Rhodes founded the De Beers Diamond Mining Company and continued to expand his commercial interest.

When diamonds were first discovered plots were sold cheaply to the first digger to lay claim to the site, but very quickly, and especially as the diggings became deeper, one or two individuals and companies managed to buy up all the shares and monopolize the buying and selling of diamonds. By the end of the 1880s, there were only really two players left in the game: Cecil Rhodes and Barney Barnato. In 1888, with the backing of British capital, Rhodes eventually bought out Barnato – with one cheque for the sum of £5,338,650.

As befits a grand imperialist Rhodes combined his hugely successful business career with a career in politics – indeed the two went very much hand in hand. He was first elected to the Cape parliament, as member for Barkly West, in 1880, and soon gained the reputation as an ardent supporter of British interests in South Africa and the expansion of British rule to the whole of southern Africa. In 1890 he became the colony's Prime Minister and continued to advocate British imperial expansion into remaining African controlled areas, such as Pondoland. This expansionism was driven partially by jingoistic pride in Britain but mainly by his commercial ambitions. This is clearly demonstrated in the expansion to the

trip on the hour every hour for R5. Trams have played an important role in the history of public transport in Kimberley. The first passenger tramway, pulled by mule, was opened in June 1887 to bring labour from the Beaconsfield township to Kimberley.

Africana Library The Africana Library is a major research centre and a rewarding place to visit for those with a particular interest in local history. There is a wealth of archive material on the diamond industry, missionary work in the region and early Tswana books. Two of its most famous books are Dr Moffat's copy of his translation of the Old Testament into Tswana, and a first edition of Schedel's Nuremburg Chronicle, 1493. ■ *Mon-Fri 0800-1630. Du Toitspan Rd. T8306247.*

William Humphreys Art Gallery In the Civic Centre on Cullinan Crescent is this gallery, housing one of the most important art collections in South Africa. It is an excellent gallery, with fine examples of 16th- and 17th-century art by British and Flemish-Dutch Old Masters. More interesting is the newer collection of contemporary South African art. There are examples of South African impressionists, an excellent graphics and prints display and a few individual gems such as the Irma Stern portraits. Also of interest is the rock engravings collection, tracing ancient San engravings dating back to 12,000 BC with photographs and some real examples. The gallery organizes some excellent nationwide initiatives, such as mobile exhibitions which aim to bring art to people empire he is best known for – the founding of a new colony that was to take his name.

Despite Rhodes' commercial genius he had made a serious miscalculation when gold was first discovered on the Witwatersrand. Taking the advice of an American prospector who told him that the gold was not even worth getting off a horse for, Rhodes decided to sit out the initial rush to buy up the best goldfields. By the time the true worth of the new reef was apparent Rhodes was too late to make an economic killing, though he did become involved with deep level mining activities. Frustrated by missing a golden opportunity, Rhodes began to look to the lands further to the north beyond the Limpopo River. Gold had been mined in these areas for centuries in small scale mines and Rhodes hoped to find another Witwatersrand. In 1888 he sent his Kimberley business partner, Charles Dunell Rudd, to secure from Lobengula, the leader of the Ndebele, mineral rights in the area they controlled. Armed with the mineral concession, Rhodes was able to secure agreement from London to set up a 'charter company' (the South Africa Company) which would not only prospect for minerals in the area but also be granted ownership of all the land and run all the administration.

In 1890 Rhodes sent out a 'Pioneer Column' to lay claim to the area. Their dreams of huge gold reserves proved illusory, but the country was still rich in minerals and many of the Pioneers indulged in the settlers' favourite activity of land speculation.

With the failure to find a second Witwatersrand, Rhodes turned his attentions back to his investments in the Transvaal. Rhodes' annoyance with President Kruger's constraints on non-Boer residents led him to make one of his worst political mistakes in backing the ill-fated Jameson Raid. This failed attempt to topple Kruger's government led to a serious breach in relations between Rhodes and Afrikaners in the Cape. He was forced to resign as Prime Minister and take a less public role in the Charter Company in Rhodesia.

At the outbreak of the Anglo-Boer War Rhodes was staying at his house in Kimberley where he remained throughout the siege. His health was poor throughout much of his life and the harsh conditions during the siege did not help. He died outside Cape Town in 1902 in his Muizenberg cottage, his body was transported by train and gun carriage to be buried in the Matopo Hills in present-day Zimbabwe.

---

who would otherwise not have the opportunity of seeing it. ■ *Mon-Sat 1000-1700, Sun 1400-1700. Small entrance charge. T8311724.*

Sitting alongside the Big Hole, this fascinating museum is made up of a collection of 40 original and model buildings dating from the late 19th century. They have been arranged to form a muddle of streets, with sound effects such as singing or snatches of conversation playing inside the shops. Each shop or office is furnished with items dating from the early days of Kimberley, and the overall result is very effective. There are a number of professions on show, including Dr JM Osborne's dental surgery, R Bodley & Son Undertakers, EHW Awty, a well-known watchmaker, the Standard Bank and A Ciring the Pawnbroker – the window display includes objects that have never been redeemed. One of the most impressive items is the original De Beers Directors' Private Pullman Railway Coach, a very plush carriage complete with a dining table laid with silverware and cut glass decanters and luxurious leather chairs. Another highlight is Sir Davis Harris' ballroom, an ingenious structure built in 1901. It is constructed entirely out of corrugated iron, with stamped steel walls made to look like smart wallpaper, fake skirting boards and metal stucco on the ceilings.

Inside the **Mining Hall** are examples of the first machines used in the diamond mining industry, some of which can be made to work for 10 cents. Look out for the early photographs of the diggings as the Big Hole gradually starts to take shape,

Kimberley Mine Museum & The Big Hole

Northern Cape

The Big Hole: the big statistics

It has a surface area of 17 ha and a perimeter of 1.6 km.

Before the consolidation of diggings, 30,000 men dug night and day. For several kilometres around Kimberley you could hear the dull noise of tapping and machinery.

These diggers went 400 m down before it became impossible to mine as a group of individuals.

In 1889 De Beers sunk the first shaft, and the hole extended to 800 m deep. Today there is over 600 m of water in the hole.

By August 1914 when the mine was closed, the mine shafts were 1,100 m deep. It is estimated that between 22 and 28 million tons of earth was removed to create the Big Hole.

All this labour resulted in the recovery of 14.5 million carats; only 2,722 kg of diamonds. Less than three metric tonnes!

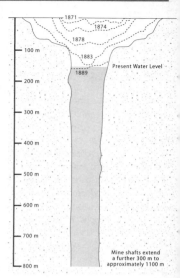

providing a vivid impression of life during the heady days of the boom. For a taste of the real thing, head to De Beers Hall close to the exit. More of a bank vault than a hall, it contains a collection of uncut stones, reproductions of the world's largest diamonds and examples of multicoloured stones.

The whole complex lies alongside the Big Hole (see below). There is a shop selling T-shirts and curios by the entrance and at the far end of the museum is a café serving toasted sandwiches and burgers. Allow at least 2 hours to see everything. ■ *Daily 0800-1800, entrance: R15, excellent value. Museum entrance on Tucker St. T8394901.*

The **Big Hole** can only be seen from inside the Kimberley Mine Museum. There are two caged viewing platforms which stick out over the rim of the hole so you can look down and see the murky green lake at the bottom. It is an astounding sight, especially when you remember that only a fraction of the hole lies above the water level, and that every piece of earth and rock was removed by hand.

Bultfontein mine On the other side of town from the Big Hole are two operational diamond mines, the Bultfontein and Dutoitspan mines, on Molyneux Road. It is possible to go on an underground tour of the Dutoitspan mine, a fascinating tour allowing a real insight into the reality of diamond mining. Tours begin in the surprisingly sparse visitors centre, where you are shown an introductory and safety video, and kitted out in protective overalls, hardhat, shoes and head torch. You then walk to the main shaft and are taken in a lift down to 820 m, a fairly unnerving experience and not for the claustrophobic. Once down, the guide walks you around key areas of the mine, including the main retrieval areas, crusher machines and mile-long conveyer belts transporting kimberlite. The most exciting part of the tour is when the miners are blasting – the ground and air shakes with the force of the explosion. You may also be taken to see 'development' sites, where the tunnels of the mines are being expanded. Here there are no luxuries such as dust extraction or electric light, so you really get a feel for how tough mining can be. Back on the surface, visitors are taken to see the mine from the surface, which is actually a far bigger hole than the Big Hole. This tour is a superb way of experiencing the heat, dust and mud of diamond mines, although you should bear in mind that you are very unlikely to see any diamonds. ■ *Surface tours are also possible, and are organized from the reception centre at the mine gate,*

T8421321. Mon-Fri 0900 and 1100, no tours on Wed, tours last up to 2 hrs. Underground tours, (you must book a day in advance; no children under 16), Mon-Fri 0745, no tours on Wed, tours last about 4 hrs, R80. You can wear contact lenses on this tour as they give you goggles to protect your eyes from dust.

Just to the east of the city centre is the residential suburb of Belgravia where many of the wealthy mines people built grand Victorian houses. There is a 2 km historical walk through the suburb which takes you past most of the old buildings; the majority can only be appreciated from the outside as they remain in private hands. The best known of the buildings open to the public are **Rudd House**, 5-7 Loch Road, and **Dunluce**, 10 Lodge Road. Both are kept closed for security reasons but they can be viewed on weekdays by prior arrangement with the McGregor Museum (see below). The first owner of Dunluce was Gustav Bonus of Dunluce, who instructed the architect to design a house fit for a member of the Diamond Syndicate. He was not disappointed; when the house was completed in 1897 it perfectly reflected the prosperity of the period. Unfortunately, it was badly damaged during the Siege of Kimberley in 1899 by a shell from the Boers' infamous 'Long Tom' gun.

Belgravia

Also in Belgravia is the **Duggan-Cronin Gallery**, set back on Egerton Road. The basis of this collection is a series of 8,000 ethnographic photographs taken between 1919-39 by Alfred Martin Duggan-Cronin, a De Beers' night watchman with an interest in photography. ■ *Mon-Sat 1000-1300, 1400-1700, Sun 1400-1700. Small entrance charge. T8420099.*

The history of this building, at 2 Egerton Road, is worth mentioning in addition to the collection it houses. The original house was built by Rhodes to serve as a hotel and a health spa, since the pure dry climate here was thought to be healthy. During the siege of Kimberley, Rhodes lived in two rooms on the ground floor. These now form part of

McGregor Museum

Kimberley

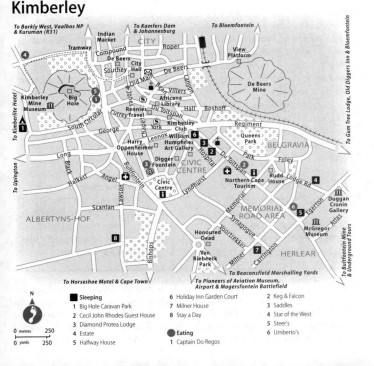

Northern Cape

■ Sleeping
1 Big Hole Caravan Park
2 Cecil John Rhodes Guest House
3 Diamond Protea Lodge
4 Estate
5 Halfway House
6 Holiday Inn Garden Court
7 Milner House
8 Stay a Day

● Eating
1 Captain Do Regos
2 Keg & Falcon
3 Saddles
4 Star of the West
5 Steer's
6 Umberto's

Siege of Kimberley

During the Anglo-Boer War Kimberley was laid siege to by some 4,000 Boer soldiers from the 15 October 1899 to the 16 February 1900. Hemmed inside the town were 500 British troops under Colonel Kekewich and about 50,000 civilians including the town's most famous resident Cecil Rhodes whose capture was a particularly enticing prospect for the Boers. They were never able to break through some carefully mounted British defences. The surrounding countryside made an attack difficult. There were few nearby hills on which to place siege guns or snipers and the British were able to use the mine dump heaps to build secure gun placements overlooking the flat and sparsely vegetated plain on the town's outskirts.

The Boers, therefore, had to content themselves with trying to starve the town into surrender. However, the extensive stores owned by De Beers Diamond Mining Company meant that the town did not suffer from food shortages to the same extent as Ladysmith or Mafeking and Kekewich prudently passed a military law that all food prices were to remain at pre-siege levels. Nevertheless, the town's inhabitants did suffer, and inevitably the African population suffered the most. There were widespread reports of scurvy and very high rates of infant mortality. By the end of the siege horse meat was the main item on many menus.

Rhodes, nearing the end of his life, put the full resources of De Beers into defending the town. This included manufacturing ammunition in the mine's workshops and most impressively a big gun, inevitably nicknamed 'Long Cecil', that could return fire on the Boer siege guns. The main mine tower was also invaluable as a lookout post and messages about any Boer movements could be relayed by telephones to the outer perimeter of the British defences. This lookout also proved invaluable as an early warning

post for incoming shells – when a lookout spotted a puff of smoke from the main Boer siege gun (sited 4 miles away) a flag would be waved and buglers sited around the town would sound a warning for people to take cover. The system gave about 15 seconds' notice and undoubtedly saved many lives – though the shelling did take a heavy toll.

Relations between Colonel Kekewich and Rhodes were very poor. Rhodes was used to getting what he wanted and in early 1900 he wanted the town relieved. Rhodes could not understand why a large British army located just 20 miles away at Modder River was unable to break through and relieve the town. To the ire of Kekewich he managed to get out to the South African and British press increasingly critical statements about the performance of the British military. In February 1900 Rhodes threatened to call a public meeting, where Kekewich was convinced he would call for the town to surrender, unless they were given specific information about plans to relieve the town. Kekewich was determined that the meeting would not take place so instead Rhodes and 12 other leading citizens demanded that Kekewich send a message to the British Commander-in-Chief, General Roberts, calling for their immediate relief. When Kekewich refused, the two of them almost ended in a fist fight.

Relief was not far off, however. General Roberts' arrival at Modder River with reinforcements had revitalized the British efforts. A bold plan of attack was evolved. The British cavalry completely outflanked General Cronje's Boer forces, unblocking the main advance and allowing Roberts to relieve Kimberley. With it the whole impetus of the war turned against the Boers. On the 16 February Kimberley was at last relieved and Cecil Rhodes (and many London stock brokers) were able to celebrate.

the museum and are furnished as he had them; note the austere surroundings preferred by Rhodes. During the next period of use, the building was converted into the very elegant *Hotel Belgrave*. One of the rooms upstairs has been furnished as it would have been in the 1920s. As the diamond industry fell into decline, the wealthy customers disappeared and the hotel was forced to close. In 1933 it was taken over by the

Sisters of the Holy Family and turned into a school and convent. Forty years later the McGregor Museum moved its displays and offices here.

The collection is a mix of objects depicting the history of Kimberley and the northern region, and standard displays of natural history. While the latter are of little interest, the displays relating to Kimberley are reasonably absorbing. Downstairs is a display of Kimberley personalities on a street map of the town. To the right of the entrance are a couple of rooms devoted to the Siege of Kimberley, including the two small rooms occupied by Rhodes. Upstairs is a room relating the history of the Kimberley Regiment, from the days of the Du Toit Span Hussars (1876) to fighting counter insurgence in Namibia.

There is a café in the central courtyard serving drinks and simple snacks, closed at the weekend. On the first floor is a museum shop, stocking the usual collection of trinkets and postcards. Public entrance from Atlas St. ■ *Mon-Sat 0900-1700, Sun 1400-1700. Small entrance charge. T8420099, www.museumsnc.co.za*

Galeshewe

Kimberley was the first town in South Africa to establish on its outskirts 'locations' for housing non-white mine labourers. Galeshewe, the resulting township, rose significantly in importance during the struggle against Apartheid, and was second only to Soweto as a centre of political activism. It was home to **Robert Sobukwe**, the leader of the Pan African Congress (PAC), who spent the last days of his life, following his imprisonment on Robben Island, under house arrest in Galeshewe. ■ *For tours of Galeshewe, contact the Kimberley Tourist Office, T8327298.*

Memorial to the Pioneers of Aviation

On General van der Spuy Drive, 4 km from the airport and on the site of South Africa's first flying school, is the Memorial to the Pioneers of Aviation. The memorial comprises a reconstructed hangar and a replica of the Biplane used in the early days of flight training. The flying school was set up here in 1913 and the graduates went on to become the first pilots of the newly formed South African Aviation Corps, which in turn saw its first action over Walvis Bay in May 1915. ■ *Mon-Sat 0900-1700, Sun 1400-1700. Small entrance charge. T8420099.*

Excursions

Kamfers Dam

Kamfers Dam is 5 km out of town on the N12 towards Johannesburg, partially hidden from the road by the raised railway line. This is a natural heritage site and an important area for greater and lesser flamingos – just driving past the dam allows views of the carpet of pink created by the resident flamingos. Sadly the waters are under threat from continual agricultural pollution, and it has been predicted that the flamingos may soon disappear from here. Look out for a gravel track leading from the road under the railway line, where there is a small parking area.

Magersfontein Battlefield

On 11 December 1899 one of the most famous battles of the Anglo-Boer War took place here. The British force, under the command of Lt-General Lord Methuen, was defeated by a Boer force under General Piet Cronje, while attempting to come to the aid of besieged Kimberley. This was the first appearance of trench warfare, and the first major defeat suffered by the British (in the first encounter the British had 239 killed and 663 wounded). The Boer trenches can still be seen from the hilltop. There are nine memorials commemorating the dead, including a Celtic cross in memory of the Highland Regiment, a granite memorial to the Scandinavians who fought with the Boers, and a marble cross in memory of the Guards Brigade. In 1971 the area was declared a national monument. There is a tea room and a small museum at the site containing weapons, uniforms and photographs which tell the story of the battle. ■ *For information, call T8357115. Magersfontein Battlefield is 32 km from Kimberley. To get there, follow Oliver Rd towards the airport and the Aviation Memorial. Turn on to a gravel road opposite Jack Hindon Officers' Club and then follow the signs for Modder River.*

Northern Cape

Noitgedacht Open-air Museum

Noitgedacht Open-air Museum is 24 km from town on the Barkly West road, followed by 8 km on gravel. This open-air site displays glacial geological rock formations, which have been covered in ancient San rock engravings, thought to be 1,500 years old. It is an important engravings site, and a small open-air museum was being built at time of writing to explain the different images. For those interested in the modern-day San, there is a local community of !Xu and Khwe people who were granted 1,200 ha of land under the Land Reform Programme. The community shares this land, from where they produce traditional and progressive arts and crafts. ■ *For more information, contact the !Xu and Khwe Vereniging, T053-8337069, xkpft@iafrica.com*

Rafting

River rafting is not what you might expect looking out over the dry, flat countryside around Kimberley, but to the south flows the **Orange River**, one of South Africa's largest rivers. It is possible to raft the rapids between Hopetown, on the N12, and Douglas. The river flows through beautiful dolerite hills past old farms and orchards. Two companies organize rafting trips here: *Aquarush*, T083-5861795 (mob); and *Adventure Bound*, T053-8312659, adventurebound@iafrica.com

Vaalbos National Park

Vaalbos National Park has been under international scrutiny in recent years as diamond mining activities have been given permission to begin within the park boundaries. For a time it was thought that the park would be de-proclaimed but at the time of writing it remains open. Set along the Vaal River, the main attraction here is rhino, both black and white, as well as giraffe and a range of antelope. There is a gravel road providing access to the further reaches of the park, as well as several picnic spots. Accommodation in the park is in **D** *Cottages*, sleeping 6, 2 bedrooms, bathroom, fully equipped kitchen, no electric plugs, all power is solar. There are no shops or restaurants in the park. Reservations, Mon-Fri; Pretoria, T012-3431991, F3430905, reservations@parks-sa.co.za Bookings can also be made in person at two offices in Cape Town, either at the Clocktower Centre office at the V&A Waterfront, or at the main tourist office at the corner of Castle and Burg streets.

Game farms

Within 75 km of Kimberley are a number of game farms, mostly private farms stocked with wildlife which have been developed into tourist destinations. They generally have very comfortable lodges and high standards of service. Some also offer self-catering facilities. In addition to game viewing they offer horse riding and hunting, the latter being a major source of income but not to most people's taste – call ahead to check what is on offer. The list below is a selection of farms which are within a couple of hours' drive of Kimberley.

Koedoesrand Game Lodge, T053-8315538. 27 km from Kimberley off the Bloemfontein road, luxury chalets, emphasis on hunting. *Marrick Game Farm*, T053-8611530, marrick@kimnet.co.za Game drives, mountain biking and hiking, range of accommodation. *Rooipoort Nature Reserve*, T053-8316742. A well-established hunting concession, 40,000 ha, tented accommodation. *Withuis Safaris*, T053-8921212. 50 km from Kimberley, primarily hunting on foot but also organize birdwatching and photographic safaris.

Essentials

Sleeping
■ *on map, page 697*
Price codes:
see inside front cover

B-C *Cecil John Rhodes Guest House*, 138 Du Toitspan Rd, T8318318, ceciljohnrhodes@freemail.absa.co.za Luxurious old-style guesthouse set in converted house built in 1895. 7 comfortable rooms, en suite bathrooms, a/c, TV, shady tea garden, friendly management, dining room has a good reputation. Recommended. **B-C** *Edgerton House*, 5 South Edgerton Rd, T8311150, F8311785. 13 double rooms with en suite bathroom, all meals available, swimming pool, gardens, secure parking, a relatively large guesthouse with plenty of home comforts. **B-C** *Diamond Protea Lodge*, 124 Du Toitspan Rd, T8311281, F8311284. 34 a/c rooms, large rooms, mini bar, clean and modern, restaurant, bar, swimming pool, good service. **C** *Holiday Inn Garden Court*, 120 Du Toitspan Rd, T8331751, F8321814. Bland hotel with 135 a/c rooms, disabled access, restaurant is an attached franchise steakhouse, bar, swimming pool, sauna, falls short of the standard you'd expect for the main town hotel. **C The Estate**, 7 Lodge Rd, T8322668, tjoef@kimnet.co.za Guesthouse set in building designed for Sir Ernest Oppenheimer in 1907, 7 en suite rooms, comfortable furnishings, gardens with pool, close to sights. **C Kimberlite**, 162 George St, T8311968, F8311967. 30 double a/c rooms, close to the Big Hole, restaurant, bar, swimming pool, secure parking. **C-D Horseshoe Motel**, Cape Town Rd, T8325267. Large roadside motel, 58 a/c rooms, restaurant, bar, swimming pool, popular conference venue thus can be very busy or empty, airport transfer service.

D Carrington Lodge, 60 Carrington Rd, T8316448, spanhc@kingsley.co.za A comfortable guesthouse with clean en suite rooms, TV, ceiling fans, mini bar, spacious gardens with pool, meals on request. Secure parking, central location. **D Halfway House**, 229 Du Toitspan Rd, T8316324. Has seen better days but good atmosphere and value, better known for the drive-in bar and lively pub. **D Milner House**, 31 Milner St, T/F8316405, fires@kimnet.co.za Well-run guesthouse in a good location in Belgravia, 5 luxurious double rooms with en suite bathroom, fans, TV, phone, swimming pool, large gardens, log fires in the winter evenings, good breakfasts, run by the very helpful van Vuuren family, an excellent B&B. Highly recommended. **D-F Stay a Day**, 72 Lawson St, T8327239. Functional building with a range of rooms, from en suite with TV to dorms sleeping 8, TV lounge, breakfast room, secure parking, spotless throughout, friendly owners, but sterile and completely lacking atmosphere. One of the few budget options in town.

E-F Gum Tree Lodge, Bloemfontein Rd, T8328577, F8315409. Large complex 4 km out of town, dorms and doubles, communal kitchen, some self-contained flats, lounge, restaurant, shop, TV room, swimming pool, probably still the best option for budget travellers, quiet location, but inconvenient for the sights. **F Big Hole Caravan Park**, West Circular Rd, T8306322. Medium sized site, grassy, a few young thorn trees provide limited shade, smart central washblock, clean grounds, fenced off swimming pool, pay phones, an easy walk to the 'Big Hole' museum, 20-min walk from town centre.

Eating
● on map, page 697

Kimberley is better served by pubs and bars than restaurants

There are the usual collection of pie and fast food outlets by the taxi stand behind the City Hall. **King Pie**, York St. Mix of meat and vegetarian pies, above average pies, best when warm, ideal for picnics. Further up from here is **Steer's**, serving good burgers, and **Captain Do Regos**, with Portuguese-style chicken. **Halfway House**, Du Toitspan Rd, T8316324. Historical pub with bizarre drive-in section, claiming to be where Cecil Rhodes used to ride-in on to sip a quick beer on his horse. Good atmosphere, simple pub meals, can get very busy at weekends. Also has rooms. **Keg & Falcon**, Du Toitspan Rd, T8332075. Popular pub serving decent meals. Part of a chain that is slightly more upmarket than most bars. Good for a lunch. **Mohawk Spur**, Du Toitspan Rd, T8326472. Acts as the restaurant for the Holiday Inn Garden Court. Standard quality steak restaurant, good value, generous portions. **Old Diggers Inn**, Bloemfontein Rd, next to the Gum Tree Lodge, T8328577. Large restaurant frequented by backpackers staying next door, good value meals, hearty portions. **Saddles**, Sidney St, T8315506. Franchise steak house, good steaks and burgers, always busy. **Star of the West**, North Circular Rd. The oldest pub in South Africa, dating from 1873. Bit of a tourist trap but characterful, with a long wooden bar. Tram to the mine museum stops outside across the road (on request). Enjoy a cool beer and a pub lunch before visiting the Big Hole. **Umberto's**, Du Toitspan Rd, T8325741. Excellent Italian restaurant just next to the *Halfway House*. Superb pizza and home-made pasta dishes, friendly service. Recommended.

Sports

Cricket International matches are played at the *Kimberley Country Club*. Watching a game here makes a pleasant change from the large stadiums found in the cities. The atmosphere is very relaxed and if you're lucky you may meet the players in the hotel bar. During the domestic season, Kimberley is home to Griqualand West. **Kimberley Country Club**, PO Box 297, Dickenson Av, Cassandra, Kimberley, 8300. Ticket enquiries: T8323775, F8322196.

Tour operators

Rennies Travel, Nedbank Building, corner of Chapel and Currey streets, T8311825. Bureau de Change and travel agent. **Aquarush**, in Hopetown, 120 km south of Kimberley, but can organize trips from Kimberley, T083-5861795 (mob). Organizes whitewater rafting trips on the

Northern Cape

nearby Orange River, as does *Adventure Bound*, based on the Egerton Game Ranch, about 20km upriver from Hopetown (120 km south of Kimberley). Again, they can organize trips from, and be contacted in, Kimberley, T053-8312659, adventurebound@iafrica.com

Transport   **Local Car hire**: all are based at the airport and are open throughout the day during the week, but only when flights arrive over the weekend. *Avis*, T8511082. *Budget*, T8511182. *Imperial*, T8511131. **Taxis**: *AA Taxis*, T8614015. The main rank is behind the City Hall. *Rikki's*, T083-3422533 (mob).

Air The airport is 10 km south of the town centre. There is 1 flight a day to **Cape Town**, except for Sat. There are 6 flights a day to **Johannesburg** during the week, a single flight on Sat and 3 on Sun. Flight information, T85111241. *SA Express*, T8383337.

Rail For **steam enthusiasts** there is a collection of locomotives in perfect condition in the Beaconsfield Marshalling Yards to the south of the city centre. Three main line trains stop in Kimberley each week. Reservations and information, T8382631.
The *Diamond Express* runs between **Bloemfontein** and **Pretoria**. Bloemfontein (3 hrs), daily except Sat, 0530. **Pretoria** (11½ hrs), daily except Sat, 2020, via **Johannesburg**.
The *Trans Karoo* runs between **Cape Town** and **Pretoria**. Cape Town (17¼ hrs), daily 2110, via **Beaufort West**, **Worcester** and **Wellington**. Pretoria (9½ hrs), daily 0212, via **Johannesburg**.
The *Trans Oranje* runs between **Cape Town** and **Durban**. Cape Town (17 hrs), Wed 1315, via **Beaufort West** and **Worcester**. Durban (19 hrs), Mon 1153, via **Bloemfontein**, **Bethlehem**, **Harrismith** and **Pietermaritzburg**.

Shell Ultra City bus terminus is inconveniently 6 km from town, making it necessary to take a taxi to/from town

Road 485 km to **Johannesburg**, 979 km to **Cape Town**, 238 km to **Kuruman**, 401 km to **Upington. Bus** *Greyhound*, T8314548. The local booking agent is *Tickets for Africa* at the *Tourist Information Centre* on Bultfontein Rd, T8326040. Coaches depart from outside here. All services also stop at the Shell Ultra City on the Transvaal Rd (N12) in the northern suburbs. **Cape Town** (13 hrs), daily 2000, 2240. **Pretoria** and **Johannesburg** (7 hrs), daily 0700, 0130. *Intercape*, coaches depart from the Shell Ultra City, Transvaal Rd. 24-hr information, T021-3804400. **Pretoria** and **Johannesburg** (6 hrs), Thu 0015. **Plettenberg Bay** (9 hrs), Mon, Tue, Fri, Sat, 2115, via **Garden Route**. *Translux*, T012-3348000. Coaches depart from the Shell Ultra City, Transvaal Rd. **Cape Town** (13 hrs) daily 1900. **Johannesburg** and **Pretoria** (6½ hrs), daily 1900; Tue, Wed, Fri, Sun, 0155. **Plettenberg Bay** (11 hrs), Tue, Wed Fri, 0020, via **Oudsthoorn** and **Knysna**.

Directory   **Banks** *Standard Bank*, 10 Old Main St, T8384800. *ABSA*, 69 Du Toitspan Rd, T8397109. **Communications** Internet: *Small World Net Café*, 42 Sidney St, T8313484. **Useful services** 24-hr Medi-City Private Hospital: T8381111. Pharmacy: 142 du Toitspan Rd, T8311737.

Routes west from Kimberley

Barkly West   The R31 passes through Barkly West, 32 km from Kimberley en route to Kuruman.
Phone code: 053   The first site of the diamond rush in South Africa, the town is named after Sir Henry
(NB Always use   Barkly, Governor of the Cape when diamonds were discovered here. This is also the
3-figure prefix)   town Cecil Rhodes represented when he was first elected to the Cape parliament.
Colour map 4, grid A2   Today, the town is tatty and rundown, and you may still see prospectors using manual methods to work their claims along the **Vaal River**. In 1869, the first diamond digging area was known as Klipdrift. The following year the diggers at *Canteen Kopje* took the unexpected step of establishing the independent Republic of Klipdrift. In 1871 the Cape government took the decision to annexe the territory to keep it out of the hands of the Transvaal government. For **tourist information**, T5310673.

Sleeping D *Die Zinkhuys*, T5310264. Small town hotel, some en suite rooms. **E** *Barkly West Holiday Resort*, T5310673. Camping and caravan park.

Wonderwerk Cave, signposted 42 km before Kuruman, is an important archaeological site on a private farm, set back from the road in the Kuruman Hills, T082-327226 (mob). The main attraction here is some rock paintings and the evidence of early human habitation, such as fire. You may have to stop at the homestead to collect a key as the cave is usually kept locked. A small display centre, café, and toilets have been built close to the entrance. The display contains some interesting background material on the prehistory of the region. The cave itself has been extensively examined by the Kimberley museum; the majority of the floor has been divided into squares for research purposes. It stretches back 700 m into the hillside, with a level path leading into it. The rock paintings are near the entrance. The grandparents of the current owners lived in the cave when they first settled in the region and started farming. **D-E** *Chalet & Campsite*, T082-327226 (mob). Self-catering for up to six people, close to the cave and the farm homestead. Allow one hour for a visit.

Wonderwerk Cave

The Kalahari

The Kalahari, like all great deserts, evokes images of vast lapis skies, shimmering horizons and cruel heat. It is at once enthralling and intimidating, begging to be explored but overwhelming in its sheer size and harshness. The area is one of semi-desert, of rolling red sand dunes, salt pans, dry river beds and endless scrub, stretching from the Orange River to northern Botswana and west into Namibia. Despite the arid conditions, there is some of the best game viewing here in South Africa, in the magnificent Kgalagadi Transfrontier Park (Kalahari Gemsbok Park). But the main draw of the Kalahari is its vast open spaces and the true wilderness of the desert – even today, travelling here fills one with a real sense of adventure.

The name Kalahari is derived from the term Kgalagadi, the San term for 'place without water'

Ins and outs

Kuruman is the principal town in this corner of the Kalahari. If you plan on travelling north from here, make sure you stock up on all supplies and check the condition of your car, especially water, oil and fuel. The R31 north is one of only two routes to the Kgalagadi Transfrontier Park (Kalahari Gemsbok Park). The only other road into the park is from Upington. Each route involves stretches on gravel, although much of the road between Upington and Askam is now tarred. **NB** Driving on loose gravel and sand can be dangerous and these are not the conditions to break down in. Do not be tempted to drive too fast if the roads are empty and straight. If you have an accident you could be waiting a long time for help.

Getting around

Kuruman

This isolated northern town has two reasons for being on the tourist map: the Moffat family and their mission station; and a natural spring known as The Eye. Neither take up much time and the town itself is scruffy and unappealing, so half a day should be more than enough. Once you've made it this far north it is well worth exploring the rest of the beautiful area. Kuruman is an important local centre, so stock up on supplies here.

Phone code: 053 (NB Always use 3-figure prefix) Colour map 1, grid C4

Tourist Office, Main St, T7121001, F7123581. In an old cottage next to The Eye. This is in fact the old *Drostdy House*, once home to the local magistrate. Part of the building is given over to a Tea Room which serves light lunches and tea/coffee throughout the day.

Tourist offices

The Eye, on Main Street, is an amazing spring which has continuously produced almost 20 million litres of fresh water per day, with little variance between the wet and the dry season. It was the presence of this water and the resultant river that made settlement possible in this area. The site was proclaimed a National Monument in 1992. There is little to see of the spring, but the gardens around the pond are a popular picnic

Sights

Northern Cape

Robert Moffat

Robert Moffat is known in southern Africa for two reasons, firstly for translating the Bible into Tswana and secondly for his association with David Livingstone, the great Victorian explorer of the region. Moffat was born at Ormiston in Scotland into a poor family, left school at the age of 11, and then worked as a gardener for 10 years – hardly a background to prepare him for 50 years of scholarly work in remotest Africa. After a brief theological training he was accepted by the London Missionary Society on 30 September 1816. His first posting was to Namaqualand where he immediately made a name for himself by converting an outlaw called Jager Afrikaner. In 1819 he married Mary Smith, his employer's daughter, in St George's Church in Cape Town. The first days of their marriage were spent in a wagon crossing the Karoo to Kuruman. In 1824 Moffat persuaded the missionaries to move to the present site which he considered to be far more suitable because of the abundant water supply, and the fertile level land was ideal for farming.

It took four years to build the Moffat Homestead and a house for his colleague, Robert Hamilton. Fine materials were used, and neat gardens were laid out. They wanted to show what Christianity could do. The homestead is still standing today and is the oldest building north of the Orange River. An important part of the missionary's work was teaching. And it was when Moffat was confronted with a class of 23 "of

Batswanas, Hottentots, two Bushmen and two Mantatees", that he realized the problem of language. The next 40 years his life was dominated by translation and printing. He was the first person to print the language of the Matabele people, on his press in Kuruman, and so lay the foundation for their modern education system. His greatest feat was the translation of the Bible into Tswana. In 1857 he printed a thousand copies despite a whole range of problems. To help the people understand the Bible he then had to teach them to read their own language. It was the first time the Bible had been printed anywhere in Africa, and the first time in a previously unwritten African tongue.

It was beyond their capacity to print the New Testament at Kuruman, and Moffat could find no one in South Africa to help. So the couple had no choice but to return to England, only to find out that they were famous. This helped them raise vital funds, and get the printing done, but after three years away they both yearned for Africa. They worked in Kuruman until 1870, when the Missionary Society persuaded them to return to England. Mary died within six months of their return and Robert Moffat continued to work for the LMS from Britain. He died 13 years later on 9 August 1883. In 1983 a bronze bust of Moffat was moved from a church in Brixton, London, and erected at Kuruman close to the school to mark the centenary of his death.

spot – the pond is full of large goldfish, fattened by breadcrumbs. Unfortunately the grounds are not quite as peaceful as they might appear – there is a constant background noise of buried pumping equipment. The gardens around town rely on the spring water, giving Kuruman the feel of an oasis during the dry season when the surrounding farmlands are burnt brown. ■ *Open daylight hours. Minimal entrance fee.*

Moffat Mission Under the guidance of Robert Moffat, the Kuruman Mission Station, 5 km north of town, became one of the best-known mission stations in Africa. To get there, follow Voortrekker Street out of town past the police station. The mission is today run by the United Congregational Church of Southern Africa, and the complex is an atmospheric and fascinating place.

The first building you come to is the **stable**, with a few portraits on the walls and an early wagon used by the mission. Turning left out of the stable, you find yourself walking parallel to a **furrow** that Moffat had dug to bring water from the 'Eye', 5 km away (see above). Across the furrow is a small garden created by Mary Moffat – it was here that explorer David Livingstone proposed to the Moffat's daughter, after she had nursed him back to health following an attack by a lion. Opposite the garden is the **Moffat Homestead**, built in 1824 and fully restored in the 1980s. Inside, the main room has a few objects on display, but overall it is disappointing. The kitchen has been turned into a tea room and curio shop. Just beyond the homestead is the original **Mission Church**, for many years the largest building in the interior of South Africa. Despite having only nine converts when he designed the T-shaped church, Moffat planned for it to seat 800 people. The stone walls stood for seven years before timber of sufficient length could be found for the roof. Moffat found the trees on one of his journeys 350 km away in the Marico Valley; it was given to him by the Matabele chief of the region, Mizilikatzi. The building still has a thatch roof, dung floor and wooden pews and the acoustics are surprisingly good.

At the far end of the mission is the **Hamilton House**, built between 1826 and 1828 for Robert Hamilton, an artisan missionary who worked with Moffat. The house was in continuous use by missionaries until the Mission was forced to close following the passing of the Group Areas Act. The structure is a perfect record of building methods and materials from the early days of settlement in South Africa, but unfortunately it is not open to the public.

This was the first house that Livingstone lived in when he came to Africa

The final building of note is the **School Classroom**; inside are the original wooden school benches and desks. The room is now home to the original printing press Moffat used to print the first Tswana Bible. The press was also used to print school books and publications for the church.

■ *There's no public transport to the mission, which is a few kilometres out of town. Allow at least a couple of hours for a complete visit. Mon-Sat 0800-1700, Sun 1500-1700. Small entrance charge. T7121242.*

This privately owned centre has a wealth of information on raptors and a chance to see the rehabilitation work on injured birds. They can also advise on the best areas for birdwatching in the Kalahari. There is also a small selection of rescued and hand-raised mammals, such as young impalas, meerkats and bat eared foxes. ■ *Visitors by appointment only. The entrance gate is kept locked to contain the young game in care which roam freely on the farm. Small entrance charge. T7123576. 15 km from Kuruman, along the Upington road. Look out for a side road on the right signposted Ulster; the farm is a further 12 km from here.*

Kalahari Raptor Rehabilitation Centre

A little further out of town, off the Hotazel Road, is a small Bird sanctuary in 7 ha of wetlands. There are over 115 species of bird here, including the duck, ibis and heron families. Collect gate keys from the waterworks next door.

Bird sanctuary

B *Eldorado Motel*, Main St, T7122191, F7122194. Bland 1960s roadside motel on the outskirts of town, 25 double rooms, 52 single rooms, a/c rooms are a bit frayed, 4 blocks arranged around swimming pool, large airy dining room with plenty of light, quiet but overpriced, more suited to business travellers. **C** *Riverfield*, 12 Seodin Rd, T7120003. Modern house set in large well-kept gardens, 6 clean double rooms, TV, some en suite, lounge, braai area at the back, swimming pool, self-service bar, good breakfasts, well-run, the best option in Kuruman. **C** *Savoy Hotel*, Beare St, T7121121. Small hotel in good condition, best cheaper option in town. **D** *AJ's Guest Flat*, 8 Gemsbok St, T7122754. Simple self-catering option. **D** *Shalom Guesthouse*, 20 Cunningham St, T7120729. Small guesthouse with bed and breakfast. **E-F** *Die Oog*, T7120645. Off the Kimberley road in the centre of town, self-catering cottages have 3 beds in single rooms, small kitchen area with fridge, plus bathroom, campsite has more shade, electric points, laundry, braai area, walking distance of all shops and The Eye. Run by the municipality.

Sleeping

Price codes:
see inside front cover

Kalahari Pub, 63 Main Rd, T7121271. Pub and grill serving predictable pub lunches. *Over-de-voor*, 31 Main St, T7122773. The best option in town, tables divided by high walls, low seats, a superior steakhouse with a varied menu with a few continental dishes. *Savoy*, Beare St. Hotel restaurant offering steaks, salads and pasta at medium prices. *Pizza Den*,

Eating

Main St. Quick cheap meals and takeaways. There is also a café in the tourist information centre building, recommended for a light lunch.

Sports **Golf** *Kuruman Country Club*, T7321242, 9-hole course, also offers tennis, squash and bowls. **Paragliding** The country around Kuruman produces the ideal conditions for flying. The world record for a long distance flight was set in the district. If you'd like to try paragliding here, call T083-4489201 (mob), T7231471. Daily trips can be organized.

Transport **Road** 238 km to Kimberley, 263 km to Upington. **Bus**: *Intercape*, T012-65441154. Buses leave from the Caltex Garage on Mark's St. **Johannesburg** and **Pretoria** (7½ hrs), daily 1015. **Upington** (3 hrs), daily 1415. *Intercape* buses depart from the *Eldorado Motel*.

Directory **Banks** *First National* and *ABSA Bank*, Beare St. *Standard Bank*, Voortrekker St. **Communications** Post Office: School St. **Medical Services** Hospital: Main St, T7120044. **Useful services** Police: Voortrekker St, T10111.

Northwest from Kuruman

Hotazel & Travelling on the R31 from Kuruman allows you to explore more of the Kalahari
Black Rock region. This is a good road but it is only surfaced as far north as Hotazel, 61 km; 25 km
Phone code: 053 further on is Black Rock. These are both **manganese ore mining** centres. ■ *Visits to*
(NB Always use *the mine in Hotazel, Samancor, have to be arranged 2 weeks in advance, contact*
3-figure prefix) *T7422000. Black Rock can also be visited, but you must book visits a week in advance,*
T7511291. From Hotazel, follow the signs for Sonstraal and Van Zylsrus, 105 km.

Tswalu Private Tswalu is a magnificent 100,000 ha reserve created by the late Stephen Boler, and
Desert Reserve known as an upmarket oasis of designer ecotoursim. Over $US7 million was spent in
establishing the enterprise, reputedly South Africa's largest private reserve. At the foot
of the Korannaberg mountains, off the R31 between Hotazel and Sonstraal, this is a
region of stunning red sand dunes and typical savannah dotted with acacia trees.

The park has been well-stocked with wildlife, including lion, buffalo, three types
of zebra, red hartebeest, blue and black wildebeest, giraffe, gemsbok, kudu and
impala. A breeding programme for the rare desert black rhino has been set up and
there are now eight within the park.

Price codes: **Sleeping** **L4** *Tswalu Lodge*, T053-7819311, F7819316, tswalu@kimberley.co.za Top-notch
see inside front cover luxury lodge. Guests stay in beautifully appointed stone cottages with private viewing decks,
swimming pool. Excellent service and meals. Air transfers direct from Johannesburg can be
arranged. Recommended as a serious extravagance.

Van Zylsrus Van Zylsrus is a typical Kalahari town, one dusty street is lined with all the shops in
Phone code: 053 town. Although there is little of interest here, it is a sensible place to stop for the night if
(NB Always use en route to Kgalagadi. The *Oasis Café* is famous for its 'fairy garden', a glorious patch
3-figure prefix) of shady green, a welcome spot in the heat of the day. If you don't stop for the night,
Colour map 1, grid C3 have a snack here and fill up with petrol before pushing on. Between Hotazel and Van
Zylsrus are some very smart **game ranches** which cater for trophy hunters and also
accept overnight guests. The other major hunting area is due north from Hotazel in
the **Severn** district on the border with North West Province. **Tourist information**,
the best source in this isolated region, is available on Livingstone Street, T7121001.

Price codes: **Sleeping** **B** *Ruimsig Guest Farm*, T7810458. Spacious farmhouse just outside town, range
see inside front cover of accommodation, plus horse riding and exploring the dunes. **D** *Gemsbok Hotel*, town centre, T7810238. Friendly small town hotel, rather rundown, restaurant, good local informa-
tion. **F** *Caravan Park*, T7810238. Washblock and braai area. **E** *Newton Hunting Farm*, 46 km
west of Van Zylsrus, T7813712. This is a hunting setup, but also has 2 cheap dormitory huts,
self-catering, meals can be provided at very reasonable rates.

From Van Zylsrus the road follows the dry course of the Kuruman River as far as **Askam**. At this point the route combines with the road from Upington, and just one (gravel) road leads a further 61 km to the gates of the Kgalagadi Transfrontier Park (Kalahari Gemsbok National Park). A short distance out of Van Zylsrus there is a road off to the right to the Middelputs border post. This is an alternative route for visitors wishing to visit the Botswana side of the park. After a long and dusty drive, the national park camp at **Twee Rivieren** is a welcome sight, especially the swimming pool. The total distance from Kuruman to the park gates is 385 km. It is an undeniably tiring journey, but allows you to experience the vast southern fringes of the Kalahari desert.

Van Zylsrus to Kgalagadi Transfrontier Park

Kgalagadi Transfrontier Park (Kalahari Gemsbok National Park)

Although probably one of the least visited national parks in the country, the Kgalagadi Transfrontier Park has some of the finest game viewing in Africa. It is remote and relatively undeveloped, with uncomfortably high summer temperatures, but few visitors begrudge the hot dusty roads once they've glimpsed their first lion. The roads follow the scrubby valleys of two seasonal rivers, the Auob and Nossob, and cut across red sand dunes typical of the Kalahari.

Colour map 1, grid B1

A major advantage, much repeated in promotional literature, is that Kgalagadi is malaria-free

Getting there From Upington, the first 190 km is an excellent tarred road followed by 61 km of fairly good gravel. Allow 3-3½ hrs to the park gates. It is 385 km from Kuruman, via Hotazel, Sonstraal and Van Zylsrus, to the park gates. Petrol is available at Noenieput and Andriesvale. There is no access from **Namibia** since the Mata Mata border gate is closed. The easiest access from Namibia is via the Aroab/Rietfontein border.

Ins & outs

Until the new entrance gate and border post are built (due some time in 2003), visitors wishing to visit the **Botswana** side have 2 options. It is possible to enter Botswana at the Gemsbok/Bokspits border post (60 km south of Twee Rivieren), and then enter the park at the Botswana Twee Rivieren Gate, just across the riverbed from the South African gate – a frustratingly roundabout route. A valid passport, but no visa, is required. The other option is to enter/exit Botswana at Middleputs or McCarthy's Rest via Makopong border posts, allowing access to the Mabuasehube section of the park. For both of these, you must have a 4-wheel drive vehicle. There are campsites on the Botswana side. Bookings for the campsites have to be made through the Botswana parks authority, T0926-7580774, dwnp@gov.bw, PO Box 131, Gaborone. The approximate distance from Twee Rivieren to Mabuasehube via Van Zylsrus (R31), McCarthy's Rest border post and Tshabong, is 450 km.

Park information Twee Rivieren is the only entrance (on the South African side) and the hours vary almost every month, open Jan-Feb, 0600-1930; Mar, 0630-1900; Apr, 0700-1830; May, 0700-1800; Jun-Jul, 0730-1800; Aug, 0700-1830; Sep, 0630-1830; Oct, 0600-1900; Nov-Dec, 0530-1930. Office and shop hours: as for entrance gate, T054-5612000. There is an **entrance fee** per person (R30) and per vehicle. The three main rest camps (Twee Rivieren, Nossob and Mata Mata) have shops which stock basic groceries. Given their remoteness, none stock fresh vegetables, although meat and bread are available at Twee Rivieren. **Petrol** is available at all three camps. There are two more remote camps, **Bitterpan** and **Grootkolk**, neither of which have shops. It is possible to **hire a car** through *Avis* and pick it up at Twee Rivieren, but there is no public transport to get you here. Nossob and Mata Mata generate their own **electricity** (220V). Power is available for a few hours in the early morning, and from 1700 to 2300. Because of the remoteness of the region a close record is kept of your movements and you have to sign in and out of every camp. There is a **curfew** on returning to the camps in the evening – if you do not make it back to the gates on time, you will be fined R500.

NB Although the park authorities and the Upington tourist office insist that 4-wheel drive vehicles are not necessary, saloon vehicles can be uncomfortable on the gravel roads and prone to flat tyres. If you don't have an off-road vehicle, be sure that your car is in good condition and can deal with several days on gravel – one of our researchers suffered a breakdown in the park and spent two hot and frustrating days retrieving and fixing her car. Although Twee Rivieren has a car workshop, there is no system in place to cope with breakdowns. In the event of a breakdown, stay in the car and wait for passing cars to assist you. You will have to make

Northern Cape

your way back to Twee Rivieren, from where a mechanic can drive out to your car. You should also never leave the gravel roads, it is easy to get stuck in the soft sand.

Best time to visit Between Feb and May, but most of the accommodation is fully booked during these months, especially at weekends and around Easter. Camping is usually possible, although the main camp, Twee Rivieren, is likely to be very busy. This is an arid region with less than 200 m of rainfall a year, falling between the summer months of Jan and Apr. In the summer it gets very hot and you should carry at least 10 litres of drinking water in your vehicle. Camping in winter requires warm sleeping bags as temperatures fall below zero. **Always** check the availability of rooms in advance – this is the end of the road, and even space for tents gets fully booked. If you plan on visiting during the main season, try and arrange your accommodation as soon as you arrive in South Africa.

History The area was proclaimed a national park on 3 July 1931 as part of a progressive initiative to combat the problem of poachers. Known until a few years ago as the Kalahari Gemsbok National Park, the area was adjacent to the Gemsbok National Park in Botswana. On 7 April 1999 the two parks were formally merged into a single ecological unit, now known as the Kgalagadi Transfrontier Park. There are plans to build a new entrance gate and border post to facilitate movement between the two sections, but for the time being, visiting the Botswana side of the park is fairly complicated (see above).

Landscape
The combined protected area is over 3.6 million ha, nearly twice the size of Kruger National Park and one of the largest protected areas in the world

The first camp for tourists was built in 1940 near the confluence of the Auob and Nossob rivers. Most of the game viewing is along these riverbeds where most of the vegetation is concentrated. Thanks to the aridity of the region, vegetation remains sparse and mostly close to the ground, which is why game viewing is so good here. The rivers rarely flow but rainwater collects in the bed under the sand, which is sufficient for grasses and plants to survive on. Both of the rivers were once thundering waterways, evident by the great width of their valleys in some areas. Look out for the windmills which pump the boreholes – these waterholes are usually frequented by some form of wildlife. Between the two rivers stretch mighty red sand dunes, aligned from north to south and covered in yellow grass following good rains. These are fossil dunes, and their red tint is produced by an iron oxide coating on the white grains of sand. Between the 20 m high dunes are level valleys known as streets. Two roads cross the dunes; do not venture off them as you will get stuck in sand.

Wildlife The park is famous for its predators, particularly the dark-maned Kalahari lion which can sometimes be spotted lazing in the shade of trees found along the river beds. Other predators to look out for include cheetah, wild dog, spotted hyena, bat-eared fox, black-backed jackal and the honey badger. Leopard are, as always, elusive but are seen relatively regularly in the park. The park's prize antelope is the gemsbok, a beautiful creature with a dark glossy coat, strong frame and characteristic long, straight horns. You should also see giraffe, red hartebeest, Burchell's zebra and huge herds of wildebeest and springbok.

The birdlife, too, is impressive. Over 200 species have been recorded in the park. The best viewing months are between February and May, especially if the rains have been good. The park is known for its variety of raptors, which prey upon the smaller mammals. Ones to look out for include tawny eagles, martial eagles, chanting goshawks, white-backed vultures and eagle owls. Other birds you might see include Burchell's courser, Namaqua sandgrouse, the kalahari robin and the pink-billed lark. You also frequently see pairs of secretary birds strutting along the dry riverbeds.

Sleeping
Price codes see inside front cover

Check in is from 1200, but all rooms must be vacated by 0900. There are 3 main camps in the park: Twee Rivieren, the main camp at the entrance gate; Mata Mata, a more remote camp; and Nossob, on the Botswana border. Two new, more remote camps have also been opened (see below). At each main camp there is a mix of self-catering cottages plus a campsite with washing and braai facilities. There are no electric points in the campsites, but lighting is provided by generator until 2300. **Reservations**: Mon-Fri, Pretoria, T012-3431991, F3430905, reservations@parks-sa.co.za Bookings can also be made in person at 2 offices in Cape Town, either at the Clocktower Centre office at the V&A Waterfront, or at the main tourist office at the corner of Castle and Burg streets. You can also contact the park direct, T054-5612000 (Botswana, T+267-580774). Credit card bookings are accepted over the telephone. If the park is full there are several options just outside the park limits (see below).

Twee Rivieren All the accommodation and administrative buildings are lined up on a sandy slope. There is a shop selling groceries, meat and fresh bread, wine, beer and souvenirs. There is also a takeaway selling snacks, a bar with TV and an overpriced (and frankly awful) restaurant. Self-catering is a far more preferable option. **B-C** *Chalets*, self-contained thatched cottages with a/c, sleeping 2 to 4 people, shower, fully equipped kitchen, no oven, braai area. **F** *Campsite*, dusty site but with good pre-fabricated shade, some trees, plus good ablutions including a laundry but no cooking facilities other than braais. Swimming pool. Can be very busy with noisy families.

Mata Mata 118 km from entrance gate, allow at least 2½ hrs travelling time. This road is one of the most beautiful in the park with some of the best game-viewing opportunities. Look out for a few signs of past settlement; a couple of families lived here during the First World War to watch over the waterholes in case the Germans invaded from Namibia. The Germans did enter South Africa, but by a different route, and the families were forgotten for several years after the war had finished. The camp has a small shop selling groceries and firewood. Electricity is generated from 0500 for a few hours, and again from 1700-2300. **C** *Chalets*, self-contained chalets sleeping up to 6, bed in dining room, shower, kitchen, no oven, braai area. **E** *Huts*, 3 beds in 1 room, washbasin, private veranda, communal washblock and kitchen with gas stove and fridge, cooking utensils. **F** *Campsite*, sandy plots in front of the chalets, little shade but fantastic setting just metres from a viewpoint, good ablution facilities, but no cooking.

Nossob 152 km from the entrance gate, allow at least 3½ hrs travelling time; the first sign of the camp is a pair of white gates and a few battered trees beside the white buildings. This is the most remote camp and probably provides the best opportunity of hearing lions roar at night. The facilities are, however, more basic than elsewhere. Range of accommodation including a **B** *House* with 3 bedrooms, one a/c bedroom, bathroom, dining room, lounge, fully equipped kitchen, enclosed veranda, good value for a group. **C** *Cottage*, sleeps 6, 2 bedrooms, 2 bathrooms, dining room, kitchen with gas stove and fridge. **C-E** *Hut*, sleeps 3, with or without kitchen and bathroom, communal facilities as at Mata Mata. **F** *Camp Site*, separate facilities from the huts, the whole camp overlooks a broad section of the river bed and a waterhole.

Bitterpan This new camp is the most luxurious in the park, but is only accessible by 4-wheel drive as all access is along sand roads. The camp is situated in the dunes, about 3 hrs from Nossob. Accommodation is in 4 **C** *Stilted Huts*, sleeping 2 with en suite bathroom, built with natural materials such as reed and canvas. There are walkways linking the huts to a communal kitchen/entertainment/braai area. There is also a 6-m-high tower allowing excellent views out over the dunes. Electricity is solar-powered. This is an unfenced camp, but there is an armed ranger on site at all times.

Grootkolk 100 km north of Nossob, this new camp is again set in red sand dunes but is more basic. Accommodation is in 4 **D** *Sand Huts*, simple en suite chalets sleeping 2, built out of sandbags and canvas. There is a communal kitchen with fridge and hotplates, plus a braai. This camp can be accessed by saloon car.

Outside the park During the peak season the park's accommodation is fully booked for weeks on end. There are several other accommodation options before you reach Twee Rivieren, but these too are likely to be booked at peak times. **B-D** *Molopo Kalahari Lodge*, T054-5110088, www.molopo.com 15 km from Askham, on the gravel road to the park (60 km). Well-run lodge on the edge of the park, rondavels and chalets set in dusty grounds, restaurant, bar, swimming pool, permanent tents set up in front of main lodge with shared facilities. The owners organize all-in tours around the region. **D** *Koppieskraal*, off the R31 towards Rietfontein on Namibian border, T083-3843315 (mob). Self-catering cottage for 4 people, camping, meals on request, peaceful remote setting, camel safaris, good last stop in South Africa if heading for Namibia. **D** *Loch Brom*, Askham, T082-3511834 (mob), off the Kuruman road. Prices include dinner and breakfast, rondavel for 4 people and a family room on a farm, secluded setting, swimming pool. **D** *Klipkolk Guest House*, Opstaan, call T054902 and ask for 104. A simple B&B with attached tea room set on a typical Kalahari farm. Evening meals available on request. Very close to the border post at Rietfontein. Follow the R360 from Upington, take the R31 turning. Run by Gertuida and Hendrik. **D** *Rooipan Guest House*, PO Box 2214, Upington, T082-4151579 (mob). Old farmhouse which has been converted into a guesthouse and tea room. Swimming pool, braai area. Evening meals on request. Located midway between Upington and the Kgalagadi Transfrontier Park (Kalahari Gemsbok Park). **F** *Witdraai Farm*, just opposite the *Molopo Kalahari Lodge* (no phone). This area is owned by local Nama (San) people who were given back some of their ancestral lands in 1999. They open up their land for backpackers who want to camp out under the stars in true wilderness. Turn left at the entrance (you won't miss the Nama men dressed in loincloths selling handicrafts) and ask for Abraham. He will direct you about 3 km into the veld, where there is a toilet and shower – be sure to bring all your drinking and washing water as these don't work if there is no water available. There are no other facilities; you simply set up camp under some thorn trees. Abraham may bring some firewood if requested. Recommended for a taste of camping in wilderness, while supplementing local Nama initiatives.

Southwest from Kuruman

From Kuruman the R27 runs 263 km west to Upington via Kathu and Olifantshoek. The only reason for stopping en route is to refuel and buy something to eat and drink, unless you wish to marvel at an open cast mine in the midst of a beautiful and fragile environment.

Kathu
Phone code: 053
(NB Always use 3-figure prefix)
Colour map 1, grid C4

Just off the main road (N14), this modern settlement has grown up entirely around the mining industry, first started in 1972. This is the location of **Sishen mine**, a massive scar in the earth and one of the largest open iron ore mines in the world. Everything associated with the mine is giant – the trucks that move the ore look oversized, and can carry over 170 metric tonnes. The mine is connected to **Saldanha** ore terminal on the west coast by a single railway line which you can see in the vicinity of Elands Bay and Velddrif. Guided tours of the mine are held on the first Saturday of the month. **Tourist information**: T7232261.

Price codes:
see inside front cover

Sleeping B-C *Gamagara Lodge*, Hendrik van Eck Rd, T7232285. 24 single rooms, 4 double rooms, restaurant, bar, swimming pool, popular with business visitors to the mine, hence most are single rooms. In the Kathu Shopping Centre is the *Gourmet Steakhouse*, a pleasant choice for a lunch break.

Upington

Phone code: 054
(NB always use 3-figure prefix)
Colour map 3, grid A5
Altitude: 805 m

Despite Upington's attractive setting on the banks of the Orange River, it is a bland and modern town with searing summer temperatures and little in the way of sights. It is, however, the largest town in the region, making it a welcome stop for those who've been off the beaten track for a while. It is a major service centre with all the major South African shops and high-street chains, and as such is an excellent place to re-stock your supplies. As a major entry point to the Kalahari, Upington is also a good spot to organize trips to the Kgalagadi Transfrontier Park and Augrabies Falls National Park.

The origin of the town is rather more disreputable than one might expect. In the mid-19th century the northern reaches of the Cape Colony were home to a colourful variety of outlaws and rustlers – there were no settlements, making it impossible for the police to track people into the uncharted wilderness. By 1879 the Cape government had had enough, and founded a small settlement on the Orange River to try and exercise some control over the area. In 1884 Sir Thomas Upington, the new Prime Minister of the colony, visited the settlement, which was renamed in his honour.

Getting there There are daily flights from Cape Town and Johannesburg and buses from Cape Town, Clanwilliam, Johannesburg and Pretoria. There is a train station, but no passenger trains stop here. There is, however, a train which runs from Johannesburg to Windhoek, called the *Desert Express*, although it is unclear where the closest stop is. For more information, contact the Upington train station, T3382203. **Ins & outs**

Tourist offices The *Upington Tourist Office* is in the Kalahari Oranje Museum on Schröder St, T3326064. Open Mon-Fri 0800-1730, Sat 0900-1200. This helpful and professional office deals only with information on the town. For information on the Kgalagadi Transfrontier Park (Kalahari Gemsbok Park) and the Kalahari in general you'll have to visit the *Green Kalahari Information Centre*, Siyanda District Building, corner of Rivier and Le Roux streets, T3372826, www.greenkalahari.co.za This office has a good selection of brochures on the Kalahari area, although not quite as much information as one would expect on the Kgalagadi Transfrontier Park.

The fortunes of the new settlement, and the subsequent development of the district, can be attributed to the pioneering works of two men, the **Rev Christiaan Schröder** **History**

Upington

To Airport, Kalahari Gemsbok National Park (Kgalagadi Transfrontier Park) & Namibia - (N10)

Orange River

To Namibia
To Augrabies Falls (120 km)
To Kuruman & Vryburg
To Groblershoop & Kimberley

Northern Cape

N

0 metres 200
0 yards 200

■ **Sleeping**
1 Affinity Guest House
2 Eiland Holiday Resort
3 Kalahari Junction
4 Libby's Lodge
5 Le Must Guest Manor
6 Oasis Protea
7 Oranje
8 River City Inn
9 Three Gables Guest House
10 Upington Protea & Spur
11 Yebo!

● **Eating**
1 Dros
2 Le Must
3 O'Hagan's
4 Saddles
5 Sakkie se Arkie

and **Johann 'Japie' Lutz**. Together they built the first irrigation canal, constructed a pump on the river and started a pontoon ferry. After the Anglo-Boer War, Lutz built canals at Kakamas, Marchand and Onseepkans. These irrigated areas now produce cotton, lucerne, vegetables, grapes and sultanas. Today the *SA Dried Fruit Co-operative* and the *Orange River Wine Cellars Co-operative* are responsible for handling most of the agricultural produce in the region.

Sights The main building of the town museum is the restored **Manse** where the Rev Schröder lived in the 1870s. This houses a collection of Victorian furniture and household objects. Look out for item #20, a fine old compendium of games. The doorways are all very low on account of the Rev Schröder being somewhat vertically challenged! Inside the church are some odd bits and pieces from Upington's past. They are poorly displayed, although worth seeking out are the photographs of Augrabies Falls in 1957 when they were dry. The building also houses the town tourist office. ■ *Schröder St, overlooks the road bridge. Mon-Fri 0900-1230, 1400-1700. Small entrance charge.*

Excursions Upington is a convenient centre for trying some of the wines produced on the vineyards which make up the **Orange River Valley Wine Route**. There is only one vineyard which allows visits, *Keimos Wines*, T4911597, on the N14 about 12 km out of town. You must phone ahead for tastings and cellar tours. Although its buildings have none of the character of the estates found in the Western Cape, the wines are still worth tasting. All of the vineyards on the wine route belong to the same co-operative. If you're particularly interested in trying wines of the area, visit the co-operative shop, in Upington's industrial area, T3378800. Ask at the town tourist office for more information.

Upington also acts as a major entry point to the Kalahari, and is the nearest town to **Augrabies Falls National Park**, a visit to which is possible in a day trip (see page 716). The highlight of the Northern Cape, the **Kgalagadi Transfrontier Park** (Kalahari Gemsbok Park), is also relatively near, lying 358 km to the north (see page 707), but you'll definitely need a few days to fully appreciate the park.

A popular day trip is the **Witsand Nature Reserve**, about 200 km from Upington off the R14 towards Kuruman. The reserve is a beautiful area of desert landscape, but the highlight is a collection of white sand dunes, set incongruously on the typical red sand of the Kalahari. The dunes are up to 60 m high and stretch for 9 km, making them an impressive sight. The reserve is also home to the well-known 'Brulsand', the phenomenon of roaring sand dunes, thought to be caused by shifting sand lacking the usual red coating of iron oxide, plus the dry air. Visitors can walk freely around the reserve. There is also a concealed bird-hide dug into the ground, allowing an eye-level view of a waterhole. **Accommodation** is in comfortable self-catering **B** *Chalets*, with 3 bedrooms, all a/c, 1 bathroom, 'safari' décor. There is also some **E** *Camping*, basic facilities, swimming pool. ■ *Information and bookings, T053-3131061.*

Closer to town, about 15 km north of Upington off the R360 (follow Swartmodder Street past the swimming pool), is the **Spitskop Nature Reserve**. The 5,000 ha reserve makes for a pleasant day trip and acts as a good introduction to the flora and fauna that lie further north. Here you can view a variety of wildlife commonly found throughout the Kalahari region, including springbok, eland, zebra, gemsbok and camels – the latter were once used by the local police force as transport. In the centre of the reserve is a *kopjie* with an observation platform. **Accommodation** There are a few simple self-catering **E** *Chalets*, within the park, with 4 beds, as well as **F** *Camping*, both basic, at the base of the kopjie. Hiking, mountain bike trails and canoeing are also available. ■ *Information and bookings, T3321336.*

Sleeping
■ *on map, page 711*
Price codes:
see inside front cover

B *Oasis Protea Lodge*, 26 Schröder St, T3378500, F3378599. Usual bland building with 32 double rooms, a/c, TV, non-smoking room, designed for regular business travellers, the other *Protea* next door is better value. **B-C** *Oranje*, Scott St, T3324177, F3323612. 50 a/c rooms, restaurant, bar, swimming pool, characterless modern building, often full with coach groups.

B-C *River City Inn*, Scott and Park streets, T/F3311971. 28 a/c rooms, TV, bar, breakfast area but no restaurant, a popular newish mid-range hotel in the centre of town. **B-C** *Upington Protea*, 24 Schröder St, T3378400, F3378499. 53 clean and spacious a/c rooms some with river view, TV, 4-bed rooms are good value, breakfasts served in the bar lounge, no restaurant, attached is the *Totem Creek Spur* and the gaudy *Desert Casino*, pool at back in secluded grounds overlooking the river. A well-run hotel.

C *Affinity Guest House*, 4 Budler Southeast, T3312101, piet@weathersa.co.za 17 en suite rooms, all a/c with TV and refrigerator. Secure parking, swimming pool, good views of the river. Recommended. **C** *Le Must Guest Manor*, 12 Murray Av, T3323971, manor@lemust.co.za An elegant guest house set in a mock Cape Dutch style building overlooking the river. Double a/c rooms with en suite facilities. Also home to the excellent restaurant of the same name. **C** *Three Gables Guest House*, 34 Bult St, T3322041, piet@pastationers.co.za Small guesthouse with shady balconies, swimming pool.

C-F *Eiland Holiday Resort*, T3340286. Good location on a large island opposite the town, a mix of 58 self-catering chalets and rondavels, good value for 4 people, campsite has plenty of large trees and grass, well-kept, clean, electric points, swimming pool, restaurant, shop, telephones, a well-run municipal camp site. The camp is famous for having what is claimed to be the longest palm avenue in the southern hemisphere. Recommended. Sundowner cruises on the river depart from here whenever there is sufficient demand.

D *Libby's Lodge*, 140 Schröder St, T3322661, libbyslodge@mweb.co.za Peaceful B&B in the town centre, en suite rooms, swimming pool, covered parking, breakfast not included in price. **E-F** *Kalahari Junction*, 3 Oranje St, T082-4350007 (mob). Excellent new backpackers, 1 dorm, 2 doubles and camping, good kitchen and TV room/lounge. 'San' décor, small garden with animals and tiny pool. Homely, friendly atmosphere, also a tour operator organizing budget trips to the Khalagadi Transfrontier park, Augrabies Falls and Witsand Nature Reserve. Recommended. **D-F** *Yebo!*, 21 Morant St, T3312496, teuns@intekom.co.za A welcoming guesthouse and backpackers, dorms and double rooms plus camping in attractive gardens. Self catering facilities and laundry. Gardens have a small swimming pool and braai facilities. Just out of the town centre, (10 mins walk), close to shopping centre.

Eating
● *on map, page 711*

Dros, Kalahari Pick 'n' Pay Centre, T3313331. Popular wine-cellard-themed chain, good selection of beers, usual steak-and-chips menu, small portions. *Le Must*, 11 Schröder St, T3323971. Probably the best restaurant in town. Sophisticated menu, well-prepared dishes, good service, interesting local wine list, priced with overseas visitors in mind. Book ahead. Recommended. *O'Hagan's*, Schroeder St. Irish themed pub and restaurant, usual steaks and pies, good selection of beers. *Saddles*, Market St, T3324664. Quality steakhouse, usual choice of good steaks, popular with families. *Sakkie se Arkie*, T3340286. Sundowner cruise with a braai departing from the *Eiland Holiday Resort*. *Totem Creek Spur*, Schroeder St, T3311240. Standard chain (part of Protea Hotel) with good value steaks, chicken and Tex-Mex dishes.

Sports

Golf 18-hole golf course on the N14 to Kuruman, take a left turn after the Drive-In. **Swimming** There is an Olympic size municipal swimming pool, in the park off Borcherd St.

Tour operators

Note that trips into the Kalahari are not cheap, as 4-wheel drives are often essential and all equipment and provisions (including water) has to be taken along. Logistically, this can take quite a bit of organization, but the rewards are well worth it. If you wish to visit the Richtersveld National Park, organize a tour from Springbok. *Kalahari Tours & Travel*, PO Box 113, Upington 8800, T082-4935041 (mob), www.kalahari-tours.co.za Well-organized local operator organizing range of tours into the Kalahari, including to the Khalagadi Transfrontier Park, Augrabies and Namaqualand, also river rafting on the Orange River. *Kalahari Adventure Centre*, T054-4510177, www.kalahari.co.za Based close to the Augrabies Falls, offer range of rafting trips, including half-day 8 km trips, plus longer 2 and 5 day trails involve rafting on rapids in 2-man inflatables. Also offer 4-wheel drive tours to the Khalagadi Transfrontier Park. Recommended. *Kalahari Junction*, 3 Oranje St, T082-4350007 (mob). Budget tours including 2-5 day trips to the Khalagadi Transfrontier Park, 1 day trip to Augrabies Falls, rafting on the Orange River and trips to Witsand and Spitskop nature

Northern Cape

reserves. Pieter really knows and loves the area, making him a great guide. Recommended. *Spitskop Tours & Safaris*, T3321336. Rafting tours and trips to the local national parks, run by folks with excellent local knowledge. Call in advance to discuss possible tours and prices. Great introduction to the region.

Transport **Local Car hire**: there are several local companies catering specifically for the wilderness regions of the Northern Cape. *Tempest*, T3378500. *Kalahari 4x4*, Elron Motors, Scott St, T3323099. *Avis*, T3324746. *Venture 4x4*, 24 Schroeder St, T3378400. Based at the *Oasis Protea*. Expect to pay in the region of R750 per day, although some packages have additional kilometre costs, which can make it very expensive.

Air The town airport, T3377900, has one of the longest runways in southern Africa. *SA Airlink* have daily flights to **Cape Town** and **Johannesburg**. Reservations, T3322161. Fares are in the region of US$180 one way. These are very useful services if your time is short and you wish to visit the magnificent Khalagadi Tranfrontier Park – you can fly in, hire a car at the airport, and be in the park by the end of the day.

Road 894 km to **Cape Town**, 804 km to **Johannesburg**, 401 km to **Kimberley**, 263 km to **Kuruman**, 374 km to **Springbok**, 120 km to **Augrabies Falls National Park**, 80 km to **Kakamas**, 50 km to **Keimoes**. **Bus**: *Big Sky Coaches*, T053-8322006/7, kby@bigskycoaches.co.za City-to-city service between major Northern Cape towns, weekend service to **Upington** from **Kimberley**. *Intercape* leave from their town office in Lutz St, T3326091. Coaches arrive/depart from here, this is a short walk from the *Oasis Protea Lodge*. **Cape Town** (10 hrs), daily 1830. **Clanwilliam** (7 hrs), daily 1830. **Johannesburg** and **Pretoria** (10 hrs), daily 0715. **Kuruman** (3 hrs), daily 0715. **Vryburg** (5 hrs): Mon, Tue, Thu, Sat, 0530. **Long distance taxis**: there are a variety of local companies running services to **Cape Town**, **Kimberley**, **Johannesburg**, **Springbok** (and other local towns) and **Windhoek** (Namibia). Check on the state of the vehicle; if in doubt don't travel. Run to flexible timetables depending upon numbers. Depart from the railway station or the taxi rank on Market St, 2 blocks from the museum. For information on all the taxi companies, contact the *Upington Taxi Association*, T3390430. *VIP Taxis*, T027-7122006. A weekday shuttle service between **Upington** and **Port Nolloth** via **Springbok**, departs early morning. *Douglas Taxis*, T3391017. Runs to **Cape Town** 4 days a week.

Directory **Banks** *First National* and *ABSA* have branches in Schroeder St, close to the hotels. **Communications** **Internet**: *Café de Net*, Le Roux St, T3312252. In the Pick 'N' Pay Centre. *Lyndi's Bookshop*, Schröder St, T3324393. **Useful services** **Ambulance**: T10177. **Hospital**: T3388900. **Police**: Schroeder St, T3321793. Opposite Camel and Rider Statue.

West to Namaqualand

Driving across the Northern Cape between Upington and Springbok, stop for a moment and look out over the endless horizons and stillness of the desert. Here one gets a real sense of how large South Africa is, pausing in countryside that has barely changed in thousands of years. Although stark and deserted, the emptiness has a certain beauty. The first part of the journey is particularly striking as the road follows the Orange River, with its band of lush vegetation along either bank.

Cannon Island (Kanoneiland)
Phone code: 054
(NB Always use 3-figure prefix)
Colour map 3, grid A5

Between Upington and Keimoes there is a choice of two roads along the banks of the Orange River. The main road follows the northern bank, but if you take the southern road you can stop off at Cannon Island (Kanoneiland). This is the largest island on the river, 14 km long and 3 km at its widest point. These days 1,700 ha out of a total area of 2,500 ha is under irrigation. Before the Cape government had managed to establish control over the region, the island was a stronghold for Korana tribes who continually harassed the early white sheep farmers. The island was named after a terrible incident when the Korana tried to fire a cannon made from the hollowed-out trunk of a quiver tree – when the smoke cleared, six of them lay dead amongst the debris. In 1928 private settlers landed on the island and started to clear the dense vegetation. At first the government opposed the illegal settlement, but then granted them land rights after the police had failed to move them on. It was only in 1940 that the first bridge was built on the southern side of the island. **E** *Kanoneiland Guest House*, T4911223. Simple self-catering on the island, an ideal base if you wish to explore the irrigated fields and view some of the water birds.

Keimoes is the local farming centre at the junction with the R27, the main road south across the Karoo to Calvinia. This is the quickest route to Cape Town but it means missing out Namaqualand. Look out for the Persian waterwheel in the centre of town, still in use on an irrigation canal. A short drive from the centre takes you to **Tierberg Nature Reserve**, a municipal reserve covering some 160 ha. It is centred around a rocky outcrop which is notable for the aloes and succulents. Most of the flowers are in bloom between August and September. It is possible to visit some wineries in the vicinity of Keimons – call T4611006 for details. The local **tourist information** office is on Main Rd, T4611016, F4611230.

Keimoes
Phone code: 054
(NB Always use 3-figure prefix)
Colour map 3, grid A5

Sleeping **D** *De Watervoor*, T4612710. B&B. **D** *De Werf*, T4611635. Small guesthouse, B&B. **F** *Caravan Park*, T4611016. A small neat site alongside some irrigated fields, shady gravel pitches, electric points, laundry, washblock.

Price codes:
see inside front cover

Transport **Bus:** *Intercape*, 24-hr information T021-3804400. Coach leaves from *Rainbow Take Aways*. **Upington** (1 hr), daily 0545. **Cape Town** (9½ hrs), daily 1930, via **Calvinia** (4 hrs) and **Clanwilliam** (6½ hrs).

Kakamas

The second most important farming centre along this stretch of the Orange River is Kakamas. The settlement was founded in 1893 by the Cape Parliament, as a centre for the Dutch Reformed Church to establish a colony for poor farmers who had lost everything following periods of drought and an outbreak of *rinderpest*. For many years the lives of the settlers were strictly regulated by the church, and it was not until 1964 that they were finally granted property rights when the church's interests in the settlement were liquidated. The **tourist office**, T4310838, F4310836, is in the Waterwiel Lodge on Voortrekker Rd

Phone code: 054
(NB Always use 3-figure prefix)
Colour map 3, grid A4

There is little of interest in the town itself, although it has a relaxed, rural atmosphere and there are several sites nearby which relate to the early history of Kakamas. Most of the town is strung out along the main road which runs parallel to the southern canal. The canal is one of several canals fed by the **Neus Weir** which irrigate the surrounding vineyards and fruit farms. The wier is 936 m long and was the first cylindrical weir with a smooth overflow to be built in South Africa.

Sights

Driving along Voortrekker Road in the town centre, look out for the set of fine, giant **water-wheels**. These nine wheels were built by a local farmer, Piet Burger, to help lift water from the canals into his fields. They are still in use today and considerably more economical to operate than modern lifting methods such as pumps. Along the route of the northern irrigation canal are a couple of **water tunnels**. One tunnel is 97 m long; the second is an incredible 172 m long, and both are 2 m high and between 3 and 4 m wide. They were built between 1889 and 1901 by Cornish tin miners.

Close to the north bank of the Orange River, just off the N14 to Upington, is a sign for some **German graves**. They are, in fact, the graves of six German soldiers who were killed during the Battle of Kakamas on the morning of 4 February 1915. The bodies were reburied here in 1960 by a German war graves organization. The battle was between the forces of the Union of South Africa and the German army in German Southwest Africa (now Namibia).

Northern Cape

There are a number of **wine cellars** and **dried fruit co-operatives** who welcome visitors for tours and tastings. *Orange River Wine Cellars Co-Op*, off the N14, direction of Augrabies Falls. ■ *Mon-Fri 0830-1245, 1400-1700, Sat 0830-1130. Guided tours available, T4310830.*

Sleeping
Price codes:
see inside front cover

D *Waterwiel Lodge*, Voortrekker Rd, T4310838, F4310836. 25 a/c rooms, restaurant, bar, swimming pool in pleasant palm setting, comfortable, good value hotel, camping and caravan park on the site. **F** *Die Mas Resort*, T082-9244719 (mob).

Augrabies Falls National Park

Colour map 3, grid A4

The remote location of the Augrabies Falls park has saved it from mass development, and it remains one of the highlights of the north. The falls are the main reason for coming here, although the surrounding landscape is equally impressive, a bizarre moonscape of moulded rock formations surrounded by shimmering semi-desert. There is good hiking here, and the Orange River above and below the falls has some excellent whitewater rafting. The name *Augrabies* is derived from the Khoi term *!oukurubes,* Place of Great Noise.

Ins & outs

Getting there There is only one route into the park, the R359. From Upington, take the N14 and turn off at Alheit. From Springbok, there is a left turning before you reach Alheit. All are clearly signposted. The park is 120 km from Upington and 304 km from Springbok.

Information Entrance gates open: Apr-Sep, 0630-2200; Oct-Mar, 0600-2200. Office hours: 0700-1900, T054-4529200. There is a large shop stocking a selection of groceries including meat and a few fresh vegetables, plus beer and wine; open office hours. In the same building there is a restaurant with views of the falls. Petrol is available by the entrance and there are public telephones (cards only) by the reception desk.

Best time to visit Mar to Oct are the best times to visit. This area has a typical arid climate, with very hot summer days. Rain falls in autumn and in winter conditions are ideal for walking, although it gets very cold at nights.

Landscape & wildlife

There are some dangerous spots at the edge of the gorge. Take care when approaching it, especially if you are with small children

The park was created in 1966 to protect the waterfall and conserve the surrounding area, a unique ecosystem of riverine and desert environments. The landscape is typical of the arid north, seemingly barren but rich in wild plants and with a growing population of small mammals.

The centrepiece of the park is an impressive waterfall – the sixth largest in the world. Above the falls, the Orange River passes over a series of impressive cataracts, dropping about 100 m. From here the main channel passes over a 56 m drop into a narrow gorge of steep, smooth rock, the water churning below like melted milk chocolate. The falls can be viewed from a number of viewpoints along the southern side of the gorge. Thanks to the slippery surface of the rock, and the number of over-curious visitors who slid to their deaths, the edge of the gorge is today lined with a small fence.

Following heavy rains, a number of smaller waterfalls drop into the main gorge along the sides of the main fall – a tremendous sight, but fairly rare. After exceptional rains the gorge has been known to fill with water, cutting off the whole camp. This is less likely to happen today since several large dams were built upstream to control river flow for irrigation.

Walking along the cliffs above the river, you pass a number of **unusual plants** which have adapted to the harsh desert environment. Some of the more notable trees include the quiver tree, camel thorn, tree fuschia and the wild olive – there are some informative displays on these by the reception centre. There is also a fair range of **fauna**, including klipspringer, eland, kudu, gemsbok and springbok, although these all tend to be elusive. You are more likely to see ground squirrels foraging between the rocks. A good time of day to visit is around sunset, when the swallows flitting through the gorge are slowly replaced by small bats which stream from cracks in the rock faces surrounding the falls.

Hiking

There is a popular two-day hiking trail, the **Klipspringer Trail**, which is always booked up during local school holidays. There are also several one-hour hikes which you don't have to book, each leading to a scenic point close to the camp. The walk to **Arrow Point** from the campsite is perhaps the best, leading to a promontory with a canyon on each side. The views along the gorge downstream are superb. You need to wear shoes with a good grip, but the walk does not involve any climbing. The **Klipspringer Trail** is 40 km long and takes 3 days to complete. There are two overnight stone huts, **E** *Fish Eagle* and *Mountain*; each can sleep 12 and is fitted with bunks, mattresses, toilets, drinking water, firewood and simple cooking utensils. There are no showers or lamps. Hikers must carry their own food, cooking pots, sleeping bag and light. Numbers are limited to 12 hikers per day so it is always advisable to book in advance. Reservations, T054-4529200 or T012-3431991, reservations@parks-sa.co.za The trail is closed between the middle of October and the end of March due to high temperatures.

Rafting

An excellent way of experiencing the gorge is by rafting its rapids. The most popular stretch is known as the **Augrabies Rush**, an 8 km section covering grade two and three rapids and pulling out just 300 m above the falls. Longer two and five day trails involve rafting on some excellent rapids as well as calmer stretches in two-man inflatables. The river is still relatively uncommercial, which means that you're unlikely to see anyone on the longer trails. For more details, contact *Kalahari Adventure Centre*, T054-4510177, www.kalahari.co.za Prices start at around R225 for the 3-hour Augrabies Rush.

The park also organizes the **Gariep 3-in-1 Adventure**. This involves descending into the gorge, canoeing for 3 km downriver, and then hiking the 4 km out of the gorge. The final 11 km back to the rest camp is completed by mountain bike. Contact the reception for details.

Game drives

There are several short game drives from the campsite; ask at reception for a map. The gravel roads take you to Echo Corner, Oranjekom, Ararat and Moon Rock. The only game you're likely to see is klipspringer and eland, but the birdlife is very rewarding, as is the unusual desert plantlife. The park also organizes guided night drives in an open four-wheel drive, which may be a better way of learning about the flora and fauna found in the park. Ask at reception for details.

Augrabies Falls National Park

Sleeping & eating

Monkeys are a real pest here, so lock up any food in your car and leave nothing in the tent

Check in is from 1200, but all rooms must be vacated by 0900. The cottages and campsite are well-spaced out amongst the thorn trees, allowing for a degree of privacy. There are three small swimming pools, ideal for hot summer days when temperatures can rise above 40°C. The campsite is located at the far end of the complex from the office. In between are a mix of 2, 3 and 4-bed cottages. These are self-catering, but many guests choose to eat in the restaurant in the evening. Overall the park's accommodation here is particularly good, and while the campsite can get crowded, it is in a beautiful setting. Reservations, Mon-Fri; Pretoria, T012-3431991, F3430905, reservations@parks-sa.co.za Bookings can also be made in person at two offices in Cape Town, either at the Clocktower Centre office at the V&A Waterfront, or at the main tourist office at the corner of Castle and Burg streets. **Reservations** are also possible through the Warden, Augrabies Falls National Park, Private Bag X1 Augrabies 8874, T054-4529200. Credit card bookings are accepted over the telephone.

B-C *Chalets*. All a/c and fully equipped, clean, comfortable units with views towards gorge, typical parks style, good value for 4 people. **F** *Camp Site*, not all pitches have electricity, grass patches are preserved for recreational use, which means you have to pitch your tent in the dust. The best shady spots get occupied quickly. Kitchen block has electric hot plates, laundry and an ironing room.

The shop is in the main reception centre, as is *Shibula* restaurant, open 1200-1400, and 1800-2200. A surprisingly good and smart dining room given the location, with a choice of pricey continental dishes. Last orders are at 2030. Next to the restaurant is the cosy *Gariep* ladies bar. Downstairs is a cafetería, serving drinks and light meals throughout the day.

Pofadder

Phone code: 054 (NB Always use 3-figure prefix) Colour map 3, grid A3

The dusty town of Pofadder lies on in a particularly arid stretch of road, and were it not for a small natural spring it would never have come into being. The country around here is exceptionally dry, receiving less rain in a year than most northern European towns receive in a day. For the couple of weeks a year that is does rain, the surrounding countryside is transformed into a vibrant carpet of wild flowers and succulents, attracting its fair share of visitors. For the rest of the year the town has little to offer other than petrol and a cold drink, and it suffers a rather scornful reputation amongst South Africans who snigger at its odd name – Afrikaans for puff adder. Although the town is not actually named after the venomous snake, the reality isn't much better. It is named after Klaas Pofadder, a cattle rustler who based himself here during the 1860s. He was killed with his gang in 1875 after a gunfight; a mission station was then established by the spring. There is a small **tourist office**, T9330046, in the municipality building – follow the signs to the right from the town petrol station on the N14.

A few houses offer occasional B&B accommodation; contact the tourist office for details

Sleeping C-D *Pofadder*, Voortrekker St, T/F9330063. Squat, orange building on the main street, 23 basic rooms, restaurant, lively bar, swimming pool, secure parking, the only hotel in town. **D** *Pofadder Flats*, T9330019. 14 self-catering flats, all fully equipped, popular during flower season. **F** *Caravan Park*, T9330056. Small, dusty site with electric points, hot showers, braai spots, some grass.

Out of town: **D** *Diepvlei Farm Guest House*, PO Box 175, Pofadder, T/F027-7121578. A working sheep farm situated 125 km from Pofadder and Springbok off the Gamoep Rd. 3 double rooms with shared bathrooms plus a honeymoon suite. TV lounge with log fireplace. Rates include dinner and afternoon tea served on the veranda. Although hardly local, this farm is an excellent spot to explore the countryside, and is especially good for birdwatching and fossil hunting. Recommended.

Pella

Colour map 3, grid A3

Founded by the London Missionary Society in 1814, Pella it was named after the village which provided refuge for Christians in Macedonia. In 1878 the running of the station was taken over by the Catholic church. Of particular interest is the original **mission church**, which has been consecrated as a cathedral. It was designed and built by Father LM Simon and Father Leo Wolf – neither had any experience or knowledge of building, so they used an encyclopaedia for reference. The venture took seven years and the building is still standing today. Surrounded by scorched countryside, the cathedral comes as a welcome cool refuge, standing in a neat walled

Northern Cape

garden fringed with date palms. Classrooms and a convent make up the rest of this peaceful station. ■ *Call in advance to arrange visits, T073-1918986.*

Pofadder Hiking Trail

This is a fascinating trail into the surrounding desert, but should not be treated lightly. If you plan on walking the full 72 km, allow at least four days and pay particular attention to the advice offered at the start of your walk. The trail is closed from 1 October through to 30 April because of high summer temperatures, but even in autumn and spring the daytime temperatures can reach 35°C. The hike should not be attempted in groups of less than three. You can start/finish in either Pella or Onseepkans, but there is the perennial problem of transport. If you finish walking in Onseepkans, close to the Namibian border, there is a good chance of hitching a lift back to Pofadder with traffic entering South Africa from Namibia. If you wish to make a more definite arrangement to be collected at the end of your walk, the local hotel can help, at a price.

The trail is made up of two connected loops and for much of the way follows the banks of the Orange River, a reassuring and refreshing sight. Away from the river, the trail heads along isolated, arid mountains and you will need to carry all your drinking water. If you start in Pella, it is about another 8 km to the river, from where you can follow the cool waters all the way to Onseepkans. Look out for Ritchie Falls and the birdlife in the reed beds. The scenery is very similar to that along the **Klipspringer Trail**, a short distance upstream in Augrabies Falls National Park. If you are heading towards Namibia and plan to walk the well-known Fish River Canyon, a couple of days hiking around here is ideal preparation. Wear sturdy boots – these provide both support on the rocky terrain and protection from snakes. Other essential items include a hat, sunglasses, sunscreen and warm clothes for the cold nights. Permits and advance booking are required. For more information, contact JG Louw, T054-9330066 or the **Pofadder Municipality**, T054-9330046. There is a minimal daily fee per person, but no accommodation costs.

Canoe trails & rafting on the Orange River

One of the best ways of exploring the region is by rafting along the Orange River, which for the most part is blissfully deserted and wild. Several companies organize canoe or rafting safaris below the Augrabies Falls and explore the lower reaches of the river. A popular tour is known as the Black Eagle Canoe Trail, covering on average around 75 km over a period of five days. Each night is spent camping on the riverbanks under the stars. There are a couple of sets of rapids which are relatively straightforward (grade 2 to 3). Two-man inflatable or fibreglass canoes are used. *Kalahari Tours & Travel*, PO Box 113, Upington 8800, T082-4935041 (mob), www.kalahari-tours.co.za Well-organized operator organizing range of tours including river rafting on the Orange River. *Kalahari Adventure Centre*, T054-4510177, www.kalahari.co.za Based close to the Augrabies Falls, offer range of rafting trips, including half-day 8 km trips, plus longer two and five day trails involve rafting on rapids in two-man inflatables. Also offer four-wheel drive tours to the Khalagadi Transfrontier Park. Recommended. *Kalahari Junction*, 3 Oranje St, T082-4350007 (mob). Budget tours including half-day rafting trips on the Orange River. and trips to Witsand and Spitskop nature reserves. Pieter really knows and loves the area, making him a great guide. Recommended.

Namaqualand

Namaqualand is the name given to the arid northwest corner of the Northern Cape, starting in the south at the Doorn River bridge near Klawer, and extending north to the Namibian border. The area is best known for its magnificent wild flowers which transform the barren, rocky countryside every spring. The regional centre is Springbok, the most viable base for exploring the area.

Namaqualand flowers

At present there are insufficient hotel rooms to cope with the peak seasonal demand. If you are planning on coming here during Sep and Oct, book your hotel rooms as far in advance as possible

The region of Namaqualand is a scorched area of semi-desert which for much of the year holds little more than shimmering dust and rock-strewn mountains. Following the spring rains, however, the ground explodes in a riot of colour, literally carpeting the region with wild flowers. The Namaqualand flowers have become a major tourist attraction, and during flower season the still valleys and sleepy towns are transformed into busy hubs crowded with tour buses.

Nevertheless, the very nature of the attraction – in that the flowers appear in different locations from year to year – prevents the flower-viewing industry from getting too over the top. The conditions which govern where flowers appear have been the subject of long-term research in Pretoria University. Under normal conditions, rains are expected in July and August; the further north you travel, the less rain the land receives. The occurrence and distribution of the wild flowers is determined by the interaction between temperature, light, and the timing and intensity of rainfall. As climatic factors vary from year to year, so too does the composition of the vegetation change. A late frost or intense sand storms can cause a sudden end to the flower season in an area overnight, while some blooms last until the end of October in the mountains. For more information on the study by Pretoria University, visit the **Goegap Nature Reserve** outside Springbok where there is an interesting display charting the university project. Before travelling to the region call the **Flower Hotline** which can advise on the location of the best blooms, T083-9101028 (mob).

Over 4,000 species have been discovered in the area, the most common of which is the **orange and black gousblom**, a large daisy. These flowers look their best when they occupy a valley floor, forming a stunning carpet of orange. On the mountainsides or rocky hills you will see **mesembryanthemums**, commonly known as vygies or sour figs. Their blossoms can be pink, scarlet, blue or yellow. Closer to Springbok are **quiver trees** (*Aloe dichotoma*), the tree from which the San made their quivers. This is a slow growing plant which reaches a height of 7 m when fully grown. Another interesting plant to look out for is the **halfmens** (*Pachypodium namaquanum*), a strange looking succulent which has a long spine with a clump of leaves at the top – some specimens are thought to be several hundred years old. These are usually seen along the Orange River and on isolated granite kopjies.

Springbok

Phone code: 027 (NB Always use 3-figure prefix) Colour map 3, grid B2 Altitude: 1,000 m

The capital of Namaqualand is set in a narrow valley surrounded by the *Klein Koperberge* (Small Copper Mountains), and hemmed in by *kopjies* littered with rough butter-coloured rocks. It is a modern town with little of interest within its confines, but it is a good base from which to explore the countryside north to the Namibian border, and west to the Atlantic coast. Although quiet for most of the year, the town is totally transformed when the spring wild flowers start to bloom.

Namaqualand Tourism Information, the main office for the Namaqualand region, on Voortrekker St, on the left just as you enter town is open Mon-Fri 0730-1615, and (flower season only) Sat and Sun 0830-1600, T7122011, F7121421, www.northerncape.org.za The staff here are very knowledgeable about the area and have a good selection of pamphlets and maps on the region.

Sights　In the past, the fortunes of the town were closely linked with the **copper industry**. In 1852 the first copper mine started production – this was the first commercial mining operation of any type in South Africa. Despite several other discoveries further north, Springbok was able to develop into an important regional centre because of its abundant supply of drinking water from a spring, a rare and valuable commodity in the region before dams and pipelines were built. There is a small town **museum** outlining local history, housed in what was the synagogue, just off Van der Stel St.

During spring, from Aug to Oct, you should reserve accommodation well in advance, even for the campsite. As with many of South Africa's popular destinations, the domestic market reserves the best value rooms up to a year in advance. Fortunately, it is impossible to predict when and where the best blooms occur from year to year, so you may be able to view early or late displays of colour without the usual coach loads of day trippers. If you are unable to find a room, try to join a tour to the region; there are plenty advertised in Cape Town.

C *Annie's Cottage*, 4 King St, T/F7121451, T083-4541252 (mob), anniescottage@ intekom.co.za Finely restored old farmhouse with immaculate polished floors, comfortable furnishings. 3 double rooms with en suite bathrooms, also studio flats. Neat and mature gardens, swimming pool, secure off-street parking. Annatjie can also organize stays on farms in the surrounding area. Recommended. **C** *Masonic Hotel*, 3 van Riebeeck St, T7121505, F7121730. 26 a/c rooms, some without bathroom, TV, restaurant, bar, homely rooms, plenty of character, retains much of the original 1940s décor, helpful and friendly management. **C** *Springbok Hotel*, 87 van Riebeeck St, T7121161, F7121932. Principal hotel in town, comfortable and clean, central setting, 28 rooms, most a/c, popular à la carte restaurant, bar. **C-D** *Old Mill Lodge*, 69 van Riebeeck St, T7181705. 6 a/c rooms with queen size bed and TV, a comfortable B&B. **D** *Springbok Lodge*, Voortrekker St, T7121321, F7122718, sblodge@ intekom.co.za 45 rooms of various formats, most of the houses in neighbouring streets are outbuildings belonging to the lodge, look out for the deep yellow paintwork, some are double rooms, others are self-catering flats. A bizarre local institution run by Jopie Kotze, who spends his day at a table surrounded by mirrors so he can watch all the goings-on of his mini empire. The reception area is also an information centre, newsagent and curio shop, with an interesting semi-precious stone display. In the middle of all this is the restaurant (see below).

Sleeping
■ *on map*
Price codes:
see inside front cover

Springbok

■ Sleeping
1 Annie's Cottage
2 Masonic
3 Old Mill Lodge
4 Richtersveld Challenge
5 Springbok
6 Springbok Lodge

● Eating
1 Arkade
2 BJ's Steakhouse
3 Carne Casa
4 Godfather's
5 Melboschkuil
6 Titbits
7 Wimpy

N
Not to scale

Northern Cape

This popular lodge has a prime central location and is good value when compared with the larger hotels. **E** *Richtersveld Challenge*, Voortrekker St, just opposite the tourist office, T7181905. Local adventure tour operator, also has rooms for backpackers. Some very comfortable rooms with 4 beds, 1 double room, very clean, shared bathrooms, kitchen. Also has a 'Bunkhouse', basically a large garage with pull-down beds, but more comfortable than it sounds. Friendly management, still quite new so everything is in very good condition, gardens, braai area. Best choice for backpackers in town. **E** *Namastat*, 2 km from town centre, T7122435. Chance to stay in traditional Nama huts made of grass matting, 2 single beds in each hut, also some chalets, communal meals, bar, modern washblock, good set-up but isolated on a barren stretch outside of town. **E** *Springbok Caravan Park*, 2 km from town centre, on the left off the road to Goegap Park, T7181584. Small, 1 chalet and 2 caravans for hire, limited shade, few power points, swimming pool, shop.

Eating
● *on map*

Considering the size of Springbok, there is a good choice of restaurants, all of which are found on Voortrekker St

Arkade, Voortrekker St, T7122271. Quick lunch snacks and toasted sandwiches, next to shopping precinct overlooking petrol station. *BJ's Steakhouse*, Hospital St, T7122701. Basement restaurant with spaghetti western theme, generous portions, German dishes, boozy bar and dancing, pleasant change to hotel food. Recommended. *Carne Casa*, Voortrekker St, just before the Springbok Lodge. New steakhouse with a vague Portuguese theme, nice outdoor seating under thatch, excellent steaks, also chicken dishes, schnitzels and seafood. *Godfather's*, Voortrekker St, T7181877. Simple, family-run restaurant serving good pizzas and other dishes. *Melboschkuil*, Voortrekker St, T7181600. Attractive, brightly painted restaurant with a pleasant outdoor deck, serves a range of steaks, pasta dishes, some vegetarian options, good wine list. *Springbok Lodge*, Voortrekker St, T7121321. Part of the reception area and the curio shop is the hotel restaurant, popular given that most residents seem to eat here, good selection, bland but generous portions, laid back and slow service, settle for breakfast here and have a more hearty meal elsewhere in the evenings. *Titbits*, Voortrekker St, T7181455. A friendly pizzeria with excellent stone-baked pizzas, also range of other dishes such as pasta and steaks, breezy outdoor seating overlooking the main road. There are a few fast food options along Voortrekker St and by the petrol stations. *Southern Fried Chicken* and *Wimpy*, are the most popular.

Shopping
As a regional centre, Springbok has all of South Africa's main high street shops, and supermarkets can be found here. Most shops are within walking distance of the car park below the small kopjie in the centre of town. *CNA Books*, Van der Stel St. Stock some glossy coffee table books showing the flowers at their best.

Sports
Mountain biking *Pedroskloof Farm*, T6721666. Organizes mountain biking in the Kamiesberg area. There are several trails ranging in length and difficulty, but you have to bring your own bike. Closer to Springbok, there are 2 cycle routes in the **Goegap Nature Reserve**. One is 20 km and the other is 14 km long. In all districts drinking water is scarce. You should travel with at least 2 litres per person, and drink plenty just before you start off.

Tour operators
Richtersveld Challenge, T7181905, just opposite the tourist office on Voortrekker St. Good value local operator organizing a range of tours throughout the area, including overland trips, 4-wheel drive tours of Richtersveld National Park, and boat trips on motorized inflatables on the Orange River.

Transport
Local Car hire: *Tempest*, T7181600, behind *Melkboschkuil Restaurant*. You can hire 4-wheel drive vehicles from *Richtersveld Challenge*, T7181905, opposite the tourist office on Voortrekker St.

Air There is a small airfield close to the entrance to Goegap Park. *National Airlines*, T021-9340350. Fly once a day during the week between **Cape Town** and **Alexander Bay** via **Springbok**. **Cape Town** (90 mins): Mon-Fri, 1500.

Road 554 km to **Cape Town**, 1,274 km to **Johannesburg**, 374 km to **Upington**, 401 km to **Lamberts Bay**, 256 km to **Van Rhynsdorp**, 239 km to **Ai-Ais** (Namibia), 941 km to **Windhoek** (Namibia). **Bus**: *Intercape*, 24-hr enquiries T021-3804400. Buses depart from the *Springbok Café*. **Cape Town**: daily, 0600. **Windhoek** and **Namibia**: daily, 1830.

Banks *Standard*, Voortrekker St. *ABSA*, Van der Stel St. **Internet** *Melkboschkuil Restaurant*, Voortrekker St. Has speedy internet access. **Medical Services** Chemists: *Namaqualand Pharmacy*, Voortrekker St, T7121169. Plus *Foto First*, 1 hr film processing, open Sun am. **Directory**

Goegap Nature Reserve

The local O'Okiep Copper Company donated the area in 1960 to the government to establish a reserve to help protect the wild flowers of the region. The park has since been added to, including the opening of the **Hester Malan Wild Flower Garden** in 1966, a beautiful spot in August and September. The entire area was proclaimed as the Goegap Nature Reserve in 1990; the name 'Goegap' was derived from the Nama word for waterhole. The reserve is a mix of granite kopjies and dry valleys, with a good cross-section of typical Namaqualand vegetation. Although the area looks parched and barren, it supports a surprising number of species – 581 plant species have been recorded in the reserve. The area is classified as semi-desert with rain usually falling during the winter months, but this is very unpredictable and can vary between 80 and 160 mm per year. During the summer temperatures soar and it is unwise to walk under these conditions.

Colour map 3, grid B2

This is a popular little reserve with a well-known aloe collection and a couple of mountain bike trails, and a 4X4 route

Getting there The reserve is out of town, beyond the airport. From the centre of Springbok, pass under the N7 and turn right. Just before the airport, take a left turn; it is 15 km to the gates. You have to sign in at the gate, and then drive up to the office and information centre. **Ins & outs**

Information Open 0800-1600. Small fee per car and per person. Next to the reception centre is a snack bar which serves braai lunches and home-made cakes and drinks. Before you venture into the park, have a look at the information on display in the reception area. There is also a video which introduces you to the unique Namaqualand environment. Beyond the office on the edge of the hill are a number of picnic spots. Enquiries: Manager, Goegap Nature Reserve, Private Bag XI, Springbok, T027-7121880.

Like much of the area, the park becomes carpeted with wild flowers after the rains, making it very popular during spring. For the rest of the year, there is a famous succulents garden, the **Hester Malan Wild Flower Garden**, with a display of over 100 different species of aloes and succulents. Plants and seeds can also be purchased here. **Sights**

   In the areas which are only accessible to four-wheel drive vehicles, there is a good chance of seeing game – the most common species are gemsbok, mountain zebra, springbok, klipspringer, duiker and steenbok.

   Visitors can drive around a 17 km loop which wends into the hills, offering opportunities of seeing game and birdlife. The longer four-wheel drive route can only be visited by booking a trip through the reserve office. The route travels through more remote and dramatic corners of the reserve and lasts for three hours.

Starting from the reception centre are a couple of hiking trails, a mountain bike route and a trail for horse riders. While these are all excellent ways to explore the park, you have to bring your own horses and bicycles. The hiking trails are 6 km and 12 km long. Both involve a climb to the hilltops behind the offices, from where a level path leads to several viewpoints. When the flowers are in full bloom the walks allow visitors to gain some height, providing excellent views of the colourful carpets below. **Hiking**

Northern Cape

Port Nolloth &
Alexander Bay
Phone code: 027
(NB Always use
3-figure prefix)
Colour map 3, grid A1

Port Nolloth is an odd little town on the windswept West Coast, an important fishing centre, but more interestingly an area renowned for attracting fortune-seekers who trade (often, it is said, illegally) in diamonds. The town was established as a harbour and railway junction for the copper industry in 1854, but it proved too shallow for the bulk ore carriers, and the trade moved north to Alexander Bay. These days it has developed into a small holiday centre – the only one on this stretch of the coast – with crayfishing and diamonds supplementing local income. The beaches have a certain wild, windswept beauty to them, although the long stretches of sun-bleached sand can appear rather bleak at times. **Tourist office**, T8518229.

The diamond industry becomes more apparent in **Alexander Bay**, further north by the Namibian borderi. Diamonds were first found here in 1925, and today the town is run by the mining company *Alexkor Ltd*. Alexander Bay was closed to visitors until a few years ago – today visitors can take part in diamond mine tours, although most people come here for easy access to the **Richtersveld National Park** (see below).

If you wish to explore more of the region contact Alexkor Ltd in Alexander Bay, T027-8311330. They conduct three-hour tours of the alluvial diamond mines and diamond museum. Tours are held twice a week; booking is essential. Included on the tour is a visit to an oyster farm and a seal colony. There is a town museum open weekday mornings. *Alexkor* also run the local tourist information office, T8311330.

Price codes:
see inside front cover

Sleeping **C-D** *Scotia Inn Hotel*, Coastal Rd, Port Nolloth, T8518353. Single and double rooms, cheaper rooms without attached bathroom. Restaurant, bar. **D-F** *Brandkaros*, Private Bag X5, T8311856, F8311464. Fully furnished self-catering rondavels on the banks of the Orange River, caravan and camping sites with electric points, well-grassed and plenty of shade, a beautiful spot surrounded by irrigated farmland. If you have a permit you can drive down to the mouth of the Orange River from here. This camp is 65 km from the Richtersveld National Park, close enough to enjoy a day visit. Good value, recommended. **E-F** *Peace of Paradise Campsite*, 22 km from the Namibia border at Vioolsdrift, turn left at the border post just after the police station, T7618968. Beautiful shady camping on the Orange River, hot/cold showers, canoes to rent for R100 per day, meals available on request, close to the camp are a few engravings to admire. Recommended. **F** *McDougall's Bay Caravan Park*, 4 km south of Port Nolloth, T8518657, F8518366. A delightful caravan park with chalets right on the beach front, beautiful clean beach to walk along. This is an area well-known for its lobster and crayfish, so you should be able to enjoy a delicious seafood braai while staying here. Don't be deceived by the calm, attractive sea; it's very cold all year round.

Richtersveld National Park

Colour map 3, grid A1

The magnificent national park of Richtersveld covers some of the most remote and starkly beautiful scenery in Namaqualand. This is rough country, much of which can only be reached by four-wheel drive – the park is both isolated and inaccessible, but this is much of its appeal.

Ins & outs

Getting there The easiest route is to drive north from Springbok on the N7 to Steinkopf (49 km). Take the Port Nolloth turning and follow the R382 to the coast via Annienous Pass. In Port Nolloth take the coast road north towards Alexander Bay. Look out for restricted areas – a lot of the diamond mining roads are closed to the public. The park is signposted from Alexander Bay. For **tourist information** for the Alexander Bay area, and any questions concerning local access, T027-8311506, F8311364. It is a further 93 km of gravel along the Orange river, curving back inland to the park's office at Sendelingsdrif. Entry permits are issued here. The total distance from Springbok to the parks office is 330 km. Visitors must arrive before 1600 in order to reach the designated campsites before dark.

Information Gate and office hours: 0730-1730. Visitor numbers are strictly controlled; always call in advance. The contact address is: Warden, Richtersveld National Park, PO Box 406, Alexander Bay, 8290, T027-8311506, F8311175. None of the routes within the reserve are suitable for normal cars – a **four-wheel drive is essential** when driving in the park. It is also not recommended to visit the park alone, so try and organize at least a couple of vehicles. Fuel is available at reception at Sendelingsdrif, Mon-Fri 0730-1800, Sat 0800-1600, Sun, 0830-1400. A small general store is also open at Sendelingsdrif (weekdays only), selling cool drinks and basic provisions are available. The nearest shops are at Kuboes and Alexander Bay. Petrol and diesel are also available in the latter.

Fresh drinking water is only available at Sendelingsdrif. Make sure you have containers which can hold up to 20 litres. The park authorities advise visitors to bring gas stoves for cooking as there can be strong winds at the end of the day.

If possible, buy a copy of the 1:250,000 map of the area, as the park's map leaves off many of the roads making it easy to get lost. Keep clear of all 'no entry' signs, most of which denote mining and security areas.

Best time to visit Visits in the spring and autumn avoid the climatic extremes. The region receives virtually no rainfall in the east, while the western margin is frequently covered by coastal fog known as the 'malmokkie'. In summer the daytime temperatures can exceed 50°C – definitely a time to avoid the area.

Sights

Richtersveld was proclaimed a national park on 16 August 1991. In order to try to deflect some of the local opposition, herders are still allowed to graze their animals within the park limits. The northern boundary is the Orange River and the international border with Namibia.

The park encompasses a mountainous desert, seemingly barren but full of sturdy succulents, many of them endemic. These, coupled with the surreal rugged terrain, are the principal attractions of the park. Some of the most visible plants include the kokerboom and halfmens trees, while hidden in the mountains are hundreds of different succulents. None of the larger mammals are able to survive in such a hostile environment, but you may come across klipspringer, grey rhebok, steenbok, duiker, and mountain zebra; consider yourself very fortunate if you see leopard, jackal, brown hyena or caracal. Swimming and fishing (with a permit) are allowed in the Orange River, but you need always to be wary of the current.

Hiking

Three **Hiking trails** are open from 1 April to 30 September: *Vensterval Trail* (four days, three nights); *Lelieshoek-Oemsberg Trail* (three days, two nights) and the *Kodaspiek Trail* (two days, one night). Conditions are tough and only experienced hikers should consider attempting these. It is also possible to walk a little in the vicinity of the campsites.

Sleeping

Price codes:
see inside front cover

There are several **D** *Guest Houses* at Sendelingsdrift, T027-8311506, F8311175. *Arieb Guest Cottage*, 5 bedrooms with ceiling fans, 2 bathrooms, lounge, dinning room and fully equipped kitchen; *Kokerboom Guest Cottage*, 4 bedrooms and *Fish Eagle Guest Cottage*, 2 bedrooms. They all have similar facilities and bedding, towels and soap are also provided. **F** *Camping*, there are 5 designated sites, Potjiespram, De Hoop, Richtersberg (all close to the river), Ou Koei and Kokerboomkloof. Do not sleep on the bare ground, as there are many scorpions in the park, and be prepared for heavy dew. At present there are no shelters, washblocks, toilets or supplies – you must bring everything you might need with you, including containers to carry drinking and washing water. If you have all the right equipment, a visit to the park is a great experience.

Springbok to Cape Town

As you travel south from Springbok, the N7 winds through rugged granite scenery. There are no settlements of note until you reach Van Rhynsdrop. After 66 km the road passes the small settlement of **Kamieskroon**, which has little more than a petrol station, a shop, a few houses and a couple of places to stay. During the spring many visitors stop in this area to admire the wild flowers.

Northern Cape

Price codes:
see inside front cover

Sleeping **C** *Kamieskroon*, T027-6721614, F6721675, kamieshotel@kingsley.co.za Well-run family hotel with 15 rooms plus a caravan and camping park, rates include dinner and breakfast, tasty country meals, good source of information when the flowers are in bloom, has an excellent reputation for its photographic courses which are run during the flower season. **C-D** *Olienpoort*, 5 km from N7, T027-6721683. B&B on a quiet farm with 6 double rooms, dinners on request, caravans welcome, craft shop as part of the farm, during the day you can stop over for home-made snacks. Recommended. **D** *De Hoek*, T027-6721632, PO Box 132. 4 double rooms, TV, good value guesthouse serving meals to order, walking distance of village, ask for Sannie Gagiano. **D** *Rand Spaar*, 25 Church St, T027-6721604. Self-catering rooms, some with en suite bathroom. Booking essential during flower season.

**Namaqua
National Park**
Colour map 3, grid B2

*Best time for viewing
flowers: 1030-1600
The reserve is open
daily, 0800-1700
during the flower
season. Outside of the
flower season there is
little to see here*

Formerly known as the Skilpad Wildflower Reserve, the Namaqua National Park was officially opened in 1999, and has some of the best flower displays in Namaqualand. The reserve has been incorporated into a larger area designed to protect the fragile ecosystem of this unique region. Lying to the west of the N7 highway between Garies and Kharkams, it covers the area between the Spoeg and Groen rivers, allowing for the protection of the Atlantic seaboard marine ecosystems as well as the associated estuaries.

Its fine flowers have much to do with the park's location, set on the first ridge of hills in from the coast, which ensures that it receives the first rains of the season. When the conditions are right the wild flowers here are the best in Namaqualand – even in poor years, the displays are better than in most areas. Visitors can expect to see various bulb species: *babianas, lapeirousias,* and *romuleas* plus duikerwortel (*Grielum humifusum*) and orange mountain daisies (*Ursinia cakilefolia*).

Access is via a gravel road, heading north and then west from the *Kamieskroon Hotel*. The entrance is 17 km from the N7. From here, a 5 km gravel road winds in a loop around the hill, which during the flower season is a carpet of orange. Visitors can either walk around the park or ride a mountain bike. There is also a slight chance of seeing some wildlife; klipspringer, steenbok, duiker and the black-backed jackal. Note that the park is popular and can get very crowded. For further details, call T027-6721948. Entrance fee, R10. There is an information centre with a shop, tea room and toilets.

Continuing south on the N7 there is little of interest until you are past Van Rhynsdorp and enter the Olifants River Valley. From here you can explore the **West Coast** fishing villages or the beautiful **Cederberg Mountains**, (see page 193). Cape Town (495 km) can easily be reached in a single day.

Northern Cape

Background

13

Background

History

History, and not just modern history, is often a very contentious issue in South Africa. During the apartheid era schoolchildren, both black and white, were taught a particularly lopsided version of the country's history. In recent years there have, of course, been massive moves towards rewriting the history books, but it remains a field of conflict between left and right. Not all the myths, or misconceptions, come from racist apartheid historians and we will try to be even-handed in our approach. However, we start with one of the most important myths taught by apartheid historians; that Europeans arrived at the Cape at just about the same time as African people were crossing the Limpopo River and migrating into present-day South Africa. It is one of the easier myths to dismiss.

Early humans in South Africa

South Africa is actually home to some of the oldest fossil human remains in the world. Three million-year-old fossil remains of an early human-like species *Australopithecus africanus*, have been discovered at a number of sites on the highveld. The exact way in which the evolution of the early human-like species into modern human took place is a matter of considerable debate amongst archaeologists. Whatever the exact timing and process of this evolution, by one million years ago a species that looked and behaved very much like modern humans, called *Homo erectus*, ranged far and wide across Asia, Africa and Europe. Within the last 100,000 years some of these groups seem to have developed still further into *Homo sapiens*, or modern humans. According to some archaeologists the earliest fossil remains anywhere in the world of modern man come from Klasies River mouth in Eastern Cape and Border Cave on the KwaZulu Natal border. They are dated as being more than 50,000 years old.

As elsewhere in the world, early humans in southern Africa were hunter-gatherers. They had stone tools to help with basic tasks. At first these tended to be large and multi-purpose but over time they became increasingly specialized and usually smaller. Early humans tended to live in small nomadic groups and their activities were largely dependent upon the particular environment they occupied. It is often assumed that the life of hunter-gatherers is necessarily harsh with very little leisure time, but anthropological studies of present-day hunter-gatherers indicates that this is probably not the case.

The fossil evidence of early humans in present-day South Africa confirms that the apartheid myth of an unpopulated land is indeed simply fiction. However, apartheid historians were too sophisticated in telling their particular stories to be put off by the presence of a few fossils. The argument was not so much that the land was totally empty when Europeans arrived but that it was not populated by the ancestors of the present-day African population of South Africa. The fossil remains, according to this argument, were of the ancestors of a totally separate race of people who were killed by the ancestors of the present-day African population as they migrated south.

Physical anthropologists working early in the 20th century believed that all humans fell into a small number of distinct race groups that had evolved independently from early human-like species. The Khoi and San people of southern Africa, called Hottentots or Bushmen by the European settler, were believed to have been one of these totally distinct race groups and to be the direct descendants of the early humans whose fossils are found across South Africa. More recent scientific studies, especially studies of the gene pools of present-day populations, indicate that this was not the case. While Khoi and San people may look racially distinct from other African peoples, they share many of the same genes (as do Europeans with Africans and so on). However, the perception that Khoi and San people were very different from other human groups and stuck in some sort of stone-age

The Khoi & the San

Background

past where nothing ever changed, has lived on. While Khoi and San technologies had remained relatively unsophisticated, political units small and populations sparse, it is wrong to think that when Europeans first arrived at the tip of Africa they somehow encountered primitive stone-age people. These communities had changed and adapted over time and had long established trading contacts with other groups in southern Africa.

Up until about 20,000 years ago the ancestors of the Khoi and San people were all hunter-gatherers living in small egalitarian communities of about 20-30 people. They were nomadic and moved with the herds of wild game as they undertook seasonal migrations. Their tools were made out of stone, water was stored in ostrich shells rather than pottery and they lived in caves or simple tents. As they were nomadic they had few personal possessions and there was no concept of personal possession of land or wealth. They spoke a whole series of similar languages distinctive for the large number of clicks and even whistling noises included in their speech. Linguists say that in terms of tongue and lip movements these clicks, which can still be heard in the language of their descendants, are very similar to any other consonants but to the outsider they sound strange and rather wonderful.

Given their lifestyle, few of their remains have been discovered by the archaeologist, with one notable exception: their famous and beautiful **cave paintings**. These are found throughout southern Africa and usually depict hunting expeditions or the trance dances through which the San believed they could communicate with their dead ancestors. These paintings were at first monochrome but over time some artists began to experiment with colour. The contents also changed over time with later paintings showing domesticated animals, especially cattle and, after the arrival of Europeans, people holding guns.

Sometime about 20,000 years ago some of these hunter-gatherer communities underwent a huge and relatively rapid change that was to have far reaching effects on their lifestyles. At this time a number of groups, probably sited in present-day northern Botswana, acquired domesticated livestock. The first livestock they had were fat-tailed sheep. These were probably originally domesticated in North Africa and the Middle East and the southern African hunter-gatherers traded for them with the Sudanic tribes who then occupied much of eastern Africa. Later they were able to acquire cattle from Bantu groups who migrated from the forest margins of West Africa into East and southern Africa.

The arrival of domesticated livestock radically altered the social relations within hunter-gatherer communities. With livestock came the concept of ownership of property and it was possible for one or two individuals to amass wealth and prestige. The people that acquired cattle also became more politically powerful and formed into larger groups under one or two chiefs. These groups, who became known as the Khoi, migrated south from present-day Botswana and occupied the coast zone of the Cape region from the Fish River right round to Namibia. The interior was occupied by San hunter-gatherers who maintained the smaller social units and a more egalitarian society. There was a large degree of interchange between these two peoples. The San hunters often raided the livestock herds of the Khoi, especially if these herds had displaced the wild animals upon which they relied and there is some evidence that the Khoi had San working for them as servants. There was also probably a large flow of people backwards and forwards between the two categories – if San acquired livestock they could become Khoi and if Khoi fell on hard times and lost all their cattle they could end up as San.

Arrival of the Bantu speakers There was also a large degree of contact between the Khoi and San and other African peoples living in southern Africa. Apartheid history was right when it taught that these other African peoples had migrated into southern Africa from the north but got the dates wrong by some 1,000 years. These newer arrivals, the ancestors of the vast majority of South Africa's present-day population, spoke a group of languages known as the Bantu group of languages. The people themselves are sometimes called Bantu people but this word is now associated with the racist institutions of the 1960s that used the name.

Bantu-speaking peoples began migrating into present-day South Africa about the period 500 AD, bringing with them new technologies, especially iron smelting and new domesticated livestock. The migration was not one big trek southwards but a whole series of small movements by groups of individuals setting off in search of new pastures and looking to establish new villages. Where they came into contact with San and Khoi groups occupying good pasture they tended to displace them, pushing them into the more marginal desert and mountain areas. Some groups occupied the highveld areas whilst others spread out along the fertile coastal strip that was later to become KwaZulu Natal and the Eastern Cape. The peoples who settled along the coastal strip were known as **Nguni** and were the ancestors of the present-day Zulu and Xhosa people, whilst those who settled on the highveld were eventually to become the Sotho, Tswana and other related people. When the Bantu speakers came up against organized and established coastal Khoi groups in the area between the Fish and Sundays rivers, in present-day Eastern Cape, and the drier interior Karoo and Kalahari areas on the highveld, the migration came to a halt.

Like the Khoi these newer arrivals were essentially herders and cattle were the mainstay of their economy. But they were also keen agriculturists and raised crops of millet, sorghum and other cereals and vegetables. In good rainfall years any surplus was exchanged for cattle with other people not so fortunate and in bad years cattle could in turn be exchanged for cereals. The Bantu-speaking peoples tended to form larger and more politically organized groups with clear hierarchical structures. In the dry interior they tended to form large villages around regular water supplies, whilst on the better-watered coastal strip they tended to live in more isolated homesteads. Iron smelting was an important activity and iron goods were traded over long distance exchange networks. In present-day Zimbabwe some Bantu-speaking peoples were especially successful with smelting gold and this was traded with Arabs along the east African coast and later with Europeans.

There is a good deal of trading contact between the Bantu speakers and the Khoi. The Khoi were particularly keen to get hold of iron which they used in their tools and also the *dagga* (marijuana) that they enjoyed eating or drinking in tea and which did not grow well in the dry Cape. Both Khoi, San and Bantu speakers only started smoking the *dagga* after being introduced to pipes by Europeans. This large degree of contact is reflected in the fact that some Bantu speakers incorporated the Khoi-San clicks into their language – today these clicks can be heard in both Xhosa and Zulu. There was also a degree, small but significant, of intermarrying between the Khoi and Bantu-speakers, the Xhosa in particular.

Arrival of the Europeans

The first Europeans to make contact with these three different social groups in southern Africa were Portuguese sailors attempting to find routes to the spice islands of Asia. For many years the Portuguese had been pushing further and further south along Africa's western coastline and in 1487 a ship captained by Bartholomeu Dias made it around the Cape of Good Hope and sailed up the eastern coast of southern Africa as far as Algoa Bay. Ten years later another Portuguese sailor, Vasco da Gama, rounded the Cape and continued up the continent's eastern coast before heading further east, eventually to India. Over the next 200 years increasing numbers of Portuguese traders and their Dutch and British competitors began to make the journey to the east via the Cape of Good Hope. Though they occasionally stopped for fresh water and supplies in some of the more sheltered Cape bays and river mouths the Portuguese usually tried to give a wide berth to the territory that is now South Africa. Apart from the treacherous coastline they also often encountered a hostile reception from the local inhabitants. Instead the Portuguese had trading and supply posts in present-day Angola and Mozambique where they were able to both resupply their ships on the way to their eastern empire and capture slaves to send to their American colonies.

The Dutch were the first European trading power to set up a permanent settlement in South Africa. In 1652 the powerful **Dutch East India Company** built a fort and established a supply station under the command of Jan Van Reibeck on a site that later became Cape

Dutch, Khoi & slave society at the Cape

Background

Town. The idea was that this was to be simply a point where passing Dutch ships could drop in to get fresh supplies and to rest sick members of their crew. The company did not envisage the settlement growing into a larger community and at first, every inhabitant was a company servant. This situation soon altered, however, when the company decided that it would allow a group of servants who had worked out their contracts to settle close by as independent farmers and supply the post with their produce. Prior to this decision all fresh supplies had been either delivered by sea or brought from the Khoi groups living in and around the Cape Peninsula. These independent settlers were known as burghers and their number was soon increased by the freeing of more servants and the arrival of new settlers from Holland and, after 1685, Huguenots fleeing French anti-protestant legislation.

With the advent of free burghers, the size of the settlement began to increase and some farmers moved out into outlying districts. This brought them into increased conflict with Khoi herders. There were a series of small skirmishes which the Dutch, with their superior weapons, easily won and the Khoi found themselves displaced from more and more land and their herds of cattle diminished. Under these circumstances some began to work for the burghers on their farms, theoretically as free labourers but in effect as little more than slaves. In this early expansion and subjection of the Khoi the seeds of a whole long history of dispossession of the established population of South Africa are apparent. As the settler farming areas expanded they came into contact with San groups whom they systematically slaughtered in revenge for their raids on settler livestock. European and Asian diseases, especially smallpox, also killed many more San and Khoi and by the end of the 18th century they had almost all been either absorbed into the settler economy as servants, pushed into the most marginal mountain and desert areas, such as the Kalahari, or exterminated.

As the settlers moved further to the east and north they encountered environments less conducive to settled agriculture and more suited to pastoralism. Many settlers adopted a life as semi-nomadic *trekboers* living exclusively by trading their livestock and the products of hunting with the settled colonists in the western Cape. As they moved east they also began to come into contact with Bantu-speaking Africans, in particular the Xhosa in what is now the Eastern Cape. Trading relations were established between the settlers and Xhosa and some Xhosa also came to work on settler farms in return for guns and other European imports. As well as trade, however, the settlers and Xhosa also interacted through warfare. Cattle raiding was especially common and some historians also argue that settlers also indulged in widespread slave raiding (see Mfecane section for more details about this). These battles were, however, inconclusive and a fluid and unstable boundary between the *trekboers* and Xhosa persisted for many years.

The other factor that began to alter the original function of the settlement was the arrival, in 1658, of a group of slaves captured from the Portuguese in Angola. The company had originally intended that there would be no slaves at the settlement but the company servants and free burghers soon became accustomed to avoiding the hardest and most menial manual tasks and demanded that they be supplied with more slaves. Unlike in the Americas most of these slaves did not come from West Africa but from Asia and Madagascar. They tended not to be owned in large numbers on huge plantations but in small groups, often less than 10, by individual farmers. The balance between the slave and free population of the Cape remained much more even than in West Indian and South American colonies.

There was, however, always a big gender imbalance in both the settler and slave populations, with far more men than women. Sexual encounters between slave owners and their female slaves, or Khoi servants, were frequent and a number of slave owners married freed slaves. Apartheid history taught that the present-day Coloured population are the descendants of slaves and passing sailors, but even a cursory reading of the contemporary Dutch and other European reports of the settlement show that it it is probably more accurate to see the present-day Afrikaner and Coloured population as having the same ancestry. Another fact about the present-day Coloured population that is seldom recognized is that they are frequently the direct descendants of original Khoi inhabitants of the area. This is especially so in the Eastern and Northern Cape, where there was never a large slave population and certainly no sailors!

A number of slaves managed to escape from their captivity and joined up with still independent groups of Khoi and miscellaneous European and mixed race adventurers beyond the frontiers of the Dutch colony. Here they formed new and unusual political groupings who often existed by raiding both European settlers and African groups in the interior. The best-known of these bands were known as the **Griquas**. With European horses and guns they became an important political force in the South African interior right through until the mid-19th century.

During the 18th century Dutch economic and political power began to wane. Just as the Dutch had superseded the Portuguese they were themselves challenged by the rising power of the British. In 1795 the British sailed into False Bay and annexed the Dutch colony (The Battle of Muizenberg). The British were concerned that the French, with whom they were fighting in Europe, would take over the strategic port. In a general peace settlement of 1803 the colony was returned to the Dutch but in 1806 the British reconquered the territory and their sovereignty was finally accepted by other European powers in the peace settlement of 1816.

Arrival of the British

The British were only really interested in the Cape as a staging post and strategic port to protect trade with their new Asian empire. The colony was not profitable and neither the British government nor business took much interest in the new possession. There were, however, two important events in the early years of British rule that were to have crucial impacts on the subsequent history of South Africa.

The first factor was the British authorities' concern over persistent and inconclusive fighting along the colony's eastern frontier with the Xhosa. Some Xhosa groups had taken advantage of the instability in the colony to re-establish themselves to the west of the Fish River. The British decided that the only way to stop the persistent battles was to push the Xhosa back across the Fish River and establish a secure and clear frontier. During the first years of their rule they cleared the Xhosa occupying this area and tried to ban *trekboers* from having any contact with them. It was decided that what was needed was a group of permanent settlers on new farms in the area from which the Xhosa had been cleared in order to keep them apart from the *trekboers*.

In 1820 the British parliament agreed to release £50,000 to transport settlers from Britain to occupy this area. The money was used to send out 4,000 settlers, with an additional 1,000 paying their own passage to the region. These people became known as the **1820 Settlers** and formed the nucleus of the subsequent British settler community. Though the British authorities had intended that they should become farmers and hence occupy the disputed territory, most of the settlers were from urban artisan backgrounds and few had the skills or inclination necessary to become successful cultivators in the difficult and unfamiliar environment of the Eastern Cape. Most of them quickly gravitated towards the small towns, especially Port Elizabeth and Grahamstown, where they used their previous experience to become traders or skilled artisans. Their presence introduced an important new element to the equation, not least cultural, and 1820 Settler attitudes towards things such as the freedom of the press and towards the proper role of government played an important part in shaping 19th-century Cape settler society.

It soon became apparent that the British attempts to create a permanent border between the Xhosa and settlers had failed and cattle raiding backwards and forwards across the border continued. The Xhosa tried on numerous occasions to reclaim their land, occupied now by the settlers, but these attempts always failed, despite many initial successes. The **Frontier Wars** between Xhosa and settler continued for the next half century with Xhosa independence and land occupation being progressively eroded until their remaining areas (which became known as Transkei), were eventually incorporated into the Cape Colony.

The other fundamental change that British rule brought about was the **ending of the slave trade** and then the total banning of slavery. The peripheral role of South Africa in the British colonial empire and the dispersed nature of its slave population meant that it was seldom considered in debates about slavery, which instead concentrated on the massive slave plantations of the West Indies. Nevertheless, when the British parliament eventually decided to call an end to the institution that many felt was both inhumane and, more importantly, not beneficial to the empire's economy, it was also banned in South Africa. In 1834 slaves throughout the British Empire were officially emancipated, though they were to remain with their owners as apprentices until 1838. Slave owners were also offered compensation of one third of the value of their slaves. Though emancipation provided some slaves with new opportunities, in reality many of them continued to live very similar lives, carrying out the same heavy manual labour, under extremely harsh conditions, on the same Cape farms.

Nevertheless, many of the original Dutch settlers were extremely unhappy about the emancipation of slaves. To make things worse the British government, after extensive lobbying by British missionaries working in South Africa, also prevented them from introducing legislation aimed at tying both freed slaves and Khoi servants to individual farms as indentured labourers. The Dutch settlers had already been annoyed by the way their extremely loose system of administration had been reformed by the British, making it more difficult for individual farmers to impose their own law on their particular district. Many *trekboers* in the eastern districts also felt that the British were not quick enough in coming to their support when they had cattle raided by Xhosa groups to the east. Now they were not only losing a large proportion of their 'property' (slaves) but were being prevented from making sure they had a captive (cheap) labour supply. Though they were offered compensation at one third of the value of their slaves this had to be claimed in London. Many slave owners, therefore, sold their compensation rights to agents at usually about one fifth of the slave's value.

In response to these complaints a number of Dutch settlers decided that they would set out with their families and servants in search of new land beyond the British colonial boundaries. Between 1835 and 1840 around 5,000 people left the Cape colony and headed east in a movement that later became known as the **Great Trek**. It tended to be the *trekboers* from the eastern areas, who had fewer possessions and little investment in established farms who took part in this movement. The settlers taking part in the trek became known as *voortrekers* and their experiences beyond the colonial frontiers have become fertile ground for 20th century Afrikaner nationalism. One thing not often celebrated in the national myths that grew up around the Great Trek is that accompanying the treks were a large number of Khoi servants and a small number of freed slaves still economically and socially bound to their masters/patrons.

African States and the Mfecane

The area the *voortrekers* were entering into was the home of numerous Bantu-speaking African chiefdoms, but at the very time they made their appearance on the scene these political groupings were undergoing unprecedented political upheaval. The causes and indeed the very nature of this upheaval is a matter of considerable debate amongst historians and for once this is not a debate between apartheid historians and their opponents. Rather the debate is between those who believe that the turmoil was caused by wholly internal African political manoeuvrers and those who believe that external parties, especially slave raiders from Mozambique and the Cape, were to blame. Inevitably the truth is probably somewhere between the two. External factors, such as the presence of European traders interested in products such as ivory, may have lead to increased competition amongst African chiefdoms for lucrative resources, but the dynamics of the upheaval probably had more to do with internal African state formation. On balance, the evidence used by those who argue for a basically internal dynamic to the process seems to be stronger than those arguing the opposite.

Prior to the early 19th century African political units tended to be small and loyalty fluid. If there was disagreement within a chiefdom one section would simply set off and establish a new village in a new area. In the early 19th century, however, new larger and more strictly organized African political groupings (something closer to European nations), were formed. The epicentre of this new process of state formation was between the Tugela and Pongola rivers in present-day northern KwaZulu Natal and involved one of the best known pre-colonial African personalities: **Shaka Zulu**.

In 1886 there was a further mineral discovery in South Africa; this time it was gold on the Witwatersrand in the Transvaal Republic. Miners from across the world rushed to the new reef and capitalists were quick to make sure they got a slice of the pie. The deep level and relatively poor grade of the ore meant that it was only large capitalist organizations that could secure the investment necessary to succeed and, just as at Kimberley, mine ownership was quickly consolidated into a few hands. The main town on the Rand, Johannesburg, grew rapidly from nothing to about 75,000 white residents and many more Africans by the turn of the century.

These mineral discoveries fundamentally altered South African society. It was at the mines that many of the features that dominated life in 20th century South Africa first came into existence, in particular the pass laws, the migrant labour system, the compounds and the colour bar. The deep level diggings and the complicated process of extraction from poor gold ores meant that production expenses were high and, as the gold price was fixed internationally, the one way mining companies could ensure high profits was to hold down or reduce labour costs. The diamond mines at Kimberley provided the model of how this was to be done.

At first all labour at Kimberley was able to demand a high wage, but as the number of companies were rationalized there were fewer and fewer opportunities. White labourers began to realize that they were losing out to cheaper African labourers and pressurized the government to reduce this competition. Whilst government was unwilling to institute too overtly racist legislation, they did introduce a pass law that required all Africans present in the town to carry a pass signed either by a magistrate or a mine owner showing that they had legitimate employment. This legislation was aimed at preventing large numbers of Africans arriving at Kimberley in hope of jobs and hence pushing down wage rates.

The mines' owners, however, wanted to keep wages as low as possible and therefore to substitute more expensive white labour with cheaper African labour. The solution to this problem lay in the migrant labour system, where only male Africans came to the mines leaving their families at home on the reserves. The DeBeers mining company had quickly introduced a system whereby all African labour had to live in a single compound above the mine from which they were prohibited to leave for the duration of their contract. The official reason was that this was to prevent diamond thefts, but there were also many other advantages for the employers. As the compounds were only to house single male African labourers the company did not have to pay adequate wages to support the miner's family, who usually remained in the reserves and farmed to meet their own subsistence needs. Furthermore the mine owners could be assured of economies of scales in buying in provisions and therefore were able to feed African labourers on the site. If Africans had to buy their own food they would have needed higher wages. At first DeBeers wanted to introduce a compound system for white labourers, but because they had a political voice they were able to resist these plans.

For white labour the migrant labour system meant that they were being squeezed out of the job market by cheaper African labour. The mining companies were always nervous that white and African labour would unite, especially as many of the white labourers were experienced trade union activists. Over time there developed a sort of tacit agreement between white labour and capitalists that in exchange for the political support of labour, the capitalists would introduce a colour bar that reserved the more skilled and better paid jobs for Whites only. At times this arrangement broke down, especially in the years after the First World War, but on the whole White labour never rocked the boat.

While capitalists on the Rand were able to develop a labour system that ensured wages were kept low, they were not able always to secure African labour in the quantities they required. They were, therefore, always pressurizing the respective governments to introduce policies to push more African men out of the reserves. They also went to great extents to get labour from wherever it was available, including beyond the borders of South Africa as far away as Malawi. The mine owners also decided to co-operate with one another to keep wages low and formed a Witwatersrand Native Labour Association that was to look after all recruitment of African labour. When mine owners experienced a particular shortage of labour early in the 20th century, they recruited 63,000 Chinese

Background

labourers on fixed contracts who undermined the wage levels demanded by Africans. Once the wage rate had been forced down, the Chinese labourers were simply repatriated.

One reason the capitalists felt that Africans were not entering the labour market in the numbers they required was the success that African peasant farmers were having at this time. African farmers were the first to react to the new markets created by the mines at Kimberley and on the Rand and, using new farming techniques learnt from missionaries, they increased their output of grains tremendously. Many of the successful African peasant farmers lived in the reserves, but others had managed to buy or rent land outside these areas. White farmers were not usually able to cope with the competition these new African peasants presented and lobbied government for support. This was forthcoming in the form of subsidies, soft loans and technical advice and after the turn of the century these African peasant farmers began to lose out against their white competitors. In 1913 legislation was introduced that made it impossible for Africans to buy or rent land in many 'White' areas. The depression of the 1930s was the final nail in the coffin for many peasant farmers and after that date very few struggled on. Today it seems hard to believe that there was once a highly successful African peasant class, outperforming their White neighbours, and that it was deliberately ruined by government action. The success of African farmers at this time was ignored by all school history textbooks during the apartheid era and even today few South Africans, black or white, know that African farmers were at one time much more successful than their white competitors.

Anglo-Boer War

When diamonds were discovered at Kimberley it was not quite clear who had sovereignty over the area, with a Tswana chiefdom, the Orange Free State, the Transvaal Republic and the Griquas all claiming the area. Britain pressurized the rival claimants to undergo a process of arbitration under their direction. At the arbitration it was decided that the Griqua's claim was strongest, but the British immediately offered the Griqua leader substantial compensation if he agreed that the territory should be administered by the British. Not surprisingly, the Orange Free State, which had the strongest claim out of the two republics, was annoyed by this sleight of hand, especially as the British soon incorporated the area into the Cape Colony, but there was little they could do about it.

The Rand, on the other hand, was clearly within the Transvaal Republic. The British had annexed the Transvaal in 1877 but after a brief Boer uprising they handed control back. They must have regretted the decision when gold was discovered just five years later. The government of the Republic was primarily concerned with looking after the interests of its richer Boers, the vast majority of whom were farmers. They were a little unsure about how to treat the new mining economy. On the one hand the extra revenue from taxing the operations was clearly to be welcomed, whilst on the other they were nervous about the implications of having a large number of new immigrants, known by them as *uitlanders*, or foreigners, in their midst. They therefore introduced legislation restricting the franchise to white adult male naturalized citizens who had lived in the Republic for at least 14 years.

While most *uitlanders* were too busy trying to make their fortune to worry about politics, they did complain about the inefficiency of the Transvaal government in meeting the conditions necessary for an efficient capitalist system. British Imperialist forces were keen to get their hands on the Republic and in 1895 tried to manipulate *uitlander* dissatisfaction in a plot to overthrow the Transvaal government. In 1895, with the backing of the Colonial Office in London, Cecil Rhodes, then Prime Minister of the Cape Colony, tried to organize a committee of leading *uitlanders* to seize control of Johannesburg and declare a new government. Rhodes also arranged for a column of British police, under the control of his old friend Leander Starr Jameson, based in the Bechuanaland Protectorate, to come to their assistance. The plot, later known as the Jameson Raid, was a fiasco. The *uitlander* committee in Johannesburg bickered amongst themselves and did not command any mass following. Realizing this, Rhodes called off the proposed intervention by Jameson's force, but Jameson ignored his command and entered the Transvaal. When the committee learnt of this, they did belatedly declare that they had taken over Johannesburg but even in the process of doing so they entered into negotiations with the Transvaal Republic and came to an agreement. Jameson's column, therefore, had no crisis in which to intervene and were simply met and arrested by a Transvaal commando. This embarrassing incident marked the end of Rhodes' political career and helped to alienate British and Afrikaners across South Africa.

Despite the failures of the Jameson Raid the British were still keen to gain control of the Transvaal. Just four years after, Britain mounted a far better equipped, more sustained and ultimately successful bid to gain control of the whole of South Africa; the Anglo-Boer (or South African) War of 1899 to 1902. There is some disagreement among historians about the underlying cause of the war. Afrikaner Nationalist historians tend to view it simply as an example of British Imperial expressionism. Some historians of the British Empire, on the other hand, argue that it was more to do with British strategic concerns; they were worried that the Transvaal Republic could inspire Afrikaners in the Cape to rebel against the British who would, therefore, lose control of ports such as Simon's Town which were vital for protecting her sea routes. Most historians, however, see gold as being the key. The British were not surprisingly keen to control the world's largest supply of gold and make sure heavy British investment in the mines was profitable.

During the late 1890s the Colonial Office in London and the British High Commissioner in the Cape both lobbied for direct British military intervention to overthrow the Transvaal and the Orange Free State Republics. The situation grew more and more tense and in September 1899 Britain sent a large party of British soldiers to reinforce their troops. Sensing that Britain was about to invade the Transvaal, the Orange Free State decided to strike before the reinforcements arrived and on 11 October 1899 declared war on Britain in an attempt to preserve their independence. Deciding that attack was the best form of defence, they invaded both the Cape and Natal colonies.

At first the Boer Republics had great success and achieved victories in both northern Natal and the northeastern Cape. They drove back British forces and laid siege to Ladysmith, Kimberley and Mafikeng. They were, however, unable to advance much further in either colony and the general uprising of Afrikaners in the Cape that they had hoped for never materialized. Initially they held off British attempts to relieve the three towns, but with the arrival of huge numbers of British troops the fortunes changed. During 1900 the British set off on a triumphant and unstoppable advance on Pretoria and Paul Kruger, the president of the Transvaal Republic, escaped into exile via the Portuguese colony of Mozambique.

British victory seemed secure, but a number of die-hard Boers had other ideas. For the next two years they indulged in a continuous and, for the British, exceptionally frustrating, guerrilla war. The British were unable to capture the small bands of highly skilled Boer commandos so set about instituting a scorched earth policy to deny the guerrillas any help from local populations. Large numbers of Boers from areas with a guerrilla presence were rounded up and placed in concentration camps to prevent them from supplying the commandos in the field with provisions. Though it was by no means a deliberate policy of the British, poor administration meant that food and medical supplies in the camps often ran out and many Boers, including many women and children, died of disease or starvation. Memories of the British scorched earth policy were often revived by Afrikaner politicians throughout the 20th century, though they conveniently forgot that the Boers tended to use very similar techniques in their battles against African chiefdoms. Also forgotten is the British policy of rounding up any African workers on Boer farms and placing them in similar concentration camps during the war.

The British scorched earth policy and the sheer hopelessness of their situation eventually lead many Boers to abandon the fight and return to their farms. The remaining guerrilla bands, who became known as the *bitterenders*, eventually surrendered to the British under the Treaty of Vereeniging in April 1902. The British were keen to ensure that the two defeated Boer republics were fully incorporated into a unified South Africa and therefore agreed a number of concessions for the defeated army. One of the key issues that the British were willing to concede was that any discussion of political rights for Africans be delayed until some unspecified future date.

Peace & union

Background

The British hoped that after the war they would be able to substantially Anglicize the country by enforcing English as an official language and encouraging mass immigration from Britain. This policy proved to be a failure but they were successful in encouraging the four territories to agree to Union just seven years after the end of the war. One of the key sticking points in discussions over Union was the issue of African voting rights. In the Cape Africans and Coloureds had the right to vote as long as they owned above a set value in property. While this excluded most Africans it did give at least some an opportunity to vote and therefore a political voice, however weak. Natal also had a property qualification but the figure was set so high for Africans that only a handful ever managed to vote. The other two Boer republics had never allowed Africans any political rights whatsoever. During the discussions over Union, which only Natal had reservations about, it was decided that the issue of voter representation for Africans would be side-stepped by entrenching a constitutional clause maintaining the pre-Union franchise arrangements in each of the four territories. With this issue solved and agreement on things such as dual official languages (English and Dutch), all sides agreed on the **Act of Union**, which was passed by the British Houses of Parliament in 1909 and the Union of South Africa came into being in 1910.

The rise of nationalism

First stirrings of African nationalism The Act of Union, and particularly the entrenchment of the Boer republics' voting arrangements, felt like a powerful slap in the face for very many Africans. Most Africans had supported the British during the Anglo-Boer War and had assumed that their loyalty would be recognized in the post-war settlement. Though Africans in the Cape had their voting rights entrenched in the Constitution they feared that the Cape government's willingness (with British backing) to placate the two northern former republics was a very bad omen. This proved all too correct; in 1935 they had their voting rights removed by an Act which amended the Constitution.

In the early 20th century African political opposition to racist policies tended to be exceptionally moderate. During the 19th century there had been small but steady growth of the African educated middle class. They were mostly educated in mission schools, were committed Christians and employed as teachers or government clerks. They tended to look to London for support and were especially concerned about preserving their voting rights. Not surprisingly these early African political leaders were dismayed about the proposals for Union and sent a delegation to London to try to urge the British House of Commons to amend the Act. Despite receiving some support from Labour politicians they failed in this venture. In 1912 a group of African leaders called for a national convention for all African political groups in the country. This gathering in Bloemfontein marked the formation of a more organized phase in African opposition to racist legislation and lead to the South African Native National Congress, later renamed the **African National Congress**.

Despite the formation of a national opposition organization, African protest still tended to be extremely moderate. Many African leaders placed a special emphasis on education as a means to achieving political recognition. Many still believed in the old Cape liberal ideology of 'equal rights for all civilized men' and therefore went to great lengths to prove just how civilized they were. London remained the Mecca for these early leaders and the most common form of protest was appeals to the Imperial authorities.

Over the next few decades, however, there were also a number of shorter lived, more radical, opposition movements. The most successful of these was the Industrial and Commercial Union (ICU) established by the very colourful figure, Clements Kadalie. The ICU spread rapidly through South Africa in the 1920s and was especially successful amongst farm workers. It demanded fairer wages for African workers and full political rights for all. The organization of the ICU left much to be desired, however, and just as quickly as it grew it subsided.

After the First World War a few white communists also made attempts to forge links between the white union movements and African workers. Though there were many influential Africans who came up through these Communist Party links the movement was never able to reach out to a wide range of Africans, especially Africans in the rural areas. The Party also suffered from numerous internal splits, often caused by contradictory statements coming from the international Communist leadership and from continual harassment from the police. White Unionists also resisted the attempts to form a non-racial movement and in 1922 the South African Labour Party, which represented the interests of white working class voters, entered into an election pact with the Afrikaner nationalists in the National Party.

While the 1920s had seen a great deal of protest from African peoples, especially from the ICU, the 1930s were a period of relative quiet. The international depression also affected the South African economy and many Africans found themselves unemployed or on low wages. To make matters worse the early years of the decade also saw one of the worst ever droughts, ruining the residual African farming economy in the reserves. Under these circumstances political protest seemed to be secondary to the tough job of simply surviving. During the Second World War, however, there was an upswing of African protest culminating in a series of protest movements amongst squatters outside Johannesburg and a massive African mineworkers strike. After the war African protest entered a more radical phase as younger leaders came to the forefront.

It is a common misconception that Afrikaner nationalist sentiments existed right from the arrival of Van Reibeck and that the 'Afrikaner spirit' somehow grew out of the harsh conditions of the frontier. This is a misconception that has often been fuelled by Afrikaner nationalists' versions of history. The reality is very different and, whilst Afrikaners have used the imagery of the Great Trek to help create a sense of nationalism, it was by no means an event in which all Afrikaners took part. **Rise of Afrikaner nationalism**

Class divisions were strong amongst both the descendants of the original settlers who remained in the Cape and those who migrated to the north. The established richer Western Cape farmers looked down both on the people who migrated to the new Republics and their poorer neighbours. Because of these deep rooted divisions it is not really correct to talk about Afrikaners as a single category prior to the 20th century, when there were potent political forces that led to increased collective nationalism. It is, therefore, somewhat of an anachronism to talk about Afrikaners, which simply means African in Dutch, prior to the 20th century. In the Western Cape it is possible to see an earlier sense of Afrikaner nationalism, but this might more accurately be called a Dutch settler identity, whilst in the two Republics the sense of nationalism was firmly tied up with an extremely local (agricultural) identity, hence the use of the term *Boer*, which simply means farmer in Dutch.

In the 19th century the Afrikaans language, later to become a potent symbol of Afrikaner nationalism, was regarded by the more élite settlers as a bit of an embarrassment. Because the language had developed out of a mixture between Dutch and the various languages spoken by the Khoi and slaves, it was regarded as a rather low form of dialect and its association with coloured servants was apparently the common description of a language known as kitchen Dutch. There had been one attempt to raise the profile of Afrikaans in the 1870s but it had not spread much beyond the movement's base in Paarl. During the negotiations over Union, Boer leaders were not arguing for Afrikaans to be a dual official language, they were arguing for Dutch. At the very time these negotiations were taking place, however, there was a second attempt to gain respectability for the Afrikaans language. The political climate was much more conducive to the movement and it quickly spread throughout the Cape and the two former Boer Republics.

The ravages of the war and the development of mechanized agriculture meant that many poorer Afrikaner tenant farmers were being forced off the land in the early decades of this century. They migrated to the new towns in search of work, but had few skills to offer and often ended up poor and unemployed. Their plight, often labelled 'the poor white problem', was a continual worry for Afrikaner politicians. They were especially fearful that their marginal position in the new towns was pushing them into closer contact with the growing band of African urban poor. The 'poor white problem' was a key motivation behind the deepening of segregationist policies in the urban areas, designed to keep black and white apart. During the first half of the century the nitty-gritty of segregation tended to be largely left up to local authorities to implement, with central government simply providing the legislative framework for local regulations. Nevertheless, in almost every town residential segregation and pass laws strictly regulated the daily lives of Africans.

The 'poor white problem' was also an important force behind the development of Afrikaner nationalism. As poorer Afrikaners moved to the towns they became immersed in a very different working class culture to the one they had experienced in the countryside. The Afrikaner leaders realized that if these new urban residents became part of this new urban culture they may well lose much of their separate Afrikaner identity and the Afrikaner politicians would find their support base undermined. They therefore decided that they needed to create a stronger sense of Afrikaner nationalism that would incorporate all Afrikaners, rich and poor. Historical events, such as the Great Trek, were deliberately resurrected and celebrated, the Afrikaans language was encouraged and, crucially, the Afrikaner leaders developed exclusively Afrikaner economic institutions that deliberately helped Afrikaner small businesses.

Afrikaner politics

Despite the deliberate fostering of Afrikaner nationalism the Afrikaner leadership was constantly fighting amongst itself and political parties frequently split and reformed. One of the key issues of disagreement was over the relationship between the new Union and the British Empire. After Union the British asked an ex-Boer General, Louis Botha to form the first government. He, and his close ally and successor General Jan Smuts, both strongly believed that the Afrikaners should strive to have good relations with the Imperial government and unite English and Dutch/Afrikaans-speaking white South Africans. Their **South Africa Party**, built on a coalition between the Transvaal and Cape ruling parties easily won the first election, but another important ex-Boer General, Hertzog, felt that they were too keen on maintaining good relations with the British government and formed a rival **National Party**. At first the National Party only had support in Hertzog's home province, the Orange Free State, but later he was joined by DF Malan, an ardent anti-British Afrikaner from the Cape province.

The First World War caused a further and more vicious split in Afrikaner ranks. A number of important generals resisted Botha's strong support for Britain in the war and his commitment to send South African troops to Europe. Their attempted coup failed and Botha quickly put the rebellion down, but the issue resurfaced again and again over the next few decades. A strike by white miners in 1922, which grew into a mini revolt as workers seized power in Johannesburg, was dealt with in a similar fashion by Botha's successor, Smuts. This time, however, white workers were able to gain a measure of revenge: in 1924 their support was crucial in electing a coalition Labour/Nationalist government.

Under Hertzog, Afrikaner nationalist sentiment was given an important boost by the replacement of Dutch by Afrikaans as one of the two official languages. In 1934 there even seemed a chance of forging a united Afrikaner leadership when Hertzog and Smuts joined together under a new United Party banner during the crisis caused by the great depression. This, however, was not to be, as Malan led a breakaway group to form a new 'Purified' National Party. The decision whether or not to join the Second World War caused a further split and Hertzog resigned as Prime Minister to join Malan in opposition, in so doing creating yet another version of the National Party – this time the *Herenigde* (Reunited) National Party. Smuts, the ardent supporter of close ties with Britain, became the new Prime Minister and took South Africa into the war. He won an election in 1943 on the back of a wave of pro-British feeling and his international reputation grew and grew. After the war, however, he found his popularity at home waning. The economic boom caused by the war had lead to massive African urban migration and the National Party were able to use this to stir up fear amongst white, especially Afrikaner, voters. In 1948 they voted in Malan's Nationalists on an election platform promising a new ideology of apartheid.

The apartheid programme

What exactly was meant by apartheid was not exactly clear in 1948; and the full programme of legislation was only really finalized in the mid-1950s. In fact the real beauty of the concept in 1948 was that it meant different things to different sections of the white voting population. The word simply means 'apart', and as such can be seen as simply a refinement of segregationist ideas that had dominated in the first half of the century. Despite the image of apartheid created by many popularist historians and journalists, it was by no means or exclusively Afrikaner ideology. Indeed the roots of the idea can be traced back to English-speaking liberals in the early years of the century.

There was a distinct group of white South Africans who were very concerned about the plight of Africans and saw the solution as being total separation of the two races. They believed that rapid urbanization was destroying the basis of African culture and that they needed to be protected from the evils of white urban civilization. This ideology was tied up with ideas of both paternalism, that Whites should be like parents to child-like Africans, and ideas of Social Darwinism, that different races were at different points along an evolutionary scale. In the middle decades of the century these ideas began to be considered by a group of Afrikaner intellectuals who saw the total separation of the races as being the only way in which whites could maintain political power over South Africa. They began to argue that if Africans were allowed to take part in the white capitalist economy they could rightly expect to be given political rights, so the solution was to keep them in a totally separate political and economic sphere where they could exercise their own rights.

This political philosophy was obviously not at all popular amongst white factory owners and farmers who relied upon cheap African labour to run their business. To these people apartheid should be simply a way of maintaining a cheap supply of African labour with few employment or political rights that would allow the demand of higher wages. There was, therefore, a clear conflict between the ideology of apartheid as expressed by Afrikaner intellectuals and the wishes of the average Afrikaner voter. During the early 1950s this conflict was solved by the nationalists stating that their long term aim was the total separation of races, but in the meantime they had to be practical and recognize the economic reality that white industry relied upon African labour.

Apartheid became in essence a way of ensuring a continual supply of cheap African labour whilst denying Africans any political rights. Legislation such as the Group Areas Act tightened previous segregation regulations and the government set about a massive national campaign to remove Africans from urban areas or squatter camps close to urban centres. Africans living in vibrant urban communities such as Sophiatown in Johannesburg found their homes bulldozed as they were ordered out. Those without passes were returned to the reserves, now restyled as homelands, whilst those with rights to reside in urban areas were removed to distant townships such as Soweto. Segregation of all amenities was also tightened and there became no areas of African life where the state did not intervene. In the countryside, Africans who had retained access to land either as freeholders or tenant farmers, in areas that were labelled 'black spots', were also forcibly removed to the homelands.

African opposition

Africans did not take these new assaults lying down, and the 1950s saw an unprecedented display of African political opposition to the white state. The ANC was revitalized and radicalized by the rise of a group of young militant activists, including Nelson Mandela, who had joined the ANC's Youth League in the 1940s. The organization saw that their attempts to appear moderate had not done them any favours and they could clearly not rely upon Britain to look after their interests. In 1952 the ANC launched a Defiance Campaign that used Gandian tactics of peaceful resistance to the new apartheid legislation. The ANC, in alliance with Indians, Coloureds and a few radical Whites, took the lead in deliberately breaking racist laws and offering themselves up for arrest. These peaceful protests were often met with violence from the police and many ANC members were harshly treated after arrest. Though the campaign failed, the ANC's membership mushroomed in its aftermath.

The National Party met this increased opposition with new legislation that firstly banned the South African Communist Party and then increased restrictions on the ANC and other political organizations. The banning of the Communist Party meant that many Communists now looked to the ANC as their main political organization. Some within the ANC were worried about the increased prominence of communists within the organization, especially as they tended to have very strong links with white communists, many of whom joined a newly formed white organization called the Congress of Democrats. These people were also concerned about the developing alliances with Indian and Coloured organizations and wanted to maintain the ANC as an exclusively African organization. Uniting under the slogan "Africa for the Africans", they formed a splinter group within the ANC and finally broke off to form a rival Pan African Congress (PAC) under Robert Sobukwe.

Apartheid policies also made themselves felt in the homelands where the government introduced 'betterment' policies designed to shore up the faltering subsistence economy in the areas which provided food for the families of migrant workers and for the workers themselves when unemployed. The plans consisted of regulations to consolidate small plots of land and setting aside areas for farming and areas for grazing. A crucial element of the plans was the compulsory culling of African cattle when there were deemed to be too many head of livestock on grazing land. This was really the first time that the White state had intervened in the daily lives of Africans living in the reserves and many resented the fact that there was now no area of their life free from the control of the racist authorities. The compulsory culling regulations were especially resented and when the government tried to implement them there was violent resistance in a number of areas. These outbreaks were inevitably dealt with extremely harshly.

A number of urban areas also experienced bouts of violence, with African protesters displaying their frustration through rioting. In response to the growing protest the government moved to break the ANC-led alliance and put 156 of its leaders on trial for treason. The mammoth trial lasted from 1956 to 1960, eventually resulting in their acquittal. Despite the acquittal it was important in diverting the accuseds' energy away from organizing opposition. Furthermore, by the time the trial was over it had also been overtaken by other events.

In late 1959 the newly formed PAC decided to launch a massive anti-pass law campaign. The pass laws were one of the most hated apartheid policies as they strictly controlled African mobility and were also used by the police as an excuse to stop and search any African. Their campaign was to start on 21 March 1960, in order to pre-empt an ANC led campaign due to start on 31 March 1960. The PAC called on all African men to leave their passes at home and present themselves for arrest at the nearest police station. They believed that the prison system would be swamped and the pass laws would have to be revoked. One of the main areas of PAC activity on the morning of 21 March was the southern Transvaal. At Evaton and Vanderbijlpark police stations large crowds were dispersed by police baton charges and low flying jets, but at Sharpville the crowd stayed put when they were buzzed by the jets. At 1315 there was a small scuffle and a small section of the wire fence surrounding the police station was knocked over. The police later claimed they were under extreme danger and were being stoned but this is denied by almost all eyewitness accounts. What is clear, however, is that the police suddenly opened fire on the crowd with machine guns. The terrified crowd ran for cover but the police continued to fire on the fleeing protesters. Most of the 69 dead and 180 wounded were shot in the back.

Moves towards armed resistance The Sharpville Massacre marked a turning point in African political opposition to apartheid. As news of the killings spread around the country Africans rioted and refused to go to work. In Cape Town there was a series of huge marches from the townships into the city centre which created panic amongst the white residents and police. The march leaders were, however, insistent that they passed off peacefully and had negotiations with the local police chief to ensure this was the case. They were rewarded with arrest and the Cape Town townships also erupted into rioting. A nationwide state of emergency was declared

African political activists organizing the union and student protests of the 1970s knew little of the older generation, and the likes of Mandela. Internationally, however, the imprisonment of Mandela and other ANC leaders was kept in the media by the constant lobbying and speech making of Oliver Tambo, who had gone into exile in the early 1960s to do just that job. It was not really until the massive 1982 international 'Release Mandela Campaign' that people inside South Africa began to take notice. By 1988, his 70th birthday, the international Mandela bandwagon was really rolling and his face adorned a thousand student walls and his name was borrowed by countless bars.

The personality cult that spread around Mandela also extended to his second wife, Winnie. Winnie and Nelson Mandela had married in 1958 whilst he was on trial for treason. During her husband's imprisonment Winnie was an active member of the banned ANC and she too suffered detention and banning orders keeping her within the Orlando district of Soweto. In 1977 she was sent into virtual internal exile in the small Free State town of Brandfort. Along with Nelson her suffering for the struggle got international recognition and she was ascribed the image of a long suffering and loyal partner.

This image first began to slip in April 1986 when she made a statement to the press that appeared to offer support to the spate of 'necklacings' (see page 751) occurring at that time in many South African townships. Winnie later claimed she had been misquoted but her virtuous image had begun to slip. It slipped still further when news about the activities of her 'Football Club' began to seep out of Soweto into the national and international press. The accusations of beatings and terrorization had existed for some time in Soweto before the murder of 14-year-old Stoompie Moeketse Seipei brought the activities of the Mandela Football Club to international prominence. Though Winnie has been able to avoid prosecution for the incident, on appeal, few people in South Africa believe she is innocent and internationally she went from saint to villain almost overnight. Where their pictures had been hung side by side on the walls of student bars Nelson now hangs alone.

Meanwhile, Mandela, by now moved to a warden's cottage in the grounds of Victor Vester Prison near Paarl, was involved in extensive talks with the South African government and with senior members' opposition groups and trade union organizations. On the 9 February 1990, with the ANC now a legal organization, Mandela was at last released and made a series of celebratory public addresses. The next few years saw Mandela involved in a whirl of international and national trips and the nitty-gritty of detailed negotiations with the Nationalist government. At first he returned to live with Winnie but it was soon clear she had become a political liability, not to mention her personal infidelity. In April 1992 they formally separated and were eventually divorced.

His public life, however, was a triumph. When negotiations were perilously close to collapse, for example after the June 1992 Boipatong massacre, it often seemed that Mandela's strength of personality alone kept them on the road. Not everything was rosy, however; Mandela's personal appeals to ANC supporters to end violence in KwaZulu Natal fell on deaf ears. Nevertheless once elections were certain the only obstacle to Mandela becoming the country's first democratically elected President seemed to be ill health.

On the 10 May 1994 Mandela was inaugurated President at a huge gathering, attended by countless world leaders, in front of the Union Buildings in Pretoria. Since the elections Mandela's reputation has remained untarnished, despite numerous scandals that have befallen the ANC, and he is hugely popular throughout the country, not least with many of the white South Africans who once regarded him as a terrorist. The hectic pace of political life has taken its toll on a man in his late 70s. In August 1996 he confirmed that he would be standing down after the next elections. Following the successful elections in May 1999 he retired from political life and was succeeded by his deputy Thabo Mbeki.

The economic divide between white and black, however, widened. Whilst wages in manufacturing for Whites increased, Africans found theirs held down. With organized opposition smashed, the government set about fully implementing its apartheid policies. Forced removals increased as the government set about dividing the country into clear White, Indian, Coloured and African zones. The official policy was that all Africans should live within the homelands though the presence of large townships like Soweto made this policy look unlikely. Nevertheless Africans living in cities such as Pretoria with homeland areas within daily commuting distance (in reality huge distances), found themselves removed to new townships within the homeland. On occasions the government also altered the borders of homelands so that townships on the outskirts of cities were absorbed into a new administrative structure. Forced removals and natural population growth meant that the populations of the homelands increased rapidly and though these areas were officially rural, their population densities were closer to urban areas.

Apart from the insidious change of name there were important differences between the previous reserve system and the homelands. The apartheid government attempted to allocate each and every African to one of eight tribes and then allocated them to a homeland. This proved very difficult, partly because many Africans, especially those who were long term residents in urban areas, did not identify themselves as belonging to a particular tribe and partly because, as the history of pre-colonial African groups discussed above indicates, tribal identity was often fluid and somewhat confused. Many people resisted attempts to define them as belonging to one of eight hard and fast categories and the government tacitly admitted this problem when it increased the number of possible tribes to which people could be allocated to 10.

Under the apartheid system all Africans were supposed to express their political rights through the homeland administration. The government established totally separate bureaucracies in each homeland and then began a process of encouraging the areas to become increasingly autonomous. A number of African leaders saw that they could gain power and economic wealth through the new system and actively collaborated with the apartheid state.

During the 1970s the South African government encouraged the homeland administrations to become independent states. They argued that this was a process that would allow Africans to enjoy full political rights in their own area. The first homeland to take independence was Transkei in 1976 and over the next five years Ciskei, Bophuthatswana and Venda followed suit. Transkei was at least a more or less unified block of land with a long coastline, but the other three were divided into numerous small blocks totally surrounded by South Africa. Their independence was never recognized by any country other than the Republic of South Africa: and they even refused to recognize each other's independence! The borders of Bophuthatswana were so complicated that neither South Africa's nor the homeland government were ever quite sure exactly where they were. Indeed just before independence the borders had to be altered when it was discovered that the South African embassy to Bophuthatswana was not actually inside the homeland. Though homeland independence was a farce it had great significance for the South Africans labelled as belonging to that particular tribe. They were now considered foreigners in the land of their birth.

The developing apartheid programme had not just material effects on the African population but also psychological. In the late 1950s and early 1960s many African people felt that the overthrow of the racist white state was imminent. But the apartheid state had managed to break African opposition and for almost a decade renewed resistance seemed impossible. The effects on many Africans' morale was not surprisingly extremely bad.

Union & student opposition In the early 1970s South Africa entered a new era of opposition to apartheid, but this time not led by organized political groups such as the ANC and PAC but by the trade unions. During the 1960s there had been very little labour unrest; only about 2,000 workers went on strike each year. Then in early 1973 there was suddenly a huge rise in strike activity and in the first three months of the year there were 160 strikes involving something like 61,000 workers. The epicentre for the strike activity was Durban but they quickly spread to other areas such as

East London and then on to the Rand. These strikes were unusually successful in gaining the workers' demands; almost always this was for increased wages to reflect the recent sharp rises in the inflation rate. One reason they were surprisingly successful was that the workers refused to elect leaders to enter into negotiations with their employers, rather they simply published their demands and then struck for short periods, usually staying in the vicinity of the factory. This meant that the employers had no target on which to aim reprisals and the police could not be called in to arrest strike leaders.

The early 1970s also saw the rise of a more vocal African student protest movement. This was spearheaded by the South Africa Students Organization (SASO), which had broken away from the white dominated National Union of South African Students in 1968, under the leadership of Steve Biko. SASO had a Black Consciousness ideology which stressed the need for all Black people in South Africa, Africans, Indians and Coloureds, to free themselves from the mental oppression that taught them white people were somehow innately superior to blacks. SASO took this message out into the country at large and played particular attention to spreading the ideology amongst school pupils.

With the example of the striking workers before them and a Black Consciousness message in their minds school pupils began to rebel against an education system designed to make them fit only for un-skilled and semi-skilled occupations. The immediate issue around which they organized their protest was the new rules enforcing the Afrikaans language as a medium of instruction. On the 16 June 1976 a Soweto school pupils' committee organized a mass march to deliver their complaints to the local authorities. This peaceful march was met with a violent response and the police shot two of the pupils. At first the pupils fled but then many turned and started throwing stones at the police. They then went on a rampage throughout the township destroying every symbol of their oppression that they could get to, including the government-run beer halls which many pupils felt bought off their fathers' opposition to state oppression with cheap beer. The **Soweto Uprising**, as the incident soon became known, marked an important turning point in the history of opposition to apartheid: from 16 June 1976 onwards there was constant and violent unrest across South Africa, lead by school pupils but gaining widespread support.

Rioting erupted around the country when news of the Soweto Uprising spread. The government was hard pressed to stop the unrest spreading beyond the townships but in a nationwide clampdown they eventually managed to quieten some of the protest. The SASO and school pupil leaders found themselves under arrest or harassed by the police. Many of the young people involved in the uprising escaped across the border.

Though the ANC had not been involved in the organization of the school pupils' protest, their underground cells, which had been carefully and quietly organizing in the early 1970s, it did help channel escaping pupils towards the guerrilla training camps they had set up in countries like Tanzania, Algeria and the newly independent Angola. The ANC benefited greatly from this new arrival of activists and managed effectively to amalgamate them into their organization. The ANC had made better use of their time in exile than the PAC, who suffered from poor organization and internal splits. Many of the pupils were ideologically closer to the PAC but they nevertheless ended up in ANC camps. In recent years these camps have been revealed to have often been pretty brutal places and people who disagreed with the camps' leaders were sometimes dealt with extremely harshly.

ANC re-enters the scene

Despite the government crackdown, protests continued and a generalized culture of resistance was fostered. The ANC made use of this new climate of opposition to begin to reinfiltrate South Africa. In the late 1970s they began a new campaign of sabotage, but now there was less care to avoid civilian casualties and the ANC released a statement saying they were at war with the apartheid state and, whilst their attacks were aimed at apartheid and economic targets, they could not promise that civilians would not be caught up in the struggle. A number of Unkhonto cells seemed to ignore these commands and bombs were set off in shopping centres and similar locations.

The ANC quickly regained legitimacy amongst Africans, many of whom had been disillusioned with the organization during its long dormant period. Black Consciousness

Background

organizations, smashed apart by the police after the Soweto Uprising, lost support to the ANC, though it could be argued that the movement had achieved its aim of increasing African pride. In August 1983 there was a large gathering of 575 community, church and similar non-governmental organizations which resulted in the formation of the United Democratic Front (UDF) which spearheaded protest throughout the 1980s. The government argued that the organization was simply a front for the ANC. This was an exaggeration but it is true that the UDF did have strong links with the ANC and that they regarded it as the government in exile and the imprisoned Mandela as the legitimate president of the country.

'Total onslaught' & destabilization

The apartheid state was not only coming under attack from internal protest but from international criticism of the Pretoria regime. The ANC in exile had managed to foster anti-apartheid groups in Europe and North America that began to put pressure on their governments to institute economic sanctions against South Africa. Most Commonwealth governments supported these sanctions and also instituted sporting and cultural sanctions on South Africa. The anti-apartheid movement also started campaigns detailing the working conditions inside branches of multi-national companies in South Africa and asking individuals to boycott companies with large investments in South Africa. Despite the resistance of Margaret Thatcher and Ronald Reagan, during the 1980s these campaigns began to take effect and a number of important companies withdrew from South Africa.

This international isolation of Pretoria added to their gradual geopolitical isolation in southern Africa during the 1970s. Up until the mid-1970s South Africa had been surrounded either by states run by white settler régimes or by small states that rarely criticized their actions. However, independence for Angola and Mozambique in 1976 and Zimbabwe in 1980 changed all that. Now South Africa had hostile, left-wing, neighbours right on its doorstep, and even the previously compliant weaker states, such as Lesotho, began actively to oppose the apartheid state. White South Africa felt increasingly vulnerable and the government argued that they were now facing a 'total onslaught' led by communists that were intent on bringing them down.

The apartheid government reacted to this 'total onslaught' with a careful mixture of economic, diplomatic and military foreign policy designed to neutralize the threat. The exact mix of the different elements varied in each country and over time. In Angola, for example, intervention was in the form of a direct military invasion designed to overthrow the communist government. When the invasion faltered they concentrated on supplying an armed opposition movement and therefore helped to fuel a bloody civil war that has gone on more or less ever since. In Mozambique they also intervened militarily, but this time through another opposition organization that had originally been set up by Ian Smith's settler régime in Rhodesia/Zimbabwe. They encouraged their clients in Mozambique to blow up railways and pipelines running from Zimbabwe to their nearest ports. With these out of action, Zimbabwe and other landlocked central African states were forced to continue trading with South Africa in order to get access to the sea. This, in turn, gave the South Africans an important economic hold over the countries to the north.

Across the region South African guerrilla troops carried out occasional raids designed both to knock out ANC camps and to keep their neighbours in political and economic turmoil and therefore as less effective opponents. South Africa's proxy war with the rest of the region caused a huge amount of suffering to very many people, especially in Mozambique and Angola. Though these states did receive some international support the international media tended to concentrate more on events unfurling in the South African townships than on these regional events.

Reform or revolution?

In the mid-1980s South Africa's townships, simmering since the Soweto Uprising, exploded into violence. The primary target of the violence were Africans who had taken jobs as administrators in the 'homelands' or townships and African policemen. Many had their families killed and their houses burnt down and a new and horrendous form of execution was invented, called 'necklacing'. This involved placing a car tyre full of petrol over the victim's torso and then setting fire to it. The police reacted violently to unrest in the townships and shot, arrested and beat many protesters. Bus boycotts, strikes and 'stay aways' (where Africans remained at home), were frequent and often met with violence by the police.

Violence became endemic to the townships and there was a fine line between political violence and general crime. Many of the young ANC supporting comrades decided that they should take the law into their own hands and kangaroo courts were frequent occurrences. Older Africans sometimes found it hard to take orders from the youngsters and inter-generational battles broke out on a number of occasions, most violently at Crossroads squatter camp on the outskirts of Cape Town. The violence was fanned by massive new flows of illegal migrants into the towns. The government was unable to cope with the new influx of people and eventually was forced into the withdrawal of the hated pass laws. The growth of squatter camps was spectacular and no sooner had the government removed squatters from one site than they appeared somewhere else. During the 1970s wage increases in established industry had been generous, partly reflecting the move towards a more capital intensive economy and partly a result of the strikes. The downside of this was massive and endemic unemployment, especially among the young. A whole generation of young people missed all their formal education because of their involvement in 'the struggle' and their chances of employment were extremely remote. Inevitably this fuelled the violence and crime.

The worst violence took place in the townships surrounding Pietermaritzburg and Durban. These areas were within the KwaZulu 'homeland' run by Gatsha Buthelezi. Originally Buthelezi had been an ANC supporter and had even received the organization's (reserved) blessing in the establishment of a Zulu cultural organization called Inkatha. The organization, however, began to act much more like a political party and ran the KwaZulu 'homeland' administration. When ANC supporters began to challenge the 'homelands' authority this lead to violent clashes as the two organizations vied for control of the townships. This conflict has continued until the present and has involved numerous atrocities committed by both sides.

By the late 1980s the South African state had more or less lost control of large portions of the townships. The unrest and international sanctions were hitting the economy hard and South African businesses were feeling the pinch. While the state security apparatus was strengthened and numerous crackdowns were attempted, the government, fearing revolution, also undertook a programme of reform.

To some extent this programme had begun in the 1970s but it was accelerated in the early 1980s under the presidency of PW Botha. One strand of the reform process was to pull Coloureds and Indians into the political process under a new tri-cameral parliament. Under a new constitution there were to be three houses in the parliament, one for white voters, one for Coloureds and one for Indians. Most Coloureds and Indians saw this move as an attempt to drive a wedge between them and the African population and refused to vote for the new parliament. The National Party's reform policy also lead to a new split in Afrikaner ranks and the creation of a new, more right-wing, Conservative Party. Over the 1980s the new Party was to attract more and more Afrikaner support and the National Party became increasingly reliant upon English-speaking supporters.

Botha also set about dismantling some of the segregationist policies, in particular the 'petty apartheid' legislation that divided up facilities such as beaches. These did very little to assuage the unrest in the townships and were probably more to do with creating an international impression of reform to hold off further sanctions. Under these circumstances the National Party began to do the unthinkable and sat down to negotiate with the ANC. Business leaders were the first South African establishment figures to talk with the ANC in exile, in September 1985. With sanctions and unrest big business was being squeezed hard and apartheid was no longer making them good profits as it had in the 1960s. The business leaders were therefore keen for a political settlement, but were obviously nervous about the intentions of an ANC strongly influenced by communist ideology. South African ministers and eventually Botha himself met with Mandela, offering him his freedom if he place De Klerk announced that the NP would be leaving the GNU to become the official opposition and try to rebuild itself in order to fight the next national elections due in 1999. The NP ministers selected in 1994 left the cabinet in June 1996 and were replaced by members of the ANC. No new Deputy President was selected; effectively increasing the power of Thabo Mbeki. The IFP remained within the GNU.

In the aftermath of the election the most pressing political problem was the continuation of violence in KwaZulu Natal between supporters of the ANC and supporters of the IFP. Unprovoked attacks, revenge killings and political intrigue all continued to haunt the townships and villages of the province. Peace talks between the leaderships of the provincial parties and high-level discussions between Mandela and Buthelezi were frequently called off and when they did take place made no impact on the rate of violence. Local elections for new unitary local government structures took place throughout the country in mid-1995 but were frequently delayed in KwaZulu Natal because of the violence and allegations over fraudulent electoral rolls. The elections did eventually take place, about one year after the rest of the country and marked the beginnings of a period of significantly reduced levels of violence in the province. Buthelezi and the IFP continue to be primarily interested in provincial issues, though Buthelezi's reputation nationally has somewhat improved from its dire position in 1995-96. The local elections in KwaZulu Natal indicate that the IFP has continued to command widespread support in the rural areas, though the urban townships returned ANC local governments by big majorities.

Mandela commanded huge popular support amongst the African population and won the backing of many of South Africa's white population as well. Mbeki lacked the same mass popularity, but was seen as having aa good grasp of the major issues and is credited with being a key player in bringing peace to KwaZulu Natal. Mandela's punishing international schedule meant that Mbeki was left with many of the domestic political chores, especially dealing with the ANC's internal problems. His position as Mandela's chosen successor left him vulnerable to accusations of manipulating internal ANC politics to strenthen his position over some of his colleagues. This was particularly the case with the easing out of Cyril Ramaphosa, who had led the ANC negotiating team during initial negotiations with the NP. Prior to the election he was seen by many as Mandela's likely successor and his decision to leave politics and join a commercial company was seen as evidence that his leadership ambitions had been frustrated.

The ANC has had its fair share of internal wranglings. In 1995 the most serious of these was over the role of Winnie Mandela (or since her divorce, Winnie Madikizela-Mandela). Since mid-1995 she has been effectively sidelined by the ANC leadership. Though she was sacked from her cabinet position she retains her seat as an ordinary member of the National Assembly and has some support from the more radical wings of the party. She was re-elected to her post as leader of the ANC's Women's League, but the organization's influence has plummeted amidst stories of mismanagement and financial impropriety. It seems Madikizela-Mandela's fast lifestyle has caught up with her: she has suffered from ill health and her own financial problems.

Provincial ANC governments have also had their share of problems. The Free State party was subject to a bitter split during 1996 between the then provincial premier Patrick Lekota and his Finance executive, who was investigated for corruption. The national ANC leadership stepped into the battle and redeployed Lekota as a member of the National Assembly. In the midlands region of KwaZulu Natal the local ANC leader, Sifiso Nkabinde, was expelled after he was accused of having been an informer during the apartheid era. He has since joined Holomise's National Consultative Forum and accused the ANC of fostering violence and stockpiling weapons in the region. The Eastern Cape ANC has also had more than its fair share of problems and the national executive have intervened on more than one occasion.

The NP has not had too much success in repositioning itself as a non-racial centrist party. Its efforts to change its image have not been helped by the continual unearthing of more and more horror stories from the apartheid years. Particularly damaging to the NP are the stories about covert actions taking place right up to the evening of the 1994 execution was invented, called 'necklacing'. This involved placing a car tyre full of petrol over the victim's torso and then setting fire to it. The police reacted violently to unrest in the townships and shot, arrested and beat many protesters. Bus boycotts, strikes and 'stay aways' (where Africans remained at home), were frequent and often met with violence by the police.

Violence became endemic to the townships and there was a fine line between political violence and general crime. Many of the young ANC supporting comrades decided that they should take the law into their own hands and kangaroo courts were frequent occurrences. Older Africans sometimes found it hard to take orders from the youngsters and inter-generational battles broke out on a number of occasions, most violently at Crossroads squatter camp on the outskirts of Cape Town. The violence was fanned by massive new flows of illegal migrants into the towns. The government was unable to cope with the new influx of people and eventually was forced into the withdrawal of the hated pass laws. The growth of squatter camps was spectacular and no sooner had the government removed squatters from one site than they appeared somewhere else. During the 1970s wage increases in established industry had been generous, partly reflecting the move towards a more capital intensive economy and partly a result of the strikes. The downside of this was massive and endemic unemployment, especially among the young. A whole generation of young people missed all their formal education because of their involvement in 'the struggle' and their chances of employment were extremely remote. Inevitably this fuelled the violence and crime.

The worst violence took place in the townships surrounding Pietermaritzburg and Durban. These areas were within the KwaZulu 'homeland' run by Gatsha Buthelezi. Originally Buthelezi had been an ANC supporter and had even received the organization's (reserved) blessing in the establishment of a Zulu cultural organization called Inkatha. The organization, however, began to act much more like a political party and ran the KwaZulu 'homeland' administration. When ANC supporters began to challenge the 'homelands' authority this lead to violent clashes as the two organizations vied for control of the townships. This conflict has continued until the present and has involved numerous atrocities committed by both sides.

By the late 1980s the South African state had more or less lost control of large portions of the townships. The unrest and international sanctions were hitting the economy hard and South African businesses were feeling the pinch. While the state security apparatus was strengthened and numerous crackdowns were attempted, the government, fearing revolution, also undertook a programme of reform.

To some extent this programme had begun in the 1970s but it was accelerated in the early 1980s under the presidency of PW Botha. One strand of the reform process was to pull Coloureds and Indians into the political process under a new tri-cameral parliament. Under a new constitution there were to be three houses in the parliament, one for white voters, one for Coloureds and one for Indians. Most Coloureds and Indians saw this move as an attempt to drive a wedge between them and the African population and refused to vote for the new parliament. The National Party's reform policy also lead to a new split in Afrikaner ranks and the creation of a new, more right-wing, Conservative Party. Over the 1980s the new Party was to attract more and more Afrikaner support and the National Party became increasingly reliant upon English-speaking supporters.

Botha also set about dismantling some of the segregationist policies, in particular the 'petty apartheid' legislation that divided up facilities such as beaches. These did very little to assuage the unrest in the townships and were probably more to do with creating an international impression of reform to hold off further sanctions. Under these circumstances the National Party began to do the unthinkable and sat down to negotiate with the ANC. Business leaders were the first South African establishment figures to talk with the ANC in exile, in September 1985. With sanctions and unrest big business was being squeezed hard and apartheid was no longer making them good profits as it had in the 1960s. The business leaders were therefore keen for a political settlement, but were obviously nervous about the intentions of an ANC strongly influenced by communist ideology. South African ministers and eventually Botha himself met with Mandela, offering him his freedom if he repudiated the use of violence as a weapon in the fight against apartheid. Mandela refused the offer and for a time it seemed further reform was impossible.

The late 1980s, however, saw a crucial shift in the global political scene that opened up an important window to allow a negotiated settlement. The unexpected collapse of the Soviet block suddenly made Botha's image of a 'total onslaught' seem meaningless and the ANC was no longer seen by Whites as a front for Soviet-backed communist expansion into South Africa. These changes coincided with a change in leadership of the National Party and the replacement of Botha with FW de Klerk. Even though de Klerk had been regarded as a conservative he soon made it clear he was embarking on a bold new policy. The ANC was unbanned, Mandela and other political leaders were released and the process of negotiating a political settlement got underway.

Modern South Africa

Politics

Constitution

South Africa's first democratic constitution was passed by the Constitutional Assembly in May 1996, the 1994 elections being held under an interim version. After ratification by the Supreme Court most of it passed into law, since some elements were returned to the Constitutional Assembly for reconsideration. The Constitutional Assembly is made up of both Houses of Parliament sitting together and constitutional provision needs to be passed by a two-thirds majority. The bi-cameral Parliament consists of a directly elected lower house (the National Assembly) and an upper house (the Senate) appointed by provincial assemblies. The National Assembly is elected via a system of proportional representation. The President, who combines the role of chief and head of state, is elected by members of the National Assembly and chooses his cabinet from those members.

Parliament sits in Cape Town and government ministries are in Pretoria. This geographical division dates from the Act of Union in 1910 as a way of balancing power between the two former British colonies and the two former Boer republics. This division has been criticized in recent years as government representatives have to waste time and money travelling backwards and forwards to opposite ends of the country. There are moves to relocate Parliament in Pretoria, though this will require a change in the constitution and would be strongly opposed by delegates from the Western Cape.

Significant powers are devolved to the nine provincial administrations. Provincial assemblies are also elected via proportional representation and in turn they elect members to the Senate who are specifically charged with looking after provincial interests against the power of central Government.

Provincial governments have significant scope over things such as regional planning, investment policies, social services and education. Provincial leaders are, therefore, powerful political figures and a number of politicians of national standing have decided to serve as provincial representatives rather than seek election to Parliament.

1994 elections The African National Congress (ANC), together with its alliance partners, the South African Communist Party (SACP) and the Congress of South African Trade Unions (Cosatu) won the national vote in South Africa's first democratic elections in April 1994 by a huge majority. They gained 63% of the total vote giving them 252 seats in the National Assembly. The only other parties to win significant numbers of votes were the National Party (NP) (20.5%) and Inkharta Freedom Party (IFP) (10.8%). The ANC's victory was based upon widespread support from the majority African population throughout the country. The only area in which its support amongst Africans was threatened was in KwaZulu Natal where the IFP received significant support from rural Zulu speakers. The IFP were unable to convert their popularity in their political heartland to any other parts of the country. The NP received widespread support from the white population and, more surprisingly, from a majority of Coloured voters in the Western Cape.

Four other parties managed to secure seats, though with tiny proportions of the total vote. The Freedom Front (FF), an alliance of right-wing Afrikaner Nationalists, won nine seats with a 2.3% share of the vote, coming mainly from working-class Afrikaners fearful of the new political dispensation. The Democratic Party (DP), traditionally the party of liberal English-speaking white South Africans, were unable to expand their attraction and won a paltry 1.7% of the vote. The Pan African Congress (PAC) fared particularly badly; an organization which in the 1950s had seriously challenged the ANC's position as the most popular political organization amongst the African population received only 1.2% of the national vote, giving them just five seats. The remaining two seats were won by a newly formed political organization called the African Christian Democratic Party (ACDP) which called for the enactment of policies in line with the gospels.

In line with the interim Constitution, the leader of the ANC, Nelson Mandela, was duly elected President and set about choosing his cabinet. The constitution stated that any party who gained more than 20% of the vote was eligible to have its leader instated as a Deputy President. Mandela, therefore had two deputy presidents, Thabo Mbeki from the ANC and FW de Klerk, the leader of the NP. The selection of Thabo Mbeki as Deputy President effectively marked him as Mandela's likely successor. All other parties were invited to join the ANC in a Government of National Unity (GNU). Despite the continued antagonism between the ANC and IFP, Mongosuthu Buthelezi was given the important post of Minister of Home Affairs. A number of cabinet posts were also filled by delegates from the NP. The only party to stay out of the GNU were the DP who felt they could have more of an impact as the official opposition.

The elections for provincial assemblies resulted in the ANC winning control of seven out of the nine provinces. In a number of provinces they won huge majorities: 80% of the vote in the Free State, 83% in Mpumalanga, 85% in the Eastern Cape, 87% in North West Province, and a staggering 95% in Northern Province. Though many of these areas are associated with hardline Afrikaner nationalism it has to be born in mind that the vast majority of the population in these areas are poor, rural Africans who solidly support the ANC.

In the more populous provinces of Gauteng and KwaZulu Natal the ANC fared less well. In KwaZulu Natal the ANC were beaten into second place by the IFP who won just over half of the votes. In Gauteng the ANC still won an impressive overall majority of 58%, but they lost seats to the NP (24%) who gained the support of the urban middle-class Whites and to smaller parties such as the FF and DP. Three seats in Gauteng also went to the IFP: their only seats outside KwaZulu Natal.

In the Western and Northern Cape the NP did better than many people had expected. Their 40% in the Northern Cape was still substantially behind the ANC's 50% but in the Western Cape they managed to gain 55% to the ANC's 33%. In both these provinces the NP vote was based upon widespread support amongst Coloured voters who feared an ANC government would put the interests of Africans ahead of their own. The irony of the only NP election victory being built on the back of Coloured voters is quintessentially South African!

Politics since the 1994 election

The GNU's first task was to set about ratifying the interim constitution. Debate on some issues was intense. Labour rights proved to be a bone of contention between the NP and ANC while the ANC and IFP frequently clashed over the division of power between central government and the provinces. Despite their official position as part of the GNU and Buthelezi's cabinet seat the IFP boycotted much of the debate on the constitution on the grounds that the ANC had gone back on a pre-election promise to allow international mediation on the issue of KwaZulu Natal ceding from the rest of the country. Nevertheless by May 1996 all the clauses of the new constitution had been agreed and the Constitutional Assembly voted to ratify the new constitution. With the new constitution in place De Klerk announced that the NP would be leaving the GNU to become the official opposition and try to rebuild itself in order to fight the next national elections due in 1999. The NP ministers selected in 1994 left the cabinet in June 1996 and were replaced by members of the ANC. No new Deputy President was selected; effectively increasing the power of Thabo Mbeki. The IFP remained within the GNU.

In the aftermath of the election the most pressing political problem was the continuation of violence in KwaZulu Natal between supporters of the ANC and supporters of the IFP. Unprovoked attacks, revenge killings and political intrigue all continued to haunt the townships and villages of the province. Peace talks between the leaderships of the provincial parties and high-level discussions between Mandela and Buthelezi were frequently called off and when they did take place made no impact on the rate of violence. Local elections for new unitary local government structures took place throughout the country in mid-1995 but were frequently delayed in KwaZulu Natal because of the violence and allegations over fraudulent electoral rolls. The elections did eventually take place, about one year after the rest of the country and marked the beginnings of a period of significantly reduced levels of violence in the province. Buthelezi and the IFP continue to be primarily interested in provincial issues, though Buthelezi's reputation nationally has somewhat improved from its dire position in 1995-96. The local elections in KwaZulu Natal indicate that the IFP has continued to command widespread support in the rural areas, though the urban townships returned ANC local governments by big majorities.

Mandela commanded huge popular support amongst the African population and won the backing of many of South Africa's white population as well. Mbeki lacked the same mass popularity, but was seen as having aa good grasp of the major issues and is credited with being a key player in bringing peace to KwaZulu Natal. Mandela's punishing international schedule meant that Mbeki was left with many of the domestic political chores, especially dealing with the ANC's internal problems. His position as Mandela's chosen successor left him vulnerable to accusations of manipulating internal ANC politics to strenthen his position over some of his colleagues. This was particularly the case with the easing out of Cyril Ramaphosa, who had led the ANC negotiating team during initial negotiations with the NP. Prior to the election he was seen by many as Mandela's likely successor and his decision to leave politics and join a commercial company was seen as evidence that his leadership ambitions had been frustrated.

The ANC has had its fair share of internal wranglings. In 1995 the most serious of these was over the role of Winnie Mandela (or since her divorce, Winnie Madikizela-Mandela). Since mid-1995 she has been effectively sidelined by the ANC leadership. Though she was sacked from her cabinet position she retains her seat as an ordinary member of the National Assembly and has some support from the more radical wings of the party. She was re-elected to her post as leader of the ANC's Women's League, but the organization's influence has plummeted amidst stories of mismanagement and financial impropriety. It seems Madikizela-Mandela's fast lifestyle has caught up with her: she has suffered from ill health and her own financial problems.

Provincial ANC governments have also had their share of problems. The Free State party was subject to a bitter split during 1996 between the then provincial premier Patrick Lekota and his Finance executive, who was investigated for corruption. The national ANC leadership stepped into the battle and redeployed Lekota as a member of the National Assembly. In the midlands region of KwaZulu Natal the local ANC leader, Sifiso Nkabinde, was expelled after he was accused of having been an informer during the apartheid era. He has since joined Holomisa's National Consultative Forum and accused the ANC of fostering violence and stockpiling weapons in the region. The Eastern Cape ANC has also had more than its fair share of problems and the national executive have intervened on more than one occasion.

The NP has not had too much success in repositioning itself as a non-racial centrist party. Its efforts to change its image have not been helped by the continual unearthing of more and more horror stories from the apartheid years. Particularly damaging to the NP are the stories about covert actions taking place right up to the evening of the 1994 elections, a time when the party had supposedly thrown off its old ways and embraced democracy. The Steyn Report into the actions of the Third Force includes many disturbing allegations, including reports that SADF operatives initiated the spate of train massacres that took place on the Witwatersrand in the run up to the 1994 election. Other allegations in the report included reports that the SADF used chemical bombs against Frelimo troops in Mozambique in the late 1980s and that they stockpiled weapons in game reserves in countries as far away as Kenya.

Other reports of atrocities have come out of the hearings of the Truth and Reconciliation Commission (TRC) chaired by Desmond Tutu. These hearings were intended to be a process of national healing, but many of the wounds revealed look more like running sores. Reports of apartheid era death camps in the South African countryside have resulted in the media putting huge pressure on De Klerk to say exactly what he, and other senior NP members, knew about. Instead De Klerk has gone on the offensive, denying any knowledge of the camps and attacking the TRC for being 'political'. His image has been tarnished by both the allegations and his reaction: his claims that ANC members had attacked his fundamental human rights by saying they did not believe his denials made him look petty, especially in the context of the gross human rights violations being continually reported in the TRC.

De Klerk also dithered over restructuring the NP. There have been two basic visions for the party's future within the organizations. Firstly a more conservative wing, centred around the hard-line Western Cape Premier, Hernus Kriel, want to develop the NP as the 'party of minorities' and look to maintain control of Western Cape and perhaps make in-roads in the Northern Cape and KwaZulu Natal. They argued that this approach might leave the party in constant opposition nationally but that it would allow them to retain control of at least one province. The other vision, associated with a more liberal section of the party, centred around former secretary general Roelf Meyer, wanted radically to restructure the party, looking for support amongst the African population and sought to challenge the ANC for national power. De Klerk's attempt to accommodate both visions proved to be untenable and in mid-1997 he appeared to opt for the first. Meyer was first dismissed as secretary general and then he had his task team (trying to find viable African NP leaders) disbanded.

Not surprisingly Meyer left the party and formed an alternative organization known as the New Movement Process. He took a number of members of the Gauteng Provincial Assembly (his home province) with him to the new organization. There was some speculation at the time that he might team up with Holomise's National Consultative Forum or the Democratic Party.

In June 1999 Nelson Mandela passed the mantle of power over to his long time deputy Thabo Mbeki. In the national elections the ANC won a large victory despite a widespread feeling that they had still to deliver on promises they made when they first came to power in 1994. Although there was some violence associated with the elections it was a great triumph for the country on a continent which has so rarely witnessed fair and peaceful democratic elections.

The outcome of the election showed that people still saw the ANC as the only party capable of providing for their needs. Mbeki was always going to find Mandela a hard act to follow. He surrounded himself with a cabinet of loyal supporters, and he is regarded as an efficient if not dynamic party leader. Keeping the ANC-SACP-Cosatu alliance intact has been one of Mbeki's biggest challenges. Following the 1999 election, relations between the ANC and its alliance partners became increasingly strained over the issues of privatization, the neo-liberal growth, employment and redistribution (Gear) policy, and the government's approach to dealing with HIV/AIDS. Much to Mbeki's embarrassment, Cosatu timed a two-day general strike against privatization to coincide with the International Conference on Racism in Durban during August-September 2001. Cosatu also publicly supported a court challenge to the Governent's AIDS policy by the HIV/AIDS NGO, *Treatment Action Campaign*. However, by February 2002 there were signs of rapprochement between the government and Cosatu, and rumours of a split seem premature.

Thabo Mbeki has been keen to see South Africa expand its scope of activity in regional and international affairs. Infused with Mbeki's vision for an African Renaissance, South Africa has been a driving force behind restructuring the Southern African Development Community (SADC), establishing the new African Union, and developing the New Partnership for Africa's Development (Nepad). South Africa has also been involved in efforts to solve a number of conflicts and political crises on the continent, such as the long-running war in the DRC; former president Nelson Mandela has led efforts to bring an end to political instability in Burundi. South Africa has become an articulate advocate for Third World interests and has helped to reinvigorate the Non-Aligned Movement. South Africa is usually careful to balance the concerns of smaller countries with those of the broader international community. After September 11 for example, the country voiced its opposition to terrorism, but demurred from supporting US military action. South Africa also courted controversy by declaring the contentious 2002 Zimbabwean elections free and fair, but Mbeki ultimately decided, along with the leaders of Australia and Nigeria, to recommend Zimbabwe's suspension from the Commonwealth.

Mbeki's views on AIDS have cast a shadow over the first four years of his presidency. Going against the weight of medical opinion, he has questioned the link between HIV and AIDS, and the effectiveness of anti-retroviral drugs. The Department of Health's refusal to provide anti-AIDS drugs to pregnant women and rape survivors has angered AIDS activists and drawn widespread criticism of the government. The Treatment Action Campaign won a High Court case against the Department of Health in 2001, forcing it to provide the anti-retroviral drug Nevirapine to all HIV-positive pregnant women.

The 1999 election did not dramatically alter South Africa's political landscape, except for some growth in support for the Democratic Party (DP). The DP's line on crime and tough talk from its leader, Tony Leon, won it a substantial proportion of the White vote. In an effort to unite opposition to the government in the lead up to the 2000 local elections, the DP joined forces with the NP to form the Democratic Alliance. The Alliance was however short-lived and fell apart following in-fighting about the party's administration in the Western Cape. Martinus van Schalkwyk, the NP leader has continued to develop his party as a 'party of minorities', but efforts to expand the NP's profile beyond the Western Cape have proved largely unsuccessful. Support for other parties such as the IFP and the PAC remains small, but individuals such as the firebrand PAC politician, Patricia de Lille continue to be vocal critics of the government's policies.

Economy

South Africa is often referred to as being a First and Third World economy within one country. While it is true that parts of South African society are extremely rich and the majority are extremely poor this situation is not actually that different from many other countries classified as Third World (or developing or South countries). The well-off sections of society are bigger than in other African countries but they are not dissimilar in size and wealth to countries such as Brazil or Argentina. The overall per capita levels of wealth in South Africa are also pretty much similar to these Latin American economies (referred to as the Higher Middle Income nations in World Bank league tables).

Structure of the economy The economy is dominated by the industries exploiting the country's extremely rich mineral resources. The mineral sector of the economy accounts for something like two thirds of export earnings, though it employs less than 10% of the labour force. Apart from the gold and diamonds for which the country is famous it also produces a range of other mineral products, including platinum and chromium (of which it is the major world producer).

The country lacks oil, though it does have some reserves of natural gas. The scarcity of oil was a key issue in the apartheid days, hence the conversion of coal into oil by SASOL.

Agricultural production also continues to make a significant contribution to the economy, especially if you add the food preparation secondary industries based on primary agricultural products. Almost one third of the workforce is in agriculture, though employment in this sector is characterized by extremely low wages and seasonal unemployment. The agricultural base is very diverse and in non-drought years, the country is a net food exporter.

The manufacturing sector of the economy has tended to suffer from low productivity levels, meaning that South Africa has found it difficult to break into lucrative export markets. The southern African regional market, where South Africa does have an advantage, is constrained by low levels of consumption and is, in any case, already pretty much saturated with South African goods. The most important local manufacturing sectors include automobile assembly, machinery, textiles, iron and steel, chemicals and fertilizers.

The tourism sector has been highlighted as one area of potential growth. Though there have been positive developments in some sectors of the tourism economy the country has been hampered both by a shortage of reasonably priced hotel rooms in the main cities and the reputation for high crime rates, especially with the centre of Johannesburg being a virtual no-go area for many visitors. Crime is thought to be a fairly significant drain on the economy in general and is the major political issue in the country.

The ANC came to power in 1994 with the economy in a mess. Throughout much of the 1980s and early 1990s the economy had grown slower than population growth rates and in some years had contracted in absolute terms. Inflation rates were high, the rand was slipping against the major currencies, investment rates were low, productivity was low and unemployment rates were extremely high. Much of this was due to global isolation which had led the country down an economic dead end. Growth was low because of the limitations of the domestic market and the inaccessibility of export markets, difficulties in obtaining technology due to sanctions and an unskilled labour force due to the poor state of African education. Probably the only area in which South Africa was better placed than comparable economies was in the level of external debt: sanctions by international banks and development finance organizations had prevented the government from borrowing heavily. Despite its stated objectives of reducing poverty, increasing equality and providing basic social services for all, the new ANC government also signalled its intentions to ensure macro-economic stability. The first post-Apartheid Minister of Finance, Derek Keys, was appointed from outside party politics and the subsequent budgets did not include the heavy public borrowing and increased taxation that many observers predicted before the election. Macro-economically the economy has been a qualified success. Economic growth rates have been running at around three to four percent per annum, inflation has been controlled and deficit spending and public borrowing have only risen slowly. The rand has continued to slip on the international currency markets, though not as catastrophically as might have been expected when currency dealing and profit repatriation legislation were revoked. A significant development for South Africa's export industries was the signing of the EU-South Africa Trade, Development and Co-operation Agreement (TDCA) in October 1999. The benefits of increased access to European markets for South African goods have become immediately apparent; South Africa's trade surplus with the EU increased four-fold between 1999 and 2001.

The major problem area for the economy has been unemployment. Despite the fact that the economy is growing there are still more young people entering the employment market than there are new jobs being created. Calculations by some economists indicate that the country needs a five to six percent growth rate just to keep up with these new entrants, let alone meet the backlog of unemployed. Actual figures for unemployment vary considerably, but most of them indicate unemployment rates somewhere in the region of 30 percent of the labour force.

In terms of meeting its objectives to provide basic social services for all, the government's record has been mixed. Some ministries have performed well while others barely seem to have got programmes off the ground. The much vaulted Reconstruction and Development Programme collapsed under its own weight and its functions were parcelled out to various government agencies. The provision of clean drinking water and rural electrification programmes have both been making steady progress. Provision of new housing to meet the huge urban backlog, on the other hand, is moving at a snail's

Recent economic developments

Background

pace. International development organizations have shown a huge amount of interest in the country and there have been some significant flows of new capital into the country from these sources.

The ANC government is beginning to show signs of reassessing the growth, employment and redistribution policy (Gear), which was criticised by trade unions as being a 'home-grown structural adjustment programme'. The 2001 budget showed a significant increase in public expenditure on social services. This may be an acknowledgment that Gear has not delivered the expected levels of economic growth. Crucially, South Africa's fiscal discipline had not attracted significant foreign investment, which in 2001, fell to its lowest level in years. Ultimately, it is Aids that may have the greatest impact on South Africa's economic future; a recent study predicts that by 2010, the disease may have shrunk the South African economy by between 17% and 20%.

Culture

Population

Figures from South Africa's 1996 census show the total population to be about 38 million. This figure is significantly lower than those generated by the previous census. Before the census data became available the population in 1996 was estimated to be just under 43 million people, based on projections from the 1991 census. The lower figure indicates that previous census data had significant errors, which were then compounded by errors in the calculation of population growth rates.

In 1991 the census figures were adjusted upwards because of the belief that the actual census had missed out large numbers of Africans. These adjustments were made by multiplying the census figures for 1970, the last census believed to have accurately counted the African population, by a calculation of the African population growth rate. It now appears that the population growth rate used to adjust the 1991 figures was too high and that the difference between the African and white growth rates was not as great as had been assumed. This meant that the 1991 figure and subsequent projections have all overestimated the size of the population, though some demographers have suggested that it is the 1996 census that gets the figures wrong. This also means that previous calculations of the proportion of the population falling into different racial groups may also be flawed.

Population distribution The two most populous provinces are KwaZulu Natal and Gauteng. KwaZulu Natal contains a major urban area, Durban, but higher rainfall figures also means that the KwaZulu Natal countryside is able to support a greater population density than other rural areas of the country. The legacy of apartheid means that former homeland areas have much higher population densities than other rural areas: the scattered fragments of what was the homeland of KwaZulu Natal stretch across the province and account for much of the region's 7.7 million people.

Gauteng, the country's smallest province in area (1.4% of the total), contains 19% of the total population, the vast majority of whom are urban residents living in the towns and cities around Johannesburg.

The Eastern Cape's 5.9 million people are less urbanized. Though the province contains a major city, Port Elizabeth, many of its people live in the area that used to comprise the homelands of Transkei and Ciskei.

The Western Cape, by contrast, never contained any homeland areas. Its 4.1 million people mainly live in and around Cape Town though there is also a significant population of farmworkers and residents of small rural towns and villages.

The next four provinces in terms of population size, Northern Province, North West, Mpumalanga and the Free State, all have their population divided between smaller

Background

industrial centres, sparsely populated white rural areas and densely populated fragments of former homelands.

Finally, the Northern Cape, the largest province in area (361,830 sq km), has a tiny population of just 700,000 people widely dispersed across this semi-arid region.

Ethnic groups

Ethnicity is a very sensitive issue in South Africa. For many years the majority of South Africa's population were classified by race and tribe in order to deprive them of access to resources or political rights. Not surprisingly many people resent being classified in terms of ethnicity.

The most recent census did include questions about ethnic group and home language, but as these are based on people's classifications of themselves, rather than official classifications, they are less contentious. This does mean, however, that the data from this census will probably not be comparable with data from previous censuses.

The apartheid system recognized four major population groups (races) in the country: African, Asian, Coloured and white (the terminology has changed over time). Despite the avowed non-racial nature of the present South African state this fourfold classification remains profoundly important to South African life. This does not mean, however, that everyone fits neatly into these four categories: during the apartheid era huge numbers of people had their race altered by official decree. This could have profound impacts and often resulted in people being evicted from their homes and their children thrown out of schools. Within each of the four racial categories it is possible to make further sub-divisions on the basis of home language, tribe and geography – these sub-divisions (especially tribe) are even more fluid and open to debate than the fourfold racial classification.

African

The African population makes up something like 75% of South Africa's total population. The terminology used to describe this section of the population has changed over the years: in the 19th and early 20th century they tended to be referred to as 'natives' while in the 1960s the apartheid authorities adopted the term 'Bantu'. Both these names have strong connotations of racism. The word Bantu simply comes from the Zulu and Xhosa words for people but it is resented by most South Africans because of its connection to the apartheid institutions who adopted it in the 1960s , especially in the field of education. Today it is only acceptable to use the term when discussing languages; the Bantu group of languages includes all the African languages spoken in South Africa and related Bantu languages are spoken as far away as Somalia. The African population are also often termed black, though this can be confusing as Coloureds and Indians have also been called black in the past.

The apartheid system also designated the African population on the basis of tribe. This was not as straightforward as it might seem. Many Africans, especially those living in urban areas and those who were long-term residents on white farms, had only weak links with any tribal authority and often did not describe themselves in terms of their tribal background. Under the apartheid system every African was allocated to one of nine different tribes, each with a designated tribal authority and a homeland. This classification system lead to many complaints and many people claimed that they did not belong to any of the tribes or that their clan constituted a separate tribe – originally there were eight designated tribes but complaints of this nature lead to the creation of a ninth.

In terms of population the biggest African tribal group is the Zulu. The majority of Zulu live in KwaZulu Natal or in the industrial centres of Gauteng. Rural Zulu probably have the greatest ethnic identity out of the entire African population and this has been fuelled by the IFP calls for more autonomy for KwaZulu Natal. The second biggest ethnic group is the Xhosa. Under the apartheid system they were ascribed two separate homelands: the Ciskie and Transkie, now incorporated into Eastern Cape province. There is a large Xhosa population in Cape Town and on the farms of the Western Cape. Many of the ANC's leaders are Xhosa from the Eastern Cape, reflecting the area's long history of resistance politics and the education provided in the large number of mission schools in the region. These two groups together account for about 40% of the African population.

There are three ethnic groups in the country who are closely related to the populations of three neighbouring countries dominated by people of that tribe: the Tswana (Botswana), the Swazi (Swaziland) and the Southern Sotho (Lesotho). These three and the other four ethnic groups, the Shangana or Tsonga, the Ndebele, the Venda and the Northern Sotho have their populations dispersed in the previous homeland areas or mixed together in the towns and cities of the highveld.

Each one of the nine ethnic groups has an official language. Many of these are more or less mutually intelligible. The major distinction is between the Nguni languages (Xhosa, Zulu, Swazi and Ndebele) and those closely related to SeSotho and SeTswana. There are distinctive cultural activities associated with each ethnic group, though these usually only come into play at times like weddings and funerals. In the urban areas, where the majority of Africans live, many of these ethnic tribal customs have been replaced by generic amalgams of different practices. Similarly a distinctive urban African language containing words from all the languages plus English and Afrikaans has evolved in the urban areas.

White South Africa's white population accounts for something like 13% of the total. It can be sub-divided into two main groups on the basis of home language: English speakers and Afrikaans-speaking people. The ancestors of English-speaking white South Africans first arrived in the country in 1820 and since then there has been a steady stream of new immigrants. The first English settlers to arrive were concentrated in the Eastern Cape but today they are to be found in every town and city. They tend to be more urbanized and more metropolitan in outlook than the Afrikaners, though this is a generalization that does not always match up to reality.

The Afrikaner population are descended from the original Dutch and Huguenot settlers who came with the Dutch East India Company. The word Afrikaner simply means African in Dutch. They account for just over half of the white population. They have a reputation for being conservative, rural and more racist than the English-speaking population. In reality the vast majority live in town and you can very often only tell the difference between an English-speaking and Afrikaans-speaking white South African from their surnames.

There are a number of other smaller communities of white South Africans, including a Jewish community descended from early 20th century immigrants from eastern Europe and a Portuguese community, many of whom came to South Africa from Moçambique and Angola in the 1970s.

Asian South Africa has a small Asian population, accounting for about three percent of the total. It is descended from two main groups: indentured labourers brought to the sugar cane farms of Natal in the 19th century and a number of traders and their families who followed the indentured labourers. The vast majority of the Asian population are originally from South Asia and they are also often referred to as Indian. The majority of Asians still live in KwaZulu Natal though there are small Asian communities in most towns and cities across the country, especially in Gauteng. About 70% of the Asian population are Hindu and 20% Muslim. Almost all Asians speak English as their home language.

Coloured This is probably the most contentious of the four basic racial categories used in South Africa. In some ways the Coloured category just represents the rest lumped together into one group. There is a distinctive Coloured cultural identity – though by no means all people classified as Coloured during apartheid would subscribe to it. Under apartheid about 9% of the population was classified as Coloured. The Coloured population is concentrated in the Western Cape. Many of them are descended from slaves brought to work on the farms of the Cape during the era of rule by the Dutch East India Company and from slave owners and other white settlers. There are also many Coloured people who are descended from the pre-colonial San and Khoi populations of the Cape. This is especially so in the Northern and Eastern Cape which never had large slave populations. Some Coloured people, especially the 200,000 strong Malay community in Cape Town, have retained elements of their pre-slavery culture, including Islam.

On the whole, the Coloured community is very closely linked (both culturally and through descent) with the Afrikaner community. About 80% of the Coloured population speak Afrikaans as their home language: it surprises many visitors to discover that Coloured Afrikaans speakers outnumber White Afrikaans speakers. Some people refer to the Coloured population as 'Brown Afrikaners'. In post-apartheid South Africa the links between the Coloured and Afrikaner communities have been increasingly stressed by people on both sides.

Music and dance

South Africans love to sing and the country's music is world-renowned. Its most famous musical export, Hugh Masekela, is one of the true giants of World Music and has brought the irresistable sounds of this great country to a mass audience., while Abdullah Ibrahim (Dollar Brand) is regarded as one the greatest living jazz pianists, whose legendary musical landscapes make the listener believe they are actually travelling across the country instead of sitting in their front room with the headphones on.

Though the likes of Hugh Masekela have been preaching to the converted for many years, South African music first came to the attention of most people with Paul Simon's *Graceland* album which melded South African rythms with a western pop idiom. The recent resurgence of the World Music scene, with festivals such as Womad in the UK becoming part of the mainstream, has further helped placed South African music firmly on the map. One of the most recent groups to make it onto the world stage is Ladysmith Black Mambazo, whose haunting melodies even featured in a TV as for a certain brand of baked beans!

If music is the very heartbeat of this country, then dance also features as an integral part of life for many South Africans. In KwaZula Natal many tourists will be treated to a traditional Zulu ceremony, while the fantastically-talented *Gumboots* dance company have toured the world with their unforgettable mix of music, dance and showmanship.

Western music is hugely popular with many young South Africans. Durban has been dubbed the Seattle of South Africa and is the best place to see live rock bands. Johannesburg is a great place to go clubbing and experience why this is the country's most vibrant city, but please note that Jo'burg is a dangerous place and going out late at night carries a government health warning.

Cape Town is currently the hot ticket on the South African club scene and is now regarded as one of the great clubbing cities in the world with a fast-growing reputation for uninhibited hedonism. The backdrop of Table Mountain makes this a very special place in the hearts of clubbers, many of whom finish off a wild night out with the unforgettable experience of watching the sun rise. All the top DJs from the UK regularly make trips to play the city's main venues, particularly black DJs who would have been prevented from doing so only a decade ago.

Some of the best clubs in Cape Town are on Long Street. This is also where most of the backpackers hostels are located and at weekends this is party central.

Cape Town club scene

Land and environment

South Africa is a big country with an extremely diverse physical environment. The country's total land area amounts to 1,219,912 sq km (1,267,462 sq km including Swaziland and Lesotho). Contained within this land area are a wide mix of environments, ranging from tropical moist forest, through high mountains, rolling grasslands and temperate woodlands to sparsely vegetated areas of semi-desert. South Africa's natural scenery is world famous and rightly so. There are some amazingly beautiful areas which can take the breath away from even the most world weary traveller. The wild and empty beaches of the south coast, the panoramic views of the Drakensberg mountains, the wide open spaces of the Karoo and many other stunning landscapes can all leave a lasting impression on the visitor.

There are also, however, some big areas of undistinguished natural scenery and the impacts of both industrialization and apartheid have also had their toll. This is obviously worth bearing in mind when you are planning a holiday, especially if you are only going to be there for a short period of time. If your primary interest is in South Africa's natural beauty read the following sections carefully before planning your route.

Landscape

South Africa's physical geography is dominated by one feature: a massive escarpment that runs right around the subcontinent dividing a thin coastal strip from a huge inland plateau. This escarpment is clearest in the east, where it is marked by the spectacular Drakensberg mountains, running in an arc from the Eastern Cape round to northern Mpumalanga. To the west the escarpment is confused by a jumble of beautiful mountain chains (the Cape Folded Mountains), such as the Cederberg, the Tsitsikamma, the Swartberg and the Hottentot-Hollands. The inland plateau, usually known as the highveld, is a relatively flat plain sloping gently down towards the west and north. This plain is, however, broken up by numerous geological features, resulting in isolated steep-sided hills or longer chains of higher ground.

This interior plateau forms the southernmost tip of the massive Africa continental plateau which stretches as far north as Ethiopia. This plateau was part of the ancient landmass of Pangaea (c200 million years ago), which split in two to form Gondwanaland in the southern hemisphere and Laurasia in the north. Gondwanaland later broke up to form the continents of South America, Australasia and Africa, around 135 million years ago. As it is made up of an old continental plate many of South Africa's rocks are very old and some rocks found in the Limpopo valley, Northern Province, rank with the oldest yet discovered anywhere in the world.

Other areas, such as the Witwatersrand and Barberton complexes, are also made up of ancient Precambrian rocks, about 3,000 million years old. This contrasts with rock formations in places such as the Western Cape coast which were only formed in the past 250,000 years, during the Quaternary era. Most of the country is, however, made up of sandstone and slates laid down in the Carboniferous to Jurassic periods (when Pangaea began to break up). These are commonly referred to as the Karoo sequence of rocks. The eastern portions of the Karoo sequence have been covered by an intrusion of basalt. This harder layer of rock has protected the softer Karoo sandstones from erosion and stands out as a highland area, especially in Lesotho.

The Karoo sequence is particularly rich in fossil remains. Contained in the sandstones and shales are the remains of many reptilian creatures who lived in the low-lying areas of swamps and shallow lakes. Some of these fossils have been crucial to scientists' attempts to reconstruct the way in which reptiles evolved into mammals. The best places to look for fossils is along the sides of the many steep-sided hills or *koppies* that dominate the Karoo landscape. The best fossils are usually found in the dull red shales, which erode easily to reveal the fossil remains.

Climate

Over most of South Africa rain falls during the southern hemisphere summer months (November-March). Rainfall tends to be in the form of intense cloud bursts, often accompanied by thunderstorms, though there can also be periods of longer rainfall. During the summer months warm and wet easterly winds sweep in from over the Indian Ocean. As these winds flow over the southeastern coast and the Drakensberg they drop much of their moisture, making these areas the wettest parts of the country with annual totals over 1,000mm. Over the highveld the moisture-bearing winds trigger rain showers and thunderstorms. In the east of the highveld these tend to be more regular but towards the west, especially in the Northern Cape, they are infrequent. Here average annual rainfall figures are usually below 200 mm per annum. The summer rains never reach the western coast of the Northern Cape province and rainfall levels here can be as low as 20mm per annum. South Africa is, on the whole, a very dry country, with something like 30 percent of the land area receiving below 250 mm a year on average. Rain may be unpopular with visitors but it is almost always welcomed by South Africans.

The only part of the country where the major rainfall does not come from summer easterlies is the Western Cape and the extreme west of Northern Cape province. Here most rain falls during the winter months as depressions over the southern Atlantic sweep north and east bringing with them frontal systems and cool rains. Late in the winter and early spring an occasional winter storm will travel further north than usual and bring with it much needed rain to the arid northwestern coastal belt. Apart from these occasional storms this area receives its moisture from mists that roll in from the cold Atlantic during the summer months.

The winter weather systems can also sometimes skirt up along the southern coast bringing rain and even snow to the Eastern Cape, Lesotho and KwaZulu Natal. Snowfalls tend to be minor and confined to light dustings of the highest peaks, though there are occasionally significant falls of a few inches or more. In the winter of 1996 a number of people had to be rescued after large snow storms in the Drakensberg.

This seasonal pattern is also highly variable from year to year. This variability tends to be most pronounced in the lowest rainfall areas: here there can be some years where the rains fail entirely. The exact reasons for this variability are a matter of considerable academic debate. There does appear to be a cycle of wet and dry years in South Africa over a period of about four to eight years. This cycle is related to a frequent, but irregular, event known as the El Niño, in which ocean and air currents in the South Pacific are reversed. This, in turn, triggers changes in the circulation of air around the southern hemisphere and results in weaker easterlies and drought in South Africa. The weather system is, however, extremely complex and involves the interaction of global and local variables, so predicting exactly how something like the El Niño will affect South African rainfall is impossible with any degree of accuracy. Global warming may also be further complicating the already complex weather systems. Beyond short range forecasting all that meteorologists can predict with any degree of accuracy is that the climate is very unpredictable.

Temperatures vary according to season, altitude and distance from the moderating influence of the oceans. During the summer months the inland plateau tends to heat up considerably, especially if the rains fail. The highest daytime temperatures are to be found in the lower lying semi-desert areas of the Northern Cape and the lowveld regions of Mpumulanga. On the highveld temperatures can also soar in summer, though they tend to be moderated by the higher altitudes. Fortunately in these inland regions the evenings tend to be significantly cooler, especially under clear skies. Travelling at night or in the early morning is a sensible and popular option in these regions during summer. The coastal fringes of Natal are also hot and sticky in summer and don't expect too much relief at night. The most pleasant area of the country during the summer months is the Western Cape, with hot but often breezy days and comfortable evenings.

During the winter the Western Cape can get very chilly, with frequent blustery storms and heavy rain. On the highveld and in the Karoo stable high pressure systems result in clear skies, warm days and cold nights. It is a combination many visitors find very comfortable especially for travelling long distances. In the highest areas of the Drakensberg winter temperatures can plummet to way below freezing at night: the best time to visit these areas is during the autumn or spring. The Natal coast remains warm throughout the year, especially in the northern subtropical areas near the Moçambique border. Winter is a good time to visit the lowveld game parks: the drier conditions make it easier to spot wildlife, especially around water holes.

Vegetation

There are a number of different ways of categorizing South Africa's vegetational zones, which are sometimes called biomes or ecozones. All these categorizations are simplifications of complex and dynamic patterns of vegetation and rarely are there clear boundaries between the different zones. Even without the influence of humans this pattern has constantly shifted with long-term trends in climate: when you add in millenniums of human impacts, mapping a set pattern of different biomes becomes an extremely difficult task.

One vegetational zone that is not difficult to classify as distinctive is the fynbos of the Western Cape. Although fynbos covers only a relatively small area it comprises one of the earth's six separate floral kingdoms. The other five floral kingdoms cover huge areas such as most of the northern hemisphere or the whole of Australia. The Cape floral kingdom is both the smallest and the richest floral kingdom in the world, with the highest known concentration of plant species per unit area. There are over 7,700 different plant species within the fynbos biome and of these over 5,000 are endemic to the Western Cape (ie they do not occur naturally anywhere else). The 470 sq km of the Cape Peninsula is home to 2,256 different plant species – more than the whole of the UK, an area 5,000 times bigger! The 60 sq km of Table Mountain alone supports 1,470 species. The richness of the fynbos is well demonstrated by its *ericas* or heaths, of which there are over 600 different species. There are just 26 in the rest of the world. Not surprisingly the Western Cape is a magnet for plant enthusiasts.

The word fynbos comes from the Dutch for fine-leaved plants. Almost all of the woody plants have small leaves (microphyllous) which are hard, tough and leathery (sclerophyllous). True grasses are also relatively rare and as much as five percent of the biome is covered by Cape reeds (of the *Restionaceae* family). Most of the plants that fill the niches usually taken up by grasses have small, thin (*ericoid*) leaves. Additionally, the fynbos biome contains proteas, ericas and members of seven plant families found nowhere else in the world. These include the King Protea, South Africa's national flower, the beautiful Red Disa, symbol of the Cape Province and the popular garden plants, *pelargoniums*, commonly known as geraniums. The largest family in number of species is *Asteraceae* (daisy family), with just under 1,000 species of which more than 600 are endemic. Fynbos is very rich in bulbous plants (*geophytes*) and many species from the family *Iridaceae* have become household names such as babiana, freesia, gladiolus, iris, moraea, sporaxis and watsonia.

As many of the endemic fynbos species have amazingly small ranges (sometimes as small as a football field), they are extremely vulnerable to extinction. One small housing project, for example, could wipe out a whole species. Given this and the fact that the Western Cape has fairly dense human population, it is not surprising that many of South Africa's threatened and rare plants are found in the fynbos. Almost 500 species are classified as rare, threatened or endangered. Fynbos species tend to grow fairly slowly. This is because they are in a winter rainfall region so during the summer months there is not enough water available and during the winter low temperatures restrict plant growth. The hot dry summer months also make fire a common occurrence in the biome. The fynbos plants are well adapted to fire and the biome is adapted to quickly re-establish itself after naturally occurring burns. If fire is totally restricted fynbos often loses out to plant species from surrounding biomes. If fires are too frequent, however, the fynbos plants do not have time to re-establish themselves and this can lead to local extermination of species.

Soils under fynbos tend to be extremely infertile, due partially to the chemical make-up of the underlying rocks and partially to heavy leaching that has occurred over long periods. The nutrient-poor soils produce plants that are also low in nutrients and therefore of low feeding potential for grazing animals. This means that there is a relatively low density and diversity of mammals and birds in the fynbos biome.

The western coast of South Africa also has a large number of endemic plant species. This area, stretching north into Namibia, has extremely low and erratic rainfall and the plant life reflects this. Many of the plants in this region are succulents and about 200 of these are classified as rare or endangered. When rains do come to the area there is a dramatic transformation of the vegetation. Hundreds of flowering plants lying dormant during the long dry periods burst into bloom covering the whole of the landscape in a carpet of brightly coloured flowers. This is a spectacular annual event and attracts many visitors to the region every spring, but as the flowers are reliant upon unpredictable rainfall it is impossible to say exactly when and where they will appear. The rains are expected in the spring, and once the first blooms start to appear a 'Flower Hotline' can be called for the latest information, see page 765 in the Northern Cape for full details. After a brief period of flowering the plants drop their seeds which then lie dormant until the next rainfall event.

The inland plateau of the Cape is dominated by Karoo types of vegetation. This is made up mainly from low lying shrubs and succulents, though in good rainfall years grasses can also make an appearance. There tends to be a lot of open soil between the shrubs so much of the region takes on the red tinge of the underlying soils and this can lead to some wonderful sunsets and sunrises. The low density of vegetation also makes fires a less common occurrence than in better watered regions. There are occasional areas of green along side streams and rivers and these are the only places you will see trees in the biome.

The northern highveld areas (along the Botswana border) and the lowveld areas of Northern Province, Mpumalanga and Swaziland, by contrast, have a fair number of trees. This is the classic savanna formation: areas of grassland interspersed by occasional trees. In the highveld areas the vegetation is dominated by thorny acacia woodland, often referred to as bushveld. In valley bottoms and in lowveld areas the vegetation is often dominated by mopane, which can tolerate the extremes of waterlogging and drying encountered on heavy soils. This region tends to have fertile soils and grasses have a high nutrition content. They are, therefore, heavily populated by grazing animals (both wild and domestic). The major wildlife viewing areas fall within this biome.

The remaining highveld, the KwaZulu Natal midlands, Lesotho and the inland areas of Eastern Cape are taken up by grasslands with few naturally occurring trees. The grasses grow vigorously during the hot and wet summer months and then remain dormant during the dry, cold winter. The grasslands are often divided into two different categories: sweet and sour veld. Sweetveld occurs in the areas with lower rainfall figures (400-600 mm per annum), especially on heavier clay soils. It tends to be more nutritious than the sour velds and is therefore popular for grazing, especially during the summer months. Sourveld tends to occur in the areas with rainfall above 600 mm per annum. Greater availability of water means that sourveld grasses grow rapidly, though they tend to have a lower nutritional content. Both these veld types intermingle and it is hard to draw a clear distinction between the two. The division between the Karoo and grassland areas is also hazy. During dry spells and in areas which have been overgrazed, Karoo-type shrubs expand into the grasslands while in wetter years or if grazing pressure is reduced they will retreat. On the highveld much of this grassland has been converted to agriculture or covered with factories, roads and cities.

The densely populated narrow coast strip of the Eastern Cape and KwaZulu Natal was once heavily wooded. The closed canopy subtropical forests of KwaZulu Natal can still be found in a few isolated patches but most of the area has been converted to agriculture. In the Eastern Cape the evergreen temperate forest has also been largely cut down, though some small patches are left around Knysna. The forests here give some idea of what the environment would have been like before the arrival of Europeans with commercial logging: there are some beautiful trees such as the stinkwood, Cape chestnut, yellowwood and the white and red alder. In total, indigenous closed canopy woodland accounts for only 1% of South Africa's land area, with a similar amount under commercial plantations (many of these on the Drakensberg escarpment in Mpumalanga).

Urban and rural environments

Any description of the South African landscape that leaves out the impact of humans would not give a visitor any real idea about what the place actually looks like. Though apartheid has now come to an end its legacy is often apparent in the South African landscape and the pattern of South African cities and towns. For many years some of the most striking features of apartheid social engineering, such as the huge rural slums that sprang up around the country, were never shown on official maps. Visitors were often shocked to suddenly encounter a massive area of slum housing way out in the countryside which they could not find on their road maps and which did not appear on any road signs. Official maps and guides are now slowly catching up with reality but the landscape itself will take much longer to transform.

Agriculture   While large areas of South Africa are given over to wildlife or wilderness areas most of the countryside is dominated by farming. The nature of the country's agricultural sector, therefore, has a huge impact on the landscape. The pattern of agriculture in South Africa is determined by two major factors: the physical environment and the legacy of apartheid. Low and variable rainfall figures make arable farming an extremely risky business and only about 10% of the country is covered by arable crops. Maize is the country's staple crop. It is mainly grown in the Free State, the southern and eastern portions of North West, the western portions of Mpumalanga and those parts of Gauteng not covered by towns and industry. These areas comprise some of the least eventful countryside in South Africa. Maize and other grain crops, such as sorghum or millet, are also grown in the Eastern Cape and KwaZulu Natal. In these wetter areas the constraining factor is often not availability of water, but of sufficient flat land to plough amongst the broken topography. The most rewarding landscapes for a tourist are inevitably very different from the most rewarding landscapes for a farmer.

Other arable crops include wheat, grown mostly in the Western Cape and sugar cane, grown mostly in KwaZulu Natal. The Western Cape is also well known for its vineyards and fruits, such as peaches and nectarines. The lowveld areas of Mpumalanga and Northern Province are also major fruit growing areas.

The majority of the countryside is, however, given over to extensive grazing land. This accounts for something like 65% of the country's total land area, the vast majority of this given over to large enclosures of naturally occurring veld plants rather than improved and carefully managed paddocks. The wetter areas in the east, where grasses dominate over woodier Karoo shrubs, are given over mainly to cattle. The rolling hills of the KwaZulu Natal Midlands are particularly good cattle rearing country: well watered but with sufficiently cool evenings and winters to kill off disease-bearing insects that flourish in the more tropical coastal fringes and the lowveld regions. Further west, especially in the Karoo, livestock rearing is dominated by sheep and in the very driest areas by goats.

This pattern of agriculture is confused, however, by the legacy of apartheid. Until very recently African farmers were not allowed to own or buy land outside certain prescribed areas. These areas, known as the homelands, comprised only 13% of the country and were supposed to provide land for an African population comprising 75% of the total. In these areas the population density is high and plots of land for agriculture are very small. Most of these plots are unproductive and yields from agricultural crops very low. Grazing in these areas is on common land owned by the local community. Though individual herds tend to be small the total animal population is high and includes a mixture of goats, sheep and cattle. As the grazing land is unfenced and communal herds will usually be looked after by a shepherd – usually a teenage boy, livestock are usually brought back to the village at night where they are *kraaled* to stop them wandering and to reduce the risk of theft.

This contrasts with the white farming areas where farms tend to be huge. Arable agriculture is highly mechanized and produces high yields. Some farms, such as the fruit growing areas, employ large numbers of seasonal labour but on the whole the number of people employed permanently on each farm is not high. On the white farms livestock are grazed in large fenced paddocks at a lower density than on the former homeland areas. Except on the dairy farms, livestock are only checked up on periodically.

These different patterns of farming produce very different looking landscapes. The former homeland areas are more densely populated with small plots of unhealthy looking maize interspersed amongst scattered homesteads. The grazing areas often look barren, especially towards the end of the winter dry season when all available forage has been eaten by livestock. The white farming areas, on the other hand, have large fields of arable crops or huge areas of grazing land. On the grazing land there will tend to be more vegetation available to the livestock, though in drought years these areas can also look pretty barren. It is unusual to see many people in the fields and paddocks of the white farming areas.

Though the restrictions on buying or renting land have now been lifted this pattern will remain for many years. Some African farmers who were evicted from white farming areas during the apartheid era have been resettled on their original farms, but this process is very slow and the geography of agriculture is unlikely to change significantly in the conceivable future.

South Africa's urban geography has been largely shaped by segregation: this pattern is now changing rapidly but the legacy of residential segregation will be apparent for a very long time to come. Under the Group Areas Act different areas of each city were reserved for one of the four major population groups (White, Indian, Coloured or African). Prior to the passing of the Group Areas Act in 1950 most cities and towns were already segregated to an extent. The pattern of segregation was complicated however and there were in most cities a number of areas in which the different population groups intermingled. Under the Group Areas Act the government attempted to consolidate this pattern of segregation into bigger, clearly defined blocks of land and to do away with any areas where there was a mixture of the different races. This process continued right through to the mid-1980s. The urban environment that this system created is distinctive.

Living in the city

Prior to the Group Areas Act much of the poorer urban population lived in slum areas near the central business areas of industrial centres. These areas were home to large numbers of Africans, Indians and Coloureds and a few 'poor Whites'. Under the Group Areas Act these slum areas were knocked down and new housing for Whites was built in their place. The African, Indian and Coloured populations were moved to new, racially segregated, planned settlements on the outskirts of cities, known as townships. These areas tend to be some distance from the city centre and are divided from the white suburbs by areas of unoccupied land. There are often only one or two access routes into the township and the streets are wide and straight: both factors were deliberately intended to make the control of unrest and protest easier to handle. The best known of these township areas is the vast residential area called Soweto, which originally stood for South Western Townships, on the outskirts of Johannesburg.

The vast majority of Africans living in urban areas still live in these townships. They tend to be made up of large areas of small uniform houses with few local urban amenities. Many of the roads in township areas are not tarred, rubbish is strewn across the streets and air pollution is horrendous. In recent years there have been a proliferation of squatter camps within the townships on areas of open ground and many of the residential plots include not just the original house but a large number of additional shacks. These townships contrast sharply with the suburbs reserved for white populations during the apartheid years. Houses in these areas are usually large, streets are clean and often tree-lined. The fear of crime means that in areas like Johannesburg's northern suburbs many of these houses look like mini-forts.

This pattern of residential segregation will remain for many years to come. A few rich Africans, Coloureds and Indians have moved into formerly all white suburbs, but on the whole these middle-class groups tend to live in small richer enclaves in the townships. The major change in the pattern of residential segregation over the past decade or so has been the rebirth of inner city African housing, resulting in areas such as Hillbrow in Johannesburg.

Not surprisingly the pattern of industry and infrastructure has also been affected by apartheid. Obviously industrial development has also been influenced by matters such as the proximity to raw materials but industrial development planning has also had an influence. The main industrial centre is Gauteng where the South African industrial revolution was centred around the gold mines on the Wit watersrand. Other important

Industry & infrastructure

industrial centres are in the major coastal port cities of Cape Town, Port Elizabeth and Durban and around secondary mining centres in the Free State and Mpumalanga.

During the apartheid years some efforts were made to decentralize industrialization in order to provide jobs for the African population in areas closer to the homelands. The idea behind this policy was to try to prevent rural to urban migration amongst the African population and to foster the plan of overall segregation. On the whole these decentralization policies were unsuccessful, though a number of labour intensive industries, such as garment manufacturers, did relocate to the borders of homeland areas to take advantage of the low wages prevalent in these areas of high unemployment.

Infrastructural development tends to reflect the pattern of racial segregation. The major cities and the smaller towns and villages of the former white rural areas are well served by roads, railways and other economic infrastructure. The former homeland areas tend to be badly served by roads and railways and other infrastructure, such as piped water, is also lacking. This pattern will again take many years to rectify.

Lesotho

14

Lesotho

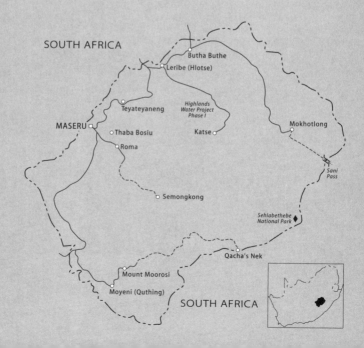

Lesotho is often referred to as the 'Kingdom in the Sky'. A small independent country completely surrounded by South Africa, none of its 30,000 sq km lies below 1,000 m and some of its peaks reach as high as 3,480 m. This scenery is very different to anything you may have already experienced in South Africa and the rural life of its people is intriguing. Despite its underdeveloped physical infrastructure (climate and corresponding road conditions are subject to extreme weather conditions in these high altitudes) and minuscule tourism industry, it has much to offer the adventurous traveller. Trout fishing in clear mountain streams; pony trekking through remote mountain valleys; and hiking in a country with no fences. Whilst it is the mountain scenery that will attract most visitors, the country's friendly atmosphere often leaves the biggest impression. If you love being outdoors and are willing to put up with a bit of discomfort to see some of southern Africa's most outstanding natural scenery, than Lesotho is well worth the effort.

Essentials

Planning your trip

When to go The spring or autumn months (October-November and March-May) are the best times of the year to visit, whilst skies are clear and temperatures warm. Mid-winter is also popular with richer South Africans if there has been snow in the mountains.

Language **Sesotho** is the official language and is spoken everywhere. **English** is widely spoken in Maseru and the bigger towns, even in remote areas there will usually be somebody, often a school child, who speaks at least some English.

Before you travel

Visas & immigration Visas are not required by most nationalities, however passport holders from the following countries do require a visa only obtainable in advance: Australia, Canada, Ghana, India, Mozambique, New Zealand, and Nigeria. People not requiring a visa will normally be given a one month permit with their entry stamp, although it is possible to ask for longer with proof of funds. To extend your permit, go to the *Lesotho Immigration Department*, Transport Building, Assissi Rd, Maseru, T317339. Visitors who require a visa can wait until they are in the region and then contact the Lesotho High Commission in Pretoria or in a few cases contact the Lesotho Overseas High Commission in their own country, see box. When applying for a visa you must fill in an application form with one photo. In Pretoria the visa office hours are Mon-Fri 0900-1300. *Lesotho High Commission*, 391 Menlo Park, Pretoria 0001, T4607648, F4607649. A single entry, valid for one month, costs about R300, multi-entry visas can be requested.

Vaccinations If arriving from tropical African countries you may be asked for a Yellow Fever vaccination card.

Money

Currency Lesotho's standard unit of currency is the **Maloti**, divided into 100 **lisente**. It is exactly equivalent to the Rand. Indeed one of the curious things about Lesotho is that the Rand and the Maloti are actually interchangeable, you can pay in either currency. This can get a bit confusing sometimes when you have three different coins (old Rand, new Rand and Maloti) for the same unit of currency. Old Rand coins are still used in Lesotho but are not generally accepted back in South Africa so try to dispose of these before returning, and while the Rand is interchangeable with the Maloti in Lesotho this is not the case in South Africa. If you are due to leave Lesotho in a few days, try to get change in Rand and when you change money ask for the cash in Rand. If you have Maloti left when you leave Lesotho simply ask one of the street traders or someone travelling in the other direction to do a swap for Rand notes and coins.

Bank opening hours: Mon-Fri, 0830-1530, Sat, 0830-1100

Banks There are three main banks in Lesotho, the *Lesotho National Bank*, *Nedbank* and *Standard Bank*. The *Lesotho National Bank* charges no commission on forex transactions, though it involves plenty of paperwork and long queues. Rather use your credit card to withdraw forex from the specific *Standard Bank*, SA bank account ATM on Kingsway in Maseru, or bring sufficient Rand with you. Outside Maseru most banks do not have a separate forex counter. You are strongly advised to avoid changing money on a Friday and especially the last Friday of the month when many people get paid. On these days the queues can be enormous.

Credit cards Accepted at the large international *Sun* hotels and can be used at the South African ATM of the *Standard Bank*, on Kingsway in Maseru. Otherwise they are of little use.

Getting there

Air **Moshoeshoe I International Airport** is 21 km south of Maseru along the Main South Road. Since the liquidation of *Lesotho Air* several years ago, *SA Airlink*, has been operating the route between Moshoeshoe I International Airport and Johannesburg International Airport. There are 2-3 flights per day in each direction. There is a M20 departure tax for international flights

Kingdom of Lesotho missions overseas

Denmark, *Bogevej 17, 2900 Hellerup, Copenhagen, T2369449, F621538.*
Germany, *Goldersberger Alle 50, Bonn, 53175, T3084300, F3084322.*
Italy, *Via Di Porta Pertusa 4, Rome 00165, T8542419, F8542527.*

South Africa, *391 Menlo Park, Pretoria 0001, T4607648, F4607649.*
UK, *7 Chesham Place, Belgravia, London SW1 8HN, T7355686, F7355023.*
USA, *2511 Massachusetts Av, Washington, DC 20008, T7975533-6, F2346815.*

Road

As very few people visit Lesotho without also going to South Africa, the commonest way of entering and leaving the country is by road. In total there are eight road crossings from South Africa into Lesotho. **Calendonspoort** border post, open 0600-2200, is close to the town of Botha Bothe and the South African town of Fouriesburg and is the logical border post for visitors arriving in their own transport from Gauteng or northern KwaZulu Natal. **Maputsoe Bridge** border post, open 24 hours, is close to Ficksburg on the South African side and is one of the busiest crossings used by most of the mineworkers returning from the Witwatersrand. Long distance taxis also run the route from Maputsoe Bridge to and from Johannesburg but as they arrive and depart in Johannesburg's Hillbrow district it is not advised to use these. (**NB** For a number of years, the South African taxi industry was plagued by extreme violence and the accident rate on South African roads, caused by irresponsible taxi drivers is still appallingly high. Think very carefully before embarking on a long taxi trip.)

Maseru Bridge border crossing, open 24 hours, is the crossing used by visitors arriving from Bloemfontein. This border post is usually less crowded than Maputsoe Bridge so if you have your own transport and are going straight to Maseru, you might find it quicker to use the South African Ficksburg-Ladybrand road and cross at Maseru Bridge rather than Maputsoe Bridge. If you are travelling by taxi from Bloemfontein you may have to change

Lesotho

★ **Things to do in Lesotho**

- **Pony trek** deep into the mountains without doing the hard work yourself.
- Celebrate the tremendous view of the uKhahlamba-Drakensberg National Park with a glass of steaming mulled wine at **Sani Top Lodge** – the highest pub in Africa.
- Try the local variety of **beer** in Sani Top village. A white flag is hung outside the house when this beer is for sale, it has a thick, almost porridge-like head – quite an experience!
- Talk to the experts. There is not much that Ashley and Jennifer Thorn at the **Trading Post** in Roma, and Mike and Di at **Malealea Lodge** do not know about Lesotho.
- Take a walk from Semongkong to the **Maletsunyane Falls**, at 192 m the highest single drop falls in southern Africa.
- Get into the Basotho culture at the **Morija Arts and Cultural Festival**, held each year over the weekend nearest to 1st October.

taxis in Botshabelo Township. This was a notorious dumping ground for Basotho people kicked off farms in the Orange Free State during the Apartheid era. It remains a large sprawling slum, but the taxi terminus has been redeveloped and is well-run and policed.

Taxis to and from Bloemfontein leave several times throughout the day and depart when full. The taxi terminus in Bloemfontein itself is conveniently located next to the railway station not far from the town centre. There has been very little violence associated with taxis along the route between Bloemfontein and Maseru. This route, rather than direct from Johannesburg, is the one we would recommend for visitors going to Maseru via public transport.

Alternatively *Naval Hill Backpackers*, in Bloemfontein (see page 674), offer a shuttle service to *Malealea Lodge* in Lesotho, (2 hours' drive) Monday and Friday, minimum four people. This returns on the same days so it is quite feasible to stay at Malealea for three nights to undertake the activities on offer and return to Bloemfontein on the next shuttle. If you are short of time and are travelling between Cape Town and Johannesburg this is a good way to visit Lesotho.

Van Rooyen's gate border post, 0600-2000, is between Mafeteng and the small Free State town of Wepener. The **Makhaleng** border post, 0800-1600, is close to Mohales Hoek and on the South African road to Zastron. The southernmost border crossing at **Tele Bridge**, 0800-2200, is close to the town of Quthing/Moyeni and joins up with South African roads to Sterkspruit, Lady Grey and other small Eastern Cape towns. It is possible to catch taxis to and from each of these crossings, and the nearest respective town in Lesotho.

There are two road crossings into the eastern mountains of Lesotho: **Qachas Nek** open 0800-1800, which is rarely used except by local traffic mostly on foot, and as there is no public transport you will need to hitch or walk; and **Sani Pass** open 0800-1600, the well-known scenic crossing that passes through the uKhahlamba-Drakensberg Park on the South African side. Both of these are on poor roads only passable by four-wheel drive vehicles. Unless you have your own vehicle hitchhiking is the only way of getting to and from Sani Pass by road on the Lesotho side of the border, though it is possible to arrange a pick-up from the border crossing to the nearest South African backpackers, *Sani Lodge*.

There is a R5 road tax on all vehicles As Lesotho is part of the **Customs Union** visitors with South African registered vehicles do not need a Carnet de Passages en Douanes. They should, however, ensure that their insurance will be valid in Lesotho and, if in a hire car, that it does not contravene the terms of the hire agreement. Visitors with vehicles registered outside the Customs Union will obviously need the normal temporary import documentation.

Touching down

Local customs & laws Greetings are very important in Sesotho culture. It is considered very rude if you do not formally greet people before addressing them and, except on busy town streets, people will expect you to greet them if you are simply passing them on a street or path. Ask somebody to

Touching down

Business hours Banks: Monday-Friday, 0900-1530; Saturday, 0830/0900 to 1030/1100. ***Businesses***: Monday-Friday, 0830-1700; Saturday, 0830-1400. ***Government offices***: Monday-Friday, 0830-1630. Most shut for lunch between 1300-1400. ***Post Offices***: weekdays 0830-1600; Saturday, 0800-1200. ***Shops***: Monday-Friday, 0800-1800; Saturday, 0800-1300; Sunday, 0900-1300.

IDD code 266

Official time Two hours ahead of GMT, seven hours ahead of eastern USA standard time, one hour ahead of Europe; eight hours behind Australian Eastern Standard Time.

Voltage 220/230 volts AC at 50 Hz.

Weights and measures The metric system is used.

teach you greetings in Sesotho if possible but if you can't remember the vocabulary a simple "hello" will suffice – *'lumela'*.

Where to stay

Most main centres have one or two formal and rather soulless hotels. These often look dilapidated from the outside but are usually kept reasonably clean inside. They rarely have more than a handful of guests, so you are usually able to benefit from close attention from hotel staff. Most will happily arrange tours of local sights, though prices are sometimes a little steep. As these hotels are often the centre of local nightlife for local professionals it is usually best to ask for a room away from the bar area, especially at weekends. Maseru has two international standard hotels (part of the *Sun* chain). Neither are outstanding, but they are clean and comfortable.

Hotels
See the inside front cover of the book for hotel grade price guides

There are few budget travellers' hostels in Maseru and the lowland urban centres and what are available are not recommended. There are, however, a number of lodges in the mountains and foothills that provide excellent value accommodation. For the independent traveller, it is a good idea to arrive in Maseru early in the morning, spend the day in the city before heading out to cheaper accommodation in the outlying districts, some of which is only 20-30 km away. This avoids having to pay the high prices for the city hotels.

Hostels

Away from the main towns camping is very easy. You should always try to get permission to set up camp from the chief of the nearest village. Apart from the obvious courtesy, getting permission can also be to your advantage: you may be offered space in one of the village huts or allocated a young boy to guard your equipment. You should not pass up the opportunity of staying in a village hut: you will often be offered a fascinating experience. Make sure you are carrying small gifts, such as disposable lighters, pens or boiled sweets. You do also need to be prepared to sleep through the noise of mice and rats scurrying around the roof and floor.

Camping

In the densely populated lowlands it is more difficult to find a suitable camping site and you also run the risk of losing your belongings to the crowds of children who inevitably gather. Ask around at the churches and missions for permission to camp in their grounds or at the local police station.

Getting around

The charter company, ***Mission Aviation***, T310347, runs in conjunction with the Lesotho Flying Doctors and sometimes has space for extra passengers.

Air

The main route running north-south along the lowland strip is tarred and in good repair. Other tarred routes include the road from Maseru to Roma, Leribe/Hlotso to Katse dam, and Botha Bothe to Mokhotlong. The quality of gravel roads varies considerably: the 'mountain road' to Thaba Tseke and the road to Semongkong are both in good condition whilst the routes from Thaba Tseke to Mokhotlong or Qacha's Nek are very poor and get very slippery in the wet.

Road

Lesotho

Petrol is readily available in the lowland centres but if you are travelling into the mountains make sure you have plenty of fuel before you leave. Distances between filling stations are long and supplies are not always assured.

Road safety in Lesotho usually leaves a lot to be desired, as the death of the King in an accident a few years ago on the Main South Road indicates. Taxi drivers are often in direct competition for passengers so rush to get to stops ahead of other drivers – this often means they take huge risks. Be especially careful when driving behind taxis as they often brake extremely sharply to pick up passengers. Drink driving is also a huge problem, especially at weekends, bank holidays and at the end of the month when people have just been paid. It is probably best to avoid driving at these times. Any valid driving licence is accepted as long as it is in English or accompanied by a certified translation. Wear your seat belt at all times, occasionally the police will use this as an excuse for imposing a fine.

Taxis, buses and hitchhiking The lowland towns and villages are linked together by an effective and cheap taxi service. These taxis consist of minibuses with about 16 seats, or sometimes in remote districts of converted four-wheel drive vehicles. There is no set timetable for taxis, they simply set off when they are full. It is important to remember, however, that taxis stop running very early in the evening and it is more or less impossible to get one after sunset. There is very little space for baggage in the taxis and you will usually end up with your bags on yours, or your neighbour's, lap. The first passengers to arrive get the most comfortable seats next to the driver, though the downside is that you get a full view of some crazy driving habits. Luckily there is none of the violence in Lesotho so associated with the South African taxi industry. Also unlike most of South Africa, people in taxis talk to each other in Lesotho.

Larger buses do the longer routes especially over the gravel mountain roads. To most towns there is at least one bus a day to and from Maseru or another larger lowland centre. They usually leave about 0900 or 1000 but timetables vary with the number of passengers.

As taxis are cheap and frequent and most drivers will charge the same fare as a taxi anyway, hitchhiking in the lowlands is not usually worth the trouble. In more remote areas more or less every passing vehicle acts as a de facto taxi service – somewhat blurring the distinction between hitching and taking a taxi. There are certain routes, however, where hitchhiking is the only alternative to walking, for example over Sani Pass into KwaZulu Natal or from Qacha's Nek into the Eastern Cape. If you are hitchhiking in the mountains make sure you have a jacket or blanket (or both) to hand – most lifts will be on the back of a pick-up or a truck and it can get very cold, especially on winter evenings.

Other transport Horses and ponies are the main form of transport other than foot for most Basotho in the mountains. You can hire ponies from a number of centres.

Keeping in touch

Internet Internet facilities are only available in Maseru in offices next to the *Basotho Hat* craft shop, and at the Maseru Sun Hotel (see page 783). Internet speed is painfully slow so you should try and catch up with your emails before arriving in Lesotho.

Post The international postal service is fairly quick and reliable – letters to Europe take between five and 10 days. The central post office in Maseru has a poste restante service, letters are kept for 6 months. The *American Express* travel centre will also act as a poste restante.

Telephone
The international code for Lesotho is 266
The local telephone system is reasonable in the lowlands but there is poor coverage in the mountain areas. International calls are very expensive and only possible to make from the larger centres. It is possible to send telegrams from all post offices.

Media Lesotho TV has news and current affairs programmes that are broadcast, in Sesotho, every evening, and South African TV channels are available at the larger hotels that have satellite dishes. The BBC World Service has a relay station near Maseru.

Food and drink

Maize is the staple food of most Basotho. It is usually made into a stiff porridge, *pap*, and eaten with stew twice or even three times a day. It is fairly tasteless but if properly cooked and accompanied by a flavoursome stew it is enjoyable and very filling. Poorer households, however, are generally unable to afford any condiments and eat plain *pap*.

In the mountain areas where wheat is grown, bread forms an important part of the staple diet. The bread is baked in huge saucepans greased with mutton fat over fires – delicious.

Food

As in the rest of southern Africa vegetarians will have a hard time, unless they are addicted to cheese and tomato toasties

There are a couple of very good restaurants in Maseru with international menus. But their versions of traditional Basotho meals do not add much for the additional expense and you are usually better off going to local cafés or street stalls. Outside Maseru most restaurants serve boring but filling Western-style meals. After experiencing excellent high levels of service in restaurants in South Africa, you may find the pace somewhat slower in Lesotho. Rather than complaining, enjoy the more laid back atmosphere.

All the major South African **beers** are available throughout the country and there is also a decent commercial local variety, *Maluti Beer*. Maize beer is brewed by many women as an additional source of income: a white flag (usually made from a faded maize bag) is hung outside the house when this beer is for sale. The beer has a thick, almost porridge-like head, and is usually not enjoyed by visitors, though it is well worth the experience!

South African **wine** can be purchased in Maseru and some of the larger towns but is not widely drunk by Basotho. **Whisky** is also popular and sold at many bars.

Drink

Sport and special interest travel

As all land in Lesotho is theoretically owned 'by the nation' there are very few fences and certainly none outside the densely inhabited lowland towns and villages. This makes walking in Lesotho a unique experience – you can efectively walk anywhere you choose.

The mountains are criss-crossed by numerous footpaths and bridle tracks, but by no means all of them are shown on even the best maps. The physical geography of the country means that most routes consist of long level stretches on either the plateaus tops or valley bottoms interspersed by very steep ascents and descents – this should obviously be borne in mind when planning routes. Maps (1:50,000 and 1:25,000) can be bought from the Department of Lands, Surveys and Physical Planning, PO Box 876, Maseru (on Lerotholi Rd behind the police station). For more practical hints on hiking in Southern Africa's mountain areas, see page 469.

For much of the year the mountain skies are clear and the air crisp. Rain, snow and low cloud can close in very rapidly, however, and you should go equipped for these eventualities. For example, very heavy snowfalls in July 1996 resulted in a number of hikers being trapped in remote areas and having to be rescued by South African military helicopters. The following year there were similar heavy snowfalls as early as May. People planning adventurous hikes should bring equipment with them as it is not readily available in Lesotho.

Some hikers entering Lesotho from South Africa stick to the highest and uninhabited peaks along the Drakensberg escarpment. While these routes cover some of the most beautiful scenery in southern Africa they exclude one of the major joys of hiking in Lesotho; unlike in carefully managed South African wilderness areas you are walking through a landscape where most people are simply going about their day-to-day lives. We highly recommend that you plan routes that include sections in the mountain valleys as well as the high peaks. People in the mountain villages are almost always very pleased to see outsiders and will often offer them places to sleep and food: indeed the hospitality is sometimes overwhelming. You must, therefore, make sure you carry some small gifts to reciprocate this hospitality.

In the past there have been stories about some hikers being attacked by herd boys in the remote mountains. While it is true that some of the herd boys are a fairly lawless bunch, if they are involved in crime it is usually either stock theft or *dagga* (marijuana) growing and dealing (marijuana grows especially well in the mountain valleys and is obviously a potentially very

Hiking

If you want to hike in a challenging but unspoilt and stunning landscape the mountains of Lesotho cannot be too highly recommended

Lesotho

valuable source of income). Many herd boys are actually very lonely and only too pleased for any company, though as they very rarely ever go to school they do not speak any English. Care should be taken, however, when approaching the cattle post where herd boys live; they often have dogs that are trained to go for any unknown passers-by as a guard against stock theft. *Malealea Lodge* and *Semonkong Lodge* (see below) both organize hikes.

Mountain pony trekking The Basotho are renowned as a nation of horsemen, and for generations the strong Basotho pony has been bred as the ideal form of transport in the rugged mountains. A cross between a European full mount and short Javanese horses, the first ponies were captured from the invading Griqua people in the early 1800s. Gentle and extremely sure-footed, they are ideal for people who have not sat on a horse for many years or even at all. Discovering Lesotho on the back of a pony is one of the greatest attractions for visitors. Pony trekking centres have a number of tours that take you wandering through the magnificent scenery, with plenty of stops to enjoy the views. Treks on offer range from 1 hour to 6 days with overnight stops in local villages, mountain lodges, and campsites. Don't expect mad gallops across open spaces, much of the trekking goes up and down steep and rocky mountainsides, where the ponies pick out a route with their feet, often side stepping or following the course of a mountain stream. It is quite extraordinary how these strong little ponies cope with the terrain. This is a highly recommended excursion and gentle way to explore the landscapes of Lesotho. The main pony trekking centres are: *Basotho Pony Trekking Centre*, Molimo Nthuse, Private Bag A82, Maseru 100, T314165/317284; *Malealea Lodge*, PO Box 12118, Brandhof 9324, SA T/F+27-(0)51-4473200, malealea@mweb.co.za (see page 791); and *Semongkong Lodge*, PO Box 243, Ficksburg 9730, South Africa, SA T/F+27-(0)51-9333106 (see page 790).

Trout fishing A popular sport amongst visitors to Lesotho, there are good accessible sites on **Malibamat'so River** near *Oxbow Lodge,* on the Khubelu in Mokhotlong district and the upstream sections of Mokhotlong River itself; on the **Tsoelikane River** in and around Sehlabethebe National Park; and on the **Makhalaneng River** near *Molimo-Nthuse Lodge*. There are also two well-stocked dams near **Thaba Tseka**. There are many other excellent sites, though these are often only accessible via long treks on foot or horseback. During the rainy season rivers tend to be very silty and fishing is badly affected. There is a daily quota of 12 trout over 30 cm imposed on fishermen. Permits and further information about good sites and regulations can be obtained from the *Ministry of Agriculture*, Livestock Division, Private Bag A82, Maseru 100, T323896, beyond the old airfield on Airport Rd.

Other sports Other outdoor sports such as **hang gliding** and **kayaking** are possible for the experienced, but no organized facilities exist within Lesotho.

Holidays and festivals

New Year's Day, Moshoeshoe's Day (11 Mar), Good Friday, Easter Monday, Heroe's Day (4 Apr), Workers' Day (1 May), King's Birthday (17 Jul), Ascension Day, Morija Arts and Cultural Festival (1 Oct), Independence Day (4 Oct), Christmas Day and Boxing Day.

Health

See also health section on page 65 Its high altitude makes Lesotho a healthier place than many African countries. Malaria is non-existent and other tropical diseases are rare. There are, nevertheless, many health risks that visitors need to consider. Water-borne microbes often cause **diarrhoea** and care should be taken to boil or purify drinking water. As livestock and herd boys are often found in even the highest areas great care should be taken in using water from mountain streams. In the rural areas milk is often un-pasteurized so tea and coffee is served with boiled milk – if it isn't boiled, take it black.

Across southern Africa recent years have seen an epidemic of **tuberculosis**. Lesotho has suffered from this epidemic, especially as the disease is often associated with mine workers. **AIDS** is also a big problem. Blood products and medical equipment in the main hospital should be safe, but in smaller clinics there are no guarantees. If you plan to travel to remote areas, take a sterilized medical pack but make sure it is clearly marked with an official hospital stamp to avoid suspicion of intravenous drug use.

Some visitors to the **highest mountain areas** may feel short of breath, tired and even dizzy, especially if they arrive via Sani Pass from the coast. If you are not particularly fit take the first couple of days in the mountains easy.

Maseru

Maseru must be one of the world's sleepiest capital cities – though in comparison to the rest of the country life here seems almost frantic. The city centre sprawls along the Clarendon River and most of the important shops, offices, hotels and restaurants are located along one long central street, called Kingsway. This main road is choked with minibus taxis and people milling in and out of the various offices, many of the buildings are unfinished and in a perpetual state of incompleteness, but it is a good place for a wander. Basotho people are outstandingly friendly, and it's not uncommon for people to approach you in the street simply to ask how you are and where you come from. Unlike many South African city centres where safety is in question, Maseru is a pleasant place to walk around in and to appreciate the vibrant African city street atmosphere. Approaching from the rural farmland on the South African side, the city centre appears unexpectedly and even the newer tower blocks look pretty behind the numerous trees of the more affluent suburbs above the river. In the other direction the city sprawls for mile upon mile of poorer, often unplanned, suburbs.

Phone code: 266
Colour map 4,
grid B4

Lesotho

Ins and outs

Moshoeshoe I International Airport is 21 km south of Maseru along the Main South Rd. There are buses or taxis to most centres in Lesotho. Buses depart from the **bus station** about 500 m along the Main South Rd from Cathedral Circle, and the **main taxi stand** is on Market St one block from Cathedral Circle where taxis depart randomly to all centres in the country.

Getting there

There is a constant stream of taxis up and down Kingsway from Cathedral Circle down to the Border Post. If you ask for the bus or taxi station you may get taken to the old railway station; rather ask for 'stopo', meaning the main bus and taxi terminals (stop) near Cathedral Circle. See transport section page 782 for more details.

Getting around

The *Lesotho Tourist Board Office* (under *Victoria Hotel*), PO Box 1378, Maseru 100, T312896 or 313760, F310108, ltbhq@ltb.org.is, are very helpful, but do not act as a booking agent. However they are ready with advice and information on accommodation and local tour operators. The *Tourism Office* at the Ministry of Tourism, 7th floor of the New Post Office Building, T323734, can also provide general information, but this is not really a walk-in office and it is necessary to make an appointment in advance. If you are crossing into the country through Maseru Bridge be sure to drop in at the *Maloti Tourist Office* in Ladybrand which also covers Lesotho in its jurisdiction. (See Free State chapter page 677 for details.)

Tourist offices

History and sights

Maseru was founded in 1869 when Lesotho's second colonial leader, Commandant JH Bowker, sited his headquarters at this strategically important site overlooking a good fording point on the Clarendon. Shortly afterwards the first traders were also established, on the site now occupied by the *Lancer's Inn*. In the early years the city grew only very slowly and up to independence in 1966 the city centre underwent few changes. The main street was only tarred when King George VI visited in 1947 (when it was also renamed Kingsway) and by the mid-1960s there were still no buildings over two storeys.

Since then the city has grown rapidly, both in terms of population and urban development. Along central Kingsway there are modern office and shopping buildings with further complexes under construction. Despite the redevelopment a number of buildings have managed to maintain their more attractive original façades. While some of the individual buildings are quite nice as a whole the centre is not especially inspiring and certainly not in the area at the top of Kingsway near Cathedral Circle and around the old pitso ground – now the taxi terminus. However, it is a place where you can stock up on supplies, information and fuel for more adventurous excursions into the mountainous regions.

Despite the city's recent growth it is possible to see most of it on foot

There are very few immediately obvious 'sights' for the visitor to Maseru. There are really no buildings that are of any great architectural significance, though there are a couple which are interesting for historical reasons.

In front of *Lancer's Inn*, on Central Kingsway, is **St John's Church**. Built in 1912 the small church's interior has a number of inscriptions to some of Maseru's more important past residents.

Behind the Lesotho **National Bank Tower** is a park, which houses a statue of **Moshoeshoe I**, the founder of the Basotho nation. It was unveiled in 1976 to mark 10 years of independence. To the north of Kingsway and along Constitution and Parliament roads there are many of the main government departments, usually in colonial sandstone one-storey buildings.

The new **parliament** building is at the far end of Parliament Road and is a fairly impressive modern structure in well-maintained grounds.

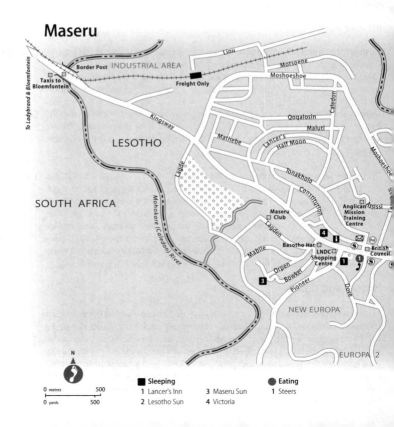

Maseru

Sleeping		Eating
1 Lancer's Inn	3 Maseru Sun	1 Steers
2 Lesotho Sun	4 Victoria	

Lesotho (side margin)

Essentials

B *Lesotho Sun*, off Nightingale Rd, behind *Queen Elizabeth Hospital*, Private Bag A68, T313111, F310104. 194 a/c rooms, 2 bars, casino, slot machines, restaurant, gym, sauna, swimming pool, tennis courts, cinema, some rooms have good views across Maseru. **B** *Maseru Sun*, Orpen Rd, Private Bag A84, T312434, F310158. 115 a/c rooms, slot machines, restaurant, 2 bars, sauna, swimming pool, tennis courts, internet facilities at the office next to the front gate. **B** *Victoria*, Kingsway, PO Box 212, T312922. A/c, 2 bars, nightclub, restaurant, swimming pool (not always open), central location, bars/nightclub popular and noisy. **C-D** *Lancer's Inn*, central Kingsway, Private Bag A216, T312114, F310223. 21 rooms, 2 popular bars, gym, restaurant, relaxed atmosphere. **F** *Phomolong Youth Hostel*, 5 km out of Maseru on Main North Rd. 60 beds, often full, especially during term time, self-catering, hot water rare, not recommended. **F** *Anglican Mission Training Centre*, Assissi Rd, T322900 or 324046. Can sometimes find accommodation for budget travellers, but you need to persevere.

Hotel Victoria, T312992. Hotel dining room, food is of a reasonable standard and service good. *Lancer's Inn*, T312114. Popular restaurant, serving standard and usually boring international dishes, the service is notoriously bad. *Le Haha Grill*, T313111. A la carte restaurant in *Lesotho Sun Hotel*, good food and service, at lunch eat by the pool, popular with Maseru's richer residents, reservations necessary at weekends and public holidays. *China Garden*, LNDC shopping centre, reasonable Chinese food, central location, pleasant, popular early evening bar attached. *Hut*, next door to the *Basotho Hat* craft shop. Over ambitious menu including steaks and seafood, but only open during the day until 1830, safer options are the usual toasted sandwiches and coffees. There are a few South African chain burger and chicken places popping up such as *Steers*, opposite the post office.

There are **street vendors** all along Kingsway and around the taxi station, they sell two main dishes, the staple Basotho meal of stiff maize porridge (pap) and stew, or roasted maize, both are usually very tasty, though the meat is sometimes rather tough.

The main bars are either attached to the big hotels or to restaurants. The small public bar at *Lancer's Inn* is often referred to as the alternative Parliament; it is monopolized by a regular clientèle of (male) civil servants, teachers and lecturers from the National University and newcomers will often be quizzed about their political opinions. The lounge bar has a more relaxed atmosphere, especially for women and there are 2 pool tables; ignore the sign that says the bar is for hotel residents only – everybody else does. The most lively bars in central Maseru are at the *Victoria Hotel*. The bar and beer garden on the first floor is usually packed and noisy, and men will find themselves approached by numerous prostitutes; the bar on the top floor is quieter. There is a dirty and dingy nightclub but it's cheap and keeps going late. The casino at the *Lesotho Sun Hotel* used to be very popular with visiting South Africans, but since the relaxing of the gaming laws in South Africa, they are now able to gamble closer to home and come less frequently.

Entertainment **Cinemas** *Parkway Cinema*, corner of Airport and Parliament roads, but the most up to date films are shown at the cinema in the *Lesotho Sun*.

Shopping Most of the shops in central Maseru are branches of the main South African chain stores and supermarkets and they are mostly in and around the **LNDC Centre** on central Kingsway. The main hotels all have craft or curio shops but inevitably these are very expensive. There are two good craft shops on central Kingsway opposite *Victoria Hotel*, the **Basotho Hat** craft shop (a thatched building in the shape of a Basotho hat) is best known and is a useful landmark. The *Hut Restaurant* is also located here. Both shops have a fairly good selection of local crafts but prices are higher than in smaller towns and rural areas. Mohair, woollen, sheepskin and leather products and jewellery (all important local craft industries) can be bought from a number of workshops and studios around Maseru. Most of these are in the outskirts, with a number in the industrial area near the old railway station. Ask at the Lesotho Tourist Board Office for details (outside here you will find some ladies selling the traditional wicker Basotho hats).

Sports There is little scope for participant sport outside of the facilities provided by the main hotels. Football is played at the National Stadium, near the old airport.

Tour operators The **Lesotho Tourist Board** can recommend a number of operators to areas of scenic, historic or artistic interest within easy reach of Maseru. Unfortunately many of these tours involve spending much of the day in a minibus. The major hotels also organize their own tours. **American Express Travel**, central Kingsway, PO Box 294, Maseru T312554, F310216. Useful for international travel, flight confirmations, but not local tours. **Cimex Travel**, T313111. **Lesotho tours**, T857805. Can provide guides for trips from Maseru. **Maluti Travel**, CHAL House, behind the *Victoria Hotel*, T327172. **Thabo Tours**, T340678, F310275, tours@ thabotours.de English and German speaking local tours.

Transport **Local Car hire**: *Avis* at the *Lesotho Sun*, T314325, and at Moshoeshoe I International Airport, T350328. **Budget**, at the *Maseru Sun*, T316344, and **Hertz** at the *Lesotho Sun*, T314460, F315945. Both of these can arrange pick up and drop off at the airport.

    Taxi: there is a constant stream of taxis up and down Kingsway from Cathedral Circle down to the Border Post. The taxis doing this route will usually have a sign saying 'R/Station' in the window, meaning the old railway station near Maseru Bridge. If you ask for the bus or taxi station you may get taken to the old railway station; rather ask for 'stopo', meaning the main bus and taxi terminals (stop) near Cathedral Circle. As well as the minibus taxi routes there is a conventional taxi service that will take you wherever you want in Maseru, **Moonlight Telephone Taxis**, T312695. Minibus taxis will take you off their set route for a negotiable price as long as they do not have other passengers.

NB *There is an Airport Departure Tax of M20 for all international flights* **Air** Since the liquidation of *Lesotho Air* several years ago, **SA Airlink**, has been operating the route between Moshoeshoe I International Airport and Johannesburg International Airport. The office is at the airport, T350418-9, central reservations, Johannesburg, T011-9781111. Flights to **Johannesburg** depart Mon-Sat at 0825, 1055 and 1725, Sun at 1055 and 1725. Flights to **Lesotho** depart from **Johannesburg** Mon-Sat at 0645, 0915 and 1545, Sun at 0915 and 1545. Flying time is 1 hr. By regional standards flights are not cheap, expect to pay around R1750 one-way.

    Road Bus: Buses depart from the bus station about 500 m along the Main South Rd from Cathedral Circle and **taxis** from the maze of streets around the Pitso ground. Taxis heading north tend to leave from the northern end of the area, near the *Kentucky Fried Chicken*, taxis to the suburbs and surrounding villages leave from the central area, taxis heading towards Roma leave from near the small post office and taxis and buses heading south leave from the Cathedral end of the area. **Taxis**: heading towards **Bloemfontein** and **Ficksburg** in South Africa leave from the South African side of Maseru Bridge border post.

    NB In recent years there have been numerous cases of muggings, sometimes associated with violent assault, in the area around the Cathedral Circle and taxi terminus. During daylight the area is totally safe but it should be avoided after dark; as taxis do not run during the evening there is little reason for most visitors to be in this area after dark in any case.

Banks *Standard Chartered Bank*, *Lesotho National Bank* and *Nedbank* are on central Kingsway. **Directory** The *Lesotho National Bank* charges no commission on forex transactions, but the process takes much longer than at the 2 international banks. Foreign exchange departments are open 0900-1600 Mon-Fri. Credit card withdrawals possible at the ATM of the *Standard Bank*. **Communications** Post Office: New Post Office Building, central Kingsway opposite *Steers*, open Mon-Fri 0800-1430. **Telephone**: it is possible to send and receive faxes at the main Post Office. Local telephone calls and calls to South Africa can be made from the phone boxes outside, but for international calls it is necessary to go to the LTC offices (open Mon-Fri 0830-1430) on Main North Rd, opposite the main taxi terminus. Calls are expensive and during the hours of peak taxi activity it is almost impossible to hear. The main hotels will make international connections but these are even more expensive. **Internet**: available at *Leo Internet Services*, T322772. There is one office next to the *Basotho Hat*, which is open during normal office hours, and another next to the boom gate of the *Maseru Sun*, which also has international phones. Open Mon-Fri 0800-2200, Sat 0900-2200, Sun 1000-2200. Internet speed is painfully slow. **Embassies** Many countries have closed their Maseru missions in recent years as they have opened up embassies in South Africa. Those remaining include: **UK**, T313961, Linare Rd, PO Box 521, Maseru. **USA**, PO Box 333, 254 Kingsway, T312666, F310116. Remaining **Consulates** include: **Germany**, PO Box 75, T314426, F310058. **Ireland**, T314068, 2nd Flr, Christie House, Private Bag A647, Maseru. **Netherlands**, T312144, c/o *Lancer's Inn*, Maseru. **South Africa** (High Commission), 10th Floor, Lesotho Bank Centre, Kingsway, Private Bag A206, Maseru, T315758, F310127; (visa section) T314700, F310270. **Libraries** The *Central Library* is on central Kingsway next to *Standard Chartered Bank*. The staff are helpful and friendly, though unfortunately their stock of books is poor and very dated. **Medical Services** Hospital: *Queen Elizabeth Hospital*, Kingsway, T322501. Is reasonably well-equipped and staffed, but patients with serious illness or injuries will be transported to a South African hospital. **Pharmacies**: *Cathedral Pharmacy*, Main North Rd, near Cathedral Circle, T324351. **Useful services** Police: *Lesotho Mounted Police*, Constitution Rd, between Lerotholi and Palace roads, T124 or 123.

Excursions from Maseru

Roma is about 30 km east of Maseru along the road to Semongkong. It is the site of **Roma** the National University of Lesotho and a large number of churches, presbyteries and *Colour map 4, grid B5* schools. The town itself is little more than a few houses scattered around these institutions in a pretty, wooded valley at the foothills of the Maluti. The University was founded in 1945 by the Catholic Church. It became part of the combined university of Botswana, Lesotho and Swaziland in the 1960s until that institution collapsed and it was brought under the sole control of the Lesotho Ministry of Education. The entrance to the University is on the left as you enter the town from Maseru. Few of the University buildings are of any historical interest but the campus is green and well maintained and visitors are welcome to wander around.

Sleeping and eating **F** *Trading Post Guest House*, PO Box 64, Maseru, T340678, F340630. *Price codes:* Offers comfortable backpackers accommodation in an original sandstone trading post *see inside front cover* building, rondavels, dorms, camping, self-catering or meals by prior arrangement, if arriving from Maseru turn right about 2 km before Roma at the Aids awareness sign. There is not much that Ashley and Jennifer Thorn do not know about Lesotho and many of the sights are within an easy distance from here. Close to local weavers. Recommended. **F** *Roma Roman Catholic Mission*, T340204. Will sometimes accommodate visitors in shared rooms and allow camping in the grounds, if you ask the father in charge nicely and leave a suitable donation. The mission is behind the large Catholic Church on the right about 1 km further on from the University entrance.

Roberto's, restaurant and bar, opposite University entrance. Has a limited but fairly cheap menu, the bar is popular in the evening and a good place to meet students or staff of the University. It is also possible to eat lunch at the *University dining room* which serves one, usually tasty, dish a day.

Chief Moshoeshoe and Thaba Bosiu

Chief Moshoeshoe, often regarded as the founder of the Basotho nation, was born in about 1786 at Menkhoaneng in the north of present day Lesotho. Though he was later to become one of the most powerful chiefs in southern Africa, he was by birth no more than a village headman. According to oral tradition, however, even as a young man he had dreams of becoming a great chief. Fearing that his short temper and overweening ambition would lead him into trouble Moshoeshoe's father sent him for instruction from the famous chief Mohlomi. Mohlomi impressed on the young Moshoeshoe the need for a ruler to gain loyalty from his followers not just through violence but by ensuring they were materially reliant upon his protection.

Moshoeshoe learnt his lessons well and realized that control of large numbers of cattle was the key to political power. With many cattle he could afford the brideprice needed to marry many wives (eventually over 40) and therefore bind other lineages and clans to his own, and by lending some of his cattle to his supporters he was able to make them materially reliant upon his power. The young Moshoeshoe therefore set about building up his herds by both careful management and raiding his neighbours. His reputation soon grew and with his followers he broke away from his previous clan to establish a new chieftainship on Butha-Buthe mountain.

Through a careful strategic balance of making alliances with stronger chiefs and attacking weaker ones (and raiding their cattle), Moshoeshoe soon built up his power base. He never went into any battle he could risk losing and often managed to buy off enemies with gifts of cattle – sometimes raiding the same herds back if his rival fell upon hard times. Nevertheless the interior of South Africa in the early 19th century was a violent and complex political world and Moshoeshoe came under increasing military pressure from nearby chiefs. Realizing Butha-Buthe was not easy to defend Moshoeshoe sent out his brother to find a new stronghold. He returned with news of a larger flat topped mountain with plenty of water resources two days' journey to the south. In June 1824 Moshoeshoe and his followers set off on the dangerous trek to their new headquarters. Despite coming under attack during the move and losing Moshoeshoe's grandfather to a band of cannibals he and his followers managed to secure themselves in their new stronghold. From this new position Moshoeshoe was able to extend his power and controlled the whole of the Clarendon Valley and a large number of followers.

Later in his reign he came under intense pressure from the new Boer republics and lost much of his kingdom, eventually turning to the British for protection. Nevertheless this remarkable leader had managed to build a powerful and unified kingdom during a time of intense strife and continual conflict out of an initial handful of followers. He died at Thaba Bosiu in 1870.

Transport Buses: the daily bus between Maseru and Semongkong passes through Roma (twice a day at weekends). **Taxi**: taxis to and from Maseru leave throughout the day, but stop soon after dark.

Directory Banks: *Lesotho National Bank*, opposite the main University entrance. Will make foreign transactions, open 0900-1300.

Thaba Bosiu
Colour map 4, grid B4

Thaba Bosiu, 20 km outside Maseru, was the mountain stronghold of the founder of the Basotho nation, Chief Moshoeshoe. It is an isolated and steep sided mountain with a large flat plateau at the top. From this secure defensive position Moshoeshoe was able to launch raids against his neighbours before retreating to safety. He, and many other important Basotho (including King Moshoeshoe II who died a few years ago in a car accident), are buried at the mountain's summit. Not surprisingly it is today regarded as a national monument.

There are a number of pathways up the mountain but visitors usually use the steep Rafutho's Pass. The walls of the defensive wall built by Moshoeshoe's men when they first arrived at the mountain can still be seen. The views are lovely, and nearby is **Qiloane**, a strangely formed mountain, the shape of which is supposed to have inspired the Basotho Hat.

Tour guides can usually be found at the car park at the base of the mountain, most are fairly knowledgeable and will give visitors a fascinating (if not altogether accurate) account of the role of the Thaba Bosiu stronghold and much of Lesotho's early history. The tours usually take about two hours in total and the price will depend on your skills of negotiation.

Some of the guides may offer visitors accommodation and meals in their homes. Unlike most offers of accommodation in Lesotho you will be expected to pay, and a fairly high charge at that.

There are frequent taxis to and from Thaba Bosiu directly from Maseru along a good tarred road. If you are arriving from Roma or the mountain road taxis will drop you off at the junction with the Thaba Bosiu road from where it is fairly easy to pick up a connecting taxi. There is a lodge selling cold drinks and snacks near the bottom of the main path. The main hotels in Maseru organize frequent half-day trips to the mountain, though it is just as easy and cheaper to go under your own steam.

Route north

The main route north out of Maseru is along the well-maintained Main North Road that runs along Lesotho's narrow lowland strip. The countryside on either side of the route is heavily populated and unremarkable, but there are some good views across to the mountains and some interesting smaller towns.

Teyateyaneng

Teyateyaneng, 'TY' as it is referred to, or 'Berea', another local name, was founded as an administrative centre by the British colonial authorities in 1886. Teyateyaneng, meaning 'shifting sands', takes its name from the quicksand in the river that runs past the town.

Colour map 4, grid B5

TY is well-known as an important handicraft centre and this is the primary reason most people visit the town. Traditional Sesotho goods tend to be cheaper than in Maseru and there are well-established centres that are run to ensure that profits return to the artists and not middle-men (see details under Shopping). Other than shopping there is not a huge amount of interest in TY, though it is a pleasant town to have a wander around.

D *Blue Mountain Inn*, PO Box 7, Teyateyaneng (signposted from Main North Rd), T500362. Recently refurbished, 16 rooms, en suite, restaurant, bar, TV in rooms, pleasant gardens, friendly staff, secure parking, will arrange trips to local handicraft centres. **D** *Palace Hotel*, 15 km south of TY on the road to Mateka, T853838, F851395. A modern motel popular as a conference location for businesses from Maseru. Basic en suite rooms with TV, phone, restaurant, bar.

The *Blue Mountain Inn* has a decent restaurant and 2 bars and there are numerous basic cafés and bars around the main road junction of the Main North Rd.

Sleeping & eating
Price codes:
see inside front cover

Helang Basali Handicrafts (on Main North Rd to the south of town centre) is run by a local mission and sells reasonably priced rugs, blankets, tapestries and other handicrafts. Visitors can watch the weaving taking place. *Letlutlo Handicrafts* and *Elleloang Weavers* (opposite *Blue Mountain Inn*) and *Sesotho Design* (near the post office) all sell good quality woven products. About 10 km north of TY on the Main North Rd is *Beadazzeled Jewellery*, selling high quality and beautiful handicrafts, but prices reflect the fact it is a popular tourist stop.

Shopping

Lesotho

Transport There are frequent taxis, leaving from near the main junction, in both directions along the Main North Rd. If you are going to **Hlotse/Leribe** it is usually necessary to change taxis at the junction for Maputsoe where most turn off the Main North Rd for the Ficksburg border crossing.

Directory **Banks** The 3 main banks all have branches in the town centre not far from the *Blue Mountain Inn*.

Leribe (Hlotse)

Colour map 4, grid B5 Hlotse is the administrative centre of Leribe district (and is often also known simply as Leribe). Founded in 1876, it was an important town in the 1880 Gun War. Still to be seen today are the remains of a British fort and a primitive statue of a kneeling British soldier. About 5 km north on the old Botha-Botha road, in the Subeng stream, are three and five-toed dinosaur tracks estimated to be 108-200 million years old. Ask for directions in the village.

Sleeping **D** *Leribe*, PO Box 14, Leribe, town centre, T312922. 33 rooms, en suite, restaurant, bar, TV in
& eating rooms, dilapidated exterior but pleasant inside. **D** *Sekekete*, town centre, T312922. Small but neat en suite rooms, pleasant gardens. Often used for the overflow of the more popular Leribe Hotel but just as adequate. The **F** *Anglican Mission*, will sometimes allow visitors to camp in their grounds, no charge but leave a donation. The *Leribe Hotel* has a passable restaurant and 2 bars. As in all towns in Lesotho there are a number of small cafés scattered around town serving pap and stew.

Shopping The *Leribe Craft Centre*, T400323, on the northern outskirts of the town, sells blankets, baskets, hats and beadwork.

Transport **Road** **Taxis**: to **Botha Bothe** leave throughout the day from the south end of the main street. Taxis towards **Teyateyaneng** and **Maseru** leave from the same area, though passengers usually have to change at **Maputsoe** (where the approach road to the Ficksburg Border crossing turns off from the Main North Rd).

Botha Bothe

Colour map 4, grid A5 Botha Bothe is the most northern town in the lowlands. From here you can either continue north into South Africa or turn east on to the mountain road. Botha Bothe gets its name from the mountain that dominates the town; the name means 'place of lying down' or 'place of security' and it is here that Moshoeshoe had his first **mountain stronghold**. Towering above the town, this is the main attraction. The walk to the top is fairly strenuous but is worth it for the fine views across the town and surrounding countryside. Beyond Botha Bothe, towards Oxbow is the scenic **Moteng Pass**. Travelling northeast, spending much of the journey over 3,000 m, the tightly twisting road climbs up gradients of over 35% and the summit offers excellent views of the authentic Basotho homesteads in the valley below. This is the original 'Roof of Africa' motor rally route that takes place annually at the beginning of summer.

Sleeping **D** *Crocodile Inn*, PO Box 72, Botha Bothe, in southern suburbs of town, signposted from
& eating main road, T460223, F460506. 29 rooms, en suite bathroom and TV, restaurant that will serve good quality Basotho food if requested, 2 bars, pool table, secure parking, camping allowed. **F** *Botha Bothe Youth Hostel*, PO Box 96, Botha Bothe, about 3 km outside town, near St Paul's Mission, ask directions, T460223. 8 beds, basic facilities, communal kitchen.

There are numerous small, cheap eating and drinking places on the main road near the bus stop. There are also lots of street vendors, often selling pretty dreadful 'russian and chips'.

Transport **Road** **Bus**: the bus towards **Oxbow** and **Mokhotlong** leaves from the far side of the petrol station near the main junction. This is a steep bus journey so your nerves need to be up to it. Taxis heading towards **Leribe** and **Maseru** leave from the other end of the main street.

Route south

The main route south from Maseru runs along the southern lowland strip. The mountain escarpment is not as clear in the south and the lowland strip wider. This is one of the main farming regions, but it tends to be drier than further north. There are a number of important urban centres along the route, none of them could be thought of as tourist attractions but there are places of interest in each town.

Morija is the site of Lesotho's oldest church and a well-run museum. The French Protestant missionaries who established the church named the town after **Mount Moriah** in Palestine. Lesotho's first printing press was established here and the village is still an important centre for culture, theology and printing. The **museum** is the only museum in Lesotho, and has a number of important historic and pre-historic exhibits and a well organized archive of personal and church papers. The annual Morija Arts and Cultural Festival takes place here in the first week of October. Concerts, traditional dance, choirs, and horse racing.

Morija/ Matsieng
Colour map 4, grid B4

About 7 km from Morija is the royal family's country home, **Matsieng**. The royal court met at Matsieng more or less throughout the colonial period and, in theory, all decisions taken by the colonial authorities in Maseru had to be agreed to by the monarch. Though the village is of great historical interest there is unfortunately not a great deal to see or anywhere to stay.

Mafeteng

This is the main commercial and administrative centre for the southern lowlands. The name means 'place of Lefeta's people'; Lefeta, meaning 'one who passes by'. There are pleasant views from the town across the lowlands towards the Thaba-Putsoa range of mountains. The **British War Memorial**, erected in memory of members of Cape Mounted Rifles who died during the 'Gun War', is located near St John's Primary School on the road from Mafeteng towards the Van Rooyens border post.

Colour map 4, grid B4

D *Golden Hotel*, PO Box 36, Mafeteng (on main Maseru Rd), T700566, F312922. 16 rooms en suite, restaurant, bar, swimming pool, can organize local tours. **D** *Mafeteng Hotel*, PO Box 109, Mafeteng (in town centre), T700236. 27 rooms en suite, restaurant, 3 bars, swimming pool, slightly run down and can get very noisy at the weekends.

Sleeping & eating

Apart from the 2 hotel restaurants there is *Le Joint Restaurant* in the town centre which serves reasonable and good value meals. There are a large number of street vendors in the town centre and some cafés in the area just to the south. There is a popular open air restaurant and a *Kentucky Fried Chicken* near the taxi terminal.

The bar at the *Hotel Mafeteng* is popular with guests and locals alike, particularly on Fri (pay day) when there is a lively late night disco. There are numerous smaller bars in the area to the south of the town centre.

Bars

There are **buses** and **taxis** to and from Maseru and to and from Mohales Hoek and Moyeni.

Transport

Banks *Standard Chartered*, and *Lesotho National Bank* have branches in the town centre.

Directory

This is a pleasant town named after King Moeshoeshoe's younger bother. There are **San cave paintings** in the cliffs beside the Main South Rd as you enter town from the north, but they are difficult to get to. There are also cave paintings in various caves about 10 km from the Main South Rd up the Maphutseng Valley. Although there is nothing to see, the most interesting story behind this region are the **cannibal caves** 2 km south. Found throughout Lesotho, they are a reminder of *'lifaqane'*, 'the terrible time', when in the 1820s roving bands of warriors fleeing the Zulu attackers prevented farmers from growing crops, and people resorted to cannibalism in order to survive.

Mohales Hoek
Colour map 4, grid B4

Lesotho

Price codes:
see inside front cover

Sleeping and eating C *Mount Maluti Hotel*, PO Box 10, Mohales Hoek, north of town centre, T785224. 35 rooms en suite, restaurant, bars, tennis courts, swimming pool, nice gardens,
one of the better small town hotels, reservations recommended. There are few places to eat
other than the hotel restaurant. There are a couple of cafés and street vendors on Mafoso Rd.

Transport Taxis: leave from either side of Mafoso Rd. People hitchhiking south may find it
easier to get a lift if they first get a taxi about 4 km out of town to the turn off to the
Makhaleng Bridge border post.

Directory Banks: *Standard Bank* is on Mafoso Rd and *Lesotho National Bank* is on Maluti Ring Rd
near the post office.

Moyeni (Quthing)

Colour map 4, grid B5

Moyeni (meaning 'place of the wind') is the administrative centre of Quthing district
(the town itself is often also called Quthing). It was established as an administrative centre by the British in 1877 but was abandoned three years later during the Gun War, being
rebuilt later. It straggles along one main street running uphill from the Main South Road.
The town is in the far south of the lowlands at the point where the Senqu (Orange) River
leaves the mountains and winds out across the flatter central South African plateau.

Sights   There are a number of good sets of **dinosaur footprints** on the river bank on the
northern outskirts of Moyeni. There are also some dinosaur footprints further up
the **Qomoqomong valley** though they are hard to find without a guide. The
Qomoqomong valley is also the home to some of the best preserved **San cave paint-
ings** in Lesotho; follow the small road east out of Moyeni towards the village of
Qomoqomong (where the road ends), the caves are in the hills to the southwest.
There are local children who will act as guides. **Masitise Cave House** is about 5 km
to the west of Moyeni near Masitise Primary School. The cave house was home to the
Rev DF Ellenberger who established a mission in the area in the late 19th century.
There is a small display of objects from that time in the house, but it has not been
well-maintained. Ask at the school and someone will accompany you with the keys.

Sleeping
& eating
Price codes:
see inside front cover

D *Orange River Hotel*, PO Box 37, Moyeni 700, near radio mast, T750252. 16 rooms en suite,
restaurant, bar, good views, has an atmosphere of having seen better days, will organize
guided tours of San paintings and dinosaur footprints. The **F** *The Quthing Merino Stud
Farm*, locally known as the sheep stud, 2½ km from town where the tar road ends, some
rooms with en suite or shared bathrooms, meals on request, quiet with a lovely view.

The *Orange River Hotel* has the town's only restaurant though there are numerous street
vendors and cafés especially around the taxi terminus in lower Moyeni. There are a number
of popular and noisy bars in lower Moyeni.

Transport   **Road**   Buses and taxis towards **Qacha's Nek** and **Mohales Hoek** leave from near the petrol
station in lower Moyeni. Hitchhikers will find it easier to get a lift if they walk the 2 km or so to
the junction of the Main South Rd.

Directory   **Banks**   There is a branch of the *Lesotho National Bank* in upper Moyeni.

Central Mountains

*The central mountain areas are the most accessible highland region from Maseru. The
Lesotho government hopes that the construction of the huge Katse Dam will make this
area an important tourist destination. This is the best area to visit if you want to see the
mountains but do not have the time to travel in the more challenging areas to the north
and less accessible areas to the south.*

There is a new tarred road to the Katse Dam so access is possible for visitors in their own vehicles who do not want to drive on gravel surfaces (though the road is steep with many hairpin bends). There are lots of beautiful walks and pony treks in the valleys and mountains of the area, some ending at lovely waterfalls including the Maletsunyane Falls, the longest single drop falls in southern Africa.

Thaba Tseka

This new town was established in 1980 as the administrative centre for a new mountain district. There have been a large number of aid projects established in and around Thaba Tseka and there are, therefore, a disproportionate number of government and aid organization offices in the town. Because it is a new town there is little of interest in the town itself for visitors, but it is a place through which most visitors to the central mountains will pass.

Colour map 4, grid B5

It is occasionally possible to buy ponies from the centre and trek around the mountain area on your own transport

The official **Basotho Pony stud farm** is to the south of the main town on the road towards Mokhotlong. Though it is not established as a pony trekking centre it is possible to rent ponies and a guide for a few hours and the manager will show you around the farm.

Until very recently there has been no accommodation in this town, but two new lodges with simple overnight rooms are expected to be open soon. **E** *Mashai Guest House*, T853003, and **F** *Mountain Star Lodge*, T900415. Reports are welcome. There is also the **F** *Farmer's Training Centre*, PO Box 125, Thaba Tseka, behind the Police Station in the south of town, T900304/857605. 12 rooms, communal showers and kitchen, often full with students during the week but empty at weekends.

Sleeping & eating

There are numerous small, cheap eating and drinking places in the older section of town on the north side of the stream running through the town.

Road There are 3 roads into Thaba Tseka, one from Leribe via the Katse Dam (tarred as far as the dam), one from Maseru, via the Basotho Pony Project and a badly maintained road from Mokhotlong. There are daily buses to and from **Maseru** and a taxi to and from **Katse Dam**, from where there are buses and taxis to **Leribe**. There is an occasional bus to **Mokhotlong** but without your own transport you will probably have to hitchhike this route.

Transport

Banks The *Lesotho National Bank* has a branch in a trailer in the new town area, opening times seem to vary considerably.

Directory

Katse Dam

The massive **Highlands Water Project**, one of the biggest of its kind in the world, is currently under construction. The first phase of the project, the construction of a huge dam at Katse, has been completed. It is ambitiously claimed to be the second largest in Africa after Ghana's Lake Volta Akosombo Dam. Water from this dam is pumped through a huge tunnel and into the South African river system to help meet the demand of thirsty mines and industry in Gauteng.

Colour map 4, grid B5

The next two phases of the project consist of two more dams further downstream, and the one at Mahole is presently under construction and completion is expected in 2003. Once it is operational, Mahole Dam will double the water supply to South Africa through an interconnecting tunnel into Katse reservoir.

The project has been largely funded by South Africa, which maintains a large degree of control over the project's administration; a consequently has led to many complaints in Lesotho that the project will not benefit local people

The **Lesotho Highlands Development Authority** (LHDA) has stressed tourism development as a major part of the project and has promised the development of water-based recreational facilities, camp sites and new lodges and hotels. At the time of writing the LHDA was in the process of establishing the Ts'ehlanyane Nature Reserve, the Bokong Nature Reserve, both north of the Katse Dam, and the Liphofung Cultural and Historical Site near Oxbow. What will be provided at these places still remains to be seen, but visitors' centres, ablution blocks, tarred access roads, and marked hiking trails are currently under construction, so development looks promising. We would be interested in hearing from anyone who visits these places once they are open to the public. For more information contact the LHDA, T/F460723, www.lhda.org.is

The dam itself is an impressive structure and worth seeing for its own sake and its views. As you enter Katse you will see the modern yellow building with a blue roof of the Lesotho Highlands Development Authority. There is an information officer on duty Mon-Fri, 0800-1700, and he will be happy to talk to you.

Sleeping **D** *Katse Lodge*, is in Katse village, a sprawling ex-construction worker settlement, and provides basic accommodation in what were until recently site managers' rooms.

Maseru-Thaba Tseka Mountain Road

This is a beautiful route through the mountains, crossing the lowlands before ascending the first range of the Maluti Mountains via Bushman's Pass. It is commonly known as the Mountain Road simply because it was the first road into the mountains that could be negotiated by a saloon car.

The *Basotho Pony Project*, PO Box 1027, Maseru, T314165, about 60 km from Maseru (mostly tarred or good gravel road) can arrange **pony treks** of anything from a few hours to a week. It was set up in 1983 as a breeding centre to protect the gene pool of the Basotho pony. There are also pony racing events organized in May each year. There no accommodation at the project but it is possible to camp, there is a toilet and shower but no cooking facilities, otherwise come with the earliest bus from Maseru.

From the village of **Nazareth** there is a walk of 7 km to **Ha Barona**, the site of some good **San cave paintings**. Local children are often willing to act as a guides.

Semongkong

Colour map 54 grid B5 This small town historically had a reputation for being a secret hideout of outlaws. It is of interest mainly because of the nearby **Maletsunyane Falls**. Semongkong means 'place of smoke' and was so named because of these falls. Under normal conditions, the journey from Maseru (120 km) is about 2½ hours, a four-wheel drive vehicle is not vital. However, most people visit these falls on a pony trek from *Semongkong Lodge* or *Malealea Lodge*. There is broad range of outdoor activities on offer here, weather permitting. You can walk, follow motorbike trails, watch birds, go trout fishing – or do nothing.

Sights Though the volume of water is usually small, the **Maletsunyane Falls** are very
At 192 m these falls are impressive and drop into a huge gorge that winds through the mountains for many
the highest single drop kilometres. Part of the attraction is that there are absolutely no tourist facilities
falls in southern Africa around the falls. They are about 4 km south of Semongkong, it is possible to drive part of the way but the walk from Semongkong is easy and pleasant. They are best seen during the late rainy season when they are full. At the end of very dry periods they are often reduced to little more than a trickle and occasionally in winter they freeze, forming spectacular ice pinnacles. They are also known as the **Lebinhan Falls** after Father Francois Le Binhan, the first European to see them in 1881.

Sleeping **D** *Semongkong Lodge*, Reservations: through a South African contact, PO Box 243,
& eating Ficksburg 9730, South Africa, T/F051-9333106. Double rooms with an en suite bathroom, for
Price codes: a little less guests can have a double room, but share the bathroom. There are also some fam-
see inside front cover ily rooms which can sleep up to 4, with or without an en suite bathroom, self-catering kitchen, all recently refurbished. **F** *Campsite & Dormitory*, 20 beds in the 'bunkhouse' dorm, shared bathrooms, 10 rondavels, clean, à la carte restaurant, bar, well-equipped communal kitchen, barbecue pits, gas braai, plenty of hot water (unless pipes freeze in which case boiling water provided in kitchen), pool table. After a visit to the waterfalls the next major

attraction is to go and explore the surrounding countryside on horseback. The lodge offers a variety of packages from a day ride for a single person to a 5-day safari with a group of 5, prices vary depending on group size and length of trek. If you have prior knowledge of the area you can make up your own route – the final price includes the services of a pack horse, guide and any special requirements. The overnight rides are quite strenuous and involving 6-7 hrs riding each day but they can be attempted by novices. Accommodation is in Basotho huts along the way, equipped with cooking equipment. Pack horses are also available for hire to hikers. The more popular sites visited include the unusual spiral cactuses on top of Mt Qong, the Ketane Falls, and various gorges away from it all.

Apart from the lodge restaurant there are a couple of bars near the main bus stop which also serve meals.

Road The gravel road to Semongkong is fairly good except for the last 10 km or so. There **Transport** are daily buses to and from **Maseru** (twice daily at weekends), the timetable is flexible but buses usually leave Maseru at about 0700 and the journey takes about 4 hrs. If you just miss the bus in Maseru it is worth catching a taxi to Roma which will inevitably overtake the slow moving bus. If you miss the daily bus at the Semongkong end ask about lifts at the bar next to the bus stop.

Malealea

This popular pony trekking and hiking centre is in the foothills of the Thaba Putsoa *Colour map 4, grid B4* range. There are **San rock paintings**, isolated waterfalls, cool rock pools ideal for swimming and peaceful hikes in the surrounding mountains. This is a real opportunity to appreciate fully the clean, fresh mountain air and rural life. Most budget travellers end up here and for good reason.

If you only go to one place in Lesotho, make it Malealea Lodge

D-E *Malealea Lodge*, T27-51-4473200, F27-51-4473100, T082-5524215 (mob), 7 km east of **Sleeping** the B40, PO Box 12118, Brandhof, 9324, Bloemfontein, malealea@mweb.co.za A collection of *Price codes:* en suite rooms, self-catering rondavels, and dorms in the old farmhouse, will provide full board *see inside front cover* if sufficient notice given, camping allowed in grounds, honesty bar, general store, lovely surroundings, built around old trading post, established in 1905. A lovely place to stay in a friendly village that you are welcome to wander through and meet the charming Basotho people.

The owners of the *Malealea Lodge*, Mike and Di who were born in Lesotho, can organize pony **Local tours** treks, no experience necessary, hikes or 4-wheel drive vehicles to all the local sites. These include day treks to the **Botsoela Waterfalls** and **Pitseng Gorge** and rock pools plus 1, 2, 3 or 5 night treks to the **Ribaneng** (2 days), **Ketane** (4 days) and **Maletsunyane** waterfalls, the 3 highest in Lesotho. This is one of the best places to visit if you are keen on pony trekking. Treks are priced on a daily basis, expect to pay in the region of M135 per person for day treks, and R185 per person for small groups on overnight treks, prices come down for a larger group.

You will spend on average 7 hrs riding each day, be prepared for some sore backsides. If riding is not your scene then there are plenty of walks in the area, these take you to some beautiful natural features as well as remote mountain villages. Once again ask at *Malealea Lodge* for advice on routes and sights. Mike and Di can also arrange informal performances by the village youth choir, which is a real treat.

Road *Malealea Lodge* is about 7 km down a decent track to the east of the road marked B40 **Transport** on the map. The road goes over the spectacular **Gate of Paradise Pass**, an escarpment that opens out to a broad panorama over the plains below, dotted with Basotho villages. In the spring the sides of the road are covered in flowering alpine plants.

Bus: there is a daily bus between Malealea and Mafeteng (leaving at about 0600 in both directions). If travelling from Maseru you can intercept the bus at Motsekuoa where the B40 turns off from the Main South Rd (about 10 km south of Morija); this obviously involves setting out early from Maseru. If travelling from Mohales Hoek or if you miss the bus at Motsekuoa you can catch one of the taxis going along the road marked B40 on most maps

National Dress of Lesotho

As the Basotho people are one of the few African tribes living in a mountainous environment, they have had to make adaptations to their living conditions. The Basotho blanket is one example. Most people in the rural areas wear colourful blankets attached at the shoulder by giant pins to form a sort of coat to provide warmth and keep the rain off. These are usually worn with

well-patched gumboots, essential in the cool mountain climate. However, neither garment is produced locally. The gumboots come from South Africa, and the blankets are mostly imported from the textile regions of England around Leicester and Coventry. Lesotho's national dress has developed simply out of necessity rather than tradition; they are worn to keep one warm.

(though not on signposts). **Taxi**: some taxis go all the way to *Malealea Lodge*. If none of these are running get dropped off at the Malealea turn off (about 25 km from the Main South Rd) and walk or hitchhike the last 7 km.

Shuttle *Naval Hill Backpackers*, T082-5796509 (mob), in Bloemfontein, and *Amphitheatre Backpackers*, T036-4386106 (on the *Baz Bus* route) at Oliviershoek Pass in the Northern Drakensberg, offer regular shuttle services directly to and from Malealea lodge. See under the Free State and KwaZulu Natal chapters for details.

Southern Mountains

The southern mountain area is dominated by the Senqu or Orange River Valley that winds through the area, to the north of the area between steep cliffs but further south in a wider valley.

Mount Moorosi
Colour map 4, grid B5

This is an important historical site. In the mid-19th century it was the home of the Chief of the Baphuthi clan (Moorosi) who carried out numerous raids against white settlers in nearby areas. After the British made Moyeni the district capital in 1877 they tried to subdue Moorosi by taking his son captive, but Moorosi resisted and managed to free his son. The British then spent over two years trying to eliminate the threat of Moorosi, eventually succeeding in capturing his mountain stronghold and massacring him and about 500 of his followers, including many children. Nearby to the village is Letsie Lake, a reeded wetlands area that attracts waterbirds. A wildlife conservation project has recently been set up here involving the local people in the protection of the bearded vulture.

Sleeping and eating There is no official accommodation in Mount Moorosi, but, as elsewhere in Lesotho, it should be possible to find somewhere to stay by simply asking around and camping is permitted throughout the valley. There is a good café next to the *Mitchell Brothers' Trading Store*.

This is the last assured place to get fuel before Qacha's Nek, 130 km

Transport There are fairly frequent taxis running the route between Moyeni and Mount Moorosi and the daily bus between Moyeni and Qacha's Nek passes through the town. The road towards Qacha's Nek becomes very challenging beyond Mount Moorosi. The steepest sections of the road are still tarred as far as Mphaki, after which the tar ends and the road becomes gravel.

Qacha's Nek

Colour map 4, grid B5
Population: 64,000

This border town at the southeastern corner of Lesotho is on the only road pass from the southern mountain area into South Africa's Eastern Cape. Its location means that, unlike most of the country, there are residents from a number of southern

African tribal groups and visitors are as likely to hear Xhosa being spoken in the street as Sesotho. *Qacha*, meaning hideaway, was the name of a local 19th-century chief who was apparently able to disappear into the mountains for months at a time. The British established an administrative centre at the location in an attempt to maintain control of this region which had a reputation of lawlessness. This is one of the few regions of Lesotho that is heavily forested and of particular interest are the Giant California Redwood trees that exceed 25 m and are over 50 years old.

D *Nthatuoa Hotel*, PO Box 167, Qacha's Nek, near the airfield, T950260. Recommended. 18 rooms en suite, restaurant, bar, can arrange pony treks or trout fishing, camping in grounds, reservations necessary. **D** *Qacha Nek Guest House*, T950224. Small secure guest rooms in the centre of town. **F** *St Joseph's Mission*, in a wooded valley to the north of the town centre. The father will allow visitors to camp in the grounds or stay in one of the outbuildings.

    The *Nthatuoa Hotel* dining room has a varied menu and a good reputation, reservations often needed. There are a number of smaller cafés selling cheap and filling meals near the bus and taxi terminal.

Sleeping & eating

Air Given Qacha's Nek's distance from the main towns and the poor roads, air travel is a popular form of transport and the airfield has a tarred runway and is relatively busy. There are no scheduled flights but it is possible to pay for a seat on one of the many charter flights that operate between here and **Maseru**, weather permitting. Ask at the airfield for information on flights. **Road** **Bus**: there are daily buses between Qacha's Nek and both **Moyeni** and **Sehlabethebe**. The drive to Qacha Nek border post is very steep and winding and recommended for 4x4s only. Visitors without their own transport wanting to cross into **South Africa** will have to walk across the border and then hitchhike.

Transport

Banks There is a branch of the *Lesotho National Bank* on the western outskirts of town.

Directory

Sehlabethebe National Park

Lesotho's only national park is isolated, inaccessible and rugged and this is its main attraction, particularly for self-sufficient South African holiday makers in their 4x4s. It is situated in the far east of Lesotho on the border with South Africa and has more than 6,500 ha of sub alpine grasslands and the average elevation is 2,400 m. There is little large game, except for the occasional hardy eland or baboon, but plenty of birdlife including the rare bearded vulture and black eagle. There is excellent trout fishing and the park is also home to the **water lily of the Sehlabethebe** and the tiny **Maluti minnow**, a flower and fish both thought to be extinct for many years. The park was gazetted in 1970. The Prime Minister of the time, Leabua Jonathan, loved trout fishing, which may explain the park's existence. The park lodge used to be called Jonathan's Lodge, and when he stayed all the other guests had to leave. Jonathan's successors haven't been fishing enthusiasts so you are now unlikely to be disturbed.

Colour map 4, grid B6

Getting there There are 2 routes into the park, one via Sehlabethebe village and one across the border from South Africa. Access to Sehlabethebe village is either from **Qacha's Nek** about 100 km to the southwest or from **Thaba Tseka** about 120 km to the northwest. Both roads are difficult, but the route from Thaba Tseka is especially challenging. There is usually a daily bus from Qacha's Nek and it is possible to hitchhike from Thaba Tseka but expect long waits between lifts as there is little traffic. The route from South Africa is possible on foot or horse only; the path crosses the border at **Nkonkoana Gate** and then heads down to the South African border post at **Bushman's Nek**. Sehlabethebe Lodge is a 10 km walk or ride from Bushman's Nek. It is possible to arrange to do the journey on horseback. If you are going down you can arrange it at the lodge, but if you are going up from the South African side you need to arrange for the horses to meet you at the bottom through Lesotho National Parks in Maseru, T323600, at least a week in advance.

Ins & outs

Lesotho

Sleeping
Price codes:
see inside front cover

E *Sehlabethebe Lodge*, c/o Lesotho National Park, Ministry of Agriculture, PO Box 92, Maseru, T323600. 5 rooms, communal showers, toilets and kitchen, a little faded but well looked after and clean, horse riding available. Camping is allowed but you have to get a permit from the park reception. There is no food available and very little in Sehlabethebe village, so bring your own supplies. **F** *The Range Management Education Centre*, in Sehlabethebe village. Offers dormitory beds if you arrive too late to walk the 11 km to the park lodge, meals available.

Northern Mountains

Commonly referred to as 'The Roof of Africa', the northern mountains are the highest, harshest and most inaccessible in southern Africa. The high mountain tops have a harsh beauty, unpopulated except for the occasional herd boy during summer. In winter the peaks are frequently under snow. There is one main road that runs across the area, from Botha Bothe to Sani Pass, the highest road in all of Africa. This road has recently been upgraded which has helped make the whole area much more accessible.

Oxbow
Colour map 4, grid A5

This is the centre of the southern African ski industry. This may sound grand but it actually consists of one lodge that happens to have an ancient collection of skis for hire. Hardy skiers still pitch up here occasionally but there are no ski lifts or facilities. However, this may change soon as the skiing concession is up for tender and it is hoped that an international company will move in and build a resort, which will enhance the tourism opportunities in this region.

This is the last petrol
stop until Mokhotlong
(about 115 km on
poor roads)

Sleeping C *Oxbow Lodge*, PO Box 43, Maputsoe, T27-51-9332247 (South Africa). 16 rooms, restaurant, great bar overlooking the river, camping allowed in grounds, skiing equipment, pony trekking, guides and trout-fishing arranged, popular especially when there is snow, so make reservations in advance.

Leiseng Le Trai

Leiseng Le Trai consists of a small cluster of huts housing a community of people who make a living from mining for diamonds in the waste tips of a now abandoned **Anglo-American diamond mine**. It is a wild lawless place high in the mountains and conjures up images of the 'Wild West'. Prospectors will try to sell diamonds to visitors; these are very cheap but, unless you really know what you are doing, you are very likely to be ripped off, ie, you'll be buying broken beer bottles or bits of quartz. The diamond selling is illegal and buyers run many risks. **Don't be tempted**.

About 2 km walk east of the main village along the original airstrip, is the abandoned mine, a huge grey hole. Most diamond prospecting goes on in the stream beds down the hill from the mine; it is a fascinating sight. There is a small bar in the village, but it is rough and ready and not the sort of place many visitors would want to spend time in.

Mokhotlong

Colour map 4, grid B6
Population: 75,000

The road between Oxbow and Mokhotlong (114 km) snakes and twists higher until almost at the half way point it reaches the Tlaeeng Pass. The summit of the highest road in Africa is 3,275 m above sea level. As you can imagine, the views here are truly outstanding. Mokhotlong Town or Camp is one of Lesotho's remotest towns and is the administrative and economic centre of the northern mountain area. The town's name means 'the place of the bald ibis', and these birds can still be seen along the river and in the surrounding valleys. The town was established as a police post in 1905 and grew as a trading centre supplied by pack ponies coming over the Drakensberg from KwaZulu Natal. Until the 1950s it had no road connection with the outside world.

There is little of great interest in the town itself, but it retains something of an isolated outpost atmosphere with plenty of interesting characters arriving by horse or on foot from the surrounding villages. An interesting sight is the Basotho in their striking blankets, hitching their horses outside and entering the modern computerized bank to do their banking! It is, however, the logical place from which to start exploring the remote valleys and high mountains of this area. The main supply stores are either near the bank or next to the airfield. There is a petrol station opposite the bank.

Sleeping & eating

E *Mokhotlong Hotel*, PO Box 13, Mokhotlong, T920212, at the eastern end of the main road. 16 rooms en suite, bar, restaurant, dilapidated, but one of the only options. **D** *Senqu Hotel*, PO Box 23, Mokhotlong (on left hand side of road as you enter town from west), T920330. 10 rooms en suite, restaurant, bar, clean, can arrange pony treks or guides. **F** *Farmers Training Centre*, past the *Mokhotlong Hotel*. Rooms with 3 beds, linen supplied, cold showers.

The *Senqu Hotel* has a reasonable restaurant with a fairly varied menu. There are a large number of small eating and drinking houses and street vendors along the main street, selling mutton stew and *pap* or the delicious local brown bread with a hot sauce; this heavy moist bread is highly recommended and almost constitutes a meal in itself.

Transport

Air There used to be several charter airlines that had regular flights between Mokhotlong and Maseru, but since the road has been upgraded this no longer seems to be the case. It still maybe worth inquiring at the airfield.

Road The road from Mokhotlong on to **Sani Pass** is very poor and should only be attempted by 4-wheel drive vehicles. It is a spectacular road that winds over the Black Mountain pass (3,240 m) then down to the Sani Flats and Sani Top village. Travellers without their own transport should find it fairly easy to hitch a lift over Sani Pass into South Africa (see pages 492 and 494). **Taxi**: there is a daily taxi from the Lesotho Border Post to **Molhakhe** in South Africa (the turn-off for Sani Pass Hotel). It leaves at 0700 when the border post opens. From Molhakhe there is a very slow local bus to **Underberg**, **Himeville** and **Pietermaritzburg**. There is also a regular minibus service from *Sani Lodge* backpackers hostel on the South African side, to Pietermaritzburg. **Bus**: there is a twice daily bus to and from **Botha Bothe**, one usually departs at about 0800 and one a few hours later, but the timetable is very flexible. There is also a slightly more expensive, but much faster, taxi service, that sometimes does the route. A bus also occasionally does the route from Mokhotlong to **Thaba Tseka**, but there is no guarantee that it will be running. There are trucks and pick-ups so hitchhiking is possible. The road is poor.

Directory

Banks *Lesotho National Bank* on the north side of the main street, foreign exchange transactions. **Communications** Next to the police station is the post office and LTC Office. Local and international calls can be made from the LTC Office, but the lines are very bad. **Useful services** Police: the *Lesotho Mounted Police* is at the east end of the main street, near the large radio mast.

Sani Pass

Colour map 4, grid B6

This torturous steep cork-screwing road is the only road pass from the northern mountains into South Africa and is only open to 4x4s. The views across the mountains of KwaZulu Natal are awe inspiring. The Sani Pass was originally a bridle track for pack horses and was opened to vehicular transport in the 1950s. About 12 km from Sani Pass is the highest mountain in southern Africa, Thabana-Ntlenyana (3482 m). There are some beautiful walks in this rugged area, for details of hikes see page 492.

Sleeping
Price codes:
see inside front cover

C *Sani Top Chalet*, c/o *Himeville Arms Hotel*, PO Box 105, Himeville 4583, South Africa, T033-7021158, T082-7151131 (mob). 8 rooms, camping possible, hot water, bar, communal kitchens, 10-bed backpacker dorm with kitchen equipment, skiing equipment available, pony treks and guides can be arranged, very popular, especially during snowy weather, book well in advance during winter. Stop here for a celebratory drink even if not staying as it claims to be the highest pub in Africa and the views down the valley to KwaZulu Natal are awe-inspiring. On the South African side, 18 km down the escarpment you will find **B** *Sani Pass Hotel*, T/F033-7021320, and the excellent backpackers, **F** *Sani Lodge Backpackers*,

Lesotho

T033-7020330, run by Russell and Simone. This is a relaxing base from which to explore the mountains and they operate 4x4 tours up Sani Pass so it is possible just to go up for the day from the South African side to experience the monumental views. Recommended.

Background

History

This brief section is not a history of all Basotho, but rather of the separate Basotho state. As the history of Lesotho is so tied up in that of South Africa, you should also refer to that section (see page 752).

The rise of the Basotho state The roots of modern day Lesotho were in the era of intense political upheaval known to the Basotho as the *difaqane* (and the Zulu and Xhosa as the *mfecane*). The exact causes of the *difaqane* are a subject of considerable debate (see pages 735 and 735) but what is clear is that out of this intense upheaval a new and powerful Basotho state was forged under the influential ruler Moshoeshoe. Before this time there had not been such a thing as a Basotho state, but simply a whole set of clans speaking similar dialects and with similar cultural practices. These clans formed constantly shifting sets of loose alliances and rivalries and their fortunes tended to wax and wane over time.

During the early 19th century these clans came under attack from highly organized and militarily ruthless Zulu and Ndebele armies (*impis*). Instead of uniting against these new enemies most clans ended up attacking their neighbours in an attempt to raid back cattle and grain lost to the *impis*. Moshoeshoe, chief of the insignificant Koena clan, however, had a more sophisticated approach. He carefully sued for peace with all the more powerful clans or marauding *impis* with whom he came into contact and would send them tribute gifts of cattle. At the same time he attacked and stole the cattle of weaker clans and then invited them to join with him in a new alliance. Using this strategy, Moshoeshoe was able to build up the power and influence of the Koena clan, especially after moving his headquarters to the strong defensive position at Thaba Boisiu (see box on page 784). Soon his influence spread over the whole of the southern highveld with his chiefdom centred on the fertile Clarendon Valley. Unlike Shaka and Dingane, kings of the Zulu, Moshoeshoe did not insist that all his followers give up their previous clan identity and indeed his new Basotho state was more an alliance of a number of different clans than a united and centralized kingdom.

Wars with the Free State During the 1830s two new forces entered into the Basotho sphere from the south and west: Voortrekkers leaving the Cape Colony in search of new territory (see page 735); and missionaries looking for converts. Both these groups offered both threats and opportunities for the new Basotho state. The first missionaries to arrive in Lesotho were French Protestants. Moshoeshoe was keen to have them in Lesotho, partially because he wanted to learn more about the powerful Europeans impinging more and more on his state and partially to help him gain access to European guns. Their presence also presented a threat, however, as the converts' loyalty could sometimes be divided.

A more obvious threat came from the Voortrekkers. They wanted land and, unlike other new African arrivals, were unwilling to show allegiance to a Basotho state. With their guns and wagons they were a powerful military force and over the next 30 years slowly gained more and more control over areas formerly belonging to the Basotho. By the end of the 1860s the Basotho had lost half of their best arable land in the Clarendon Valley to the new Voortrekker Free State republic. But despite this major setback the Voortrekkers also provided the Basotho with an opportunity. Most were unable or unwilling to survive by farming, instead relying on hunting, trading and land speculating as their economic mainstay. They, therefore, had to buy food, especially grain, and the Basotho were able to provide them with it. Using new techniques, often learnt from the missionaries, and the new grain crop maize, brought by Europeans from the Americas, the Basotho developed a

Sotho: what's in a name?

Lesotho is one of the few countries in Africa in which the vast majority of people belong to the same ethnic ('tribal') group: the Basotho. Many people in South Africa will talk about 'the Sotho' but in Lesotho you will rarely hear the phrase: rather people will use the word

Basotho, meaning 'the Sotho people'. The singular of Basotho is Mosotho, Sesotho is the language spoken by the Basotho and Lesotho means the place, or home, of the Basotho. Today there are as many Basotho living in South Africa as in Lesotho.

thriving agricultural economy. They soon began to trade not just with the Voortrekkers but also further afield, especially with the eastern districts of the Cape Colony. In exchange for grain the Basotho bought new European goods, especially guns.

Moshoeshoe realized, however, that their booming economy did not make them immune to attack from the Free State and he decided to turn to the British for help. At first the British refused to become involved but over time they began to realize that it was in their interests to have peace between the Boers and Basotho. In 1868, with Voortrekker commandos laying siege to Thaba Bosiu and burning acres of the Basotho's maize, the British declared Lesotho a British Protectorate. At a peace convention the following year the boundaries of Lesotho, or 'Basutoland' as the British named the area, were firmly established. The Basotho had lost huge swathes of their territory to the Free State but British protection did allow them to maintain a degree of political independence. This was more or less the last big political manoeuvre by Moshoeshoe, who died just two years later.

British Protection & the Gun War

At first the sole concern of the British was to maintain peace along the new boundaries, but that changed when administration was handed over from direct British rule to rule by the Cape Colony. The Cape Colony began to intervene in a more direct way in the government of the country. Chiefs found their powers reduced and everybody found themselves subject to a new hut tax. Not surprisingly, many Basotho were unhappy about these new arrangements. There were also tensions between the new Paramount Chief Letsie and his two brothers and also between the main Koena lineage and other clans who had been integrated into the Basotho state. One of these clans, the Phuti in southern Lesotho, refused to recognize the authority of the local Cape magistrate. When the magistrate tried to arrest the son of the Phuti's chief, Moorosi, open conflict broke out. To the disgust of many Basotho, Letsie sided with the Cape Colony and assisted in putting down the rebellion. In November 1879 after months of fighting the Cape forces finally stormed Moorosi's stronghold, slaughtering him and many of his people.

The following year there was another, more serious, outbreak of fighting. The immediate cause was the attempts by the Cape Colony to enforce a general policy of disarming all Basotho. For most Basotho, already unhappy about the way they were being administered and worried about rumours that the south of the country would be opened to white settlement, this was too much. The so-called Gun War of 1880-81 saw the Cape forces verging on the brink of outright defeat and there were numerous bloody battles. Not all chiefs agreed with the war, however, and Letsie himself never publicly supported the attacks on the Cape authorities. Fighting broke out, especially in the north, between elements in favour of the war and those against it. Peace only returned when the British agreed to suspend the policy of enforced disarmament and agree that administration should be taken away from the Cape Colony and returned to rule from London.

Colonial era

The return to British rule also saw a return to the much less interventionist policy, and the country was basically administered through the chiefs, not white magistrates. The British continued with the policy right through until the 1930s and there were few significant political developments. Economically and socially, however, the country changed drastically. The early years of British rule saw the agricultural economy continue to thrive, especially as the new diamond mines at Kimberley gave the Basotho a new and profitable market to serve. Over time, however, these markets became less and less lucrative. The arrival of railways meant that Basotho farmers had to compete with cheap imported grain from places like the USA and Canada. And as time went on, white farmers were also providing more and more competition, especially after they began to receive vast quantities of state subsidies and other assistance. The agricultural economy began to falter and during the first decades of the 20th century the country no longer managed to produce enough food for export and indeed became a major importer. Part of the problem was also the migrant labour system that the Basotho found themselves tied into. Basotho men began to travel to the mines to earn wages to buy European goods and to pay taxes, but as the agricultural economy faltered it became more important for simple survival. This created a vicious cycle, as more Basotho men went to the mines there were fewer of them to help their wives with agriculture which, as a consequence, became less productive.

The early decades of the 20th century also saw the growth of a small but important educated class within Lesotho. They resented the continued political power of the chiefs and, through their Progressive Association, lobbied the British to introduce a more democratic system of administration. Another more radical political organization also began to make a mark. Known as *Lekhotla la Bafo* (Council of Commoners) this group was highly critical of both the British and of the chiefs, who they claimed were corrupt, and conniving with the British to impoverish the Basotho nation. Whilst criticizing the chiefs for their individual actions they strongly supported the institution of chieftainship and advocated a return to pre-colonial systems of government.

One of the key reasons the British never bothered to intervene (and certainly not invest any money) in Lesotho was their belief that the country would at some stage be incorporated into the rest of South Africa. Over time, however, this eventuality became less and less likely, especially with the enactment of increasingly racist segregation legislation in South Africa. The British colonial authorities realized that transferring the country's administration to South Africa would not only encounter stiff opposition in Lesotho but also from the increasing number of people in Britain criticizing the South African government. From the mid-1930s and especially after 1945 the British colonial authorities, therefore, began to take a more active interest in the internal affairs of Lesotho, and even began to invest some capital into development schemes for the country.

The Progressive Association lobbied the British hard for the introduction of a more democratic government, believing that they, the educated élite, should be the country's natural leaders not the chiefs. Starting in the late 1930s, the British started to reform the system of government. These reforms at first had the effect of increasing the power of a few of the most important chiefs, to the detriment of some of the less important ones. This was one of the major causes of an outbreak of 'medicine murders' in which people were killed in order to use parts of their bodies in 'medicines' believed to bring power or protection. A number of the most important chiefs were implicated in these murders, which were seen by many as further proof that the chiefs were incapable of running the country. From the mid-1950s onwards new reforms led to a decrease in all chiefs' political powers and the gradual handing over of the national administration to the developing political parties.

The first of these new political parties was the Basutoland Congress Party (BCP). The BCP had many of its roots in the *Lekhotla la Bafo* organization and strong links with the ANC in South Africa, especially with the 'Africanist' wing of the ANC who later split to form the PAC (see pages 744-752). Not unlike *Lekhotla la Bafo*, which withered away as the BCP grew, the BCP did not call for a return to 'traditional' Basotho political systems but for a new democratic and independent nation. One of the key elements of its platform was strong criticism of the racist South African regime. This stance was opposed by some more conservative elements within the organization and they split to form a rival Basutoland National Party (BNP). The BNP was more traditional in outlook and received substantial support from the Catholic Church. The first elections in the country were held in 1960 to elect members to District Councils who then sent representatives to the National Council. These elections returned BCP candidates around the country, but the turnout was extremely low and women had still not been granted suffrage.

The British colonial authorities entered into wide-ranging discussions with the members of the National Council about writing a new national constitution under which the country would be granted its independence. After numerous wranglings a new constitution, based on the Westminster model, was produced. There would be a directly elected lower house from which the prime minister and cabinet would be chosen and an appointed upper house (Senate) consisting of the most important chiefs. The Senate's powers were limited to delaying legislation. Much to the dismay of the new and young incumbent, Moshoeshoe II, the monarch was to be no more than a ceremonial Head of State. Under this new constitutional framework elections were held in 1965 to form the government to take Lesotho to independence. To the surprise of many these were won by a tiny majority by the BNP. Their leader, Leabua Jonathan, therefore became the country's first Prime Minister and on 4 October 1966 Lesotho became an independent country.

Independence

Most Basotho had high expectations for this new system of government; expectation which the BNP proved incapable of fulfilling. The civil service was dominated by BCP members and the BNP was unwilling to work with them and instead relied on many expatriate workers, including a number from South Africa. The BNP's inability to deliver once in power helped the BCP regroup and in the 1970 elections they won a clear majority, maintaining their urban powerbase and managing to gain widespread support in the mountains as well. To the surprise of just about everyone Leabua Jonathan refused to hand over power, declared a state of emergency and arrested hundreds of BCP supporters. At first it looked as if he would have to come to an agreement with the BCP especially when Britain suspended all aid to Lesotho but as the crisis dragged on and Britain and other countries resumed their aid programmes the BNP's position became stronger.

Under pressure from Britain the BCP split, with some moderates entering into a new national assembly appointed by Jonathan to write a new constitution and others turning to more radical methods. An attempted counter-coup by elements of the BCP in January 1974 was a fiasco and the BNP tightened their grip on power. BCP civil servants were purged and activists arrested or sent into exile. Jonathan concentrated more and more power into his hands and developed many of the state security policies of other dictators. His attitude towards South Africa, however, shifted somewhat unexpectedly. From having been an advocate of close and cordial relations with the Apartheid regime he began to be more and more outspoken in his opposition. He developed close links with the ANC, who were offered support within Lesotho. This stance in turn brought him into confrontation with South Africa and led to attempts by South Africa to destabilize his regime. On the other hand the changed stance gave him increased legitimacy in the eyes of the international community and the government benefited from a generous influx of development aid.

The BCP, meanwhile, tried to build on its links with the PAC and some of their members received guerrilla training at camps in Libya. Elements within the South African security apparatus actively courted members of the BCP and offered them assistance in their attempts to wage a guerrilla war against Jonathan's regime. Some BCP members seemed willing to drink from this poison chalice and during much of the 1980s the country suffered a very low-level guerrilla war. Some members of the military were very unhappy with the situation and in 1986 the South Africans managed to topple Jonathan's government.

At first the new government was a coalition between the military and Moshoeshoe II. Though they promised to hold new elections under a new constitution in the near future things moved very slowly and if anything the new regime was more corrupt than the previous one. Relations soon broke down between the military and Moshoeshoe II, who went into exile. In the early 1990s the military government began to make arrangements for new elections, with the process being spurred on by outbreaks of rioting and by the negotiation process across the border in South Africa. These long awaited elections finally took place in March 1993 and the BCP won a huge majority and every single seat in the national Parliament. Twenty three years after being denied his position the leader of the BCP, Ntsu Mokhehle, at last became Prime Minister.

Modern Lesotho

Politics With the March 1993 election Lesotho returned to a system of parliamentary democracy, suspended in 1970 after Chief Jonathan refused to hand over power to the Basotho Congress Party. Ntsu Mokhele, the leader of the Basotho Congress Party, is the Prime Minister and chairs a Cabinet made up of members of Parliament. In addition to the main elected legislative lower house there is an upper house, with the power to delay and comment upon legislation, made up of the most senior chiefs and a number of appointed members. The monarch again fulfils the largely ceremonial role of Head-of-State, with a limited political role.

Despite sweeping the board in the 1993 election the Basotho Congress Party has failed to build on its strong political position. Many people in the country feel that after so many years in the wilderness the BCP came to power with surprisingly few new policies in the pipeline. The government has failed to deal with the country's many structural economic difficulties and with many issues seems to be simply drifting along with the tide.

Periodic political unrest has continued despite the advent of democratic elections. The most serious was in August 1994 when King Letsie III (who had succeeded his father, Moshoeshoe II, when he was exiled in November 1990) dismissed the BCP government. Though the exact links between this royal coup and the military and the opposition BNP are a little hazy it is clear that Letsie III was not acting on his own. His excuse for declaring the suspension of the government was the allegation that the leader of the BCP, Ntso Mokhele, had entered into talks with neighbouring heads of government to deploy a peace-keeping force because of his fears about political interference from the military. In the ensuing political unrest a number of people were shot dead and many more injured when the police and the military broke up demonstrations against Letsie's actions. Mokhele and the BCP refused to acknowledge that the head-of-state had dismissed their government and, after direct involvement from regional heads-of-government, Letsie III eventually backed down and re-instated the elected government.

Another element in this confused political situation was that Letsie III wanted to abdicate in favour of his father, Moshoeshoe II. Moshoeshoe II had returned to Lesotho shortly before the return to democracy, but had not taken over the throne. Moshoeshoe had fairly wide domestic support and was respected by many individuals in the international development community because of his pronouncements on human rights whilst in exile in the early 1990s (although some of his actions whilst in coalition with the first military government painted a slightly different picture). This popularity explained the reason why the BCP were not altogether keen on seeing him re-instated as King, despite Letsie's actions in August 1994. Nevertheless, in February 1995, after another bout of intense political activity, Letsie did abdicate in favour of his father. Moshoeshoe II's reign on the throne proved to be short-lived, on the 16 January 1996 he was killed in a car accident.

The BCP itself has been plagued by internal political wranglings, which came to a surprising climax in June 1997. Soon after the BCP came to power two tendencies emerged within the party: one became known as the Pressure Group and the other as Majelathoko. The Pressure Group, who saw themselves as more progressive, were led by Molapo Qhobela, whilst the more conservative faction organized itself around Prime Minister Mokhele. The division became wider when Mokhele sidelined Qhobela in both government and the party.

In retaliation, the Pressure Group attempted to remove Mokhele from his position as leader of the BCP, a move that under the 'Westminster system' of government would have also forced him to stand down as Prime Minister. In mid-1997 the Pressure Group seemed to be on the verge of winning this political battle when Mokhele totally outflanked them with a cunning political move. While Mokhele knew there was a good chance that the party as a whole would vote against him he also calculated that he had the support of the majority of BCP members of Parliament. He therefore resigned from the BCP, registered a new political party (the Lesotho Congress of Democrats) – with him as leader, and managed to persuade 40 of the 63 elected BCP parliamentarians to join him in the new party. After a vote of confidence, his position as Prime Minister and a Lesotho Congress of Democrats (LDC) government were both confirmed, and the BCP became the official opposition party. While this move was unprecedented, it did not appear to be unconstitutional.

The other political parties tried to restructure and re-position themselves to contend the 1998 general elections, which were won by the LDC who claimed almost all of the seats. This led to calls of vote rigging by the opposition who called for fresh elections. The government refused and the opposition began a long-running protest outside the King's palace. The Southern African Development Community (SADC) became involved in mediation, but with the military becoming restive, Prime Minister Mosisili, (Mokhehle having retired), appealed to SADC to send in troops to prevent a military coup. South African troops entered Lesotho in September 1998 and encountered stiff resistance from the Lesotho Defence Force. Confusion spread throughout the country as most people did not know exactly what was going on and were under the mistaken impression that South Africa was invading Lesotho. The South African shops in Maseru were looted and a large number of commercial buildings burnt down. Eventually South African and Botswana forces restored order and a long process of trying to bring together the various parties began. An interim council was established to prepare a new electoral system, under which future elections will be processed. SADC troops left Lesotho in May 2000. Given apartheid era tensions, South Africa was uneasy about deploying troops in Lesotho, but the SADC intervention was ultimately successful in helping to maintain political stability. South Africa has set about improving relations with its smaller neighbour, and is keen to emphasize Lesotho's sovereign equality. In 2001 the foreign ministers of Lesotho and South Africa met to begin mapping out a new relationship for the two countries. Elections in Lesotho in 2002 passed peacefully. The ruling LDC swept to victory and there were no signs of the instability that had followed the elections four years earlier.

Culture

Lesotho's population, of just under two million, is made up almost exclusively of Basotho people and Sesotho is the language spoken by the vast majority. There are a few Xhosa speakers in Qacha's Nek district and a handful of Asian and European settlers in the lowland towns. One of the key reasons why there are few non-Basotho settlers in Lesotho is that (officially) all land is owned communally 'by the nation'. Unofficially there is a market in land but it is very difficult for a non-Basotho to own or even lease land.

Population density in the lowlands is very high and the urban sprawl around Maseru merges into neighbouring towns and villages. In contrast the population in the mountain regions is very low and concentrated into the valleys. The high mountain tops are more or less uninhabited with the exception of the occasional herd boy. Over 80% of the population is rural, though the high density of population sometimes makes the rural/urban distinction a little hazy.

The vast majority of **Basotho**, over 80%, would classify themselves as Christians. The Catholic church is the largest and richest church in the country. In the past it received generous external funding, especially from Quebec, and indeed many of its priests were French Canadian. This has, however, dried up in recent years and efforts have been made to localize all the clergy. The Catholic Church was strongly associated with the establishment of the BNP and, though many priests were uneasy with the stance, it rarely voiced opposition to the autocratic regime of Chief Jonathan. The largest Protestant church, the Lesotho Evangelical Church (LEC), has received far less external funding and is much poorer, though its position as the first major autonomous church in Lesotho has given it prestige and strong local support. It was the first major church to ordain women and a growing number of its trainee clergy are female. The LEC frequently criticized the actions of Chief Jonathan and in return its leaders were persecuted by the government and many forced into exile. The Anglican church is also well represented in Lesotho and, as it is a diocese of the South African Anglican structure, it has good external contacts. There are also a large number of smaller churches and spiritualist movements which are receiving growing support, such as the Methodists, Pentacostalists, Zionists and Seventh Day Adventists. Whatever the specific church,

Lesotho

Christianity plays an important part in the lives of most Basotho and the church is a focal point of many communal activities.

As in all societies, however, Christianity in Lesotho co-exists with other (sometimes contrary) beliefs and rituals. Many Basotho continue to include some elements of 'ancestor worship' in their religious practice and there is a strong belief in the power of witchcraft. Initiation ceremonies, including circumcision lodges for young men, still exist in many areas of Lesotho, indeed there is some evidence they have made something of a comeback in recent years.

Land and environment

Geography Lesotho is a small country of 30,350 square km totally surrounded by South Africa. The country is made up of a thin lowland strip along the Clarendon River valley in the west and a high mountain plateau cut into by numerous deep valleys. The lowland strip is in reality part of the great central plateau of southern Africa and hence the lowest altitude in Lesotho is over 1,000 feet above sea level – the highest 'low point' in the world.

The vast majority of the country's rivers drain south and east. The headwaters of the famous Orange River (known as the Senqu in Lesotho) are in the far northwest of the country and its deeply incised valley runs diagonally across the mountain area, eventually flowing into South Africa across the southeastern border. Water is one of the few resources Lesotho has in abundance and, given the growing constraints of water shortages on South Africa's economy, it is a resource that is becoming increasingly valuable. The headwaters of a number of tributaries of the Senqu River are currently being developed in the massive Highlands Water Project to allow water to be transferred to economically important South African river systems. Phase I of the scheme was successfully completed in 1996. The huge weight generated by filling up the dam triggered a number of minor local earth tremors, but these problems now seem to have been overcome. Phase II is due for completion in 2003, when the new Mohale Dam will be filled. Lesotho has few other natural resources. Some diamonds have been discovered but not in profitable quantities and there is little hope of any lucrative mineral deposits.

With the exception of a few willows and fruit trees in sheltered kloofs and government sponsored woodlots, Lesotho is treeless. The lowlands and mountain valleys are planted with maize and, in the higher areas, wheat. The vast majority of the country is given over to communal grazing: the mountain grasses are considered to be some of the best sheep pasture in southern Africa.

Wildlife Lesotho's large mammalian fauna has been decimated by hunting and displaced by agriculture. If you are very lucky you may see an eland in Sehlabethebe National Park or perhaps the occasional baboon or jackal, but there is none of the large game generally associated with southern Africa. There are, however, a number of interesting and unusual bird species, such as the bald ibis, found particularly in Mokhotlong district. The natural flora is dominated by grasses.

Swaziland

15

Swaziland

With an area of just over 17,000 sq km (smaller than the Kruger National Park), Swaziland may be the smallest country in the southern hemisphere but it has myriad African landscapes – all of which can be seen from the top of **Mlembe**, 1,862 m, a mountain on the country's western border. Before independence in 1968, Swaziland was plundered by European gold prospectors in the 19th century but, unlike South Africa, huge fortunes were never really made here and even throughout the colonial period, the government was more or less left in the hands of the royal family. (Today Swaziland remains one of only three monarchies left in Africa.)

On the whole, Swaziland is an accessible country to visit; it has moderate temperatures all year round, you can travel between the highveld and the lowveld in a day, and none of the major sights are more than a two-hour drive away. The tourist industry in Swaziland developed during the Apartheid years when South African tourists left their rather puritanical regime to visit Swaziland's casinos and nightclubs. Unfortunately, as a consequence, the country developed a reputation for seedy sex and gambling holidays, but since the change of government in South Africa, this market has decreased considerably, and thanks to some pioneering conservationists, effective anti-poaching initiatives and animal restocking, Swaziland's **game parks** have improved dramatically in recent years. The Swazi people are friendly and expert **craft makers**, producing a wealth of high quality African curios and compared to South Africa, Swaziland is a country where tribal values, craftsmanship, and royal loyalty have withstood the test of encroaching modernization.

Essentials

Planning your trip

When to go The climate varies between the different geographical regions but all the areas are affected by high summer rainfall. The mountains in the northwest are cooler than the southeast lowveld where temperatures can become swelteringly hot. The coolest time of year is April to September, the high summer temperatures and the rainy season are from October to March.

Tourist information *Ministry of Tourism*, PO Box 2652, Mbabane, Kingdom of Swaziland, T4046420, F4045415. There are 2 tourist information offices, one in the Swazi Plaza at Mbabane, T4042531, and the other at the Ngwenya border, T4424206.

Language The two main languages are **Siswati** and **English**. English is the language used in education and business whilst Parliament works with both languages. English is widely spoken and understood in urban areas, in the more isolated rural areas Siswati is more prevalent.

Before you travel

Visas & immigration Nationals of the following countries do not need a visa: Austria, Belgium, Botswana, Canada, Denmark, France, Germany, Finland, Israel, Ireland, Italy, Kenya, Lesotho, Malawi, Namibia, Netherlands, New Zealand, Norway, Portugal, South Africa, Spain, Switzerland, Sweden, United Kingdom, United States, Zambia and Zimbabwe.

For details of foreign embassies and consulates in Swaziland, see Directory, Mbabane on page 812 Visas are obtainable free of charge on arrival at any of the borders to nationals from Australia and all other countries not listed above. If you wish to stay for more than 60 days you must obtain a Temporary Residence Permit from the Chief Immigration Office, PO Box 372, Mbabane.

Visiting Swaziland for a few days is not a means of extending your South African visa for a further 90 days (the maximum permitted on entry) – you will get the same departure date as was on the original South African visa.

Money

Swaziland's currency is equivalent to the South African Rand Swaziland's currency is the **Lilangeni** (plural **Emalangeni**, E). Travellers' cheques can be changed in Mbabane but the process is very slow. You are better off bringing in cash in the form of South African Rand. Both the Rand and the Emalangeni are accepted currencies just about everywhere. However, you may find old South African coins still being used as legal tender in Swaziland, which are no longer in use back in South Africa.

Make sure you change any Emalangeni back into Rand or other currencies before leaving the country, ask nicely at the service stations on the Swaziland side of the major borders who will usually swap Emalangeni for Rand. Emalangeni is not a convertible currency. There are no restrictions on the import/export of local and foreign currency, and it is not worthwhile changing your Rand into Emalangeni for just a short visit, the Rand is accepted almost everywhere. Travellers' cheques can be changed at the following **banks**: *First National Bank*, *Nedbank*, *Standard Bank*, and *Swaziland Development & Savings*.

Major **credit cards** such as Visa, Mastercard and American Express are accepted in hotels and restaurants. ATMs have been installed in Mbabane and Manzini, credit cards can be used to withdraw cash, either through the machine or from the teller. However, most of the other ATMs around the country do not as yet accept foreign credit cards.

Getting there

See pages 810 and 811 for information on how to get to Swaziland There are 12 border posts in total, 11 of which are with South Africa, Namaacha Border Post in the north west near Hlane is with Mozambique. **NB** Visas for Mozambique are now issued at this border, US$25 or R170. The road on the Swaziland side is fine and the road on the Mozambique side towards Maputo is presently being upgraded, it is now very easy to travel between the two countries. The four principal entry points from South Africa are

Swaziland missions overseas

Canada, 111 Echo Drive Suite, 270 Melaren St, Ottawa, Ontario K2P OM3
Germany, Honorary Consul, 59 Worringer Strasse, D-4 Düsseldorf 1
Italy, Honorary Consul, 262 Via del Carso, Rome, T6-6786481, F6-6796201
Kenya, Swaziland High Commission, Trans-National Plaza, 3rd Flr, Nairobi, T339231, F330540
Mozambique, Swaziland High Commission – Chancery, 608 Av do Zimbabwe, PO Box 4711, Maputo, T492451, F492117
Norway, Honorary Consul, Postboks 5 Okern, 0508 Oslo 5

Republic of South Africa, Infotech Building, 1090 Arcadia St, Hatfield, Pretoria, T021-3425782, F021-3425682; Trade Mission – Johannesburg, T011-4032050
Sweden, Honorary Consul, Munksjo Wood AB, 37 Birger Jarlsgatan, Stockholm S-11145
Switzerland, Honorary Consul, 58 Tal Strasse, Zürich, CH-8039
UK, Swaziland High Commission, 20 Buckingham Gate, London SW1E 6LB, T020-7630 6611, F020-7630 6564
US, Embassy of the Kingdom of Swaziland, 3400 International Drive, Suite 3M, Washington DC 20008, USA, T3626683, F2448059

Swaziland

Swaziland

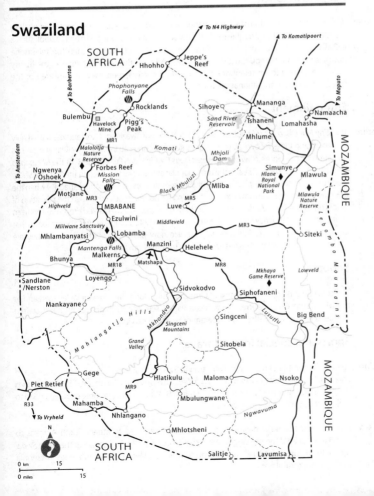

Swaziland

Touching down

Police T42221
Business hours Banks: Monday-Friday
0830-1400, Saturday 0830-1100. **Post**
Offices: Monday-Friday 0800-1600, Saturday
0800-1100. **Shops**: Monday-Friday
0830-1700, Saturday 0830-1300. Some larger

supermarkets are open on Sunday mornings.
IDD code 268
Time GMT +5
Voltage 220-240v
Weights and measures The metric
system is more common than Imperial.

Ngwenya/Oshoek (to Ermelo and the most convenient for Gauteng), the largest and busiest border, open: 0700-2200; **Mahamba** (to Piet Retief in Mpumalanga), open: 0700-2200; **Lavumisa** (KwaZulu Natal and most convenient for Durban), open: 0700-2200; and **Lomahasha/Namaacha**, (Mozambique) open: 0700-2000. Minor entry points tend to have shorter opening hours (eg Bulembu, 0800-1600).

Keeping in touch

Telephone When making a call within the country there are no area codes to remember. Direct dialling for international calls is possible in Mbabane, but in rural areas you will need to book such a call. If you are calling from South Africa the code is (09) (268), and then the telephone number, from the UK you must dial (00) (268) and then the number. While all the luxury hotels have an efficient telephone system, calls are very expensive and they are not the place to make an international call from.

Entertainment

Nightlife The *Why Not Disco & Nightclub* in the Ezulwini Valley is a Swazi institution and has remarkably been pumping tunes for over 25 years, nightly live music and cabaret. Three well-known casinos operate in various places in Swaziland: *Protea Pigg's Peak* in Pigg's Peak (page 814), the *Nhlangano Sun* in Nhlangano (page 823), and the most popular at the *Royal Swazi Sun* in the Ezulwini Valley (page 815). For a touch of sophisticated nightlife these still provide a lot of fun, especially when the favourable exchange rate allows plenty of playing for not too much cost. Since the relaxation of gambling laws in South Africa the casino business has experienced a marked drop in visitors from South Africa, consequently some of the large and lavish hotel complexes will appear somewhat overdone. Although more international tours are now passing through Swaziland, they are unlikely ever to replace the business which used to come from South Africa.

Shopping

The concentration of craft outlets and farm shops are along the Ezulwini Valley road and at the *Mantenga Craft Centre*, which has a varied selection of high-quality hand-crafted clothes, screen prints, leather goods, ceramics, rugs and carvings.

Sports and special interest travel

Fishing There are a number of dams and rivers around Swaziland suitable for fishing trout, bass and tigerfish. Les Deakin at his shop *The Flyfisher*, Coventry Cres, Mbabane, T6031948, issues permits on behalf of the Ministry of Agriculture. **NB** When fishing in some rivers you need to seek permission from the local chief.

Golf courses Part of the major hotel development which was designed to attract South Africans to Swaziland included the building of some superb golf courses. The course at the *Royal Swazi Sun* hotel holds an annual championship, while smaller country club ones present a challenge to most players.

Things to do in Swaziland

- Take a tour with *Swazi Trails*, and try out some adrenaline-pumping white-water rafting, or scary caving tours. You couldn't be in better hands.
- Share a few beers in the bars along the **Malkerns** and **Ezulwini Valleys**, and don't miss the sleazy *Why Not Disco & Night Club* and *If Not Go-Go Bar*, a Swazi institution.
- Shop for **crafts** and support the local economy. Swaziland has an excellent selection of curios and you will be better off buying here than in South Africa.
- Sleep in a traditional Swazi beehive hut in **Mlilwane Wildlife Sanctuary**, and hike, bike, or horse ride amongst the zebra, giraffe, warthog, and wildebeest.
- Be pampered at the *Swazi Spa Health & Beauty Studio* and try out the intriguingly named Cuddle Puddle.

National parks

There are six reserves in Swaziland which are all worth a visit for different reasons, one common factor is that they are the only areas where you will be able to appreciate the landscape in an unspoilt state. Population pressure has meant that most of the countryside has suffered from overgrazing, the felling of indigenous forests for firewood, and in the lowveld large plantations dominate the landscape. Three of the reserves are privately run, the other three are managed by the government.

National Trust Commission, National Museum, PO Box 100, Lobamba, T4161179, F4161875, manage **Malolotja Nature Reserve**, **Mantenga Nature Reserve** and **Mlawula Nature Reserve**.

Big Game Parks, PO Box 311 Malkerns, T5283944/3, F5283924, after hours T4161591-3, reservations@biggame.co.sz, www.biggame.co.sz, manage **Hlane Royal National Park**, **Mlilwane Wildlife Sanctuary** and **Mkhaya Game Reserve**.

Big Game Parks is owned and managed by the Reilly family. With the former King Sobhuza's support, Ted Reilly was instrumental in the gazetting of Swaziland's National Parks and is founder of the Nature Conservation Association. His 37 years crusade has seen former species of large game, that had become extinct in Swaziland, re-introduced to the parks. We heard an interesting story about this formidable man during our research. A few years ago poachers shot and killed a number of rhino in the Swazi parks. Ted Reilly and his team tracked the international poachers, who were armed and had rhino horn in their possession, to one of the *Sun International* hotels in Mbabane. During a scuffle, Ted shot and killed one of the poachers inside the hotel and a further two in the car park. Although Swazi law permits armed response to poaching within the national parks, but it does not cover areas outside of the parks, least of all a private hotel in the capital city. However, the King who in reality is owner of these rhino, and in recognition of Ted Reilly's conservation successes, personally pardoned him and no charges were made against him for the incident.

Whitewater rafting & caving

Operated by *Swazi Trails*, whitewater rafting is offered year-round on the Great Usutu River. With a new stretch of river opened in the remote Bulunga Gorge, a couple of adrenaline-pumping Grade IV and V rapids are a feature on what is on average a Grade III stretch of river. Two-man rafts are used, shepherded by guides in kayaks. All equipment is provided as well as safety and technique instruction. During winter months the day is split into half-day rafting and half-day abseiling, where a 15 m high cliff alongside the Bulunga Falls is negotiated using mountaineering techniques. A picnic lunch and sundowner drinks are included. Trips normally depart from Matenga Craft Centre with pick-ups from most hostels and hotels.

Swazi Trails also run 4-6-hour guided **caving** excursions to the largely unexplored Gobholo cave system near Mbabane, described by them as a 'crouching, crawling, climbing thing'. The caves are full of bats and pitch black and you are supplied with a protective overall, headlamp, battery pack and helmet. Not for the claustrophobic who is afraid of the dark, but otherwise a fun experience and the evening tour ends with a dip in the *Cuddle Puddle* (see page 815). *Swazi Trails*, T4162180 or T6020261, tours@swazitrails.co.sz

Swaziland

Holidays and festivals

1 January: New Year's Day; Good Friday; Easter Monday; 19 April: King's Birthday; 25 April: National Flag Day; Ascension; 22 July: Public Holiday; August-September: Umhlanga Dance; 6 September: Independence; 25 December: Christmas; December-January: Incwala Day.

Mbabane

Colour map 2, grid C5
Altitude: 1,250 m

Mbabane is a small modern town built on the site of a trading station on the busy route between Mozambique and the Transvaal. After the Boer War the British established their administrative headquarters here and the town grew up around them. The main street is named after Allister Miller, a journalist who moved from Barberton. He founded the Times of Swaziland and helped to deal with the fiasco caused by the concessions (see Background, page 825). But Mbabane never benefited architecturally from these eras. Over the last few decades, development has been in the form of a disorganised collection of unattractive concrete blocks and a snarled traffic system, new shopping malls, hotels and the main business district located around a few streets in the centre of town. But it is a useful place to get things done and close enough to the far more attractive Ezulwini Valley to the south.

Ins and outs

Getting there & around
See page 811 for full transport details

Mbabane is a day's drive from most of South Africa's major cities. **Matsapha Airport** is Swaziland's main airport where all international passenger flights arrive. The airport is 8 km from Manzini and 34 km from Mbabane. Buses, and minibus taxis ply the route between the airport and both towns. No banking exchange facilities at the airport. *Swazi Trails*, T4162180, can arrange airport pickups and transfers throughout Swaziland.

Bus There is an efficient modern service with departures from Mbabane to all major centres in Swaziland. Although most towns can be reached by bus there may only be a couple of buses per day, arrive early at the bus station. Minibus taxis run regular short routes: but the drivers are generally poor, making them very dangerous. Do not use. The South African backpackers bus service, *The Baz Bus*, now includes Swaziland on its route.

Tourist offices *Swaziland Information Office*, Swazi Plaza, T4042531, information on hotels, nature reserves, tours, craft centres and casinos, open Mon-Fri, 0800-1600, Sat, 0800-1300.

Essentials

Sleeping
■ on map
Price codes:
see inside front cover

B *Mountain Inn*, PO Box 223, 2 km out of town on the road to Ezulwini Valley, T4042781, F4045393. 60 rooms, en suite bathrooms, telephone, TV, swimming pool, à la carte restaurant, spectacular views. **C** *City Inn*, Allister Miller St, in city centre,

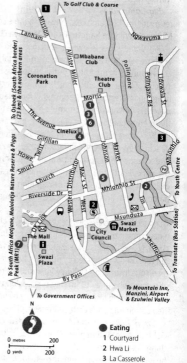

Mbabane

To Golf Club & Course

Sleeping
1 Chillage Backpackers
2 City Inn
3 Thokoza Youth Centre

Eating
1 Courtyard
2 Hwa Li
3 La Casserole
4 Lourenço Marques
5 Marco's Trattoria
6 Mediterranean
7 Phoenix Spur

T4042406, F4045855. 28 rooms, en suite bathroom, some a/c, TV, laundry service, *Pablo's* restaurant. Big difference between the new rooms and the originals in the old part of the hotel. Advisable to look at the room on offer before making your mind up. **C** *Khula Guest House*, Moba St, 3 km from town in an upmarket suburb, T/F4045095. Self-catering units for visiting students, tourists and businessmen, breakfasts available, swimming pool, secure parking. **D** *Kapola Guest House*, T/F4043449, phone Annette for directions, 6 km in a suburb to the west of town, 6 en suite rooms, TV lounge, B&B, secure parking. **F** *The Chillage Backpackers*, 18 Mission St, T404885. 4 Dorms, 1 double room, camping. Décor becomes more pleasing the more stoned you get. Described by one reader as 'a smoker's dream'. Enjoy the cheap, safe accommodation and then check out the rest of the country while your fellow inmates skin up again, they may still be in the same seat on your return. You know the setup. **F** *Thokoza Youth Centre*, Polinjane Rd, T4046682. Basic and clean rooms with locks, some with attached bathroom. Recommended, but often full. A fine alternative if the local backpackers is not your scene.

La Casserole, Omni Centre, Allister Miller St, T4046426. German and cosmopolitan cuisine, fully licensed, pizza oven, outside patio, relaxed charming atmosphere. *Courtyard*, 112 Johnson St, T/F4046213. Courtyard restaurant serving African dishes, the gallery also sells baskets, jewellery and other handicrafts. *Friar Tuck's*, at the *Mountain Inn*, T4042781. Good quality hotel restaurant in a vaulted cellar, great views from the outside tables. *Hwa Li*, Mhlonhlo St, T4045986. Open Mon-Sat, Chinese restaurant, spicy and flavoursome dishes, specialities are spring rolls, spicy soups and chow mein, very popular, takeaway service available. *Valentino's*, Swazi Plaza, T4041729. Lively local bar, frequented by the staff from the shops in the Plaza Centre after work, smoky pool hall. *Lourenço Marques*, corner of Gilfillan and Allister Miller streets, T4043097. Portuguese-style, chicken peri-peri, King and Queen prawns, good wines, continental atmosphere with tables in individual booths. *Marco's Trattoria*, Allister Miller St, T4045029. Italian restaurant, pizza, pasta and grills, upstairs location, fully licensed, friendly atmosphere. *The Mediterranean*, Allister Miller St, T4043212. 'Indian Cuisine', curries, seafood, snacks, fully licensed, good South African and Portuguese wines, takeaway service, all food is Halal. *Phoenix Spur*, The Mall, T4049103. Part of the South African chain, popular family venue, good value meals, large steaks, ribs and choice of salads.

Eating
● *on map*

Curios African Fantasy, The Mall, has a wide selection of curios. Look out for Swazi candles, these are made in the Malkerns Valley and are an excellent souvenir unique to Swaziland. Don't miss a visit to the *Swazi Market*, Msunduza Rd, at the end of Allister Miller St, here you will come across the full range of curios from all over the country, although you will have to haggle for the best bargains. The fruit and vegetable market is here too and is an excellent place to buy fresh guavas, mangoes, litchis and other tropical fruits.

Shopping malls *Swazi Plaza*, *The Mall* and *New Mall*, are all within walking distance of each other on OK Link Rd. They are large, covered, modern malls with department stores, banks, chemists, travel agents, cafés and restaurants.

Shopping
There are plenty of craft stalls in Swaziland, but if you don't want to bargain beside the road then there are several outlets in the capital

Air *Royal Swazi National Airways*, T4042672, fly to **Johannesburg**, daily return flights, 2 on Thu; and **Maputo**, return flights on Tue, Wed, Sat and Sun. *Steffen Air Charter Service/Swazi Express*, Matsapha Airport, T5186848, F3636531. Daily scheduled flights between **Swaziland**, **Durban** and **Maputo**. *SA Airlink*, reservations South Africa, T011-9781111. Fly 4 times a day between **Johannesburg** and **Matsapha**.

Charter Airlines: *Scan Air Charter*, Matsapha Airport, T5184474. A small private operator, which runs flights to/from Swaziland and the luxury lodges on the islands off the coast of Maputo in Mozambique. The following companies fly between South Africa and Swaziland-Matshapa International Airport, most of the departures in South Africa are from Johannesburg-Lanseria Airport, 41 km from Johannesburg centre, T011-6592750, *Executive Aerospace*, T011-3952800; *Million Air Charter*, T011-6592683; *Streamline Air Charter*, T011-2675100. **NB** All the phone numbers are Johannesburg code.

Transport
There is an airport departure tax, E20

Swaziland

See the Baz Bus timetable on page 831

Road 635 km to **Durban**, 370 to **Johannesburg**, 235 km to **Maputo (Mozambique)**, 425 km to **Pretoria**. **Bus**: the South African backpackers bus service, *Baz Bus*, T021-4392323, info@bazbus.com, www.bazbus.com, now includes Swaziland on its route. The bus departs from **Durban** on Mon, Wed, and Fri, and runs up the coast through **Zululand**, to **Manzini**, arriving at about 1830. The bus then overnights close to **Manzini** (at *Swaziland Backpackers*, T5187225) and continues on to **Malkerns** (*Sondzela Backpackers*), arriving at Mbabane at 0830 the next day. From Mbabane the bus goes to **Nelspruit** (1130-1200) and then to **Johannesburg** and **Pretoria** (1830). The bus also runs 3 times a week from **Pretoria** to **Durban** via Swaziland and **Zululand** – departs Pretoria 0700, Mon, Wed, and Sat – arrives: Mbabane (1645), Manzini (1715), Malkerns (1730 – overnight stop). The *Swazi Trails Shuttle Bus* departs from the *Royal Swazi Sun* (see page 815) at 1700 daily. The service runs through **Lobamba** to *Sondzela Backpackers Lodge*. Call T4-4162180 to arrange for a pickup anywhere along this route. On the return journey the shuttle leaves Sondzela at 0730 for the Mlilwane Rest Camp, Lobamba and Ezulwini.

All of the towns and settlements are within an easy drive of the capital. It only takes 2 hrs to drive from Lavumisa to Mbabane

Car hire: the easiest way to see Swaziland is by car. *Affordable Car Hire*, Mbabane Plaza, T4049136/7. *Avis*, Matsapha Airport Office, T5186266, F5186227; *Imperial Car Rental*, Matsapha Airport Office, T5184393, F5184396, Mbabane Office (at Engen petrol, Main Rd), T/F4040459. It is also possible to drive South African hire cars in the country as long as you have a covering letter from the company you hired the car from, so remember to mention that you plan to take the car into Swaziland when you hire it.

Directory

It may be easier contacting embassies in South Africa, check under Directory, Pretoria, for a full listing of countries in the region

Embassies & consulates *Austria*, PO Box 3340, Manzini, T5054368. *Denmark & Norway*, PO Box 815, Sokhamlilo Building, Johnson St, T4043547, F4043548. *France*, Coca Cola Swaziland, PO Box 2040, Manzini, T5185053, F5184538. *Germany*, PO Box 1507, Dhlan'ubeka House, Tin and Mhlonhlo streets, T4043174. *Italy*, 219 Tenbergen St, Manzini, T5052436. *Mozambique*, PO Box 1212, Alister Miller St, T4043700. *Portuguese Consulate*, Portuguese Club, OK Rd, T4046780. *South Africa*, New Mall, OK Rd, T4044651-4. *UK*, Lilunga House, Gilfillan St, T4042581, F4042585. *USA*, PO Box 199, Central Bank Building, Warner St, T4046441, F4045959. **Medical Services** Chemists: *Philani*, Swazi Plaza, T4046460. *Mbabane*, Allister Miller St, T4042817. Hospitals: *Mbabane Clinic Service*, T4042423. *Mbabane Government Hospital*, T4042111. **Useful services** Police: T4042221.

Northern districts

Mbabane to South Africa

The only settlement of note between Mbabane and the border is **Motjane**, where the MR1 branches north to Malolotja Nature Reserve and Pigg's Peak. This is a good centre for curio items. The **Ngwenya glass factory**, 5 km before the border, T4424053, is a popular stop-off point for coach parties. All the items for sale are made from 100% recycled glass. A kilometre or so on the road behind the glass factory is **Endlotane Studios**, T4424196, a varied collection of crafts from mohair tapestries, to rugs, wall hangings, paintings, woodcrafts, and pottery.

Tourist information for the whole country is available at this border post

The border with South Africa is at **Ngwenya/Oshoek**, 23 km from Mbabane (open daily, 0700-2200). Close to the border post are numerous curio stalls, only really worth a glance if you are leaving Swaziland. There are plenty of similar stalls throughout the country. Buses to the capital and the rest of the country depart from Ngwenya.

The road north from Motjane is the MR1, 9 km along this road is the small **Hawane Nature Reserve** and dam. As the surfaced road heads north it passes through the small settlement of **Forbes Reef**. A general store is the centre of activity here, hidden close by are the remains of a long abandoned gold mine.

Price codes: see inside front cover

Sleeping C-F *Hawane Trails*, T4043375, 9 km from Motjane on the MR1 towards Pigg's Peak. Accommodation is in simple grass hut village close to small dam, Swazi-style meals are included in the rates, we would be interested to hear from anyone who has stayed here.

Malolotja Nature Reserve

Malolotja is a wild region of mountains and forest along the northwestern border with Mpumalanga. This reserve has been designed as a wilderness area where most of the park is only accessible on foot. Mgwayiza, Ngwenya, 1,829 m, and Silotfwane, 1,680 m, are three of Swaziland's highest peaks and the hikes around these ranges cross deep forested ravines, high plateaux and grasslands. Archaeological remains show that this region has been inhabited for thousands of years and the site of the world's oldest mine thought to be 43,000 years old is within the park. The diggings were used to excavate red and black earth possibly for use as pigments.

Colour map 2, grid C5

This is a challenging landscape for hikers with altitudes rising from 615 m to 1,800 m

Getting there From the MR3 there is a turning at Motjane on to the MR1 heading north to Pigg's Peak. The turning into the reserve, easily identified by the collection of curio sellers – look out for some fine soapstone sculptures, is 7 km from the junction of the two roads and the park gates are a further 18 km from the MR1. Be wary of traffic along this road, there are a few precipitous drops and the buses tend to drive down in the middle of the road.

Ins & outs

Best time to visit The weather can change suddenly with rain and fog closing in without warning. The summers here are hot and humid with heavy rains. Winter is warm and dry but the nights can be bitterly cold with occasional frost.

There are chances of seeing blesbok, klipspringer, oribi, zebra and both blue and black wildebeest. The rare plants here include aloes, Barberton and Kaapasche Hoop cycads, proteas, orchids and fever trees. The small herbarium at the main camp has a good collection of unusual plants.

Malolotja is an excellent area for **birdwatching**, over 280 species have been recorded here. There is a breeding colony of the rare bald ibis at the Malolotja Falls which drop an impressive 90 m into the Nkomati River. This is also a site for breeding blue swallows and the blue crane. Other species to look out for are the African fin foot, kurrichane button quail and striped fluff tail. There is a short 25 km network of gravel roads for self-guided **game drives** but the best way to see the park is on foot by going on one of the many **hiking trails**, the longest is 7 km and leads up to the 95 m **Malolotja Falls**. Maps for the overnight hiking trails, information brochures and wildlife lists are all available from the camp office.

Wildlife
The wildlife in Malolotja is not the main attraction, although surplus game from other reserves is gradually being introduced

Reservations: **National Trust Commission**, National Museum, PO Box 100, Lobamba, T4161178, F4161875. Last minute bookings can also be arranged through the Senior Warden, Malolotja Nature Reserve, T4043060. **C** *Log cabins*, 5 self-catering, sleeping 6, fully equipped, set in a beautiful mountain location. Recommended. **F** *Campsite*, the main site has room for 15 tents or caravans, an ablution block and a communal cooking area, firewood available; there are very basic campsites along the hiking trails but you will need to be totally self-sufficient.

Sleeping
*Price codes:
see inside front cover*

Game meat is occasionally for sale at the camp shop, this is excellent for braais

Phophonyane Nature Reserve

On leaving Malolotja Reserve, instead of rushing north to the South African border, look out for a signpost for *Phophonyane Lodge and Reserve* about 15 km after the mountain community of Pigg's Peak. In a country where everywhere you look land is being cleared and put to some use, it is a pleasant change to find large tracts of natural vegetation full of bird and animal life. The precise location of this 500 ha reserve contributes to its unique environment. The lands lie on the middleveld escarpment where there is a dramatic change in the environment over a relatively small area. There is dense riverine forest, home to small mammals such as duiker, bushbuck and the clawless otter. In the mountains, the peace is filled with the sound of waterfalls and more than 200 species of bird. Within the boundaries of the reserve are the **Phophonyane Falls** – some of the best known falls in Swaziland.

This is one of the most beautiful and relatively unspoilt patches of Swazi countryside

You can explore the forest and mountains on foot or by four-wheel drive vehicle. The forest trails lead you to the river and a series of small waterfalls where there are clean rock pools ideal for bathing in during the heat of the day. If you are lucky you may see the elusive forest bird, the Narina Trogon. An artificial swimming pool has been created in the rocks just below the lower Phophonyane Falls. Sitting in the water you have a regal view of the valley below.

Sleeping
Price codes:
see inside front cover

About 3 km off the MR1 is the reserve lodge, a small establishment and reservations are strongly recommended. **B** *Phophonyane Lodge*, PO Box 199, Pigg's Peak, T4371429, F4371319, lungile@phophonyane.co.sz The lodge is designed for peace and privacy and can only accommodate 23 guests. There is a luxury 'top cottage', double-storey thatched cottages, a suite and a safari tented camp. Although each unit is self-catering there is an excellent à la carte restaurant, the *Driftwood* bar has the prime location on a balcony over-looking the river as it flows across the ancient rocks. A few days here will quickly make you forget about the rest of Swaziland and Africa, strongly recommended – far better than the glitzy garish giant hotels in the Ezulwini Valley.

Pigg's Peak
Colour map 2, grid C5

This small town was named after William Pigg, a French gold prospector who came here in 1884. There was a working gold mine here until 1954, although no great fortunes were ever recovered. The ore was processed just below the waterfalls. Another mining operation, which is now presented as a tourist attraction, is **Havelock**, a huge asbestos mine. It is known locally as Bulembu (20 km). This mine is linked with Barberton by an aerial cableway.

Price codes:
see inside front cover

Sleeping B *Protea Pigg's Peak*, PO Box 385, Pigg's Peak, T4371104/5, F4371382. 106 rooms, en suite bathrooms, TV, telephone, great views from every balcony, 2 restaurants – the *Egumeni*, and the *Forest* where pianists add to the atmosphere – swimming pool, tennis courts, squash courts, bowls, horse stables, casino, live entertainment most nights, set in beautiful highlands 10 km northeast of Pigg's Peak. Worth its 5-star rating, book in advance.

Bulembu &
Jeppe's Reef
border posts

From Pigg's Peak the MR20, a dirt road, heads west to the border post at Bulembu. Border times, open daily 0800-1600. There is another scenic route north on a tarred road through Rocklands and Hhohho to the border post at Jeppe's Reef (to Barberton in South Africa). Border times 0800-1800.

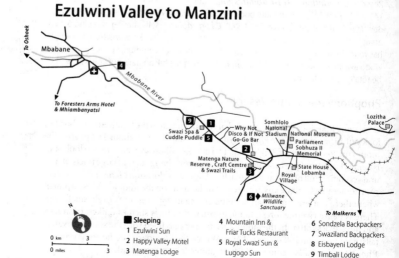

Ezulwini Valley to Manzini

Sleeping
1 Ezulwini Sun
2 Happy Valley Motel
3 Matenga Lodge

4 Mountain Inn &
Friar Tucks Restaurant
5 Royal Swazi Sun &
Lugogo Sun

6 Sondzela Backpackers
7 Swaziland Backpackers
8 Eisbayeni Lodge
9 Timbali Lodge

Ezulwini Valley

Colour map 2, grid C5

Clearly signposted from Mbabane the Ezulwini Valley (the Valley of Heaven) is the centre of most tourist activity in Swaziland. The completion of a double-lane highway between Mbabane and Manzini has greatly improved travel on this road. The tourist route follows the old main road through Ezulwini. Take the fly-off at the bottom of Malagwane Hill. In the daytime there are superb views as you leave the highveld and drop into the middleveld. The valley itself has no real centre, but every few hundred metres you will pass either a smart hotel, craft shop or a restaurant. During the weekend everyone in Swaziland seems to come here to play. The 30 km long valley ends at **Lobamba**, the Royal Village of the King. Just past the Caltex service station at Lobamba is the new entrance to **Mlilwane Wildlife Sanctuary**. Turn right and travel 4 km to Sangweni Gate at eSitjeni.

Swazi Trails end their night time caving excursion here with a midnight swim, beers, and pizza

The **Swazi Spa Health & Beauty Studio**, T4161164, makes an interesting diversion if you are staying in the region. It is a hugely popular resort, mainly for the intriguingly named **Cuddle Puddle**, a swimming pool fed by a hot natural mineral spring, to which tours from hotels and hostels are run at all times of the day and night. The spa is 400 m before the turn off to the *Royal Swazi Sun Hotel*. There are 2 large ladies and gents saunas, 2 indoor hot mineral pools, cold plunge pools, whirl and bubble bath, an aromatherapy steam-tube, and the outside Cuddle Puddle. This place is famous for its Oxygen Multistep Therapy, which we cannot comment on, as we did not try this and quite frankly have no idea what it is, as well as a range of beauty treatments and a gym. If you are on holiday this is a good place to spoil yourself, as the cost of massages, facials and the like, are a fraction to what they probably are at home.

Swaziland

Sleeping

■ on map
Price codes:
see inside front cover

Assuming you have your own car there are plenty of places to enjoy the nightlife and this is not the place to spend a quiet evening in your hotel room. The top end of the price range is dominated by 3 hotels all owned by the Sun Group, these are all next to each other.

AL *Royal Swazi Sun*, T4161001, F4161606. 122 a/c rooms, TV, bar, restaurant, gym, sauna, swimming pool, bowls, squash, tennis, horse riding, golf, *Gigi's* restaurant, casino, every room has magnificent views of the valley and mountains, probably the most luxurious hotel in Swaziland, an amazing contrast to life in the rest of the country, if you have the money this is the place to come and spend it. **A** *Ezulwini Sun*, PO Box 123, T4161201, F4161782. 120 a/c rooms, TV, restaurant, coffee shop, swimming pool, sauna, tennis, horse riding, volleyball, casino next door. **B** *Lugogo Sun*, in the grounds of the *Royal Swazi*, T4161101, F4161111. 202 a/c rooms, restaurant, bar, a large establishment which has set itself up as a popular weekend family venue, frequently caters for conferences and large tour groups, 'Pub Night' on Wed has a live band – you will find many ex-pats and locals from all over the country turning up for the fun. **D-E** *Happy Valley Motel*, T4161061, F4161050. Good value and lots going on, next door to the *Why Not Disco*, and *If Not Go-Go Bar!* There are several restaurants, bars, and nightclubs in and around the motel so it's the place to go if you want to live it up, probably not suitable for children though. Rooms have a/c, fridge, phone, TV, rates include breakfast and entry to the disco and the *Royal Swazi Casino*, ask for special 3-day weekend specials. **C-D** *Mantenga Lodge*, T4161049,

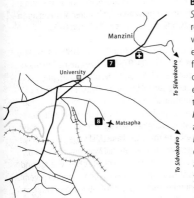

The world's most dangerous road?

The road to Manzini and the Ezulwini Valley from Mbabane has to be one of the world's most dramatic roads. It is very straight and alarmingly steep. Before the recent completion of a double-lane highway, which involved whole sides of the mountain being blasted away, this road was little more than a narrow track going straight down a cliff face. All other traffic had to get out of the way if the royal family's motorcade was going up or down between Mbabane and the Royal Palace in the Ezulwini Valley. It once made a listing in the Guinness Book of World Records as having the highest car accident rate in the world. The father of Ted Reilly, (the man who was instrumental in re-introducing wildlife in Swaziland's parks), owned the first car in Swaziland, a Model T Ford. This road was so steep for the rudimentary car that the only way he could get back up to the top was in reverse.

F4162516. 14 double rooms, restaurant, vegetarians should find something pleasant to eat here, lively bar, swimming pool, sauna, hidden amongst the trees this is a pleasant country hotel next to the Mantenga Craft Centre and in the Mantenga Nature Reserve, with easy access to the Mlilwane Wildlife Sanctuary. **C-F** *Timbali Lodge & Country Park*, PO Box 1, Ezulwini, T09-268-4161156. 9 nicely decorated en suite rooms, fridge, TV, and 3 self-catering family cottages. The campsite has 30 sites and is well-grassed and shady, the best pitches are furthest from the main road and fence. Pool, dinner is served in a boma, braais or a variety of *potjies* (stews cooked in iron pots over the fire). *Joy's Coffee Shop* serves breakfasts and light lunches. Recommended for anyone on a tight budget, popular in all circles, close to the *Royal Swazi Sun*.

Eating *Calabash*, T4161187, close to *Timbali Lodge*. Delicious German and Austrian meals, special Austrian beers on draught, not what you would expect to find in this corner of Africa, a very popular venue, Swaziland's leading à la carte restaurant for the last 20 years, booking advised at weekends. *First Horse*, close to Timbali Lodge, T4161137, an excellent restaurant serving a mix of continental dishes and Indian meals, enjoy a cool beer at the bar before your meal, run by a Swiss chef. *The Sir Loin Steakhouse*, in the *Happy Valley Motel*, T4161061. Late night steakhouse, open until 2am, good atmosphere, booth seating, closed Sun.

Entertainment *Why Not Disco & Night Club*, and *If Not Go-Go Bar* (adult cabaret), T4161061. Don't be put off by the slightly unsavoury reputation, this is an institution in Swaziland and at the weekend many top bands and performers come to put on a show here, good entertainment and a great atmosphere. Open nightly at 2200, live bands/cabaret acts at 2345 and 0100.

Tour operators *Swazi Trails*, Mantenga Craft Centre, PO Box 2197, Mbabane, T4162180, F4161040, tours@swazitrails.co.sz From South Africa phone T011-7041975 for a free international connection. A local tour operator specializing in culture, wildlife and adventure tours, plus a few unique activities. Caving, whitewater rafting, mountain biking, and paragliding. Using minibus combis and small coaches for groups, the company visits most local attractions including Swazi homesteads, a royal homestead where the chief of an area is the host, and clients get to view many of the sustainable craft industries using natural resources plus a visit to the secret caves in the Mdzimba Mountains. There are tours to Hlane, Mlilwane and Mkhaya along with a special historic trail which includes a visit to the National Museum, the Sobhuza Monument and a Swazi village. All the guides are local Swazis with plenty of knowledge and enthusiasm. All of the above-mentioned tours are no more than a day long – tours of several days can be arranged, but then you must remember that all places of interest are within an easy drive of the luxury/tourist hotels along the Ezulwini Valley. Clients will be collected from all hotels and establishments within the Mbabane-Manzini area.

Mlilwane Wildlife Sanctuary

Mlilwane is one of the most popular of Swaziland's nature reserves and covers a varied landscape of highveld and lowveld along a section of the Ezulwini Valley. The land which now makes up the sanctuary was originally used as farmland and for tin mining. The hydraulic sluicing used to mine the tin with high pressure water jets had caused massive damage to the landscape leaving it scarred with ravines. The mine operators had simply abandoned the land after the mine closed leaving a wasteland of slag heaps and open excavations behind.

The land has been regenerated into a wildlife sanctuary where it is now possible to see a wide variety of birds and animal species including: hippo, giraffe, crocodile, eland, zebra, blue wildebeest, blesbuck, kudu, nyala, klipspringer, waterbuck, impala, steenbuck, duiker, warthog, many species of waterfowl and purple-crested lourie, the brilliantly coloured national bird of Swaziland. Mlilwane is ideal for birdwatching and several hides have been specially built overlooking the dams.

Getting there The reserve is signposted from Lobamba. From the turning the new Sangweni gatehouse is 4 km. 24-hr access is available to all the reserve's facilities. **Entrance fee:** R20 per person, which covers the whole length of your stay within the sanctuary. The Interpretorium in the rest camp, the Sangweni Gate complex and the newly opened Craft Centre for Sustainable Resource Use all offer interesting information on nature conservation in Swaziland. **Ins & outs**

There are over 100 km of dirt roads, with some marked for four-wheel drive vehicles only. The wildlife is quite relaxed enabling close viewing and quiet viewpoints, along with the possibility of tranquil sunsets. Alternatives for exploring the sanctuary include guided horse rides, open Land Rover game drives, guided mountain bike rides, all of which depart from the Rest Camp at hourly intervals and an extensive system of self-guided walking trails including the Macobane, Sondzela, Hippo and Mhlambanyatsi Trails. The 8-km Macobane Trail offers an easy gradient and particularly spectacular views of the Ezulwini Valley as it winds its way along the contours of an old aqueduct on the Nyonyane Mountain, 1,136 m. Horse riding, E90 per person per hour. Overnight hikes, E150, overnight mountain biking, E350 and overnight Real Africa Horse Trails, E550. Ask about multi-day horse riding treks to remote rural areas of Swaziland, which were being planned at the time of writing. In all cases a minimum of two people necessary. **Sights**

Mlilwane has 5 different types of accommodation. All have communal self-catering facilities, there is also a restaurant, the *Hippo Haunt*, barbecued game dishes a speciality, open to all guests, the deck of the restaurant overlooks a small pool which is home to a resident hippo that was actually born in London Zoo and relocated here, watch it being fed every afternoon. Rooms must be vacated by 1000 on the day of departure but you may spend the rest of the day in the park. Mlilwane's famous traditional dancing team perform on a nightly basis in *The iNkhundla*, boma in the rest camp. Manned entirely by park staff, who enjoy the aerobic workout, this display is energetic and full of fun. **B** *Reilly's Rock Hilltop Lodge* or '*kaGogo*', this is a new exclusive 6-room period guesthouse, and 4-bed family cottage, recently refurbished and brimming with local history, en suite facilities, fully equipped kitchenette, set in a lush tract of botanical gardens with fabulous views of the game sanctuary. Recommended. **E** *Beehive Village*, thatched huts and dorms, camping ground, self-catering facilities, bedding provided. **E** *Nyonyane Camp*, on the park's eastern periphery, self-catering in wooden cottages. **E** *Rest Camp*, huts with en suite ablutions, B&B. **E-F** *Sondzela Backpackers*, Mlilwane Wildlife Sanctuary, PO Box 311, Malkerns, T5283117, F5283924, can also be booked through the *Big Game* email address (above). The hostel is just inside Mlilwane Wildlife Sanctuary, offering high security and the advantage of easy access to self-guided trails, mountain bikes and horses. Dorms, twin rooms and double rooms, pool, *Hog 'n' Wart* bar, probably the best option for budget travellers in Swaziland. With IYHF standards and a stunning setting overlooking the Nyonyane Mountains the 2 cottages could be mistaken for a luxury lodge. The *Baz Bus*, T021-4392323, from South Africa calls in here 3 days a week

Sleeping
Price codes:
see inside front cover

Reservations for all accommodation through Big Game Parks, PO Box 311 Malkerns, T5283944/3, F5283924, after hours T4161591-3, reservations@ biggame.co.sz

Swaziland

enroute to either Pretoria or Durban. The tour company, *Swazi Trails*, pick up from the hostel for whitewater rafting, caving, and abseiling. There is a community guide who offers daily walking trails around Lobamba and to the nearby Royal Village.

Lobamba At the eastern end of the Ezulwini Valley before the airport is the royal village of Lobamba, set amongst typical open bush countryside. All of the royal buildings are closed to the public, but the Somhlolo National Stadium is the venue for major celebrations, including sports events, musical shows and royal events. On no account try to take any photographs of the **Lozitha Palace**, you will end up in trouble with some rather unpleasant military characters. The parliament buildings are open to visitors but the effort to gain admittance is not worth the tour. Of much greater interest is the **National Museum**, T4161178, which has some excellent displays relating to Swazi life throughout history. If you wish to find out more ask for a guided tour, well worth it for an insight into local life and customs. The offices for the **National Trust Commission** are in the museum, they are responsible for the management of Malolotja, Mantenga, and Mlawula Nature Reserves. Opposite the museum is a memorial to King Sobhuza II and a small museum depicting his life. His statue stands under a domed cover with open arches and an immaculate white tiled floor.

Mantenga Nature Reserve

Close to the *Mantenga Lodge* is an area of outstanding beauty and mature patches of forest. The area between the main road and the Mantenga Falls was recently proclaimed a Nature Reserve. The Little Usutu River flows through the area and the well-known waterfalls are about a 2-km walk away. The first phase of the reserve's development was the creation of an authentic cultural village, and picnic spots and walking trails have been marked out.

Mantenga Cultural Village Every aspect of this 'show' village is based upon traditional methods and materials. This is exactly how a medium-sized Swazi homestead would have looked 100 years ago. There are 16 beehive-shaped huts built from local materials – local trees provided the poles for the framework, dried grasses were used for thatching and ropes, hard earth collected from termite mounds and ant nests was mixed with cow dung to make the floors, tree bark and strips of leather were used to bind all the parts together, and finally reeds were collected from the river beds to act as windbreaks.

At first glance the layout of the huts may appear to be random, but they are in fact laid out in a plan that can be seen throughout rural Swaziland. The huts form a semi-circle partly surrounded by a cattle kraal. The focal point is a larger hut, the 'great hut', and the kraal. This is a polygamous homestead, each wife has her own circle of different huts for cooking, making beer and sleeping in. Slightly separate are the huts for unmarried mature boys and girls and for the married sons.

The whole complex is brought to life by people performing traditional dances and songs as the guides show visitors around the compound. You will also see food being prepared, clothes and household objects being made, and if you are very lucky an authentic marriage ceremony. You are unlikely to be disappointed with a visit to Mantenga Cultural Village. The whole set up is quite informal and you can just turn up at any time. Guides are always available for a small fee, T4161178. The Swazi River Café, is located here, specializing in African dishes, there's late bar, and it's great place for a sundowner on the wooden deck.

Mantenga Craft Centre One of the principal attractions along the Ezulwini Valley road has always been the concentration of curio outlets and farm shops. Over the years the former has evolved into a well-organized and thriving industry. Back in 1974 the Mantenga Foundation was formed to retail the finished works of local artists in the Mantenga Craft Centre, T4161136. From the outset the project has been managed on the basis of long term self-sufficiency. The centre stocks an excellent range of crafts; clothes, screen prints, leather goods, ceramics, rugs and carvings, their T-shirts are worth buying, there are a whole range of concessions under the one roof. There is also a snack bar and a small **tourist information** desk with a selection of brochures.

Shopping *African Fantasy*, collection of T-shirts and sweat shirts with conservation as a central theme, some delightful children's objects. *Little Silver Shop*, T4161136, the opportunity to buy some unique designs in gold and silver, pieces can be made to suit your own tastes, recommended for anyone who appreciates metal work.

In general Swaziland has an excellent selection of curios. You are better off buying them here than in South Africa

Malkerns Valley

About 5 km beyond the National Museum is a right turning for Malkerns, M18. This makes for an enjoyable circuit from Mbabane which can easily be covered on a day trip, although most people choose to stay overnight in Mlilwane Wildlife Sanctuary. Between the junction and Malkerns are a number of roadside shops and farmstalls. The most interesting stop is at *Swazi Candles*, T5283219, only 1 km out of Malkerns. The candles are famous throughout the region, but they are not cheap. If you are on a tight budget there are 'seconds' at a reduced price, it is difficult to see where the flaws lie in most cases. Close by are two other craft shops, *Baobab Batik Shop* and *Gone Rural*. Many of their products are available in Mbabane but here you have a chance to see how they are made and meet some of the artists. At *Gone Rural*, over 600 women work on creating pots and grass matting, the shop upstairs over looks the dyeing procedure. If you are planning on camping or staying at a self-catering complex then you may be tempted to call in at the *Emangweni Farm Shop* where there are some excellent fresh vegetables and fruit.

This is a typical rural Swazi town which has grown up around the pineapple plantations. The town itself can easily be explored on foot, there is a post office and a branch of the *Nedbank*. This is the ideal place to introduce yourself to a more typical Swazi lifestyle than you encounter along the Ezulwini Valley. A meal at the *Mangozeni Restaurant* or a drink in the *Ekuthuleni Bar* will provide you with a few tales to take home. On Friday and Saturday nights one of the best places to be is *Malandela's* restaurant-cum-pub in Malkerns. There is plenty of good food, lots of drinking and a fun time is had by all. This is a typical African party scene and you will meet plenty of local boozers.

Malkerns
All around the settlement the Malkerns Valley is lined with fields full of spiky pineapple plants

The road south from Malkerns towards Bhunya is now tarred and you will frequently encounter groups of schoolchildren, the odd stray donkey and a few cattle. As the road climbs up into the highlands the forest closes in and it can get quite cool out of the sunlight. For part of this route the road follows the Great Usutu River as you pass through rolling farmlands. 26 km from Malkerns is the factory town of Bhunya, the centre of the local timber industry. The local pulp mill is responsible for much of the local pollution. From Bhunya there is a choice of two routes; one road crosses the Lusutfu River and then climbs steeply for 2 km into the coniferous plantations, the road to the South African border (34 km), **Sandlane/Nerston**, open 0800-1800. If you are arriving in Swaziland at this border there are plenty of buses which depart from in front of the church. Hitching may be a problem here. All along this road are numerous lookout towers protecting Swaziland's forests. This is the important **Usutu Forest** which extends for over 65,000 ha. At first sight it is an impressive expanse, but plantations are dead compared to the indigenous forests, there is little birdlife and very little colour in the form of wild flowers or flowering trees.

Bhunya & around

The second road out of Bhunya heads north towards **Mhlambanyatsi** and Mbabane. About 12 km out of Bhunya is the **B** *Forester's Arms*, T4674177, F4674051. This is a delightful hotel set in the cool highlands with a number of pretty waterfalls and surrounded by forest in its own colourful garden, recommended for anyone looking for a quiet retreat and well worth the journey. It has 23 rooms all with en suite bathrooms, restaurant which serves excellent fresh meals and caters for the vegetarian,

Swaziland

cosy pub with log fire, people from all around come here for a meal at the weekend. Swimming pool, sauna, golf course, trout and bass fishing in the local dams, tennis, squash, hiking, horseriding and mountain biking. The road from Mbabane (27 km), is now tarred and it will take less than 30 minutes to reach the capital from here although there is still a great sense of being out in the country.

Central and southern Swaziland

Manzini

Colour map 2, grid C5 This town is an industrial centre with a brewery, a meat processing plant and electronics factories, that attract commuter labourers from the outlying areas. The industrial atmosphere is not desperately pleasant but most of the accommodation options are outside Manzini in the more attractive rural regions. There is little of interest for the visitor but the markets that bring in the local farming communities into town once a week are worth a browse.

Ins & outs Swaziland's main airport, **Matsapha Airport**, is 8 km west of Manzini. There are buses, combis and taxis going to Manzini and Mbabane.

History The first trading station was opened here in 1885 and was originally run from a tent. The plot was later sold on to Alfred Bremer who built a hotel and a shop. Manzini was originally known as Bremersdorp after Alfred Bremer, but it was renamed Manzini after the Boers burnt the settlement to the ground during the Anglo Boer War. The administrative centre then moved to Mbabane. Whilst Swaziland was being administered by a provisional government composed of representatives of the Transvaal, the British government, and the king during 1894, the headquarters were in the local hotel.

Sights The **Bhunu Mall** on Ngwane Street and **The Hub** on Mhlakuzane Street are Manzini's newest shopping centres. **Tiger-City** on Villiers St is a small complex where the cinema and a couple of restaurants are located. The **market** on the corner of Mhlakuvane Street and Mancishane Road takes place on Friday and Saturday mornings. This is one of the busiest local markets in Swaziland selling fresh fruit and vegetables, clothes, a good selection of curios and freshly cooked snacks.

Sleeping C-D *Eisbayeni Lodge*, 8 km from Manzini next to the airport, T5184848, F5184849. Used to be
Price codes a simple roadside bar but has recently extended in new thatched buildings to what is the clos-
see inside front cover est accommodation to Matsapha Airport. Bland but modern en suite rooms with TV, pool, restaurant, several bars with frequent live entertainment, still used to catering for functions and conferences rather than paying attention to individual guests. D *Madonsa Guest House*, signposted off Central Distirbution Rd, T5055725, F5054331. Large modern house, B&B in rather frilly but spacious rooms, some with balconies, pool, evening meals on request, quiet suburb. F *Woza Nawe Hostel/Myxo's Place*, 6 km from town off the Siteki Big Bend Rd, ask for directions to the *Big Surprise Bottle Store*, PO Box 2140, Manzini, T/F5058363, T6044102 (mob). A relatively new hostel, the only one managed by a Swaziland resident, pick-ups/drop-offs from Manzini and Swaziland Backpackers (for the *Baz Bus*), bike hire, live music at the weekend, drumming lessons on request. A great and rare opportunity to really find out about life in the region. Dorms, double rooms and camping. Setup as a traditional Swazi home, including the meals on offer. Two-day trips to Myxo's home village in the mountains can be arranged for around R300, this is a very special rural experience. So far has received good reports from overseas visitors, we hope the place will continue to succeed in this competitive business. F *Swaziland Backpackers*, PO Box 1975, Matsapha, T/F5187225, info@swazilandbackpackers.com Located 12 km out of Manzini on the road to Mbabane, next to the *Salt & Pepper Club*. Dorms, double rooms, email and laundry facilities. Currently the overnight stop for the *Baz Bus* in Swaziland. A well-organized setup, which can provide plenty of local advice and information on

Swaziland and further travel into Mozambique. Easy access to shops, nightlife and restaurants, nightly trips to the *Cuddle Puddle* hot springs, R30.

China Palace, Tiger City, Villeirs St, T5055388. Good value Chinese and take-away. *Fontana di Trevi Pizzeria*, The Hub, corner of Villiers and Mhlakuvane streets, T5053608. *Gil Vicente*, Martin St, T5053874, Ilanga Centre. Portuguese dishes. *Nando's*, The Hub, corner of Villiers and Mhlakuvane streets, T5052330. Portuguese chicken dishes.

The Travel Centre, The Hub, Mhlakuvane St, T5053955, F5053829.

Air Most visitors travel to Mbabane and the Ezulwini Valley directly from **Matsapha Airport**. There are buses, combis and taxis going to Manzini and Mbabane. There is an airport departure tax of E20. *Royal Swazi National Airways*, T4043486, fly to **Johannesburg**, daily return flights, 2 on Thu, and **Maputo**: return flights on Tue, Wed, Sat and Sun. *Steffen Air Charter Service/Swazi Express*, Matsapha Airport, T5186848, F3636531. Daily scheduled flights between Swaziland, **Durban** and **Maputo** (Mozambique). *SA Airlink*, central reservations (Johannesburg), T011-9781111, fly 4 times a day between **Johannesburg** and Matsapha.

Road **Bus**: buses and combis leave from the bus station on Louw St to Mbabane, Big Bend, Lavumisa, Nhlangano and Mahamba. **Car hire**: there are offices at the airport for *Avis*, T5186266 and *Imperial*, T5184393.

Medical services Hospital: *Raleigh Fitkin Hospital*, T5052211.

Hlane Royal National Park

Formerly a royal hunting ground, Hlane was declared a protected area in 1967 by King Sobhuza II. Following heavy poaching in the 1960s, the park has been restocked by the *Big Game Parks*, with wildlife from neighbouring countries as well as species propagated at Mkhaya Game Reserve. At 30,000 ha in extent and the kingdom's largest area, Hlane has been selected for predator reintroductions with healthy numbers of lion, cheetah and leopard already visible, a project supported by the European Union. Today the park supports these big cats as well as elephant, white rhino, herds of wildebeest, and zebra, kudu, steenbuck, bushbuck, giraffe and impala. In the past poaching was a serious problem and the rhino had to have their horns removed for their own protection. Hlane supports the densest population of raptors in the kingdom, with vultures in particular being very visible at kills and waterholes. Birdlife in and around the two camps is also prolific.

Colour map 2, grid C5

Getting there The park is 67 km from Manzini along the road to Simunye, where the main road bisects the park. Turn left into the Ngongoni Gate, where all arrivals need to report. **Entrance fee**: R18 per person. A 2 hr game drive will cost R1,000 per person. Park gates close at sunset, notify in advance if you think your arrival will be after dark.

The western area of the Park is linked with a network of roads which the visitor can use for game viewing, the area around the Black Mbuluzi River attracts animals during the dry winter season. Close to Ndlovu camp is an Endangered Species area, where elephant and rhino have been concentrated for security reasons, the Mahlindza waterhole with its hippo, crocodile and waterbird population is one of the most peaceful picnic sites in the country. Guided game walks can be booked through the park office. The best game viewing walks are in the northern sectors of the reserve.

There are 2 camps in the park, overnight visitors must be fully self-sufficient. Traditional dancing is performed by the staff on request, there is a new open air bar and restaurant at Ndlovu. **D** *Bhubesi Camp*, 6 self-catering cottages, 2 bedrooms, bathroom, kitchenette, bedding and towels provided, electricity, a beautiful setting overlooking the Umbuluzana

Swaziland

River. **D-E** *Ndlovu Camp*, 6 thatched rondavels – 2 large cottages sleeping 8, 3 sleeping 4 and 1 sleeping 2, bedding, towels, cutlery, crockery provided, Ndlovu Camp has no electricity, paraffin lanterns provide light, the fridges are gas powered and cooking is carried out over an open fire, there is a nearby waterhole which is good for game viewing and birdwatching. Reservations for all accommodation are made through *Big Game Parks*, PO Box 311 Malkerns, T5283944/3, F5283924, after hours T4161591-3, reservations@biggame.co.sz Credit cards cannot be used to pay for accommodation. All accommodation must be vacated by 1000 on the day of departure.

Simunye

Colour map 2,
grid C5

Simunye is a small town that is quite unusual in that the centre lies behind the boom gate of the Royal Swazi Sugar Corporation that owns the surrounding sugar plantations, giving the settlement a rather institutional feel. There is nothing much here but it is a stop off en route through Hlane, Mlawula and the border with Mozambique at Lomahasha/Namaacha. The main road to Simunye coming north skirts Hlane Game Sanctuary and there are amusing if not sober signposts telling cyclists and pedestrians to be aware of lion and elephant.

Sleeping
Price codes:
see inside front cover

C-D *Simunye Country Club*, once through the boom gate turn right, T3838600, F3838600. Owned by the Royal Swazi Sugar Corporation, accommodation in a variety of rooms, self-catering houses & flats. Pool, nice restaurant, 3 bars, TV lounge. Tennis, squash, gym available if you pay the nominal temporary membership fee. Accommodation is nothing special but conveniently located, 15-min drive to Mozambique, and 30 mins to South African borders. If you cannot take your vehicle into Mozambique, say a hired car, and have negotiated a lift from here, it is possible to park the car here for a couple of days.

Mlawula Nature Reserve

Colour map 2, grid C5

Mlawula is signposted after Simunye and Hlane. The nature reserve covers an area extending from the Lebombo Mountains down to the lowveld, and is part of the new greater Lubombo Conservancy. The Siphiso Valley and the Mbuluzi Gorge are good areas for game viewing on hiking trails or game drives.

Ins & outs

Getting in Daily entrance charge, E15 per person, E35 per vehicle. For reservations contact: *National Trust Commission*, National Museum, PO Box 100, Lobamba, T4161178, F4161875. Information is also available from The Senior Warden, Mlawula Nature Reserve, PO Box 312, Simunye. There is a leaflet on trails and the reserve available from the camp shop.

Best time to visit Summers are hot and humid with high rainfall, the winters warm and dry although they can be cold at night with the occasional frosts. The best season for birdwatching is between Sep and Oct.

Sights

This is a region of amazing and varied scenery of Lebombo Mountain forest descending to dry thorn savanna and coastal thickets. Over 1,000 species of plant have been identified here although this region is best known for its birdlife as 350 species have been recorded here including African fin foot, crested guinea fowl and yellowspotted nicator. There are good facilities here with the vulture feeding area and the bird hide. The Mbuluzi Gorge is an excellent area for birdwatching but the road is not always in good condition. The game likely to be seen in the reserve includes kudu, oribi, mountain reedbuck, samango monkeys, Sharpe's grysbok and white rhino. The Mbuluzi and Mlawula rivers are good for seeing crocodiles. Many of the animals which are protected here are particularly difficult to spot and include rare species of reptile and amphibian. The interesting plantlife includes the rare Lebombo ironwood and the *encephalartos umeluziensis*, a cycad that only grows in the deep mountain valleys of the reserve.

Early traces of *homo sapiens* dating back 100,000 years have been found in the riverbeds of the Lebombo Mountains, although these are protected archaeological sites, there are plans to lay out a trail in the Timphisini area with an archaeological theme. Visitors to the reserve are encouraged to hike on the new network of trails. More information is available from the camp office at the entrance gate. The trails open up new areas of the reserve passing through beautiful areas of gorges, pools, waterfalls and rapids with views over Mozambique from the top of the escarpment.

E *Sara Camp*, the only accommodation here is 3 tents sleeping 2 people each. You must be totally self-sufficient. **F** *Ndzindza Cottage*, is a trail hut exclusively for the use of hikers. **F** *Siphiso*, is a nearby campsite with an ablution block and cooking facilities, firewood is available from both camps.

Sleeping
Price codes:
see inside front cover

Swaziland

Shewula Nature Reserve

The community-owned Shewula Nature Reserve just north of Mlawula is also part of the Lebombo Conservancy. An interesting new tourist initiative has recently been established here. Shewula is a new reserve established by the local community, straddling the 500-m high Lebombo Mountains on the border with Mozambique and covering an escarpment of ancient ironwood mountain forest stretching down the Mbuluzi River. We hear the views from the Shewula Mountain Camp, which is literally perched on top of a mountain, are incredible, Maputo can be seen to the east, and there is an uninterrupted 100-km view across Swaziland.

Colour map 2, grid C6

The Shewula turnoff is 10 km south of the Lomahasha/Namaacha border with Mozambique, the camp is a 30 mins drive from the turnoff. Apart from during heavy rains (Dec-Feb) it is accessible by 2 wheel drive cars, when the road is too muddy, it is possible to leave your vehicle at the chief's office in the village, and be transported in a 4x4.

Ins & outs

E-F *Shewula Mountain Camp*, reservations are arranged by *Swazi Trails*, T4162180. 4 huts sleeping up to 6 people, camping ground, shared ablution block and kitchen, there is no electricity, but there are gas stoves and fridge, paraffin lamps, hot showers. Bedding is not supplied so you will need a sleeping bag. Traditional meals can be ordered, prepared by local families. Activities include guided nature walks, swimming in the river, cultural tours around the villages, even helping the mountain herd boys driving their cattle to the dip. This sounds like an interactive experience that should be supported, we would be interested to hear reports.

Sleeping
Price codes:
see inside front cover

Manzini to Mahamba

The drive down through Grand Valley passes through beautiful mountain scenery with cliff faces rising above the Mkhondvo River and the forests on either side of the road. The MR9 passes through the village of **Hlatikulu** before reaching **Nhlangano**. The weather here is often misty with drizzle, which for many is a welcome relief to the hot and humid plains.

Grand Valley

This used to be a popular resort with South African tourists who crossed the border to gamble and watch films which were banned at home. Since the end of Apartheid gambling and censorship are not the problems they used to be and the number of South African visitors has fallen sharply. There is a small shopping centre in town and a market. Buses depart from the station next to the mall to Manzini, Mahamba and Lavumisa.

Nhlangano
Colour map 2, grid C5

Sleeping **A-B** *Nhlangano Sun*, 4 km out of town, T2078211, F2078402. 45 chalet-style rooms, TV, restaurant, bar, swimming pool, horse riding, disco, casino, tennis, it will be interesting to see how these hotels survive following the changes in South Africa, to appeal to the broader tourist market they may well have to reduce their prices. **C** *Phumula Farm Guest House*, PO Box 4 Nhlangano, T2079099. B&B, pretty gardens, en suite rooms with TV, dinner on request.

Price codes:
see inside front cover

Mahamba The MR9 continues south to the border at Mahamba, open 0700-2200. The routes into South Africa from here lead to **Piet Retief** in Mpumalanga.

Manzini to Lavumisa

Mkhaya Game Reserve
Colour map 2, grid C5

This small reserve is now one of the best places in Southern Africa to see black rhino. It is Swaziland's most exclusive reserve in an area of acacia lowveld southeast of Manzini. It is an excellent place for game viewing and many species have been re-introduced including black and white rhino, tsessebe, roan, sable and elephant. At present the only large cat you might see is the leopard. The birdlife here is interesting and there are chances of seeing a good number of raptors including bateleur, booted, martial and tawny eagles. The summers here are very hot and humid with potentially heavy thunderstorms, whilst in winter the climate is warm during the day and cool at night.

Getting there Travelling from Mbabane and Ezulwini Valley go through Manzini. 8 km after Manzini take a right turn and continue towards Big Bend, the reserve is signposted to the left after about 44 km. If you are approaching from Durban via the Lavumisa border follow the road to Big Bend and then Siphofaneni, the turning is on the right, 22 km after Big Bend. All visitors are met at the locked gates by a ranger. This is a private reserve and guests must arrange to arrive between 1000 and 1600. Alternatively the rangers will pick you up or drop you off in Phuzamoya at 1000 and 1600.

Information Access only by prior reservation. Reservations for accommodation and day visits are made through *Big Game Parks*, PO Box 311, Malkerns, T5283944/3, F5283924, after hours T4161591-3, reservations@biggame.co.sz, www.biggame.co.sz Day visits, E60 per person entrance fee, and activities: guided walks lasting 3 hrs, R110 per person sharing; guided Land Rover tour, a full day including lunch, R200 per person (minimum 2 people).

Sights Because Mkhaya is a private reserve it can only be visited by prior reservation, either on a day tour between 1000 and 1600 or as an overnight visitor staying at a tented safari camp. Open Land Rover game drives are the main activity, interspersed with the opportunity to take guided bush walks, all promising close contact with a variety of big game. Overnight visitors have the option of early morning drives as well as sundowner excursions, but strangely, the midday drive, in the heat of the day remains the most popular, due to the presence of rhino, buffalo and elephant at the waterholes.

Price codes: see inside front cover

Sleeping Overnight rates include entry, 3 full meals and 3 guided game viewing trips – walking or driving. In addition to the main camp there is a private camping ground – **A** *Stone Camp*, 12 semi-open self-contained stone and thatched cottages shaded by hardwood forest, thatched summerhouse, meals are prepared for you by the camp staff and often include barbecued game, freshly baked bread, fresh salads and South African wines. This is currently the most comfortable game viewing experience in Swaziland, compared to the private reserves in South Africa it represents very good value, although it may seem a bit expensive for some visitors.

Big Bend
Colour map 2, grid C5

Big Bend is named after the loop of the Lusutfu River that passes by the town. The land around Big Bend is covered in sugar plantations and the Ubombo Ranches sugarmill in town is the area's main processing centre. The town is a quiet neatly laid out settlement with a small shopping centre.

Sleeping and eating **C-D** *The Bend Inn*, T3636337, F3636725. 16 a/c rooms, some with en suite bathroom, restaurant, indoor and outdoor bars, TV lounge, swimming pool, snooker. **C-D** *Riverside*, 2 km south of town on the MR25 T3636012, F3636032. 18 rooms, en suite bathroom, restaurant serving Portuguese-style dishes, bar, roof garden, nightclub, swimming pool, motel overlooking Usutu River, private car ports. *Lubombo Lobster*, south of Big Bend off MR25, T3536308. Portuguese-style restaurant with quality seafood meals and wide choice of Portuguese wines. People come from KwaZulu Natal to eat here. Recommended.

Transport Bus: regular departures west to Manzini and Mbabane and south to Lavumisa.

Nisela Safari's, Swaziland's newest private game lodge development is nestled at the foot of the Lebombo Mountains, near the village of Nsoko, 30 km south from Big Bend on the road to the Lavumisa border. This is a small private reserve where game including lion, wilderbeest, giraffe, and zebra has recently been introduced, existing populations of nyala, red and grey duiker, jackal, bushbuck, reedbuck, and steenbok are also present. There are also a number of hand-reared lion cubs to visit near the entrance gate. Day visitors are welcome for a small entry fee, for game drives and walks. *Nisela Safaris*, PO Box 8, Nsoko, T3030318, F3030354, nisela@africaonline.co.sz

Sleeping There is a variety of accommodation here to suit all budgets. Card carrying backpackers (ISAC, YHA), staying in the beehive village, qualify for a discount and get the 4th night free. **B-C** *Game Lodge*, 5 luxury rooms sleeping 2-4. The pool, bar, and restaurant here is used by guests in all the facilities. **C** *Guest House*, 10 rooms in a very pleasant colonial house, B&B. **D-E** *Overland Camp*, 2 4-bed rustic self-catering chalets, 22 km into the bush on a dirt road, only accessible by 4x4. **F** *Beehive Village*, traditional Swazi grass huts with 4 beds, shared ablution block and kitchen. Also available is the **F** *Campsite*.

*Price codes:
see inside front cover*

Lavumisa is a busy border post which most travellers pass through on their way to Big Bend or into KwaZulu Natal. There is one main street lined with snack bars and petrol stations. The border is open from 0700-2200. The bus station is on the main street and buses regularly depart for Big Bend, Manzini and Mbabane. The road that runs the entire length of Swaziland from Lavumisa border to Lomahasha border with Mozambique is due to be upgraded to a highway. It is intended that this will be the main truck route from the port in Durban all the way through to Maputo in Mozambique. It will be a shame to see the expected increase in heavy traffic ploughing through the Swazi countryside, but this development appears to be inevitable.

Background

History

The precolonial history of Swaziland started with the Dlamini clan in the late 16th century when they migrated south settling in the region around what is now Delagoa Bay. Approximately two centuries later, in 1750, Ngwane III migrated to what is now Swaziland. The land was a well-watered mountain area with fertile soils and good pastures for raising cattle. The mountainous territory also offered good protection from Zulu raids.

By the 19th century, Swaziland had become a major power in the region controlling a much larger area than it does today. Europeans arrived in 1836, and called the place Swaziland after the leader at the time Mswasi II. After gold was discovered at Pigg's Peak and Forbes' Reef, large numbers of foreigners were attracted to the area and pressure for land concessions increased. The 'concession rush' occurred during the reign of Mbandeni when speculators believed there was about to be a great boom in Swaziland. Five hundred concessions were eventually granted on which the king received a payment. When the gold rush ended without any great results most of the concessionaires left the country.

The Transvaal administered Swaziland from 1894-1903. After the Anglo Boer War the British took control of the country leaving the traditional forms of government in the hands of the royal family. One of the country's major problems was that most of the land had been granted to foreigners in concessions. The Swazis believed that the concessions were only temporary but a government commission recognized the concessions as valid as long as the rents continued to be paid. In 1907 a third of the land under concession was expropriated to give the Swazis somewhere to live. Sobhuza II, the grandson of Mbandeni, became king in 1921 and spent his resources on regaining the land for the Swazi nation. Over 60% of the land has now been bought back from the concession holders.

Political activity in modern Swaziland began in the 1960s with the formation of the Swaziland Progressive Party by younger educated Swazis. The party later split into three factions of which the Ngwane National Liberatory Congress (NNLC), became the most influential. Swazi royalists formed the Imbokodvo National Movement in 1964. They formed an alliance with the European Advisory Council which had been established to look after the interests of European farmers and miners. The elections held before independence in 1964 were won by Imbokodvo who controlled all the seats.

Modern Swaziland

Politics Swaziland became independent in 1968 and although the constitution guaranteed a parliamentary system when the NNLC won three seats in the 1972 election the Swazi royal family dissolved parliament and banned all political parties. Since then political opponents have regularly been imprisoned and until 1993 attempts to reintroduce a parliamentary constitution have failed. The government is now headed by the king, who is assisted by the Prime Minister; there are two legislative houses, the Senate and the House of Assembly. Non-party elections were held in September and October 1993, and the power of the king has been slightly reduced. A Constitutional Review Commission was appointed by King Mswati in 1996 and while Swazis were promised that the new constitution would contain a bill of rights, it was assumed that power would remain in the hands of the king. Labour unions, banned political parties and human rights organisations boycotted the Commission's work, arguing that it was undemocratic and open to manipulation by the authorities. In the absence of formal political opposition, the labour movement and the media have led the call for democratisation. The Swaziland Federation of Trade Unions represents 83,000 people out of a total population of 1 million. Tensions between the government and the pro-democracy movement reached boiling point in 2000/2001. Protest meetings were moved to neighbouring South Africa after they were banned by Prime Minister Sibusiso Dlamini. Leaders of the trade union movement were put on trial for organizing a strike, restrictions were placed on the media, and the independence of the judiciary was effectively ended. Internal opposition and a threat by the US to take away Swaziland's trade privileges however pressured Mswati into lifting these restrictions in July 2001. This move was greeted with cautious optimism, but Swazis await a return to the multiparty democracy they were guaranteed in their 1968 constitution.

Culture This is a traditional African society preserving many ancient ceremonies and customs. The *Umhlanga* dance is celebrated every two years at Loamba where the nation's young girls dance and sing in homage to the Queen Mother. One of the attractions of Swaziland is the African atmosphere which pervades the country. After South Africa it can be a pleasant change to relax in a country free from the tensions which plague South African society.

Economy Swaziland is virtually surrounded by South Africa and is dependent on this market for much of its external trade. It is a prosperous country with iron, coal and asbestos mines. Much of the higher western mountainous regions have been planted with timber plantations, whilst the central and eastern lowveld regions are dedicated to cotton, tobacco, citrus fruits, sugar cane and cattle ranching. Subsistence farming is the main occupation for the majority of Swazis and much of the landscape is devoted to small scale agricultural plots and cattle pastures. Cattle are highly valued as a source of wealth, and the outbreak of Foot and Mouth Disease in South Africa in 2000 was a significant concern for Swazis, not least because it meant a temporary ban on meat exports from the region. One of the largest foreign direct investments in Swaziland in years came in 2000 when a Taiwanese firm opened a textile factory which employed thousands of workers. Swaziland is one of the few countries that has diplomatic relations with Taiwan.

Land and environment

The **Highlands** in the northwest are Swaziland's most important economic region with extensive forestry plantations and mining development. This is the coolest region of the country where the mountains, forests and streams of Malolotja and Pigg's Peak attract many visitors. The road descending through the Ezulwini Valley from Mbabane to Manzini is Swaziland's most popular region for tourists. The **Middleveld** runs through the centre of the country and is the major agricultural region covered in rolling grasslands. The **Lowveld** is a hot dry region of typical African savanna where pineapples and sugarcane are cultivated. Hlane National Park is a good example of this landscape. The **Lebombo** region is part of the escarpment rising up to 600 m which runs from Maputaland through the eastern boundaries of Swaziland and on into Mpumalanga. This is the least-populated area with only two notable settlements at Big Bend and Siteki.

Landscape

The game reserves in Swaziland are rather overwhelmed by Kruger which is only a short drive away. However, the private game reserve at **Mkhaya** is one of the best places in Africa to see black rhino and **Malolotja** offers some challenging opportunities for hikers. Malolotja is a wilderness area developed for hikers with only the most basic facilities. The amazing mountain scenery is a relatively undiscovered, top hiking area, where a good network of trails has been developed in recent years. The Mbuluzi Gorge in **Mlawula Nature Reserve** is a little visited region with over 300 recorded species of birds and a new network of hiking trails.

Game & nature reserves

Swaziland

Swaziland

Footnotes

16

830

Footnotes

Baz Bus routes (March 2002)

Passengers must be ready to leave 15 minutes prior to the earliest pick-up times.

NB This timetable is subject to change without prior notification. Please enquire at your hostel for any changes.

Cape Town - Port Elizabeth

	Out	Return
Cape Town	0715-0830	2130-2215
Stellenbosch[1]	0900-0915	2015-2045
Hermanus[2]	0945-1000	1930-2000
Swellendam	1145-1200	1800-1815
Mossel Bay	1415-1445	1530-1545
Oudtshoorn[3]	shuttle	
George[4]	1515-1525	1445-1500
Wilderness[4]	1545-1600	1345-1415
Knysna[4]	1630-1700	1245-1315
Plettenberg Bay	1745-1800	1200-1215
Nature's Valley	1815-1840	1115-1130
Storms River	1900-1915	1015-1045
Jeffreys Bay	2030-2100	0830-0900
Port Elizabeth	2145-2215	0645-0730

Daily service

[1] *Hostels will meet you at Lord Charles Hotel, Somerset West.*
[2] *Shuttle bus from the Bot River Hotel. Telephone hostel in advance to confirm pick-up and costs.*
[3] *A shuttle bus departs from Oudtshoorn at 1230 for George. The shuttle departs from George between 1515-1530 for Oudtshoorn. Return fare R25 per person. Telephone hostel in advance to confirm pick-up.*
[4] *An alternative to the Baz Bus is to take the steam train between George and Knysna, known as the Outeniqua Choo-Tjoe. Fare R50. The service stops in Wilderness. No train service on Sundays.*

Port Elizabeth - Durban

	Out[1]	Return[2]
Port Elizabeth	0700-0730	2130-2230
Grahamstown	0845-0900	2000-2010
East London/Hogsback[3]	1115	1730
Cintsa[3]	1145-1200	1645-1700
Mazeppa Bay[4]	1300-1315	1545
Coffee Bay/Mpande/Port St Johns[5]	1445	1415
Port St Johns[5]	1520	1345
Kokstad[6]	1700	1115-1145
Port Edward/Margate/Port Shepstone[7]	1930	0900
Umzumbe/Banana Beach	1950	0830
Warner Beach	2045	0745
Durban	2115-2145	0645-0730

[1] *Daily except Wednesday and Saturday*
[2] *Daily except Tuesday and Friday*
[3] *Shuttle from Sugarshack in East London and from Buccaneers in Cintsa.*
[4] *Hostels will meet you at Butterworth Spar. One way fare R30 per person.*
[5] *Hostels will meet the bus at Shell Ultra City, Umtata and take passengers directly to the hostel. Fare R35-45 per person*
[6] *Telephone hostel in advance to confirm pick-up and costs.*
[7] *Hostels will collect you from the Spur Silver Lake in Port Shepstone.*

Durban - Swaziland

	Out[1]	Return[2]
Durban	0730-0830	1715-1745
Ballito	0915-0930	1645
Gingindlovu	1015	1530-1600
Eshowe	1030-1100	1515
Empangeni	1200	1430
Kwambonambi	1230-1300	1330-1400
St Lucia	1345	1245
Bushlands	1430	1100
Mkuzi	1500	1030
Manzini	1830	0730

[1] Departs Monday, Wednesday & Friday

[2] Departs Tuesday, Thursday & Sunday

Swaziland - Johannesburg/Pretoria

	Out[1]	Return[2]
Manzini	0730	1715
Malkerns	0745	1730
Mbabane	0830	1645
Nelspruit[3]	1130-1200	1415
Waterval Onder	1245-1300	1300-1330
Johannesburg	1700-1745	0800-0930
Pretoria	1815-1845	0645-0715

[1] Departs Tuesday, Thursday & Saturday

[2] Departs Monday, Wednesday & Saturday

[3] For hostels in Graskop, Hazyview and Hoedspruit, telephone in advance to arrange pick-up in Nelspruit.

Durban-Johannesburg/Pretoria (via Northern Drakensberg)

	Out[1]	Return[2]
Durban	0730-0830	1715-1745
Pietermaritzburg[3]		
	0930-1000	1615
Mooi River[4]	1100	1500
Winterton[5]	1215	1330
Amphitheatre	1310	1240
Flicksburg/Lesotho[6]		
	shuttle	
Johannesburg	1700-1745	0800-0930
Pretoria	1815-1845	06466-0715

[1] Tuesday, Friday & Sunday

[2] Wednesday, Friday & Sunday

[3] Telephone hostel in advance to confirm pick-up and costs.

[4] Pick-up from the Wimpy.

[5] Pick-up from the First National Bank, Winterton.

[6] A shuttle bus services is available from Amphitheatre (Northern Drakensberg). Contact the hostel to find out departure days and cost.

Shorts

Index

Footnotes

Footnotes

Footnotes

Map index

Footnotes

Map symbols

Administration
- ⌁ International border
- ─·─ State / Province border
- ☐ CAPITAL CITY
- ○ Other town

Roads and travel
Urban
- Main through route
- Main street
- Minor street
- Pedestrianized street
- → One way street

Regional
- Motorway
- Main road (National highway)
- Other road
- 4WD track
- Footpath
- Railway with station

Sights and services
- ■ Sleeping
- ● Eating
- ▫ Sight
- Building
- Steps
- Park, garden, stadium
- ✈ Airport
- ☐ Bus station
- Ⓜ Metro station
- ➕ Hospital
- ☎ Market
- 🏛 Museum
- ✝ Cathedral, church
- ✡ Synagogue
- Mosque
- 🛕 Temple
- Petrol station
- Police station

- Ⓢ Bank
- ✉ Post office
- ♪ Telephone office
- @ Internet
- Tourist office
- ⋈ Bridge
- Vineyard/wine cellar
- Archaeological site
- ✕ Historic battlefield
- Golf course
- Viewing point
- ♦ National park, wildlife sanctuary
- National park boundary
- Hide
- ▲ Camp site
- Palm trees
- A Detail map
- C Related map

Water features
- River
- Lake, reservoir, tank
- Seasonal marshland
- Sand bank, beach, dry river bed
- ~~~ Coral reef
- Ocean
- Waterfall
- Ferry
- Shipwreck

Topographical features
- Contours (approx), rock outcrop
- Mountain/kopjie
- Mountain Pass
- Gorge
- Escarpment
- Salt pan
- Rocks

Weights and measures

Weight
1 kilogram = 2.205 pounds
1 pound = 0.454 kilograms

Length
1 metre = 1.094 yards
1 yard = 0.914 metres

Capacity
1 litre = 0.220 gallons
1 gallon = 4.546 litres
1 pint = 0.863 litres

1 kilometre = 0.621 miles
1 mile = 1.609 kilometres

Footnotes

Acknowledgements

Firstly, many thanks are due to Sebastian Ballard, for his work on the original and previous five editions of the South Africa Handbook.

Dr Charlie Easmon wrote the health section. His aid and development work has included: Raleigh International (Medical Officer in Botswana), MERLIN (in Rwanda his team set up a refugee camp for 12,000 people), Save the Children (as a consultant in Rwanda), ECHO (The European Community Humanitarian Office review of Red Cross work in Armenia, Georgia and Azerbaijan), board member of International Care and Relief and previously International Health Exchange. In addition to his time as a hospital physician, he has worked as a medical adviser to the Foreign and Commonwealth Office and as a locum consultant at the hospital for tropical diseases travel clinic, as well as being a specialist registrar in Public Health. He now also runs Travel Screening services (www.travelscreening.co.uk) based at 1 Harley Street.

Thanks to Mark Durham and Charlie Graham for their thorough and detailed diving section and to Dawn Nell for updating the history and politics in the background chapters.

Francisca Kellett thanks:
First and foremost, I'd like to thank Hugo Rifkind for his constant support and unwavering good humour during our travels. Not only was he uncomplaining of our hectic schedule during what was meant to be his holiday, he was an amazing help, both with research on the road and dealing with the dreaded maps.

Thank you also to everyone at 3 Fairfield Road for making living in Cape Town what it was, especially Robert Dersely for introducing me to braais and the finer details of the city's nightlife, and the German doctors for dragging me up Lion's Head. I'd also like to thank my parents and brother Dan for letting me show off Cape Town and the Garden Route, and Jess Lipson, Laura Ferguson and Caroline Wright for taking the time to visit and helping me explore the more enjoyable aspects of the Winelands.

On my travels I was assisted by an extraordinary number of people, without whom my job would have been impossible. I'm particularly indebted to the following for their invaluable advice and thoughtfulness: Johan and Liz for saving us from a night stranded in the Kalahari; Brian at the Old Goal in Grahamstown; Mike at Gekko Backpackers in Citrusdal; Andrea and Aranxa at North South Backpackers in Pretoria; the team at Stumble Inn in Stellenbosch; and SATOUR, particularly the staff in Cape Town, Ceres, East London, George, Grahamstown, Oudtshoorn, Springbok, Stellenbosch and Tulbagh.

Finally, a big thank you to all the readers who took the time to write or email Footprint HQ with useful information, including: Richard Killpack; David and Erica Clapp; Lennart Bjernfalk; Mike Brown; Claudia Ruettimann; Alexander Horn; Tanja Schlienz; Andrea Zeus; Manuelle Prunier; Kodzo Selormey; Stefanie Grünberg; Janine Taylor; Elizabeth Wright; Martin Evans; Pauline Tremlett; John Wardle.

Lizzie Williams thanks:
I would like to thank Mark and Astrid, Steve and Mignon, Peter and all the little additions of the Baines family from the Backpackers Ritz for their help and exceptionally generous hospitality in Johannesburg. Thanks to Mike and Tracey from Wagon Trails for the wheels and Neo Mnisi from Karabo Tours for being an entertaining and informative guide of Pretoria, Johannesburg and Soweto. It was great to have my good friends Patch and Kerry come down from Zimbabwe to keep me company, read the map, and share a few good bottles of South African wine in St Lucia, Swaziland and Mpumalanga. Thanks to my Aunt and Uncle, Rene and Hanif for providing a few home comforts in Durban, and FB Logging for being great hosts in

KwaZulu Natal. In Swaziland, Anne Rielly from Mlilwane is an enthusiastic ambassador for tourism in this tiny country, and there is little Russell from Sani Lodge doesn't know about Lesotho and the Drakensberg. My job was made easier by the excellent tourist offices that are found in even the smallest of dorps, staffed by friendly people who really are keen to promote their regions. In particular the Panorama offices in Mpumalanga, Louise in Bloemfontein, Clara in Pietersburg, the Tourist Junction in Durban, and the Maluti office in Ficksburg. Thanks to the Bam family at the Lions Head Lodge and Aardvark Backpackers in Cape Town for putting up with me once again, particularly Kathy for being my laptop doctor. And finally thanks to all my friends and colleagues in the backpacker's industry with whom I have worked over the last few years for their great company and updates. Because of them South Africa has an excellent network of hostels, tours and transport that rivals Europe and provides a fun and easy way of exploring the country for the budget traveller. Finally thanks for Sarah Thorowgood for making it all make sense.

Footnotes

Footprint feedback

We try as hard as we can to make each Footprint Handbook as up-to-date and accurate as possible but, of course, things always change. Many people email or write to us with corrections, new information, or simply comments. If you want to let us know about your experiences and adventures – be they good, bad or ugly – then don't delay; we're dying to hear from you. And please try to include all the relevant details and juicy bits. Your help will be greatly appreciated, especially by other travellers. In return we will send you details about our special guidebook offer.

email Footprint at:
saf06_online@footprintbooks.com

or write to:
Elizabeth Taylor
Footprint Handbooks
6 Riverside Court
Lower Bristol Road
Bath   BA2 3DZ
UK

Advertisers index

Travel the World
with Putumayo

These legendary artists from South Africa
have created an extraordinary musical legacy.
Featuring Miriam Makeba, Huge Masekela,
Johnny Clegg and more.

PUTUMAYO
World Music
Guaranteed to make you feel good!
www.putumayo.com

South Africa

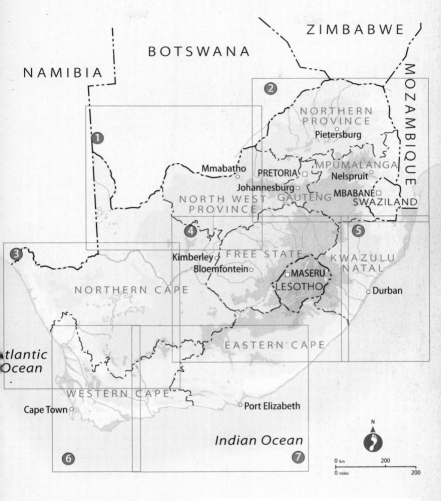

ZIMBABWE

BOTSWANA

NAMIBIA

MOZAMBIQUE

① ②

NORTHERN PROVINCE
Pietersburg ○

MPUMALANGA

Mmabatho ●
PRETORIA □
Nelspruit ○
Johannesburg ○
MBABANE □
GAUTENG
SWAZILAND

NORTH WEST PROVINCE

④ ⑤

③

Kimberley ○
FREE STATE
KWAZULU NATAL

Bloemfontein ○
□ MASERU
LESOTHO
Durban ○

NORTHERN CAPE

Atlantic Ocean

EASTERN CAPE

WESTERN CAPE

Cape Town ○
Port Elizabeth ○

Indian Ocean

⑥ ⑦

N

0 km 200
0 miles 200

	Altitude in metres
	3000
	2000
	1500
	1000
	500
	200
	100
	0
	Neighbouring Country

PRETORIA □ Capital
Durban ○ Provincial capital
Upington ○ Other town
——— Main roads
——— Minor roads
——— Tracks
N14 Route number
——— Railways
–·–·– International border
–··–··– Province border

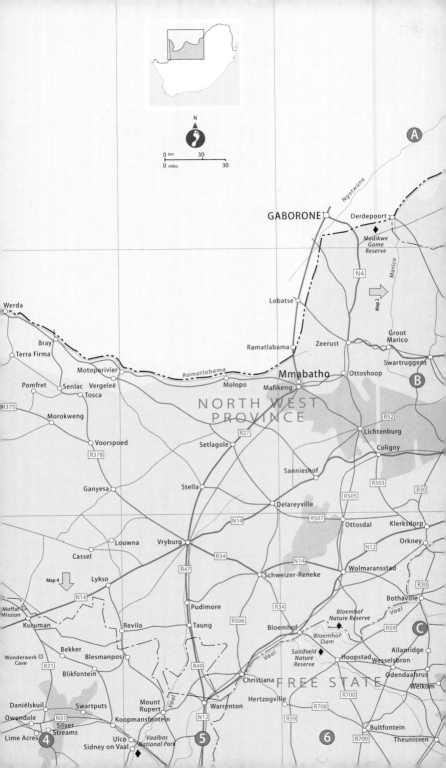

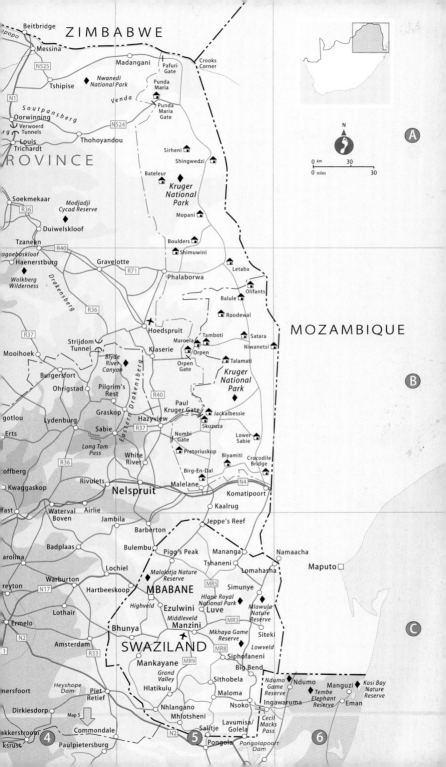

Map 3

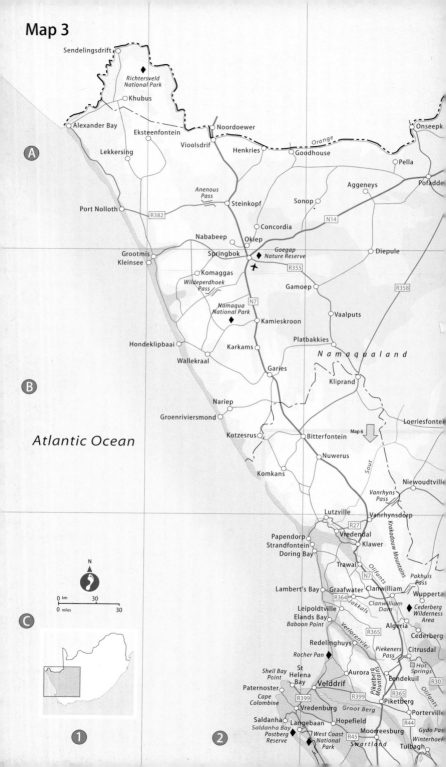

Sendelingsdrift

Richtersveld National Park

Khubus

Alexander Bay

Eksteenfontein

Noordoewer

Vioolsdrif

Orange

Onseepk

A

Lekkersing

Henkries

Goodhouse

Pella

Pofadde

Port Nolloth

R382

Anenous Pass

Steinkopf

Sonop

Aggeneys

Concordia

N14

Diepule

Nababeep

Okiep

Goegap Nature Reserve

R355

Grootmis

Springbok

Kleinsee

Komaggas

Wildeperdhoek Pass

Gamoep

R358

N7

Vaalputs

Namaqua National Park

Kamieskroon

Platbakkies

Hondeklipbaai

Karkams

N a m a q u a l a n d

Wallekraal

Garies

Kliprand

B

Nariep

Loeriesfonte

Groenriviersmond

Kotzesrus

Bitterfontein

Map 6

Atlantic Ocean

Nuwerus

Sout

Komkans

Niewoudtville

Vanrhyns Pass

Lutzville

Vanrhynsdorp

Papendorp

R27

Krakadouw Mountains

Strandfontein

Vredendal

Doring Bay

Klawer

Trawal

Olifants

Pakhuis Pass

N7

Lambert's Bay

Graafwater

Clanwilliam

Wupperta

R364

Jakkals

Clanwilliam Dam

Leipoldtville

Algeria

Cederberg Wilderness Area

Elands Bay

Baboon Point

R365

Cederberg

Redelinghuys

Verlorenvlei

Citrusdal

Rocher Pan

Piekeners Pass

N

Shell Bay Point

St Helena Bay

Aurora

Hot Springs

Bendekuil

0 km 30

0 miles 30

Paternoster

Piketberg Mountains

Velddrif

R30

C

Cape Colombine

R399

Groot Berg

Piketberg

Porterville

Vredenburg

R399

Hopefield

R365

Olifants

Saldanha

Langebaan

Mooreesburg

R44

Gydo Pa

Saldanha Bay Postberg Reserve

West Coast National Park

R45

Swartland

Winterhoek

Tulbagh

1

2

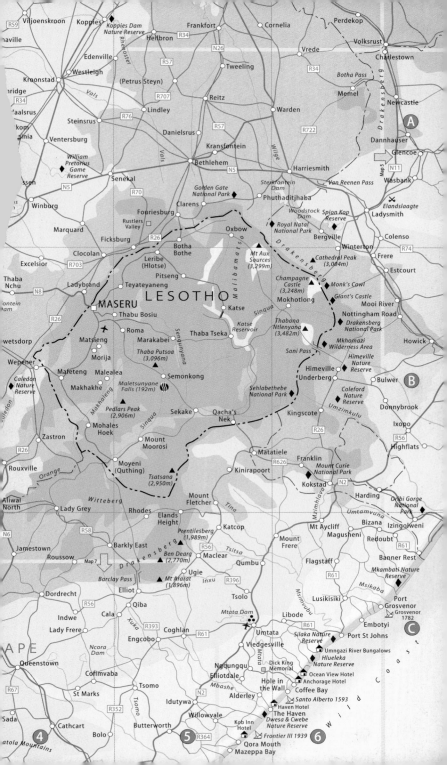

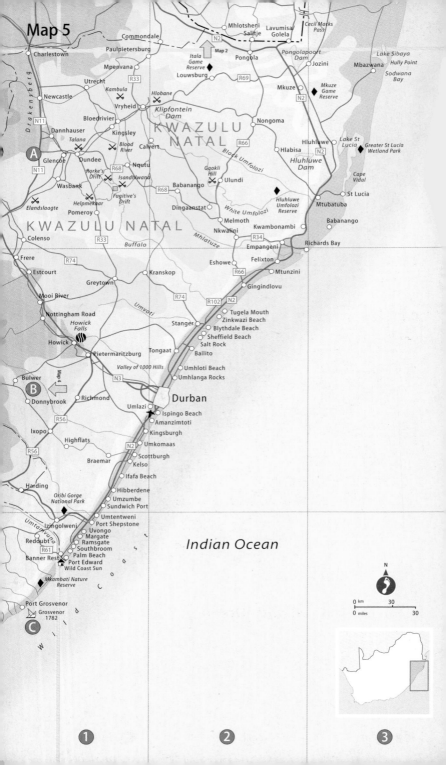

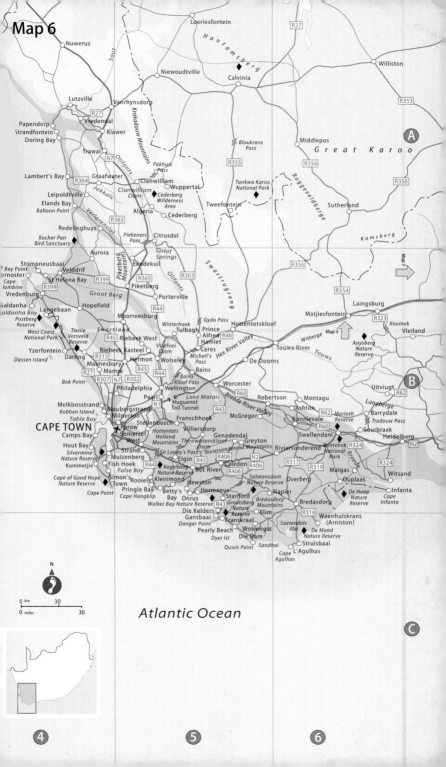

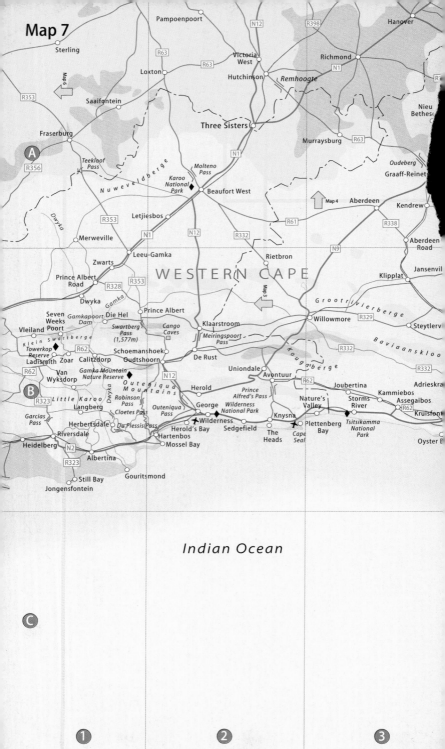

www.footprintbooks.com
70 travel guides, 100s of destinations, 5 continents and 1 Footprint...